This volume of the
METSUDAH KITZUR SHULCHAN ARUCH
is reverently dedicated
to the memory of my grandparents

THE ROTHNERS

נתנאל ב"ר אברהם דוד ע"ה
כ' שבט תרצ"ו
February 13, 1936

שרה בת יעקב מאיר ע"ה
כ"ט טבת תשכ"ח
January 29, 1968

THE STEINBERGS

יעקב צבי ב"ר יהודה ליב הכהן ע"ה
כ"ד אלול תשל"ג
September 21, 1973

פריידל מלכה בת אברהם דוד ע"ה
ד' ניסן תשכ"ד
March 17, 1964

By their grandson
Eric Rothner and Family
Chicago, IL

Contents

Volume I

סִימָן צז
הִלְכוֹת רֹאשׁ־חֹדֶשׁ וְקִדּוּשׁ־לְבָנָה

א) יֵשׁ נוֹהֲגִין לְהִתְעַנּוֹת בְּעֶרֶב רֹאשׁ־חֹדֶשׁ. וְאוֹמְרִים סֵדֶר יוֹם כִּפּוּר קָטָן, לְפִי שֶׁבּוֹ מִתְכַּפְּרִין כָּל הָעֲוֹנוֹת שֶׁל כָּל הַחֹדֶשׁ, דּוּמְיָא דִּשְׂעִיר רֹאשׁ־חֹדֶשׁ. וּכְמוֹ שֶׁאָנוּ אוֹמְרִים בְּמוּסָף, זְמַן כַּפָּרָה לְכָל תּוֹלְדוֹתָם. וְכָל מָקוֹם לְפִי מִנְהָגוֹ.

ב) מִצְוָה לְהַרְבּוֹת בִּסְעוּדָה בְּרֹאשׁ־חֹדֶשׁ. וְאִם חָל בְּשַׁבָּת, יַעֲשֶׂה תַּבְשִׁיל אֶחָד יוֹתֵר מִבִּשְׁאָר שַׁבָּתוֹת.

ג) רֹאשׁ־חֹדֶשׁ, מֻתָּר בַּעֲשִׂיַּת מְלָאכָה. וְנָשִׁים נוֹהֲגוֹת שֶׁלֹּא לַעֲשׂוֹת בּוֹ מְלָאכָה, וּמִנְהָג הָגוּן הוּא וְאֵין לְהָקֵל לָהֶן.

ד) הַלֵּל צָרִיךְ לְאָמְרוֹ בַּעֲמִידָה וְלֹא יַפְסִיק בּוֹ. וְיִשְׁתַּדֵּל לְאָמְרוֹ עִם הַצִּבּוּר. וְלָכֵן אִם בָּא לְבֵית־הַכְּנֶסֶת סָמוּךְ לַהַלֵּל, יֹאמַר הַלֵּל עִם הַצִּבּוּר וְאַחַר כָּךְ יִתְפַּלֵּל. וְאִם הוּא עוֹמֵד בִּפְסוּקֵי דְזִמְרָה, (דְּהַיְנוּ מִן הוֹדוּ עַד לְאַחַר אָז יָשִׁיר), יִקְרָא הַלֵּל עִם הַצִּבּוּר וְלֹא יְבָרֵךְ לֹא בַּתְּחִלָּה וְלֹא בַּסּוֹף, כִּי בִּרְכַּת בָּרוּךְ שֶׁאָמַר וּבִרְכַּת יִשְׁתַּבַּח, עָלוּ לוֹ גַּם לַהַלֵּל. וְדַוְקָא בְּרֹאשׁ־חֹדֶשׁ יָכוֹל לַעֲשׂוֹת כֵּן, שֶׁאוֹמְרִים הַהַלֵּל רַק בְּדִלּוּג, וְכֵן בְּחֹל־הַמּוֹעֵד וְיָמִים אַחֲרוֹנִים שֶׁל פֶּסַח. אֲבָל כְּשֶׁאוֹמְרִים הַלֵּל שָׁלֵם, אֵינוֹ יָכוֹל לַעֲשׂוֹת כֵּן. וּמִי שֶׁאָמַר הַלֵּל שֶׁלֹּא בְּצִבּוּר, אִם יֵשׁ שְׁנַיִם אֲחֵרִים, יֹאמַר לִפְנֵיהֶם הוֹדוּ לַה' וְגוֹ', כְּדֵי שֶׁיַּעֲנוּ הֵם. דְּכֵיוָן שֶׁאוֹמֵר הוֹדוּ, מַשְׁמַע שֶׁאוֹמֵר לַאֲחֵרִים. (דין אמירת הלל בבית האבל, ר"ל, ע"ל סי' רז).

ה) לְאַחַר הַלֵּל, אוֹמְרִים קַדִּישׁ שָׁלֵם, וּמוֹצִיאִין סֵפֶר־תּוֹרָה וְקוֹרִין אַרְבָּעָה. הַכֹּהֵן קוֹרֵא שְׁלֹשָׁה פְּסוּקִים, שֶׁהֵם: וַיְדַבֵּר, צַו, וְאָמַרְתָּ. וְהַלֵּוִי

1. *Mogein Avraham* 417:3. *Bach, Minhagim.*

2. *Pri Chodosh, Rav Moshe Kordaviro.* It is, therefore, called *Yom Kippur Kattan* which means a small day of atonement. The order of prayers include various *slichos* and themes on repentance.

3. The he-goat was brought as a sin-offering every *Rosh Chodesh.*

4. *Shulchan Aruch* 417.

5. *Biur Halacha* says it is forbidden for women to do *melacha* on Rosh Chodesh in the manner they do every day. Each woman must choose for herself at least one *melacha* she will not do on Rosh Chodesh.

Chapter 97

The Laws of Rosh Chodesh and Sanctification of the Moon

1) Some people are accustomed to fast on Erev Rosh Chodesh[1] and recite the order of *Yom Kippur Kattan,* for on this day we are forgiven for all the sins committed in the past month.[2] It is likened to the *Seir*[3] [goat offering] of Rosh Chodesh, and as we say in the Mussaf service, "It is a time of atonement for all their generations." Each communifty should follow its own custom.

2) It is a Mitzvah to have an elaborate meal on Rosh Chodesh, and if it occurs on Shabbos, an extra cooked dish should be prepared in addition to those prepared on other *Shabbasos.*

3) It is permissable to do *Melacha*[4] on Rosh Chodesh, but women customarily refrain from doing *melachah* on this day.[5] This is a proper custom and it should not be made trivial for them.

4) *Hallel* should be said while standing, and without interruption. You should try to say it with the congregation.[6] Therefore, if you arrive at the synagogue when the congregation is about to say *Hallel,* you should say *Hallel* with the congregation and recite the other prayers later. And if you are saying *Pesukei Dezimrah* (that is from *Hodu* until after *Az Yashir),*[7] you should read Hallel with the congregation without saying the berachah before or after the *Hallel,* because the berachah of *Baruch Sheamar* and the berachah of *Yishtabach* also fulfill the berachah for *Hallel.* And only on Rosh Chodesh can this be done, because then parts of the *Hallel* are omitted. This is also true for *Chol Hamoed* and the last days of *Pesach.* But when the entire *Hallel* is recited, this cannot be done.[8] And if you recite *Hallel* without the congregation, and two [or more] other persons are present, you should say *Hodu* in their presence[9] in order that they may respond, for the expression *Hodu* (thank Hashem) implies that you are addressing others [to do so]. The law of saying *Hallel* in the house of a mourner, may the Merciful save us, is found further in Chapter 207.

5) After *Hallel* the whole Kaddish[10] is recited, a *Seifer* Torah is taken out, and four (men) are called (to the Torah).

---

6. According to *Rif,* the berachah of *Hallel* is said on Rosh Chodesh only when it is said with a *minyan,* a quorum of ten adult men.

7. According to Nusach Sfard from *Mizmor Lesodah* until after *Az Yashir.*

8. For then you must make a berachah on the *Hallel* according to all the *poskim,* for it is an obligation, not a custom.

9. But you do not have to try and find them if they are not in front of you. (*Mishnah Berurah, Eliyohu Rabbah*)

10. On a day when there is a *Mussaf* service, the whole Kaddish is said after *Hallel* because *Hallel* marks the completion of the *Shacharis* (morning) prayer. Therefore on Chanukah, only the half-Kaddish is said after *Hallel,* as there is no *Mussaf* service. (*Mishnah Berurah* 423:1, *Achronim*)

חוֹזֵר וְקוֹרֵא וְאָמַרְתָּ, וְקוֹרֵא אֶת־הַכֶּבֶשׂ אֶחָד, וַעֲשִׂירִית הָאֵיפָה. וְיִשְׂרָאֵל קוֹרֵא עוֹלַת תָּמִיד עַד וּבְרָאשֵׁי חָדְשֵׁיכֶם. וּרְבִיעִי קוֹרֵא וּבְרָאשֵׁי חָדְשֵׁיכֶם וְגוֹ'.

ו) רֹאשׁ־חֹדֶשׁ, אָסוּר בְּתַעֲנִית וּבְהֶסְפֵּד, וְאֵין אוֹמְרִים בּוֹ צִדּוּק הַדִּין.

ז) חַיָּבִין לְקַדֵּשׁ אֶת הַלְּבָנָה בְּכָל חֹדֶשׁ. וְאֵין מְקַדְּשִׁין אוֹתָהּ, אֶלָּא כְּשֶׁהוּא וַדַּאי לַיְלָה, שֶׁנִּרְאֵית זְרִיחָתָהּ עַל גַּבֵּי הַקַּרְקַע וְרָאוּי לֵהָנוֹת מֵאוֹרָהּ. אִם נִתְכַּסְּתָה בְּעָב, אֵין מְקַדְּשִׁין אוֹתָהּ, אֶלָּא אִם כֵּן הוּא דַק וְקָלוּשׁ. וְאִם הִתְחִיל לְבָרֵךְ וְאַחַר כָּךְ נִתְכַּסְּתָה בְעָב, גּוֹמֵר אֶת הַבְּרָכָה. אֲבָל אִם הוּא מְשַׁעֵר שֶׁלֹּא יוּכַל לִגְמוֹר אֶת הַבְּרָכָה קֹדֶם שֶׁתִּתְכַּסֶּה, אָסוּר לוֹ לְהַתְחִיל.

ח) אֵין לְקַדְּשָׁהּ רַק תַּחַת הַשָּׁמַיִם וְלֹא תַחַת גַּג. אֲבָל אִם אֵין לוֹ מָקוֹם נָקִי אוֹ מֵחֲמַת אֹנֶס אַחֵר, יָכוֹל לְקַדְּשָׁהּ גַּם בְּתוֹךְ הַבַּיִת בְּעַד הַחַלּוֹן.

ט) מִצְוָה מִן הַמֻּבְחָר לְקַדְּשָׁהּ בְּמוֹצָאֵי שַׁבָּת כְּשֶׁהוּא מְבֻסָּם וּמְלֻבָּשׁ בִּבְגָדִים נָאִים. אַךְ אִם מוֹצָאֵי שַׁבָּת יִהְיֶה לְאַחַר עֲשָׂרָה יָמִים מִן הַמּוֹלָד, אוֹ שֶׁיֵּשׁ אֵיזֶה חֲשָׁשׁ שֶׁמָּא לֹא יוּכַל לְקַדְּשָׁהּ, אֵין מַמְתִּינִין לְמוֹצָאֵי שַׁבָּת. מִצְוָה לְקַדְּשָׁהּ בַּאֲסֵפַת עָם, מִשּׁוּם דִּבְרָב־עָם הַדְרַת מֶלֶךְ. אֲבָל אַל יִתְעַכֵּב בִּשְׁבִיל זֶה, כִּי מִצְוַת זְרִיזִין מַקְדִּימִין, דָּחֵי לְמִצְוַת בְּרָב־עָם.

י) אֵין מְקַדְּשִׁין אוֹתָהּ עַד שֶׁיַּעַבְרוּ עָלֶיהָ לְכָל הַפָּחוֹת שְׁלֹשָׁה יָמִים מִן הַמּוֹלָד. וְיֵשׁ מַמְתִּינִין עַד שִׁבְעָה יָמִים. וּכְשֶׁחָל מוֹצָאֵי שַׁבָּת קֹדֶם שִׁבְעָה יָמִים, אֵין לְהַמְתִּין, אֶלָּא יְקַדְּשׁוּהָ בְּמוֹצָאֵי שַׁבָּת. וְאֵין מְקַדְּשִׁין

---

11. The reason for this is because at least three verses must be read, for each *aliyah* and also we must not stop less than three verses before the end of a *parsha* (sections). The *parsha* of the *Tamid* (the first parsha read on Rosh Chodesh) has only eight verses, and, therefore, in order to divide it into three *aliyahs,* some repetition is required. The *parsha* of Rosh Chodesh cannot be divided into two *aliyahs* because it has only five verses. Repetition cannot be used there because we must not start less than three verses in a *parsha,* nor stop less than three verses before the end of the *parshah.*

12. *Gaonim, Shulchan Aruch* 423:2. But in Eretz Yisroel, the opinion of the *Gra* is widely accepted. He says the *kohein* reads the first three verses, the *levi* reads the next five, the third

The *kohein* reads three *pesukim* (verses), which are *Vayedaber, Tzav, Veamarta.* The Levi repeats the verse of *V'amarta,*[11] and adds: *Es hakkeves echad, veasiris haeifah.* The Yisroel reads from *olas tamid* until *uverashei chodsheychem.* And the fourth person reads from *uverashai chodsheychem.*[12]

6) On Rosh Chodesh it is forbidden to fast and to eulogize someone, and the prayer *Tziduk Hadin*[13] is not said.

7) It is obligatory to sanctify the moon each month.[14] It should not be sanctified until it is definitely night, which is when its light is visible on the ground, so that you can derive some use from its light. If the moon is covered by a cloud, it should not be sanctified[15] unless the cloud is thin and scanty.[16] If you began the berachah, and afterwards it was covered by the cloud, you should complete the berachah. But if you estimate that you will not be able to complete the berachah before it is covered, it is forbidden to begin (the berachah).

8) The moon must be sanctified only under the heavens (open sky) and not under a roof.[17] If, however, there is no clean place [outside] or because of another situation beyond your control [you cannot go outside]; you may sanctify it inside the house through the window.[18]

9) It is a mitzvah performed in its excellence to sanctify the moon on *Motzai Shabbos* when you are in high spirits and dressed in fine clothes. But if *Motzai Shabbos* will occur after ten days from the appearance of the new moon, or if it is feared that you will then be unable to sanctify it, you needn't wait until *Motzai Shabbos.* It is a mitzvah to sanctify the moon in the gathering of a multitude of people, since in the multitude of the people is the glory of the King. But it should not be postponed because of this, because the mitzvah to "perform precepts promptly" overrides the mitzvah of "in the multitude of people."

10) The moon should not be sanctified until the passage of at least three days from the appearance of the new moon, and some wait seven days. And when *Motzai Shabbos* occurs before seven days, you should not wait,[19] but you should sanctify it on *Motzai Shabbos.* The moon may be sanctified only up to the expiration of half the

---

person repeats the last three verses read by the levi plus the two verses about Shabbos, and the fourth person reads the five verses about Rosh Chodesh.

13. This is a prayer expressing acceptance of the Divine judgment.

14. *Sanhedrin* 42.

15. Ramah 426:1, *Mishnah Berurah.*

16. *Radvaz.*

17. *Ramah* 426:4—*Rif.* Since the mitzvah is akin to greeting the Divine Presence (*shechina*), it is disrespectful not to go outside and do it. However, if you have a slight cold or illness, you may do it from your house. (*Mogen Avraham, Bach*)

18. It is preferable to do it through an open window if possible. (*Shaar Hatziyun* 426:25, *Pri Megadim*)

19. In the winter season it is definitely better not to wait because you may not be able to see it later. (*Mishnah Berurah*)

אוֹתָהּ אֶלָּא עַד חֲצִי כ"ט, י"ב, תשצ"ג, שֶׁהוּא אַרְבָּעָה עָשָׂר מֵעֵת לְעֵת וּשְׁמוֹנֶה עֶשְׂרֵה שָׁעוֹת וְעֶשְׂרִים וּשְׁתַּיִם דַּקּוֹת (מִינוּטִין) מִן הַמּוֹלָד.

יא) אֵין לְקַדְּשָׁהּ קֹדֶם תִּשְׁעָה בְּאָב, וְכֵן כְּשֶׁהוּא אָבֵל אֶלָּא אִם כֵּן לֹא יַשְׁלִים אֲבֵלוּתוֹ עַד שֶׁיִּהְיוּ עֲשָׂרָה מֵעֵת לְעֵת מִן הַמּוֹלָד, אָז יְקַדְּשָׁהּ בִּימֵי אֶבְלוֹ. וְאֵין לְקַדְּשָׁהּ כְּשֶׁהוּא בְּתַעֲנִית עַד שֶׁיִּטְעַם מִקֹּדֶם. וּמִכָּל מָקוֹם בְּמוֹצָאֵי יוֹם הַכִּפּוּרִים, כֵּיוָן שֶׁאָז יוֹצְאִים מִבֵּית־הַכְּנֶסֶת בְּשִׂמְחָה עַל מְחִילַת הָעֲוֹנוֹת, מְקַדְּשִׁין אוֹתָהּ מִיָּד.

יב) אֵין לְקַדְּשָׁהּ לֹא בְּלֵיל שַׁבָּת וְלֹא בְּלֵיל יוֹם־טוֹב אֶלָּא בִּשְׁעַת הַדְּחָק, כְּשֶׁבְּמוֹצָאֵי שַׁבָּת יַעֲבוֹר הַזְּמָן.

יג) סוּמָא מֻתָּר לְקַדְּשָׁהּ.

יד) אִם הַלְּבָנָה זוֹרַחַת בִּתְחִלַּת הַלַּיְלָה קֹדֶם שֶׁהִתְחִילוּ לְהִתְפַּלֵּל מַעֲרִיב, אִם יֵשׁ עוֹד זְמַן אֵיזֶה לֵילוֹת לְקַדְּשָׁהּ, מִתְפַּלְּלִין תְּחִלָּה מַעֲרִיב וְאַחַר כָּךְ מְקַדְּשִׁין אוֹתָהּ, מִשּׁוּם דְּתָדִיר וְשֶׁאֵינוֹ תָדִיר, תָּדִיר קוֹדֵם, וְעוֹד, דִּקְרִיאַת־שְׁמַע הֲוֵי דְּאוֹרָיְתָא, אֲבָל אִם אֵין עוֹד זְמַן רַק שְׁנַיִם אוֹ שְׁלֹשָׁה לֵילוֹת, בִּזְמַן קָצָר כָּזֶה יֵשׁ לָחוּשׁ שֶׁמָּא תִתְכַּסֶּה בֶּעָבִים. וּבְעֵת הַגְּשָׁמִים, גַּם כְּשֶׁיֵּשׁ עוֹד זְמַן אַרְבָּעָה לֵילוֹת, יֵשׁ לָחוּשׁ לְכִסּוּי עֲנָנִים, וְיֵשׁ לְהַקְדִּים קִדּוּשׁ לְבָנָה. וְאִם נִרְאֲתָה הַלְּבָנָה בְּעֵת שֶׁאוֹמְרִים קְרִיאַת־שְׁמַע וּבִרְכוֹתֶיהָ, אִם הַזְּמַן מְצֻמְצָם כָּל כָּךְ שֶׁבְּעוֹד שֶׁיִּגְמְרוּ שְׁמוֹנֶה־עֶשְׂרֵה יַעֲבוֹר זְמַן קִדּוּשָׁהּ, יְכוֹלִין לְהַפְסִיק אֲפִלּוּ בְּאֶמְצַע בִּרְכוֹת קְרִיאַת־שְׁמַע אוֹ בְּאֶמְצַע קְרִיאַת־שְׁמַע לְקַדֵּשׁ אוֹתָהּ. אַךְ אִם אֶפְשָׁר, יִגְמְרוּ אֶת הַפֶּרֶק, לְקַדְּשָׁהּ בֵּין הַפְּרָקִים.

---

20. An hour is divided into 1,080 *chelakim* (parts). (see *Rambam* 6:2)

21. *Ramah* 426:2. Because sanctifying the moon is a mitzvah fulfilled with joy.

22. *Mogein Avraham.*

23. Ten 24 hour periods.

24. *Mogein Avraham.* But the *Biur Halachah* 426:2 says a mourner may not sanctify the moon unless the entire allotted time to sanctify the moon will elapse before the end of the seven days of mourning.

25. *Chayei Adam.* After you taste something, you may sanctify the moon even immediately after *Tisha B'av.* (*Mishnah Berurah, Achronim*) If there is a *minyan* sanctifying the moon now and there will be none later, you should do it with them even if you have not yet broken your fast. (*Sha'ar Hatziyun* 426:9, *Eliyohu Rabba*)

26. Even before breaking your fast or putting on shoes. After *Tisha B'av,* however, you should first put on your shoes.

period of twenty-nine days twelve hours and 793 *chalakim*[20] (29 days, 12 hours, 793/1080) that is fourteen twenty-four hour days and eighteen hours and twenty two minutes from the appearance of the new moon.

11) The moon should not be sanctified before *Tisha B'av,*[21] and not when one is a mourner,[22] unless his mourning period will not end within the ten full days[23] after the appearance of the new moon. In such a situation, it may be sanctified during the days of mourning.[24] The moon should not be sanctified on a fast day until some food has been eaten. But in any case after Yom Kippur, since we leave the synagogue in a joyous spirit, confident that our sins were forgiven, we sanctify it[25] immediately.[26]

12) The moon should not be sanctified on Friday night,[27] nor on the night of Yom Tov[28] except in extenuating circumstances, as when by *Motzai Shabbos,* the prescribed time will have passed.

13) A blind person is permitted to sanctify the moon.[29]

14) If the moon is visible at the beginning of the night, before you began the *Maariv* prayer, and there is still time, [i.e., there are still] a few more nights in which to sanctify it, you should say the *Maariv* prayer first, and then sanctify the moon, because a mitzvah that is constant takes precedence over one that is only periodic,[30] and also the reading of the *Shemah* is a Biblical precept.[31] If, however, there remains only two or three nights [to the end of the period], since the time is short, it may happen that the moon will be covered by clouds. And in the rainy season even if there remain yet four nights [to the end of the period], it may happen that it will become covered by clouds, and therefore you should first sanctify the moon (and then say *Maariv*). If the moon becomes visible at the time you are saying *Kerias Shema* and its *berachos,* and the time is so limited that before you complete *Shemoneh Esrei* the time of sanctification will have passed, you may interrupt even in the middle of the *berachos* of *Kerias Shema,* or in the middle of *Kerias Shema* in order to sanctify it. But if possible, you should complete the section [you are reading,[32]] and sanctify the moon between the sections.[33]

---

27. *Radvaz.* The *Sha'ar Hatziyun* 426:11 says the reason is because it is a custom to dance at the sanctifying of the moon and, if possible, you should avoid this on Shabbos. There are also many other reasons.

28. *Ramah* 426:2. See *Shvuss Yaakov* (vol. 3, resp. 31). The reason is because one should not merge one *simcha* with another. (see *Masechet Moed Katan* 8b)

29. *Mishnah Berurah* 426:1 rules that a blind person is obligated to sanctify the moon because he benefits from the light that others have (to guide him). However, since the *Radvaz* and *Maharikash* say that he may not sanctify the moon, *Biur Halachah* rules that it is better to have someone make the berachah for him.

30. *Maseches Zevachim* 90a.

31. And thus it has precedence over sanctifying the moon which is not Biblically ordained.

32. See *Kitzur Shulchan Aruch* Chapter 16.

33. You may only say the (berachah) sanctifying the moon, but not the verses we are accustomed to say after the berachah. [*Lechem Haponim* (author of the *Kitzur Shulchan Aruch)*]

טו) אִם בְּחֹדֶשׁ אֲדָר לֹא נִרְאֲתָה הַלְּבָנָה עַד לֵיל אַרְבָּעָה עָשָׂר שֶׁהוּא זְמַן קְרִיאַת הַמְּגִלָּה, יְקַדֵּשׁ תְּחִלָּה אֶת הַלְּבָנָה וְאַחַר כָּךְ יִקְרָא אֶת הַמְּגִלָּה וְאִם נִרְאֲתָה בְּאֶמְצַע קְרִיאַת הַמְּגִלָּה, אִם הוּא בִּזְמַן שֶׁגַּם לְאַחַר שֶׁיִּגְמְרוּ אֶת הַקְּרִיאָה, יִהְיֶה עוֹד שָׁהוּת לְקַדְּשָׁהּ, אֵין מַפְסִיקִין בְּאֶמְצַע קְרִיאַת הַמְּגִילָּה. אֲבָל אִם עַד שֶׁיִּגְמְרוּ אֶת הַמְּגִלָּה יַעֲבוֹר זְמַנָּהּ, אֲזַי אִם כָּל הַקָּהָל עֲדַיִן לֹא קִדְּשׁוּ אוֹתָהּ, יַפְסִיקוּ לְקַדֵּשׁ אוֹתָהּ, וְאַחַר כָּךְ יִגְמְרוּ אֶת הַמְּגִלָּה. אֲבָל אִם רַק יָחִיד לֹא קִדֵּשׁ אוֹתָהּ, שֶׁאִם יַפְסִיק לְקַדְּשָׁהּ, יִצְטָרֵךְ אַחַר כָּךְ לִגְמוֹר אֶת הַמְּגִלָּה בִּיחִידוּת, לֹא יַפְסִיק, מִשּׁוּם דְּפִרְסוּמֵי נִסָּא עָדִיף.

סִימָן צח
הִלְכוֹת יוֹם־טוֹב

א) כָּל מְלָאכָה שֶׁאָסוּר לַעֲשׂוֹתָהּ בַּשַּׁבָּת, אָסוּר לַעֲשׂוֹתָהּ בְּיוֹם־טוֹב. וּכְמוֹ שֶׁבְּשַׁבָּת אָסוּר לַעֲשׂוֹת אֲפִלּוּ עַל יְדֵי גוֹי, כְּמוֹ כֵן בְּיוֹם־טוֹב. וּכְשֵׁם שֶׁאָדָם מְצֻוֶּה עַל שְׁבִיתַת בְּהֶמְתּוֹ בַּשַּׁבָּת, כָּךְ הוּא מְצֻוֶּה בְּיוֹם־טוֹב. וְאֵין בֵּין יוֹם־טוֹב לַשַּׁבָּת, אֶלָּא אֹכֶל נֶפֶשׁ בִּלְבָד, שֶׁנֶּאֱמַר, אַךְ אֲשֶׁר יֵאָכֵל לְכָל נֶפֶשׁ הוּא לְבַדּוֹ יֵעָשֶׂה לָכֶם, דְּהַיְנוּ, לִישָׁה, אֲפִיָּה, שְׁחִיטָה וּבִשּׁוּל. וְהוֹצָאָה וְהַבְעָרָה מֻתָּרוֹת בְּיוֹם־טוֹב גַּם שֶׁלֹּא לְצֹרֶךְ אֹכֶל נֶפֶשׁ אֶלָּא לְצֹרֶךְ אַחֵר, כְּמוֹ שֶׁקִּבְּלוּ רַבּוֹתֵינוּ זִכְרוֹנָם לִבְרָכָה, דְּאָמְרִינָן בְּהוּ, מִתּוֹךְ שֶׁהֻתְּרוּ

---

34. Because a mitzvah that is constant has precedence, and also it may get cloudy and you will not be able to sanctify the moon, but the Megillah can be read later as well. (*Nodah B'Yehudah*).

35. Precedence to a *mitzva d'rabonon.*

1. This includes all rabbinically prohibited work.(*Peri Megadim M.Z.* 308, *Chayei Adam* 80:1)

2. However, the penalty of death applies to the desecration of Shabbos, but not Yom Tov.

3. See Chapter 87 for details.

4. Meiri *Maseches Beitzah* 36, *Beis Yosef* 305, *Magein Avraham* 246:12, *Vilna Gaon, Mishnah Berurah* 246:19. The *Remah* 246:3, *Rashi, Riva* and *Peri Chadash,* however, maintain that this is not prohibited on Yom Tov.

5. *Maseches Megillah* 7b.

6. *Exodus* 12:16.

7. Many types of *melachah* in the preparations of food are forbidden on Yom Tov (e.g. harvesting, grinding, squeezing grapes etc., threshing, sifting etc.). *Shulchan Aruch* 495:2 rules

15) If in the month of *Adar* (the moon) was not visible until the night of the fourteenth which is the time for the reading of the *Megillah,* the moon should be sanctified first and the *Megillah* read afterwards.[34] And if it became visible during the reading of the *Megillah,* then if there will be time even after the reading is concluded to sanctify the moon, the reading of the *Megillah* is not interrupted; but if by the time the *Megillah* is concluded, the time for sanctification will pass, and the entire congregation has not yet sanctified the moon, the reading is interrupted for the sanctifying, and afterwards the *Megillah* is concluded. But if only one person has not yet sanctified the moon, and if he stops to sanctify it, he will have to finish the *Megillah* alone, he must not interrupt, because the public reading of the miracle takes precedence.[35]

Chapter 98

The Laws of Yom Tov

1) Any[1] *melachah* (work) that may not be done on Shabbos, is also forbidden on Yom Tov.[2] And just as on Shabbos it is forbidden to have work done even by a non-Jew, so it is forbidden on Yom Tov. And just as a person is commanded to allow his animals to rest[3] on Shabbos, so, too, is he commanded on Yom Tov.[4] Yom Tov differs from Shabbos only with regard to the preparation of food,[5] for it says (concerning Yom Tov), "Only that which is eaten by any soul, that alone may be prepared by you."[6] This[7] includes kneading, baking, slaughtering, and cooking. Carrying,[8] and lighting a fire[9] are permitted on Yom Tov, even if not needed for preparing food, but for some other necessity.[10] Our Sages, of Blessed Memory,[11] had this rule by tradition regarding these (two *melachos*),[12] of which it is said: "Since these labors are permitted for the purpose of preparing

---

that these types are prohibited rabbinically, while the *Yerushalmi, Rashba, Reshal, Taz, Vilna Gaon* etc. rule that they are prohibited *de'oraisa.* They maintain that the Torah permitted only the kind of labor needed for one day's needs, but not the kind of labor usually done on a large scale.

8. See Chapter 82 for details.

9. You may only light a fire from an existing flame but you are not allowed to produce a new fire. See paragraph 31.

10. Most *poskim* maintain it is a *de'oraisa* prohibition to carry on Yom Tov if there is no necessity. *Rashi, Riaz* and possibly *Rif* and *Rambam* hold it is *derabanan.* (See *Biur Halachah* 518:1)

11. See *Maseches Beitzah* 12a.

12. Even though carrying and lighting a fire are not *melachos* performed directly on the food itself, they are necessary for its preparation. *Melachos* that are synonymous with food preparation such at baking and cooking are certainly included in this ruling and are permitted for other necessities. (*Maggid Mishneh, Magein Avraham, Vilna Gaon, Machatzis Hashekel, Mishnah Berurah* 518:1)

לְצֹרֶךְ אֹכֶל נֶפֶשׁ, הֻתְּרוּ נַמִּי שֶׁלֹּא לְצֹרֶךְ אֹכֶל נֶפֶשׁ, אֶלָּא לְצֹרֶךְ אַחֵר. וְנֵר שֶׁל יָארְצַייט, אֵין לְהַדְלִיק בְּיוֹם־טוֹב.

ב) אֵין עוֹשִׂין גְּבִינָה בְּיוֹם־טוֹב, וְאֵין עוֹשִׂין חֶמְאָה בְּיוֹם־טוֹב. וְכֵן אֵין מַעֲמִידִין חָלָב עַל יְדֵי קֵבָה אוֹ שְׁאָר דְּבָרִים, שֶׁיִּתְקַבֵּץ הֶחָלָב וְיִקָּפֶה. וְכֵן אָסוּר לִקְלוֹט שֶׁמֶן הֶחָלָב (סמעטן) מִן הֶחָלָב, אֶלָּא שֶׁיַּנִּיחַ מְעַט עַל הֶחָלָב הַתַּחְתּוֹן, כְּמוֹ בְּשַׁבָּת. וְגַם זֶה, אֵינוֹ מֻתָּר אֶלָּא מַה שֶּׁהוּא צָרִיךְ לְבוֹ בַּיּוֹם. אֲבָל לְצֹרֶךְ מָחָר, אָסוּר. מִשּׁוּם הֲכָנָה וְאִם חוֹשֵׁשׁ לְהֶפְסֵד, מֻתָּר לִקְלוֹט בְּעִנְיָן הַנִּזְכָּר עַל יְדֵי גוֹי.

ג) תְּבָלִין שֶׁאִם יִטְחַן אוֹתָם קֹדֶם יוֹם־טוֹב יָפִיגוּ טַעְמָן, מֻתָּר לְדוּכָן בְּיוֹם־טוֹב עַל יְדֵי שִׁנּוּי, כְּגוֹן שֶׁיַּטֶּה אֶת הַמַּכְתֶּשֶׁת לִצְדָדִין אוֹ שֶׁיָּדוּךְ עַל הַשֻּׁלְחָן וְכַיּוֹצֵא בוֹ. וְכֵן תַּמְכָא (קריין) שֶׁגּוֹרְרִין אוֹתוֹ עַל הַמּוֹרָג (ריב אייזען), לֹא יִגְרוֹר לְתוֹךְ קְעָרָה כְּדַרְכּוֹ בְּחֹל, אֶלָּא עַל מַפָּה. וְקָפֶה אֵין לִטְחוֹן בָּרֵיחַיִם, אֶלָּא יְדוּכוֹ בִּמְדוֹכָה וְעַל יְדֵי שִׁנּוּי. אֲבָל טוֹב יוֹתֵר לַעֲשׂוֹת הַכֹּל מֵעֶרֶב יוֹם־טוֹב. וּדְבָרִים שֶׁאֵינָם מְפִיגִין טַעְמָם, וַדַּאי צְרִיכִין לִזָּהֵר לְדוּכָן מֵעֶרֶב יוֹם־טוֹב. אַךְ אִם שָׁכַח, יֵשׁ לְהַתִּיר גַּם כֵּן עַל יְדֵי שִׁנּוּי. וְכָל הַנִּזְכָּר, אֵינוֹ מֻתָּר אֶלָּא מַה שֶּׁהוּא צָרִיךְ לְאוֹתוֹ הַיּוֹם וְלֹא לְמָחָר. וְיֵשׁ לְהַחְמִיר, שֶׁלֹּא לַעֲשׂוֹת אֶלָּא מַה שֶּׁצָּרִיךְ לוֹ עַתָּה לְאוֹתָהּ סְעוּדָה. וְגַם בִּדְכִיכַת מַצָּה, יֵשׁ לִזָּהֵר בָּזֶה.

ד) אָסוּר לְבַקֵּעַ עֵצִים אוֹ אֲפִלּוּ לְשַׁבְּרָן בְּיָד. וְאָסוּר לְלַקֵּט עֵצִים מִמָּקוֹם שֶׁהֵם מְפֻזָּרִין.

---

13. *Shulchan Aruch* 495:1 implies that *Melachah* is permitted for food requirements, even if it could have been done before Yom Tov and would have the same taste. Most *poskim*, however, *Rema, Maharil, Eliyahu Rabbah, Peri Chadash* etc. maintain that this is forbidden rabbinically, but permit it when done in an unconventional way (*shinui*). (*Rema, Ran*) If you were unable to prepare it before Yom Tov, due to an extreme emergency, you may prepare it on Yom Tov in the usual manner. (*Shulchan Aruch Harav, Mishnah Berurah*) If, however, you just didn't have time to do it before Yom Tov, you must do it in an unconventional way.

14. The *Rema* 518:1 rules that it is permitted to carry something because you fear it will get stolen or lost. *Mishnah Berurah* 518:6 rules it proper to be stringent, like the *Rosh, Tur, Maharil, Reshal* etc., who hold the necessity must be for a *mitzvah* or for something you need that day in particular (such as an ornament).

15. The *Kesav Sofer* responsum 65 permits this, but says it is still better to light it in the synagogue where you may light candles on Yom Tov, as it is an honor to the synagogue. (see *Kitzur Shulchan Aruch* 101:2) The *Misgeres Hashulchan* says the custom is to light them even at home but it is best to do it in the synagogue. This is also the view of *Biur Halachah* 514:5, who adds if you light it in your house, you should do it in the room where you eat.

food,[13] they are also permitted for purposes other than preparing food,"[14] but for some other necessity. However, a *yahrzeit* candle may not be lit on Yom Tov.[15]

2) You may not make cheese on Yom Tov, neither may you make butter on Yom Tov. Likewise, you may not curdle milk, by putting it in a stomach or by putting a substance into it to cause the milk to thicken and coagulate. Also,[16] you may not skim off the cream from the milk, unless you leave a little on the milk, the same way it must be done on Shabbos. This, too, is permitted only for as much as you need for that day, but not for the following day, because it amounts to preparing [on Yom Tov for a weekday, which is forbidden]. But if you fear that it will spoil, you may have it skimmed off in the aforementioned manner by a non-Jew.

3) Should spices that are ground before Yom Tov lose their flavor, [before Yom Tov,] they may be ground on Yom Tov, if done in an unconventional manner: such as inclining the mortar on its side,or by pounding them on the table, or similar unconventional procedures. Horseraddish that is grated on a (hand-)grater may not be grated into a dish as is usually done on weekdays, but onto a tablecloth.[17] You may not grind coffee with a grinder,[18] but you may pound it with a mortar in an unconventional manner. It is best to prepare everything on the day before Yom Tov. Foods that do not lose their flavor, certainly should be crushed the day before Yom Tov,[19] but if you forgot (to do it before), you are permitted to do it in an unconventional manner on Yom Tov. All that was mentioned is only permitted for as much as you need for that day, but not for the next day, and you should be stringent to prepare only as much as you need for that particular meal. When grinding matzoh,[20] you should also be careful about this.[21]

4) You may not split wood,[22] or even break it by hand.[23] It is also forbidden to gather wood from a place[24] where it is scattered about.

---

16. *Magein Avraham* 510:13, *Mishnah Berurah* 510:23.

17. *Chayei Adam* 83:3, *Mishnah Berurah* 504:19. You may not grind it in a grinding mill, even in an unusual manner, for it is an *uvdah de'chol,* which is forbidden, even in an unconventional fashion. (general rule of the *Magein Avraham* 504:7)

18. Not even in an unconventional manner. (*Panim Meiros, Peri Megadim, M.Z.* 504:1)

19. This is a rabbinical ordinance, so that Yom Tov is not spent working in the kitchen. (*Shulchan Aruch Harav* 495:7)

20. The matzoh is made from ground flour, and you are permitted to grind something that was previously ground, even in the usual manner. (*Mishnah Berurah* 504:20)

21. Not to grind more than you need for that meal.

22. If the logs are too large to use for fuel, you may cut them with a knife or by hand. (*Shulchan Aruch* 501:1) The *Kitzur Shulchan Aruch* refers to such wood that can be burned for fuel as is. See *Shulchan Aruch* 501:2. It is prohibited because it is a bother.

23. Cutting small pieces (like match sticks) is a *melachah de'oraisa* of grinding. (*Shulchan Aruch Harav,* see *Taz*)

24. I.e. in your yard, because it appears as though you are doing it for your weekday needs. If they are scattered in the field, gathering them is a *melachah de'oraisa* (*me'ameir*-gathering). You may not take wood from a field, even if it is not scattered. This is a rabbinical prohibition lest you gather scattered wood. (see *Magein Avraham* 501:6, *Shulchan Aruch Harav*)

ה) כְּשֶׁהוּא עוֹרֵךְ אֶת הָעֵצִים עַל הָאֲבָנִים לְהַבְעִיר אֵשׁ, אָסוּר, מִשּׁוּם דְּעוֹשֶׂה אֹהֶל, דַּהֲוֵי כְּמוֹ שְׁתֵּי מְחִצּוֹת וְגַג עַל גַּבֵּיהֶן. וְצָרִיךְ שֶׁיַּעֲשֶׂה שִׁנּוּי, דְּהַיְנוּ שֶׁיֹּאחַז אֶת הָעֵצִים בְּיָדוֹ וְיִתֵּן אֶת הָאֲבָנִים תַּחְתֵּיהֶם. וְכֵן כְּשֶׁמַּעֲמִיד קְדֵרָה עַל אֲבָנִים לְהַבְעִיר תַּחְתֶּיהָ, צָרִיךְ שֶׁיֹּאחַז אֶת הַקְּדֵרָה בְּיָדוֹ וְיַכְנִיס אֶת הָאֲבָנִים תַּחְתֶּיהָ, אֲבָל לֹא יַנִּיחֶנָּה עַל גַּבֵּי הָאֲבָנִים.

ו) אֵין נוֹפְחִין אֵשׁ בְּמַפּוּחַ, כְּדֵי שֶׁלֹּא יַעֲשֶׂה כְּדֶרֶךְ שֶׁהָאֻמָּנִין עוֹשִׂין. וְהָעוֹלָם נוֹהֲגִין הֶתֵּר בְּמַפּוּחַ שֶׁל בַּעֲלֵי־בָתִּים עַל יְדֵי שִׁנּוּי לְהָפְכוֹ מִלְמַעְלָה לְמַטָּה. אֲבָל בְּמַפּוּחַ שֶׁל אֻמָּנִין, אֲפִלּוּ עַל יְדֵי שִׁנּוּי, אָסוּר.

ז) מֻתָּר לִבְרֹר קִטְנִיּוֹת מַה שֶּׁהוּא צָרִיךְ לְאוֹתוֹ הַיּוֹם, אֲבָל לֹא בְּנָפָה ילֹא בִּכְבָרָה, וְגַם לֹא יִתְּנֵן לְתוֹךְ הַמַּיִם כְּדֵי שֶׁיָּצוּף הַפְּסֹלֶת אוֹ הָאֹכֶל, יָדוֹ וִילַקֵּט מַה שֶּׁהוּא נוֹחַ לוֹ יוֹתֵר. אִם נוֹחַ לְלַקֵּט הַפְּסֹלֶת, יְלַקֵּט הַפְּסֹלֶת. וְאִם נוֹחַ לוֹ לְלַקֵּט הָאֹכֶל, יְלַקֵּט הָאֹכֶל.

ח) קֶמַח שֶׁכְּבָר הָיָה מְרֻקָּד אֶלָּא שֶׁהוּא רוֹצֶה לְרַקְּדוֹ שֵׁנִית, יֵשׁ לְרַקְּדוֹ עַל יְדֵי גּוֹי אוֹ עַל יְדֵי שִׁנּוּי, דְּהַיְנוּ שֶׁיְּרַקֵּד בַּאֲחוֹרֵי הַנָּפָה. וְכֵן יַעֲשֶׂה בְּמַצּוֹת דּוּכוֹת. וְקֶמַח שֶׁעֲדַיִן לֹא הָיָה מְרֻקָּד, אָסוּר לְרַקְּדוֹ אֶלָּא עַל יְדֵי גּוֹי וּבְשִׁנּוּי. אָסוּר לִבְרֹר פְּסֹלֶת מִתּוֹךְ הַקֶּמַח, כְּגוֹן שֶׁנָּפְלוּ לְתוֹכוֹ צְרוֹרוֹת וְכַדּוֹמֶה וַאֲפִלּוּ לִבְרֹר מִתּוֹךְ מַצּוֹת כְּתוּתוֹת אֶת הַפֵּרוּרִים הַגְּדוֹלִים, אָסוּר.

ט) לִישָׁה מֻתֶּרֶת בְּיוֹם טוֹב. וּמִכָּל מָקוֹם לֹא יִמְדּוֹד אֶת הַקֶּמַח, אֶלָּא יִקַּח בְּאֹמֶד הַדַּעַת. וְאִם אֵינוֹ מְצַמְצֵם אֶת הַמִּדָּה, אֶלָּא פּוֹחֵת אוֹ מוֹסִיף, מֻתָּר.

י) בָּצֵק מְחֻתָּךְ (אִטְרִיּוֹת, פְּתִיתִים) שֶׁמְּבַשְּׁלִים לְאָכְלוֹ עִם רֹטֶב, יֵשׁ לָלוּשׁ בְּעֶרֶב יוֹם טוֹב, כִּי הַיְשָׁנִים, יוֹתֵר טוֹבִים. וְאִם לֹא לָשׁ מֵעֶרֶב יוֹם טוֹב, יָלוּשׁ בְּיוֹם טוֹב עַל יְדֵי שִׁנּוּי. דְּהַיְנוּ שֶׁאִם דַּרְכּוֹ לָלוּשׁ עַל דַּף,

---

25. These halachos apply only when the sides were set up on Yom Tov. If they were standing from before Yom Tov it is permitted. (*Eliyahu Rabbah, Mishnah Berurah* 502:13)

26. It looks as if you are making a tent. (*Shulchan Aruch* 502:1)

27. *Shulchan Aruch* 502:1.

28. Unlike Shabbos when, unless it is for immediate use, even separating food from refuse is a *melachah de'oraisa*. On Yom Tov, separating (*boreir*) is a *melachah de'oraisa* only when separating grain (from chaff etc.), which is usually done on a large scale. (*Shulchan Aruch Harav*

5) Arranging wood on top of the stones to start a fire is prohibited,[25] because you are[26] making a tent; for it is like erecting two walls upon which you are placing a roof. But you can do it in an unconventional manner, that is by holding the wood in your hand and placing the stones underneath. Similarly, when you place a pot on stones to light a fire underneath, you must hold the pot in your hand and place the stones under it; but you may not place it (the pot) on top of the stones.

6) You may not fan a fire with a bellow, because it is forbidden to do so in a professional manner. It is customary to permit (the use of) a domestic-type bellows by operating it in an unconventional manner,[27] holding it in an upside down position, but with a professional bellows it is forbidden, even in an unconventional manner.

7) You may sort all the legumes you need for that day,[28] but not with a sieve or strainer.[29] Neither may you put them in water so that the refuse or the edible part will float. But you may separate them by hand and pick out whatever is easier for you; if it is easier to pick out the refuse,—pick out the refuse,[30] and if it is easier to pick out the edible part,—pick out the edible part.

8) Flour that has already been sifted, but you wish to sift it a second time, should be sifted by a non-Jew or you may do it in an unconventional manner, turning the sieve upside down. Do the same when sifting crushed matzos. Flour that has never been sifted, may be sifted only by a non-Jew, in an unconventional way. It is forbidden to pick out refuse from flour; for example, if pebbles or something similar fell into it. It is forbidden to separate the large crumbs even from ground matzoh.[31]

9) Kneading is permitted on Yom Tov.[32] However, you should not measure the flour but should take it by estimate.[33] If you do not measure exactly, but take less or more, it is permitted to (use a measuring utensil).[34]

10) Dough for noodles and farfel used in soups should be kneaded on *erev* Yom Tov, for if they are older they taste better. But if you did not knead it *erev* Yom Tov, you may knead it on Yom Tov in an unconventional way.[35] For example, if you usually knead it on a board, you should knead it on a tablecloth or on something

---

510:3) The *Yeshuos Yaakov* 500:2 rules that separating two types of foods, even on Yom Tov is permitted only for immediate use.

29. Since usually a large quantity is separated with these utensils, it looks as though you are doing it for tomorrow's needs. (*Taz* 510:1, *Mishnah Berurah*)

30. *Taz* and *Shulchan Aruch Harav* say this is forbidden if you were able to do it before Yom Tov. *Biur Halachah* 510:2 says since you are not using a sieve etc., it is considered doing it in an unusual manner, and it is permitted even if you could have done it before Yom Tov. But, in such a case it is better to take the food from the refuse; and this is the prevailing custom.

31. *Magein Avraham* 504:9, *Maharil.* Because they are like two different foods.

32. Also see paragraph 23.

33. If inaccurate measuring will affect the quality, you may use a measuring utensil. (*Peri Megadim, Mishnah Berurah* 6:2)

34. *Bach, Tur.*

35. See footnote 13.

יָלוּשׁ עַל מַפָּה וְכַדּוֹמֶה. וְגַם תַּבְשִׁיל שֶׁאֵינוֹ מִתְקַלְקֵל, כְּגוֹן פֵּרוֹת יְבֵשִׁים וְכַדּוֹמֶה, יֵשׁ לְבַשְּׁלָם בְּעֶרֶב יוֹם טוֹב.

יא) עִסָּה שֶׁלָּשָׁהּ בְּיוֹם־טוֹב, מֻתָּר לְהַפְרִישׁ מִמֶּנָּה חַלָּה. אֲבָל אָסוּר לְשָׂרְפָהּ, דְּאֵין שׂוֹרְפִין קָדָשִׁים בְּיוֹם־טוֹב. וְגַם אָסוּר לַאֲפוֹתָהּ, מִשּׁוּם דְּאֵינָהּ רְאוּיָה לַאֲכִילָה, שֶׁהֲרֵי כֻּלָּנוּ טְמֵאֵי מֵתִים. וַאֲסוּרָה גַּם בְּטִלְטוּל. רַק בְּעוֹדָהּ בְּיָדוֹ, יַנִּיחֶנָּה בְּמָקוֹם הַמִּשְׁתַּמֵּר עַד מוֹצָאֵי יוֹם־טוֹב וְיִשְׂרְפֶנָּה. וְעִסָּה שֶׁלָּשׁ בְּעֶרֶב יוֹם־טוֹב, אָסוּר לְהַפְרִישׁ מִמֶּנָּה חַלָּה בְּיוֹם־טוֹב, אֶלָּא אוֹפֶה וְאוֹכֵל וּמַנִּיחַ קְצָת פַּת שֶׁיַּפְרִישׁ מִמֶּנּוּ בְּמוֹצָאֵי יוֹם־טוֹב. וְצָרִיךְ שֶׁיַּנִּיחַ פַּת כְּדֵי שֶׁיַּפְרִישׁ מִמֶּנּוּ וְיִשָּׁאֵר עוֹד קְצָת.

יב) אָסוּר לְגַבֵּל טִיט בְּיוֹם־טוֹב, וַאֲפִלּוּ עַל יְדֵי גוֹי. וְלָכֵן אִם צָרִיךְ לִסְתּוֹם אֶת הַתַּנּוּר שֶׁמַּטְמִינִין בּוֹ לְצֹרֶךְ שַׁבָּת, צָרִיךְ שֶׁיָּכִין לוֹ טִיט מְגֻבָּל מֵעֶרֶב יוֹם־טוֹב. גַּם לִקַּח רֶפֶשׁ מֵהָרְחוֹב אָסוּר, אֶלָּא אִם כֵּן הֱכִינוֹ בְּעֶרֶב יוֹם־טוֹב וְהִנִּיחוֹ בְּקֶרֶן זָוִית. וְנָכוֹן לִזָּהֵר שֶׁלֹּא לָטוּחַ אֶת הַטִּיט אוֹ הָרֶפֶשׁ, אֶלָּא יִסְתְּמוּהוּ בְּלֹא טִיחָה, מִשּׁוּם דְּיֵשׁ אוֹסְרִים אֲפִלּוּ לְצֹרֶךְ אֹכֶל נֶפֶשׁ.

יג) עוֹפוֹת שֶׁהֵם בְּבֵיתוֹ אוֹ בֶּחָצֵר הָעוֹמְדִים לַאֲכִילָה, וְהֵם כְּבָר הֻרְגְּלוּ בַּבַּיִת, שֶׁאֲפִלּוּ יוֹצְאִין לַחוּץ, בָּאִים לָעֶרֶב לְבֵיתוֹ, מֻתָּר לְצוּדָן אֲפִלּוּ חוּץ לֶחָצֵר לְצֹרֶךְ יוֹם־טוֹב לְשָׁחֳטָן. אֲבָל שֶׁלֹּא לְצֹרֶךְ אֲכִילָה, אָסוּר לְצוּדָן. וְאִם הֵם חֲדָשִׁים שֶׁלֹּא הֻרְגְּלוּ, אָסוּר לְצוּדָן אֲפִלּוּ לְצֹרֶךְ אֲכִילָה, אֲפִלּוּ כְּשֶׁהֵן בְּבֵיתוֹ. אַךְ בַּלַּיְלָה כְּשֶׁהֵן יוֹשְׁבִין, מֻתָּר לְקַחְתָּן. וּבְכָל עִנְיָן יֵשׁ לִזָּהֵר שֶׁיִּבְרוֹר מֵעֶרֶב יוֹם־טוֹב אֵיזֶה שֶׁהוּא רוֹצֶה לִשְׁחוֹט בְּיוֹם־טוֹב, כִּי שֶׁמָּא זֶה שֶׁיִּטּוֹל יִמָּצֵא כָּחוּשׁ, וְנִמְצָא שֶׁטִּלְטֵל שֶׁלֹּא לְצֹרֶךְ. וְעוֹפוֹת שֶׁאֵינָן עוֹמְדִין לַאֲכִילָה אֶלָּא לְבֵיצִים, הֵן מֻקְצִים.

---

36. (*Chayei Adam* 85:7).

37. See footnote 13. You are allowed to schedule these *melachos* for Yom Tov if you will do them in an unconventional manner. (*Magein Avraham, Chayei Adam*) The *Bigdei Yesha* questions this. (See *Mishnah Berurah 495:10)*

38. *Shulchan Aruch* 506:4.

39. Or with people who have been in contact with corpses. (See chapter 202 for details.)

40. When kneaded before Yom Tov, it is prohibited, rabbinically, because it looks like you are fixing it. When kneaded on Yom Tov, however, they did not prohibit it. (see *Mishnah Berurah* 506:17)

similar.[36] Cooked food that does not spoil, like dried fruits and similar food should be cooked on *erev* Yom Tov.[37]

11) If you knead dough on Yom Tov, you may take *challah* from it. But you may not burn (the *challah* portion), because holy things may not be burned on Yom Tov. It is also forbidden to bake (the *challah* portion)[38] because it is not fit to be eaten, for we are all considered as ritually unclean due to having come in contact with corpses.[39] And it is forbidden to handle (the *challah* portion), but while it is still in your hand, you should put it in a safe place until after Yom Tov, and then burn it. If you knead dough on *erev*Yom Tov, it is forbidden to take *challah* from it on Yom Tov,[40] but you may bake (the bread) and eat it, leaving a little bread from which to take (*challah*)[41] right after Yom Tov. The portion you leave should be sufficient for separating *challah* and have some left over.

12) It is forbidden to mix clay on Yom Tov, even if done by a non-Jew. Therefore if you (need clay) to seal the oven in which you warm your food, for Shabbos, you must prepare clay that was mixed, before Yom Tov. Also taking mud from the street is forbidden, unless it was prepared on *erev* Yom Tov, and placed in a corner. You should be careful not to smear the clay or mud, but you should seal the oven with it without smearing, for some authorities prohibit this (on Yom Tov) even to keep food warm.

13) Domesticated poultry that is kept in the house or in the yard for food, are permitted to be caught[42] so that you may slaughter them for your Yom Tov needs. But if not needed for food, it is forbidden to catch them.[43] And if they are new and not accustomed to (the house or yard), it is forbidden to catch them even for food, even while they are in the house.[44] But at night, when they are roosting, it is permitted to take them.[45] In any event, you must be careful to select those you intend to slaughter on Yom Tov before Yom Tov, lest the one you will take will prove to be too lean and you will have handled it needlessly.[46] Poultry, not kept for food, but for laying eggs, are *muktzeh*.[47]

---

41. This is only permitted outside of *Eretz Yisrael,* where separating *challah* is a rabbinic ordinance. In *Eretz Yisrael,* where it is a *de'oraisa,* you may not eat from it before separating *challah.* (*Mishnah Berurah* 506:21) If you want, you may knead a new dough on Yom Tov, put it next to the other dough, and separate the *challah* of both from the Yom Tov dough, (*Rema* 506:3)

42. Even with a trap. (*Mishnah Berurah* 497:17, *poskim*)

43. *Magein Avraham* 497:8.

44. Unless they enter a very narrow space. (*Mishnah Berurah* 497:17)

45. *Chayei Adam* 88:2.

46. This is a needless bother on Yom Tov. (*Mishnah Berurah* 497:18) Also if you catch it in an open space, it is considered a *melachah* of catching, without valid purpose. (*Sha'ar Hatziyun* 497:40)

47. *Mishnah Berurah* 497:16.

יד) יוֹנֵי שׁוֹבָךְ וְיוֹנֵי עֲלִיָּה, אַף־עַל־פִּי שֶׁכְּבָר הֻרְגְּלוּ לָבוֹא לְקִנֵּיהֶן, אָסוּר לְצוּדָן, אֲפִלּוּ הִזְמִינָן מֵעֶרֶב יוֹם־טוֹב.

טו) הָאֶגֶד שֶׁעַל רַגְלֵי הָעוֹפוֹת, מֻתָּר לְאַחַר שְׁחִיטָה לַחְתְּכוֹ אוֹ לְשָׂרְפוֹ. וּמֻתָּר לִתְפּוֹר עוֹפוֹת שֶׁמְּמַלְּאִין אוֹתָן, אַךְ צָרִיךְ לִזָּהֵר לְהַכְנִיס אֶת הַחוּט בְּתוֹךְ הַמַּחַט בְּעֶרֶב יוֹם־טוֹב. וְאִם לֹא הִכְנִיסוֹ מֵעֶרֶב יוֹם־טוֹב, אָסוּר לְהַכְנִיסוֹ בְּיוֹם־טוֹב. לְאַחַר שֶׁתְּפָרוֹ, מֻתָּר לִשְׂרוֹף אֶת הַחוּט הַנִּשְׁאָר.

טז) דָּגִים שֶׁבְּבִיבָר, אִם אִי אֶפְשָׁר לְתָפְסָן בְּיָדַיִם אֶלָּא בִּכְלִי, אָסוּר לְתָפְסָן אֲבָל אִם אֶפְשָׁר לְתָפְסָן בְּיָדַיִם, מֻתָּר לְתָפְסָן אֲפִלּוּ בִּכְלִי. וְאִם יֵשׁ שָׁם דָּגִים הַרְבֵּה, צָרִיךְ שֶׁיַּזְמִין בְּעֶרֶב יוֹם־טוֹב אֶת זֶה שֶׁהוּא רוֹצֶה לָקַחַת בְּיוֹם־טוֹב, שֶׁיַּעֲשֶׂה בּוֹ אֵיזֶה סִימָן. וְאִם צָרִיךְ לְכֻלָּם, יַזְמִין אֶת כֻּלָּם, דְּהַיְנוּ שֶׁיֹּאמַר בְּעֶרֶב יוֹם־טוֹב, כָּל אֵלּוּ הַדָּגִים אֲנִי מַזְמִין לְיוֹם־טוֹב.

יז) סָפֵק צֵידָה וְסָפֵק מוּכָן, אָסוּר. וּלְצֹרֶךְ גָּדוֹל, יֵשׁ לְהָקֵל בְּיוֹם־טוֹב שֵׁנִי, אַךְ לֹא בְּרֹאשׁ־הַשָּׁנָה.

יח) כָּל בַּעֲלֵי־חַיִּים שֶׁהֵן מֻקְצִין, אָסוּר לְהַשְׁקוֹתָן אוֹ לִתֵּן לָהֶם מְזוֹנוֹת בְּסָמוּךְ לָהֶם, אֶלָּא בְּרִחוּק קְצָת.

יט) שָׁחַט עוֹף וְנִמְצָא טְרֵפָה, אָסוּר לְטַלְטְלוֹ, כְּמוֹ שְׁאָר מֻקְצֶה. אֲבָל אִם שָׁחַט בְּהֵמָה וְנִמְצֵאת טְרֵפָה, מֻתָּר לְהַצְנִיעָהּ בְּמָקוֹם שֶׁלֹּא תִתְקַלְקֵל. וְאִם אִי אֶפְשָׁר לְהַצְנִיעָהּ שֶׁלֹּא תִתְקַלְקֵל, מֻתָּר לְמָכְרָהּ לְגוֹי בְּאֹפֶן שֶׁלֹּא יִקְצוֹץ דָּמִים וְלֹא יִשְׁקוֹל. וְאוּלַי גַּם בְּאַוָּזִים מְפֻטָּמִים דִּשְׁכִיחַ בְּהוּ טְרֵפוֹת, יֵשׁ לְהָקֵל.

כ) אֵין לִשְׁחוֹט בְּהֵמָה בְּיוֹם־טוֹב אֶלָּא לְצֹרֶךְ גָּדוֹל. וְאָסוּר לִמְכּוֹר

---

48. Wild birds that do not belong to anyone.

49. Because they are not domesticated, they are hard to catch and are not considered as though they are already caught. Even if they are easy to catch, you may not catch them. Since they find their food elsewhere, they are like other wild fowl. (*Magein Avraham.* (see *Mishnah Berurah* 497:28)

50. If they are small and not able to fly and escape, it is sufficient to designate the ones you want before Yom Tov. (see *Shulchan Aruch* 497:9–10)

51. So you will not desecrate Yom Tov by cutting the string to the proper length. (*Magein Avraham, Rabbeinu Yerucham*)

14) It is forbidden to catch doves of a dove-cote or doves living in an attic,[48] even though they are accustomed to return to their nests[49] and even if you selected them before Yom Tov.[50]

15) It is permitted to cut or burn the rings around the legs of poultry after slaughtering. You may also sew up poultry when you stuff them, but you must be careful to thread the needle on *erev* Yom Tov.[51] If you did not thread it before Yom Tov, it is forbidden to thread it on Yom Tov.[52] After the poultry is sewn up, you may burn the leftover thread.[53]

16) It is forbidden to catch fish in a pond, that cannot be caught with your hands, but (only) with a utensil. But if you can catch them with your hands, you may catch them, even with a utensil.[54] If there are many fish in the pond you must designate before Yom Tov the one you wish to take on Yom Tov, by making a mark on it; and if you need all of them, you must designate all of them by saying before Yom Tov: "I am designating all of these fish for Yom Tov."

17) If you are in doubt whether something was caught or prepared on Yom Tov, it is forbidden to be used. If it is very urgent, you may be lenient on the second day of Yom Tov, but not on [the second day] Rosh Hashanah.

18) Living creatures that are *muktzeh*[55] may not be given drink, nor may their food be placed within a close reach, but it should be placed a short distance away.

19) If you slaughtered poultry, and it was found to be *tereifah,*[56] you are forbidden to handle it, similar to other *muktzeh* (items). But if you slaughtered an animal and it was found to be *tereifah,* you may put it in a place where it will not spoil. But if it is impossible to put it away, so that it will not spoil, you may sell it to a non-Jew, provided that no price is set, and it is not weighed. Perhaps with regard to fattened geese among which *tereifos* are generally found, you may be lenient.[57]

20) You may not slaughter an animal on Yom Tov[58] unless it is absolutely

52. *Magein Avraham, Mishnah Berurah* 509:16.

53. Burning it and cutting it are halachically identical, but the custom is to burn it. (*Magein Avraham* 509:9, *Mishnah Berurah* 509:18)

54. *Taz, Eliyahu Rabbah.* But the *Mishnah Berurah* 497:14 says you should consider the opinion of the *Peri Chadash* and *Shulchan Aruch Harav,* who do not permit the use of a utensil. See *Shulchan Aruch* 497 for details of these *halachos.*

55. *Shulchan Aruch* 497:12, *Shulchan Aruch Harav.* This is so that you will not inadvertantly take them for eating in violation of *muktzeh.* This *halachah,* therefore, applies only to kosher species. The *Shulchan Aruch* 497:7 says this prohibition applies only to living creatures in a situation where catching them is a *melachah* and we fear you might do so if you put food near them. But your domestic creatures, even if *muktzeh,* should be fed on Yom Tov. This is the ruling of the *Peri Chadash* and *Mishnah Berurah* (497:4.)(see also *Biur Halachah*)

56. Anyone of the eighteen types of bodily injuries or defects that prohibit eating it.

57. It is not clear if the *Kitzur Shulchan Aruch* is referring to selling them in the manner described or even to handling them. The *Sha'ar Hatziyun* 497:76, and *Chemed Moshe* permit handling them also.

58. But poultry is permitted. (*Chayei Adam, Mishnah Berurah* 495:50)

אֶת הַבָּשָׂר בְּמִשְׁקָל וְלֹא בִּקְצִיצַת דָּמִים, אֶלָּא נוֹתֵן לוֹ אֵיזֶה חֵלֶק סְתָם וּלְאַחַר יוֹם־טוֹב יְשַׁלֵּם לוֹ.

כא) הַשּׁוֹחֵט בְּהֵמָה בְּיוֹם־טוֹב, טוֹב שֶׁלֹּא לִבְדֹּק אֶת הָרֵאָה עַד לְאַחַר שֶׁיַּפְשִׁיט אֶת הָעוֹר, כִּי אִם יִבְדֹּק וְתִמָּצֵא טְרֵפָה, אָסוּר לְהַפְשִׁיטָהּ. מֻתָּר לְטַלְטֵל אֶת הָעוֹר מִבְּהֵמָה שֶׁשְּׁחָטָהּ הַיּוֹם כְּדֵי לְהַצְנִיעָהּ, אֲבָל לֹא לְשָׁטְחָהּ עַל גַּבֵּי יְתֵדוֹת. וּשְׁאָר עוֹרוֹת, אֲסוּרִין בְּטִלְטוּל. וְכֵן הַנּוֹצוֹת מֵעוֹף שֶׁשְּׁחָטוּ הַיּוֹם, מֻתָּר לְטַלְטְלָן לְהַצְנִיעָן. אֲבָל שְׁאָר נוֹצוֹת, אָסוּר לְטַלְטְלָן.

כב) מֻתָּר לִמְלוֹחַ בָּשָׂר לְהַכְשִׁירוֹ מִדָּמוֹ, אֲפִלּוּ הָיָה אֶפְשָׁר לְמָלְחוֹ מֵאֶתְמוֹל. וְדַוְקָא אִם יֵשׁ בּוֹ לְצֹרֶךְ הַיּוֹם. וְאִם יֵשׁ לוֹ בָּשָׂר יוֹתֵר וְהוּא מִתְיָרֵא שֶׁלֹּא יִתְקַלְקֵל, מֻתָּר לִמְלוֹחַ הַכֹּל בְּיַחַד אֲפִלּוּ הַרְבֵּה, גַּם מַה שֶּׁאֵינוֹ לְצֹרֶךְ הַיּוֹם, דְּהַכֹּל חֲדָא טִרְחָא הִיא. אֲבָל בָּשָׂר שֶׁכְּבָר נִמְלַח מִדָּמוֹ, וְכֵן דָּגִים שֶׁהָיָה אֶפְשָׁר לְמָלְחָן בְּעֶרֶב יוֹם־טוֹב, אָסוּר לְמָלְחָן בְּיוֹם־טוֹב.

כג) כְּשֶׁעוֹשֶׂה מַעֲשֵׂה אוֹפֶה בְּיוֹם־טוֹב, אָסוּר לַעֲשׂוֹת בּוֹ צִיּוּרִים עַל יְדֵי דְפוּס אוֹ בַּיָּד לַעֲשׂוֹת מִן הָעִסָּה אֵיזֶה צִיּוּרִים כְּעוֹפוֹת וְכַדּוֹמֶה.

כד) אָסוּר לְמָרֵחַ שׁוּם דָּבָר בְּיוֹם־טוֹב כְּמוֹ בְּשַׁבָּת. וְלָכֵן אָסוּר לְחַמֵּם נֵר שֶׁל שַׁעֲוָה אוֹ שֶׁל חֵלֶב לְדַבְּקוֹ בַּמְּנוֹרָה אוֹ בַכֹּתֶל, שֶׁמָּא יְמָרֵחַ. וְאִם הַשְּׁפוֹפֶרֶת מְמֻלֵּאת בְּחֵלֶב, יָכוֹל לְנַקוֹתָהּ בְּדָבָר שֶׁאֵינוֹ מֻקְצֶה.

---

59. *Magein Avraham* 498:16. This is the custom, even when *treifos* are not very common. (*Mishnah Berurah* 498:49)

60. *Shulchan Aruch* 497:16. Because it is a *melachah* not for the purpose of food. (*Mishnah Berurah*)

61. That is clearly done to dry the hide, and we are concerned you may salt it, too, which is a *melachah de'oraisa*. (*Mishnah Berurah* 499:5, *Magein Avraham* etc.)

62. This applies only when attached to their stems. But when detached, they are soft, and can be used to lie on, and are not *muktzeh*. (*Shulchan Aruch Harav* 302:3)

63. See Chapter 36 for details.

64. *Ramah* 500:5. Because after the *kashering* process, the meat must be kept salted in order to keep it from spoiling, and this is detrimental to its taste.(*Shulchan Aruch Harav*) This is true when it is warm and you have no access to refrigeration.

65. See *Shulchan Aruch* 500:5.

66. *Rashi*. We maintain that you have to salt both sides of the meat, so there is a little more labor when there is more meat. Even so, since the prohibition involved is not *de'oraisa*,

necessary.[59] It is forbidden to sell meat by weight and at a set price. But you may give someone a piece of meat to be paid for after Yom Tov.

21) When you slaughter an animal (on Yom Tov) it is best not to examine the lungs until after you have skinned it; for if you examine it and it is found to be *tereifah,* it is forbidden to skin it.[60] You are allowed to handle the hide of an animal that was slaughtered that day in order to put it away. But not to spread it on posts.[61] Other hides are absolutely forbidden to be handled. Also, feathers from a bird that was slaughtered that day, may be handled in order to put them away. But it is forbidden to handle any other feathers.[62]

22) It is permited to salt meat to draw off the blood,[63] even if it could have been salted the day before Yom Tov,[64] provided you need it for that day. If you have more meat (than you need) and fear it might spoil, you may salt all the meat together,[65] no matter how much there is, and even that which is not needed for today, for it involves the same labor.[66] But meat that has already been salted and its blood (drawn off),[67] and fish that could have been salted[68] on *erev* Yom Tov, is forbidden to be salted on Yom Tov.

23) When baking pastry on Yom Tov, it is forbidden to shape it into figures either by using a mold or by hand.[69]

24) Levelling [or smearing] is forbidden[70] on Yom Tov as on Shabbos. Therefore, it is forbidden to warm[71] a candle of wax or of tallow to make it stick to the candlestick or the wall, for you might inadvertently smear it.[72] If the socket (of the candlestick) is full of tallow,[73] you may clean it with an object that is not *muktzeh.*

---

the Sages were lenient, if there is concern that the meat will spoil. (*Mishnah Berurah* 500:22, *Shulchan Aruch Harav*)

67. *Magein Avraham.* Because it is obvious that you are not salting it to eat it now, for then you would cook it and you wouldn't re-salt it. But you may resalt it on the second night of Yom Tov, for it could be you want it for the Yom Tov morning meal. The first night of Yom Tov, you may not re-salt it because you should have done it before Yom Tov. (see *Machatzis Hashekel* 500:17)

68. Small fish that spoil after a while, when salted, may be salted on Yom Tov. (*Mishnah Berurah* 500:26, *poskim*) Even fish that do not get spoiled in salt may be salted on Yom Tov if they were cut open before Yom Tov. (*Machatzis Hashekel* 500:11)

69. *Chayei Adam* 92:3.

70. A *toladah* of scraping (מְמַחֵק). It is forbidden to spread or smear something in order to make it level.

71. *Eliyahu Rabbah* 514 says if it is not warmed, it is permitted. The *Pri Megadim* maintains it is not.

72. *Magein Avraham* 514:6.

73. The piece of tallow is not *muktzeh* on Yom Tov because you can put on a wick and light it. (*Magein Avraham* 499:9) But the *Shulchan Aruch Harav* 499:11 says not to move it unless it is urgent.

כה) אָסוּר לְכַבּוֹת אֵשׁ בְּיוֹם־טוֹב. וַאֲפִלּוּ לִגְרוֹם כִּבּוּי, אָסוּר. וְלָכֵן אָסוּר לְהַעֲמִיד נֵר דּוֹלֵק בְּמָקוֹם שֶׁיָּכוֹל לְנַשֵּׁב הָרוּחַ וּלְכַבּוֹתוֹ. וְאַף־עַל־פִּי שֶׁעַתָּה אֵין הָרוּחַ מְנַשֶּׁבֶת. וְכֵן אָסוּר לִפְתּוֹחַ דֶּלֶת אוֹ חַלּוֹן כְּנֶגֶד הַנֵּר הַדּוֹלֵק, כִּדְלְעֵיל סִימָן פ סָעִיף ב'.

כו) מֻתָּר לְכַסּוֹת אֶת הָאֵשׁ בִּכְלִי אוֹ בְּאֵפֶר מוּכָן. וְאַף־עַל־פִּי שֶׁאֶפְשָׁר שֶׁיִּכְבֶּה קְצָת עַל יְדֵי הַכִּסּוּי, מִכָּל מָקוֹם כֵּיוָן שֶׁאֵינוֹ מְכַוֵּן לְכִבּוּי (וְגַם הָוֵי מְלָאכָה שֶׁאֵינָהּ צְרִיכָה לְגוּפָהּ). מֻתָּר לְצֹרֶךְ יוֹם־טוֹב. וְדַוְקָא לְצֹרֶךְ אוֹתוֹ הַיּוֹם. אֲבָל לְצֹרֶךְ הַלַּיְלָה, אָסוּר, דְּהָא הַלַּיְלָה שַׁיָּךְ לְיוֹם שֵׁנִי.

כז) אֵין מַגְעִילִין וְאֵין מְלַבְּנִין כֵּלִים שֶׁנֶּאֶסְרוּ. וְדִין טְבִילַת כֵּלִים עַיֵּן לְעֵיל סוֹף סִימָן לז.

כח) דִּין הֲדָחַת כֵּלִים בְּיוֹם־טוֹב, כְּמוֹ בְּשַׁבָּת. וְאָסוּר לַהֲדִיחָן מִיּוֹם־טוֹב רִאשׁוֹן לְיוֹם־טוֹב שֵׁנִי.

כט) אָסוּר לְהַסִּיק כְּדֵי לְחַמֵּם אֶת הַבַּיִת, אֶלָּא אִם הַקּוֹר גָּדוֹל, שֶׁהַמַּאֲכָלִים נִקְרָשִׁים, וַהֲוֵי צֹרֶךְ אֹכֶל נֶפֶשׁ. אֲבָל אִם אֵין הַקּוֹר גָּדוֹל, אָסוּר. רַק עַל יְדֵי גוֹי, מֻתָּר.

ל) מֻתָּר לְחַמֵּם מַיִם לִרְחוֹץ יָדָיו, אֲבָל לֹא כָּל גּוּפוֹ. וּלְצֹרֶךְ תִּינוֹק, אִם צְרִיכִין לְרָחֲצוֹ, אָסוּר גַּם כֵּן לְחַמֵּם מַיִם בִּשְׁבִילוֹ, אֲפִלּוּ עַל יְדֵי גוֹי. אַךְ יְכוֹלִין לְהַרְבּוֹת בִּשְׁבִילוֹ, דְּהַיְנוּ כְּשֶׁצְּרִיכִין קְצָת מַיִם לְבַשֵּׁל, מֻתָּר לְחַמֵּם אֲפִלּוּ יוֹרָה גְדוֹלָה, רַק שֶׁיִּתֵּן כָּל הַמַּיִם קֹדֶם שֶׁהֶעֱמִידָהּ עַל הָאֵשׁ,

---

74. Unless it is life threatening or for the purpose of food. For example, if your food will burn, or your only dishes etc. will burn, and you haven't any other way to alleviate the situation. (see *Shulchan Aruch* 514:1)

75. *Magein Avraham, Biur Halachah.*

76. To preserve the fire for later use.

77. See Chapter 99:4.

78. *Vilna Gaon.* Even though you are allowed to roast meat on coals, which will surely extinguish some of the coals, in that case, it is done for the immediate preparation of food, while, here, you are merely preserving it for later preparation; and therefore it is forbidden, if extinguishing it is inevitable (*Magein Avraham*). But some *poskim* permit this, even though you will inevitably extinguish part of it, since this is not your intention and is for the sake of food preparations (*Peri Chadash, Reshal*). The *Mishnah Berurah* 502:9 mentions both opinions.

79. And is, therefore, not a *de'oraisa* violation according to most *poskim.*

80. *Ramah* 509:5. Because boiling the water for this purpose is only a preparation to prepare food, and should have been done before Yom Tov (*Or Zarua, Magein Avraham*), or

25) It is forbidden to extinguish a fire on Yom Tov.[74] It is even forbidden to extinguish it indirectly. Therefore, it is forbidden to place a burning candle where the wind may blow it out, even though when you place it no wind is blowing.[75] It is also forbidden to open a door or a window opposite a burning candle. See above chapter 80:2

26) It is permitted to cover a fire (on Yom Tov)[76] with a vessel or ashes that have been prepared (before Yom Tov).[77] Even though it may be slightly extinguished by being covered,[78] nevertheless since your intention is not to extinguish it, (and it is a *melachah* not needed for its own sake),[79] it is permitted for the needs of the Yom Tov. But it is permitted only when you need it for that day. But for the needs of the (following) night it is forbidden, for the night belongs to the second day.

27) You may not kasher utensils by placing them in boiling water,[80] nor by heating them until red hot,[81] once they have become forbidden for use.[82] For the laws of immersing (new) utensils on Yom Tov, see Chapter 37 above.

28) The law regarding washing dishes on Yom Tov is the same as on Shabbos.[83] It is forbidden to wash dishes on the first day Yom Tov to be used on the second day of Yom Tov.

29) It is forbidden to make a fire in order to heat the house, unless the cold is so severe that the food congeals; then it is considered as required for the preparation of food. But if the cold is not so severe, it is forbidden.[84] If done by a non-Jew, it is permitted

30) It is permitted to heat water to wash your hands[85] but not for bathing your whole body.[86] If you need (warm) water to bathe a child, it is also forbidden to heat the water for him, even through a non-Jew.[87] But you may heat a larger quantity because of him; thus when you need a little water for cooking, it is permitted to heat even a large kettle,[88] provided you pour in all the water before placing it on the fire

---

because it looks like fixing vessels, which is only a preparation of preparing etc. (*Eliyohu Rabbah, Vilna Gaon*) (see *Mishnah Berurah, Sha'ar Hatziyun* 509:31)

81. *Shulchan Aruch* 509:5.

82. Having absorbed a non-kosher product.

83. *Ramah* 509:7. (see Chapter 80:26)

84. The prevailing custom is that even a Jew is permitted to light the furnace, even if just slightly cold. (*Rema, Vilna Gaon, Mishnah Berurah* 511:7)

85. Face, hands, and feet, (*Mishnah Berurah* 511:9, *poskim)* Because this is something everyone needs to do. In our times, when people wear shoes, washing the feet may not be in this category.

86. Warming the water just enough to take the chill out is permitted according to some *poskim*. (see *Sha'ar Hatziyun*)

87. *Rema.* This is true according to all *poskim*. (*Mishnah Berurah* 511:13) In the event it was warmed on Yom Tov for this purpose, even by a Jew, you may bathe the child in it if he is normally bathed every day. This is forbidden for an adult, even if the water was warmed for cooking. (See *Ramah, Magein Avraham* and *Mishnah Berurah* 511:12)

88. And use the extra water to bathe the child.

וְלֹא יוֹסִיף אַחַר כָּךְ. וְאִם הַתִּינוֹק חוֹלֶה קְצָת, מֻתָּר לְחַמֵּם בִּשְׁבִילוֹ עַל יְדֵי גּוֹי.

לא) אָסוּר לְהוֹצִיא אֵשׁ בֵּין מֵאֶבֶן בֵּין מִזְּכוּכִית (ברענגלאז) בֵּין מֵעֵצִים הַנַּעֲשִׂים בְּגָפְרִית (צינדהעלצעל).

לב) אֵין עוֹשִׂין מֻגְמָר, דְּהַיְנוּ לְפַזֵּר מִינֵי בְשָׂמִים עַל הַגֶּחָלִים, בֵּין לְהָרִיחַ בֵּין לְגַמֵּר אֶת הַבַּיִת אוֹ כֵלִים, דִּכְתִיב לְכָל נֶפֶשׁ, וּבָעִינַן דָּבָר הַשָּׁוֶה לְכָל נֶפֶשׁ. אֲבָל מֻגְמָר, אֵינוֹ נִצְרָךְ אֶלָּא לִמְפֻנָּקִים וּמְעֻנָּגִים. וּבְעִנְיַן עִשּׁוּן הַטִּיטוּן, נֶחְלְקוּ הַפּוֹסְקִים זִכְרוֹנָם לִבְרָכָה. וְגַם לְהַמְּקִלִּים צְרִיכִין לִזָּהֵר שֶׁלֹּא לְהַדְלִיק בִּנְיָר וְלֹא בְגַחֶלֶת, מִשּׁוּם דִּכְשֶׁזּוֹרְקָן עַל הָאָרֶץ נַעֲשֶׂה כִּבּוּי, וּבְנָקֵל יוּכַל לִטְעוֹת לַעֲשׂוֹת כֵּן בְּיוֹם־טוֹב, כֵּיוָן שֶׁרָגִיל לַעֲשׂוֹת כֵּן בַּחֹל. וְאִם כְּתוּבִים עַל הַנְּיָר אוֹתִיּוֹת בִּכְתָב אוֹ בִדְפוּס וְהוּא שׂוֹרְפוֹ, אִכָּא גַּם אִסּוּר מְחִיקָה, אֶלָּא צָרִיךְ לְהַדְלִיק מִשַּׁלְהֶבֶת. וְגַם אֵין לְעַשֵּׁן מִתּוֹךְ כְּלִי (פייף) חֲדָשָׁה. גַּם אָסוּר לַחְתּוֹךְ אֶת הַטִּיטוּן בְּיוֹם־טוֹב. וְנִרְאֶה דְּהוּא הַדִּין דְּאָסוּר לְהָסִיר אֶת הַקְּצָווֹת מִן סִיגָרִין.

לג) דָּבָר שֶׁאֵינוֹ מְלָאכָה גְמוּרָה וְאָסוּר לַעֲשׂוֹת בְּשַׁבָּת מִשּׁוּם רְפוּאָה לְחוֹלֶה שֶׁאֵין בּוֹ סַכָּנָה, גַּם בְּיוֹם רִאשׁוֹן שֶׁל יוֹם־טוֹב וְכֵן בִּשְׁנֵי יָמִים טוֹבִים שֶׁל רֹאשׁ־הַשָּׁנָה, אָסוּר לַעֲשׂוֹתוֹ כִּי אִם עַל יְדֵי גוֹי. אֲבָל בְּיוֹם־טוֹב שֵׁנִי (חוּץ מֵרֹאשׁ־הַשָּׁנָה), מֻתָּר לַעֲשׂוֹתוֹ גַּם עַל יְדֵי יִשְׂרָאֵל. אֲבָל מְלָאכָה גְמוּרָה, אָסוּר לַעֲשׂוֹתָהּ לְחוֹלֶה שֶׁאֵין בּוֹ סַכָּנָה, אֲפִלּוּ בְּיוֹם־טוֹב שֵׁנִי, כִּי אִם עַל יְדֵי גוֹי (וְיֵשׁ לַעֲשׂוֹת שְׁאֵלַת חָכָם).

לד) הוֹצָאָה מֻתֶּרֶת בְּיוֹם־טוֹב, אֲפִלּוּ מַה שֶּׁאֵינוֹ לְצֹרֶךְ אֹכֶל נֶפֶשׁ, וּבִלְבַד שֶׁיְּהֵא בָּהּ אֵיזֶה צֹרֶךְ אַחֵר. אֲבָל שֶׁלֹּא לְצֹרֶךְ כְּלָל, אָסוּר לְהוֹצִיא,

---

89. *Chayei Adam, Mishnah Berurah.*

90. It is a preparation for preparing food and could have been done before Yom Tov. (*Rambam, Rashba, Mishnah Berurah* 502:1) In the event you made a fire on Yom Tov, the *Taz* and *Toras Hashmarim* (*Yoreh Dei'ah* 197) rule that you may not use it, but the *Rashbah, Magein Avraham, Shulchan Aruch Harav, Mishnah Berurah* 502 permit it.

91. The prohibition involved is that of extinguishing fire. The *Magein Avraham* 514:4, *Korban Nessanel* (*Maseches Beitzah* Chapter 2) and *Chayei Adam* 95:13 prohibit smoking on Yom Tov, for it is not necessary for everyone. Some halachic authorities rule that you are not

and do not add any water after that. If the child is slightly ill, it is permitted to have the water heated for him through a non-Jew.[89]

31) It is forbidden[90] to touch off a fire either from a flintstone, a glass or a match.

32) You may not make *mugmar,* that is to scatter various spices over coals, either in order to smell its fragrance, or to perfume the house or clothing, for it is written "For everyone," (Ex. 12:16). meaning, it must be of a nature that everyone requires. But perfuming is only a necessity for dainty and indulgent people. With regard to smoking tobacco, the *poskim,* of blessed memory, disagree.[91] Even according to those who are lenient, you must be careful not to light it with a (burning) piece of paper or a coal, because when you throw these on the ground, they will be extinguished.[92] It is easy to make the mistake of doing it on Yom Tov, since you are used to doing so during the week. If there are letters on the paper, either written or printed, and you burn it, the prohibition of erasing also applies. Rather, you must light it from a (pre-existing) flame. You also may not smoke a new pipe.[93] It is also forbidden to grind the tobacco on Yom Tov. It would seem that it is also forbidden to cut off the tips of cigars.[94]

33) Something which is not a full-scale *melachah*[95] and yet is forbidden on Shabbos in order to cure a patient who is not critically ill, is also forbidden even on the first day of Yom Tov, or on both days of Rosh Hashanah, unless it is done by a non-Jew. But on the second day of Yom Tov, (except for the second day of Rosh Hashanah), it may be done, even by a Jew.[96] But a full-scale *melachah* may not be performed for a patient who is not critically ill, even on the second day of Yom Tov unless it is done by a non-Jew. (You should consult a halachic authority before taking any actions in this matter.)

34) Carrying is permitted on Yom Tov. It is permitted to carry even things that are not needed for preparing food, provided there is some other need for it, but if it is totally unnecessary, it is forbidden to be carried out [of the house] unless it is to

---

allowed to smoke at all because it is a proven health hazard. On Yom Tov there is more reason to be stringent.

92. You may not light a cigarette from another cigarette because it partially extinguishes the first one. (*Minchas Yom Tov*)

93. This refers only to an unglazed potsherd pipe, which becomes stronger from heat. It does not apply to wooden pipes. (see *Kerem Shlomoh* and *Misgeross Hashulchan*)

94. To open its ends. You may also not bite off the ends and, maybe, not even burn them when you begin smoking, because it may be considered making a vessel (in this case a cigar) on Yom Tov. (see *Minchas Yom Tov, Mikra Kodesh*)

95. This means it is a rabbinic prohibition, not a *de'oraisa.* See Chapter 91 for details of this *halachah.*

96. It is permitted, even if done in the usual manner, and even if the illness is local and does not affect the whole body. On the first day of Yom Tov, a Jew may do it only in an unconventional manner, even if the illness affects the whole body. (*Shulchan Aruch Harav* 496:45)

כִּי אִם בְּמָקוֹם שֶׁמֻּתָּר לְהוֹצִיא בַּשַּׁבָּת. וְגַם לְצֹרֶךְ אֹכֶל נֶפֶשׁ, כְּגוֹן כַּדֵּי יַיִן, לֹא יִשָּׂא מַשָּׂא גָדוֹל כְּמוֹ שֶׁהוּא עוֹשֶׂה בַּחֹל, אֶלָּא יְשַׁנֶּה. וְאִם אִי־אֶפְשָׁר לְשַׁנּוֹת, כְּגוֹן שֶׁיֵּשׁ לוֹ הַרְבֵּה אוֹרְחִים, עוֹשֶׂה כְּדַרְכּוֹ.

לה) כָּל הַמְּלָאכוֹת הַמֻּתָּרוֹת לַעֲשׂוֹת בְּיוֹם־טוֹב, זֶהוּ דַוְקָא לְצֹרֶךְ אָדָם, אֲבָל לֹא לְצֹרֶךְ בְּהֵמָה, דִּכְתִיב, יֵעָשֶׂה לָכֶם, וְדָרְשִׁינָן, לָכֶם וְלֹא לִבְהֵמָה. וְלָכֵן אָסוּר לְבַשֵּׁל אוֹ לְהוֹצִיא אֵיזֶה דָּבָר לְצֹרֶךְ בְּהֵמָה, כְּמוֹ בַּשַּׁבָּת.

לו) אָסוּר לְבַשֵּׁל אוֹ לֶאֱפוֹת לְצֹרֶךְ גּוֹי. אַךְ מִי שֶׁיֵּשׁ לוֹ מְשָׁרֵת גּוֹי, יָכוֹל לְהוֹסִיף וּלְבַשֵּׁל בִּקְדֵרָה אַחַת, שֶׁיְּהֵא בָּהּ גַּם בִּשְׁבִיל הַמְשָׁרֵת. אֲבָל בִּשְׁבִיל גּוֹי מְכֻבָּד, אָסוּר אֲפִלּוּ לְהוֹסִיף. וְלֹא עוֹד, אֶלָּא אֲפִלּוּ אִם בִּשֵּׁל הַיִּשְׂרָאֵל אוֹ אָפָה בִּשְׁבִיל עַצְמוֹ, אָסוּר לְהַזְמִין גּוֹי שֶׁיֹּאכַל עִמּוֹ. וְאַךְ גּוֹי שֶׁאֵינוֹ מִתְכַּבֵּד בּוֹ, מֻתָּר לָתֵת לוֹ אֵיזֶה דָּבָר מִמַּה שֶּׁבִּשֵּׁל אוֹ אָפָה. וְלֶאֱפוֹת פַּת, אֲפִלּוּ בִּשְׁבִיל גּוֹי מְשָׁרְתוֹ, אָסוּר.

לז) אָסוּר לְהוֹצִיא שׁוּם דָּבָר בִּשְׁבִיל גּוֹי, כִּי אִם בַּמָּקוֹם שֶׁמֻּתָּר לְהוֹצִיא בַּשַּׁבָּת.

סִימָן צט
דִּינֵי מֻקְצֶה בְּיוֹם־טוֹב

א) כָּל מֻקְצֶה הָאָסוּר בְּטִלְטוּל בַּשַּׁבָּת, אָסוּר גַּם בְּיוֹם־טוֹב. וְיֵשׁ אוֹמְרִים, דְּגַם מֻקְצֶה מִדַּעַת וּמֻקְצֶה מֵחֲמַת מִאוּס, אַף־עַל־פִּי שֶׁמֻּתָּרִין בַּשַּׁבָּת, אֲסוּרִין בְּיוֹם־טוֹב. וְלָכֵן פֵּרוֹת שֶׁהִקְצָה אוֹתָם לִסְחוֹרָה, אֲסוּרִין

---

97. See Chapter 94 about requirements of *Eruv Chatzeiros* (courtyards) and partnership in alleys. According to the *Rif, Rambam, Rosh* and *Shulchan Aruch* 528, you may carry in the courtyards and alleyways on Yom Tov, even without an *eruv.* The *Rashbah* and *Rema* 518:1 rule that it is not permitted. The *Reshal* says it is best to include Yom Tov in your *erev chatzeiros* etc., even though the *halachah* is like the *Shulchan Aruch* in this case.

98. See *Shulchan Aruch* 510:8. If you are accustomed to carry four or five pitchers of wine, you should only carry one or two and you should not carry them in a basket made for carrying wine etc. This applies only when moving the wine etc. through alleyways where people frequent and may see you, but within your house or courtyard, you may carry it as you wish.

99. And you are in a hurry to serve them.

100. *Masechet Beitzah* 21.

101. See *Biur Halachah* 512:1.

102. It is permitted to add more to the pot at one time, but if your food was already in the pot, you may not add more for your servant. (*Mishnah Berurah* 512:12)

a place where you are permitted to carry on Shabbos.[97] Concerning things that are needed for food, like kegs of wine, you should not carry as heavy a burden as you do on weekdays; but you should do it in a different way.[98] If it is impossible to do it differently, as when you have many guests,[99] you may carry it the usual manner.

35) All work that is permitted to be done on Yom Tov, may be performed only for the needs of man, but not for animals, for it is written, "Shall be done for you," (Ex. 12:16) and it is expounded[100] "For you, but not for animals." Therefore it is forbidden to cook or carry out anything for the needs of an animal, just as it is forbidden on Shabbos.

36) It is forbidden to cook or bake for the needs of a non-Jew[101] but if you have a non-Jewish servant, you are allowed to add food[102] and cook it in the same pot so that there should be enough for the servant too. But for a distinguished non-Jew, it is even forbidden to add (food).[103] Moreover, even if you cooked or baked anything for yourself, you are forbidden to invite a non-Jew[104] to eat with you.[105] But if the non-Jew is an ordinary person, you may give him something of what you cooked or baked. Baking bread, even if for your non-Jewish servant, is forbidden.[106]

37) It is forbidden to carry out anything on Yom Tov for a non-Jew unless to a place where you may carry on Shabbos.

Chapter 99

The Laws of Muktzeh on Yom Tov

1) *All Muktzeh,* that is forbidden to be handled on Shabbos, is also forbidden to be handled on Yom Tov. Some authorities say, things that are purposely excluded from use and things excluded from use because of their filth, even though they may be handled on Shabbos, they may not be handled on Yom Tov.[1] Therefore,

---

103. The reason is in order to make sure that you do not cook specially for him. (see *Shulchan Aruch* 512:1)

104. If he dropped in uninvited, and the food is already prepared (*Rashbah, Tur*), you may also give him food. (*Shulchan Aruch* 512:1) Some *poskim* disagree. *Shulchan Aruch Harav* and *Mishnah Berurah* cite the *Taz* who rules that you may give him food, but not if you have to urge him to dine with you.

105. You are allowed to send food to his house if it is to promote peaceful relations. See *Shulchan Aruch* and *Mishnah Berurah* 512:8 (provided you do not violate laws of carrying). *Chayei Adam* 98:1–2 rules that even this is permitted only for food you prepared for your personal use, but not food added for him. You may not invite him to dine with you, even to prevent his hard feelings. (*Biur Halachah, Rashbah*)

106. For each bread is an extra bother. (*Shulchan Aruch Harav*) If necessary, you may be lenient and rely on the *Reshal* that more bread in the oven will improve your bread, too. (*Mishnah Berurah* 512:12)

1. *Shulchan Aruch* 495:4. Since some *melachos* are permitted for preparation of food on Yom Tov, the Sages feared people might not view Yom Tov with the proper seriousness, and, therefore, were more stringent regarding *muktzeh* on Yom Tov than on Shabbos. (see *Mishnah Berurah* 495:15)

בְּיוֹם־טוֹב, אֶלָּא צָרִיךְ שֶׁיַּזְמִינֵם בְּעֶרֶב יוֹם־טוֹב, דְּהַיְנוּ שֶׁיֹּאמַר, מִפֵּרוֹת אֵלּוּ אֹכַל לְמָחָר. וּבְפֵרוֹת הָעוֹמְדִין לִמְכֹּר מְעַט מְעַט, יֵשׁ לְהָקֵל.

ב) בֵּיצָה שֶׁנּוֹלְדָה בְּיוֹם־טוֹב, אֲסוּרָה אֲפִלּוּ בְּטִלְטוּל. אֲבָל מֻתָּר לִכְפּוֹת עָלֶיהָ כְּלִי שֶׁלֹּא תִשָּׁבֵר. וְאִם נוֹלְדָה בְּיוֹם רִאשׁוֹן, מֻתֶּרֶת בְּיוֹם שֵׁנִי. וְאִם יוֹם־טוֹב שֵׁנִי הוּא שַׁבָּת, אֲסוּרָה גַּם בְּשַׁבָּת. וְכֵן אִם יוֹם רִאשׁוֹן הוּא שַׁבָּת וְנוֹלְדָה בּוֹ, אֲסוּרָה גַּם לְמָחָר שֶׁהוּא יוֹם־טוֹב שֵׁנִי. וְכֵן שַׁבָּת הַסָּמוּךְ לְיוֹם־טוֹב, בֵּין לְפָנָיו בֵּין לְאַחֲרָיו, נוֹלְדָה בָּזֶה אֲסוּרָה בָּזֶה. וּבְרֹאשׁ־הַשָּׁנָה, גַּם אִם נוֹלְדָה בְּיוֹם רִאשׁוֹן, אֲסוּרָה גַּם בַּשֵּׁנִי (כִּי שְׁנֵי הַיָּמִים שֶׁל רֹאשׁ־הַשָּׁנָה, כְּיוֹמָא אֲרִיכְתָּא דַּמְיָא. וְהַיְנוּ לְחֻמְרָא כְּמוֹ הָכָא. אֲבָל לְעִנְיַן מַה שֶּׁבִּשְׁאָר יָמִים טוֹבִים אָסוּר לַעֲשׂוֹת מִיּוֹם הָרִאשׁוֹן לְיוֹם הַשֵּׁנִי כִּדְלְקַמָּן בְּסִימָן ק"א, אֵין חִלּוּק בֵּין שְׁאָר יָמִים טוֹבִים לְרֹאשׁ־הַשָּׁנָה, דְּגַם בְּרֹאשׁ־הַשָּׁנָה אָסוּר, דִּלְקֻלָּא לָא אָמְרִינַן כְּיוֹמָא אֲרִיכְתָּא דַּמְיָא). וְאִם חָל רֹאשׁ־הַשָּׁנָה בְּיוֹם הַחֲמִישִׁי וּבְיוֹם הַשִּׁשִּׁי, אֲפִלּוּ נוֹלְדָה בְּיוֹם הַחֲמִישִׁי, אֲסוּרָה גַּם בַּשַּׁבָּת. שָׁחַט תַּרְנְגֹלֶת וּמָצָא בָּהּ בֵּיצִים, אֲפִלּוּ הֵן גְּמוּרוֹת, מֻתָּרוֹת אֲפִלּוּ בּוֹ בַּיּוֹם.

ג) עֵצִים, לֹא הִתִּירוּ בְּטִלְטוּל אֶלָּא לְצֹרֶךְ הַסָּקָה. אֲבָל שֶׁלֹּא לְצֹרֶךְ הַסָּקָה, אֲסוּרִים בְּטִלְטוּל. וְלָכֵן אֵין סוֹמְכִין לֹא אֶת הַקְּדֵרָה וְלֹא אֶת הַדֶּלֶת בִּבְקַעַת.

ד) אֵפֶר כִּירָה שֶׁהֻסְּקָה מֵעֶרֶב יוֹם־טוֹב, מֻתָּר לְטַלְטְלוֹ בְּיוֹם־טוֹב, מִפְּנֵי שֶׁהוּא מוּכָן לְכָל צָרְכֵי הָאָדָם, לְכַסּוֹת בּוֹ צוֹאָה אוֹ רֹק וְכַדּוֹמֶה. וְאִם הֻסְּקָה בְּיוֹם־טוֹב, אִם הוּא עֲדַיִן חַם שֶׁרָאוּי לִצְלוֹת בּוֹ בֵּיצָה, מֻתָּר לְטַלְטְלוֹ לְכָל צָרְכֵי הָאָדָם. אֲבָל אִם נִצְטַנֵּן, אָסוּר בְּטִלְטוּל, מִשּׁוּם דַּהֲוֵי לֵהּ נוֹלָד, אֶתְמוֹל הָיָה עֵצִים וְהַיּוֹם אֵפֶר, וְגָרוּעַ מִמֻּקְצֶה.

---

2. Even though you may handle *muktzeh* for preparation of food, it is permitted only to remove the *muktzeh* in order to take the food etc., but you may not use the *muktzeh* itself, even for food or its preparation. (*Magein Avraham, Mishnah Berurah* 508:31)

3. The *Ramah* 495:4 rules that only *livestock* must be designated, but regarding fruits etc., it is sufficient to say you will take from the pile. The *Rif, Rambam, Rosh, Meiri, Magein Avraham* etc. rule that even fruits must be designated and that it is necessary to make some sign or notation to this effect. The *Meiri* explains that the purpose of a sign is to remember which ones were selected; therefore, one who has a good memory need not make a sign. (see *Biur Halachah* 495:4)

4. *Ramah* 513:1. But the *Mishnah Berurah* 513:3 rules as the *Shulchan Aruch, Taz, Magein Avraham* and *Vilna Gaon* that since it is round and moves very easily, you are not even allowed to touch it.

fruits[2] that were set aside for sale, are forbidden to be handled on Yom Tov, unless you designate them on *erev* Yom Tov by saying: "I will eat from this fruit[3] tomorrow." Concerning fruit that is scheduled to be sold a little at a time, you may be lenient.

2) It is forbidden to handle an egg that was laid on Yom Tov,[4] but you may cover it with a vessel so that it should not break.[5] If it was laid on the first day (of Yom Tov), you may eat it on the second day, but if the second day of Yom Tov occurs on Shabbos, it is forbidden on Shabbos as well. Similarly, if the first day occurs on Shabbos, and it was laid on that day, it is forbidden also on the following day, which is the second day of Yom Tov. Whenever Shabbos borders on Yom Tov, whether before or after it, if it is laid on either of these days, it is forbidden on the other (also). And on Rosh Hashanah, even if it was laid on the first day, it is forbidden on the second day. (The two days of Rosh Hashanah are considered one long day, only concerning restrictive measures, as in this case. In reference to the law regarding the other *yomim tovim,* [however] when it is forbidden to prepare [food] on the first day for the second day, there is no difference between other *yomim tovim* and Rosh Hashanah. It is also forbidden to do so on Rosh Hashanah, because to effect a relaxation of the law we do not say it is considered one long day.)[6] And if Rosh Hashanah occurs on Thursday and Friday, even if it was laid on Thursday, it is forbidden on Shabbos as well. If a hen was slaughtered and eggs found inside it, even if they are fully developed, they are permitted even on that day.

3) Wood may not be handled except to burn as fuel, but (if) not for burning, it is forbidden to handle it. Therefore, you may not support a pot or a door with a piece of wood.[7]

4) Ashes (of wood) that was burned before Yom Tov may be handled on Yom Tov because it was fit (before Yom Tov) for all the necessities of man; such as to cover excrement with it or (to cover) saliva and similar things. If the ashes are made from a fire that burned on Yom Tov, then if it is still so hot that an egg can be roasted on it, it may be handled for all the necessities of man. But if it has cooled off, it is forbidden to be handled because it is *nolad* [newly created],[8] (that is) yesterday it was wood and today it is ashes, and this is more stringent than *muktzeh.*

---

5. But care must be taken not to touch it with the vessel. (*Shulchan Aruch* 513:4, see footnote 4)

6. See Chapter 101:6 and footnote.

7. *Shulchan Aruch* 502:3. This refers to dry wood which is fit for fuel and thus can be handled and used for fuel. (*Magein Avraham, Eliyohu Rabbah, Vilna Gaon, Mishnah Berurah*) However, the *Mishnah Berurah* 502:21 cites *Beis Meir*'s ruling that in a pressing situation, you may rely on the *Taz* and others who maintain the *Shulchan Aruch* refers to damp wood that is not fit for fuel and is, therefore, considered *muktzeh,* and this type of *muktzeh* is forbidden on Yom Tov.

8. Anything that is no longer fit for the purpose it had at twilight of the eve of Yom Tov, or anything that has come into being this day is *nolad* (like a chair that was broken on Yom Tov). (see *Shulchan Aruch* 501:6, *Magein Avraham* 308:15 and *Shulchan Aruch Harav* 495:13)

ה) אֱגוֹזִים שֶׁאֲכָלָן קֹדֶם יוֹם־טוֹב, מֻתָּר לְהַסִּיק בִּקְלִפֵּיהֶן. אֲבָל אִם אֲכָלָן בְּיוֹם־טוֹב, אָסוּר לְהַסִּיק בִּקְלִיפֵּיהֶן. וַאֲפִלּוּ לְטַלְטְלָן, אָסוּר. וְכֵן שְׁאָר קְלִפּוֹת אַף־עַל־פִּי שֶׁרְאוּיוֹת לִבְהֵמָה, מִשּׁוּם דַּהֲוֵי לֵהּ נוֹלָד, דְּאֶתְמוֹל הָיוּ עוֹמְדוֹת לָאָדָם.

סִימָן ק
הִלְכוֹת נְשִׂיאַת־כַּפַּיִם

א) מִצְוַת עֲשֵׂה מִן הַתּוֹרָה עַל הַכֹּהֲנִים שֶׁיְּבָרְכוּ אֶת הָעָם, שֶׁנֶּאֱמַר, כֹּה תְבָרְכוּ אֶת־בְּנֵי יִשְׂרָאֵל. וְכָל כֹּהֵן שֶׁאֵין בּוֹ מִדְּבָרִים הַמְעַכְּבִים אוֹתוֹ וְאֵינוֹ עוֹלֶה לַדּוּכָן, עוֹבֵר בַּעֲשֵׂה. וְאֵינוֹ עוֹבֵר אֶלָּא כְּשֶׁקּוֹרְאִין אוֹתוֹ, שֶׁנֶּאֱמַר, אָמוֹר לָהֶם, וְתִרְגֵּם אוּנְקְלוֹס, כַּד תֵּימְרוּן לְהוֹן. וְהַמִּנְהָג בִּמְדִינוֹתֵינוּ, שֶׁאֵין נְשִׂיאַת־כַּפַּיִם אֶלָּא בְּיוֹם־טוֹב, מִשּׁוּם דְּאָז שְׁרוּיִים בְּשִׂמְחַת יוֹם־טוֹב, וּבְיוֹם הַכִּפּוּרִים יֵשׁ בּוֹ שִׂמְחַת מְחִילָה וּסְלִיחָה, וְטוֹב לֵב הוּא יְבָרֵךְ, מַה שֶּׁאֵין כֵּן בִּשְׁאָר יָמִים, אֲפִלּוּ בְּשַׁבְּתוֹת הַשָּׁנָה, שֶׁטְּרוּדִים בְּהִרְהוּרִים עַל מִחְיָתָם וְעַל בִּטּוּל מְלַאכְתָּם. וַאֲפִלּוּ בְּיוֹם־טוֹב, אֵין נוֹשְׂאִין כַּפֵּיהֶם אֶלָּא בִּתְפִלַּת מוּסָף, שֶׁיּוֹצְאִין אַחַר כָּךְ מִבֵּית־הַכְּנֶסֶת וְיִשְׂמְחוּ בְּשִׂמְחַת יוֹם־טוֹב. עוֹד נוֹהֲגִין בִּמְדִינוֹתֵינוּ, שֶׁבְּיוֹם־טוֹב שֶׁחָל לִהְיוֹת בְּשַׁבָּת, אֵין נְשִׂיאַת־כַּפַּיִם אֶלָּא בְּיוֹם הַכִּפּוּרִים, שֶׁאֲפִלּוּ חָל בְּשַׁבָּת, נוֹשְׂאִין כַּפֵּיהֶם. וְיֵשׁ מְקוֹמוֹת שֶׁנּוֹהֲגִין שֶׁבְּכָל יוֹם־טוֹב, אֲפִלּוּ חָל בְּשַׁבָּת, נוֹשְׂאִין כַּפֵּיהֶם, וְכֵן נָכוֹן יוֹתֵר.

ב) אֵין נְשִׂיאַת כַּפַּיִם אֶלָּא בַּעֲשָׂרָה, וְהַכֹּהֲנִים מִן הַמִּנְיָן, לְפִי שֶׁגַּם הֵם בִּכְלַל הַבְּרָכָה, שֶׁנֶּאֱמַר, וַאֲנִי אֲבָרְכֵם.

---

1. Even in our times. (See *Magein Avraham* 128:41, *Peri Megadim* etc., unlike the *Penei Yehoshua, Maseches Kesubos* 24b and *Yeshuos Yaakov,* who assert that it is *de'oraisa* only in the *Beis Hamikdash.*)

2. *Numbers* 6:23.

3. Platform. It is traditionally built in front of the Holy Ark on the East side of the synagogue. The platform is not essential for the mitzvah, but the *Eshel Avraham (Butchatch)* says it is preferable. However, the *Rambam* makes no mention of it in the laws concerning the architecture of a synagogue.

4. *Shulchan Aruch* 128:2. (*Rambam*)

5) If you ate nuts before Yom Tov, you may burn their shells (for fuel). But if you ate them on Yom Tov, you may not burn their shells and it is forbidden to even handle them. Similarly, other peels, even though they are fit for animals, (may not be handled them) because they are *nolad;* for yesterday they were fit for human consumption.

Chapter 100

The Laws of the Priestly Blessing

1) It is a positive commandment of the Torah[1] for the *kohanim* to bless the people, as it is said: "This is how you must bless the Children of Israel."[2] Any *kohein* who is not disqualified and does not go up to the *duchan*[3] violates a positive commandment.[4] But he is not in violation, unless he is called upon to do so,[5] as it is said: "Say to them,"[6] and the *Targum* translates: "When they tell you." It is the custom in our regions[7] that the *kohanim* bless the people only on Yom Tov because then, people rejoice Yom Tov,[8] and it is said that a happy heart will bless, and on Yom Kippur there is (also) rejoicing over the forgiveness and pardon [of our sins]. This is not true on other days. Even on the Shabbos days of the whole year, people are worried about their livelihood and about being idle from work. And even on Yom Tov, they only bless the people during the *musaf* service, because they will soon leave the synagogue and rejoice in the joy of Yom Tov. We are accustomed in our regions that [even] when Yom Tov occurs on Shabbos, the *kohanim* do not bless the people[9] except on Yom Kippur; for even if it occurs on Shabbos, they bless the people. There are communities that have the custom, that on every Yom Tov, even when it occurs on Shabbos, the *kohanim* bless the people; and this is more correct.[10]

2) The *Birkas Kohanim* is pronounced only in a congregation of at least ten adult males,[11] including the *kohanim,* because they also are included in the blessing, as it is said: "And I will bless them" (*Numbers* 6:27).

---

5. *Maseches Sotah* 38a. It is sufficient to call out *kohanim* or to tell them to wash their hands (at the appropriate time).

6. The command is stated in the plural. Therefore, they are to be summoned only when there are at least two *kohanim.* But if there is only one *kohein,* he pronounces the blessings without being summoned. (*Shulchan Aruch* 128:10.)

7. This is the custom throughout most of the Diaspora. In Eretz Yisroel, some cities have the blessings on Shabbos, too, while in Jerusalem they are pronounced daily. The custom of the Jews of Seforad is to have the blessings daily. It is also the custom of the Yeshivos, even those not in Jerusalem.

8. The source for the *Kitzur Shulchan Aruch*'s ruling is the *Ramah* 128:44.

9. See *Magein Avraham* 128:70, *Yeshuos Yaakov, Yosef Da'as* (responsa) for various explanations for this custom.

10. *Taz* 128:38, *Shulchan Aruch Harav.*

11. *Shulchan Aruch* 128:1.

ג) קֹדֶם נְשִׂיאַת כַּפַּיִם, לֹא יִשְׁתֶּה הַכֹּהֵן לֹא יַיִן וְלֹא שְׁאָר מַשְׁקֶה מִמַּשְׁקִים הַמְשַׁכְּרִין. וְאִם לִבּוֹ חָלוּשׁ וְרוֹצֶה לֶאֱכוֹל פַּת כִּסְנִין קֹדֶם מוּסָף, יִשְׁמַע קִדּוּשׁ מֵאַחֵר.

ד) קֹדֶם הַדּוּכָן, צָרִיךְ הַכֹּהֵן לִטּוֹל יָדָיו עַד הַפֶּרֶק, שֶׁהוּא חִבּוּר הַיָּד עִם הַזְּרוֹעַ, כְּדֶרֶךְ שֶׁהָיוּ מְקַדְּשִׁין אֶת יְדֵיהֶם בַּמִּקְדָּשׁ לַעֲבוֹדָה, שֶׁנֶּאֱמַר, שְׂאוּ יְדֵיכֶם קֹדֶשׁ וּבָרְכוּ אֶת ה׳. וְיֵשׁ סָפֵק אִם צְרִיכִין לְבָרֵךְ עַל נְטִילָה זוֹ אוֹ אֵין צְרִיכִין לְבָרֵךְ, כֵּיוָן שֶׁבֵּרַךְ עַל נְטִילַת יָדַיִם בְּקוּמוֹ מִמִּטָּתוֹ. וּמִסְּפֵקָא נוֹהֲגִין שֶׁלֹּא לְבָרֵךְ. וְאִם נָגַע בֵּינְתַיִם בְּמָקוֹם מְטֻנָּף, הָיָה רָאוּי לְבָרֵךְ עַל נְטִילָה זוֹ, אֶלָּא שֶׁלֹּא נָהֲגוּ. וְרָאוּי לְכָל כֹּהֵן יְרֵא־שָׁמַיִם, לִשְׁמוֹר הֵיטֵב יָדָיו מִנְּטִילַת יָדַיִם שַׁחֲרִית, שֶׁלֹּא יִגַּע בְּמָקוֹם הַמְלֻכְלָךְ, כְּדֵי שֶׁלֹּא יִצְטָרֵךְ לְבָרֵךְ שֵׁנִית.

ה) הַלֵּוִי יוֹצֵק אֶת הַמַּיִם עַל יְדֵי הַכֹּהֲנִים, עַל שֵׁם שֶׁנֶּאֱמַר, וְגַם אֶת־אַחֶיךָ מַטֵּה לֵוִי וְגוֹ׳ הַקְרֵב אִתָּךְ וְיִלָּווּ עָלֶיךָ וִישָׁרְתוּךָ. וְאִם אֵין שָׁם לֵוִי, יִצּוֹק בְּכוֹר פֶּטֶר רֶחֶם שֶׁהוּא קָדוֹשׁ, עַל יָדוֹ. וְאִם גַּם בְּכוֹר אֵינוֹ, מוּטָב שֶׁהַכֹּהֵן בְּעַצְמוֹ יִצֹּק, וְלֹא יִצֹּק יִשְׂרָאֵל. הַלֵּוִי אוֹ הַבְּכוֹר אֲשֶׁר יִצֹּק מַיִם עַל יְדֵי הַכֹּהֲנִים, אִם אֵין יָדָיו נְקִיּוֹת, יֵשׁ לוֹ לִרְחוֹץ יָדָיו תְּחִלָּה.

ו) אָסוּר לַעֲלוֹת לַדּוּכָן בְּמִנְעָלִים. וְיַחֲלֹץ הַמִּנְעָלִים קֹדֶם נְטִילַת יָדַיִם. וְטוֹב לִזָּהֵר לְהַצְנִיעַ הַמִּנְעָלִים תַּחַת הַסַּפְסָלִים שֶׁלֹּא יִהְיוּ מְגֻלִּין וְנִרְאִין, מִפְּנֵי כְּבוֹד הַצִּבּוּר.

ז) כְּשֶׁשְּׁלִיחַ־הַצִּבּוּר מַתְחִיל רְצֵה, צְרִיכִין כָּל הַכֹּהֲנִים לַעֲקֹר מִמְּקוֹמוֹתֵיהֶם לַעֲלוֹת לַדּוּכָן. וְעַל כֵּן יִטְּלוּ אֶת יְדֵיהֶם קֹדֶם לָכֵן, כְּדֵי

---

12. He is forbidden to drink a *revi'is* of undiluted wine without pausing. However, if he drinks more than a *revi'is* of wine, even if diluted with water, and even if he paused many times while drinking, he may not pronounce the priestly blessings. (*Shulchan Aruch* 128:38)

13. *Magein Avraham* 128:55 rules if he drank other intoxicating beverages, he may *duchan* so long as he is not stone drunk; even if he is not sober enough to speak before a king. The *Eliyahu Rabbah* and *Derech Hachaim* rule that he must be sober enough to speak before a king (as by *tefillah*). *Taz* rules that he may not drink any amount of an intoxicating beverage before he *duchans,* because the minumum of a *revi'is* applies only to wine.

14. *Maseches Sotah* 39a.

15. The priestly service in the *Beis Hamikdash.* This comparison is found in the *Rambam.* (Laws of *Tefillah* 15a Psalms 134:2)

3) Before pronouncing the *Birkas Kohanim* the *kohein* may not drink[12] wine or any other intoxicating[13] beverage. And if he feels faint, and wants to eat some cake before *musaf,* he should listen to someone else's kiddush.

4) Before going up to the *duchan* the *kohein* must wash his hands[14] up to the wrist, that is the junction of the hand and the arm, just as the *kohanim* sanctified their hands in the *Beis Hamikdash* before the *avodah,*[15] as it is said: "Raise your hands in holiness and bless Hashem." It is questionable if they have to recite a berachah on this washing, or if they do not have to say a berachah, since he made a berachah on washing his hands when he got up in the morning. Because of the doubt, the custom is not to recite a berachah. In the meantime[16] if he touched an unclean spot, it would be proper to say a berachah on this washing, but this is not the custom.[17] Every God-fearing *kohein* should watch his hands carefully after washing his hands in the morning, not to touch an unclean spot, so that he would need not repeat the berachah.

5) A *levi* pours the water[18] on the hands of the *kohanim*[19] as it is said: "And also your brothers, the tribe of *Levi* bring near to you, and they will accompany you and serve you."[20] If no *Levi* is present, a first born of the mother, who is holy, should pour the water on his hands, and if there is no firstborn[21] present, it is better that the *kohein* himself pour it rather than a Yisrael. If the *Levi* or firstborn who pours water on the hands of the *kohanim*, has unclean hands,[22] he must wash them first.

6) The *kohanim* are forbidden to go up to *duchan* wearing shoes.[23] They should remove their shoes before washing their hands.[24] They should be careful to hide their shoes under the benches, so that they cannot be seen, out of respect for the congregation.

7) When the *Chazzan* begins *Retzeih,* all the *kohanim* must leave their places[25] to go up to the *duchan.* Therefore, they should wash their hands before this, so that

---

16. From the time he washed his hands in the morning until he goes to *duchan.*

17. *Magein Avraham* 128:9. See *Eliyahu Rabbah* that perhaps a berachah is never made on this handwashing.

18. Only water may be used (*Beis Yosef, Peri Chadash*), but the *Shevus Yaakov* Vol. 3:2 rules that anything that cleans may be used (if no water is available).

19. *Shulchan Aruch* 128:6. (*Zohar*)

20. *Numbers* 18:2.

21. See *Sefer Massah Chaim* (cited in *Orchos Chaim*) that if there are no first-born, the *shamash* (sexton) of the synagogue should pour the water.

22. *Shulchan Aruch* rules as the *Zohar* that even if their hands are clean, they should wash again. *Ramah* says this is not the custom. *Bach* and *Mishnah Berurah* 128:23 rule that if they were distracted from their previous handwashing, they should wash again, even if they don't remember touching anything unclean.

23. See *Maseches Sotah* 41a. He may not go up barefoot, either because it is considered disrespectful in our times. He should go up in stockings. (*Mishnah Berurah* 128:18)

24. If they are sure they can remove them without touching them, they may remove them after they wash. (*Mishnah Berurah* 128:15, *Acharonim*)

25. *Maseches Sotah* 38b. *Shulchan Aruch* 128:8.

שֶׁכְּשֶׁיֹּאמַר שְׁלִיחַ־הַצִּבּוּר רְצֵה, יַעַקְרוּ מִמְּקוֹמָם לַעֲלוֹת לַדּוּכָן עִם יָדַיִם רְאוּיוֹת לִבְרָכָה. וּבְדִיעֲבַד גַּם אִם נָטְלוּ יְדֵיהֶם אַחַר כָּךְ, שַׁפִּיר דָּמֵי.

ח) כְּשֶׁעָלוּ לַדּוּכָן, עוֹמְדִים וּפְנֵיהֶם כְּנֶגֶד אֲרוֹן הַקֹּדֶשׁ שֶׁבַּמִּזְרָח, וְאוֹמְרִים מוֹדִים דְּרַבָּנָן עִם הַצִּבּוּר, וְאַחַר כָּךְ אוֹמְרִים, יְהִי רָצוֹן מִלְּפָנֶיךָ ה׳ אֱלֹקֵינוּ וֵאלֹקֵי אֲבוֹתֵינוּ, שֶׁתְּהֵא בְּרָכָה זוֹ שֶׁצִּוִּיתָנוּ לְבָרֵךְ אֶת עַמְּךָ יִשְׂרָאֵל, בְּרָכָה שְׁלֵמָה, וְלֹא יְהֵא בָהּ שׁוּם מִכְשׁוֹל וְעָוֹן מֵעַתָּה וְעַד עוֹלָם. וּמַאֲרִיכִין בִּתְפִלָּה זוֹ עַד שֶׁיְּכַלֶּה שְׁלִיחַ־הַצִּבּוּר וּלְךָ נָאֶה לְהוֹדוֹת, כְּדֵי שֶׁיַּעֲנוּ הַצִּבּוּר אָמֵן גַּם עַל תְּפִלָּה זֹאת. שְׁלִיחַ־הַצִּבּוּר אוֹמֵר, אֱלֹקֵינוּ וֵאלֹקֵי אֲבוֹתֵינוּ, בָּרְכֵנוּ בַּבְּרָכָה וְכוּ׳ בְּלַחַשׁ, וְתֵבַת כֹּהֲנִים אוֹמֵר בְּקוֹל רָם, וּבָזֶה הוּא קוֹרֵא אֶת הַכֹּהֲנִים- שֶׁיְּבָרְכוּ. וְשׁוּב אוֹמֵר בְּלַחַשׁ, עַם קְדוֹשֶׁךָ כָּאָמוּר. וּלְאַחַר שֶׁקָּרָא שְׁלִיחַ־הַצִּבּוּר כֹּהֲנִים, מַתְחִילִים וּמְבָרְכִים כֻּלָּם בְּיַחַד, בָּרוּךְ אַתָּה ה׳, אֱלֹקֵינוּ מֶלֶךְ הָעוֹלָם, אֲשֶׁר קִדְּשָׁנוּ בִּקְדֻשָּׁתוֹ שֶׁל אַהֲרֹן, וְהוֹפְכִין פְּנֵיהֶם כְּלַפֵּי הָעָם, וּמְסַיְּמִים אֶת הַבְּרָכָה, וְצִוָּנוּ לְבָרֵךְ אֶת עַמּוֹ יִשְׂרָאֵל בְּאַהֲבָה, וְעוֹנִין הַצִּבּוּר אָמֵן. אֲבָל שְׁלִיחַ־הַצִּבּוּר לֹא יַעֲנֶה אָמֵן, מִשּׁוּם דַּהֲוֵי הֶפְסֵק. מַה שֶּׁאוֹמְרִים בְּאַהֲבָה, הוּא לְאַפּוּקֵי שֶׁאִם הַצִּבּוּר שׂוֹנְאִים אֶת הַכֹּהֵן אוֹ הַכֹּהֵן שׂוֹנֵא אֶת הַצִּבּוּר, לֹא יִשָּׂא אֶת כַּפָּיו, וְסַכָּנָה הִיא לַכֹּהֵן אִם יִשָּׂא אֶת כַּפָּיו, וְעַל כֵּן יֵשׁ לוֹ לָצֵאת מִבֵּית־הַכְּנֶסֶת. אִם אֵין בְּבֵית־הַכְּנֶסֶת אֶלָּא כֹּהֵן אֶחָד, אֵינוֹ אוֹמֵר שְׁלִיחַ הַצִּבּוּר כֹּהֲנִים בְּקוֹל רָם, אֶלָּא הוּא מֵעַצְמוֹ מַחֲזִיר אֶת פָּנָיו.

ט) מַגְבִּיהִים אֶת יְדֵיהֶם נֶגֶד כִּתְפֵיהֶם, וּפוֹשְׁטִים אוֹתָן, וְחוֹלְקִין אֶצְבְּעוֹתֵיהֶם שֶׁיִּהְיוּ בֵינֵיהֶן חֲמִשָּׁה אֲוִירִים, דְּהַיְנוּ בֵּין שְׁתֵּי אֶצְבָּעוֹת לִשְׁתֵּי אֶצְבָּעוֹת אֲוִיר אֶחָד, וּבֵין שְׁתֵּי אֶצְבָּעוֹת לַאֲגוּדָל גַּם כֵּן אֲוִיר אֶחָד, וְכֵן בַּיָּד הַשְּׁנִיָּה, הֲרֵי אַרְבָּעָה אֲוִירִים. וּבֵין אֲגוּדָל לַאֲגוּדָל גַּם כֵּן אֲוִיר אֶחָד, הֲרֵי חֲמִשָּׁה אֲוִירִים. וְצָרִיךְ לַעֲשׂוֹת כֵּן, מִשּׁוּם דִּכְתִיב, מֵצִיץ

26. They must move up towards the *duchan* during the berachah of *Retzeih*. If they did not wash before *Retzeih*, they should go to the *duchan* and water should be brought to them for washing at the *duchan*. (*Mishnah Berurah* 128:27)

27. *Magein Avraham* etc. (*Rema*), unlike the *Shulchan Aruch* 128:9, who rules that they say this on their way up to the *duchan*.

when the *Chazzan* says *Retzeih,* they will leave their places to go up to the *duchan* with hands fit for the blessing. If post facto they washed their hands afterwards (after *Retzeih*), it is acceptable.[26]

8) When they go up to the *duchan,* they stand facing the Holy Ark (which is) in the East, and they say *Modim Derabanan* with the congregation, and after[27] that they say: "May it be your will Adonoy, our God, and God of our fathers, that this blessing which you have commanded us to bless your people, Israel, be a perfect blessing; that there be in it neither stumbling nor iniquity from now and forever." And they should prolong this prayer until the *Chazzan* concludes with: *Ulecha na'eh lehodos,* so that the congregation may respond *amein* also to this prayer. The *Chazzan* says: *Elokainu v'Eilokei avoseinu barecheinu vaberachah* etc. quietly, but the word *kohanim* he says in a loud voice, for with this he calls the *kohanim* to bless (the people). And then he says quietly: *am kedoshecha ka'amur* "Your holy people, as it is said." And after the *Chazzan* proclaims: *kohanim,* they begin the berachah, all saying in unison "*Baruch atah Adonoy, Elokeine Melech ha'olam, asher kiddeshanu, bikedushaso shel Aharon,*" then, turning around facing the people[28] they complete the berachah "*vetsivanu levareich es amo Yisrael be'ahavah,*" and the congregation responds *amein.* But the *Chazzan* should not respond *amein,* for this would constitute an interruption (in his prayer). From the words "With love," it is infered, that if the worshippers hate the *kohein,* or the *kohein* hates the worshippers, he should not bless them. In fact, it is dangerous for the *kohein* to bless them (under such circumstances). Therefore, he should leave the synagogue (at that time). If there is only one *kohein*[29] in the synagogue, the *Chazzan* should not say, *kohanim* in a loud voice, but the *kohein* should, on his own, turn around to face the congregants.

9) They raise their hands to the level of their shoulders[30] and stretch them out, and separate their fingers in such a way that there are five spaces between them. That is, between two fingers and two fingers there is one space, and between the two fingers and the thumb, there is another space, and the same with the other hand; making four spaces. And between the two thumbs there is another space, which makes a total of five spaces.[31] This must be done, because it is written, "He is peering through the lattices,"[32] five open spaces.[33] He must be careful that his

---

28. See *Rambam.* (*Laws of Tefillah* 14:11) The *poskim* rule that this is essential. But the *Peri Megadim* 128:9 says it is not. See paragraph 11.

29. See footnote 6.

30. *Maseches Sotah* 38a.

31. *Shulchan Aruch* 128:12.

32. *Shir Hashirim 2:9.*

33. *Rosh, Maseches Megillah* 3:21, *Midrash.* (*Tanchuma Parshas Nasso*) Metaphorically, Hashem watches over His people through those five spaces between the fingers of the *kohanim* at the *duchan.* (*Hei Charakim, hei,* is the equivalent of the number five, and *Charakim* means openings)

מִן־הַחֲרַכִּים, ה' חֲרַכִּים. וְצָרִיךְ לִזָּהֵר מְאֹד, שֶׁלֹּא יִגְּעוּ רָאשֵׁי הָאֲגוּדָלִין זֶה בָּזֶה, שֶׁלֹּא יִתְקַלְקֵל הַחַלּוֹן. וְצָרִיךְ לְהַגְבִּיהַּ אֶת הַיָּד הַיְמָנִית קְצָת לְמַעְלָה מֵהַשְּׂמָאלִית, וִיהֵא אֲגוּדָל יָמִין עַל אֲגוּדָל שְׂמֹאל. וּפוֹרְשִׂין כַּפֵּיהֶם, שֶׁיִּהְיֶה תּוֹךְ כַּפֵּיהֶם כְּנֶגֶד הָאָרֶץ, וַאֲחוֹרֵי יְדֵיהֶם כְּנֶגֶד הַשָּׁמָיִם.

י) בְּשָׁעָה שֶׁהַכֹּהֲנִים מְבָרְכִים אֶת הָעָם, לֹא יַבִּיטוּ וְלֹא יַסִּיחוּ דַעְתָּם, אֶלָּא יִהְיוּ עֵינֵיהֶם כְּלַפֵּי מַטָּה, כְּמוֹ בִּתְפִלָּה, וְהָעָם יְכַוְּנוּ לַבְּרָכָה, וְיִהְיוּ פְנֵיהֶם כְּנֶגֶד פְּנֵי הַכֹּהֲנִים, אֲבָל לֹא יִסְתַּכְּלוּ בָּהֶם. וְגַם הַכֹּהֲנִים בְּעַצְמָם לֹא יִסְתַּכְּלוּ בִּידֵיהֶם. וְנָהֲגוּ לְשַׁלְשֵׁל אֶת הַטַּלִּית עַל פְּנֵיהֶם, וִידֵיהֶם חוּץ לַטַּלִּית. וְגַם הַצִּבּוּר מְשַׁלְשְׁלִין אֶת הַטַּלִּיתִים עַל פְּנֵיהֶם שֶׁלֹּא יִסְתַּכְּלוּ.

יא) הָעָם שֶׁאֲחוֹרֵי הַכֹּהֲנִים, אֵינָם בִּכְלַל הַבְּרָכָה, אֶלָּא אִם כֵּן הָיוּ אֲנוּסִים. אֲבָל הָעָם שֶׁמִּן הַצְּדָדִים לִפְנֵיהֶם, הֵמָּה בִּכְלַל הַבְּרָכָה. וּבְמָקוֹם שֶׁאֲרוֹן הַקֹּדֶשׁ בּוֹלֵט מִן הַכֹּתֶל, אִם כֵּן הָאֲנָשִׁים שֶׁעוֹמְדִין אֵצֶל הַכֹּתֶל הַמִּזְרָחִי, הֵמָּה מִן הַצְּדָדִין שֶׁאֲחוֹרֵי הַכֹּהֲנִים, צְרִיכִין לָלֶכֶת מִשָּׁם וְלַעֲמוֹד בְּמָקוֹם שֶׁיִּהְיוּ לְכָל הַפָּחוֹת מִן הַצְּדָדִין שֶׁלִּפְנֵי הַכֹּהֲנִים. וְאִם אִי אֶפְשָׁר, הֲרֵי הֵן כְּמוֹ אֲנוּסִים, וְהֵם בִּכְלַל הַבְּרָכָה.

יב) שְׁלִיחַ־הַצִּבּוּר מַקְרֵא אוֹתָם בִּרְכַּת כֹּהֲנִים מִלָּה בְּמִלָּה, וְהֵם אוֹמְרִים אַחֲרָיו כָּל מִלָּה, עַד שֶׁמְּסַיְּמִים פָּסוּק רִאשׁוֹן, וְעוֹנִין הַצִּבּוּר אָמֵן, וְכֵן אַחַר הַפָּסוּק הַשֵּׁנִי וְאַחַר הַפָּסוּק הַשְּׁלִישִׁי. לֹא יַקְרֵא שְׁלִיחַ־הַצִּבּוּר בְּעַל־פֶּה אֶלָּא מִתּוֹךְ הַסִּדּוּר, שֶׁלֹּא יִתְבַּלְבֵּל. וְיָכוֹל לוֹמַר גַּם הוּא הָאֲמֵנִים שֶׁלְּאַחַר הַפְּסוּקִים וְלֹא הֲוֵי הֶפְסֵק, שֶׁזֶּהוּ צֹרֶךְ תְּפִלָּה. אֵלּוּ תֵּבוֹת שֶׁהַכֹּהֲנִים הוֹפְכִים בָּהֶן לַדָּרוֹם וְלַצָּפוֹן, יְבָרֶכְךָ וְיִשְׁמְרֶךָ, אֵלֶיךָ, וִיחֻנֶּךָּ, אֵלֶיךָ, לְךָ, מִשּׁוּם דְּתֵבוֹת אֵלּוּ הֵן לְנֹכַח, לָכֵן הוֹפְכִין אֶת עַצְמָם

---

34. If the *kohein* is too weak to raise his hands properly without resting them on something, he may not *duchan.* This is essential to fulfilling the mitzvah. See *Nodah Biyehudah* Responsum 5. He should step outside until the *kohanim* complete the blessings.(*Mishnah Berurah* 128:50, *Acharonim*) Some say if he is tired, it is sufficient to keep the fingers separated when he says the words and may relax his fingers between words (*Mishnah Berurah* 128:43) and the same applies to raising the hands. (see *Ksav Sofer* 13, *Mishnah Berurah* 128:55) The *kohein* must stand. If he is too weak, and must lean on something, he may not *duchan* (*Panam Meiros, Noda Biyehudah,* etc.) unlike the *Shvus Yaakov,* who says if he is unable to stand, he may lean (or sit).

35. *Shulchan Aruch* 128:23.

36. They are praying that Hashem will bless His people. (*Levush*)

thumbs should not touch each other, so that there will be five spaces. He must raise his right hand slightly above the left and the right thumb should be above the left thumb. They should spread out their hands in such a way that the palms of their hands are turned toward the ground, and the back of their hands toward Heaven.[34]

10) When the *kohanim*[35] bless the people, they should not look around, nor should they cause their mind to stray; but their eyes should be directed downward as in prayer.[36] The people should concentrate on the blessing, and face the *kohanim*, but they should not gaze at them,[37] neither should the *kohanim* gaze at their hands. It is [therefore] their custom to lower the *tallis* over their faces, extending their hands outside the *tallis*. The worshippers also lower their *tallissim* over their faces in order not to gaze at the *kohanim*.[38]

11) The people standing behind the *kohanim*, are not included in the blessing,[39] unless they were compelled to stand there, but those standing on the sides facing (the *kohanim*) are included in the blessing. In a synagogue where the Holy Ark projects from the wall, the men standing near the eastern wall, on the sides behind the *kohanim*, should leave their places and stand in a place where they will be at least on the sides facing the *kohanim*. If this is not possible, they are considered as being compelled to do so, and are included in the blessing.

12) The *Chazzan* reads[40] to them the *Birkas Kohanim* word for word, and they repeat each word after him until the conclusion of the first verse, whereupon the congregation responds *amein*. [In this manner, the *Chazzan* reads the second and third verses as well.] After the second verse and after the third verse, [the congregation also responds *amein*.] The *Chazzan* should not recite (these verses) from memory but should read them from the *Siddur* in order not to get confused. The *Chazzan*, too, may respond *amein* after these verses.[41] It is not considered an interruption because it is necessary to the prayer. When reciting the following words, the *kohanim* turn (partially) toward the South and then to the North: *yevarechecha, veyishmerecha, eilecha* ["May He bless you" "and safeguard you," "to you"] *vichuneka, eilecha,* and *lecha,* ["and be gracious to you" to you" "you"] because

---

37. Staring at them is forbidden, for you distract yourself from the berachah. Seeing or looking was only forbidden in the *Beis Hamikdash,* where the Divine Presence rested on their hands at the *duchan*. Now it is a custom not to look, in remembrance of the *Beis Hamikdash*. (*Magain Avraham, Mishnah Berurah* 128:89) The *Neziras Shimshon, Zohar* says in our times, too, there is Divine Presence on their hands and, out of respect, you should not look.

38. *Darkei Moshe.*

39. Because they show the blessing is not important to them. (see *Rashi* and *Tosafos Sotah* 38b)

40. *Shulchan Aruch* 128:13. If this was not done, the blessings are still valid. (*Peri Chadash, Mishnah Berurah* 128:49)

41. Only if he prompts from a *siddur* so he will not get confused. (see *Chayei Adam, Sha'ar Hatziyon* 128:61)

גַּם לַצְּדָדִין, כְּדֵי לְבָרֵךְ אֶת כֻּלָּם. וְכֵן הוֹפְכִין גַּם בְּתֵבַת שָׁלוֹם, לְפִי שֶׁהִיא סִיּוּם הַבְּרָכוֹת. וּבְשָׁעָה שֶׁמַּאֲרִיכִין בְּנִגּוּן שֶׁל הַתֵּבוֹת שֶׁבְּסוֹף הַפְּסוּקִים, דְּהַיְנוּ, וְיִשְׁמְרֶךָ, וִיחֻנֶּךָּ, שָׁלוֹם, אוֹמְרִים הַצִּבּוּר, רִבּוֹנוֹ שֶׁל עוֹלָם וְכוּ'. וְהַמַּקְרֵא, אֲפִלּוּ אֵינוֹ שְׁלִיחַ־הַצִּבּוּר, לֹא יֹאמַר, רִבּוֹנוֹ שֶׁל עוֹלָם, מִפְּנֵי הַטֵּרוּף. וּמִכָּל־שֶׁכֵּן שֶׁאִם הוּא שְׁלִיחַ־הַצִּבּוּר, שֶׁלֹּא יֹאמְרוֹ, מִפְּנֵי הֶפְסֵק בַּתְּפִלָּה וְלֹא יְנַגְּנוּ הַכֹּהֲנִים אֶלָּא נִגּוּן הַמְיֻחָד, מִפְּנֵי טֵרוּף הַדַּעַת.

יג) בְּשָׁעָה שֶׁהַכֹּהֲנִים אוֹמְרִים אֶת הַתֵּבוֹת, אֵין לַצִּבּוּר לוֹמַר שׁוּם פָּסוּק, רַק יִשְׁמְעוּ הֵיטֵב בְּכַוָּנָה אֶת הַתֵּבוֹת מִפִּי הַכֹּהֲנִים, כִּי כְּלוּם יֵשׁ עֶבֶד שֶׁמְּבָרְכִים אוֹתוֹ וְאֵינוֹ מַאֲזִין וּמְכַוֵּן לַבְּרָכָה. וְאִם אוֹמְרִים הַפְּסוּקִים, אֵינָם יְכוֹלִים לְכַוֵּן לַבְּרָכָה. אַךְ קְצָת, נוֹהֲגִים לוֹמַר פְּסוּקִים. וְיִזָּהֲרוּ שֶׁלֹּא לְאָמְרָם אֶלָּא בְּשָׁעָה שֶׁשְּׁלִיחַ־הַצִּבּוּר אוֹ הַכֹּהֲנִים מְנַגְּנִים, וְלֹא בְּשָׁעָה שֶׁאוֹמְרִים אֶת הַתֵּבוֹת.

יד) אַחַר כָּךְ מַתְחִיל שְׁלִיחַ־הַצִּבּוּר שִׂים שָׁלוֹם, וְאָז הַכֹּהֲנִים מַחֲזִירִים אֶת פְּנֵיהֶם כְּלַפֵּי אֲרוֹן הַקֹּדֶשׁ שֶׁבַּמִּזְרָח, וְאוֹמְרִים, רִבּוֹן הָעוֹלָמִים וְכוּ', וְיַאֲרִיכוּ בִּתְפִלָּה זוֹ עַד שֶׁיְּסַיֵּם שְׁלִיחַ־הַצִּבּוּר, הַמְבָרֵךְ אֶת עַמּוֹ יִשְׂרָאֵל בַּשָּׁלוֹם, כְּדֵי שֶׁיַּעֲנוּ הַצִּבּוּר אָמֵן גַּם עַל תְּפִלָּתָם. וְאִם אֵינָם יְכוֹלִים לְהַאֲרִיךְ כָּל־כָּךְ, יֹאמְרוּ עוֹד, אַדִּיר בַּמָּרוֹם וְכוּ'. וּבְרֹאשׁ־הַשָּׁנָה וְיוֹם־הַכִּפּוּרִים שֶׁמְּנַגְּנִים הַיּוֹם תְּאַמְּצֵנוּ וְכוּ', לֹא יַתְחִילוּ הַכֹּהֲנִים רִבּוֹן הָעוֹלָמִים וְכוּ', עַד קָרוֹב לַסּוֹף, כְּדֵי שֶׁיְּסַיְּמוּ בְּשָׁוֶה עִם שְׁלִיחַ־הַצִּבּוּר.

טו) אֵין הַכֹּהֲנִים רַשָּׁאִים לְהַתְחִיל בִּרְכַּת אֲשֶׁר קִדְּשָׁנוּ וְכוּ', עַד שֶׁתִּכְלֶה לִגְמְרֵי תֵּבַת כֹּהֲנִים מִפִּי הַמַּקְרֵא. וְאֵין הַמַּקְרֵא רַשַּׁאי לְהַתְחִיל יְבָרֶכְךָ, עַד לְאַחַר שֶׁיִּכְלֶה אָמֵן מִפִּי כָּל הַצִּבּוּר. וְכֵן בְּאָמֵן שֶׁעוֹנִים אַחַר וְיִשְׁמְרֶךָ, וִיחֻנֶּךָּ, שָׁלוֹם, יַמְתִּין הַמַּקְרֵא וְלֹא יַתְחִיל יָאֵר, יִשָּׂא, שִׂים שָׁלוֹם, עַד לְאַחַר שֶׁיִּכְלֶה אָמֵן מִפִּי כָּל הַצִּבּוּר. וְאֵין הַכֹּהֲנִים רַשָּׁאִים

42. See *Maseches Sotah* 40a.

43. The *kohanim,* too, should probably answer *amein* to the berachah of the *Chazzan.* (*Mishnah Berurah* 128:52)

44. The *Mishnah Berurah* 128:65 rules that it is sufficient if most of the congregation answered *amein.*

these words are in the second person. therefore, the *kohanim* turn also toward the sides, in order to bless the entire congregation. They also turn thus when saying the word *shalom,* because it is the conclusion of the blessings. While the *kohanim* prolong the slow chant before saying the concluding words of each verse, which are *ve'yishmerecha, vichuneka* and *shalom,* the congregation recites (the prayer) *Ribono shel olam* etc. "Master of the Universe . . ." The one who prompts the *kohanim,* even though he is not the *Chazzan,* should not recite *Ribono shel olam,* in order not to get confused. Certainly the *Chazzan* should not recite it because it would be considered an interruption of the *Shemoneh esreih.* The *kohanim* should chant only the customary melody in order to avoid confusion.

13) When the *kohanim* recite the words (of the *Birkas Kohanim*),the congregants should not recite any verse, but should listen very attentively to the words pronounced by the *kohanim;* for is there a slave who, while receiving a blessing, would not listen attentively to his blessing?[42] But if the worshippers recite verses, they cannot concentrate on the blessing. However, some are accustomed to recite various verses, and they must be careful to recite them only when the *Chazzan* or *kohanim* are chanting but not when they are saying the words.

14) After the conclusion of the *Birkas Kohanim, the Chazzan* begins reciting *Sim shalom,* and then the *kohanim* turn their faces toward the Holy Ark in the East, and say, *Ribon Ha'olamin* etc. "Master of the Universe," and they prolong this prayer until the *Chazzan* concludes the berachah *Hamevareich es Amo Yisrael bashalom* ["Who blesses His people Israel with peace,"] so that the congregation should respond *amein* to their prayer as well.[43] If they are unable to prolong this prayer until then, they should also recite, *Adir bamarom.* ["Mighty One on high."] On Rosh Hashanah and Yom Kippur when everyone sings *Hayom te'amtzeinu* ["Strengthen us this day,"] the *kohanim* should not begin reciting *Ribon Ha'olamim* until that prayer is nearly ended, in order to finish at the same time as the *Chazzan.*

15) The *kohanim* are not permitted to begin the berachah *Asher kiddeshanu* etc. until the *Chazzan* completely finishes the word *kohanim.* The *Chazzan* is not permitted to begin saying *yevarechecha* until the entire[44] congregation finishes answering *amein.* The same applies to the *amein* the congregation says after *Veyishmerecha, Vichuneka* and *Shalom.* The *Chazzan* must wait and may not begin saying *Ya'eir, Yissa* and *Sim Shalom* until after the entire congregation has said[45] *amein.*[46] The *kohanim* are not permitted to turn their faces away from the congregation to the Holy Ark

---

45. Similarly, the *kohanim* and the one who prompts them must wait for each other to complete the words, and the congregation must wait for the *kohanim* to complete the words before answering *amein.* See *Shulchan Aruch* 128:18; because the congregation must hear the blessings from the *kohanim.* (*Shulchan Aruch Harav* 128:29)

46. *Mishnah Berurah* 128:60 says, since the custom is (in the Diaspora), to thank the *kohanim* after their blessings, the *kohanim* should stay at the *duchan* until after *kaddish* to ensure that *kaddish* be answered properly.

לְהַחֲזִיר פְּנֵיהֶם מִן הַצִּבּוּר לַהֵיכָל, עַד שֶׁיַּתְחִיל שְׁלִיחַ־הַצִּבּוּר שִׂים שָׁלוֹם. וְאֵינָם רַשָּׁאִים לָכֹף אֶצְבְּעוֹתֵיהֶן מִפְּשִׁיטָתָן, עַד שֶׁיַּחֲזִירוּ פְּנֵיהֶם מִן הַצִּבּוּר. וְאֵינָם רַשָּׁאִים לַעֲבוֹר מִן הַדּוּכָן, עַד שֶׁיְּסַיְּמוּ הַצִּבּוּר אָמֵן לְאַחַר הַמְבָרֵךְ אֶת עַמּוֹ יִשְׂרָאֵל בַּשָּׁלוֹם.

טז) כְּשֶׁמַּחֲזִירִין הַכֹּהֲנִים אֶת פְּנֵיהֶם בֵּין בַּתְּחִלָּה בֵּין בַּסּוֹף, לֹא יַחֲזִירוּ אֶלָּא דֶּרֶךְ יָמִין. לָכֵן בַּתְּחִלָּה כְּשֶׁעוֹמְדִים וּפְנֵיהֶם לַמִּזְרָח, יִפְנוּ לַדָּרוֹם וְאַחַר כָּךְ לַמַּעֲרָב. וְאַחַר הַדּוּכָן כְּשֶׁהוֹפְכִין פְּנֵיהֶם לַמִּזְרָח, פּוֹנִים דֶּרֶךְ צָפוֹן. וּכְשֶׁהֵם יוֹרְדִין מִן הַדּוּכָן, יִהְיֶה פְּנֵיהֶם קְצָת לְנֶגֶד אֲרוֹן הַקֹּדֶשׁ, וְיִפְסְעוּ לַאֲחוֹרֵיהֶם כְּתַלְמִיד הַנִּפְטָר מִלִּפְנֵי רַבּוֹ. כְּשֶׁנּוֹעֲלִין הַמִּנְעָלִים, לֹא יִגְּעוּ בָּהֶם. וְאִם נָגְעוּ, צְרִיכִין לִטּוֹל יְדֵיהֶם.

יז) מִשְׁתַּדְּלִים שֶׁשְּׁלִיחַ־הַצִּבּוּר לֹא יִהְיֶה כֹּהֵן. וְאִם הוּא כֹּהֵן, לֹא יַעֲלֶה לַדּוּכָן, וְגַם לֹא יִקְרָא לִפְנֵי הַכֹּהֲנִים, אֶלָּא אִישׁ אַחֵר יַעֲמֹד אֶצְלוֹ שֶׁיִּקְרָא כֹּהֲנִים, וְגַם יַקְרֵא לִפְנֵיהֶם אֶת הַתֵּבוֹת יְבָרֶכְךָ וְגוֹ׳, וּשְׁלִיחַ־הַצִּבּוּר עוֹמֵד וְשׁוֹתֵק עַד שִׂים שָׁלוֹם וְאֵינוֹ עוֹבֵר בְּמַה שֶּׁאֵינוֹ עוֹלֶה לַדּוּכָן, אַף שֶׁזֶּה קָרָא כֹּהֲנִים בְּקוֹל, כִּי אֵין הַכַּוָּנָה אֶלָּא עַל מִי שֶׁאֵינוֹ עוֹמֵד בִּתְפִלָּה וְעָקַר רַגְלָיו בִּרְצֵה. וְאִם אֵין שָׁם כֹּהֵן אַחֵר אֶלָּא הוּא, אֲזַי כְּדֵי שֶׁלֹּא תִתְבַּטֵּל מִצְוַת נְשִׂיאַת כַּפַּיִם, יַעֲלֶה הוּא לַדּוּכָן וְסוֹמֵךְ עַל נְטִילַת יָדַיִם שֶׁל שַׁחֲרִית. כֵּיצַד עוֹשֶׂה. עוֹקֵר רַגְלָיו קְצָת כְּשֶׁאוֹמֵר רְצֵה, וְאוֹמֵר עַד וּלְךָ נָאֶה לְהוֹדוֹת, וְאַחַר אוֹמֵר, אֱלֹקֵינוּ וֵאלֹקֵי אֲבוֹתֵינוּ בָּרְכֵנוּ בַּבְּרָכָה וְכוּ׳, וּשְׁלִיחַ־הַצִּבּוּר עוֹלֶה לַדּוּכָן, וְזֶה הָאַחֵר מַקְרֵא לוֹ, וְחוֹזֵר שְׁלִיחַ־הַצִּבּוּר וְאוֹמֵר שִׂים שָׁלוֹם, וְלֹא יֹאמַר רִבּוֹן הָעוֹלָמִים וְכוּ׳, עַד לְאַחַר הַקַּדִּישׁ. וְאִם לֹא עָקַר רַגְלָיו בִּרְצֵה, אֵינוֹ רַשַּׁאי לַעֲלוֹת.

יח) צִבּוּר שֶׁכֻּלָּם כֹּהֲנִים, אִם אֵין שָׁם אֶלָּא עֲשָׂרָה, כֻּלָּם עוֹלִים לַדּוּכָן. לְמִי מְבָרְכִין. לַאֲחֵיהֶם שֶׁבַּשָּׂדוֹת. וּמִי עוֹנֶה אַחֲרֵיהֶם אָמֵן. נָשִׁים וָטַף. וַאֲפִלּוּ אֵין נָשִׁים וָטַף, עֲנִיַּת אָמֵן אֵינָהּ מְעַכֶּבֶת. וְאִם יֵשׁ יוֹתֵר מֵעֲשָׂרָה, הַיְתֵרִים מֵעֲשָׂרָה יַעֲלוּ לַדּוּכָן, וַעֲשָׂרָה יִשָּׁאֲרוּ לַעֲנוֹת אָמֵן.

יט) כֹּהֵן שֶׁנָּשָׂא אֶת כַּפָּיו וְאַחַר כָּךְ הָלַךְ לְבֵית־כְּנֶסֶת אַחֵר, אִם רוֹצֶה.

---

47. *Shulchan Aruch* 128:17, *Mishnah Berurah.*
48. In order to continue their *tefillah.* (*Ramah* 128:17)

until the *chazzan* begins *Sim Shalom.* They are not permitted to relax their fingers from their extended position until they turn their faces away from the congregation. They are not permitted to leave the *duchan* until the congregation[47] responds *amein* after the berachah *Hamevoreich es amo Yisrael bashalom.*

16) Whenever the *kohanim* turn around, either at the beginning or at the end of (the *Birkas Kohanim*), they must always turn towards the right. Therefore, at the beginning, when they are standing facing to the East, they should first turn South and then West. After concluding *Birkas Kohanim*, when they turn to face East, they should do so by first turning North. When going down from the *duchan,* their faces should be somewhat towards the Holy Ark, and they should walk backwards, like a pupil taking leave of his master. When putting on their shoes, they should not touch them. If they did touch them, they must wash their hands.[48]

17) An effort should be made to have a *Chazzan,* who is not a *kohein.* If he is a *kohein,* he should not go up to *duchan,* and should not prompt the *kohanim,* but someone else should stand alongside him to call *kohanim.* He should also read to them the words *Yevarechecha* etc. and the *Chazzan* should remain silent, until *Sim Shalom.* He commits no sin by not going up to bless the people, even though the other man called out *kohanim,* because this call is intended only for a *kohein* who is not engaged in prayer, and who moved from his place during *Retzeih.* If he is the only *kohein* present, then, in order not to forego the mitzvah of the priestly blessings, he should go up to the *duchan,*[49] relying on his hand-washing in the morning. How should he act? He should move his feet slightly while saying *Retzeih,* and continue until *Ulecha na'eh lehodos.* ["And to You it is fitting to give thanks."] Then someone else says, *Elokeinu veilokei avoseinu barecheinu vaberachah;* the *Chazzan* then goes up to the *duchan,* while the other man prompts him. After this, the *Chazzan* resumes and recites *Sim Shalom,* but does not say *Ribon Ha'olamim* until after reciting the *kaddish.* If he did not move his feet while reciting *Retzeih,* he is not permitted to go up to the *duchan.*

18) If a congregation consists of *kohanim* only, then, if there are no more than ten men, they all go up to the *duchan.* Whom do they bless? Their brethren in the fields (countryside). And who responds, *amein?* The women and the little children. Even if there are no women and children, the lack of the *amein* response is not an obstacle. If there are more than ten *kohanim* present, then as many as there are in excess of ten go up to the *duchan,* and ten should remain to respond *amein.*[50]

19) A *kohein* who had already blessed the congregation, and, afterwards, went to

---

49. This is so only if he is sure he will not get confused in his *tefillah.* (*Shulchan Aruch* 128:20) Even if they call him, he may go up only if he is sure he will not get confused. (*Peri Megadim*)
But the Eliyahu Rabbah, Derech Hachaim and Chayei Adam hold, if called, he must go up, even if he is not sure of himself. Now that we use a siddur, there is no concern of confusion. (Mishnah Berurah 128:75)

50. When there are no *Yisraeilim* [Israelites] in the congregation, the priestly blessings is a *de'rabbonon* mitzvah, not a *de'oraisa.* (*Peri Megadim.* See *Biur Halachah* 128:25)

יָכוֹל לַעֲלוֹת לַדּוּכָן גַּם כָּאן. וְאִם אֵינוֹ רוֹצֶה, אַף שֶׁשּׁוֹמֵעַ קוֹרְאִין כֹּהֲנִים, אֵינוֹ צָרִיךְ לַעֲלוֹת, כֵּיוָן שֶׁכְּבָר עָלָה.

כ) מִי שֶׁיֵּשׁ לוֹ מוּם בְּפָנָיו, בִּמְדִינוֹתֵינוּ שֶׁנּוֹהֲגִים שֶׁכָּל הַכֹּהֲנִים מְשַׁלְשְׁלִים אֶת הַטַּלִּיתִים עַל פְּנֵיהֶם, מֻתָּר לִשָּׂא אֶת כַּפָּיו. אֲבָל מִי שֶׁיֵּשׁ לוֹ מוּם בְּיָדָיו, כְּגוֹן שֶׁהֵן בַּהֲקָנִיּוֹת (פי' מִין נֶגַע לָבָן) אוֹ מְנֻמָּרוֹת בִּנְקֻדּוֹת דַּקּוֹת אוֹ שֶׁהֵן עֲקֻמּוֹת, אוֹ שֶׁאֵינוֹ יָכוֹל לְחַלֵּק אֶת אֶצְבְּעוֹתָיו, לֹא יִשָּׂא אֶת כַּפָּיו, מִפְּנֵי שֶׁהָעָם יִסְתַּכְּלוּ בוֹ וְיַסִּיחוּ דַעְתָּם. וְאִם הוּא רָגִיל בְּעִירוֹ, שֶׁכְּבָר שָׁהָה שָׁם שְׁלֹשִׁים יוֹם וּמַכִּירִים אוֹתוֹ, נוֹשֵׂא אֶת כַּפָּיו. הָיוּ יָדָיו צְבוּעוֹת, לֹא יִשָּׂא אֶת כַּפָּיו, מִפְּנֵי שֶׁהָעָם מִסְתַּכְּלִין בָּהֶם. וְאִם רֹב הָעִיר מְלַאכְתָּן בְּכָךְ, יִשָּׂא אֶת כַּפָּיו. וּמִי שֶׁאֵינוֹ יוֹדֵעַ לַחְתֹּךְ הָאוֹתִיּוֹת הֵיטֵב, וְקוֹרֵא שִׁי"ן יְמָנִית כְּמוֹ שְׂמָאלִית, לֹא יִשָּׂא אֶת כַּפָּיו, אִם לֹא שֶׁכָּל הַקָּהָל קוֹרֵא כֵּן. וְכָל כֹּהֵן שֶׁאֵינוֹ נוֹשֵׂא אֶת כַּפָּיו, יֵצֵא קֹדֶם רְצֵה מִבֵּית־הַכְּנֶסֶת לַחוּץ, עַד שֶׁיִּגְמְרוּ נְשִׂיאַת־כַּפַּיִם.

כא) הָרַג אֶת הַנֶּפֶשׁ בְּמֵזִיד, אֲפִלּוּ עָשָׂה תְשׁוּבָה, לֹא יִשָּׂא אֶת כַּפָּיו. וְאִם הָרַג בִּשְׁגָגָה וְעָשָׂה תְשׁוּבָה, נוֹשֵׂא אֶת כַּפָּיו. וְכֵן מוּמָר שֶׁעָשָׂה תְשׁוּבָה, נוֹשֵׂא אֶת כַּפָּיו. נָשָׂא גְרוּשָׁה אוֹ חֲלוּצָה אוֹ שֶׁנִּטְמָא לְמֵת שֶׁאָסוּר לוֹ לְטַמֵּא אֵלָיו, לֹא יִשָּׂא אֶת כַּפָּיו, עַד שֶׁיַּעֲשֶׂה תְשׁוּבָה עַל פִּי תַלְמִיד חָכָם. וּשְׁאָר עֲבֵרוֹת, אֵינָן מוֹנְעוֹת מִנְּשִׂיאַת־כַּפַּיִם. חָלָל, אֵינוֹ נוֹשֵׂא אֶת כַּפָּיו.

כב) אוֹנֵן אֵינוֹ נוֹשֵׂא אֶת כַּפָּיו. וַאֲבָל תּוֹךְ שְׁנֵים־עָשָׂר חֹדֶשׁ עַל אָבִיו וְאִמּוֹ אוֹ תּוֹךְ שְׁלֹשִׁים עַל שְׁאָר קְרוֹבִים, אֵינוֹ נוֹשֵׂא אֶת כַּפָּיו, וְצָרִיךְ

51. Unless they follow the custom of covering their hands with their *tallis.* (Shulchan Aruch, Remah 128:31)

52. Only if he intends to stay there for at least six months or so. But if he just happened to be there for thirty days, he may not go up. (*Shulchan Aruch* 128:30)

53. *Radvaz, Maharit.* See *Mishnah Berurah* 128:120, that if many people say it that way, he may *duchan.*

54. In all these cases, if he went to the *duchan,* he need not step down. (*Peri Chadash,* also see *Chayei Adam*)

55. *Peri Chadash, Eliyahu Rabbah.* But the *Ramah* 128:35 permits him. *Shulchan Aruch* forbids him, even if it was accidental. *Biyur Halachah* remains undecided, but if he went up, he shouldn't step down.

56. An idol worshipper or one who publicly desecrates Shabbos may not go up to *duchan.* (*Mishnah Berurah* 128:134, see *Igros Moshe* 1:33)

another synagogue, if he wishes to do so, he may go up to the *duchan* again, but if he does not wish to do so, even if he heard the call *kohanim,* he is not obligated to go up, since he has already gone up [and fulfilled his obligation.]

20) In our communities where it is customary for all *kohanim* to lower their *tallisim* over their faces, a *kohein* who has a blemish on his face, is permitted to pronounce the *Birkas Kohanim.* But a *kohein* who has a defect on his hands, like *bahakaniyos,* i.e. a white lesion, or they are speckled with small spots, or they are deformed, or he is unable to separate his fingers, may not bless the people,[51] because the people might look at him, and be distracted. If he is well-known in his town, having lived there for thirty days,[52] and people recognize him, he may raise his hands to bless the people. If his hands are discolored from dye or paint, he may not raise his hands to bless the people because the people will look at them. If most of the people of the town follow this trade [of dyeing or painting], he is permitted to raise his hands in blessing. If he does not know how to pronounce the letters properly, or if he pronounces the letter *shin* like the letter *sin,* he may not raise his hands to bless the people, unless the entire congregation[53] pronounces it like that. Any *kohein,* who does not raise his hands for the *Birkas Kohanim,* should leave the synagogue before *Retzeih* is said, [and stay outside] until the end of the priestly blessing.[54]

21) A *kohein,* who once intentionally killed someone, even though he has repented, may not raise his hands to bless the people.[55] If he accidentally killed someone, and has repented, he may raise his hands. Similarly, an apostate[56] who repented, may raise his hands to bless the people. A *kohein* who married a divorcee, or a *chalutzah*[57], or who became ritually unclean by contact with a corpse,[58] for whom he is forbidden to defile himself, may not raise his hands until he repents under the direction of a Torah scholar. Other transgressions do not disqualify a *kohein* from raising his hands. A *chalal*[59] may not raise his hands to bless the people.[60]

22) A mourner, before burial takes place, may not raise his hands.[61] A mourner, during the twelve months of mourning for his father or mother, or, during the thirty

---

57. According to *Deut.* 25:5–10, a brother-in-law has the obligation to marry his brother's childless widow. If he declines, he must perform the *chalitzah* ceremony, whereby the widow attains the status of *chalutzah.* A *kohein* is forbidden to marry a chalutzah or a divorcée.

58. Even a non-Jewish corpse, which is not a *de'oraisa* prohibition. (*Mahari Assad* 47) A *kohein* who is a medical student or doctor and exposes himself to this, may not *duchan.* (*Ksav Sofer* 16, *Maharam Shick* 303) This is only if he does this on purpose, but if by accident (out of ignorance), he may *duchan.* (*Beis Yosef, Mishnah Berurah* 128:150)

59. A *chalal* is a person born from a marriage forbidden only to *kohanim.*

60. If he went up to the *duchan,* he must step down. (*Peri Chadash*)

61. Even on Yom Tov, when the laws pertaining to the mourning period do not take effect. (see Chapter 198) He may not *duchan* because he is not in a state of happiness. (*Magein Avraham, Mishnah Berurah* 128:158)

לָצֵאת מִבֵּית־הַכְּנֶסֶת קֹדֶם רְצֵה עַד אַחַר נְשִׂיאַת־כַּפַּיִם. וְאִם אֵין בְּבֵית־הַכְּנֶסֶת שְׁנֵי כֹהֲנִים אֲחֵרִים, מֻתָּר לְאָבֵל לִשָּׂא אֶת כַּפָּיו תּוֹךְ שְׁנֵים־עָשָׂר חֹדֶשׁ עַל אָבִיו וְאִמּוֹ וְתוֹךְ שְׁלֹשִׁים עַל שְׁאָר קְרוֹבִים. אֲבָל תּוֹךְ שִׁבְעָה, כְּגוֹן הַקּוֹבֵר מֵתוֹ בָּרֶגֶל, אֲפִלּוּ אִם אֵין שָׁם שְׁנֵי כֹהֲנִים אֲחֵרִים, אֵינוֹ נוֹשֵׂא אֶת כַּפָּיו.

סִימָן קא
דִּין הֲכָנָה מִיּוֹם־טוֹב רִאשׁוֹן לְיוֹם־טוֹב שֵׁנִי אוֹ לַחֹל

א) כָּל הַמְּלָאכוֹת הַמֻּתָּרוֹת לַעֲשׂוֹתָן בְּיוֹם־טוֹב, זֶה דַוְקָא לְצֹרֶךְ אוֹתוֹ הַיּוֹם. אֲבָל לְהָכִין מִיּוֹם רִאשׁוֹן לְיוֹם שֵׁנִי (אֲפִלּוּ בְּרֹאשׁ־הַשָּׁנָה), וּמִכָּל־שֶׁכֵּן לְיוֹם חֹל, אָסוּר. אַךְ אִם הוּא צָרִיךְ לְבַשֵּׁל בִּשְׁבִיל הַיּוֹם, מֻתָּר לוֹ לָקַחַת קְדֵרָה יוֹתֵר גְּדוֹלָה וּלְמַלֵּא אוֹתָהּ בָּשָׂר וְכַיּוֹצֵא בוֹ, אַף־עַל־פִּי שֶׁאֵינוֹ צָרִיךְ הַיּוֹם כָּל־כָּךְ, וְיוֹתִיר גַּם לַלַּיְלָה אוֹ לְמָחָר. וְדַוְקָא בְּתַבְשִׁיל בִּקְדֵרָה מֻתָּר, מִפְּנֵי שֶׁהַתַּבְשִׁיל מֵטְעָם יוֹתֵר כְּשֶׁמִּתְבַּשֵּׁל הַרְבֵּה בָּשָׂר בְּיַחַד, וּבִלְבַד שֶׁלֹּא יֹאמַר בַּפֶּה, שֶׁהַמּוֹתָר יִהְיֶה לְצֹרֶךְ הַלַּיְלָה אוֹ לְצֹרֶךְ מָחָר, אֶלָּא יְבַשֵּׁל סְתָם. אֲבָל בִּשְׁאָר מַאֲכָלִים, אָסוּר לְהוֹסִיף בְּדָבָר שֶׁיֵּשׁ קְצָת טִרְחָא בְּמַה שֶּׁהוּא מוֹסִיף.

ב) אֲפִלּוּ דָּבָר שֶׁאֵינוֹ מְלָאכָה, כְּגוֹן לְהָבִיא מַיִם אוֹ אֲפִלּוּ יַיִן לְקִדּוּשׁ אוֹ לְהַבְדָּלָה, אָסוּר לְהָכִין. וְכֵן אָסוּר לְהַעֲמִיד אֶת הַנֵּרוֹת בַּמְּנוֹרָה אוֹ לְתַקֵּן אֶת הַפְּתִילוֹת וְהָעֲשָׁשִׁיּוֹת בְּיוֹם־טוֹב רִאשׁוֹן לְצֹרֶךְ הַלַּיְלָה, אֶלָּא אִם הוּא צָרִיךְ לְהִשְׁתַּמֵּשׁ בָּהֶם גַּם קֹדֶם הַלַּיְלָה, אוֹ לִכְבוֹד בֵּית־הַכְּנֶסֶת.

ג) גּוֹי שֶׁהֵבִיא בְּיוֹם־טוֹב רִאשׁוֹן דָּגִים אוֹ פֵּרוֹת שֶׁיֵּשׁ לָחוּשׁ שֶׁמָּא נִצּוֹדוּ הַיּוֹם, אוֹ נִתְלְשׁוּ הַיּוֹם, אוֹ הוּבְאוּ מִחוּץ לַתְּחוּם, אֲסוּרִים הַיּוֹם

---

62. If he were called upon to *duchan,* he should not go up. (*Peri Chadash*) If he went up, he does not have to step down. (*Rav Ephraim Zalman Margalios Z"l* [Laws of *Onein*], *Ba'eir Heiteiv, Peri Chadash*) The *Peri Megadim* 128:64 says he should step down. The *Mishnah Berurah* 128:158 seems to be inclined to say if he were called upon, he should go up, but he also mentions the ruling of *Peri Chadash,* also see *Chayei Adam.*

1. This includes even such chores that are not halachically considered *melachos.* See paragraph 2. (*Magein Avraham, Mishnah Berurah* 503:1)

2. *Maseches Beitzah* 2b.

3. *Shulchan Aruch* 503:1.

4. The *halachah* is, that if you put it on the fire at one time, you are permitted to do so with all foods, since you are not performing additional labor, once it is on the fire. Regarding

days of mourning for other relatives, may not raise his hands.[62] He must leave the synagogue before *Retzeih* is said, and stay outside until after *Birkas Kohanim.* In the event there are no other *kohanim* in the synagogue, the mourner is permitted to raise his hands during the twelve month period of mourning, for his father or mother, or during the thirty days of mourning for other relatives. But during the seven days of mourning, for example, if he buried his dead on the Festival, even if there are no other *kohanim,* he may not raise his hands to bless the people.

Chapter 101

Laws Concerning Preparation on the First Day of Yom Tov for the Second Day or for a Weekday

1) All *Melachah*[1] that is permitted on Yom Tov is permitted only if it is necessary for that day. But to prepare on the first day of Yom Tov for the second day,[2] (even of Rosh Hashanah), and certainly for a weekday, is forbidden. However, if you need to cook for that day, you are permitted to take a larger pot and fill it with meat or something similar, even though you do not need so much for that day, and leave some for the evening, or for the next day.[3] Only in the case of cooked food, is this permitted. because it tastes better when a large quantity of meat is cooked in one pot.[4] This is permitted provided you do not expressly state that the leftovers will be for the night, or for the following day. It should be cooked without mentioning anything at all.[5] In the case of other foods, it is forbidden to add (to that day's needs), if even a little additional labor is entailed. because of adding to it.

2) Even something that is not actual work, such as bringing in water, or even wine for *kiddush* and *havdalah,* is forbidden if it is for the next day. It is also forbidden to put the candles in the candlesticks, or to prepare the wicks and lamps on the first day of Yom Tov, for the night (of the second day of Yom Tov), unless they are needed also before the night,[6] or they are lit in honor of the synagogue.

3) If a non-Jew brings fish or fruit on the first day of Yom Tov, and there is reason to suspect that the fish were caught, or the fruit was picked on that day, or brought in from outside the *Techum,*[7] it is forbidden to handle them on that day. In the

---

meat dishes, however, you are permitted to add to the pot even after it is on the fire. (*Magein Avraham* 503:2)

5. If you have already eaten that day, you may not cook a pot for the following day, even if you eat a piece of it today. (*Shulchan Aruch* 503:1) If you intentionally did it anyway, you may use it if you eat a piece of it today. (*Magein Avraham, Beis Meir, Shulchan Aruch Harav*) *Eliyahu Rabbah* rules that it is permitted, even if you intended to eat a piece of it, but ended up not doing so. *Peri Chadash* and *Vilna Gaon* rule, even if you eat a piece of it, it is forbidden, for it was done with dishonest intent.

6. If it will be difficult to obtain wine at night, you may bring it when it is still day, if it is for a *mitzvah.* (second night of Yom Tov or Shabbos) (*Chayei Adam* 153:6.)

7. See glossary and Chapter 65. If the non-Jew is living in your city and is known to have the items in stock within the *techum,* you may assume what he has brought is from within the *techum.* (*Shulchan Aruch* 515:7)

בְּטִלְטוּל, וְלָעֶרֶב מֻתָּרִים. שֶׁאִם הַגּוֹי מַכִּירוֹ וְנוֹתְנָם לוֹ בְּלֹא קְצִיצַת דָּמִים, מֻתָּר לְקַחְתָּם וּלְאָכְלָם, חוּץ מִיּוֹם־טוֹב שֶׁל רֹאשׁ־הַשָּׁנָה, שֶׁאֲפִלּוּ אִם הוּבְאוּ בְּיוֹם רִאשׁוֹן, אֲסוּרִים גַּם בְּיוֹם שֵׁנִי.

ד) אִם הֱבִיאָם הַגּוֹי בִּשְׁבִיל יִשְׂרָאֵל לְדוֹרוֹן אוֹ לְמָכְרָם לוֹ, יֵשׁ לֶאֱסוֹר גַּם בְּיוֹם־טוֹב שֵׁנִי. וְאַף אִם חָל יוֹם־טוֹב בַּיּוֹם הַחֲמִישִׁי וּבַיּוֹם הַשִּׁשִּׁי וְהֵבִיא בַּיּוֹם הַחֲמִישִׁי, אִם יֵשׁ צֹרֶךְ גָּדוֹל, מֻתָּר לְטַלְטְלָן בַּיּוֹם הַשִּׁשִּׁי וּלְבַשְּׁלָם לִכְבוֹד שַׁבָּת. וּבְיוֹם־טוֹב שֶׁל רֹאשׁ־הַשָּׁנָה, גַּם זֶה אָסוּר.

ה) חָלָב שֶׁחֲלָבוֹ גוֹי בְּיוֹם רִאשׁוֹן וְיִשְׂרָאֵל רוֹאֵהוּ, מֻתָּר בְּיוֹם שֵׁנִי. וְאִם חֲלָבוֹ בְּשַׁבָּת, וְיוֹם רִאשׁוֹן הוּא יוֹם־טוֹב, אָסוּר בְּיוֹם רִאשׁוֹן. וּבְרֹאשׁ־הַשָּׁנָה, אִם חֲלָבוֹ בְּיוֹם רִאשׁוֹן שֶׁל יוֹם־טוֹב, אָסוּר גַּם בְּיוֹם שֵׁנִי, וְגַם בְּשַׁבָּת הַסְּמוּכָה לוֹ.

ו) פְּתִילוֹת שֶׁהִדְלִיק בָּהֶן בְּיוֹם־טוֹב רִאשׁוֹן וְכָבוּ, מֻתָּר לְהַדְלִיק בָּהֶן בְּיוֹם־טוֹב שֵׁנִי. אַךְ בִּשְׁנֵי יָמִים טוֹבִים שֶׁל רֹאשׁ־הַשָּׁנָה, אָסוּר לְהַדְלִיק בְּיוֹם־טוֹב שֵׁנִי בִּפְתִילָה שֶׁכָּבְתָה בְּיוֹם רִאשׁוֹן, וַאֲפִלּוּ בַּקָּצֶה הַשֵּׁנִי. וּמִכָּל מָקוֹם מֻתָּרוֹת בְּטִלְטוּל לַהֲסִירָן וְלָתֵת חֲדָשׁוֹת. וְכֵן בְּיוֹם־טוֹב שֶׁלְּאַחַר שַׁבָּת.

---

8. Immediately after nightfall. (*Mishnah Berurah* 515:59)

9. This refers only to where it may have been harvested or caught on that day for these are *melachos.* But if there is only concern that they may have been brought in from outside the *techum,* they are permitted on the second day, even if they were brought for a Jew and even if it is *Rosh Hashanah* or Shabbos, but you must wait for the time it would take the non-Jew to bring it from that place after nightfall.(see *Shulchan Aruch* 515:8, *Vilna Gaon, Mishna Berurah* 515:66)

10. *Ramah* 515:1, *Rabbeinu Tam.* However, it is permitted for guests who were unexpected when the non-Jew brought it, or for out-of-town guests. In such a case, you may also eat from it with them in their honor. (*Magein Avraham, Mishnah Berurah* 515:12)

11. This is only in cases where a *melachah* is involved, but where the *techum* is concerned, the *poskim* are lenient, as is the *Shulchan Aruch.* (*Ramah* 515:5, *Mishnah Berurah)* The *Misgeros Hashulchan* says the grouping together of *techum* and *melachah* in paragraphs 3 and 4 may be a

evening on the second night of Yom Tov[8] it is permitted to use them. Thus, if the non-Jew knows you, and gives them to you without quoting a price, you may take them and eat them; except on Rosh Hashanah, when, even if they were brought on the first day, they are forbidden on the second day.[9]

4) If the non-Jew brings these things, as a gift for a Jew or to sell them to him, they are forbidden even on the second day of Yom Tov.[10] [11] If Yom Tov occurs on Thursday and Friday, and the non-Jew brings them on Thursday, if it is very urgent,[12] you are permitted to handle them[13] on Friday, and cook them in honor of Shabbos.[14] On the Yom Tov of Rosh Hashanah, even this, is forbidden.

5) Milk which non-Jew milks on the first day of Yom Tov, in the presence of a Jew, may be used on the second day of Yom Tov. If the milking was done on Shabbos, and Sunday is the first day of Yom Tov, it is forbidden on Sunday. Milk that was milked on the first day of Rosh Hashanah, is also forbidden on the second day, and also on the Shabbos if it follows immediately.

6) Wicks that were lit on the first (night of) Yom Tov and were extinguished, may be lit on the second day of Yom Tov. But, on the two days of Rosh Hashanah it is forbidden to light a wick on the second day that was extinguished on the first day. It is forbidden to light them even at the other end.[15] However, you are allowed to handle them in order to remove and replace them.[16] The same law applies when Yom Tov occurs the day after Shabbos.[17]

---

typographical error in the *Kitzur Shulchan Aruch,* for it is explicit in the *Talmud* and *poskim* that they are not the same. See footnote 9.

12. *Mishnah Berurah* 515:42 says if you need it in honor of Shabbos, and you have no other food of this type in your house, it is also permitted.

13. If you do have more of this type of food in your house, you may still have it cooked for Shabbos by a non-Jew, but you should not handle it. (*Magein Avraham, Eliyahu Rabbah, Mishnah Berurah*)

14. You must wait on Friday night, however, until after "due time" elapses. (*Beis Yosef, Mishnah Berurah* 515:40)

15. *Taz* 501:7. The reason is, since a charred wick lights better than an uncharred one, the wick has been prepared from one day *Rosh Hashanah* to the second day. The *Ramah, Rosh, Or Zarua, Meiri* etc. permit it because it is possible to light an uncharred wick so it is not considered preparation. The *Peri Chadash* and *Eliyahu Rabbah* say those who are stringent will be blessed. The *Mishnah Berurah* says that you should try to be stringent and prepare different wicks in advance (before *Rosh Hashanah)* and if not, at least light the other end. *The Shaar Hatziyun* 501:43 permits lighting the uncharred end. The *Taz* forbids this to ensure you do not light the charred tip.

16. You may handle them in order to use them or if you need the space they occupy. (*Shulchan Aruch Harav* 501) According to one opinion in the *Peri Megadim M.Z.* 501:7, you may not handle the remnants of the wick, even for the space it occupies.

17. When the first day of Yom Tov follows Shabbos. (*Taz*)

סִימָן קב
דִּינֵי עֵרוּב תַּבְשִׁילִין

א) יוֹם־טוֹב שֶׁחָל לִהְיוֹת בְּעֶרֶב שַׁבָּת, אָסוּר לֶאֱפוֹת אוֹ לְבַשֵּׁל בִּקְדֵרָה מְיֻחֶדֶת לַשַּׁבָּת, אֶלָּא עַל יְדֵי עֵרוּב תַּבְשִׁילִין שֶׁעוֹשֶׂה בְּעֶרֶב יוֹם־טוֹב, דְּהַיְנוּ שֶׁלּוֹקֵחַ אֵיזֶה תַּבְשִׁיל אוֹ צְלִי שֶׁרָאוּי לְלַפֵּת בּוֹ אֶת הַפַּת, וְגַם פַּת, וּמְבָרֵךְ, אֲשֶׁר קִדְּשָׁנוּ בְּמִצְוֹתָיו וְצִוָּנוּ עַל מִצְוַת עֵרוּב. וְאוֹמֵר, בַּהֲדֵין עֵרוּבָא יְהֵא שָׁרֵא לָנָא לַאֲפוּיֵי, לְבַשּׁוּלֵי, וּלְאַטְמוּנֵי, וּלְאַדְלוּקֵי שְׁרָגָא, וּלְמֶעְבַּד כָּל צָרְכָּנָא מִיּוֹמָא טָבָא לְשַׁבְּתָא. וְאִם אֵינוֹ מֵבִין לָשׁוֹן זֶה, יֹאמַר בְּלָשׁוֹן שֶׁהוּא מֵבִין.

ב) צָרִיךְ שֶׁיְּהֵא הַתַּבְשִׁיל דָּבָר שֶׁדַּרְכּוֹ לְאָכְלוֹ עִם פַּת, כְּגוֹן בָּשָׂר, דָּגִים, וּבֵיצִים. אֲבָל דָּבָר שֶׁאֵין דַּרְכּוֹ לְאָכְלוֹ אִם פַּת, לֹא מַהֲנֵי. שִׁעוּר הַתַּבְשִׁיל, כַּזַּיִת. וְהַפַּת כַּבֵּיצָה. וְיֵשׁ לְהַדֵּר אַחַת מָנָה יָפָה לִכְבוֹד הַמִּצְוָה. וְגַם הַפַּת תְּהֵא שְׁלֵמָה, וְיַנִּיחָהּ בְּשַׁבָּת לְלֶחֶם מִשְׁנֶה, וּבִסְעוּדָה שְׁלִישִׁית יִבְצַע עָלֶיהָ, שֶׁכֵּיוָן דְּאִתְעֲבִיד בַּהּ מִצְוָה חֲדָא זִמְנָא, יִתְעֲבֵיד בַּהּ נַמִּי מִצְוָה אַחֲרִיתָא.

ג) אֵין עֵרוּב תַּבְשִׁילִין מוֹעִיל אֶלָּא לְהַתִּיר לַעֲשׂוֹת כָּל צָרְכֵי שַׁבָּת בְּיוֹם־טוֹב בְּעוֹד הַיּוֹם גָּדוֹל, דְּהַיְנוּ שֶׁיֵּשׁ שָׁהוּת בַּיּוֹם, שֶׁאִם הָיוּ מִזְדַּמְּנִים לוֹ אוֹרְחִים שֶׁלֹּא אָכְלוּ הַיּוֹם, הָיוּ אוֹכְלִים וְנֶהֱנִים בּוֹ־בַּיּוֹם קֹדֶם בֵּין־הַשְּׁמָשׁוֹת מִמְּלַאכְתּוֹ שֶׁעָשָׂה בְּיוֹם־טוֹב. אֲבָל אִם אֵין שָׁהוּת בַּיּוֹם לֵהָנוֹת מִמְּלַאכְתּוֹ, אֵינוֹ מוֹעִיל עֵרוּב הַתַּבְשִׁילִין. וְלָכֵן נוֹהֲגִין כְּשֶׁחָל יוֹם־טוֹב בְּעֶרֶב שַׁבָּת, מַקְדִּימִין לְהִתְפַּלֵּל עַרְבִית שֶׁל שַׁבָּת מִבְּעוֹד יוֹם, שֶׁיִּהְיוּ זְרִיזִין לְמַהֵר לִגְמוֹר הַכֹּל קֹדֶם שֶׁאוֹמְרִים מִזְמוֹר שִׁיר לְיוֹם הַשַּׁבָּת.

---

1. Even at twilight. (*Ramah* 527:1) After the congregation says *Barechu* at *Maariv,* you may no longer make an *eiruv,* even if it is not yet dark. (*Magein Avraham, Derech Hachaim*) In an urgent situation, you may make the *eiruv* until the congregation says the Yom Tov *Shemoneh Esrei,* according to the ruling of the *Taz.* (*Chayei Adam, Mishnah Berurah* 527:4) If you, accepted the holiness of Yom Tov, on your own, some hold that you may still make an *eiruv.* (see *Mishnah Berurah* and *Sha'ar Hatziyun* 527:9)

2. This is preferable, but it also helps if you made it many days before, in which case you should still recite the declaration at the end of this paragraph (without a berachah). (*Taz, Magein Avraham* 527:13)

3. You only need to take bread if you wish to bake for Shabbos. (*Beis Yosef, Vilna Gaon, Mishnah Berurah* 527:6) In any event, if you only used a cooked food for your *eiruv,* it is sufficient. (*Shulchan Aruch* 527:2)

Chapter 102

The Laws of Eiruv Tavshilin

1) When Yom Tov occurs on Friday, it is forbidden to bake or cook in a separate pot for Shabbos, unless you make an *eiruv tavshilin* on *erev* Yom Tov.[1] [2] This is done as follows: Take some cooked or roasted food that is eaten with bread, and take bread with it,[3] and recite the berachah *Asher kideshanu bemitzvosav* ["Who has sanctified us with the commandments] *vetzivanu al mitzvas eiruv.* ["and commanded us concerning the mitzvah of *eiruv.*"] And declare: "By means of this *eiruv* it will be permissible for us to bake, cook, keep food warm, kindle a light and do anything necessary on Yom Tov for the sake of Shabbos." If you do not understand this language, you should say it in the language you understand.

2) The cooked food[4] must be the kind usually eaten with bread, like meat, fish or eggs. But food not usually eaten with bread[5] is not acceptable (for *eiruv tavshilin*). The required amount of the food is a *kazayis,*[6] and of the bread, a *kebeitzah.*[7] [8] You should take a generous portion in honor of the mitzvah. The bread you use should be a whole[9] loaf and should be placed [on the table], for *lechem mishneh*[10] on Shabbos. You should eat it at the third Shabbos meal; since one mitzvah was performed with it, it is appropriate to use it for another mitzvah.

3) An *eiruv tavshilin* is effective in permitting you to prepare all your Shabbos needs on Yom Tov [only when you make the *eiruv*] early in the day; that is, there must be enough time in the day, that should guests arrive, who had not yet eaten that day, they would have enough time to eat and enjoy the food that was prepared on Yom Tov before the onset of twilight. But if there is not enough time (left in the day) to enjoy the benefit of the labor, the *eiruv tavshilin* is not effective.[11] Therefore, it is customary, when Yom Tov occurs on Friday, to begin *Maariv* prayers Friday night earlier than usual, while it is still daytime,[12] so that people will hurry to complete all their work before the congregation recites, *Mizmor shir leyom haShabbos.* The cooked dishes that you want to keep warm for Shabbos, should be put in the

---

4. You may not use foods that are merely salted, such as salted herring. [*Shulchan Aruch Harav, Chayei Adam* 102:6, *Korban Nessanel* (*Beitzah* 2:9), *Mishnah Berurah*] The *Maharsham* 528:7 rules that in the event you used salted fish etc., you may rely on the ruling of the *Chacham Tzvi* 130, *Tz'lach* and *Derech Hachaim* who rule that it is sufficient.

5. For example, cooked grain cereals. (*Maseches Beitzah* 16, *Shulchan Aruch* 527:4)

6. See glossary.

7. See glossary.

8. If you used a *kazayis,* it is also enough, but a *kebeitzah* is better. (*Ramah* 527:3)

9. In order to perform the mitzvah in its excellence. (*Tanya Rabassi* 56)

10. See glossary.

11. *Mishnah Berurah* 527:3 rules that if you were late in your preparations, you may be lenient on the second day of Yom Tov, and if it is urgent, you may be lenient even on the first day of Yom Tov and rely on the ruling of the *Rambam* and *Ritva.*

12. *Eliyahu Rabbah, Levush.*

וְהַתַּבְשִׁילִין שֶׁמַּטְמִינִים לַשַּׁבָּת, צְרִיכִין לְהַטְמִינָם בְּעוֹד הַיּוֹם גָּדוֹל, שֶׁיִּתְבַּשְּׁלוּ קֹדֶם בֵּין הַשְּׁמָשׁוֹת לְכָל הַפָּחוֹת שְׁלִישׁ בִּשּׁוּלָן.

ד) לֹא הֻתַּר לֶאֱפוֹת וּלְבַשֵּׁל עַל יְדֵי עֵרוּב תַּבְשִׁילִין אֶלָּא בְּעֶרֶב שַׁבָּת. אֲבָל אִם חָל יוֹם־טוֹב בְּיוֹם הַחֲמִישִׁי וּבְיוֹם הַשִּׁשִּׁי, אָסוּר לְבַשֵּׁל אוֹ לֶאֱפוֹת בְּיוֹם הַחֲמִישִׁי בִּשְׁבִיל שַׁבָּת.

ה) צָרִיךְ שֶׁיְּהֵא הָעֵרוּב קַיָּם עַד שֶׁהֵכִין כֹּל צָרְכֵי־שַׁבָּת. אִם נֶאֶבְדָה אוֹ נֶאֶכְלָה הַפַּת, אֵין בְּכָךְ כְּלוּם, וּמֻתָּר אֲפִלּוּ לֶאֱפוֹת. וְאִם נֶאֱבַד אוֹ נֶאֱכַל הַתַּבְשִׁיל, אִם נִשְׁאַר כַּזַּיִת, גַּם כֵּן לֹא הִפְסִיד. אֲבָל אִם לֹא נִשְׁתַּיֵּר מִמֶּנּוּ כַּזַּיִת, אָסוּר לוֹ לְבַשֵּׁל, כְּאִלּוּ לֹא עֵרַב כְּלָל. וְכֵיצַד עוֹשֶׂה מִי שֶׁלֹּא עֵרַב. אִם לֹא נִזְכַּר עַד אַחַר סְעוּדַת שַׁחֲרִית, וְאֵין שָׁם בַּמָּקוֹם הַהוּא יִשְׂרָאֵל אַחֵר שֶׁעֵרַב, אֵינוֹ מֻתָּר לוֹ אֶלָּא לְבַשֵּׁל קְדֵרָה אַחַת, וְלֶאֱפוֹת פַּת אַחַת. וּלְהַדְלִיק נֵר אֶחָד לַשַּׁבָּת. וְאִם נִזְכַּר קֹדֶם שֶׁמְּבַשֵּׁל לִסְעוּדַת שַׁחֲרִית, יָכוֹל לְבַשֵּׁל מִכָּל מִין בִּקְדֵרָה גְּדוֹלָה וּלְהוֹתִיר לַשַּׁבָּת. וְאִם יֵשׁ שָׁם מִי שֶׁעֵרַב, יִתֵּן לָזֶה בְּמַתָּנָה קִמְחוֹ וּבְשָׂרוֹ וְכָל הַשַּׁיָּךְ לָזֶה, וְהוּא יִזְכֶּה בִּדְבָרִים אֵלּוּ בְּהַגְבָּהָה, וִיבַשֵּׁל וְיֹאפֶה עֲבוּרוֹ, וַאֲפִלּוּ בְּבֵיתוֹ שֶׁל זֶה שֶׁלֹּא עֵרַב.

ו) כָּל בַּעַל־הַבַּיִת צָרִיךְ לַעֲשׂוֹת עֵרוּב תַּבְשִׁילִין בְּעַצְמוֹ. וַאֲפִלּוּ אִשָּׁה שֶׁאֵין לָהּ בַּעַל, אִם יוֹדַעַת, מְחֻיֶּבֶת לַעֲשׂוֹת בְּעַצְמָהּ, וְאָסוּר לִסְמוֹךְ עַל הָעֵרוּב שֶׁל גְּדוֹל הָעִיר. וּמִי שֶׁשָּׁכַח מֵחֲמַת אֹנֶס וְלֹא עָשָׂה עֵרוּב תַּבְשִׁילִין, אוֹ שֶׁעָשָׂה וְנֶאֱבַד, אִם יֵשׁ בָּעִיר מִי שֶׁמְּעָרֵב בִּשְׁבִיל כָּל בְּנֵי הָעִיר, (דְּהַיְנוּ שֶׁמְּזַכֶּה לָהֶם אֶת הַתַּבְשִׁיל וְאֶת הַפַּת, כִּמְבֹאָר בְּשֻׁלְחָן־עָרוּךְ), יָכוֹל זֶה לִסְמוֹךְ עַל עֵרוּב זֶה. אֲבָל מִי שֶׁשָּׁכַח מֵחֲמַת עַצְלוּת אוֹ שֶׁסָּמַךְ עַצְמוֹ לְכַתְּחִלָּה עַל עֵרוּב זֶה, לֹא מַהֲנֵי לֵהּ וְדִינוֹ כִּדְלְעֵיל סָעִיף ה׳.

13. *Peri Megadim.* See Chapter 72.

14. *Shulchan Aruch* 527:13. If you did, you may eat it on Shabbos. (*Taz, Eliyahu Rabbah, Mishnah Berurah*)

15. If you started preparing food (like cutting vegetables to cook) and then, the *eiruv* was lost, you may continue and complete the preparation of that food.

16. From this it seems that you may not bake, even though the bread was left. If you made a proper *eiruv,* but the cooked component was lost and you are left with the bread alone, *Sha'arei Teshuvah* 527:13, and *Penei Yehoshua's* (Responsum 15) rule that if you are lenient and rely on it, you have not done anything wrong. The *Semak* also rules that you may rely on the baked component.

17. *Shulchan Aruch* 527:2. The *Magein Avraham, Darkei Moshe* say that if there is another

oven to warm while it is still broad daylight, so that before twilight, at least one third of the cooking[13] should be done.

4) You are permitted to bake and to cook by means of an *eiruv tavshilin* only on Friday. If Yom Tov occurs on Thursday and Friday, you are forbidden to cook or bake anything on Thursday for Shabbos.[14]

5) The *eiruv* must remain in tact until you have prepared all your Shabbos needs.[15] If the bread (of the *eiruv*) was lost or eaten, it also does not matter; and you are allowed even to bake for Shabbos. But if the cooked food was lost or eaten, if a *kazayis* is left it doesn't matter. But if less than a *kazayis* is left, it is forbidden to cook [for Shabbos,] just as if you had made no *eiruv*.[16] What should you do if you made no *eiruv?* If you thought of it after the morning (Yom Tov) meal, and in that community there is no other Jew who made an *eiruv*,[17] you are perrmitted to cook only one pot,[18] bake only one loaf of bread, and light one[19] candle for Shabbos. If you thought of it before cooking the morning (Yom Tov) meal, you may cook all kinds of foods in a large pot[20] and leave some over for Shabbos. If there is someone there who made an *eiruv*, you should give him as a gift, your flour, meat and all other ingredients. The one who made the *eiruv* acquires possession of these items by lifting them up,[21] and then he may cook and bake for you, even in your house though you did not make an *eiruv*.

6) The head of every household is required to make an *eiruv tavshilin* for himself. Even a woman who has no husband, if she knows how to make an *eiruv tavshilin*, is required to make one for herself. It is forbidden to rely on the *eiruv* made by the rabbi of the city. If, because of unavoidable circumstances, you forgot to make an *eiruv tavshilin*, or you made one, but it was lost, then if someone in the city makes an *eiruv*, for everyone in the city, (that is, he gives them a share in the cooked dish and the bread, as is explained in the *Shulchan Aruch*) you may rely on such an *eiruv*. But if you forgot out of laziness,[22] or if you meant to rely on this *eiruv* from the start, it is ineffective[23] and you must conduct yourself, according to the laws laid down in paragraph 5 above.

Jew, you must do as prescribed (at the end of this paragraph) and may not cook even one dish etc., but the *Mishnah Berurah* 527:61 (*Acharonim* (*Reshal* etc.) hold that the choice is yours.

18. Large enough for all your Shabbos needs. Even if you have *challah* in the house, but it is not enough for Shabbos, you may bake one more to meet those needs. (*Sha'ar Hatziyun* 527:89)

19. This is in accordance with most *Rishonim* who require an *eiruv* in order to light the Shabbos candles. *Rambam, Bach, Knesses Hagedolah, Birkei Yosef* etc. permit the lighting of candles even without an *eiruv*. *Mishnah Berurah* 527:55 rules that it is proper to be stringent.

20. This means each kind may be cooked in a pot large enough to suffice for both Yom Tov and Shabbos.

21. One *tefach* high. (*Shulchan Aruch Harav* 527:28)

22. If you deliberately relied on his *eiruv*, *Shulchan Aruch* 527:7 rules that it does not help. But *Rambam, Rashba, Ran* etc. say it does. *Mishnah Berurah* 527:26 rules that if your (*simchas* Yom Tov) rejoicing on Yom Tov, will be impaired, you, may be lenient and rely on this opinion.

23. This applies also to a person who heard that he is obligated to make an *eiruv tavshilin*,

ז) אִם חָל יוֹם־טוֹב בַּיּוֹם הַחֲמִישִׁי וּבַיּוֹם הַשִּׁשִּׁי, וְנִזְכַּר בַּיּוֹם הַחֲמִישִׁי שֶׁלֹּא עָשָׂה עֵרוּב תַּבְשִׁילִין, יָכוֹל לַעֲשׂוֹת הַיּוֹם, וִיבָרֵךְ אֶת הַבְּרָכָה, וְאַחַר כָּךְ יֹאמַר, אִם הַיּוֹם קֹדֶשׁ, אֵינִי צָרִיךְ לַעֲשׂוֹת עֵרוּב. וְאִם הַיּוֹם חֹל, בַּהֲדֵין עֵרוּבָא וְכוּ׳. אֲבָל בְּרֹאשׁ־הַשָּׁנָה, אֵינוֹ יָכוֹל לַעֲשׂוֹת כֵּן.

סִימָן קג
דִּינֵי שִׂמְחַת יוֹם־טוֹב

א) כְּשֵׁם שֶׁמִּצְוָה לְכַבֵּד אֶת הַשַּׁבָּת וּלְעַנְּגוֹ, כָּךְ מִצְוָה לְכַבֵּד כָּל יָמִים־טוֹבִים וּלְעַנְּגָן, שֶׁנֶּאֱמַר, לִקְדוֹשׁ ה׳ מְכֻבָּד. וְכָל יָמִים טוֹבִים, נֶאֱמַר בָּהֶם מִקְרָא קֹדֶשׁ.

ב) אֵיזֶהוּ כִּבּוּד. זֶה שֶׁאָמְרוּ רַבּוֹתֵינוּ זִכְרוֹנָם לִבְרָכָה, שֶׁמִּצְוָה עַל הָאָדָם לְגַלֵּחַ בְּעֶרֶב יוֹם־טוֹב, כְּדֵי שֶׁלֹּא יִכָּנֵס לָרֶגֶל כְּשֶׁהוּא מְנֻוָּל. וְכֵן מִצְוָה לִרְחוֹץ בְּחַמִּין וְלָחֹף רֹאשׁוֹ וְלִטּוֹל צִפָּרְנָיו בְּעֶרֶב יוֹם־טוֹב כְּמוֹ בְּעֶרֶב שַׁבָּת, וְכֵן מִצְוָה לָלוּשׁ פַּת בְּבֵיתוֹ בְּעֶרֶב יוֹם־טוֹב לִכְבוֹד יוֹם־טוֹב כְּמוֹ בְּעֶרֶב שַׁבָּת. וְכֵן אָסוּר לֶאֱכוֹל בְּעֶרֶב יוֹם־טוֹב מִן הַמִּנְחָה וּלְמַעְלָה כְּמוֹ בְּעֶרֶב שַׁבָּת, כְּדֵי שֶׁיֹּאכַל סְעוּדַת יוֹם־טוֹב לְתֵאָבוֹן. וְאִם חָל עֶרֶב יוֹם־טוֹב בְּשַׁבָּת, יֹאכַל סְעוּדָה שְׁלִישִׁית קֹדֶם מִנְחָה קְטַנָּה. וְכֵן הַדִּין בְּיוֹם־טוֹב רִאשׁוֹן שֶׁהוּא עֶרֶב יוֹם־טוֹב שֵׁנִי.

ג) אֵיזֶהוּ עֹנֶג. זֶה שֶׁאָמְרוּ רַבּוֹתֵינוּ זִכְרוֹנָם לִבְרָכָה, שֶׁחַיָּב לֶאֱכוֹל בְּיוֹם־טוֹב בְּכָל יוֹם שְׁתֵּי סְעוּדוֹת, אַחַת בַּלַּיְלָה וְאַחַת בַּיּוֹם. אֲבָל סְעוּדָה שְׁלִישִׁית, אֵין נוֹהֲגִים בּוֹ. וְחַיָּב לְקַדֵּשׁ עַל הַיַּיִן קֹדֶם סְעוּדָה, וְיִבְצַע עַל

---

but does not know how to make one. He should have asked someone to make it for him. Since he did not, he may not rely on someone else's *eiruv.* (*Radvaz* 3:475) If he thought he was allowed to rely on someone else's *eiruv,* he may rely on it, unless he is a Torah scholar and should have known better. (*Shulchan Aruch Harav* 527:14, *Magein Avraham*)

24. But the *Chacham Tzvi, Lechem Setarim, Rabbi Akiva Eiger Ya'avetz* (Siddur), *Birkei Yosef* rule that a berachah should not be recited when making a conditional *eiruv,* for it is a *safeik* (doubt) and a berachah is not made when there is a doubt.

1. *Isaiah* 58:13. This verse mentions taking delight in Shabbos, God's holy day.

2. Yom Tov is, therefore, like Shabbos in this regard. (*Rambam)*

3. *Ramah* 529:1. The term forbidden is not to be taken literally, for it is not forbidden; it is just better not to eat then. (*Mishnah Berurah, Eliyahu Rabbah*)

4. See *Rambam*. This includes doing work. (*Eliyahu Rabbah, Biur Halachah* 529:1)

7) If Yom Tov occurs on Thursday and Friday, and on Thursday you remember that you did not make an *eiruv tavshilin,* you may make it on that day, and recite the berachah.[24] Afterwards you should say, "If this day is Holy (Yom Tov), then I do not need to make an *eiruv.* And if today is really a weekday, then by means of this *eiruv* etc." On Rosh Hashanah, this cannot be done.

Chapter 103

Laws of Rejoicing on Yom Tov

1) Just as it is a mitzvah to honor the Shabbos and delight in it, so it is a mitzvah to honor all the *Yomim Tovim* and delight in them, as it is said,[1] "God's holy and honored" (day). And with regard to all *Yomim Tovim* it is said, "A holy convocation."[2]

2) What is meant by honor? As our Rabbis, of blessed memory, said, "It is a mitzvah for a man to take a haircut on *erev* Yom Tov so that he does not enter the festival looking untidy. It is also a mitzvah to bathe in warm water, to wash your hair, and to cut your nails on *erev* Yom Tov, the same as on erev Shabbos. It is also a mitzvah to bake challos in your house on *erev* Yom Tov in honor of Yom Tov, just as it is on *erev* Shabbos. It is forbidden to[3] eat[4] on *erev* Yom Tov after[5] *Minchah,*[6] just as on *erev* Shabbos, so that you will be able to eat the Yom Tov meal with good appetite. And if *erev* Yom Tov occurs on Shabbos, you must eat the third meal before *Minchah ketanah.*[7] This law also applies to the first day of Yom Tov, since it is the *eve* of the second day of Yom Tov.[8]

3) What is meant by delight? As our Rabbis, of blessed memory, said on each Yom Tov day you must have two meals, one at night and one during the day,[9] but it is not our custom to have a third meal.[10] You are obligated to say *kiddush* over a cup of wine before the meal. You should say *Hamotzi* on two whole loaves as you do

---

5. This refers to *Minchah Ketanah* which starts 9-1/2 hours into the day. (*Mishnah Berurah, Eliyahu Rabbah, Vilna Gaon*) You should not eat a meal from a half an hour before this time. (*Biur Halachah, Shulchan Aruch Harav*) The *Ramah* 639:3 and *Chok Yaakov* 471 rule that on *erev* Sukkos you may not eat bread from noon onward. The *Matteh Ephraim* rules, if you were unable to eat before noon, you may eat bread before noon.

6. You may eat meat, fish,or fruit even after *Minchah ketanah.* Even on *erev* Sukkos and *erev* Pesach. (*Matteh Ephraim* 625:7)

7. If you did not, you should eat only a little bread, that is slightly more than a *kebeitzah* (see glossary). (*Machatzis Hashekel, Sha'ar Hatziyun* 529:10)

8. *Magein Avraham.* See *Biur Halachah* 529:1 who questions this.

9. If you did not eat at night, you must eat two meals during the day and say the night *kiddush* at the morning meal. (see *Magein Avraham, Mishnah Berurah* 529:13)

10. Some *Acharonim* hold it is best to eat at least some fruit. Some people add an extra dish in the morning meal to represent a third meal. However, this does not suffice for the third meal on Shabbos. (*Mishnah Berurah* 529:13)

שְׁתֵּי כִּכָּרוֹת שְׁלֵמוֹת כְּמוֹ בְּשַׁבָּת. וְיַרְבֶּה בְּבָשָׂר וְיַיִן וּמִגְדָּנוֹת כְּפִי יְכָלְתּוֹ.

ד) בְּכָל יוֹם־טוֹב, בְּקִדּוּשׁ שֶׁבַּלַּיְלָה אוֹמְרִים לְאַחֲרָיו בִּרְכַּת שֶׁהֶחֱיָנוּ עַל שִׂמְחַת הֶחָג, חוּץ מִלֵּיל שְׁבִיעִי שֶׁל פֶּסַח וְלֵיל שְׁמִינִי, שֶׁאֵין מְבָרְכִין שֶׁהֶחֱיָנוּ, כֵּיוָן שֶׁאֵינוֹ רֶגֶל בִּפְנֵי עַצְמוֹ. וְהַנָּשִׁים, בִּשְׁעַת הַדְלָקַת הַנֵּרוֹת אֵין לָהֶן לְבָרֵךְ שֶׁהֶחֱיָנוּ בְּשׁוּם יוֹם־טוֹב, וּקְצָתָן נוֹהֲגוֹת לְבָרֵךְ שֶׁהֶחֱיָנוּ, (חוּץ מִלֵּיל שְׁבִיעִי וְלֵיל שְׁמִינִי שֶׁל פֶּסַח), וְלָא מְחַיְּנָן לְהוּ.

ה) חַיָּב לְשַׂמֵּחַ אֶת אִשְׁתּוֹ וּבָנָיו וְכָל הַנִּלְוִים אֵלָיו, כָּל אֶחָד כָּרָאוּי לוֹ. הַקְּטַנִּים, נוֹתֵן לָהֶם אֱגוֹזִים וּמִגְדָּנוֹת. וְהַנָּשִׁים, בִּבְגָדִים וְתַכְשִׁיטִים כְּפִי יְכָלְתּוֹ. וְהָאֲנָשִׁים, בְּבָשָׂר וָיַיִן. וְנוֹהֲגִין לְהַרְבּוֹת בְּמִינֵי מַאֲכָלִים בְּיוֹם־טוֹב יוֹתֵר מִבְּשַׁבָּת, כִּי בְּיוֹם־טוֹב נֶאֱמַר בּוֹ שִׂמְחָה וְלֹא בְּשַׁבָּת. וְגַם בִּגְדֵי יוֹם־טוֹב יִהְיוּ יְקָרִים יוֹתֵר מִשֶּׁל שַׁבָּת.

ו) בְּיוֹם שֵׁנִי שֶׁל פֶּסַח, יֵשׁ לַעֲשׂוֹת בִּסְעוּדָה אֵיזֶה דָּבָר, לְזֵכֶר סְעוּדַת אֶסְתֵּר שֶׁהָיְתָה בְּיוֹם זֶה, שֶׁבּוֹ־בַּיּוֹם נִתְלָה הָמָן.

ז) בְּיוֹם רִאשׁוֹן שֶׁל שָׁבוּעוֹת, נוֹהֲגִין לֶאֱכֹל מַאַכְלֵי חָלָב. וְיֵשׁ בָּזֶה כַּמָּה טְעָמִים. וְרֶמֶז, מִנְחָה חֲדָשָׁה לַה' בְּשָׁבֻעֹתֵיכֶם, רָאשֵׁי תֵבוֹת, מֵחָלָב. וְיֵשׁ לֶאֱכוֹל גַּם מַאַכְלֵי דְבַשׁ, מִפְּנֵי שֶׁהַתּוֹרָה נִמְשְׁלָה לָהֶם, שֶׁנֶּאֱמַר, דְּבַשׁ וְחָלָב תַּחַת לְשׁוֹנֵךְ. וְכֵיוָן שֶׁאוֹכְלִים מַאַכְלֵי חָלָב וּצְרִיכִין גַּם כֵּן לֶאֱכוֹל בָּשָׂר, שֶׁהֲרֵי מִצְוָה לֶאֱכוֹל בָּשָׂר בְּכָל יוֹם־טוֹב, צְרִיכִין לִזָּהֵר שֶׁלֹּא יָבוֹאוּ לִידֵי אִסּוּר.

ח) אַף־עַל־פִּי שֶׁהָאֲכִילָה וְהַשְּׁתִיָּה בַּמּוֹעֲדוֹת הִיא מִצְוַת עֲשֵׂה, לֹא יְהֵא אוֹכֵל וְשׁוֹתֶה כָּל הַיּוֹם כֻּלּוֹ, שֶׁהֲרֵי כְּבָר נֶאֱמַר, עֲצֶרֶת לַה' אֱלֹהֶיךָ. וְאַף־עַל־פִּי שֶׁנֶּאֱמַר, עֲצֶרֶת תִּהְיֶה לָכֶם, כְּבָר פֵּרְשׁוּ רַבּוֹתֵינוּ זִכְרוֹנָם לִבְרָכָה, חֶצְיוֹ לַה', וְחֶצְיוֹ לָכֶם. לְפִיכָךְ צְרִיכִין לַעֲסוֹק גַּם בַּתּוֹרָה.

---

11. *Shulchan Aruch* 529: Because a double portion of manna was sent down on *erev* Yom Tov, as on *erev* Shabbos. (*Beis Yosef, Rif*)

12. Rejoicing is an obligation on *Chol Hamoed* also, but, honoring and taking delight is only an obligation of the actual Yom Tov. (*Shulchan Aruch Harav, Mishnah Berurah* 529:16)

13. This is the husband's obligation, but women are not commanded to rejoice on Yom Tov and may even fast if they want to. (*Rabbi Akiva Eiger* Responsum 1) But *Sha'agas Aryeh* rules that women, too, are obligated to rejoice on Yom Tov. *Toras Avigdor* says they are forbidden to fast on Yom Tov.

on Shabbos,[11] and you should be lavish with meat, wine and sweets, according to your means.

4) On every Yom Tov, at the conclusion of the *kiddush* at night we say the berachah of *Shehecheyanu* on the joy of the holiday, except on the seventh and eighth nights of Pesach when *shehecheyanu* is omitted, since they are not a separate Yom Tov in themselves. When lighting the candles, women should not say the berachah *shehecheyanu* on any Yom Tov. Some women follow the custom of saying *shehecheyanu* on all *Yomim Tovim* (except on the seventh and eighth nights of Pesach), and we do not protest their practice.

5) Every man is obligated to gladden the hearts[12] of his wife, his children, and all who are dependent on him, in a way suitable for each. To the little children you should give nuts and candy, to the women,[13] clothing and jewelry according to your means,[14] and to the men, meat and wine.[15] It is the custom to serve a greater variety of foods on Yom Tov than on Shabbos, because with regard to Yom Tov, the Torah mentions "rejoicing," but it is not mentioned with regard to Shabbos. Also Yom Tov clothes should be more expensive than Shabbos clothes.

6) On the second day of Pesach, you should add an extra dish to the meal to remember the feast of Esther which took place on this day, for it was on this day that Haman was hanged.

7) On the first day of Shavuos it is customary to eat dairy foods. There are several reasons for this. A hint of this custom is found in the words, *Minchah chadashah LaShem beshavuoseichem.*[16] The initials of these words spell *meichalav*—"of milk." You should also eat foods with honey, because the Torah is compared to milk and honey, as it is said,[17] "Honey and milk are under your tongue." Now, since we eat dairy foods and we must also eat meat, because it is a mitzvah to eat meat on every Yom Tov, care must be taken not to violate the law of mixing the dairy and meat foods.

8) Even though eating and drinking on festivals is a positive commandment, you should not spend all day eating and drinking, because it is said, "(A day of) restraint (in honor) of Adonoy, your God." Even though it is said, "(A day of) restraint it shall be for *you*," our Rabbis, of blessed memory, explained:[18] The day should be divided, half devoted to Hashem and half to yourself. Therefore, it is your duty to engage also in the study of Torah.

---

14. At least new shoes. (*Eliyahu Rabbah, Maharil, Biur Halachah*)

15. In our times, when our meat is not from a *shelamim* offering (peace-offering), eating meat is a mitzvah and drinking wine an obligation. (*Biur Halachah* 529:2, *Shulchan Aruch Harav* 529:7) *Chayei Adam* rules that even now, you may fulfill your obligation with meat or wine.

16. *Numbers* 25:26.

17. *Shir Hashirim* 4:11.

18. *Maseches Beitzah* 15.

ט) וּכְשֶׁהוּא אוֹכֵל וְשׁוֹתֶה, חַיָּב לְהַאֲכִיל גַּם לַגֵּר לַיָּתוֹם וְלָאַלְמָנָה עִם שְׁאָר הָעֲנִיִּים הָאֻמְלָלִים, שֶׁנֶּאֱמַר, וְהַלֵּוִי וְהַגֵּר וְהַיָּתוֹם וְגוֹ׳. אֲבָל מִי שֶׁנּוֹעֵל דַּלְתֵי חֲצֵרוֹ וְאוֹכֵל וְשׁוֹתֶה הוּא וְאִשְׁתּוֹ וּבָנָיו וְאֵינוֹ מַאֲכִיל וּמַשְׁקֶה לָעֲנִיִּים וּלְמָרֵי נֶפֶשׁ, אֵין זוֹ שִׂמְחַת מִצְוָה, אֶלָּא שִׂמְחַת כְּרֵסוֹ, וְעַל אֵלּוּ נֶאֱמַר, זִבְחֵיהֶם כְּלֶחֶם אוֹנִים לָהֶם, כָּל אוֹכְלָיו יִטַּמָּאוּ כִּי לַחְמָם לְנַפְשָׁם. וְשִׂמְחָה כָּזֹאת, קָלוֹן הִיא לָהֶם, שֶׁנֶּאֱמַר, וְזֵרִיתִי פֶרֶשׁ עַל פְּנֵיכֶם פֶּרֶשׁ חַגֵּיכֶם.

י) כְּשֶׁאָדָם אוֹכֵל וְשׁוֹתֶה וְשָׂמֵחַ בָּרֶגֶל, לֹא יִמָּשֵׁךְ בַּיַּיִן וּבִשְׂחוֹק וּבְקַלּוּת־רֹאשׁ וְיֹאמַר כָּל מַה שֶּׁיּוֹסִיף בָּזֶה, יַרְבֶּה בְּמִצְוַת שִׂמְחָה. כִּי הַשִּׁכְרוּת וְהַשְּׂחוֹק וְקַלּוּת־הָרֹאשׁ, אֵינָהּ שִׂמְחָה. אֶלָּא הוֹלֵלוּת וְסִכְלוּת. וְלֹא נִצְטַוֵּינוּ עַל הַהוֹלֵלוּת וְהַסִּכְלוּת, אֶלָּא עַל הַשִּׂמְחָה שֶׁיֵּשׁ בָּהּ עֲבוֹדַת יוֹצֵר הַכֹּל, שֶׁנֶּאֱמַר, תַּחַת אֲשֶׁר לֹא עָבַדְתָּ אֶת־ה׳ אֱלֹהֶיךָ בְּשִׂמְחָה וּבְטוּב לֵבָב מֵרֹב כֹּל. הָא לָמַדְתָּ, שֶׁהָעֲבוֹדָה הִיא בְּשִׂמְחָה, וְאִי אֶפְשָׁר לַעֲבוֹד אֶת ה׳, לֹא מִתּוֹךְ שְׂחוֹק וְלֹא מִתּוֹךְ קַלּוּת־רֹאשׁ וְלֹא מִתּוֹךְ שִׁכְרוּת.

יא) מִדַּת הַחֲסִידִים אֲשֶׁר ה׳ לְנֶגְדָּם תָּמִיד וּבְכָל דַּרְכֵיהֶם יְדָעוּהוּ, בְּעֵת שִׂמְחָתָם אָז יוֹתֵר וְיוֹתֵר הֵם מְבָרְכִין וּמְשַׁבְּחִין לְהַקָּדוֹשׁ־בָּרוּךְ־הוּא אֲשֶׁר שִׂמַּח אוֹתָם. וְיֹאמַר הָאָדָם בְּלִבּוֹ בְּעֵת שִׂמְחָתוֹ וַהֲנָאָתוֹ, אִם כָּךְ הִיא שִׂמְחַת הָעוֹלָם הַזֶּה אֲשֶׁר הִיא הֶבֶל, כִּי יֵשׁ אַחֲרֶיהָ תּוּגָה וָצַעַר, מַה תִּהְיֶה שִׂמְחַת הָעוֹלָם הַבָּא הַתְּמִידִית, שֶׁאֵין אַחֲרֶיהָ תּוּגָה. וְיִתְפַּלֵּל לְהַקָּדוֹשׁ־בָּרוּךְ־הוּא, שֶׁיַּטֶּה לִבּוֹ לְעָבְדוֹ וְלַעֲשׂוֹת רְצוֹנוֹ בְּלֵב שָׁלֵם, וְשֶׁיְּשַׂמְּחֵנוּ בְּשִׂמְחַת עוֹלָם, וִיזַכֵּנוּ לְחַיֵּי הָעוֹלָם הַבָּא לֵאוֹר בְּאוֹר פְּנֵי מֶלֶךְ חַיִּים.

יב) חַיָּב כָּל אָדָם לְהַשְׁגִּיחַ עַל בְּנֵי־בֵיתוֹ שֶׁלֹּא יְטַיְּלוּ בְּמָקוֹם שֶׁיָּבוֹאוּ חַס וְשָׁלוֹם לִידֵי קַלּוּת־רֹאשׁ בְּהִתְעָרְבָם עִם קַלֵּי הַדַּעַת, רַק יִהְיוּ קְדוֹשִׁים, כִּי קָדוֹשׁ הַיּוֹם.

יג) בְּמוֹצָאֵי יוֹם־טוֹב לַחֹל אוֹ לְחֹל־הַמּוֹעֵד, אוֹמֵר בַּתְּפִלָּה, אַתָּה חוֹנַנְתָּנוּ, וּמַבְדִּיל עַל הַכּוֹס, אֲבָל לֹא עַל הַנֵּר וְלֹא עַל הַבְּשָׂמִים.

יד) נוֹהֲגִין לְהַרְבּוֹת קְצָת בַּאֲכִילָה וּשְׁתִיָּה בְּיוֹם שֶׁלְּאַחַר הֶחָג בְּכָל שָׁלֹשׁ רְגָלִים, וְהוּא אִסְרוּ חַג. וְנוֹהֲגִין שֶׁאֵין מִתְעַנִּין בּוֹ, אֲפִלּוּ חָתָן וְכַלָּה

9) And when you eat and drink, it is your duty to provide also for the orphan, the widow and other needy people, as it is said, "And the Levite, the proselyte, and the orphan etc. . . ." (*Deuteronomy* 16:14). He who locks the doors of his courtyard, and eats and drinks with his wife and children and does not give food and drink to the poor and unhappy souls, is not rejoicing in a mitzvah, but rejoicing in his gluttony. Concerning such people it is said,[19] "Their sacrifices will be to them like the bread of mourners; all who eat of them will be unclean; for their bread will be for their souls." And such rejoicing is a disgrace for them as it is said,[20] "I will spread dung on your faces, the dung of your festival offerings."

10) When a person eats and drinks, and rejoices on the festival, he should not overindulge in drinking wine, in laughter and lightheadedness, thinking that the more he indulges, the greater will be the mitzvah of rejoicing. For drunkenness, mockery and lightheadedness is not rejoicing, but licentiousness and foolishness. And we were not commanded to act licentiously and foolishly, but to rejoice in the service of the Creator of all things, as it is said, "Because you did not serve Adonoy, your God, with happiness and a glad heart, when you had plenty of everything."[21] From this we infer that the service of God must be done with joy, but you cannot serve God in frivolity, or lightheadness or in drunkenness.

11) It is the way of the pious, who constantly have God before them, and who are mindful of Him in all their ways, when they rejoice, to greatly bless and praise the Holy One Blessed is He Who enabled them to rejoice. A man should say to himself at the time of his rejoicing and pleasure, "If the happiness of this world is so great, (a world) which is vanity because it ends in grief and sorrow, how great will be the eternal joy of the World to Come which is not followed by grief." And he should pray to the Holy One Blessed is He that He bend his heart to serve Him and to do His will wholeheartedly, and that He should gladden us with everlasting joy, and make us worthy of the life of the World to Come, to be enlightened by the light of the presence of the Living King.

12) Every man is obligated to prevent[22] the members of his household from congregating in places which, Heaven forbid, could lead to levity, through association with lightheaded people. They should be encouraged to be holy because the day is holy.

13) At the conclusion of a Yom Tov that is followed by a weekday or *Chol Hamoed, Atah chonantanu* is said in the *Shemoneh Esrei,* and *Havdalah* is said over a cup [of wine.] However, the berachah is not said over the candle, or over the spices.

14) It is customary to eat and drink a bit more lavishly [than usual] on the day after all three festivals. That day is called *Isru chag,* and it is customary not to fast

19. *Hosea* 9:4.
20. *Malachi* 2:3.
21. *Deuteronomy* 28:47.
22. When *Beis Din* (Jewish courts) were empowered, it was their duty to dispatch officers to patrol and prevent the gathering of men and women for social eating and drinking etc. (*Rambam, Shulchan Aruch* 529:4)

בְּיוֹם חֻפָּתָן, וְלֹא יָארְצַייט. וּבְאִסְרוּ חַג שֶׁלְּאַחַר חַג הַשָּׁבוּעוֹת, גַּם מִצַּד הַדִּין אָסוּר לְהִתְעַנּוֹת בּוֹ, לְפִי שֶׁבִּזְמַן שֶׁבֵּית־הַמִּקְדָּשׁ הָיָה קַיָּם, אִם חָל שָׁבוּעוֹת בְּשַׁבָּת. הָיָה יוֹם טְבוֹחַ הַקָּרְבָּנוֹת בְּיוֹם שֶׁלְּאַחֲרָיו. אֲבָל שֶׁל פֶּסַח וְשֶׁל סֻכּוֹת, הָיוּ מַקְרִיבִין בְּיוֹם רִאשׁוֹן דְּחֹל הַמּוֹעֵד.

סִימָן קד
דִּינֵי חֹל־הַמּוֹעֵד

א) חֹל־הַמּוֹעֵד אָסוּר בִּקְצָת מְלָאכוֹת וּמֻתָּר בִּקְצָתָן, דְּהַיְנוּ כָּל מַה שֶּׁהוּא לְצֹרֶךְ אֲכִילָה לְחֹל־הַמּוֹעֵד אוֹ לְיוֹם־טוֹב. וְכֵן מְלָאכָה בְּדָבָר הָאָבֵד, דְּהַיְנוּ שֶׁאִם לֹא יַעֲשֶׂנָּה יָבוֹא לִידֵי הֶפְסֵד, מֻתָּר לַעֲשׂוֹתָהּ. וּצְרִיכִין לִזָּהֵר מְאֹד, שֶׁלֹּא לַעֲשׂוֹת בְּחֹל־הַמּוֹעֵד מְלָאכָה הָאֲסוּרָה, כִּי אָמְרוּ רַבּוֹתֵינוּ זִכְרוֹנָם לִבְרָכָה, הַמְחַלֵּל אֶת חֹל־הַמּוֹעֵד, כְּאִלּוּ עוֹבֵד עֲבוֹדָה־זָרָה.

ב) עוֹד אָמְרוּ רַבּוֹתֵינוּ זִכְרוֹנָם לִבְרָכָה, הַמְבַזֶּה אֶת חֹל־הַמּוֹעֵד, אַף־עַל־פִּי שֶׁיֵּשׁ בְּיָדוֹ תּוֹרָה וּמַעֲשִׂים טוֹבִים, אֵין לוֹ חֵלֶק לָעוֹלָם הַבָּא. וְהַמְבַזֶּה, הַיְנוּ, שֶׁאֵינוֹ מְכַבְּדוֹ בְּמַאֲכָל וּבְמִשְׁתֶּה וּבִכְסוּת. וְלָכֵן כָּל אָדָם חַיָּב לְכַבְּדוֹ כְּפִי כֹחוֹ, וְלִלְבּוֹשׁ בְּגָדִים מְכֻבָּדִים.

ג) מְלֶאכֶת דָּבָר הָאָבֵד יָכוֹל לַעֲשׂוֹת גַּם עַל יְדֵי יִשְׂרָאֵל אַחֵר, אֲפִלּוּ בְּשָׂכָר. אֲבָל מַה שֶּׁאֵינוֹ דָּבָר הָאָבֵד אֶלָּא שֶׁהוּא לְצֹרֶךְ הַמּוֹעֵד, אֵין לַעֲשׂוֹת עַל יְדֵי יִשְׂרָאֵל אַחֵר בְּשָׂכָר, אֶלָּא עַל יְדֵי גּוֹי. וְאִם אֵינוֹ מוֹצֵא

---

1. Concerning the halachic status of the prohibition against *melachah* on *Chol Hamoed*, there are two basic views among the early *poskim*. *Rif*, *Rashi* and others consider it to be a *de'oraisa* (a Scriptural prohibition), while *Rambam*, *Rabeinu Tam* and *Rosh* regard it as an *issur de'rabbanan* (A Rabbinic prohibition). It is interesting to note that even *Rif* and *Rashi* concede that this prohibition is unique in that the Sages were granted full authority to determine which forms of work to permit and which to prohibit on *Chol Hamoed*) (see *Maseches Chagigah* 18:a).

2. The preparation of food for Yom Tov may be done even in a professional manner. (*Mishna Berurah*) 530:1

3. *Nishmas Adam* 105:1 says that according to *Beis Yosef*, if there is only a possibility of incurring a loss, you are not allowed to do a *melachah* to protect yourself. In *Chayei Adam* 106:5, he says that it should be done through a non-Jew in this case. *Magein Avraham* 537, *Ke'Sav Sefer* 102, *Maharam Shick* rules that you may do it yourself. *Peri Megadim* rules that it depends if the *melachah* is *de'oraisa* or Rabbinic. *Mishnah Berurah* 537:1 maintains that if it is likely that you will incur a loss, you may do the *melachah*, but it should be done in private, if possible.

on that day. Even a groom and bride on their wedding day [do not fast] ,and a person observing *yahrzeit* [should also not fast on *Isru chag*]. On *Isru chag* following Shavuos, even according to *halachah,* it is forbidden to fast, because when the *Beis Hamikdash* was in existence, if Shavuos occurred on Shabbos, the sacrifices were offered on the following day. But on Pesach and Sukkos, they were offered on the first day of *Chol Hamoed.*

Chapter 104

Laws of Chol Hamoed (Intermediate Days of a Yom Tov)

1) On *Chol Hamoed* it is forbidden to do certain *melachos,*[1] while others are permitted, namely, all work that is necessary for the preparation of food[2] for *Chol Hamoed* or Yom Tov. Any *melachah* that is done to prevent a loss, that is, if by not doing it you will incur a loss,[3] may be done.[4] But you should be very careful not to do any *melachah* that is forbidden on *Chol Hamoed* because our Rabbis, of blessed memory, said: "He who desecrates *Chol Hamoed* is considered as though he worshipped idols."[5]

2) In addition, our Rabbis, of blessed memory, said:[6] "He who disgraces *Chol Hamoed,* even though he has to his credit Torah and good deeds, has no share in the World to Come." Disgracing *Chol Hamoed* implies not honoring it with better food and wearing better clothes.[7] Therefore, every man is obligated to honor it according to his means,[8] and to wear dignified clothing.

3) Work, which, if not done, would result in a loss, may be done even by another Jew, even for payment.[9] But, if no loss would result, but the work is needed for the festival, it should not be done by another Jew for pay, but by a non-Jew.[10] And if

---

4. This is true only if it does not involve a major imposition. (*Shulchan Aruch* 537:2) If it does, it is forbidden only if it is a *melachah de'oraisa*. (*Machatzis Hashekel* 536:3, *Magein Avraham*) To prevent a major loss, perhaps it is permitted, even if major imposition is involved. (*Peri Magadim* 540:7)

5. This applies even according to those who maintain that a *melachah* on *Chol Hamoed* is a Rabbinic prohibition. (see *Magein Avraham* 530 and *Chayei Adam* 106:1)

6. *Pirkei Avos* 3:11.

7. *Rashi* and *Bartenura* (*Pirkei Avos*). *Rabbeinu Yonah* and *Sha'ar Hakedushah* explain that it means not desecrating *Chol Hamoed* by doing a *melachah.*

8. See *Sha'ar Hatziyun* 530:4. You are obligated to honor it, but not to the extent that you are obligated on Yom Tov. Therefore, although it is meritorious to eat two meals a day with bread, it is not an actual obligation. Also your clothing should be nicer than during the weekdays, but need not be Shabbos clothing. (see *Magein Avraham* 664:3) In our times, many people including Chassidim and Bnei Torah, wear their Shabbos clothing on *Chol Hamoed,* especially in Eretz Yisroel. This was also the custom of the *Maharil.*

9. *Ramah* 542:1, *Kol Bo. Rabbeinu Yerucham,* permits this only when done without pay. *Ritva* and *Levush* rule that if you have no other option, you may even pay a Jew. This is also the ruling of *Mishnah Berurah* 542:1.

10. Or a Jew without pay.

גּוֹי, וְגַם בְּעַצְמוֹ אֵינוֹ יָכוֹל לַעֲשׂוֹת, מֻתָּר אֲפִלּוּ עַל יְדֵי יִשְׂרָאֵל בְּשָׂכָר.

ד) הָא דְמֻתָּר לַעֲשׂוֹת דָּבָר הָאָבֵד, זֶהוּ דַוְקָא אִם לֹא הָיָה אֶפְשָׁר לוֹ לַעֲשׂוֹתוֹ קֹדֶם יוֹם־טוֹב. אֲבָל אִם הָיָה אֶפְשָׁר לוֹ לַעֲשׂוֹתוֹ קֹדֶם יוֹם־טוֹב וְהִנִּיחוֹ עַד חֹל־הַמּוֹעֵד, אָסוּר לַעֲשׂוֹתוֹ בְּחֹל־הַמּוֹעֵד.

ה) כָּל מְלָאכוֹת הָאֲסוּרוֹת לַעֲשׂוֹת בְּחֹל־הַמּוֹעֵד, אִם יֵשׁ כָּאן יִשְׂרָאֵל שֶׁאֵין לוֹ מַה לֶּאֱכֹל כָּרָאוּי לְחֹל־הַמּוֹעֵד וְיוֹם־טוֹב, מֻתָּר לַעֲשׂוֹתָן עַל יָדוֹ, כְּדֵי שֶׁיְּהֵא לוֹ מַה לֶּאֱכוֹל. וּמִכָּל מָקוֹם יַעֲשֶׂה בְּצִנְעָא, וְאָסוּר לַעֲשׂוֹתָן עַל יְדֵי גוֹי. אַךְ לְצֹרֶךְ מִצְוָה, מֻתָּר.

ו) אֲפִלּוּ מְלָאכוֹת הַמֻּתָּרוֹת, אָסוּר לַעֲשׂוֹתָן בִּשְׁבִיל גּוֹי.

ז) אָסוּר לְזַבֵּל שָׂדֵהוּ. וַאֲפִלּוּ לְהַכְנִיס שָׁם צֹאן בִּשְׁבִיל שֶׁיַּעֲשׂוּ שָׁם זֶבֶל, אָסוּר. וַאֲפִלּוּ עַל יְדֵי גוֹי, אָסוּר.

ח) זְרִיעָה, אֲסוּרָה. וְאִם יֵשׁ לוֹ זְרָעִים, שֶׁאִם לֹא יַשְׁקֵם בְּמַיִם יִפָּסְדוּ לְגַמְרֵי, מֻתָּר לְהַשְׁקוֹתָם.

ט) אָסוּר לִתְלוֹשׁ אוֹ לִקְצוֹץ שׁוּם דָּבָר מִן הַמְחֻבָּר אִם לֹא יִתְקַלְקְלוּ הַפֵּרוֹת עַד לְאַחַר יוֹם־טוֹב, כִּי אִם מַה שֶּׁהוּא צָרִיךְ לֶאֱכוֹל בַּמּוֹעֵד. וְאֵינוֹ צָרִיךְ לְצַמְצֵם, אֶלָּא תוֹלֵשׁ בְּהַרְוָחָה, וְאִם יוֹתִיר, יוֹתִיר. וְכֵן עֵצִים שֶׁהוּא צָרִיךְ לְהַסָּקָה בַּמּוֹעֵד, מֻתָּר לְקַצְּצָם מִמְּחֻבָּר. וְאִם צָרִיךְ לִתְלוֹשׁ בִּשְׁבִיל לְהַאֲכִיל לַבְּהֵמָה, יַעֲשֶׂה בְּשִׁנּוּי. וְאָסוּר לְלַקֵּט עֵצִים מִן הַשָּׂדֶה לְיַפּוֹתוֹ לַחֲרִישָׁה. וְאִם נִכָּר שֶׁמְּכַוֵּן לְצָרְכּוֹ שֶׁצָּרִיךְ לְעֵצִים, כְּגוֹן שֶׁנּוֹטֵל הַגְּדוֹלִים וּמַנִּיחַ הַקְּטַנִּים, מֻתָּר. וְכֵן אָסוּר לִקְצוֹץ עַנְפֵי הָאִילָן לְתַקְּנוֹ. וְאִם נִכָּר שֶׁמְּכַוֵּן בִּשְׁבִיל הָעֲנָפִים לְהַאֲכִילָן לִבְהֶמְתּוֹ וְלֹא לְתַקְּנוֹ, כְּגוֹן שֶׁקּוֹצֵץ כֻּלָּן מִצַּד אֶחָד, מֻתָּר.

---

11. *Ritva, Mishnah Berurah* 542:2.

12. This is also true if you mistakenly thought it could wait until after Yom Tov (*Shulchan Aruch* 538:1), or you forgot it was *erev* Yom Tov. (*Peri Megadim M.Z.* 540)

13. This applies even if you thought you are allowed to do this and even if you thought you would get around to it later and then forgot about it. (*Maharsham*)

14. *Shulchan Aruch* 538:6. This does not apply to a *melachah* for the preparation of food. (see *Shulchan Aruch* 533:1 and *Mishnah Berurah* 533:2)

15. *Eliyahu Rabbah, Nishmas Adam* 105.

16. If this is not possible, he may do it in public if he does not have even bread and water.

you cannot find a non-Jew, and you are unable to do it yourself, it is permitted[11] to have it done, even by a Jew for pay.

4) The law that permits *melachah* in order to prevent a loss, applies only if it was impossible[12] for you to do it before Yom Tov, but if it was possible for you to do it before Yom Tov, and you left it for *Chol Hamoed,*[13] you are forbidden to do it on *Chol Hamoed.*[14]

5) Any work that is forbidden on *Chol Hamoed,* [is permitted in the following circumstances,] if a Jew does not have enough food for *Chol Hamoed* and Yom Tov,[15] it is permitted to give him work, so that he will have something to eat, but he should do it in private.[16] It is forbidden to have such work done by a non-Jew,[17] but if it is needed for a mitzvah, it is permitted.[18]

6) Even *melachos* that are permitted, are forbidden to be done for a non-Jew.[19]

7) It is forbidden to fertilize a field.[20] Even to put sheep in a field to fertilize it with manure is forbidden.[21] Even to have it done by a non-Jew is forbidden.

8) Planting is forbidden. However if you have seeds that will spoil completely, unless they are put into water, you are permitted to water [soak] them.[22]

9) It is forbidden to pluck or cut off anything that is growing, unless the fruit will spoil[23] [if left] until after Yom Tov. It is permitted to pluck what you need to eat on Yom Tov, and you do not have to skimp. You may pick a generous quantity, and if there is some left over, it does not matter.[24] Also, wood that is needed for heating on the festival, is permitted to be cut from a growing tree. If it is necessary to pick something in order to feed your animals, it should be done in an irregular way. It is forbidden to collect wood from a field in order to improve it for plowing. But if it is obvious that you intend it for your own need, because you need the wood, for example, if you take the big pieces and leave the small ones, it is permissible. Similarly, it is forbidden to cut off the (soft) branches of a tree in order to trim it. But if it is obvious that your purpose is to feed the branches to your animals, and not to trim the tree, for example, if you cut all the branches from one side of the tree, it is permitted.[25]

But if he has bread and water, none of the *poskim* permit him to work in public in order to eat properly on Yom Tov. (*Peri Megadim* 542, *Mishnah Berurah, Sha'ar Hatziyun* 542:14)

17. *Shulchan Aruch* 543:1.
18. *Magein Avraham.*
19. *Chayei Adam* 106:11.
20. It is a *toldah* of the *melachah* of plowing. (*Levush*)
21. *Shulchan Aruch* 537:14.
22. See *Shulchan Aruch* 537 for details.
23. If they will spoil, it is for the prevention of loss and is permitted, if there is not much bother. In order to prevent the loss of profit, you may only do a *melachah* that is of Rabbinic status, and only if no bother is involved. (*Peri Megadim* 533:6)
24. See *Shulchan Aruch* 533:1.
25. See *Shulchan Aruch* 537. The rule is that your intent must be for something permissible, and this intent must be obvious. (*Mishnah Berurah* 537:34, *Levush, Gra*)

י) מִי שֶׁיֵּשׁ לוֹ גַּן אֵצֶל גַּן גּוֹי, וְהַגּוֹי לוֹקֵט פֵּרוֹתָיו, וְאִם הַיִּשְׂרָאֵל לֹא יִלְקֹט, יָבוֹא לִידֵי הֶפְסֵד, מֻתָּר לוֹ לְלָקְטָם. וְאִם הֵמָּה דְּבָרִים שֶׁיִּתְקַלְקְלוּ בְּתָלוּשׁ אִם לֹא יַעֲשֶׂה לְצָרְכָּם גַּם מְלָאכָה אַחֶרֶת, מֻתָּר לַעֲשׂוֹת הַכֹּל, אֲפִלּוּ לִדְרוֹךְ עֲנָבִים לַעֲשׂוֹת יַיִן וְכַדּוֹמֶה לָזֶה, וּבִלְבַד שֶׁלֹּא יַנִּיחַ בְּכַוָּנָה מְלַאכְתּוֹ לְחֹל־הַמּוֹעֵד.

יא) אָסוּר לְגַלֵּחַ בְּחֹל־הַמּוֹעֵד, אֲפִלּוּ גִּלַּח אֶת עַצְמוֹ גַּם בְּעֶרֶב יוֹם־טוֹב, אֶלָּא מִי שֶׁיָּצָא מִבֵּית הָאֲסוּרִים. וַאֲפִלּוּ יָצָא בְּעֶרֶב יוֹם־טוֹב, אֶלָּא שֶׁלֹּא הָיָה לוֹ פְּנַאי לְגַלֵּחַ אָז.

יב) וְלִקְצוֹץ הַצִּפָּרְנַיִם, גַּם כֵּן אָסוּר. אַךְ אִם קְצָצָן בְּעֶרֶב יוֹם־טוֹב, מֻתָּר לְקָצְצָן גַּם בְּחֹל־הַמּוֹעֵד. וְכֵן אִשָּׁה לְצֹרֶךְ טְבִילָה, מֻתֶּרֶת.

יג) אָסוּר לְכַבֵּס שׁוּם דָּבָר, אֲפִלּוּ לְצֹרֶךְ הַמּוֹעֵד, אֶלָּא אִם לֹא הָיָה אֶפְשָׁר לוֹ בְּשׁוּם אֹפֶן לְכַבֵּס קֹדֶם יוֹם־טוֹב. וְכֵן מִטְפָּחוֹת שֶׁמְּלַפְּפִין בָּהֶן אֶת הַתִּינוֹקוֹת, כֵּיוָן שֶׁמַּשְׁתִּינִין תָּדִיר וּצְרִיכִין לָהֶם הַרְבֵּה, מֻתָּר לְכַבְּסָן, וְיִזָּהֲרוּ לְכַבְּסָן בִּצְנְעָא.

יד) כָּל דָּבָר שֶׁהוּא לְצֹרֶךְ רְפוּאָה, מֻתָּר לַעֲשׂוֹת, בֵּין לְאָדָם בֵּין לִבְהֵמָה.

טו) חֶשְׁבּוֹנוֹת וְכַיּוֹצֵא בָּזֶה, שֶׁאִם לֹא יִכְתְּבֵם, יִשְׁכָּחֵם, מֻתָּר לְכָתְבָם, מִשּׁוּם דַּהֲוֵי דָּבָר הָאָבֵד. וְכֵן מַה שֶּׁהוּא לְצֹרֶךְ הַמּוֹעֵד, מֻתָּר לִכְתּוֹב. אֲבָל שְׁאָר דָּבָר, אָסוּר לִכְתֹּב. וְאִגֶּרֶת שְׁלוֹמִים שֶׁכּוֹתֵב אָדָם לַחֲבֵרוֹ, נוֹהֲגִין לִכְתֹּב בְּשִׁנּוּי קְצָת, דְּהַיְנוּ שֶׁכּוֹתְבִין שׁוּרָה רִאשׁוֹנָה עֲקֻמָּה. וּלְכָל מַה שֶׁמֻּתָּר לִכְתּוֹב, מֻתָּר גַּם לְתַקֵּן קֻלְמוֹס וּדְיוֹ.

---

26. A prominent person should be stringent, even when the prevention of loss is concerned. (see *Mishnah Berurah* 533:53, *Beis Yosef* and *Taz-Rokeach*)

27. To take a haircut is also forbidden.

28. *Maseches Moed Katan* 14b. This is a Rabbinic prohibition to make sure that you shave *erev* Yom Tov so you will not enter Yom Tov looking disheveled. (see *Taz, Magein Avraham* 531:1)

29. *Shulchan Aruch* 531:2. Because people may not know you shaved before Yom Tov and will think everyone is permitted to shave on *Chol Hamoed.* (*Beis Yosef*)

30. This includes all situations where everyone knows you were not able to shave before Yom Tov. (see *Sha'ar Hatziyun* 531:7, *Ritva*)

31. The *Mishnah Berurah* 531:7 disagrees with the ruling and permits it only if he was released from jail (etc.) near nightfall when there was no time. (see *Sha'ar Hatziyun* 531:9)

10) If you have a garden adjacent to a garden of a non-Jew, and the non-Jew is gathering his fruit, and if you do not gather (your fruit), you will incur a loss, you are permitted to gather them.[26] And if they are fruits that will spoil when they are picked, unless you do additional *melachah,* you are permitted to do everything [that is necessary] even to press grapes to make wine or similar *melachos,* provided you did not intentionally leave this work to be done on *Chol Hamoed.*

11) It is forbidden to shave[27] on *Chol Hamoed,*[28] even if you shaved on *erev* Yom Tov.[29] But a person who has been released from jail,[30] even if he was released *erev* Yom Tov, but had no time[31] to shave then, is permitted to shave on *Chol Hamoed.*

12) Cutting your nails is also[32] forbidden,[33] but if you cut them on *erev* Yom Tov, you are permitted to cut them also on *Chol Hamoed.*[34] A woman is also permitted (to cut her nails) for the ritual immersion.[35]

13) It is forbidden to launder anything, even (clothes) needed for the festivals,[36] unless it was impossible to wash them before Yom Tov.[37] Since (babies) urinate all the time, and you need many diapers,[38] you are permitted to wash them, but you should be careful to wash them in privacy.[39]

14) Anything required to restore health, is permitted to be done, either for man[40] or beast.

15) It is permitted to record bills and similar records which, if not recorded will be forgotten because it is considered prevention of a loss.[41] You are permitted to write[42] whatever is necessary for the needs of Yom Tov, but it is forbidden to write anything else. Social letters that friends write to each other, should be written with a slight change,[43] like writing the first line unevenly.[44] For everything that you are permitted to write, you are also permitted to prepare a pen and ink.

---

32. For the same reason as shaving. (*Levush*) Those allowed to shave are also allowed to cut their nails. (*Magein Avraham, Mishnah Berurah* 532:2)
33. It is forbidden only if done with a utensil. (*Ramah* 532:1)
34. *Magein Abraham*
35. *Ramah*
36. For the same reason that shaving is forbidden.
37. For example, it got soiled during the holiday, and you have nothing else to wear.
38. Four or five at a time. (*Ramah* 534:1) This *halachah* applies also to hand towels that are changed daily. (*Magein Avraham*)
39. If it will wash better in the public area, you may wash it in public. (*Ramah* 534:1)
40. *Shulchan Aruch* 532:2.
41. *Shulchan Aruch* 545:4.
42. This, however, is only permitted if the writing is commonplace and not professional. (*Mishnah Berurah* 545:18)
43. *Rema* 545:5. However, you may not purposely leave your letter writing for *Chol Hamoed.* (*Shibolei Haleket, Mishnah Berurah* 545:31) The reason some permit writing letters to a friend is because it makes them happy and is, therefore, considered a need of *Chol Hamoed.* (*Ritva, Peri Megadim,* see *Sha'ar Hatziyun* 545:30) This would mean the letter would have to be received before Yom Tov is over. It is best not to write about things pertaining to business. (see *Biur Halachah* 545:5)
44. *Bach, Taz* etc. But *Magein Avraham* says to make all the lines uneven.

טז) מִי שֶׁצָּרִיךְ לְמָעוֹת אֲפִלּוּ שֶׁלֹּא לְצֹרֶךְ הַמּוֹעֵד, אֶלָּא שֶׁהוּא חוֹשֵׁשׁ פֶּן לֹא יִמְצָא לִלְווֹת לְאַחַר הַמּוֹעֵד, וְהַמַּלְוֶה אֵינוֹ רוֹצֶה לְהַלְווֹת לוֹ בְּלִי שְׁטָר, מֻתָּר לוֹ לִכְתּוֹב אֶת הַשְּׁטָר.

יז) אֵין נוֹשְׂאִין נָשִׁים בְּחֹל־הַמּוֹעֵד, מִשּׁוּם דְּאֵין מְעָרְבִין שִׂמְחָה בְּשִׂמְחָה. אֲבָל מֻתָּר לְהַחֲזִיר גְּרוּשָׁתוֹ. וּמֻתָּר לַעֲשׂוֹת מִשְׁתֶּה לִבְרִית מִילָה וּלְפִדְיוֹן הַבֵּן. גַּם מֻתָּר לַעֲשׂוֹת מִשְׁתֶּה לִכְתִיבַת תְּנָאִים.

יח) מֻתָּר לִשְׂכּוֹר פּוֹעֲלִים, וַאֲפִלּוּ יִשְׂרְאֵלִים, שֶׁיַּעֲשׂוּ מְלַאכְתּוֹ לְאַחַר הַמּוֹעֵד.

יט) מֻתָּר לָלֶכֶת חוּץ לַתְּחוּם, בֵּין בְּרַגְלָיו בֵּין בְּקָרוֹן בֵּין רָכוּב.

כ) אֵין מַעֲלִין בְּהֵמָה זָכָר עַל נְקֵבָה לְהַרְבִּיעָהּ, מִשּׁוּם דְּלֹא הֲוֵי דָּבָר הָאָבֵד.

כא) אֵין מוֹשִׁיבִין תַּרְנְגֹלֶת עַל בֵּצִים לְגַדֵּל אֶפְרוֹחִים. וְאִם הוֹשִׁיבָהּ קֹדֶם הַמּוֹעֵד וּבָרְחָה, אִם זֶה בְּתוֹךְ שְׁלֹשָׁה יָמִים לִבְרִיחָה, מֻתָּר לְהַחֲזִירָהּ. אֲבָל לְאַחַר שְׁלֹשָׁה יָמִים, אָסוּר לְהַחֲזִירָהּ, אֲפִלּוּ אִם יִפָּסְדוּ הַבֵּיצִים. וּלְהוֹשִׁיב אַחֶרֶת תַּחְתֶּיהָ, אֲפִלּוּ תּוֹךְ שְׁלֹשָׁה יָמִים, אָסוּר.

סִימָן קה
דְּבָרִים הָאֲסוּרִים מִשּׁוּם טִרְחָא

א) אָסוּר לְהַסִּיעַ וְלִשָּׂא מִטַּלְטְלָיו וּכְלֵי בֵיתוֹ בְּחֹל־הַמּוֹעֵד מִדִּירָה שֶׁבְּחָצֵר זוֹ לְדִירָה שֶׁבְּחָצֵר אַחֶרֶת, אֲפִלּוּ מִדִּירָה כְּעוּרָה לְדִירָה נָאָה. אֲבָל מִבַּיִת לְבַיִת בְּחָצֵר אַחַת, מֻתָּר. וְכֵן אִם שְׁתֵּי הַחֲצֵרוֹת סְמוּכוֹת וְיֵשׁ פֶּתַח בֵּינֵיהֶן, מֻתָּר לְהוֹצִיא הַחֲפָצִים דֶּרֶךְ שָׁם. וּבִמְקוֹם פְּסֵידָא, מֻתָּר

45. *Magein Avraham* 545:23.
46. Even without a meal. (*Maharsha, Ra'anach Magein Avraham* etc) But if it is made with a meal, it then becomes a *de'oraisa* prohibition. (*Eliyahu Rabbah* 546)
47. *Maseches Moed Katan* 8b.
48. *Shulchan Aruch* 546:2. *Beis Yosef* holds you should not make the meal on the same day. *Kesav Sofer* Responsum 79 says according to *Tosafos* and *Rosh* you may. (see *Mishnah Berurah* 546:7)

16) A person who needs money, even if not for Yom Tov needs, and is afraid that he might not get a loan after Yom Tov, and the lender refuses to give a loan without receiving a note, is permitted to write such a note.[45]

17) Weddings are not performed on *Chol Hamoed*[46] because one kind of rejoicing[47] should not be mixed with another. But one is permitted to remarry the woman he divorced.[48] It is permitted to make a feast for a circumcision, or the redemption of a firstborn. It is also permitted[49] to make a feast for an engagement.[50]

18) It is permitted to hire workers, even Jews,[51] to do work for you after Yom Tov.

19) You are permitted to go outside the *techum,* either on foot or in a vehicle,[52] or on horseback.

20) It is not permitted to mate a male animal with a female animal, because no loss is sustained [by delaying it]

21) You are not allowed to set a chicken on eggs to hatch them. If you set her before the festival and she ran away, if it is within three days from the time she ran away, you are permitted to put her back, but after three days, you are forbidden to put her back, even if the eggs will be spoiled. And to set another in her place, even within three days is forbidden.

Chapter 105

Things Forbidden Because They are Bothersome

1) It is forbidden to move and carry movable belongings and household utensils on *Chol Hamoed,* from an apartment in one courtyard to an apartment in another courtyard, even from an unattractive apartment to a nice one.[1] But to move these items from one house to another in the same courtyard, is permitted.[2] Similarly, if the two courtyards are adjacent to each other, and there is a door between them, it is permitted to take things out through that door. However, if you would otherwise incur a loss, you are permitted to move these articles even from one city

---

49. *Shulchan Aruch* 546:4.

50. *Eliyahu Rabbah, Chayei Adam* 117:11. *Mishnah Berurah* 546:2 rules that if you are not serving a whole meal, but just cake etc., there is certainly no need to be stringent.

51. *Rambam, Magein Avraham.* (*Eliyahu Rabbah,* however, permits hiring only non-Jewish workers).

52. You are allowed to repair your vehicle for travel to meet a friend or to profit in order to purchase holiday necessities. But you may not do so in order to profit for other needs. (*Peri Megadim* 536:1) Going on an outing is considered a Yom Tov need, and you may repair your vehicle to go on one. (*Shulchan Aruch, Ramah* 536:1)

1. *Shulchan Aruch* 535:1. If these items are necessary for the *Moed,* and it is obvious that it is so, you may do it even openly. (*Eliyahu Rabbah, Mishnah Berurah* 535:4)

2. Because there is less bother and less publicity. (*Mishnah Berurah*)

אֲפִלּוּ מֵעִיר לְעִיר. וְכֵן מִדִּירָה שֶׁאֵינָהּ שֶׁלּוֹ לְדִירָה שֶׁהִיא שֶׁלּוֹ, מֻתָּר מִשּׁוּם שִׂמְחַת יוֹם־טוֹב, שֶׁ.מְחָה הִיא לוֹ לָדוּר בְּדִירָה שֶׁהִיא שֶׁלּוֹ.

ב) אִם צָרִיךְ לְהַכְנִיס פֵּרוֹתָיו אוֹ שְׁאָר סְחוֹרָה מִפְּנֵי שֶׁהוּא יָרֵא מִפְּנֵי גַנָּבִים אוֹ מִשְּׁאָר הֶפְסֵד, כָּל מַה שֶׁאֶפְשָׁר לַעֲשׂוֹת בְּצִנְעָא, יַעֲשֶׂה. וְאִם אִי אֶפְשָׁר לַעֲשׂוֹת בְּצִנְעָא, מֻתָּר לַעֲשׂוֹת אֲפִלּוּ בְּפַרְהֶסְיָא.

סִימָן קו
דִּינֵי מִקָּח וּמִמְכָּר בְּחֹל־הַמּוֹעֵד

א) כָּל סְחוֹרָה, אֲסוּרָה, בֵּין לִקְנוֹת בֵּין לִמְכּוֹר. רַק אִם נִזְדַּמֵּן לוֹ רֶוַח מְרֻבֶּה, יָכוֹל לִקְנוֹת וְלִמְכּוֹר בְּצִנְעָא, וְיוֹצִיא לִכְבוֹד יוֹם־טוֹב יוֹתֵר מִמַּה שֶּׁהָיָה בְּדַעְתּוֹ לְהוֹצִיא.

ב) אִם יֵשׁ לוֹ סְחוֹרָה שֶׁיֵּשׁ לָחוּשׁ שֶׁאִם לֹא יִמְכְּרֶנָּה עַתָּה יַפְסִיד מִן הַקֶּרֶן, מֻתָּר לְמָכְרָהּ, מִשּׁוּם דַּהֲוֵי דָּבָר הָאָבֵד. אֲבָל אִם אֵין לָחוּשׁ שֶׁיַּפְסִיד אֶלָּא שֶׁלֹּא יַרְוִיחַ אַחַר כָּךְ, אָסוּר לְמָכְרָהּ. כִּי מְנִיעַת רֶוַח, לֹא מִקְּרֵי הֶפְסֵד.

ג) אִם חָל יָרִיד, שֶׁהוּא יוֹם הַשּׁוּק הַבָּא לִפְרָקִים, אוֹ יוֹם הַשּׁוּק שֶׁבְּכָל שָׁבוּעַ, אֶלָּא שֶׁעַתָּה הוּא קֹדֶם הַחַגָּאוֹת שֶׁמִּתְאַסְּפִים קוֹנִים הַרְבֵּה, מֻתָּר לִמְכּוֹר. דְּכֵיוָן שֶׁהוּא דָּבָר שֶׁאֵינוֹ תָּדִיר, חָשְׁבִינָן גַּם מְנִיעַת הָרֶוַח כְּמוֹ הֶפְסֵד. אֲבָל בְּיוֹם הַשּׁוּק שֶׁבְּכָל שָׁבוּעַ, אָסוּר. וּכְשֶׁבָּאִים לִפְעָמִים סוֹחֲרִים אוֹ סְפִינוֹת שֶׁמּוֹכְרִים בְּזוֹל אוֹ קוֹנִים בְּיֹקֶר, מַה שֶּׁאֵינוֹ שָׁכִיחַ תָּמִיד, גַּם כֵּן מֻתָּר לִקְנוֹת מֵהֶם וְלִמְכּוֹר לָהֶם.

ד) וְכֵן מִי שֶׁצָּרִיךְ לִקְנוֹת יַיִן בְּעֵת הַבָּצִיר, שֶׁיְּהֵא לוֹ לְצָרְכֵי בֵיתוֹ

---

3. *Ramah.*

4. *Shulchan Aruch* 535:2 says this applies, even if you move from a nice one to an unattractive one. If you shared a rented room with someone, you may move to a private rented room. (*Peri Megadim* 535:2) If you already live in your own house and want to bring your belongings from another house, this reason (happiness of moving into your own house) does not apply (*Minchas Pittim*) and you should not be lenient. (*Mishnah Berurah* 535:7)

5. *Shulchan Aruch* 538:2.

1. The Sages prohibited commerce on *Chol Hamoed,* since it often involves physical or mental stress which detracts from the festival. (*Magein Avraham* 539:1, *Mishnah Berurah*) It is also prohibited because of the fear that you might write something that is not permitted to be written on *Chol Hamoed.* (see *Yeshuos Ya'akov*)

to another.[3] Moving from a house that doesn't belong to you to your own house, is permitted, for this is considered rejoicing on Yom Tov, because it is a joy to live in your own home.[4]

2) If you must take in fruit, or other merchandise because you fear it will be stolen, or damaged, it should be done in a secluded manner if possible. If you cannot do it in a secluded manner, you are permitted to do it openly.[5]

Chapter 106

Buying and Selling During Chol Hamoed

1) All commerce is forbidden,[1] whether buying or selling.[2] However if you have an opportunity to make a big profit,[3] you may buy and sell in private.[4] You should then spend more in honor of Yom Tov than you had previously intended.[5]

2) If you have merchandise and you are afraid that if you don't sell it now, its value will become less than its cost, you are permitted to sell it, because you prevent a loss thereby. However, if there is no fear of sustaining a loss, except that you will not make a profit later, you are forbidden to sell it, because unearned profit is not considered a loss.[6]

3) If a fair occurs on (*Chol Hamoed*), that is, a market day which occurs infrequently, or even the weekly market day, which occurs before the non-Jewish holidays,[7] when many buyers come together, you are permitted to sell in that market. Since it is an irregular occasion, even a lack of profit is considered a loss. But to sell in a regular weekly market is forbidden. Merchants or ships that arrive occasionally, and sell merchandise cheaply, or buy at a high price, which is something that does not happen often, you are then also permitted to buy from them and sell to them.

4) If you need to purchase wine at the time of vintage, for the needs of your household for the entire year, because later the price of wine will go up, you are

---

2. *Shulchan Aruch* 539:1.

3. In this case, even if the opportunity may be there afterwards, it is permitted, for if the opportunity will be lost, it would be permitted even without the conditions listed. See paragraph 3.

4. *Ramah* 539:1. This restriction is only in a situation when you have sufficient money, or, according to the *Taz*, when you are extremely wealthy. But if you are not, then you may buy or sell, even openly and for a modest profit; provided you use some of this profit for enjoying the Yom Tov. You also should keep your store gate closed until a customer arrives. (see *Mishnah Berurah* 539:5, 6, 17, 18, *Sha'ar Hatziyun* 539:7, *Biur Halachah* 539:4, and *Chayei Adam* 112:2)

5. *Ramah*. See footnote 4. (*Biur Halachah* 539:5) You are not permitted to do a *melachah* (like cutting material to sell) even under these conditions.

6. See footnotes 4 and 5.

7. Before the non-Jewish holidays there is usually heavy trade.

לִשְׁתּוֹת כָּל הַשָּׁנָה, וְאַחַר כָּךְ יִתְיַקֵּר הַיַּיִן, מֻתָּר לוֹ לִקְנוֹת בְּחֹל־הַמּוֹעֵד. אֲבָל לְמַשָּׂא וּמַתָּן, אָסוּר לִקְנוֹת.

ה) דְּבָרִים הַנִּצְרָכִים לַמּוֹעֵד, כְּגוֹן פֵּרוֹת וְתַבְלִין, מוֹכְרִין כְּדַרְכָּן אֲפִלּוּ בְּפַרְהֶסְיָא. וְכֵיוָן שֶׁמֻּתָּרִין לִפְתֹּחַ הַחֲנוּת בִּשְׁבִיל יִשְׂרָאֵל, מֻתָּרִין לִמְכֹּר גַּם לַגּוֹי.

ו) לִתְבֹּעַ חוֹבוֹת, נָהֲגוּ לְהָקֵל אֲפִלּוּ מִיִּשְׂרָאֵל, מִשּׁוּם דְּחוֹשְׁבִין זֶה לְדָבָר הָאָבֵד.

ז) לְהַלְווֹת בְּרִבִּית לַגּוֹי הָרָגִיל אֶצְלוֹ, מֻתָּר, מִפְּנֵי דַּהֲוֵי דָּבָר הָאָבֵד, שֶׁלֹּא יַרְגִּיל אֶת עַצְמוֹ אֵצֶל אַחֵר. וְאִם מַלְוֶה לַגּוֹי שֶׁאֵינוֹ רָגִיל אֶצְלוֹ, יוֹצִיא הָרִבִּית מִשָּׁבוּעַ אֶחָד לְשִׂמְחַת יוֹם־טוֹב. וְלִמְכֹּר סְחוֹרָה לְמִי שֶׁאֵינוֹ רָגִיל אֶצְלוֹ, אָסוּר, וְלֹא מַהֲנֵי מַה שֶּׁיּוֹסִיף לְשִׂמְחַת יוֹם־טוֹב. אֲבָל לְמִי שֶׁרָגִיל אֶצְלוֹ, מֻתָּר, מִשּׁוּם דַּהֲוֵי דָּבָר הָאָבֵד, שֶׁלֹּא יַרְגִּיל אֶת עַצְמוֹ אֵצֶל אֲחֵרִים.

ח) חִלּוּף מַטְבְּעוֹת, אָסוּר.

סִימָן קז
דִּינֵי חֹדֶשׁ נִיסָן

א) כָּל חֹדֶשׁ נִיסָן אֵין אוֹמְרִים תַּחֲנוּן, וְלֹא צִדּוּק הַדִּין, וְאֵין אוֹמְרִים צִדְקָתְךָ, בַּשַּׁבָּת בְּמִנְחָה. נוֹהֲגִין מֵרֹאשׁ־חֹדֶשׁ וְאֵילָךְ לִקְרוֹת בְּכָל יוֹם

---

8. You may not purchase more than one year's supply because it can be purchased again the following year. (*Beis Yosef, Bach, Mishnah Berurah* 539:31)

9. See *Shulchan Aruch* and *Ramah* 539:9. *Eliyahu Rabbah* rules that buying wine in order to profit is permitted, and only buying large quantities for your own use is prohibited because it is an unnecessary bother. See *Biur Halachah* who says not to protest against those who rely on this opinion.

10. *Shulchan Aruch* 539:10 permits their sale because they are perishable. *Magein Avraham* and *Mishnah Berurah* include non-perishable items as well, provided they are obviously for Yom Tov needs. Anything for Yom Tov that is not obvious, must be done in private. (see *Shulchan Aruch* 533:5)

11. See *Shulchan Aruch* 539:2–3. This reason is only necessary for commercial debts such as payment for merchandise (already delivered). These have the *halachah* of commerce, and are allowed only when classified as prevention of loss. Debts from loans, however, are not considered business and you may try to collect them on *Chol Hamoed*, even in court. (see *Taz, Mishnah Berurah* 539:7–11) If you have a good security (מַשְׁכּוֹן) you may not make your claim

allowed to buy it on *Chol Hamoed,*[8] but it is forbidden to buy it for business purposes.[9]

5) Things that are needed for the Yom Tov, like fruits and spices,[10] may be sold regularly, even openly. And since you are allowed to open your store to sell to a Jewish customer, you may also sell to a non-Jewish customer.

6) It is customary to be lenient about collecting debts, even when the debt is owed by a Jew, because we consider this the prevention of a loss.[11]

7) Lending money on interest to a regular non-Jewish customer is permitted, because it would be a loss, if he took his business elsewhere.[12] If you lend money to a non-Jew, who is not your regular customer, you should spend the interest[13] of one week for [the mitzvah of] rejoicing on Yom Tov.[14] Selling merchandise to someone who is not a regular customer is forbidden, and it is of no avail even if you spend more of your profits for [the mitzvah of] rejoicing on Yom Tov.[15] But you are permitted to sell to a regular customer, because it is considered prevention of a loss, so that he will not get accustomed to purchase elsewhere.

8) It is forbidden to exchange money[16] (on *Chol Hamoed).*

Chapter 107

The Month of Nisan

1) During the entire month of *Nisan* we do not say *Tachanun*[1] or *Tzidduk Hadin*[2] (burial service), and we do not say *Tzidkasecha* on Shabbos at *Minchah.*[3] It is customary[4] from *Rosh Chodesh* on, to read (from the *Seifer Torah*) the *parashah* of the *Nasi*[5] who brought his offering on that day. On the thirteenth day of the month, we

---

in *Beis Din* (court) on *Chol Hamoed.* (*Eliyahu Rabbah*) When claiming outstanding loans, etc., if they are not considered prevention of loss, you may not do *melachah* (like writing) in the process.

12. *Rabbeinu Tam, Rosh.*

13. If it was a large loan and you find it difficult to spend so much, you should do the best you can. *(Ba'eir Heiteiv, Maharil)*

14. This is in addition to what you had intended to spend. (*Mishnah Berurah* 539:45)

15. See paragraphs 1–2 and footnotes 4–5. Lending is less restricted than business because it does not involve the bother of pricing or the disappointment of overpaying. (*Magein Avraham* 539:17, *Mishnah Berurah* 539:45)

16. *Shulchan Aruch* 539:14. Because it is considered business. (*Vilna Gaon, Mishnah Berurah* 539:47)

1. See Chapter 22.
2. See Chapter 198:14.
3. *Shulchan Aruch* 429.
4. This custom is not very widespread in our times, except among Chassidim.
5. The leader of each tribe was called *Nasi.* On *Rosh Chodesh Nisan* the *Tabernacle* was erected, and in honor of its dedication, during the ensuing twelve days, each *Nasi* had his day on which he brought a special offering, as is written in *Numbers* 7:10–7:89.

פָּרָשַׁת הַנָּשִׂיא שֶׁהִקְרִיב בּוֹ־בַיּוֹם. וּבַיּוֹם הַשְּׁלֹשָׁה־עָשָׂר קוֹרִין פָּרָשַׁת בְּהַעֲלֹתְךָ, עַד כֵּן עָשָׂה אֶת הַמְּנוֹרָה, שֶׁהִיא כְּנֶגֶד שֵׁבֶט לֵוִי.

ב) אֵין מִתְעַנִּין בּוֹ אֲפִלּוּ תַּעֲנִית יָארְצַייט. אֲבָל תַּעֲנִית חֲלוֹם, מִתְעַנִּין. וְהַבְּכוֹרִים, מִתְעַנִּין בְּעֶרֶב פֶּסַח, כַּאֲשֶׁר יְבֹאַר אִם יִרְצֶה הַשֵּׁם בְּסִימָן קי"ג. וְחָתָן וְכַלָּה גַּם כֵּן מִתְעַנִּין בּוֹ, וַאֲפִלּוּ בְּרֹאשׁ־חֹדֶשׁ נִיסָן.

ג) בְּשַׁבָּת הַגָּדוֹל לְמִנְחָה, נוֹהֲגִין שֶׁאֵין אוֹמְרִים בָּרְכִי נַפְשִׁי, אֶלָּא עֲבָדִים הָיִינוּ וְכוּ', לְפִי שֶׁבְּשַׁבָּת הַגָּדוֹל הָיְתָה הַתְחָלַת הַגְּאֻלָּה וְהַנִּסִּים.

סִימָן קח
דִּינֵי הַחִטִּין וְהַקֶּמַח לַמַּצּוֹת

א) כְּתִיב, וּשְׁמַרְתֶּם אֶת הַמַּצּוֹת, מִכָּאן, שֶׁצְּרִיכִין לִשְׁמוֹר אֶת הַחִטִּין לְשֵׁם מַצּוֹת מִצְוָה, שֶׁלֹּא יָבוֹאוּ עֲלֵיהֶן מָיִם. וּלְדַעַת קְצָת מִגְּדוֹלֵי הַפּוֹסְקִים זִכְרוֹנָם לִבְרָכָה, צְרִיכִין שְׁמִירָה זוֹ מִיָּד מִשְּׁעַת קְצִירָה וְאֵילָךְ. אֲבָל הַמִּנְהָג הוּא כַּפּוֹסְקִים דְּסַגֵּי לְהוּ בִּשְׁמִירָה מִשָּׁעָה שֶׁמּוֹלִיכִין אוֹתָן לִטְחוֹן וְאֵילָךְ. וְאַךְ הַמְדַקְדְּקִין בְּמִצְוֹת, חוֹשְׁשִׁין לִשְׁמִירָה מִשְּׁעַת קְצִירָה, וְכֵן נָכוֹן לַעֲשׂוֹת. וְרָאוּי לְדַקְדֵּק שֶׁלֹּא יַעַמְדוּ הַשִּׁבֳּלִים בִּמְחֻבָּר עַד שֶׁיִּתְיַבְּשׁוּ כָּל צָרְכָּן וְיַלְבִּינוּ, כִּי אָז אִם יֵרְדוּ עֲלֵיהֶן גְּשָׁמִים, יַחְמִיצוּ אֲפִלּוּ בִּמְחֻבָּר, כֵּיוָן שֶׁאֵינָן צְרִיכוֹת עוֹד לַקַּרְקַע. עַל כֵּן רָאוּי וְנָכוֹן לִקְצוֹר בְּעוֹד שֶׁיֵּשׁ בָּהֶן עוֹד קְצָת מַרְאֶה יְרָקוּת. וּמִי שֶׁאֶפְשָׁר לוֹ בְּחִטִּין שְׁמוּרוֹת מִשְּׁעַת קְצִירָה לְכָל יְמֵי הֶחָג, מַה־טּוֹב. וְאִם לָאו, רָאוּי לוֹ עַל־כָּל־פָּנִים לְהַדֵּר בָּזֶה לַמַּצּוֹת שֶׁעַל הַסֵּדֶר בִּשְׁנֵי הַלֵּילוֹת.

---

6. Aaron, the High Priest, and *Nasi* of the tribe of *Levi* did not take part in the offering of the *Nesi'im.* His lighting of the *Menorah* was his part in the dedication. See Rashi. (*Numbers* 8:2)

7. The anniversary of the death of one's father or mother. (See *Ramah* 429:2) This is our custom; but *Shulchan Aruch* permits a private individual to fast during *Nisan.*

8. If one has a particularly onimous and disturbing dream, fasting with repentance helps to nullify the decree indicated by the dream.

9. Since it is a day of atonement for them, they fast the day of the wedding until the marriage ceremony takes place. (*Magein Avraham* 573) Refraining from fasting during *Nisan* is not a *halachah,* but a custom, and this fast overrides it. (*poskim*)

10. *Ramah* 573. This is so only on *Rosh Chodesh Nisan,* because two of Aaron's sons (Nadav

read in *parashas Beha'alosechah* until *"Kein asah es hamenorah"* "So did he make the Menorah" which is fitting for the tribe of Levi.[6]

2) [During the month of *Nisan,]* we do not fast even the fast of a *Yahrzeit,*[7] but we may fast because of a dream.[8] The firstborn (males) fast on *erev Pesach,* as will be explained, God willing, in Chapter 113. A groom and a bride also fast during *Nisan,*[9] even on *Rosh Chodesh Nisan.*[10]

3) On *Shabbos Hagadol*[11] at *Minchah* it is customary not to recite *Barchi Nafshi,* but to say instead *Avadim Hayinu*[12] etc., because on *Shabbos Hagadol* the redemption from Egypt and the miracles began.[13]

Chapter 108

The Wheat and Flour for the Matzos

1) It is written, "And you must guard the matzos" (Exodus 12:17). From this we learn that we must guard the wheat [from which we make] the matzos with which we perform the mitzvah, to see that no water comes upon them. According to some of the great *halachic* authorities, of blessed memory, this watchfulness is to begin from the time the wheat is harvested. The prevailing custom is to follow the opinion of the authorities, who maintain it is sufficient to guard it from the time it is brought to the mill, and thereafter. However, people who are meticulous in their performance of mitzvos, are concerned that [the wheat] should be guarded from the time it is harvested, and this is the proper thing to do. Special care must be taken that the stalks do not remain attached to the earth until they completely dry out and turn white, because then if rain falls on them they will become *chametz,* even though they are still attached to the soil,[1] since they no longer need the soil's (nourishment). It is, therefore, fitting and proper to harvest them when they are still slightly green. If you can obtain wheat that was guarded from the time of harvesting for all the days of Yom Tov, so much the better. If this is impossible, you should at least be scrupulous about this for the matzos of both Seder nights.

---

and Avihu) died on that day. On any other *Rosh Chodesh,* the bride and groom may not fast. (*Magein Avraham, Mishnah Berurah* 573:9)

11. The Shabbos before *Pesach* is so called because in Egypt, the Jews were commanded to take a lamb on the tenth day of *Nisan* and designate it for the paschal offering. They did so, and tied the sheep to their bedposts. The Egyptians, upon hearing the Jews were bringing the sheep as a sacrifice, did not protest, even though the lamb was the Egyptian idol. That year, the tenth day of *Nisan* occurred on Shabbos, and in commemoration of this miracle, we call it *Shabbos Hagadol*—the Great Shabbos. (*Tur* 430 etc.)

12. This is found in the *Hagaddah* of *Pesach.* It is customary to recite until *Lechappeir al Kol Avonoseinu* (to atone all our sins). (*Ramah* 430) The *Vilna Gaon* did not agree with this custom, and many people follow his ruling and do not say it.

13. See note 11.

1. This is so only if there was a huge downpour of rain, but a slight rain or drizzle does not disqualify the wheat and it may be used even for the required matzo of the Seder. (*Mishnah Berurah* 467:18)

ב) חִטִּים שֶׁנִּמְצְאוּ בָהֶן מְבֻקָּעוֹת אוֹ מְצֻמָּחוֹת, הַשְּׁאָר מֻתָּר. וּבִלְבַד שֶׁיִּבְרְרוּ אוֹתָן, אוֹ צְרִיכִין לְדַקְדֵּק הֵיטֵב, אִם יֵשׁ שָׁם עַל־כָּל־פָּנִים שִׁשִּׁים כְּנֶגֶד הַמְבֻקָּעוֹת וְהַמְצֻמָּחוֹת. וּלְכַתְּחִלָּה יֵשׁ לְהַדֵּר לִבְרֹר גַּם מִן הַחִטִּים שֶׁאָכְלוּ מֵהֶן עַכְבָּרִים אוֹ שֶׁיִּהְיֶה שִׁשִּׁים כְּנֶגְדָּן. וְהַחִטִּים שֶׁבָּאוּ בִּסְפִינָה אוֹ שֶׁהָיוּ מֻנָּחוֹת בְּבוֹרוֹת, אִם הֵן יְבֵשׁוֹת וְקָשׁוֹת וְלֹא נִשְׁתַּנָּה מַרְאֵיהֶן, כְּשֵׁרוֹת. וְאִם הָיוּ מֻנָּחוֹת בַּעֲלִיָּה וְיָרְדוּ עֲלֵיהֶן גְּשָׁמִים דֶּרֶךְ הַגַּג בִּקְצָת מְקוֹמוֹת, אֲסוּרוֹת. אֲבָל אִם נָפַל עֲלֵיהֶן קְצָת שֶׁלֶג אוֹ קְצָת מַיִם בְּמָקוֹם אֶחָד, מְסַלֵּק אוֹתָן שֶׁיֵּשׁ לְהִסְתַּפֵּק בָּהֶן, וְהַשְּׁאָר מֻתָּרוֹת.

ג) כְּבָר נָהֲגוּ יִשְׂרָאֵל לְדַקְדֵּק בְּהֶכְשֵׁר הָרֵחַיִם, לְנַקֵּר הֵיטֵב וּלְנַקּוֹת בְּכָל הָאֶפְשָׁרִי. וְכִיסִים, לוֹקְחִים חֲדָשִׁים. וּבִמְקוֹם שֶׁיֵּשׁ תַּלְמִידֵי חֲכָמִים, הֵמָּה הוֹלְכִים אֶל הָרֵחַיִם לְהַשְׁגִּיחַ, שֶׁיְּהֵא הַהֶכְשֵׁר כָּרָאוּי. וּבִמְקוֹם שֶׁאֵין תַּלְמִידֵי חֲכָמִים, רָאוּי לְכָל יְרֵא־שָׁמַיִם שֶׁיֵּלֵךְ בְּעַצְמוֹ לְהַשְׁגִּיחַ עַל הַהֶכְשֵׁר, דְּמִצְוָה בּוֹ יוֹתֵר מִבִּשְׁלוּחוֹ. וְנוֹהֲגִין כִּי הַקֶּמַח הָרִאשׁוֹן שֶׁנִּטְחַן לְאַחַר הַהֶכְשֵׁר, אֵין אוֹכְלִין אוֹתוֹ בְּפֶסַח. אִם טוֹחֲנִים בְּרֵחַיִם גַּם תְּבוּאָה לְתוּתָה, צְרִיכִין לְהַפְסִיק בִּמְחִצָּה שֶׁלֹּא יִתְעָרְבוּ בּוֹ מִן הָאָבָק הַהוּא.

ד) שַׂק עִם קֶמַח שֶׁנִּתְלַחְלַח מִמַּיִם, אִם הוּא בְּמָקוֹם אֶחָד, בֵּין שֶׁהוּא עֲדַיִן לַח, בֵּין שֶׁנִּתְיַבֵּשׁ, יֹאחַז אֶת הַמָּקוֹם הַזֶּה בְּיָדוֹ וְיָרִיק הַשְּׁאָר, וּמֻתָּר. רַק זֶה שֶׁנִּתְלַחְלַח, אָסוּר. וְאִם נִתְלַחְלַח בְּכַמָּה מְקוֹמוֹת שֶׁאִי אֶפְשָׁר לוֹ לַעֲשׂוֹת כֵּן, אֲזַי אִם עֲדַיִן הוּא לַח, יְרַקֵּד אֶת הַקֶּמַח. וּמַה שֶּׁנִּשְׁאַר עַל הַנָּפָה פֵּרוּרִין, זֶה לְבַד חָמֵץ, וְהַשְּׁאָר מֻתָּר. וְכֵן אִם אָכְלוּ עַכְבָּרִים מִן הַקֶּמַח, יְרַקְּדֶנּוּ. אֲבָל אִם כְּבָר נִתְיַבֵּשׁ, לָא מַהֲנֵי לֵהּ הַרְקָדָה, וְכָל הַקֶּמַח אָסוּר.

ה) בְּיוֹם שֶׁטָּחֲנוּ אֶת הַקֶּמַח, אָסוּר לְאָפוֹתוֹ, מִפְּנֵי שֶׁאָז הַקֶּמַח הוּא חַם וּמְמַהֵר לְהַחְמִיץ כְּשֶׁנּוֹתְנִים בּוֹ אֶת הַמַּיִם, עַל כֵּן יִשְׁהֶה אַחַר הַטְּחִינָה לְכָל־הַפָּחוֹת מֵעֵת־לְעֵת.

ו) הַשַּׂקִּים שֶׁמַּנִּיחִים בָּהֶם אֶת הַקֶּמַח, טוֹב לַעֲשׂוֹתָן חֲדָשִׁים, אוֹ לְכָל־הַפָּחוֹת לְהַתִּיר אֶת הַתְּפִירוֹת וּלְכַבֵּס הֵיטֵב בְּחַמִּין וּבְאֵפֶר וּבְשִׁפְשׁוּף וַחֲבִיטָה.

ז) אָסוּר לְהַנִּיחַ שַׂק עִם קֶמַח עַל גַּבֵּי בְּהֵמָה, אֶלָּא אִם יֵשׁ עוֹר

2) If in some of the wheat there was found kernels that were split open or sprouted; the rest may be used for matzah, provided the unfit ones were separated or carefully measured to make sure that there is at least sixty times as much (of the good wheat) as the split and sprouted (wheat). Initially, you should be scrupulous to sort out even wheat from which mice have eaten, or to make sure that there is at least sixty times as much of the good wheat. Wheat that arrived by ship or was stored in pits, if it is dry and hard, and its color has not changed, is kosher for *Pesach*. If it was stored in an attic and rain dripped upon it in several places, through the roof, it is forbidden. But if a little snow fell on it or a little water, in one place only, you must remove those kernels which are doubtful, and the rest may be used.

3) It is a long established custom in Yisroel, in preparing the mill, to clean it thoroughly, and scrub it in every possible way and to purchase new bags [for the flour.] In a community where there are Torah scholars, they should go to the mill to supervise the cleansing, and to see that the preparations are done properly. In a community where there are no Torah scholars, every God-fearing person should go himself to supervise the preparation of the mill, for it is a greater mitzvah to do it yourself, than if an agent does it for you. It is customary that the first flour milled after this preparation, is not eaten on *Pesach.* If moist grain is also ground at that mill, it should be separated with a partition, so that none of its powder should mix with it.

4) If a bag of flour has become wet, if only one part became wet, whether it is still moist or already dry, you may take that part in your hand while you empty the rest of the flour, which you are permitted to use. Only the part that has become wet is forbidden. However, if the bag of flour has become wet in several places so that it is impossible to take these steps, then, if it is still moist, the flour is sifted and only the pieces that remain in the sieve are *chametz,* but the rest may be used. If mice have eaten some of the flour, it should be sifted. However, if the bag of flour has become dry, sifting is of no use, and the entire flour is forbidden to be used.

5) On the day the flour has been ground it is forbidden to be baked,[2] because the flour is then warm and will quickly become *chametz* when water is poured on it. Therefore, you should postpone using it for at least twenty-four hours after the grinding.

6) The bags for holding the flour preferably should be made new, or at least the seams of the old bags should be opened, and they should be washed thoroughly with warm water and ashes, and by rubbing and beating them.

7) It is forbidden to load a bag of flour on an animal, unless thick leather is

---

2. If, however, it was already kneaded with water, it may be baked, but special care must be taken that it not be allowed to become *chametz.* This is done by speeding up the process and getting into the oven even quicker than other matzos. (*Mishnah Berurah* 453:43)

עָבֶה תַּחְתָּיו, דְּאִם לֹא כֵן יִתְחַמֵּם וְיִתְלַחְלֵחַ מִן הַזֵּעָה. וְאִם אֶפְשָׁר, יִזָּהֵר גַּם כֵּן שֶׁלֹּא לְהַנִּיחַ הַרְבֵּה שַׂקִּים זֶה עַל זֶה, מִפְּנֵי שֶׁעַל יְדֵי זֶה מִתְחַמֵּם וַיַּחְמִיץ בַּלִּישָׁה.

סִימָן קט
דִּינֵי הַמַּיִם

א) אֵין לָשִׁין אֶת הַמַּצּוֹת אֶלָּא בְּמַיִם שֶׁלָּנוּ הַלַּיְלָה, דְּהַיְנוּ שֶׁיִּשְׁאַב אוֹתָם בֵּין הַשְּׁמָשׁוֹת וְיַעַמְדוּ בְּתָלוּשׁ כָּל הַלַּיְלָה. וַאֲפִלּוּ אִם הַלַּיְלָה אָרֹךְ יוֹתֵר מִשְּׁתֵּים עֶשְׂרֵה שָׁעוֹת, אָסוּר לָלוּשׁ בָּהֶן עַד אוֹר הַיּוֹם. וְאִם הַלַּיְלָה קָצָר וְאֵין שְׁתֵּים עֶשְׂרֵה שָׁעוֹת עַד אוֹר הַיּוֹם, צְרִיכִין לְהַמְתִּין עַד שֶׁיַּעַבְרוּ שְׁתֵּים־עֶשְׂרֵה שָׁעוֹת מִשָּׁעָה שֶׁנִּשְׁאָבוּ. וְעַמָּא דְאַרְעָא נוֹהֲגִין שֶׁמִּיָּד בְּאוֹר הַיּוֹם לָשִׁין בְּמַיִם שֶׁלָּנוּ, אַף שֶׁעֲדַיִן לֹא עָבְרוּ שְׁתֵּים־עֶשְׂרֵה שָׁעוֹת. וְאַף שֶׁיֵּשׁ לָהֶם עַל מַה שֶּׁיִּסְמֹכוּ, אֲבָל רֹב הַפּוֹסְקִים מַחְמִירִים בָּזֶה. וְעַל כֵּן צָרִיךְ לִזָּהֵר בַּדָּבָר.

ב) אִם לֹא יוּכַל לְשַׁעֵר אֶת זְמַן בֵּין הַשְּׁמָשׁוֹת, יַקְדִּים קְצָת, וּבִלְבַד שֶׁלֹּא יִשְׁאַב קֹדֶם שְׁקִיעַת הַחַמָּה. וְהַמִּנְהָג לְסַנֵּן אֶת הַמַּיִם וּלְכַסּוֹתָן. וּצְרִיכִין לְהַעֲמִידָם בְּמָקוֹם קַר. וּכְשֶׁהוּא נוֹשְׂאָם בַּיּוֹם לַבַּיִת, יִזָּהֵר שֶׁלֹּא יָבֹא עֲלֵיהֶם הַשֶּׁמֶשׁ.

ג) יָכוֹל לִשְׁאוֹב בְּפַעַם אַחַת לְכַמָּה יָמִים, אֲבָל הַמִּצְוָה הִיא לִשְׁאוֹב בִּשְׁבִיל כָּל יוֹם וָיוֹם בִּפְנֵי עַצְמוֹ. וְנוֹהֲגִין שֶׁלֹּא לִשְׁאוֹב בִּכְלִי חֶרֶס יָשָׁן אֲפִלּוּ הוּא שֶׁל פֶּסַח, אֶלָּא אִם כֵּן הוּא מְצֻפֶּה. דִּכְלִי חֶרֶס יָשָׁן שֶׁאֵינוֹ מְצֻפֶּה, אֵינוֹ הִדּוּר מִצְוָה. וְאֵין לְשַׁנּוֹת הַמִּנְהָג.

ד) הַנְּהָרוֹת בִּימֵי נִיסָן עַל פִּי הָרֹב הֵן יוֹתֵר קָרִים מִן הַבְּאֵרוֹת, וְעַל כֵּן יִשְׁאַב מִן הַנָּהָר. אַךְ לִפְעָמִים הַנְּהָרוֹת גְּדוֹלִים מֵהַפְשָׁרַת שְׁלָגִים וְאֵינָם קָרִים כָּל כָּךְ, וְאָז טוֹב יוֹתֵר לִשְׁאוֹב מִן הַבְּאֵרוֹת.

ה) לֹא יִשְׁאָבֵם עַל יְדֵי גוֹי, אֶלָּא עַל יְדֵי יִשְׂרָאֵל.

ו) לֹא יִתְּנֵם בִּכְלִי שֶׁהָיָה בּוֹ דְּבַשׁ אוֹ שְׁאָר מֵי פֵּרוֹת, אֶלָּא אִם

---

3. If, however, they were placed one on top of the other, it is necessary to wait at least twenty-four hours before using the wheat. One should also not sit on the bags of flour. (*Mishnah Berurah* 453:35)

placed underneath the bag, as otherwise, it will get warm and moist from perspiration. If possible, you should also be careful not to place many bags one on top of the other, because as a result of that, the flour will be heated, and become *chametz* in the kneading.[3]

Chapter 109

The Laws Concerning the Water (Used for Kneading the Matzos)

1) The flour for the matzos should be kneaded only with water that has stayed overnight,[1] that is to say, it should be drawn during twilight, and left standing overnight. Even if the night is longer than twelve hours, it is forbidden to use it for kneading until daylight, and if the night is short and there are no twelve hours until daylight, we must wait until twelve hours will have passed from the time it has been drawn. Ordinary people are accustomed to begin kneading as soon as it grows light, with water that stayed overnight, even though, as yet twelve hours have not passed. Although there are some authorities who permit this, most of the authorities take the more stringent view. It is necessary, therefore, to be watchful in this matter.

2) If you are unable to estimate the exact time of twilight, you may draw water a little earlier, provided you do not draw it before sunset.[2] It is the custom to strain the water and to cover it, and it must be placed in a cool place. When bringing the water into the house in the morning, you must be careful to keep it out of the sun.

3) You are permitted to draw enough water at one time to last for several days, but the proper way of fulfilling the mitzvah is to draw water daily for the needs of that day. It is the custom not to draw water in an old earthen vessel, even though it is used only for Pesach, unless it is glazed, for the use of an old unglazed vessel cannot be considered an enhancement of the mitzvah. This custom should not be changed.

4) Rivers in the month of Nissan are generally cooler than wells. You should, therefore, draw water from a river. Sometimes, however, the rivers are swollen from the melting snow and the water is not so cold; it is then preferable to draw water from a well.

5) The water should not be drawn by a non-Jew, but by a Jew.[3]

6) You should not put the water in a vessel that has contained honey or fruit

---

1. This applies both to the *matzah shel mitzvah* (which is required eating at the Seder) and to the regular matzos eaten during Pesach. See Chapter 110:15. (*Mishnah Berurah* 455:1)

2. Many *Poskim* rule that twilight begins at sunset and according to them, you may draw the water even before sunset.

3. Drawing water for baking matzah is considered part of the mitzvah and should be done only by a Jew. This *halachah* also applies to regular matzos and certainly to *matzo shel mitzvah.* The one who draws the water should say: "This is being done for *matzah shel mitzvah.*" (*Mishnah Berurah* 455:21–23)

הִגְעִילוֹ קֹדֶם. מִכָּל־שֶׁכֵּן שֶׁלֹּא יִתֵּן בִּכְלִי שֶׁהָיָה בוֹ דָבָר חָרִיף אֲפִלּוּ לֹא הָיָה חָמֵץ, מִשּׁוּם דְּעַל יְדֵי דָּבָר חָרִיף, מְמַהֵר לְהַחְמִיץ, וַאֲפִלּוּ הַגְעָלָה לָא מַהֲנֵי לָזֶה. גַּם לֹא יִתֵּן בִּכְלִי נְחֹשֶׁת, שֶׁאֵינוֹ מְצַנֵּן כְּמוֹ שְׁאָר כֵּלִים.

ז) אִם רוֹאֶה שֶׁלֹּא יַסְפִּיקוּ לוֹ הַמַּיִם שֶׁלָּנוּ, מֻתָּר לְהוֹסִיף לְתוֹכָן שְׁאָר מַיִם, וּבִלְבַד שֶׁיִּהְיֶה הָרֹב מִמַּיִם שֶׁלָּנוּ, וּלְכַתְּחִלָּה טוֹב שֶׁיִּהְיוּ שְׁנֵי שְׁלִישִׁים מִמַּיִם שֶׁלָּנוּ. וְיֵשׁ לְהַדֵּר, אִם אֶפְשָׁר, לִשְׁאוֹב אֶת הַמַּיִם שֶׁמּוֹסִיפִין מִתּוֹךְ [מַשְׁאֵבָה] (פְּלוּמְפּ), אוֹ שְׁאָר בְּאֵר מְכֻסָּה, שֶׁאֵין הַשֶּׁמֶשׁ בָּאָה עַל הַמָּיִם.

ח) כְּשֶׁאוֹפִין בְּיוֹם רִאשׁוֹן, צְרִיכִין לִשְׁאוֹב בְּיוֹם חֲמִישִׁי בָּעֶרֶב, כִּי בְּעֶרֶב שַׁבָּת אִי אֶפְשָׁר לְצַמְצֵם בֵּין הַשְּׁמָשׁוֹת. וּבִשְׁעַת הַדְּחָק אִם לֹא שָׁאַב בְּיוֹם חֲמִישִׁי, יִשְׁאַב בְּעֶרֶב שַׁבָּת לְאַחַר מִנְחָה אוֹ בַּשַּׁבָּת עַל יְדֵי גּוֹי.

ט) אֵין לִשְׁפֹּךְ אֶת הַמַּיִם מִפְּנֵי הַמֵּת, וְלֹא מִפְּנֵי הַתְּקוּפָה, שֶׁנֶּאֱמַר, שׁוֹמֵר מִצְוָה לֹא יֵדַע דָּבָר רָע. וּמִכָּל מָקוֹם לְכַתְּחִלָּה כְּשֶׁיּוֹדֵעַ שֶׁהַתְּקוּפָה תִּפּוֹל, יַנִּיחַ בְּתוֹךְ הַמַּיִם חֲתִיכַת בַּרְזֶל קְטַנָּה וּנְקִיָּה, כְּמוֹ מַחַט, וּתְהֵא תְלוּיָה בְּחוּט, שֶׁלֹּא יִצְטָרֵךְ אַחַר כָּךְ לְהַכְנִיס אֶת הַיָּד לְתוֹךְ הַמַּיִם לִקַּח אוֹתָהּ, אֶלָּא יִמְשְׁכֶנָּה עִם הַחוּט.

סִימָן קי
דִּינֵי הַלִּישָׁה וַאֲפִיַּת הַמַּצּוֹת

א) תַּנּוּר שֶׁאָפוּ בוֹ חָמֵץ, כְּשֶׁרוֹצֶה לֶאֱפוֹת בּוֹ מַצּוֹת, צָרִיךְ לְהַכְשִׁירוֹ עַל יְדֵי לִבּוּן בָּאוּר, דְּהַיְנוּ שֶׁיַּסִּיקֶנּוּ כָּל כָּךְ עַד שֶׁיִּהְיוּ נִיצוֹצוֹת נִתָּזִין מִמֶּנּוּ, כִּי בְּפָחוֹת מִזֶּה לֹא הָוֵי לִבּוּן גָּמוּר. וְצָרִיךְ לִזָּהֵר שֶׁיֵּלְכוּ הַגֶּחָלִים עַל פְּנֵי כֻלּוֹ. וְטוֹב וְיָשָׁר הוּא, לְגָרְפוֹ וּלְנַקּוֹתוֹ הֵיטֵב אַחַר הַהֶסֵּק וּלְהַמְתִּין עַד שֶׁיִּצְטַנֵּן קְצָת, וְאַחַר כָּךְ יַחֲזוֹר וְיַסִּיקֵהוּ לַאֲפִיַּת הַמַּצּוֹת, וְלֹא מִיָּד אַחַר הַלִּבּוּן.

ב) יֵשׁ נוֹהֲגִין לָטוּחַ אֶת הַתַּנּוּר בְּקַרְקַע חָדָשׁ, כְּדֵי שֶׁלֹּא יִצְטָרְכוּ לְהַכְשִׁירוֹ עַל יְדֵי הֶסֵּק. שֶׁהֶחָמֵץ הַבָּלוּעַ בְּגַגּוֹ וּבְקִירוֹתָיו, הוּא נִפְלָט עַל

juice, unless it has been *kashered* with boiling water. You surely should avoid placing the water into a vessel that had contained food with a sharp taste, even if it was not *chametz,* because on account of the sharpness, the dough will rise faster, and even *kashering* with boiling water will be of no use in such a case. Neither should you put the water into a copper vessel,[4] because it does not keep it as cool as other vessels.

7) If you notice that the water kept overnight is not sufficient, you may add other water,[5] provided most of the water is that which stayed overnight. Initially, it is best that two thirds of the total should consist of the water that stayed overnight. If possible, try to draw the added water from a pump or a covered well, where the sun does not reach.

8) If the matzah is baked on Sunday, the water must be drawn on Thursday evening, because on Friday it is impossible to fix the exact time of twilight. In an extreme circumstance, if the water was not drawn on Thursday, it should be drawn on Friday after the Minchah service, or on Shabbos by a non-Jew.

9) The water held overnight should not be poured out on account of a death that has occurred, or on account of the vernal equinox, because it is said, "He who keeps the commandment shall know no evil thing" (Ecclesiastes 8:5). Nevertheless, if you know that the vernal equinox will occur, you should put into the water a small, clean piece of metal, something like a needle attached to a thread, so that afterwards you will not have to put your hands into the water to get it out, but you will be able to pull it out by the thread.[6]

Chapter 110

Laws Concerning the Kneading and Baking of the Matzos

1) If you want to bake matzos in an oven in which *chametz* has been baked, it must be *kashered* by heating it until it becomes red hot, that is, heating it to such a degree that sparks fly from it, for anything less than that does not constitute true glowing. You should be careful to spread the coal over the entire area of the oven. The correct thing to do is to remove the ashes and clean it thoroughly after heating, and wait until it cools off somewhat; and then make a new fire for baking the matzos. This should not be done immediately after the heating process.

2) Some people have the custom to plaster the oven with fresh clay to avoid the necessity of *kashering* it through heating, for the *chametz* absorbed in the roof and

---

4. The flour may be kneaded, however, even initially in a copper vessel. (*Mishnah Berurah* 455:25)

5. According to some later *Poskim* (*Tshubiner Rav*) you may not add water if it contains chlorine.

6. According to *Ramah,* (*Yoreh Deiah* 116) water should not be drawn at the time of the vernal equinox. Many of the later *Poskim* maintain that in our times, we are lenient in these matters.

יְדֵי לִבּוּן מֵהַשַּׁלְהֶבֶת שֶׁמַּסִּיקִין לַאֲפִיַּת הַמַּצּוֹת, וּמִנְהָג יָפֶה הוּא, וּבִלְבַד שֶׁיְּטוּחוּ אוֹתוֹ בְּקַרְקַע עָבֶה כְּעֳבִי אֶצְבַּע אוֹ יוֹתֵר עַל פְּנֵי כֻלּוֹ. אֲבָל טִיחַ מוּעָט, אֵינוֹ מוֹעִיל כְּלוּם.

ג) אֵין לָשִׁין וְאֵין עוֹשִׂין אֶת הַמַּצּוֹת אֶלָּא בְּבַיִת מְקֹרֶה, וְלֹא כְּנֶגֶד חַלּוֹן פָּתוּחַ, אֲפִלּוּ אִם אֵין הַחַמָּה זוֹרַחַת שָׁמָּה. אֲבָל אִם הַחַלּוֹנוֹת נְעוּלִים וְיֵשׁ בָּהֶן זְכוּכִית, מֻתָּר אִם אֵין הַחַמָּה זוֹרַחַת שָׁמָּה. אֲבָל אִם הַחַמָּה זוֹרַחַת שָׁמָּה, לָא מַהֲנֵי חַלּוֹן זְכוּכִית, אֶלָּא צָרִיךְ לִפְרוֹס וִילוֹן בִּמְקוֹם זְרִיחַת הַחַמָּה. וְכֵן צְרִיכִין לִזָּהֵר שֶׁלֹּא יְהֵא הַבַּיִת מֻסָּק וְחָם.

ד) אֵין לָשִׁין עִסָּה גְדוֹלָה יוֹתֵר מִשִּׁעוּר חַלָּה. וְטוֹב לְמַעֵט, כִּי שִׁעֲרוּ רַבּוֹתֵינוּ זִכְרוֹנָם לִבְרָכָה. שֶׁאִם הָעִסָּה גְדוֹלָה יוֹתֵר מִשִּׁעוּר חַלָּה, אִי אֶפְשָׁר לַעֲסוֹק בָּהּ בְּפַעַם אַחַת, וְחֵלֶק מִמֶּנָּה מֻנָּח בְּלֹא עֵסֶק. וְיֵשׁ לָחוּשׁ פֶּן יִתְחַמֵּץ. אִם לָשׁ עִסָּה רַכָּה, לֹא יוֹסִיף בָּהּ קֶמַח לְעַבּוֹתָהּ.

ה) לֹא יִדְחוֹק אֶת הַקֶּמַח לְתוֹךְ הַמִּדָּה, כִּי יֵשׁ לָחוּשׁ שֶׁלֹּא יְהֵא נִלּוֹשׁ יָפֶה וְיִשָּׁאֵר בְּתוֹךְ הַמַּצָּה מַשֶּׁהוּ קֶמַח. וּכְשֶׁיָּבוֹא אַחַר כָּךְ בְּתַבְשִׁיל, יִתְחַמֵּץ. גַּם יִזָּהֲרוּ שֶׁלֹּא לְהַנִּיחַ אֶת הַקֶּמַח סָמוּךְ לַמַּיִם, שֶׁלֹּא יִפּוֹל מֵאֲבַק הַקֶּמַח לְתוֹךְ הַמַּיִם. וְכֵן הַמּוֹדֵד אֶת הַקֶּמַח, לֹא יִתְקָרֵב אֶל הָעִסָּה אוֹ אֶל הַמַּיִם. וְטוֹב לִזָּהֵר שֶׁלֹּא לְהַנִּיחַ אֶת הַיָּד עַל הַקֶּמַח שֶׁלֹּא לְצֹרֶךְ, כִּי הַיָּד מְחַמֶּמֶת קְצָת.

ו) הַכְּלִי שֶׁלָּשִׁין בּוֹ, צְרִיכִין לְהַשְׁגִּיחַ שֶׁלֹּא יְהֵא בוֹ שׁוּם נֶקֶב אוֹ סֶדֶק שֶׁיּוּכַל לְהִשָּׁאֵר שָׁם מַשֶּׁהוּ עִסָּה וְתִתְחַמֵּץ. וְלֹא יַנִּיחַ הַכְּלִי בִּשְׁעַת לִישָׁה עַל כָּרִים וּכְסָתוֹת, פֶּן יִתְחַמֵּם. וְיִזָּהֵר שֶׁלְּאַחַר כָּל שְׁמוֹנֶה־עֶשְׂרֵה דַקָּה, יְנַקֶּה אֶת הַכְּלִי הֵיטֵב, וְגַם יִרְחַץ יָדָיו הֵיטֵב. וְכֵן הַדַּפִּין וְהָעֵצִים שֶׁמְּגַלְגְּלִין בָּהֶם, יַשְׁגִּיחוּ עֲלֵיהֶם שֶׁלֹּא יְהֵא בָּהֶם שׁוּם נֶקֶב אוֹ סֶדֶק. וּלְכָל־הַפָּחוֹת, לְאַחַר כָּל שְׁמוֹנֶה־עֶשְׂרֵה דַקָּה, יְנַקּוּ אוֹתָם הֵיטֵב. וְכֵן הַכֵּלִים שֶׁמְּנַקְּבִים בָּהֶם, שֶׁלֹּא יְהֵא עֲלֵיהֶם אֲפִלּוּ מַשֶּׁהוּ עִסָּה. וְכֵן הַמַּרְדֶּה שֶׁמַּכְנִיסִין בּוֹ אֶת הַמַּצּוֹת לְתוֹךְ הַתַּנּוּר, צְרִיכִין לְהַשְׁגִּיחַ שֶׁלֹּא יְהֵא בוֹ שׁוּם סֶדֶק, שֶׁלֹּא תִכָּנֵס בּוֹ קְצָת עִסָּה וְתִתְחַמֵּץ.

ז) אִם נָפַל לְתוֹךְ הָעִסָּה אֵיזֶה דָבָר חָרִיף, כְּגוֹן מֶלַח אוֹ תַבְלִין אוֹ

1. A quantity of flour that equals forty-three and one-fifth eggs is subject to the law of *challah.* (see Chapter 35:2)

walls of the oven is emitted by the heat of the flame that is lit for the purpose of baking the matzos. It is a good custom, provided the oven is plastered with a coating of clay, the thickness of a finger or more, over its entire area. But a thin coating is of no use.

3) Matzos should be kneaded and prepared only in a house that has a roof, and not before an open window, even if the sun does not shine through it. But if the windows are closed and have panes, it is permitted to knead the matzos, if the sun does not shine through them. But if the sun shines through them, the glass panes are of no use, but a curtain must be spread over the windows on the sunny side of the room. Care must be taken that the house should not be heated and warm.

4) No dough should be kneaded that is larger than the quantity of dough that is subject to the separation of *challah.*[1] It is better to make it smaller, for our Rabbis of blessed memory estimated, that if the dough is larger than the quantity of dough that is subject to *challah,* it cannot be worked at one and the same time;[2] thus part of it will be left unworked, and there is reason to fear that it may become *chametz.* If the dough you are kneading is loose, flour should not be added to thicken it.

5) When the flour is measured, it should not be stuffed into the measuring vessel because there is reason to fear that the dough might not be kneaded well, and particles of flour will be found in the matzah, and when put into the soup, it will become *chametz.* Care should be taken not to put the flour near the water, so that flour dust should not fall into the water. Similarly, the person who measures the flour should not go near the dough or the water. It is good to be careful not to handle the flour needlessly, because the hands will warm it slightly.

6) It should be watched that the vessel used for kneading should not have any holes or cracks where particles of dough might remain and become *chametz.* While kneading, the vessel should not be placed on pillows or pads, lest it become warm. Care must be taken that every eighteen minutes the vessel is thoroughly cleaned, and the hands thoroughly washed. The boards and rolling pins must be carefully inspected to make sure that they have no holes or cracks. They should be thoroughly cleaned at least every eighteen minutes. The tools that make the perforations must also be cleaned of even the smallest particle of dough. The peel (a shovel-like tool), with which the matzos are put into the oven, must be carefully inspected for any cracks[3] where a particle of dough might be caught and become *chametz.*

7) If anything with a sharp flavor fell into the dough, such as salt, spices or even

---

2. There are some *Poskim* that are lenient and permit even larger quantities, since in our times there are large ovens and many people are involved in production which makes it unlikely that it will become *chametz. Mishnah Berurah* says, however, that it is best to be stringent, even in these times and to follow the opinions of the *Shulchan Aruch.* (*Mishnah Berurah* 456:7, *Shaarei Tzion* 10)

3. The proper custom is to appoint a supervisor (*Mashgiach*) in the matzah bakery to oversee the entire process. (*Ibid.* 459:33)

סִיד חַי, אֲפִלּוּ מַשֶּׁהוּ, וְנִלּוֹשׁ בְּתוֹכָהּ, כָּל הָעִסָּה אֲסוּרָה, מִשּׁוּם דְּמִתְחַמֶּמֶת שָׁם. וְאִם נִמְצָא בְּתוֹךְ הָעִסָּה גַּרְעִין תְּבוּאָה, יִטּוֹל מִן הָעִסָּה כָּעֳבִי אֶצְבַּע סְבִיב הַגַּרְעִין וְיַשְׁלִיךְ, וְהַשְּׁאָר מֻתָּר.

ח) יִזָּהֲרוּ שֶׁלֹּא לְהָנִיחַ אֶת הָעִסָּה אֲפִלּוּ רֶגַע אֶחָד בְּלִי עֵסֶק. וּמִיָּד כְּשֶׁנִּגְמְרָה הָעִסָּה, יְחַלְּקָהּ כֻּלָּהּ לַמְגַלְגְּלִים. וְעַל כֵּן יֵשׁ לְהַשְׁגִּיחַ שֶׁלֹּא לַעֲשׂוֹת עִסָּה גְדוֹלָה רַק כְּפִי עֶרֶךְ הַמְגַלְגְּלִים. וְאִם נִשְׁאַר מִן הָעִסָּה בִּידֵי הַמְחַלֵּק, יְלוּשֶׁנָּה וְיַעֲסוֹק בָּהּ, שֶׁלֹּא תָנוּחַ אֲפִלּוּ רֶגַע בְּלִי עֵסֶק.

ט) הַמְגַלְגְּלִים יְגַלְגְּלוּ בִּזְרִיזוּת, וְאַל יִשְׁהוּ לַעֲשׂוֹת אֶת הַמַּצָּה בִּדְמוּת אֵיזוֹ צוּרָה. וְיַשְׁגִּיחוּ שֶׁלֹּא יִהְיוּ פֵּרוּרִין מִן הָעִסָּה עַל הַדַּף. וְגַם שֶׁלֹּא תְהֵא מְדֻבֶּקֶת בִּידֵיהֶם שׁוּם עִסָּה. וּמִיָּד כְּשֶׁרוֹאִין שֶׁנִּדְבְּקָה בָּהֶן קְצָת עִסָּה, יִרְחֲצוּ יְדֵיהֶם הֵיטֵב.

י) מִיָּד לְאַחַר שֶׁנִּגְמְרָה הַמַּצָּה, יְנַקְּבוּהָ בִּזְרִיזוּת. וְלֹא יַעֲשׂוּ אֵיזֶה צִיּוּר בְּמַה שֶּׁמְּנַקְּבִים, אֶלָּא יְמַהֲרוּ בְּכָל מַה דְּאֶפְשָׁר, וּמִיָּד יִתְּנוּהָ לְתוֹךְ הַתַּנּוּר. וְיִזָּהֵר מְאֹד שֶׁלֹּא יַשְׁהֶה אוֹתָהּ אֲפִלּוּ מְעַט נֶגֶד פִּי הַתַּנּוּר, כִּי שָׁם תְּמַהֵר לְהַחְמִיץ. וְעַל כֵּן צְרִיכִין לְהַדֵּר שֶׁזֶּה שֶׁהוּא מוֹשִׁיט אֶת הַמַּצּוֹת לָאוֹפֶה, יִהְיֶה בַּעַל תּוֹרָה וִירֵא שָׁמַיִם, שֶׁיְּדַקְדֵּק בָּזֶה.

יא) הַיָּרֵא אֶת דְּבַר ה׳, יִזָּהֵר שֶׁקֹּדֶם אֲפִיַּת הַמַּצּוֹת שֶׁלּוֹ, יַסִּיקוּ הֵיטֵב מֵחָדָשׁ אֶת הַתַּנּוּר וִיפַזְּרוּ אֶת הַגֶּחָלִים עַל פְּנֵי כֻלּוֹ, כִּי מִי יוֹדֵעַ אִם זֶה אֲשֶׁר אָפָה קֹדֶם לוֹ הָיָה נִזְהָר בְּכָל הַזְּהִירוּת.

יב) הָאוֹפֶה יִזָּהֵר מְאֹד לְהַשְׁגִּיחַ שֶׁלֹּא תִתְכַּפֵּל אֵיזוֹ מַצָּה, וְגַם שֶׁלֹּא תִגַּע אַחַת בַּחֲבֶרְתָּהּ, כִּי בִּמְקוֹם הַנְּגִיעָה, וְכֵן בְּמָקוֹם שֶׁמִּתְכַּפֶּלֶת, אֵינָהּ נֶאֱפֵית מַהֵר וּמִתְחַמֶּצֶת. וְאִם אֵרַע שֶׁנִּתְכַּפְּלָה אוֹ שֶׁנִּתְנַפְּחָה אֵיזוֹ מַצָּה, צְרִיכִין לִשְׁבּוֹר [וּלְהַשְׁלִיךְ] אֶת הַמָּקוֹם הַהוּא וְהוּא חָמֵץ, וְהַשְּׁאָר מֻתָּר. אֲבָל אִם נָגְעוּ זוֹ בָּזוֹ בַּתַּנּוּר כְּשֶׁהֵן עֲדַיִן לַחוֹת, יֵשׁ לְהַתִּיר בְּדִיעֲבַד. מַצָּה נְפוּחָה, הַיְנוּ שֶׁנִּכָּר שֶׁנִּתְחַלְּקָה הַמַּצָּה בְּעָבְיָהּ, וְהֶחָלָל הוּא כְּמוֹ רֹחַב אֲגוּדָל.

יג) צְרִיכִין לִזָּהֵר שֶׁלֹּא לְהוֹצִיא מַצָּה מִן הַתַּנּוּר כָּל זְמַן שֶׁלֹּא נֶאֶפְתָה קְצָת עַד שֶׁאִם הָיוּ פּוֹרְסִין אוֹתָהּ לֹא הָיוּ כְּעֵין חוּטִין נִמְשָׁכִין. כִּי קֹדֶם שִׁעוּר זֶה, הֲרֵי הִיא עֲדַיִן כְּמוֹ עִסָּה. וּכְשֶׁהִיא חוּץ לַתַּנּוּר, תְּמַהֵר לְהַחְמִיץ. וְגַם הַמַּרְדֶּה שֶׁהוֹצִיאוּהָ עָלָיו, גַּם כֵּן אָסוּר עוֹד לַמַּצּוֹת. וְאִם

if the smallest quantity fresh lime and was kneaded into it, the use of the entire dough is forbidden, because it has become heated by it. If a grain of wheat is found in the dough, you should remove from it a quantity of dough as thick as your finger, all around that grain, and throw it away; and the rest of the dough may be used.

8) Care must be taken not to leave the dough, even for a moment without working it. As soon as the dough is completed, it should be divided into portions and handed to the rollers. Care should be taken, therefore, to make the dough only as large as can be handled by the rollers. If some of the dough is left with the person who hands out the portions, he should keep kneading it so that it should not lie idle even for a moment.

9) The rollers should do their work at full speed and not waste time on giving the matzos a specific shape. They should pay close attention that no particles of the dough are left on the board, and also that no dough clings to their hands. As soon as they notice any dough sticking to their hands, they must wash them thoroughly.[4]

10) As soon as the matzah is ready, it should be perforated quickly. They should not make any design with the perforations, but they should rush at top speed, and put it into the oven immediately. Great care should be taken not to hold it even for a moment in front of the opening of the oven, for it will become *chametz* quickly. It is necessary, therefore, to make sure that the person handing the matzos to the baker should be a Torah scholar, a God-fearing man, who will be meticulously vigilant.

11) A God-fearing person should take care, before baking his matzos, to have the oven well heated again, and the coals spread over the entire oven, for who knows if the person who baked matzos before him was scrupulously careful about it.

12) The baker should be very careful to see to it that none of the matzos are folded over, and that one matzah does not touch the other, for in the place where one matzah touches another or where it is folded over it does not bake quickly and it becomes *chametz.* In the event that a matzah is folded over or becomes blown up, it is necessary to break off and throw away that piece; that piece is *chametz,* but the rest may be eaten. However, if the matzos touched each other in the oven while still moist, they may be eaten, since it is already done. A blown up matzah is one in which it is evident that the matzah has separated in its thickness, and the bubble is as wide as a thumb.

13) Care should be taken not to take a matzah out of the oven before it is slightly baked; that is, if you would break it, there should be no threads of dough [between the pieces.] Before this stage it is still like dough, which when taken out of the oven will become *chametz* very quickly. The peel with which this matzah was taken out of the oven is forbidden to be used for baking matzos. If it is impossible

4. They should also wash their hands every eighteen minutes. (*Ibid.* 459:33)

אִי אֶפְשָׁר לֵדַע אִם הָיוּ חוּטִין נִמְשָׁכִין מִמֶּנָּה אוֹ לֹא, יֵשׁ לְהַחְמִיר מִסָּפֵק. אַךְ אִם קָרְמוּ פָּנֶיהָ, יֵשׁ לְהָקֵל.

יד) רָאוּי לְכָל יְרֵא־שָׁמַיִם, שֶׁיְּהֵא הוּא בְּעַצְמוֹ עוֹמֵד וּמַשְׁגִּיחַ בַּעֲשִׂיַּת וַאֲפִיַּת הַמַּצּוֹת שֶׁלּוֹ וּלְהַזְהִירָם שֶׁיַּעֲשׂוּ בִּזְרִיזוּת וּבְהַשְׁגָּחָה. וְכָךְ הָיוּ עוֹשִׂים גְּדוֹלֵי יִשְׂרָאֵל הָרִאשׁוֹנִים זִכְרוֹנָם לִבְרָכָה, וְכֵן עוֹשִׂין גַּם בִּזְמַנֵּנוּ.

טו) הַמַּצּוֹת שֶׁהֵן לָצֵאת בָּהֶן יְדֵי חוֹבַת אֲכִילַת מַצָּה בִּשְׁנֵי לֵילוֹת הָרִאשׁוֹנִים, נִקְרָאוֹת מַצּוֹת מִצְוָה. וּצְרִיכִין לַעֲשׂוֹתָן לְשֵׁם מִצְוָה עַל יְדֵי יִשְׂרָאֵל גָּדוֹל בֶּן־דַּעַת, שֶׁהוּא בֶּן שְׁלֹשׁ־עֶשְׂרֵה שָׁנָה וְיוֹם אֶחָד, וְאִשָּׁה בַּת שְׁתֵּים־עֶשְׂרֵה שָׁנָה וְיוֹם אֶחָד. וּבְכָל הָעֲשִׂיּוֹת יֹאמַר הָעוֹשֶׂה, לְשֵׁם מַצַּת מִצְוָה, אֲפִלּוּ בִּשְׁאִיבַת הַמַּיִם. (כָּל הַדִּינִים שֶׁכָּתַבְנוּ בְּעִנְיַן אֲפִיַּת הַמַּצּוֹת, זֶהוּ לְמִנְהָגֵנוּ שֶׁאוֹפִין הַכֹּל לִפְנֵי הַפֶּסַח. אֲבָל בִּמְקוֹם הַדְּחָק שֶׁאוֹפִין גַּם בַּפֶּסַח, יֵשׁ בָּזֶה עוֹד חֻמְרוֹת יְתֵרוֹת עַל מַה שֶּׁכָּתַבְנוּ. וְכֵן הַנּוֹהֲגִין לֶאֱפוֹת מַצּוֹת מִצְוָה בְּעֶרֶב פֶּסַח לְאַחַר חֲצוֹת הַיּוֹם, צְרִיכִין זְהִירוּת יְתֵרָה.)

סִימָן קיא
הִלְכוֹת בְּדִיקַת חָמֵץ וּבִטּוּלוֹ

א) בַּלַּיְלָה שֶׁלִּפְנֵי עֶרֶב פֶּסַח בּוֹדְקִין אֶת הֶחָמֵץ. וְחַיָּבִין לִבְדּוֹק מִיָּד בִּתְחִלַּת הַלָּיְלָה. וְאָסוּר לְהַתְחִיל לֶאֱכֹל אוֹ לַעֲשׂוֹת שׁוּם מְלָאכָה חֲצִי שָׁעָה קֹדֶם הַלָּיְלָה.

ב) אֵין בּוֹדְקִין אֶלָּא בְּנֵר שֶׁל שַׁעֲוָה יְחִידִי, וְלֹא קָלוּעַ, מִשּׁוּם דַּהֲוֵי כַּאֲבוּקָה. וּבִשְׁעַת הַדְּחָק שֶׁאֵין לוֹ נֵר שֶׁל שַׁעֲוָה, יִבְדּוֹק בְּנֵר שֶׁל חֵלֶב.

ג) בּוֹדֵק כָּל הַחֲדָרִים שֶׁיֵּשׁ לָחוּשׁ שֶׁמָּא הִכְנִיסוּ בָּהֶם חָמֵץ, אֲפִלּוּ הַמַּרְתְּפִים וְהָעֲלִיּוֹת וְהַחֲנֻיּוֹת וּבֵית־הָעֵצִים. כֹּל שֶׁיֵּשׁ לָחוּשׁ שֶׁמָּא הִכְנִיסוּ שָׁם חָמֵץ, צְרִיכִין לְבָדְקָן. וְכֵן צְרִיכִין לִבְדּוֹק כָּל הַכֵּלִים שֶׁמַּחֲזִיקִים בָּהֶם חָמֵץ. וְקֹדֶם הַבְּדִיקָה, יְכַבְּדוּ הֵיטֵב כָּל הַמְּקוֹמוֹת וִינַקּוּ אוֹתָם מִכָּל חָמֵץ, לְמַעַן יְהֵא נָקֵל לוֹ אַחַר כָּךְ לְבָדְקָם.

---

5. According to *Rambam,* all the precautions that must be taken for *matzos mitzvah* must be taken for all the matzos that are eaten on Pesach. *Magid Mishnah* maintains that *Rambam's* ruling was only said on an initial stringency, and only regarding violations of these precautions disqualifying the matzos. *Chayei Adam* writes that the *Vilna Gaon* insisted that all matzos eaten on Pesach be made with these precautions. (see *Biyur Halachah* 460:1)

6. There is a dispute among the *Poskim* regarding grinding the wheat. Some maintain that the grinding, too, must be done by Jews, but the custom today is to be lenient and permit it

to determine whether or not this matzah, had threads of dough when taken out of the oven, because of the uncertainty, we are strict. But if the matzah has formed a crust, we may take a lenient view.

14) Every God-fearing man should personally supervise the preparation and baking of his own matzos, and urge the workers, to work with speed and care. This was how it was done by the early, great Sages of Yisrael of blessed memory, and this is what is done also at the present time.

15) The matzos with which we fulfill the mitzvah of eating matzah on the first two nights of Pesach are referred to as *matzos mitzvah,*[5] and they must be prepared for the sake of the mitzvah by an adult, male Jew of intelligence,[6] aged at least thirteen years and one day, or a female aged at least twelve years and one day. At each stage in the preparation the worker says, *leshem matzas mitzvah,* ["For the sake of the matzah of the mitzvah."] (This should be said) even when drawing the water. (All the foregoing laws regarding the baking of the matzos refer to our custom that all matzos are baked before Pesach. In an emergency, when matzos are baked on Pesach, there are other stringencies in addition to the ones mentioned above. Those who follow the custom of baking *matzos mitzvah* in the afternoon of *erev Pesach* must take special precautions).

Chapter 111

The Search and Nullification of the Chametz

1) On the evening before *erev Pesach* the search for *chametz* must be made. You must make the search immediately after nightfall.[1] It is forbidden to begin a meal[2] or do any work one half-hour before nightfall.[3]

2) The search should be made with only one wax candle, not with several candles intertwined, for that would be like a torch.[4] In a predicament when you have no wax candle, you may use a tallow candle.

3)You must search all rooms in which you suspect that someone carried *chametz,* even cellars, attics, stores and woodsheds; any places in which you think that *chametz* may have been brought must be searched. You must also search all vessels in which you keep *chametz.* Before making the search, you should carefully sweep all these places and clean all *chametz* out of them, in order to make it easy for you to search the rooms afterwards.

---

even when done by a non-Jew, so long as a Jew is present to watch that it does not become *chametz.* Nevertheless, where possible, the grinding should be done by a Jew and it is considered a praiseworthy deed when done so. (*Ibid.* 460:1)

1. I.e. immediately after the appearance of the stars. (*Mishnah Berurah* 431:1)
2. A small snack is permitted. (*Ibid.* 431:6)
3. Even if you began the meal earlier than one half hour, you must interrupt the meal when the time for searching begins. (*Ibid.* 431:11, 12)
4. If you used a torch or even a candle with several wicks, the search is invalid and you must repeat it with a single candle. (*Ibid.* 433:10)

ד) רֶפֶת שֶׁל בָּקָר שֶׁנּוֹתְנִים שָׁמָּה תְּבוּאָה לִבְהֵמוֹת לֶאֱכֹל, וְכֵן לוּל שֶׁל תַּרְנְגוֹלִים שֶׁנּוֹתְנִים לָהֶם שָׁם תְּבוּאָה. אֵינָן צְרִיכִין בְּדִיקָה, כִּי שֶׁמָּא לֹא נִתְחַמְּצָה כְּלָל הַתְּבוּאָה. וְאִם תִּמְצָא לוֹמַר נִתְחַמְּצָה, שֶׁמָּא אָכְלוּ הַכֹּל וְלֹא שִׁיְּרוּ כְּלוּם. אֲבָל אִם נָתְנוּ לָהֶם שָׁמָּה תְּבוּאָה חֲמוּצָה, שֶׁאֵין כָּאן אֶלָּא סָפֵק אֶחָד, שֶׁמָּא אָכְלוּ הַכֹּל, אֵין סוֹמְכִין עַל זֶה, וּצְרִיכִין בְּדִיקָה.

ה) צְרִיכִין לִבְדּוֹק בְּכָל הַמְּקוֹמוֹת בְּחוֹרִין וּבִסְדָקִין כָּל מַה שֶּׁאֶפְשָׁר. וְגַם הַכִּיסִים שֶׁבִּבְגָדִים שֶׁלּוֹ וְשֶׁל תִּינוֹקוֹת, שֶׁלִּפְעָמִים נוֹתְנִים בָּהֶם חָמֵץ, צְרִיכִין בְּדִיקָה. וִינַעֲרֵם הֵיטֵב לְמָחָר בִּשְׁעַת הַבִּעוּר.

ו) הַחֲדָרִים שֶׁמּוֹכְרִים לַגּוֹי עִם הֶחָמֵץ, כֵּיוָן שֶׁאֵין מוֹכְרָן עַד לְמָחָר, אִם כֵּן חָל עָלָיו בַּלַּיְלָה חִיּוּב בְּדִיקָה וְחַיָּב לְבָדְקָם.

ז) קֹדֶם שֶׁמַּתְחִיל לִבְדֹּק, יְבָרֵךְ, בָּרוּךְ אַתָּה ה׳, אֱלֹקֵינוּ מֶלֶךְ הָעוֹלָם, אֲשֶׁר קִדְּשָׁנוּ בְּמִצְוֹתָיו וְצִוָּנוּ עַל בִּעוּר חָמֵץ. וְאַף־עַל־פִּי שֶׁעַתָּה עֲדַיִן אֵינוֹ מְבַעֲרוֹ, מִכָּל מָקוֹם מְבָרֵךְ עַל בִּעוּר, לְפִי שֶׁמִּיָּד לְאַחַר הַבְּדִיקָה יְבַטֵּל אֶת הֶחָמֵץ שֶׁאֵינוֹ יָדוּעַ לוֹ, וְהוּא הַבִּעוּר לְחָמֵץ שֶׁאֵינוֹ יָדוּעַ לוֹ. וְלֹא יַפְסִיק בֵּין הַבְּרָכָה לִתְחִלַּת הַבְּדִיקָה. וְטוֹב שֶׁלֹּא יַפְסִיק עַד גְּמַר כָּל הַבְּדִיקָה אֶלָּא בְּמַה שֶּׁהוּא מֵעִנְיַן הַבְּדִיקָה. וְיָכוֹל לִבְדּוֹק כַּמָּה בָּתִּים בִּבְרָכָה אַחַת.

ח) יֵשׁ נוֹהֲגִין שֶׁקֹּדֶם הַבְּדִיקָה מַנִּיחִין פְּתִיתֵי לֶחֶם בִּמְקוֹמוֹת שֶׁיִּמְצָאֵם הַבּוֹדֵק, כִּי חוֹשְׁשִׁין שֶׁמָּא לֹא יִמְצָא כְּלוּם וּתְהֵא בְּרָכָה לְבַטָּלָה. וּפְשִׁיטָא כִּי מִי שֶׁאֵינוֹ בּוֹדֵק כָּרָאוּי, אֶלָּא שֶׁהוּא מְקַבֵּץ אֵלּוּ הַפְּתִיתִים, לֹא קִיֵּם מִצְוַת בְּדִיקָה, וּבֵרַךְ בְּרָכָה לְבַטָּלָה.

ט) הֶחָמֵץ שֶׁהוּא מְשַׁיֵּר לַאֲכִילָה אוֹ לִמְכִירָה, יַנִּיחַ קֹדֶם הַבְּדִיקָה בְּמָקוֹם מְשֻׁמָּר הֵיטֵב. וְכֵן הֶחָמֵץ שֶׁהוּא מוֹצֵא בִּבְדִיקָתוֹ וְצָרִיךְ לְשָׂרְפוֹ

---

5. Even if you say you are certain that you did not put any *chametz* in your pockets, you are, nevertheless, required to search them, because often people place things in their pockets and forget they did so. (*Ibid.* 433:47)

6. This is also the opinion of *Mekor Chaim* and *Chayei Adam.* In their responsa, *Binyan Olam* and *Chasam Sofer* disagree and rule that you may be lenient so long as you searched the other rooms. This is also the opinion of *Aishel Avrohom.* (*Ibid.* 436:32, 433:23)

7. If you did interrupt with something unrelated to the search, you must repeat the berachah, since there was an interruption between the berachah and the mitzvah. (*Ibid.* 432:5)

4) A cowshed where the cattle are fed grain, and a chicken coop where the chickens are fed with grain do not require searching; [first of all,] because the grain may never have become *chametz,* and even if it did become *chametz,* it is possible that all of it was eaten and nothing was left. But if the grain you put there was *chametz,* you then have only one uncertainty, whether all of it was eaten; we do not rely on this possibility, and you are required to make a search.

5) You must search everywhere, every nook and cranny, as best as you can. You must also search the pockets of your garments and those of your children's garments; for since sometimes *chametz* gets into them,[5] they have to be searched. You should shake them thoroughly the next morning when you burn the *chametz.*

6) [This is the law concerning] the rooms you sell to a non-Jew together with the *chametz* in them. Since the sale is not valid until the morning, you are obliged to search them in the evening,[6] and you must do so.

7) Before beginning the search you recite the berachah: *Baruch ata Hashem, Elokeinu melech haolam asher kideshanu bemitzvosav vetzivanu al biur chameitz* "Blessed are you, Hashem, our God, King of the universe, Who has sanctified us with His commandments, and has commanded us concerning the removal of *chametz.*" Even though you do not yet remove it, you still say the berachah "concerning the removal," since immediately after the search, you nullify the *chametz* that is unknown to you, and this, in effect, is the removal of such *chametz.* Do not make any interruption between the berachah and beginning the search.[7] It is a good thing not to interrupt until the search is completed, except for things relating to the search.[8] You may search many houses on the basis of the one berachah you recited.

8) Some people have the custom, before beginning the search, to deposit small pieces of bread in places where the searcher will find them. They are fearful, if he finds no *chametz,* the berachah will have been said in vain.[9] Needless to say, however, anyone who does not search properly, but only gathers up these pieces of bread, has not fulfilled the mitzvah of searching, and his berachah was said in vain.

9) The *chametz* you leave for food or for sale, should be put away in a safe place, before making the search. The *chametz* you find in the search, which must be burned in the morning, should be put away in a safe place and tied so that it won't get lost.

---

8. If you did interrupt, you need not repeat the berachah since you began the search, and thus there was no interruption between the berachah and the mitzvah. (*Ibid.* 432:6)

9. It is, however, not a "blessing in vain" because the mitzvah is specifically to search for *chametz* and even if no *chametz* is found, the mitzvah is fulfilled. Nevertheless, it is not proper to negate a custom of the Jewish people. According to the *Arizal,* it is customary to place ten pieces of bread around the house. Special care must be taken that none of these pieces of *chametz* go lost. It is best to use the sort of bread that will not create crumbs. (*Ibid.* 432:12, 13)

לְמָחָר, יַנִּיחַ בְּמָקוֹם מְשֻׁמָּר וּמְקֻשָּׁר, שֶׁלֹּא יֹאבַד מִמֶּנּוּ, וְיַנִּיחֶנּוּ בְּמָקוֹם שֶׁיִּרְאֵהוּ לְמָחָר וְלֹא יִשְׁכַּח לְשָׂרְפוֹ.

י) אַחַר הַבְּדִיקָה מִיָּד יְבַטְּלֶנּוּ. וְעִקַּר הַבִּטּוּל הוּא בַּלֵּב, שֶׁיִּגְמוֹר בְּלִבּוֹ שֶׁכָּל חָמֵץ שֶׁבִּרְשׁוּתוֹ, הֲרֵי הוּא כְּאִלּוּ אֵינוֹ, וְאֵינוֹ חָשׁוּב כְּלוּם, וַהֲרֵי הוּא כְּמוֹ עָפָר, וּכְדָבָר שֶׁאֵין בּוֹ צֹרֶךְ כְּלָל. וְתִקְּנוּ חֲכָמִים שֶׁיּוֹצִיא דְבָרִים אֵלּוּ גַּם בְּפִיו, וְיֹאמַר כָּל חֲמִירָא וְכוּ׳. וּמִי שֶׁאֵינוֹ יוֹדֵעַ פֵּרוּשׁוֹ, יֹאמַר בְּלָשׁוֹן שֶׁהוּא מֵבִין, כָּל שְׂאוֹר וְכָל חָמֵץ שֶׁבִּרְשׁוּתִי, שֶׁלֹּא רְאִיתִיו וְלֹא בִעַרְתִּיו, יְהֵא בָּטֵל וְהֶפְקֵר וְחָשׁוּב כַּעֲפַר הָאָרֶץ.

יא) אַף־עַל־פִּי שֶׁבִּטֵּל אֶת הֶחָמֵץ בַּלַּיְלָה לְאַחַר הַבְּדִיקָה, מִכָּל מָקוֹם גַּם בַּיּוֹם לְאַחַר שֶׁשָּׂרַף אוֹתוֹ יַחֲזוֹר וִיבַטְּלֶנּוּ, וְיִכְלוֹל כָּל הֶחָמֵץ וְיֹאמַר כָּל חֲמִירָא וְכוּ׳, אוֹ בְּלָשׁוֹן שֶׁהוּא מֵבִין, כָּל שְׂאוֹר וְכָל חָמֵץ שֶׁבִּרְשׁוּתִי שֶׁרְאִיתִיו וְשֶׁלֹּא רְאִיתִיו, שֶׁבִּעַרְתִּיו וְשֶׁלֹּא בִעַרְתִּיו, יְהֵא בָטֵל וְהֶפְקֵר וְחָשׁוּב כַּעֲפַר הָאֲדָמָה.

יב) חֶדֶר שֶׁצָּרִיךְ בְּדִיקַת חָמֵץ, וְרוֹצֶה לַעֲשׂוֹתוֹ אוֹצָר, פֵּרוּשׁ, שֶׁרוֹצֶה לֶאֱצוֹר בְּתוֹכוֹ פֵּרוֹת אוֹ עֵצִים אוֹ שְׁאָר דְּבָרִים, שֶׁמֵּחֲמַת זֶה לֹא יוּכַל לְבָדְקוֹ כְּשֶׁיַּגִּיעַ לֵיל אַרְבָּעָה עָשָׂר, צָרִיךְ לִבְדּוֹק תְּחִלָּה אֶת הֶחָמֵץ שָׁם בַּלַּיְלָה, כְּמוֹ שֶׁבּוֹדְקִין אֶת הֶחָמֵץ לֵיל אַרְבָּעָה עָשָׂר. וַאֲפִלּוּ יֵשׁ עוֹד זְמַן רַב עַד הַפֶּסַח, וַאֲפִלּוּ מִיָּד לְאַחַר פֶּסַח שֶׁעָבַר. וּבְדִיעֲבַד אִם לֹא בְּדָקוֹ קֹדֶם שֶׁעֲשָׂאוֹ אוֹצָר, אִם דַּעְתּוֹ לְפַנּוֹתוֹ קֹדֶם שֶׁיַּגִּיעַ זְמַן בְּדִיקַת חָמֵץ, אֵינוֹ צָרִיךְ לִטְרוֹחַ עַתָּה לְפַנּוֹתוֹ וּלְבָדְקוֹ. אֲבָל אִם דַּעְתּוֹ לְפַנּוֹתוֹ בְּתוֹךְ יְמֵי פֶּסַח, צָרִיךְ לְפַנּוֹתוֹ עַתָּה וּלְבָדְקוֹ, וְאַף־עַל־פִּי שֶׁיֵּשׁ טֹרַח רַב וְחֶסְרוֹן כִּיס.

יג) וְאִם עוֹשֶׂה אֶת הָאוֹצָר עַל דַּעַת שֶׁלֹּא לְפַנּוֹתוֹ עַד לְאַחַר הַפֶּסַח, אֲזַי יֵשׁ חִלּוּק בִּזְמָן. אִם הוּא קֹדֶם שְׁלשִׁים יוֹם שֶׁלִּפְנֵי הַפֶּסַח, אֵינוֹ צָרִיךְ לְבָדְקוֹ, (אֶלָּא שֶׁאִם יֵשׁ שָׁם חָמֵץ יָדוּעַ, יְבַעֲרֶנּוּ תְּחִלָּה) וְיוֹעִיל לוֹ הַבִּטּוּל, שֶׁיְּבַטֵּל כָּל חָמֵץ בִּזְמַנּוֹ. אֲבָל אִם הוּא תּוֹךְ שְׁלשִׁים יוֹם שֶׁלִּפְנֵי

10. Someone who understands absolutely nothing of the text of this declaration and thinks he is merely reciting some sort of prayer, has not fulfilled his obligation. (*Ibid.* 434:9)

11. Regarding a person who embarks on a journey before the night of the fourteenth, who is required to search his home before leaving, *Mishnah Berurah* writes that he must also nullify the *chametz* that is not visible to him. (This may also apply in our case as well). (Ibid. 436:3)

It should be put it in a place where you will notice it in the morning, so that you will not forget to burn it.

10) Immediately after the search, you should nullify the *chametz.* The actual nullification takes place in your heart, when you decide in your heart that you consider all *chametz* in your possession as non-existent, as worthless, as compared to dust, as something utterly useless. Our sages ordained that you should express these thoughts verbally by declaring *kol chamira* (all *chametz)* etc. Anyone who does not understand it in the Aramaic, should say it in a language he understands.[10] [The English translation of the Aramaic text is]: "Any leaven or *chametz* that is in my possession, that I have not seen and have not removed, should be nullified and become ownerless, like the dust of the earth."

11) Even though you have already nullified the *chametz* at night after the search, nevertheless, in the morning after burning it, you must nullify it again. In this declaration you include all the *chametz,* and you say, *Kol chamira*—(all *chametz*) etc., or in a language you understand. [The English translation of the Aramaic text is:] Any leaven or *chametz* that is in my possession whether I have seen it or not, whether I have removed it or not, should be nullified and become ownerless like the dust of the earth."

12) If you have a room that must be searched, that you want to use as a storage room; that is to say, you want to store, fruit, wood or other articles, which would make it impossible to search the room on the night of the fourteenth of Nisan, then you should search that room before[11] you convert it to a storeroom, making the search at night,[12] in the same manner as you search for *chametz* on the night of the fourteenth of Nisan.[13] [This holds true] even if there is still plenty of time before Pesach, and even if this is immediately after the *Pesach* that has just passed. However, if you did not search the room before turning it into a storage room, if you intend to remove the stored articles, before the time of the search will come, you do not have to go to the trouble at this time to empty the room and search it. But if you intend to remove the articles during the week of *Pesach,* you must remove them now and make the search, even though it involves great trouble and loss of money.

13) If you fill up a storage room with the intention of not emptying it until after *Pesach,* then it depends on the time you fill it up. If you do it more than thirty days before *Pesach,* you need not search the room. However if there is any *chametz* you know of, you must first remove it. The declaration of nullification will then effectively nullify all your *chametz* at the proper time (*erev Pesach*). However, if it is within thirty days before *Pesach,* you are subject to the laws of searching for *chametz*

---

12. Regarding a person who embarks on a journey before the night of the fourteenth who is required to search his home before leaving, *Mishnah Berurah* writes that if he forgot to search at night, he should do so by day. (*Ibid.*)

13. However, the berachah is not recited when the search is made before the night of the fourteenth. (See *Mishnah Berurah* 436:4 and also *Biyur Halachah* who writes that there are opinions that a berachah is said when the search is made within thirty days of the fourteenth).

הַפֶּסַח, חָל עָלָיו חִיּוּב בְּדִיקָה, (כֵּיוָן שֶׁשּׁוֹאֲלִין וְדוֹרְשִׁין בְּהִלְכוֹת פֶּסַח קֹדֶם לַפֶּסַח שְׁלֹשִׁים יוֹם), וְצָרִיךְ לְבָדְקוֹ. וַאֲפִלּוּ בְדִיעֲבַד אִם שָׁכַח וְלֹא בְדָקוֹ, צָרִיךְ לְפַנּוֹת אֶת הָאוֹצָר וּלְבָדְקוֹ בַּלַּיְלָה תֵּכֶף לְאַחַר שֶׁנִּזְכָּר.

יד) וְאִם עוֹשֶׂה אוֹצָר בַּבּוֹר מֵחִטִּים שֶׁאֵינָן מְחֻמָּצוֹת, וְאַחַר כָּךְ מֵחֲמַת לַחוּת הַבּוֹר נִתְחַמְּצוּ הַחִטִּים שֶׁבְּקַרְקָעִית הַבּוֹר וְשֶׁבְּקִירוֹתָיו, אַף־עַל־פִּי שֶׁאֲצָרָן בְּתוֹךְ שְׁלֹשִׁים יוֹם, אֵינוֹ צָרִיךְ לְפַנּוֹת אֶת הַבּוֹר בְּלֵיל אַרְבָּעָה עָשָׂר וּלְבָדְקוֹ, אֶלָּא דַי לוֹ בְּבִטּוּל, כֵּיוָן שֶׁבְּשָׁעָה שֶׁאָצַר, אָצַר בְּהֶתֵּר. וְאִם יֵשׁ בֵּינֵיהֶם חִטִּים מְחֻמָּצוֹת, יֵשׁ בָּזֶה כַּמָּה חִלּוּקֵי דִינִים, וְיַעֲשֶׂה שְׁאֵלַת חָכָם.

טו) לֹא יַשְׁלִיךְ גַּרְעִינֵי תְבוּאָה לַתַּרְנְגוֹלִים בְּמָקוֹם לַח תּוֹךְ שְׁלֹשִׁים יוֹם, שֶׁמָּא יִשְׁכַּח מִלְּבַעֲרָם.

טז) הַיּוֹצֵא לַדֶּרֶךְ, קֹדֶם לֶכְתּוֹ יְמַנֶּה שָׁלִיחַ שֶׁיִּבְדּוֹק וִיבַטֵּל חֲמֵצוֹ, וְיֹאמַר לוֹ בְּפֵרוּשׁ, שֶׁהוּא מְמַנֶּה אוֹתוֹ לְשָׁלִיחַ עַל הַבְּדִיקָה וְגַם עַל הַבִּטּוּל. וְהַשָּׁלִיחַ יֹאמַר בַּבִּטּוּל, חֲמֵצוֹ שֶׁל פְּלוֹנִי וְכוּ'. וּמִכָּל מָקוֹם גַּם הוּא בַּאֲשֶׁר הוּא שָׁם, בְּעֶרֶב פֶּסַח בַּבֹּקֶר יְבַטֵּל חֲמֵצוֹ שֶׁבִּרְשׁוּתוֹ.

יז) מָצָא חָמֵץ בְּבֵיתוֹ בְּחֹל־הַמּוֹעֵד, יוֹצִיאֶנּוּ וְיִשְׂרְפֶנּוּ. וְאִם יֵשׁ בּוֹ כַּזַּיִת, יְבָרֵךְ מִתְּחִלָּה עַל בִּעוּר חָמֵץ. אֲבָל עַל פָּחוֹת מִכַּזַּיִת, לֹא יְבָרֵךְ. וְאִם מְצָאוֹ בְּיוֹם־טוֹב אוֹ בְּשַׁבַּת־חֹל־הַמּוֹעֵד, וְכֵן בְּשַׁבָּת שֶׁחָל בְּעֶרֶב פֶּסַח דְּאָסוּר לְטַלְטְלוֹ מִשּׁוּם דַּהֲוֵי מֻקְצֶה, יִכְפֶּה עָלָיו כְּלִי עַד מוֹצָאֵי יוֹם־טוֹב אוֹ מוֹצָאֵי שַׁבָּת, וְאָז יִשְׂרְפֶנּוּ. וְאִם מְצָאוֹ בַּיָּמִים הָאַחֲרוֹנִים, שֶׁאָז בְּמוֹצָאֵי יוֹם־טוֹב כְּבָר עָבַר הַפֶּסַח, אֵינוֹ מְבָרֵךְ עָלָיו, אֶלָּא שׂוֹרְפוֹ בְּלֹא בְרָכָה אֲפִלּוּ יֵשׁ בּוֹ כַּזַּיִת.

---

14. According to *Mishnah Berurah* (436:9) this refers to one who is going on a long trip or a sea journey. Even though he plans to return in ample time before *Pesach,* we are concerned that he might be delayed. One who leaves on a short trip and plans to return before the night of the fourteenth, need not take these measures. If, however, he plans to return within a short time before the search must begin, we are concerned that he may be delayed and, therefore, he should take the steps outlined in this paragraph.

(because we ask questions and explain the laws of *Pesach* thirty days before *Pesach*), thus you must search the room. Even if, inadvertently, you forgot to make the search, you must empty the storeroom, and make the search in the night, immediately after you become aware of your oversight.

14) If you store wheat that has not become *chametz*, in a pit, but afterwards, because of the dampness of the pit, the wheat at the bottom of the pit and at the sides became *chametz*; then, even if it was stored there within thirty days, you need not empty the pit on the night of the fourteenth and search it, rather reciting the nullification is enough, since it was stored in a permissible manner. If some of the wheat was *chametz* (when stored); there are many differing opinions about this, and in such case you should consult a qualified *posek.*

15) You should not throw grain to the chickens in a moist place during the thirty days before *Pesach,* for you may forget to burn it.

16) Before starting on a trip,[14] you should appoint an agent to search and nullify your *chametz.* You should tell him explicitly, that you appoint him as your agent to make the search and the nullification. When making the nullification the agent says, "The *chametz* of so-and-so etc." Nevertheless, wherever you happen to be on the morning of *erev Pesach,* you should nullify the *chametz* on your premises.

17) If you find *chametz* in your house on *Chol Hamoed,* you should take it out and burn it, and if it is the quantity of a *kazayis,*[15] you should first say the berachah: *Al biur chametz,*[16] but if it is less than a *kazayis,* you do not say a berachah. If you find the *chametz* on Yom Tov or on the Shabbos of *Chol Hamoed,* or on the Shabbos which occurs on *erev Pesach,*[17] when it is forbidden to handle the *chametz* because it is *muktzeh,* you should cover it with a vessel until the conclusion of Yom Tov, or the conclusion of Shabbos, and then you should burn it. If you find *chametz* on the last two days of *Pesach,* in which case at the conclusion of Yom Tov, *Pesach* has already ended, you do not say the berachah when burning it. You should burn it without saying the berachah, even though its quantity is as much as a *kazayis.*

---

15. See glossary.

16. If, however, you searched your house properly and nullified all *chametz* before Pesach, and then found *chametz* on *Chol Hamoed,* according to some later *Poskim,* the original berachah you made before *Pesach* suffices even for the *chametz* you found on *Chol Hamoed.* Other *Poskim* maintain that a new berachah should be recited. Since there is a question, the rule of "doubtful *berachos*" applies and the berachah should not be recited. (*Ibid.* 435:5)

17. After the fifth hour of the day has passed.

סִימָן קיב
אֵיזֶה חָמֵץ אָסוּר לְהַשְׁהוֹתוֹ בְּפֶסַח וְאֵיזֶה מֻתָּר לְהַשְׁהוֹתוֹ

א) כָּל דָּבָר שֶׁיֵּשׁ בּוֹ תַּעֲרֹבֶת חָמֵץ, וַאֲפִלּוּ אֵין בּוֹ חָמֵץ בָּעַיִן, רַק הַטַּעַם מֵחָמֵץ, כְּגוֹן שֶׁהֵסִירוּ אֶת הֶחָמֵץ, מִכָּל מָקוֹם אָסוּר לְהַשְׁהוֹתוֹ בְּפֶסַח. אֲבָל דָּבָר שֶׁלֹּא הָיָה בּוֹ חָמֵץ כְּלָל, אֶלָּא שֶׁנִּתְבַּשֵּׁל בִּכְלִי חָמֵץ, אֲפִלּוּ הָיָה הַכְּלִי בֶּן־יוֹמוֹ, אוֹ שֶׁנִּכְבַּשׁ בִּכְלִי חָמֵץ, מֻתָּר לְהַשְׁהוֹתוֹ בְּפֶסַח. וְדַוְקָא שֶׁנִּתְבַּשֵּׁל אוֹ נִכְבַּשׁ קֹדֶם הַפֶּסַח. אֲבָל אִם נִתְבַּשֵּׁל אוֹ נִכְבַּשׁ בְּפֶסַח בִּכְלִי חָמֵץ, חַיָּבִין לְבַעֲרוֹ.

ב) תְּבוּאָה שֶׁיֵּשׁ בָּהּ גַּרְעִינִים צְמוּחִים אוֹ מְבֻקָּעִים, וַאֲפִלּוּ הֵם מְעֹרָבִים מְעַט בְּהַרְבֵּה. וְכֵן תְּבוּאָה שֶׁנָּפְלוּ עָלֶיהָ מַיִם אוֹ שֶׁרְחָצָהּ בְּמַיִם, אָסוּר לְהַשְׁהוֹתָהּ. וְכֵן כָּל הַדְּבָרִים שֶׁנַּעֲשׂוּ מִתְּבוּאָה זוֹ, אָסוּר לְהַשְׁהוֹתָן. וּמִי שֶׁמּוֹכֵר לַחֲבֵרוֹ תְּבוּאָה שֶׁנִּתְלַחְלְחָה, צָרִיךְ לְהוֹדִיעַ לוֹ שֶׁלֹּא יַשְׁהֶה אוֹתָהּ בְּפֶסַח. וּלְנָכְרִי אָסוּר לְמָכְרָהּ בְּמָקוֹם שֶׁיֵּשׁ חֲשָׁשׁ שֶׁיִּמְכְּרֶנָּה הַנָּכְרִי לְיִשְׂרָאֵל וְיַשְׁהֶה אוֹתָהּ בְּפֶסַח.

ג) בְּגָדִים שֶׁנִּתְכַּבְּסוּ, וְנִתְקְנוּ בְּחֵלֶב חִטָּה [עֲמִילָן], מֻתָּר לְלָבְשָׁן בְּפֶסַח. אֲבָל אֵין לְהַצִּיעָן עַל הַשֻּׁלְחָן אִם יֵשׁ עֲלֵיהֶם אֵיזֶה מַמָּשׁוּת שֶׁיֵּשׁ לָחוּשׁ שֶׁיִּתְפָּרֵר מֵהֶם אֵיזֶה פֵּרוּר, וְכָל־שֶׁכֵּן שֶׁאָסוּר לָתֵת לְתוֹכָן קֶמַח שֶׁל פֶּסַח.

ד) מֻתָּר לְדַבֵּק נְיָרוֹת בַּחַלּוֹן, אֲפִלּוּ בְּתוֹךְ שְׁלשִׁים יוֹם לַפֶּסַח, וּבִלְבַד שֶׁלֹּא יְהֵא הֶחָמֵץ נִרְאֶה, דְּכֵיוָן שֶׁהַדֶּבֶק אֵינוֹ חָמֵץ גָּמוּר, וְגַם הוּא מְכֻסֶּה, לֹא הֶחְמִירוּ בּוֹ. אֲבָל אִם נִרְאֶה בַּחוּץ, אָסוּר. וְקֹדֶם שְׁלשִׁים יוֹם, בְּכָל עִנְיָן מֻתָּר.

ה) דְּיוֹ שֶׁנִּתְבַּשְּׁלָה בְּשֵׁכָר קֹדֶם פֶּסַח, מֻתָּר לִכְתּוֹב בָּהּ בְּחֹל־הַמּוֹעֵד פֶּסַח, כֵּיוָן שֶׁנִּפְסְלָה מֵאֲכִילַת הַכֶּלֶב קֹדֶם הַפֶּסַח. וְכֵן כֹּל כַּיּוֹצֵא בָּזֶה שֶׁנִּפְסַל וְנִפְסַד הֶחָמֵץ לְגַמְרֵי קֹדֶם הַפֶּסַח, מֻתָּר בְּפֶסַח בַּהֲנָאָה וּבִשְׁהִיָּה. אֲבָל גּוֹי שֶׁבִּשֵּׁל בְּפֶסַח דְּיוֹ בְּשֵׁכָר, אָסוּר לְיִשְׂרָאֵל בַּהֲנָאָה, מִשּׁוּם דְּחָמֵץ שֶׁל גּוֹי גַּם כֵּן אָסוּר לְיִשְׂרָאֵל בַּהֲנָאָה בְּפֶסַח.

ו) כָּל הַכֵּלִים שֶׁאֵינוֹ מַכְשִׁירָן לַפֶּסַח, צָרִיךְ לְשַׁפְשְׁפָן הֵיטֵב בְּעֶרֶב פֶּסַח קֹדֶם שָׁעָה שִׁשִּׁית וּלְהַדִּיחָן בְּעִנְיָן שֶׁלֹּא יְהֵא חָמֵץ נִכָּר, וְיַצְנִיעֵם

Chapter 112

Chametz That is Forbidden to be Kept on Pesach and That Which May be Kept on Pesach

1) Any food that contains a mixture of *chametz* even if the *chametz* is not actually present, but only the taste of the *chametz* remained after the *chametz* itself was removed, is forbidden to be kept during *Pesach*. However, if the food never contained *chametz* but was cooked in a vessel used for *chametz,* even if *chametz* was cooked in the vessel that day, or if an item was pickled in a vessel used for *chametz,* you are permitted to keep it during *Pesach,*[1] provided it was cooked or pickled before *Pesach;* but if the cooking or pickling was done on *Pesach* in a vessel used for *chametz,* the food item must be burned.

2) If grain contains some seeds that have sprouted or were split open, even if only a few of them were mixed in a large quantity, or if water has fallen on the grain, or it was washed with water, it is forbidden to keep (such grain during *Pesach*), and anything that was prepared from such grain, is forbidden to be kept during *Pesach.* If you sell your neighbor grain that has become wet, you must let him know this, so that he will not keep it in his possession during *Pesach.* You are forbidden to sell it to a non-Jew, when you are concerned that the non-Jew will sell it to a Jew who will keep it during *Pesach.*

3) Clothes that were laundered and starched with wheat starch are permitted to be worn on *Pesach,* but you should not spread a tablecloth if there is any starch on it, for there is concern that some particles may flake off, and most certainly it is forbidden to put the *Pesach* flour into such a cloth.

4) You are allowed to paste paper on a window even during the thirty days before *Pesach,* provided the *chametz* is not visible. Since the paste is not absolute *chametz,* and it is also covered up, the Sages did not rule stringently in this case. But, if the paste is visible, it is forbidden. But before the thirty days, it is permitted in any case.

5) If ink was prepared with beer before *Pesach,* you are permitted to write with it on *Chol Hamoed Pesach,* because it has become unfit even for dog food before *Pesach.* The same law applies to all similar cases where *chametz* has become spoiled and totally unfit before *Pesach.* You may derive benefit from such *chametz* and keep it on *Pesach.* But if a non-Jew prepared ink with beer on *Pesach,* a Jew is forbidden to derive benefit from it, because the *chametz* belonging to a non-Jew is also forbidden for a Jew to benefit from on *Pesach.*

6) All vessels that you are not kashering for *Pesach* must be scrubbed thoroughly on *erev Pesach* before the sixth hour, and rinsed in such a way that no *chametz* is

---

1. This is permitted only if it is removed from the *chametz* vessel and put into a *Pesach* vessel. You should take care to put the food in a place where you or others do not usually go, in order to prevent anyone from eating the food on *Pesach.* (*Mishnah Berurah* 442:1)

בְּמָקוֹם צָנוּעַ שֶׁאֵינוֹ רָגִיל לֵילֵךְ לְשָׁם בַּפֶּסַח. וְטוֹב לְסָגְרָם בְּחֶדֶר מְיֻחָד וּלְהַצְנִיעַ אֶת הַמַּפְתֵּחַ עַד לְאַחַר הַפֶּסַח.

סִימָן קיג
דִּינֵי עֶרֶב פֶּסַח וַאֲפִיַּת הַמַּצּוֹת

א) אֵין אוֹמְרִים מִזְמוֹר לְתוֹדָה וְלֹא לַמְנַצֵּחַ.

ב) מֻתָּר לֶאֱכוֹל חָמֵץ רַק עַד שְׁלִישׁ הַיּוֹם, (וְהַיּוֹם נֶחְשָׁב מִן עֲלוֹת הַשַּׁחַר עַד צֵאת הַכּוֹכָבִים). וּבַהֲנָאָה מֻתָּר עוֹד שָׁעָה אֶחָת. וּמֻתָּר לְמָכְרוֹ אָז לַגּוֹי, אֲבָל אַחַר כָּךְ אָסוּר גַּם בַּהֲנָאָה. וְצָרִיךְ לִשְׂרוֹף אֶת הֶחָמֵץ וּלְבַטְּלוֹ כָּל זְמַן שֶׁהוּא מֻתָּר בַּהֲנָאָה.

ג) מֵחֲצוֹת הַיּוֹם וְאֵילַךְ אָסוּר בַּעֲשִׂיַּת מְלָאכָה. וְאֵינוֹ מֻתָּר לַעֲשׂוֹת, רַק מַה שֶּׁמֻּתָּר לַעֲשׂוֹת בְּחֹל־הַמּוֹעֵד. וְעַל יְדֵי גוֹי, נוֹהֲגִין לְהַתִּיר. וְיֵשׁ מְקוֹמוֹת שֶׁנּוֹהֲגִין לֶאֱסוֹר כָּל הַיּוֹם בִּמְלָאכָה.

ד) לְהִסְתַּפֵּר וְכֵן לִקְצֹץ הַצִּפָּרְנַיִם, צְרִיכִין קֹדֶם חֲצוֹת. וְאִם שָׁכַח, יָכוֹל לִקְצֹץ צִפָּרְנָיו גַּם לְאַחַר חֲצוֹת. אֲבָל לְהִסְתַּפֵּר, אָסוּר, כִּי אִם עַל יְדֵי גוֹי.

ה) אָסוּר לֶאֱכוֹל מַצָּה כָּל הַיּוֹם. וַאֲפִלּוּ הַקְּטַנִּים וְהַקְּטַנּוֹת, כֹּל שֶׁמְּבִינִים עִנְיַן יְצִיאַת מִצְרַיִם, אָסוּר לָתֵת לָהֶם מַצָּה. אֲבָל תַּבְשִׁילִין שֶׁעוֹשִׂין מִמַּצּוֹת טְחוּנוֹת, מֻתָּר כָּל אָדָם לֶאֱכוֹל עַד תְּחִלַּת שָׁעָה עֲשִׂירִית, דְּהַיְנוּ עַד הָרְבִיעִית הָאַחֲרוֹנָה שֶׁל הַיּוֹם. וּמִשָּׁם וְאֵילַךְ, אָסוּר לֶאֱכוֹל כִּי אִם לְעֵת הַצֹּרֶךְ מְעַט פֵּרוֹת אוֹ בָּשָׂר וְדָגִים. וְיִזָּהֵר שֶׁלֹּא יְמַלֵּא כְּרֵסוֹ, כְּדֵי שֶׁיֹּאכַל בַּלַּיְלָה לְתֵאָבוֹן.

ו) הַבְּכוֹרִים, בֵּין בְּכוֹר לָאָב בֵּין בְּכוֹר לָאֵם, מִתְעַנִּים בְּעֶרֶב פֶּסַח, אֲפִלּוּ חָל בְּעֶרֶב שַׁבָּת, וְגַם הַבָּא אַחַר הַנְּפָלִים, צָרִיךְ לְהִתְעַנּוֹת. וְכָל זְמַן

---

1. In cases where large financial losses may occur, it is permitted to sell the *chametz* up to an hour (60 minutes) before midday. (*Mishnah Berurah* 443:9)

2. A worker who will not have food to eat unless he works is permitted to work even after midday. (*Ibid.* 468:46)

3. All those who are permitted to take a haircut and to wash clothing on *Chol Hamoed,* are also permitted to do so on *erev Pesach* after midday. (See Chapter 104:11) (*Ibid.* 468:7)

visible on them. They should be stored in a secluded place where you do not ordinarily go on *Pesach*. It is best to lock them up in a separate room and to hide the key until after *Pesach*.

Chapter 113

Laws Concerning Erev Pesach and the Baking of Matzos

1) On *erev Pesach* we do not say *Mizmor lesodah*—"A psalm of thanksgiving" (Psalm 100), neither do we say *Lamenatzei'ach*—"For the Conductor" (Psalm 20).

2) You are permitted to eat *chametz* only during the first third of the day, (the day is calculated as extending from dawn until the stars appear). But you may derive benefit from it for another hour. Thus, you are permitted to sell it to a non-Jew[1] during that hour, but after that time it is forbidden to derive any benefit from it. You must burn the *chametz* and nullify it while you are still permitted to derive benefit from it.

3) After midday it is forbidden to do any work.[2] However, you are permitted to do such work as is permitted on *Chol Hamoed*. But it is customary to permit a non-Jew [to do work for you.] In some communities it is the custom to forbid doing work the entire day.

4) You should take a haircut and cut your nails before midday.[3] If you forget to do so, you may cut your nails in the afternoon, but it is forbidden to take a haircut, unless it is done by a non-Jew.

5) It is forbidden to eat matzah the entire day.[4] It is forbidden to give matzah even to small children once they are able to understand the meaning of the Exodus. However, everyone is permitted to eat[5] food made of matzah meal, until the beginning of the tenth hour, that is until the beginning of the final quarter of the day. From that time on it is forbidden to eat, except when it is necessary, in which case you may eat some fruit, or a little meat and fish You should be careful not to overeat, so that you will eat the matzah in the evening with appetite.

6) The firstborn sons either of the father or of the mother must fast on *erev Pesach*,[6] even if it occurs on Friday. A firstborn who was born after a miscarriage

---

4. Some have the custom not to eat matzo from *Rosh Chodesh Nissan*. (*Ibid.* 471:12)

5. Cakes made with matzah meal are forbidden, but knodel made with matzah meal is permitted. See *Ramah* 671. The difference between cake and knodel is that cake is baked whereas knodel is cooked, and in cooking the taste of matzah is not as strong.

6. However, if you had a severe headache or your eyes hurt you, you need not complete the fast. Similarly, if fasting affects you so that after the fast you are unable to eat, except light foods, and it is possible you will be unable to eat matzah, marror and drink four cups of wine at night, it is better not to fast. (*Ibid.* 470:2)

שֶׁהַבְּכוֹר קָטָן, הָאָב מִתְעַנֶּה תַּחְתָּיו. בִּסְעוּדַת מִצְוָה אִם מֻתָּרִים לֶאֱכוֹל, תַּלְיָא בְּמִנְהַג הַמְּקוֹמוֹת.

ז) בְּכוֹר הַמִּתְעַנֶּה, אוֹמֵר בִּתְפִלַּת הַמִּנְחָה, עֲנֵנוּ. וְאִם הֵם כַּמָּה בְּכוֹרִים וּמִתְפַּלְּלִין בְּצִבּוּר, לֹא יֵרֵד בְּכוֹר לִפְנֵי הַתֵּבָה, כִּי אֵין לוֹמַר עֲנֵנוּ בַּחֲזָרַת הַתְּפִלָּה בְּקוֹל, כֵּיוָן שֶׁהוּא חֹדֶשׁ נִיסָן.

ח) הַמְהַדְּרִים אוֹפִין הַמַּצּוֹת שֶׁל מִצְוָה בְּעֶרֶב פֶּסַח אַחַר חֲצוֹת הַיּוֹם, שֶׁהוּא זְמַן הַקְרָבַת קָרְבַּן פֶּסַח. וְכֵיוָן שֶׁאָז הוּא אַחַר זְמַן אִסּוּר חָמֵץ, טוֹב שֶׁיְּבַטֵּל בְּפֵרוּשׁ אֶת הַפֵּרוּרִים, וְיֹאמַר בְּלָשׁוֹן שֶׁהוּא מֵבִין, עִנְיָן זֶה, כָּל פֵּרוּרִים שֶׁיִּפְּלוּ בִּשְׁעַת לִישָׁה וַעֲרִיכָה, וְכֵן הַבָּצֵק שֶׁיִּדָּבֵק בַּכֵּלִים, אֲנִי מְבַטֵּל וּמַפְקִיר אוֹתָם.

ט) וְהַמַּיִם שֶׁרוֹחֲצִין בָּהֶם אֶת הַכֵּלִים, צְרִיכִין לְשָׁפְכָן בְּמָקוֹם מִדְרוֹן, וְשֶׁלֹּא תִהְיֶה רִצְפַּת אֲבָנִים, כְּדֵי שֶׁיִּבָּלְעוּ מְהֵרָה בַּקַּרְקַע, שֶׁאִם יִשְׁפְּכֵן שֶׁלֹּא בְּמָקוֹם מִדְרוֹן אוֹ אֲפִלּוּ בְּמָקוֹם מִדְרוֹן וְהוּא רִצְפַּת אֲבָנִים, יֵשׁ לָחוּשׁ שֶׁמָּא יִתְקַבְּצוּ בְּמָקוֹם אֶחָד וְיַחְמִיצוּ קֹדֶם שֶׁיִּבָּלְעוּ בַּקַּרְקַע, וְנִמְצָא שֶׁיִּהְיֶה חָמֵץ בִּרְשׁוּתוֹ.

סִימָן קיד
דִּינֵי מְכִירַת חָמֵץ

א) יִשְׂרָאֵל שֶׁהָיָה לוֹ חָמֵץ שֶׁלּוֹ בִּרְשׁוּתוֹ בַּפֶּסַח, עוֹבֵר בְּכָל רֶגַע וָרֶגַע עַל בַּל יֵרָאֶה וּבַל יִמָּצֵא. וְהֶחָמֵץ אָסוּר בַּהֲנָאָה לְעוֹלָם, וַאֲפִלּוּ בִּטְּלוֹ קֹדֶם פֶּסַח. וְלָכֵן מִי שֶׁיֵּשׁ לוֹ הַרְבֵּה חָמֵץ שֶׁאֵינוֹ יָכוֹל לְבַעֲרוֹ מִן הָעוֹלָם, צָרִיךְ לְמָכְרוֹ לַגּוֹי קֹדֶם הַפֶּסַח בְּשָׁעָה שֶׁהוּא עֲדַיִן מֻתָּר בַּהֲנָאָה. וְלֹא יְהֵא עִנְיַן מְכִירַת חָמֵץ אֵצֶל הָאָדָם כְּמוֹ מִצְוַת אֲנָשִׁים מְלֻמָּדָה, אֶלָּא צָרִיךְ שֶׁיִּגְמוֹר בְּדַעְתּוֹ שֶׁהוּא מוֹכְרוֹ בֶּאֱמֶת לַגּוֹי מְכִירָה גְמוּרָה וַחֲלוּטָה. וְלֹא יִמְכּוֹר בְּיֹקֶר מִן הַמְּחִיר הָרָאוּי. וּלְאַחַר הַפֶּסַח יְבַקֵּשׁ מֵאֵת הַגּוֹי שֶׁיְּשַׁלֵּם לוֹ אֶת הַחוֹב. וְכַאֲשֶׁר יְשִׁיבֵהוּ שֶׁאֵין לוֹ כֶּסֶף, יְבַקֵּשׁ מִמֶּנּוּ שֶׁיַּחֲזוֹר וְיִמְכּוֹר לוֹ אֶת הֶחָמֵץ עִם (הַחֶדֶר) בְּעַד כָּךְ וְכָךְ. וְלֹא יְהֵא הַדָּבָר כְּחוּכָא בְּעָלְמָא, אֶלָּא כְּדֶרֶךְ הַסּוֹחֲרִים מַמָּשׁ.

ב) הֶחָמֵץ שֶׁהוּא מוּכָר לַגּוֹי, צָרִיךְ שֶׁלֹּא יְהֵא בְּבֵיתוֹ שֶׁל יִשְׂרָאֵל.

must also fast. When the firstborn is a minor, his father fasts instead of him. Whether firstborn are permitted to eat at a mitzvah meal depends on the local custom.[7]

7) A firstborn who fasts should say *Aneinu* in the *Shemoneh esre* of *Minchah.* If there are many firstborn and they pray with the congregation, none of the firstborn should be the Chazzan, since *Aneinu* should not be said loud during the repetition of the *Shemoneh esre,* since it is the month of Nisan.

8) People who do the mitzvah meticulously bake the mitzvah-matzos in the afternoon of *erev Pesach,* which is the time when the Paschal lamb was offered. And because at that time *chametz* is forbidden, it is best to nullify the crumbs explicitly, by making the following statement: "All the crumbs that will fall off during the kneading and preparing, as well as the dough that will cling to the vessels, I hereby nullify and render ownerless."

9) The water with which the vessels are washed should be poured on a sloping place where there is no stone floor, so that it will be quickly absorbed in the ground; for by pouring it on level ground, or even in a sloping place with a stone floor, there is reason to be concerned that the water will gather in one place and become *chametz* before it is absorbed in the ground; thus there will be *chametz* in your possession.

Chapter 114

The Laws Concerning the Selling of Chametz

1) A Jew who has *chametz* in his possession on *Pesach,* continually transgresses the law, "No *chametz* must be seen in your possession" (Ex. 13:7) and "No *chametz* may be found in your home" (Ex. 12:19). Benefit of such *chametz* is forever forbidden, even if he nullified it before *Pesach.*[1] Therefore, if you own a great deal of *chametz* that you cannot do away with, you must sell it to a non-Jew before *Pesach,* while you are still permitted to derive benefit from it. You should not treat the matter of selling *chametz* as a routine formality. Rather, it should be your firm intention to actually sell the *chametz* to the non-Jew, in a firm and binding sale. You should not sell it for more than it is worth. After *Pesach* you demand from the non-Jew that he pay his debt, and when he replies that he has no money, you ask of him to resell the *chametz* to you (together with the room) for so-and-so-much. You should not make a mockery out of this matter, rather, it should be handled in a business-like manner.

2) The *chametz* sold to the non-Jew, may not remain in the house of the Jew. If

7. Our custom is to permit the first born to eat at a *Siyum* (the completion) of a *Maseches,* even though they, themselves, did not study it. (*Ibid.* 470:10)

1. Many later *Poskim* rule that this law applies, even if you made the search for *chametz* and also nullified the *chametz,* but others are lenient and rule that if you both searched for and nullified the *chametz,* it is not forbidden for benefit, since you fulfilled all that was required of you. Therefore, in a situation where there is a potential for great losses, this lenient opinion may be relied on. (*Mishnah Berurah* 448:25; also *Biyur Halachah*)

וְאִם הַגּוֹי לוֹקֵחַ אֶת הֶחָמֵץ לְתוֹךְ בֵּיתוֹ, מַה טּוֹב. וְאִם אִי אֶפְשָׁר שֶׁיִּקָּחֵהוּ לְבֵיתוֹ, צָרִיךְ לְהַשְׂכִּיר לוֹ אֶת הַחֶדֶר שֶׁהֶחָמֵץ מֻנָּח בּוֹ. וְצָרִיךְ לִכְתּוֹב בַּשְּׁטָר שֵׁם הַקּוֹנֶה, וּבְכַמָּה הִשְׂכִּיר לוֹ אֶת הַחֶדֶר, וְשֶׁאַגַּב קַרְקַע הִקְנָה לוֹ אֶת הֶחָמֵץ הַמֻּנָּח שָׁם, וִיפָרוֹט אֶת כָּל הֶחָמֵץ בְּכַמָּה מָכַר לוֹ, אֲבָל אֵינוֹ צָרִיךְ לִפְרוֹט סְכוּם הַמִּדּוֹת, וְיוּכַל לִכְתֹּב רַק בְּעַד כַּמָּה כָּל מִדָּה עַד לְמִדִידָה. וְכָל מַה שֶּׁכָּתוּב בַּשְּׁטָר, יְדַבֵּר עִם הַקּוֹנֶה גַּם בְּעַל־פֶּה. וִיקַבֵּל מִמֶּנּוּ עֵרָבוֹן, וּשְׁאָר הַמָּעוֹת יִזְקוֹף עָלָיו בְּמִלְוֶה, וִיהֵא הַכֹּל כָּתוּב בַּשְּׁטָר, וְגַם יִמְסוֹר לוֹ אֶת הַמַּפְתֵּחַ מִן הַחֶדֶר. חָמֵץ שֶׁהוּא בְּתוֹךְ כְּלִי הַצָּרִיךְ טְבִילָה (כְּשֶׁלּוֹקְחוֹ מִגּוֹי), לֹא יִמְכְּרֶנּוּ עִם הַכְּלִי, כִּי לְאַחַר הַפֶּסַח כְּשֶׁיַּחֲזוֹר וְיִקְנֵהוּ מִן הַגּוֹי, יִצְטָרֵךְ טְבִילָה מֵחָדָשׁ.

ג) לְאַחַר שֶׁמָּכַר לוֹ אֶת הֶחָמֵץ, אִם יָרֵא פֶּן יְקַלְקֵל שָׁם הַקּוֹנֶה, יָכוֹל גַּם הוּא לִתְלוֹת שָׁם מַסְגֶּרֶת לִשְׁמִירָה, אוֹ אִם הַקּוֹנֶה רוֹצֶה לְהַפְקִיד אֵצֶל הַיִּשְׂרָאֵל אֶת הַמַּפְתֵּחַ, רַשָּׁאִי. אֲבָל אָסוּר שֶׁיַּנִּיחַ הַיִּשְׂרָאֵל חוֹתָם עַל הֶחָמֵץ.

ד) אִם אֵינוֹ יָכוֹל לְהַשְׂכִּיר לוֹ כָּל הַחֶדֶר, מִפְּנֵי שֶׁהוּא צָרִיךְ גַּם כֵּן לְהִשְׁתַּמֵּשׁ בּוֹ, יַעֲשֶׂה מְחִצָּה לִפְנֵי הֶחָמֵץ, וְיַשְׂכִּיר לוֹ אֶת הַמָּקוֹם שֶׁעַד הַמְּחִצָּה, וְיִכְתֹּב כֵּן בְּתוֹךְ הַשְּׁטָר. גַּם יִכְתֹּב שֶׁיֵּשׁ לְהַקּוֹנֶה דְּרִיסַת הָרֶגֶל לָלֶכֶת כִּרְצוֹנוֹ אֶל הַמָּקוֹם הַהוּא, וְגַם שֶׁאִם יִרְצֶה הַגּוֹי הַזֶּה הַקּוֹנֶה לִמְכּוֹר אֶת הֶחָמֵץ לְגוֹי אַחֵר בְּתוֹךְ הַפֶּסַח אוֹ לְיִשְׂרָאֵל בְּאִסְרוּ חַג דְּפֶסַח, יֵשׁ לְכֻלָּם דְּרִיסַת הָרֶגֶל לָלֶכֶת שָׁמָּה. וְכֵן אִם מַשְׂכִּיר אוֹ מוֹכֵר לַגּוֹי חֶדֶר שֶׁצְּרִיכִין לָלֶכֶת שָׁמָּה דֶּרֶךְ רְשׁוּתוֹ שֶׁל הַמּוֹכֵר, צָרִיךְ לִכְתּוֹב כֵּן בַּשְּׁטָר, שֶׁיֵּשׁ לַגּוֹי הַקּוֹנֶה וּלְכָל הַקּוֹנִים שֶׁיָּבִיא שָׁמָּה, דְּרִיסַת הָרֶגֶל לָלֶכֶת שָׁמָּה.

ה) אִם הַבַּיִת הוּא אֵצֶל הַיִּשְׂרָאֵל רַק בִּשְׂכִירוּת מִיִּשְׂרָאֵל אַחֵר, אֲזַי אֵינוֹ יָכוֹל לְהַשְׂכִּירוֹ לַגּוֹי לְבֵית דִּירָה בְּלִי רְשׁוּת הַמַּשְׂכִּיר, לָכֵן יַתְנֶה בְּפֵרוּשׁ עִם הַגּוֹי, שֶׁאֵינוֹ מַשְׂכִּירוֹ לוֹ לָדוּר בּוֹ, רַק לְהַחֲזִיק בּוֹ כֵּלָיו וּמִטַּלְטְלָיו. אֲבָל לֹא יַשְׂכִּירוֹ בְּפֵרוּשׁ לְהַחֲזִיק בּוֹ אֶת הֶחָמֵץ, רַק סְתָם לְהַחֲזִיק בּוֹ כֵּלָיו וּמִטַּלְטְלָיו כִּרְצוֹנוֹ. וּמִכָּל מָקוֹם אִם הַמַּשְׂכִּיר בָּעִיר,

---

2. Most later *Poskim* rule that ownership of *chametz* in the room can also be transferred to the non-Jew, by means of the rental or sale of the room. This particular form of *kinyan* (ownership transferred), called *kinyan agav,* is considered, by many *Poskim*, the best form of *kinyan,* and it does not require that the articles, which are sold, actually be in the room. (*Ibid.* 448:17,19)

the non-Jew takes the *chametz* into his own house, so much the better. But if he cannot take it to his home, then you must rent to him the room in which the *chametz* is (stored). You must mention in the bill of sale the name of the buyer and the amount for which the room was rented, and that by means of the rental of the room, you are transferring to him the ownership of the *chametz* that is contained in it.[2] You should list all the *chametz*, stating the price of each item,[3] but you need not mention their weights and measures. You may simply write how much you charge per measure. All that is written in the contract should be discussed orally with the buyer. You should take a deposit from him, and the balance of the purchase price should be considered as a loan. All of the above should be written in the contract. You must also deliver to the buyer the key to the room.[4] If any *chametz* is in a vessel that requires *tevilah* (ritual immersion) when bought from a non-Jew, you should not sell it with the vessel, because (if you do sell it), then, after *Pesach*, when you buy it back from the non-Jew, you will have to immerse it again.

3) If, after you sold the *chametz*, you are afraid that the buyer may damage it, you are permitted to put an additional lock on the door to protect it;[5] or, if the buyer wants to deposit the key with the Jew, he may do so. But it is forbidden for a Jew to put a seal on the *chametz*.

4) If you are unable to rent the whole room because you need part of it for your own use, you should make a partition[6] in front of the place where the *chametz* is kept, and rent to the non-Jew the space (where the *chametz* is kept) up to the partition, and write this in the contract. You should also state that the buyer has the right of access to enter this place at will. You should also stipulate, that if this non-Jew, the buyer, wishes to sell the *chametz* to another non-Jew during *Pesach*, or to a Jew, the day after *Pesach*, all of these have the right to access there. If a Jew rents or sells to a non-Jew a room that is accessible only through the premises of the seller, it must be written in the contract that the non-Jew, the buyer, and any other buyers that he may bring there, should have the right to enter there.

5) If the house you live in was rented from another Jew, you cannot rent it to the non-Jew as a residence without the permission of the landlord. Therefore, you should expressly tell the non-Jew that you are not renting it to him as a residence, but only to keep his vessels and belongings there. You should not rent it with the stipulation that you are doing so to keep the *chametz* there, but generally to keep his vessels and belongings as he sees fit. Nevertheless, if the landlord is in town,

---

3. According to *Choshen Mishpat* 200:7, it is not necessary to list or state the price of each item. It is sufficient if the buyer agrees to rely on the evaluation of three people or even one person. This is the custom that is prevalent in our form of selling *chametz*.

4. It is also acceptable, if you tell him that you will make the key available to him, whenever he desires to enter to take his *chametz*. (*Ibid.* 448:12)

5. But if you lock the room, at the time of sale, in order to prevent the non-Jew from taking the *chametz*, the *chametz* is forbidden after Pesach, as stated in Paragraph 1. (See *Mishnah Berurah* 448:12; *Biyur Halachah* 448:3, *Shaar Hatzion* 28)

6. The partition should be at least ten *tefachim* high, and it should not be made with a sheet that moves to and fro. (*Mishnah Berurah* 440:12)

יִקַּח מִמֶּנּוּ רְשׁוּת לְהַשְׂכִּירוֹ. וְכֵן מִי שֶׁנּוֹסֵעַ לַדֶּרֶךְ קֹדֶם פֶּסַח, וְאִשְׁתּוֹ תִּמְכֹּר אֶת הֶחָמֵץ, יִתֵּן לָהּ רְשׁוּת בְּפֵרוּשׁ שֶׁתַּשְׂכִּיר אֶת הַחֶדֶר.

ו) אָסוּר לַעֲשׂוֹת תְּנַאי עִם הַגּוֹי, שֶׁלְּאַחַר הַפֶּסַח מְחֻיָּב הַגּוֹי לְמָכְרוֹ לוֹ, אוֹ שֶׁהַיִּשְׂרָאֵל מְחֻיָּב לַחֲזוֹר וְלִקְנוֹתוֹ מִמֶּנּוּ. אֲבָל יָכוֹל לְהַבְטִיחוֹ, שֶׁיַּחֲזוֹר לִקְנוֹתוֹ מִמֶּנּוּ וְשֶׁיִּתֶּן לוֹ רֶוַח.

ז) אָסוּר לִמְכּוֹר אֶת הֶחָמֵץ לְמוּמָר אוֹ לְמוּמֶרֶת, וְלֹא לְבֶן מוּמֶרֶת, אַף־עַל־פִּי שֶׁיְּלָדַתּוּ מִגּוֹי לְאַחַר שֶׁהֵמִירָה, כִּי לְעִנְיָן זֶה דִּינָם כְּמוֹ יִשְׂרָאֵל, וַהֲוֵי לֵהּ חֲמֵצוֹ שֶׁל יִשְׂרָאֵל שֶׁעָבַר עָלָיו הַפֶּסַח דְּאָסוּר בַּהֲנָאָה.

ח) מִי שֶׁיֵּשׁ לוֹ חָמֵץ בְּמָקוֹם אַחֵר אוֹ בַּדֶּרֶךְ בָּעֲגָלוֹת אוֹ בִּסְפִינָה, יָכוֹל לְמָכְרוֹ גַּם כֵּן אַגַּב קַרְקַע שֶׁבִּמְקוֹמוֹ. וּמִכָּל מָקוֹם יַפְקִירוֹ גַּם כֵּן בִּפְנֵי בֵּית־דִּין אוֹ שְׁלֹשָׁה אֲנָשִׁים. וְאִם הוּבָא לוֹ הֶחָמֵץ בְּפֶסַח, הַגּוֹי הַקּוֹנֶה הוּא יְשַׁלֵּם שְׂכַר הָעֲגָלָה וְיֶתֶר הַהוֹצָאוֹת. וְאִם הוּבָא לוֹ חָמֵץ אֲשֶׁר שָׁלַח לוֹ גּוֹי סְחוֹרָה, וְהוּא לֹא בִקְשָׁהּ וְלֹא יָדַע, יְקַבְּלָהּ גַּם כֵּן הַגּוֹי וִישַׁלֵּם מַה שֶּׁמַּגִּיעַ לְהַמֵּבִיא, וְהַיִּשְׂרָאֵל לֹא יִתְעַסֵּק בָּהּ כְּלָל, וְאַדְּרַבָּה יַפְקִירֶנָּה גַּם כֵּן בִּפְנֵי בֵּית־דִּין אוֹ בִּפְנֵי שְׁלֹשָׁה אֲנָשִׁים.

ט) מִי שֶׁיֵּשׁ לוֹ רֵחַיִם, וְהַטּוֹחֲנִים נוֹתְנִים מֶכֶס תְּבוּאָה מְחֻמֶּצֶת, צָרִיךְ לִמְכֹּר אוֹ לְהַשְׂכִּיר אֶת הָרֵחַיִם קֹדֶם פֶּסַח לַגּוֹי.

י) בְּעִנְיַן מְכִירַת בְּהֵמוֹת שֶׁיַּאֲכִילֵם הַגּוֹי חָמֵץ, יֵשׁ מַחֲלֹקֶת בֵּין הַגְּדוֹלִים זִכְרוֹנָם לִבְרָכָה. וּמִי שֶׁאֶפְשָׁר לוֹ לְהִזָּהֵר, טוֹב לוֹ. וְאִם אִי אֶפְשָׁר לוֹ, יַעֲשֶׂה עַל פִּי הוֹרָאַת חָכָם.

יא) מֻתָּר לְהַלְווֹת לְיִשְׂרָאֵל כִּכַּר חָמֵץ קֹדֶם הַפֶּסַח שֶׁיַּחֲזִיר לוֹ לְאַחַר הַפֶּסַח. וְיֵשׁ מְקוֹמוֹת שֶׁנּוֹהֲגִין בָּזֶה אִסּוּר.

יב) אִם חֲמֵצוֹ שֶׁל יִשְׂרָאֵל הוּא בִּרְשׁוּת גּוֹי, אוֹ בְּהִפּוּךְ, חֲמֵצוֹ שֶׁל גּוֹי בִּרְשׁוּת יִשְׂרָאֵל, יַעֲשֶׂה שְׁאֵלָה הֵיאַךְ יִתְנַהֵג בּוֹ, כִּי יֵשׁ בָּזֶה הַרְבֵּה חִלּוּקֵי דִינִים.

יג) צְרִיכִין לִזָּהֵר שֶׁלֹּא לֵהָנוֹת לְאַחַר הַפֶּסַח מֵחֲמֵצוֹ שֶׁל יִשְׂרָאֵל שֶׁהוּא חָשׁוּד שֶׁלֹּא מְכָרוֹ כַּדָּת.

you should obtain his permission to rent it. If you go on a trip before *Pesach,* and your wife is going to sell the *chametz,* you should give her express permission to rent the room.

6) It is forbidden to stipulate with the non-Jew that after *Pesach,* he must sell the *chametz* back to you, or that you, are obligated to buy it back from him, but you are permitted to assure him that you will buy it back from him, and give him some profit.

7) It is forbidden to sell the *chametz* to an apostate Jewish man or woman, or to the son of an apostate woman, even if she gave birth to him from a non-Jew after she became an apostate; for regarding this matter, they are Jews in the eyes of halachah, and the *chametz* will be considered as chametz that was in the possession of a Jew during *Pesach,* the benefit of which is forbidden forever.

8) If you own *chametz* in another place, or en route in wagons or on ships, you can also sell it [to a non-Jew] by means of selling him a place in your town.[7] Nevertheless, you should also renounce your ownership to it before a Rabbinic Court or before three laymen. If the *chametz* is delivered to you on *Pesach,* the non-Jewish buyer should pay the cost of the wagon and the other expenses. If *chametz* is delivered to you, which was shipped by a non-Jew, and you had not ordered it, and knew nothing about it, the non-Jew should also receive it and pay whatever is due to the one who brought it. You should have nothing at all to do with it; on the contrary, you should renounce ownership to it before a Rabbinical Court or before three laymen.

9) A person owning a mill, whose customers, grind their grain, and pay their fee in grain, which is *chametz,* must either sell or lease the mill, to a non-Jew, before *Pesach.*

10) Regarding the sale of cattle to a non-Jew, who will feed them *chametz,* there are differing opinions among the Sages of blessed memory. If possible, it is best to avoid selling them, but if it is impossible, it should be done with advice of a qualified *Posek.*

11) You are permitted to lend a loaf of bread to another Jew before *Pesach,* with the understanding that he should return (a loaf of bread) after *Pesach.* In some communities, it is the custom to forbid such loans.

12) If the *chametz* of a Jew is in the possession of a non-Jew, or conversely, the *chametz* of a non-Jew is in the possession of a Jew, you should consult (a qualified *Posek*) how to act in this matter, for there are many differing opinions regarding it.

13) You should be careful, not to benefit after Pesach of the *chametz* of a Jew, who is suspected of not having sold it properly.

---

7. See notes 2,3.

נֹסַח שְׁטַר מְכִירַת חָמֵץ

אָנֹכִי הֶחָתוּם מַטָּה מָכַרְתִּי לַגּוֹי (פְּלוֹנִי) אֶת כָּל סְפִּירְט שֶׁיֵּשׁ לִי בַּמַּרְתֵּף בַּדִּירָה שֶׁאֲנִי דָר בָּהּ, וְהַמַּרְתֵּף הוּא בְּתוֹךְ הֶחָצֵר מִצַּד צָפוֹן, הַשֵּׁנִי מִצַּד מִזְרָח. וְכָל סְפִּירְט שֶׁיֵּשׁ לִי שָׁם, הֵן בַּחֲבִיתִין בֵּינוֹנִיּוֹת הֵן בַּחֲבִיתִין גְּדוֹלוֹת, הַכֹּל מָכַרְתִּי לְהַנִּזְכָּר לְעֵיל עִם הַכֵּלִים בְּעַד מָאתַיִם וְעֶשְׂרִים זְהוּבִים. וְגַם אַרַאק שֶׁיֵּשׁ לִי שָׁם בִּצְלוֹחִית גְּדוֹלָה לְעֶרֶךְ שֶׁבַע מִדּוֹת מָכַרְתִּי לוֹ בְּעַד חֲמִשָּׁה זְהוּבִים בְּלִי הַכֵּלִים. וְגַם (שליוואוויטץ) שֶׁיֵּשׁ לִי שָׁם בֶּחָבִית קְטַנָּה מָכַרְתִּי לוֹ בְּעַד שְׁנֵים־עָשָׂר זְהוּבִים וַחֲמִשִּׁים עִם הַכֶּלִי. וְגַם מָכַרְתִּי לוֹ שֵׁשׁ חָבִיּוֹת רֵיקָנִיּוֹת שֶׁהָיָה בָּהֶן סְפִּירְט, וּשְׁתֵּי חָבִיּוֹת גְּדוֹלוֹת בַּחֲשׁוּקֵי בַּרְזֶל גַּם כֵּן רֵיקָנִיּוֹת מִסְּפִּירְט שֶׁיֵּשׁ לִי שָׁם, כֻּלָּן מָכַרְתִּי לוֹ בְּעַד שְׁמוֹנָה זְהוּבִים וַחֲמִשִּׁים צ״ל. גַּם חֲמִשָּׁה שַׂקִּים קֶמַח חִטִּים שֶׁיֵּשׁ לִי בְּתוֹךְ הַחֶדֶר הַנִּקְרָא שפייז הַשַּׁיָּךְ לַדִּירָה שֶׁאֲנִי דָר בָּהּ, מָכַרְתִּי לְהַנִּזְכָּר לְעֵיל עִם הַשַּׂקִּים בְּעַד שְׁלֹשִׁים וְתִשְׁעָה זְהוּבִים. וְגַם כָּל הַכֵּלִים מֵחָמֵץ שֶׁיֵּשׁ לִי שָׁם, דְּהַיְנוּ עֲרֵבוֹת וְתֵבוֹת מִקֶּמַח מָכַרְתִּי לוֹ בְּעַד אַרְבָּעָה זְהוּבִים וַחֲמִשִּׁים צ״ל. גַּם גְּרִיסֵי שְׂעוֹרִים בְּשַׂק קָטָן שֶׁיֵּשׁ לִי שָׁם, מָכַרְתִּי לוֹ בְּעַד זָהוּב אֶחָד וַחֲמִשִּׁים צ״ל עִם הַשַּׂק. וְקִבַּלְתִּי מֵאִתּוֹ עֵרָבוֹן עֲשָׂרָה זְהוּבִים וְהַמּוֹתָר זָקַפְתִּי עָלָיו בְּמִלְוֶה. וּזְמַן הַפֵּרָעוֹן לֹא יְאֻחַר מִן עֲשָׂרָה יָמִים מִיּוֹם הָרָשׁוּם דִּלְמַטָּה. וְהִשְׂכַּרְתִּי לְהַקּוֹנֶה הַנִּזְכָּר לְעֵיל אֶת הַמַּרְתֵּף הַנִּזְכָּר לְעֵיל וְאֶת הַחֶדֶר הַנִּזְכָּר לְעֵיל, מֵעַכְשָׁו עַד עֲשָׂרָה יָמִים מִיּוֹם הָרָשׁוּם דִּלְמַטָּה בְּעַד אַרְבָּעָה זְהוּבִים, וְקִבַּלְתִּי עֵרָבוֹן שְׁלֹשָׁה זְהוּבִים וְהַמּוֹתָר זָקַפְתִּי עָלָיו בְּמִלְוֶה, שֶׁיְּשַׁלֵּם לִי לֹא יְאֻחַר מֵעֲשָׂרָה יָמִים מִיּוֹם הָרָשׁוּם דִּלְמַטָּה, וְאַגַּב קַרְקַע הַמֻּשְׂכָּר לוֹ, דְּהַיְנוּ הַמַּרְתֵּף וְהַחֶדֶר הַנִּזְכָּרִים לְעֵיל, הִקְנֵיתִי לוֹ כָּל הַמִּטַּלְטְלִין הַנִּזְכָּרִים לְעֵיל. וַאֲנִי מוֹדֶה בְּהוֹדָאָה גְּמוּרָה, שֶׁהִשְׂכַּרְתִּי לוֹ הַמַּרְתֵּף וְהַחֶדֶר הַנִּזְכָּרִים לְעֵיל, וְהִקְנֵיתִי לוֹ כָּל הַמִּטַּלְטְלִין הַנִּזְכָּרִים לְעֵיל בְּכָל מִינֵי קִנְיָנִים הַמּוֹעִילִים בְּאֵיזֶה מֵהֶם שֶׁיִּהְיֶה הַקִּנְיָן חָל עַל פִּי דִּין תּוֹרָתֵנוּ הַקְּדוֹשָׁה וְעַל פִּי נִימוּסֵי הַקֵּיסָ״ה וְהַמְּדִינָה בְּלִי שׁוּם טַעֲנָה וּמַעֲנֶה. וּרְשׁוּת בְּיָדוֹ לַעֲשׂוֹת בְּכָל הַנִּזְכָּר לְעֵיל כְּכָל חֶפְצוֹ וּרְצוֹנוֹ לִמְכּוֹר וְלִתֵּן בְּמַתָּנָה, וּלְהַשְׂכִּיר בְּלִי שׁוּם מוֹחֶה. וְכֵן יֵשׁ רְשׁוּת בְּיָדוֹ לִקַּח מִיָּד כָּל הַנִּזְכָּר לְעֵיל לְבֵיתוֹ. וְאַף אִם יַשְׁאִיר אוֹתָם כַּאֲשֶׁר הֵמָּה שָׁמָּה, מֵעַתָּה הַכֹּל הוּא בְּאַחֲרָיוּתוֹ שֶׁל הַקּוֹנֶה, וְאֵין עָלַי שׁוּם אַחֲרָיוּת, וַאֲפִלּוּ אַחֲרָיוּת אֹנֶס. וְנָתַתִּי לוֹ דְּרִיסַת הָרֶגֶל דֶּרֶךְ חֲצֵרִי וְדֶרֶךְ בֵּיתִי לֵילֵךְ לַמַּרְתֵּף וְלַחֶדֶר הַנִּזְכָּרִים לְעֵיל הַמֻּשְׂכָּרִים לוֹ. וְכֵן אִם יִרְצֶה בְּתוֹךְ מֶשֶׁךְ יְמֵי הַשְּׂכִירוּת לִמְכּוֹר מֵהַמִּטַּלְטְלִין לְאִישׁ אַחֵר, לְכָל הַבָּאִים מִדַּעְתּוֹ, לְכֻלָּם יֵשׁ לָהֶם דְּרִיסַת הָרֶגֶל. גַּם מָסַרְתִּי לוֹ אֶת הַמַּפְתְּחוֹת שֶׁל הַמַּרְתֵּף

Form of Contract for the Sale of Chametz

I, the undersigned, have sold hereby to the non-Jew (so-and-so) all the whiskey that I have in the cellar of my residence. The cellar is on the north side of the courtyard, another cellar is situated on the east side. All the whiskey that I have there, whether in medium-size barrels, or in large ones, I have sold to the above-mentioned party, together with the vessels for one hundred and twenty dollars. Also the arak-brandy that I have there, in a big bottle, about seven measures in size, I sold to him for five dollars, without the bottle. Also, the slivovitz, that I have there in a small barrel, I sold him for twelve dollars and fifty cents, together with the vessel. I also sold him six empty barrels, that once contained whiskey, and two large barrels with iron hoops, that once contained whiskey. I sold all of these for eight dollars and fifty cents. Also, five bags of wheat flour, that I have in a room called storage room, which is part of my residence, I sold to the above-mentioned party, together with the bags, for thirty-nine dollars, as well as all chametz vessels that I have there, such as kneading troughs and flour boxes, which I sold to him for four dollars and fifty cents. Also, barley, in a small bag that I have there, I sold to him for one dollar and fifty cents, together with the bag. I received a deposit from him of ten dollars; the balance I charge him as a loan. The time for payment to be no later than ten days from the date mentioned below. I rented to the said buyer, the above-mentioned cellar and the above-mentioned room, from now until the end of ten days, from the day mentioned below, for the amount of four dollars. I received a deposit of three dollars. The balance I charged as a loan, to be paid to me, no later than ten days from the date mentioned below. By means of the real estate rented to him, that is, the cellar and the room mentioned above, I conferred ownership to him of all the goods mentioned above. I hereby declare, truthfully, that I leased to him the cellar and the room mentioned above, and I conferred ownership to him of all goods mentioned above, by any and all means of acquisition that may be effective, whichever it may be; that the acquisition be binding, according to the laws of our holy Torah, and according to the civil law, without any claim or counterclaim. He has the right to do with all the above-mentioned, as he sees fit, to sell it or to give it as a gift, or to rent it, without any interference. He also has the right to move all the above-mentioned into his house; and even if he leaves them where they are at present, he assumes the responsibility for everything as of now, and I assume no responsibility whatsoever, not even the responsibility for accidental loss. I have given the buyer the right of access, to go through my courtyard and my house, to the above-mentioned cellar and room, that are leased to him. Also, if he wishes, during the term of the lease, to sell some of the goods to someone else, to all those who come with his consent, likewise have the right of access. I also surrendered to him the keys to the above-mentioned cellar and

וְשֶׁל הַחֶדֶר הַנִּזְכָּרִים לְעֵיל. כָּל זֶה נַעֲשָׂה בְּכָל אֹפֶן הַיּוֹתֵר מוֹעִיל עַל פִּי דִין תּוֹרָתֵנוּ הַקְּדוֹשָׁה, וְעַל פִּי נִימוּסֵי הַקֵּיסָר"ה וְהַמְּדִינָה.

אונגוואר י"ד תרל"ד

ראובן בר' שמעון איזראעלאוויטש

סִימָן קטו

דִּינֵי עֶרֶב פֶּסַח שֶׁחָל לִהְיוֹת בְּשַׁבָּת

א) עֶרֶב פֶּסַח שֶׁחָל לִהְיוֹת בְּשַׁבָּת, בּוֹדְקִין אֶת הֶחָמֵץ בְּלֵיל שְׁלֹשָׁה־עָשָׂר, דְּהַיְנוּ בַּלַּיְלָה הַשַּׁיָּךְ לְיוֹם הַשִּׁשִּׁי. וְאַחַר הַבְּדִיקָה מְבַטְּלוֹ, וְאוֹמֵר, כָּל חֲמִירָא וְכוּ', כְּמוֹ בְּפַעַם אַחֶרֶת, וּבְיוֹם הַשִּׁשִּׁי שׂוֹרְפוֹ גַּם כֵּן בַּזְּמַן שֶׁהוּא שׂוֹרְפוֹ בְּכָל עֶרֶב פֶּסַח. אֲבָל אֵינוֹ צָרִיךְ לוֹמַר, כָּל חֲמִירָא, אֶלָּא בְּשַׁבָּת לְאַחַר הָאֲכִילָה מְבַטְּלוֹ וְאוֹמֵר, כָּל חֲמִירָא וְכוּ'.

ב) הַבְּכוֹרִים מִתְעַנִּין בְּיוֹם הַחֲמִישִׁי. וְאִם קָשֶׁה לְהִתְעַנּוֹת עַד לְאַחַר בְּדִיקַת חָמֵץ, יָכוֹל לִטְעֹם אֵיזֶה דָּבָר מוּעָט קֹדֶם הַבְּדִיקָה אוֹ יַעֲשֶׂה שָׁלִיחַ לִבְדֹּק.

ג) אֵין מְבַשְּׁלִין לְשַׁבָּת זוֹ תַּבְשִׁילֵי קֶמַח וּגְרִיסִין, שֶׁיְּכוֹלִין לְהִדָּבֵק בַּקְּדֵרוֹת, וְאָסוּר לַהֲדִיחָן. עַל כֵּן יְבַשֵּׁל רַק מַאֲכָלִים שֶׁאֵינָם מִתְדַּבְּקִים. וְאַחַר הָאֲכִילָה מְנַעֵר הֵיטֵב אֶת הַמַּפָּה וּמַצְנִיעַ אוֹתָהּ עִם כָּל כְּלֵי הֶחָמֵץ בְּחֶדֶר שֶׁאֵינוֹ רָגִיל לָלֶכֶת שָׁמָּה בַּפֶּסַח. וְאִם נִשְׁאַר לוֹ מְעַט פַּת יִתְּנֶנָּה לְגוֹי, רַק יִזָּהֵר מֵאִסּוּר הוֹצָאָה (עַיֵּן לְעֵיל סִימָן פ"ב סָעִיף ט'). וּמְכַבְּדִין אֶת הַבַּיִת עַל יְדֵי גוֹי אוֹ בְּדָבָר הַמֻּתָּר.

ד) בַּבֹּקֶר, מִתְפַּלְּלִין בְּהַשְׁכָּמָה שֶׁלֹּא לְאַחֵר הַזְּמַן שֶׁמֻּתָּרִין בַּאֲכִילַת חָמֵץ. וְנָכוֹן לְחַלֵּק סְעוּדָתוֹ לִשְׁתַּיִם, דְּהַיְנוּ שֶׁיְּבָרֵךְ בִּרְכַּת־הַמָּזוֹן וּמַפְסִיק מְעַט בַּהֲלִיכָה וּבְדִבְרֵי תוֹרָה אוֹ בְּטִיּוּל, וְחוֹזֵר וְנוֹטֵל יָדָיו וְאוֹכֵל קְצָת וּמְבָרֵךְ שֵׁנִית בִּרְכַּת־הַמָּזוֹן, כְּדֵי לְקַיֵּם מִצְוַת סְעוּדָה שְׁלִישִׁית.

ה) נוֹהֲגִין לְהַפְטִיר בְּמַלְאָכִי וְעָרְבָה וְגוֹ', לְפִי שֶׁכָּתוּב שָׁם, הָבִיאוּ אֶת־כָּל־הַמַּעֲשֵׂר אֶל־בֵּית הָאוֹצָר וְגוֹ', וְהוּא מֵעִנְיָנָא. כִּי (לְפִי יֵשׁ אוֹמְרִים), הָיָה זְמַן הַבִּעוּר בְּעֶרֶב פֶּסַח שֶׁל הַשָּׁנָה הָרְבִיעִית שֶׁבַּשְּׁמִטָּה, וּבְעֶרֶב פֶּסַח שֶׁל הַשָּׁנָה הַשְּׁבִיעִית שֶׁבַּשְּׁמִטָּה, שֶׁכָּל הַמַּעַשְׂרוֹת שֶׁהִפְרִישׁ כָּל שָׁלֹשׁ שָׁנִים מִתְּבוּאָתוֹ וְהָיוּ מֻנָּחִים בְּבֵיתוֹ, מְחֻיָּב אָז לִתְּנָם לַלֵּוִי.

room. This was executed in the most expedient manner, according to the law of our holy Torah, and in accordance to the law of the land.

Ungvar 14th of Nisan 5634/1874

Reuvein ben Reb Shimon Israelovitz.

Chapter 115

The Laws of Erev Pesach When it Occurs on Shabbos

1) If *erev Pesach* occurs on Shabbos, we make the search for *chametz* on the eve of the thirteenth of *Nisan,* that is, on Thursday night. After concluding the search, you nullify the *chametz* by saying *Kol chamira* etc., as in other years, and on Friday, you burn it, at the same time that you burn it every *erev Pesach,* but you do not say *Kol chamira.* On Shabbos, after the meal, you nullify it and say *Kol Chamira* etc.

2) The firstborn fast on Thursday; and if it is difficult for a firstborn to fast, until after the search for the *chametz,* he may have a small snack before making the search, or else, he may appoint someone as his agent to make the search (and eat a full meal).

3) For this Shabbos, you should not cook dishes made with flour and grits, because they may stick to the pots, and it is forbidden to clean them on Shabbos. Therefore, you should cook only dishes that will not stick (to the pot). After the meal, you should shake the tablecloth well, and hide it away, together with the vessels used for *chametz,* in a room, where you do not usually go on *Pesach.* If any bread is left over, you should give it to a non-Jew; but you should be careful not to violate the law against removing things from one domain to another (see Chapter 82, par. 9 above). The house should be swept, either by a non-Jew, or with a sweeper that may be used on Shabbos.

4) On Shabbos morning, the *Shacharis* service should be said at an early hour, so that there should be enough time to eat a meal with *chametz,* while it is still permissible to do so. It is proper to divide the meal into two parts, that is (after eating one course) recite *Birkas Hamazon.* Make a short pause by discussing Torah thoughts or taking a walk,[1] then wash your hands again, eat and say *Birkas Hamazon* again. Thereby, you will have fulfilled the mitzvah of eating three meals on Shabbos.

5) It is customary to read the *Haftarah* from Malachi 3:4, *Ve'arvah* etc. because it is written there, "Bring all the tithes into the storehouse etc." That is appropriate for the day, for (according to some authorities), the time at which all tithes had to be removed from the house was on *erev Pesach* of the fourth year of the *Shemitah* cycle, and on *erev Pesach* of the seventh year of the *Shemitah* cycle. All the tithes which were separated from your grain during the three years, and which were kept in your house, had to be given to the *Levi* at the above-mentioned times.

1. If there is not sufficient time to pause between them, the meal should not be divided, as this will cause you to recite unnecessary berachos. It is, therefore, better to fulfill the mitzvah of eating the third meal, by eating meat, fish or fruits. (*Mishnah Berurah* 444:8).

ו) בְּעֶרֶב שַׁבָּת [זה] יִזָּהֵר כָּל אָדָם בִּמְאֹד מְאֹד לִשְׁאֹל, אִם הִפְרִישׁוּ חַלָּה מִן הַחַלּוֹת שֶׁאָפוּ לִכְבוֹד שַׁבָּת. כִּי אִם לֹא הִפְרִישׁוּ חַלָּה וְנִזְכְּרוּ בְּשַׁבָּת, יֵשׁ בָּזֶה מְבוּכָה גְדוֹלָה מַה לַּעֲשׂוֹת, כִּי אָסוּר לְהַפְרִישׁ חַלָּה בְּשַׁבָּת, וְגַם אָסוּר לְהַשְׁהוֹת אֶת הַחַלּוֹת. וְדַעַת הַ"מָּגֵן אַבְרָהָם", שֶׁצָּרִיךְ לִתֵּן כָּל הַחַלּוֹת לַגּוֹי בְּמַתָּנָה גְמוּרָה קֹדֶם שָׁעָה שֶׁנֶּאֱסָרוֹת בַּהֲנָאָה. וְיֵשׁ חוֹלְקִין וְכָתְבוּ תַּקָּנוֹת אֲחֵרוֹת וְכֻלָּן דְּחוּקוֹת. וְעַל כֵּן צְרִיכִין לִזָּהֵר בַּדָּבָר.

סִימָן קטז
דִּינֵי הַגְעָלָה

א) כָּל כְּלִי חֶרֶס שֶׁנִּשְׁתַּמֵּשׁ בּוֹ חָמֵץ, לָא מַהֲנֵי לֵהּ לֹא הַגְעָלָה וְלֹא לִבּוּן. אֲבָל הַתַּנּוּרִים וְהַכִּירוֹת הַבְּנוּיִים מֵאֲבָנִים וּלְבֵנִים, מַהֲנֵי לְהוּ לִבּוּן (וְעַיֵּן לְעֵיל סִימָן קי סָעִיף א וְסָעִיף ב). בְּתַנּוּרִים שֶׁיֵּשׁ בְּבֵית הַחֹרֶף, נוֹהֲגִין דְּלָא מַהֲנֵי לְהוּ הֶכְשֵׁר. וּכְשֶׁרוֹצִים לְהַעֲמִיד עַל הַתַּנּוּר אֵיזוֹ קְדֵרָה בְּפֶסַח, צְרִיכִין לְהָנִיחַ תְּחִלָּה טַס שֶׁל בַּרְזֶל וְעָלָיו מַעֲמִידִין הַקְּדֵרָה, וְזֶה מַהֲנֵי גַּם בְּתַנּוּר הֶעָשׂוּי מֵחֲרָסִים.

ב) כְּלֵי עֵץ וּכְלֵי מַתָּכוֹת וּכְלֵי אֶבֶן וּכְלֵי עֶצֶם מַהֲנֵי לְהוּ הַגְעָלָה. אַךְ אִם הוּא דָבָר שֶׁמִּתְקַלְקֵל בָּרוֹתְחִין, כְּגוֹן כֵּלִים הַמְדֻבָּקִים בְּדֶבֶק, וַאֲפִלּוּ אִם רַק הַקַּתָּא מְדֻבֶּקֶת בְּאֵיזֶה דֶבֶק, לָא מַהֲנֵי לֵהּ הַגְעָלָה, מִשּׁוּם דְּחַיְשִׁינָן שֶׁמָּא לֹא יַגְעִילוּ יָפֶה.

ג) קֹדֶם שֶׁמַּגְעִיל אֶת הַכְּלִי, צָרִיךְ לְנַקּוֹתוֹ הֵיטֵב מִן הַחֲלוּדָה וְכַדּוֹמֶה, שֶׁיְּהֵא נָקִי לְגַמְרֵי. אֲבָל מַרְאוֹת כְּתָמִים, אֵין בָּהֶם קְפִידָא. וְאִם יֵשׁ גּוּמוֹת בַּכְּלִי, צָרִיךְ לְנַקְּרָן הֵיטֵב. וְאִם הוּא כְּלִי מַתֶּכֶת, יָשִׂים עַל הַגּוּמוֹת גֶּחָלִים לְלַבֵּן שָׁם, וְאַחַר כָּךְ יַגְעִילוֹ. וְאִם אִי אֶפְשָׁר לְנַקּוֹת הֵיטֵב הַגּוּמוֹת וְהַסְּדָקִים, וְגַם אִי אֶפְשָׁר לְלַבֵּן שָׁם, אֵין לוֹ תַּקָּנָה. וְלָכֵן בְּסַכִּינִים עִם קַתּוֹת, צְרִיכִין לְדַקְדֵּק הֵיטֵב אִם מוֹעִילָה לָהֶן הַגְעָלָה. וּמִצְוָה מִן הַמֻּבְחָר לְמִי שֶׁאֶפְשָׁר לוֹ, שֶׁיִּקְנֶה לוֹ סַכִּינִים חֲדָשִׁים לַפֶּסַח.

ד) כֵּלִים שֶׁמִּשְׁתַּמְּשִׁים בָּהֶם עַל יְדֵי הָאוּר בְּלִי מַיִם, צְרִיכִין לִבּוּן.

---

1. This also applies, if the handle is made of any substance, that will be damaged by immersion in boiling water. (*Mishnah Berurah* 451:23)

6) On this Friday, every man should be very careful to ask whether *challah* has been separated from the *challah* loaves that were baked in honor of Shabbos, for if *challah* has not been separated, and you become aware of that on Shabbos, there is a great deal of confusion as to what should be done; because it is forbidden to separate *challah* on Shabbos, and it is also forbidden to keep the *challah* loaves because of Pesach. The *Magein Avraham* contends that all the loaves must be given to a non-Jew as an outright gift, before the time that their benefit is forbidden. Other authorities disagree and offer different solutions, but they all involve serious problems. Therefore, you must be careful about this.

Chapter 116

Laws of Kashering

1) Vessels made from earthenware that were used for *chametz* cannot be *kashered* by immersion in boiling water, nor by heating with charcoal or blow torch. Ovens and stoves made of stone and bricks can be *kashered* by heating with charcoal (or a blow torch) (see above Chapter 110, par. 1 and 2). It is customary not to *Kasher* stoves used for heating the house during the winter. If you want to place any kind of a dish on the stove, during *Pesach,* you must first put a metal plate on the stove and then place the dish on it. This method may be used also with an oven made of tiles.

2) Vessels made of wood, metal, stoneware or bone, can be *kashered* by immersing them in boiling water. But vessels that will be damaged by boiling water, such as vessels that are glued together, even if only the handle is glued on, cannot be *kashered* by immersion in boiling water,[1] because we are concerned that they will not be *kashered* properly.

3) Before *kashering* a vessel, you must clean it thoroughly to remove any rust,[2] or similar residue, making it perfectly clean; but rust stains do not matter.[3] If the vessel has dents, they should be scraped carefully (with steel wool etc.). If it is made of metal, you should place hot charcoal on the dents (or use a blow torch) to "glow" them, and then *kasher* the vessel with boiling water. If it is impossible to thoroughly clean the dents and the cracks, and if it is also impossible to "glow" them, then the vessel cannot be *kashered.*[4] Therefore, knives with handles must be carefully examined[5] to determine whether they can be *kashered.* The best way to do the mitzvah, if you can afford it, is to buy new knives for *Pesach.*

4) Vessels that are used over fire (or heat), without water, require glowing.

---

2. If, however, you are *kashering,* by using charcoal or a blow-torch, you need not remove the rust, because the flame or heat will also remove the rust. (*Ibid.* 451:24)

3. This refers to other stains as well.

4. Similarly, vessels, with a very narrow opening, that have rust in them, cannot be *kashered.* (*Ibid.* 451:26; See also *Kitzur Shulchan Aruch,* paragraph 10)

5. Handles, that are attached with nails or screws, cannot be *kashered.* (*Ibid.* 451:23)

וְלָכֵן הָאַגָּנוֹת וְהַמַּחֲבָתוֹת שֶׁאוֹפִין בָּהֶן חָמֵץ, צְרִיכִין לִבּוּן. וְהַלִּבּוּן צָרִיךְ לִהְיוֹת לְכַתְּחִלָּה לִבּוּן חָזָק עַד שֶׁיִּהְיוּ נִיצוֹצוֹת נִתָּזִין מִמֶּנּוּ. וְהַמַּרְדֶּה שֶׁל עֵץ אֵין לוֹ תַּקָּנָה.

ה) כְּלִי שֶׁיֵּשׁ בּוֹ טְלַאי, אִם הוּא בְּעִנְיָן שֶׁיֵּשׁ לָחוּשׁ שֶׁמָּא יֵשׁ תַּחַת הַטְּלַאי מַשֶּׁהוּ חָמֵץ בְּעַיִן, אֲזַי צָרִיךְ מִקֹּדֶם לְלַבֵּן אוֹתוֹ מָקוֹם עַד שֶׁיֵּדַע בְּבֵרוּר, שֶׁאִם הָיָה שָׁם מַשֶּׁהוּ חָמֵץ הָיָה נִשְׂרָף, וְאַחַר כָּךְ יַגְעִילוֹ. וְאִם אֵין חֲשָׁשׁ שֶׁיְּהֵא שָׁם חָמֵץ בְּעַיִן, אֲזַי אִם הָיָה הַטְּלַאי נַעֲשֶׂה קֹדֶם שֶׁהִשְׁתַּמְּשׁוּ בּוֹ חָמֵץ, יָכוֹל לְהַגְעִילוֹ כְּמוֹ שֶׁהוּא, דִּכְמוֹ שֶׁבָּלַע אֶת הֶחָמֵץ, כָּךְ יִפְלְטֶנּוּ בְּהַגְעָלָה. אֲבָל אִם נִשְׁתַּמֵּשׁ תְּחִלָּה בִּכְלִי חָמֵץ, וְאַחַר כָּךְ שָׂמוּ אֶת הַטְּלַאי, אֲזַי לָא מַהֲנֵי לֵהּ הַהַגְעָלָה לַמָּקוֹם שֶׁתַּחַת הַטְּלַאי, אֶלָּא צָרִיךְ לִתֵּן גַּם כֵּן קֹדֶם הַהַגְעָלָה גֶּחָלִים עַל הַטְּלַאי לְלַבֵּן אֶת הַמָּקוֹם הַהוּא. וְאִם הַטְּלַאי נִתְחַבֵּר בְּהַתָּכַת בְּדִיל אוֹ כֶּסֶף וְכַדּוֹמֶה, יָכוֹל לְהַגְעִילוֹ כְּמוֹ שֶׁהוּא, כִּי בְּלִיעַת הֶחָמֵץ נִשְׂרְפָה אָז בַּהַתָּכָה.

ו) מְדוֹכָה בְּמָקוֹם שֶׁדַּרְכָּן לָדוּךְ בָּהּ דְּבָרִים חֲרִיפִים עִם חָמֵץ בְּיַחַד, צְרִיכָה לִבּוּן קַל, דְּהַיְנוּ שֶׁמְּמַלְּאִין אוֹתָהּ גֶּחָלִים בּוֹעֲרוֹת שֶׁתִּרְתַּח כָּל כָּךְ עַד שֶׁהַקַּשׁ נִשְׂרָף עָלֶיהָ מִבַּחוּץ. וּבְמָקוֹם שֶׁאֵין דַּרְכָּן לָדוּךְ בָּהּ רַק פִּלְפְּלִין וְכַדּוֹמֶה, סַגֵּי בְּהַגְעָלָה.

ז) כֵּלִים שֶׁהֶחֱזִיק בָּהֶם יֵין־שָׂרָף לְקִיּוּם, אֵין טַעַם וְרֵיחַ יֵין־הַשָּׂרָף נִפְלָט עַל יְדֵי הַגְעָלָה, רַק אִם בִּשֵּׁל אוֹתָן הֵיטֵב בְּמַיִם עִם אֵפֶר עַד שֶׁנִּסְתַּלֵּק מֵהֶם הָרֵיחַ לְגַמְרֵי, מוֹעִילָה לָהֶם אַחַר כָּךְ הַגְעָלָה.

ח) הַגְעָלַת הֶחָבִית יַעֲשֶׂה בְּדֶרֶךְ זֶה, יְלַבֵּן אֲבָנִים וְיָשִׂימַן בָּהּ, וִיעָרֶה עֲלֵיהֶן מַיִם רוֹתְחִין מִכְּלִי רִאשׁוֹן, וִיגַלְגֵּל אֶת הֶחָבִית כְּדֵי שֶׁתַּגִּיעַ הַהַגְעָלָה לְכָל מָקוֹם. וַחֲבִיּוֹת שֶׁלָּנוּ שֶׁהֵן עֲשׂוּיוֹת מִכַּמָּה דַּפִּים מְחֻבָּרִים בַּחֲשׁוּקִים, אִם עָמַד בָּהֶן חָמֵץ, כְּגוֹן יֵין־שָׂרָף אוֹ שֶׁהֶחֱזִיק בָּהֶן קֶמַח, לָא מַהֲנֵי לְהוּ הַגְעָלָה.

ט) כָּל דָּבָר שֶׁצָּרִיךְ הַגְעָלָה, לָא מַהֲנֵי לֵהּ קְלִיפָה, אֶלָּא דַּוְקָא הַגְעָלָה.

י) כָּל כְּלִי שֶׁאִי אֶפְשָׁר לְנַקּוֹתוֹ הֵיטֵב, כְּגוֹן הַנָּפָה, וְכִיס שֶׁל רֵחַיִם, וְכֵן סַלִּים שֶׁמִּשְׁתַּמְּשִׁים בָּהֶם חָמֵץ, וְכֵן מְגֶרֶדֶת, וְכֵן כְּלִי שֶׁפִּיו צַר וְאִי אֶפְשָׁר לְשַׁפְשְׁפוֹ מִבִּפְנִים, אוֹ שֶׁיֵּשׁ לוֹ קָנִים, לָא מַהֲנֵי לֵהּ הַגְעָלָה.

Therefore, baking and frying pans, in which *chametz* was baked,[6] require glowing. Initially, the vessel must be heated so intensely, that it shoots off sparks. A wooden peel cannot be *kashered.*

5) If a vessel has a patch, and there is reason to suspect that underneath the patch, some *chametz* may have become trapped, that place must first be glowed until you are certain, that if there was a trace of *chametz,* it was burned; and then it should be *kashered* in boiling water. But if there is no reason to suspect that a trace of *chametz* was trapped there, then, if the patch was put on before the vessel was used for *chametz,* you may *kasher* it as is, because, just as the vessel absorbed the *chametz,* so it will expel it with the boiling water (used in the *kashering*). However, if the vessel was first used for *chametz,* and the patch was put on afterwards, then the *kashering* has no effect on the place underneath the patch, and in this case, too, before *kashering,* you must place hot charcoal on the patch, to glow that spot. If the patch was soldered with lead, silver, or similar solder, it may be *kashered* as is, since the *chametz* that has been absorbed, was burned by soldering.

6) A mortar, which is ordinarily used for pounding sharp tasting spices together with *chametz,* requires *libun kal* —"simple glowing", that is, it should be filled with burning charcoal, until it is hot enough to burn a piece of straw placed on the outside of the vessel. But in a community, where it is customary to pound in it, only pepper and similar spices, *kashering* with boiling water is sufficient.

7) In vessels that were used to age whiskey, the taste and aroma of the whiskey is not eliminated by *kashering* with boiling water. Only if you first boil them thoroughly in water and ashes, until the aroma has disappeared completely, can they then be *kashered* in boiling water.

8) The *kashering* of a barrel, should be done as follows: place heated stones in it, and pour boiling water on them out of the vessel, in which the water was boiled; then roll the barrel, so that the hot water will reach every part of it. The type of barrels which we use, are made of many planks hooped together and if they contained *chametz,* such as whiskey, or if flour, *kashering* is of no avail.

9) When a vessel requires *kashering* with boiling water, merely scouring the surface is of no avail,[7] it must be immersed in boiling water.

10) *Kashering* is of no avail regarding vessels that cannot be thoroughly cleaned, such as a sieve, the receptacle of a grinder, baskets used for keeping *chametz,* a grater, as well as any vessel that has a narrow opening, which is impossible to clean on the inside, (or a vessel) that has a spout.

---

6. If, however, they were used for meat or fish and you are certain that *chametz* was never baked in them, it is sufficient to immerse them in boiling water. (*Ibid.* 451:27)

7. Because the entire thickness of the walls have absorbed the *chametz.* (*Ibid.* 451:26)

יא) הַתֵּבוֹת שֶׁמַּצְנִיעִים בָּהֶן מַאֲכָלִים כָּל הַשָּׁנָה, וְלִפְעָמִים נִשְׁפָּךְ שָׁם מָרָק מִן הַקְּדֵרוֹת, צְרִיכִין הֶכְשֵׁר קַל, דְּהַיְנוּ שֶׁמְּעָרִין עֲלֵיהֶן רוֹתְחִין. וְדַוְקָא מִתּוֹךְ הַכְּלִי שֶׁהִרְתִּיחוּ בּוֹ אֶת הַמַּיִם. וְלֹא יִזְרוֹק אֶת הַמַּיִם, אֶלָּא יִשְׁפְּכֵם עֲלֵיהֶן בְּקִלּוּחַ. וְהַשֻּׁלְחָנוֹת, נוֹהֲגִין גַּם כֵּן לְלַבֵּן אֲבָנִים וּמַנִּיחָן עַל הַשֻּׁלְחָן, וְשׁוֹפְכִין עֲלֵיהֶן רוֹתְחִין, וּמוֹלִיכִין אֶת הָאֲבָנִים מִמָּקוֹם לְמָקוֹם בְּאֹפֶן שֶׁיִּהְיוּ מַיִם רוֹתְחִים עַל פְּנֵי כֻלּוֹ. וּצְרִיכִין לְשַׁפְשְׁפָן מִקֹּדֶם, וְאַחַר מְעַט־לְעֵת יַכְשִׁירוּם. וּמִכָּל מָקוֹם יֵשׁ נוֹהֲגִין שֶׁלֹּא לְהִשְׁתַּמֵּשׁ גַּם אַחַר הַהֶכְשֵׁר בְּשֻׁלְחָנוֹת וּבְתֵבוֹת, אֶלָּא בִּפְרִיסַת מַפָּה אוֹ דָבָר אַחֵר.

יב) יְדוֹת הַכֵּלִים צְרִיכוֹת גַּם כֵּן הֶכְשֵׁר. וּמִכָּל מָקוֹם אִם אֵין הַיָּד נִכְנֶסֶת לְתוֹךְ הַיּוֹרָה, יָכוֹל לְהַכְשִׁיר אֶת הַיָּד בִּשְׁפִיכַת רוֹתְחִין עָלֶיהָ.

יג) כָּל כְּלֵי שְׁתִיָּה וּכְלֵי הַמִּדּוֹת, צְרִיכִין גַּם כֵּן הַגְעָלָה. וּכְלֵי זְכוּכִית, נוֹהֲגִין בִּמְדִינוֹת אֵלּוּ דְּלָא מַהֲנֵי לְהוּ הַגְעָלָה. וְכֵן כְּלֵי מַתֶּכֶת שֶׁהֵן מֻתָּכִין מִבִּפְנִים בְּהִתּוּךְ זְכוּכִית, אֵין לָהֶם תַּקָּנָה בְּהַגְעָלָה, אֲבָל סַגֵּי לְהוּ בְּלִבּוּן קַל, כְּמוֹ מְדוּכָה בְּסָעִיף ו'.

יד) אֵין מַגְעִילִין אֶלָּא בְּמַיִם וְלֹא יְהֵא בָהֶם שׁוּם תַּעֲרֹבֶת, אֲפִלּוּ אֵפֶר וְכַדּוֹמֶה. אִם הִגְעִיל הַרְבֵּה בְּיוֹרָה עַד שֶׁנֶּעְכְּרוּ הַמַּיִם כְּעֵין צִיר, אֵין מַגְעִילִין עוֹד בָּהֶם.

טו) אִם מַגְעִיל עַל יְדֵי צְבָת שֶׁמַּחֲזִיק בָּהּ אֶת הַכְּלִי, צָרִיךְ לְרַפּוֹת אֶת הַכְּלִי וְלַחֲזוֹר וּלְתָפְסוֹ. דְּאִם לֹא כֵן, הֲרֵי לֹא בָּאוּ מֵימֵי הַהַגְעָלָה בִּמְקוֹם הַצְּבָת. וְטוֹב יוֹתֵר לָשִׂים אֶת הַכְּלִי בְּמַחֲרוֹזֶה אוֹ בְּתוֹךְ סָל. וְלֹא יַנִּיחַ כֵּלִים הַרְבֵּה בְּפַעַם אַחַת לְתוֹךְ הַכְּלִי שֶׁהוּא מַגְעִיל בּוֹ, כְּדֵי שֶׁלֹּא יִגְּעוּ זֶה בָּזֶה. דְּאִם כֵּן, בִּמְקוֹם נְגִיעָתָן אֵינָן מֻגְעָלִין.

טז) אֵין לְהַגְעִיל אֶלָּא כְּלִי שֶׁאֵינוֹ בֶּן־יוֹמוֹ, דְּהַיְנוּ שֶׁכְּבָר עָבַר

8. This is only when hot foods are kept in them, but otherwise, they do not require *kashering*. (*Ibid.* 451:113)

9. Others hold that since hot puddings, that contain *chametz,* are sometimes placed there, they require that hot stones be placed on them, (similar to *kashering* tables, that are discussed in this paragraph). (*Ibid.* 451:114)

10. You must not use another vessel to dip into the vessel containing the boiling water and then pour it onto the surface from the second vessel. (*Ibid.* 451:20)

11) A cabinet, in which food is kept[8] the entire year, and soup is sometimes spilled there from the pots, requires simple *kashering,* that is pouring boiling water on it;[9] but it must be poured out of the vessel, in which the water was boiled.[10] The water should not be thrown, but it should be poured in a steady stream. (As for *kashering*) tables, it is also customary to place glowing hot stones on the table, and pour boiling water on them, and then to move the stones from place to place in such a manner, that the boiling water covers the entire surface. The table must be scrubbed first, and after twenty-four hours, it should be *kashered,* in the manner described above. Nevertheless, some people are accustomed, not to use tables and chests even after *kashering*, without covering them with a cloth or something else.

12) Handles of vessels also require *kashering.* However, if the handle does not fit into the *kashering* pot, you should *kasher* the handle, by pouring boiling water on it.[11]

13) Vessels used for drinking or measuring, also require *kashering.*[12] As for glassware, it is the custom in these regions not to *kasher* them.[13] Vessels made of metal, glazed on the inside, cannot be kashered by immersion in boiling water; but "simple glowing" is sufficient, just as with a mortar, see par. 6.

14) Only water should be used for *kashering,* and nothing should be mixed with it, not even ashes or similar substances. If you *kashered* many vessels in one *kashering* kettle, so that the water became thick and filmy like soup, you should not continue to *kasher* with it.

15) If you *kasher,* using a pair of tongs, to hold the vessel, you should relax your hold on the vessel, and then grip it firmly again; otherwise, the *kashering* water would not reach the spot held by the tongs. It is better to put the vessel in a net or in a basket. You should not put many vessels at one time into the kettle in which you *kasher,* so that they should not touch each other; otherwise, the place where they touch, would not be *kashered.*

16) You should not *kasher* a vessel that has been used the same day, that is, unless

---

11. However, if you know, for certain, that the handles were immersed in boiling liquid, containing *chametz*; pouring hot water over them will not help, but they must be *kashered* in the regular way by immersion, then in boiling water. (*Ibid.* 451:71)

12. There is another method for *kashering* drinking glasses. If they have not been used during a twenty-four hour period, you may fill them, even with cold water, allowing the water to overflow, and then leave the water in the glasses for twenty-four hours. After twenty-four hours, you spill out the water and refill the glasses with new water. After twenty-four hours, you spill out the water and repeat the process a third time. This need not be done in consecutive days, so long as it was repeated thrice, as outlined. (*Ibid.* 451:150)

13. In a situation where new glasses cannot be purchased, and you have no other drinking vessels, the *Chayei Adam* writes that you may rely on the *kashering,* described in note 12 above. (*Ibid.* 451:156)

מֵעֵת־לְעֵת מִשָּׁעָה שֶׁבִּשְּׁלוּ בּוֹ חָמֵץ. וְכֵן הַיּוֹרָה שֶׁמַּגְעִילִין בָּהּ, לֹא תְהֵא בַּת־יוֹמָהּ. וְיַשְׁגִּיחַ שֶׁבְּכָל פַּעַם שֶׁהוּא נוֹתֵן אֶת הַכְּלִי לְתוֹךְ הַיּוֹרָה, יַעֲלוּ הַמַּיִם רְתִיחוֹת. וְאִם צָרִיךְ לְהַגְעִיל אֶת הַיּוֹרָה, אֲזַי כְּשֶׁהַמַּיִם מַעֲלִין רְתִיחוֹת, תְּהֵא הַיּוֹרָה מְלֵאָה וְיִזְרוֹק בָּהּ אֲבָנִים מְלֻבָּנוֹת, כְּדֵי שֶׁיִּשְׁטְפוּ הַמַּיִם הָרוֹתְחִין עַל שְׂפָתָהּ. וְאֵין לְהַגְעִיל [בְּעֶרֶב פֶּסַח] רַק עַד חֲצוֹת הַיּוֹם.

יז) נוֹהֲגִין שֶׁאַחַר הַהַגְעָלָה שׁוֹטְפִים אֶת הַכֵּלִים בְּמַיִם קָרִים.

יח) אִם אֶפְשָׁר, יֵשׁ לְהַגְעִיל בִּפְנֵי בַּעַל תּוֹרָה הַבָּקִי בְּדִינֵי הַגְעָלָה.

סִימָן קיז
קְצָת דִּינִים מְלֻקָּטִים לְפֶסַח

א) אִם נִמְצְאָה אֵיזוֹ תַּעֲרֹבֶת חָמֵץ בְּעֶרֶב פֶּסַח עַד הַלַּיְלָה, הֲרֵי הִיא כְּמוֹ שְׁאָר אִסּוּרִין שֶׁבְּטֵלִים בְּשִׁשִּׁים. וְלָכֵן אִם נִמְצָא גַּרְעִין בְּעוֹף וּבְתַבְשִׁיל, זוֹרְקוֹ, וְהַשְּׁאָר מֻתָּר לֶאֱכוֹל אֲפִלּוּ בְּפֶסַח. אֲבָל בְּתוֹךְ הַפֶּסַח, חָמֵץ אוֹסֵר אֲפִלּוּ בְּמַשֶּׁהוּ גַּם בַּהֲנָאָה. וּבְכָל מָקוֹם שֶׁנִּמְצָא אֵיזֶה גַּרְעִין מֵחֲמֵשֶׁת מִינֵי דָגָן אוֹ מַשֶּׁהוּ חָמֵץ, צְרִיכִין לַעֲשׂוֹת שְׁאֵלָה.

ב) בְּאֵר מַיִם שֶׁנִּמְצְאוּ בָהּ גַּרְעִינֵי תְבוּאָה, אֵין לְהִסְתַּפֵּק מֵהַמַּיִם הָאֵלּוּ אֶלָּא בְּדֹחַק גָּדוֹל, כְּגוֹן שֶׁאֵין מַיִם אֲחֵרִים בְּנִמְצָא. וְאִם נִמְצְאָה בָהּ חֲתִיכַת פַּת, אָסוּר, אֲפִלּוּ אֵין מַיִם אֲחֵרִים. וְגַם סִנּוּן לָא מַהֲנֵי.

ג) נוֹהֲגִין שֶׁלֹּא לְהַבְהֵב אֶת הָעוֹפוֹת בְּקַשׁ שֶׁעִם הַשִּׁבֳּלִים, כִּי חָיְשִׁינַן שֶׁמָּא יֵשׁ בָּהֶן גַּרְעִין מְחֻמָּץ. וְלָכֵן מְהַבְהֲבִין בַּעֲשָׂבִים אוֹ חוֹתְכִין אֶת הַשִּׁבֳּלִים מִן הַקַּשׁ. וּבְדִיעֲבַד מֻתָּר. וְיִזָּהֲרוּ לִטּוֹל אֶת הַזֶּפֶק מִן הָעוֹף קֹדֶם שֶׁמְּהַבְהֲבִין אוֹתוֹ.

ד) כָּל מִינֵי קִטְנִיּוֹת, אֲסוּרִים. וְכֵן כָּל מִינֵי פֵּרוֹת יְבֵשִׁים, אֲסוּרִין,

---

14. This should be done immediately, so that the vessel will not absorb the boiling water of the *kashering* vessel. (*Ibid.* 452:34)

1. This is said, in reference to *chametz* in liquid form, that has become mixed with other liquid; or if the *chametz* has contributed to the taste of the mixture. Regarding dry *chametz*, that has been mixed with other dry foods, (see *Shulchan Aruch* and *Ramah* 447:4.)

2. This is true also if the *chametz* and the other food are of the same species, i.e. vinegar and vinegar, soup and soup. (*Biyur Halachah* 447:2)

twenty-four hours have passed, since *chametz* was cooked in it. Likewise, the kettle, in which the *kashering* is done, should not have been used that same day. You should pay attention that the water is still bubbling when you put a vessel in the kettle. If the kettle, itself, has to be *kashered,* then, when the water is boiling, it must be full and you should throw glowing stones into it, so that the boiling water will overflow its rim. On *erev Pesach, kashering* must be done, only until midday.

17) It is customary, after *kashering,* to rinse the vessels with cold water.[14]

18) If possible, the *kashering* should be done in the presence of a Torah scholar, who is well versed in the laws of *kashering.*

Chapter 117

Various Laws Concerning Pesach

1) If you find any *chametz* in food[1] on *erev Pesach,* anytime before nightfall, it is like any other forbidden substance, which is nullified if it becomes mixed (into a permitted subtance), sixty times its volume.[2] Therefore, if you find a grain of seed in poultry or in cooked food, you should throw away the seed, and you may eat the rest, even on *Pesach.*[3] But during *Pesach,* itself, even the smallest bit of *chametz* makes food forbidden (to eat) and to derive benefit from it. Thus, wherever you find a seed of the five species of grain, or a small particle of *chametz,* you should consult a competent *Posek.*

2) If grain seeds are found in a water well, you should not use this water, except in case of urgent need,[4] for example, if no other water is available. But if you find a piece of bread in the well, the water is forbidden to be used, even if no other water is available and even filtering is of no use.

3) It is the custom not to singe poultry with straw bearing ears of grain, for we are concerned that one of the seeds may be *chametz.* We, therefore, singe poultry with grass, or we cut the ears off of the straw. But, if inadvertently, (the poultry was singed with straw bearing ears of grain), the poultry may be used. You should take care to remove the crop from the poultry, before you singe it.[5]

4) All kinds of legumes are forbidden;[6] and all kinds of dried fruit are forbidden,

---

3. This is true, only when the cooked food had been cooled before *Pesach.* (If the food was still warm on *Pesach,* it had absorbed the *chametz* on *Pesach* and would be forbidden). (*Mishnah Berurah* 447:19)

4. This is certainly true if the seed is still whole, but only soft. (*Ibid.* 467:62)

5. Those who are scrupulous, in their observance, are careful to split the chicken in half, in order to examine it very carefully for any kernels of wheat or other *chametz.* (*Ibid.* 467:86)

6. They are forbidden, only so far as eating, but they may be kept over *Pesach,* and their benefit is not forbidden. When there is an urgent need, such as when there is no other food to eat, or for a sick person (who needs such food), it is permitted. (*Ibid.* 453:6,7,12; 465:4) Some of the typical legumes that we must not eat are the various species of beans, rice and peas.

אֶלָּא אִם כֵּן נוֹדַע שֶׁנִּתְיַבְּשׁוּ בְּהֶכְשֵׁר עַל גַּבֵּי קָנִים אוֹ בְּתַנּוּר שֶׁהֻכְשַׁר לְשֵׁם פֶּסַח. אֲפִלּוּ תְּאֵנִים יְבֵשׁוֹת וְצִמּוּקִים, בֵּין גְּדוֹלִים בֵּין קְטַנִּים, אֲסוּרִין. וְכֵן קְלִפּוֹת תַּפּוּחֵי זָהָב. וּמִכָּל מָקוֹם הַמַּשְׁקֶה שֶׁעוֹשִׂין מִן הַצִּמּוּקִין, נוֹהֲגִין הֶתֵּר לִשְׁתּוֹתוֹ. נוֹהֲגִין שֶׁלֹּא לִתֵּן לְתוֹךְ הַתַּבְשִׁיל צִפֹּרֶן וְכַרְכֹּם, מִפְּנֵי שֶׁיֵּשׁ בָּהֶם חֲשַׁשׁ חִמּוּץ. וַאֲפִלּוּ כַּרְכֹּם הַגְּדֵלָה בִּמְדִינָתֵנוּ בַּגַּנּוֹת, אָסוּר, מִשּׁוּם לָא פַּלוּג. וּשְׁאָר בְּשָׂמִים שֶׁאֵין בָּהֶם חֲשַׁשׁ חִמּוּץ, וְכֵן הַמֶּלַח, קֹדֶם שֶׁנּוֹתְנִים אוֹתָם לַתַּבְשִׁיל, צְרִיכִים לְבָדְקָם אִם אֵין אֵיזֶה גַּרְעִין תְּבוּאָה מְעֹרָב בָּהֶם.

ה) דְּבַשׁ, אֵין אוֹכְלִין אֶלָּא מַה שֶּׁלֹּא נִתְרַסֵּק, אוֹ שֶׁנִּתְרַסֵּק עַל יְדֵי יִשְׂרָאֵל לְשֵׁם פֶּסַח.

ו) בִּשְׁעַת הַדְּחָק, כְּגוֹן לְצֹרֶךְ חוֹלֶה, אוֹ זָקֵן, מַתִּירִין לֶאֱפוֹת מַצּוֹת עִם מֵי בֵּיצִים אוֹ שְׁאָר מֵי פֵּרוֹת, כְּגוֹן חָלָב אוֹ יַיִן וְכַדּוֹמֶה, וְהִיא נִקְרֵאת מַצָּה עֲשִׁירָה, וּבִלְבַד שֶׁיִּזָּהֲרוּ שֶׁלֹּא יִתְעָרֵב בָּהֶם אֲפִלּוּ מְעַט מַיִם. אֲבָל בִּשְׁנֵי הַלֵּילוֹת הָרִאשׁוֹנִים צְרִיכִין לֶאֱכוֹל מַצָּה מַמָּשׁ, וְאֵין יוֹצְאִין בְּמַצָּה עֲשִׁירָה. וְשֶׁלֹּא לְצֹרֶךְ גָּדוֹל, אָסוּר לֶאֱפוֹת מַצָּה עֲשִׁירָה. אֲפִלּוּ קֹדֶם פֶּסַח לְשֵׁם פֶּסַח.

ז) הַנּוֹתֵן תְּבוּאָה אוֹ מֻרְסָן לִפְנֵי עוֹפוֹת, יִזָּהֵר לְתִתָּם בְּמָקוֹם יָבֵשׁ, שֶׁלֹּא יִתְלַחְלָחוּ. אֲבָל לִבְהֵמָה, אָסוּר לִתֵּן מֻרְסָן, כִּי יִתְלַחְלַח מִן הָרֹק. וְגַם אִם נוֹתֵן לָהּ תְּבוּאָה, יִזָּהֵר לָתֵת לָהּ מְעַט מְעַט, שֶׁלֹּא תַשְׁאִיר מְלַחְלָחִים. וְאִם הִשְׁאִירָה, יְבַעֲרֵם מִיָּד.

ח) בְּעֶרֶב פֶּסַח מִשָּׁעָה שֶׁהֶחָמֵץ נֶאֱסָר בַּהֲנָאָה, וְכֵן בְּכָל יְמֵי הַפֶּסַח, אָסוּר לֵהָנוֹת אֲפִלּוּ מֵחֲמֵצוֹ שֶׁל גּוֹי. וְלָכֵן אָסוּר לְיִשְׂרָאֵל לְהוֹלִיךְ אוֹ לִשְׁמוֹר חֲמֵצוֹ שֶׁל גּוֹי. וּמִכָּל־שֶׁכֵּן דְּאָסוּר לִקְנוֹת חָמֵץ בִּשְׁבִיל גּוֹי, וַאֲפִלּוּ בִּמְעוֹתָיו שֶׁל גּוֹי.

ט) וְכֵן אָסוּר לְהַשְׂכִּיר אָז לַגּוֹי בְּהֵמָה שֶׁתָּבִיא לוֹ חָמֵץ, אוֹ חֶדֶר לָשִׂים בּוֹ חָמֵץ, מִפְּנֵי שֶׁאָסוּר לְהִשְׂתַּכֵּר בְּאִסּוּרֵי הֲנָאָה. אֲבָל מֻתָּר לְהַשְׂכִּיר לוֹ בְּהֵמָה לְשָׁבוּעַ שֶׁל פֶּסַח (חוּץ מִשַּׁבָּת וְיוֹם־טוֹב) בִּסְתָם, שֶׁאֵין הַגּוֹי מְפָרֵשׁ לוֹ שֶׁהוּא צָרִיךְ אוֹתָהּ לְהָבִיא חָמֵץ, אַף־עַל־פִּי שֶׁהוּא יוֹדֵעַ

unless it is known that they have been dried in a proper way on planks, or in a stove that has been made kosher for *Pesach* (see above 110: 1 and 2). Even dried figs and raisins, whether large or small, are forbidden to be used; orange peels are also forbidden. Nevertheless, the beverage prepared from raisins, is customarily permitted to drink. It is the custom not to put cloves or saffron into food because they are suspect of containing *chametz.* Even in our regions, where saffron is raised in gardens, it is forbidden, in order not to make an exception (to the law). There are spices, including salt, that are not suspect of containing *chametz.* However, before putting them into the food, you should examine them to see whether there are any grain seeds in them.[7]

5) You should only eat honey, that has not been removed from the comb, or honey, that has been taken out of the comb by a Jew, to be used specifically for *Pesach.*[8]

6) In case of great urgency, for example, when it is needed for a sick or elderly person, it is permissible to bake matzos with eggs, fruit juice, milk, wine, or similar beverage, and this is called *matzah ashirah* (rich matzah). Care should be taken, however, not to mix any water with it. However on the first two nights of *Pesach,* actual matzah must be eaten; you have not fulfilled your duty, if you eat *matzah ashirah.* If there is no urgent need, it is forbidden to bake *matzah ashirah,* even before *Pesach,* to be used on *Pesach.*

7) If you feed grain or meal to fowl, you should be careful to put it in a dry place, so that it should not become wet. But it is forbidden to feed meal to cattle, since it becomes wet from their saliva; and when feeding them grain, you should be careful to give them a little at a time, so that no wet grain is left over. If there is any grain left over, you must clear it away immediately.

8) On *erev Pesach,* from the time *chametz* is forbidden, as well as during the entire week of Pesach, it is forbidden to derive any benefit, even from *chametz* belonging to a non-Jew. A Jew is, therefore, forbidden to haul or to guard *chametz,* belonging to a non-Jew. It goes without saying, that a Jew is forbidden to buy *chametz* for a non-Jew, even with the money belonging to the non-Jew.

9) During Pesach, it is forbidden to rent an animal to a non-Jew for the purpose of carrying *chametz* to him, or to rent him a room for the purpose of storing *chametz* in it, because it is forbidden to make profit from things, from which you are forbidden to benefit. But you are permitted to rent him an animal for the week of *Pesach* (except for Shabbos and Yom Tov), for an unspecified purpose,[9] as when the

7. Needless to say, that dried fruits, spices, salt, etc. are permitted in our times, when they have proper, authorative kosher certification.

8. See note 7.

9. This applies only to animals, but pots or other vessels, that are usually used for cooking, may not be rented to him, under any circumstances, because he will probably cook items containing *chametz* in them. (*Ibid.* 450:11, *Shaarei Tzion* 46)

שֶׁהַגּוֹי יוֹלִיךְ עָלֶיהָ חָמֵץ, אֵין בְּכָךְ כְּלוּם. דְּכֵיוָן שֶׁאַף אִם לֹא יוֹלִיךְ עָלֶיהָ כְּלוּם, יִצְטָרֵךְ לִפְרוֹעַ לַיִּשְׂרָאֵל כָּל שְׂכָרוֹ מִשָּׁלֵם, אֵין הַיִּשְׂרָאֵל מִשְׂתַּכֵּר כְּלוּם מֵהֶחָמֵץ. וְכֵן מֻתָּר לְהַשְׂכִּיר לוֹ חֶדֶר שֶׁיָּדוּר בּוֹ בְּפֶסַח, אַף־עַל־פִּי שֶׁיּוֹדֵעַ שֶׁיַּכְנִיס לְתוֹכוֹ חָמֵץ, מִכָּל מָקוֹם הַיִּשְׂרָאֵל אֵינוֹ נוֹטֵל מִמֶּנּוּ שְׂכַר הַכְנָסַת הֶחָמֵץ, אֶלָּא שְׂכַר הַדִּירָה, שֶׁאַף אִם לֹא יַכְנִיס לְשָׁם חָמֵץ, לֹא יְנַכֶּה מִשְּׂכָרוֹ.

י) אָסוּר לִמְסוֹר אֲפִלּוּ זְמַן הַרְבֵּה קֹדֶם פֶּסַח בְּהֶמְתּוֹ לַגּוֹי, כְּשֶׁיּוֹדֵעַ שֶׁיַּאֲכִילֶנָּה חָמֵץ בְּפֶסַח.

יא) מֻתָּר לוֹמַר לִמְשָׁרְתוֹ גּוֹי, אֲפִלּוּ בְּשָׁעָה שֶׁהֶחָמֵץ אָסוּר בַּהֲנָאָה, הֵילָךְ מָעוֹת וּקְנֵה לְךָ מְזוֹנוֹת וֶאֱכוֹל, אַף־עַל־פִּי שֶׁהוּא יוֹדֵעַ שֶׁיִּקְנֶה חָמֵץ. וּבִשְׁעַת הַדְּחָק, מֻתָּר גַּם כֵּן לוֹמַר לוֹ, צֵא וֶאֱכוֹל אֵצֶל גּוֹי וַאֲנִי אֶפְרַע לוֹ, אוֹ לוֹמַר לְגוֹי אַחֵר, תֵּן לִמְשָׁרְתִי לֶאֱכוֹל וַאֲנִי אֲשַׁלֵּם לָךְ. אֲבָל אָסוּר לְהַקְדִּים לוֹ אֶת הַמָּעוֹת בִּשְׁבִיל מַה שֶּׁיִּתֵּן לִמְשָׁרְתוֹ.

יב) וְכֵן מִי שֶׁהוּא צָרִיךְ לְהַאֲכִיל לַתִּינוֹק חָמֵץ, יִשָּׂאֵהוּ אֶל גּוֹי וְיַאֲכִילֵהוּ הַגּוֹי חָמֵץ וְיִפְרַע לוֹ הַיִּשְׂרָאֵל אַחַר כָּךְ. אֲבָל הַיִּשְׂרָאֵל, לֹא יַאֲכִילֵהוּ חָמֵץ. וְאִם הַתִּינוֹק מְסֻכָּן, פְּשִׁיטָא דְּהַכֹּל מֻתָּר, כְּמוֹ שֶׁכָּתַבְתִּי סִימָן צב וּלְקַמָּן סִימָן קצב.

יג) לִשְׁתּוֹת חָלָב מִבְּהֶמַת גּוֹי הָאוֹכֶלֶת חָמֵץ בְּפֶסַח, יֵשׁ אוֹסְרִין וְיֵשׁ מַתִּירִין. וְשׁוֹמֵר נַפְשׁוֹ, יַחְמִיר. וּבִפְרָט בְּמָקוֹם שֶׁנָּהֲגוּ לֶאֱסוֹר, חָלִילָה לְהַתִּיר.

סִימָן קיח
דִּינֵי הֲכָנַת הַסֵּדֶר

א) יְהַדֵּר אַחַר יַיִן יָפֶה לְמִצְוַת אַרְבָּעָה כּוֹסוֹת. וְאִם יֵשׁ בְּנִמְצָא יַיִן אָדֹם יָפֶה כְּמוֹ הַלָּבָן, וְגַם הוּא כָּשֵׁר כְּמוֹ הַלָּבָן, מִצְוָה בּוֹ יוֹתֵר מִבְּלָבָן, שֶׁנֶּאֱמַר, אַל תֵּרֶא יַיִן כִּי יִתְאַדָּם, מַשְׁמַע שֶׁחֲשִׁיבוּתוֹ שֶׁל יַיִן הוּא כְּשֶׁהוּא

10. It is forbidden, however, to say to him, "Here is money, buy yourself some *chametz* (bread etc.) and eat." (*Ibid.* 450:15)

non-Jew does not expressly state that he needs the animal to haul *chametz.* Even if you know that the non-Jew will use it to haul *chametz,* it does not matter, because, even if the non-Jew hauls nothing with the animal, he will still have to pay you the full amount of the rental fee. Consequently, you do not profit at all from (the hauling of) the *chametz.* It is also permitted to rent him a room to live in on *Pesach,* even though you know, that he will bring *chametz* there; nevertheless, you do not receive payment for letting him bring in *chametz*; rather only rent for the room, for, even if he brought in no *chametz,* you would not reduce his rent.

10) You are forbidden to entrust, your animal to a non-Jew even a long time before *Pesach,* if you know that he will feed it *chametz* on *Pesach.*

11) You are permitted to say to your non-Jewish servant, even at a time, when it is forbidden to derive benefit from *chametz,* "Here is money, buy yourself some food and eat," even if you know that he will buy *chametz.*[10] If it is urgent, you are also allowed to say, "Go and eat at the non-Jew's place, and I will pay him for it."[11] Or you may say to another non-Jew, "Give my servant something to eat, and I will pay you for it." But you are forbidden to pay in advance for the food he will give your servant.[12]

12) If it is necessary to feed *chametz* to a baby, he should be carried to the house of a non-Jew.[13] The non-Jew should feed him the *chametz* and the Jew should pay him afterwards, but the Jew, himself, should not feed *chametz* to the baby. But if the baby's life is threatened, of course, everything is permitted, (as I have written in Ch. 92 and in Ch. 192 below).

13) Some authorities forbid drinking the milk of a cow, belonging to a non-Jew, that is fed *chametz* on *Pesach,* while others permit it. The scrupulous should follow the stricter opinion. Certainly in a community, where it is the custom to forbid it, God forbid, that anyone should permit it.

Chapter 118

The Preparation for the Seder

1) You should do your best to obtain choice wine to perform the mitzvah of drinking the Four Cups. If red wine is available, that is, of the same quality as white wine, and its *kashrus* is as reliable as white wine, the red wine is preferred for the Four Cups, for it is said, "Look not after wine when it is red," (Proverbs 23:31)

---

11. Regarding servants, that you are responsible to feed, it is best not to tell them to buy food and charge it to you, but, rather, give them money and let them buy whatever they want. (*Ibid.* 450:16,17)

12. This is so, because you are responsible for their meals.

13. If it is impossible to carry the baby to the house of the non-Jew, and, therefore, the non-Jew must come into your house and feed him there, the non-Jew should remove any leftover *chametz* to his house, and bring it back when he returns to feed the child. (*Ibid.* 450:18)

אָדֹם. וְעוֹד, לְפִי שֶׁיֵּשׁ בּוֹ זֵכֶר לְדָם, שֶׁהָיָה פַּרְעֹה שׁוֹחֵט יַלְדֵי בְּנֵי יִשְׂרָאֵל. וּבִמְדִינוֹת שֶׁהָאֻמּוֹת טִפְּשִׁים וּסְכָלִים לְהַעֲלִיל עֲלִילוֹת שְׁקָרִים, נִמְנְעוּ מִלִּקַּח יַיִן אָדֹם לַפֶּסַח.

ב) לְצֹרֶךְ טִבּוּל הָרִאשׁוֹן שֶׁהוּא כַּרְפַּס, נוֹהֲגִין הַרְבֵּה לִקַּח פֶּטְרוֹזִילְיָה. וְטוֹב יוֹתֵר לָקַחַת צֶעלֶלעֶר, שֶׁיֵּשׁ לוֹ טַעַם טוֹב כְּשֶׁהוּא חַי. וְהַמֻּבְחָר הוּא לָקַחַת צְנוֹן.

ג) לְצֹרֶךְ מָרוֹר, נוֹהֲגִין לִקַּח תַּמְכָא. וְכֵיוָן שֶׁהוּא חָרִיף מְאֹד, יְכוֹלִין לְפָרְרוֹ בִּמְגֵרֶרֶת, רַק שֶׁיִּזָּהֲרוּ שֶׁלֹּא יָפוּג לְגַמְרֵי. וְיֵשׁ לְפָרְרוֹ כְּשֶׁבָּאִין מִבֵּית־הַכְּנֶסֶת, (וְעַיֵּן לְעֵיל סִימָן צ"ח סְעִיף ג', שֶׁצְּרִיכִין לְפָרְרוֹ עַל יְדֵי שִׁנּוּי). וּבְשַׁבָּת, אֲסוּרִין לְפָרְרוֹ, אֶלָּא שֶׁצְּרִיכִין לְפָרְרוֹ קֹדֶם הַלַּיְלָה, וִיכַסֵּהוּ עַד הַלַּיְלָה. אֲבָל יוֹתֵר טוֹב לָקַחַת חֲזֶרֶת שֶׁהִיא חַסָּה שֶׁנּוֹחַ לְאָכְלָהּ וְנִקְרֵאת מָרוֹר, לְפִי שֶׁכְּשֶׁשּׁוֹהֶה בַּקַּרְקַע, נַעֲשֶׂה הַקֶּלַח מָר. וְיוֹצְאִין גַּם בְּלַעֲנָה הַנִּקְרָא וֶוערְמוּטָה. (עֻלְשִׁין וְחַרְחֲבִינָא אֵינָם שְׁכִיחִים בִּמְדִינוֹתֵינוּ). כָּל הַמִּינִים שֶׁיּוֹצְאִין בָּהֶם, מִצְטָרְפִין זֶה עִם זֶה לְכַזַּיִת. וְיוֹצְאִין בֵּין בֶּעָלִים בֵּין בַּקְּלָחִין, אֲבָל לֹא בַּשָּׁרָשִׁים, דְּהַיְנוּ שָׁרָשִׁים הַקְּטַנִּים הַמִּתְפַּצְּלִים לְכָאן וּלְכָאן. אֲבָל הַשֹּׁרֶשׁ הַגָּדוֹל שֶׁבּוֹ גְּדֵלִים הֶעָלִים, אַף שֶׁהוּא טָמוּן בַּקַּרְקַע, הֲרֵי הוּא בִּכְלַל קֶלַח. וּמִכָּל מָקוֹם טוֹב יוֹתֵר לִטּוֹל הֶעָלִים, וְהַקֶּלַח הַיּוֹצֵא חוּץ לַקַּרְקַע, כִּי יֵשׁ אוֹמְרִים, שֶׁמַּה שֶּׁהוּא בַּקַּרְקַע נִקְרָא שֹׁרֶשׁ. הֶעָלִים אֵין יוֹצְאִין בָּהֶם אֶלָּא אִם כֵּן הֵם לַחִים, אֲבָל הַקְּלָחִים יוֹצְאִין בָּהֶן, בֵּין הֵם לַחִים בֵּין יְבֵשִׁים, אַךְ לֹא בִּמְבֻשָּׁלִין אוֹ כְּבוּשִׁין.

ד) הַחֲרֹסֶת צָרִיךְ שֶׁתִּהְיֶה עָבָה, זֵכֶר לַטִּיט. וּבְשָׁעָה שֶׁהוּא צָרִיךְ לִטְבֹּל אֶת הַמָּרוֹר, יִשְׁפֹּךְ לְתוֹכָהּ יַיִן אוֹ חֹמֶץ, שֶׁתִּהְיֶה רַכָּה, וְזֵכֶר לַדָּם, וְגַם שֶׁתְּהֵא רְאוּיָה לִטְבֹּל בָּהּ. יֵשׁ לַעֲשׂוֹת אֶת הַחֲרֹסֶת מִפֵּרוֹת שֶׁנִּמְשְׁלָה בָּהֶם כְּנֶסֶת יִשְׂרָאֵל, כְּגוֹן תְּאֵנִים, שֶׁנֶּאֱמַר, הַתְּאֵנָה חָנְטָה פַגֶּיהָ. וֶאֱגוֹזִים, שֶׁנֶּאֱמַר, אֶל־גִּנַּת אֱגוֹז. וּתְמָרִים, שֶׁנֶּאֱמַר, אֶעֱלֶה בְתָמָר. וְרִמּוֹנִים, שֶׁנֶּאֱמַר, כְּפֶלַח הָרִמּוֹן. וְתַפּוּחִים, זֵכֶר לְמָה שֶׁכָּתוּב, תַּחַת הַתַּפּוּחַ

1. It should never be eaten, when it is whole, because it could be very dangerous to your health and, thus, it is not a mitzvah. (*Mishnah Berurah* 473:36)

2. After grating, it should be covered until the beginning of the *Seder,* in order that it does not lose its strength completely. (*Ibid.*)

indicating that wine is most desirable, when it is red. In addition, because it reminds us of the blood, which flowed, when Pharaoh slaughtered innocent Jewish children. In backward and ignorant countries, where people, make slanderous accusations, Jews refrain from using red wine on Pesach.

2) For the first dipping, which is called *karpas,* many people follow the custom of using parsley, but it is better to use celery, which tastes good when raw. Best of all is to use radishes.

3) For *maror* (bitter herbs), it is customary to use horseradish, which, may be grated,[1] because it is very sharp; but you should take care that it does not lose its strength completely. It should be grated, when you return home from the synagogue.[2] (see Ch. 98:3 that the grating should be in an unusual manner). On Shabbos, it is forbidden to grate the *maror,* but you should grate it before night, and keep it covered until nightfall.[3] However, it is preferable to use *chazeres,* lettuce, which is easier to eat,[4] and it is called *maror,* because when it stays in the ground for a long time, the stem becomes bitter. You can also fulfill the mitzvah with *la'anah,* (an herb called wormwood).[5] (*Alashin* and *charchevina* [mentioned in the Mishnah], are not found in our region). All the species, with which you can fulfill the mitzvah (of eating *maror*), may be combined to make up a *kazayis,* and you may fulfill your duty with either the leaves or the stems, but not with the roots, that is not with the little roots, that branch out in all directions. But the large root, out of which the leaves grow, although it is hidden in the ground, is considered a stem. Nevertheless, it is better to use the leaves and the stem that is out of the ground, because some authorities hold that the part that grows in the ground is called "root." The leaves are valid only if they are fresh, but the stems are valid whether they are fresh or dried out, but not when they are cooked or pickled.

4) The *charoses* must have a thick consistency[6] to recall the mortar from which our forefathers had to make bricks. When you are ready to dip the *maror* into it, you should add a little wine or vinegar to make it soft to represent the blood, and for the additional reason that it should become fit to dip something into it. The *charoses* should be made from fruits that symbolize the Jewish people; for example: figs, for it is said, "The fig tree has produced its green figs," (Song of Songs 2:13); nuts, because it is said, "I went down to the garden of nuts" (ibid. 6:11); dates, because it is said, "I will ascend the palm tree" (ibid. 7:9); pomegranates, because it is said, "Like a slice of pomegranate" (ibid. 6:7); apples, to commemorate what is written, "Beneath the apple tree I aroused you," (ibid. 8:5) where the women gave

---

3. Actually, until the beginning of the *Seder.* (*Ibid.*)

4. Many *Poskim* maintain that this refers to romaine lettuce. Since, however, small worms are often found in lettuce, unless it is inspected carefully by God-fearing persons, it is better to use the grated horseradish. (*Ibid.* 473:42)

5. *Mishnah Berurah* says, that according to *Ramah,* wormwood is not acceptable as a species of *maror.* Others rule that it is. (*Ibid.* 473:46)

6. The *charoses* should be prepared *erev* Yom Tov. If, however, you forgot, it may then be made on Yom Tov (*Ibid.* 473:47)

עוֹרַרְתִּיךָ, שֶׁהָיוּ הַנָּשִׁים יוֹלְדוֹת שָׁם בְּנֵיהֶן בְּלֹא עֶצֶב. וּשְׁקֵדִים, עַל שֵׁם שֶׁשָּׁקַד הַקָּדוֹשׁ־בָּרוּךְ־הוּא עַל הַקֵּץ לַעֲשׂוֹת. וְצָרִיךְ לִתֵּן בְּתוֹכָהּ תְּבָלִין הַדּוֹמִין לְתֶבֶן, כְּגוֹן קִנָּמוֹן וְזַנְגְּבִיל, שֶׁאֵינָן נְדוֹכִין הֵדֵק הֵיטֵב. וְיֵשׁ בָּהֶן חוּטִין כְּמוֹ תֶבֶן, זֵכֶר לַתֶּבֶן שֶׁהָיוּ מְגַבְּלִין בְּתוֹךְ הַטִּיט. בְּשַׁבָּת, לֹא יִשְׁפּוֹךְ אֶת הַיַּיִן אוֹ הַחֹמֶץ לְתוֹךְ הַחֲרֹסֶת, כִּי צָרִיךְ לַעֲשׂוֹת בְּשִׁנּוּי, וְיִתֵּן אֶת הַחֲרֹסֶת לְתוֹךְ הַיַּיִן וְהַחֹמֶץ. וְאֶת מֵי הַמֶּלַח, (אֲפִלּוּ כְּשֶׁלֹּא חָל יוֹם־טוֹב בְּשַׁבָּת), יַעֲשֶׂה מֵעֶרֶב יוֹם־טוֹב. וְאִם עוֹשֵׂהוּ בְּיוֹם־טוֹב, צָרִיךְ לַעֲשׂוֹתוֹ בְּשִׁנּוּי, שֶׁיִּתֵּן תְּחִלָּה אֶת הַמַּיִם וְאַחַר כָּךְ אֶת הַמֶּלַח.

ה) מִשֶּׁחָרַב בֵּית־הַמִּקְדָּשׁ, תִּקְּנוּ חֲכָמִים שֶׁיִּהְיוּ עַל הַשֻּׁלְחָן בִּשְׁעַת אֲמִירַת הַהַגָּדָה שְׁנֵי מִינֵי תַבְשִׁילִין, אֶחָד זֵכֶר לְקָרְבַּן פֶּסַח וְאֶחָד זֵכֶר לְקָרְבַּן חֲגִיגָה, שֶׁהָיוּ מַקְרִיבִין בִּזְמַן שֶׁבֵּית־הַמִּקְדָּשׁ הָיָה קַיָּם. וְנָהֲגוּ שֶׁאֶחָד מִן הַתַּבְשִׁילִין יִהְיֶה בָּשָׂר, וְיִהְיֶה מִפֶּרֶק הַנִּקְרָא זְרוֹעַ, לְזֵכֶר שֶׁגְּאָלָם הַקָּדוֹשׁ־בָּרוּךְ־הוּא בִּזְרוֹעַ נְטוּיָה. וְיִהְיֶה נִצְלֶה עַל הַגֶּחָלִים, זֵכֶר לַפֶּסַח שֶׁהָיָה צְלִי אֵשׁ. וְהַשֵּׁנִי יִהְיֶה בֵּיצָה, מִשּׁוּם דְּבֵיצָה בְּלָשׁוֹן אֲרַמִּי, בֵּיעָה. כְּלוֹמַר, דְּבָעֵי רַחֲמָנָא לְמִפְרַק יָתָנָא בִּדְרָעָא מְרוֹמְמָא. וְעוֹשִׂין הַבֵּיצָה, בֵּין צְלוּיָה בֵּין מְבֻשֶּׁלֶת. וְצָרִיךְ לִצְלוֹתָן וּלְבַשְּׁלָן מֵעֶרֶב יוֹם־טוֹב בְּעוֹד יוֹם. וְאִם שָׁכַח אוֹ שֶׁהָיָה שַׁבָּת, יִצְלֶה וִיבַשֵּׁל אוֹתָם בַּלַּיְלָה, אֲבָל צָרִיךְ לְאָכְלָן בְּיוֹם־טוֹב רִאשׁוֹן. וְכֵן בְּלֵיל שֵׁנִי, יִצְלֵם וִיבַשְּׁלֵם וְיֹאכְלֵם בְּיוֹם־טוֹב שֵׁנִי, כִּי אֵין מְבַשְּׁלִין מִיּוֹם־טוֹב לַחֲבֵרוֹ, וְלֹא מִיּוֹם־טוֹב לְחֹל. וּלְפִי שֶׁאֵין אוֹכְלִין בָּשָׂר צָלִי בִּשְׁנֵי לֵילוֹת אֵלּוּ, עַל כֵּן צָרִיךְ לֶאֱכוֹל אֶת הַזְּרוֹעַ דַּוְקָא בַּיּוֹם. וְאַף כְּשֶׁצּוֹלִין אוֹתָן בְּעֶרֶב יוֹם־טוֹב, אֵין לְזָרְקָן אַחַר כָּךְ, אֶלָּא יִתְּנֵם בְּיוֹם־טוֹב שֵׁנִי תּוֹךְ הַמַּאֲכָל שֶׁמְּבַשְּׁלִין וְיֹאכְלֵם.

ו) יָכִין מוֹשָׁבוֹ מִבְּעוֹד יוֹם בְּמַצָּעוֹת נָאִים כְּפִי יְכָלְתּוֹ, וּבְאֹפֶן שֶׁיּוּכַל לְהַטּוֹת וּלְהָסֵב בִּשְׂמֹאלוֹ. וַאֲפִלּוּ הוּא אִטֵּר, יָסֵב בִּשְׂמֹאל שֶׁל כָּל אָדָם. גַּם אֶת הַקְּעָרָה יָכִין מִבְּעוֹד יוֹם, כְּדֵי שֶׁמִּיָּד בְּבוֹאוֹ מִבֵּית־הַכְּנֶסֶת יוּכַל לַעֲשׂוֹת אֶת הַסֵּדֶר בְּלִי עִכּוּב.

---

7. According to *Maharil,* they should not be ground at all, but should be left in long pieces.

8. If, however, it does occur on Shabbos, the salt water should be prepared before Shabbos, and not on Shabbos. (*Ibid.* 473:21, 42)

9. *Mishnah Berurah* makes no mention of preparing the salt water in an unusual manner

birth to their children without pain; and almonds, (*shekeidim*, singular *shakeid*), because the Holy One, blessed is He, watched diligently (*shakad*) to end our bondage. You should put spices in it, that look like straw, such as cinnamon and ginger, that are not finely ground,[7] and have straw-like strands in them, to recall the straw, the Jews used to knead into the mortar. On Shabbos, you should not pour the wine and the vinegar into the *charoses,* for it must be done in an unusual manner, by putting the *charoses* into the wine or the vinegar. The salt water, (even when Yom Tov does not occur on Shabbos)[8] should be prepared on *erev Yom Tov*). If you do prepare it on Yom Tov, you should do it in an unusual way,[9] by pouring the water first, and adding the salt later.

5) After the *Beis Hamikdash* was destroyed, the Sages ordained that there should be two cooked foods on the table, during the reciting of the *Haggadah,* one to recall the *Korban Pesach,* (Passover sacrifice), the other to recall the *Korban Chagigah* (Festival sacrifice), which were offered in the times when the *Beis Hamikdash* was standing. It is customary that one of the foods should be meat, from the shoulder section,[10] to recall that the Holy One, blessed is He, redeemed Yisrael, with an outstretched arm. It should be roasted on fire, to recall the *Korban Pesach* (Passover sacrifice), which was roasted on fire. The second food should be an egg,[11] because an egg, in the Aramean language is *beiah,* that is to say, the Merciful One desired (*ba'ei*) to redeem us with an outstretched arm. You may prepare the egg, either roasted or boiled, but you must do the roasting or boiling on *erev Yom Tov,* while it is still daylight. If you forgot to do it (on *erev Yom Tov*), or if that day occurred on Shabbos, you should roast or boil it at night, but then you must eat it on the first day of Yom Tov. The same goes for the second night; you should roast it or boil it (at night), and you must eat it on the second day of Yom Tov, for you are not permitted to cook on the first day of Yom Tov for the second day, and neither on a Yom Tov for a weekday. Now, since it is customary not to eat roasted meats on the two nights of the *seder,* you should, therefore, eat the shoulder meat on Yom Tov during the day. Even if you roasted it on *erev Yom Tov,* you should not throw away (the meat) afterwards, but you should put it into the food that is cooked on the second day and eat it on the second day.

6) You should prepare your seat [at the table] while it is still daytime, with the nicest pillows you can afford, placing them in such a way that you can recline and lean on the left side. Even a left-handed person should recline on the left side. You should also prepare the *seder* plate while it is still day, in order that immediately on returning home from the synagogue you can begin the *seder* without delay.

---

on Yom Tov, when it *does not* occur on Shabbos. It would seem that he maintains that it is permitted to prepare it on Yom Tov in the usual manner.

10. If you cannot obtain a shoulder piece, you may use other meat, even without a bone. The *Poskim* write that when a bone is used, there should be some meat on it, to recall the *Korban Pesach.* (*Ibid.* 473.27)

11. According to *Mishnah Berurah,* you may use two kinds of meat, one roasted, to recall the *Korban Pesach,* and one boiled, to recall the *Korban Chagigah.* (*Ibid.* 473:27)

ז) אַף־עַל־פִּי שֶׁבְּכָל הַשָּׁנָה טוֹב לְמַעֵט בְּכֵלִים נָאִים זֵכֶר לְחָרְבָּן, מִכָּל מָקוֹם בְּלֵיל פֶּסַח טוֹב לְהַרְבּוֹת בְּכֵלִים נָאִים כְּפִי כֹחוֹ. וַאֲפִלּוּ הַכֵּלִים שֶׁאֵינָן צְרִיכִין לַסְּעוּדָה, יְסַדְּרֵם יָפֶה עַל הַשֻּׁלְחָן לְנוֹי, זֵכֶר לְחֵרוּת.

ח) סֵדֶר הַקְּעָרָה כָּךְ הוּא, מַנִּיחַ שָׁלֹשׁ מַצּוֹת עַל הַקְּעָרָה וּפוֹרֵס עֲלֵיהֶם מַפָּה נָאָה, וְעָלֶיהָ מַנִּיחַ אֶת הַזְּרוֹעַ נֶגֶד הַיָּמִין שֶׁלּוֹ, וְאֶת הַבֵּיצָה מִשְּׂמֹאל. הַמָּרוֹר לִבְרָכָה, בָּאֶמְצַע. חֲרֹסֶת, תַּחַת הַזְּרוֹעַ. כַּרְפַּס, תַּחַת הַבֵּיצָה. וּמָרוֹר לִכְרִיכָה, בָּאֶמְצַע. כָּזֶה,

זְרוֹעַ בֵּיצָה

מָרוֹר (לברכה)

חֲרֹסֶת כַּרְפַּס

מָרוֹר (לכריכה)

ט) הַכּוֹסוֹת יִהְיוּ שְׁלֵמִים בְּלִי שׁוּם פְּגִימָה, וּמוּדָחִים יָפֶה, וְיַחֲזִיקוּ לְכָל הַפָּחוֹת רְבִיעִית.

י) מִנְהָגֵנוּ לִלְבּוֹשׁ הַקִּיטֶל, וְיָכִינוּ גַּם כֵּן מִבְּעוֹד יוֹם. וּמִי שֶׁהוּא אָבֵל, רַחֲמָנָא לִצְלָן, אֵינוֹ לוֹבְשׁוֹ. אֲבָל בַּהֲסִבָּה, חַיָּב. רַק אִם לֹא נָהַג אֲבֵלוּת כְּלָל קֹדֶם יוֹם־טוֹב, כְּגוֹן שֶׁקָּבַר מֵתוֹ בְּיוֹם־טוֹב, נוֹהֲגִין שֶׁאֵינוֹ מֵסֵב. וְהַלֵּל, אוֹמֵר, כִּי הַהַלֵּל הוּא חִיּוּב.

יא) בֵּן אֵצֶל אָבִיו, חַיָּב בַּהֲסִבָּה. אֲבָל תַּלְמִיד אֵצֶל רַבּוֹ, אֵינוֹ צָרִיךְ.

סִימָן קיט
סֵדֶר לֵיל פֶּסַח

א) אַף־עַל־פִּי שֶׁבְּכָל שַׁבָּת וְיוֹם־טוֹב יְכוֹלִין לְקַדֵּשׁ וְלֶאֱכֹל מִבְּעוֹד יוֹם לְהוֹסִיף מֵחֹל עַל הַקֹּדֶשׁ, בְּפֶסַח אֵינוֹ כֵן, לְפִי שֶׁמִּצְוַת אֲכִילַת מַצָּה הִיא דַוְקָא בַּלַּיְלָה, כְּמוֹ קָרְבַּן פֶּסַח, דִּכְתִיב בֵּהּ, וְאָכְלוּ אֶת־הַבָּשָׂר בַּלַּיְלָה הַזֶּה. וְכֵן מִצְוַת אַרְבָּעָה כּוֹסוֹת הִיא דַוְקָא בַּלָּיְלָה. וְכֵיוָן שֶׁגַּם הַכּוֹס שֶׁל קִדּוּשׁ הוּא אֶחָד מֵאַרְבַּעַת הַכּוֹסוֹת, לָכֵן אֵין מְקַדְּשִׁין עַד שֶׁהוּא וַדַּאי לָיְלָה.

12. If they are wiped clean, with a cloth, both inside and outside, it is also acceptable. Even though you are not careful, all year, to examine the cups, used for *Kiddush*, you should take care to do so on the nights of the Seder. (*Ibid.* 183:1,2)

7) Although during the year, it is best to be moderate in displaying fine tableware, so that we remember the destruction of the *Beis Hamikdash,* nevertheless, on the night of *Pesach,* it is good to set the table with as many beautiful things as are within your means. Even vessels not used for the meal should be placed on the table for elegant decor, to symbolize freedom.

8) The *seder* plate is arranged in this manner: You place three matzos on the *seder* plate, you cover them with a beautiful cloth, you place the shankbone on your right side, and the egg on the left; the *maror,* over which you say the berachah, you place in the center; the *charoses,* you place below the shankbone; the *karpas* below the egg, and the *maror,* that is eaten together with the matzah, you place in the center; as in the diagram:

egg shankbone

maror (for berachah)

karpas *charoses*

maror (for *korech*)

9) The wine cups must be whole, without any defect, thoroughly rinsed,[12] and they must hold no less than a *revi'is.*[13]

10) It is our custom to wear a *kittel* (a white robe), which should also be prepared, while it is still day. A person, in mourning, God forbid, should not wear it, but he is required to recline. However, if he has observed no mourning at all before Yom Tov, as, for example, if the funeral was held on Yom Tov, then, it is customary that he should not recline. But he must recite *Hallel,* because the saying of *Hallel* is mandatory.

11) A son, at his father's table, is required to recline, but a student, in the presence of his *Rebbe,* is not required to recline.

Chapter 119

The Seder

1) Although on every other Shabbos and Yom Tov, you are permitted to say *kiddush* and eat a meal while it is still day, in order to add from the secular to the holy, on *Pesach,* you are not permitted to do so. The mitzvah of eating matzah must be performed only at night, as was the case with the *Pesach* sacrifice, about which it is written, "And they shall eat the meat (of the *Korban Pesach)* on this night." (Exodus 12:8). The mitzvah of the Four Cups may also be done only after nightfall. Since the cup of wine, over which we say *kiddush,* is one of the Four Cups, the

13. See Glossary.

יִלְבַּשׁ אֶת הַקִּיטֶל וְיִתְיַשֵּׁב עַל מוֹשָׁבוֹ לַעֲשׂוֹת אֶת הַסֵּדֶר. וּמִצְוָה לְחַלֵּק לַתִּינוֹקוֹת שְׁקֵדִים וֶאֱגוֹזִים וְכַדּוֹמֶה, כְּדֵי שֶׁיִּרְאוּ שִׁנּוּי וְיִשְׁאֲלוּ, וְעַל יְדֵי זֶה יִתְעוֹרְרוּ לִשְׁאוֹל גַּם כֵּן עַל מַצָּה וּמָרוֹר וַהֲסִבָּה. וְתִינוֹק וְתִינֹקֶת שֶׁהִגִּיעוּ לְחִנּוּךְ, דְּהַיְנוּ שֶׁהֵם יוֹדְעִים בִּקְדֻשַּׁת יוֹם־טוֹב וּמְבִינִים מַה שֶּׁמְּסַפְּרִים מִיצִיאַת מִצְרַיִם, נוֹתְנִים לָהֶם גַּם כֵּן כּוֹס שֶׁיִּשְׁתּוּ מִמֶּנּוּ. נוֹהֲגִין לִמְזוֹג כּוֹס אֶחָד יוֹתֵר מִן הַמְסֻבִּין, וְקוֹרִין אוֹתוֹ כּוֹס שֶׁל אֵלִיָּהוּ הַנָּבִיא.

ב) מְשָׁרְתוֹ אוֹ אֶחָד מִבְּנֵי בֵּיתוֹ, יִמְזְגוּ אֶת הַכּוֹסוֹת. וְכֵן בְּכָל פַּעַם שֶׁמּוֹזְגִין, יִמְזְגוּ הֵם וְלֹא הוּא בְּעַצְמוֹ, כְּדֵי לְהַרְאוֹת דֶּרֶךְ חֵרוּת. וְיַזְהִיר לִבְנֵי בֵיתוֹ, שֶׁיִּשְׁתּוּ מִכָּל כּוֹס לְכָל־הַפָּחוֹת אֶת הָרֹב בְּפַעַם אַחַת, וּמִכּוֹס רְבִיעִי יִשְׁתּוּ רְבִיעִית בְּפַעַם אֶחָת. וִיכַוְּנוּ כֻּלָּם לְמִצְוַת אַרְבָּעָה כּוֹסוֹת וְסִפּוּר יְצִיאַת מִצְרַיִם וַאֲכִילַת מַצָּה וּמָרוֹר, כִּי גַם הַנָּשִׁים חַיָּבוֹת בְּמִצְוֹת אֵלוּ, רַק בַּהֲסִבָּה אֵינָן נוֹהֲגוֹת. יַעֲשֶׂה קִדּוּשׁ כַּכָּתוּב בְּהַגָּדָה, וְיִשְׁתֶּה בַּהֲסִבַּת שְׂמֹאל. וְטוֹב אִם אֶפְשָׁר לַעֲשׂוֹת כְּדַעַת הַפּוֹסְקִים לִשְׁתּוֹת כּוֹס שָׁלֵם בְּכָל אַרְבַּעַת הַכּוֹסוֹת.

ג) אַחַר כָּךְ יִרְחַץ יָדָיו וְלֹא יְבָרֵךְ עֲלֵיהֶן, וּמְנַגְּבָן. וְחוֹתֵךְ מִן הַכַּרְפַּס לְעַצְמוֹ וּלְכָל בְּנֵי בֵיתוֹ לְכָל אֶחָד פָּחוֹת מִכַּזַּיִת, וְטוֹבְלִין בְּמֵי מֶלַח, וּמְבָרְכִין בּוֹרֵא פְּרִי הָאֲדָמָה, וּמְכַוְּנִין לִפְטֹר בִּבְרָכָה זוֹ גַּם אֶת הַמָּרוֹר, וְאוֹכֵל גַּם כֵּן בַּהֲסִבַּת שְׂמֹאל. אַחַר כָּךְ נוֹטֵל אֶת הַמַּצָּה הָאֶמְצָעִית וְחוֹלְקָהּ לִשְׁנֵי חֲלָקִים, וּמַנִּיחַ אֶת הַחֵלֶק הַגָּדוֹל אֵצֶל מוֹשָׁבוֹ לַאֲפִיקוֹמָן. וְנוֹהֲגִין לְכָרְכוֹ בְּמַפָּה, זֵכֶר לְמַה שֶּׁכָּתוּב, מִשְׁאֲרֹתָם צְרֻרֹת בְּשִׂמְלֹתָם. וְיֵשׁ

---

1. It is required to wait, therefore, until after the appearance of the stars. See glossary.

2. These questions are included in the text of the *Haggadah, Mah Nishtanah.* It is important to keep the children at the table until after *Avodim Hayinu* is recited and explained to them, because this section of the *Haggadah* explains the questions, previously asked by the children. (*Mishnah Berurah* 472:50)

3. It is considered a mitzvah to give them a cup of wine, but it is not required to do so, since many *Poskim* ruled that the mitzvah of the Four Cups was never ordained for children. (*Ibid.* 472:46,47)

4. It is not clearly stated, when the Cup of Elijah should be filled. The fact that the *Kitzur Shulchan Aruch* mentions it, in this paragraph, could indicate that he maintains that it be filled, when the first cups are filled for *Kiddush. Mishnah Berurah* mentions the filling of the Cup of Elijah, in the paragraph dealing with the text, שְׁפֹךְ חֲמָתְךָ (Pour out Your wrath etc.), which comes much later after *Birkas Hamazon.* (*Ibid.* 481:10)

kiddush should not be said until it is definitely night.[1] (The person who conducts the *seder*) puts on the kittel and takes his seat to conduct the *seder.* It is a mitzvah to distribute almonds, nuts and similar things to the children, so that they notice the change and ask questions, and this will also stimulate them to ask also the reasons for eating matzah, *maror* and reclining.[2] Boys and girls who have reached the age of training for mitzvos, that is, who are able to understand the holiness of Yom Tov and understand what is being told about the Exodus from Egypt, should also be given a cup of wine,[3] from which they should drink. It is customary to fill an additional cup of wine,[4] and it is called "The Cup of Elijah the Prophet."

2) A servant or a member of the household should fill the cups, and each time the cups are filled, they should fill them, rather than doing it yourself. This conveys an impression of freedom. You should instruct the members of the household to drink at least the greater part of each cup at one time,[5] and of the fourth cup, they should drink a *revi'is* at one time.[6] All should have in mind to fulfill the mitzvah of drinking the Four Cups (of wine), and of relating the story of the Exodus, and eating matzah and *maror,* because women, too, are required to perform these mitzvos, except that they do not recline. You recite the *kiddush,* as it is written in the *Haggadah,* and drink the wine while reclining on your left side. It is best, if possible, to follow the opinion of the authorities, and to drink the entire contents of all the Four Cups.

3) After that, you should wash your hands,[7] without saying the berachah, dry them, and cut the *karpas* for yourself and for all the members of the household, giving each less than a *kazayis.*[8] Each dips his portion in salt water and says the berachah *Borei peri ha'adamah* "Who creates the fruit of the ground." They should have in mind to exempt the *maror* which will be eaten later with this berachah, and while eating the *karpas,* they should also recline on the left side.[9] The person who leads the Seder then takes the middle matzah and breaks it into two parts, placing the larger part near his seat for the *afikoman.* It is customary to wrap the *afikoman* in a napkin,[10] to recall what is written, "Their leftover dough was wrapped in their

---

5. If the cup holds only a *revi'is,* you should, initially, drink the entire cup of wine. From a large cup, some *Poskim* say that it is sufficient to drink a *revi'is,* and others say you must drink the greater part of the cup, even though it holds several *revi'is. Mishnah Berurah* rules, according to the first opinion, but writes, nevertheless, that if you do not intend drinking a large quantity of wine, you should not use a large cup, but, rather, one that holds only a *revi'is,* in order to conform with the second opinion, as well. (*Mishnah Berurah* 472:30,33)

6. This means that the *revi'is* should be drunk in the time span of כְּדֵי אֲכִילַת פְּרָס. (kedei achilas peras) (*Ibid.* 472:34) See glossary.

7. The reason for washing the hands, at this point, is because the *karpas* must be dipped in salt water, and before eating food that is dipped in liquid, such as wine, honey, oil, milk, dew, blood or water it is required that you wash your hands. (*Ibid.* 473:51)

8. See glossary. We eat less than a *kazayis,* because, otherwise, it would be questionable, regarding the saying of the after-berachah. By eating less than a *kazayis,* we remove ourselves from this problem. According to the *Gra,* however, if you should eat a *kazayis,* you should say the after-berachah. (*Ibid.* 473:53,56)

9. *Mishnah Berurah* does not mention the rule that the *karpas* should be eaten in a reclining position.

10. When using a cloth napkin, care must be taken that the napkin was not starched in laundering. (*Ibid.* 473:59)

שֶׁמְּשִׂימִים אוֹתוֹ כָּךְ עַל שִׁכְמָם, זֵכֶר לִיצִיאַת מִצְרַיִם. וּלְפִי שֶׁהָאֲפִיקוֹמָן הוּא בִּמְקוֹם הַפֶּסַח, לָכֵן הוּא חָשׁוּב וְיִהְיֶה הַחֵלֶק הַגָּדוֹל. וְהַחֵלֶק הַקָּטֹן מַחֲזִירוֹ לַקְּעָרָה לִמְקוֹמוֹ, וּמְגַלֶּה קְצָת אֶת הַמַּצּוֹת, וּמַגְבִּיהַּ אֶת הַקְּעָרָה, וְאוֹמְרִים, הָא לַחְמָא עַנְיָא דִּי אֲכָלוּ וְכוּ׳, עַד לַשָּׁנָה הַבָּאָה בְּנֵי חוֹרִין. וְהָאוֹמְרִים כְּהָא לַחְמָא עַנְיָא, לֹא יֹאמְרוּ תֵּבַת דִּי.

ד) אַחַר כָּךְ מוֹזְגִין כּוֹס שֵׁנִי, וְהַתִּינוֹק שׁוֹאֵל מַה נִּשְׁתַּנָּה. וְאִם אֵין תִּינוֹק, יִשְׁאַל בֶּן אַחֵר, אוֹ בִּתּוֹ, אוֹ חֲבֵרוֹ, אוֹ אִשְׁתּוֹ, וְאַחַר כָּךְ אוֹמְרִים, עֲבָדִים הָיִינוּ וְכוּ׳. וְהַנָּכוֹן לְפָרֵשׁ לִבְנֵי בֵיתוֹ דִּבְרֵי הַהַגָּדָה בְּלָשׁוֹן שֶׁמְּבִינִים. וְאִם גַּם בְּעַצְמוֹ אֵינוֹ מֵבִין לְשׁוֹן הַקֹּדֶשׁ, יֹאמַר מִתּוֹךְ הַגָּדָה, שֶׁהוּא עִם פֵּרוּשׁ אַשְׁכְּנָז. וּלְאַחַר כָּל פִּסְקָא, יֹאמַר בִּלְשׁוֹן אַשְׁכְּנַז, וּמִכָּל־שֶׁכֵּן הַמַּאֲמָר רַבָּן גַּמְלִיאֵל הָיָה אוֹמֵר וְכוּ׳, שֶׁצְּרִיכִין לְהָבִין אֶת הַטַּעַם שֶׁל פֶּסַח מַצָּה וּמָרוֹר. כְּשֶׁמַּגִּיעַ לְוְהִיא שֶׁעָמְדָה וְכוּ׳, יְכַסֶּה אֶת הַמַּצּוֹת, (שֶׁלֹּא תִרְאֶה הַפַּת בָּשְׁתָּהּ, שֶׁמַּנִּיחִין אוֹתָהּ וְנוֹטְלִין אֶת הַכּוֹס), וְנוֹטְלִין אֶת הַכּוֹסוֹת בִּידֵיהֶם וְאוֹמְרִים וְהִיא שֶׁעָמְדָה וְכוּ׳, עַד מִיָּדָם, וְחוֹזֵר וּמְגַלֶּה אֶת הַמַּצּוֹת. וּכְשֶׁמַּגִּיעַ לְמַצָּה זוֹ, נוֹטֵל אֶת הַמֶּחֱצִית הַמַּצָּה שֶׁבַּקְּעָרָה וּמַרְאָהּ לִבְנֵי בֵיתוֹ וְאוֹמֵר, מַצָּה זוֹ וְכוּ׳. וְכֵן בְּמָרוֹר זֶה, מַגְבִּיהַּ אֶת הַמָּרוֹר. אֲבָל כְּשֶׁאוֹמֵר פֶּסַח שֶׁהָיוּ אֲבוֹתֵינוּ אוֹכְלִים וְכוּ׳, לֹא יַגְבִּיהַּ אֶת הַזְּרוֹעַ, שֶׁהִיא זֵכֶר לַפֶּסַח, שֶׁלֹּא יְהֵא נִרְאֶה כְּאִלּוּ הִקְדִּישׁוֹ לְכָךְ. וּכְשֶׁמַּגִּיעַ לִלְפִיכָךְ, מְכַסֶּה אֶת הַמַּצּוֹת, וְנוֹטֵל כָּל אֶחָד אֶת הַכּוֹס בְּיָדוֹ וּמַגְבִּיהוֹ עַד שֶׁחוֹתֵם גָּאַל יִשְׂרָאֵל, וּמְבָרְכִין עַל הַכּוֹס בּוֹרֵא פְּרִי הַגָּפֶן, וְשׁוֹתִין בַּהֲסִבַּת שְׂמֹאל.

ה) אַחַר כָּךְ רוֹחֲצִין יְדֵיהֶם וּמְבָרְכִין עַל נְטִילַת יָדַיִם, וּמְבָרֵךְ הַמּוֹצִיא עַל הַמַּצּוֹת. וּלְפִי שֶׁבְּיוֹם־טוֹב צָרִיךְ לִבְצוֹעַ עַל שְׁתֵּי כִּכָּרוֹת שְׁלֵמוֹת, וּמִצְוַת אֲכִילַת מַצָּה הִיא מִן הַפְּרוּסָה, לְפִי שֶׁהַמַּצָּה נִקְרֵאת לֶחֶם עֹנִי, וְדַרְכּוֹ שֶׁל עָנִי בִּפְרוּסָה עַל כֵּן בְּשָׁעָה שֶׁהוּא מְבָרֵךְ הַמּוֹצִיא, אוֹחֵז שְׁתֵּי

11. This declaration should be said in a loud voice. (*Ibid.* 473:61)

12. If there is no one present, you must ask these questions of yourself. Even Talmudic scholars must ask each other these questions. (*Shulchan Aruch* 473:7)

clothes" (Exodus 12:34). Some people place it on their shoulders, to recall the Exodus. Since the *afikoman* takes the place of the *Pesach* sacrifice, it is most esteemed, and the larger portion of the matzah is set aside for it. The smaller portion, is put back on the *seder* plate. He then uncovers the matzos slightly, lifts the *seder* plate, and all declare *Ha lachma anya diachalu,*[11] "This is the bread of affliction, which our forefathers ate etc. to *leshanah haba'ah benei chorin,* "Next year we shall be free men." Those who say, *Keha lachma anya* (*keha* instead of *ha*), "Such as this bread of affliction," should omit the word *di* (which).

4) The second cup is now filled, and a child asks: *Mah nishtanah* "Why is this night different." If there is no child present, then an older son or daughter should ask, or a friend or your wife should ask.[12] Then *Avadim hayinu* (we were slaves) etc. is said.[13] It is proper to explain to the members of the family[14] the contents of the *Haggadah* in the language they understand.[15] If you do not understand Hebrew, you should use a *Haggadah* with a translation, and after completing each paragraph, you should repeat from the translation, and particularly, the declaration, *Rabban Gamliel hayah omeir* (Rabban Gamliel used to say,) because it is essential to understand the reasons for the *Pesach* sacrifice, matzah and *maror.* At *Vehi she'amedah* (this promise) etc. you should cover the matzos (so that the matzah is not slighted when it seems that we are ignoring it, by lifting only the cup of wine). All take their cups in their hands and say, *Vehi she'amedah,* to *miyadam,* (from their hands), when you again uncover the matzos. When you say *Matzah zo* (this matzah) etc., you should take the half matzah from the *seder* plate, and show it to the family and say, *Matzah zo* (this matzah etc.). When saying *Maror zeh* (this *maror*), you should lift the *maror.* However, when saying *Pesach shehayu avoseinu ochelim* (the *Pesach* offering which our fathers ate etc.), you should not raise the shankbone, which is a reminder of the *Pesach* offering, for it might appear as if you had set it apart for a *Pesach* offering, (which can only be done in the *Beis Hamikdash*). When saying, *Lefichach* (Therefore), you should cover the matzos, and each person takes his cup in his hand and raises it, holding it until concluding with *Ga'al Yisrael,* (Who redeemed Israel). Everyone then says the berachah, *Borei peri hagafen,* over their cup of wine, and drink the cup, while reclining on the left side.

5) After that, everyone should wash their hands, and say the berachah, *Al netilas yadayim,* and *Hamotzi* over the matzos. Since on Yom Tov, we must say *Hamotzi* over two whole loaves of bread, and the mitzvah of matzah requires that we eat the broken one, because matzah is called "poor man's bread," and a poor man generally eats broken pieces of bread, therefore, when saying *Hamotzi,* you should take the

---

13. The entire *Haggadah* should be read with great awe and *not* while reclining. (*Mishnah Berurah* 473:11)

14. The explanations should start with the saying of *Ha lachma anya d'achalu* (this is the bread of affliction), since this is the beginning of the *Haggadah.* (*Ibid.* 473:62,63)

15. It should be explained in language, that will be understood by the women and children, as they too are obligated to fulfill the mitzvah of relating the story of the Exodus from Egypt. (*Ibid.* 473:64)

הַמַּצּוֹת הַשְּׁלֵמוֹת בְּיָדָיו וְהַפְּרוּסָה בֵּינֵיהֶן, וּמְבָרֵךְ הַמּוֹצִיא, וּמַנִּיחַ אֶת הַמַּצָּה הַתַּחְתּוֹנָה מִיָּדָיו, וְאוֹחֵז רַק בָּעֶלְיוֹנָה וְגַם בַּפְּרוּסָה וּמְבָרֵךְ עַל אֲכִילַת מַצָּה, וּבוֹצֵעַ מִן הָעֶלְיוֹנָה וְגַם מִן הַפְּרוּסָה מִכָּל אַחַת כַּזַּיִת, וְכֵן הוּא נוֹתֵן לְכָל אֶחָד מִבְּנֵי בֵיתוֹ, וְאוֹכֵל שְׁנֵיהֶם יַחַד בַּהֲסִבָּה שְׂמָאלִית. וְאִם קָשֶׁה לוֹ לְאָכְלָם בְּפַעַם אַחַת, אוֹכֵל תְּחִלָּה אֶת הַכַּזַּיִת הַמּוֹצִיא, וְאַחַר כָּךְ הַכַּזַּיִת מִן הַפְּרוּסָה, רַק שֶׁלֹּא יִשְׁהֶה בֵּינֵיהֶם כְּלָל, וְיֹאכַל שְׁנֵיהֶן בַּהֲסִבָּה. וְנוֹהֲגִין בִּמְדִינוֹת אֵלּוּ, שֶׁבְּלֵילֵי פֶּסַח אֵין טוֹבְלִין אֶת הַמַּצָּה בְּמֶלַח, לֹא שֶׁל הַמּוֹצִיא וְלֹא שֶׁל מַצָּה.

ו) מִי שֶׁאֵינוֹ יָכוֹל לִלְעֹס מַצָּה, מֻתָּר לִשְׁרוֹתָהּ בְּמַיִם לְרַכְּכָהּ, וּבִלְבַד שֶׁלֹּא תְהֵא נִמּוֹחָה לְגַמְרֵי. וּמִי שֶׁהוּא זָקֵן אוֹ חוֹלֶה וְאֵינוֹ יָכוֹל לְאָכְלָהּ שְׁרוּיָה בְּמַיִם, יָכוֹל לִשְׁרוֹתָהּ בְּיַיִן אוֹ בִשְׁאָר מַשְׁקִים. כְּשֶׁשּׁוֹרִין אֶת הַמַּצָּה לָצֵאת בָּהּ, צְרִיכִין לִזָּהֵר שֶׁלֹּא לִשְׁרוֹתָהּ מֵעֵת־לְעֵת, כִּי אָז נֶחְשֶׁבֶת כִּמְבֻשֶּׁלֶת וְאֵין יוֹצְאִין בָּהּ. וְגַם צְרִיכִין לִזָּהֵר בִּשְׁאָר דְּבָרִים, שֶׁלֹּא יַפְסִיד דִּין לֶחֶם. עַיֵּן לְעֵיל סִימָן מח סָעִיף ה.

ז) אַחַר כָּךְ נוֹטֵל כַּזַּיִת מָרוֹר, וְכֵן הוּא נוֹתֵן לְכָל אֶחָד מִבְּנֵי בֵיתוֹ, וְטוֹבְלוֹ בַּחֲרֹסֶת, וּמְנַעֵר אֶת הַחֲרֹסֶת מֵעָלָיו, שֶׁלֹּא יִתְבַּטֵּל טַעַם הַמָּרוֹר, וּמְבָרֵךְ עַל אֲכִילַת מָרוֹר, וְאוֹכְלוֹ בְּלֹא הֲסִבָּה. אַחַר כָּךְ נוֹטֵל מִן הַמַּצָּה הַתַּחְתּוֹנָה גַּם כֵּן כַּזַּיִת וְגַם כַּזַּיִת מָרוֹר, וְנָכוֹן לְטָבְלוֹ גַּם כֵּן בַּחֲרֹסֶת וּלְנַעֲרוֹ מֵעָלָיו, וּמַנִּיחַ אֶת הַמָּרוֹר תּוֹךְ הַמַּצָּה וְאוֹמֵר, כֵּן עָשָׂה הִלֵּל וְכוּ', וְאוֹכֵל בַּהֲסִבָּה. שִׁעוּר כַּזַּיִת כָּתַבְנוּ בִּכְלָלִים, שֶׁהוּא כְּמוֹ חֲצִי בֵיצָה. אָמְנָם יֵשׁ אוֹמְרִים, שֶׁהוּא קְצָת פָּחוֹת מִכְּשְׁלִישׁ בֵּיצָה. וְכֵיוָן דְּמָרוֹר בִּזְמַן

---

16. You should, simply, allow the bottom matzah to slip from your hands (rather than putting it down). (*Ibid.* 475:2)

17. You should break off a *kazayis* of each matzah, simultaneously. (*Shulchan Aruch* 475:1)

18. It is the consensus of the later *Poskim,* that it is not necessary to swallow both pieces, simultaneously. So long as you chew them together, you can swallow each *kazayis* individually. If you find this too difficult, you can swallow each *kazayis* a little at a time, so long as you consume both *kazeisim* within the time span of *kedei achilas peras* (כְּדֵי אֲכִילַת פְּרָס) (See Glossary). (*Mishnah Berurah* 475:9)

19. If you did not recline, you should, at least, eat another *kazayis* while reclining. (*Ibid.* 472:22)

20. It is also permitted to have the matzah ground up, so long as it equals a *kazayis* of unbroken matzo. (*Biyur Halachah* 461:4)

21. This leniency applies only when a whole matzah is soaked in one piece, but if it is broken into pieces and then soaked until the water becomes discolored from the matzah, it

two whole matzos in your hands and the broken one between them, and recite *Hamotzi.* You then put down the bottom matzah,[16] holding only the top, and the broken middle matzah, and say the berachah, *Al achilat matzah.* You then break off a piece the size of a *kazayis,* from the top matzah and from the broken middle matzah.[17] You distribute the same quantity to every member of the family. Then you eat both pieces simultaneously,[18] while reclining on the left side.[19] If it is difficult for you to eat both pieces of matzah at the same time, you should first eat the *kazayis* piece over which you said *Hamotzi,* and then eat the *kazayis* piece from the broken matzah. But you should not pause between eating the two pieces, and eat both pieces while reclining. It is the custom in our region, at the *seder,* not to dip the matzah in salt; neither the matzah, over which *Hamotzi* is said, nor the one over which *Al achilas matzah* is said.

6) If someone is unable to chew the matzah, he is permitted to soak it in water[20] to soften it,[21] provided it is not completely mashed. An elderly or sick person, who cannot eat matzah, when soaked in water, may soak it in wine, or in any other beverage.[22] When you soak the matzah, with which you want to fulfill the mitzvah (of eating matzah), you must be careful not to soak it for twenty-four hours, for it would then be considered as if it were cooked and you could not fulfill the mitzvah with it. You must also be careful, in other respects, that the matzah should not lose its status as bread. See Chapter 48:5 above.

7) You then take a *kazayis* of *maror,*[23] and distribute portions of the same quantity to each member of the family. You dip it in the *charoses,* and shake off the *charoses,* so that the *maror* should not lose its taste, and say the berachah, *Al achilas maror,* and eat it[24] *without* reclining.[25] You then take a *kazayis* from the bottom matzah and a *kazayis maror.* It is also proper to dip (this *maror*) in *charoses* and shake it off. You then place the *maror* between (two pieces of) matzah and say, *Kein asa Hillel* (This is the way Hillel did it) etc.[26] and eat it while reclining.[27] The size of a *kazayis,* as we have written in the general rules, is as much as half an egg.[28] However, some authorities hold, that it is a little less than one-third of

---

cannot be used to fulfill the mitzvah, as it is no longer considered bread. These rules applies only to soaking, but if the matzah was boiled, or soaked in boiling water, it is not permissible under any circumstances. (*Mishnah Berurah* 461:17,18,20)

22. A healthy, young person cannot fulfill his obligation, if the matzah was soaked in any liquid, except water. (*Ibid.* 461:18)

23. If you are using ground horseradish, you should make sure it is compacted, so that it is a *kazayis.* If you are using leaves, you must also be certain that it is compacted, as the space between leaves are not considered. (*Ibid.* 473:36,41)

24. See note 18.

25. The *maror* recalls our slavery, and is, therefore, not eaten in a leisurely manner.

26. *Mishnah Berurah* questions the custom of reciting this sentence, as it constitutes an interruption between the berachah and the eating. (*Ibid.* 475:1, *Biyur Halachah*)

27. See note 18.

28. See Glossary.

הַזֶּה מִדְּרַבָּנָן, לָכֵן מִי שֶׁקָּשֶׁה עָלָיו לֶאֱכוֹל מָרוֹר, יָכוֹל לִסְמוֹךְ עַל דֵּעָה זֹאת לֶאֱכוֹל רַק פָּחוֹת קְצָת מִכְּמוֹ שְׁלִישׁ בֵּיצָה וִיבָרֵךְ עָלָיו. וּמִי שֶׁהוּא חוֹלֶה, שֶׁאֵינוֹ יָכוֹל לֶאֱכוֹל מָרוֹר כְּלָל, יִלְעוֹס עַל־כָּל־פָּנִים קְצָת מֵהַמִּינִים שֶׁיּוֹצְאִין בָּהֶם אוֹ שְׁאָר עֵשֶׂב מַר עַד שֶׁיַּרְגִּישׁ טַעַם מְרִירוּת בְּפִיו לְזֵכֶר בְּעָלְמָא, בְּלֹא בְּרָכָה.

ח) אַחַר כָּךְ אוֹכְלִין הַסְּעוּדָה. וְיֵשׁ לֶאֱכוֹל כָּל הַסְּעוּדָה בַּהֲסִבָּה. וְנוֹהֲגִין לֶאֱכֹל בֵּיצִים. וְהֶחָכָם עֵינָיו בְּרֹאשׁוֹ, שֶׁלֹּא לְמַלֹּאת כְּרֵסוֹ, לְמַעַן יוּכַל לֶאֱכוֹל אֶת הָאֲפִיקוֹמָן כְּמִצְוָתוֹ, וְלֹא לַאֲכִילָה גַּסָּה. וְאֵין אוֹכְלִין בָּשָׂר צָלִי בִּשְׁנֵי הַלֵּילוֹת, אֲפִלּוּ שֶׁל עוֹף. וַאֲפִלּוּ בִּשְׁלוּהוּ וְאַחַר כָּךְ צְלוּהוּ בִּקְדֵרָה, אֵין אוֹכְלִין. יֵשׁ נוֹהֲגִין שֶׁלֹּא לֶאֱכוֹל בַּלֵּילוֹת אֵלּוּ שׁוּם טִבּוּל, חוּץ מִשְּׁנֵי טִבּוּלִים שֶׁל מִצְוָה, כְּדֵי שֶׁיְּהֵא נִכָּר שֶׁאֵלּוּ הֵם לְשֵׁם מִצְוָה. לְאַחַר גְּמַר הַסְּעוּדָה, אוֹכְלִין אֲפִיקוֹמָן, זֵכֶר לְקָרְבַּן פֶּסַח שֶׁהָיָה נֶאֱכָל בְּסוֹף הַסְּעוּדָה, שֶׁיְּהֵא גְּמַר כָּל הַשְּׂבִיעָה. וְיֵשׁ לֶאֱכוֹל כִּשְׁנֵי זֵיתִים, אֶחָד זֵכֶר לַפֶּסַח, וְאֶחָד זֵכֶר לַמַּצָּה שֶׁהָיְתָה נֶאֱכֶלֶת עִם הַפָּסַח. וְעַל־כָּל־פָּנִים לֹא יִפְחוֹת מִכַּזַּיִת, וְאוֹכְלוֹ בַּהֲסִבָּה. וְאַחַר הָאֲפִיקוֹמָן, אָסוּר לֶאֱכוֹל שׁוּם דָּבָר. אַחַר כָּךְ מוֹזְגִין כּוֹס שְׁלִישִׁי לְבִרְכַּת־הַמָּזוֹן. וְצָרִיךְ לְדַקְדֵּק בּוֹ אִם הוּא נָקִי מִשִּׁיּוּרֵי כוֹסוֹת, דְּהַיְנוּ אִם אֵין בּוֹ שִׁיּוּרֵי יַיִן שֶׁשָּׁרָה בּוֹ מַצָּה בִּשְׁעַת הַסְּעוּדָה. כִּי אִם אֵינוֹ נָקִי, צָרִיךְ שְׁטִיפָה וַהֲדָחָה (עַיֵּן לְעֵיל סִימָן מ"ה סָעִיף ד'). וּמִצְוָה לְהַדֵּר שֶׁיְּבָרְכוּ בְּזִמּוּן. אֲבָל לֹא יֵלְכוּ מִבַּיִת לְבַיִת לְצֹרֶךְ זִמּוּן, כִּי כָל אֶחָד צָרִיךְ לְבָרֵךְ בִּרְכַּת־הַמָּזוֹן בְּמָקוֹם שֶׁאָכַל. וְנוֹהֲגִין שֶׁבַּעַל־הַבַּיִת מְבָרֵךְ בַּזִּמּוּן, שֶׁנֶּאֱמַר, טוֹב עַיִן הוּא יְבֹרָךְ (עַיֵּן לְעֵיל סִימָן מה סָעִיף ה), וְהוּא מִקְרֵי טוֹב עַיִן, שֶׁאָמַר, כָּל דִּכְפִין יֵיתֵי וְיֵיכוֹל וְכוּ'. וְאַחַר כָּךְ מְבָרְכִין עַל הַכּוֹס וְשׁוֹתִין בַּהֲסִבָּה. וְאָסוּר לִשְׁתּוֹת בֵּין כּוֹס זֶה לְכוֹס רְבִיעִי.

ט) אַחַר בִּרְכַּת־הַמָּזוֹן מוֹזְגִין כּוֹס רְבִיעִי. וְנוֹהֲגִין לִפְתּוֹחַ אֶת הַדֶּלֶת,

---

29. Nevertheless, if you reclined only while eating the matzah and drinking the Four Cups of wine, you have fulfilled your obligation. (*Ibid.* 472:23)

30. If you are so full that any more eating is abhorent, and you eat the *Afikoman* in such a condition, you have not fulfilled your obligation. (*Ibid.* 476:6)

31. Women are also obligated to eat the *afikoman*. (*Ibid.* 476:2)

32. Since it is a reminder of the *Pesach* sacrifice, it must be eaten before midnight, as was required of the actual *Pesach* sacrifice. (*Ibid.* 476:6) Midnight does not mean 12 P.M., but is dependent on the length of the hours of daylight and night time.

an egg. Since the mitzvah of eating *maror* is in our days a rabbinical requirement, therefore, a person, who finds it difficult to eat *maror,* may rely on this (more lenient) opinion, and eat a little less than one third of an egg, and say the berachah over it. A person who is sick and cannot eat *maror* at all, should, nevertheless, chew a little of any of the species, with which the mitzvah of *maror* may be fulfilled, or any bitter tasting herb, until he feels a bitter taste in his mouth; just as a token, without saying a berachah.

8) After that the meal begins. It is proper to eat the entire meal[29] while reclining It is customary to eat eggs. It is wise to use good judgment, and not overeat, so that you will be able to eat the *afikoman,* as required, (with appetite), and not on a full stomach.[30] Roast meat should not be eaten, on the two *seder* nights, not even roast poultry. Even if it was boiled and then pot roasted, it should not be eaten. Some have the custom not to eat any food dipped in liquid, on the *seder* nights, except the two required dipped foods, so that it should be prominently recognized that these two are mitzvos. After completing the meal, the *afikoman* is eaten[31] to remind us of the *Pesach* sacrifice,[32] which was eaten at the end of the meal so that you should be completely satiated. It is proper to eat two *kazeisim* (of matzah for the *afikoman*), one to remind us of the *Pesach* sacrifice, and the other to recall the matzah that was eaten with the *korban Pesach* . At any rate, you should not eat less than a *kazayis,* and you should eat the *afikoman,* while reclining. After eating the *afikoman,* it is forbidden to eat anything.[33] [34] The third cup is then filled for *Birkas Hamazon.* You must make sure that it is clean, not containing leftover wine, that is to say, nothing is left from the wine, in which matzah may have been soaked during the meal. If it is not clean, it requires washing and rinsing (See Chapter 45:4 above). It is a mitzvah to make an effort to recite *Birkas Hamazon* with *zimun* (three males), but you should not go from house to house to look for people required for *zimun,* because each person is required to say *Birkas Hamazon* in the place where he has eaten. It is customary for the master of the house to lead the *zimun*[35] as it is said: "A man of a good eye shall bless," (Proverbs 22:9) (see Ch. 45:5) and he is called, "A man of good eye," (i.e. a generous person) because he said: "All who are hungry—let them come and eat" etc. After *Birkas Hamazon,* the berachah is said over the third cup, and you should drink it while reclining. It is forbidden to drink between this cup and the fourth cup.

9) After *Birkas Hamazon,* the fourth cup is filled. It is the custom to open

---

33. Our Sages ordained this rule, so that the taste of matzo remains with you. If you forgot and did eat something else, you must eat another *kazayis* of matzo for the *afikoman.* (*Ibid.* 476:1)

34. You are permitted to drink water. Some *Poskim* also permit tea. Other drinks, however, that are tasty or sharp, that would remove the taste of matzah are forbidden. (*Ibid.* 478:2, 481:1)

35. He takes precedence even over a guest, who is usually accorded the privilege of leading the *zimun.* (*Ibid.* 479:13)

לְזֵכֶר שֶׁהוּא לֵיל שִׁמּוּרִים, וְאֵין מִתְיָרְאִין מִשּׁוּם דָּבָר. וּבִזְכוּת הָאֱמוּנָה, יָבוֹא מָשִׁיחַ צִדְקֵנוּ, וְהַקָּדוֹשׁ־בָּרוּךְ־הוּא יִשְׁפֹּךְ חֲמָתוֹ עַל הַגּוֹיִם, וְלָכֵן אוֹמְרִים שְׁפֹךְ חֲמָתְךָ וְגוֹ'. אַחַר כָּךְ מַתְחִילִין לֹא לָנוּ, וְאוֹמְרִים כַּסֵּדֶר. וּכְשֶׁמַּגִּיעַ לְהוֹדוּ, אִם הֵם שְׁלֹשָׁה, אֲפִלּוּ עִם אִשְׁתּוֹ וּבָנָיו שֶׁהִגִּיעוּ לְחִנּוּךְ, יֹאמַר הוֹדוּ, וְהַשְּׁנַיִם יַעֲנוּ, כְּמוֹ שֶׁאוֹמְרִים בְּצִבּוּר. מִן הַכּוֹס הָרְבִיעִי, צְרִיכִין לִשְׁתּוֹת רְבִיעִית שְׁלֵמָה וּמְבָרְכִים אַחֲרָיו בְּרָכָה אַחֲרוֹנָה, וְאַחַר כָּךְ גּוֹמְרִין כְּסֵדֶר הַהַגָּדָה. וְאַחַר אַרְבַּעַת הַכּוֹסוֹת אָסוּר לִשְׁתּוֹת שׁוּם מַשְׁקֶה רַק מָיִם. אִם אֵין שֵׁנָה חוֹטַפְתּוֹ, יֹאמַר אַחַר הַהַגָּדָה שִׁיר הַשִּׁירִים. וְנוֹהֲגִין שֶׁאֵין קוֹרִין קְרִיאַת־שְׁמַע שֶׁעַל הַמִּטָּה, רַק פָּרָשַׁת שְׁמַע וּבִרְכַּת הַמַּפִּיל, לְהוֹרוֹת שֶׁהוּא לֵיל שִׁמּוּרִים מִן הַמַּזִּיקִין וְאֵינוֹ צָרִיךְ שְׁמִירָה.

י) מִי שֶׁאֵינוֹ שׁוֹתֶה יַיִן כָּל הַשָּׁנָה מִפְּנֵי שֶׁמַּזִּיק לוֹ, אַף־עַל־פִּי־כֵן צָרִיךְ לִדְחֹק אֶת עַצְמוֹ לִשְׁתּוֹת אַרְבָּעָה כּוֹסוֹת, כְּמוֹ שֶׁאָמְרוּ רַבּוֹתֵינוּ זִכְרוֹנָם לִבְרָכָה, עַל רַבִּי יְהוּדָה בַּר רַבִּי אִלְעַי, שֶׁהָיָה שׁוֹתֶה אַרְבָּעָה כּוֹסוֹת שֶׁל פֶּסַח, וְהָיָה צָרִיךְ לַחֲגוֹר צְדָעָיו עַד שָׁבוּעוֹת. וּמִכָּל מָקוֹם יָכוֹל לְמָזְגוֹ בְּמַיִם, אוֹ לִשְׁתּוֹת יַיִן צִמּוּקִים (עַיֵּן לְעֵיל סִימָן נג סָעִיף ו), אוֹ שֶׁיִּשְׁתֶּה מֶעַד אִם הֵם חֲמַר מְדִינָה.

יא) אִם נֶאֱבַד הָאֲפִיקוֹמָן, אִם יֵשׁ לוֹ עוֹד מַצָּה מֵאֵלּוּ שֶׁנַּעֲשׂוּ לְשֵׁם מַצַּת מִצְוָה, יֹאכַל מִמֶּנָּה כַּזַּיִת. וְאִם לָאו, יֹאכַל מִמַּצָּה אַחֶרֶת כַּזַּיִת.

יב) מִי שֶׁשָּׁכַח לֶאֱכוֹל אֶת הָאֲפִיקוֹמָן, אִם נִזְכַּר קֹדֶם בִּרְכַּת־הַמָּזוֹן, אַף־עַל־פִּי שֶׁכְּבָר נָטַל מַיִם אַחֲרוֹנִים אוֹ שֶׁאָמַר, הַב לָן וּנְבָרֵךְ, אוֹכְלוֹ וְאֵינוֹ צָרִיךְ לְבָרֵךְ בִּרְכַּת הַמּוֹצִיא. וְאַף־עַל־גַּב דְּאַסַּח דַּעְתֵּהּ מִלֶּאֱכוֹל, לָא חָשִׁיב הֶסַּח־הַדַּעַת, כֵּיוָן שֶׁהוּא מְחֻיָּב לֶאֱכוֹל, וְאַתְּכָא דְּרַחֲמָנָא קָסָמְכֵינַן. וּמִכָּל מָקוֹם יֵשׁ לוֹ לִטּוֹל יָדָיו, וְלֹא יְבָרֵךְ עַל נְטִילַת יָדַיִם. וְאִם לֹא נִזְכַּר עַד לְאַחַר בִּרְכַּת־הַמָּזוֹן קֹדֶם שֶׁבֵּרַךְ בּוֹרֵא פְּרִי הַגָּפֶן עַל כּוֹס שְׁלִישִׁי, יִטּוֹל יָדָיו, וְגַם כֵּן לֹא יְבָרֵךְ עַל נְטִילַת יָדַיִם, וִיבָרֵךְ בִּרְכַּת הַמּוֹצִיא, וְיֹאכַל כַּזַּיִת, וְאַחַר כָּךְ יְבָרֵךְ בִּרְכַּת־הַמָּזוֹן, וִיבָרֵךְ עַל כּוֹס שְׁלִישִׁי וְיִשְׁתֶּה. אֲבָל אִם לֹא נִזְכַּר עַד לְאַחַר שֶׁבֵּרַךְ בּוֹרֵא פְּרִי הַגָּפֶן עַל כּוֹס שְׁלִישִׁי, יִשְׁתֶּה אֶת הַכּוֹס. וְאִם רָגִיל בְּפַעַם אַחֶרֶת לְבָרֵךְ בִּרְכַּת־הַמָּזוֹן בְּלֹא כּוֹס,

---

36. You must do this, in order to be able to recite the after-berachah over the wine; for if you drink less, it is questionable if you should recite the berachah. (*Ibid.* 472:30)

the door, to remind us that tonight is a night of Divine vigil, and we are not afraid of anything. In the merit of our faith in Hashem, our righteous *Mashiach* will come, and the Holy One, blessed is He, will pour out his anger on the nations. Therefore, we recite *Shefoch chamasecha* (Pour out Your anger) etc. After that, we say, *Lo lanu* (Not for us) and continue reciting the *Hallel.* When we reach *Hodu* (Give thanks), if there are three people present, even if they are his wife and children, who have reached the age of training for mitzvos, the leader should say *Hodu,* and the other two people respond, as it is done in the synagogue. You are required to drink a full revi's[36] from the fourth cup, after which you say the after-berachah.[37] You then recite the *Haggadah* to the end. After the fourth cup, it is forbidden to drink any beverage, except water.[38] If you are not too sleepy, you should say *Shir hashirim* after the *Hagadah.* It is customary not to say the bedtime *Shema,* except for the section of *Shema* and the berachah *Hamapil,* to indicate that it is a night of divine vigil when Hashem protects us from all evil, and we need no other protection.

10) A person, who does not drink wine all year, because it causes him discomfort, nevertheless should make a special effort to drink the Four Cups, as our Rabbis, of blessed memory, relate about Rabbi Yehudah bar Rabbi Ilai, who used to drink the Four Cups of wine on *Pesach,* and then he would have to wrap his temples until *Shavuos* (because of the headache the wine gave him). However, such a person may dilute the wine with water, or drink raisin wine, (see Chapter 50:6 above), or he may drink mead, if these are the "beverage of the country"

11) If the *afikoman* was lost, and you still have matzah left of those that were made specifically for the mitzvah, you should eat a *kazayis* of that matzah, otherwise, you should eat a *kazayis* of any other matzah.

12) If you forgot to eat the *afikoman;* and reminded yourself before saying *Birkas Hamazon,* although you already had washed your hands at the end of the meal or said, "Come, let us say the blessings," you may eat the *afikoman,* and do not have to say *Hamotzi.* And even though you had not intended to eat anymore, this does not constitute a diversion of the mind, since it is your duty to eat the *afikoman,* and are sitting at Hashem's table, (and must fulfill His will; thus you were not completely distracted). Nevertheless, you should wash your hands, without saying *Al netilas yadayim.* But if you did not remind yourself, until after saying *Birkas Hamazon,* before saying *Borei peri hagafen* over the third cup, then you should wash your hands again, without saying, *Al netilas yadayim,* and recite the berachah of *Hamotzi,* eat a *kazayis* of the *afikoman,* say *Birkas Hamazon;* then say the berachah over the third cup, and drink it. But if you only reminded yourself after saying *Borei peri hagafen* over the third cup, you should drink the cup. If on other occasions you are accustomed to recite *Birkas Hamazon,* without a cup of wine, you should wash your

---

37. This berachah will also exempt the wine of the third cup. (*Ibid.* 480:7)
38. See note 34.

יִטּוֹל יָדָיו וְיֹאכַל אֲפִיקוֹמָן וִיבָרֵךְ בִּרְכַּת־הַמָּזוֹן בְּלֹא כוֹס. אֲבָל אִם הוּא נִזְהָר לְבָרֵךְ תָּמִיד בִּרְכַּת־הַמָּזוֹן עַל הַכּוֹס, וְעַתָּה לֹא יוּכַל לְבָרֵךְ עַל הַכּוֹס, מִשּׁוּם דַּהֲוֵי מוֹסִיף עַל הַכּוֹסוֹת, לָכֵן לֹא יֹאכַל אֲפִיקוֹמָן, וְיִסְמוֹךְ עַל הַמַּצָּה שֶׁאָכַל תְּחִלָּה.

סִימָן קכ
הִלְכוֹת סְפִירַת הָעֹמֶר וִימֵי הַסְּפִירָה

א) בְּלֵיל שֵׁנִי שֶׁל פֶּסַח, מַתְחִילִין לִסְפֹּר סְפִירַת הָעֹמֶר. וְסוֹפְרִין מְעֻמָּד. הַמִּצְוָה הִיא לִסְפּוֹר תֵּכֶף בְּהַתְחָלַת הַלַּיְלָה, אַחַר צֵאת הַכּוֹכָבִים. וּבְדִיעֲבַד, זְמַנָּהּ כָּל הַלַּיְלָה. בְּבֵית־הַכְּנֶסֶת, בְּלֵיל שַׁבָּת וְיוֹם־טוֹב, סוֹפְרִין לְאַחַר הַקִּדּוּשׁ, כְּדֵי לְהַקְדִּים קְדֻשַּׁת הַיּוֹם. וּבְמוֹצָאֵי־שַׁבָּת וְיוֹם־טוֹב, סוֹפְרִין קֹדֶם הַבְדָּלָה, כְּדֵי לְאַחֵר יְצִיאַת הַיּוֹם. וּכְשֶׁחָל יוֹם־טוֹב הָאַחֲרוֹן בְּמוֹצָאֵי־שַׁבָּת, שֶׁאוֹמְרִים קִדּוּשׁ וְהַבְדָּלָה עַל כּוֹס אֶחָד סוֹפְרִין גַּם כֵּן קֹדֶם, כְּדֵי לְאַחֵר אֶת הַהַבְדָּלָה.

ב) מִי שֶׁשָּׁכַח כָּל הַלַּיְלָה וְלֹא סָפַר, יִסְפּוֹר בַּיּוֹם בְּלֹא בְּרָכָה, וּבַלֵּילוֹת שֶׁאַחַר כָּךְ יִסְפּוֹר בִּבְרָכָה. וְאִם שָׁכַח גַּם כָּל הַיּוֹם, יִסְפּוֹר אַחַר כָּךְ בְּכָל הַלֵּילוֹת בְּלֹא בְרָכָה. וְאִם נִסְתַּפֵּק לוֹ אִם סָפַר בַּלַּיְלָה אוֹ לֹא, אַף־עַל־פִּי שֶׁלֹּא סָפַר בַּיּוֹם שֶׁלְּאַחֲרָיו, מִכָּל מָקוֹם יָכוֹל לִסְפּוֹר שְׁאָר הַלֵּילוֹת בִּבְרָכָה.

ג) הַשּׁוֹאֵל מֵחֲבֵרוֹ בֵּין הַשְּׁמָשׁוֹת אוֹ אַחַר כָּךְ, כַּמָּה מוֹנִים הַיּוֹם, יֹאמַר לוֹ, אֶתְמוֹל הָיָה כָּךְ וְכָךְ. שֶׁאִם יֹאמַר לוֹ כַּמָּה מוֹנִים הַיּוֹם, אֵינוֹ רַשַּׁאי לְבָרֵךְ אַחַר כָּךְ עַל הַסְּפִירָה.

ד) לְכַתְּחִלָּה קֹדֶם שֶׁיְּבָרֵךְ, צָרִיךְ שֶׁיֵּדַע עַל מָה הוּא מְבָרֵךְ, דְּהַיְנוּ שֶׁיֵּדַע כַּמָּה יָמִים הוּא בַּסְּפִירָה. וּבְדִיעֲבַד אִם לֹא יָדַע וּפָתַח וּבֵרֵךְ עַל

---

1. Since this is a mitzvah, that is done only at a certain, specific time, women are exempt from counting the *Omer. Magein Avraham* says that women have since accepted this mitzvah as an obligation, but *Mishnah Berurah* says that in our areas, women are not accustomed to count the *Omer.* He quotes from *Shulchan Shlomo* that women certainly should not say the berachah. (*Mishnah Berurah* 489:3)

2. You should also stand for the berachah. If, however, you did count while sitting, you have still fulfilled your obligation (and you need not count over again). (*Ibid.* 489:6)

hands, eat the *afikoman,* and say *Birkas Hamazon* without a cup of wine. However, if you are scrupulous, and always says *Birkas Hamazon,* over a cup of wine, and now cannot do it, because you would be adding to the four cups, (which is forbidden), then you should not eat the *afikoman,* but rely on the matzah, which you ate before.

Chapter 120

The Laws of Counting the Omer and the Days of Sefirah

1) On the second night of Pesach, we begin counting the *Omer.*[1] You should stand during the counting.[2] The mitzvah requires that the *Omer* be counted, as soon as possible after nightfall,[3] after (three medium-size star) stars begin to appear. If you did not count at the beginning of the evening, you may count the entire night. In the synagogue, on the eve of Shabbos and Yom Tov, we count after the *Kiddush* is said, in order to give precedence to the (proclamation of the) holiness of the day.[4] At the conclusion of Shabbos and Yom Tov, we count before the *Havdalah* is said, in order to delay the end of the day. If the last day of Yom Tov occurs on Shabbos night, when the *Kiddush* and the *Havdalah* are said over one [the same] cup of wine, we also count before, in order to postpone the *Havdalah.*

2) If you forgot to count during the night, you should count during the daytime, but without a berachah. On subsequent nights, you may count with a berachah. If you neglected to count an entire day, you should count on all subsequent nights, without saying the berachah.[5] If you are not sure whether or not you counted that night, even though you did not count on the following day, nevertheless, you may count the remaining days with a berachah.

3) If someone asks you, during twilight or later, "What is tonight's count?" You should tell him, "Yesterday was such-and-such," for if you would tell him today's count, you are not permitted to say the berachah, when you count the *Omer* later that night.[6]

4) Before saying the berachah, you should know what the berachah is for; that is, you should know the exact number of days of the *Omer.*[7] However, if you did not

---

3. Counting the *Omer* is done after the *Maariv* prayer, before saying *Aleinu.* Later *Poskim* rule, however, once the stars have appeared, the *Omer* may be counted even before *Maariv.* (*Ibid.* 489:2,18)

4. At home, however, we must count the *Omer* before *Kiddush,* as it is forbidden to eat before counting the *Omer.* (*Ibid.* 489:39)

5. This law also applies, if you realized you counted the wrong *Sefirah* yesterday. (*Ibid.* 489:35)

6. However, if, for example, you just said the number twelve, without saying *today is the twelfth day,* you can still count the *Omer* with a berachah. (*Ibid.* 489:22)

7. The later *Poskim* rule that it is permitted to count the *Omer* in any language you understand. If you do not understand, and, thus, you do not know what you are counting, you cannot fulfill your obligation, even if you count in Hebrew. (*Ibid.* 489:11)

דַעַת שֶׁיִּסְפּוֹר כְּמוֹ שֶׁיִּשְׁמַע מֵחֲבֵרוֹ, גַּם כֵּן יָצָא. וְכֵן אִם בֵּרֵךְ עַל דַּעַת לִסְפּוֹר אַרְבָּעָה יָמִים, וּלְאַחַר שֶׁבֵּרַךְ נִזְכַּר שֶׁצָּרִיךְ לִסְפּוֹר חֲמִשָּׁה, סוֹפֵר חֲמִשָּׁה וְאֵינוֹ צָרִיךְ לְבָרֵךְ שֵׁנִית. וְכֵן אִם טָעָה בַּסְפִירָה, כְּגוֹן שֶׁהָיָה צָרִיךְ לוֹמַר שִׁשָּׁה יָמִים וְאָמַר חֲמִשָּׁה יָמִים, אִם נִזְכַּר מִיָּד, סוֹפֵר כָּרָאוּי וְאֵינוֹ צָרִיךְ לְבָרֵךְ שֵׁנִית. אֲבָל אִם הִפְסִיק קְצָת, צָרִיךְ לְבָרֵךְ שֵׁנִית.

ה) בְּכָל יוֹם־טוֹב אִם חָל לֵיל רִאשׁוֹן בַּשַּׁבָּת שֶׁאֵין אוֹמְרִים אָז מַעֲרָבִית, אֲזַי בְּלֵיל שֵׁנִי אוֹמְרִים הַמַּעֲרָבִית מִלֵּיל רִאשׁוֹן, חוּץ מִפֶּסַח, שֶׁאֲפִלּוּ חָל לֵיל רִאשׁוֹן בַּשַּׁבָּת, מִכָּל מָקוֹם בְּלֵיל שֵׁנִי אוֹמְרִים מַעֲרָבִית שֶׁשַּׁיֶּכֶת לוֹ, מִפְּנֵי שֶׁמְּדַבֵּר מִקְּצִירַת הָעֹמֶר שֶׁהָיְתָה בְּלֵיל זֶה.

ו) בִּימֵי הַסְּפִירָה מֵתוּ תַלְמִידֵי רַבִּי עֲקִיבָא בִּשְׁלֹשָׁה וּשְׁלֹשִׁים יוֹם, וְלָכֵן נוֹהֲגִין בַּיָּמִים הָאֵלּוּ קְצָת אֲבֵלוּת, שֶׁאֵין נוֹשְׂאִין נָשִׁים וְאֵין מִסְתַּפְּרִים. וְיֵשׁ חִלּוּקֵי מִנְהָגִים בְּמִסְפַּר שְׁלֹשָׁה וּשְׁלֹשִׁים יוֹם הָאֵלֶּה, יֵשׁ מְקוֹמוֹת נוֹהֲגִין שֶׁחוֹשְׁבִין אוֹתָן מִיּוֹם רִאשׁוֹן דִּסְפִירָה, וְלָכֵן אוֹסְרִין עַד לַ״ג בָּעֹמֶר. אַךְ כְּשֶׁחָל רֹאשׁ־חֹדֶשׁ אִיָּר בַּשַּׁבָּת, דְּיֵשׁ בּוֹ שְׁתֵּי קְדֻשּׁוֹת, קְדֻשַּׁת שַׁבָּת וּקְדֻשַּׁת רֹאשׁ־חֹדֶשׁ, אָז מַתִּירִין לִשָּׂא, וְכֵן לְהִסְתַּפֵּר בְּעֶרֶב שַׁבָּת. וּבְיוֹם לַ״ג בָּעֹמֶר, וְכֵן מִשָּׁם וְאֵילָךְ מַתִּירִין, מִפְּנֵי שֶׁבְּיוֹם לַ״ג בָּעֹמֶר פָּסְקוּ מִלָּמוּת, וְלָכֵן מַרְבִּים בּוֹ קְצָת שִׂמְחָה, וְאֵין אוֹמְרִים בּוֹ תַּחֲנוּן. וְאַף שֶׁגַּם בּוֹ בַּיּוֹם מֵתוּ קְצָת, אָמְרִינָן, מִקְצָת הַיּוֹם כְּכֻלּוֹ, וְלָכֵן אֵין לְהִסְתַּפֵּר אוֹ לִשָּׂא עַד לְאַחַר שֶׁהֵאִיר הַיּוֹם, וְלֹא מִבָּעֶרֶב. אַךְ כְּשֶׁחָל לַ״ג בָּעֹמֶר בְּיוֹם רִאשׁוֹן, מִסְתַּפְּרִין בְּעֶרֶב שַׁבָּת שֶׁלְּפָנָיו, לִכְבוֹד הַשַּׁבָּת.

ז) וְיֵשׁ מְקוֹמוֹת שֶׁמַּתִּירִין עַד רֹאשׁ־חֹדֶשׁ אִיָּר וְעַד בִּכְלָל, שֶׁהֵן שִׁשָּׁה עָשָׂר יוֹם, וְנִשְׁאָרִים שְׁלֹשָׁה וּשְׁלֹשִׁים יוֹם בְּאִסּוּר עַד חַג הַשָּׁבוּעוֹת (וּמִסְתַּפְּרִין בְּעֶרֶב הֶחָג). וּמִכָּל מָקוֹם בְּיוֹם לַ״ג בָּעֹמֶר בְּעַצְמוֹ מַתִּירִין. (וּכְשֶׁחָל בְּיוֹם רִאשׁוֹן, מַתִּירִין בְּעֶרֶב שַׁבָּת, כְּמוֹ שֶׁכָּתַבְתִּי לְעֵיל). וְיֵשׁ מְקוֹמוֹת שֶׁמַּתִּירִין עַד רֹאשׁ־חֹדֶשׁ אִיָּר וְלֹא עַד בִּכְלָל, וּבְיוֹם רִאשׁוֹן

8. *Toch kedei dibur* i.e., within the time it takes to say these three words, *sholom olecha Rebbe* (Peace be with you Rebbe).

9. Ma'aravis are poetic compositions that are inserted in the Ma'ariv service of Yom Tov.

10. Should the need arise, it is permitted to say the berachah, שֶׁהֶחֱיָנוּ (*shehechiyanu*) during these days. (*Ibid.* 493:2)

know it, and began the berachah with the intention of counting the number you will hear from your neighbor, you have also fulfilled your obligation. Similarly if you say the berachah with the intention of counting four days, but after completing the berachah, you realize that you should have counted five days, you should count five [days], and need not repeat the berachah. Similarly, if you made an error in counting, for example you should have said "six days," but you said "five days," if you realize it immediately,[8] you should count the correct number, and you need not repeat the berachah; but if you made a short pause, you must repeat the berachah.

5) When the first night of the Yom Tov occurs on Shabbos, *ma'aravis* are omitted,[9] and, on the second night of Yom Tov, we say the *ma'aravis* of the first night. On Pesach, however, even if the first night occurs on Shabbos, nevertheless, on the second night we say the *ma'aravis* pertaining to that night, because it deals with the harvesting of the *Omer* which took place on that night.

6) During [the first] thirty-three days of the *Sefirah* period (the counting of the *Omer*), the disciples of Rabbi Akiva perished. Therefore, it is the custom during these days to observe a partial state of mourning:[10] Marriages should not be performed and you should not take a haircut (or shave).[11] There are various customs regarding (the day on which to begin) to count these thirty-three days. Some communities have the custom of counting them beginning with the first day of the *Omer,* and, therefore, they forbid [weddings and haircuts] until *Lag ba'omer* (the 33rd day of the *Omer*). But when *Rosh Chodesh Iyar* occurs on Shabbos, which has two levels of *kedushah* (sanctity), the *kedushah* of Shabbos and the *kedushah* of *Rosh Chodesh,* they permit marriages and haircuts on *erev Shabbos.* On *Lag ba'omer* and from that day on, the restrictions are permitted, because on *Lag ba'omer* [Rabbi Akiva's disciples] ceased to die. We, therefore, rejoice somewhat, and we do not say *Tachanun* on that day. Although on that very day some of them died (mourning need not be observed for a full day), for the *Halachah* states, a part of a day is considered as a full day; therefore, you should not take a haircut, nor should weddings be held; until after dawn (of *Lag ba'omer*), but not in the evening. But if *Lag ba'omer* occurs on Sunday, you may take a haircut on the preceding *erev Shabbos,* in honor of Shabbos.

7) In other communities, they permit (weddings and haircuts) until *Rosh Chodesh Iyar,* inclusive, which adds up to sixteen days. This leaves thirty-three days, during which these things are forbidden, [that is] until *Shavuos,* (but they permit haircuts on *erev Shavuos*). Nevertheless, on *Lag ba'omer* they permit (weddings and haircuts); (and if *Lag ba'omer* occurs on Sunday, they permit them on *erev Shabbos,* as I have written above.) In still other communities, they permit (these things) until *Rosh Chodesh Iyar,* exclusive of that day, and on the first day of *Rosh Chodesh,* the

---

11. Those that are permitted to shave on *Chol Hamoed,* are also permitted to shave during *Sefirah*. (See *Kitzur Shulchan Aruch* 104:11) (*Ibid.* 493:1)

דְּרֹאשׁ־חֹדֶשׁ מַתְחִיל הָאִסּוּר, וְיוֹם הָרִאשׁוֹן דְּהַגְבָּלָה הוּא יוֹם הַלַּ"ג, וְאָמְרֵינַן בּוֹ, מִקְצָת הַיּוֹם כְּכֻלּוֹ, וּמֻתָּרִין לִשָּׂא וּלְהִסְתַּפֵּר בָּהֶן, וְגַם בְּיוֹם לַ"ג בָּעֹמֶר מֻתָּרִין (וּכְמוֹ שֶׁכָּתַבְתִּי לְעֵיל). וּצְרִיכִין לִנְהֹג בְּכָל קְהִלָּה מִנְהָג אֶחָד, וְלֹא יַעֲשׂוּ מִקְצָתָן כָּךְ וּמִקְצָתָן כָּךְ.

ח) הַסַּנְדָּק (הוּא הַתּוֹפֵס אֶת הַתִּינוֹק בִּשְׁעַת מִילָה), וְהַמּוֹהֵל, וַאֲבִי הַבֵּן, מֻתָּרִין לְהִסְתַּפֵּר בְּיוֹם שֶׁלִּפְנֵי הַמִּילָה סָמוּךְ לָעֶרֶב קֹדֶם הֲלִיכָה לְבֵית־הַכְּנֶסֶת.

ט) לַעֲשׂוֹת שִׁדּוּכִין אֲפִלּוּ בִּסְעוּדָה, מֻתָּרִין בְּכָל הַיָּמִים. אַךְ רִקּוּדִין וּמְחוֹלוֹת, אֲסוּרִין.

י) נוֹהֲגִים שֶׁלֹּא לַעֲשׂוֹת מְלָאכָה, אֶחָד אֲנָשִׁים וְאֶחָד נָשִׁים כָּל יְמֵי הַסְּפִירָה מִשְּׁקִיעַת הַחַמָּה עַד לְאַחַר סְפִירַת הָעֹמֶר, וְרֶמֶז לָזֶה, שֶׁנֶּאֱמַר, שֶׁבַע שַׁבָּתוֹת, מִלְּשׁוֹן שְׁבוּת, שֶׁבִּזְמַן הַסְּפִירָה, דְּהַיְנוּ מִשְּׁקִיעַת הַחַמָּה וְאֵילַךְ, יֵשׁ לִשְׁבּוֹת מִמְּלָאכָה עַד לְאַחַר הַסְּפִירָה.

יא) בְּלֵיל רִאשׁוֹן דְּשָׁבוּעוֹת, מְאַחֲרִין מִלְּהִתְפַּלֵּל עַרְבִית עַד צֵאת הַכּוֹכָבִים. שֶׁאִם יִתְפַּלְּלוּ קֹדֶם וִיקַבְּלוּ קְדֻשַּׁת יוֹם־טוֹב, חָסֵר מְעַט מִתִּשְׁעָה וְאַרְבָּעִים יְמֵי הַסְּפִירָה. וְהַתּוֹרָה אָמְרָה, שֶׁבַע שַׁבָּתוֹת תְּמִימוֹת תִּהְיֶינָה.

סִימָן קכא
הִלְכוֹת תַּעֲנִית־צִבּוּר

א) מִצְוַת עֲשֵׂה מִדִּבְרֵי הַנְּבִיאִים לְהִתְעַנּוֹת בַּיָּמִים שֶׁאֵרְעוּ צָרוֹת לַאֲבוֹתֵינוּ. וְתַכְלִית הַתַּעֲנִית הִיא, כְּדֵי לְעוֹרֵר אֶת הַלְּבָבוֹת לְפַקֵּחַ עַל דַּרְכֵי הַתְּשׁוּבָה, וּתְהִי זֹאת זִכָּרוֹן לְמַעֲשֵׂינוּ הָרָעִים וּמַעֲשֵׂי אֲבוֹתֵינוּ שֶׁהָיוּ כְּמַעֲשֵׂינוּ עַתָּה, עַד שֶׁגָּרְמוּ לָהֶם וְלָנוּ אוֹתָן הַצָּרוֹת. וּבְזִכְרוֹן הַדְּבָרִים הָאֵלֶּה, נָשׁוּב לְהֵטִיב, כְּמוֹ שֶׁנֶּאֱמַר, וְהִתְוַדּוּ אֶת־עֲוֹנָם וְאֶת־עֲוֹן אֲבוֹתָם. וְלָכֵן חַיָּב כָּל אִישׁ לָשׂוּם אֶל־לִבּוֹ בְּאוֹתָן הַיָּמִים לְפַשְׁפֵּשׁ בְּמַעֲשָׂיו וְלָשׁוּב מֵהֶן, כִּי אֵין הָעִקָּר בְּתַעֲנִית, כְּמוֹ שֶׁנֶּאֱמַר בְּאַנְשֵׁי נִינְוֵה, וַיַּרְא הָאֱלֹהִים אֶת־מַעֲשֵׂיהֶם, וְאָמְרוּ רַבּוֹתֵינוּ זִכְרוֹנָם לִבְרָכָה, וַיַּרְא אֶת שַׂקָּם וְאֶת תַּעֲנִיתָם לֹא נֶאֱמַר, אֶלָּא וַיַּרְא הָאֱלֹהִים אֶת־מַעֲשֵׂיהֶם כִּי שָׁבוּ מִדַּרְכָּם

restrictions begin to apply. On the first of the three days of *Hagbalah* [the three days preceding *Shavuos*,] which is the thirty-third day (of the period the restrictions are in effect), they apply the rule, "A part of day is considered as a full day," and they, therefore, permit marriages and haircuts during these three days, as well as on *Lag ba'omer,* (as I have written above). It is essential that the entire community follow the same custom, and not that some follow one custom and others follow a different custom.

8) The *Sandak,* (the person who holds the infant during the *bris* circumcision), the *mohel,* and the father of the infant, are permitted to take a haircut (and shave) on the day before the *bris,* towards evening, before going to the synagogue.[12]

9) Engagement parties, even with a meal, are permitted during all the *Sefirah* days; but dancing is forbidden.

10) It is the custom that no work is performed, by either men or women during the *Sefirah* days, from sunset, until after the counting of the *Omer.* There is an allusion for this (in the Torah), because it is said, "Seven weeks" (Leviticus 23:15). [The word *shabbasos,* meaning weeks,] is derived from *shevos,* denoting rest, indicating that during the time we count the *Omer,* that is from sunset on, you should rest [refrain] from doing any work, until after you have counted the *Omer.*

11) On the first night of *Shavuos,* the *Maariv* service is delayed, until the stars come out, for, if we would hold the service before this time, and usher in the Yom Tov, a bit of time will be lacking from the forty-nine days of the *Sefirah,* and the Torah says, "They shall be seven *complete* weeks" (Leviticus 23:15).

Chapter 121

Laws Concerning Public Fast Days

1) It is a positive commandment, ordained by the Prophets, to fast on those days on which tragic events occurred to our forefathers. The purpose of the fast is to stir our hearts to reflect on the ways of repentance, and to serve as a reminder of our own evil deeds,and the deeds of our forefathers, which were as reprehensible as ours, and caused all these troubles for them as well as for us. By remembering these events we will improve our ways, as it has been said, "They will then confess their sins and the sins of their fathers" (Leviticus 26:4). Therefore, it is everyone's duty to take it to heart on those days to examine his past actions and to repent; for fasting is not the main thing, as it was said about the people of Nineveh, "And God saw their deeds" (Jonah 3:10), and our Rabbis, of blessed memory, have said, "It does not say, 'He saw their sackcloth and their fast,' but 'God saw their deeds, that they had turned away from their evil ways.'" Fasting is only a preparation for

12. If the *bris* (circumcision) will be held on Shabbos, they are permitted to take a haircut or shave on Friday, even before midday. (*Ibid.* 493:13)

הָרָעָה. וְאֵין הַתַּעֲנִית אֶלָּא הֲכָנָה לִתְשׁוּבָה. לָכֵן אוֹתָן אֲנָשִׁים שֶׁכְּשֶׁמִּתְעַנִּים הוֹלְכִים בְּטִיּוּל וּמְבַלִּים אֶת הַיּוֹם בִּדְבָרִים בְּטֵלִים, תָּפְסוּ אֶת הַטָּפֵל וְהִנִּיחוּ אֶת הָעִקָּר.

ב) וְאֵלּוּ הֵן הַיָּמִים, שְׁלֹשָׁה בְּתִשְׁרֵי בּוֹ נֶהֱרַג גְּדַלְיָה בֶּן אֲחִיקָם. שֶׁלְּאַחַר שֶׁחָרַב בֵּית־הַמִּקְדָּשׁ, הִשְׁאִירוֹ נְבוּכַדְנֶצַּר בְּאֶרֶץ־יִשְׂרָאֵל, וַיְשִׂימֵהוּ לְרֹאשׁ עַל יִשְׂרָאֵל. וְעַל יְדֵי שֶׁנֶּהֱרַג, גָּלוּ כֻּלָּן, וְנֶהֶרְגוּ מֵהֶם לַאֲלָפִים, וְנִכְבְּתָה גַּחֶלֶת יִשְׂרָאֵל הַנִּשְׁאֶרֶת.

ג) עֲשָׂרָה בְּטֵבֵת, בּוֹ סָמַךְ מֶלֶךְ בָּבֶל, נְבוּכַדְנֶצַּר הָרָשָׁע עַל יְרוּשָׁלַיִם וֶהֱבִיאָהּ בְּמָצוֹר וּבְמָצוֹק, וּמִזֶּה נִמְשַׁךְ הַחֻרְבָּן.

ד) שִׁבְעָה־עָשָׂר בְּתַמּוּז, בּוֹ אֵרְעוּ חָמֵשׁ צָרוֹת, נִשְׁתַּבְּרוּ הַלּוּחוֹת כְּשֶׁיָּרַד מֹשֶׁה מִן הָהָר, כְּמוֹ שֶׁכָּתוּב בַּתּוֹרָה, וְזֶה הָיָה בְּשִׁבְעָה־עָשָׂר בְּתַמּוּז. וְנִתְבַּטֵּל קָרְבַּן הַתָּמִיד. וְהָבְקְעָה הָעִיר בְּחֻרְבַּן בַּיִת שֵׁנִי. אַף־עַל־גַּב דִּבְחֻרְבָּן הָרִאשׁוֹן הָבְקְעָה בְּתִשְׁעָה לַחֹדֶשׁ, דִּכְתִיב, בַּחֹדֶשׁ הָרְבִיעִי בְּתִשְׁעָה לַחֹדֶשׁ וַיֶּחֱזַק הָרָעָב בָּעִיר וְגוֹ׳ וַתִּבָּקַע הָעִיר וְגוֹ׳. אֲבָל בְּחֻרְבָּן הַשֵּׁנִי, בְּשִׁבְעָה־עָשָׂר בּוֹ הָבְקְעָה הָעִיר. וְחֻרְבַּן בַּיִת שֵׁנִי חֲמִירָא לָן. (וְעוֹד אִיתָא בִּירוּשַׁלְמִי, דְּגַם בָּרִאשׁוֹן הָיָה בְּשִׁבְעָה־עָשָׂר, אֶלָּא שֶׁמִּפְּנֵי הַצָּרוֹת, טָעוּ בְּחֶשְׁבּוֹן). וְשָׂרַף אַפּוֹסְטוּמוּס הָרָשָׁע אֶת הַתּוֹרָה וְהֶעֱמַד צֶלֶם בַּהֵיכָל עַל יְדֵי רִשְׁעֵי יִשְׂרָאֵל, וְזֶה גָּרַם חֻרְבָּנוּ וְגָלוּתֵנוּ.

ה) וְתִשְׁעָה־בְּאָב, בּוֹ בַּיּוֹם נִגְזַר עַל אֲבוֹתֵינוּ שֶׁבַּמִּדְבָּר שֶׁלֹּא יִכָּנְסוּ לְאֶרֶץ־יִשְׂרָאֵל, כִּי אָז חָזְרוּ הַמְרַגְּלִים וּבָכוּ יִשְׂרָאֵל בְּכִיָּה שֶׁל חִנָּם, וְנִקְבַּע לִבְכִיָּה לְדוֹרוֹת וּבוֹ בַּיּוֹם הָיָה הַחֻרְבָּן הַגָּדוֹל שֶׁנֶּחֱרַב בּוֹ בֵּית־הַמִּקְדָּשׁ הָרִאשׁוֹן וְגַם הַשֵּׁנִי, וְנִלְכְּדָה הָעִיר בֵּיתָר שֶׁהָיְתָה עִיר גְּדוֹלָה, וְהָיוּ בָּהּ אֲלָפִים וּרְבָבוֹת מִיִּשְׂרָאֵל. וּבוֹ בַּיּוֹם חָרַשׁ טוּרְנוּסְרוּפוּס אֶת הַהֵיכָל וְאֶת סְבִיבָיו, וְנִתְקַיֵּם הַפָּסוּק, צִיּוֹן שָׂדֶה תֵחָרֵשׁ. (וְעוֹד יֵשׁ תַּעֲנִית צִבּוּר, תַּעֲנִית אֶסְתֵּר, לְקַמָּן סִימָן קמא סָעִיף ב).

ו) אִם חָלוּ תַעֲנִיּוֹת אֵלּוּ בְּשַׁבָּת, דּוֹחִין אוֹתָן לְאַחַר הַשַּׁבָּת. אֲבָל אִם חָל עֲשָׂרָה בְּטֵבֵת בְּעֶרֶב שַׁבָּת, מִתְעַנִּין וּמַשְׁלִימִין.

ז) חָתָן, שֶׁחָלָה אַחַת מֵאַרְבַּע תַּעֲנִיּוֹת אֵלּוּ בְּתוֹךְ שִׁבְעַת יְמֵי הַמִּשְׁתֶּה שֶׁלּוֹ, אַף־עַל־גַּב שֶׁאֵלּוּ הַיָּמִים הֵמָּה לוֹ כְּמוֹ רֶגֶל, מִכָּל מָקוֹם חַיָּב

repentance. Therefore those who while fasting, spend the time taking walks, and doing trivial things, take hold of the least important aspect of the fast, while ignoring the essence [of the fast.]

2) These are the fast days: **the third day of *Tishrei,*** when Gedaliah, the son of Achikam, was killed. After the *Beis Hamikdash* was destroyed, Nebuchadnezzar left him in *Eretz Yisrael,* and appointed him governor over Yisrael. Because he [Gedaliah] was assassinated, all Jews were exiled and thousands of them were killed; thus, the last ember of Jewish hope died.

3) **The tenth day of *Teiveis*** (is a fast day), because the king of Babylonia, the wicked Nebuchadnezzar, approached Jerusalem, and laid seige to it and crushed it; and this ultimately led to the destruction of the *Beis Hamikdash.*

4) **The seventeenth day of *Tammuz*** (is a fast day) because five tragic events occured on that day: 1) the Tablets [of the Covenant] were broken by Moses, when he came down from Mount Sinai, as it is written in the Torah, and this occurred on the seventeenth day of *Tammuz.* 2) The continual daily sacrifices were abolished. 3) (The Romans) broke through the wall of Jerusalem during the destruction of the second *Beis Hamikdash.* Although, during the destruction of the first *Beis Hamikdash,* the wall was breached on the ninth of *Tammuz,* as it is written, "In the fourth month, on the ninth of the month, the famine was growing worse in the city, etc. then a breach was made in the city," (Jeremiah 52:6), but at the destruction of the second *Beis Hamikdash,* the breach was made on the seventeenth day of *Tammuz,* and the destruction of the second *Beis Hamikdash* affects us more deeply. (Furthermore, it is stated in the Jerusalem Talmud, that even at the destruction of the first *Beis Hamikdash,* the breach was made on the seventeenth, but that because of all the troubles, they made an error in the date). 4) The wicked Apostomos burned a Torah scroll. 5) An idol was placed in the *Beis Hamikdash* by some wicked people among the Jews, and this caused the destruction of the *Beis Hamikdash* and our exile.

5) **The ninth day of *Av*** (is a fast day), because on that day the Almighty decreed that our forefathers in the wilderness, would not enter *Eretz Yisrael,* for then the spies had returned (from exploring Canaan), and Yisrael cried in vain, and it was established as a day of weeping for future generations. On that day, the first *Beis Hamikdash,* as well as the second were destroyed, the city of Betar was captured, which was a large city, in which an immense number of Jews lived. On that day, Turnus Rufus plowed the site of the *Beis Hamikdash,* and the surrounding area, and, thereby, the verse was fulfilled, "Zion shall be plowed into a field" (Jeremiah 26:18). (There is another public fast day, the fast of Esther, see Chapter 141:2 below.)

6) If any of these fast days occurs on Shabbos, it is postponed until after Shabbos. When the tenth of *Teiveis* occurs on *erev Shabbos,* we fast that entire day.

7) Should any of these four fast days occur during the bridegroom's seven days of wedding feast, although these days (of the wedding feast) are considered to him

לְהִתְעַנּוֹת. כֵּיוָן דְּהֶרְגֵּל שֶׁלּוֹ הֲוֵי רֶגֶל דְּיָחִיד, אָתֵי אֲבֵלוּת וְתַעֲנִית דְּרַבִּים וְדָחֵי לֵהּ. וְעוֹד הָא כְּתִיב, אִם־לֹא אַעֲלֶה אֶת־יְרוּשָׁלַיִם עַל רֹאשׁ שִׂמְחָתִי.

ח) חִלּוּק יֵשׁ בֵּין שָׁלֹשׁ תַּעֲנִיּוֹת הָרִאשׁוֹנוֹת לְתִשְׁעָה בְּאָב. בְּשָׁלֹשׁ תַּעֲנִיּוֹת הָרִאשׁוֹנוֹת, אוֹכְלִים בַּלַּיְלָה שֶׁלִּפְנֵיהֶן עַד שֶׁיַּעֲלֶה עַמּוּד הַשַּׁחַר, וְהוּא שֶׁלֹּא יָשַׁן שְׁנַת קֶבַע. אֲבָל אִם יָשַׁן שְׁנַת קֶבַע, אָסוּר אַחַר כָּךְ לֶאֱכֹל אוֹ לִשְׁתּוֹת, אֶלָּא אִם כֵּן הִתְנָה קֹדֶם שֶׁיָּשַׁן. וְאִם הוּא רָגִיל לִשְׁתּוֹת לְאַחַר הַשֵּׁנָה, אֵינוֹ צָרִיךְ לְהַתְנוֹת עַל הַשְּׁתִיָּה. וּבְתִשְׁעָה בְּאָב, צְרִיכִין לְהַפְסִיק מִבְּעוֹד יוֹם שֶׁלְּפָנָיו. שָׁלֹשׁ תַּעֲנִיּוֹת הָרִאשׁוֹנוֹת, מֻתָּרוֹת בִּרְחִיצָה וְסִיכָה וּנְעִילַת הַסַּנְדָּל וְתַשְׁמִישׁ הַמִּטָּה. וּבְתִשְׁעָה בְּאָב, אֲסוּרִים בְּכֻלָּן. וּמִי שֶׁהוּא בַּעַל נֶפֶשׁ וְאָדָם בָּרִיא, יַחְמִיר בְּכֻלָּן כְּמוֹ בְּתִשְׁעָה בְּאָב, וְרַק בִּנְעִילַת הַסַּנְדָּל לֹא יַחְמִיר, מִשּׁוּם חוּכָא וּטְלוּלָא. וּבְתַשְׁמִישׁ הַמִּטָּה, אִם הוּא לֵיל טְבִילָה, יְקַיֵּם עוֹנָתוֹ בְּשָׁלֹשׁ הַתַּעֲנִיּוֹת הָרִאשׁוֹנוֹת.

ט) עוֹד יֵשׁ קֻלָּא בְּשָׁלֹשׁ הַתַּעֲנִיּוֹת הָרִאשׁוֹנוֹת, דְּעֻבָּרוֹת וּמֵינִיקוֹת הַמִּצְטַעֲרוֹת, פְּטוּרוֹת מִלְּהִתְעַנּוֹת. וְכֵן חוֹלֶה, אַף־עַל־פִּי שֶׁאֵין בּוֹ סַכָּנָה, לֹא יִתְעַנֶּה. וּמִכָּל מָקוֹם אַף מִי שֶׁמֻּתָּר לוֹ לֶאֱכֹל, לֹא יְעַנֵּג אֶת עַצְמוֹ, אֶלָּא יֹאכַל מַה שֶּׁהוּא צָרִיךְ לִבְרִיאוּת גּוּפוֹ. וְכֵן הַקְּטַנִּים, אַף־עַל־פִּי שֶׁאֵינָם חַיָּבִים לְהִתְעַנּוֹת, מִכָּל מָקוֹם אִם יֵשׁ בָּהֶם דַּעַת לְהִתְאַבֵּל, רָאוּי לְחַנְּכָם, שֶׁלֹּא לְהַאֲכִילָם רַק לֶחֶם וּמַיִם, לְהִתְאַבֵּל עִם הַצִּבּוּר.

י) לִרְחוֹץ פִּיו בְּמַיִם בְּשַׁחֲרִית, אָסוּר בְּכָל תַּעֲנִית צִבּוּר. וְהָרֹק, אִם אֶפְשָׁר לִפְלֹט, יִפְלֹט. וְאִם אִי אֶפְשָׁר, בּוֹלְעוֹ אֲפִלּוּ בְּיוֹם הַכִּפּוּרִים, כֵּיוָן שֶׁאֵינוֹ מְכַוֵּן לַהֲנָאָתוֹ. לִטְעֹם הַמַּאֲכָל, אֲפִלּוּ אִם יִפְלֹט, אָסוּר בְּתַעֲנִית־צִבּוּר. אֲבָל בְּתַעֲנִית שֶׁהוּא מְקַבֵּל עַל עַצְמוֹ, מֻתָּר לִטְעֹם וְלִפְלוֹט. וְכֵן רְחִיצַת הַפֶּה, מֻתֶּרֶת בְּתַעֲנִית־יָחִיד.

יא) מִצְוָה עַל כָּל עֲדַת יִשְׂרָאֵל, שֶׁעַל כָּל צָרָה שֶׁלֹּא תָבוֹא, יִתְעַנּוּ וְיִתְפַּלְּלוּ עַל צָרָתָם לִפְנֵי ה׳ יִתְבָּרַךְ שְׁמוֹ. וְאִם אֵין הָעֵת מַכְשֶׁרֶת לְהִתְעַנּוֹת, כְּגוֹן הַנִּרְדָּפִים שֶׁאֵינָם רַשָּׁאִים לְהִתְעַנּוֹת, שֶׁלֹּא לִשְׁבֹּר כֹּחָם, יְקַבְּלוּ עֲלֵיהֶם לְהִתְעַנּוֹת כָּךְ וְכָךְ תַּעֲנִיּוֹת לִכְשֶׁיִּנָּצְלוּ, וְנֶחְשָׁב לָהֶם כְּאִלּוּ

1. This law also applies when any of these fast days is postponed, as stated in paragraph 6. A groom must fast even on a postponed fast day. (*Mishnah Berurah* 559:9,35)

2. They are permitted to eat, even if they have no discomfort; except that our women have elected to be stringent and eat only if they experience discomfort. If they are weak,

as a Yom Tov, nevertheless, he must fast.[1] Since his Yom Tov is only a personal celebration, the public mourning and fasting overrides it, and also, because it is written, ". . . if I fail to elevate Jerusalem above my foremost joy" (Psalms 137:6).

8) There is a difference between the first three fast days and *Tisha beAv* (the ninth day of Av). On the first three fast days, you are permitted to have food during the preceding night until the break of dawn, if you did not have your regular sleep. If, however, you did have your regular sleep, you are forbidden to eat or drink afterwards, unless you planned to do so before going to sleep. If you usually drink something when getting up from sleep, you need not formulate your plan to have a drink (when getting up). But on *Tishah beAv* you must begin the fast on the day before, while it is still day. On the first three fast days, you are permitted to wash, to apply cream, to wear leather shoes, and have marital relations, but on *Tishah beAv* all these are forbidden. A pious person, who is in good health, should observe these restrictions on the other fast days, just as on *Tishah beAv,* except for the wearing of leather shoes, because people might ridicule him. Concerning marital relations, if it is the night of the immersion in the *mikveh,* he should fulfill his marital obligation on the first three fast days.

9) There is still another lenient feature regarding the first three fasts: pregnant and nursing women, are exempt from fasting, if it causes them discomfort.[2] Also, a sick person, even if he is not critically ill, should not fast.[3] Nevertheless, even a person who is permitted to eat, should not enjoy an elaborate meal, but should eat only as much as he needs to preserve his health. Children, too, although they do not have to fast, nevertheless, if they understand the significance of mourning, it is proper to train them, and give them only bread and water,[4] so that they will be part of the communal mourning.

10) Rinsing your mouth in the morning is forbidden on all public fast days.[5] The saliva should be spit out, if possible. But if you cannot spit it out, you are permitted to swallow it, even on Yom Kippur, since you do not do it for enjoyment. Tasting food, even when spitting it out, is forbidden on a public fast day. But on a fast day, which you undertake voluntarily, you are permitted to taste food and then spit it out. Similarly, rinsing your mouth is permitted on a private fast day.

11) It is a mitzvah, for every Jewish community, when they are beset with trouble, God forbid, to fast and pray to Hashem, blessed is His Name, (for rescue) from their troubles. But if the time is not appropriate for fasting, for instance, if people are fleeing, they are not permitted to fast, lest their strength will be sapped. However they should resolve to fast a certain number of fast days, when they are

---

however, they should not practice this stringency, and they should not fast. (*Mishnah Berurah* 550:5)

3. It is forbidden to practice stringencies in this situation. (*Ibid* 550:4)

4. They may be given any other simple food. (*Ibid.* 550:5)

5. According to *Mishnah Berurah,* if you experience discomfort, you are permitted to rinse your mouth, except that you must be careful to bend forward, so that the liquid does not enter the throat. This is even permitted on *Tishah beAv,* if you experience *extreme* discomfort. On Yom Kippur, however, it is proper to be stringent, under all circumstances. (*Ibid.* 567:11)

הִתְעַנּוּ עַתָּה, כִּדְמָצִינוּ בְּדָנִיֵּאל, דִּכְתִיב, וַיֹּאמֶר אֵלַי אַל־תִּירָא דָנִיֵּאל כִּי מִן־הַיּוֹם אֲשֶׁר נָתַתָּ אֶת־לִבְּךָ לְהָבִין וּלְהִתְעַנּוֹת לִפְנֵי אֱלֹהֶיךָ נִשְׁמְעוּ דְבָרֶיךָ.

סִימָן קכב
דִּינִים מִן שִׁבְעָה עָשָׂר בְּתַמּוּז עַד תִּשְׁעָה בְּאָב

א) כֵּיוָן שֶׁבְּשִׁבְעָה עָשָׂר בְּתַמּוּז הִתְחִילוּ צָרוֹת הַחֻרְבָּן, לָכֵן נוֹהֲגִין קְצָת אֲבֵלוּת מִיּוֹם זֶה עַד אַחַר תִּשְׁעָה בְּאָב. וְרָאוּי לְכָל יְרֵא שָׁמַיִם לַעֲשׂוֹת תִּקּוּן חֲצוֹת בְּכָל יוֹם לְאַחַר חֲצוֹת הַיּוֹם. אֵין נוֹשְׂאִין נָשִׁים, אֲפִלּוּ מִי שֶׁעֲדַיִן לֹא קִיֵּם מִצְוַת פְּרוּ וּרְבוּ. אֲבָל לַעֲשׂוֹת שִׁדּוּכִין, אֲפִלּוּ בִּסְעוּדָה, מֻתָּר עַד רֹאשׁ־חֹדֶשׁ אָב. וּמֵרֹאשׁ־חֹדֶשׁ וְאֵילָךְ, אַף־עַל־גַּב דְּמֻתָּר גַּם כֵּן לַעֲשׂוֹת שִׁדּוּכִין, מִכָּל מָקוֹם אָסוּר לַעֲשׂוֹת סְעוּדָה, אַךְ יְכוֹלִין לֶאֱכֹל מִינֵי מִרְקַחַת וְכַדּוֹמֶה. יִשְׂרָאֵל שֶׁפַּרְנָסָה שֶׁלּוֹ בִּכְלֵי זֶמֶר, מֻתָּר לְנַגֵּן בְּבֵית גּוֹי בִּכְדֵי פַּרְנָסָתוֹ עַד רֹאשׁ־חֹדֶשׁ. אֲבָל מֵרֹאשׁ־חֹדֶשׁ עַד אַחַר הַתַּעֲנִית, אָסוּר. וְיוֹם שִׁבְעָה עָשָׂר בְּתַמּוּז עַצְמוֹ גַּם כֵּן אָסוּר, וְכֵן עֲשָׂרָה בְּטֵבֵת. וְיֵשׁ נוֹהֲגִין שֶׁלֹּא לֶאֱכֹל בָּשָׂר וְשֶׁלֹּא לִשְׁתּוֹת יַיִן מִשִּׁבְעָה עָשָׂר בְּתַמּוּז עַד אַחַר תִּשְׁעָה בְּאָב, אִם לֹא בְּשַׁבָּת אוֹ בִּסְעוּדַת מִצְוָה.

ב) נוֹהֲגִין שֶׁאֵין מְבָרְכִין שֶׁהֶחֱיָנוּ בַּיָּמִים הָאֵלּוּ. וְלָכֵן אֵין קוֹנִין וְאֵין לוֹבְשִׁין בֶּגֶד חָדָשׁ, מִשּׁוּם דְּהָיָה צָרִיךְ לְבָרֵךְ שֶׁהֶחֱיָנוּ. וְעַל פִּדְיוֹן הַבֵּן, מְבָרְכִין שֶׁהֶחֱיָנוּ, שֶׁלֹּא לְהַחְמִיץ אֶת הַמִּצְוָה. וְעַל פְּרִי, יֵשׁ לְהָקֵל לְבָרֵךְ שֶׁהֶחֱיָנוּ בְּשַׁבָּת אוֹ אֲפִלּוּ בַּחֹל, אִם לֹא יִמָּצֵא פְּרִי זֶה לְאַחַר תִּשְׁעָה בְּאָב. לֹא יַכּוּ הַתַּלְמִידִים אוֹ הַבָּנִים בַּיָּמִים הָאֵלּוּ.

ג) וְכֵן נוֹהֲגִין שֶׁאֵין מִסְתַּפְּרִין בַּיָּמִים הָאֵלּוּ, לֹא שַׂעֲרוֹת הָרֹאשׁ וְלֹא שַׂעֲרוֹת הַזָּקָן וְלֹא כָּל שֵׂעָר שֶׁבְּגוּפוֹ. וְאָסוּר לַגְּדוֹלִים לְסַפֵּר אֶת הַקְּטַנִּים.

ד) הַשָּׂפָה הָעֶלְיוֹנָה שֶׁבַּזָּקָן, כֹּל שֶׁמְּעַכֵּב אֶת הָאֲכִילָה, נִרְאֶה לִי דְּיֵשׁ

1. It is forbidden to make such a special meal, even on Shabbos, since it is in honor of the engagement. (*Mishnah Berurah* 551:16)

2. On Shabbos, however, it is not permissible to be stringent regarding meat and wine (*Ibid.* 551:59).

3. According to the *Vilna Gaon,* this is an unnecessary stringency. *Taz* is also doubtful about this custom. On Shabbos, therefore, you need not be concerned, and the berachah *Shehecheyanu* may be said over a new fruit or on new clothing. (*Ibid.* 551:98)

saved. This will be counted as if they were now fasting, as we find concerning Daniel, about whom it is written, "He said to me, 'Do not be afraid, Daniel; for from the day you resolved to understand and to fast before your God, your words were heard'" (Daniel 10:12).

Chapter 122

Laws Concerning the Three Weeks between the Seventeenth of Tammuz and Tishah beAv

1) Since the Seventeenth of *Tammuz,* marks the beginning of the anguish of the destruction of the *Beis Hamikdash,* it is customary to observe a partial mourning, from that day until after *Tishah beAv.* It is proper for every God-fearing person to recite *Tikun Chatzos* (the special midnight order), daily, in the afternoon. No weddings are performed, even for a person who has not yet fulfilled the mitzvah of *Piryah Verivyah* ("Be fertile and have many children.") But engagement parties, even with a meal, are permitted until *Rosh Chodesh Av.* Although it is permissible to make engagements after *Rosh Chodesh,* nevertheless, it is forbidden to serve a meal (at the engagement party),[1] but it is permitted to serve desserts and other delicacies. A Jew, who makes his living as a professional musician, is permitted to play in the house of a non-Jew, until *Rosh Chodesh Av,* but from *Rosh Chodesh* until after *Tishah beAv,* he is forbidden to play. On the seventeenth day of *Tammuz,* itself, as well as on the tenth of *Teiveis.* he is also forbidden to play. Some people have the custom not to eat meat, nor to drink wine from the Seventeenth of *Tammuz* until after *Tishah beAv,* except on Shabbos[2] or at a meal that is considered a mitzvah.

2) It is customary not to say the berachah, *Shehecheyanu* during these days.[3] Therefore, you should not buy or put on a new garment, since that would make it necessary for you to say the berachah, *Shehecheyanu.* But at the occasion of a *Pidyon haben,* (redemption of the firstborn), *Shehecheyanu* must be said, so as not to postpone the fulfillment of the mitzvah. Concerning a new fruit, we are lenient and say *Shehecheyanu* on Shabbos[4] or even on a weekday,[5] if this fruit will not be available[6] after *Tishah beAv.* Teachers should not strike students, and parents should not strike their children during these days.

3) It is the custom not to have the hair cut during these days, neither the hair of the head, nor of the beard nor of any part of the body. Adults are forbidden to give their children a haircut.

4) It seems to me that it should be permissible to trim the mustache, until the

---

4. See note 3.
5. According to *Rav Akiva Eiger,* this rule also applies to Rosh Chodesh. (*Shaar Hatzion* 551:98)
6. This refers to a situation where the fruit cannot be kept until Shabbos because of spoilage. If, however, the fruit can be preserved until Shabbos, it is best to do so. (*Mishnah Berurah* 551:101)

לְהַתִּיר לְגַלְּחוֹ עַד הַשָּׁבוּעַ שֶׁחָל בּוֹ תִּשְׁעָה בְּאָב. אֲבָל בַּשָּׁבוּעַ שֶׁחָל בּוֹ תִּשְׁעָה בְּאָב, יֵשׁ לֶאֱסֹר.

ה) קְצִיצַת הַצִּפָּרְנַיִם, אֵין לֶאֱסֹר, רַק בַּשָּׁבוּעַ שֶׁחָל בּוֹ תִּשְׁעָה בְּאָב. וְאִשָּׁה לְצֹרֶךְ טְבִילָתָהּ, מֻתֶּרֶת גַּם אָז. וְכֵן הַמּוֹהֵל יָכוֹל לְתַקֵּן צִפָּרְנָיו לְצֹרֶךְ הַפְּרִיעָה.

ו) בְּשָׁלֹשֶׁת הַשַּׁבָּתוֹת שֶׁבֵּין שִׁבְעָה עָשָׂר בְּתַמּוּז לְתִשְׁעָה בְּאָב, מַפְטִירִין תְּלָתָא דְפֻרְעֲנוּתָא, שֶׁהֵן, דִּבְרֵי יִרְמְיָהוּ, שִׁמְעוּ דְבַר ה', חֲזוֹן יְשַׁעְיָהוּ, וְסִימָנָךְ דַּשַׁ"ח. וְאִם טָעָה וְקָרָא בַּשַּׁבָּת הָרִאשׁוֹנָה אֶת הַהַפְטָרָה שֶׁל פָּרָשָׁה דְיוֹמָא, מַפְטִירִין בַּשַּׁבָּת הַבָּאָה, דִּבְרֵי יִרְמְיָהוּ וְגַם, שִׁמְעוּ, מִפְּנֵי שֶׁהֵן סְמוּכוֹת זוֹ לְזוֹ. חָל רֹאשׁ־חֹדֶשׁ אָב לִהְיוֹת בַּשַּׁבָּת, מַפְטִירִין הַשָּׁמַיִם כִּסְאִי. וְיֵשׁ מְקוֹמוֹת שֶׁמַּפְטִירִין שִׁמְעוּ.

ז) מִשֶּׁנִּכְנַס אָב, מְמַעֲטִין בְּשִׂמְחָה. אֵין בּוֹנִין בִּנְיָן שֶׁל שִׂמְחָה אוֹ בִּנְיָן שֶׁהוּא רַק לִרְוָחָה. וְאִם קָצַץ עִם גּוֹי לְצַיֵּר לוֹ אֶת בֵּיתוֹ, אִם יָכוֹל לְפַיְּסוֹ בְּדָבָר מְעַט שֶׁיַּמְתִּין עַד אַחַר תִּשְׁעָה בְּאָב, נָכוֹן הַדָּבָר. וְאִם לָאו, מֻתָּר. וּבַר יִשְׂרָאֵל דְּאִית לֵהּ דִּינָא בַּהֲדֵי נָכְרִי, לִשְׁתַּמִּיט מִנֵּהּ, מִשּׁוּם דְּרִיעַ מַזָּלֵהּ. אִם אֶפְשָׁר, יִשְׁתַּמֵּט כָּל הַחֹדֶשׁ, וּלְכָל־הַפָּחוֹת עַד לְאַחַר תִּשְׁעָה בְּאָב. אֵין מְקַדְּשִׁין אֶת הַלְּבָנָה עַד לְאַחַר תִּשְׁעָה בְּאָב.

ח) מִנְהָג בְּכָל יִשְׂרָאֵל שֶׁלֹּא לֶאֱכֹל בָּשָׂר וְשֶׁלֹּא לִשְׁתּוֹת יַיִן בְּתִשְׁעַת הַיָּמִים שֶׁמִּן רֹאשׁ־חֹדֶשׁ עַד לְאַחַר תִּשְׁעָה בְּאָב, וְאָסוּר אֲפִלּוּ בְּתַבְשִׁיל שֶׁנִּתְבַּשֵּׁל בּוֹ בָּשָׂר אוֹ שֶׁיֵּשׁ בּוֹ שֻׁמָּן. וַאֲפִלּוּ בְּשַׂר עוֹף, אָסוּר. אַךְ מִי שֶׁמַּאַכְלֵי חָלָב מַזִּיקִין לוֹ, יָכוֹל לֶאֱכֹל בְּשַׂר עוֹף. וּלְצֹרֶךְ חוֹלֶה, הַכֹּל מֻתָּר. וּמִכָּל מָקוֹם אִם אֵינוֹ קָשֶׁה לוֹ, יֵשׁ לוֹ לְהַפְסִיק, שֶׁלֹּא לֶאֱכֹל מִן שִׁבְעָה בְּאָב וּלְהַלָּן. וְכֵן נוֹהֲגוֹת קְצָת יוֹלְדוֹת לְהִמָּנַע מִבָּשָׂר וָיַיִן מִשִּׁבְעָה בְּאָב וְאֵילָךְ, כִּי בְּאוֹתוֹ הַיּוֹם נִכְנְסוּ גּוֹיִם לַהֵיכָל (כִּדְלְקַמָּן סִימָן קכ"ד סָעִיף ב). וּבִסְעוּדַת מִצְוָה, כְּגוֹן מִילָה וּפִדְיוֹן הַבֵּן, וְסִיּוּם מַסֶּכְתָּא גַּם כֵּן, מֻתָּרִין

---

7. *Mishnah Berurah* disagrees and rules that you need not be stringent regarding the mustache, even during the week of *Tishah beAv.* (see *Shaar Hatzion* 551:90)

8. According to *Mishnah Berurah,* you are permitted to cut your nails in honor of Shabbos, even during the week of *Tishah beAv.* (*Mishnah Berurah* 551:20)

9. According to *Magein Avrohom,* this implies a total restriction of happiness, and others maintain it implies only a partial restriction (of your usual manner of happiness). (*Ibid.* 551:1 and *Shaar Tzion*)

week in which *Tishah beAv* occurs, if it interferes with your eating, but during the week in which *Tishah beAv* occurs, it should be forbidden.[7]

5) Cuting the nails is forbidden only during the week of *Tishah beAv,*[8] but for the purpose of immersion in the *mikveh,* a woman is permitted to cut her nails during that week. Also, a *mohel* is permitted to trim his nails for the requirements of *periah* (removal of the thin membrane).

6) On the three *Shabbosos* between the seventeenth of *Tammuz* and *Tishah beAv,* we read the "Three *haftaros* of retribution," which are: *Divrei Yirmiyahu* (The words of Jeremiah) (Jeremiah 1:1), *Shim'u devar Hashem,* (Hear the word of Hashem) (Jeremiah 2:4), *Chazon Yeshayahu,* (The vision of Isaiah) (Isaiah 1:1). Their initials form the acronym *DeShaCh.* If, by mistake, the reader recited on the first Shabbos the *haftarah* of the weekly portion, on the second Shabbos, he should read the *haftarah* of both *Divrei Yirmiyahu* and *Shim'u,* because they are close to each other. If *Rosh Chodesh Av* occurs on Shabbos, he reads the *haftarah Hashamayim Kis'i* (The heaven is My throne) (Isaiah 66), but in some communities, the *haftarah Shim'u* is read.

7) When the month of *Av* arrives, we should restrict such activities that create happiness.[9] You should not build a building meant for enjoyment or strictly for relaxation. If you made a contract with a non-Jew, to have your house painted, and you can persuade him for a small compensation, to wait until after *Tishah beAv,* that would be the right thing to do, but if he cannot be persuaded, you may have the work done. If a Jew has a lawsuit against a non-Jew, he should postpone it, because it is an unlucky period. If possible, he should postpone it until after the end of the month, or at least until after *Tishah beAv.* We do not sanctify the new moon until after *Tishah beAv.*[10]

8) It is the accepted custom in all Yisrael not to eat meat or drink wine during the nine days, from *Rosh Chodesh* until after *Tishah beAv.*[11] It is even forbidden to eat food that was cooked with meat or that contains animal fat; even poultry is forbidden. However, a person, who is sensitive to dairy food, is permitted to eat poultry,[12] and for a sick person, all restrictions are lifted.[13] Nevertheless, if it is not too difficult for him, he should abstain from eating (any kind of meat) from the seventh of *Av* on. Also, some women, who have given birth, abstain from meat and wine, from the seventh of *Av* on, for on that day, the heathens entered the *Beis Hamikdash* (See Chapter 124:2 below). At a meal that is considered a mitzvah, such as a *bris* (circumcision), a *pidyon haben* (redemption of the first-born son), or the

---

10. Regarding the sanctification of the moon on the night immediately after *Tishah beAv,* see *Kitzur Shulchan Aruch* 97:11 and notes.

11. These things are forbidden until after midday of the tenth day of *Av.* (See *Kitzur Shulchan Aruch* 124:20)

12. A sick person is certainly permitted to eat food that was cooked with meat. (*Mishnah Berurah* 551:64)

13. This applies even to a person who is only slightly ill. (*Ibid.* 551:61)

בְּבָשָׂר וָיַיִן. וְחוּץ מֵאֲבוֹתָיו וְאֶחָיו וּבָנָיו, וְחוּץ מֵאֵלּוּ שֶׁיֵּשׁ לָהֶם שַׁיָּכוּת לַמִּצְוָה, יָכוֹל לְהַזְמִין עוֹד עֲשָׂרָה אֲנָשִׁים לְרֵעוּת. אֲבָל רַק אוֹתָן שֶׁגַּם בְּפַעַם אַחֶרֶת הָיוּ בָּאִין אֵלָיו אֶל הַמִּשְׁתֶּה. וְכָל זֹאת מֻתָּר אֲפִלּוּ בְּעֶרֶב תִּשְׁעָה בְּאָב קֹדֶם חֲצוֹת הַיּוֹם, אֲבָל לֹא אַחַר כָּךְ. וְהַסְּעוּדָה שֶׁנּוֹהֲגִין לַעֲשׂוֹת בַּלַּיְלָה שֶׁלִּפְנֵי הַמִּילָה, אֵינָהּ סְעוּדַת מִצְוָה (עַיֵּן לְקַמָּן סִימָן קסג סָעִיף ח) וַאֲסוּרִין בְּבָשָׂר וָיַיִן, אֶלָּא יֵשׁ לַעֲשׂוֹתָהּ בְּמַאַכְלֵי חָלָב. וְכוֹס שֶׁל הַבְדָּלָה בְּמוֹצָאֵי שַׁבָּת, אִם יֵשׁ תִּינוֹק שֶׁיִּשְׁתֶּה רֹב הַכּוֹס, נוֹתְנִין לוֹ. וְאִם לָאו, יָכוֹל הַמַּבְדִּיל בְּעַצְמוֹ לִשְׁתּוֹת.

ט) וְכֵן אֵין מְכַבְּסִין בְּתִשְׁעָה יָמִים אֵלּוּ. וַאֲפִלּוּ חָלוּק אוֹ בֶּגֶד שֶׁאֵינוֹ רוֹצֶה לְלָבְשׁוֹ עַד אַחַר הַתַּעֲנִית. וַאֲפִלּוּ לִתְּתָם לְכוֹבֶסֶת גּוֹיָה, אָסוּר. וְיִשְׂרְאֵלִית, מֻתֶּרֶת לְכַבֵּס בִּגְדֵי גוֹיִם. וּמִכָּל מָקוֹם בְּשָׁבוּעַ שֶׁחָל בּוֹ תִּשְׁעָה בְּאָב יֵשׁ לָהּ לִזָּהֵר. וְכֵן אָסוּר בְּתִשְׁעָה יָמִים אֵלּוּ לִלְבּוֹשׁ אוֹ לְהַצִּיעַ אֲפִלּוּ הַמְכֻבָּסִין מִקֹּדֶם. רַק לִכְבוֹד שַׁבָּת, מֻתָּר לִלְבּוֹשׁ בִּגְדֵי פִשְׁתָּן, וּלְהַצִּיעַ עַל הַשֻּׁלְחָנוֹת לְבָנִים, וּלְהַחֲלִיף מִטְפָּחוֹת הַיָּדַיִם וּמַגָּבוֹת, כְּדֶרֶךְ שֶׁעוֹשִׂין בִּשְׁאָר שַׁבָּתוֹת. אֲבָל סְדִינִים לְבָנִים, אָסוּר לְהַצִּיעַ. וְאִשָּׁה שֶׁצְּרִיכָה לִלְבּוֹשׁ לְבָנִים לִסְפּוֹר שִׁבְעָה נְקִיִּים, מֻתֶּרֶת לְכַבֵּס וְלִלְבּוֹשׁ. וְכֵן הַמִּטְפָּחוֹת שֶׁמְּלַפְּפִין בָּהֶן אֶת הַתִּינוֹקוֹת שֶׁמְּלַכְלְכִין אוֹתָן תָּדִיר, מֻתָּר לְכַבְּסָן.

י) אֵין עוֹשִׂין בְּתִשְׁעָה יָמִים אֵלּוּ בְּגָדִים חֲדָשִׁים, אוֹ מִנְעָלִים חֲדָשִׁים, אוֹ לֶאֱרוֹג אַנְפְּלָאוֹת, אֲפִלּוּ עַל יְדֵי אֻמָּן גּוֹי. וּלְצֹרֶךְ גָּדוֹל, כְּגוֹן לְנִשּׂוּאִין שֶׁיִּהְיוּ מִיָּד אַחַר תִּשְׁעָה בְּאָב, מֻתָּר עַל יְדֵי אֻמָּן גּוֹי, אֲבָל לֹא עַל יְדֵי יִשְׂרָאֵל. וְקֹדֶם רֹאשׁ־חֹדֶשׁ, מֻתָּר בְּכָל עִנְיָן לִתְּתָן אֲפִלּוּ לְאֻמָּן יִשְׂרָאֵל, וּמֻתָּר לוֹ לַעֲשׂוֹתָן אֲפִלּוּ אַחַר כָּךְ.

יא) נָשִׁים שֶׁנּוֹהֲגוֹת שֶׁלֹּא לְסַדֵּר הַחוּטִין לַאֲרִיגָה, מִשּׁוּם דְּזֶה נִקְרָא

---

14. *Mishnah Berurah* cautions against deliberately hurrying or delaying the conclusion of a *Talmud* tractate, in order to eat meat in the nine days. He maintains this rule is valid, only when the Tractate is concluded under normal circumstances. (*Ibid.* 551:73)

15. The *Sandek*, and the couple who bring in the child are included in those "involved in the mitzvah." (*Ibid.* 551, *Shaar Hatzion*)

16. This applies to a child who is of age so far as *chinuch* is concerned, (six or seven years old) but, nevertheless, who has not reached the age to understand the mourning over the destruction of Jerusalem. (*Ibid.* 551:70)

conclusion of a *Talmud* tractate,[14] it is permitted to eat meat and drink wine. Aside from your parents, brothers and children, and those involved with the mitzvah,[15] you may also invite ten other friends, but only such friends [who, if the meal would have been held] at any other time, would also have joined you. All these mitzvah meals are permitted even on *erev Tishah beAv* before noon, but not later than that. The festive meal, that is usually made on the night before the *bris*, is not considered a mitzvah meal (see 163:8 above). It is forbidden to have meat and wine [at such meals]; rather you should serve dairy food instead. Regarding the cup of wine for *Havdalah* on Shabbos night, if there is a child[16] who is able to drink the greater part of the cup, it should be given to him, otherwise, the person reciting the *Havdalah* may drink it.

9) You should not wash any laundry during the nine days;[17] not even a shirt or a garment that you will not wear until after the fast day. It is forbidden even to have it washed by a non-Jewish washerwoman.[18] A Jewish woman is permitted to wash the clothes of a non-Jew; nevertheless, during the week in which *Tishah beAv* occurs, she should be diligent [not to do this work].[19] During these nine days, it is also forbidden to put on laundered clothing, or to spread linen, even if they were washed before. However in honor of Shabbos, you may put on clean linen garments (undershirts and socks) and spread a fresh tablecloth on the table, and change washcloths and towels, just as you do on other *Shabbosos*.[20] But it is forbidden to spread clean sheets. A woman who is required to put on clean white undergarments when she begins to count the seven clean days, is permitted to wash her undergarments, and to put them on. Also diapers, which are dirtied constantly, may be washed.[21]

10) During these nine days, you should not have new garments, or new shoes made or socks knitted, even by a non-Jewish craftsman. However if you need them urgently, such as for a wedding that will be held immediately after *Tishah beAv*, you are permitted to use a non-Jewish craftsman, but not a Jew. Before *Rosh Chodesh Av*, you are permitted, in any case, to arrange that clothes or shoes be made, even by a Jewish craftsman, who may make them, even after (*Rosh Chodesh Av*).

11) Women who have the custom not to arrange the threads for weaving, during these nine days because this (the warp), is called in Hebrew *shesi*, and since the

---

17. See note 11.
18. If you must leave on a distant journey during the week of *Tisha beAv*, it is permitted to have the clothes needed for the trip laundered by a non-Jew. (*Ibid.* 551:39)
19. In a situation where there is a question of providing food for her family, this would be permitted. (*Ibid.* 551:42)
20. The *Vilna Gaon* permitted the wearing of regular Shabbos clothing on the Shabbos before *Tishah beAv*. *Rav Yaakov Emden* permitted wearing Shabbos clothing, even when *Tishah beAv* occured on Shabbos and was postponed until Sunday. (See *Kitzur Shulchan Aruch*, paragraph 16) (*Ibid.* 551:6)
21. Other types of infants' and children's clothing may also be washed. You should, however, not wash a large amount of clothes at one time. (*Ibid.* 551:82,83)

שְׁתִי, וְכֵיוָן שֶׁבָּטְלָה אֶבֶן הַשְׁתִיָּה שֶׁהָיְתָה בְּבֵית־הַמִּקְדָּשׁ הֶחְמִירוּ עֲלֵיהֶן בָּזֶה, אָסוּר לְהַתִּיר לָהֶן.

יב) אֵין רוֹחֲצִין בְּתִשְׁעָה יָמִים אֵלּוּ אֲפִלּוּ בְּצוֹנֵן. אַךְ לִרְפוּאָה, כְּגוֹן יוֹלֶדֶת אוֹ מְעֻבֶּרֶת שֶׁקְּרוֹבָה לָלֶדֶת, שֶׁטּוֹב לָהּ לִרְחוֹץ, וְכֵן אָדָם חָלוּשׁ שֶׁצִּוָּה אוֹתוֹ הָרוֹפֵא לִרְחוֹץ, מֻתָּרִין לִרְחוֹץ אֲפִלּוּ בְּחַמִּין. וְכֵן נִדָּה, רוֹחֶצֶת וְטוֹבֶלֶת כְּדַרְכָּהּ. וְאִם טוֹבֶלֶת בַּלַּיְלָה שֶׁלְּאַחַר תִּשְׁעָה בְּאָב וְאִי אֶפְשָׁר לָהּ לִרְחוֹץ אָז, יְכוֹלָה לִרְחוֹץ בְּעֶרֶב תִּשְׁעָה בְּאָב. וְכֵן כְּשֶׁלּוֹבֶשֶׁת לְבָנִים, יְכוֹלָה לִרְחוֹץ מְעַט כְּדַרְכָּהּ, כֵּיוָן שֶׁאֵינָהּ עוֹשָׂה לְתַעֲנוּג.

יג) רֹאשׁ־חֹדֶשׁ אָב שֶׁחָל בְּעֶרֶב שַׁבָּת, מִי שֶׁרָגִיל לִרְחוֹץ בְּחַמִּין בְּכָל עֶרֶב שַׁבָּת, מֻתָּר גַּם עַתָּה לִרְחוֹץ אֲפִלּוּ בְּחַמִּין. אֲבָל בְּעֶרֶב־שַׁבַּת־חֲזוֹן, אָסוּר לִרְחוֹץ בְּחַמִּין אֲפִלּוּ לְמִי שֶׁרָגִיל בְּכָךְ, כִּי אִם פָּנָיו יָדָיו וְרַגְלָיו. וְכֵן מִי שֶׁרָגִיל בַּחֲפִיפַת הָרֹאשׁ כָּל עֶרֶב שַׁבָּת, מֻתָּר לוֹ גַּם עַתָּה, אַךְ לֹא בְּבוֹרִית וְלֹא בְּמֵי אֵפֶר. וּמִי שֶׁרָגִיל לִטְבּוֹל כָּל עֶרֶב שַׁבָּת, מֻתָּר לוֹ גַּם עַתָּה לִטְבּוֹל בְּצוֹנֵן. אֲבָל מִי שֶׁמְּבַטְּלָהּ לִפְעָמִים, אָסוּר לוֹ.

יד) אָבֵל שֶׁחָל יוֹם שְׁלֹשִׁים שֶׁלּוֹ בִּשְׁמוֹנָה עָשָׂר בְּתַמּוּז אוֹ אַחַר כָּךְ עַד עֶרֶב רֹאשׁ־חֹדֶשׁ אָב, מֻתָּר לוֹ לְהִסְתַּפֵּר. אֲבָל מֵרֹאשׁ־חֹדֶשׁ וְאֵילָךְ, גַּם בִּכְהַאי גַּוְנָא, אָסוּר בְּכִבּוּס וּבְתִסְפֹּרֶת.

טו) מִילָה שֶׁהִיא בְּתִשְׁעָה יָמִים אֵלּוּ, נוֹהֲגִין שֶׁהַמּוֹהֵל וְהַסַּנְדָּק וַאֲבִי־הַבֵּן וְאִמּוֹ לוֹבְשִׁין בִּגְדֵי שַׁבָּת. אֲבָל הַמַּכְנִיס אֶת הַתִּינוֹק, אָסוּר. אַךְ הָאִשָּׁה הַמַּכְנֶסֶת אֶת הַתִּינוֹק, נוֹהֶגֶת לִלְבּוֹשׁ בִּגְדֵי שַׁבָּת, כֵּיוָן שֶׁזּוֹהִי כָּל מִצְוָתָהּ. וְגִלּוּחַ, יֵשׁ לְהַתִּיר לָהֶם קֹדֶם שַׁבַּת־חֲזוֹן. אֲבָל אַחַר כָּךְ אָסוּר.

טז) כְּבָר כָּתַבְנוּ בְּסָעִיף ט', כִּי בְּשַׁבַּת־חֲזוֹן לוֹבְשִׁין בִּגְדֵי פִשְׁתָּן לָבָן, דְּהַיְנוּ הַכְּתֹנֶת וּפוּזְמְקָאוֹת, שֶׁאֵינָן אֶלָּא מִפְּנֵי הַזֵּעָה. אֲבָל שְׁאָר בִּגְדֵי שַׁבָּת, תַּלְיָא בְּמִנְהַג הַמְּקוֹמוֹת אִם לְהַחֲלִיפָן אוֹ לֹא. וּבְבֵית־הַכְּנֶסֶת מַחֲלִיפִין אֶת הַפָּרֹכֶת וְהַמַּפּוֹת וְהַמְּעִילִים בְּשַׁבַּת־חֲזוֹן, אַךְ לֹא בְּשַׁבָּת שֶׁחָל בּוֹ תִּשְׁעָה בְּאָב.

22. Washing of the face, hands and feet is permitted. (*Ibid.* 551:94)
23. Only if he was ordered to bathe daily in hot water. (*Shaar Hatzion* 551:94)
24. On *Tishah beAv,* itself, however, he should refrain from doing so. (*Ibid.*)
25. Even with hot water. (see *Biyur Halachah* 551:16)

destruction of the *Even hashesiyah* (foundation stone) which was in the *Beis Hamikdash,* they imposed this stringency on themselves, (mindful of the similarity of *shesi* and *shesiyah*); it is forbidden to let them (arrange the threads).

12) You should not take a bath[22] during these nine days, even in cold water. However for medical reasons, as, for example, when a woman has given birth, or a pregnant woman, close to childbirth, for whom bathing is beneficial, or a weak person, whose physician ordered him to bathe,[23] these are permitted to bathe, even in warm water.[24] A woman, who was menstrually unclean, may bathe and immerse herself in the *mikveh* as usual.[25] If she has to immerse herself on the night after *Tishah beAv,* and it will be impossible for her to take the required bath (on *Tishah beAv*), she is permitted to bathe on *erev Tishah beAv.* Similarly, when she puts on clean undergarments, [to begin counting her seven clean days], she is permitted to bathe a little in her accustomed manner because she is not doing it for pleasure.

13) If *Rosh Chodesh Av* occurs on *erev Shabbos,* and you are accustomed to bathe in warm water every *erev Shabbos,* you are permitted to bathe, even in warm water. But on *erev Shabbos Chazon,* it is forbidden to bathe in warm water, even if you usually do so. Only the face, hands and feet (may be washed with warm water).[26] Similarly, if you are accustomed to wash your head every *erev Shabbos,* you are permitted to do so this *erev Shabbos,*[27] but not with soap or a solution of lye. If you are accustomed to immerse yourself in the *mikveh* every *erev Shabbos,* you are permitted to immerse yourself in cold water; but if you omit it occasionally, you are forbidden to do so.

14) A mourner, whose thirtieth day of mourning occurs on the eighteenth day of *Tammuz* or after that, is permitted to take a haircut, until the day before *Rosh Chodesh Av.* But from *Rosh Chodesh* on, even in such a case, he is forbidden to bathe or to take a haircut.

15) At a *bris* that occurs during the nine days, it is customary for the *mohel,* the *sandak,* and the parents of the infant to wear Shabbos clothing, but the man who brings in the child (*gefatter*) is forbidden to do so. However, the woman who brings in the child customarily wears Shabbos clothes, since this is the only part of the entire mitzvah she can fulfill. They are permitted to have their haircut before *Shabbos Chazon,* but after that, it is forbidden.

16) We wrote in paragraph 9 that on *Shabbos Chazon,* you may put on clean linen garments, that is, undershirts and socks, which (you change) only because of perspiration. But regarding other Shabbos clothing, it depends on the local custom, whether or not you may change to Shabbos clothing. At the synagogue, we change the *paroches* [coverning of the Torah ark], also the table coverings and the mantles, on *Shabbos Chazon;* but not on the Shabbos which occurs on *Tishah beAv.*

---

26. *Mishnah Berurah* 551:97.

27. This, too, is permitted, only if you do so every *erev* Shabbos. This may be done with hot water, if you are accustomed to do so. (*Mishnah Berurah* 551:97)

יז) נוֹהֲגִין בְּשַׁבַּת־חֲזוֹן לִקְרוֹת לְמַפְטִיר אֶת הָרַב שֶׁהוּא יוֹדֵעַ לְקוֹנֵן, וְלֹא יַעֲלֶה אָז לִשְׁלִישִׁי.

סִימָן קכג
דִּינֵי עֶרֶב תִּשְׁעָה בְּאָב

א) בְּרִית מִילָה וְכֵן פִּדְיוֹן הַבֵּן שֶׁחָל בְּעֶרֶב תִּשְׁעָה בְּאָב, עוֹשִׂין הַסְּעוּדָה קֹדֶם חֲצוֹת הַיּוֹם.

ב) לֹא יְטַיֵּל בְּעֶרֶב תִּשְׁעָה בְּאָב. וְנוֹהֲגִין שֶׁלֹּא לִלְמֹד אַחַר הַצָּהֳרַיִם, כִּי אִם בִּדְבָרִים שֶׁמֻּתָּרִים לִלְמֹד בְּתִשְׁעָה בְּאָב.

ג) בְּעִנְיַן סְעוּדָה הַמַּפְסֶקֶת יֵשׁ כַּמָּה דִינִים, וְהַמִּנְהָג הַיָּשָׁר הוּא לֶאֱכֹל קֹדֶם מִנְחָה סְעוּדַת קֶבַע, וְאַחַר כָּךְ מִתְפַּלְּלִין מִנְחָה, וְאֵין אוֹמְרִין תַּחֲנוּן, מִשּׁוּם דְּתִשְׁעָה בְּאָב אִקְרֵי מוֹעֵד, דִּכְתִיב, קָרָא עָלַי מוֹעֵד. וְסָמוּךְ לָעֶרֶב, יוֹשְׁבִין עַל הָאָרֶץ, וְאֵין צְרִיכִים לַחֲלֹץ הַמִּנְעָלִים. וְלֹא יֵשְׁבוּ שְׁלֹשָׁה בְּיַחַד, שֶׁלֹּא יִתְחַיְּבוּ בְּזִמּוּן. וְאוֹכְלִין רַק פַּת עִם בֵּיצָה מְבֻשֶּׁלֶת קָשָׁה וְקָרָה. וְטוֹבְלִין קְצָת פַּת בְּאֵפֶר וְאוֹכְלִין. וְצָרִיךְ לִזָּהֵר לְהַפְסִיק מִבְּעוֹד יוֹם. (אִם מֻתָּר לֶאֱכֹל אַחַר כָּךְ. עַיֵּן סִימָן קל"א סָעִיף י"ב).

ד) מִי שֶׁמִּתְעַנֶּה כָּל יְמוֹת הַשָּׁנָה שֵׁנִי וַחֲמִישִׁי, וְאֵרַע בּוֹ עֶרֶב תִּשְׁעָה בְּאָב, יִשְׁאַל עַל נִדְרוֹ. וּמִי שֶׁיֵּשׁ לוֹ יָאר־צַייט בְּעֶרֶב תִּשְׁעָה בְּאָב, יַתְנֶה בַּפַּעַם הָרִאשׁוֹנָה שֶׁלֹּא לְהִתְעַנּוֹת רַק עַד אַחַר חֲצוֹת הַיּוֹם, וְיִתְפַּלֵּל מִנְחָה גְּדוֹלָה, דְּהַיְנוּ חֲצִי שָׁעָה לְאַחַר הַצָּהֳרַיִם, וְיֹאכַל סְעוּדָה, וְאַחַר כָּךְ סָמוּךְ לָעֶרֶב יֹאכַל סְעוּדָה הַמַּפְסֶקֶת.

ה) בֵּין הַשְּׁמָשׁוֹת, אָסוּר בְּכָל מַה שֶּׁאָסוּר בְּתִשְׁעָה בְּאָב, וְלָכֵן צְרִיכִין לַחֲלֹץ אֶת הַמִּנְעָלִים קֹדֶם בֵּין הַשְּׁמָשׁוֹת.

17) It is customary on *Shabbos Chazon* to call the rabbi, who knows the special mournful chant, for the reading of the *maftir;* thus, he should not be called up (as usual), for the third *aliyah.*

Chapter 123

Laws Concerning Erev Tishah beAv

1) When a *bris* or a *pidyon haben* occur on *erev Tishah beAv,* the festive meal should be held before noon.

2) You should not go for a walk on *erev Tishah beAv;* and in the afternoon, it is the custom to study only the subjects you are permitted to study on *Tishah beAv.*[1]

3) Concerning the final meal before the fast, there are many laws. The correct custom is to eat a regular meal before the *Minchah* service. After that, you pray *Minchah,* omitting *Tachanun,* because *Tishah beAv* is called a *Moed* as it is written, "He has proclaimed a *Moed* for me" (Lamentations 1:15). Towards evening, you should sit on the floor[2] but it is not necessary to take off your shoes. Three people should not sit down (to eat) together, so that they will not be required (to recite *Birkas Hamazon*) with *zimun.* You should eat only bread and a cold hard-boiled egg.[3] You should dip a small piece of bread in ashes and eat it.[4] You should be careful to finish the meal while it is still day. (Whether you are permitted to eat after this, see 131:12 below).

4) If a person fasts throughout the year on Mondays and Thursdays, and *erev Tishah beAv* occurs on either of these days, he should have his vow annulled. If someone observes *Yahrtzeit* on *erev Tishah beAv,* he should resolve on the first *Yahrtzeit,* to fast only until noon has passed, then he should pray *Minchah gedolah* (early *Minchah*), that is, half-an-hour past noon, eat a meal, and afterwards towards evening, he should eat the final meal.

5) During twilight, you are forbidden to do all that is forbidden on *Tishah beAv.* You must, therefore, take off your shoes before twilight.

---

1. *Mishnah Berurah* cites other opinions who maintain that this custom is an extraordinary stringency, and concludes that we need not protest if someone maintains his usual course of studies, even on *erev Tishah beAv.* He cites the opinions of *Rashal, Vilna Gaon, Chayei Adam,* who permitted regular study of all subjects. (*Mishnah Berurah* 553:8)

2. A weak person is permitted to place a cushion or mat on the floor to sit on after concluding this meal. It is permitted to sit on a regular chair until nightfall. (*Ibid.* 552:18)

3. *Mishnah Berurah* does not mention that the egg must be cold.

4. Before eating it, you may say, "This is the meal of *Tishah beAv.*" (*Ibid.* 552:16)

סִימָן קכד
הִלְכוֹת תִּשְׁעָה בְּאָב

א) עַרְבִית, נִכְנָסִין לְבֵית־הַכְּנֶסֶת וְחוֹלְצִין הַמִּנְעָלִים (כְּמוֹ שֶׁכָּתַבְנוּ בְּסוֹף סִימָן הַקּוֹדֵם). וְנוֹהֲגִין לְהָסִיר אֶת הַפָּרֹכֶת מֵאֲרוֹן הַקֹּדֶשׁ, מִשּׁוּם דִּכְתִיב, בִּצַּע אִמְרָתוֹ. וְאֵין מַדְלִיקִין רַק נֵר אֶחָד לִפְנֵי שְׁלִיחַ־הַצִּבּוּר, וּמִתְפַּלְּלִין עַרְבִית בְּנַחַת וְדֶרֶךְ בְּכִי כַּאֲבֵלִים. וְאֵין אוֹמְרִים נַחֵם עַד לְמָחֳרַת בְּמִנְחָה. וְאַחַר תְּפִלַּת שְׁמוֹנֶה־עֶשְׂרֵה אוֹמְרִים קַדִּישׁ שָׁלֵם עִם תִּתְקַבֵּל, וְיוֹשְׁבִים לָאָרֶץ, וּמַדְלִיקִין קְצָת נֵרוֹת רַק בִּכְדֵי שֶׁיּוּכְלוּ לוֹמַר אֵיכָה וְקִינוֹת. וְאוֹמְרִים אֵיכָה וְקִינוֹת גַּם כֵּן בְּנַחַת וְדֶרֶךְ בְּכִי, וּמַפְסִיק בְּאֵיכָה מְעַט בֵּין כָּל פָּסוּק וּפָסוּק, וּמְעַט יוֹתֵר בֵּין כָּל אֵיכָה וְאֵיכָה. וּבְכָל אֵיכָה, מַגְבִּיהַּ שְׁלִיחַ־הַצִּבּוּר קוֹלוֹ קְצָת יוֹתֵר. וּפָסוּק הָאַחֲרוֹן שֶׁבְּכָל אֵיכָה, אוֹמְרִים בְּקוֹל רָם. וּכְשֶׁמַּגִּיעַ לְפָסוּק הֲשִׁיבֵנוּ וְגוֹ׳, אוֹמְרִים אוֹתוֹ הַקָּהָל בְּקוֹל רָם, וְאַחַר כָּךְ מְסַיֵּם שְׁלִיחַ־הַצִּבּוּר, וְחוֹזֵר הַקָּהָל וְאוֹמֵר הֲשִׁיבֵנוּ וְגוֹ׳, בְּקוֹל רָם, וְכֵן שְׁלִיחַ־הַצִּבּוּר. וְאַחַר כָּךְ אוֹמְרִים וְאַתָּה קָדוֹשׁ וְקַדִּישׁ שָׁלֵם בְּלֹא תִּתְקַבֵּל, לְפִי שֶׁאָמַר בְּאֵיכָה, שָׂתַם תְּפִלָּתִי. וְכֵן לְמָחָר בְּשַׁחֲרִית מְדַלְּגִין תִּתְקַבֵּל עַד לְמִנְחָה. גַּם מִי שֶׁהוּא בִּיחִידוּת, שֶׁאֵין לוֹ מִנְיָן, אוֹמֵר אֵיכָה וְקִינוֹת.

ב) יֵשׁ לְאָדָם לְהִצְטַעֵר בְּעִנְיַן מִשְׁכָּבוֹ, שֶׁאִם רָגִיל לִשְׁכַּב עַל שְׁנֵי כָּרִים, יִשְׁכַּב עַתָּה עַל אֶחָד. וְיֵשׁ נוֹהֲגִין לִשְׁכַּב בְּלֵיל תִּשְׁעָה בְּאָב עַל הָאָרֶץ, וְשָׂם אֶבֶן תַּחַת רֹאשׁוֹ, זֵכֶר לְמַה שֶּׁנֶּאֱמַר, וַיִּקַּח מֵאַבְנֵי הַמָּקוֹם וְגוֹ׳, שֶׁרָאָה אֶת הַחֻרְבָּן וְאָמַר, מַה נּוֹרָא וְגוֹ׳. וְהַכֹּל לְפִי מַה שֶּׁהוּא אָדָם.

ג) בְּשַׁחֲרִית אֵין מַנִּיחִין תְּפִלִּין, מִשּׁוּם דִּתְפִלִּין נִקְרָאִין פְּאֵר. וְגַם אֵין לוֹבְשִׁין טַלִּית גָּדוֹל, מִשּׁוּם דִּכְתִיב, בִּצַּע אִמְרָתוֹ, וּמְתַרְגְּמִינָן, בַּזַּע פּוּרְפִּירָא דִּילֵהּ. אֶלָּא לוֹבְשִׁין טַלִּית־קָטָן בְּלֹא בְּרָכָה, וּמַשְׁכִּימִין קְצָת

1. *Maharil* writes that shoes should be removed before leaving the house to go to the synagogue. (See *Mishnah Berurah* 553:5)

2. A pregnant woman or any weak (or sick) person is not obligated to do any of these things. (*Ibid.* 555:7)

Chapter 124

Laws of Tishah beAv

1) In the evening, upon entering the synagogue, you should remove your shoes[1] (as we have written at the conclusion of the previous chapter). It is customary to remove the covering of the Torah Ark, because it is written, "He has carried out His word" (Lamentations 2:17) (for explanation, see 124:3 below) and to have only one light in front of the *Chazzan.* We pray *Maariv* in a low and tearful voice, like mourners. We do not say *Nacheim* (comfort) until the *Shemoneh Esrei* of *Minchah* of the next day. After the *Shemoneh Esrei,* the *Chazzan* says the whole *Kaddish* including *tiskabbeil,* and everyone sits on the floor. Then a few lights are lit, sufficient for the congregation to say *Eichah* (Lamentations) and *Kinnos. Eichah* and *kinnos* are also recited in a low, tearful voice. When saying *Eichah,* a short pause should be made between one verse and the other, and a slightly longer pause between one chapter and the other. At the beginning of each chapter of *Eichah,* the *Chazzan* raises his voice a little more. The last verse of each chapter should be said in a loud voice, and when he reaches the verse *Hashiveinu* etc. (Bring us back), the congregation recites it aloud. The *Chazzan* then concludes the reading, and the congregation repeats *Hashiveinu* etc. aloud, and the *Chazzan* does the same. After that, *Ve'atah kadosh* (You are the Holy One) is recited by the congregation and the complete *Kaddish* without *tiskabbeil* is said by the *Chazan,* since it says in *Eichah,* "He shuts out My prayer" (Lamentations 3:8). The next morning at *Shacharis, tiskabbeil* is again omitted in the *Kaddish.* It is not said until *Minchah.* A person who prays by himself, because he can find no *minyan* (quorum of ten males thirteen years and older), should also recite *Eichah* and *Kinnos.*

2) You should express grief in the manner of your sleeping. For example, if you are accustomed to sleep on two pillows, you should sleep only on one. Some people have the custom to sleep on the floor during the night of *Tishah beAv,* and to put a stone underneath their head as a reminder of what was said, "And he took some of the stones of the place etc.," (Genesis 28:11). Our Sages comment that Jacob foresaw the destruction of the *Beis Hamikdash* and said, "How frightful" etc. (verse 17). It all depends on the person's attitude.[2]

3) In the morning, we do not put on the *tefillin,* because *tefillin* are called an "ornament." Neither do we put on the large *tallis,* because it is written, "*Bitza imraso*" (Lamentations 2:17), and the *Targum* translates, "He tore his purple cloak apart." But you should put on your *tallis katan* (small *tallis*) without saying a berachah.[3] You should go to the synagogue a bit earlier than usual.[4] No light should

3. If you removed your *tallis katan* at night, some maintain that you should say a berachah when you put it on in the morning. (*Ibid.* 555:2)

4. If starting *Shacharis* early will cause the congregation to conclude saying *Kinnos* much before midday, it is better not to start too early. (*Ibid.* 559:16)

לְבֵית־הַכְּנֶסֶת, וְאֵין מַדְלִיקִין נֵר תְּפִלָּה כְּלָל, וּמִתְפַּלְּלִין גַּם כֵּן בְּנַחַת וְדֶרֶךְ בֶּכִי, וְאוֹמְרִים מִזְמוֹר לְתוֹדָה. וּשְׁלִיחַ־הַצִּבּוּר, בַּחֲזָרַת הַתְּפִלָּה אוֹמֵר עֲנֵנוּ בֵּין גּוֹאֵל לְרוֹפֵא, כְּמוֹ בְּכָל תַּעֲנִית־צִבּוּר, וְאֵינוֹ אוֹמֵר בִּרְכַּת־כֹּהֲנִים. וּלְאַחַר הַתְּפִלָּה אוֹמֵר חֲצִי קַדִּישׁ. אֵין אוֹמְרִים לֹא תַחֲנוּן וְלֹא אֵל אֶרֶךְ אַפַּיִם, מִשּׁוּם דְּאִקְרֵי מוֹעֵד. וּמוֹצִיאִין סֵפֶר־תּוֹרָה וְקוֹרִין כִּי תוֹלִיד בָּנִים וְגוֹ׳, תְּלָתָא גַּבְרֵי. וְנָכוֹן שֶׁהָעוֹלֶה יֹאמַר בְּלַחַשׁ קֹדֶם הַבְּרָכָה, בָּרוּךְ דַּיַּן הָאֱמֶת. אַחַר קְרִיאַת הַתּוֹרָה אוֹמְרִים חֲצִי קַדִּישׁ, וּמַפְטִירִין אָסֹף אֲסִיפֵם בְּנִגּוּן אֵיכָה, וּמַחֲזִירִין אֶת סֵפֶר־הַתּוֹרָה, וְיוֹשְׁבִים עַל הָאָרֶץ וְאוֹמְרִים קִינוֹת, וְיֵשׁ לְהַאֲרִיךְ בָּהֶן עַד סָמוּךְ לַצָּהֳרַיִם. אַחַר כָּךְ אוֹמְרִים אַשְׁרֵי, וְאֵין אוֹמְרִים לַמְנַצֵּחַ, אֶלָּא וּבָא לְצִיּוֹן וְגוֹ׳, וּמְדַלְּגִין אֶת הַפָּסוּק וַאֲנִי זֹאת וְגוֹ׳, לְפִי שֶׁהָיָה נִרְאֶה כִּמְקַיֵּם בְּרִית עַל הַקִּינוֹת. וְעוֹד, דְּלֹא שַׁיָּךְ לוֹמַר וַאֲנִי זֹאת בְּרִיתִי וְגוֹ׳, לֹא יָמוּשׁוּ מִפִּיךָ וְגוֹ׳, כֵּיוָן שֶׁהַכֹּל בְּטֵלִים וַאֲסוּרִים בְּדִבְרֵי תוֹרָה. אֲבָל בְּבֵית הָאָבֵל, בְּכָל הַשָּׁנָה חוּץ מִתִּשְׁעָה בְּאָב, אוֹמְרִים אוֹתוֹ, שֶׁאַף־עַל־גַּב שֶׁהָאָבֵל בָּטֵל מִדִּבְרֵי תוֹרָה, הַמְנַחֲמִים אֵינָן בְּטֵלִין. וְאוֹמְרִים וְאַתָּה קָדוֹשׁ וְגוֹ׳, וְאוֹמְרִים קַדִּישׁ שָׁלֵם בְּדִלּוּג תִּתְקַבֵּל, עָלֵינוּ, קַדִּישׁ יָתוֹם, וְאֵין אוֹמְרִים לֹא שִׁיר הַיִּחוּד וְלֹא שִׁיר שֶׁל יוֹם וְלֹא פִּטּוּם הַקְּטֹרֶת. וְנָכוֹן שֶׁכָּל אֶחָד יִקְרָא אַחַר כָּךְ מְגִלַּת אֵיכָה.

ד) אִם יֵשׁ אָבֵל בָּעִיר הוֹלֵךְ לְבֵית־הַכְּנֶסֶת בַּלַּיְלָה וְגַם בַּיּוֹם עַד שֶׁיִּגְמְרוּ הַקִּינוֹת, וּמֻתָּר לוֹ לַעֲלוֹת לַתּוֹרָה וְלִקְרוֹת הַהַפְטָרָה, שֶׁהֲרֵי כֻּלָּם אֲבֵלִים הֵם.

ה) דִּבְרֵי תוֹרָה מְשַׂמְּחִין אֶת הַלֵּב, שֶׁנֶּאֱמַר, פִּקּוּדֵי ה׳ יְשָׁרִים מְשַׂמְּחֵי לֵב. וְלָכֵן אָסוּר בְּתִשְׁעָה בְּאָב לִלְמֹד תּוֹרָה, כִּי אִם בִּדְבָרִים שֶׁמַּעֲצִיבִים אֶת לִבּוֹ, כְּגוֹן בְּסֵפֶר יִרְמְיָה בַּדְּבָרִים הָרָעִים שֶׁבּוֹ, וּפְסוּקֵי נֶחָמָה שֶׁבּוֹ

---

5. At *Minchah,* however, lights may be lit. (*Ibid.* 559:15)

6. This rule is not mentioned in *Mishnah Berurah.*

7. This custom is also not mentioned in *Mishnah Berurah.*

8. During the saying of *Kinnos,* it is forbidden to walk out of the synagogue or to engage in conversation which interrupt your thoughts and feelings of mourning the destruction. Light-headedness is always forbidden in the synagogue, and certainly so on *Tishah beAv,* a day of mourning over the destruction and the consequent exile of our people. (See *Mishnah Berurah* 559:22)

be lit for the prayers.[5] Again, prayers should be said in a low and tearful voice. We do say *Mizmor Lesodah* (a Psalm of thanksgiving). In the repetition of the *Shemoneh esrei* the *Chazzan* says *Aneinu* (Answer us) between *Ga'al Yisrael* (the Redeemer of Israel) and *Refa'einu* (Heal us), as on every other public fast day. He does not say the *Birkas kohanim* (priestly blessing).[6] After the *Shemoneh esrei,* he says half-*kaddish.* We do not say *Tachanun* or *Keil erech apayim* (O' God, slow to anger), because *Tishah beAv* is called a *moed.* A *Seifer* Torah is taken out and the section *Ki solid banim* etc. is read (When you will have children) etc. (Deuteronomy 4:25), is read for three persons. It is proper for the one called up, to say quietly, *Baruch dayan ha'emes*[7] (Blessed is the true Judge) before saying the berachah. After the reading of the Torah, half-*kaddish* is said, and the *haftarah* is read of the chapter, *Asof asifeim*, [I will destroy them completely] (Jeremiah 8:13) in the tone of *Eichah.* The *Seifer* Torah is then replaced in the Ark. Everyone is seated on the floor to say *Kinnos.*[8] The saying of *kinnos* should be drawn out, until close to noon. Then *Ashrei* (Fortunate are those) is said omitting *Lamenatzei'ach,* (For the conductor), and we say *Uva letziyon go'eil* [A redeemer shall come to Zion] etc., but we omit the verse *Va'ani zos berisi* [And as for Me, this is My covenant], for it would appear, as if He established a covenant for the *Kinnos,* and, besides, it would be inappropriate to say *Va'ani zos berisi etc., Lo yamushu mipicha etc.* (My words shall not depart from your mouth), since no one is studying Torah, as Torah study is forbidden (on *Tishah beAv*). But at a mourner's house, during the entire year, except on *Tishah beAv,* the verse should be said, for, although the mourner is not studying Torah, those that come to console him are not exempt [from Torah study]. Then, *Ve'atah kadosh* is said (And You are the Holy One) etc., followed by the complete *kaddish,* omitting *tiskabbeil,* then *Aleinu* (It is our duty) is said, and the mourner's *kaddish.* We do not say *Shir hayichud* (Song of God's Unity), nor *Shir shel yom* (Song of the day), nor *Pittum haketores* (The incense mixture). It is proper for everyone to read *Eichah* afterwards

4) If there is a mourner in the town, he should go to the synagogue on the night (of *Tishah beAv*) and also during the day,[9] (and stay) until the conclusion of the *Kinnos.* He is permitted to receive an *aliyah* and to read the *haftarah,*[10] because we all are mourners (on *Tishah beAv*).

5) The words of the Torah gladden the heart, as it is said, "The precepts of Hashem are upright, gladdening the heart" (Psalms 19:9). Therefore, it is forbidden to study Torah on *Tishah beAv,* except for subjects that sadden the heart, such as the chapters of the book of Jeremiah,[11] regarding the ominous events he prophesied,

---

9. Other *Poskim* maintain that during the first three days of mourning, he should not go to the synagogue. *Rav Shlomo Kluger* ruled that he should not go at night, when only a limited *Kinnos* is said, but by day, when the majority of *Kinnos* is said, he is permitted to go. After the three days, however, he may go, even at night. (See *Mishnah Berurah* 559:24 and also *Shaar Hatzion* 22)

10. This rule is not mentioned in *Mishnah Berurah.*

11. According to *Shulchan Aruch* 554:2, it is also permitted to study commentaries on *Jeremiah* and *Job.*

יְדַלֵּג. וְכֵן פֵּרְעָנִיּוֹת עַל אֻמּוֹת הָעוֹלָם שֶׁכְּתוּבוֹת שָׁם יְדַלֵּג. וְכֵן מֻתָּר לִלְמֹד בְּסֵפֶר אִיּוֹב, וּמִדְרַשׁ אֵיכָה, וּגְמָרָא פֶּרֶק וְאֵלּוּ מְגַלְּחִין וְכוּ', דְּמַיְרֵי בְּדִינֵי אָבֵל וּמְנֻדֶּה, וּבְהַגָּדָה דְּפֶרֶק הַנִּזָּקִין, וִירוּשַׁלְמִי סוֹף מַסֶּכֶת תַּעֲנִית, דְּמַיְרֵי מֵחֻרְבָּן. וְאַף בְּאֵלּוּ שֶׁהוּא מֻתָּר לִלְמֹד, אָסוּר לְעַיֵּן בָּהֶם בְּאֵיזוֹ קֻשְׁיָא וְתֵרוּץ אוֹ דְרוּשׁ, כִּי מְשַׂמְּחִים אֶת הַלֵּב. וְכָל מַה שֶּׁמֻּתָּר הָאָדָם לִלְמֹד בְּעַצְמוֹ, מֻתָּר לִלְמֹד גַּם עִם תִּינוֹקוֹת. מֻתָּר לִקְרוֹת כָּל סֵדֶר הַיּוֹם, אֲפִלּוּ אֵיזֶהוּ מְקוֹמָן. וְסֵדֶר מַעֲמָדוֹת אֵין לוֹמַר, אֲפִלּוּ מִי שֶׁרָגִיל לְאָמְרוֹ בְּכָל יוֹם.

ו) אֲפִלּוּ עֻבָּרוֹת וּמֵינִיקוֹת, אַף־עַל־פִּי שֶׁמִּצְטַעֲרוֹת הַרְבֵּה, צְרִיכוֹת לְהַשְׁלִים הַתַּעֲנִית, אִם לֹא בְּמָקוֹם שֶׁיֵּשׁ לָחוּשׁ חַס־וְשָׁלוֹם לְסַכָּנָה. אֲבָל חוֹלֶה, אַף־עַל־פִּי שֶׁאֵין בּוֹ סַכָּנָה, יֵשׁ לְהָקֵל שֶׁלֹּא יַשְׁלִים הַתַּעֲנִית, רַק יִתְעַנֶּה אֵיזֶה שָׁעוֹת, וּמִכָּל־שֶׁכֵּן אִם הוּא חָלוּשׁ בְּטִבְעוֹ. וְיוֹלֶדֶת לְאַחַר שִׁבְעָה יָמִים עַד שְׁלֹשִׁים יוֹם נַמִּי, דִּינָהּ כְּחוֹלֶה שֶׁאֵין בּוֹ סַכָּנָה, אַף־עַל־פִּי שֶׁאֵינָהּ חוֹלָה. אַךְ אִם מַרְגֶּשֶׁת בְּעַצְמָהּ שֶׁהִיא בְּרִיאָה לְגַמְרֵי וְהַתַּעֲנִית לֹא תַזִּיק לָהּ, יֵשׁ לָהּ לְהַשְׁלִים. וְאֵלּוּ שֶׁצְּרִיכִין לֶאֱכוֹל בְּתִשְׁעָה בְּאָב, לֹא יִתְעַנְּגוּ בְּמַאֲכָלִים, אֶלָּא בִּכְדֵי צֹרֶךְ בְּרִיאוּת הַגּוּף.

ז) רְחִיצָה, אֲסוּרָה בֵּין בְּחַמִּין בֵּין בְּצוֹנֵן. וַאֲפִלּוּ לְהוֹשִׁיט אֶצְבָּעוֹ לְתוֹךְ מַיִם, אָסוּר. וְאֵינָהּ אֲסוּרָה רַק רְחִיצָה שֶׁל תַּעֲנוּג. אֲבָל שֶׁלֹּא לְתַעֲנוּג, מֻתָּר. וְלָכֵן רוֹחֵץ יָדָיו בְּשַׁחֲרִית, וְיִזָּהֵר שֶׁלֹּא יִרְחַץ רַק אֶצְבְּעוֹתָיו, שֶׁזֶּהוּ עִקַּר הָרְחִיצָה בְּשַׁחֲרִית, מִפְּנֵי שֶׁרוּחַ רָעָה שׁוֹרָה עַל הָאֶצְבָּעוֹת. וּלְאַחַר שֶׁנִּגְּבָן קְצָת וַעֲדַיִן לַחוֹת קְצָת מַעֲבִירָן עַל עֵינָיו. וְאִם עֵינָיו מְלֻכְלָכוֹת וְדַרְכּוֹ לְרָחֲצָן בְּמַיִם, רוֹחֲצָן גַּם עַתָּה כְּדַרְכּוֹ וְאֵינוֹ חוֹשֵׁשׁ. וְכֵן אִם הָיוּ יָדָיו מְלֻכְלָכוֹת בְּטִיט וְכַדּוֹמֶה, מֻתָּר לִרְחוֹץ בְּמָקוֹם הַמְלֻכְלָךְ. וְכֵן כְּשֶׁעָשָׂה צְרָכָיו, מֻתָּר לִרְחוֹץ יָדָיו קְצָת כְּדַרְכּוֹ תָּמִיד. וְכֵן לִתְפִלַּת מִנְחָה, יִרְחַץ אֶצְבְּעוֹתָיו.

---

12. The portion of prayers that deal with the order of sacrificial offerings should not be said, with the exception of the daily sacrifice. (See *Mishnah Berurah* 554:7)

13. If this, too, is difficult for him, he need not fast at all. (*Ibid.* 554:14)

14. The berachah *al netilas yadayim* (over washing the hands) should not be said, until after you have gone to the bathroom and washed your hands. (*Ibid.* 554:21)

omitting the verses of consolation. Also the verses foretelling the punishment to be meted out to the nations of the world that are written there, should be omitted. It is also permitted to study the Book of Job, as well as *Midrash Eichah*. [The following Talmudic selections may also be studied:] the Talmud, chapter *Eilu megalchin,* (Moed Katan, 3rd chapter), which deals with the laws of a mourner, and a person who was excommunicated, and the *Aggadic* portion of the chapter *Hanizakin* (*Maseches Gittin* 55b), and in the Jerusalem Talmud, the last part of the *Maseches Ta'anis,* which discusses the destruction of the *Beis Hamikdash.* But even the chapters you are permitted to study, you are forbidden to study in depth, to find an answer to a difficult question or a homiletic interpretation, for that would gladden the heart. Any subject you, yourself, are permitted to study, you are permitted to teach to children. You are permitted to read the entire order of daily prayers, even the *Mishnah* of *Eizehu mekoman*[12] (What is the location [of the offerings?]). But you should not say *Ma'amados,* even if you are accustomed to saying it every day.

6) Even if pregnant and nursing women suffer very much, they are required to complete the fast, unless, God forbid, this might endanger their health. However, a sick person, even if his condition is not critical, should be lenient, and should not complete the fast, but fast only for a few hours.[13] This is especially true if he is weak by nature. A woman, from the seventh until the thirtieth day after giving birth, is governed by the same *halachah* that applies to a sick person, whose condition is not critical, even though she is not really sick. However, if she feels that she is in perfect health and the fast will not harm her, she should complete the fast. Those who must eat on *Tishah beAv* should not enjoy an elaborate meal, but should eat no more than they need to preserve their health.

7) You are forbidden to wash yourself, whether in hot or cold water. Even dipping your fingers in water is forbidden. But only washing for pleasure is forbidden, however, when it is not for pleasure, it is permitted. You may, therefore, wash your hands in the morning. But you should be careful to wash only your fingers, for this constitutes the mitzvah of washing in the morning,[14] to remove the evil spirit, that rests on the fingers. After you dry your hands a little, while they are still slightly damp, you may pass them over your eyes.[15] If your eyes are sticky and you usually wash them in the morning, you may wash them now also, as usual, and you need not be concerned about it.[16] Similarly, if your hands are soiled with mud or other dirt, you may wash the dirty spots. After going to the bathroom, you may wash your hands lightly in the usual manner.[17] Also, for the *Minchah* service, you should wash your fingers.

---

15. You may also pass them over your face and hands as well. (*Ibid.* 554:22)
16. This is similar to removing mud or other dirt, which you are permitted to wash, as mentioned in the following *halachah.*
17. *Mishnah Berurah* rules that you may wash your hands, only till the knuckles (i.e. the fingers only). (613:6)

ח) נָשִׁים הַמְבַשְּׁלוֹת וּצְרִיכוֹת לְהָדִיחַ הַמַּאֲכָלִים, מֻתָּרוֹת, דְּהָא אֵינָן מִתְכַּוְּנוֹת לִרְחִיצָה. הַהוֹלֵךְ לְצָרְכֵי מִצְוָה וְאֵין לְפָנָיו דֶּרֶךְ אַחֶרֶת רַק לַעֲבֹר בַּמַּיִם עוֹבֵר בַּמַּיִם, בֵּין בַּהֲלִיכָתוֹ בֵּין בַּחֲזִירָתוֹ וְאֵינוֹ חוֹשֵׁשׁ, אֲבָל אִם הוֹלֵךְ בִּשְׁבִיל מָמוֹנוֹ, בַּהֲלִיכָתוֹ מֻתָּר, וּבַחֲזִירָתוֹ אָסוּר. הַבָּא מִן הַדֶּרֶךְ וְרַגְלָיו כֵּהוֹת, מֻתָּר לְרָחֳצָן בַּמַּיִם.

ט) אַף־עַל־פִּי שֶׁאֵינָהּ אֲסוּרָה כִּי אִם רְחִיצָה שֶׁל תַּעֲנוּג, מִכָּל מָקוֹם אִשָּׁה שֶׁחָלָה טְבִילָתָהּ בְּלֵיל תִּשְׁעָה בְּאָב, לֹא תִטְבֹּל, כֵּיוָן דַּאֲסוּרִין בְּתַשְׁמִישׁ. (וּלְעִנְיַן לְבִישַׁת הַלִּבּוּן, עַיֵּן לְקַמָּן סִימָן קנט).

י) סִיכָה גַּם כֵּן אֵינָהּ אֲסוּרָה אֶלָּא שֶׁל תַּעֲנוּג. אֲבָל מִי שֶׁיֵּשׁ לוֹ חֲטָטִין אוֹ לְצֹרֶךְ שְׁאָר רְפוּאָה, מֻתָּר לָסוּךְ.

יא) נְעִילַת הַסַּנְדָּל, אֵינָהּ אֲסוּרָה אֶלָּא שֶׁל עוֹר. אֲבָל שֶׁל בֶּגֶד וְכַדּוֹמֶה, אִם אֵינוֹ מְחֻפֶּה בְּשׁוּלַיִם בְּעוֹר, מֻתָּר. הַהוֹלְכִים בֵּין הַגּוֹיִם, נוֹהֲגִים לִלְבּוֹשׁ מִנְעָלִים, שֶׁלֹּא יִהְיוּ לְלַעַג. וְיֵשׁ לִתֵּן עָפָר בְּתוֹךְ הַמִּנְעָלִים. וּמִכָּל מָקוֹם בַּעַל נֶפֶשׁ יַחְמִיר עַל עַצְמוֹ. וְהַיּוֹשְׁבִים בַּחֲנֻיּוֹת, וַדַּאי אֲסוּרִים. הַמְהַלֵּךְ בְּדֶרֶךְ רְחוֹקָה בְּרַגְלָיו, כֵּיוָן שֶׁהוּא טֹרַח גָּדוֹל, לֹא אָסְרוּ חֲכָמֵינוּ זִכְרוֹנָם לִבְרָכָה, וּמֻתָּר בִּנְעִילַת הַסַּנְדָּל. אַךְ כְּשֶׁמַּגִּיעַ לָעִיר, חוֹלֵץ. וְאִם יוֹשֵׁב בַּעֲגָלָה אָסוּר בִּנְעִילַת הַסַּנְדָּל.

יב) תַּשְׁמִישׁ הַמִּטָּה, אָסוּר. וְיֵשׁ לְהַחְמִיר אֲפִלּוּ בִּנְגִיעָה בְּאִשְׁתּוֹ.

יג) אָסוּר לִשְׁאוֹל בִּשְׁלוֹם חֲבֵרוֹ בְּתִשְׁעָה בְּאָב. וַאֲפִלּוּ לוֹמַר צַפְרָא טָבָא וְכַיּוֹצֵא בוֹ, אָסוּר. וְאִם עַם הָאָרֶץ אוֹ גוֹי שׁוֹאֲלִין בִּשְׁלוֹמוֹ, מֵשִׁיב בְּשָׂפָה רָפָה שֶׁלֹּא יַקְפִּידוּ עָלָיו. וְכֵן אָסוּר לִשְׁלוֹחַ דּוֹרוֹן לַחֲבֵרוֹ, שֶׁזֶּהוּ בִּכְלַל שְׁאֵלַת שָׁלוֹם.

יד) לֹא יְטַיֵּל בַּשּׁוּק, שֶׁלֹּא יָבוֹא לִידֵי שְׂחוֹק וְשִׂמְחָה. עִשּׁוּן טַבַּק, יֵשׁ אוֹסְרִין, וְיֵשׁ מַתִּירִין לְאַחַר הַצָּהֳרַיִם בְּצִנְעָא בְּתוֹךְ בֵּיתוֹ.

---

18. You are permitted to go because it may involve monetary loss, but there is no reason to permit the return. (*Ibid.* 554:25) (The return trip is permitted, when you go to do a mitzvah because you might hesitate to go, knowing that you cannot return, but this consideration will not prevent you from going, if it means financial gain or the prevention of a loss.)

8) Women who need to rinse the foods used in cooking, are permitted to do so, because their purpose is not to wash their hands. If you are on your way to perform a mitzvah, and the only way you can get there is by crossing a stream, you may cross it on your way there and on returning, and you need not be concerned about it. However, if you are going for business, you may cross it on your way going, but on your return trip it is forbidden.[18] If you return from the road and your feet feel weak, you may bathe them in water.[19]

9) Although only bathing for pleasure is forbidden, nevertheless, a woman whose time for *tevilah* (immersion) occurs on the night of *Tishah beAv* should not do the *tevilah,* since marital relations are forbidden (on *Tishah beAv*). (Regarding the putting on of white undergarments, see chapter 159 below).

10) Applying cream, too, is forbidden only, if it is done for pleasure.[20] But a person who has pimples or needs it for any other medical treatment, may apply cream or ointment.

11) Wearing shoes is forbidden only, if they are made of leather. Shoes made of cloth or similar material, which do not have leather soles,[21] may be worn. People who have to walk among non-Jews, as a rule wear leather shoes, in order not to be ridiculed, but they should put some earth in their shoes.[22] Nevertheless, a pious person should observe the law stringently. Storekeepers are surely forbidden to wear leather shoes. Our Sages, of blessed memory, ruled that since it is very exhausting, a person who has to go a long distance on foot is permitted to wear leather shoes.[23] But when he approaches a city, he must take them off. But a person riding in a vehicle is forbidden to wear leather shoes.

12) It is forbidden to have marital relations. One should be strict about this, and not even touch his wife.

13) You are forbidden to greet your neighbor on *Tishah beAv,* even to say "good morning," or any similar greeting. If an unlearned person or a non-Jew says hello to you, you may answer in a low voice, for otherwise, they would be angry with you. It is also forbidden to send a gift to your neighbor, because this is a form of greeting.

14) You should not stroll in public places, in order to avoid laughter and frivolity. Some authorities forbid smoking the entire day, while others permit it in the afternoon, in the privacy of the home.

---

19. This is not considered pleasure, but, rather, for health reasons. (*Ibid.* 554:26)

20. It is, however, permitted to apply cream etc., in order to remove perspiration. (see *Biyur Halachah* 554:15)

21. *Mishnah Berurah* rules that if the upper shoe is leather, they are forbidden, even if the soles are wooden. Similarly, if the soles are made of cloth and the upper shoe is leather, it, too, is forbidden. (554:31)

22. This *halachah* is not mentioned in *Mishnah Berurah* in this context. See, however, following note.

23. In this situation, you should put some earth in your shoes. (*Ibid.* 554:33)

טו) בְּעִנְיַן מְלָאכָה, אָנוּ נוֹהֲגִים שֶׁכָּל מְלָאכָה שֶׁיֵּשׁ בָּהּ שִׁהוּי קְצָת, אֲפִלּוּ אֵינָהּ מַעֲשֵׂה אֻמָּן אֶלָּא מַעֲשֵׂה הֶדְיוֹט, אֲסוּרִין בַּלַּיְלָה וּבַיּוֹם עַד הַצָּהֳרַיִם. אֲבָל דָּבָר שֶׁאֵין בּוֹ שִׁהוּי, כְּגוֹן הַדְלָקַת נֵרוֹת וּקְשִׁירָה וְכַיּוֹצֵא בוֹ, מֻתָּר. וּלְאַחַר הַצָּהֳרַיִם, עוֹשִׂים כָּל הַמְּלָאכוֹת. וְכֵן מַשָּׂא וּמַתָּן נוֹהֲגִים לֶאֱסוֹר קֹדֶם הַצָּהֳרַיִם, וּלְאַחַר הַצָּהֳרַיִם מַתִּירִים. אֲבָל מִי שֶׁהוּא יְרֵא־שָׁמַיִם, יֵשׁ לוֹ לְהַחְמִיר כָּל הַיּוֹם, בֵּין בִּמְלָאכָה, בֵּין בְּמַשָּׂא־וּמַתָּן, שֶׁלֹּא יַסִּיחַ דַּעְתּוֹ מִן הָאֲבֵלוּת. וְעַל יְדֵי גוֹי, מֻתָּר לַעֲשׂוֹת כָּל מְלָאכָה. וְדָבָר הָאָבֵד, מֻתָּר לַעֲשׂוֹת גַּם בְּעַצְמוֹ. לַחֲלוֹב הַפָּרוֹת, טוֹב לַעֲשׂוֹת עַל יְדֵי גוֹי. וְאִם אִי־אֶפְשָׁר, מֻתָּר בְּעַצְמוֹ.

טז) נוֹהֲגִין שֶׁאֵין יוֹשְׁבִין עַל סַפְסָל לֹא בַּלַּיְלָה וְלֹא בַּיּוֹם עַד לְאַחַר הַצָּהֳרַיִם, כִּי אִם עַל הָאָרֶץ, וּלְאַחַר הַצָּהֳרַיִם מֻתָּרִין. אֲבָל שְׁאָר דְּבָרִים הָאֲסוּרִים, אֲסוּרִים עַד צֵאת הַכּוֹכָבִים.

יז) נוֹהֲגִין שֶׁלֹּא לְהָכִין צָרְכֵי סְעוּדָה עַד אַחַר הַצָּהֳרַיִם. אֲבָל לְצֹרֶךְ מִצְוָה, מֻתָּר.

יח) אִם יֵשׁ תִּינוֹק לָמוּל, מָלִין אוֹתוֹ אַחַר שֶׁגָּמְרוּ אֶת הַקִּינוֹת. וַאֲבִי הַבֵּן וְאִמּוֹ וְהַסַּנְדָּק וְהַמּוֹהֵל, מֻתָּרִין לִלְבּוֹשׁ בִּגְדֵי שַׁבָּת לִכְבוֹד הַמִּילָה, וְאַחַר כָּךְ פּוֹשְׁטִין אוֹתָן. וּמַדְלִיקִין נֵרוֹת לִכְבוֹד הַמִּילָה. וְהַכּוֹס נוֹתְנִים לְתִינוֹק לִשְׁתּוֹת.

יט) בְּמִנְחָה מַנִּיחִין טַלִּית וּתְפִלִּין בִּבְרָכוֹת, וְאוֹמְרִים שִׁיר שֶׁל יוֹם וּשְׁאָר הַדְּבָרִים שֶׁחִסְּרוּ בְּשַׁחֲרִית, וְאוֹמְרִים אַשְׁרֵי וַחֲצִי קַדִּישׁ, וְקוֹרִין בַּתּוֹרָה, וּמַפְטִירִין כְּמוֹ בִּשְׁאָר תַּעֲנִית צִבּוּר, וּמַכְנִיסִין אֶת סֵפֶר־הַתּוֹרָה, וְאוֹמֵר שְׁלִיחַ־הַצִּבּוּר חֲצִי קַדִּישׁ, וּמִתְפַּלְּלִין שְׁמוֹנֶה־עֶשְׂרֵה, וְאוֹמְרִים נַחֵם

---

24. Regarding writing, *Eliyahu Rabbah,* in the name of *Knesseth Hagedolah,* says that you may be lenient; and *Mateh Yehudah* says that writing on *Tishah beAv* is governed by the same rules as on *Chol haMoed.* (see *Biyur Halachah* 554:22)

25. However, it is best not to get involved in your business, to the extent that you will forget that it is a day of mourning. This also applies to working. (*Mishnah Berurah* 554:49)

26. *Shulchan Aruch* 554:24 rules that one who does work on *Tishah beAv* will not see any blessing from that work. *Mishnah Berurah* explains that he will not see blessing from the profit made from working on *Tishah beAv.* See note 25, that this refers only in a situation where he completely forgot that it is a day of mourning.

27. This does not include building or exterior work that is in the public view which is forbidden. (*Ibid.* 554:46)

15) It is our custom, that any work requiring time, even work for which no skill is required, is forbidden the night (of *Tishah beAv)*, and in the daytime, until noon. But work that does not take long to do, like lighting candles or tying a knot, is permitted.[24] In the afternoon, all work is permitted. It is also the custom to forbid doing business before noon, but to permit in the afternoon.[25] However, a God-fearing man should be stringent in his observance the entire day, and not do any work, nor do any business, so that his mind should not be distracted from mourning.[26] It is permitted, however, to instruct a non-Jew to do any kind of work for you.[27] Any work, that if not done, would entail a loss, you are permitted to do yourself. Milking the cows preferably should be done by a non-Jew, but when that is impossible, you are permitted to do it yourself.

16) It is the custom not to sit on a bench (or chair), either at night, or in the day until the afternoon; but to sit only on the floor.[28] In the afternoon, it is permitted. However, the other things that are forbidden, are forbidden until the stars appear.

17) It is customary not to start preparing the meal before noon, but (if the meal is) for the purpose of a mitzvah, it is permitted.

18) If there is to be a *bris,* the *bris* should be performed after the saying of the *Kinnos* has ended. The father and the mother (of the infant), the *sandak* and the *mohel,* may put on their Shabbos clothes in honor of the *bris.*[29] After the *bris,* they should take them off. Candles should be lit in honor of the *bris,* and the cup of wine is given to a child to drink.

19) At the *Minchah* service, we put on the *tallis* and the *tefillin,*[30] saying the berachah over them.[31] The *Shir shel yom* (Song of the day) is said, as well as the other things that were omitted in the *Shacharis* service.[32] Then *Ashrei* and half-*kaddish* are said. We read the Torah and the *maftir,* as on any other public fast day. Then the *seifer* Torah is replaced in the Ark and the *Chazzan* says half- *kaddish,* after

---

28. You are permitted, however, to sit on a mat or pillow. You may also sit on a low stool, if you find it difficult to sit on the floor. (*Ibid.* 559:11)

29. Nevertheless, they are forbidden to wear leather shoes. (*Biyur Halachah* 559:8)

30. Those who also put on the *tefillin* of *Rabeinu Tam* should put them on at this time. (*Mishnah Berurah* 555:4)

31. *Mishnah Berurah* rules that you should not say *Kerias Shemah,* or the Chapter *kadeish,* which is usually said when putting on *tefillin,* because at *Minchah* time, this would merely constitute the reading of Torah chapters, which is forbidden on *Tishah beAv.* (*Ibid.* 555:5)

32. Although some have the custom to recite *tehillim* (Psalms) in the afternoon, *Mishnah Berurah* indicates that it is best not to do so, citing the custom of Posen to recite on the following day, the portion of *tehillim,* which ordinarily would have been said, had it not been *Tishah beAv,* in addition to the regular portion of the day. *Mishnah Berurah* also maintains that the passage of *Pitum haKetoras,* which deals with the compounding of the incense-offering, as well as other passage dealing with sacrificial-offering, should not be said even at *Minchah.* (*Mishnah Berurah* 554:7) (The Psalm *Lamenatzei'ach*, the verses of *Uva Letzion go'eil,* that were omitted at *Shacharis* (see paragraph 3) are not to be said at *Minchah*, and *tachanun* is also not said at *Minchah.*)

בְּבִרְכַּת וְלִירוּשָׁלַיִם. וְאִם שְׁכָחוֹ שָׁם, אוֹמְרוֹ אַחַר עֲנֵנוּ. וְלֹא יְסַיֵּם בָּרוּךְ מְנַחֵם וְכוּ׳, אֶלָּא כִּי אַתָּה שׁוֹמֵעַ וְכוּ׳. וְאִם גַּם שָׁם לֹא נִזְכַּר עַד לְאַחַר שֶׁאָמַר בָּרוּךְ אַתָּה ה׳, גּוֹמֵר הַבְּרָכָה שׁוֹמֵעַ תְּפִלָּה וּמִתְפַּלֵּל כְּסֵדֶר, וְאֵינוֹ צָרִיךְ לַחֲזוֹר. שְׁלִיחַ־הַצִּבּוּר, בַּחֲזָרַת הַתְּפִלָּה אוֹמֵר בִּרְכַּת כֹּהֲנִים, וְאַחַר הַתְּפִלָּה קַדִּישׁ שָׁלֵם עִם תִּתְקַבֵּל, וְחוֹלְצִין הַתְּפִלִּין, וּמִתְפַּלְּלִין מַעֲרִיב. וְאִם הַלְּבָנָה זוֹרַחַת, מְקַדְּשִׁין אוֹתָהּ. וְעַיֵּן לְעֵיל סִימָן צז סָעִיף יא, שֶׁצְּרִיכִים לִטְעֹם תְּחִלָּה.

כ) תַּנְיָא, בְּשִׁבְעָה בְּאָב נִכְנְסוּ הַגּוֹיִם לַהֵיכָל, וְאָכְלוּ וְשָׁתוּ וְקִלְקְלוּ בוֹ שְׁבִיעִי וּשְׁמִינִי, וּתְשִׁיעִי לְעֵת עֶרֶב הִצִּיתוּ בוֹ אֶת הָאֵשׁ, וְהָיְתָה דוֹלֶקֶת וְהוֹלֶכֶת כָּל יוֹם הָעֲשִׂירִי עַד שְׁקִיעַת הַחַמָּה. וְהָא דְּלֹא קָבְעוּ אֶת הַתַּעֲנִית לְיוֹם הָעֲשִׂירִי, אַף שֶׁרֻבּוֹ שֶׁל הֵיכָל נִשְׂרַף בּוֹ, מִפְּנֵי שֶׁהַתְחָלַת הַפֻּרְעָנִיּוֹת חָמִיר טְפֵי. וְאִיתָא בִּירוּשַׁלְמִי, רַבִּי אָבִין הִתְעַנָּה תְּשִׁיעִי וַעֲשִׂירִי. רַבִּי לֵוִי הִתְעַנָּה תְּשִׁיעִי וְלֵיל עֲשִׂירִי, מִפְּנֵי שֶׁלֹּא הָיָה בוֹ כֹּחַ לְהִתְעַנּוֹת כָּל הַיּוֹם הָעֲשִׂירִי, הִתְעַנָּה רַק הַלָּיְלָה. וְאָנוּ תַּשׁ כֹּחֵנוּ, וְאֵין מִתְעַנִּין רַק תְּשִׁיעִי לְבַד, אַךְ מַחְמִירִין שֶׁלֹּא לֶאֱכֹל בָּשָׂר וְשֶׁלֹּא לִשְׁתּוֹת יַיִן בְּלֵיל עֲשִׂירִי וְלֹא בַּיּוֹם הָעֲשִׂירִי עַד חֲצוֹת הַיּוֹם, כִּי אִם בִּסְעוּדַת מִצְוָה. וְכֵן אֵין לְבָרֵךְ שֶׁהֶחֱיָנוּ. גַּם אֵין לִרְחוֹץ וְלֹא לְהִסְתַּפֵּר וּלְכַבֵּס עַד חֲצוֹת הָעֲשִׂירִי. וּמִי שֶׁמַּחְמִיר עַל עַצְמוֹ בְּכָל הַדְּבָרִים הַנִּזְכָּרִים כָּל הַיּוֹם הָעֲשִׂירִי, הֲרֵי זֶה מְשֻׁבָּח. אִם הַיּוֹם הָעֲשִׂירִי חָל בְּעֶרֶב שַׁבָּת, מֻתָּר לִרְחוֹץ וּלְהִסְתַּפֵּר וּלְכַבֵּס מִיָּד בְּשַׁחֲרִית, מִפְּנֵי כְּבוֹד הַשַּׁבָּת.

כא) יוֹלֶדֶת, אַף שֶׁמִּתְעַנָּה לְאַחַר שִׁבְעָה, מֻתֶּרֶת בְּלֵיל עֲשִׂירִי בְּבָשָׂר וָיַיִן.

כב) נָכוֹן שֶׁלֹּא לְשַׁמֵּשׁ מִטָּתוֹ בְּלֵיל עֲשִׂירִי, אִם לֹא כְּשֶׁהוּא לֵיל טְבִילָה, אוֹ כְּשֶׁהוּא יוֹצֵא לַדֶּרֶךְ אוֹ בָּא מִן הַדֶּרֶךְ.

---

33. *Kitzur Shulchan Aruch*'s ruling is based on *Taz,* which *Mishnah Berurah* says is only a singular opinion, citing other Poskim, who refute *Taz.* The proper way, according to *Mishnah Berurah,* based on *Mateh Yehudah* is to say insert *Nacheim* before saying *Vesechezenu* (And may our eyes behold) and to conclude with *Vesechezenu,* until its concluding berachah. (see *Mishnah Berurah* 557:2; also *Biyur Halachah* 557:1)

34. See note 33 above.

which the *Shemoneh esreih* is said. We insert *Nacheim* (Console, O God) in the berachah *Velirushalayim* (And to Jerusalem). If you forgot to say it there, you should say it after *Aneinu* (Answer us),[33] but you should not conclude the prayer, with *Baruch menacheim* [Blessed . . . Consoler] etc., but with *Ki atah shomei'a* (For You hear the prayers) etc. But if you did not realize it until after you said *Baruch atah Hashem* [Blessed are You, Hashem], you conclude the berachah *Shomei'a tefillah* [Who hears prayer][34] and continue praying according to the regular order, and you do not have to repeat [the *Shemoneh esrei*]. The *Chazzan,* in the repetition of the *Shemoneh esrei,* recites the *Birkas kohanim* (Priestly Blessing). After the *Shemoneh esrei,* he says the whole *kaddish* with *tiskabbeil.* We then take off the *tefillin* and pray *Maariv.*[35] If the moon is shining, we recite *Kiddush levanah* (Sanctification of the moon).[36] See 97:11 above, where it is stated that you must taste some food first.[37]

20) We are taught in a *Beraisa*, "On the seventh day of Av, the heathens entered the *Beis Hamikdash.* They ate and drank and wreaked havoc in it on the seventh and eighth days, and on the ninth, towards evening, they set fire to the *Beis Hamikdash,* and it continued to burn throughout the tenth day until sunset. The reason the fast was not set for the tenth day, although the greater part of the *Beis Hamikdash* was burned on that day, is because the beginning of a punishment is felt more severly. In the Jerusalem Talmud it is stated, "Rabbi Avin fasted on the ninth and on the tenth," (*Maseches Taanis* 4:6). Rabbi Levi fasted on the ninth and on the night of the tenth. Because he did not have the strength to fast the entire tenth day, he fasted during the night only. But as for us, since our strength has waned, we fast only on the ninth, but we impose a stringency on ourselves, in that we do not eat meat, nor do we drink wine, during the night of the tenth day, nor on the tenth day until noon, unless it is at a meal that is considered a mitzvah. Also, the berachah *Shehecheyanu* should not be said; neither should you take a bath, or a haircut, or wash clothes, until noon of the tenth day. A person who imposes upon himself to observe all the above-mentioned restrictions for the entire tenth day of *Av,* is to be praised.[38] If the tenth of *Av* occurs on *erev Shabbos,* you may bathe, take a haircut and wash immediately in the morning, in honor of the Shabbos.

21) A woman who has given birth, although she fasts after seven days [after giving birth], is permitted, on the night of the tenth, to eat meat and drink wine.

22) It is proper not to have marital relations on the night of the tenth, unless it is on the night of her *tevilah* (immersion), or if he is going on a trip, or returned from a trip.

---

35. This is based only on the assumption that *Minchah* will be concluded at a time, when it is permitted to pray *Maariv.*
36. *Mishnah Berurah* cautions that *Kiddush levanah* should not be recited, without wearing your shoes. (*Ibid.* 426:11)
37. However, if a large number of people will be saying *Kiddush levanah,* together, it is proper to recite it with them, even before tasting food. (*Ibid.* 426:11; *Shaar Hatzion* 9)
38. This rule is not mentioned in *Mishnah Berurah.*

סִימָן קכה
דִּינֵי תִּשְׁעָה בְּאָב שֶׁחָל בַּשַּׁבָּת אוֹ בְּאֶחָד בַּשַּׁבָּת

א) תִּשְׁעָה בְּאָב שֶׁחָל בְּאֶחָד בַּשַּׁבָּת אוֹ שֶׁחָל בַּשַּׁבָּת וְנִדְחָה לְאֶחָד בַּשַּׁבָּת, אוֹכְלִין בַּשַּׁבָּת בָּשָׂר וְשׁוֹתִין יַיִן. וַאֲפִלּוּ בִּסְעוּדָה שְׁלִישִׁית שֶׁלְּאַחַר מִנְחָה, מֻתָּר בַּכֹּל, אַךְ לֹא יֵשֵׁב אָז בִּסְעוּדַת חֲבֵרִים. וְאִם חָל בְּרִית מִילָה, יַעֲשׂוּ הַסְּעוּדָה קֹדֶם מִנְחָה. אֲבָל מֻתָּר לֶאֱכוֹל עִם בְּנֵי בֵיתוֹ, וְיָכוֹל לְבָרֵךְ בְּזִמּוּן. וְצָרִיךְ לְהַפְסִיק מִבְּעוֹד יוֹם, כִּי בְּבֵין הַשְּׁמָשׁוֹת אָסוּר בַּאֲכִילָה וּשְׁתִיָּה וּרְחִיצָה. אַךְ הַמִּנְעָלִים לֹא יַחֲלוֹץ עַד לְאַחַר בָּרְכוּ. וּשְׁלִיחַ־הַצִּבּוּר חוֹלֵץ קֹדֶם שֶׁמַּתְחִיל וְהוּא רַחוּם, כְּדֵי שֶׁלֹּא לְבַלְבֵּל דַּעְתּוֹ, וְיֹאמַר מִתְּחִלָּה בְּרְכַּת הַמַּבְדִּיל בֵּין קֹדֶשׁ לְחֹל בְּלֹא שֵׁם וּמַלְכוּת.

ב) לֵיל שַׁבָּת שֶׁחָל בּוֹ תִּשְׁעָה בְּאָב, אָסוּר בְּתַשְׁמִישׁ־הַמִּטָּה, אִם לֹא כְּשֶׁחָל אָז לֵיל טְבִילָתָהּ.

ג) אוֹמְרִים אַב הָרַחֲמִים, וּמַזְכִּירִין נְשָׁמוֹת בְּשַׁחֲרִית. אֲבָל בְּמִנְחָה, אֵין אוֹמְרִים צִדְקָתְךָ צֶדֶק.

ד) תִּשְׁעָה בְּאָב שֶׁחָל בַּשַּׁבָּת, יֵשׁ לְהַחְמִיר שֶׁלֹּא לִלְמֹד כִּי אִם דְּבָרִים הַמֻּתָּרִים לִלְמֹד בְּתִשְׁעָה בְּאָב, וְלָכֵן אֵין אוֹמְרִים פִּרְקֵי אָבוֹת. אֲבָל לִקְרוֹת הַסִּדְרָה שְׁנַיִם מִקְרָא וְאֶחָד תַּרְגּוּם, מֻתָּר, וּמִכָּל־שֶׁכֵּן קֹדֶם חֲצוֹת הַיּוֹם. וְאִם חָל (בְּ)עֶרֶב תִּשְׁעָה בְּאָב [בַּשַּׁבָּת], אָסוּר לְאַחַר חֲצוֹת הַיּוֹם בִּלְמוּד כְּמוֹ בִּשְׁאָר עֶרֶב תִּשְׁעָה בְּאָב.

ה) קֹדֶם עַרְבִית אֵין אוֹמְרִים לַמְנַצֵּחַ בִּנְגִינוֹת. וְאֵין אוֹמְרִים וִיהִי נֹעַם קֹדֶם וְאַתָּה קָדוֹשׁ, מִשּׁוּם שֶׁנִּתְיַסֵּד עַל הֲקָמַת הַמִּשְׁכָּן וְעַתָּה נֶחֱרָב. גַּם אֵין אוֹמְרִים וְיִתֶּן לְךָ, וְאֵין מְבָרְכִין אֶת הַבָּנִים.

ו) מִשֶּׁתֶּחְשַׁךְ, כְּשֶׁהוּא רוֹאֶה אֶת הַנֵּר, מְבָרֵךְ בּוֹרֵא מְאוֹרֵי הָאֵשׁ. וּבִשְׁמוֹנֶה־עֶשְׂרֵה, אוֹמְרִים אַתָּה חוֹנַנְתָּנוּ. אֲבָל אֵין מַבְדִּילִין עַל הַכּוֹס

---

1. It is forbidden to refrain from eating meat on Shabbos, because of mourning. (*Mishnah Berurah* 552:23)

2. It is said in *Shulchan Aruch,* that you are permitted to serve at this meal, even like the royal feast of King Solomon.

Chapter 125

Laws of Tishah beAv When it Occurs on Shabbos or on Sunday

1) If *Tishah beAv* occurs on Sunday, or if it occurs on Shabbos and is deferred to Sunday, you may eat meat and drink wine on Shabbos.[1] Even at the third meal, after *Minchah,* you may eat everything[2] but you should not have this meal in the company of friends.[3] If a *bris* is to be held, the meal should be served before *Minchah.* But you are permitted to eat the third meal with your family, and you may say *Birkas Hamazon* with *zimun.* You must finish the meal, while it is still daytime,[4] because at twilight you are forbidden to eat, drink or wash. However, you should not take off your shoes until after *Barechu* is said. The Chazzan takes off his shoes before saying *Vehu Rachum* [He, the Merciful One], so that he should not get confused; but before [taking off his shoes] he should say: *Baruch hamavdil bein kodesh lechol* [Blessed is He Who separates between the holy and the secular], without mentioning Hashem's Name and Kingship [*Hashem Elokeinu melech haolam*].

2) If Friday night is the night of *Tishah beAv,* it is forbidden to have marital relations, unless it is the night of her *tevilah* [immersion].

3) We say *Av harachamim* [Father of compassion], and we say memorial prayers in *Shacharis,* but in *Minchah,* we do not say *Tzidkasecha tzedek* [Your righteousness is everlasting].

4) If *Tishah beAv* occurs on Shabbos, you should be stringent and study only those subjects that you are allowed to study on *Tishah beAv;*[5] therefore, we do not say *Pirkei Avos*. Reading the *sidrah* of the week twice and the *Targum* once, is permitted, before noon. If *erev Tishah beAv* occurs on Shabbos, it is forbidden to study in the afternoon, as on any other *erev Tishah beAv.*[6]

5) Before *Maariv,* we do not say *Lamenatzei'ach bineginos,* neither do we say *Vihi no'am* before *Ve'atah Kadosh,* for this was composed for the setting up of the *Mishkan* [Tabernacle] and now it is destroyed. Neither do we say *Veyitein lecha* (May Hashem grant you), nor do parents bless their children.

6) At dark, when you see the candlelight, you should say the berachah *Borei me'orei ha'eish*[7] [Who creates the lights of fire], and in the *Shemoneh esrei* we say: *Ata*

---

3. *Bechor Shor* disagrees. He rules that if you are accustomed to eat in the company of friends every Shabbos, you may do so on this Shabbos as well, because, otherwise, it would be considered mourning in public, which is forbidden on Shabbos. (*Ibid.*)

4. I.e. before sunset. (*Ibid.* 552:24)

5. This applies only after midday, but before that, it is permitted to study whatever you usually study. *Mishnah Berurah* cites *Taz,* who says that we can rely on his opinion, since many other *Poskim* are lenient and permit Torah study after midday, even on a weekday.

6. See note 5. (*Ibid.* 553:9,10)

7. This should be done, preferably before the reading of *Eichah.* (*Ibid.* 556:1)

עַד מוֹצָאֵי תִּשְׁעָה בְּאָב, וְאָז הוּא מַבְדִּיל עַל הַכּוֹס. אֲבָל אֵינוֹ מְבָרֵךְ לֹא עַל הַבְּשָׂמִים וְלֹא עַל הַנֵּר, אֲפִלּוּ לֹא בֵרַךְ עָלָיו בְּמוֹצָאֵי שַׁבָּת. וְיַזְהִיר לִבְנֵי בֵיתוֹ שֶׁלֹּא יַעֲשׂוּ מְלָאכָה עַד שֶׁיֹּאמְרוּ הַמַּבְדִּיל בֵּין קֹדֶשׁ לְחֹל בְּלֹא שֵׁם וּמַלְכוּת. וְאִם שָׁכַח לוֹמַר אַתָּה חוֹנַנְתָּנוּ, אֵין צָרִיךְ לַחֲזוֹר, אֶלָּא גוֹמֵר תְּפִלָּתוֹ (כְּמוֹ שֶׁכָּתַבְנוּ לְעֵיל סִימָן צו), שֶׁהֲרֵי יַבְדִּיל בְּמוֹצָאֵי תִּשְׁעָה בְּאָב עַל הַכּוֹס, וְלֹא יִטְעֹם קֹדֶם. וְאִם צָרִיךְ לַעֲשׂוֹת מְלָאכָה, יֹאמַר תְּחִלָּה הַמַּבְדִּיל בֵּין קֹדֶשׁ וְכוּ׳ בְּלֹא שֵׁם וּמַלְכוּת.

ז) תִּשְׁעָה בְּאָב שֶׁחָל בַּשַּׁבָּת וְנִדְחָה לְיוֹם רִאשׁוֹן, בַּלַּיְלָה שֶׁלְּאַחַר הַתַּעֲנִית, אֲסוּרִים בְּבָשָׂר וְיַיִן כְּמוֹ בִּשְׁאָר תִּשְׁעָה בְּאָב, מִפְּנֵי אֲבֵלוּת הַיּוֹם. אֲבָל לְמָחָר, מֻתָּרִים מִיָּד בַּכֹּל.

ח) אִם יֵשׁ מִילָה בְּתִשְׁעָה בְּאָב שֶׁנִּדְחָה, מֻתָּר לְבַעֲלֵי־הַבְּרִית דְּהַיְנוּ אֲבִי־הַבֵּן וְאִמּוֹ וְהַמּוֹהֵל וְהַסַּנְדָּק לְהִתְפַּלֵּל מִנְחָה גְּדוֹלָה, הַיְנוּ חֲצִי שָׁעָה אַחַר הַצָּהֳרַיִם, וְאָז מֻתָּר לְהַבְדִּיל עַל הַכּוֹס וְלֶאֱכוֹל וְלִרְחוֹץ. אֲבָל סְעוּדָה, לֹא יַעֲשׂוּ עַד הַלַּיְלָה. וְכֵן בְּפִדְיוֹן הַבֵּן בִּזְמַנּוֹ, הָאָב וְהַכֹּהֵן לֹא יַשְׁלִימוּ.

סִימָן קכו
לַעֲשׂוֹת זֵכֶר לַחֻרְבָּן

א) מִשֶּׁחָרַב בֵּית־הַמִּקְדָּשׁ, תִּקְנוּ חֲכָמֵינוּ זִכְרוֹנָם לִבְרָכָה שֶׁבְּכָל שִׂמְחָה יְהֵא בָהּ זֵכֶר לַחֻרְבָּן, כְּמוֹ שֶׁכָּתוּב, אִם אֶשְׁכָּחֵךְ יְרוּשָׁלָיִם וְגוֹ׳, אִם לֹא אַעֲלֶה אֶת־יְרוּשָׁלַיִם עַל רֹאשׁ שִׂמְחָתִי. וְגָזְרוּ שֶׁלֹּא יִבְנֶה לוֹ יִשְׂרָאֵל בִּנְיָן מְסֻיָּד וּמְצֻיָּר כְּבִנְיַן הַמְּלָכִים. וְלֹא יְסַיֵּד אֶת כָּל בֵּיתוֹ בְּסִיד, אֶלָּא טָח בֵּיתוֹ בְּטִיט וְסָד בְּסִיד, וּמַנִּיחַ בּוֹ אַמָּה עַל אַמָּה כְּנֶגֶד הַפֶּתַח

---

8. You, yourself, are permitted to drink the wine, and you need not give it to a child. (*Ibid.* 556:3) The introductory sentences beginnng with הִנֵּה קֵל should not be said.

9. All *Poskim* agree, however, that it is permitted to take a haircut or shave.

10. The introductory sentences beginning with הִנֵּה קֵל should not be said.

1. It is, however, permitted to build a *Beis Midrash* or Synagogue without any restrictions. (*Biyur Halachah* 560:1)

2. *Tur* rules that if a house was merely painted, but not plastered, even though it was decorated, leaving an *amah* unpainted is sufficient. (see *Mishnah Berurah* 560:1)

3. If, however, the house was plastered with mud or clay, but not painted, it is not required to leave an *amah* unplastered. (Ibid. 560:2)

chonantanu [You have favored us.] We do not say *Havdalah* over the cup of wine until the conclusion of *Tishah beAv.*[8] But you should not say the berachah over the spices and over the light, even if you failed to say (the berachah over the light) on Shabbos night. You should caution your family not to do do any work before they say *Hamavdil bein kodesh lechol* [Who separates between the holy and the secular] without mentioning Hashem's Name and Kingship. If you forget to say *Ata chonantanu,* you need not repeat [the *Shemoneh esrei*], but you should finish the *Shemoneh esrei,* (as stated in Chapter 96, above), because you will say *Havdalah* over wine at the end of *Tishah beAv.* You should not taste any food before *Havdalah,* and if you find it necessary to do some work, you should first say: *Hamavdil bein kodesh* etc., without mentioning Hashem's Name and Kingship.

7) When *Tishah beAv* occurs on Shabbos, and it is deferred to Sunday, it is forbidden to eat meat or drink wine[9] on the night after the fast as it is on any other *Tishah beAv,* because of the mourning observed on that day. On the following morning, everything is permitted.

8) If a *bris* is to be held on a deferred *Tishah beAv,* it is permitted for the main participants, i.e. the father and mother of the infant, the *mohel* and the *sandak* to pray the *Minchah gedolah,* that is one half hour past midday. They may then recite the *Havdalah* over wine[10] and eat and wash, but they should not have the festive meal until the night. Similarly, when a *pidyon haben* is held, that has not been postponed, the father and the *kohen* should not complete the fast.

Chapter 126

Commemorating the Destruction of the Beis Hamikdash

1) After the *Beis Hamikdash* was destroyed, our Sages, of blessed memory, ordained that on every joyous occasion, there should be a remembrance of the destruction of the *Beis Hamikdash,* as it is written: "If I forget you, Jerusalem, if I fail to elevate Jerusalem above my foremost joy" (Psalms 137:5). They decreed that no Jew should build a house[1] for himself that is lime-plastered and decorated like a royal palace.[2] Neither should he lime plaster his entire house, but he may plaster the house,[3] with clay and then lime plaster, it (lit. whitewash it), and he should leave a space of one square *amah*[4] opposite the entrance[5] unplastered,[6] as a

---

4. See glossary.

5. Others have the custom to leave the *amah* above the door, because the main objective is that the inhabitants of the house see it and be reminded of the destruction, rather than those (strangers who enter the house on occasion). Leaving it opposite the entrance, only serves as a reminder, upon entering the house, but not as a reminder for those who spend time in the house. (*Ibid.* 560:3)

6. It is not proper to have it painted black. Those who have curtains (wall-paper) around all the walls of the house, should also leave an *amah* of bare walls. (*Ibid.* 560:3)

בְּלֹא סִיד, כְּדֵי לִזְכֹּר הַחֻרְבָּן. וּמַה שֶּׁלֹּא נָהֲגוּ כֵן עַתָּה, לֹא יָדַעְנוּ טַעַם בָּרוּר.

ב) וְכֵן תִּקְּנוּ שֶׁהָעוֹרֵךְ שֻׁלְחָן לַעֲשׂוֹת סְעוּדָה לְאוֹרְחִים, אֲפִלּוּ סְעוּדַת מִצְוָה, לֹא יִתֵּן כָּל הַתַּבְשִׁילִין הָרְאוּיִין לִסְעוּדָה. וְכֵן הָאִשָּׁה לֹא תִתְקַשֵּׁט בְּכָל תַּכְשִׁיטֶיהָ בְּפַעַם אֶחָת. וְהֶחָתָן קֹדֶם חֻפָּתוֹ, נוֹתְנִים אֵפֶר עַל רֹאשׁוֹ בִּמְקוֹם הַנָּחַת תְּפִלִּין. וְהַמִּכְסֶה שֶׁמְּכַסִּים בּוֹ אֶת הַכַּלָּה, לֹא יִהְיוּ בוֹ חוּטֵי כֶסֶף אוֹ זָהָב. גַּם נוֹהֲגִין שֶׁבִּשְׁעַת כְּתִיבַת הַתְּנָאִין, אַחַר קְרִיאָתָן, שׁוֹבְרִין קְדֵרָה לַעֲשׂוֹת זֵכֶר לַחֻרְבָּן, אֲבָל יֵשׁ לִקַּח קְדֵרָה שְׁבוּרָה. וְתַחַת הַחֻפָּה שׁוֹבֵר הֶחָתָן כְּלִי זְכוּכִית, וְזֶה יָכוֹל לִהְיוֹת כּוֹס שָׁלֵם.

ג) וְכֵן גָּזְרוּ שֶׁלֹּא לִשְׁמוֹעַ שׁוּם כְּלֵי שִׁיר, וַאֲפִלּוּ שִׁיר בַּפֶּה. וְאֵין לְשׁוֹרֵר בִּסְעוּדָה אֶלָּא הַזְּמִירוֹת שֶׁנִּתְקְנוּ, כְּמוֹ בַּשַּׁבָּת. אֲבָל פִּיּוּטִים אֲחֵרִים, אָסוּר לְשׁוֹרֵר.

ד) הִשָּׁמֶר לְךָ מִלִּרְאוֹת קְנִיגְנָאוֹת [צֵיד חַיּוֹת] שֶׁל גּוֹיִים, וְכֵן מְחוֹלָתָם אוֹ שׁוּם דָּבָר שֶׁל שִׂמְחָתָם. וְאִם תִּשְׁמַע קוֹלָם שְׂמֵחִים, תֵּאָנַח וְתִצְטַעֵר עַל חֻרְבַּן יְרוּשָׁלַיִם, וְתִתְפַּלֵּל לְהַקָּדוֹשׁ־בָּרוּךְ־הוּא עָלֶיהָ. וַאֲפִלּוּ לִקְנִיגְנָאוֹת שֶׁל יִשְׂרָאֵל, אָסוּר לָלֶכֶת, מִשּׁוּם דַּהֲוֵי מוֹשַׁב לֵצִים. וְכָל מִינֵי שִׂמְחָה, אָסוּר. אֶלָּא לְשַׂמֵּחַ חָתָן וְכַלָּה מֻתָּר, בֵּין בְּשִׁיר בַּפֶּה, בֵּין בְּכֵלִים, וְגַם שָׁם אֵין לִשְׂמֹחַ בְּיוֹתֵר. וְאָסוּר לְאָדָם שֶׁיְּמַלֵּא שְׂחוֹק פִּיו בָּעוֹלָם הַזֶּה, אֲפִלּוּ בְּשִׂמְחָה שֶׁל מִצְוָה, שֶׁנֶּאֱמַר, אָז יִמָּלֵא שְׂחוֹק פִּינוּ.

סִימָן קכז
הִלְכוֹת תַּעֲנִית יָחִיד

א) כְּשֵׁם שֶׁמִּצְוָה עַל הַצִּבּוּר לְהִתְעַנּוֹת וּלְהִתְפַּלֵּל עַל כָּל צָרָה שֶׁלֹּא תָבוֹא, כָּךְ מִצְוָה עַל כָּל יָחִיד, שֶׁאִם בָּאָה עָלָיו חַס־וְשָׁלוֹם אֵיזוֹ צָרָה, כְּגוֹן שֶׁיֵּשׁ לוֹ חוֹלֶה בְּתוֹךְ בֵּיתוֹ, אוֹ שֶׁהוּא תוֹעֶה בַּדֶּרֶךְ, אוֹ חָבוּשׁ בְּבֵית הָאֲסוּרִים עַל יְדֵי עֲלִילָה, מִצְוָה עָלָיו שֶׁיִּתְעַנֶּה וְיִתְפַּלֵּל אֶל ה׳ וִיבַקֵּשׁ רַחֲמִים מֵאִתּוֹ יִתְבָּרַךְ שְׁמוֹ שֶׁיּוֹשִׁיעַ לוֹ. וְדָבָר זֶה מִדַּרְכֵי תְשׁוּבָה הוּא, שֶׁלֹּא יֹאמַר הָאָדָם, חַס־וְשָׁלוֹם, מִקְרֶה הִיא הַצָּרָה, שֶׁנֶּאֱמַר, וַהֲלַכְתֶּם

---

7. Omitting even a minor item is sufficient. On Shabbos or Yom Tov, however, nothing should be omitted from the traditional meals. (*Ibid.* 560:5,6)

reminder of the destruction [of the *Beis Hamikdash.*] We do not know of any good reason why people do not observe this custom nowadays.

2) They also ordained that if you are setting a table, and are having guests for a meal, even for a meal that is considered a mitzvah, you should not serve all the dishes that are conventionally served at a meal.[7] They also ordained that a woman should not wear all her jewelry at one occasion,[8] and that a bridegroom before the *chuppah* [wedding ceremony], should have ashes put on his head on the place where the *tefillin* are worn, and the veil, with which the bride is covered, should not contain any silver or gold threads. It is also customary, that after the *tenaim* [engagement agreement] has been read to break a plate, as a reminder of the destruction of the *Beis Hamikdash,* but a damaged plate is used (for that purpose). Under the *chuppah* the bridegroom breaks a glass, and for this purpose, a whole glass may be used.

3) They also decreed, that we should not listen to musical instruments not even to the singing of songs. During meals, you should sing only the traditional *zemiros* [songs of praise], like those we sing on Shabbos; but it is forbidden to sing other songs.

4) Take heed not to attend animal shows presented by non-Jews[9] or their dances or any of their social functions. When you hear them giving voice to their happiness, you should sigh and agonize over the destruction of Jerusalem, and pray for it unto the Holy One blessed is He. Even animal shows presented by Jews, are forbidden because it is a "Gathering of scorners." All kinds of rejoicing are forbidden, except making a groom and a bride happy which may be done both by singing and with musical instruments. But even at a wedding, you should not overdo the merry making. It is forbidden for anybody to laugh exuberantly in this world, even when rejoicing in the performance of a mitzvah,[10] for it is said: "*Then* our mouth will be filled with laughter" (Psalms 126:2). [When Hashem will return the captivity to Zion].

Chapter 127

Laws Concerning Private Fast Days

1) Just as it is a mitzvah for the community to fast and to pray in times of trouble, so it is a mitzvah for every individual, if, God forbid, any trouble befalls him, for example, a member of his family is sick, or he lost his way, or he is confined in prison on false charges, to fast and to pray to God, and to plead for mercy from Him, may His Name be blessed, to deliver him. Suffering is one of the ways that leads to repentance. A person should not say, his troubles just happened by chance, for it is said: (Leviticus 26:23,24). "If you treat My (acts) as chance, then I will

8. *Biyur Halachah* (560:2) questions why this custom and the previous custom are not observed at all (in our time and place.)

9. This also applies to theatrical presentations, presented by Jews. (see *Mishnah Berurah* 224:3)

10. Such as at a wedding or on Purim. (*Ibid.* 560:20)

עִמִּי בְּקֶרִי, וְהָלַכְתִּי גַּם־אֲנִי עִמָּכֶם בַּחֲמַת־קֶרִי. פֵּרוּשׁ, כְּשֶׁאָבִיא עֲלֵיכֶם צָרָה כְּדֵי שֶׁתָּשׁוּבוּ, אִם תֹּאמְרוּ שֶׁהוּא קֶרִי, אוֹסִיף עֲלֵיכֶם חֲמַת אוֹתוֹ קֶרִי. אֲבָל צָרִיךְ הָאָדָם לָדַעַת כִּי בַּחֲטָאָיו הֵבִיא עָלָיו הָאֱלֹהִים אֶת כָּל הָרָעָה הַזֹּאת, וִיפַשְׁפֵּשׁ בְּמַעֲשָׂיו, וְיָשׁוּב אֶל ה' וִירַחֲמֵהוּ.

ב) יָחִיד שֶׁהוּא רוֹצֶה לְהִתְעַנּוֹת, צָרִיךְ לְקַבֵּל עָלָיו בַּיּוֹם שֶׁלְּפָנָיו בִּתְפִלַּת הַמִּנְחָה, דְּהַיְנוּ בְּבִרְכַּת שְׁמַע קוֹלֵנוּ, יְהַרְהֵר בְּלִבּוֹ שֶׁהוּא מְקַבֵּל עָלָיו לְהִתְעַנּוֹת. וְקֹדֶם יִהְיוּ לְרָצוֹן יֹאמַר, רִבּוֹן הָעוֹלָמִים, הֲרֵי אֲנִי לְפָנֶיךָ בְּתַעֲנִית וְכוּ' (כְּמוֹ שֶׁנִּדְפָּס בַּסִּדּוּרִים). וְאַף־עַל־פִּי שֶׁאוֹכֵל וְשׁוֹתֶה אַחַר כָּךְ עַד שֶׁיַּעֲלֶה עַמּוּד הַשַּׁחַר, אֵין בְּכָךְ כְּלוּם. וְכֵן אִם רוֹצֶה לְהִתְעַנּוֹת אֵיזֶה יָמִים זֶה אַחַר זֶה, אַף־עַל־פִּי שֶׁיֹּאכַל וְיִשְׁתֶּה בַּלֵּילוֹת שֶׁבֵּינֵיהֶם, סַגֵּי בְּקַבָּלָה אַחַת. אֲבָל אִם מְקַבֵּל עָלָיו אֵיזֶה יָמִים שֶׁאֵינָם רְצוּפִין, כְּגוֹן שֵׁנִי חֲמִישִׁי וְשֵׁנִי, יֵשׁ לְקַבֵּל עָלָיו כָּל יוֹם בְּמִנְחָה שֶׁלְּפָנָיו.

ג) מִי שֶׁהוּא רָגִיל לְהִתְעַנּוֹת בַּעֲשֶׂרֶת יְמֵי תְשׁוּבָה אוֹ בְּיוֹם רִאשׁוֹן דִּסְלִיחוֹת וְעֶרֶב רֹאשׁ־הַשָּׁנָה, אֵינוֹ צָרִיךְ לְקַבְּלָם, שֶׁהֵם מְקֻבָּלִים מִכֹּחַ הַמִּנְהָג. וְכֵן תַּעֲנִית חֲלוֹם, אֵינָהּ צְרִיכָה קַבָּלָה. וְכֵן תַּעֲנִית שֵׁנִי חֲמִישִׁי וְשֵׁנִי שֶׁלְּאַחַר פֶּסַח וְסֻכּוֹת, אִם עָנָה אָמֵן אַחַר מִי שֶׁבֵּרַךְ וְהָיְתָה דַעְתּוֹ לְהִתְעַנּוֹת, דַּי בְּכָךְ, וְאֵינוֹ צָרִיךְ קַבָּלָה אַחֶרֶת. וּמִכָּל מָקוֹם אִם מִתְחָרֵט וְאֵינוֹ רוֹצֶה לְהִתְעַנּוֹת, רַשַּׁאי, כֵּיוָן שֶׁלֹּא קִבֵּל עָלָיו בְּפֵרוּשׁ וְלֹא הוֹצִיא בְּפִיו שֶׁהוּא רוֹצֶה לְהִתְעַנּוֹת.

ד) אַף אִם לֹא קִבֵּל עָלָיו אֶת הַתַּעֲנִית בְּפִיו, אֶלָּא בְּהִרְהוּר קִבֵּל עָלָיו וְגָמַר בְּדַעְתּוֹ לְהִתְעַנּוֹת לְמָחָר, וַאֲפִלּוּ שֶׁלֹּא בִשְׁעַת תְּפִלַּת מִנְחָה, אֶלָּא קֹדֶם תְּפִלַּת מִנְחָה אוֹ אַחַר כָּךְ בְּעוֹד שֶׁהוּא יוֹם, הֲוֵי קַבָּלָה וְחַיָּב לְהִתְעַנּוֹת.

ה) כָּל הַשָּׁרוּי בְּתַעֲנִית, לֹא יִנְהַג עִדּוּנִין בְּעַצְמוֹ, וְלֹא יָקֵל רֹאשׁוֹ,

---

1. If you do not make this commitment, it is not considered a fast. Thus, if you are fasting to fulfill a vow, and you fasted without making a prior commitment, you have not fulfilled your vow to fast. (see *Mishnah Berurah* 562:23)

2. It is preferable to do so at a *Minchah Ketanah Shemoneh Esrei* (nine and one half hours after sunrise), but, if not, you can do so at an earlier *Minchah*. (*Ibid.* 562:27)

treat you with the fury of chance"; which means, when I bring distress on you to cause you to repent and you will say this happened by chance, then I will add to your (suffering) the fury of the same "chance." Man must know that because of his sins, God brought on him all this trouble. He should, therefore, examine his deeds and return to God, and He will have mercy on him.

2) If you wish to fast, you must make a commitment to do so[1] on the preceding day, during the *Shemoneh esrei* of *Minchah.*[2] In the berachah *Shema koleinu* [Hear our voices], you should mentally accept upon yourself, to fast and before saying *Yiheyu leratzon,* you should say, Master of the universe, I come before You to accept a fast etc.[3] (as it is written in the *siddur* [prayer book].) Even though you eat and drink, afterwards until daybreak, it does not matter. If you want to fast several days in succession, although you will eat and drink during the intervening nights, one acceptance [commitment] is sufficient for all. But if you accept upon yourself [to fast] several days that are not in succession, like Monday, Thursday, and Monday, you should make a separate commitment, for each day you fast, in the *Minchah* preceding it.[4]

3) If you are accustomed to fast[5] during the *Aseres yemei teshuvah,* [the Ten Days of Penitence] or on the first day of *Selichos* or on *erev Rosh Hashanah,* you do not have to make a formal commitment because they are accepted on the basis of the prevailing custom. Similarly, fasting because of a disturbing dream, does not require prior acceptance; neither do the fasts on Monday, Thursday and Monday following *Pesach* and *Sukkos.* If you answer *Amein* after the *Mi shebeirach* [a blessing for those who fast on these days] and you intended to fast, this is sufficient, and no other form of acceptance is needed. Nevertheless, if you change your mind, and do not wish to fast, you may [eat], since you did not expressly commit yourself[6] and did not verbally declare that you intend to fast.

4) Even if you did not commit yourself verbally, to fast; doing so, only in your mind, resolving to fast the following day, and even [if you made this resolution] not during *Minchah,* but either before or after *Mincha,* while it was still daytime, it is considered an acceptance, and you are required to fast.

5) When you fast, you should not indulge in enjoyment, nor act frivolously. You

---

3. If you forgot to say this prayer, but you did, however, make a mental commitment to fast, it is sufficient. (*Shulchan Aruch* 562:6; *Mishnah Berurah* 562:30,31)

4. See *Ramah* 562:8. The prevailing custom is, however, that one acceptance is sufficient.

5. This applies, even if this is the first time you are fasting on one of these days. So long as it is an accepted custom in your community, you may join and rely on those who have fasted. (*Biyur Halachah* 562:2)

6. See Paragraph 4, and, accordingly, it would seem that it is best to be stringent, if you had in mind to fast when you answered *Amein,* even without a verbal commitment. (See *Mishnah Berurah* 562:39)

וְלֹא יְהֵא שָׂמֵחַ וְטוֹב לֵב, אֶלָּא דּוֹאֵג וְאוֹנֵן, כְּמוֹ שֶׁנֶּאֱמַר, מַה יִּתְאוֹנֵן אָדָם חַי גֶּבֶר עַל חֲטָאָיו.

ו) בְּתַעֲנִית יָחִיד, מֻתָּר לִרְחוֹץ אֶת פִּיו בְּמַיִם בְּשַׁחֲרִית.

ז) אִם קִבֵּל עָלָיו סְתָם לְהִתְעַנּוֹת, חַיָּב לְהַשְׁלִים עַד צֵאת הַכּוֹכָבִים, אֲפִלּוּ בְּעֶרֶב שַׁבָּת.

ח) הַמִּתְעַנֶּה וּמְפַרְסֵם אֶת עַצְמוֹ לְהִתְפָּאֵר, הוּא נֶעֱנָשׁ עַל כָּךְ. אֲבָל אִם מַפְצִירִין בּוֹ לֶאֱכֹל, מֻתָּר לְגַלּוֹת שֶׁהוּא מִתְעַנֶּה.

ט) הַמִּתְעַנֶּה אֲפִלּוּ תַּעֲנִית יָחִיד, בֵּין תַּעֲנִית נְדָבָה, בֵּין תַּעֲנִית חֲלוֹם, אוֹמֵר בִּתְפִלַּת הַמִּנְחָה בִּשְׁמַע קוֹלֵנוּ, עֲנֵנוּ, כְּמוֹ בְּתַעֲנִית צִבּוּר. (וְאַף־עַל־פִּי שֶׁהוּא יָחִיד, אוֹמְרוֹ בִּלְשׁוֹן רַבִּים, וְאַל יְשַׁנֶּה מִמַּטְבֵּעַ שֶׁטָּבְעוּ חֲכָמִים). וְקֹדֶם יִהְיוּ לְרָצוֹן, אוֹמֵר, רִבּוֹן הָעוֹלָמִים וְכוּ'.

י) מִי שֶׁנָּדַר לְהִתְעַנּוֹת יוֹם אֶחָד אוֹ עֲשָׂרָה יָמִים, וְלֹא פֵּרַט אֵיזֶה יוֹם אוֹ יָמִים, אֶלָּא שֶׁאָמַר סְתָם, אַף־עַל־פִּי שֶׁקִּבֵּל עָלָיו בִּשְׁעַת מִנְחָה לְהִתְעַנּוֹת לְמָחָר, אִם אֵרַע לוֹ צֹרֶךְ גָּדוֹל לֶאֱכֹל, כְּגוֹן שֶׁקּוֹרִין אוֹתוֹ לִסְעוּדַת מִצְוָה, אַף־עַל־פִּי שֶׁאֵינוֹ שַׁיָּךְ לַסְּעוּדָה, אוֹ שֶׁאָדָם גָּדוֹל מַפְצִיר בּוֹ לֶאֱכוֹל וְקָשֶׁה לוֹ לְסָרֵב כְּנֶגְדּוֹ, אוֹ שֶׁהוּא מִצְטַעֵר, הֲרֵי זֶה לֹוֶה תַּעֲנִיתוֹ, וְיָכוֹל לֶאֱכוֹל הַיּוֹם אַף־עַל־פִּי שֶׁכְּבָר הִתְחִיל לְהִתְעַנּוֹת, וּמִתְעַנֶּה תַּחַת יוֹם זֶה, יוֹם אַחֵר. וְדַוְקָא בְּעִנְיָן זֶה. דְּמַה שֶּׁקִּבֵּל עָלָיו הַתַּעֲנִית, הָיָה רַק בִּשְׁבִיל לְקַיֵּם אֶת הַנֶּדֶר. אֲבָל אִם לֹא נָדַר מִתְּחִלָּה, רַק שֶׁקִּבֵּל עָלָיו בִּשְׁעַת מִנְחָה לְהִתְעַנּוֹת לְמָחָר, אֲפִלּוּ מִצְטַעֵר אַחַר כָּךְ הַרְבֵּה, אֵינוֹ רַשַּׁאי לִלְווֹת תַּעֲנִיתוֹ לְפָרְעָהּ בְּיוֹם אַחֵר.

יא) וְכֵן אִם בִּשְׁעַת נִדְרוֹ פֵּרַט יָמִים יְדוּעִים, וְגַם קִבֵּל עָלָיו בִּשְׁעַת מִנְחָה, שׁוּב אֵינוֹ יָכוֹל לִלְווֹת תַּעֲנִיתוֹ.

---

7. You should be careful to control your anger and to conduct your business activities in such manner, as not to become angry. (*Ibid.* 568:50)

8. *Ramah,* however, rules, according to the *Poskim,* who maintain that on *erev Shabbos,* it is sufficient to fast until the congregation leaves the synagogue, after they accepted Shabbos (*Kabbolas Shabbos*). (*Ibid.* 249:21 and also *Biyur Halachah* 249:4)

9. However, if you are asked if you are fasting, it would seem that you are permitted to acknowledge that you are. *Mishnah Berurah,* however, indicates that you should deny that you are fasting, unless you are asked to join someone in a meal, in which case you have no choice but to state you are fasting. On public fast days, however, you may say you are fasting in order to encourage others to do so. (*Mishnah Berurah* 565:14)

10. These are the words of the prayer:
רִבּוֹן כָּל הָעוֹלָמִים גָּלוּי וְיָדוּעַ לְפָנֶיךָ שֶׁבִּזְמַן שֶׁבֵּית הַמִּקְדָּשׁ הָיָה קַיָּם אָדָם חוֹטֵא מַקְרִיב קָרְבָּן וְאֵין מְבִיאִים מִמֶּנּוּ אֶלָּא

should not go around happy and cheerful, but rather with anxiety and sorrow,[7] as it is said: "Why should a living man bemoan? A man, because of his sins!" (Lamentations 3:39).

6) On a private fast day, you are allowed to rinse your mouth with water, in the morning.

7) If you committed yourself to fast without being specific, you must complete the fast until the stars come out, even on *erev Shabbos.*[8]

8) If someone fasts and publicizes the fact, bragging about it, he will be punished for it.[9] But if people urge him to eat, he may let them know that he is fasting.

9) If you observe a fast, even if it is a private fast, whether it is a voluntary fast, or a fast because of a disturbing dream, you should say in the *Shemoneh esrei* of *Minchah,* in the berachah *Shema koleinu* [Hear our voice], the prayer *Aneinu* [Answer us], the same as on any public fast day. (And although you are only one individual, you should say it in the plural, and not deviate from the formula, that was established by the Sages). Before saying *Yiheyu leratzon,* you should say *Ribbon ha'olamim* [Master of the universe] etc.[10]

10) If you vowed to fast one day or ten days, but you did not specify the particular day or days, on which you were going to fast, but you stated it in indefinite terms, even if you committed yourself in the *Minchah* prayer to fast the following day, if an urgent need arises for you to eat something, for example, if you are invited to a meal, that is considered a mitzvah, even though you are not a party to the festive meal; or an important person urges you to join him in a meal, and it is difficult for you to refuse him, or if you do not feel well [enough to fast], then you may "owe" the fast [and repay it later] and you may eat on that day,[11] even if you already began to fast, and instead of fasting that day, you should fast another day. This is permissible only if the fast, you had accepted on yourself, was meant to fulfill a vow, however, if you had made no vow, but (specifically) committed yourself during *Minchah* to fast the following day, then, even if it causes you great distress, you are not permitted to "owe" your fast and repay it another day.

11) If at the time you made the vow, you specified certain days, and you also accepted it on yourself during *Minchah,* you may no longer "owe" your fast (to be paid later.).

חֶלְבּוֹ וְדָמוֹ, וְאַתָּה בְּרַחֲמֶיךָ הָרַבִּים מְכַפֵּר. וְעַתָּה בַּעֲוֹנוֹתֵינוּ חָרַב בֵּית מִקְדָּשֶׁךָ וְאֵין לָנוּ מִקְדָּשׁ וְלֹא כֹהֵן שֶׁיְּכַפֵּר בַּעֲדֵינוּ, לָכֵן יְהִי רָצוֹן מִלְּפָנֶיךָ שֶׁיְּהֵא חֶלְבִּי וְדָמִי שֶׁנִּתְמַעֵט הַיּוֹם כְּחֵלֶב מוּנָח עַל הַמִּזְבֵּחַ לְפָנֶיךָ וְתִרְצֵנִי.

Master of the Universe, we know that during the time the Holy Temple stood, if a person sinned, he brought a sacrifice. The only part of the animal to be offered on the Altar was its blood and its fat, and in Your great compassion, You forgave him. But, now, because of our sins, the Holy Temple was destroyed, and we have no temple service to atone for us. Therefore, may it be Your will, that my blood and fat, that are diminished by fasting this day, be considered as though they were offered before You on the Altar, and, thus, may I find acceptance before you.

11. You should, however, fast a part of the day, and it is sufficient, therefore, if you eat at a later hour than you are accustomed; for example, if you usually eat at 10 A.M., you should eat at 11 A.M. In this way, at least, some of your vow will be fulfilled on the day you selected. (*Mishnah Berurah* 568:9,10)

יב) מִי שֶׁקִּבֵּל עָלָיו לְהִתְעַנּוֹת וּמִצְטַעֵר הַרְבֵּה בְּתַעֲנִיתוֹ, יָכוֹל לִפְדּוֹתָהּ בְּמָמוֹן כְּפִי עֶשְׂרוֹ, וְנוֹתֵן אֶת הַדָּמִים לַעֲנִיִּים. אֲבָל בְּתַעֲנִית שֶׁמֵּחֲמַת נֶדֶר, לָא מַהֲנֵי פִּדְיוֹן. וְכֵן בְּתַעֲנִית שֶׁגָּזְרוּ הַצִּבּוּר, לָא מַהֲנֵי פִּדְיוֹן, אֶלָּא אִם כֵּן הִתְנוּ כֵן הַצִּבּוּר.

יג) מִי שֶׁנָּדַר לְהִתְעַנּוֹת שֵׁנִי חֲמִישִׁי וְשֵׁנִי, מֻתָּר לוֹ לְהַחֲלִיף וּלְהִתְעַנּוֹת חֲמִישִׁי שֵׁנִי וַחֲמִישִׁי, אֲבָל לֹא יָמִים אֲחֵרִים, כִּי מִסְתָּמָא הָיְתָה כַּוָּנָתוֹ לָהֶם, מִפְּנֵי שֶׁהֵם יוֹמֵי דְדִינָא.

יד) תַּעֲנִית שֵׁנִי חֲמִישִׁי וְשֵׁנִי שֶׁלְּאַחַר פֶּסַח וְשֶׁלְּאַחַר סֻכּוֹת, וְכֵן בַּעֲשֶׂרֶת יְמֵי תְשׁוּבָה, שֶׁלֹּא קִבְּלָהּ בִּשְׁעַת מִנְחָה, אֶלָּא שֶׁהוּא מִתְעַנֶּה מִכֹּחַ הַמִּנְהָג, וַאֲפִלּוּ כִּוֵּן בִּשְׁעַת עֲנִיַּת אָמֵן עַל מִי שֶׁבֵּרַךְ, כֹּל שֶׁלֹּא קִבְּלָהּ בִּשְׁעַת מִנְחָה, אִם אֵרְעָה בְּרִית מִילָה אוֹ פִּדְיוֹן הַבֵּן אוֹ שְׁאָר סְעוּדַת מִצְוָה, מִצְוָה לֶאֱכוֹל וְאֵינוֹ צָרִיךְ הַתָּרָה. כִּי כָל הַמִּתְעַנֶּה בְּיָמִים אֵלּוּ, עַל דַּעַת הַמִּנְהָג הוּא מִתְעַנֶּה, וְהַמִּנְהָג לֹא נִתְיַסֵּד לְהִתְעַנּוֹת בִּמְקוֹם סְעוּדַת מִצְוָה.

טו) בְּמָקוֹם שֶׁמַּתִּירִין לֶאֱכוֹל בִּסְעוּדַת מִצְוָה, נִפְסֶקֶת הַתַּעֲנִית לְגַמְרֵי, וּמֻתָּר לֶאֱכֹל אַחַר כָּךְ גַּם בְּבֵיתוֹ. אֲבָל קֹדֶם הַסְּעוּדָה, אָסוּר לֶאֱכֹל. רַק אֲבִי הַבֵּן בְּיוֹם הַמִּילָה וְהַסַּנְדָּק, יְכוֹלִין לֶאֱכוֹל גַּם לִפְנֵי הַסְּעוּדָה, כֵּיוָן שֶׁהוּא כְּמוֹ יוֹם־טוֹב לָהֶם.

טז) אֲבָל אִם אָכַל שֶׁלֹּא בְּהֶתֵּר בְּיוֹם הַתַּעֲנִית, בֵּין בְּשׁוֹגֵג בֵּין בְּמֵזִיד, חַיָּב לְהַשְׁלִים אֶת הַתַּעֲנִית גַּם לְאַחַר הָאֲכִילָה. וְיֵשׁ לוֹ לְהִתְעַנּוֹת אַחַר כָּךְ שֵׁנִי חֲמִישִׁי וְשֵׁנִי לְכַפָּרָה עַל מַה שֶּׁאָכַל בְּיוֹם הַתַּעֲנִית. וּמִכָּל־שֶׁכֵּן, אִם הָיָה יוֹם הַתַּעֲנִית מֵחֲמַת נֶדֶר, שֶׁצָּרִיךְ לְהַשְׁלִים נִדְרוֹ אַחַר כָּךְ.

יז) יָחִיד הַמִּתְעַנֶּה עַל צָרָתוֹ וְעָבְרָה, אוֹ שֶׁמִּתְעַנֶּה בִּשְׁבִיל חוֹלֶה וְנִתְרַפֵּא אוֹ מֵת, צָרִיךְ לְהַשְׁלִים כָּל הַתַּעֲנִיּוֹת שֶׁקִּבֵּל עָלָיו. וְכֵן אִם קִבֵּל עָלָיו תַּעֲנִיּוֹת אוֹ שְׁאָר מִצְוָה, עַד שֶׁיַּעֲשֶׂה בְּנוֹ בַּר־מִצְוָה, וּמֵת הַבֵּן קֹדֶם,

12. In such a case, you need not even repay the fast on a later day. (*Ibid.* 568:17)
13. This rule applies only if you ate a *kazayis* of food, but if you ate less than that, you need not fast another day as an atonement. Similarly, in regard to drinking, if you drank less

12) If you undertook to fast, and are experiencing grave discomfort because of it, you may redeem it with money, according to your means, and you should give the money to the poor. But for a fast in fulfillment of a vow, redemption is of no avail. On a fast day, decreed by the community, redemption is also of no avail, unless the community made such a stipulation.

13) If you made a vow to fast on Monday, Thursday and Monday, you may change it to fasting on Thursday, Monday and Thursday, but not to any other days (of the week), for it is presumed, that you had these days in mind, because they are the days when the court is in session.

14) If you fast on Monday, Thursday, and Monday following *Pesach* and *Sukkos*, as well as on the *Aseres yemei teshuvah*, [the Ten Days of Penitence], and you did not commit yourself to fast during *Minchah*, but your fasting is motivated by the custom, even if you had in mind to fast, when responding *Amein* to the *Mi shebeirach*, as long as you did not resolve to fast during *Minchah*, then, if there is a *bris* [circumcision] or a *pidyon haben* [redemption of first born male] or any other meal celebrating a mitzvah, you are fulfilling a mitzvah by eating,[12] and you need not absolve your vows, for whoever fasts on these days is following the rules imposed by custom, and this custom of fasting was not intended in regard to a meal in celebration of a mitzvah.

15) In cases, where you are permitted to eat at a meal celebrating a mitzvah, the fast is, thereby, ended altogether, and you may eat afterwards, even in your own house; but before the festive meal, it is forbidden to eat. Only the father of the infant on the day of the *bris* and the *sandak* may eat even before the meal, since to them it is like a Yom Tov.

16) However, if you ate on a fast day in violation of the law, whether inadvertently or intentionally, you must complete the fast, even after having eaten. Afterwards, you must fast on Monday, Thursday and Monday, as an atonement for eating on the fast day.[13] [14] It is certainly true that you must fulfil your vow at a later time if you had to fast because of a vow you had made.

17) If you fast because of personal trouble, and the trouble passed, or if you fast for a sick person, and that person recovered or died, you must complete all the fast days that you committed yourself to observe. If someone accepted upon himself to fast or to do some other mitzvah until his son becomes Bar Mitzvah,[15] and the son died before that time, he must, nevertheless, fulfill his vow until the time his son

---

than a cheekful, you may continue the fast, and it is not required that you fast on another day. (*Ibid.* 568:5)

14. *Mishnah Berurah* makes no mention of the need to fast on Monday, Thursday and Monday as an atonement. It would seem that one day is sufficient as an atonement.

15. This rule is not mentioned in *Mishnah Berurah.* (See *Ramah, Yoreh Deiah* 220:15)

צָרִיךְ הוּא לְקַיֵּם אֶת נִדְרוֹ עַד הַשָּׁעָה שֶׁהָיָה רָאוּי לִהְיוֹת בְּנוֹ בַּר־מִצְוָה. אֲבָל אִם נוֹדַע לוֹ שֶׁקֹּדֶם שֶׁקִּבֵּל עָלָיו לְהִתְעַנּוֹת, כְּבָר עָבְרָה הַסִּבָּה, דַּהֲוָה קַבָּלָה בְּטָעוּת, אֵינוֹ צָרִיךְ לְהַשְׁלִים.

יח) יָפֶה תַּעֲנִית עִם הַתְּשׁוּבָה לְבַטֵּל חֲלוֹם רָע, כְּאֵשׁ לִנְעֹרֶת. וְדַוְקָא בּוֹ בַיּוֹם. וּמִכָּל מָקוֹם אֵינוֹ מְחֻיָּב לְהִתְעַנּוֹת, דְּאָמַר שְׁמוּאֵל, הַחֲלוֹמוֹת שָׁוְא יְדַבֵּרוּ. אֲבָל מְחֻיָּב לַעֲשׂוֹת תְּשׁוּבָה, וְלַעֲסֹק כָּל הַיּוֹם בַּתּוֹרָה וּתְפִלָּה. וּלְעִנְיַן תַּעֲנִית חֲלוֹם בַּשַּׁבָּת, עַיֵּן בְּאֹרַח חַיִּים סִימָן רפח.

סִימָן קכח
דִּינֵי חֹדֶשׁ אֱלוּל

א) מֵרֹאשׁ־חֹדֶשׁ אֱלוּל עַד אַחַר יוֹם הַכִּפּוּרִים הֵמָּה יְמֵי רָצוֹן. וְאַף כִּי בְּכָל הַשָּׁנָה הַקָּדוֹשׁ־בָּרוּךְ־הוּא מְקַבֵּל תְּשׁוּבָה מִן הַשָּׁבִים אֵלָיו בְּלֵב שָׁלֵם, מִכָּל מָקוֹם יָמִים אֵלּוּ מֻבְחָרִים יוֹתֵר וּמְזֻמָּנִים לִתְשׁוּבָה, לִהְיוֹתָם יְמֵי רַחֲמִים וִימֵי רָצוֹן, כִּי בְּרֹאשׁ־חֹדֶשׁ אֱלוּל, עָלָה מֹשֶׁה אֶל הַר סִינַי לְקַבֵּל לוּחוֹת שְׁנִיִּים, וְנִשְׁתַּהָה שָׁם אַרְבָּעִים יוֹם, וְיָרַד בַּעֲשָׂרָה בְּתִשְׁרֵי, שֶׁהָיָה אָז גְּמַר כַּפָּרָה. וּמִן אָז הֻקְדְּשׁוּ יָמִים אֵלּוּ לִימֵי רָצוֹן, וְיוֹם עֲשִׂירִי בְּתִשְׁרֵי לְיוֹם הַכִּפּוּרִים. וּמִנְהָג בְּרֹב הַמְּקוֹמוֹת לְהִתְעַנּוֹת בְּעֶרֶב רֹאשׁ־חֹדֶשׁ אֱלוּל וְלַעֲשׂוֹת סֵדֶר יוֹם כִּפּוּר־קָטָן, כְּדֵי שֶׁיָּכִינוּ לִבָּם לִתְשׁוּבָה. וְאִם חָל רֹאשׁ־חֹדֶשׁ בַּשַּׁבָּת, מַקְדִּימִים לְיוֹם חֲמִישִׁי שֶׁלְּפָנָיו. הָאֲרִ"י זִכְרוֹנוֹ לִבְרָכָה כָּתַב, וַאֲשֶׁר לֹא צָדָה וְהָאֱלֹהִים אִנָּה לְיָדוֹ וְשַׂמְתִּי לְךָ, רָאשֵׁי תֵבוֹת אֱלוּל, לוֹמַר כִּי חֹדֶשׁ זֶה, הוּא עֵת רָצוֹן לְקַבֵּל תְּשׁוּבָה עַל הַחֲטָאִים שֶׁעָשָׂה בְּכָל הַשָּׁנָה. וְגַם רֶמֶז שֶׁגַּם עַל הַשְּׁגָגוֹת צָרִיךְ לַעֲשׂוֹת תְּשׁוּבָה בַּחֹדֶשׁ הַזֶּה. עוֹד אָמְרוּ דּוֹרְשֵׁי רְשׁוּמוֹת, וּמָל ה' אֱלֹהֶיךָ אֶת לְבָבְךָ וְאֶת לְבַב זַרְעֶךָ, רָאשֵׁי תֵבוֹת אֱלוּל. וְכֵן אֲנִי לְדוֹדִי וְדוֹדִי לִי, רָאשֵׁי תֵבוֹת אֱלוּל. וְכֵן אִישׁ לְרֵעֵהוּ, וּמַתָּנוֹת לָאֶבְיוֹנִים, רָאשֵׁי תֵבוֹת אֱלוּל.

---

16. However, if the cause for fasting passed after you made the commitment, even though you had not actually started the fast, you must, nevertheless, complete the fast. (*Mishnah Berurah* 569:7)

17. A pregnant woman, or a woman after child-birth should not be told to fast, but, rather, to give charity in lieu of fasting. (*Ibid.* 220:5)

would have become Bar Mitzvah. However, if you find out that before you committed yourself to fast, the cause for fasting had already passed[16] and your commitment, thus, was made in error, then you are not required to complete it.

18) Fasting is beneficial when accompained with repentance for nullifying the portents of a bad dream,[17] just as fire consumes the refuse of flax; but only if [you fast] on the day [you had the dream]. However, you are not required to fast, for (the Amora) Samuel said: "Dreams speak falsehood," (Maseches Berachos 55b). You are, however, required to repent and to devote the entire day to the study of Torah and in prayer. Concerning fasting on Shabbos for a worrisome dream, see *Orach Chaim,* chapter 288.

Chapter 128

Laws Concerning the Month of Elul

1) [The days] from *Rosh Chodesh Elul* until after *Yom Kippur,* are days of Divine favor [and acceptance.] Even though throughout the entire year the Holy One, blessed is He, accepts the repentance of those who return to Him wholeheartedly, nevertheless, these days are unexcelled and most suitable for repentance, because they are days of mercy and favor. On *Rosh Chodesh Elul,* Moshe went up Mount Sinai to receive the Second Tablets; he remained there for forty days, and came down on the tenth day of *Tishrei* when the atonement was completed. From then on these days have been designated as days of Divine favor [and acceptance,] and the tenth day of *Tishrei* as *Yom Kippur* [Day of Atonement]. In most communities it is the custom to fast on the day before *Rosh Chodesh Elul* and to recite the prayers of *Yom Kippur Katan* [minor Yom Kippur], in order to be spiritually prepared for repentance. If *Rosh Chodesh* occurs on Shabbos, *Yom Kippur Katan* is held on the preceding Thursday. The Ari (Rabbi Yitzchak Luria), of blessed memory, wrote, "If he did not lie in ambush but Hashem made it happen, then I will provide . . ." (Exodus 21:13) The initials of the words [*ina le'yado vesamti lecha*] form the acronym *Elul,* to indicate that this month is a favorable time for repentance to be accepted for the sins committed during the entire year. It also alludes to the fact that sins done inadvertently also require repentance[1] during this month. The interpreters of allusions also commented: It is written (Deuteronomy 30:6) "And Hashem your God will circumcise your heart and the heart of your children;" the initials of the words [*es levavecho ve'es levav*] form the acronym *Elul.* Also, the initials of *Ani ledodi vedodi li,* ["I am my Beloved's and my Beloved is mine,"][2] [Song of Songs 6:3] form

1. The Scriptural verse referred to in the text deals with a homicide that was commited accidentally or inadvertently.

2. During these forty days, since repentance is more readily accepted, our repentance brings our hearts closer to our Beloved One and thus He, (our Beloved) is closer to us by accepting our repentance. (*Mishnah Berurah* preface to Chapter 581)

רֶמֶז לִשְׁלֹשָׁה דְבָרִים, שֶׁהֵם, תְּשׁוּבָה, תְּפִלָּה, וּצְדָקָה, שֶׁצְּרִיכִין לְהִזָּהֵר בָּהֶם בְּחֹדֶשׁ זֶה. וּמָל ה' וְגוֹ', רוֹמֵז לִתְשׁוּבָה. אֲנִי לְדוֹדִי וְגוֹ', רוֹמֵז לִתְפִלָּה, שֶׁהִיא רִנַּת דּוֹדִים. אִישׁ לְרֵעֵהוּ וּמַתָּנוֹת לָאֶבְיוֹנִים, רוֹמֵז לִצְדָקָה.

ב) נוֹהֲגִין לִתְקֹעַ בַּשּׁוֹפָר בְּחֹדֶשׁ זֶה. וּמַתְחִילִין בְּיוֹם שֵׁנִי דְּרֹאשׁ־חֹדֶשׁ, וְתוֹקְעִין בְּכָל יוֹם לְאַחַר תְּפִלַּת שַׁחֲרִית תְּקִיעָה שְׁבָרִים תְּרוּעָה תְּקִיעָה, חוּץ מֵעֶרֶב רֹאשׁ־הַשָּׁנָה שֶׁמַּפְסִיקִין בּוֹ, כְּדֵי לְהַפְסִיק בֵּין תְּקִיעוֹת רְשׁוּת לִתְקִיעוֹת מִצְוָה. וְטַעַם הַתְּקִיעוֹת בְּחֹדֶשׁ זֶה, כְּדֵי לְעוֹרֵר אֶת הָעָם לִתְשׁוּבָה, כִּי כֵן הוּא הַטֶּבַע שֶׁל הַשּׁוֹפָר לְעוֹרֵר וּלְהַחֲרִיד, כְּמוֹ שֶׁאָמַר הַכָּתוּב, אִם יִתָּקַע שׁוֹפָר בְּעִיר וְעָם לֹא יֶחֱרָדוּ. עוֹד נוֹהֲגִין בִּמְדִינוֹת אֵלּוּ מִיּוֹם שֵׁנִי דְּרֹאשׁ־חֹדֶשׁ אֱלוּל עַד שְׁמִינִי עֲצֶרֶת, אוֹמְרִים בַּבֹּקֶר וּבָעֶרֶב לְאַחַר הַתְּפִלָּה, אֶת הַמִּזְמוֹר לְדָוִד ה' אוֹרִי וְיִשְׁעִי. וְהוּא עַל פִּי הַמִּדְרָשׁ, ה' אוֹרִי, בְּרֹאשׁ הַשָּׁנָה. וְיִשְׁעִי, בְּיוֹם הַכִּפּוּרִים. כִּי יִצְפְּנֵנִי בְּסֻכֹּה, רֶמֶז לְסֻכּוֹת. עוֹד נוֹהֲגִין לוֹמַר תְּהִלִּים בְּצִבּוּר בְּכָל מָקוֹם לְפִי מִנְהָגוֹ. מִשֶּׁנִּכְנַס אֱלוּל עַד יוֹם הַכִּפּוּרִים, כְּשֶׁכּוֹתֵב אָדָם אִגֶּרֶת לַחֲבֵרוֹ, צָרִיךְ לִרְמֹז בָּהּ בִּתְחִלָּתָהּ אוֹ בְּסוֹפָהּ, שֶׁהוּא מְבַקֵּשׁ עָלָיו וּמְבָרְכוֹ, שֶׁיִּזְכֶּה בִּימֵי הַדִּין, הַבָּאִים לְטוֹבָה, לְהִכָּתֵב וּלְהֵחָתֵם בְּסֵפֶר חַיִּים טוֹבִים.

ג) אַנְשֵׁי מַעֲשֶׂה, נוֹהֲגִין לִבְדֹּק בְּחֹדֶשׁ זֶה תְּפִלִּין וּמְזוּזוֹת שֶׁלָּהֶן. וְכָל אֲשֶׁר יִמָּצֵא שָׁם בֶּדֶק, בִּשְׁאָר מִצְוֹת, יְתַקְּנוֹ.

ד) מִשַּׁבָּת שֶׁלְּאַחַר תִּשְׁעָה בְּאָב וּלְהַלָּן, מַפְטִירִין בְּשֶׁבַע הַשַּׁבָּתוֹת, שֶׁבַע דְּנֶחָמְתָא. וְאִם חָל יוֹם רִאשׁוֹן דְּרֹאשׁ־חֹדֶשׁ אֱלוּל בַּשַּׁבָּת, דּוֹחִין עֲנִיָּה סוֹעֲרָה וּמַפְטִירִין הַשָּׁמַיִם כִּסְאִי, מִפְּנֵי שֶׁיֵּשׁ בָּהּ גַּם כֵּן מִנֶּחָמוֹת יְרוּשָׁלַיִם. וּבְשַׁבָּת פָּרָשַׁת כִּי־תֵצֵא, שֶׁאָז מַפְטִירִין רָנִּי עֲקָרָה, מַשְׁלִימִין

---

3. Some have the custom to blow shofar even on the first day of Rosh Chodesh Elul.

4. It is permitted, however, to blow shofar in order to practice in preparation for the obligatory sounding of the shofar on Rosh Hashanah. (*Ibid* 581:24)

5. Including the day of *Shemini Atzeres.* (*Ibid* 581:2)

6. On those days when the *Musaf* service is said, the psalm is recited after *Shacharis,* before *Ein Komocha* [there is none like You] which is said before the *Seifer Torah* is taken out of the Ark. In the evening the psalm is recited after the *Minchah* service. [This is the custom of those who pray *Nusach Sfard.*] In those places where they recite the psalm after the entire service [including *Musaf*] is completed, such as on Rosh Chodesh, the psalm, *Borchi Nafshi* [Psalm 104] is recited before *LeDovid Hashem Ori.* They also have the custom to recite *LeDovid*

the acronym *Elul.* Also, the initials of *Ish lerei'eihu umatanos la'evyonim* ["One to another and gifts to the poor"] (Esther 9:22) form the acronym *Elul.* These acronyms are an allusion to three things: Repentance, Prayer and Charity which must be practiced zealously during this month. "Hashem will circumcise etc." alludes to repentance, "I am my Beloved's etc." alludes to prayer, for prayer is the song of love. "One to another and gifts to the poor," alludes to charity.

2) It is customary to blow the *shofar* during this month. Beginning the second day of *Rosh Chodesh,*[3] we blow the *shofar* each day after the *Shacharis* prayer, *tekiah, shevarim, teruah, tekiah,* except on *erev Rosh Hashanah,* when the blowing is discontinued,[4] in order to make a distinction between the voluntary blowing of the *shofar* and the blowing *shofar* in fulfillment of the mitzvah. The reason for blowing the *shofar* during this month is to arouse the people to repent; for the *shofar* sound has the quality to stir [the emotions] and to inspire fear, as Scripture says, (Amos 3:6) "If a *shofar* is sounded in a city will the people not tremble?" It is also the custom in our regions, beginning with the second day of *Rosh Chodesh Elul* until *Shemini Atzeres,*[5] to recite Psalm [27] *LeDovid Hashem ori ve'yish'i*[6] ["Of David, Hashem is my light and my salvation"] [each day] [after] the morning and evening prayers,[7] This is based on the *Midrash:* "Hashem is my light" —on *Rosh Hashanah;* "and my salvation" —on *Yom Kippur;* "for He will hide me in His shelter" —alludes to *Sukkos.* It also is customary for the congregation to recite Psalms,[8] each locality according to its custom.[9] Beginning with the month of *Elul* until *Yom Kippur,* when you write a letter to your friend you should mention, either at the beginning or at the end that you pray for him and bless him to be worthy during the forthcoming Days of Judgment to be inscribed and sealed in the Book of Good Life.

3) Pious men are accustomed to examine their *tefillin* and *mezuzos* during this month; and wherever any defect may be found in other mitzvohs, to repair it.

4) Beginning with the Shabbos following *Tishah beAv* and after that, for the next seven *Shabbosos* we read the *haftoras "sheva denechamasa"* [seven *haftoras* of consolation]. If the first day of *Rosh Chodesh Elul* occurs on Shabbos, the *haftorah, Aniyah so'arah,* is set aside ["O you afflicted, floundering in the storm,"] (Isaiah 54:11) and we read instead, *"Hashamayim kis'i,"* [The heaven is My throne] (Isaiah 66:1), because this *haftorah* also contains consolation for Jerusalem. On the Shabbos of *Parshas Ki Seitzei,* when the *haftorah Roni akarah* [Sing, O barren woman] (Isaiah 54:1)

Hashem Ori after the psalm of the day is recited. [This is the custom of those who pray *Nusach Ashkenaz.*] (*Ibid* 581:2)

7. *Kaddish* should be said after the psalm is recited. (*Ibid*)

8. *Mishnah Berurah* says that we should omit the words: בָּהֶם שִׁבְעִים שָׁנָה [until we have lived our seventy years] in the prayer recited before saying *tehillim* [Psalms]; and since we [usually] do not recite an entire book of the Psalms, we should say: בִּזְכוּת מִזְמוֹרֵי תְּהִלִּים שֶׁקָּרָאנוּ לְפָנֶיךָ [In the merit of the chapters of *tehillim* we have recited], when we say the prayer that is said following the saying of *tehillim.* After this prayer Kaddish should be recited if there is a minyan [a quorum of ten males] present. (*Ibid* 581:3)

9. The custom is to recite ten chapters each day, and during the days between *Rosh Hashanah* and *Yom Kippur,* extra chapters are recited so that the entire Book of Psalms will have been said three times. (*Ibid*)

עָלֶיהָ גַּם עֲנִיָּה סוֹעֲרָה, שֶׁהִיא סְמוּכָה לָהּ. אִם טָעָה בְּשַׁבָּת רֹאשׁ־חֹדֶשׁ אֱלוּל וְאָמַר עֲנִיָּה סוֹעֲרָה, אִם נִזְכַּר קֹדֶם שֶׁבֵּרֵךְ לְאַחֲרֶיהָ, יֹאמַר גַּם הַשָּׁמַיִם כִּסְאִי, וִיבָרֵךְ לְאַחֲרֶיהָ. וְאִם לֹא נִזְכַּר עַד לְאַחַר הַבְּרָכוֹת, יֹאמַר הַשָּׁמַיִם כִּסְאִי בְּלֹא בְּרָכוֹת. וְאִם חָל רֹאשׁ־חֹדֶשׁ אֱלוּל בָּרִאשׁוֹן בַּשַּׁבָּת, דּוֹחִין הַפְטָרַת מָחָר חֹדֶשׁ, שֶׁאֵין בָּהּ מִנֶּחָמוֹת יְרוּשָׁלַיִם, וּמַפְטִירִין עֲנִיָּה סוֹעֲרָה.

ה) מִיּוֹם רִאשׁוֹן בַּשַּׁבָּת שֶׁקֹּדֶם רֹאשׁ־הַשָּׁנָה וְאֵילָךְ, מַשְׁכִּימִין לִסְלִיחוֹת. וְאִם חָל רֹאשׁ־הַשָּׁנָה בְּיוֹם שֵׁנִי אוֹ בְּיוֹם שְׁלִישִׁי, מַתְחִילִין מִיּוֹם רִאשׁוֹן בַּשָּׁבוּעַ הַקּוֹדֵם. וּכְשֶׁמַּשְׁכִּימִין, צְרִיכִין לִטּוֹל יְדֵיהֶם וּלְבָרֵךְ עַל נְטִילַת יָדַיִם וּבִרְכַּת הַתּוֹרָה. וְאַחַר הַסְּלִיחוֹת, יִטּוֹל יָדָיו שֵׁנִית בְּלֹא בְּרָכָה.

ו) שְׁלִיחַ־הַצִּבּוּר שֶׁאוֹמֵר סְלִיחוֹת, יִתְעַטֵּף בְּטַלִּית מְצֻיֶּצֶת קֹדֶם שֶׁמַּתְחִיל אַשְׁרֵי. וּלְפִי שֶׁיֵּשׁ סָפֵק, אִם יְבָרֵךְ בְּרָכָה עַל טַלִּית שֶׁלּוֹ כְּשֶׁלּוֹבְשׁוֹ בַּלַּיְלָה אוֹ לֹא יְבָרֵךְ, עַל כֵּן לֹא יִטּוֹל אֶת שֶׁלּוֹ, וְגַם לֹא טַלִּית הַקָּהָל, אֶלָּא יִשְׁאַל לוֹ טַלִּית מֵאַחֵר. וְאִם אֵין בְּנִמְצָא טַלִּית כְּלָל, יְכוֹלִין לוֹמַר סְלִיחוֹת וּשְׁלֹשׁ־עֶשְׂרֵה מִדּוֹת גַּם בְּלֹא טַלִּית. יֵשׁ מְקוֹמוֹת נוֹהֲגִין שֶׁהַמִּתְפַּלֵּל סְלִיחוֹת, מִתְפַּלֵּל גַּם שַׁחֲרִית וּמִנְחָה וְגַם מַעֲרִיב שֶׁלְּפָנָיו, וְהוּא קוֹדֵם לְאָבֵל וּלְמוֹהֵל וּלְ„יָאר צַייט". טוֹב לַעֲמֹד בַּאֲמִירַת הַסְּלִיחוֹת. וּמִי שֶׁקָּשֶׁה לוֹ, יַעֲמֹד לְכָל־הַפָּחוֹת בַּאֲמִירַת אֵל מֶלֶךְ יוֹשֵׁב וְגוֹ' וּשְׁלֹשׁ־עֶשְׂרֵה מִדּוֹת. דִּין אֲמִירַת הַוִּדּוּי, עַיֵּן לְקַמָּן סִימָן קלא סָעִיף ט.

ז) יְדַקְדְּקוּ לִבְחוֹר שְׁלִיחַ־צִבּוּר שֶׁיִּתְפַּלֵּל סְלִיחוֹת וּבַיָּמִים הַנּוֹרָאִים, אִישׁ שֶׁהוּא הָגוּן וְגָדוֹל בַּתּוֹרָה וּבְמַעֲשִׂים טוֹבִים, כְּפִי מַה שֶּׁאֶפְשָׁר לִמְצֹא. וְגַם שֶׁיִּהְיֶה בֵּין שְׁלֹשִׁים שָׁנָה, שֶׁאָז כְּבָר נָחָה רְתִיחַת הַדָּם שֶׁל בַּחֲרוּתוֹ וְנִכְנַע לִבּוֹ. וְגַם יְהֵא נָשׂוּי וְיִהְיוּ לוֹ בָּנִים, שֶׁהוּא שׁוֹפֵךְ לִבּוֹ

---

10. Nevertheless, in a situation where there is no other *tallis* except his own, he may put on his own *tallis* without saying the berachah, and when it gets light, he should examine the *tzitzis* and say the berachah. (*Shaarei Tzion* 581:5)

11. This is the opinion of *Mogein Avrohom. Eiliyahu Rabbah,* however, rules that a person observing *yahrzeit,* who is fasting, should be permitted to lead the prayers. He also says that a mourner should be permitted to conclude the *Shacharis* prayers, after the second *"Ashrei"* is said. (See *Mishnah Berurah* 581:14)

is read, we conclude the *haftorah* with *Aniyah so'arah,* which is next to it. If, by mistake, on *Shabbos Rosh Chodesh Elul,* you said *Aniyah so'arah,* and you became aware of it before saying the concluding berachos, you should also say *Hashamayim kis'i,* and then say the concluding berachah. If you only became aware [of your error] after saying the concluding berachos, then you should recite, *Hashamayim kis'i* without the berachos. If *Rosh Chodesh Elul* occurs on Sunday, the *haftorah, Machar Chodesh* is set aside, [Tomorrow is *Rosh Chodesh*] (I Samuel 20:18), because it contains no consolation for Jerusalem, and the *haftorah Aniyah so'arah* is read.

5) Beginning with the Sunday before *Rosh Hashanah* and thereafter we rise early for *Selichos,* [special prayers for forgiveness]. If *Rosh Hashanah* occurs on Monday or Tuesday, we begin [to say *Selichos*] from the Sunday of the preceding week. When you get up early in the morning [before daylight] you must wash your hands and say the berachah *Al netilas yadayim,* [regarding washing the hands] and the berachah of the Torah. After the *Selichos* [if it is daylight], you should wash your hands again without saying a berachah.

6) The *Chazzan* who leads the *Selichos* prayers should put on a *tallis* with *tzitzis* before saying *Ashrei.* Since it is doubtful, whether a berachah should be said when putting on his own *tallis* at night or not, therefore, the *Chazzan* should take neither his own *tallis*[10] nor one belonging to the congregation, but should borrow one from someone. If no *tallis* is available, he may say *Selichos* and the *Shelosh esrei midos* ["The thirteen attributes"] without wearing a *tallis.* It is customary in some communities that the *Chazzan* who leads the *Selichos* prayers should also officiate at the *Shacharis* and *Minchah* services, as well as at the *Maariv* service of the preceding night. He takes precedence over a mourner, a mohel, and a person observing *yahrzeit.*[11] It is proper to stand while saying the *Selichos,*[12] but a person who finds it difficult to stand should at least stand while saying *keil melech yosheiv* ["God, King Who is enthroned"] etc. and the *Shelosh esrei midos* ["Thirteen attributes of mercy"]. For the laws regarding the recitation of the *Viduy* (the confession of sins, the *Al cheit*), see Chapter 131:9 below.

7) [The congregation] should be discriminating to choose as *Chazzan* to lead the services of *Selichos* and the *Yomim Noraim* [*Rosh Hashanah* and *Yom Kippur*] a man who is highly respectable, a Torah scholar, known for his good deeds. He should be no less than thirty years old, for by then moderation has calmed his youthful hot-bloodedness, and his heart is subdued. He should also be married and have children,[13] so that he will pour out his heart and pray for mercy from the bottom of his heart. [The congregation] should also be discriminating in selecting as the

---

12. *Mishnah Berurah* does not mention this *halachah.*
13. If there is a choice between one who is a God-fearing, Torah scholar but who is less than thirty and unmarried, and one who is over thirty and married but is not a Torah scholar, the position should be given to the Torah scholar. (*Ibid* 581:13)

וּמַפִּיל תַּחֲנוּנִים מִקִּירוֹת הַלֵּב. וְכֵן יְדַקְדְּקוּ לִבְחוֹר תּוֹקֵעַ שֶׁיִּתְקַע שׁוֹפָר בְּרֹאשׁ־הַשָּׁנָה, וְכֵן הַמַּקְרֵא לִפְנֵי הַתּוֹקֵעַ, שֶׁיִּהְיוּ בַּעֲלֵי תּוֹרָה וְיִרְאָה, כְּפִי מַה שֶּׁאֶפְשָׁר לָהֶם לִמְצֹא. מִיהוּ כָּל יִשְׂרָאֵל כְּשֵׁרִים לַכֹּל, רַק שֶׁיְּהֵא מְרֻצֶּה לַקָּהָל. וְאִם רוֹאֶה שֶׁיֵּשׁ מַחֲלֹקֶת בַּדָּבָר, יִמְנַע עַצְמוֹ, אַף־עַל־פִּי שֶׁיִּהְיֶה מִי שֶׁאֵינוֹ הָגוּן.

ח) אָבֵל כָּל שְׁנֵים־עָשָׂר חֹדֶשׁ אַחַר אָבִיו וְאִמּוֹ, לֹא יְהֵא שְׁלִיחַ־צִבּוּר בְּרֹאשׁ־הַשָּׁנָה וְיוֹם־הַכִּפּוּרִים, וְלֹא תּוֹקֵעַ בְּרֹאשׁ־הַשָּׁנָה, אֶלָּא אִם אֵין אַחֵר הָגוּן כָּמוֹהוּ. וְאִם הוּא תּוֹךְ שְׁלֹשִׁים עַל שְׁאָר קְרוֹבִים, אִם הֶחֱזִיק מִכְּבָר לְהִתְפַּלֵּל אוֹ לִתְקֹעַ, מֻתָּר, כֵּיוָן שֶׁרֹאשׁ־הַשָּׁנָה וְיוֹם־הַכִּפּוּרִים מְבַטְּלִין גְּזֵרַת שְׁלֹשִׁים. אֲבָל אִם לֹא הֶחֱזִיק, וְיֵשׁ אַחֵר הָגוּן כָּמוֹהוּ, יֵשׁ לְהַחְמִיר. אֲבָל כָּל יְמֵי הַסְּלִיחוֹת, אֲפִלּוּ בְּעֶרֶב רֹאשׁ־הַשָּׁנָה, מֻתָּר לְכָל אָבֵל לִהְיוֹת שְׁלִיחַ־צִבּוּר, אַךְ לֹא בְּתוֹךְ שִׁבְעָה.

ט) יָחִיד הָאוֹמֵר סְלִיחוֹת, אֵינוֹ רַשַּׁאי לוֹמַר שְׁלֹשׁ־עֶשְׂרֵה מִדּוֹת דֶּרֶךְ תְּפִלָּה וּבַקָּשָׁה, אֶלָּא דֶּרֶךְ קְרִיאָה בַּתּוֹרָה בְּנִגּוּן וּבִטְעָמִים. וְכֵן בְּמָקוֹם שֶׁנִּזְכָּרוֹת שְׁלֹשׁ־עֶשְׂרֵה מִדּוֹת, כְּגוֹן וּזְכוֹר לָנוּ הַיּוֹם בְּרִית שְׁלֹשׁ־עֶשְׂרֵה וְכַדּוֹמֶה, יֵשׁ לוֹ לְדַלֵּג. וְכֵן הַבַּקָּשׁוֹת שֶׁהֵן בְּלָשׁוֹן אֲרַמִּית, כְּגוֹן מָחֵי וּמַסֵּי וְכוּ׳, מָרָן דִּי בִשְׁמַיָּא וְכוּ׳, לֹא יֹאמְרֵן אֶלָּא בַּעֲשָׂרָה.

י) אָבֵל אָסוּר לָצֵאת מִבֵּיתוֹ לָלֶכֶת לְבֵית־הַכְּנֶסֶת לוֹמַר סְלִיחוֹת, מִלְּבַד בְּעֶרֶב רֹאשׁ־הַשָּׁנָה, שֶׁמַּרְבִּים בִּסְלִיחוֹת.

יא) שְׁלִיחַ־הַצִּבּוּר שֶׁיִּתְפַּלֵּל בַּיָּמִים הַנּוֹרָאִים וְכֵן הַתּוֹקֵעַ, צְרִיכִין לִפְרוֹשׁ אֶת עַצְמָן שְׁלֹשָׁה יָמִים לִפְנֵי רֹאשׁ־הַשָּׁנָה מִכָּל דָּבָר הַמֵּבִיא לִידֵי טֻמְאָה, וְיִלְמְדוּ כְּפִי יְכָלְתָּם פֵּרוּשֵׁי הַתְּפִלּוֹת וְהַפִּיּוּטִים וְהִלְכוֹת תְּקִיעוֹת. וְגַם יִלְמְדוּ סִפְרֵי מוּסָר הַמְּעוֹרְרִים אֶת לֵב הָאָדָם, וְיִירְאוּ מִפַּחַד ה׳ וּמֵהֲדַר גְּאוֹנוֹ בְּקוּמוֹ לִשְׁפֹּט אֶת הָאָרֶץ. אִם לֹא נִמְצָא לָהֶם תּוֹקֵעַ שֶׁהוּא בַּעַל תּוֹרָה, יִרְאוּ עַל־כָּל־פָּנִים שֶׁיְּהֵא הַמַּקְרֵא בַּעַל תּוֹרָה, וִיהֵא בָקִי בְּהִלְכוֹת תְּקִיעַת שׁוֹפָר, שֶׁאִם תֶּאֱרַע אֵיזוֹ טָעוּת בַּתְּקִיעוֹת, יֵדַע מַה לַּעֲשׂוֹת, וְגַם שֶׁיֵּדַע לִבְדֹּק אֶת הַשּׁוֹפָר אִם הוּא כָּשֵׁר.

---

14. This is not mentioned by *Mishnah Berurah.*

15. *Mishnah Berurah* rules that he is not permitted to officiate under any circumstances. (*Ibid* 581:7)

tokei'a —the person who blows the *shofar* on *Rosh Hashanah,* —and as the person who prompts him, men who are Torah scholars and God-fearing. However, any Jew is eligible to officiate at any religious function, provided he is acceptable to the congregation. But if you see that your appointment will cause quarreling you should withdraw, even though an unworthy person will be chosen.

8) During the twelve months of mourning for a father or mother, a person should not officiate as *Chazzan* on *Rosh Hashanah* and *Yom Kippur,* neither should he blow the *shofar* on *Rosh Hashanah,*[14] unless there is no one else as qualified as he is.[15] If he is in the first thirty days [of mourning] for other relatives, then, if he regularly officiated in previous years as *Chazzan* or as *tokei'a,* he is permitted to do so [now][15] because *Rosh Hashanah* and *Yom Kippur* cancel the thirty day mourning period, but if he is not the regular *Chazzan,* and there is someone else as qualified as he is, we are stringent [and do not permit him to officiate]. But during the period when we say *Selichos,* even on *erev Rosh Hashanah,*[16] any mourner may act as *Chazzan,* but not during the *shivah* [the first seven days of mourning].

9) A person who says *Selichos* privately is not permitted to recite the "Thirteen Attributes of mercy" as a prayer or as a plea, but as if he were reading them from the Torah, with the appropriate cantillation chant. Wherever there is mention made of the "Thirteen Attributes," such as, "And remember for us this day the covenant of the thirteen [attributes]," and similar passages, he should omit them. Also the supplications that are written in the Aramaic language, such as, *Machei umasei* [He strikes and He heals] etc., and *Maran di vishemeya* [Master in heaven] etc. should only be said with a *minyan.*

10) A mourner [during the *shiva*] is forbidden to leave his house to go to the synagogue in order to say *Selichos,* except on *erev Rosh Hashanah,* when many *Selichos* are said.

11) The *Chazzan* who will officiate on the "Days of Awe", as well as the *tokei'a,* should abstain three days before *Rosh Hashanah* from anything that may cause *tum'ah* —(impurity). They should study the meaning of the prayers and the special liturgical poems and the laws concerning the blessing of the *shofar* to the best of their ability. They should also study books on devoutness and ethics that arouse man's heart to fear God and the splendor of His grandeur when He rises to judge the world. If the congregation is unable to find a *tokei'a* who is a Torah scholar, they should at least see to it that the prompter is a Torah scholar, well versed in the laws of the blowing of the *shofar,* so that if an error is made in the sounds of the *shofar,* he should know what to do; and he should also know how to examine the *shofar* to determine if it is fit to be used.

---

16. He may also lead the *selichos* during the days between *Rosh Hashanah* and *Yom Kippur.* (*Ibid*)

יב) הַרְבֵּה נוֹהֲגִין לְהִתְעַנּוֹת בַּעֲשֶׂרֶת יְמֵי תְשׁוּבָה, וּלְפִי שֶׁחֲסֵרִים אַרְבָּעָה יָמִים שֶׁאֵינָם מִתְעַנִּים בָּהֶם, דְּהַיְנוּ שְׁנֵי יָמִים שֶׁל רֹאשׁ־הַשָּׁנָה, שַׁבָּת, וְעֶרֶב יוֹם־הַכִּפּוּרִים, עַל כֵּן מִתְעַנִּין תְּמוּרָתָן אַרְבָּעָה יָמִים בִּימֵי הַסְּלִיחוֹת שֶׁקֹּדֶם רֹאשׁ־הַשָּׁנָה, דְּהַיְנוּ יוֹם רִאשׁוֹן דִּסְלִיחוֹת, וְעֶרֶב רֹאשׁ־הַשָּׁנָה, וְעוֹד שְׁנֵי יָמִים בֵּינָתַיִם, וּבוֹחֲרִים בְּיוֹם שֵׁנִי וַחֲמִישִׁי. וְאִם אֵרְעָה לָהֶם סְעוּדַת מִצְוָה, יְכוֹלִין לֶאֱכוֹל, וְיִתְעַנּוּ יוֹם אַחֵר תְּמוּרָתוֹ. אוֹ אִם יוֹדְעִים שֶׁתִּהְיֶה לָהֶם סְעוּדַת מִצְוָה, יִתְעַנּוּ מִקֹּדֶם יוֹם אֶחָד תְּמוּרָתוֹ.

יג) נוֹהֲגִין לֵילֵךְ בְּעֶרֶב רֹאשׁ־הַשָּׁנָה אַחַר תְּפִלַּת שַׁחֲרִית לְבֵית הַקְּבָרוֹת לְהִשְׁתַּטֵּחַ עַל קִבְרֵי הַצַּדִּיקִים, וְנוֹתְנִים שָׁם צְדָקָה לַעֲנִיִּים, וּמַרְבִּים תַּחֲנוּנִים לְעוֹרֵר אֶת הַצַּדִּיקִים הַקְּדוֹשִׁים אֲשֶׁר בָּאָרֶץ הֵמָּה, שֶׁיַּמְלִיצוּ טוֹב בַּעֲדֵנוּ בְּיוֹם הַדִּין. וְגַם מֵחֲמַת שֶׁהוּא מְקוֹם קְבוּרַת הַצַּדִּיקִים, הַמָּקוֹם הוּא קָדוֹשׁ וְטָהוֹר, וְהַתְּפִלָּה מְקֻבֶּלֶת שָׁם בְּיוֹתֵר, בִּהְיוֹתָהּ עַל אַדְמַת קֹדֶשׁ, וְיַעֲשֶׂה הַקָּדוֹשׁ־בָּרוּךְ־הוּא חֶסֶד בִּזְכוּת הַצַּדִּיקִים. אֲבָל אַל יָשִׂים מְגַמָּתוֹ נֶגֶד הַמֵּתִים הַשּׁוֹכְנִים שָׁם, כִּי קָרוֹב הַדָּבָר שֶׁיִּהְיֶה בִּכְלַל וְדוֹרֵשׁ אֶל הַמֵּתִים. אַךְ יְבַקֵּשׁ מֵהַשֵּׁם, יִתְבָּרַךְ שְׁמוֹ, שֶׁיְּרַחֵם עָלָיו בִּזְכוּת הַצַּדִּיקִים שׁוֹכְנֵי עָפָר. כְּשֶׁבָּא אֶל בֵּית־הַקְּבָרוֹת, אִם לֹא רָאָה אֶת הַקְּבָרִים שְׁלֹשִׁים יוֹם, צָרִיךְ לְבָרֵךְ, אֲשֶׁר יָצַר אֶתְכֶם בַּדִּין וְכוּ' (לְעֵיל סִימָן ס סָעִיף יא). כְּשֶׁבָּא אֶל הַקֶּבֶר, יֵשׁ לוֹ לוֹמַר, יְהִי רָצוֹן שֶׁתְּהֵא מְנוּחָתוֹ שֶׁל פְּלוֹנִי הַקָּבוּר פֹּה בְּכָבוֹד, וּזְכוּתוֹ יַעֲמֹד לִי. כְּשֶׁמְּמַשֵּׁשׁ יָדוֹ עַל הַקֶּבֶר, יֵשׁ לָשׂוּם יַד שְׂמֹאלוֹ דַּוְקָא וְלֹא יְמִינוֹ, וְיֹאמַר אֶת הַפָּסוּק, וְנָחֲךָ ה' תָּמִיד וְהִשְׂבִּיעַ בְּצַחְצָחוֹת נַפְשֶׁךָ וְעַצְמוֹתֶיךָ יַחֲלִיץ וְהָיִיתָ כְּגַן רָוֶה וּכְמוֹצָא מַיִם אֲשֶׁר לֹא יְכַזְּבוּ מֵימָיו. תִּשְׁכַּב בְּשָׁלוֹם, וְתִישַׁן בְּשָׁלוֹם, עַד בּוֹא מְנַחֵם מַשְׁמִיעַ שָׁלוֹם. (וּכְשֶׁשָּׂם יָדוֹ, יְכַוֵּן בַּפָּסוּק וְנָחֲךָ, שֶׁיֵּשׁ בּוֹ חֲמֵשׁ עֶשְׂרֵה תֵּבוֹת כְּמִנְיַן קִשְׁרֵי הַיָּד). אֵין לֵילֵךְ עַל קֶבֶר אֶחָד שְׁתֵּי פְעָמִים בְּיוֹם אֶחָד. הַקּוֹרֵא כְּתָב שֶׁעַל גַּבֵּי הַמַּצֵּבָה, אִם הוּא כְּתָב בּוֹלֵט, קָשֶׁה לְשִׁכְחָה. וּסְגֻלָּה לוֹמַר, אַהֲבָה רַבָּה עַד וּלְיַחֶדְךָ בְּאַהֲבָה.

יד) בְּעֶרֶב רֹאשׁ־הַשָּׁנָה נָהֲגוּ כֻּלָּם לְהִתְעַנּוֹת עַד אַחַר מִנְחָה, שֶׁאָז טוֹעֲמִין אֵיזֶה דָבָר, שֶׁלֹּא לִכָּנֵס לְיוֹם־טוֹב כְּשֶׁהוּא מְעֻנֶּה. וְכָל הַיּוֹם, יַעֲסֹק בַּתּוֹרָה וּבְמִצְוֹת וּבִתְשׁוּבָה, וּמִכָּל־שֶׁכֵּן מַעֲבֵרוֹת שֶׁבֵּין אָדָם לַחֲבֵרוֹ. וְלֹא יַמְתִּין עַד עֶרֶב יוֹם־הַכִּפּוּרִים, אֶלָּא יַקְדִּים אֶת עַצְמוֹ הַיּוֹם לְבַקֵּשׁ מֵחֲבֵרוֹ מְחִילָה.

12) Many people are accustomed to fast during the Ten Days of Penitence, but since this period includes four days on which fasting is not permitted, namely, the two days of *Rosh Hashanah,* Shabbos, and *erev Yom Kippur,* they make up for them by fasting four of the *Selichos* days before *Rosh Hashanah,* that is, the first day of *Selichos, erev Rosh Hashanah* and two other intervening days, preferably Monday and Thursday. If a meal that is considered a mitzvah occurs [on one of these days] they are permitted to eat at the meal and compensate by fasting on another day. If they know beforehand that they are invited to a meal celebrating a mitzvah, they should fast the day before [the meal], to make up for it.

13) It is customary to go to the cemetery *erev Rosh Hashanah* after the *Shacharis* prayers and bow prayerfully at the graves of *tzaddikim* [righteous men]. Charity should be given to the poor, and many fervent supplications offered to arouse the saintly *tzaddikim,* in their eternal resting place to intercede for us on the Day of Judgement. An additional reason for going to the cemetery is that the place where *tzaddikim* are buried is sacred and pure, and prayers are more readily accepted when they are offered on sacred ground, and the Holy One, blessed is He, will show us kindness for the sake of the *tzaddikim.* But it should not be your intention to appeal to the dead who rest there, for that would be tantamount to "Inquiring of the dead," (Deuteronomy 18:11), which is forbidden, but you should ask of Hashem, blessed is His name, to have mercy on you for the sake of the *tzaddikim* who rest in the dust. When you arrive at the cemetery, if you have not seen graves within the past thirty days, you must say the berachah: *Asher yatzar eschem badin* [Who has formed you in judgement etc.] (see Chapter 60:11. above) When you approach the grave, you should say, "May it be Your will, that the repose of [so-and-so] who is buried here, be in peace, and may his merit aid me." When placing your hand on the grave, the left hand only should be placed, —not the right hand. You should recite the verse, "Hashem will always guide you, and satisfy your soul with splendor, and make your bones strong, you will be like a watered garden and like a spring of water whose water will not fail." (Isaiah 58:11) "May you lie in peace, and may you sleep in peace until *Menachem* (the Comforter, *Moshiach*) comes, announcing peace." (When placing your hand [on the grave] you should have in mind the verse, "Hashem will always guide you," which contains fifteen words the same as the number of joints in the hands.) You should not visit the same grave twice on the same day. Reading the inscription on a headstone, if it is protruding, causes forgetfulness. A remedy for that is to say the prayer *Ahavah rabbah* (With abundant love) up to *uleyachedcha be'ahavah* [and to proclaim Your Oneness with love].

14) On *erev Rosh Hashanah* it is the universal custom to fast[17] until after *Minchah,* at which time you may eat something so that you do not welcome the Yom Tov in a state of affliction. The entire day should be spent learning Torah, performing mitzvos and in repentance, especially of sins committed against your fellow man. You should not wait until *erev Yom Kippur,* but, promptly, without delay, you should ask forgiveness of your friends, [neighbors, and family.]

---

17. *Mogein Avrohom* writes that if one is even slightly ill, he should not fast.

טו) מְכַבְּסִין וּמִסְתַּפְּרִין בְּעֶרֶב רֹאשׁ־הַשָּׁנָה לִכְבוֹד יוֹם־טוֹב, וְיֵשׁ לְהִזָּהֵר לְגַלֵּחַ קֹדֶם חֲצוֹת הַיּוֹם. וְטוֹבְלִים וְלוֹבְשִׁים בִּגְדֵי שַׁבָּת בְּרֹאשׁ־הַשָּׁנָה, לְהַרְאוֹת שֶׁאָנוּ בְּטוּחִים בְּחַסְדּוֹ יִתְבָּרַךְ שְׁמוֹ, שֶׁיוֹצִיא לָאוֹר מִשְׁפָּטֵנוּ.

טז) נוֹהֲגִין לַעֲשׂוֹת הַתָּרַת נְדָרִים בְּעֶרֶב רֹאשׁ־הַשָּׁנָה. (וְהָרֶמֶז, לֹא יַחֵל דְּבָרוֹ כְּכָל, סוֹפֵי תֵבוֹת אֱלוּל). וּמִי שֶׁאֵינוֹ מֵבִין מַה שֶּׁהוּא אוֹמֵר בִּלְשׁוֹן־הַקֹּדֶשׁ, יֹאמַר בִּלְשׁוֹן לַעַז, כְּמוֹ שֶׁהוּא מֵבִין.

סִימָן קכט
הִלְכוֹת רֹאשׁ־הַשָּׁנָה

א) בְּכָל הַקַּדִּישִׁים שֶׁאוֹמְרִים מֵרֹאשׁ־הַשָּׁנָה עַד יוֹם־הַכִּפּוּרִים, כּוֹפְלִין תֵּבַת לְעֵלָּא, הַיְנוּ שֶׁאוֹמְרִים, לְעֵלָּא לְעֵלָּא, (וְלֹא בְּוָא"ו וּלְעֵלָּא). וְכֵיוָן שֶׁבַּקַּדִּישׁ צְרִיכוֹת לִהְיוֹת שְׁמוֹנֶה וְעֶשְׂרִים תֵּבוֹת, וּבְכָל הַשָּׁנָה אוֹמְרִים, לְעֵלָּא מִן כָּל בִּרְכָתָא, אוֹמְרִים עַתָּה, לְעֵלָּא לְעֵלָּא מִכָּל בִּרְכָתָא.

ב) יֵשׁ נוֹהֲגִין לְהִתְפַּלֵּל בְּרֹאשׁ־הַשָּׁנָה וּבְיוֹם־הַכִּפּוּרִים כָּל תְּפִלּוֹת שְׁמוֹנֶה־עֶשְׂרֵה בִּכְרִיעָה וּבִכְפִיפַת הָרֹאשׁ. וְאָמְנָם כֵּיוָן שֶׁצְּרִיכִין לִכְרוֹעַ בְּבִרְכַּת מָגֵן אַבְרָהָם וּבְמוֹדִים בַּתְּחִלָּה וּבַסּוֹף, עַל כֵּן קֹדֶם שֶׁמַּגִּיעַ לִמְקוֹמוֹת אֵלּוּ, צָרִיךְ לִזְקֹף אֶת עַצְמוֹ, כְּדֵי שֶׁיִּכְרַע כְּמִצְוַת חֲכָמֵינוּ זִכְרוֹנָם לִבְרָכָה. גַּם אָסוּר לִכְרוֹעַ בִּתְחִלַּת בְּרָכָה וּבְסוֹף בְּרָכָה בְּמָקוֹם שֶׁלֹּא תִקְּנוּ חֲכָמֵינוּ זִכְרוֹנָם לִבְרָכָה. וְטוֹב יוֹתֵר לְהִתְפַּלֵּל בְּאֵבָרִים זְקוּפִים וּבְלֵב כָּפוּף וּבְדִמָעוֹת. וּמַה שֶּׁנּוֹהֲגִין לְהִתְפַּלֵּל בְּקוֹל רָם, יֵשׁ לְבַטֵּל, כִּי יֵשׁ לְהִתְפַּלֵּל בְּלַחַשׁ כְּמוֹ בְּכָל הַשָּׁנָה. וְיֵשׁ מַתִּירִין לְהַגְבִּיהַּ קוֹלוֹ מְעַט, אֲבָל לֹא הַרְבֵּה. יִזָּהֵר לְדַקְדֵּק בִּתְפִלָּתוֹ הֵיטֵב, שֶׁלֹּא יְשַׁנֶּה שׁוּם נְקֻדָּה. וִיהַדֵּר אַחַר סִדּוּר אוֹ מַחֲזוֹר שֶׁהוּא מְדֻיָּק הֵיטֵב, לְהִתְפַּלֵּל מִתּוֹכוֹ.

ג) כָּל הַשָּׁנָה, אוֹמְרִים בַּתְּפִלָּה, הָאֵל הַקָּדוֹשׁ, מֶלֶךְ אוֹהֵב צְדָקָה וּמִשְׁפָּט, חוּץ מִן רֹאשׁ־הַשָּׁנָה עַד לְאַחַר יוֹם־הַכִּפּוּרִים, שֶׁצְּרִיכִין לוֹמַר, הַמֶּלֶךְ הַקָּדוֹשׁ, הַמֶּלֶךְ הַמִּשְׁפָּט. לְפִי שֶׁבַּיָּמִים הָאֵלּוּ הַקָּדוֹשׁ־בָּרוּךְ־הוּא מַרְאֶה מַלְכוּתוֹ לִשְׁפֹּט אֶת הָעוֹלָם. אִם טָעָה וְאָמַר הָאֵל הַקָּדוֹשׁ, אוֹ

---

18. *Mishnah Berurah* says that you should not immerse yourself in the *mikvah* until an hour before mid-day. (*Ibid* 581:26)

15) You should bathe and have your hair cut on *erev Rosh Hashanah* in honor of Yom Tov. You should have your haircut before midday. You should immerse yourself in the *mikvah.*[18] We wear our Shabbos clothes[19] on *Rosh Hashanah,* to indicate that we trust in the kindness of Hashem, blessed is His Name, to bring forth our judgement as a shining light.

16) It is customary to do *hataras nedarim* [to annul certain vows] on *erev Rosh Hashanah.* (An allusion [for this can be found in the words] *Lo yacheil devaro kechol,* [He must not break his word (Numbers 30:3)]; the last letters of which form the acronym *Elul.*) A person who does not understand what he is reciting in Hebrew, should say it in the language he understands.

Chapter 129

Laws of Rosh Hashanah

1) In all the *kaddish* prayers recited from *Rosh Hashanah* through *Yom Kippur,* you should repeat the word *le'eila* [He is higher]; thus you should say *le'eila le'eila,* [He is exceedingly higher], (without adding the *vav, ule'eila*). Since the *kaddish* must contain twenty-eight words [from *yehei shemei rabba* until *be'alema*] and the entire year you say *le'eila min kol birchasa* [He is beyond any blessing], you say now *le'eila le'eila mikol birchasa.*

2) Some people have the custom when praying on *Rosh Hashanah* and *Yom Kippur* [to pray] every *Shemoneh esrei* with their bodies bent and their heads bowed. However, since you must bow at the berachah, *Magein Avraham* [Shield of Abraham] and *Modim* [we give thanks], at the beginning and at the end, therefore, before reaching these *berachos* it is necessary to straighten up in order to bow as required by our Sages of blessed memory. It is also forbidden to bow at the beginning and at the end of any berachah that was not instituted by our Sages of blessed memory. It is best [therefore] to pray while standing erect,[1] but with a humble heart and with tears. The practice of praying in a loud voice should be abolished, because you should pray quietly as you do the entire year. Some authorities permit to raise the voice slightly, but not too much. You should be careful to pronounce your prayers correctly; not to change even one vowel. You should try to obtain a *Siddur* or *Machzor* that is carefully edited, from which to pray.

3) All through the year you say in the *Shemoneh Esrei, hakeil hakadosh* [the Almighty, the Holy One], and *melech oheiv tzedakah umishpat* [King Lover of righteousness and justice] except from *Rosh Hashanah* until after *Yom Kippur,* when you must say instead *Hamelech hakadosh* (the King, the Holy One) and *Hamelech hamishpat* (the King of Justice), because on these days the Holy One blessed is He manifests His dominion by judging the world. If, by mistake, you said *Hakeil*

---

19. Nevertheless, says *Mishnah Berurah,* you should not wear overly fine and expensive clothing. (*Ibid* 581:25)

1. This *halachah* is not mentioned in *Mishnah Berurah.*

שֶׁהוּא מְסֻפָּק אִם אָמַר הָאֵל הַקָּדוֹשׁ אוֹ הַמֶּלֶךְ הַקָּדוֹשׁ, אִם נִזְכַּר תּוֹךְ כְּדֵי דִבּוּר, אוֹמֵר הַמֶּלֶךְ הַקָּדוֹשׁ, וְאֵינוֹ צָרִיךְ לַחֲזוֹר לְרֹאשׁ, וְכֵן הַדִּין בְּהַמֶּלֶךְ הַמִּשְׁפָּט. אֲבָל אִם לֹא נִזְכַּר עַד לְאַחַר כְּדֵי דִבּוּר, אֲזַי בְּהַמֶּלֶךְ הַקָּדוֹשׁ צָרִיךְ לַחֲזוֹר לְרֹאשׁ הַתְּפִלָּה, (אֲפִלּוּ מִסְּפֵקָא), מִפְּנֵי שֶׁשָּׁלֹשׁ הַבְּרָכוֹת הָרִאשׁוֹנוֹת נֶחְשָׁבוֹת כְּאֶחָת (כְּמוֹ שֶׁכָּתוּב בְּסִימָן יט סָעִיף ב). וַאֲפִלּוּ שְׁלִיחַ־הַצִּבּוּר בַּחֲזָרַת הַתְּפִלָּה צָרִיךְ לַחֲזוֹר לָרֹאשׁ, וּצְרִיכִין לוֹמַר קְדֻשָּׁה שֵׁנִית. אֲבָל בְּהַמֶּלֶךְ הַמִּשְׁפָּט, אֲפִלּוּ יָחִיד אֵינוֹ צָרִיךְ לַחֲזוֹר אֲפִלּוּ לְאוֹתָהּ בְּרָכָה, כֵּיוָן שֶׁהִזְכִּיר תֵּבַת מֶלֶךְ בִּבְרָכָה זֹאת. בְּכָל הַשָּׁנָה אִם טָעָה וְאָמַר, הַמֶּלֶךְ הַקָּדוֹשׁ, הַמֶּלֶךְ הַמִּשְׁפָּט, אֵינוֹ צָרִיךְ לַחֲזוֹר.

ד) בְּשַׁבָּת עַרְבִית, בְּבִרְכַּת מֵעֵין־שֶׁבַע, מָגֵן אָבוֹת וְכוּ', אוֹמְרִים גַּם כֵּן בִּמְקוֹם הָאֵל הַקָּדוֹשׁ, הַמֶּלֶךְ הַקָּדוֹשׁ. וְאִם טָעָה שְׁלִיחַ־הַצִּבּוּר וְאָמַר הָאֵל הַקָּדוֹשׁ, אִם נִזְכַּר מִיָּד תּוֹךְ כְּדֵי דִבּוּר, חוֹזֵר וְאוֹמֵר הַמֶּלֶךְ הַקָּדוֹשׁ וְכוּ'. אֲבָל לְאַחַר כָּךְ, אֵינוֹ חוֹזֵר.

ה) אִם שָׁכַח זָכְרֵנוּ, אוֹ מִי כָמוֹךָ, וּכְתֹב, בְּסֵפֶר חַיִּים, וְלֹא נִזְכַּר עַד שֶׁאָמַר בָּרוּךְ אַתָּה ה', כֵּיוָן שֶׁאָמַר אֶת הַשֵּׁם, גּוֹמֵר אֶת הַבְּרָכָה וּמִתְפַּלֵּל כַּסֵּדֶר, וְאֵינוֹ צָרִיךְ לַחֲזוֹר. וְכֵן אִם שָׁכַח לוֹמַר וּבְכֵן תֵּן פַּחְדְּךָ וְחָתַם הַמֶּלֶךְ הַקָּדוֹשׁ, וַאֲפִלּוּ לֹא אָמַר עֲדַיִן רַק בָּרוּךְ אַתָּה ה', חוֹתֵם הַמֶּלֶךְ הַקָּדוֹשׁ וְאוֹמֵר אַתָּה בְחַרְתָּנוּ וְכוּ'.

ו) בְּסִיּוּם הַשְּׁמוֹנֶה־עֶשְׂרֵה, יֵשׁ מְסַיְּמִים עוֹשֶׂה הַשָּׁלוֹם, וְיֵשׁ שֶׁאֵינָם מְשַׁנִּין אֶלָּא אוֹמְרִים הַמְבָרֵךְ אֶת עַמּוֹ יִשְׂרָאֵל בַּשָּׁלוֹם. וְאַף בַּקַּדִּישִׁים, אוֹמְרִים עוֹשֶׂה הַשָּׁלוֹם בִּמְרוֹמָיו וְכוּ'.

ז) אִם חָל רֹאשׁ־הַשָּׁנָה בְּשַׁבָּת, יֵשׁ מְקוֹמוֹת שֶׁאוֹמְרִים לְכוּ נְרַנְּנָה,

---

2. This is so only if you did not yet begin the next *berachah,* but if you began the next *berachah,* even if it is still within *toch kedei dibur,* you must start from the beginning of *Shemoneh Esrei.* (*Mishnah Berurah* 582:7)

3. However, if you are certain that you *intended* to say *Hamelech hakadosh,* and then much later you became doubtful if you actually said it or not, you need not repeat the *Shemoneh Esrei.* If, however, the doubt came into mind *immediately* after you completed *Shemoneh Esrei,* you must repeat the *Shemoneh Esrei.* (*Ibid* 114:38) If on Rosh Hashanah or Yom Kippur there is a doubt if you said Hamelech hakadosh, you need not repeat the Amidah, since you can assume that you said it as part of the special prayers of Yom Tov. (Ibid 582:4)

hakadosh, or if you are in doubt whether you said *Hakeil hakadosh* or *Hamelech hakadosh;* if you become aware of the error within the time needed to utter a short greeting, [*Shalom Alecha Rebbe*] you should say *Hamelech hakadosh*[2] and you need not start again from the beginning. The same law applies to *Hamelech hamishpat.* But, if you only became aware of it after the time needed for a short greeting, then, at *Hamelech hakadosh* you must repeat *Shemoneh Esrei* from the beginning, (even if in doubt),[3] because the first three *berachos* are considered as one (as is written in Chapter 19:2). Even the *Chazzan* during the repetition of the *Shemoneh Esrei,* must repeat from the beginning [if he did not say *Hamelech hakadosh*], and the *kedusha* must be said again. But at *Hamelech hamishpat,* even an individual need not repeat, even that berachah, since he mentioned the word *melech* "King" in that berachah. During the entire year, if you said, by mistake, *Hamelech hakadosh* or *Hamelech hamishpat,* you need not repeat the *Shemoneh Esrei.*

4) In the *Maariv* service on Friday night, in the abridged form of the seven berachos, in *Magein avos* (Shield of our forefathers etc.) you also say, instead of *Hakeil hakadosh* the words *Hamelech hakadosh.* If the *Chazzan* made an error and said *Hakeil hakadosh,* then, if he becomes aware of it immediately, within the time span needed for a short greeting, he should say *Hamelech hakadosh etc.;* but if he becomes aware of it later he need not repeat the berachah.

5) If you forgot to say *Zochreinu* [Remember us], or *Mi chamocha* [Who is like You], or *Uchsov* [And inscribe], or *Beseifer chayim* [In the book of life] and you do not become aware of it until you said *Baruch ata Hashem,* [Blessed are You, Hashem], since you mentioned *Hashem,* you should conclude the berachah,[4] and continue the *Shemoneh Esrei,* and you need not repeat it. Similarly, if you forgot to say [the entire section beginning with] *Uvechein tein pachdecha* [And so, grant that Your awe] and you concluded the berachah, *Hamelech hakadosh,* even if you only said *Baruch ata Hashem,* you should conclude *Hamelech hakadosh,* and then say *Ata vechartanu* [You have chosen us] etc.

6) At the conclusion of the *Shemoneh esrei,* some are accustomed to say *Oseh* ha *shalom* [He Who makes *the* peace], while others do not change, and say [the usual text], *Hamevareich es amo Yisrael ba shalom,* [Who blesses His people Israel with peace]. But in the *kaddish,* we say *Ose* ha *shalom bimeromav* [He Who makes *the* peace in His high heavens.]

7) If *Rosh Hashanah* occurs on Shabbos, in some communities they say *Lechu neranenah* [Come, let us sing], the same as on any other Shabbos; in other commu-

---

4. However, if you did not yet say the Hashem of the berachah, you may go back and say whatever you omitted. (*Ibid* 582:15)

כְּמוֹ בִּשְׁאָר שַׁבָּת. וְיֵשׁ מְקוֹמוֹת שֶׁמַּתְחִילִין, מִזְמוֹר לְדָוִד. וְיֵשׁ מְקוֹמוֹת שֶׁמַּתְחִילִין, מִזְמוֹר שִׁיר לְיוֹם הַשַּׁבָּת. וְכָל מָקוֹם יַחֲזִיק מִנְהָגוֹ.

ח) לְאַחַר גְּמַר תְּפִלַּת מַעֲרִיב בְּלֵיל רִאשׁוֹן, נוֹהֲגִין לוֹמַר כָּל אֶחָד לַחֲבֵרוֹ, לְשָׁנָה טוֹבָה תִּכָּתֵב וְתֵחָתֵם. וְלִנְקֵבָה אוֹמְרִים, תִּכָּתְבִי וְתֵחָתֵמִי. אֲבָל בַּיּוֹם, אֵין אוֹמְרִים, לְפִי שֶׁכְּבָר נִגְמְרָה הַכְּתִיבָה קֹדֶם חֲצוֹת הַיּוֹם. וּבְלֵיל שֵׁנִי, יֵשׁ נוֹהֲגִין לְאָמְרוֹ, כִּי לִפְעָמִים נִדּוֹנִין בְּיוֹם שֵׁנִי.

ט) בִּסְעוּדַת הַלַּיְלָה, נוֹהֲגִין לַעֲשׂוֹת סִימָנִים לְשָׁנָה טוֹבָה. טוֹבְלִין פְּרוּסַת הַמּוֹצִיא בִּדְבַשׁ. וְאַחַר שֶׁאָכַל כַּזַּיִת, אוֹמֵר, יְהִי רָצוֹן שֶׁתְּחַדֵּשׁ עָלֵינוּ שָׁנָה טוֹבָה וּמְתוּקָה. וְאַחַר כָּךְ טוֹבֵל קְצָת תַּפּוּחַ מָתוֹק בִּדְבַשׁ וּמְבָרֵךְ עָלָיו בּוֹרֵא פְּרִי הָעֵץ וְאוֹכְלוֹ, וְאַחַר כָּךְ אוֹמֵר גַּם כֵּן יְהִי רָצוֹן וְכוּ׳. וְנוֹהֲגִין לֶאֱכֹל רֹאשׁ שֶׁל בַּעַל־חַי וְאוֹמְרִים, יְהִי רָצוֹן שֶׁנִּהְיֶה לְרֹאשׁ. וְיֵשׁ לְהַדֵּר אַחַר רֹאשׁ כֶּבֶשׂ, שֶׁיִּהְיֶה גַּם כֵּן זֵכֶר לְאֵילוֹ שֶׁל יִצְחָק. גַּם אוֹכְלִים אוֹתָן־הַיְרָקוֹת שֶׁיֵּשׁ לָהֶם בַּמְּדִינָה הַהִיא שֵׁם הַמּוֹרֶה לְטוֹבָה, כְּמוֹ בִּמְדִינָתֵנוּ גֶּזֶר (מעהרען), וְאוֹמְרִים, יְהִי רָצוֹן שֶׁיִּרְבּוּ זְכֻיּוֹתֵינוּ. וְיֵשׁ נוֹהֲגִין גַּם כֵּן לְהַדֵּר לֶאֱכֹל דָּגִים, שֶׁיֵּשׁ רֶמֶז לִפְרוֹת וְלִרְבּוֹת כְּמוֹ הַדָּגִים. וְאֵין לְבַשֵּׁל אוֹתָם בְּחֹמֶץ, כִּי אֵין אוֹכְלִים דְּבָרִים חֲמוּצִים אוֹ מְרִירִים בְּרֹאשׁ־הַשָּׁנָה. וְאוֹכְלִים בָּשָׂר שָׁמֵן וְכָל מִינֵי מְתִיקָה. גַּם נוֹהֲגִין שֶׁלֹּא לֶאֱכוֹל אֱגוֹזִים וְלוּזִים, כִּי אֱגוֹז בְּגִימַטְרִיָּא חֵ״ט, וְגַם מַרְבִּים כִּיחָה וְנִיעָה הַמְבַטְּלִים אֶת הַתְּפִלָּה. וְיֵשׁ לִלְמֹד עַל הַשֻּׁלְחָן תּוֹרָה. וְנוֹהֲגִין קְצָת לִלְמֹד מִשְׁנָיוֹת מַסֶּכֶת רֹאשׁ־הַשָּׁנָה.

י) נָכוֹן שֶׁלֹּא לְשַׁמֵּשׁ מִטָּתוֹ בִּשְׁנֵי לֵילוֹת דְּרֹאשׁ־הַשָּׁנָה, אֲפִלּוּ כְּשֶׁחָל בַּשַּׁבָּת. אַךְ אִם הוּא לֵיל טְבִילָתָהּ, לֹא יְבַטֵּל עוֹנָתָהּ. וְיִטְבֹּל אֶת עַצְמוֹ בַּבֹּקֶר מִטֻּמְאָתוֹ.

יא) בְּרֹאשׁ־הַשָּׁנָה, כְּשֶׁאוֹמֵר אָבִינוּ מַלְכֵּנוּ חָטָאנוּ לְפָנֶיךָ, אֵין לְהַכּוֹת

5. *Magein Avrohom* says these wishes may be extended until midday. (*Mishnah Berurah* 582:25)

6. This is the opinion of *Taz,* however, *Eliyahu Rabbah* argues against this and maintains that this blessing is not said on the second day. (*Ibid*)

7. *Mishnah Berurah* does not mention *kazayas,* but only that the prayer should be said after you eat some of the bread. (*Ibid* 583:4) He does rule however that you should not speak until you have eaten a *kazayis.*

nities they begin with *Mizmor leDovid* [A psalm of David]; still in other communities they begin with *Mizmor shir leyom haShabbos* [A Psalm, a song for the Shabbos day]. Every community should follow its custom.

8) After the *Maariv* service on the first night of *Rosh Hashanah,* it is customary for people to wish each other *Leshanah tovah tikaseiv veseichaseim* [May you be inscribed and sealed for a good year], and to a woman [you use the feminine form] *tikaseivi veseichaseimi.* But you do not extend these wishes in the daytime,[5] because the writing has been finished before midday. On the second night, some have the custom of saying [*Leshanah tovah*] because sometimes we are judged on the second day.[6]

9) At the evening meal it is customary to prepare symbolic dishes [as auspicious omens] for a good year: you dip the piece of *challah* of *Hamotzi* in honey, and after eating a *kazayis* of *challah*[7] you should say: *Yehi ratzon shetechadeish aleinu*[8] *shanah tovah umesukah* [May it be Your will to renew for us a good and sweet year]. After this you should dip a piece of apple in honey, say the berachah, *Borei peri ha'eitz,* and eat it. Then you say again *Yehi ratzon etc.* It is customary to eat the head of an animal and say *Yehi ratzon shenih'yeh lerosh* [May it be Your will] that we will be heads (leaders). You should try to obtain the head of a sheep, which will also serve as a remembrance of the ram of Isaac. You should also eat vegetables the names of which, in the language of your country, allude to good things,[9] such as in our country, carrots (*mehren*) [*mehren* means to increase] and you should say *Yehi ratzon sheyirbu zechuyoseinu* [May it be Your will that our merits increase.] Some people have the custom to eat an elaborate fish course, symbolizing the blessing of fertility like the fish. The fish should not be cooked in vinegar because we must not eat sour or bitter foods on *Rosh Hashanah.* You should eat choice meats and all kinds of sweets. It is also customary not to eat nuts and almonds,[10] because the numerical value of אֱגוֹז *egoz* (nut) is 17, the same as חֵט *cheit,* which means sin. Also, nuts increase phlegm and mucus which interferes with praying. It is proper to study Torah during the meal. Some have the custom of studying the *Mishnah, Maseches Rosh Hashanah.*

10) It is proper to abstain from marital relations during the two nights of *Rosh Hashanah* even if [the first night] occurs on Shabbos. But if it is the night of her immersion in the *mikvah,* you should not withold her conjugal rights, and you should immerse yourself in the *mikvah,* in the morning.

11) On *Rosh Hashanah,* when you say *Avinu malkeinu chatanu lefanecha* [Our Father, our King, we have sinned before You] you should not beat your breast as on

---

8. You should say: יְהִי רָצוֹן מִלְּפָנֶיךָ ה׳ אֱלֹקַי וֵאלֹקֵי אֲבוֹתַי שֶׁתְּחַדֵּשׁ עָלֵינוּ שָׁנָה טוֹבָה וּמְתוּקָה "May it be Your will Almighty, my G-d, and G-d of my fathers" etc. (*Ibid* 583:21)

9. You should certainly avoid any semblance of anger during these days. You should be of good cheer and have full confidence in the Almighty's acceptance of your repentance and good deeds. (*Ibid* 583:5)

10. *Mishnah Berurah* quotes form *Maaseh Rav* that the *Vilna Gaon* did not eat grapes on Rosh Hashanah. (*Ibid* 600:4)

בָּאֶגְרוֹף עַל הֶחָזֶה כְּמוֹ בְּחֹל וּבְיוֹם־הַכִּפּוּרִים, כִּי אֵין אוֹמְרִים וִדּוּי בְּרֹאשׁ־הַשָּׁנָה, שֶׁהוּא יוֹם־טוֹב. אֶלָּא יְכַוֵּן הַפֵּרוּשׁ, אָבִינוּ מַלְכֵּנוּ חָטָאנוּ לְפָנֶיךָ, כְּלוֹמַר, אֲבוֹתֵינוּ חָטְאוּ לְפָנֶיךָ שֶׁעָבְדוּ עֲבוֹדָה־זָרָה, אֲבָל אֲנַחְנוּ אֵין לָנוּ מֶלֶךְ אֶלָּא אָתָּה. לָכֵן אָבִינוּ מַלְכֵּנוּ, עֲשֵׂה עִמָּנוּ לְמַעַן שְׁמֶךָ.

יב) בִּשְׁעַת הוֹצָאַת סֵפֶר־תּוֹרָה, נוֹהֲגִין לוֹמַר שְׁלֹשׁ עֶשְׂרֵה מִדּוֹת, וְיֵשׁ לְהַתְחִיל מִן, וַיַּעֲבֹר. וְיֹאמַר, וַיַּעֲבֹר ה' עַל פָּנָיו וַיִּקְרָא, ה', ה' וְגוֹ'. וּבְשַׁבָּת, יֵשׁ מְקוֹמוֹת שֶׁאֵין אוֹמְרִים שְׁלֹשׁ־עֶשְׂרֵה מִדּוֹת, וְלֹא רִבּוֹנוֹ שֶׁל עוֹלָם.

יג) שִׁעוּר הַתְּקִיעוֹת, לְכַתְּחִלָּה צָרִיךְ לִהְיוֹת כָּךְ, הַתְּרוּעָה הִיא תִּשְׁעָה כֹּחוֹת קְצָרִים. וְהַשְּׁבָרִים יַעֲשֶׂה שְׁלֹשָׁה שְׁבָרִים זֶה אַחַר זֶה, וְכָל שֶׁבֶר יְהֵא אָרוֹךְ כְּמוֹ שְׁלֹשָׁה כֹּחוֹת קְצָרִים מִן הַתְּרוּעָה, וְנִמְצָא שֶׁגַּם הַשְּׁבָרִים הֵם כְּמוֹ תִּשְׁעָה כֹּחוֹת. וְיִזָּהֵר מְאֹד שֶׁלֹּא לְהַאֲרִיךְ בִּשְׁבָרִים עַד שֶׁיְּהֵא כָּל שֶׁבֶר כְּמוֹ תִּשְׁעָה כֹּחוֹת. כִּי בָזֶה, אֲפִלּוּ בְּדִיעֲבַד אֵינוֹ יוֹצֵא. וְהַתְּקִיעוֹת הִנֵּה הֲבָרוֹת פְּשׁוּטוֹת. וּבְסֵדֶר תְּקִיעָה שְׁבָרִים תְּרוּעָה תְּקִיעָה, תְּהֵא כָּל תְּקִיעָה, אֲרֻכָּה כְּמוֹ הַשְּׁבָרִים עִם הַתְּרוּעָה, דְּהַיְנוּ כְּמוֹ שְׁמוֹנָה־עָשָׂר כֹּחוֹת. וּבְסֵדֶר תְּקִיעָה שְׁבָרִים תְּקִיעָה, תְּהֵא כָּל תְּקִיעָה, אֲרֻכָּה כְּמוֹ הַשְּׁבָרִים, דְּהַיְנוּ כְּמוֹ תִּשְׁעָה כֹּחוֹת. וְכֵן בְּסֵדֶר תְּקִיעָה תְּרוּעָה תְּקִיעָה. בַּתְּקִיעוֹת שֶׁקֹּדֶם תְּפִלַּת מוּסָף, יֵשׁ לַעֲשׂוֹת הַשְּׁבָרִים עִם הַתְּרוּעָה בִּנְשִׁימָה אֶחָת. וְלָכֵן הַמַּקְרֵא יַקְרֵא בְּפַעַם אַחַת שְׁבָרִים־תְּרוּעָה. וּבַתְּקִיעוֹת שֶׁבְּתוֹךְ חֲזָרַת הַתְּפִלָּה, יֵשׁ לַעֲשׂוֹתָם בִּשְׁתֵּי נְשִׁימוֹת. וּמִכָּל מָקוֹם לֹא יַפְסִיק בֵּינֵיהֶם, אֶלָּא יִהְיוּ תְּכוּפִים זֶה לָזֶה, וְהַמַּקְרֵא יַקְרֵא גַם כֵּן שְׁנֵיהֶם בְּפַעַם אֶחָת.

יד) כְּשֶׁהַתּוֹקֵעַ אוֹמֵר אֶת הַבְּרָכוֹת, אַל יֹאמְרוּ הַקָּהָל, בָּרוּךְ הוּא וּבָרוּךְ שְׁמוֹ (עַיֵּן לְעֵיל סִימָן ו סָעִיף ח), אַךְ יִשְׁמְעוּ הֵיטֵב אֶת הַבְּרָכוֹת, וְאַחַר כָּל בְּרָכָה יֹאמְרוּ בְּכַוָּנָה אָמֵן. וְאָסוּר לְהַפְסִיק מִכָּאן עַד לְאַחַר כָּל הַתְּקִיעוֹת שֶׁבַּחֲזָרַת הַתְּפִלָּה. וְעַל כֵּן אֵין לַשַּׁמָּשׁ לְהַכְרִיז, שְׁתִיקָה יָפָה בִּשְׁעַת הַתְּפִלָּה, אַף שֶׁהוּא נוֹהֵג כֵּן בְּפַעַם אַחֶרֶת.

טו) נוֹהֲגִין הָעוֹלָם לוֹמַר בֵּין הַסְּדָרִים יְהִי רָצוֹן וְכוּ', כְּמוֹ שֶׁנִּדְפַּס בְּמַחֲזוֹרִים. וּצְרִיכִין לִזָּהֵר מְאֹד, שֶׁלֹּא לְהוֹצִיא בַּפֶּה שְׁמוֹת הַמַּלְאָכִים

weekdays and on *Yom Kippur,* because we do not say *vidui* —confession, on *Rosh Hashanah,* which is a Yom Tov. You should have this interpretation in mind [when saying *Avinu malkeinu*]: Our Father, our King, we have sinned before You, meaning, our forefathers sinned before You, because they worshiped idols, but as for us, we have no King but You. Therefore, our Father, our King, deal [kindly] with us for Your Name's sake.

12) When the *Seifer Torah* is removed from the Ark, it is customary to recite the Thirteen Attributes. You should begin with *Vaya'avor* [and He passed by], and say *Vaya'avor Hashem al panav vayikra*[11] [Hashem passed by before him and He proclaimed] Hashem, Hashem, etc. On Shabbos, in some communities they say neither the Thirteen Attributes nor *Ribbono shel olam* [Master of the Universe].

13) The lengths of the various *shofar* tones, initially must be as follows: the *Teruah* consists of nine short sounds. The *Shevarim* should be blown as three consecutive sounds, each to be as long as three short *Teruah* sounds, so that the *Shevarim* is also equal to nine sounds. You should be very careful not to draw out the *Shevarim* until each [of the three] *Shevarim* sounds equals nine *Teruah* sounds, for in that case, even ex post facto, after it is already done, you have not fulfilled your duty. The *Tekios* are simple blasts. In the order of *Tekiah, Shevarim, Teruah, Tekiah,* each *Tekiah* should be as long as the *Shevarim* and the *Teruah,* combined, which is as long as eighteen sounds.[12] In the order of *Tekiah, Shevarim, Tekiah,* the sound of each *Tekiah* should be as long as the *Shevarim,* which is as long as nine sounds;[13] this is also true for the order of *Tekiah, Teruah, Tekiah.* In the sounding of the *shofar* before the *Musaf* service the *Shevarim* and the *Teruah* should be blown in one breath. Therefore, the prompter should call them at the same time, *Shevarim-Teruah.* In the blowing of the *shofar* during the repetition of the *Shemoneh Esrei,* they should be sounded in two breaths. Nevertheless, there should be no pause between them, but they should be sounded in immediate succession, and the prompter should also call them at the same time.

14) When the one blowing the *shofar* recites the *berachos,* the congregation should not respond *Baruch hu uvaruch shemo* [Blessed is He and blessed is His Name] (see chapter 6:8, above), but they should listen attentively to the *berachos* and after each berachah they should respond *Amein,* with concentration. It is forbidden to make any interruption from that point until after all the *Tekios* that are blown during the repetition of the *Shemoneh Eesrei.*[14] Therefore, the *Shammos* should not announce: "Silence please during the services!" even if he usually does so at other times.

15) People have the custom to recite *Yehi ratzon* [May it be the will] etc., between the three sets of *shofar* tones, as it is printed in the *Machzor.* You should be very

11. This is not mentioned in *Mishnah Berurah* nor is it the custom in many communities.
12. *Mishnah Berurah* says that it should be a bit longer than eighteen sounds. (*Ibid* 590:14)
13. *Mishnah Berurah* says that it should be a bit longer than nine sounds. (*Ibid* 590:13)
14. Between the *tekios* blown before *Shemoneh Esrei,* and those blown during the repetition of *Shemoneh Esrei,* it is permitted to interrupt if it concerns either the prayers or the *tekios.* (*Ibid* 592:12)

הַנִּזְכָּרִים שָׁם. וּבְהַרְבֵּה קְהִלּוֹת אֵין אוֹמְרִים כְּלָל אֶת הַיְּהִי רָצוֹן, וְכֵן נָכוֹן יוֹתֵר. וְהָעִקָּר הוּא לְהִתְעוֹרֵר אָז בִּתְשׁוּבָה בְּלֵב שָׁלֵם. וּכְמוֹ שֶׁכָּתַב הָרַמְבַּ"ם זִכְרוֹנוֹ לִבְרָכָה (בְּהִלְכוֹת תְּשׁוּבָה פֶּרֶק ג הֲלָכָה ד), וְזֶה לְשׁוֹנוֹ, אַף־עַל־פִּי שֶׁתְּקִיעַת שׁוֹפָר בְּרֹאשׁ־הַשָּׁנָה גְּזֵרַת הַכָּתוּב, רֶמֶז יֵשׁ בָּהּ, כְּלוֹמַר, עוּרוּ יְשֵׁנִים מִשְּׁנַתְכֶם, וְנִרְדָּמִים הָקִיצוּ מִתַּרְדֵּמַתְכֶם, וְחַפְּשׂוּ בְּמַעֲשֵׂיכֶם, וְחִזְרוּ בִּתְשׁוּבָה, וְזִכְרוּ בּוֹרַאֲכֶם אֵלּוּ הַשּׁוֹכְחִים אֶת הָאֱמֶת בְּהַבְלֵי הַזְּמָן וְשׁוֹגִים כָּל שְׁנָתָם בְּהֶבֶל וָרִיק אֲשֶׁר לֹא יוֹעִיל וְלֹא יַצִּיל, הַבִּיטוּ לְנַפְשׁוֹתֵיכֶם, וְהֵטִיבוּ דַּרְכֵיכֶם וּמַעַלְלֵיכֶם. יַעֲזֹב כָּל אֶחָד מִכֶּם דַּרְכּוֹ הָרָעָה וּמַחֲשַׁבְתּוֹ אֲשֶׁר לֹא טוֹבָה וְכוּ', עַד כָּאן לְשׁוֹנוֹ.

טז) בַּחֲזָרַת הַתְּפִלָּה, כְּשֶׁאוֹמֵר שְׁלִיחַ־הַצִּבּוּר וַאֲנַחְנוּ כּוֹרְעִים, נוֹהֲגִין שֶׁגַּם הַצִּבּוּר אוֹמְרִים עִמּוֹ, וְגַם כּוֹרְעִים וּמִשְׁתַּחֲוִים, אֲבָל אֵין נוֹפְלִים עַל פְּנֵיהֶם, רַק בְּיוֹם־הַכִּפּוּרִים בְּסֵדֶר הָעֲבוֹדָה. וְגַם שְׁלִיחַ־הַצִּבּוּר כּוֹרֵעַ עַל בִּרְכָּיו, אֲבָל אָסוּר לַעֲקֹר מִמְּקוֹמוֹ בִּשְׁעַת הַתְּפִלָּה. וְלָכֵן נוֹהֲגִין שֶׁיַּעֲמֹד קְצָת רָחוֹק מִן הָעַמּוּד, כְּדֵי שֶׁיּוּכַל לִכְרוֹעַ עַל בִּרְכָּיו בְּלִי עֲקִירָה מִמְּקוֹמוֹ, וְהָעוֹמְדִים אֶצְלוֹ מְסַיְּעִים אוֹתוֹ לַעֲמוֹד, שֶׁלֹּא יִצְטָרֵךְ לַעֲקֹר רַגְלָיו. הַתְּקִיעוֹת שֶׁבְּתוֹךְ חֲזָרַת הַתְּפִלָּה, אֵין לִשְׁלִיחַ־הַצִּבּוּר לִתְקֹעַ, אֶלָּא אִם הוּא בָּטוּחַ שֶׁלֹּא תִתְבַּלְבֵּל דַּעְתּוֹ עַל יְדֵי כָּךְ.

יז) בַּתְּקִיעוֹת שֶׁבְּתוֹךְ חֲזָרַת הַתְּפִלָּה, יֵשׁ מִנְהָגִים שׁוֹנִים כַּמָּה תוֹקְעִין, וְכָל מָקוֹם יַחֲזִיק מִנְהָגוֹ. וְכֵן בַּתְּקִיעוֹת שֶׁלְּאַחַר הַתְּפִלָּה, יֵשׁ מִנְהָגִים שׁוֹנִים. וּלְאַחַר שֶׁגָּמְרוּ כָּל הַתְּקִיעוֹת כְּפִי מִנְהַג הַמָּקוֹם, יֵשׁ לְהַצְנִיעַ אֶת הַשּׁוֹפָר וְלֹא יִתְקְעוּ יוֹתֵר. אֲפִלּוּ מִי שֶׁרוֹצֶה לִהְיוֹת תּוֹקֵעַ בְּיוֹם שֵׁנִי, אֵין לוֹ לִתְקֹעַ בְּיוֹם רִאשׁוֹן לְהִתְלַמֵּד.

יח) אִם יֵשׁ מִילָה, מָלִין לְאַחַר הַהַפְטָרָה קֹדֶם תְּקִיעַת שׁוֹפָר. וְהָרֶמֶז, זְכֹר בְּרִית אַבְרָהָם (זוֹ מִילָה). וַעֲקֵדַת יִצְחָק (זֶה שׁוֹפָר). וּבְשַׁבָּת, מָלִין אַחַר אַשְׁרֵי. וְאִם צְרִיכִין לָמוּל אֵצֶל הַיּוֹלֶדֶת, מָלִין אַחַר הַיְצִיאָה מִבֵּית־הַכְּנֶסֶת.

יט) מִי שֶׁיָּצָא בִּתְקִיעַת שׁוֹפָר וְצָרִיךְ לִתְקֹעַ בִּשְׁבִיל אֲחֵרִים, יָכוֹל גַּם

---

15. It is our custom, however, that the people in the congregation do fall on their faces even on *Rosh Hashanah.* We must be careful to place a mat, towel or another object on the floor because it is forbidden to fall on our faces directly on the floor. (See *Shaarei Tzion* 131:44; *Mishnah Berurah* 621:14; *Ibid* 131:40)

careful not to articulate the names of the angels mentioned there. In many communities the *Yehi ratzon* is omitted entirely, and this is preferable. The main [reason for blowing the *shofar*] is to stir the people to wholehearted repentance. The *Rambam,* of blessed memory wrote, (Laws of Repentance 3:4) and these are his words: "Although the blowing of the *shofar* on *Rosh Hashanah,* is ordained by Scriptural verse, it has an underlying message, as if the *shofar* were telling us, 'Wake up from your sleep, you slumberers, and you who are soundly asleep, awake from your deep sleep, scrutinize your deeds and repent, and remember your Creator. You, who are oblivious of the truth in your futile pursuit of transitory values, and engrossed all your years in the pursuit of vain and hollow things that are useless and will not save you, — look at the state of your souls, and improve your ways and your deeds. Let each of you abandon his evil ways and his thoughts which are not good.'"

16) During the repetition of the *Shemoneh Esrei* when the *Chazzan* recites [the prayer] *Va'anachnu kore'im* [But we bow], it is customary for the congregation to say it along with him, and the people also bow and prostrate themselves, but they do not fall on their faces,[15] except on *Yom Kippur,* during the *Avodah* [the service of the *Kohein gadol.*] The *Chazzan* also bows, but since he is forbidden to move from his place during the *Shemoneh Esrei;* therefore, he stands slightly removed from the *amud* [*Chazzan's* desk] so that he can fall to his knees without moving from his place, and those who stand near him help him stand up so that he will not have to move his feet. The *Tekios* during the repetition of the *Shemoneh Esrei* should not be blown by the *Chazzan* unless he is sure that he will not be confused [in his prayers][16] as a result of it.

17) Regarding the *Tekios* in the repetition of the *Shemoneh Esrei,* there are different customs regarding the number of sounds to be blown. Each community should maintain its custom. Regarding the *Tekios* at the conclusion of the prayers, there are also different customs.[17] After the conclusion of all the *Tekios,* according to the local custom, the *shofar* should be hidden, and it should not be blown any more. Even a person wishing to officiate as *tokei'a* on the second day of *Rosh Hashanah* may not blow it on the first day in order to practice.

18) If a *bris* is to be held in the synagogue it should be performed after the reading of the *haftarah,* before the blowing of the *shofar.* An allusion [to this sequence can be found in the *Selichos* prayer] "Remember the covenant with Abraham (this refers to *bris milah*) and the binding of Isaac" (this alludes to the *shofar*). On Shabbos the *bris* is performed after *Ashrei.* If the *bris* must be performed at the house of the infant's mother, it should be held after leaving the synagogue.

19) If you already fulfilled your obligation of blowing the *shofar,* and you must

---

16. In our time, since the *Chazzan* uses the *Siddur* or *Machzor,* he is considered as one who is sure not to become confused in his prayers. (*Ibid* 585:14)

17. These *tekios* are blown in order to complete a hundred sounds.

כֵּן לְבָרֵךְ אֶת הַבְּרָכוֹת. וּמִכָּל מָקוֹם יוֹתֵר נָכוֹן שֶׁזֶּה שֶׁצָּרִיךְ לָצֵאת, הוּא יְבָרֵךְ אֶת הַבְּרָכוֹת. וְהַתּוֹקֵעַ בִּשְׁבִיל נָשִׁים, אִם הוּא כְּבָר יָצָא, לֹא יְבָרֵךְ אֶת הַבְּרָכוֹת, אֶלָּא הָאִשָּׁה תְּבָרֵךְ, כֵּיוָן דְּמִצַּד הַדִּין נָשִׁים פְּטוּרוֹת מִתְּקִיעַת שׁוֹפָר, מִשּׁוּם דַּהֲוֵי מִצְוַת עֲשֵׂה שֶׁהַזְּמָן גְּרָמָהּ. וְיֵשׁ אוֹמְרִים, דְּמִי שֶׁיָּצָא, לֹא יִתְקַע כְּלָל בִּשְׁבִיל נָשִׁים. וְהָרוֹצֶה לִתְקֹעַ בִּשְׁבִיל נָשִׁים, יִתְקַע קֹדֶם שֶׁיִּשְׁמַע הַתְּקִיעוֹת בְּבֵית־הַכְּנֶסֶת, וִיבָרֵךְ עַל הַתְּקִיעוֹת וִיכַוֵּן שֶׁיֵּצֵא בָּהֶן, וּבִלְבַד שֶׁלֹּא יִהְיֶה זֶה בְּשָׁלֹשׁ הַשָּׁעוֹת הָרִאשׁוֹנוֹת שֶׁל הַיּוֹם, כִּי אָז אֵין לִתְקֹעַ בִּיחִידוּת, אוֹ שֶׁיִּתְקַע לָהֶן בְּשָׁעָה שֶׁתּוֹקְעִין בְּבֵית־הַכְּנֶסֶת, אוֹ לְאַחַר הַתְּקִיעוֹת שֶׁבְּבֵית־הַכְּנֶסֶת, אֶלָּא שֶׁיְּכַוֵּן שֶׁלֹּא לָצֵאת בִּתְקִיעוֹת אֵלּוּ, אֶלָּא בַּתְּקִיעוֹת שֶׁהוּא יִתְקַע לִפְנֵי הָאִשָּׁה וִיבָרֵךְ עֲלֵיהֶן. וְאַף־עַל־גַּב שֶׁהוֹלֵךְ אַחַר כָּךְ לְבֵית־הַכְּנֶסֶת לְהִתְפַּלֵּל מוּסָף וְלִשְׁמֹעַ הַתְּקִיעוֹת שֶׁבַּתְּפִלָּה, אֵין הַהֶפְסֵק מַצְרִיכוֹ לְבָרֵךְ שֵׁנִית, דְּכֻלְּהוּ תְּקִיעוֹת חֲדָא מִצְוָה נִינְהוּ. וְאִם הָאִשָּׁה חֲלוּשָׁה וּצְרִיכָה לֶאֱכוֹל קֹדֶם הַתְּקִיעוֹת, יְכוֹלָה לֶאֱכוֹל.

כ) כְּשֶׁיּוֹצְאִין מִבֵּית־הַכְּנֶסֶת, יֵשׁ לָלֶכֶת בְּשׁוּבָה וָנַחַת, שָׂמֵחַ וְטוֹב לֵב, בְּבִטָּחוֹן כִּי שָׁמַע ה׳ בְּקוֹל תְּפִלָּתֵנוּ וּתְקִיעוֹתֵינוּ בְּרַחֲמִים, וְאוֹכְלִין וְשׁוֹתִין כְּיַד ה׳ הַטּוֹבָה. וּמִכָּל מָקוֹם יִזָּהֵר שֶׁלֹּא לֶאֱכֹל אֲכִילָה גַּסָּה, וּתְהֵא יִרְאַת ה׳ עַל פָּנָיו. וְיֵשׁ לִלְמֹד תּוֹרָה עַל הַשֻּׁלְחָן. לְאַחַר בִּרְכַּת־הַמָּזוֹן, אֵין לִישׁוֹן, אֶלָּא הוֹלְכִין לְבֵית־הַכְּנֶסֶת וְאוֹמְרִים תְּהִלִּים בְּצִבּוּר עַד תְּפִלַּת מִנְחָה. וְאַךְ מִי שֶׁרֹאשׁוֹ כָּבֵד עָלָיו, יָכוֹל לִישׁוֹן מְעַט קֹדֶם שֶׁיֵּלֵךְ לְבֵית־הַכְּנֶסֶת.

כא) לְאַחַר תְּפִלַּת מִנְחָה הוֹלְכִין אֶל הַנָּהָר (לִזְכֹּר זְכוּת הָעֲקֵדָה, דְּאִיתָא בְּמִדְרָשׁ, כְּשֶׁהָלַךְ אַבְרָהָם אָבִינוּ עִם יִצְחָק בְּנוֹ לָעֲקֵדָה, עָשָׂה הַשָּׂטָן אֶת עַצְמוֹ כְּמוֹ נָהָר לְעַכְּבוֹ, וְעָבַר אַבְרָהָם אָבִינוּ, עָלָיו הַשָּׁלוֹם, בַּנָּהָר עַד צַוָּארוֹ וְאָמַר, הוֹשִׁיעֵנִי אֱלֹהִים כִּי בָאוּ מַיִם עַד נָפֶשׁ. וְעוֹד יֵשׁ טַעַם, מִפְּנֵי שֶׁאָנוּ מַמְלִיכִין הַיּוֹם אֶת הַקָּדוֹשׁ־בָּרוּךְ־הוּא עָלֵינוּ, וְהַדֶּרֶךְ הוּא לִמְשֹׁחַ אֶת הַמְּלָכִים אֵצֶל הַנָּהָר, לְרֶמֶז שֶׁתִּמָּשֵׁךְ מַלְכוּתָם). וְטוֹב

---

18. *Shulchan Aruch* (589:6) says that it is permitted to blow shofar for women even if you have already fulfilled your obligations. *Mishnah Berurah* does not even mention any authority that says it is not permitted.

19. *Ari Z'l* says that it is permitted to nap after midday. He adds that one who sits idle,

blow it for other people, you may also say the *berachos*. Nevertheless, it is best, that the person who has to fulfill his obligation [by virtue of listening to you blowing the *shofar*], should say the *berachos* himself. If you blow *shofar* for women, then, if you already fulfilled your obligation, you should not say the *berachos*, but the women should say the *berachos*, because, according to the law, women are exempt from blowing the *shofar*, since it is a positive precept dependent on a particular time. Other authorities say that a person who has already fulfilled his duty should not blow the *shofar* at all for women.[18] If you wish to blow the *shofar* for women you should do it before hearing the *Tekios* at the synagogue; and you should say the *berachos* on the *Tekios* with the intention of fulfilling your obligation thereby, but you should not do it during the first three hours of the day, for at that time you may not blow the *shofar* privately. You should either blow the *shofar* for the women at the time it is blown in the synagogue or after that; but you should have in mind [when you are in the synagogue] not to fulfill your duty with these *Tekios* but only with the *Tekios* which you will sound for the women, and [on these *Tekios*] you should say the *berachos*. Although you will go to the synagogue afterwards to pray *Musaf*, and hear the *Tekios* sounded during the *Shemoneh Esrei*, the interruption does not require you to repeat the *berachos*, since all the *Tekios* constitute one mitzvah. If a woman feels weak and needs to eat before the *Tekios*, she is permitted to eat.

20) When leaving the synagogue, we should walk unhurried and relaxed, happy and cheerful, confident that God has heard our prayers and the sounds of the *shofar* with compassion. You should eat and drink [in generous measure] enjoying the bountiful gifts of God. You should, nevertheless, take care not to overeat and the fear of God should be upon you. It is proper to study Torah at the table. After saying *Birkas Hamazon* you should not go to sleep,[19] but rather go to the synagogue and recite Psalms with the congregation[20] until the *Minchah* service. Only a person who has a headache may sleep a little before going to the synagogue.

21) After the *Minchah* service[21] you should go to a river [or stream] (to recall the merit of the *Akeidah*, [the binding of Yitzchak] for the *Midrash* relates that when our Father Avraham went to the *Akeidah* with his son Yitzchak, Satan transformed himself into a river to deter him. But our Father Avraham, peace be upon him, walked into the river until [the water reached] his neck and said, "Deliver me, O God, for the waters have reached until my soul." (Psalm 69:2) There is another reason [for this custom]; for on this day we proclaim the kingship of the Holy One, blessed is He, over us, and it was the custom to anoint kings near a river bank as a sign that their kingdom may endure without end.)[22] It is preferable that [this river]

---

not engaged in Torah study or reciting Psalms, is considered as one who is asleep. (*Mishnah Berurah* 583:9)

20. If possible, you should study Torah. It is also customary, to recite the entire book of Psalms. (*Ibid*)

21. This should be done before *sunset*. (*Ibid*)

22. *Maseches Horayos* 12a.

שֶׁיִּהְיֶה מִחוּץ לָעִיר וְיֵשׁ בּוֹ דָּגִים (לְזֵכֶר שֶׁאָנוּ מְשׁוּלִים כְּדָגִים חַיִּים הַלָּלוּ שֶׁנֶּאֱחָזִים בִּמְצוֹדָה, כָּךְ אָנוּ נֶאֱחָזִים בִּמְצוֹדַת הַמָּוֶת וְהַדִּין, וּמִתּוֹךְ כָּךְ נִהְרְהֵר יוֹתֵר בִּתְשׁוּבָה. עוֹד טַעַם, לְסִימָן שֶׁלֹּא תִשְׁלֹט בָּנוּ עַיִן רָעָה, כְּמוֹ בַּדָּגִים, וְנִפְרֶה וְנִרְבֶּה כַּדָּגִים. וְיֵשׁ אוֹמְרִים, הַטַּעַם, כִּי לַדָּגִים אֵין גְּבִינִים, וְעֵינֵיהֶם תָּמִיד פְּתוּחוֹת, כְּדֵי לְעוֹרֵר עֵינָא פְּקִיחָא דִּלְעֵלָּא). וְאִם אֵין שָׁם נָהָר שֶׁיֵּשׁ בּוֹ דָגִים, הוֹלְכִין לְנָהָר אַחֵר אוֹ לִבְאֵר, וְאוֹמְרִים הַפְּסוּקִים מִי אֵל כָּמוֹךָ וְכוּ', כַּכָּתוּב בַּסִּדּוּרִים בְּסֵדֶר תַּשְׁלִיךְ. וּמְנַעֲרִים שׁוּלֵי הַבְּגָדִים, וְהוּא לְרֶמֶז בְּעָלְמָא, לִתֵּן לֵב לְהַשְׁלִיךְ אֶת הַחֲטָאִים וּלְחַפֵּשׂ וְלַחֲקֹר דְּרָכָיו מֵהַיּוֹם וָהָלְאָה שֶׁיִּהְיוּ בְגָדָיו לְבָנִים וּנְקִיִּים מִכָּל חֵטְא. אִם חָל יוֹם רִאשׁוֹן בַּשַּׁבָּת, הוֹלְכִין בְּיוֹם שֵׁנִי.

כב) לְאַחַר שֶׁחוֹזְרִין לְבֵית־הַכְּנֶסֶת וַעֲדַיִן לֹא הִגִּיעַ זְמַן עַרְבִית, יִזָּהֵר מֵחֶבְרַת מְרֵעִים, שֶׁלֹּא יָבוֹא, חַס וְשָׁלוֹם, לִדְבָרִים בְּטֵלִים. אַךְ יַעֲסֹק בַּתּוֹרָה אוֹ בִּתְהִלִּים אוֹ בְּסִפְרֵי מוּסָר, כִּי קָדוֹשׁ הַיּוֹם לַאֲדוֹנֵנוּ.

כג) שְׁנֵי יָמִים טוֹבִים שֶׁל רֹאשׁ־הַשָּׁנָה, כְּיוֹם אֶחָד אָרֹךְ הֵן חֲשׁוּבִים, וּקְדֻשָּׁה אַחַת הֵן. (עַיֵּין לְעֵיל סִימָן צ"ט סְעִיף ב') וְלָכֵן נֶחְלְקוּ הַפּוֹסְקִים, אִם לְבָרֵךְ בְּלֵיל שֵׁנִי בַּקִּדּוּשׁ וְכֵן בְּהַדְלָקַת הַנֵּרוֹת וְכֵן בִּתְקִיעוֹת שֶׁל יוֹם שֵׁנִי שֶׁהֶחֱיָנוּ אוֹ לֹא, כִּי יֵשׁ אוֹמְרִים, כֵּיוָן דִּקְדֻשָּׁה אַחַת הֵן וּכְבָר בֵּרַךְ שֶׁהֶחֱיָנוּ בָּרִאשׁוֹן, אֵינוֹ צָרִיךְ לְבָרֵךְ עוֹד בַּשֵּׁנִי. וְעַל כֵּן נוֹהֲגִים שֶׁבַּקִּדּוּשׁ לֵיל שֵׁנִי, מַנִּיחִין עַל הַשֻּׁלְחָן פְּרִי חָדָשׁ, שֶׁתְּהֵא בִרְכַּת שֶׁהֶחֱיָנוּ שֶׁבַּקִּדּוּשׁ גַּם עַל הַפְּרִי, אוֹ שֶׁלּוֹבֵשׁ בֶּגֶד חָדָשׁ. וְאִם אֵין לוֹ, אֵינוֹ מְעַכֵּב, וְאוֹמֵר שֶׁהֶחֱיָנוּ בַּקִּדּוּשׁ, (כִּי אָנוּ תוֹפְסִין הָעִקָּר כְּהַפּוֹסְקִים שֶׁאוֹמְרִים שֶׁצָּרִיךְ לְבָרֵךְ שֶׁהֶחֱיָנוּ). וְכֵן הָאִשָּׁה בְּהַדְלָקַת הַנֵּרוֹת בְּלֵיל שֵׁנִי (אִם נוֹהֶגֶת לְבָרֵךְ שֶׁהֶחֱיָנוּ, אֲזַי עַל־כָּל־פָּנִים) אִם אֶפְשָׁר, תִּלְבַּשׁ בֶּגֶד חָדָשׁ אוֹ תַּנִּיחַ פְּרִי חָדָשׁ, שֶׁתְּהֵא בִּרְכַּת שֶׁהֶחֱיָנוּ גַּם עַל זֶה. וְאִם אֵין לָהּ, אֵינוֹ מְעַכֵּב. וְכֵן הַתּוֹקֵעַ בְּיוֹם שֵׁנִי, אִם אֶפְשָׁר, יֵשׁ לוֹ לִלְבּוֹשׁ בֶּגֶד חָדָשׁ. וְאִם חָל יוֹם רִאשׁוֹן בַּשַּׁבָּת, אֵינוֹ צָרִיךְ, דְּהָא עֲדַיִן לֹא בֵּרְכוּ שֶׁהֶחֱיָנוּ עַל הַשּׁוֹפָר.

should be outside the city limits and it should contain fish (as a reminder that we are compared to living fish who are caught in a net. We too, are caught in the net of death and judgment, and as a result [we will be inclined] to think more of repenting. Another reason is to symbolize that the evil eye shall have no power over us, just as [it has no power] over fish, and that we may be fruitful and multiply as the fish. Others say the reason is that fish have no eyelids, and their eyes are always open, the purpose is thus to arouse the compassion of the All-Seeing Eye above us.) But if there is no river that contains fish you may go to any river, or to a well, and you should recite the verses, *Mi keil kamocha* [Who, Almighty, is like you] etc. as it is written in the prayer books in the text of *Tashlich*. You should then shake the ends of your clothes, symbolizing your resolve to cast away your sins, and to examine and scrutinize your ways, from now on; so that your "clothes" will be white and innocent of all sin. If the first day of *Rosh Hashanah* is on Shabbos you go [to the stream for *Tashlich*] on the second day.

22) After returning to the synagogue, if it is not yet time for *Maariv* you should avoid the company of friends in order not to engage, Heaven forbid, in idle talk. But you should study Torah or recite Psalms or study books on ethics, because this is a holy day unto our Master.

23) The two days of *Rosh Hashanah* are considered as one long day, and as one [extended period of] holiness (see Chapter 99:2 above). Therefore, the authorities differ whether in the *Kiddush* of the second night, or when lighting candles, or when blowing the *shofar* on the second day, you should say the berachah *Shehecheyanu* or not. For some authorities say, since both days are one [extended period of] holiness and you already said *Shehecheyanu* on the first day, you need not say it again on the second day. Therefore, it is the custom, when you recite the *Kiddush* on the second night, that a new fruit is placed on the table, in order that the *Shehecheyanu* in the *Kiddush* should also apply to the fruit; You might also put on a new garment. If you have neither [a new fruit nor a new suit], it does not matter; you should still say *Shehecheyanu* in the *Kiddush*, for the *Halachah* is decided according to the authorities who say that we must say *Shehecheyanu* on the second night. A woman, too, when lighting the candles on the second night, (if she follows the custom of saying *Shehecheyanu*,)[23] should nevertheless, put on a new garment if possible, or place a new fruit [on the table], so that the *Shehecheyanu* should apply also to these. But if she has neither of these it does not matter; she should still say *Shehecheyanu*. Also the person who blows the *shofar* on the second day should, if possible, put on a new garment. However, if the first day occurs on Shabbos there is no need for this, for he has not yet said *Shehecheyanu* on the *shofar*.

23. See *Kitzur Shulchan Aruch* 103:4

סִימָן קל

דִּינֵי עֲשֶׂרֶת יְמֵי תְשׁוּבָה

א) עֲשֶׂרֶת יְמֵי תְשׁוּבָה, שְׁמָם מוֹרֶה עֲלֵיהֶם, שֶׁהֵם מְיֻחָדִים לִתְשׁוּבָה. וְכָל אָדָם מְחֻיָּב אָז לָשׁוּב בִּתְשׁוּבָה שְׁלֵמָה לִפְנֵי ה׳, יִתְבָּרַךְ שְׁמוֹ, קֹדֶם בּוֹא הַיּוֹם הַגָּדוֹל וְהַנּוֹרָא יוֹם־הַכִּפּוּרִים, שֶׁנֶּאֱמַר, לִפְנֵי ה׳ תִּטְהָרוּ. וְנֶאֱמַר, דִּרְשׁוּ ה׳ בְּהִמָּצְאוֹ, וְאָמְרוּ רַבּוֹתֵינוּ זִכְרוֹנָם לִבְרָכָה, אֵלּוּ עֲשָׂרָה יָמִים שֶׁבֵּין רֹאשׁ־הַשָּׁנָה לְיוֹם־הַכִּפּוּרִים. לָכֵן צָרִיךְ הָאָדָם בַּיָּמִים הָאֵלּוּ לְפַשְׁפֵּשׁ בְּמַעֲשָׂיו וְלָשׁוּב מִמַּעֲשָׂיו הָרָעִים. וּסְפֵק עֲבֵרָה צָרִיךְ יוֹתֵר תְּשׁוּבָה מֵעֲבֵרָה וַדָּאִית, כִּי יוֹתֵר מִתְחָרֵט הָאָדָם כְּשֶׁהוּא יוֹדֵעַ שֶׁעָשָׂה עֲבֵרָה מֵאִם אֵינוֹ יוֹדֵעַ, וְלָכֵן קָרְבַּן אָשָׁם תָּלוּי צָרִיךְ לִהְיוֹת יוֹתֵר בְּיֹקֶר מִקָּרְבַּן חַטָּאת. וְיַרְבֶּה בַּתּוֹרָה וּבְמִצְוֹת וּבִצְדָקָה, וִימַעֵט בַּעֲסָקָיו. וְכָתַב הָרַב רַבֵּנוּ מֹשֶׁה קוֹרְדוֹבֵרוֹ, זִכְרוֹנוֹ לִבְרָכָה, שֶׁיִּהְיוּ יָמִים אֵלּוּ כְּמוֹ חֹל הַמּוֹעֵד, שֶׁלֹּא יַעֲשֶׂה בָהֶם אֶלָּא מְלָאכָה הֶכְרֵחִית. וּבְיוֹתֵר צָרִיךְ הָאָדָם לְתַקֵּן דְּבָרִים שֶׁבֵּינוֹ לְבֵין חֲבֵרוֹ, אֲשֶׁר עֲלֵיהֶם אֵין כַּפָּרָה עַד שֶׁיַּחֲזִיר אֶת הַגָּזֵל וְאֶת הָעֹשֶׁק, וִיפַיְּסוֹ שֶׁיִּמְחוֹל לוֹ.

ב) רָאוּי לְאָדָם שֶׁיִּתְנַהֵג בַּיָּמִים הָאֵלּוּ גַּם בַּחֲמְרוֹת שֶׁאֵינוֹ נוֹהֵג בָּהֶם כָּל הַשָּׁנָה, כִּי גַּם אָנוּ מְבַקְשִׁים מֵאֵת ה׳, יִתְבָּרַךְ שְׁמוֹ, שֶׁיִּתְנַהֵג עִמָּנוּ בַּחֲסִידוּת. וְהָאוֹכֵל כָּל הַשָּׁנָה פַּת פַּלְטֵר, לֹא יֹאכַל בַּיָּמִים הָאֵלּוּ כִּי אִם פַּת יִשְׂרָאֵל, וְכַדּוֹמֶה לָזֶה.

ג) בְּבִרְכַּת־הַמָּזוֹן, יֵשׁ נוֹהֲגִין לוֹמַר הָרַחֲמָן הוּא יְחַדֵּשׁ וְכוּ׳, כְּמוֹ בְּרֹאשׁ־הַשָּׁנָה.

ד) נוֹהֲגִין שֶׁלֹּא לַעֲשׂוֹת נִשּׂוּאִין בַּיָּמִים הָאֵלּוּ.

ה) בְּשַׁבַּת שׁוּבָה, יֵשׁ לִקְרוֹת לַמַּפְטִיר, אָדָם חָשׁוּב.

ו) יֵשׁ נוֹהֲגִין שֶׁאֵין מְקַדְּשִׁין אֶת הַלְּבָנָה עַד מוֹצָאֵי יוֹם־הַכִּפּוּרִים, שֶׁאָז שְׂמֵחִים, וּמִקֹּדֶם הָיוּ בִּדְאָגָה. וְיֵשׁ אוֹמְרִים, דְּאַדְּרַבָּה, טוֹב לְקַדְּשָׁהּ קֹדֶם, כְּדֵי לְהוֹסִיף בִּזְכֻיּוֹת. וְהַכֹּל לְפִי הַזְּמַן. בְּמָקוֹם שֶׁמָּצוּי לִקְנוֹת

---

1. It is also sufficient if you present the case in all honesty before a Rav or *Posek* and ask him to decide what you should do. It is, however, by no means proper for you to decide on your own, for regarding matters of money, the *Yeitzer Harah* (evil inclination) will help you find many loopholes. (*Mishnah Berurah* 606:1)

Chapter 130

Laws Relating to the Ten Days of Repentance

1) The Ten Days of Repentance, as characterized by their name, are designated for repentance. During this time everyone is obligated to repent wholeheartedly before God, blessed is His Name, before the coming of the great and awesome day, of *Yom Kippur,* as it is said, "Before God you will be cleansed" (Leviticus 16:30). It is also said, "Seek God when He may be found", (Isaiah 55:6) and our Rabbis of blessed memory said, that this refers to the ten days between *Rosh Hashanah* and *Yom Kippur.* Therefore, during these days you must examine your conduct and repent of your bad deeds. Sins about which you are in doubt require greater repentance than transgressions of which you are certain, for a person is more regretful when he knows that he committed a sin, than when he is uncertain of it. Therefore, the guilt offering brought in case of doubtful sin must be of greater value than a regular sin offering. During these days You should study more Torah, perform more mitzvohs, give more charity, and spend less time on your business. It was written by Rabbi Moshe Cordovero, of blessed memory, that you should consider these days as if they were *Chol Hamoed,* by performing only necessary work. Above all, you must set right the wrongs you committed against your fellow man, for which there is no atonement unless you compensate him for any stolen articles or withheld funds[1] in your possession, and patch things up and placate him so that he will forgive you.

2) It is proper to observe stringencies during these days that you do not observe the rest of the year, for we also ask of God, blessed is His Name, that He deal with us with exceptional kindness. For example, if during the rest of the year, you eat bread from a non-Jewish bakery, during these days you should eat only bread baked by a Jew; and you should observe similar stringencies.

3) When reciting *Birkas Hamazon,* there are some who have the custom of saying *Harachaman hu yechadeish* [the Compassionate One, may He renew] etc. as we do on *Rosh Hashanah.*

4) It is customary not to get married during these days.

5) On Shabbos *Shuvah* [the Shabbos during the Ten Days of Repentance] an eminent person should be called up for *maftir.*[2]

6) Some people have the custom not to sanctify the moon before the conclusion of *Yom Kippur,* for then everybody is joyful, whereas before *Yom Kippur* they are apprehensive about the outcome of their judgment Others maintain that, on the contrary, it is better to sanctify the moon before *Yom Kippur* in order to add to our merits with this mitzvah. It all depends on the prevailing custom. In a region where

---

2. *Mishnah Berurah* merely states that a youth should not be called up for *Maftir* on this Shabbos. (*Mishnah Berurah* 602:11)

אֶתְרוֹגִים, לוּלָבִין וַהֲדַסִּים, נוֹהֲגִין אַנְשֵׁי מַעֲשֶׂה לִהְיוֹת זְרִיזִין מַקְדִּימִים לִקְנוֹת בַּיָּמִים הָאֵלּוּ, כְּדֵי שֶׁתִּצְטָרֵף גַּם הַמִּצְוָה הַיְקָרָה הַזֹּאת לִזְכֻיּוֹתֵינוּ.

סִימָן קלא
דִּינֵי עֶרֶב יוֹם־כִּפּוּר

א) נוֹהֲגִין לַעֲשׂוֹת כַּפָּרוֹת בְּעֶרֶב יוֹם־הַכִּפּוּרִים בְּאַשְׁמֹרֶת הַבֹּקֶר, שֶׁאָז הָרַחֲמִים גּוֹבְרִין. לוֹקְחִין תַּרְנְגוֹל שֶׁאֵינוֹ מְסֹרָס, לְזָכָר, וְתַרְנְגֹלֶת לִנְקֵבָה. וּלְאִשָּׁה מְעֻבֶּרֶת, תַּרְנְגוֹל וְתַרְנְגֹלֶת. תַּרְנְגוֹל, שֶׁמָּא הַוָּלָד הוּא זָכָר. וְאִם הַוָּלָד הוּא נְקֵבָה, דַּי לְאִמָּהּ וּלְבִתָּהּ בְּתַרְנְגֹלֶת אַחַת. וַאֲפִלּוּ שְׁאָר בְּנֵי אָדָם, יְכוֹלִין שְׁנַיִם לִקַּח כַּפָּרָה אַחַת. וּבוֹחֲרִים בִּלְבָנִים, עַל שֵׁם שֶׁנֶּאֱמַר, אִם יִהְיוּ חֲטָאֵיכֶם כַּשָּׁנִים כַּשֶּׁלֶג יַלְבִּינוּ. אֲבָל אֵין לַחֲזֹר בְּפֵרוּשׁ בִּשְׁעַת קְנִיָּה אַחַר לְבָנִים וְלִקְנוֹתָם בְּיֹקֶר, כִּי זֶהוּ כְּעֵין דַּרְכֵי הָאֱמוֹרִי, אֶלָּא כְּשֶׁיִּזְדַּמֵּן לוֹ לָבָן, שֶׁקָּנָה אוֹתוֹ בֵּין אֲחֵרִים, יִבְחַר בּוֹ. לוֹקֵחַ כָּל אֶחָד כַּפָּרָתוֹ בְּיָדוֹ הַיְמָנִית, וְאוֹמֵר הַפְּסוּקִים, בְּנֵי אָדָם וְגוֹ', וּמְסַבְּבָהּ סָבִיב רֹאשׁוֹ וְאוֹמֵר, זֶה חֲלִיפָתִי וְכוּ' שָׁלֹשׁ פְּעָמִים. אִם מְסַבֵּב לְאַחֵר, אוֹמֵר, זֶה חֲלִיפָתְךָ. וְיֵשׁ לוֹ לְסַבֵּב תְּחִלָּה לְעַצְמוֹ וְאַחַר כָּךְ לַאֲחֵרִים. וְטוֹב שֶׁתְּהֵא הַשְּׁחִיטָה גַּם כֵּן בְּאַשְׁמֹרֶת הַבֹּקֶר תֵּכֶף לְאַחַר הַסִּבּוּב. וְאַל יַחְשֹׁב הָאָדָם שֶׁזּוֹהִי כַּפָּרָתוֹ מַמָּשׁ, אֶלָּא יַחְשֹׁב כִּי כָל מַה שֶּׁעוֹשִׂין בָּעוֹף הַזֶּה, הָיָה רָאוּי לָבוֹא עָלָיו בַּעֲוֹנוֹתָיו. וְיִתְאוֹנֵן עַל חֲטָאָיו, וְהַקָּדוֹשׁ־בָּרוּךְ־הוּא בְּרַחֲמָיו יְקַבֵּל תְּשׁוּבָתוֹ. וְנוֹהֲגִין לִזְרוֹק בְּנֵי הַמֵּעַיִם וְהַכָּבֵד וְהַכְּלָיוֹת שֶׁל הַכַּפָּרוֹת עַל הַגַּגּוֹת אוֹ בֶּחָצֵר, מְקוֹם שֶׁהָעוֹפוֹת יְכוֹלִים לָקַחַת מִשָּׁם, לְפִי שֶׁרָאוּי לְרַחֵם עַל הַבְּרִיּוֹת בְּיוֹם זֶה, כְּדֵי שֶׁיְּרַחֲמוּ עָלָיו מִן הַשָּׁמַיִם. וְעוֹד, מִפְּנֵי שֶׁאָכְלוּ גָּזֵל, כְּדֵי שֶׁיִּתֵּן הָאָדָם אֶל לִבּוֹ לְהַרְחִיק אֶת עַצְמוֹ מִן הַגָּזֵל. אִם אֵין תַּרְנְגוֹלִים מְצוּיִים, יָכוֹל לִקַּח אַוָּז אוֹ שְׁאָר בַּעַל חַי שֶׁאֵינוֹ רָאוּי לְהַקְרָבָה. וְיֵשׁ אוֹמְרִים, אֲפִלּוּ דָגִים, אַךְ לֹא תּוֹרִין וּבְנֵי יוֹנָה, שֶׁהֵם רְאוּיִין לְהַקְרָבָה, וִיהֵא נִרְאֶה כְּאִלּוּ מַקְדִּישׁ קָדָשִׁים בַּחוּץ. יֵשׁ נוֹהֲגִים לִתֵּן אֶת הַכַּפָּרוֹת לַעֲנִיִּים, אֲבָל יוֹתֵר טוֹב לִפְדּוֹת אֶת הַכַּפָּרוֹת בְּמָמוֹן וְלִתֵּן אֶת הַמָּמוֹן לַעֲנִיִּים.

---

1. Others say that she should take two hens, one for herself and one should she be carrying a girl. (*Mishnah Berurah* 605:3

2. Where there are many chickens to be killed and a large number of people present, who pressure the *shochet* to do their chicken, it is best to do the *kapparah* ritual several days *before*

esrogim, lulavim and *hadassim* are for sale, it is the custom of pious men to purchase them ahead of time, so that during these days this precious mitzvah may be added to their merits.

Chapter 131

Laws of Erev Yom Kippur

1) It is customary to perform the *kapparos* ritual *erev Yom Kippur,* early in the morning, for then God's compassion is at its height. Men take roosters and women take hens, and a pregnant woman takes a rooster and a hen. The rooster is taken in case she is carrying a male; and if the child is a girl, one hen suffices for the mother and the child.[1] Even for other people, one *kapparah* is sufficient for two persons. You should select white chickens, for it is said, "Though your sins will be like scarlet they will become white as snow." (Isaiah 1:18). But when buying, you should not express preference for white fowl and pay a higher price for it, for this resembles the customs of the Amorites [superstition]. But if you happen to find a white one among the fowl you bought, you should choose [the white one.] You take the *kapparah* in your right hand, and recite the verses *Benei Adam* [children of man] etc., move it around your head, and say: *Zeh chalifasi* [This is instead of me] etc. three times. If you move it around someone else's head, you say *Zeh chalifasecha* [This is instead of you]. You should first move it around your own head and then do it for others. It is preferable that the *shechitah* is done also early in the morning, immediately after the *kapparos* ritual.[2] You should not think that this *kapparah* ritual is an actual atonement, but you should consider that what is done to the fowl should be rightfully done to you, because of your sins. You should agonize over your sins, and the Holy One blessed is He, in His compassion, will accept your repentance. It is customary to throw the intestines, the liver and the kidneys of the *kapparos,* on the roof or into the courtyard, where the birds can take them, for it is appropriate to take pity on living creatures on that day, so that Heaven will take pity on us. Another reason is that birds usually steal the seeds they eat [we, therefore, throw away their digestive organs] so that we should be mindful to keep away from theft. If you cannot obtain chickens for *kapparos*, you can take a goose or some other living thing that is not ritually acceptable as a sacrifice on the altar in the *Beis Hamikdash*. Some authorities say that even fish [may be used], but not pigeons or young doves, because these were acceptable as altar sacrifices, and it would appear as if you were bringing sacrifices outside the *Beis Hamikdash* [which is forbidden]. Some people follow the custom of giving the *kapparos* chickens to the poor, but it is better to redeem the *kapparos* with money, and give the money to the poor.[3]

Yom Kippur, rather than cause the *shochet* to kill the chicken improperly. He will be unable to inspect his knife properly before killing each chicken and this could cause the chicken to be *treife* (not kosher). It is also possible to avoid this problem by using money rather than chickens to do the *kapporos* ritual. (*Ibid* 605:2)

3. The poor person might be humiliated by the thought that you rid yourself of your sins through this chicken and now are sending it to him. (*Ibid* 605:5)

ב) אֵין אוֹמְרִים מִזְמוֹר לְתוֹדָה, וְלֹא תַּחֲנוּן, וְלֹא לַמְנַצֵּחַ. גַּם אֵין אוֹמְרִים אָבִינוּ מַלְכֵּנוּ. וְרַק כְּשֶׁחָל יוֹם־הַכִּפּוּרִים בַּשַּׁבָּת, אָז אוֹמְרִים עֶרֶב יוֹם־הַכִּפּוּרִים בְּשַׁחֲרִית אָבִינוּ מַלְכֵּנוּ.

ג) מִצְוָה לְהַרְבּוֹת בִּסְעוּדָה וְלֶאֱכֹל וְלִשְׁתּוֹת. וְכָל הָאוֹכֵל וְשׁוֹתֶה בְּעֶרֶב יוֹם־הַכִּפּוּרִים לְשֵׁם מִצְוָה, נֶחְשָׁב לוֹ כְּאִלּוּ הִתְעַנָּה גַּם הַיּוֹם. וּמִצְוָה לֶאֱכֹל דָּגִים בַּסְּעוּדָה הָרִאשׁוֹנָה.

ד) עֲבֵרוֹת שֶׁבֵּין אָדָם לַחֲבֵרוֹ, אֵין יוֹם־הַכִּפּוּרִים מְכַפֵּר עַד שֶׁיְּרַצֶּה אֶת חֲבֵרוֹ, שֶׁנֶּאֱמַר, מִכֹּל חַטֹּאתֵיכֶם לִפְנֵי ה׳ תִּטְהָרוּ. כְּלוֹמַר, חַטֹּאתֵיכֶם שֶׁהֵם לִפְנֵי ה׳ בִּלְבַד, יוֹם־הַכִּפּוּרִים מְכַפֵּר. אֲבָל מַה שֶּׁבֵּין אָדָם לַחֲבֵרוֹ, אֵין יוֹם־הַכִּפּוּרִים מְכַפֵּר, עַד שֶׁיְּרַצֶּה אֶת חֲבֵרוֹ. לָכֵן צָרִיךְ כָּל אָדָם לְדַקְדֵּק, שֶׁאִם יֵשׁ בְּיָדוֹ מָמוֹן שֶׁל אֲחֵרִים שֶׁלֹּא כַּדִּין, יַחֲזִיר לוֹ וִיפַיֵּס אוֹתוֹ. וְאִם יֵשׁ בְּיָדוֹ מָמוֹן שֶׁהוּא מְסֻפָּק בּוֹ, אִם הוּא שֶׁלּוֹ עַל פִּי הַדִּין אוֹ לֹא, יוֹדִיעַ לַחֲבֵרוֹ שֶׁהוּא רוֹצֶה לַעֲמֹד עִמּוֹ מִיָּד לְאַחַר יוֹם־הַכִּפּוּרִים לְדִין הַתּוֹרָה הַקְּדוֹשָׁה, וִיקַבֵּל עָלָיו בֶּאֱמֶת לְקַיֵּם כַּאֲשֶׁר יֵצֵא מִפִּי בֵּית־הַדִּין. וְגַם אִם לֹא חָטָא כְּנֶגֶד חֲבֵרוֹ אֶלָּא בִּדְבָרִים, צָרִיךְ לְפַיְּסוֹ, וּמְחֻיָּב לָלֶכֶת בְּעַצְמוֹ לְפַיְּסוֹ. אַךְ אִם קָשֶׁה עָלָיו, אוֹ שֶׁהוּא מֵבִין כִּי יוֹתֵר קָרוֹב שֶׁיִּתְפַּיֵּס עַל יְדֵי אֶמְצָעִי, יַעֲשֶׂה עַל יְדֵי אֶמְצָעִי. וְהָאִישׁ אֲשֶׁר מְבַקְשִׁין מִמֶּנּוּ מְחִילָה, יִמְחוֹל בְּלֵב שָׁלֵם וְלֹא יְהֵא אַכְזָרִי, כִּי אֵין זֶה מִמִּדַּת יִשְׂרָאֵל, אֶלָּא מִמִּדַּת עֵשָׂו, שֶׁעָלָיו נֶאֱמַר, וְעֶבְרָתוֹ שְׁמָרָה נֶצַח. וְכֵן הוּא אוֹמֵר עַל הַגִּבְעוֹנִים, לְפִי שֶׁלֹּא מָחֲלוּ וְלֹא נִתְפַּיְּסוּ, וְהַגִּבְעוֹנִים לֹא מִבְּנֵי יִשְׂרָאֵל הֵמָּה. אֲבָל דַּרְכָּן שֶׁל זֶרַע יִשְׂרָאֵל הוּא לִהְיוֹת קָשֶׁה לִכְעֹס וְנוֹחַ לִרְצוֹת. וּכְשֶׁהַחוֹטֵא מְבַקֵּשׁ מִמֶּנּוּ לִמְחוֹל, יִמְחוֹל בְּלֵב שָׁלֵם וּבְנֶפֶשׁ חֲפֵצָה. וַאֲפִלּוּ הֵצֵר לוֹ הַרְבֵּה, לֹא יִקֹּם וְלֹא יִטֹּר. וְאַדְּרַבָּה, אִם הַחוֹטֵא אֵינוֹ מִתְעוֹרֵר לָבוֹא אֵלָיו לְבַקֵּשׁ מְחִילָה, יֶשׁ לוֹ לְהָאִישׁ הֶעָלוּב לְהַמְצִיא אֶת עַצְמוֹ לְאוֹתוֹ שֶׁחָטָא, כְּדֵי שֶׁיְּבַקֵּשׁ מִמֶּנּוּ מְחִילָה. וּמִי שֶׁאֵינוֹ מַעֲבִיר שִׂנְאָה בְּיוֹם־הַכִּפּוּרִים, אֵין תְּפִלָּתוֹ נִשְׁמַעַת, חַס וְשָׁלוֹם. וְכָל הַמַּעֲבִיר עַל מִדּוֹתָיו, מַעֲבִירִין לוֹ עַל כָּל פְּשָׁעָיו.

ה) אִם מֵת זֶה הָאִישׁ אֲשֶׁר חָטָא כְּנֶגְדּוֹ, מֵבִיא עֲשָׂרָה אֲנָשִׁים וּמַעֲמִידָן עַל קִבְרוֹ, וְאוֹמֵר, חָטָאתִי לֵאלֹהֵי יִשְׂרָאֵל וּלְזֶה הָאִישׁ פְּלוֹנִי שֶׁחָטָאתִי לוֹ. וְהֵם יָשִׁיבוּ לוֹ, מָחוּל לָךְ, מָחוּל לָךְ, מָחוּל לָךְ. וְיֵשׁ לוֹ לֵילֵךְ יָחֵף. גַּם יֵשׁ לוֹ לְפָרֵט אֶת הַחֵטְא אִם אֵינוֹ בִּזָּיוֹן לְהַמֵּת. אִם קֶבֶר

2) We do not say *Mizmor lesodah* [a Psalm of thanksgiving], nor *Tachanun,* nor *Lamenatzei'ach* on *erev Yom Kippur* . Neither do we recite *Avinu malkeinu* [our Father, our King]. Only when *Yom Kippur* occurs on Shabbos, do we say *Avinu malkeinu* on *erev Yom Kippur* in the *Shacharis* service.

3) It is a mitzvah to have elaborate meals and to eat and drink [abundantly]. The person who eats and drinks on *erev Yom Kippur* in order to fulfill this mitzvah, it is regarded to him, as if he fasted on that day also. It is a mitzvah to eat fish at the first meal.

4) Sins committed against your fellow man are not atoned for on Yom Kippur unless you placate him, as it is said, "You will be cleansed of all your sins before God." This means, only sins against God are atoned for on *Yom Kippur,* but sins committed against your neighbor are not atoned for on *Yom Kippur,* unless you placate your neighbor. Everyone must, therefore, be very careful, if he has in his possession illegally acquired property, to return it and placate [the rightful owner]. If you are holding property of which you are not certain whether or not it legally belongs to you, you should let your neighbor know that you wish to appear with him, immediately after *Yom Kippur,* before a *Beis Din* Rabbinical court to be judged according to the holy Torah; and you should firmly resolve to abide by the verdict pronounced by the *Beis Din.* If you sinned against your neighbor, even if only with words, you must appease him. It is your duty to go personally to appease him. However, if it is difficult for you to do so, or if you understand that he will be reconciled more easily through an intermediary, you should appease him through an intermediary. The person whose forgiveness is asked should forgive wholeheartedly and should not be ruthless, for this is not a Jewish characteristic, but a trait of Esau of whom it is said, "And he kept his anger forever" (Amos 1:11). It is also said of the Gibeonites, because they did not forgive and would not be appeased, "The Gibeonites were not of the Children of Israel." (II Samuel 21:2) The characteristic of the Children of Israel is to be slow to anger and easy to be appeased. And when the sinner asks for forgiveness you should grant forgiveness wholeheartedly and willingly. Even if he tormented you a great deal you should not take revenge nor bear a grudge. On the contrary, if the offender does not take the initiative to come to you asking for forgiveness, you should present yourself to the offender in order that [the offender] should ask your forgiveness. If a person does not banish hatred [from his heart] on *Yom Kippur,* his prayers will not be heard, God forbid; but if you are tolerant and forgiving, all your sins will be forgiven.

5) If the wronged person has died, the offender should gather ten men at his grave, and say, "I have sinned against the God of Israel and against this man" and they respond, "You are forgiven, you are forgiven, you are forgiven." He should walk barefoot, and spell out in detail the nature of the offense, unless it

הַמֵּת הוּא חוּץ לְשָׁלֹשׁ פַּרְסָאוֹת מִן הַמָּקוֹם שֶׁדָּר בּוֹ הַחוֹטֵא, אֵינוֹ צָרִיךְ לֵילֵךְ בְּעַצְמוֹ לְשָׁם, אֶלָּא יִשְׁלַח שְׁלִיחוֹ, וְהַשָּׁלִיחַ יִקַּח שָׁם עֲשָׂרָה אֲנָשִׁים וְיֵלֵךְ עַל קִבְרוֹ, וְיֹאמַר, הִנְנִי שָׁלִיחַ שֶׁל פְּלוֹנִי, מוֹדֶה בָרַבִּים, שֶׁשְּׁלָחַנִי פְלוֹנִי לְבַקֵּשׁ מְחִילָה עַל מַה שֶּׁחָטָא וְכוּ'. אִם חֵרֵף אָדָם לְאַחַר מוֹתוֹ, אֵינוֹ צָרִיךְ לֵילֵךְ עַל קִבְרוֹ, אֶלָּא יְבַקֵּשׁ מִמֶּנּוּ מְחִילָה בְּמָקוֹם שֶׁחֵרְפוֹ. וְאִם הוֹצִיא עָלָיו שֵׁם רָע, צָרִיךְ לְקַבֵּל עַל עַצְמוֹ תְּשׁוּבָה, עַל שֶׁעָבַר חֵרֶם הַקַּדְמוֹנִים שֶׁלֹּא לְהוֹצִיא שֵׁם רָע עַל מֵתִים.

ו) מִצְוָה עַל כָּל אָדָם לִטְבֹּל אֶת עַצְמוֹ בְּעֶרֶב יוֹם־הַכִּפּוּרִים לִטַהֵר מִטֻּמְאַת קֶרִי. וְעוֹד, מִשּׁוּם תְּשׁוּבָה, וּכְמוֹ גֵר שֶׁנִּתְגַּיֵּר שֶׁצָּרִיךְ טְבִילָה. וְלָכֵן גַּם נְעָרִים וּבְתוּלוֹת, יֵשׁ לָהֶם לִטְבֹּל. וְיֵשׁ לְדַקְדֵּק שֶׁלֹּא תְהֵא עָלָיו שׁוּם חֲצִיצָה (עַיֵּן לְקַמָּן סִימָן קסא). וְעִקַּר זְמַן הַטְּבִילָה הוּא לְאַחַר חֲצוֹת הַיּוֹם. אִשָּׁה שֶׁשִּׁמְּשָׁה מִטָּתָהּ, יְכוֹלָה לִפְלֹט שִׁכְבַת־זֶרַע בְּתוֹךְ שְׁלֹשָׁה יָמִים לְאַחַר כָּךְ, וַהֲרֵי הִיא כְּמוֹ בַּעַל קֶרִי, וְלֹא הוֹעִילָה לָהּ הַטְּבִילָה לְעִנְיָן זֶה. וְהַתַּקָּנָה הִיא, שֶׁקֹּדֶם הַטְּבִילָה תִּרְחַץ הֵיטֵב בְּחַמִּין וְלֹא תִפְלֹט אַחַר כָּךְ עוֹד. וְאָמְנָם אִם שִׁמְּשָׁה מִטָּתָהּ סָמוּךְ לִטְבִילָה אוֹ סָמוּךְ לְוֶסְתָּהּ, שֶׁאָז רְגִילָה לְהִתְעַבֵּר, אָסוּר לָהּ לְהַשְׁחִית זֶרַע הַהֵרָיוֹן, וְלָכֵן לֹא תִרְחַץ בְּחַמִּין. וּמִכָּל מָקוֹם יֵשׁ לָהּ לִטְבֹּל בְּצוֹנֵן. מִי שֶׁהוּא אָבֵל, רַחֲמָנָא לִצְלַן, אֲפִלּוּ בְּתוֹךְ שִׁבְעָה, יָכוֹל לִרְחוֹץ וְלִטְבּוֹל אֶת עַצְמוֹ כְּמוֹ שָׁעָה אוֹ שְׁתֵּי שָׁעוֹת קֹדֶם הַלַּיְלָה, אֲפִלּוּ קֹדֶם מִנְחָה. אֲבָל שְׁאָר כָּל דִּינֵי אֲבֵלוּת, כְּגוֹן יְשִׁיבָה עַל גַּבֵּי קַרְקַע וּבְלֹא מִנְעָלִים. נוֹהֵג עַד הַלָּיְלָה.

ז) נוֹהֲגִין שֶׁכָּל בַּעַל־הַבַּיִת עוֹשֶׂה נֵר לְבֵיתוֹ, מִפְּנֵי שֶׁבְּיוֹם־הַכִּפּוּרִים יָרַד מֹשֶׁה עִם הַלּוּחוֹת הַשְּׁנִיּוֹת, וְהַתּוֹרָה נִקְרֵאת נֵר, וְעוֹד נֵר אֶחָד בִּשְׁבִיל נִשְׁמוֹת אָבִיו וְאִמּוֹ שֶׁמֵּתוּ, לְכַפֵּר עֲלֵיהֶם. וְנוֹהֲגִין שֶׁמַּדְלִיקִין אֶחָד בְּבֵיתוֹ, שֶׁיִּדְלַק עַד שְׁעַת הַבְדָּלָה וְיַבְדִּיל עָלָיו (עַיֵּן לְקַמָּן סִימָן קלג סָעִיף כח), וְאֶחָד מַדְלִיקִין בְּבֵית־הַכְּנֶסֶת. וְלֹא יַעֲשׂוּ נֵרוֹת אֵלּוּ מִשַּׁעֲוָה שֶׁל בָּתֵּי עֲבוֹדָה־זָרָה. וּמֵהְיוֹת שֶׁקְּצָת מַקְפִּידִים אִם אֵרַע שֶׁכָּבָה נֵרוֹ בְּיוֹם־הַכִּפּוּרִים, אַף כִּי בֶּאֱמֶת אֵין בָּזֶה שׁוּם חֲשָׁשׁ, מִכָּל מָקוֹם טוֹב

---

4. See glossary

5. It is best to do so before the *Minchah* prayers because the *Vidui,* (confession of sins) is said at *Minchah.* Others have the custom to immerse after the final meal because then it is closer to *Yom Kippur.* (*Ibid* 606:18)

6. This refers to boys of thirteen years of age and girls who are twelve years old. (*Ibid* 606:23)

is humiliating to the dead. If the grave is more than three *parsa*[4] away from the residence of the offender, he does not have to go there in person, but may send a representative. The representative should gather ten men to go to the grave, and say, "I, the agent of so-and-so publicly declare that so-and-so has sent me to ask forgiveness for his sin," etc. If he insulted a dead person he does not have to go to his grave, but he should ask for his forgiveness at the place where he insulted him. But if he had defamed his character, he must accept upon himself to repent, for transgressing the prohibition of the early sages, against slandering the dead.

6) It is a mitzvah for every man to immerse in a mikvah on *erev Yom Kippur,*[5] to purify himself from nocturnal emission, and also as an element of repentance, just as a convert is required to immerse in a *mikvah.* Therefore, even boys and girls[6] should immerse themselves in a *Mikvah.* You should be certain that there is no *chatzitzah* on your body [a particle intervening between the body and the water] (see Chapter 161 below). The most appropriate time for the immersion is after midday. A woman after intercourse is likely to discharge semen within three days. She is then considered as one who has had a nocturnal emission, and the immersion is pointless in this case. The practical thing for her to do, is before immersing, to wash herself well with warm water; she will then experience no further discharge. However, if she had intercourse soon after her monthly immersion in the *mikvah,* or immediately before her menstrual period, when she is likely to become pregnant, then she is forbidden to destroy the semen of conception, and she should, therefore, not wash herself in warm water. Nevertheless, she should immerse in cold water. A mourner, may the Merciful One protect us, even during the first seven days of mourning[7], may wash and immerse himself[8] about one or two hours before nightfall, even before the *Minchah* service, but all the other laws of mourning, such as sitting on the floor, and not wearing [leather] shoes, must be observed until nighttime.

7) It is the custom that every head of the household prepares a candle for his house, as a reminder that on *Yom Kippur* Moshe came down from Mount Sinai with the Second Tablets, of the Torah, and the Torah is called "light"; and he prepares another candle for the soul of his deceased father and mother, to make atonement for them.[9] It is customary that one candle is lit in the house to burn until the close of *Yom Kippur,* and *Havdalah* is said over it, (see Chapter 133:28 below) and one candle is lit in the synagogue. These candles should not be made out of wax taken from houses of idol worship. Some people become upset if their candle is extinguished on *Yom Kippur,* although in reality there is no reason to worry about this, still it is best to avoid it. It is best therefore to give the candle

---

7. Even if the funeral was held on *erev Yom Kippur.* (*Ibid* 606:23)
8. He may even wash with warm water in order to be sure that there is no *chatzitzah* on his body. (*Ibid* 606:24)
9. For the deceased are also judged in this period and thus require atonement.See chapter 133:21.

לִמְנוֹעַ מִזֶּה, וְיִתֵּן אֶת הַנֵּר לַשַּׁמָּשׁ, שֶׁהוּא יַעֲמִידוֹ בְּמָקוֹם שֶׁיִּרְצֶה, וְהָאִישׁ לֹא יֵדַע כְּלָל מְקוֹם נֵרוֹ. וְיֵשׁ לָשֵׂאת אֶת הַנֵּר לְבֵית־הַכְּנֶסֶת, כְּשֶׁהוֹלֵךְ לִתְפִלַּת מִנְחָה לְהַעֲמִידוֹ עַל מְכוֹנוֹ וּלְהַדְלִיקוֹ אַחַר כָּךְ קֹדֶם בֵּין־הַשְּׁמָשׁוֹת, כִּי בְּעֵת שֶׁבָּאִים אַחַר כָּךְ לְבֵית־הַכְּנֶסֶת לְעַרְבִית, הַזְּמַן בָּהוּל.

ח) כְּשֶׁהוֹלְכִין לְבֵית־הַכְּנֶסֶת לִתְפִלַּת מִנְחָה, נוֹהֲגִין לִלְבּוֹשׁ בִּגְדֵי שַׁבָּת. בִּתְפִלַּת הַמִּנְחָה, אוֹמְרִים לְאַחַר שְׁמוֹנֶה־עֶשְׂרֵה אֶת הַוִּדּוּי. דְּהַיְנוּ, קֹדֶם אֱלֹהַי נְצֹר, אוֹמְרִים אֶת הַפָּסוּק יִהְיוּ לְרָצוֹן וְגוֹ׳, וּמַתְחִילִין אֱלֹהֵינוּ וֵאלֹהֵי אֲבוֹתֵינוּ תָּבוֹא לְפָנֶיךָ, עַד וָחֳלָיִים רָעִים, וְאַחַר כָּךְ אוֹמְרִים אֱלֹהַי נְצֹר וְכוּ׳, וְאוֹמְרִים עוֹד הַפַּעַם הַפָּסוּק יִהְיוּ לְרָצוֹן וְגוֹ׳. אִם בְּעוֹד שֶׁהוּא אוֹמֵר אֶת הַוִּדּוּי, חוֹזֵר שְׁלִיחַ־הַצִּבּוּר אֶת הַתְּפִלָּה, כֵּיוָן שֶׁהוּא כְּבָר אָמַר אֶת הַפָּסוּק יִהְיוּ לְרָצוֹן, יָכוֹל לַעֲנוֹת אָמֵן וְלוֹמַר קְדֻשָּׁה וּמוֹדִים (עַיֵּן לְעֵיל סִימָן יח סָעִיף יד).

ט) צָרִיךְ לוֹמַר אֶת הַוִּדּוּי מְעֻמָּד, וְיִשְׁחֶה כְּמוֹ בְּמוֹדִים. וּכְשֶׁמַּזְכִּיר אֶת הַחֵטְא, יַכֶּה בְּאֶגְרוֹף עַל הַלֵּב, כְּלוֹמַר, אַתָּה גָּרַמְתָּ לִי שֶׁחָטָאתִי. סֵדֶר הַוִּדּוּי כַּכָּתוּב בַּסִּדּוּרִים, אוֹמְרִים כֻּלָּם בְּשָׁוֶה. וּמִי שֶׁהוּא יוֹדֵעַ בְּעַצְמוֹ חֵטְא שֶׁלֹּא נִזְכַּר בַּוִּדּוּי, כֵּיוָן שֶׁהוּא אוֹמֵר אֶת הַוִּדּוּי בְּלַחַשׁ, נָכוֹן שֶׁיְּפָרֵט אֶת הַחֵטְא הַהוּא וְיִתְוַדֶּה עָלָיו בִּמְרִירוּת הַלֵּב וּבִדְמָעוֹת שָׁלִישׁ. וְכֵן אִם הַחֵטְא הוּא אֶחָד מֵהַמְפֹרָשִׁים בַּוִּדּוּי, אֲזַי כְּשֶׁמַּגִּיעַ אֵלָיו, יִתְמַרְמֵר עָלָיו בְּיוֹתֵר. עֲוֹנוֹת שֶׁהִתְוַדָּה עֲלֵיהֶם בְּיוֹם הַכִּפּוּרִים שֶׁעָבַר, אַף־עַל־פִּי שֶׁהוּא יוֹדֵעַ שֶׁלֹּא עָשָׂה אוֹתָם יוֹתֵר, מִכָּל מָקוֹם יָכוֹל לַחֲזוֹר וּלְהִתְוַדּוֹת עֲלֵיהֶם, וַהֲרֵי זֶה מְשֻׁבָּח, שֶׁנֶּאֱמַר, וְחַטָּאתִי נֶגְדִּי תָמִיד.

י) לְאַחַר תְּפִלַּת הַמִּנְחָה, אֵין אוֹמְרִים אָבִינוּ מַלְכֵּנוּ, בֵּין שֶׁחָל יוֹם־הַכִּפּוּרִים בַּחֹל בֵּין שֶׁחָל בַּשַּׁבָּת.

יא) אַחַר תְּפִלַּת הַמִּנְחָה נוֹהֲגִין לְהַלְקוֹת, וְאַף־עַל־פִּי שֶׁאֵין מַלְקוֹת אֵלּוּ מַלְקוֹת מַמָּשׁ, מִכָּל מָקוֹם מִתּוֹךְ כָּךְ יָשִׂים אֶל לִבּוֹ לָשׁוּב מֵעֲבֵרוֹת שֶׁבְּיָדוֹ. וְיֵשׁ לִקַּח רְצוּעָה שֶׁל עֵגֶל, אַף־עַל־פִּי שֶׁאֵינָהּ רְחָבָה טֶפַח. הַנִּלְקֶה יְהֵא מֻטֶּה וְשׁוֹחֶה עַל בִּרְכָּיו, פָּנָיו לַצָּפוֹן וַאֲחוֹרָיו לַדָּרוֹם. וְנוֹהֲגִין לוֹמַר

10. *Minchah* should be said prior to eating the last meal before the fast begins. Some authorities are of the opinion that *Vidui* should also be said after the meal. *Mishnah Berurah* concurs with this opinion and says it is for this reason we recite the *Tefiloh Zakkah* (Prayer for purification) before the *Kol Nidrei* service. (*Ibid* 607:1)

to the *shamash* (sexton), who will put it wherever he wishes, so that no one will know which is his candle. You should take the candle to the synagogue, when you go there for the *Minchah* service to be put in its proper place, and to be lit before twilight, because later, when people come to the synagogue for the *Maariv* service they are pressed for time.

8) When you go to the synagogue for the *Minchah* service it is the custom to put on Shabbos clothes. In the *Minchah* service, at the conclusion of the *Shemnoneh Esrei*, the *Vidui* [confessional] is said,[10]. Before *Elokai netzor,* [My God, guard my tongue] you say the verse, *Yih'yu leratzon,* [May. . . they be acceptable] etc., and then you say, *Elokeinu v'Elokei avoseinu,* [Our God and the God of our forefathers] *tavo lefanecha* [may our prayer come before You], until *vecholayim ra'im* [or serious illness]; then you say *Eloka netzor* etc. and you repeat the verse *Yih'yu leratzon.* If, while you are saying the *Vidui* the *Chazzan* is repeating the *Shemoneh Esrei,* since you already said the verse *Yih'yu leratzon,* you may respond *Amein,* and say the *Kedusha* and *Modim,* (see Chapter 18:14 above).

9) You must say the *Vidui* while standing in a bowed position, as when you say *Modim,*[11] and when mentioning each sin you should beat your heart[12] as if to say, "You (the heart) caused me to sin. The order of the *Vidui,* set down in the *Siddur,* should be said by all alike. If you are aware of an individual sin not enumerated in the *Vidui,* since the *Vidui* is recited in an undertone, you should specify that sin, and confess it with a grieving heart, and profuse tears. If that sin is one that is mentioned in the *Vidui,* then, when you come to it, you should burst out in bitter self-reproach. Sins you confessed on the previous *Yom Kippur* may be confessed again, although you know that you did not commit them again,[13] and you are to be praised for doing so, as it is said, "And my sin is always before me." (Psalms 51:15)

10) After the *Minchah* prayer, *Avinu Malkeinu* is not recited, regardless if *Yom Kippur* occurs on a weekday or on Shabbos.

11) After the *Minchah* service it is customary to receive [symbolic] lashes. Although these lashes are not real lashes, nevertheless, it will inspire the recipient to repent of his sins. A strap of calf's leather should be used, even though it is less than a *tefach* wide.[14] The one receiving the lashes should bend down and kneel with his face towards the North and his back towards the South. It is customary to recite

---

11. You should not lean on something when saying *Vidui.* If you do lean your full weight on something to the extent that you would fall if that object were removed it may be necessary for you to repeat the *Vidui.* (*Ibid* 607:10)

12. Or the breast. (*Ibid* 607:11)

13. *Mishnah Berurah* writes that if you had wronged someone with verbal abuse, and you had asked for and received his forgiveness, and confessed on the previous *Yom Kippur,* it is not necessary to repeat your confession. (*Ibid* 607:13)

14. See glossary.

וְדוּיִים בְּשָׁעָה שֶׁלּוֹקֶה. וְהַמַּלְקֶה אוֹמֵר וְהוּא רַחוּם וְגוֹ׳ שָׁלֹשׁ פְּעָמִים, שֶׁהֵן שְׁלֹשִׁים וָתֵשַׁע תֵּבוֹת כְּנֶגֶד שְׁלֹשִׁים וָתֵשַׁע מַלְקוֹת.

יב) לְעֵת הָעֶרֶב אוֹכְלִין סְעוּדָה הַמַּפְסֶקֶת. וְנוֹהֲגִין לִטְבּוֹל פְּרוּסַת הַמּוֹצִיא בִּדְבַשׁ, כְּמוֹ בְּרֹאשׁ־הַשָּׁנָה. וְאֵין לֶאֱכֹל אֶלָּא דְבָרִים שֶׁהֵם קַלִּים לְהִתְעַכֵּל, כְּגוֹן בְּשַׂר עוֹף. וְנוֹהֲגִין שֶׁאֵין אוֹכְלִים דָּגִים בִּסְעוּדָה זוֹ. וְלֹא יֹאכַל וְלֹא יִשְׁתֶּה דְבָרִים הַמְחַמְּמִים, כְּגוֹן מַאֲכָלִים הַמְתֻבָּלִים בִּבְשָׂמִים וְכַרְכֹּם. וְצָרִיךְ לִזָּהֵר מְאֹד לְהוֹסִיף מֵחֹל עַל הַקֹּדֶשׁ, דְּהַיְנוּ שֶׁיַּפְסִיק מִלֶּאֱכֹל בְּעוֹד יוֹם, קְצָת קֹדֶם בֵּין־הַשְּׁמָשׁוֹת. וּזְרִיזִין מַקְדִּימִין לְהַפְסִיק כְּמוֹ שָׁעָה קֹדֶם הַלַּיְלָה. וְאִם מַפְסִיק מִלֶּאֱכֹל בְּעוֹד הַיּוֹם גָּדוֹל וְדַעְתּוֹ לֶאֱכֹל אוֹ לִשְׁתּוֹת אַחַר כָּךְ, צָרִיךְ שֶׁיַּתְנֶה קֹדֶם בִּרְכַּת־הַמָּזוֹן וְיֹאמַר בְּפֵרוּשׁ אוֹ לְכָל־הַפָּחוֹת יְהַרְהֵר בְּלִבּוֹ, שֶׁאֵינוֹ מְקַבֵּל עָלָיו עֲדַיִן אֶת הַתַּעֲנִית.

יג) הַמִּנְהָג בִּמְדִינוֹת אֵלּוּ, שֶׁאֵין מַטְמִינִין בְּעֶרֶב יוֹם־הַכִּפּוּרִים לְצֹרֶךְ מוֹצָאֵי יוֹם־הַכִּפּוּרִים כְּדֶרֶךְ שֶׁמַּטְמִינִין מֵעֶרֶב שַׁבָּת לְשַׁבָּת, מִשּׁוּם דַּהֲוֵי כְּמֵכִין מִיּוֹם־הַכִּפּוּרִים לַחֹל, וְגַם מִשּׁוּם דְּמִחְזֵי כְּרַעַבְתָנוּתָא.

יד) כְּתִיב, לִקְדוֹשׁ ה׳ מְכֻבָּד, וְדָרְשִׁינָן, זֶה יוֹם־הַכִּפּוּרִים, שֶׁאֵין בּוֹ אֲכִילָה וּשְׁתִיָּה, מִצְוָה לְכַבְּדוֹ בִּכְסוּת נְקִיָּה וּבְנֵרוֹת. לָכֵן מַצִּיעִין גַּם בְּבֵית־הַכְּנֶסֶת מַצָּעוֹת נָאוֹת וּמַרְבִּין בְּנֵרוֹת, שֶׁנִּקְרָאוּ כָבוֹד, שֶׁנֶּאֱמַר, בָּאֻרִים כַּבְּדוּ ה׳, וּמְתַרְגְּמִינָן, בְּפַנָּסַיָּא יַקְּרוּ ה׳. קֹדֶם בֵּין־הַשְּׁמָשׁוֹת, פּוֹרְשִׂין מַפּוֹת עַל הַשֻּׁלְחָנוֹת, וּמַדְלִיקִין נֵרוֹת בַּבַּיִת כְּמוֹ בְּעֶרֶב שַׁבָּת. וְיֵשׁ לְהַדְלִיק נֵר בְּחֶדֶר שֶׁאִשְׁתּוֹ שׁוֹכֶבֶת שָׁם, כְּדֵי שֶׁלֹּא יָבוֹא לִידֵי תַשְׁמִישׁ. וּמְבָרְכִין עַל הַנֵּרוֹת, לְהַדְלִיק נֵר שֶׁל יוֹם־הַכִּפּוּרִים. וְאִם חָל בְּשַׁבָּת, מְבָרְכִין לְהַדְלִיק נֵר שֶׁל שַׁבָּת וְשֶׁל יוֹם־הַכִּפּוּרִים. (וּלְעִנְיַן בִּרְכַּת שֶׁהֶחֱיָנוּ, עַיֵּן לְעֵיל סִימָן קנ סָעִיף ד).

טו) נוֹהֲגִין לִלְבּוֹשׁ אֶת הַקִּיטֶל, שֶׁהוּא בֶּגֶד מֵתִים, וְעַל יְדֵי זֶה לֵב הָאָדָם נִכְנָע וְנִשְׁבָּר. וְגַם הָאָבֵל יָכוֹל לְלָבְשׁוֹ. וְכֵיוָן שֶׁהוּא בֶּגֶד מְיֻחָד

15. You should not drink wine at this meal. (*Ibid* 607:15)

16. The meal should be completed before sunset. Women who light candles, and those who refrain from doing any work a half hour or at least twenty minutes before sunset, are considered virtuous. (*Ibid* 608:2)

confessions while receiving the lashes. The one who administers the lashes says *Vehu rechum* (He, the Merciful One) three times, which amounts to thirty-nine words, analogous to the thirty-nine lashes.

12) Towards evening you eat the closing meal, and it is customary to dip the piece of *challah* for *Hamotzi* in honey, just as you do on *Rosh Hashanah*. You should eat only food that is easy to digest, such as fowl. It is the custom not to eat fish at the meal. You should not eat or drink anything that raises the body temperature, such as foods seasoned with spices and saffron.[15] You should be very careful to add from the secular to the sacred, that is, you should end the meal while it is still day, a little before twilight.[16] The zealous finish their meal early, about an hour before sunset. If you ended your meal while it is still the middle of the day, and you intend to eat or drink after that, you must stipulate before *Birkas Hamazon* and say explicitly, or at least have in mind that you do not yet accept the fast on yourself.

13) It is the custom in these regions not to store food to warm on *erev Yom Kippur*, to be used at the conclusion of *Yom Kippur*, as it is done on *erev Shabbos* for Shabbos, because it is equivalent to preparing food on *Yom Kippur* for the weekday; and it also gives the impression of gluttony.

14) It is written, (Issiah 58:13), "The holy [day] of Hashem should be honored" and the Sages explain[17] that this refers to *Yom Kippur* for on that day there is no eating or drinking. It is a mitzvah to honor this day with clean clothes and with candlelight. Therefore, in the synagogue we spread beautiful covers and light many candles, which are called "honor", as it is said, "Honor Hashem, *ba'urim*," (Isaiah 58:13) and the *Targum* translated it, "Honor Hashem with lights." Before twilight, the tables should be covered with cloths, and candles should be lit in the house, as on *erev Shabbos*. A candle should be lit in the bedroom to prevent the occurence of marital relations.[18] Over the candles, the berachah[19] *Lehadlik neir shel Yom haKippurim* is said [to kindle the light of *Yom Kippur*]. If *Yom Kippur* occures on Shabbos, the berachah, *Lehadlik Neir shel Shabbos and Yom Kippur* is said. (Concerning the berachah of *Shehecheyanu* see Chapter 103:4 above)

15) It is the custom to put on a *kittel* (white robe) which is a garment of the dead. The wearing of such a garment causes the heart of man to be subdued and broken. A mourner may also wear a *kittel*.[20] Since it is a garment that is worn only at prayer,

---

17. *Maseches Shabbos* 119.

18. *Magein Avrohom* justifies the custom of many who do not light candles in the bedroom. He says, however, that it is good to be stringent in this matter, to light a candle. In the event that the woman is in the status of *niddah* (menstrual period) it is not necessary, as marital relations are forbidden under any circumstances. (*Ibid* 610:5, *Shaarei Tzion* 4)

19. *Pri Chadash* and *Vilna Gaon* rule according to those who say that a *berachah* is not recited on these candles. (*Shaarei Tzion* 610:5)

20. In some communities it is the custom that a mourner does not wear a *kittel*. (*Mishnah Berurah* 610:18)

לַתְּפִלָּה, לֹא יֵלֵךְ בּוֹ לְבֵית־הַכִּסֵּא. גַּם הַנָּשִׁים לוֹבְשׁוֹת בְּגָדִים לְבָנִים וּנְקִיִּים לִכְבוֹד הַיּוֹם, אַךְ לֹא יְקַשְּׁטוּ אֶת עַצְמָן בְּתַכְשִׁיטִין, מִפְּנֵי אֵימַת הַדִּין.

טז) הַמִּנְהָג שֶׁהָאָב וְהָאֵם מְבָרְכִין אֶת הַבָּנִים וְאֶת הַבָּנוֹת קֹדֶם שֶׁנִּכְנָסִין לְבֵית־הַכְּנֶסֶת, שֶׁאָז כְּבָר חָלָה קְדֻשַּׁת הַיּוֹם, וְשַׁעֲרֵי רַחֲמִים נִפְתָּחוּ. וּמִתְפַּלְּלִים בִּבְרָכָה זוֹ, שֶׁיֵּחָתְמוּ לְחַיִּים טוֹבִים, וְשֶׁיְּהֵא לִבָּם נָכוֹן בְּיִרְאַת ה׳, וּמִתְחַנְּנִים בִּבְכִי וּבִדְמָעוֹת שֶׁתִּתְקַבֵּל תְּפִלָּתָם. וְגַם הַבָּנִים וְהַבָּנוֹת מִתְעוֹרְרִים שֶׁיֵּלְכוּ בְּדֶרֶךְ טוֹבִים וְאָרְחוֹת צַדִּיקִים יִשְׁמֹרוּ. וְיֵשׁ שֶׁהוֹלְכִים גַּם לִקְרוֹבֵיהֶם שֶׁהֵם תַּלְמִידֵי חֲכָמִים וְצַדִּיקִים שֶׁיְּבָרְכוּ אוֹתָם, וּמְבַקְשִׁים מֵהֶם, שֶׁיִּתְפַּלְּלוּ גַם בַּעֲדָם בְּיוֹם הַקָּדוֹשׁ וְהַנּוֹרָא. וְיֵשׁ לְהַקְדִּים לַעֲשׂוֹת כֵּן בְּעוֹד הַיּוֹם גָּדוֹל, כִּי לְעֵת עֶרֶב רָאוּי שֶׁיִּהְיוּ נְכוֹנִים לְקַבֵּל קְדֻשַּׁת הַיּוֹם בְּהַשְׁקֵט וְיִשּׁוּב הַדַּעַת. נֹסַח הַבְּרָכָה, יְשִׂימְךָ וְגוֹ׳, יְבָרֶכְךָ וְגוֹ׳, וְעוֹד מוֹסִיף כָּל אֶחָד כְּפִי צַחוּת לְשׁוֹנוֹ. וְיֵשׁ לוֹמַר תְּפִלָּה זֹאת, וִיהִי רָצוֹן מִלִּפְנֵי אָבִינוּ שֶׁבַּשָּׁמַיִם, שֶׁיִּתֵּן בְּלִבְּךָ אַהֲבָתוֹ וְיִרְאָתוֹ, וּתְהֵא יִרְאַת ה׳ עַל פָּנֶיךָ כָּל יְמֵי חַיֶּיךָ שֶׁלֹּא תֶחֱטָא, וִיהֵא חֶשְׁקְךָ בַּתּוֹרָה וּבַמִּצְוֹת, עֵינֶיךָ לְנֹכַח יַבִּיטוּ, פִּיךָ יְדַבֵּר חָכְמוֹת, וְלִבְּךָ יֶהְגֶּה אֵימוֹת, יָדֶיךָ תִּהְיֶינָה עוֹסְקוֹת בְּמִצְוֹת, רַגְלֶיךָ יָרוּצוּ לַעֲשׂוֹת רְצוֹן אָבִיךָ שֶׁבַּשָּׁמַיִם, וְיִתֶּן לְךָ בָּנִים וּבָנוֹת צַדִּיקִים וְצִדְקָנִיּוֹת עוֹסְקִים בַּתּוֹרָה וּבְמִצְוֹת כָּל יְמֵיהֶם, וִיהִי מְקוֹרְךָ בָּרוּךְ, וְיַזְמִין לְךָ פַּרְנָסָתְךָ בְּהֶתֵּר וּבְנַחַת וּבְרֶוַח מִתַּחַת יָדוֹ הָרְחָבָה, וְלֹא עַל יְדֵי מַתְּנַת בָּשָׂר־וָדָם, פַּרְנָסָה שֶׁתְּהֵא פָּנוּי לַעֲבוֹדַת ה׳, וְתִכָּתֵב וְתֵחָתֵם לְחַיִּים טוֹבִים וַאֲרֻכִּים בְּתוֹךְ כָּל צַדִּיקֵי יִשְׂרָאֵל, אָמֵן.

יז) נוֹהֲגִין לִלְבּוֹשׁ אֶת הַטַּלִּית. וְיֵשׁ לִזָּהֵר לְלָבְשׁוֹ בְּעוֹד יוֹם וּלְבָרֵךְ עָלָיו. וְאִם נִתְאַחֵר עַד בֵּין־הַשְּׁמָשׁוֹת, לֹא יְבָרֵךְ עָלָיו.

סִימָן קלב
סֵדֶר לֵיל יוֹם־הַכִּפּוּרִים

א) בִּמְדִינוֹת אֵלּוּ נוֹהֲגִין, שֶׁקֹּדֶם כָּל־נִדְרֵי, מוֹצִיא הַגָּדוֹל שֶׁבַּקָּהָל סֵפֶר־תּוֹרָה וּמְסַבֵּב עִמּוֹ סְבִיב הַבִּימָה, וְהָאֲנָשִׁים מְחַבְּקִים וּמְנַשְּׁקִים אֶת סֵפֶר־הַתּוֹרָה, וּמְבַקְשִׁים מְחִילָה וּסְלִיחָה עַל מַה שֶּׁפָּגְמוּ בִּכְבוֹד הַתּוֹרָה,

..., too, should wear clean, white
wear jewelry, because of the awe of

mother to bless their sons and daughters
the holiness of the day has already begun,
...ady open. They implore in this blessing that
...d life, and that their hearts be steadfast in the
, with tearful eyes, that their prayers be accepted.
... and resolve to walk in the ways of the righteous
...t. Some people visit their relatives who are Torah
sch... receive blessings from them, and ask them to pray for
them on ... ome day. You should do this early, while it is still the
middle of the ... rds evening everyone should be ready to receive the holy
day in a quiet and ... e frame of mind. The text for blessing the children is: *Yesimecha* [May God make you] etc., *Yevarechecha* [May God bless you] etc., and everyone may add to this prayer according to his eloquence of speech. It is proper to say also the following prayer: May it be the will of our Father in heaven to place in your heart love and fear of Him, and may the fear of God be upon your face all the days of your life, so that you will not sin. May your desire be for Torah and mitzvos. May your eyes look straightforward, may your mouth speak wisdom, and your heart meditate with reverence. May your hands be engaged in the performance of mitzvos; may your feet hasten to do the will of your Father in heaven. May He grant you righteous sons and daughters occupying themselves with Torah and mitzvos all their days. May your wellspring be blessed, [May you be blessed with many children]. May He grant that your livelihood, come with honesty, ease, and abundance, from His generous hand, and not from the gifts of men; a livelihood that will free you to serve God. May you be inscribed and sealed for a good and long life among all the righteous of Israel. Amein.

17) It is customary to put on the *tallis.* You should be careful to put it on while it is still day, and to say the berachah over it. But if you waited [to put it on] until twilight you should not say the berachah.

Chapter 132

The Order of Yom Kippur Eve

1) It is the custom in our regions before saying *Kol nidrei* that the most eminent man of the congregation takes out a *Seifer Torah* [from the Ark][1] and walks around the *bimah* with it and the people embrace and kiss the *Seifer Torah,* and beg for pardon and forgiveness for having offended the Torah. They resolve, from now on

---

21. According to *Mishnah Berurah* it is not necessary to remove the *kittel* when urinating. (*Ibid* 610:18)

1. In some communities all the *Sifrei Torah* are taken, in others three are taken, and in some seven are taken.

וְאֵילָךְ לָלֶכֶת בְּדַרְכָּהּ, וְאוֹמְרִים כַּמָּה פְּעָמִים
עַ וְגוֹ', וְעוֹמֵד עִם סֵפֶר־הַתּוֹרָה אֵצֶל שְׁלִיחַ־הַצִּבּוּר
ד אֶחָד מֵחֲשׁוּבֵי הַקָּהָל עוֹמֵד אֶצְלוֹ מִשְּׂמֹאלוֹ גַּם כֵּן עִם
הַתּוֹרָה, וְאוֹמְרִים שְׁלָשְׁתָּן, בִּישִׁיבָה שֶׁל מַעְלָה וְכוּ', וּשְׁלִיחַ־הַצִּבּוּר
אוֹמֵר כָּל־נִדְרֵי שָׁלֹשׁ פְּעָמִים בְּנִגּוּן הַיָּדוּעַ, וְיֵשׁ לְכָל אָדָם לוֹמַר עִם
שְׁלִיחַ־הַצִּבּוּר בְּלַחַשׁ. וְיֵשׁ לְהַתְחִיל כָּל־נִדְרֵי בְּעוֹד יוֹם, וּלְהַמְשִׁיךְ בּוֹ עַד
הַלַּיְלָה. וּלְאַחַר שֶׁאָמַר שְׁלִיחַ־הַצִּבּוּר בָּרְכוּ, וְעָנוּ בָּרוּךְ וְכוּ', מַחֲזִירִין אֶת
סֵפֶר־הַתּוֹרָה לַהֵיכָל וְחוֹזְרִין לִמְקוֹמָן. וּבְשַׁבָּת, יְכוֹלִין לַחֲזוֹר לִמְקוֹמָן
בְּהַתְחָלַת מִזְמוֹר שִׁיר לְיוֹם הַשַּׁבָּת.

ב) כְּשֶׁשְּׁלִיחַ־הַצִּבּוּר אוֹמֵר בִּרְכַּת שֶׁהֶחֱיָנוּ, יְכַוֵּן לְהוֹצִיא אֶת הַצִּבּוּר. וּמִכָּל מָקוֹם נָכוֹן שֶׁהַשּׁוֹמֵעַ יְכַוֵּן שֶׁלֹּא יֵצֵא בְּבִרְכַּת שְׁלִיחַ־הַצִּבּוּר, אֶלָּא יְבָרֵךְ בְּעַצְמוֹ בְּלַחַשׁ, וִימַהֵר לְסַיֵּם קֹדֶם שְׁלִיחַ־הַצִּבּוּר, כְּדֵי שֶׁיַּעֲנֶה אָמֵן. וְהַנָּשִׁים שֶׁבֵּרְכוּ בְּהַדְלָקַת הַנֵּרוֹת שֶׁהֶחֱיָנוּ, וְכֵן אִישׁ אִם הִדְלִיק וּבֵרַךְ אָז שֶׁהֶחֱיָנוּ, לֹא יְבָרְכוּ עַתָּה שֶׁהֶחֱיָנוּ.

ג) לֵיל יוֹם־הַכִּפּוּרִים וְיוֹמוֹ, אוֹמְרִים, בָּרוּךְ שֵׁם כְּבוֹד מַלְכוּתוֹ לְעוֹלָם וָעֶד, בְּקוֹל רָם.

ד) יֵשׁ שֶׁעוֹמְדִים עַל רַגְלֵיהֶם בְּכָל סֵדֶר תְּפִלַּת עַרְבִית וְכָל הַיּוֹם. וְאִם נֶחְלָשׁוּ, יְכוֹלִים לִסְמֹךְ לְאֵיזֶה דָּבָר. וְטַעַם הָעֲמִידָה, לִהְיוֹת דֻּגְמַת הַמַּלְאָכִים. וְלָכֵן הַנָּשִׁים לֹא תַעֲמֹדְנָה. מִי שֶׁעָמַד פַּעַם אַחַת עַל דַּעַת לַעֲשׂוֹת כֵּן כָּל יָמָיו וְאַחַר כָּךְ רוֹצֶה לַחֲזוֹר, צָרִיךְ הַתָּרָה.

ה) יֵשׁ נוֹהֲגִין לָלוּן בְּבֵית־הַכְּנֶסֶת וְלוֹמַר שִׁירוֹת וְתִשְׁבָּחוֹת כָּל הַלַּיְלָה. וּכְשֶׁצָּרִיךְ לִישׁוֹן, יַרְחִיק אֶת עַצְמוֹ מִן אֲרוֹן הַקֹּדֶשׁ. וְהַחַזָּנִים לֹא יֵעוֹרוּ, כִּי עַל יְדֵי זֶה מְאַבְּדִין קוֹלָן. קֹדֶם הַשְּׁכִיבָה יֹאמַר אַרְבָּעָה מִזְמוֹרֵי תְהִלִּים הָרִאשׁוֹנִים, שֶׁהֵם מְסֻגָּלִים לְהִנָּצֵל מִקֶּרִי, רַחֲמָנָא לִצְלָן, כִּי יֵשׁ בָּהֶם שְׁלֹשׁ מֵאוֹת וְשֵׁשׁ תֵּבוֹת וְאַרְבָּעָה מִזְמוֹרִים, עוֹלִין שְׁלֹשׁ מֵאוֹת וָעֶשֶׂר כְּמִנְיַן קֶרִי. וְרָאשֵׁי וְסוֹפֵי הַמִּזְמוֹרִים, עוֹלִים מֵאָה עֶשְׂרִים וָשֵׁשׁ, וְאַרְבָּעָה

---

2. If it is still too early to recite the *Kerias Shemah,* the congregation should recite chapters from the Psalms until the proper time to recite *Kerias Shemah.* (*Mishnah Berurah* 619;6)

3. You must be sure that standing throughout the evening will not cause you to lose concentration of the prayers, because if it does inhibit your concentration, it is a sin to stand.

to live according to its laws. They recite the verse *Or zaru'a* [Light is sown for the righteous] etc. a number of times (Psalms 97:11). Then he places himself, with the *Seifer Torah,* to the right of the *Chazzan,* and another prominent member of the congregation stands on the *Chazzan's* left, also carrying a *Seifer Torah,* and the three say together: *Biyishivah shel malah* [By the authority of the Court on High] etc. The *Chazzan* then recites *Kol nidrei* three times, in the familiar melody. All the congregants should say it quietly along with the *Chazzan.* It is proper to begin *Kol nidrei* while it is still day, and to draw it out until night.[2] After the *Chazzan* said *Barechu* and the congregation responded *Baruch* etc. the Torah scrolls are returned to the Ark, [and the two men who carried them] return to their seats. On Shabbos they may return to their seats when the congregation recites *Mizmor shir leyom haShabbos* [a Psalm, a song for the Shabbos day].

2) When the *Chazzan* says the berachah *Shehecheyanu* he should have in mind to exempt the congregation. Nevertheless, each worshipper should have in mind not to be exempted by the *Chazzans's* berachah, but he should say the berachah quietly by himself, and say it quickly, concluding it before the *Chazzan,* so that he can respond Amein. The women who said the berachah *Shehecheyanu* when lighting candles, or a man who lit the candles and said *Shehecheyanu,* should not say it with the *Chazzan.*

3) On *Yom Kippur,* both in the evening and during the day, you should say, *Baruch sheim kevod malchuso le'olam va'ed,* [Blessed [is His] Name, Whose glorious kingdom is forever and ever], in a loud voice.

4) Some people stand on their feet[3] during the entire evening service and the entire day of *Yom Kippur.* If they feel faint they may lean against something. The reason for standing is to emulate the angels; therefore, women should not stand. A person who has stood up once with the intention to do so for the rest of his life, and afterwards wishes to retract, needs an annulment [of his personal obligation].

5) Some people have the custom to stay in the synagogue reciting songs of praise all night.[4] When they feel the need to sleep[5] they should move away from the Ark. The *Chazzanim* should not stay awake for it will cause them to lose their voice. Before going to sleep you should say the first four Psalms,[6] for they are particularly beneficial in preventing nocturnal emission, may the Merciful One save us. For [these four Psalms] contain a total of three hundred and six words. By adding four, [to the number of the] Psalms, you arrive at a total of three hundred and ten, which is the numerical equivalence of קרי, *keri,* [nocturnal emission]. [The numerical value]

Similarly if standing during the day will cause you to become tired and weak and disturb your concentration, it is a sin to stand. (*Sha'ar Hatzion* 619:18)

4. *Levush* writes that it is better to go home and sleep, for a person who is up all night will doze off by day and pray without proper concentration. (*Mishnah Berurah* 619:14)

5. It is not permitted to sleep in the synagogue, however, unless you actually intended to recite "Songs of praise" all night. (*Ibid* 619:6)

6. This is in addition to the regular *Kerias Shemah* prayer that is recited at night. (*Ibid* 619:4)

מִזְמוֹרִים וְהַכּוֹלֵל, בְּיַחַד עוֹלִים מֵאָה שְׁלֹשִׁים וְאַחַת, כְּמִנְיַן סמאל, וִיכַוֵּן לְסַלְּקוֹ מֵעָלָיו. וְטוֹב שֶׁלֹּא יִתְעַטֵּף בְּכָרִים וּכְסָתוֹת הַמְחַמְּמִין, וְעַל־כָּל־פָּנִים לֹא יְכַסֶּה רַגְלָיו.

סִימָן קלג
הִלְכוֹת יוֹם־הַכִּפּוּרִים

א) יוֹם־הַכִּפּוּרִים, אָסוּר בַּאֲכִילָה וּבִשְׁתִיָּה, בִּרְחִיצָה, בְּסִיכָה, בִּנְעִילַת הַסַּנְדָּל, וּבְתַשְׁמִישׁ־הַמִּטָּה. וְאָסוּר בְּכָל מְלָאכָה וְטִלְטוּל, כְּמוֹ בְּשַׁבָּת. וְכֵיוָן שֶׁצְּרִיכִין לְהוֹסִיף מֵחֹל עַל הַקֹּדֶשׁ, לָכֵן אֲסוּרִים בְּכָל אֵלּוּ מִבְּעוֹד יוֹם אֵיזֶה זְמַן קֹדֶם בֵּין־הַשְּׁמָשׁוֹת, וְכֵן בְּמוֹצָאֵי יוֹם־הַכִּפּוּרִים, זְמַן מְעַט לְאַחַר צֵאת הַכּוֹכָבִים.

ב) לִגַּע בָּאֳכָלִין וּמַשְׁקִין כְּשֶׁצְּרִיכִין לָתֵת לִקְטַנִּים, יֵשׁ מַתִּירִין, וְיֵשׁ מַחְמִירִין. וְאִם אֶפְשָׁר, יֵשׁ לִזָּהֵר.

ג) אִסּוּר רְחִיצָה, עַיֵּן סִימָן קכד סָעִיף ז, ח, ט. וְגַם בְּיוֹם־הַכִּפּוּרִים אֵינוֹ אָסוּר רַק בִּרְחִיצָה שֶׁל תַּעֲנוּג (וְעַיֵּן עוֹד בְּסִימָן קנט). וְצָרִיךְ לִזָּהֵר מְאֹד שֶׁלֹּא יִרְחַץ יוֹתֵר מִמַּה שֶּׁמֻּכְרָח לוֹ. וְלִתְפִלַּת נְעִילָה וּמִנְחָה וּמַעֲרִיב, כֵּיוָן שֶׁעוֹמֵד כָּל הַיּוֹם בְּבֵית־הַכְּנֶסֶת וְעוֹסֵק בִּתְפִלּוֹת וּפִיּוּטִים, הֲרֵי הוּא מְשַׁמֵּר יָדָיו, וְלֹא יִרְחָצֵן.

ד) הַכֹּהֲנִים שֶׁעוֹלִים לַדּוּכָן, כֵּיוָן שֶׁלַּדּוּכָן צְרִיכִין נְטִילַת־יָדַיִם עַד הַזְּרוֹעַ, וְאִם לֹא נָטְלוּ יְדֵיהֶם בְּשַׁחֲרִית רַק הָאֶצְבָּעוֹת, אַף שֶׁבֵּרְכוּ אָז עַל נְטִילַת יָדַיִם, מִכָּל מָקוֹם כֵּיוָן שֶׁהַנְּטִילָה הַהִיא לֹא הוֹעִילָה לָהֶם לַדּוּכָן, אִם כֵּן כְּשֶׁנּוֹטְלִין עַתָּה עַד הַזְּרוֹעַ, צְרִיכִין לְבָרֵךְ שֵׁנִית עַל נְטִילַת יָדַיִם. וְטוֹב יוֹתֵר, שֶׁיִּטְּלוּ יְדֵיהֶם גַּם בְּשַׁחֲרִית עַד הַזְּרוֹעַ, וְלֹא יִצְטָרְכוּ עַתָּה לְבָרֵךְ שֵׁנִית.

ה) הַחוֹלֶה, אֲפִלּוּ אֵין בּוֹ סַכָּנָה, רוֹחֵץ כְּדַרְכּוֹ. כַּלָּה בְּתוֹךְ שְׁלֹשִׁים יוֹם מִשֶּׁנִּשֵּׂאָה, רוֹחֶצֶת פָּנֶיהָ, כְּדֵי שֶׁלֹּא תִתְגַּנֶּה עַל בַּעְלָהּ.

---

1. According to *Mishnah Berurah* it is not necessary to be stringent even if the child is able to take the food by himself. (*Mishnah Berurah* 612:32)

of the first and last letters of the four Psalms amounts to one hundred and twenty-six, plus the four of the four Psalms, plus one, the general binding factor which unites the word, together makes a total of one hundred and thirty-one, the numerical equivalence of סמאל, [malevolent angel] and you should have in mind to shake off his evil influence. It is best not to cover yourself with pillows and blankets that make you feel hot; but at any rate you should not cover your legs.

Chapter 133

Laws of Yom Kippur

1) On *Yom Kippur* it is forbidden to eat, to drink, to wash, to anoint, to wear shoes, and to have marital relations. It is forbidden to do any work or to carry, just as on Shabbos. Since it is necessary to add from the secular to the sacred, all of the above are forbidden [on *erev Yom Kippur*] while it is still day, beginning a short time before twilight; and at the end of *Yom Kippur,* until a short time after the stars appear.

2) Some authorities permit touching food or drink when it is necessary to feed the children, while others forbid it. If possible, you should be careful[1] [not to touch any food].

3) For the prohibition of washing, see chapter 124, paragraphs 7, 8 and 9. On *Yom Kippur* only washing for pleasure is forbidden (see also chapter 159). You should be very careful not to wash more than actually necessary. Since you spend the entire day in the synagogue engaged in prayer and hymns, you have probably kept your hands clean, and should not wash them for the *Ne'ilah, Minchah* and *Maariv* services.[2]

4) The *kohanim* who go up to bless the people, for *Birkas Kohanim* must wash their hands up to their wrists. If they did not wash their entire hands in the morning, but only their fingers, even though they said the berachah *Al netilas yadayim,* nevertheless, since this washing is not valid for *Birkas Kohanim,* they must wash their hands this time up to the wrists, and repeat the berachah *Al netilas yadayim.*[3] It is best that they should wash their hands in the morning up to the wrists, so they will not need to repeat the berachah.

5) A sick person, even one whose condition is not critical, may wash in the usual manner. A bride, within thirty days of her wedding day, may wash her face so that she should not look unattractive to her husband.[4]

---

2. You are required to wash your hands (up to the knuckle) after using the bathroom to urinate or to move the bowels. Similarly if you touch any part of your body that perspires, you must wash your hands. (*Mishnah Berurah* 613:4,6)

3. According to *Eliyohu Rabbah,* the *Kohanim* need never say the berachah on washing their hands [and certainly on *Yom Kippur* they should not say it]. (*Mishnah Berurah* 128:24)

4. According to *Chayei Adam* this does not apply in our times, since the entire day is spent in the synagogue and her husband will not have the opportunity of seeing her. (*Mishnah Berurah* 613:26)

ו) הָרוֹאֶה, חַס־וְשָׁלוֹם, קֶרִי בְּיוֹם־הַכִּפּוּרִים, אִם לַח הוּא, מְקַנְּחוֹ בְּמַפָּה. וְאִם כְּבָר נִתְיַבֵּשׁ, רוֹחֵץ מְקוֹמוֹת הַמְלֻכְלָכִים לְבַד, דְּדִינוֹ כְּצוֹאָה. וְלֹא יִרְחַץ בְּבֶגֶד, שֶׁלֹּא יָבוֹא לִידֵי סְחִיטָה. וְאָסוּר לִטְבֹּל, אַף־עַל־פִּי שֶׁהוּא רָגִיל לִטְבֹּל בִּשְׁאָר יְמוֹת הַשָּׁנָה. וִיגַלֶּה צַעֲרוֹ לְתַלְמִיד־חָכָם מַה שֶּׁאֵרַע לוֹ בַּיּוֹם הַקָּדוֹשׁ וְהַנּוֹרָא, וְהוּא יוֹרֵהוּ מַה לַּעֲשׂוֹת, שֶׁיִּתְכַּפֵּר לוֹ וְיַאֲרִיךְ יָמִים.

ז) סִיכָה, אֲסוּרָה, אֲפִלּוּ בִּשְׁבִיל לְהַעֲבִיר הַזֻּהֲמָה, וַאֲפִלּוּ עַל מִקְצָת גּוּפוֹ. אַךְ חוֹלֶה, אֲפִלּוּ אֵין בּוֹ סַכָּנָה, סָךְ כְּדַרְכּוֹ. וּמִי שֶׁיֵּשׁ בּוֹ חֲטָטִים, בִּמְדִינוֹתֵינוּ שֶׁאֵין נוֹהֲגִין הַבְּרִיאִים לָסוּךְ בַּחֹל, אָסוּר לוֹ לָסוּךְ, מִשּׁוּם דְּמוּכָח שֶׁהִיא מִשּׁוּם רְפוּאָה.

ח) נְעִילַת הַסַּנְדָּל, יֵשׁ אוֹסְרִין אֲפִלּוּ בְּסַנְדָּל שֶׁל עֵץ שֶׁאֵינוֹ חָפוּי בְּעוֹר. אֲבָל שֶׁל גֶּמִי אוֹ קַשׁ אוֹ בֶגֶד, מֻתָּר. וְיֵשׁ לְהַחְמִיר בִּנְעִילַת הַסַּנְדָּל אֲפִלּוּ בִּמְקוֹם רֶפֶשׁ וְטִיט וּגְשָׁמִים. וַאֲפִלּוּ הוֹלֵךְ בֵּין הַגּוֹיִם, אָסוּר. וְאִם הוּא מִצְטַעֵר הַרְבֵּה לֵילֵךְ בִּמְקוֹם רֶפֶשׁ וְטִיט וּגְשָׁמִים בְּלִי סַנְדָּל, יִנְעֹל סַנְדָּלִים שֶׁהֵם בְּלִי עָקֵב, אוֹ מִנְעָלִים שֶׁהֵם עִם עָקֵב אֶלָּא יַחֲלִיפֵם שֶׁל שְׂמֹאל לְיָמִין וְשֶׁל יָמִין לִשְׂמֹאל אִם יֵשׁ חִלּוּק בֵּינֵיהֶם, וְלִפְנֵי פֶּתַח בֵּית־הַכְּנֶסֶת יַחֲלֹץ אוֹתָם וְיַצְנִיעֵם. וְיִזָּהֵר שֶׁלֹּא לִגַּע בָּהֶם לֹא בִנְעִילָה וְלֹא בַחֲלִיצָה, שֶׁלֹּא יִצְטָרֵךְ לִרְחוֹץ יָדָיו.

ט) מֻתָּר לַעֲמֹד עַל כָּרִים וּכְסָתוֹת, אֲפִלּוּ הֵן שֶׁל עוֹר, אֲבָל בִּתְפִלַּת שְׁמוֹנֶה־עֶשְׂרֵה, אָסוּר לַעֲמֹד עַל שׁוּם דָּבָר. אַךְ מִי שֶׁהוּא אִישׁ מְצֻנָּן, מֻתָּר לוֹ לַעֲמֹד עַל קְצָת עֲשָׂבִים.

י) כָּל חוֹלֶה, אַף־עַל־פִּי שֶׁאֵין בּוֹ סַכָּנָה, אוֹ מִי שֶׁיֵּשׁ לוֹ מַכָּה בְּרַגְלוֹ, וְכֵן הַיּוֹלֶדֶת כָּל שְׁלֹשִׁים, מֻתָּרִין בִּנְעִילַת הַסַּנְדָּל.

יא) אָסוּר לִגַּע בְּאִשְׁתּוֹ, אֲפִלּוּ בַּיּוֹם, וְיַחֲזִיקֶהָ כָּל יוֹם־הַכִּפּוּרִים כְּמוֹ נִדָּה.

יב) מְעֻבָּרוֹת וּמֵינִיקוֹת מִתְעַנּוֹת וּמַשְׁלִימוֹת כְּכָל אָדָם. וּמֵינִיקָה

---

5. You need not be concerned with their ridicule.

6) If someone has a nocturnal emission, God forbid, on *Yom Kippur,* if it is still moist, he should wipe it off with a cloth. If it has dried, he should wash only the soiled areas, for *Halachah* considers it as excrement. It should not be washed with a garment, so that he should not squeeze the garment by mistake. He is forbidden to immerse in a *mikvah,* even though he regularly immerses himself on the other days of the year. He should reveal his anguish to a Torah scholar and tell him what happened to him on this holy and awe-inspiring day, and he will instruct him what to do in order to be forgiven and live long.

7) Anointing is forbidden, even if only to remove dirt. Even to anoint only part of the body is forbidden. But a sick person, even if his condition is not critical, may anoint himself in the usual manner. In our regions, where people in normal health do not usually anoint themselves on weekdays, a person who has pimples is forbidden to anoint himself, because it is obvious he is doing it as a cure.

8) Some authorities forbid wearing even shoes made of wood that are not covered with leather; but shoes made of reed grass, or straw or cloth are permitted. You should be stringent and not wear shoes even when walking through mud and clay or in the rain. Even if you have to walk among non-Jews[5] it is forbidden to wear shoes. But if it is very painful for you to walk through mud and clay, or in the rain without shoes, you may wear shoes without heels, and if they have heels, you should change them around, putting the left shoe on the right foot[6] and the right shoe on the left foot, if there is a difference between them. Before the entrance of the synagogue you should take them off and put them away. You should be careful not to touch them with your hands either when putting them on or removing them, so that you will not have to wash your hands.

9) You are permitted to stand on a pillow or a pad, even if they are made of leather, but during the *Shemoneh Esrei* it is forbidden to stand on anything. But a person who feels chilled may stand on some grass.

10) A person who is sick, even if his condition is not critical, or one who has an injured foot, or a woman within thirty days after childbirth, is permitted to wear shoes.[7]

11) It is forbidden to touch your wife[8] even during the daytime; and you should consider her, as though she is menstrually unclean during the entire day of *Yom Kippur.*

12) Pregnant and nursing women should fast the entire day, the same as other people. A nursing woman should not fast if her child is critically ill, and will not

---

6. It is best to acquire shoes without heels rather than to exercise this option. (*Ibid* 614: *Shaarei Tzion* 18)
7. For in these conditions, cold is harmful to them. (*Ibid* 614:100)
8. Excessive conversation is also forbidden. (*Ibid* 615:1)

שֶׁוְּלָדָהּ חוֹלֶה וּמְסֻכָּן וְאֵינוֹ רוֹצֶה לִינֹק כִּי אִם מִמֶּנָּה, וְאִם תִּתְעַנֶּה, תְּהֵא סַכָּנָה לַוָּלָד, לֹא תִתְעַנֶּה.

יג) מְעֻבֶּרֶת שֶׁהֵרִיחָה אֵיזֶה מַאֲכָל וּמִתְאַוָּה לוֹ, וְיָדוּעַ שֶׁאִם אֵין נוֹתְנִין לָהּ מִמַּה שֶׁהִיא מִתְאַוָּה, הִיא וּוְלָדָהּ מְסֻכָּנִים, לָכֵן אִם אָמְרָה צְרִיכָה אֲנִי לֶאֱכֹל, אַף־עַל־פִּי שֶׁאֵין פָּנֶיהָ מִשְׁתַּנִּים, אוֹ שֶׁרוֹאִים שֶׁפָּנֶיהָ מִשְׁתַּנִּים, אַף־עַל־פִּי שֶׁאֵינָהּ אוֹמֶרֶת כְּלוּם, לוֹחֲשִׁין לָהּ בְּאָזְנָהּ, שֶׁהַיּוֹם יוֹם־הַכִּפּוּרִים, כִּי לִפְעָמִים מִתְיַשֶּׁבֶת דַּעְתָּהּ בְּכָךְ. וְאִם לֹא נִתְיַשְּׁבָה דַעְתָּהּ, מַאֲכִילִין אוֹתָהּ בְּעִנְיָן זֶה, מִתְּחִלָּה נוֹתְנִין לָהּ דָּבָר מְעַט, שֶׁטּוֹבְלִין אֶצְבַּע בְּרֹטֶב וְכַדּוֹמֶה וְנוֹתְנִין לְתוֹךְ פִּיהָ, כִּי לִפְעָמִים בְּטִפָּה אַחַת מִתְיַשֶּׁבֶת דַּעְתָּהּ. וְאִם לָאו, נוֹתְנִין לָהּ פָּחוֹת מִכַּשִּׁעוּר (עַיֵּן לְקַמָּן סָעִיף טו). וְאִם עֲדַיִן לֹא נִתְיַשְּׁבָה, נוֹתְנִין לָהּ דֵּי צָרְכָּהּ. וְכֵן כָּל אָדָם שֶׁהֵרִיחַ מַאֲכָל וְנִשְׁתַּנּוּ פָּנָיו, מְסֻכָּן הוּא (וְעַיֵּן לְעֵיל סִימָן לג סָעִיף ד), וְנוֹהֲגִין בּוֹ כְּמוֹ שֶׁכָּתַבְתִּי. אֲבָל כָּל זְמַן שֶׁלֹּא נִשְׁתַּנּוּ פָּנָיו, אֵין מַאֲכִילִין אוֹתוֹ, אַף־עַל־פִּי שֶׁאוֹמֵר שֶׁצָּרִיךְ אֲנִי.

יד) יוֹלֶדֶת וְכֵן חוֹלֶה שֶׁיֵּשׁ בּוֹ סַכָּנָה, לְעִנְיַן אֲכִילָה וּשְׁתִיָּה וְחִלּוּל יוֹם־הַכִּפּוּרִים, דִּינָם כְּמוֹ בְּחִלּוּל שַׁבָּת (עַיֵּן לְעֵיל סִימָן צב וְסִימָן צג). אֶלָּא דִּלְעִנְיַן אֲכִילָה וּשְׁתִיָּה, אֲפִלּוּ כַּמָּה רוֹפְאִים אוֹמְרִים שֶׁאֵינוֹ צָרִיךְ, וַאֲפִלּוּ אוֹמְרִים שֶׁהָאֲכִילָה אוֹ הַשְּׁתִיָּה תַּזִּיק לוֹ, וְהַחוֹלֶה אוֹמֵר שֶׁהוּא צָרִיךְ, וַאֲפִלּוּ הוּא אוֹמֵר שֶׁעֲדַיִן אֵינוֹ מְסֻכָּן, אֶלָּא שֶׁאִם לֹא יֹאכַל, יִכְבַּד עָלָיו הַחֹלִי וְיִסְתַּכֵּן, שׁוֹמְעִין לוֹ וּמַאֲכִילִין אוֹתוֹ. כִּי לְעִנְיַן אֲכִילָה וּשְׁתִיָּה, הוּא יוֹתֵר מֵבִין עַל עַצְמוֹ, וְלֵב יוֹדֵעַ מָרַת נַפְשׁוֹ.

טו) כְּשֶׁמַּאֲכִילִין אֶת הַמְעֻבֶּרֶת אוֹ אֶת הַיּוֹלֶדֶת אוֹ אֶת הַחוֹלֶה, מַנִּיחִין לִפְנֵיהֶם אֶת הַמַּאֲכָל וְאוֹמְרִים לָהֶם, אִם יוֹדֵעַ אַתָּה שֶׁאֶפְשָׁר שֶׁתִּסְתַּכֵּן אִם לֹא תֹאכַל דֵּי מַחְסוֹרְךָ, תֹּאכַל כְּסֵדֶר, עַד שֶׁתָּבִין כִּי דַי לָךְ. אֲבָל אִם אֶפְשָׁר לְךָ שֶׁלֹּא תֹאכַל בְּפַעַם אַחַת כַּשִּׁעוּר, עֲשֵׂה כָּךְ.

---

9. It makes no difference whether she is in the beginning or at the end of her pregnancy. (*Ibid* 617:11)

10. It need not be a finger. You may use a straw or any other utensil to give her a few drops.

11. This is true even if he says that his heart feels faint and he needs to eat. *Chasam Sofer* is of the opinion that while we should not give him food, he is, nevertheless, permitted to take food on his own if he feels the need to eat because of his weak heart. If, however, a person is

nurse from anyone else but her; for if she would fast, the child's life would be threatened.

13) It is an established fact, that if you do not give a pregnant woman[9] the food she craves, she and the child will be in danger. Therefore if she smelled food and it stimulated a craving for it, this precedure should be followed: If she says "I must eat," even though her facial color has not changed, or if it did visibly change, even if she does not say anything, you should whisper in her ear that today is *Yom Kippur,* because sometimes that will calm her. But if this does not calm her, she should be fed in the following manner: At first give her just a taste, by dipping your finger[10] in the soup, etc., and putting it into her mouth, because sometimes even one drop will calm her. But if that does not help, you should give her a little less than the *halachic* quantity, (see paragraph 15 below). If her mind still is not calmed, you should give her as much as she needs. The same applies to any person who caught a smell of food and his face turned [ashen]. Such a person is considered critically ill, (see chapter 33:4 above) and should be treated as I wrote [above]. But as long as his color has not changed you should not give him any food, even if he says "I must eat."[11]

14) A woman who has given birth[12] or a person who is critically ill, with regard to eating, drinking and the desecration of *Yom Kippur,* are governed by the same *Halochos* that apply in the case of desecration of Shabbos. (see chapters 92 and 93 above) However, with regard to eating and drinking, even if several doctors say that the patient is not required [to take food,] and even if they say that eating and drinking will be harmful to him, but the patient says that he does require food, and even if he says that his life is not yet in danger, but if he does not eat, his sickness will get worse, and his life will be threatened, you should obey his wishes[13] and give him food; for in regard to food and drink he is the best judge of his own condition, [as it is written, (Proverbs 14:10)] "The heart knows its own bitterness."

15) When you give food to a pregnant woman or to a woman who has given birth[14] or to a sick person, you should place the food before them, and say to them, "If you feel that you may be in danger unless you eat as much as you need, then you may eat normally, until you are satisfied.[15] However if it is possible for you to eat only the halachic quantity at one time, then do as follows: Eat at one time a

---

actually ill or if the doctor says he must eat, we should give him food immediately according to his needs. (*Ibid* 617:6)

12. *Sedei Chemed* writes that a woman who has suffered a miscarriage is in the same category as one who gave birth. (*Ibid* 617 *Biur Halachah*)

13. Before giving him food, he should be reminded that it is *Yom Kippur* for he may have forgotten. (*Ibid* 618, *Mishnah Berurah* 5)

14. A woman within three days after giving birth should not fast at all; even if she says she does not need to eat, we tell her to eat. (*Ibid* 617:10)

15. Great care must be taken not to eat more than the *halachic* quantity at one time, unless it is absolutely necessary. For if less than the *halachic* quantity will suffice, it is a grave sin to eat more than this. (*Ibid* 618, *Biur Halachah*)

וְיֹאכַל בְּפַעַם אַחַת כְּשִׁעוּר שְׁנֵי שְׁלִישֵׁי בֵיצָה, (כִּי שִׁעוּר אֲכִילָה לְהִתְחַיֵּב כָּרֵת בְּיוֹם־הַכִּפּוּרִים הוּא כַּכּוֹתֶבֶת הַגַּסָּה, שֶׁהוּא פָּחוֹת מְעַט מִכַּבֵּיצָה בֵינוֹנִית בְּלֹא קְלִפָּתָהּ). וְיִשְׁהֶה קְצָת וְשׁוּב יֹאכַל כָּךְ, וְיִשְׁהֶה בֵּין אֲכִילָה לַאֲכִילָה עַד שֶׁיְּהֵא מִסּוֹף הָאֲכִילָה הָרִאשׁוֹנָה עַד תְּחִלַּת הָאֲכִילָה הַשְּׁנִיָּה לְכָל־הַפָּחוֹת שִׁעוּר כְּדֵי אֲכִילַת פְּרָס. וְכֵן יָכוֹל לֶאֱכֹל אֲפִלּוּ הַרְבֵּה פְּעָמִים, רַק שֶׁלֹּא יִהְיוּ שְׁתֵּי אֲכִילוֹת בְּתוֹךְ שִׁעוּר אֲכִילַת פְּרָס אִם אֶפְשָׁר, וְדַי לוֹ, (כִּי שְׁתֵּי אֲכִילוֹת, שֶׁהֵן בִּכְדֵי אֲכִילַת פְּרָס, מִצְטָרְפוֹת וְנֶחְשָׁבוֹת כַּאֲכִילָה אֶחָת). וּבִשְׁתִיָּה, יִשְׁתֶּה בְּפַעַם אַחַת קְצָת פָּחוֹת מִמְּלֹא לֻגְמָיו, וְיִשְׁהֶה גַּם כֵּן קְצָת וְיַחֲזוֹר וְיִשְׁתֶּה. וּשְׁהִיּוֹת אֵלּוּ תִּהְיֶינָה גַּם כֵּן לְכָל־הַפָּחוֹת כְּדֵי אֲכִילַת פְּרָס, אוֹ עַל־כָּל־פָּנִים לַפָּחוֹת כְּדֵי שְׁתִיַּת רְבִיעִית. וְיֵשׁ לְשַׁעֵר קֹדֶם יוֹם־הַכִּפּוּרִים שִׁעוּרִים אֵלּוּ לְפִי כְּלִי שָׁעוֹת, כְּדֵי שֶׁיֵּדְעוּ אוֹתָם עַל נָכוֹן.

טז) מִי שֶׁאֲחָזוֹ בֻּלְמוּס, וְהוּא חֹלִי מֵחֲמַת רְעָבוֹן, וְסִימָנָיו שֶׁעֵינָיו כֵּהוֹת וְאֵינוֹ יָכוֹל לִרְאוֹת, מַאֲכִילִין אוֹתוֹ עַד שֶׁיֵּאוֹרוּ עֵינָיו.

יז) בְּכָל אֵלּוּ שֶׁמַּאֲכִילִין אוֹתָן מִשּׁוּם סַכָּנָה, אִם אֵין שָׁם מַאֲכָל הֶתֵּר, מַאֲכִילִין אוֹתָן מַאֲכָל אִסּוּר. (וְעַיֵּן בְּשֻׁלְחָן־עָרוּךְ סִימָן תריח סָעִיף ט). וְאִם מַאֲכִילִין אוֹתָן דְּבַר אִסּוּר, נִרְאֶה דְּיֵשׁ לְהַאֲכִילָן פָּחוֹת פָּחוֹת מִכַּזַּיִת, אִם דַּי לָהֶם בְּכָךְ.

יח) אִם דַּעְתּוֹ מְיֻשֶּׁבֶת, מְבָרֵךְ לִפְנֵיהֶם וּלְאַחֲרֵיהֶם, אֲבָל קִדּוּשׁ לֹא יַעֲשֶׂה, וּבְבִרְכַּת־הַמָּזוֹן אוֹמֵר יַעֲלֶה וְיָבוֹא. וְאִם חָל בַּשַּׁבָּת, אוֹמֵר גַּם רְצֵה. וְאִם שָׁכַח, אֵינוֹ צָרִיךְ לַחֲזוֹר וּלְבָרֵךְ, שֶׁאֵין חִיּוּב הַיּוֹם לֶאֱכוֹל פַּת.

יט) קָטָן וּקְטַנָּה פְּחוּתִים מִתֵּשַׁע שָׁנִים, אֲפִלּוּ אִם רוֹצִים לְהִתְעַנּוֹת קְצָת, אֵין מַנִּיחִין אוֹתָן, שֶׁלֹּא יָבוֹאוּ, חַס־וְשָׁלוֹם, לִידֵי סַכָּנָה. אֲבָל מִשֶּׁיֵּשׁ לָהֶם תֵּשַׁע שָׁנִים שְׁלֵמוֹת וְהֵם בְּרִיאִים, מְחַנְּכִין אוֹתָן שֶׁיִּתְעַנּוּ קְצָת, וְלֹא יֹאכְלוּ עַד לְאַחַר אֵיזוֹ שָׁעוֹת מִמַּה שֶּׁהֵם רְגִילִים לֶאֱכוֹל. וּבִנְעִילַת הַסַּנְדָּל וּרְחִיצָה וְסִיכָה, יֵשׁ לְחַנְּכָם גַּם קֹדֶם תֵּשַׁע שָׁנִים.

כ) טוֹב לְהָרִיחַ אֵיזֶה פְּעָמִים בִּבְשָׂמִים וּלְבָרֵךְ עֲלֵיהֶם, כְּדֵי לְהַשְׁלִים מֵאָה בְּרָכוֹת. וְאָמְנָם כָּל זְמַן שֶׁלֹּא הִסִּיחַ דַּעְתּוֹ, אָסוּר לְבָרֵךְ שֵׁנִית, דַּהֲוֵי

16. See Glossary

quantity the size of two-thirds of an egg.[16] (The quantity of food, for which a person is punished by *kareis* [premature death] [if he eats it] on *Yom Kippur* is the size of a large date which is a little less than a medium-size egg with the shell.) Then take a short pause, and eat the same quantity again. The pause between eatings should be sufficiently long[17] so that from the end of one meal to the beginning of the next should be at least as long as the time needed for *achilas peras.*[18] In this manner you may eat even many times, provided the interval between two meals is at least as long as *achilas peras*[18] if you can wait that long, [and the small quantity] is sufficient for you. (Two meals that are separated by a lesser pause, are combined, and considered one meal.) With regard to drinking, you may drink at one time a little less than a mouthful,[19] pause a bit and drink again. These pauses should be at least as long as the time needed for *achilas peras,* or in any case at least [as long as it takes] to drink a *reve'is.*[16] Before Yom Kippur you should measure the lengths of these intervals by timing them with a [stop] watch, so that you will know them exactly."

16) If someone is overcome by a voracious, ravenous hunger, and he is famished to the point of being sick, his symptoms being weakening eyesight and impaired vision, you may give him food until he regains his clear eyesight.[20]

17) All those who are given food because their health is in danger, if no permitted food is available, may be fed forbidden food. (see Shulchan Aruch 618:9) If they are given forbidden food, it seems that they should be fed less than a *kazayis*[16] at a time if that is sufficient for them.

18) If your mind is at ease you should say a berachah before and after eating, but you should not recite *kiddush.* In *Birkas Hamazon* you should say *Ya'aleh veyavo,* and if it occurs on Shabbos you should say *Retzeih.* But if you forgot to say it, you need not repeat *Birkas Hamazon,* because it is not a mitzvah to eat bread on this day.

19) Even if boys and girls less than nine years old want to fast for a while, they should not be permitted to do so, because it may, God forbid, endanger their health. But when they are nine years old and in good health, they should be trained to fast a little, and they should not eat until a few hours past their regular mealtime. Concerning wearing shoes, washing and anointing, children should be trained [to abstain] even before they are nine years old.

20) It is a good practice to smell spices several times [during the day] and to say the berachah over them, in order to fulfill the required number of one hundred

---

17. This must be done in order that these eatings not be combined and be considered as one. (*Ibid* 618:19)

18. According to *Chasam Sofer* the interval should be at least nine minutes. If this is too difficult, it is sufficient to wait 6 3/4 minutes.

19. This amount varies according to each individual. Before *Yom Kippur* a sick person should determine the actual quantity it takes to fill one of his cheeks and thus he will know how much he is permitted to drink at one time. (*Ibid* 618:21)

20. In this circumstance, the previous qualifications concerning amounts and time intervals need not be followed. (*Ibid* 618:26)

בְּרָכָה לְבַטָּלָה. עַל כֵּן צָרִיךְ לְהַפְסִיק בֵּינְתַיִם זְמַן רַב, שֶׁיְּהֵא הֶסַּח־הַדַּעַת בֵּינְתַיִם. וְטוֹב שֶׁיָּרִיחַ בְּכָל פַּעַם בִּבְשָׂמִים אֲחֵרִים, אַף שֶׁהֵן מִמִּין אֶחָד. וּמִכָּל־שֶׁכֵּן אִם יֵשׁ לוֹ שְׁלֹשָׁה מִינִים, כְּגוֹן עֲצֵי בְשָׂמִים, עִשְׂבֵּי בְשָׂמִים, וּמִינֵי בְשָׂמִים. וְאִם יְכַוֵּן לְכָל בִּרְכוֹת שְׁלִיחַ־הַצִּבּוּר וְהַקּוֹרְאִים בַּתּוֹרָה וְהַמַּפְטִירִין, לֹא יַחְסְרוּ לוֹ רַק שָׁלֹשׁ בְּרָכוֹת לְתַשְׁלוּם מֵאָה, וְיַשְׁלִים בְּאֵלּוּ שֶׁעַל הַבְּשָׂמִים.

כא) מַזְכִּירִין נְשָׁמוֹת בְּיוֹם־הַכִּפּוּרִים, מִשּׁוּם דִּזְכִירַת הַמֵּתִים מְשַׁבֶּרֶת וּמַכְנִיעָה לִבּוֹ שֶׁל אָדָם. וְעוֹד, לְפִי שֶׁגַּם הַמֵּתִים צְרִיכִין כַּפָּרָה, כִּדְאִיתָא בְּסִפְרֵי, כַּפֵּר לְעַמְּךָ יִשְׂרָאֵל, אֵלּוּ הַחַיִּים. אֲשֶׁר פָּדִיתָ, אֵלּוּ הַמֵּתִים. מְלַמֵּד, שֶׁהַמֵּתִים צְרִיכִין כַּפָּרָה. וְנוֹדְרִים צְדָקָה בַּעֲבוּרָם (וְעַיֵּן לְעֵיל סִימָן סז סָעִיף ג, שֶׁיֵּשׁ לוֹמַר בְּלִי נֶדֶר). וְסֶמֶךְ לָזֶה בְּסוֹף פָּרָשַׁת תְּצַוֶּה כְּתִיב, אַחַת בַּשָּׁנָה יְכַפֵּר, וְסָמִיךְ לֵהּ, וְנָתְנוּ אִישׁ כֹּפֶר נַפְשׁוֹ לַה'. וּמוֹעִילָה הַצְּדָקָה בַּעֲבוּר הַמֵּתִים, כִּי ה' בּוֹחֵן לְבָבוֹת, שֶׁאִם הָיָה זֶה הַמֵּת חַי, גַּם כֵּן הָיָה נוֹתֵן צְדָקָה. וְהַחַי יָכוֹל לְבַקֵּשׁ לְהָקֵל דִּין הַמֵּת, כְּמוֹ דָוִד שֶׁהִתְפַּלֵּל עַל אַבְשָׁלוֹם. וְהַמֵּתִים הַצַּדִּיקִים מְלִיצִים עַל צֶאֱצָאֵיהֶם. גַּם בְּיוֹם אַחֲרוֹן שֶׁל פֶּסַח וּבְיוֹם שֵׁנִי דְשָׁבוּעוֹת וּבִשְׁמִינִי־עֲצֶרֶת, מַזְכִּירִין נְשָׁמוֹת, לְפִי שֶׁקּוֹרִין בָּהֶם כָּל הַבְּכוֹר, וּכְתִיב שָׁם, אִישׁ כְּמַתְּנַת יָדוֹ. לָכֵן נוֹדְרִין מַתָּנוֹת לִצְדָקָה. וְכֵיוָן שֶׁנּוֹדְרִין לִצְדָקָה, נָהֲגוּ לִתְּנָהּ בַּעֲבוּר הַנְּשָׁמוֹת, שֶׁיִּזְכֹּר אוֹתָן אֱלֹקִים לְטוֹבָה, וְגַם אוֹתָנוּ יִזְכֹּר עִמָּהֶן לְטוֹבָה בִּזְכֻיּוֹתֵיהֶן. וְנוֹהֲגִין כִּי מִי שֶׁיֵּשׁ לוֹ אָב וָאֵם, יוֹצֵא מִבֵּית־הַכְּנֶסֶת בִּשְׁעַת הַזְכָּרַת נְשָׁמוֹת. גַּם נוֹהֲגִין שֶׁבְּתוֹךְ שָׁנָה רִאשׁוֹנָה לְמִיתַת הָאָב אוֹ הָאֵם, יוֹצֵא גַם כֵּן מִבֵּית־הַכְּנֶסֶת.

כב) אִם יֵשׁ תִּינוֹק לָמוּל, מָלִין קֹדֶם אַשְׁרֵי, וּמְבָרְכִין בִּרְכַּת הַמִּילָה בְּלֹא כּוֹס. וּבִמְדִינוֹתֵינוּ נוֹהֲגִין לְבָרֵךְ עַל הַכּוֹס, וְנוֹתְנִין מִמֶּנּוּ מְעַט לַתִּינוֹק הַנִּמּוֹל, מִלְּבַד מַה שֶּׁנּוֹתְנִים לוֹ כְּשֶׁאוֹמְרִים בְּדָמַיִךְ חֲיִי. אֲבָל לְתִינוֹק אַחֵר, אֵין לִתֵּן לִטְעֹם מִן הַכּוֹס, (דְּחָמִיר מִתִּשְׁעָה בְּאָב). הַנּוֹהֵג לִמְצֹץ בְּיַיִן, לֹא יְזַלְּפוֹ בַּפֶּה אֶלָּא בַּיָּד, וּמוֹצֵץ בַּפֶּה כְּדַרְכּוֹ.

---

21. Many *Poskim* disagree, and rule that *Yizkor* must be said even during the first year. (*Penei Baruch* 38, *Penei Hachaim* 31)

berachos a day. However, as long as your mind has not been diverted [from inhaling the fragrance], you are forbidden to repeat the berachah, for that would be a berachah in vain. It is necessary, therefore, to let a long time pass between inhalations in order that you be distracted. It is best to smell different spices each time, even if they are of the same species, and surely this is true if you have three different species such as fragrant woods, fragrant herbs, and spices, [each of which has a different berachah]. If you concentrate on all the *berachos* said by the *Chazzan,* and by those who are called to the Torah, and the two readings of the *Haftarah,* you will be missing only three *berachos* of the one hundred, and you will reach that number with the *berachos* you say over the spices.

21) *Yizkor,* the memorial service for the departed is recited on *Yom Kippur,* because remembering the departed saddens and humbles a man's heart, and for the additional reason, that the dead, too, need atonement, as expounded in *Sifri:* "Forgive Your people Yisrael," (Deuteronomy 21:8) refers to the living, "whom You have redeemed," refers to the dead, this teaches us that the dead need atonement. We pledge to give charity on their behalf, (see chapter 67:3 and when doing so you should say "without making a vow"). A support for this practice is found at the end of the portion of *Tetzaveh* (Exodus 30:10) where it is written, "He shall make atonement once each year," and this is followed by the verse (verse 12) "Each shall give an atonement offering to God." The charity is credited to the departed, because God, Who tests the hearts, knows that if this man were alive, he, too, would have given charity. The living can pray to make the judgment of the dead less severe, just as David did when he prayed for [his son] Absalom (*Maseches Sotah* 10b); and the righteous dead appeal to God on behalf of their offspring. Also on the last day of *Pesach,* on the second day of *Shavuos,* and on *Shemini Atzeres, Yizkor* is said, because on these days we read *Kol habechor* [Every male first-born], (Deuteronomy 15:19), where it is written, "Each person according to the gift of his hand" (16:17). Because of that, people pledge money for charity. Since pledges are made to charity, it became the accepted custom to make these pledges on behalf of the departed souls, that God may remember them for good, and that He may also remember us along with them for good, through their merits. It is customary for those whose father and mother are living to leave the synagogue during the *Yizkor* service. It is also the custom, during the first year after the death of one's father or mother to leave the synagogue [during *Yizkor*].[21]

22) If there is to be a *bris,* it should be performed before *Ashrei.* The berachah over the circumcision should be said without a cup of wine. In our regions it is customary to say the berachah over the cup of wine, and give a taste of it to the circumcised infant, in addition to what is given to him when saying *Bedama'yich cha'yi* [In your blood, live] (Ezekiel 16:6). But another child should not be given any of the wine, (for [the laws of *Yom Kippur*] are more stringent than those of *Tishah beAv.*) [A mohel] who is accustomed to use wine when doing the *metzitzah* [sucking blood from the wound] should not spray the wine with his mouth but with his hand, and then suck the blood with his mouth in the usual manner.

כג) נוֹהֲגִין לִשְׁטֹחַ עֲשָׂבִים בְּבֵית־הַכְּנֶסֶת. וְהַטַּעַם הוּא, לְפִי שֶׁנּוֹהֲגִין לְהִשְׁתַּחֲווֹת וְלִפֹּל עַל הַפָּנִים בִּשְׁעַת הָעֲבוֹדָה, זֵכֶר לַמִּקְדָּשׁ. וּבְמָקוֹם שֶׁהַקַּרְקַע מְרֻצָּף בַּאֲבָנִים, אָסוּר לְהִשְׁתַּחֲווֹת כֵּן. וַאֲפִלּוּ בְּמָקוֹם שֶׁאֵינוֹ מְרֻצָּף, יֵשׁ קְצָת אִסּוּר, עַל כֵּן שׁוֹטְחִין עֲשָׂבִים לְהַפְסִיק בֵּין הַקַּרְקַע. וְאִם אֵין שָׁם עֲשָׂבִים, יַפְסִיק בְּטַלִּיתוֹ אוֹ בְּדָבָר אַחֵר.

כד) זְמַן תְּפִלַּת נְעִילָה הוּא, כְּשֶׁהַחַמָּה הִיא בְּרֹאשׁ הָאִילָנוֹת, כְּדֵי שֶׁיַּשְׁלִים אוֹתָהּ עִם צֵאת הַכּוֹכָבִים. וְלִפְעָמִים נִמְשֶׁכֶת קְצָת בְּתוֹךְ הַלַּיְלָה, וַאֲפִלּוּ הָכִי אוֹמְרִים חָתְמֵנוּ, לְפִי שֶׁאֵין הַדִּין מִסְתַּלֵּק עַד שֶׁיִּגְמְרוּ יִשְׂרָאֵל אֶת סִדְרֵיהֶם לְמַטָּה. וְהֶחָרוּז הַיּוֹם יִפְנֶה וְכוּ׳, אִם יָצְאוּ הַכּוֹכָבִים, לֹא יֹאמַר כֵּן, מִשּׁוּם דַּהֲוֵי דּוֹבֵר שְׁקָרִים. אֶלָּא יֹאמַר, הַיּוֹם פָּנָה, הַשֶּׁמֶשׁ בָּא וּפָנָה. שְׁלִיחַ־הַצִּבּוּר אוֹמֵר בִּרְכַּת כֹּהֲנִים וְשִׂים שָׁלוֹם, אַף־עַל־פִּי שֶׁהוּא לַיְלָה.

כה) יֵשׁ לְבַטֵּל הַמִּנְהָג שֶׁהַגּוֹי מַדְלִיק נֵרוֹת לְצֹרֶךְ אֲמִירַת הַפִּיּוּטִים בִּנְעִילָה, אֶלָּא הַנֵּרוֹת הַדּוֹלְקִים, יְפַזְּרֵם בְּכָל בֵּית־הַכְּנֶסֶת, דְּזֶה הֲוֵי שְׁבוּת דִּשְׁבוּת.

כו) לְאַחַר תְּפִלַּת נְעִילָה, אֲפִלּוּ חָל בְּשַׁבָּת וּגְמָרָהּ בַּיּוֹם, מִכָּל מָקוֹם אוֹמְרִים אָבִינוּ מַלְכֵּנוּ. וְאוֹמְרִים שְׁמַע יִשְׂרָאֵל, פַּעַם אֶחָת. בָּרוּךְ שֵׁם כְּבוֹד מַלְכוּתוֹ לְעוֹלָם וָעֶד, שָׁלֹשׁ פְּעָמִים. ה׳ הוּא הָאֱלֹהִים, שֶׁבַע פְּעָמִים, לְלַוּוֹת אֶת הַשְּׁכִינָה, שֶׁמִּתְעַלָּה לְמַעְלָה מִשִּׁבְעָה רְקִיעִים. וְאוֹמֵר שְׁלִיחַ־הַצִּבּוּר קַדִּישׁ שָׁלֵם בְּנִגּוּן שֶׁל שִׂמְחָה, וְאַחַר כָּךְ תּוֹקְעִין תְּקִיעָה אַחַת וְהִיא סִימָן לְסִלּוּק שְׁכִינָה לְמַעְלָה, כְּמוֹ שֶׁהָיָה בְּמַתַּן תּוֹרָה, שֶׁכְּשֶׁעָלְתָה הַשְּׁכִינָה, נֶאֱמַר, בִּמְשֹׁךְ הַיֹּבֵל וְגוֹ׳. וְנֶאֱמַר, עָלָה אֱלֹהִים בִּתְרוּעָה. וְגַם הוּא זֵכֶר לִתְקִיעַת יוֹם־הַכִּפּוּרִים בַּיּוֹבֵל. וִיכוֹלִין לִתְקֹעַ אַף־עַל־פִּי שֶׁעֲדַיִן לֹא יָצְאוּ כּוֹכָבִים, אֶלָּא שֶׁהוּא בֵּין־הַשְּׁמָשׁוֹת, וַאֲפִלּוּ הוּא שַׁבָּת. אֲבָל בְּעוֹד יוֹם אֵין לִתְקֹעַ. לְאַחַר הַתְּקִיעָה, אוֹמְרִים כֻּלָּם שָׁלֹשׁ פְּעָמִים, לַשָּׁנָה הַבָּאָה בִּירוּשָׁלָיִם.

כז) לְאַחַר צֵאת הַכּוֹכָבִים, מִתְפַּלְּלִין מַעֲרִיב. וְיֵשׁ לְהַעֲמִיד שְׁלִיחַ־

22. This is shortly before the beginning of sunset.

23) It is customary to spread grass on the floor of the synagogue. The reason for this is, that you bow down and prostrate yourself during the *Avodah,* as a reminder of the service in the *Beis Hamikdash,* and in a place where the ground is covered with stone it is forbidden to bow down. Even in a place that is not tiled [with stone], it involves some prohibition. Therefore, grass is spread to form a separation between [you and] the ground. But if there is no grass, you should make the separation with your *tallis* or use something else.

24) The time for beginning the *Ne'ilah* service is when the sun is over the tree-tops,[22] so that you will conclude it when the stars begin to appear. Sometimes, the *Ne'ilah* service is drawn out into the night, but even so, you may say *Chosmeinu* [seal us], because the heavenly judgment is not concluded until Yisrael concludes the order of prayers below. If the stars have already come out the verse *Hayom yifneh* [The day is drawing to a close] etc. should not be said, because you would be speaking an untruth. You should say, instead, *Hayom panah* [the day has ended], *hashemesh bo ufanah* [the sun has set]. The *Chazzan* says *Birkas Kohanim* and *Sim shalom,* even though it is already night.

25) We should abolish the custom of having a non-Jew light candles for the purpose of saying the special poetic prayers in *Ne'ilah,* but he should distribute the burning candles throughout the synagogue, because the prohibition involved in this is only a derivation of a Rabbinical injunction.

26) After the conclusion of *Ne'ilah,* even if it is Shabbos, and *Ne'ilah* ended while it is still daytime, nevertheless, we say *Avinu Malkeinu.* We then say "*Shema Yisrael*" one time, *Baruch sheim kevod malchuso le'olam va'ed,* [Blessed is His name, whose glorious kingdom is forever and ever] is said three times; *Hashem hu haElokim* [Hashem is God] is said seven times, to honor the departure of the Divine Presence as it ascends to the spiritual heights upward of above the seven heavens. The *Chazzan* then sings the whole kaddish with a joyous melody. After that,[23] one *Tekiah* is sounded on the *shofar,* as a sign that the *Shechinah* has risen on high, as was done at the Giving of the Torah. For when the *Shechinah* ascended, it is said, "When the ram's horn is blown" etc. (Exodus 19:13), and it is also said, "God ascended amidst *Teruah* sounds." It is also a reminder of the blowing of the *shofar* on the *Yom Kippur* of the Jubilee Year. It is permitted to blow the *shofar* even though the stars have not yet appeared and it is still twilight, even on Shabbos. But when it is yet daytime, the *shofar* should not be blown. After the *Tekiah* everyone says three times,[24] *Leshanah haba'ah birushalayim* [Next year [may we be] in Jerusalem].

27) After the stars have come out the *Maariv* service is said. A respected person

23. In some places the *shofar* is sounded before the *Kaddish* is said. (*Ramah* 623:6)
24. In many places it is said only once. (*Mateh Ephraim*)

צִבּוּר הָגוּן, וְיִתְפַּלְּלוּ בְּנַחַת וּבְכַוָּנָה, וְיֵשׁ לִגְעֹר בַּחוּטְפִים. אוֹמְרִים בִּתְפִלַּת שְׁמוֹנֶה־עֶשְׂרֵה אַתָּה חוֹנַנְתָּנוּ. אִם חָל בַּשַּׁבָּת, אוֹמְרִים וְיִתֶּן־לְךָ, אֲבָל אֵין אוֹמְרִים וִיהִי נֹעַם, וְאַתָּה קָדוֹשׁ. וּלְאַחַר הַתְּפִלָּה, מְקַדְּשִׁין אֶת הַלְּבָנָה, וּפוֹקְדִין אִישׁ אֶת רֵעֵהוּ בְּשִׂמְחָה וְטוּב לֵב, כְּמוֹ בְּיוֹם־טוֹב.

כח) בְּהַבְדָּלָה שֶׁל מוֹצָאֵי יוֹם־הַכִּפּוּרִים, צְרִיכִין לְבָרֵךְ דַּוְקָא עַל נֵר שֶׁשָּׁבַת, וְלֹא עַל נֵר שֶׁהוֹצִיאוּ עַתָּה מִן הָאֲבָנִים וְכַדּוֹמֶה, וְלֹא בְּמַה שֶּׁהֻדְלַק מִמֶּנּוּ וְהַמֻּבְחָר הוּא, לְהַדְלִיק נֵר אַחֵר מִן הַנֵּר שֶׁהִדְלִיק אֶתְמוֹל בְּבֵיתוֹ וּלְבָרֵךְ עַל שְׁנֵיהֶם. וְאִם אֵין לוֹ נֵר בְּבֵיתוֹ, יָבִיא אֶת הַנֵּר הַדּוֹלֵק מִבֵּית־הַכְּנֶסֶת, וּלְהַדְלִיק עוֹד אֶחָד מִזֶּה הַנֵּר וּלְבָרֵךְ עֲלֵיהֶם. וּבִשְׁעַת הַדְּחָק, מְבָרְכִין עַל הַנֵּר שֶׁהֻדְלַק מִנֵּר שֶׁל גּוֹי, אוֹ מֵהָאוּר שֶׁהוֹצִיאוּ מֵאֲבָנִים וְכַדּוֹמֶה. וְאֵין מַתְחִילִין הִנֵּה אֵל יְשׁוּעָתִי, אֶלָּא מְבָרְכִין עַל הַכּוֹס וְעַל הַנֵּר וְהַמַּבְדִּיל, וְאֵין מְבָרְכִים עַל הַבְּשָׂמִים. וְאִם הָיְתָה שַׁבָּת, מְבָרְכִין גַּם עַל הַבְּשָׂמִים, וְגַם מַתְחִילִין הִנֵּה אֵל יְשׁוּעָתִי כְּמוֹ בִּשְׁאָר מוֹצָאֵי שַׁבָּת.

כט) אוֹכְלִים וְשׁוֹתִים וּשְׂמֵחִים בְּמוֹצָאֵי יוֹם־הַכִּפּוּרִים, דְּאִיתָא בְּמִדְרָשׁ, בְּמוֹצָאֵי יוֹם־הַכִּפּוּרִים, בַּת־קוֹל יוֹצֵאת וְאוֹמֶרֶת, לֵךְ אֱכֹל בְּשִׂמְחָה לַחְמֶךָ וּשְׁתֵה בְלֶב־טוֹב יֵינֶךָ כִּי כְבָר רָצָה הָאֱלֹהִים אֶת מַעֲשֶׂיךָ.

ל) הַמְדַקְדְּקִין בַּמִּצְוֹת, מַתְחִילִין מִיָּד בְּמוֹצָאֵי יוֹם־הַכִּפּוּרִים בַּעֲשִׂיַּת הַסֻּכָּה, לְקַיֵּם יֵלְכוּ מֵחַיִל אֶל חָיִל.

לא) בַּיּוֹם שֶׁלְּאַחַר יוֹם־הַכִּפּוּרִים, נוֹהֲגִין לְהַשְׁכִּים לְבֵית־הַכְּנֶסֶת. וּבַיָּמִים שֶׁבֵּין יוֹם־הַכִּפּוּרִים לְסֻכּוֹת, אֵין מִתְעַנִּין אֲפִלּוּ תַּעֲנִית יָאר־צַייט. וְאֵין אוֹמְרִים תַּחֲנוּן, לְפִי שֶׁהֵם יְמֵי שִׂמְחָה, שֶׁהָיוּ מְחַנְּכִין בָּהֶם אֶת הַמִּזְבֵּחַ בִּימֵי שְׁלֹמֹה. וְגַם אֲנַחְנוּ עוֹסְקִים בְּמִצְוַת בִּנְיַן סֻכָּה וַהֲכָנַת אֶתְרוֹג וּשְׁאָר הַמִּינִים, לִכְבוֹד אֲדוֹן הָאֲדוֹנִים, מְקַדֵּשׁ יִשְׂרָאֵל וְהַזְּמַנִּים.

should be chosen as *Chazzan,* and the prayers should be said slowly and intently. Those who pray in a hurry should be scolded. In the *Shemoneh Esrei* you should say *Ata chonantanu* [You have favored us]. If *Yom Kippur* occurred on Shabbos you should say *Veyiten lecha* [May God give you], but you do not say *Vihi no'am* [May the pleasantness] and *Ve'ata kadosh* [You are the Holy One]. After the prayers, *Kiddush levanah* [Sanctification of the moon] is said, and people exchange good wishes with one another, with happiness and a glad heart, as on a Yom Tov.

28) In the *Havdalah* of *Yom Kippur* night, you must say the berachah only over a candle that was lit before *Yom Kippur,* and not over a light that is produced now by means of a match or something similar, nor over a light that has been lit from such a light. The best way is to light a candle from the flame of the candle you lit in your house the day before, and to say the berachah over both of them. If you have no burning candle in your house you should bring a burning candle from the synagogue, light another candle from it and say a berachah over both of them. In extreme circumstances, you may say the berachah over a candle that was lit from a candle of a non-Jew, or from a flame that was produced by means of a match, or something similar. You should not begin the *Havdalah* with *Hinei keil yeshuasi* [Behold the Almighty is my deliverance], [rather you should begin] and say the berachah over a cup of wine, over the candle, and then say *Hamavdil.* You should not say a berachah over spices. If it is Shabbos night you should say the berachah over spices, and then you also begin with *Hinei keil yeshuasi,* as on any other Shabbos night.

29) We eat and drink and we rejoice at the conclusion of *Yom Kippur,* as it is said in the *Midrash,* "At the conclusion of *Yom Kippur* a heavenly voice goes forth and says: 'Go, eat your bread with gladness, and drink your wine with a cheerful heart, for God has already accepted your deeds with favor.'"

30) People who are meticulous in observing the mitzvos begin to build the *sukkah,* immediately after the end of *Yom Kippur,* fulfilling the verse, "They go from strength to strength" (Psalms 84:8).

31) On the day after *Yom Kippur* it is customary to rise early to go to the synagogue. On the days between *Yom Kippur* and *Sukkos,* we do not fast even the fast of a *Yahrtzeit.* We do not say *Tachanun* [on these days], because they are days of rejoicing during which the Altar was dedicated in the days of King Solomon, and also because we are occupied with the mitzvah of building the *sukkah,* and preparing the *esrog,* and the other species in honor of the Master of masters, the sanctifier of Yisrael and the seasons.

סִימָן קלד
הִלְכוֹת סֻכָּה

א) מִצְוָה לִבְנוֹת הַסֻּכָּה מִיָּד בַּיּוֹם שֶׁלְּאַחַר יוֹם־הַכִּפּוּרִים, וַאֲפִלּוּ הוּא עֶרֶב שַׁבָּת, דְּמִצְוָה הַבָּאָה לְיָדוֹ אַל יַחְמִיצֶנָּה. וְיִבְחַר מָקוֹם נָקִי לְהַעֲמִידָהּ שָׁם. וּמִצְוָה עַל כָּל אָדָם שֶׁיַּעֲסֹק בְּעַצְמוֹ בַּעֲשִׂיַּת הַסֻּכָּה וּבְהַנָּחַת הַסְּכָךְ. וְאַף־עַל־פִּי שֶׁהוּא אָדָם נִכְבָּד, זֶה כְּבוֹדוֹ, שֶׁעוֹסֵק בְּעַצְמוֹ בַּמִּצְוָה. וּמִן הָרָאוּי הָיָה לְבָרֵךְ שֶׁהֶחֱיָנוּ עַל עֲשִׂיַּת הַסֻּכָּה, אֶלָּא שֶׁאָנוּ סוֹמְכִין עַל שֶׁהֶחֱיָנוּ שֶׁאוֹמְרִים בַּקִּדּוּשׁ. וִיהַדֵּר לְיַפּוֹת אֶת הַסֻּכָּה וּלְהַנְאוֹתָהּ בְּכֵלִים נָאִים וּמַצָּעוֹת נָאוֹת כְּפִי כֹחוֹ.

ב) בְּעִנְיַן דָּפְנוֹת הַסֻּכָּה, יֵשׁ הַרְבֵּה חִלּוּקֵי דִינִים, וְאֵין הַכֹּל בְּקִיאִים. עַל כֵּן צְרִיכִין לַעֲשׂוֹת דְּפָנוֹת שְׁלֵמוֹת וַחֲזָקוֹת, שֶׁלֹּא יְהֵא הָרוּחַ מֵנִיעַ אוֹתָן, וְגַם שֶׁלֹּא יְכַבֶּה הָרוּחַ אֶת הַנֵּרוֹת. וּמִי שֶׁאֵין לוֹ דֵּי צָרְכּוֹ לִדְפָנוֹת, מוּטָב שֶׁיַּעֲשֶׂה שָׁלֹשׁ שְׁלֵמוֹת, מֵאַרְבַּע שֶׁאֵינָן שְׁלֵמוֹת. וּמִי שֶׁיָּדוֹ מַשֶּׂגֶת, מִצְוָה לוֹ שֶׁתִּהְיֶה לוֹ סֻכָּה בְּנוּיָה עִם גַּגּוֹת, שֶׁנִּפְתָּחִים וְנִסְגָּרִים עַל יְדֵי צִירִים, לְסָגְרָם בִּשְׁעַת הַגְּשָׁמִים, וּכְשֶׁפָּסְקוּ הַגְּשָׁמִים, נִפְתָּחִים הַגַּגּוֹת, וְהַסְּכָךְ הוּא נָגוּב, וְיָכוֹל לְקַיֵּם מִצְוַת סֻכָּה כָּרָאוּי.

ג) גַּם בַּסְּכָךְ יֵשׁ כַּמָּה דִינִים. וְכֵיוָן שֶׁאָנוּ נוֹהֲגִין לְסַכֵּךְ בְּעַנְפֵי אִילָנוֹת אוֹ בְּקָנִים, כֵּיוָן שֶׁהֵם גְּדוּלֵי קַרְקַע וְהֵמָּה תְלוּשִׁים וְאֵינָם מְקַבְּלִים טֻמְאָה וְאֵינָם קְשׁוּרִים יַחַד, אֵין בָּהֶם שׁוּם חֲשָׁשׁ.

ד) לְכַתְּחִלָּה רָאוּי לְהַחְמִיר, שֶׁלֹּא לְהַנִּיחַ עַל הַסֻּכָּה דָּבָר הַמְקַבֵּל טֻמְאָה שֶׁיַּנִּיחַ עָלָיו אֶת הַסְּכָךְ, כְּגוֹן סֻלָּמוֹת שֶׁיֵּשׁ בָּהֶם בֵּית קִבּוּל הַשְּׁלִיבוֹת, וְכָל־שֶׁכֵּן שְׁאָר כֵּלִים, כְּגוֹן מָרָה וּמַגְרֵפָה, וַאֲפִלּוּ לִתֵּן אוֹתָם עַל הַסְּכָךְ לְהַחֲזִיקוֹ, יֵשׁ לְהַחְמִיר. וּבְדִיעֲבַד אוֹ שֶׁאֵין לוֹ שְׁאָר דְּבָרִים, הַכֹּל מֻתָּר, דְּקַיְמָא לָן, דְּמֻתָּר לְהַעֲמִיד אֶת הַסְּכָךְ בְּדָבָר הַמְקַבֵּל טֻמְאָה.

ה) צָרִיךְ לְהַנִּיחַ סְכָךְ, עַד שֶׁתְּהֵא צִלָּתָהּ מְרֻבָּה מֵחַמָּתָהּ, שֶׁאִם הָיְתָה חַמָּתָהּ מְרֻבָּה מִצִּלָּתָהּ, פְּסוּלָה מִן הַתּוֹרָה. וְלָכֵן צְרִיכִין לִזָּהֵר לְהַנִּיחַ כָּל

---

1. Even though it was mentioned in the previous chapter (Paragraph 30) that it is a mitzvah to begin building the *sukkah* immediately after *Yom Kippur* at night, it is sufficient to make a symbolic beginning at night, whereas on the next day you should erect the entire *sukkah* if possible. (*Mishnah Berurah* 652:2)

Chapter 134

The Laws of the Sukkah

1) It is a mitzvah to build the *sukkah* immediately, on the day after *Yom Kippur,*[1] even if it is *erev Shabbos,*[2] because when a mitzvoh presents itself you should not put it off. You should select a clean location to build it.[3] It is a mitzvah for everyone to be personally involved in building the *sukkah* and laying the *sechach* (covering). Even though he is a distinguished person, it is considered an honor to be personally involved in the mitzvah. It would have been appropriate to say the berachah *Shehecheyanu* when building the *sukkah,* but we rely on the *Shehecheyanu* that is said in the *Kiddush.* You should endeaver to decorate the *sukkah* and to adorn it with beautiful things and elegant spreads, according to your means.

2) Concerning the walls of the *sukkah,* there are many different *halachos,* and not everyone is familiar with them. Therefore, you must make the walls full-length (complete) and strong, so that the wind cannot shake them[4] or blow out the candles. If you do not have enough [lumber] for [four] walls, it is better to make three complete walls than four incomplete ones. If you can afford it, it is a mitzvah to build a *sukkah* with a roof, that can open and close on hinges, so that you can close it when it rains; and when the rain is over, you can open it again. This way, the *sechach* is kept dry, and you can fulfill the mitzvah of *sukkah* properly.

3) With regard to *sechach,* there are also many *halachos.* It is our custom to cover the *sukkah* with branches of trees or with reeds. Since they grow in the earth, and are detached from the soil, and do not absorb ritual impurity, and are not tied together, you have no reason at all to hesitate [using them].

4) Initially, you should be stringent, and avoid placing anything that absorbs ritual impurity to serve as a supporting beam for the *sechach,* such as ladders which have [in their side pieces] holes in which the rungs are inserted, and certainly other utensils, such as a spade or a rake. Even placing them on top of the *sechach* to reinforce it, should be avoided. However, if they are in place already, or you have nothing else [to serve the purpose], all these are permitted for we have an established rule that it is permitted to support the *sechach* with something that absorbs ritual impurity.

5) You must put enough *sechach* on the *sukkah* to provide more shade than sun,[5] for if there is more sun than shade, the *sukkah* is invalid, according to Torah law. Care

---

2. You may work on the *sukkah* only until midday on *erev Shabbos* but afterwards it is forbidden. (*Ibid.,* see also *Kitzur Shulchan Aruch* 72:9)

3. You must not build a *sukkah* in an area which is affected by bad odors (garbage etc.) because this will cause you to leave the *sukkah.* (See *Mishnah Berurah* 630:4, *Biur Halachah* 637:3)

4. This refers to a normal, usual wind. If the walls move to and fro because of the wind, they are not considered valid walls. (*Mishnah Berurah* 630:48)

5. If there are equal amounts of shade and sun at the bottom part of the *sukkah* it is valid. (*Ibid* 631:1)

כָּךְ, שֶׁאֲפִלּוּ כְּשֶׁיִּתְיַבֵּשׁ, תְּהֵא צִלָּתָהּ מְרֻבָּה. גַּם צְרִיכִין לִזָּהֵר, שֶׁלֹּא יְהֵא בְּמָקוֹם אֶחָד אֲוִיר שְׁלשָׁה טְפָחִים. וּלְכַתְחִלָּה צְרִיכָה שֶׁיְּהֵא אֲוִיר קְצָת בֵּין הַסְּכָךְ, כְּדֵי שֶׁיֵּרָאוּ הַכּוֹכָבִים. וּמִכָּל מָקוֹם, אִם הָיְתָה מְעֻבָּה, שֶׁאֵין הַכּוֹכָבִים נִרְאִים, כְּשֵׁרָה. אֲבָל אִם הָיְתָה מְעֻבָּה כָּל־כָּךְ, שֶׁאֲפִלּוּ אִם יוֹרְדִים גְּשָׁמִים הַרְבֵּה, אֵינָם יוֹרְדִים לְתוֹכָהּ, אִם כֵּן הַוְיָא כְּעֵין בַּיִת, וּפְסוּלָה.

ו) בְּסֻכּוֹת הַבְּנוּיוֹת, לִפְעָמִים בּוֹלְטִים דַּפִּים לְמַעְלָה עַל הַכְּתָלִים, וְעַל דַּפִּים אֵלּוּ מַנִּיחִים הַכְּלוֹנְסָאוֹת שֶׁעֲלֵיהֶם הַסְּכָךְ. וּמֵאַחַר שֶׁאֵין הַדַּף רָחָב אַרְבַּע אַמּוֹת, אֵינוֹ פּוֹסֵל אֶת הַסֻּכָּה מִשּׁוּם סְכָךְ פָּסוּל, כִּי הֲלָכָה לְמשֶׁה מִסִּינַי הִיא, דִּבְפָחוֹת מֵאַרְבַּע אַמּוֹת, אָמְרִינָן דֹּפֶן עֲקֻמָּה. פֵּרוּשׁ, שֶׁנֶּחְשָׁב אֶל הַדֹּפֶן, וְחָשְׁבִינָן לֵהּ כְּאִלּוּ הַדֹּפֶן נִתְעַקְּמָה שָׁם לְמַעְלָה, אֶלָּא שֶׁאֵין יוֹשְׁבִים וְאֵין יְשֵׁנִים שָׁם תַּחַת הַדַּף, כִּי שָׁם אֵין לוֹ דִּין סֻכָּה, וַאֲפִלּוּ אֵינוֹ רָחָב אֶלָּא אַרְבָּעָה טְפָחִים. אֲבָל יֶתֶר הַסֻּכָּה, כְּשֵׁרָה. אַךְ אִם מַנִּיחִים אֵצֶל הַדֹּפֶן דַּפִּים בְּרֹחַב אַרְבַּע אַמּוֹת אוֹ יוֹתֵר, זֶהוּ נִקְרָא סְכָךְ פָּסוּל, וּפוֹסֵל אֶת כָּל הַסֻּכָּה. וּמִכָּל מָקוֹם אִם אֵינוֹ כֵן אֶלָּא בְּצַד אֶחָד, כְּמוֹ שֶׁהַדֶּרֶךְ הוּא בִּקְצָת סֻכּוֹת בְּנוּיוֹת שֶׁעוֹשִׂין קְצָת תִּקְרָה מִצַּד אֶחָד (כְּדֵי לְפַנּוֹת לְשָׁם אֶת הַכֵּלִים תֵּכֶף בְּהַתְחָלַת הַגְּשָׁמִים), זֶה אֵינוֹ מַזִּיק, דְּכֵיוָן שֶׁאֵינוֹ אֶלָּא מִצַּד אֶחָד, הֲרֵי יֵשׁ כָּאן עוֹד שָׁלשׁ דְּפָנוֹת כְּשֵׁרוֹת שֶׁמֻּנָּח עֲלֵיהֶן סְכָךְ כָּשֵׁר, וְסֻכָּה מִשָּׁלשׁ דְּפָנוֹת גַּם כֵּן כְּשֵׁרָה, וּבִלְבַד שֶׁיְּהֵא שָׁם שִׁעוּר סֻכָּה, דְּהַיְנוּ לְכָל־הַפָּחוֹת שִׁבְעָה טְפָחִים עַל שִׁבְעָה טְפָחִים בִּמְרֻבָּע, וְלֹא יֵשְׁבוּ תַּחַת הַתִּקְרָה.

ז) הָעוֹשֶׂה סֻכָּתוֹ תַּחַת עַנְפֵי אִילָן, הֲרֵי הִיא פְּסוּלָה. וַאֲפִלּוּ אִם מֵחֲמַת הָעֲנָפִים בִּלְבַד הָיְתָה חַמָּתָהּ מְרֻבָּה מִצִּלָּתָהּ, וְאִם כֵּן בַּסְּכָךְ שֶׁהִנִּיחַ עָלֶיהָ, עָשָׂה אֶת הַסֻּכָּה, מִכָּל מָקוֹם פְּסוּלָה. וַאֲפִלּוּ אִם יִקְצֹץ אַחַר כָּךְ עַנְפֵי הָאִילָן, מִכָּל מָקוֹם הַסֻּכָּה נִשְׁאֶרֶת בִּפְסוּלָהּ, דִּכְתִיב, חַג הַסֻּכּוֹת תַּעֲשֶׂה לְךָ, וְדָרְשִׁינָן, תַּעֲשֶׂה, וְלֹא מִן הֶעָשׂוּי (עַיֵּן לְעֵיל סִימָן ט סָעִיף ו). וְלָכֵן לְאַחַר שֶׁקָּצַץ אֶת הָעֲנָפִים, צָרִיךְ הוּא לְהַגְבִּיהַּ כָּל עָנָף

---

6. See glossary. Even though less than three *tefachim* does not disqualify the *sukkah*, nevertheless, you should not eat or sleep under that opening. (*Ibid* 632:12)

7. *Mishnah Berurah* writes that if for any reason it is impossible to remove some of the

must be taken, therefore, to put on enough *sechach*; that, even if it dries out, there will still be more shade than sun. You must also be careful not to leave an open space of three *tefachim* in any one place.[6] Initially, it is necessary to leave a slight space between the branches of the *sukkah,* so that the stars can be seen. Nevertheless, if the *sechach* is so thick that the stars cannot be seen, the *sukkah* is still valid. But if the *sechach* is so thick, that even a heavy rain cannot come through, then it is almost like a house, and the *sukkah* is invalid.[7]

6) When *sukkos* are solidly constructed, sometimes boards jut out along the top of the walls, and on these boards, the beams are placed on which the *sechach* rests. If this board is less than four *amos*[8] wide, the *sukkah* does not become invalid, because of invalid *sechah,* for there is a *halachic* tradition from Mount Sinai, that when a board projects less than four *amos,* we say that it is a curved wall, which means that the protruding board is considered part of the wall, and we regard the wall as if it is bent at the top.[9] But you may not sit or sleep underneath that board, for *Halachah* does not recognize that area as part of the *sukkah,* even if the board is only four *tefachim* wide; but the rest of the *sukkah* is valid. But if protruding from the *sukkah* wall, there are boards that are four *amos* or more wide, then they are called invalid *sechach* which invalidates the entire *sukkah.* Nevertheless, if the boards protrude into the *sukkah* only on one side, as is the style in some of the built [permanent] *sukkos,* where a small shelf is installed on one side (to put the dishes there when it starts to rain), then it does not matter; since it is only on one side, there are still three valid walls on which there is valid *sechach;* and a *sukkah* made of three walls is also valid, provided it has the minimum size required for a *sukkah,* which is no less than seven *tefachim*[10] by seven *tefachim* square. But you must not sit underneath the shelf.

7) If you build a *sukkah* underneath the branches of a tree[11] it is invalid. Even if the branches alone would have allowed more sun than shade, and consequently, by placing the *sechach* on the *sukkah,* you, in fact, made it into a *sukkah* [by providing the required shade], it is, nevertheless, invalid. Even if you cut off the branches of the tree afterwards, the *sukkah* still remains invalid, for it is written, "Make [*ta'aseh*] the festival of *Sukkos* for yourself" (Deuteronomy 16:13), and it is expounded, "A *sukkah* must be made, and not come into being by itself." (see chapter 9:6 above) Therefore, after cutting the branches of the tree, you must pick up each branch of

---

sechach, you can rely on those authorities who rule that the *sukkah* is valid even with such thick *sechach.* (*Ibid* 631:6)

8. See glossary.

9. In practice it is advisable to consult a competent *halachic* authority in such situations, for there are various ramifications regarding this rule.

10. Both the length and width of the *sukkah* must be at least seven *tefachim.* Therefore, if one is seven *tefachim* and the other is less or much longer, it is invalid even though the total area is equal to an area of seven by seven *tefachim.* (*Ibid* 634:1)

11. This rule applies only when the branches of the tree actually overhang the *sukkah* itself, but if the branches are adjacent to the *sukkah,* even though they provide the shade for the *sukkah,* the *sukkah* is valid. (*Ibid* 626:1, see *Biur Halachah*)

מִן הַסְּכָךְ וְיַחֲזוֹר וְיַנִּיחֶנּוּ לְשֵׁם סֻכָּה. וְכֵן אָסוּר לְהַנִּיחַ אֶת הַסְּכָךְ קֹדֶם שֶׁעָשָׂה אֶת הַדְּפָנוֹת, דִּבְעֵינָן שֶׁבְּהַנָּחַת הַסְּכָךְ תְּהֵא סֻכָּה כְּשֵׁרָה.

ח) וְכֵן בְּסֻכָּה הָעֲשׂוּיָה בְּגַגּוֹת הַנִּפְתָּחִים, צָרִיךְ לִפְתֹּחַ אֶת הַגַּגּוֹת קֹדֶם שֶׁמַּנִּיחַ אֶת הַסְּכָךְ, וְאַף שֶׁאַחַר כָּךְ סוֹגֵר אֶת הַגַּג וְחוֹזֵר וּפוֹתֵחַ, אֵינוֹ מַזִּיק, דַּהֲוֵי כְּאִלּוּ פּוֹרֵס עָלֶיהָ סָדִין וְחוֹזֵר וְנוֹטְלוֹ. וּמִכָּל מָקוֹם יֵשׁ לְהַחְמִיר, שֶׁיְּהֵא הַגַּג פָּתוּחַ בְּהִכָּנְסַת הֶחָג. עוֹד צְרִיכִין לִזָּהֵר בְּאֵלּוּ הַסֻּכּוֹת, שֶׁיְּהֵא הַגַּג פָּתוּחַ הֵיטֵב עוֹמֵד בְּשָׁוֶה עִם דֹּפֶן הַסֻּכָּה. שֶׁאִם אֵינוֹ עוֹמֵד בְּשָׁוֶה, אֶלָּא נוֹטֶה קְצָת עַל הַסְּכָךְ, אֲפִלּוּ אֵינוֹ שִׁעוּר גָּדוֹל שֶׁתִּפָּסֵל הַסֻּכָּה בְּכָךְ, מִכָּל מָקוֹם צָרִיךְ לִזָּהֵר שֶׁלֹּא יֵשֵׁב בַּמָּקוֹם הַזֶּה שֶׁהַגַּג מְשֻׁפָּע, שֶׁנִּמְצָא יוֹשֵׁב תַּחַת הַגַּג (עַיֵּן לְעֵיל סָעִיף ו). אַף־עַל־פִּי שֶׁסֻּכַּת הֶחָג בֶּחָג פְּטוּרָה מִן הַמְּזוּזָה, מִכָּל מָקוֹם אֵלּוּ הַסֻּכּוֹת הַבְּנוּיוֹת שֶׁמִּשְׁתַּמְּשִׁים בָּהֶן כָּל הַשָּׁנָה וְנִתְחַיְּבוּ בִּמְזוּזָה, גַּם בֶּחָג לֹא נִפְטְרוּ, וְאֵין צְרִיכִין אַחַר הֶחָג לִקְבֹּעַ אֶת הַמְּזוּזָה מֵחָדָשׁ.

ט) יוֹצְאִין בְּסֻכָּה שְׁאוּלָה, אֲבָל לֹא בְסֻכָּה גְזוּלָה. וְלָכֵן אָסוּר לַעֲשׂוֹת סֻכָּה בִּרְשׁוּת הָרַבִּים. וּבִשְׁעַת הַדְּחָק שֶׁאֵין לוֹ סֻכָּה אַחֶרֶת בְּשׁוּם אֹפֶן, יוֹשֵׁב בָּהּ וּמְבָרֵךְ עָלֶיהָ.

י) יֵשׁ לִזָּהֵר שֶׁלֹּא יִקְצֹץ הַיִּשְׂרָאֵל בְּעַצְמוֹ סְכָךְ לְסֻכָּתוֹ, אֶלָּא יִקְנֶה מֵאַחֵר. וּבִשְׁעַת הַדְּחָק יָכוֹל לִקְצֹץ בְּעַצְמוֹ, אֶלָּא שֶׁיִּטּוֹל רְשׁוּת מִבַּעַל הַקַּרְקַע.

יא) מֻתָּר לַעֲשׂוֹת סֻכָּה בְּחֹל־הַמּוֹעֵד.

יב) עֲצֵי סֻכָּה, בֵּין מֵהַדְּפָנוֹת בֵּין מֵהַסְּכָךְ, אֲסוּרִין בַּהֲנָאָה עַד לְאַחַר שִׂמְחַת תּוֹרָה, כֵּיוָן שֶׁהֻקְצוּ לְמִצְוָה. וַאֲפִלּוּ לִטֹּל מֵהֶם קֵיסָם לַחֲצֹץ שִׁנָּיו, אָסוּר. וַאֲפִלּוּ אִם נָפְלוּ, אֲסוּרִין, וְלָא מַהֲנֵי בְּהוּ תְּנַאי. וְאִם חָל שִׂמְחַת־תּוֹרָה בְּעֶרֶב שַׁבָּת, אֲסוּרִין גַּם בְּשַׁבָּת. וְכֵן נוֹיֵי סֻכָּה אֲסוּרִין בַּהֲנָאָה אֲפִלּוּ אִם נָפְלוּ. וְכֵיוָן שֶׁאֲסוּרִין בַּהֲנָאָה, לָכֵן בְּשַׁבָּת וּבְיוֹם־טוֹב, אֲסוּרִין בְּטִלְטוּל מִשּׁוּם מֻקְצֶה. וּמִכָּל מָקוֹם אֶתְרוֹג הַתָּלוּי בַּסֻּכָּה לְנוֹי, מֻתָּר לַהֲרִיחַ בּוֹ, דְּלֹא הֻקְצָה מֵרֵיחַ. וּבְנוֹי הַתָּלוּי בַּסְּכָךְ, נוֹהֲגִין שֶׁאֲפִלּוּ תְּנַאי לָא מַהֲנֵי. אֲבָל בְּנוֹי הַתָּלוּי בַּדְּפָנוֹת, מַהֲנֵי תְּנַאי. וְהַסְּדִינִין

the *sechach* and a new act of placing it down must be performed, for the purpose of fulfilling the mitzvah of *sukkah.*[12] It is also forbidden to lay down the *sechach* before making the walls for it is required that with the laying of the *sechach* the *sukkah* should become valid for use.

8) Similarly when you build a *sukkah* with a roof that can be opened [and closed], you must open the roof before you put down the *sechach,* and if afterwards you close the roof and open it again, it does not matter, for it is the same as if you spread a sheet over it and then remove it. Nevertheless, you should be stringent, and have the roof open at the onset of the Yom Tov. You must also take care with these *sukkos* that the roof is wide open, straight in line with the wall of the *sukkah.* For if it is not perfectly straight, but inclines slightly over the *sechach,* even if the area covered is not large enough to make the *sukkah* invalid, nevertheless, you should be careful not to sit under the area over which the roof protrudes, for you would then be sitting underneath the roof. (see paragraph 6 above) Although a *sukkah* is exempt from a *mezuzah* during the Yom Tov, nevertheless, the permanently built *sukkos,* that are used all year and are required to have a *mezuzah,* are not exempt during *Sukkos,* and it is not necessary after *Sukkos* to affix the *mezuzah* again.

9) You may fulfill your obligation with a borrowed *sukkah,* but not with a *sukkah* that was stolen. It is forbidden, therefore, to build a *sukkah* in a public domain. In extreme situations when there is no other *sukkah* available under any circumstance you may sit in it and say the berachah in it.

10) You should be careful not to cut the *sechach* for your *sukkah* yourself, but you should buy it from someone else. In exterme situations, you may cut it yourself, but you should get permission from the owner of the land.

11) You are permitted to build a *sukkah* during *Chol Hamo'ed.*

12) The wood of the *sukkah,* either of the walls or of the *sechach,* is forbidden to be used [for any purpose] until after *Simchas Torah,* because they were set aside for the performance of a mitzvah. Even to take a splinter from it to use as a toothpick is forbidden. Even if [a piece of wood] fell down you are forbidden to use it; and it is of no avail [if you had made] a stipulation [before Yom Tov] [to use such wood.] If *Simchas Torah* occurs on Friday, the wood is forbidden also on Shabbos. The *sukkah* decorations are also forbidden to be used, even if they fell down. Since it is forbidden to derive any benefit from them, consequently, on Shabbos and Yom Tov it is forbidden to handle them because they are *muktzeh.* Nevertheless, if an *esrog* is hanging in the *sukkah* as a decoration, you are permitted to inhale its fragrance, for it was not set aside in regard to its fragrance. With regard to decorations hanging from the *sechach,* it is generally accepted that even if you made a stipulation [to use them on Yom Tov], it is of no avail. However, regarding decorations hanging on the walls, this stipulation is effective. Tapestries that are hung in the *sukkah* as decora-

12. *Mishnah Berurah* writes that the *sechach* must be placed down for the sake of providing shade but not necessarily for the mitzvah of *sukkah.* (*Ibid* 626:14)

הַמְצֻיָּרִים שֶׁתְּלוּיִים בַּסֻּכָּה לְנוֹי, נוֹהֲגִין לְטַלְטְלָן, שֶׁלֹּא יִתְקַלְקְלוּ מִן הַגְּשָׁמִים, וַאֲפִלּוּ לֹא הִתְנָה בְּפֵרוּשׁ, כִּי מִסְתָמָא מִתְּחִלָּה אַדַּעְתָּא דְהָכִי תְּלָאָן. וּמִכָּל מָקוֹם טוֹב לְהַתְנוֹת תְּחִלָּה בְּפֵרוּשׁ, דְּהַיְנוּ קֹדֶם בֵּין־הַשְּׁמָשׁוֹת הָרִאשׁוֹן יַעֲמֹד שָׁם וְיֹאמַר, אֲנִי מַתְנֶה שֶׁאֱהֵא מֻתָּר לֶאֱכֹל וּלְהִשְׁתַּמֵּשׁ בְּנוֹי סֻכָּה זוֹ מָתַי שֶׁאֶרְצֶה. וְצָרִיךְ לִזָּהֵר בְּנוֹי סֻכָּה אֲשֶׁר בְּדַעְתּוֹ לִטְּלוֹ בְּתוֹךְ יוֹם־טוֹב, שֶׁלֹּא לְקָשְׁרוֹ בְּקֶשֶׁר, אֶלָּא בַּעֲנִיבָה (עַיֵּן לְעֵיל סִימָן פ סָעִיף מה־מו).

יג) גַּם לְאַחַר הֶחָג, כְּשֶׁסָּתַר אֶת הַסֻּכָּה, לֹא יִפְסַע עַל הָעֵצִים, וְלֹא יִשְׁתַּמֵּשׁ בָּהֶם לְדָבָר מְגֻנֶּה, מִשּׁוּם דְּתַשְׁמִישֵׁי מִצְוָה נִינְהוּ, כְּמוֹ צִיצִית (עַיֵּן לְעֵיל סִימָן ט סָעִיף יט).

יד) אָסוּר לַחֲקוֹק פָּסוּק בַּסֻּכּוֹת תֵּשְׁבוּ וְגוֹ' אוֹ שְׁאָר פָּסוּק עַל דֶּלֶת וְכַיּוֹצֵא בָּהּ לְנוֹי סֻכָּה, מִשּׁוּם דְּיָבוֹא אַחַר כָּךְ לִידֵי בִּזָּיוֹן. וְעוֹד, דְּאָסוּר לִכְתֹּב פָּסוּק שֶׁלֹּא לְצֹרֶךְ.

טו) עֶרֶב סֻכּוֹת לְאַחַר חֲצוֹת הַיּוֹם, לֹא יֹאכַל פַּת, כְּדֵי שֶׁיֹּאכַל בַּסֻּכָּה לְתֵאָבוֹן. וְיֵשׁ לְהַרְבּוֹת בִּצְדָקָה בְּעֶרֶב סֻכּוֹת.

סִימָן קלה
דִּינֵי יְשִׁיבַת סֻכָּה

א) כְּתִיב, בַּסֻּכֹּת תֵּשְׁבוּ שִׁבְעַת יָמִים, פֵּרוּשׁ, תָּדוּרוּ בַּסֻּכּוֹת. אָמְרָה תוֹרָה, שֶׁיָּדוּר בַּסֻּכָּה שִׁבְעַת יָמִים. כְּמוֹ שֶׁהוּא דָר בְּבֵיתוֹ כָּל הַשָּׁנָה, כֵּן תְּהֵא עַתָּה עִקַּר־דִּירָתוֹ בַּסֻּכָּה, שֶׁיַּכְנִיס לְתוֹכָהּ כֵּלָיו הַנָּאִים וּמַצָּעוֹת הַנָּאוֹת, וְאוֹכֵל וְשׁוֹתֶה וְלוֹמֵד וּמְטַיֵּל וְיָשֵׁן בַּסֻּכָּה. וַאֲפִלּוּ אִם מְסַפֵּר עִם חֲבֵרוֹ, יְסַפֵּר בַּסֻּכָּה. וְכֵן אִם מִתְפַּלֵּל בִּיחִידוּת, יִתְפַּלֵּל בְּתוֹךְ הַסֻּכָּה. כְּתִיב, לְמַעַן יֵדְעוּ דֹרֹתֵיכֶם כִּי בַסֻּכּוֹת הוֹשַׁבְתִּי אֶת־בְּנֵי יִשְׂרָאֵל בְּהוֹצִיאִי אוֹתָם מֵאֶרֶץ מִצְרָיִם, וְלָכֵן צְרִיכִין לְכַוֵּן בִּישִׁיבַת הַסֻּכָּה, שֶׁצִּוָּנוּ הַקָּדוֹשׁ־בָּרוּךְ־הוּא לֵישֵׁב בַּסֻּכָּה זֵכֶר לִיצִיאַת מִצְרָיִם. וְסֻכּוֹת אֵלּוּ שֶׁאָמַר

---

13. *Shaarei Tzion* (638:26) writes: "Therefore, it is permitted to remove them whenever you want, even when it is not raining, and even when there is no threat of rain."

14. According to *Mishnah Berurah* this stipulation must be made before sunset. (638:21)

15. These restrictions apply to the *sechach* as well. We must rebuke those who throw the boards or *sechach* to places where they will be stepped upon or otherwise misused. (*Ibid* 638:24)

tions, it is the accepted practice to remove them so that they should not get ruined by an impending rain, even if you had made no express stipulation; for we assume that initially you had that in mind when you hung them.[13] Nevertheless, it is best to express prior stipulation, that is, before twilight on the eve of *Sukkos,*[14] you should stand [in the *sukkah*] and say, "I hereby stipulate that I am permitted to eat, and to use the decorations of this *sukkah* whenever I wish." You must be careful about those *sukkah* decorations that you intend to remove during Yom Tov, not to tie them with a knot, but only with a loop, (see chapter 80:45, 46 above).

13) Even after *Sukkos,* when you dismantle the *sukkah,* you should not step on the boards, and you should not use them in a degrading manner,[15] because they are articles that were used for a mitzvah, the same as *tzitzis.* (see chapter 9:19)

14) It is forbidden to carve out the verse "You must live in *sukkos*" etc. or any other verse on a pumpkin or similar fruit as a *sukkah* decoration, because it will subsequently be degraded, and besides, it is forbidden to write a verse needlessly.

15) On *erev Sukkos,* after midday you should not eat bread, so that you will eat your meal in the *sukkah* with good appetite. You should give generous amounts of charity on *erev sukkos.*

Chapter 135

Laws of Dwelling in the Sukkah

1) It is written "For seven days *teishvu* in *sukkos,*" (Leviticus 23:42), which means "you must dwell" in *sukkos.* The Torah teaches that you should make the *sukkah* your home for seven days. Just as you live in your home all year, so now [on *Sukkos*] the *sukkah* should be your principal residence. There you should bring your fine china and elegant tablecloths. You should eat, drink, study,[1] spend your leisure, and sleep in the *sukkah.* Even conversation with friends[2] should be held in the *sukkah,* and if you pray alone[3] you should also pray in the *sukkah.* It is written, "This is so that future generations will know that I caused the Israelites to live in *sukkos* when I brought them out of Egypt," (Leviticus 23:43). Therefore, you should keep in mind when you live in the *sukkah,* that the Holy One, blessed is He, commanded us to live in the *sukkah* as a memorial of the Exodus from Egypt. Regarding the *sukkos* of which the verse says "That I caused [the Israelites] to live in *sukkos,* there is

---

1. You must study Torah in the *sukkah* only if you are able to concentrate with total peace of mind. However, when because of cold weather you are unable to remain there for an extended period, to study with concentration, you are exempt, and may study in your home or in the *Beis Midrash.* (*Mishnah Berurah* 639:29)

2. However, because of the sacred nature of the *sukkah,* you must be very careful not to speak about forbidden subjects, gossip or slander. (*Ibid* 639:2)

3. If however there is a synagogue in your area, you must leave the *sukkah* and attend the synagogue because during the rest of the year, you also leave your house to pray in the synagogue. (*Ibid* 639:30)

הַכָּתוּב כִּי בַסֻּכּוֹת הוֹשַׁבְתִּי, נֶחְלְקוּ בָהֶם תַּנָּאִים. רַבִּי אֱלִיעֶזֶר אוֹמֵר, הֵמָּה עַנְנֵי הַכָּבוֹד, שֶׁהִקִּיף בָּהֶם הַקָּדוֹשׁ־בָּרוּךְ־הוּא אֶת אֲבוֹתֵינוּ, לְבַל יַכֵּם שָׁרָב וָשֶׁמֶשׁ. וְרַבִּי עֲקִיבָא אוֹמֵר, סֻכּוֹת מַמָּשׁ, שֶׁעָשׂוּ לָהֶם בִּשְׁעַת חֲנִיָּתָן מִפְּנֵי הַחַמָּה. וְאַף־עַל־פִּי שֶׁיָּצָאנוּ מִמִּצְרַיִם בְּחֹדֶשׁ נִיסָן, לֹא צִוָּנוּ לַעֲשׂוֹת הַסֻּכָּה בְּאוֹתוֹ הַזְּמַן, לְפִי שֶׁהוּא הַתְחָלַת יְמוֹת הַקַּיִץ, וְדֶרֶךְ כָּל אָדָם לַעֲשׂוֹת אָז סֻכָּה לְצֵל, וְלֹא הָיְתָה נִכֶּרֶת שֶׁהִיא בְּמִצְוַת הַבּוֹרֵא יִתְבָּרַךְ שְׁמוֹ. לָכֵן צִוָּה אוֹתָנוּ לַעֲשׂוֹתָהּ בַּחֹדֶשׁ הַשְּׁבִיעִי, שֶׁהוּא זְמַן הַגְּשָׁמִים, וְדֶרֶךְ כָּל אָדָם לָצֵאת מִסֻּכָּתוֹ וְלֵישֵׁב בְּבֵיתוֹ. וַאֲנַחְנוּ יוֹצְאִין מִן הַבַּיִת לֵישֵׁב בַּסֻּכָּה, בָּזֶה יֵרָאֶה לַכֹּל, כִּי מִצְוַת הַמֶּלֶךְ הִיא עָלֵינוּ לַעֲשׂוֹתָהּ.

ב) צָרִיךְ לְהַחֲזִיק אֶת הַסֻּכָּה בְּכָבוֹד, שֶׁלֹּא תִהְיֶינָה מִצְוֹת בְּזוּיוֹת עָלָיו. וְלָכֵן לֹא יַכְנִיס לְתוֹכָהּ כֵּלִים שֶׁאֵינָם מְכֻבָּדִים, כְּגוֹן קְדֵרוֹת, וְכַד שֶׁשּׁוֹאֲבִים בּוֹ מַיִם, וְכֵלִים שֶׁמַּשְׁהִים בָּהֶם קֶמַח, וַעֲרֵבָה וְיוֹרָה וּמַחֲבַת וּמַכְתֶּשֶׁת וְכַיּוֹצֵא בָהֶן. וְגַם הַקְּעָרוֹת, לְאַחַר הָאֲכִילָה צָרִיךְ לְהוֹצִיאָן לַחוּץ. אֲבָל כְּלֵי שְׁתִיָּה, יִהְיוּ בַּסֻּכָּה. וְנוֹהֲגִין שֶׁלֹּא לְהַכְנִיס לְתוֹכָהּ נֵר שֶׁל חֶרֶס, מִשּׁוּם דְּמָאִיס. וְכֵן לֹא יַעֲשֶׂה בָהּ תַּשְׁמִישׁ בָּזוּי, כְּגוֹן שְׁטִיפַת קְדֵרוֹת וּקְעָרוֹת. אֲבָל כּוֹסוֹת, מֻתָּר לִשְׁטֹף. וְכָל־שֶׁכֵּן דְּאָסוּר לְהַשְׁתִּין בָּהּ, אֲפִלּוּ לְתוֹךְ כֶּלִי, אַף־עַל־פִּי שֶׁעוֹשֶׂה כֵּן בְּתוֹךְ בֵּיתוֹ. אֲבָל תַּשְׁמִישׁ־הַמִּטָּה, מֻתָּר בַּסֻּכָּה, שֶׁהֲרֵי עִקַּר מִצְוָתָהּ אִישׁ וְאִשְׁתּוֹ. אִם הִכְנִיס לְתוֹכָהּ כֵּלִים בְּזוּיִים, אֵינָהּ נִפְסֶלֶת בְּכָךְ. אַךְ בְּשָׁעָה שֶׁהֵם בָּהּ, אֵין לְבָרֵךְ לֵישֵׁב בַּסֻּכָּה, עַד שֶׁיּוֹצִיאוּם.

ג) אֲכִילָה בַּסֻּכָּה בַּלַּיְלָה הָרִאשׁוֹן הִיא חוֹבָה, שֶׁצָּרִיךְ לֶאֱכֹל בַּסֻּכָּה פַּת לְכָל־הַפָּחוֹת כַּזַּיִת. וַאֲפִלּוּ מִצְטַעֵר, חַיָּב לֶאֱכֹל בַּסֻּכָּה. וְאִם יוֹרְדִים גְּשָׁמִים (עַיֵּן לְקַמָּן סָעִיף ט), אִם מְדַמֶּה שֶׁיִּפָּסְקוּ לְאַחַר שָׁעָה אוֹ שְׁתֵּי שָׁעוֹת, יַמְתִּין וְאַחַר כָּךְ יְקַדֵּשׁ וְיֹאכַל בַּסֻּכָּה כָּרָאוּי. וְאִם רוֹאֶה שֶׁלֹּא יִפָּסְקוּ הַגְּשָׁמִים, אוֹ שֶׁהִמְתִּין וְלֹא פָּסְקוּ, מְקַדֵּשׁ בַּסֻּכָּה וּמְבָרֵךְ שֶׁהֶחֱיָנוּ, וּמְכַוֵּן בְּשֶׁהֶחֱיָנוּ גַּם עַל הַסֻּכָּה, אֲבָל אֵינוֹ מְבָרֵךְ לֵישֵׁב בַּסֻּכָּה. וְנוֹטֵל יָדָיו וּמְבָרֵךְ הַמּוֹצִיא, וְאוֹכֵל שָׁם כַּזַּיִת פַּת בְּלִי הֶפְסֵק, וְהוֹלֵךְ לְתוֹךְ הַבַּיִת וְגוֹמֵר סְעוּדָתוֹ. וְיֵשׁ לוֹ לְכַוֵּן בִּשְׁעַת נְטִילַת יָדַיִם וּבִשְׁעַת בִּרְכַּת הַמּוֹצִיא, שֶׁדַּעְתּוֹ לֶאֱכֹל גַּם בַּבַּיִת (עַיֵּן לְעֵיל סִימָן מב סָעִיף יט, כא). וְאִם פָּסְקוּ

4. *Mishnah Berurah* rules that if you have sufficient bread, you should eat at least a

disagreement among *Taanaim.* Rabbi Eliezer says that it refers to the Clouds of Glory with which the Holy One, blessed is He, surrounded our forefathers, to shield them from the heat and the sun. Rabbi Akiva, says that it means actual *sukkos* that they built for themselves when they camped [in the desert] as a protection from the sun. Although we departed from Egypt in the month of *Nisan,* He did not command us to build the *sukkah* during that season, because it is the beginning of the summer, when people usually build booths for the shade, and it would not be recognized as being built in order to fulfill the mitzvah of the Creator, blessed is His Name. He, therefore, commanded us to make it in the seventh month, which is the rainy season, when people usually move out of their booths to live in their homes; but we move out of our houses to live in the *sukkah;* which makes it clear to all that we are fulfilling the King's command.

2) You should maintain the *sukkah* with dignity so that *mitzvos* should not be treated with disrespect. Therefore, you should not bring into it vessels that are unbecoming to a *sukkah,* such as pots, pitchers used for drawing water, vessels in which you keep flour, kneading troughs, kettles, frying pans, mortars, or similar utensils. After the meal, the dishes should be cleared away from the *sukkah,* but drinking glasses may remain in the *sukkah.* People usually do not bring earthen candlesticks into the *sukkah* because they are repulsive. You should not do undignified work in the *sukkah* like washing pots and dishes. But you are allowed to rinse a wine cup. Of course, it is forbidden to urinate there, even in a vessel, even if one usually does so in his house. But marital relations are permitted in the *sukkah,* for the underlying principle of the mitzvah is for husband and wife to be together. If you bring offensive vessels into the *sukkah* it does not become invalid, but while they are there you should not say the berachah *Leisheiv basukkah,* until they have been removed.

3) Eating in the *sukkah* on the first night of *Sukkos,* is an obligation. It is required that you eat in the *sukkah* not less than a *kazayis* of bread;[4] and even if you suffer discomfort you are obligated to eat it in the *sukkah.* If it rains, (see paragraph 9 below) and it seems that it will stop in an hour or two, you should wait and then say the *Kiddush*[5] and eat in the *sukkah,* in the appropriate way. But if it appears that the rain is not stopping, or you waited and it did not stop, then you should say the *Kiddush* in the *sukkah* and say *Shehecheyanu,* and have in mind when saying *Shehecheyanu* that this berachah also applies to the *sukkah,* but you should not say *Leisheiv basukkah.* You then wash your hands and say *Hamotzi* and eat a *kazayis* of bread in the *sukkah* without interruption; and then go into your house to complete the meal. You should bear in mind when washing your hands and when saying *Hamotzi* that you also intend to eat in the house. (See chapter 42:19, 21 below) If

---

kebeitzah (see glossary) in order to fulfill the mitzvah even according to those authorities who maintain that a *kebeitzah* is the minimum amount that must be eaten. (*Ibid* 639:22)

5. *Mishnah Berurah* rules that if you are distraught through hunger, or lack of sleep because of waiting, and certainly if you have poor guests at your table who probably have not eaten all day and are famished, you should not wait. (*Ibid* 639:35)

הַגְּשָׁמִים קֹדֶם שֶׁבֵּרַךְ בִּרְכַּת־הַמָּזוֹן, הוֹלֵךְ שׁוּב לְתוֹךְ הַסֻּכָּה וּמְבָרֵךְ לֵישֵׁב בַּסֻּכָּה, וְאוֹכֵל קְצָת יוֹתֵר מִכַּבֵּיצָה פַּת, וּמְבָרֵךְ בִּרְכַּת־הַמָּזוֹן. וְאִם פָּסְקוּ הַגְּשָׁמִים לְאַחַר שֶׁבֵּרַךְ בִּרְכַּת־הַמָּזוֹן, הוֹלֵךְ גַּם כֵּן לְתוֹךְ הַסֻּכָּה, וְנוֹטֵל יָדָיו שֵׁנִית, וְאוֹכֵל יוֹתֵר מִכַּבֵּיצָה פַּת בְּבִרְכַּת לֵישֵׁב בַּסֻּכָּה, וּמְבָרֵךְ בִּרְכַּת־הַמָּזוֹן. אִם בְּסֻכָּה שֶׁלּוֹ אַף לְאַחַר שֶׁפָּסְקוּ הַגְּשָׁמִים עֲדַיִן הַמַּיִם מְטַפְטְפִין מִן הַסְּכָךְ, וְיֵשׁ בִּשְׁכוּנָתוֹ סֻכָּה שֶׁהָיְתָה מְסֻגֶּרֶת בְּגַג, וּלְאַחַר הַגְּשָׁמִים נִפְתְּחָה, יֵלֵךְ שָׁמָּה וְיֹאכַל פִּתּוֹ בְּטוּב לֵבָב.

ד) בַּלַּיְלָה הַשֵּׁנִי גַּם כֵּן חוֹבָה לֶאֱכֹל בַּסֻּכָּה, וַאֲפִלּוּ הוּא מִצְטַעֵר, וְדִינוֹ כְּמוֹ בַּלַּיְלָה הָרִאשׁוֹן, וּכְמוֹ שֶׁכָּתַבְנוּ, אֶלָּא חִלּוּק אֶחָד יֵשׁ בֵּינֵיהֶן, שֶׁאִם רָאָה שֶׁלֹּא יִפָּסְקוּ הַגְּשָׁמִים, אוֹ הִמְתִּין וְלֹא פָּסְקוּ, מְקַדֵּשׁ בַּבַּיִת וְאוֹכֵל שָׁם, וְקֹדֶם בִּרְכַּת־הַמָּזוֹן הוֹלֵךְ לְתוֹךְ הַסֻּכָּה וְאוֹכֵל שָׁם לְכָל־הַפָּחוֹת כַּזַּיִת פַּת בְּלֹא בִּרְכַּת לֵישֵׁב בַּסֻּכָּה, וְחוֹזֵר לְבֵיתוֹ וּמְבָרֵךְ בִּרְכַּת־הַמָּזוֹן.

ה) עַרְבִית, כְּשֶׁבָּא מִבֵּית־הַכְּנֶסֶת, נִכְנָס לַסֻּכָּה וּמְקַדֵּשׁ מִיָּד, רַק לֹא יְקַדֵּשׁ אֶלָּא כְּשֶׁהוּא וַדַּאי לַיְלָה. וּכְשֶׁהוּא מְבָרֵךְ בַּקִּדּוּשׁ לֵישֵׁב בַּסֻּכָּה, יְכַוֵּן לִפְטֹר בִּבְרָכָה זוֹ, סְעוּדָה זוֹ וְגַם הַשֵּׁנָה וּשְׁאָר צְרָכָיו שֶׁיַּעֲשֶׂה בַּסֻּכָּה, עַד הַקִּדּוּשׁ שֶׁבְּיוֹם הַמָּחֳרָת. וּבְבִרְכַּת שֶׁהֶחֱיָנוּ יְכַוֵּן, שֶׁהוּא מְבָרֵךְ שֶׁהֶחֱיָנוּ עַל הֶחָג וְגַם עַל הַסֻּכָּה. וְלָכֵן בַּלַּיְלָה הָרִאשׁוֹן מְבָרְכִין תְּחִלָּה לֵישֵׁב בַּסֻּכָּה וְאַחַר כָּךְ שֶׁהֶחֱיָנוּ, שֶׁתְּהֵא בִּרְכַּת שֶׁהֶחֱיָנוּ גַּם עַל הַסֻּכָּה. וּבַלַּיְלָה הַשֵּׁנִי מְבָרֵךְ תְּחִלָּה שֶׁהֶחֱיָנוּ, וְאַחַר כָּךְ לֵישֵׁב בַּסֻּכָּה.

ו) כְּשֶׁאוֹכְלִים כַּמָּה בַּעֲלֵי־בָתִּים בְּסֻכָּה אַחַת, וְיֵשׁ שָׁם גַּם הַנָּשִׁים וּשְׁאָר בְּנֵי בַיִת שֶׁצְּרִיכִין לִשְׁמֹעַ הֵיטֵב אֶת הַקִּדּוּשׁ לָצֵאת בּוֹ, אִם יְקַדְּשׁוּ כָּל בַּעֲלֵי הַבָּתִּים בְּיַחַד, תְּרֵי קָלֵי לָא מִשְׁתַּמְעֵי, וְלֹא יִשְׁמְעוּ הֵיטֵב אֶת הַקִּדּוּשׁ. עַל כֵּן טוֹב יוֹתֵר שֶׁיְּקַדְּשׁוּ בָּזֶה אַחַר זֶה. וְאִם מְקַדְּשִׁין בְּיַחַד, כְּגוֹן אִם אֵין שָׁם מִי שֶׁצָּרִיךְ לָצֵאת בִּשְׁמִיעַת קִדּוּשׁ, אִם קָדַם אֶחָד וְסִיֵּם בִּרְכַּת בּוֹרֵא פְּרִי הַגָּפֶן אוֹ בְּרָכָה אַחֶרֶת, וְאַחַר כָּךְ סִיֵּם חֲבֵרוֹ, אֵין לְהָרִאשׁוֹן לַעֲנוֹת אָמֵן אַחַר בִּרְכַּת חֲבֵרוֹ, מִשּׁוּם דְּאָמֵן, הֲוֵי הֶפְסֵק בֵּין

---

6. If you eat less than this amount you must not say the berachah *Leisheiv basukkah.* (*Shaar Hatzion* 639:69)

it stops raining before you said *Birkas Hamazon,* you should go back to the *sukkah,* say the berachah *Leisheiv basukkah,* eat slightly more than a *kebeitzah* of bread,[6] and say *Birkas Hamazon.* If it stops raining after you said *Birkas Hamazon,* you should also return to the *sukkah,* wash your hands again, eat more than a *kebeitzah* of bread, saying the berachah *Leisheiv basukkah,* and then say *Birkas Hamazon.* If after the rain has stopped, water is still dripping from the *sechach* in your own *sukkah,* and there is a *sukkah* in your neighborhood that was closed with a roof, and after the rain they opened it, you should go there and eat your meal in good spirits.

4) On the second night of *Sukkos* it is also mandatory to eat in the *sukkah,* even if you suffer discomfort. It is governed by the same *halachos* that apply to the first night, as we have written, except for one difference, that if it appears that the rain is not going to stop, or if you waited and it did not stop, you should recite the *Kiddush* in the house and eat your meal there, and before saying *Birkas Hamazon,* you should go to the *sukkah* and eat at least a *kazayis* of bread without saying *Leisheiv basukkah.* You then return to the house and say *Birkas Hamazon.*

5) In the evening, on returning from the synagogue you should enter the *sukkah* and immediately say the *Kiddush,* but you should not say *Kiddush* unless you are sure that it is night. When you say *Leisheiv basukkah* you should be mindful to exempt with this berachah, the meal you are eating now, your sleeping [in the *sukkah*], and other necessities you will do in the *sukkah,* until you say *Kiddush* again the next morning. When saying *Shehecheyanu* you should be mindful that this berachah applies to the Yom Tov as well as to the *sukkah.* Therefore, on the first night you should say first *Leisheiv basukkah,* and then *Shehecheyanu,* so that the *Shehecheyanu* applies to the *sukkah* as well; but on the second night you should first say *Shehecheyanu* and then *Leisheiv basukkah.*[7]

6) When several heads of families eat in one *sukkah* and there are also women, and other members of the family who must listen attentively to the *Kiddush* in order to fulfill their obligation; and, if all the men recite the *Kiddush* at the same time since two voices cannot be heard simultaneously, [their voices would become unintelligible,] and the family members would not hear the *Kiddush* clearly. It is best, therefore, that they should say the *Kiddush* one at a time. If they do recite the *Kiddush* simultaneously, [for example] in a situation when there is no one who has to fulfill his obligation by listening to the *Kiddush;* then if one of them finished saying the berachah *Borei peri hagafen,* or one of the other berachos, before the others, then the one who finishes early should not respond *Amein* to the berachah of the other, because saying *Amein* constitutes an interruption between the *Borei*

---

7. There are other authorities who rule that *Leisheiv basukkah* is recited first on both nights. However, if several people eat together in the same *sukkah,* everyone should follow the same custom. (*Mishnah Berurah* 661:2)

בִּרְכַּת בּוֹרֵא פְּרִי הַגָּפֶן לִשְׁתִיָּה. וְהָעוֹלָם נוֹהֲגִים לְהַמְתִּין זֶה עַל זֶה וְעוֹנִין אָמֵן, וְזֶהוּ שֶׁלֹּא כַּדִּין, אֶלָּא יֵשׁ לָהֶם לוֹמַר הַכֹּל בְּיַחַד.

ז) בִּשְׁאָר הַלֵּילוֹת וְכֵן בְּכָל הַיָּמִים, אֵין חִיּוּב לֶאֱכֹל בַּסֻּכָּה, אֶלָּא שֶׁאִם הוּא רוֹצֶה לֶאֱכֹל אֲכִילַת קֶבַע אוֹ לִישַׁן, צָרִיךְ לֶאֱכֹל אוֹ לִישַׁן בַּסֻּכָּה. וּמַהִי אֲכִילַת קֶבַע. פַּת יוֹתֵר מִכַּבֵּיצָה, אֲפִלּוּ לֹא קָבַע עָלֶיהָ, וַאֲפִלּוּ הִיא פַּת כִּסְנִין. וְכֵן תַּבְשִׁיל הֶעָשׂוּי מֵחֲמֵשֶׁת מִינֵי דָגָן יוֹתֵר מִכַּבֵּיצָה וְקָבַע עָלָיו, חַיָּב בַּסֻּכָּה וּלְבָרֵךְ עָלָיו לֵישֵׁב בַּסֻּכָּה. אֲבָל פֵּרוֹת, אֲפִלּוּ אָכַל הַרְבֵּה וְקָבַע עֲלֵיהֶם, מֻתָּר לֶאֱכוֹל חוּץ לַסֻּכָּה. וְכֵן יַיִן אוֹ שְׁאָר מַשְׁקִין אוֹ בָשָׂר וּגְבִינָה, מֻתָּר לֶאֱכוֹל וְלִשְׁתּוֹת חוּץ לַסֻּכָּה. וְדַוְקָא כְּשֶׁלֹּא קָבַע עֲלֵיהֶם. אֲבָל אִם רוֹצֶה לִשְׁתּוֹת יַיִן אוֹ שְׁאָר מַשְׁקִים בְּדֶרֶךְ קֶבַע, אוֹ שֶׁרוֹצֶה לֶאֱכֹל בָּשָׂר אוֹ גְבִינָה דֶּרֶךְ קֶבַע, צָרִיךְ סֻכָּה, וְלֹא יְבָרֵךְ עֲלֵיהֶם לֵישֵׁב בַּסֻּכָּה. וְטוֹב שֶׁיֹּאכַל קֹדֶם, פַּת, כְּדֵי שֶׁיְּבָרֵךְ. וְכָל זֹאת, מִדִּינָא. אֲבָל מִי שֶׁמַּחְמִיר עַל עַצְמוֹ שֶׁאֲפִלּוּ מַיִם אֵינוֹ שׁוֹתֶה חוּץ לַסֻּכָּה, הֲרֵי זֶה מְשֻׁבָּח.

ח) שֵׁנָה, אֲפִלּוּ אַרְעַי, מִדִּינָא צְרִיכָה סֻכָּה. וְכֵן עוֹשִׂין הַמְדַקְדְּקִין בַּמִּצְוֹת, שֶׁאֲפִלּוּ שְׁנַת אַרְעַי אֵינָם יְשֵׁנִים חוּץ לַסֻּכָּה. וְעַתָּה שֶׁנּוֹהֲגִים הַרְבֵּה לְהָקֵל בַּשֵּׁנָה, כָּתְבוּ הָאַחֲרוֹנִים, זִכְרוֹנָם לִבְרָכָה, כַּמָּה טְעָמִים, לְלַמֵּד קְצָת זְכוּת עֲלֵיהֶם. אֲבָל כָּל יְרֵא שָׁמַיִם, רָאוּי לוֹ לְהַחְמִיר וְלַעֲשׂוֹת סֻכָּה, שֶׁיּוּכַל לָדוּר שָׁם עִם אִשְׁתּוֹ, כְּמוֹ שֶׁהוּא דָר בְּכָל הַשָּׁנָה כֻּלָּהּ, אִם אֶפְשָׁר לוֹ. וּלְכָל הַפָּחוֹת שֶׁתְּהֵא רְאוּיָה לִישַׁן שָׁם הוּא לְבַדּוֹ. וְאִם אֵינָהּ כֵּן, אֲפִלּוּ בְּדִיעֲבַד, הִיא פְּסוּלָה.

ט) יָרְדוּ גְשָׁמִים, פָּטוּר מִן הַסֻּכָּה. בְּאֵיזֶה גְשָׁמִים פָּטוּר. אִם יָרְדוּ כָּל כָּךְ, שֶׁהוּא מְשַׁעֵר, שֶׁאִם הָיוּ נוֹפְלִים כָּךְ לְתוֹךְ הַתַּבְשִׁיל, הָיָה מִתְקַלְקֵל, אֲפִלּוּ אֵין לְפָנָיו הַתַּבְשִׁיל, אוֹ שֶׁהוּא מְשַׁעֵר, שֶׁאִם הָיוּ נוֹפְלִים לְתוֹךְ הַחֶדֶר שֶׁהוּא בוֹ, הָיָה יוֹצֵא מִשָּׁם לְחֶדֶר אַחֵר, אָז יוֹצֵא גַּם מִן הַסֻּכָּה לַבַּיִת. וְאִם הִתְחִיל לֶאֱכֹל בַּסֻּכָּה, וְאַחַר כָּךְ יָרְדוּ גְשָׁמִים וְנִכְנַס לְתוֹךְ הַבַּיִת, וְהִתְחִיל לֶאֱכֹל גַּם בַּבַּיִת, אוֹ שֶׁמֵּחֲמַת הַגְּשָׁמִים הִתְחִיל

8. See glossary.

9. *Mishnah Berurah* writes, "In places where the climate is cold [during this time of year], you still fulfill your obligation by eating in the *sukkah* even though you are unable to sleep

peri hagafen [he just now said] and the drinking of the wine. Some people are accustomed to wait for the others to finish the *Kiddush* and to respond *Amein*. This is not according to *Halachah;* but they should all say it together.

7) On the other nights and days of *Sukkos,* you are not obligated to eat in the *sukkah;* but if you want to eat a regular meal or to sleep, you must do so in the *sukkah.* What is meant by a "regular meal?" If you eat more than a *kebeitzah*[8] of bread, even if you do not schedule it as a "meal," and even if it is pastry, [similar to a blintz or a strudel it must be eaten in the sukkah]. Similarly, any dish made of [one of] the five species of grain, if it is more than a *kebeitzah* and you scheduled it as a "meal," you must eat it in the *sukkah* and say the berachah *Leisheiv basukkah.* But even if you eat a large quantity of fruit and you scheduled it as a meal, you are allowed to eat the fruit outside the *sukkah.* Also wine or other beverages, or meat and cheese may be eaten and drunk outside the *sukkah,* provided you do not schedule it as a meal. But if you want to drink wine or other beverages as a scheduled "meal," or you want to eat meat or cheese as a scheduled "meal," you must have it in the *sukkah,* but without saying the berachah *Leisheiv basukkah.* It is best to eat some bread first, so that you can say the berachah. All this is as required by *Halachah,* but those who are more meticulous and do not even drink water outside the *sukkah* are considered praiseworthy.

8) Sleeping, or even taking a nap, according to *Halachah,* must be in the *sukkah.* And this is the practice of those who are scrupulous in observing the mitzvos; they, indeed, do not even take a nap outside the *sukkah.* But nowadays, many people are lenient with regard to sleeping [in the *sukkah*]. The later authorities, of blessed memory, wrote a number of reasons to justify this leniency to an extent. However, every God-fearing person, should be stringent and build a *sukkah* in which he and his wife can dwell in the same manner they live the entire year, if possible. At minimum, [the *sukkah*] should be suitable for him to sleep in, for if it does not meet these standards it is not valid, even post factum[9] [even after it was already built].

9) If it rains, you are exempt from [staying in] the *sukkah.*[10] How heavy a rain must it be for you to be exempt? If it rains so much, that in your judgment, if that much rain would drip into your cooked food,[11] it would be spoiled, even if the food is not actually in the *sukkah,* or if you estimate,[12] that if it would rain that much into the room where you are sitting, you would move into another room, then you

---

there. Since it is impossible otherwise, it is therefore considered that you are living in the *sukkah* in the same manner as in your home. (*Ibid* 640:18, 20)

10. However, if the rain does not drip through to the place where you are sitting, you must remain in the *sukkah* until it rains on you and on the table where you are sitting. It is also possible that you are even obligated to say the berachah *Leisheiv basukkah* under these circumstances. (*Mishnah Berurah* 639:33)

11. This is true even if the food is of the kind that spoils quickly because of a little water. (*Mishnah Berurah* 639:34)

12. If you are unable to make such a judgment, you should use the next example quoted in the text as a criterion. (*Ramah* 639:5)

מִתְחִלָּה לֶאֱכֹל בַּבַּיִת, וְאַחַר כָּךְ פָּסְקוּ הַגְּשָׁמִים, גּוֹמֵר סְעוּדָתוֹ בַּבַּיִת וְאֵינוֹ מְחֻיָּב לָלֶכֶת בְּאֶמְצַע הַסְּעוּדָה מִבֵּיתוֹ לְתוֹךְ הַסֻּכָּה. וְכֵן כְּשֶׁהָעֵת קָרָה וְהַמַּאֲכָלִים נִקְרָשִׁים בְּתוֹךְ הַסֻּכָּה, פָּטוּר מִן הַסֻּכָּה וְאוֹכֵל בַּבַּיִת.

י) וּלְעִנְיַן שֵׁנָה בַּסֻּכָּה, גַּם גְּשָׁמִים מֻעָטִין הֲוֵי צַעַר לִישַׁן, וְיָכוֹל לָצֵאת. וְאִם יָצָא לְבֵיתוֹ וְשָׁכַב לִישַׁן, וְאַחַר כָּךְ פָּסְקוּ הַגְּשָׁמִים, אוֹ שֶׁמִּתְחִלָּה שָׁכַב בְּבֵיתוֹ לִישַׁן מִפְּנֵי הַגְּשָׁמִים, וְאַחַר כָּךְ פָּסְקוּ, אֵין מַטְרִיחִין אוֹתוֹ לֵילֵךְ לַסֻּכָּה כָּל הַלַּיְלָה, אֶלָּא יָשֵׁן בְּבֵיתוֹ עַד הַבֹּקֶר.

יא) כְּשֶׁהוּא פָּטוּר מִן הַסֻּכָּה, וְאֵינוֹ יוֹצֵא מִשָּׁם, נִקְרָא הֶדְיוֹט, וְאֵינוֹ מְקַבֵּל שָׂכָר עָלֶיהָ, וְאֵינוֹ רַשַּׁאי לְבָרֵךְ, מִשּׁוּם דַּהֲוֵי בְּרָכָה לְבַטָּלָה. וּכְשֶׁיּוֹצֵא מִן הַסֻּכָּה בִּשְׁבִיל הַגְּשָׁמִים, לֹא יִבְעַט בְּסֻכָּתוֹ וְיֵצֵא, אֶלָּא יֵצֵא בְּהַכְנָעָה, כְּעֶבֶד שֶׁמָּזַג כּוֹס לְרַבּוֹ, וְשָׁפַךְ לוֹ רַבּוֹ קִיתוֹן עַל פָּנָיו.

יב) נוֹהֲגִין שֶׁאֵין מְבָרְכִין לֵישֵׁב בַּסֻּכָּה אֶלָּא בַּאֲכִילַת קֶבַע. וְנוֹהֲגִין שֶׁמְּבָרְכִין תְּחִלָּה הַמּוֹצִיא, וְאַחַר כָּךְ לֵישֵׁב בַּסֻּכָּה, קֹדֶם שֶׁטּוֹעֵם. וּשְׁאָר דְּבָרִים שֶׁהוּא אוֹכֵל בַּסֻּכָּה כָּל הַיּוֹם, וְכָל מַה שֶּׁהוּא יוֹשֵׁב וְעוֹשֶׂה שָׁם, וַאֲפִלּוּ אִם יָשֵׁן שָׁם, נִפְטָר הַכֹּל בַּבְּרָכָה שֶׁבֵּרַךְ בִּשְׁעַת אֲכִילַת קֶבַע, עַד שֶׁיֹּאכַל שֵׁנִית בְּקֶבַע. וְאִם לֹא יָצָא מִן הַסֻּכָּה לַעֲסָקָיו אוֹ לְבֵית־הַכְּנֶסֶת בֵּין סְעוּדָה לִסְעוּדָה, כֵּיוָן שֶׁבֵּרַךְ פַּעַם אַחַת, שׁוּב אֵינוֹ צָרִיךְ לְבָרֵךְ בִּסְעוּדָה שְׁנִיָּה שֶׁאוֹכֵל. וַאֲפִלּוּ כָּל שִׁבְעַת יְמֵי הֶחָג, אִם יָשַׁב וְאָכַל וְלָמַד וְהִתְפַּלֵּל וְיָשֵׁן תּוֹךְ סֻכָּתוֹ, אֵינוֹ צָרִיךְ לְבָרֵךְ רַק פַּעַם אַחַת. כֵּיוָן שֶׁלֹּא הִסִּיחַ דַּעְתּוֹ מִן הַסֻּכָּה. וַאֲפִלּוּ יָצָא יְצִיאַת אַרְעַי וְדַעְתּוֹ לַחֲזוֹר מִיָּד, לֹא הֲוֵי הֶסַּח־הַדַּעַת, וְאֵינוֹ צָרִיךְ לְבָרֵךְ בִּסְעוּדָה שְׁנִיָּה, רַק כְּשֶׁיָּצָא לַעֲסָקָיו אוֹ לְבֵית־הַכְּנֶסֶת וְכַדּוֹמֶה. וַאֲפִלּוּ הָלַךְ לְתוֹךְ בֵּיתוֹ לִלְמֹד שָׁם אוֹ לַעֲשׂוֹת שָׁם אֵיזֶה דָּבָר שֶׁהוּא שׁוֹהֶה בּוֹ, גַּם כֵּן הֲוֵי הֶסַּח־הַדַּעַת, וְצָרִיךְ לְבָרֵךְ בִּסְעוּדָה שְׁנִיָּה.

---

13. This is certainly true if you are troubled because of the cold. (*Shaar Hatzion* 639:59)

14. This *halachah* also holds true if the climate is so intensely hot or if there are many insects that cause you to be uncomfortable, or will cause the food to become inedible. (*Mishnah Berurah* 639:31)

15. You need not go into the *sukkah* to sleep even if you wake up during the night. (*Ibid* 639:32)

may leave the *sukkah* and go into the house. If you started to eat in the *sukkah,* and then it began to rain, so that you went into the house and started to eat there; or because of the rain you began initially to eat in the house, and then it stopped raining, you may finish your meal in the house, and you are not obligated to leave while the meal is in progress, to go from your house into the *sukkah.* When it is so cold that the food in the *sukkah* jells,[13] you are exempt from sitting in the *sukkah,* and you may eat in the house.[14]

10) As for sleeping in the *sukkah,* even a slight rain causes discomfort when you sleep, and you may leave [the *sukkah* when it rains]. If you left the *sukkah* to sleep in the house, and then it stopped raining; or if you initially went to sleep in the house because of the rain and then the rain stopped, you do not have to bother to go to the *sukkah* during the night,[15] but you may sleep in the house until morning.

11) Anyone who is exempt from staying in the *sukkah* and does not leave is called a simpleton, and will receive no reward for it. And he is not permitted to say the berachah [*Leisheiv basukkah]*, because it would be a berachah said in vain. When you leave the *sukkah* because of rain, you should not complain [in anger] as you leave, but go out feeling humbled, like a servant who poured a cup [of wine] for his master, and the master poured a pitcher [of water] into his face.

12) It is the custom to say the berachah *Leisheiv basukkah* only when you eat a regular meal.[16] And it is the custom to say the *Hamotzi* first, and then *Leisheiv basukkah,* before you begin to eat. Everything that you eat in the *sukkah* the entire day, and whatever you do while staying there, even if you sleep there, is exempt with the berachah you said before eating the regular meal, [and it exempts everything] until you eat your next regular meal. If you did not leave the *sukkah* to go to business or to the synagogue between meals, since you once said the berachah, you need not repeat it at the next meal. Even if during the entire week of *Sukkos,* you would dwell in the *sukkah* eating, studying, praying and sleeping there, you would need to say the berachah only one time, because your thoughts were never diverted from the *sukkah.* Even if you left the *sukkah* temporarily, with the intention of returning immediately, it is not considered a diversion, and you need not say the berachah at the following meal. However, if you went out to do business, or to go to the synagogue, or for similar reasons; even if you went into your house to study, or to do something which is time consuming, it also constitutes a distraction, and you must say the berachah at the next meal.

---

16. It is the custom of many not to say the berachah until they eat the meal even though they gather in the *sukkah* and sit there for an hour or so before eating. The rationale is that the berachah which will be said at mealtime exempts even the time spent in the *sukkah* before the meal. The later *Poskim,* however, write that in order to comply with those *halachic* authorities who maintain that it is not proper to sit for a length of time without saying the berachah, it is best to say the berachah *Borei minei mezonos* and eat a piece of cake larger than a *kebeitzah* as soon as you enter the *sukkah* and to say the berachah *Leisheiv basukkah.* This will make it unnecessary to say the berachah when you eat the regular meal. (*Ibid* 639:46)

יג) מִי שֶׁהוֹלֵךְ אֲפִלּוּ בְּאֶמְצַע סְעוּדָתוֹ לְסֻכַּת חֲבֵרוֹ וְאוֹכֵל שָׁם שִׁעוּר דְּחַיָּב בַּסֻּכָּה, צָרִיךְ לְבָרֵךְ גַּם שָׁם לֵישֵׁב בַּסֻּכָּה.

יד) מִי שֶׁשָּׁכַח לְבָרֵךְ לֵישֵׁב בַּסֻּכָּה, וְנִזְכַּר בְּאֶמְצַע הַסְּעוּדָה, אוֹ אֲפִלּוּ לְאַחַר שֶׁגָּמַר אֲכִילָתוֹ, צָרִיךְ לְבָרֵךְ, כִּי גַּם הַיְשִׁיבָה שֶׁיֵּשֵׁב שָׁם אַחַר כָּךְ, הִיא מִצְוָה.

טו) נָשִׁים, פְּטוּרוֹת מִסֻּכָּה, וְאַף־עַל־פִּי־כֵן רַשָּׁאִין לְבָרֵךְ. קְטַנִּים, גַּם כֵּן פְּטוּרִים. וּמִכָּל מָקוֹם כָּל שֶׁהוּא מִבֶּן חָמֵשׁ שָׁנִים וּלְמַעְלָה, חַיָּב אָבִיו לְחַנְּכוֹ שֶׁיֹּאכַל בַּסֻּכָּה. וַאֲפִלּוּ אֵין אָבִיו בְּבֵיתוֹ, אֵין לְהַנִּיחוֹ שֶׁיֹּאכַל חוּץ לַסֻּכָּה.

טז) חוֹלֶה וּמְשַׁמְשָׁיו, פְּטוּרִים מִסֻּכָּה. וְאִם הוּא חוֹלֶה שֶׁאֵין בּוֹ סַכָּנָה, אֵין הַמְשַׁמְשִׁין פְּטוּרִין אֶלָּא בְּשָׁעָה שֶׁהוּא צָרִיךְ לָהֶם. אִם הוּא חוֹלֶה שֶׁיֵּשׁ בּוֹ סַכָּנָה, פְּטוּרִין גַּם בְּשָׁעָה שֶׁאֵינוֹ צָרִיךְ לָהֶן כָּל כָּךְ.

יז) מִצְטַעֵר, גַּם כֵּן פָּטוּר מִן הַסֻּכָּה בִּשְׁאָר הַלֵּילוֹת, וְכֵן בְּכָל הַיָּמִים. וְהַיְנוּ שֶׁמִּצְטַעֵר מֵחֲמַת צִנָּה אוֹ מֵרוּחַ אוֹ מֵרֵיחַ רָע וְכַיּוֹצֵא בוֹ. וְכֵן אִם כָּבוּ לוֹ הַנֵּרוֹת בְּסֻכָּתוֹ בְּשַׁבָּת וְיֵשׁ לוֹ טֹרַח גָּדוֹל לֵילֵךְ לְסֻכַּת חֲבֵרוֹ, יָכוֹל לֵילֵךְ לְבֵיתוֹ בְּמָקוֹם שֶׁיֵּשׁ לוֹ נֵרוֹת דּוֹלְקִים. וְדַוְקָא אִם מִתְּחִלָּה עָשָׂה סֻכָּתוֹ כָּרָאוּי, וְאַךְ בְּמִקְרֶה בָּא לוֹ הָעִנְיָן שֶׁהוּא מִצְטַעֵר לֵישֵׁב אוֹ לִישֹׁן בְּתוֹכָהּ. אֲבָל אִם מִתְּחִלָּה עֲשָׂאָהּ בְּמָקוֹם רֵיחַ רָע וְכַדּוֹמֶה, אוֹ בְּמָקוֹם שֶׁיִּתְיָרֵא לִישֹׁן בָּהּ, אֵינוֹ יוֹצֵא בָהּ אֲפִלּוּ בַּאֲכִילָה בַּיּוֹם. אִם בָּא הָרוּחַ לְכַבּוֹת הַנֵּרוֹת דֶּרֶךְ הַדְּפָנוֹת, מֻתָּר לִפְרוֹשׂ שָׁם סָדִין אוֹ בֶגֶד.

יח) הוֹלְכֵי דְּרָכִים בַּיּוֹם, פְּטוּרִין מִן הַסֻּכָּה בַּיּוֹם, כֵּיוָן שֶׁאֵין לָהֶם שָׁהוּת לִטְרֹחַ אַחַר סֻכָּה, כֵּיוָן שֶׁצְּרִיכִין לֵילֵךְ תֵּכֶף לְדַרְכָּן. אֲבָל אִם יְכוֹלִים לֵישֵׁב בְּסֻכָּה בְּלִי טֹרַח, חַיָּבִים לֵישֵׁב בַּסֻּכָּה. וּבַלַּיְלָה, כְּשֶׁהֵם בְּמָלוֹן שֶׁהֵם רוֹצִים לָלוּן שָׁם, צְרִיכִים לְהַטְרִיחַ אֶת עַצְמָם לֵישֵׁב בַּסֻּכָּה.

---

17. Many later *Poskim* maintain that this is not considered an interruption if you had intended to go to another *sukkah* when you initially said the berachah, and that it is not necessary to say another berachah in the second *sukkah*. *Beis Meir* writes that you need not say another berachah even if you had no intention to eat in another *sukkah*. In situations where there is a doubt regarding *berachos*, the rule is that we are lenient and do not say the berachah. It is the best practice, therefore, not to leave the *sukkah* in the middle of the meal. (*Ibid* 639:48)

13) If you leave the *sukkah* even in the middle of your meal, to go to a friend's *sukkah,* and you eat a quantity of food which must be eaten in the *sukkah,* you must say *Leisheiv basukkah* there too.[17]

14) If you forgot to say *Leisheiv basukkah,* and you become aware of it in the middle of the meal, or even after you finished the meal, you must still say the berachah, because by staying in the *sukkah* after the meal you are also fulfilling the mitzvah.

15) Women are exempt from the mitzvah of *sukkah,* nevertheless, they are permitted to say the berachah. Children also, are exempt, Nevertheless, if a boy is five years and over, his father must train him to eat in the *sukkah.* Even if the father is not at home, he should not be permitted to eat outside the *sukkah.*

16) A sick person and his attendants are exempt from the mitzvah of *sukkah.* However, if the patient is not critically ill, the attendants are exempt only when he needs them. If he is critically ill, they are exempt even when he does not need them so urgently.

17) [If staying in the *sukkah*] causes you discomfort, that is if you are troubled by the cold weather or the wind, or by a bad odor or similar annoyances, you are exempt from the mitzvah of *sukkah* on all nights other [than the first night], and on all the days of *Sukkos.* Similarly, if the light in the *sukkah* went out on Shabbos, and it is a great bother for you to go to a friend's *sukkah,* then you may go to your house, if the candles are burning there. This only applies if initially you made your *sukkah* properly, and it was only an accident that caused you to be uncomfortable while sitting or sleeping there. But if initially you made the *sukkah* in a place where there is an offensive odor, or similar [irritation], or in a place where you are afraid to sleep, then you cannot fulfill your obligation even when you eat there in the daytime. If the wind threatens to blow out the candles [on Shabbos], as it passes through the walls, you are permitted to spread a sheet or a garment on the wall.

18) People traveling in the daytime[18] are exempt from eating in the *sukkah* during the day,[19] because they have no time to look for a *sukkah,* since they must move along.[20] But if they are able to sit in a *sukkah* without too much trouble, they are obligated to do so. At night, when they are at the lodging where they intend to stay overnight, they must make an effort to [find] a *sukkah* in which to dwell. Even

---

18. According to *Mishnah Berurah,* you need not curtail your travel even if you know that you will not find a *sukkah* enroute. (*Ibid* 640:42)

19. You need not delay eating until you are able to find a *sukkah.* Needless to say, however, if there is a *sukkah* nearby, that you can use without too much bother, you are not exempt, and you must eat in the *sukkah.* (*Ibid* 640:42)

20. This rule applies only to those traveling for business. However those who travel for pleasure are forbidden to travel to places where they will have no *sukkah.* (*Igros Moshe, Orach Chaim,* volume III Responsa 93.)

וַאֲפִלּוּ אִם הֵם בְּמָקוֹם שֶׁאֵין שָׁם סֻכָּה, אִם יְכוֹלִים לַעֲשׂוֹת סֻכָּה בִּמְעַט מָמוֹן, חַיָּבִים לְהִשְׁתַּדֵּל שֶׁתְּהֵא לָהֶם סֻכָּה לִישׁוֹן בְּתוֹכָהּ. וְאִם הוֹלְכִים גַּם בַּלַּיְלָה, דִּינָם כְּמוֹ בַּיּוֹם. וְהַהוֹלְכִים בַּכְּפָרִים לִגְבּוֹת חוֹבוֹת בְּחֹל־הַמּוֹעֵד, אִם אֵינָם יְכוֹלִין לַעֲשׂוֹת לָהֶם סֻכָּה, יַחְמִירוּ עַל עַצְמָם לַחֲזוֹר לְבָתֵּיהֶם בְּכָל לַיְלָה לְקַיֵּם מִצְוַת סֻכָּה.

יט) שְׁלוּחֵי מִצְוָה, אֲפִלּוּ בַּלַּיְלָה, כְּשֶׁהֵם בַּמָּלוֹן, אִם צְרִיכִים לִטְרֹחַ אַחַר סֻכָּה אוֹ שֶׁאֵין נוֹחַ לָהֶם לִישׁוֹן בַּסֻּכָּה, וְאִם יִישְׁנוּ, יִהְיוּ לְמָחָר יְגֵעִים וְיִתְעַכְּבוּ מִן הַמִּצְוָה, פְּטוּרִין מִן הַסֻּכָּה. אֲבָל בְּלָאו הָכִי, חַיָּבִים.

כ) שׁוֹמְרֵי גַּנּוֹת וּפַרְדֵּסִים וּתְבוּאָה וְכַיּוֹצֵא בָזֶה, אִם אֶפְשָׁר לִשְׁמֹר הַכֹּל בְּמָקוֹם אֶחָד, יַעֲשֶׂה לוֹ שָׁם סֻכָּה וְיֵשֵׁב בָּהּ.

כא) הָעוֹשִׂים יַיִן אֵצֶל גּוֹיִם, פְּטוּרִין מִן הַסֻּכָּה, בֵּין בַּיּוֹם בֵּין בַּלַּיְלָה, מִשּׁוּם דִּצְרִיכִים לִשְׁמוֹר שֶׁלֹּא יִגַּע בּוֹ גּוֹי. וְאִם הוּא בְּעִנְיָן שֶׁאֵינוֹ צָרִיךְ שִׁמּוּר, חַיָּבִין.

כב) הַיּוֹשְׁבִים בַּחֲנוּת, אַף־עַל־פִּי שֶׁהֵם דָּרִים חוּץ לָעִיר וְהַחֲנוּת הִיא בָּעִיר וּרְגִילִין כָּל הַשָּׁנָה בְּרֹב פְּעָמִים לֶאֱכוֹל שָׁם בַּיּוֹם, מִכָּל מָקוֹם בַּסֻּכּוֹת חַיָּבִים לֶאֱכוֹל בַּסֻּכָּה.

סִימָן קלו
הִלְכוֹת לוּלָב וּשְׁאָר הַמִּינִים

א) כְּבָר נָהֲגוּ יִשְׂרָאֵל, שֶׁמִּי שֶׁהוּא קוֹנֶה אֶתְרוֹג וְלוּלָב וְהוּא אֵינוֹ מֵבִין, מַרְאֶה אוֹתָן לְמוֹרֶה הוֹרָאָה אִם הֵם כְּשֵׁרִים אוֹ לֹא, כִּי יֵשׁ הַרְבֵּה חִלּוּקֵי דִּינִים. וְיֵשׁ לְהַדֵּר לִקְנוֹת לוּלָב חָדָשׁ, כִּי לוּלָב הַיָּבֵשׁ אֵינוֹ כָּשֵׁר אֶלָּא בִּשְׁעַת הַדְּחָק. וְיֵשׁ אוֹמְרִים, דְּכֹל שֶׁכָּלְתָה הַיַּרְקוּת שֶׁבּוֹ, הֲוֵי יָבֵשׁ. שִׁעוּר הַלּוּלָב, שֶׁתְּהֵא הַשִּׁדְרָה חוּץ מִן הֶעָלִין הָעֶלְיוֹנִים, אַרְבָּעָה טְפָחִים. וּבִשְׁעַת הַדְּחָק, שְׁלֹשָׁה־עָשָׂר אֲגוּדָלִין וּשְׁלִישׁ אֲגוּדָל סַגֵּי.

21. This is not an actual obligation but those who do so will be blessed. If you intend to remain at any one place for three or four days, you must then make a *sukkah*. (*Ibid* 640:44)

22. *Mishnah Berurah* citing Responsa of *Chasam Sofer* writes that this is true only if the mission is one hundred percent for the purpose of fulfilling a mitzvah. If, however, there is any personal gain of pleasure involved, there is no exemption. (*Ibid* 640:7, *Biur Halachah*)

if they are in a place where there is no *sukkah,* if they can make one at a small cost,[21] they must endeavor to have a *sukkah* for sleeping. If they are also traveling at night they are governed by the same *Halachos* that apply in the daytime. People who travel to villages on *Chol Hamoed* to collect debts, and cannot make a *sukkah* there, must assume the inconvenience of returning home every night in order to fulfill the mitzvah of *sukkah.*

19) People traveling for the sake of doing a mitzvah,[22] and would find it bothersome to find a *sukkah,* or if it is not convenient for them to sleep in the *sukkah,* and if they would sleep there they would be tired the next morning, and would be hampered in the performance of the mitzvah, are exempt from the mitzvah of *sukkah;* otherwise, they are obligated to fulfill it.

20) If watchmen who guard gardens, orchards, grain and other produce, find it possible to watch everything from one location, they should make a *sukkah* there, in which to stay.

21) Men who make wine in non-Jewish areas are exempt of the mitzvah of *sukkah,* whether by day or by night, because they must watch continuously that a non-Jew should not touch the wine. But if the situation is such that no watching is needed, then they are required to stay in the *sukkah.*

22) People who stay in a store, even if they live out of town, and the store is in town, and during the year they eat most of their daily meals there, nevertheless, on *Sukkos* they are required to eat in the *sukkah.*

Chapter 136

Laws of the Lulav and the other Species

1) It is a time-honored custom in Yisrael that when you buy an *esrog* and a *lulav,* and you are not an expert in these *Halachos,* you should show it to an halachic authority to determine if they are valid, because there are many different *Halachos* regarding them. You should do your best to buy a fresh *lulav,* because a dry *lulav* may be used only in extreme circumstances.[1] Some authorities say,[2] that [a *lulav*] that is no longer green is considered dry. The required length of a *lulav* is that it's main stem besides the upper leaves should measure four *tefachim.*[3] In extreme circumstances, a length of 13⅓ *egudlin*[3] is sufficient.

1. See *Mishnah Berurah* [649:58] for definition of what constitutes "extreme circumstances."
2. Most authorities are of this opinion and therefore you must not be lenient in this matter. (See *Mishnah Berurah* 645:25)
3. See glossary.

ב) הַהֲדַס צָרִיךְ לִהְיוֹת מְשֻׁלָּשׁ, דְּהַיְנוּ שֶׁיּוֹצְאִין בּוֹ מִכָּל קֵן וָקֵן שְׁלֹשָׁה עָלִין בְּשׁוּרָה אַחַת בְּשָׁוֶה, שֶׁלֹּא יִהְיֶה אֶחָד גָּבוֹהַּ אוֹ נָמוּךְ מֵחֲבֵרָיו. וּצְרִיכִין שֶׁיִּהְיוּ הֶעָלִין חוֹפִין אֶת עֵצוֹ, דְּהַיְנוּ שֶׁרֹאשׁ כָּל עָלֶה, יַגִּיעַ לְמַעְלָה מֵעֻקְצוֹ שֶׁל הֶעָלֶה שֶׁלְּמַעְלָה. וּבְתוֹךְ אֵלּוּ הַהֲדַסִּים הַמּוּבָאִים מִמֶּרְחָק, בְּדֹחַק שֶׁיִּמָּצְאוּ כְּשֵׁרִים, וּצְרִיכִין לְבָדְקָם. וְהַיָּרֵא דְּבַר ה', יְהַדֵּר לִקְנוֹת הֲדַסִּים לַחִים יְרֻקִּים מְשֻׁלָּשִׁים וּמְהֻדָּרִים. וְהַגְּדֵלִים בִּמְדִינָתֵנוּ, צְרִיכִין לְדַקְדֵּק בָּם אִם אֵינָם מֻרְכָּבִים, וְאִם לֹא גָּדְלוּ בְּעָצִיץ שֶׁאֵינוֹ נָקוּב. וְכֵן צְרִיכִין לְדַקְדֵּק בָּזֶה בַּלּוּלָבִין הַגְּדֵלִים בִּמְדִינָתֵנוּ. אִם אֵין בְּנִמְצָא הֲדַסִּים מְשֻׁלָּשִׁים, יִטֹּל שֶׁאֵינָם מְשֻׁלָּשִׁים, וְלֹא יְבָרֵךְ.

ג) שִׁעוּר הַהֲדַס, שְׁלֹשָׁה טְפָחִים. וּבִשְׁעַת הַדְּחָק, סַגֵּי בְּעֶשְׂרָה אֲגוּדָלִין. וְיִהְיֶה כָּל הַהֲדַס מִלְּמַטָּה עַד לְמַעְלָה, מְשֻׁלָּשׁ. וּבִשְׁעַת הַדְּחָק, אִם לְמַטָּה הַמְּעַט אֵינוֹ מְשֻׁלָּשׁ, וְהָרֹב שֶׁלְּמַעְלָה מְשֻׁלָּשׁ, גַּם כֵּן כָּשֵׁר. צְרִיכִין לְדַקְדֵּק, שֶׁלֹּא יִשְׁרוּ הֶעָלִין מִן הַהֲדַס, כִּי אִם נָשְׁרוּ אֲפִלּוּ מִקְצָת עָלִין, יֵשׁ כַּמָּה חִלּוּקֵי דִינִים, וּצְרִיכִין לַעֲשׂוֹת שְׁאֵלַת חָכָם.

ד) צְרִיכִין לְהַשְׁגִּיחַ, שֶׁלֹּא יְהֵא נִקְטָם רֹאשׁוֹ, דְּהַיְנוּ רֹאשׁ הָעֵץ. וְאִם אֵין לוֹ רַק קְטוּמִים, יַעֲשֶׂה שְׁאֵלַת חָכָם. אֲבָל הָעֲנָפִים הַקְּטַנִּים שֶׁיּוֹצְאִין בֵּין הַקִּנִּים, צְרִיכִים לִקְטוֹם אוֹתָם, שֶׁלֹּא יַפְסִיקוּ בֵּין הַקִּנִּים.

ה) הָעֲרָבָה, יְדוּעָה. הֶעָלֶה מָשׁוּךְ, וּפִיו חָלָק, וְהַקָּנֶה אָדֹם. וַאֲפִלּוּ בְּעוֹדוֹ יָרוֹק, כָּשֵׁר, כֵּיוָן שֶׁכְּשֶׁהוּא שׁוֹהֶה בָּאִילָן, מִתְאַדֵּם. וְרֹב מִין זֶה גָּדֵל אֵצֶל הַנְּחָלִים, וְעַל כֵּן נִקְרָא עַרְבֵי נָחַל. וַאֲפִלּוּ הַגְּדֵלִים בְּמָקוֹם אַחֵר, כְּשֵׁרִים, אֶלָּא שֶׁאִם אֶפְשָׁר, יֵשׁ לְהַדֵּר לִקַּח מֵאוֹתָן הַגְּדֵלִים אֵצֶל נָחַל. שִׁעוּר הָעֲרָבָה, כְּשִׁעוּר הַהֲדַס.

ו) עֲרָבָה שֶׁיָּבְשָׁה, אוֹ שֶׁנָּשְׁרוּ רֹב הֶעָלִין שֶׁלָּהּ, אוֹ שֶׁנִּקְטַם רֹאשׁ הָעֵץ שֶׁלָּהּ, פְּסוּלָה, וְיֵשׁ אוֹמְרִים, דְּגַם אִם נִדַּלְדְּלוּ הֶעָלִין מִן הַקָּנֶה וּתְלוּיִים לְמַטָּה, פְּסוּלָה. וּצְרִיכִין לְהַשְׁגִּיחַ מְאֹד גַּם בָּעֲרָבָה, כִּי לִפְעָמִים מֵחֲמַת שֶׁתּוֹחֲבִין אוֹתָהּ אֶל הַלּוּלָב אוֹ עַל יְדֵי הַנִּעְנוּעִין, נוֹשְׁרִין הֶעָלִין, וְאָז פְּסוּלָה.

ז) צָרִיךְ לִזָּהֵר שֶׁלֹּא יִקְצֹץ הַיִּשְׂרָאֵל בְּעַצְמוֹ מִן הָאִילָן אֶחָד מֵאַרְבַּעַת

2) The *hadas* (myrtle twig) must have leaves growing in groups of three, that is, each set of leaf buds should produce three leaves on the same horizontal level, none should be higher or lower than the others. Also it is essential that the leaves cover the twig, that is, that the tip of each leaf should overlap the stem of the leaf above it. Among the *hadassim* that are imported from distant places you rarely find valid ones, and you must, therefore, examine them. A God-fearing person should do his best to buy *hadassim* that are fresh, green and have leaves "in a threesome," and are beautiful. You must make sure that those grown locally have not been grafted, and have not been grown in a pot that has no hole [in the bottom]. Similarly, we must be concerned regarding the *lulavim* that grow in our region. If *hadassim* with "threesome" leaves are unavailable you may take those without "threesome" leaves, but you should not say the berachah.

3) The required length of a *hadas* is three *tefachim*. In extreme circumstances ten *egudlin* is sufficient. The entire *hadas*, from bottom to top, should have leaves growing in "threesomes." In extreme circumstances, however, if at the bottom there are a few leaves not in "threesomes," but on top the majority are "threesomes," it is also valid. You should be careful that the leaves of the *hadas* should not fall off; for even if some of the leaves fall off, there are many differing *Halachos*, and you must consult an *halachic* authority.

4) You should make sure that the top [of the *hadas*] is not broken off, that is, the top of the wooden stem. If you have only *hadassim* with broken-off tops, you should consult an *halachic* authority. But the small side-branches that grow between the leaf-buds must be broken off so that they should not form a separation between the leaf-buds.

5) The *aravah* (willow) is well-known, it has lengthy leaves that have smooth edges, and it has a red stem. Even when the stem is still green, the *aravah* is valid, because if it stays on the tree it turns red. Most of this species grow near a brook, therefore, they are called *arvei nachal* [willows of the brook] (Leviticus 23:40). But even if they grow elsewhere they are valid, but if it is possible, you should try to get those that grow near a brook. The required size of the *aravah* is the same as that of the *hadas*.

6) An *aravah* that is dried up, or if most of its leaves have fallen off, or if its stem is broken off, is invalid. Some authorities say, that if the leaves are partially torn from the stem and are hanging limp it is also invalid. You should be extremely careful also with regard to the *aravah*, because sometimes when you insert it in its place among the *lulav* [and the *hadas*], or because of the waving, the leaves fall off and then it becomes invalid.

7) Care should be taken that a Jew should not personally cut off any of the four species from a tree for his own use, even if the owner of the land gives him

הַמִּינִים לְצָרְכּוֹ, אֲפִלּוּ נָתַן לוֹ בַּעַל הַקַּרְקַע רְשׁוּת, אֶלָּא גּוֹי אוֹ יִשְׂרָאֵל אַחֵר יִקְצְצֵם וְיִקַּח מִמֶּנּוּ.

ח) לוֹקְחִין שְׁלֹשָׁה בַּדֵּי הֲדַס וּשְׁנֵי בַדֵּי עֲרָבָה, (וְאֵין לְהוֹסִיף), וְאוֹגְדִין אוֹתָם עִם הַלּוּלָב, שֶׁיִּהְיוּ כֻּלָּן אֲגֻדָּה אַחַת. וּצְרִיכִין לְהַשְׁגִּיחַ שֶׁיִּהְיוּ כֻּלָּם כְּדֶרֶךְ גְּדִילָתָן, דְּהַיְנוּ מְקוֹם הַחִתּוּךְ לְמַטָּה, שֶׁאִם נִתְהַפֵּךְ אֲפִלּוּ רַק בַּד אֶחָד, גַּם בְּדִיעֲבַד אֵינוֹ יוֹצֵא. וְיֵשׁ לֶאֱגוֹד אֶת הַהֲדַס מִימִין הַשִּׁדְרָה אֶל הַלּוּלָב, וְאֶת הָעֲרָבָה מִשְּׂמֹאלוֹ, דְּהַיְנוּ שֶׁכְּשֶׁיִּטֹּל אֶת הַלּוּלָב וְהַשִּׁדְרָה נֶגֶד פָּנָיו, יִהְיֶה הַהֲדַס נֶגֶד יְמִינוֹ, וְהָעֲרָבָה נֶגֶד שְׂמֹאלוֹ. וְיִהְיוּ לְמַטָּה כֻּלָּם שָׁוִים, כְּדֵי שֶׁכְּשֶׁיִּטּוֹל אֶת הַלּוּלָב, יֹאחַז כֻּלָּם. וּמִכָּל מָקוֹם יֵשׁ לִרְאוֹת שֶׁיִּהְיֶה הַהֲדַס מְעַט גָּבוֹהַּ מִן הָעֲרָבָה. וְצָרִיךְ לְהַשְׁגִּיחַ שֶׁתֵּצֵא הַשִּׁדְרָה מִן הַלּוּלָב לְמַעְלָה מִן הַהֲדַס לְכָל־הַפָּחוֹת טֶפַח. קוֹשֵׁר כֻּלָּם בְּיַחַד בְּקֶשֶׁר גָּמוּר, דְּהַיְנוּ שְׁנֵי קְשָׁרִים זֶה עַל גַּב זֶה. וּמִלְּבַד מַה שֶּׁקָּשַׁר אֵלּוּ הַמִּינִים בְּיַחַד, יַעֲשֶׂה עוֹד בַּלּוּלָב שְׁלֹשָׁה קְשָׁרִים, וְרַק טֶפַח אֶחָד מִן הַלּוּלָב לְמַעְלָה יִהְיֶה בְּלִי קֶשֶׁר, כְּדֵי לְכַסְכֵּס בּוֹ בִּשְׁעַת הַנִּעְנוּעִים. אִם יֵשׁ חוּט כָּרוּךְ עַל הַהֲדַס, צָרִיךְ לַהֲסִירוֹ קֹדֶם הָאִגּוּד, שֶׁלֹּא תְהֵא חֲצִיצָה. אִם הֻתְּרָה הָאֲגֻדָּה בְּיוֹם־טוֹב, אָסוּר לְאָגְדָהּ בְּיוֹם־טוֹב בְּקֶשֶׁר, אֶלָּא בַּעֲנִיבָה, אוֹ כְּמוֹ שֶׁנּוֹהֲגִין שֶׁכּוֹרְכִין סְבִיבוֹתָם וְתוֹחֲבִין רֹאשׁ הַכְּרִיכָה לְתוֹךְ הָעִגּוּל הַכָּרוּךְ.

ט) עֲרָבָה שֶׁנִּתְלְשָׁה בְּיוֹם־טוֹב, בֵּין בְּיוֹם־טוֹב רִאשׁוֹן בֵּין בְּיוֹם־טוֹב שֵׁנִי, אֲסוּרָה הַיּוֹם אֲפִלּוּ בְּטִלְטוּל בְּעָלְמָא, כִּי הִיא מֻקְצֶה גָּמוּר. וְאִם נִתְלְשָׁה בְּיוֹם־טוֹב רִאשׁוֹן, כְּשֵׁרָה בְּיוֹם־טוֹב שֵׁנִי. אַךְ אִם חָל יוֹם רִאשׁוֹן בַּשַּׁבָּת וְנִתְלְשָׁה, אֲסוּרָה גַּם בְּיוֹם שֵׁנִי. אִם הוּבְאוּ מִחוּץ לַתְּחוּם אֶתְרוֹג אוֹ שְׁאָר מִינִים, מֻתָּרִין לְטַלְטְלָן וְלָצֵאת בָּהֶם. אַךְ אִם אֵין הָעִיר מְתֻקֶּנֶת בְּעֵרוּבִין, אֲסוּרִין לְטַלְטֵל לַחוּץ מִן הַבַּיִת שֶׁהֵם שָׁם, וְיֵלְכוּ כֻּלָּם שָׁמָּה לָצֵאת בָּהֶם.

י) מִי שֶׁאֵין לוֹ כָּל אַרְבַּעַת הַמִּינִים מְבֻחָרִים, טוֹב לוֹ יוֹתֵר לָצֵאת

---

4. This halachah is based on the concern that the non-Jew possessed the land illegally by stealing it from its Jewish owner. Therefore if you personally take these species from the land,

permission;[4] but a non-Jew or another Jew should cut them off and then he should buy it from him.

8) You should take three *hadas* branches and two *aravah* branches, (no more than that), and bind them together with the *lulav,* so that they become one bundle. You should make sure that they are all [bound together] in the direction they grow, that is, with the cut edges downward. For, if only one branch is upside down, it is invalid, even ex post facto, [after it is already done]. You should bind the *hadas* on the right of the stem of the *lulav* and the *aravah* on its left side,[5] that is, when you take the *lulav,* with its stem facing you, the *hadas* should be opposite your right and the *aravah* opposite your left.[6] On the bottom they should all be even, so that when you take the *lulav* you should hold all the species [in your hand]. Nevertheless, you should see to it that the *hadas* should be slightly higher than the *aravah.* And you should make sure that the stem of the *lulav* protrudes at least a *tefach* above the *hadas.* You should tie all of them together with a complete knot, that is, two knots one on top of the other. Besides binding these [three] species together you should also fasten three more bands on the *lulav.*[7] However, at least only one *tefach* at the top of the *lulav*[8] should remain without a band, in order to make a rustling sound when you shake it. If there is a string tied around the *hadassim,* you must remove it before binding it with the *lulav,* so that nothing intervenes between [the *hadassim* and the *lulav*]. If the *lulav*-bundle becomes undone on Yom Tov, it is forbidden to tie it on Yom Tov with a knot, but you may make a loop, or as the custom is, to wind the strip around the *lulav* and insert the end of the strip into the ring you made.

9) An *aravah* that was cut off the tree either on the first day of Yom Tov or on the second day is forbidden to be handled on that day, because it is absolutely *muktzeh.* If it was cut on the first day, it may be used on the second day. But if the first day occurs on Shabbos, and it was cut then, it is also forbidden on the second day. If an *esrog* was brought in, from outside the Shabbos boundary, or if any of the other species were brought in, you may handle them and fulfill the mitzvah with them. But if the city has no *eiruv,* you may not move them outside the house where they are found; and all must go to this house to fulfill the mitzvah with them.

10) Should you not have been able to obtain choice specimens of all four species,

---

you may be actually acquiring them illegally. It is best therefore that you acquire them from a non-Jew who took them from the land and possessed them, for once he becomes the owner, you may legally purchase them from him. *Mishnah Berurah* questions if this ruling applies to our times. (See *Biur Halachah* 649:1 and *Mishnah Berurah* 649:10)

5. See *Shaar Hatzion* (651:11) who mentions that there are those who follow the custom of *Ari Zal* which is different than the custom stated here.

6. This ruling also applies to one who is left-handed. (*Ibid* 651:12)

7. According to *Taz* the band that is tied around the species at the bottom of the *lulav* is counted as one of the three bands. *Eliyohu Rabbah* rules, however, that there must be three bands in addition to the one holding the species together. (See *Mishnah Berurah* 651:14)

8. This refers to the stem of the *lulav.* A *tefach* of the stem should remain without a band.

בְּשֶׁל חֲבֵרוֹ (וְעַיֵּן סִימָן שֶׁלְּאַחַר זֶה סָעִיף ח). וּמִכָּל מָקוֹם מִצְוָה לוֹ שֶׁיִּהְיוּ לוֹ גַּם כֵּן אַרְבָּעָה מִינִים כְּפִי הַשָּׂגַת יָדוֹ לַעֲשׂוֹת בָּהֶם הַנִּעְנוּעִים בְּהַלֵּל וְהַקָּפוֹת.

סִימָן קלז
דִּינֵי נְטִילָתָן וְסֵדֶר הַהַקָּפוֹת

א) נוֹטֵל אֶת הַלּוּלָב עִם הָאִגּוּד וְשִׁדְרַת הַלּוּלָב כְּנֶגֶד פָּנָיו בִּימִינוֹ, וְאֶת הָאֶתְרוֹג בִּשְׂמֹאלוֹ. וְכֵיוָן שֶׁבְּכָל הַמִּצְוֹת צְרִיכִין לְבָרֵךְ עֲלֵיהֶן קֹדֶם עֲשִׂיָּתָן, וְגַם הָאֶתְרוֹג צְרִיכִין לְהַחֲזִיק דֶּרֶךְ גְּדִילָתוֹ, דְּהַיְנוּ שֶׁהָעֹקֶץ שֶׁבּוֹ נֶחְתַּךְ מִן הָאִילָן יִהְיֶה לְמַטָּה, וְהַשּׁוֹשַׁנְתָּא לְמַעְלָה, עַל כֵּן כְּשֶׁהוּא נוֹטֵל אֶת הָאֶתְרוֹג קֹדֶם שֶׁמְּבָרֵךְ, יִטְּלֵהוּ בְּהִפּוּךְ, הָעֹקֶץ לְמַעְלָה וְהַשּׁוֹשַׁנְתָּא לְמַטָּה, שֶׁלֹּא יֵצֵא בּוֹ. וּמְבָרֵךְ מְעֻמָּד עַל נְטִילַת לוּלָב. (לְפִי שֶׁהַלּוּלָב גָּבוֹהַּ מִכֻּלָּן, חָשׁוּב הוּא וְנִקְרֵאת כָּל הָאֲגֻדָּה עַל שְׁמוֹ). וּבַיּוֹם הָרִאשׁוֹן, מְבָרֵךְ גַּם שֶׁהֶחֱיָנוּ. וְאִם חָל הַיּוֹם הָרִאשׁוֹן בְּשַׁבָּת, שֶׁאֵין נוֹטְלִין בּוֹ לוּלָב, אֲזַי מְבָרֵךְ שֶׁהֶחֱיָנוּ בַּיּוֹם הַשֵּׁנִי. וּלְאַחַר שֶׁבֵּרַךְ, מְהַפְּכוֹ בְּיָדוֹ וּמְקָרְבוֹ אֶל הַלּוּלָב, שֶׁלֹּא יִהְיֶה פֵּרוּד בֵּינֵיהֶם, וּמְנַעְנֵעַ לְאַרְבַּע רוּחוֹת כַּסֵּדֶר הַזֶּה, מִזְרָח, דָּרוֹם, מַעֲרָב, צָפוֹן, מַעְלָה, מַטָּה. וְכֵן בַּנִּעְנוּעִים שֶׁבַּהַלֵּל, וְכֵן בַּהַקָּפָה, יִזָּהֵר לְקָרֵב אֶת הָאֶתְרוֹג אֶל הַלּוּלָב, שֶׁלֹּא יִהְיֶה פֵּרוּד בֵּינֵיהֶם. אִם הִפֵּךְ וְנָטַל אֶת הָאֶתְרוֹג בַּיָּמִין וְאֶת הַלּוּלָב בִּשְׂמֹאל, יַחֲזוֹר וְיִטְּלֵם בְּלֹא בְרָכָה.

ב) אִטֵּר, נוֹטֵל אֶת הַלּוּלָב בִּימִינוֹ שֶׁהִיא שְׂמֹאל כָּל אָדָם, וְאֶת הָאֶתְרוֹג בִּשְׂמֹאלוֹ. וְאִם הִפֵּךְ, חוֹזֵר וְנוֹטְלָם בְּלֹא בְּרָכָה. וּמִי שֶׁהוּא שׁוֹלֵט בִּשְׁתֵּי יָדָיו, הֲרֵי הוּא כְּכָל אָדָם.

9. According to *Mishnah Berurah,* it is better to use your own even if they are not as beautiful as your friends. (*Ibid* 658:39)

1. If you take both of them in one hand, according to some *poskim* you have not fulfilled your obligation and you must take them again with two hands as prescribed. According to *Mishnah Berurah* we should be stringent and follow this ruling but another berachah should not be said. (*Mishnah Berurah* 651:15)

2. According to *Beis Yosef* there is another option—to have in mind that you are not fulfilling the mitzvah until you have them all in your hand. *Vilna Gaon* writes that this is the best way. (*Ibid* 651:25)

you should rather fulfill the mitzvah with a set belonging to a friend,[9] [who has obtained choice specimen,] (see following chapter, par. 8). Nevertheless, it is a mitzvah for you to obtain for yourself the best four species you can afford, in order to wave with them when you say *Halleil* and also for the *Hakafos.*

Chapter 137

Laws of Taking the Lulav and the Hakafos

1) You should take the *lulav,* together with the bundle, the stem [spine] of the *lulav* facing you—in your right hand, and the *esrog* in your left hand.[1] As in all mitzvos, you must say the berachah on the *lulav* before performing the mitzvah. You must also hold the *esrog* in the manner it grows, that is, that the stem from where it was cut off the tree should point downward and the *pitam* [knob on top] upward. Therefore, when you pick up the *esrog* before saying the berachah, you should hold it upside down, with the stem facing upward and the *pitam* downward, in order not to fulfill the mitzvah[2] before saying the berachah. Then, while standing, you should say the berachah *Al netilas lulav* [Concerning the taking of the *lulav*]. (Because the *lulav* is taller than any of the other species, it is considered more important, and the entire bundle is called by that name.) On the first day of *Sukkos* you should also say *Shehecheyanu.*[3] If the first day of *Sukkos* occurs on Shabbos, when we do not take the *lulav,* then you say *Shehecheyanu* on the second day. After the berachah you turn the *esrog* around,[2] and holding it close to the *lulav,* so that there is no separation between them, you wave [the species][4] towards the four points of the earth, in this sequence: East, South, West, North, up and down.[5] When waving during *Halleil* and during the *Hoshanos,* you should also be careful to hold the *esrog* close to the *lulav,* so that there is no separation between them. If you did it in the opposite manner, and took the *esrog* with the right hand and the *lulav* with the left hand you should take them again, without saying the berachah.

2) A left-handed person should take the *lulav* with *his* "right" hand, which is everyone else's left hand, and the *esrog* with his [so-called] "left" hand. If he did it in the opposite manner he should take them again without saying a berachah. A person who is ambidextrous is considered as any [right-handed] person.

---

3. If you did not say the berachah *Shehecheyanu* on the first day, you may say it on any of the other days. (*Ibid* 651:29)

4. In addition to holding the *Four Species* together—which is sufficient for the fulfillment of the mitzvah—you should also perform the waving (or shaking) of the Species in the same manner. (*Ibid* 651:49)

5. It is preferable to face east while waving the Species. The sequence followed in most *Ashkenaz* congregations is: straight ahead (i.e., east), right (south), back (west), left (north), up and down. The generally followed manner of waving is to stretch out the arms and shake the bundle enough to rustle the leaves of the *lulav,* and then draw the bundle close to the chest and shake again. This procedure is repeated three times in each direction. (*Ibid* 651:47)

ג) נָכוֹן שֶׁיַּחֲלֹץ אֶת הַתְּפִלִּין קֹדֶם נְטִילַת לוּלָב. לְכָל־הַפָּחוֹת יָסִיר אֶת הָרְצוּעָה מֵעַל יָדוֹ, שֶׁלֹּא תְהֵא חֲצִיצָה. גַּם נָכוֹן לְהָסִיר הַטַּבָּעוֹת שֶׁבְּאֶצְבְּעוֹתָיו.

ד) סֵדֶר הַנִּעְנוּעִים בְּהַלֵּל, כָּךְ הוּא, בְּהוֹדוּ יֵשׁ שֵׁשׁ תֵּבוֹת חוּץ מִן הַשֵּׁם, וִינַעְנֵעַ בְּכָל תֵּבָה לְרוּחַ אֶחָד, וּבַשֵּׁם לֹא יְנַעְנֵעַ. בְּהוֹדוּ, לַמִּזְרָח. כִּי, לַדָּרוֹם. טוֹב, לַמַּעֲרָב. כִּי, לַצָּפוֹן. לְעוֹלָם, לְמַעְלָה. חַסְדּוֹ, לְמָטָּה. שְׁלִיחַ־הַצִּבּוּר אֵינוֹ מְנַעְנֵעַ אֶלָּא בְּהוֹדוּ וּבְיֹאמַר נָא־יִשְׂרָאֵל. וְהַצִּבּוּר, בְּכָל פַּעַם שֶׁאוֹמְרִים הוֹדוּ. וּבְאָנָּא שְׁלִיחַ־הַצִּבּוּר גַּם הַצִּבּוּר, מְנַעְנְעִים רַק בְּאָנָּא ה׳ הוֹשִׁיעָה־נָּא. וְכֵיוָן שֶׁמִּלְּבַד הַשֵּׁם יֵשׁ בּוֹ שָׁלֹשׁ תֵּבוֹת, מְנַעְנְעִים בְּכָל תֵּבָה לִשְׁתֵּי רוּחוֹת. וּבְהוֹדוּ שֶׁבְּסוֹף הַלֵּל גַּם כֵּן מְנַעְנְעִים שְׁלִיחַ־הַצִּבּוּר וְהַצִּבּוּר. כְּשֶׁמְּנַעְנֵעַ לְמַטָּה, יַשְׁפִּיל רַק יָדָיו לְמַטָּה, וְהַלּוּלָב עִם שְׁאָר הַמִּינִים יִשָּׁאֲרוּ כְּדֶרֶךְ גְּדִילָתָן. וְיֵשׁ נוֹהֲגִין שֶׁמְּהַפְּכִין אֶת הַלּוּלָב לְצַד מַטָּה. וְאַל יְשַׁנֶּה אָדָם מִן הַמִּנְהָג. אֵינוֹ צָרִיךְ לַהֲפֹךְ פָּנָיו לַצַּד שֶׁהוּא מְנַעְנֵעַ, רַק רֹאשׁ הַלּוּלָב יַטֶּה. וְהַנִּעְנוּעַ אֵינוֹ צָרִיךְ שֶׁיִּהְיֶה בְּחֹזֶק, אֶלָּא כִּסְכּוּס מְעַט כְּדֵי שֶׁיִּתְנַעְנְעוּ הֶעָלִין, סַגֵּי.

ה) אָסוּר לֶאֱכֹל קֹדֶם נְטִילַת לוּלָב. וּמִי שֶׁהוּא בַּדֶּרֶךְ וּמְצַפֶּה שֶׁיָּבוֹא לְמָקוֹם שֶׁיֵּשׁ שָׁם אֶתְרוֹג וְלוּלָב, וְכֵן הַדָּרִים בְּיִשּׁוּבִים וּמְשַׁלְּחִים לָהֶם אֶתְרוֹג וְלוּלָב, צְרִיכִין לְהַמְתִּין עַד חֲצוֹת הַיּוֹם וְלֹא יוֹתֵר, כִּי אָסוּר לְהִתְעַנּוֹת בְּיוֹם־טוֹב וּבְחֹל־הַמּוֹעֵד, יוֹתֵר. וּמִי שֶׁחָלַשׁ לִבּוֹ לְהַמְתִּין עַד חֲצוֹת הַיּוֹם, יָכוֹל לִטְעֹם אֵיזֶה דָּבָר קֹדֶם. אֲבָל מִי שֶׁאֵין לִבּוֹ חַלָּשׁ, יֵשׁ לוֹ לְהַחְמִיר אֲפִלּוּ בִּטְעִימָה.

ו) מֻתָּר לְהַחֲזִיר הַלּוּלָב בְּיוֹם־טוֹב לַמַּיִם וּלְהוֹסִיף עָלָיו מַיִם, אֲבָל לֹא יַחֲלִיף. וּבְחֹל־הַמּוֹעֵד, מִצְוָה לְהַחֲלִיף אֶת הַמַּיִם, כְּדֵי שֶׁיִּשָּׁאֵר הַלּוּלָב לַח וּמְהֻדָּר. וְנוֹהֲגִין לִקַּח בְּחֹל־הַמּוֹעֵד בְּכָל יוֹם עֲרָבָה חֲדָשָׁה לַלּוּלָב, וְהוּא הִדּוּר מִצְוָה.

ז) הֲדַס שֶׁל מִצְוָה, אָסוּר לְהָרִיחַ בּוֹ בְּכָל שִׁבְעַת יְמֵי הֶחָג, אֲפִלּוּ בַּשַּׁבָּת. אֲבָל בְּאֶתְרוֹג, מֻתָּר לְהָרִיחַ בּוֹ בַּשַּׁבָּת, וּמְבָרְכִין עָלָיו, הַנּוֹתֵן רֵיחַ טוֹב בַּפֵּרוֹת. וּבִשְׁאָר יְמֵי הֶחָג, אֵין לְהָרִיחַ בּוֹ אֲפִלּוּ שֶׁלֹּא בִשְׁעַת נְטִילָתוֹ לָצֵאת בּוֹ, מִשּׁוּם דְּיֵשׁ סְפֵק בְּרָכָה. הַלּוּלָב, אָסוּר לְטַלְטְלוֹ בַּשַּׁבָּת אֲפִלּוּ

3) It is proper to take off the *tefillin* before taking the *lulav* in hand, or at least remove the strap from your hand, so that nothing intervenes between [your hand and the *esrog*.] It is also proper to remove the rings from your fingers.

4) The order of the waving in *Halleil* is as follows: There are six words in *Hodu* [Give thanks] besides the Name *Hashem;* and at each word you should wave in a different direction; but when saying Hashem, you should not wave. At *Hodu* you wave towards the East (straight ahead), at *ki* towards the South (right), at *tov* towards the West (back), at *ki* towards the North (left), at *le'olam,*—upward; at *chasdo,* —downward.[6] The *Chazzan* waves only at *Hodu* and at *Yomar na Yisrael.* The congregation waves each time they say *Hodu.*[7] At *Ana,* both the *Chazzan* and the congregation wave only when saying *Ana Hashem hoshiah na,* [Please Hashem, save now!] But since this verse has only three words besides *Hashem,* you should wave at each word in two directions. In the *Hodu* at the conclusion of *Halleil* both the *Chazzan* and the congregation wave again. When waving downward you should lower only your hands, while the *lulav* and the other species should remain [in an upright position] the same way they grow. People who have the custom to turn the *lulav* downwards should not change their custom. It is not necessary to turn your face in the direction in which you are waving; you should only point the top of the *lulav,* [in that direction]. You do not have to wave the *lulav* forcefully, just shaking it slightly to rustle the leaves is sufficient.

5) It is forbidden to eat before fulfilling the mitzvah of *lulav.* If you are traveling and anticipate to arrive at a place where there is an *esrog* and a *lulav;* or people who live in small villages, [and must wait until] an *esrog* and *lulav* is sent to them, must wait until midday, but no later, because it is forbidden to fast longer than that on Yom Tov and *Chol Hamoed.* If you feel faint and cannot wait until noon, you may have something to eat before; but if you do not feel faint you should be stringent and abstain from tasting any food.

6) You are permitted to replace the *lulav* in water on Yom Tov, and add water to the vessel [in which it is placed], but you may not change the water. However, on *Chol Hamoed* it is a mitzvah to change the water for the purpose of keeping the *lulav* fresh and beautiful. It is customary to buy fresh *aravos* on each day of *Chol Hamoed,* for the *lulav;* for thereby you enhance the beauty of the mitzvah.

7) It is forbidden to inhale the fragrance of the *hadassim* during the seven days of *Sukkos,* even on Shabbos. But you may inhale the aroma of the *esrog* on Shabbos, and you should say the berachah *Hanosein rei'ach tov bapeiros,* [Who places a good aroma into fruit]. But on the other days of *Sukkos,* you should not smell it, even

---

6. Many congregations have adopted the custom of the *Ari Zal* which is South (right), North (left), East (straight ahead), upward, downward, West (back). There are also different customs regarding the verses at which the congregation waves the *lulav.*

7. If you are praying individually (not with a congregation) you wave only at the first and last *Hodu* of the *Halleil* and also at *Ana Hashem Hoshiah na.* (*Ibid* 651:41)

לְצֹרֶךְ גּוּפוֹ וּמְקוֹמוֹ, מִשּׁוּם דַּהֲוֵי מֻקְצֶה. אֲבָל הָאֶתְרוֹג, כֵּיוָן שֶׁיְּכוֹלִין לְהָרִיחַ בּוֹ, אֵינוֹ מֻקְצֶה, וּמֻתָּר לְטַלְטְלוֹ. וּמֻתָּר לִתְּנוֹ לְתוֹךְ הַמּוֹכִין שֶׁהָיָה בָּהֶם קֹדֶם יוֹם־טוֹב, שֶׁכְּבָר קָלְטוּ הָרֵיחַ. אֲבָל לֹא יִתְּנֶנּוּ לְתוֹךְ מוֹכִין חֲדָשִׁים אוֹ לְבֶגֶד, מִשּׁוּם דְּמוֹלִיד רֵיחָא.

ח) בְּיוֹם־טוֹב הָרִאשׁוֹן, אֵין יוֹצְאִין בְּלוּלָב וּשְׁאָר מִינִים שְׁאוּלִים, אֶלָּא צְרִיכִין שֶׁיִּהְיוּ שֶׁלּוֹ מַמָּשׁ, דִּכְתִיב, וּלְקַחְתֶּם לָכֶם בַּיּוֹם הָרִאשׁוֹן, וְדָרְשִׁינַן, לָכֶם, מִשֶּׁלָּכֶם, לְהוֹצִיא אֶת הַשָּׁאוּל. וּבְנֵי חוּץ־לָאָרֶץ שֶׁעוֹשִׂין שְׁנֵי יָמִים טוֹבִים מִסְּפֵקָא, גַּם בְּיוֹם־טוֹב שֵׁנִי אֵין מְבָרְכִין עָלָיו. וְאִם אַחֵר נוֹתְנָם לוֹ בְּמַתָּנָה עַל מְנָת לְהַחֲזִיר, הֲוֵי מַתָּנָה וְיוֹצֵא בָהֶם, וַאֲפִלּוּ נוֹתְנִים לוֹ סְתָם לָצֵאת בָּהֶם, נֶחְשָׁב כְּאִלּוּ אָמַר לוֹ בְּפֵרוּשׁ שֶׁהוּא נוֹתְנָם לוֹ בְּמַתָּנָה עַל מְנָת לְהַחֲזִיר. אִם אֵין הָאִישׁ בְּבֵיתוֹ וְהָאִשָּׁה רוֹצָה לִתְּנָם לְאַחֵר לָצֵאת בָּהֶם, תַּלְיָא בְּאֻמְדַּן דַּעַת הַבַּעַל, אִם הוּא גַבְרָא דְקָפִיד אוֹ לָא.

ט) שֻׁתָּפִים שֶׁקָּנוּ לָהֶם אֶתְרוֹג וּשְׁאָר הַמִּינִים, מִסְתָמָא אַדַּעְתָּא דְהָכִי קְנָאוּם, דִּבְשַׁעַת מִצְוָתוֹ כָּל אֶחָד מַקְנֶה חֶלְקוֹ לַחֲבֵרוֹ. וְלָכֵן הַמִּנְהָג שֶׁהַקָּהָל קוֹנִים אֶתְרוֹג, וְכָל הַקָּהָל יוֹצְאִין בּוֹ. וְכָל מִי שֶׁיָּדוֹ מַשֶּׂגֶת, מְחֻיָּב לָתֵת דְּמֵי אֶתְרוֹג. וְעִם כָּל זֹאת, מוּטָב לָצֵאת בְּאֶתְרוֹג שֶׁל יָחִיד, אֲשֶׁר לוֹ כָּל הַמִּינִים מְהֻדָּרִים. כִּי מַה שֶׁהַיָּחִיד מַקְנֶה לַחֲבֵרוֹ, עָדִיף טְפֵי.

י) בַּיּוֹם הָרִאשׁוֹן לֹא יִתְּנוּ לִקְטַנִּים לִטּוֹל לוּלָב וְאֶתְרוֹג עַד לְאַחַר שֶׁיִּטְּלוּ הַגְּדוֹלִים, כִּי הַקָּטָן קוֹנֶה וְאֵינוֹ מַקְנֶה מִן הַתּוֹרָה.

יא) בְּכָל יְמֵי הֶחָג לְאַחַר תְּפִלַּת מוּסָף, נוֹהֲגִים לְהַעֲלוֹת סֵפֶר־תּוֹרָה עַל הַבִּימָה, וּמַנִּיחִין אֶת אֲרוֹן הַקֹּדֶשׁ פָּתוּחַ עַד לְאַחַר אֲמִירַת הַהוֹשַׁעְנוֹת, שֶׁאָז מַחֲזִירִין אֶת סֵפֶר־הַתּוֹרָה. וְכָל מִי שֶׁיֵּשׁ לוֹ אֶתְרוֹג וְלוּלָב, מַקִּיף אֶת הַבִּימָה שֶׁעָלֶיהָ סֵפֶר־הַתּוֹרָה בִּשְׁעַת אֲמִירַת הַהוֹשַׁעְנוֹת.

---

8. In a case where the donor does not know that you cannot fulfill the mitzvah unless it is considered completely yours, you cannot fulfill the mitzvah unless he expressly gives it to you as a returnable gift. (*Ibid* 649:15)

9. *Mishnah Berurah* writes that it is nevertheless better for each partner to actually say that he is giving his share to the person who is fulfilling the mitzvah. (*Ibid* 658:32)

when you are not taking it to fulfill the mitzvah, because it is *halachically* doubtful whether you should say a berachah on it. It is forbidden to handle the *lulav* on Shabbos, even if you need the *lulav* itself or the space it occupies, because it is *muktzeh*. However, since you are permitted to smell the *esrog*, it is not *muktzeh*, and you may handle it. And you are permitted to put it back in the cotton where it was kept before Yom Tov, because it already absorbed the fragrance. However you should not place it in new cotton or in a garment, because you are creating fragrance in the garment, [which is forbidden on Shabbos].

8) On the first day of *Sukkos*, you cannot fulfill the mitzvah with a *lulav* and other species that were borrowed, but they must actually belong to you, for it is written, "And take for yourself on the first day." (Leviticus 23:40) And [our Rabbis] expound "For yourself" means "from that which is yours," which excludes a borrowed [*lulav* or other species] Those living outside *Eretz Yisrael* who observe Yom Tov two days, because of a doubt [about the date], even on the second day should not say a berachah [over a borrowed *lulav*]. If someone gives you his *lulav* as a gift, on condition that you return it, it is considered [*halachically* as] a gift and you may fulfill the mitzvah with it. Even if he gives it to you unconditionally for the purpose of fulfilling the mitzvah, it is considered as if he had expressly stipulated[8] that he is giving it to you as a gift on condition that you return it. If the husband is not at home and the wife wants to give the *lulav* to someone to fulfill the mitzvah, the validity depends on the judgment of the husband's disposition, whether or not he would mind.

9) If people joined to buy an *esrog* and the other species [in partnership], we presume that they bought it with the understanding, that when it is time to perform the mitzvah, each partner would transfer his share to the other.[9] Therefore, it is customary for the congregation to buy an *esrog*, and the entire congregation fulfills the mitzvah with it,[10] and whoever can afford it must contribute to the "*esrog* fund." Still, it is better to fulfill the mitzvah with an *esrog* belonging to an individual, if all his species are superbly beautiful, because an individual's transfer of ownership is more effective.

10) On the first day of *Sukkos*[11] minor children should not be permitted to take the *lulav* and *esrog* before the adults have fulfilled the mitzvah, for a minor can acquire an object but cannot transfer ownership, according to Torah law.

11) On all the days of *Sukkos*, after the *Musaf* service,[12] it is customary to carry a *Seifer Torah* to the *bimah*. The Ark remains open until the conclusion of the *Hoshana* service, when the *Seifer Torah* is returned to the Ark. All men who possess an *esrog* and *lulav* circle the *bimah*, where the *Seifer Torah* is held, while the *Hoshanos*

---

10. Here too, it is best that an announcement be made that each person gives his share to the one fulfilling the mitzvah. (*Ibid* 658:40)

11. To those living outside *Eretz Yisrael*, this law applies to the second day of *Sukkos* as well. (*Ibid* 658:23)

12. This is according to the *Ashkenazi* custom. The *Sephardic* custom is to say the *Hoshanos* after the Halleil service.

בְּכָל יוֹם, מַקִּיפִין פַּעַם אֶחָת. וּבַיּוֹם הַשְּׁבִיעִי שֶׁהוּא הוֹשַׁעְנָא רַבָּה, מוֹצִיאִין אֶת כָּל סִפְרֵי הַתּוֹרָה וּמַעֲלִין אוֹתָן עַל הַבִּימָה, וּמַקִּיפִין שֶׁבַע פְּעָמִים, זֵכֶר לַמִּקְדָּשׁ, שֶׁבְּכָל יוֹם הָיוּ מַקִּיפִין אֶת הַמִּזְבֵּחַ פַּעַם אַחַת, וּבַיּוֹם הַשְּׁבִיעִי שֶׁבַע פְּעָמִים. הַהַקָּפוֹת צְרִיכוֹת לִהְיוֹת לְצַד יָמִין. וּלְפִי שֶׁסֵּפֶר־הַתּוֹרָה עַל הַבִּימָה, וְכָל הַצִּבּוּר צְרִיכִין לַהֲפֹךְ פְּנֵיהֶם כְּלַפֵּי סֵפֶר־הַתּוֹרָה שֶׁעַל הַבִּימָה קֹדֶם שֶׁיַּתְחִילוּ לְהַקִּיף, וְאָז הֲוֵי צָפוֹן, יָמִין שֶׁלָּהֶם, לָכֵן מַקִּיפִין דֶּרֶךְ צָפוֹן. כָּל מִי שֶׁיֵּשׁ לוֹ אֶתְרוֹג וְלוּלָב וְאֵינוֹ מַקִּיף, רָעָה הוּא עוֹשֶׂה. בִּקְצָת מְקוֹמוֹת נוֹהֲגִין בְּהוֹשַׁעְנָא רַבָּה וּבְשִׂמְחַת תּוֹרָה, שֶׁלְּאַחַר שֶׁהוֹצִיאוּ אֶת כָּל סִפְרֵי־הַתּוֹרָה מִן אֲרוֹן הַקֹּדֶשׁ, מַעֲמִידִין לְתוֹכוֹ נֵר דוֹלֵק, (לְרַמֵּז תּוֹרָה אוֹר, שֶׁכְּשֶׁאֵין שָׁם תּוֹרָה, צְרִיכִין לְאוֹר אַחֵר). וְאֵין זֶה מִנְהָג יָפֶה, וְיֵשׁ לְבַטְּלוֹ, כִּי אָסוּר לְהִשְׁתַּמֵּשׁ בַּאֲרוֹן הַקֹּדֶשׁ תַּשְׁמִישׁ חֹל, אֲפִלּוּ לְפִי שָׁעָה.

יב) בַּשַּׁבָּת, אֵין מַקִּיפִין, שֶׁגַּם בַּמִּקְדָּשׁ לֹא הָיוּ מַקִּיפִין, וְלָכֵן אֵין מַעֲלִים סֵפֶר־תּוֹרָה עַל הַבִּימָה, אֶלָּא פּוֹתְחִין אֶת אֲרוֹן הַקֹּדֶשׁ עַד לְאַחַר אֲמִירַת הַהוֹשַׁעְנוֹת.

יג) מִי שֶׁאֵרַע לוֹ אֵבֶל בֶּחָג, וְכֵן אָבֵל כָּל שְׁנֵים עָשָׂר חֹדֶשׁ עַל אָבִיו אוֹ אִמּוֹ, נוֹהֲגִין שֶׁאֵינוֹ מַקִּיף. וְיֵשׁ לוֹ לְכַבֵּד בְּאֶתְרוֹג וְלוּלָב שֶׁלּוֹ אֶת מִי שֶׁאֵין לוֹ, שֶׁיַּקִּיף הוּא.

סִימָן קלח
דִּינֵי הוֹשַׁעְנָא רַבָּה וּשְׁמִינִי עֲצֶרֶת וְשִׂמְחַת תּוֹרָה

א) בַּיּוֹם חֲמִישִׁי (וּבְאֶרֶץ יִשְׂרָאֵל בַּיּוֹם הַשִּׁשִּׁי) שֶׁל חֹל־הַמּוֹעֵד, הוּא הוֹשַׁעְנָא רַבָּא, נוֹהֲגִין לִהְיוֹת נֵעוֹרִים בַּלַּיְלָה שֶׁלְּפָנָיו לַעֲסֹק בַּתּוֹרָה, כְּמוֹ שֶׁנִּדְפַּס הַסֵּדֶר, לְפִי שֶׁבֶּחָג נִדּוֹנִין עַל הַמַּיִם, שֶׁכָּל חַיֵּי הָאָדָם תְּלוּיִים בַּמַּיִם, וְהַיּוֹם הוּא יוֹם הָאַחֲרוֹן שֶׁל הֶחָג, וְהַכֹּל הוֹלֵךְ אַחַר הַחִתּוּם. בְּשַׁחֲרִית, מַרְבִּים קְצָת בְּנֵרוֹת בְּבֵית־הַכְּנֶסֶת כְּמוֹ בְּיוֹם־הַכִּפּוּרִים, וּשְׁלִיחַ־הַצִּבּוּר לוֹבֵשׁ אֶת הַקִּיטֶל. אוֹמְרִים לַמְנַצֵּחַ כְּמוֹ בְּיוֹם־טוֹב, וְאוֹמְרִים גַּם מִזְמוֹר לְתוֹדָה, וְאֵין אוֹמְרִים נִשְׁמַת. אוֹמְרִים אֵין כָּמוֹךָ, שְׁמַע יִשְׂרָאֵל, כְּמוֹ בְּיוֹם־טוֹב. וּבִקְדֻשַּׁת מוּסָף, נַעֲרִיצְךָ.

ב) מִנְהַג נְבִיאִים, שֶׁכָּל אֶחָד יִטּוֹל בְּיוֹם זֶה עֲרָבָה מְיֻחֶדֶת, מִלְּבַד

are recited. Each day they circle the *bimah* once. But on the seventh day [of *Sukkos*] which is *Hoshana Rabbah,* all the *Sifrei Torah* are removed from the Ark and brought to the *bimah.* The *bimah* is circled seven times, in remembrance of the *Beis Hamikdash,* where each day [of *Sukkos*] they would circle the altar once and on the seventh day, seven times. The *hakafos* (circuits) should be made, [starting] to the right. Since the *Seifer Torah* is on the *bimah,* and the entire congregation must turn towards the *Seifer Torah* on the *bimah* before beginning the *hakafah,* their right side thus faces North; therefore, the circle moves in a northerly direction. A person who owns an *esrog* and *lulav* and does not encircle the *bimah* manifests poor conduct. In some communities it is customary on *Hoshana Rabbah* and *Simchas Torah,* after they remove all the *Sifrei Torah* from the Ark, to place a burning candle in it (to indicate that Torah is light, and when the Torah is not there, another light is needed). This is not a proper custom and should be abolished, for it is forbidden to use the Holy Ark for secular purposes, even temporarily.

12) On Shabbos no circuits are made because even in the *Beis Hamikdash* they did not circle the altar [on Shabbos]. Therefore, a *Seifer Torah* is not brought to the *bimah,* but the Holy Ark is left open until after the *Hoshanos* are said.

13) A person who becomes a mourner on *Sukkos,* or a mourner during the twelve months after the death of his father or mother, according to custom, should not encircle the *bimah,* but he should give his *esrog* and *lulav* to someone who does not own a *lulav,* to circle the *bimah.*

Chapter 138

Laws of Hoshana Rabbah, Shemini Atzeres and Simchas Torah

1) The fifth (in Eretz Yisrael, the sixth) day of *Chol Hamoed* is *Hoshana Rabbah.* It is customary to stay awake the preceding night and to study Torah, according to the order printed [in the *Tikkun*], because on *Sukkos* we are judged with regard to water, upon which human life depends, and this day is the last day of *Sukkos,* and all depends upon the conclusion [of judgment.] At *Shacharis* additional candles are lit in the synagogue, as on *Yom Kippur,* and the *Chazzan* wears a *kittel. Lamenatzei'ach* [for the choirmaster] is said as on Yom Tov, and *Mizmor lesodah* [a psalm of thanksgiving] is also said, but *Nishmas* [the soul] is not said. We say *Ein kamocha* [There is none like you], and *Shema Yisrael,* as on Yom Tov. In the *Kedusha* of *Musaf* we say *Na'aritzecha* [We will revere].

2) The prophets instituted the custom, that each person should take a special *aravah,* on that day besides the *aravah* in the *lulav* bundle. Whatever disqualifies the

הָעֲרָבָה שֶׁבַּלּוּלָב. וְכָל הַפּוֹסֵל בַּעֲרָבָה שֶׁבַּלּוּלָב, פּוֹסֵל גַּם בַּעֲרָבָה זוֹ. לָכֵן לֹא יִקְצְצָהּ הַיִּשְׂרָאֵל בְּעַצְמוֹ לְצָרְכּוֹ, (כְּמוֹ שֶׁכָּתַבְתִּי לְעֵיל סִימָן קלו סָעִיף ז׳), אֶלָּא שֶׁאִם נָשְׁרוּ אֲפִלּוּ רֹב הֶעָלִין, כְּשֵׁרָה. וַאֲפִלּוּ נִשְׁאַר רַק עָלֶה אֶחָד בְּבַד אֶחָד, כְּשֵׁרָה. וּמִכָּל מָקוֹם הִדּוּר מִצְוָה הוּא, שֶׁיִּהְיוּ בָהּ עָלִין הַרְבֵּה, וְהַבַּדִּים אֲרֻכִּים. וְהַמִּנְהָג הַיָּפֶה, לָקַחַת חֲמִשָּׁה בַדִּין, וְאוֹגְדִין אוֹתָם בַּעֲלֵי לוּלָב.

ג) אֵין לוֹקְחִין אוֹתָהּ עִם הַלּוּלָב בְּיַחַד, אֶלָּא כְּשֶׁמַּגִּיעִין לְתַעֲנֶה אֱמוּנִים, מַנִּיחִין אֶת הַלּוּלָב וְהָאֶתְרוֹג וְנוֹטְלִין אוֹתָהּ, לְפִי שֶׁאָז מִתְפַּלְּלִין עַל הַמַּיִם. וּלְאַחַר גְּמַר הַהוֹשַׁעְנוֹת, מְנַעְנְעִין בָּהּ, וְאַחַר כָּךְ חוֹבְטִין אוֹתָהּ בַּקַּרְקַע חָמֵשׁ פְּעָמִים, וְדַי בָּזֶה, אֲפִלּוּ אִם לֹא נֶחְסְרוּ עָלֶיהָ. וּלְאַחַר הַחֲבָטָה, לֹא יִזְרְקֶנָּה עַל הַקַּרְקַע, מִשּׁוּם בִּזּוּי מִצְוָה. וְטוֹב לְהַצְנִיעָהּ לְהַשְׁלִיכָהּ בְּתוֹךְ הָאֵשׁ שֶׁאוֹפִין מַצּוֹת, הוֹאִיל וְאִתְעֲבַד בָּהּ חֲדָא מִצְוָה, לִתְעֲבֵד בָּהּ מִצְוָה אַחֲרִיתָא.

ד) בְּלֵיל שְׁמִינִי עֲצֶרֶת, יֵשׁ לְהַמְתִּין שֶׁלֹּא לְקַדֵּשׁ עַד הַלָּיְלָה. וּמְבָרְכִין בַּקִּדּוּשׁ שֶׁהֶחֱיָנוּ, לְפִי שֶׁהוּא רֶגֶל בִּפְנֵי עַצְמוֹ. וְאֵין מְבָרְכִין לֵישֵׁב בַּסֻּכָּה, לְפִי שֶׁבַּתְּפִלָּה וּבַקִּדּוּשׁ אוֹמְרִים, יוֹם הַשְּׁמִינִי חַג הָעֲצֶרֶת הַזֶּה. וְאִם הָיוּ מְבָרְכִין לֵישֵׁב בַּסֻּכָּה, הֲוֵי תַּרְתֵּי דְסַתְרֵי.

ה) לֵיל שְׁמִינִי עֲצֶרֶת וְכָל הַיּוֹם, אוֹכְלִין בַּסֻּכָּה, אֶלָּא שֶׁאֵין מְבָרְכִין, כְּמוֹ שֶׁכָּתַבְנוּ. וּלְאַחַר הַגְּמָר, אוֹמְרִים יְהִי רָצוֹן וְכוּ׳. וּבְעִנְיַן הַשֵּׁנָה בַּסֻּכָּה, יֵשׁ מְקִלִּין, וְכֵן נוֹהֲגִין. אֲבָל הַנָּכוֹן, לְהַחְמִיר.

ו) בַּשְּׁמִינִי סָמוּךְ לַחֲשֵׁכָה, יָכוֹל לְפַנּוֹת אֶת הַכֵּלִים מִן הַסֻּכָּה לְתוֹךְ הַבָּיִת. אֲבָל לֹא יְסַדְּרֵם בַּיּוֹם, מִשּׁוּם דַּהֲוֵי כְּמֵכִין מִיּוֹם טוֹב לַחֲבֵרוֹ.

ז) יוֹם אַחֲרוֹן שֶׁל הֶחָג, שֶׁהוּא גַּם כֵּן שְׁמִינִי עֲצֶרֶת, נִקְרָא שִׂמְחַת־תּוֹרָה, לְפִי שֶׁמְּסַיְּמִין בּוֹ אֶת הַתּוֹרָה וּשְׂמֵחִים בָּהּ. עַרְבִית, לְאַחַר הַתְּפִלָּה, עוֹשִׂין הַקָּפוֹת, וְאַחַר כָּךְ מַכְנִיסִין סִפְרֵי הַתּוֹרָה, וּמְשַׁיְּרִין אֶחָד שֶׁקּוֹרִין בּוֹ תְּלָתָא גַבְרֵי בְּפָרָשַׁת וְזֹאת הַבְּרָכָה. וְיֵשׁ מְקוֹמוֹת שֶׁנּוֹהֲגִין לִקְרוֹת בְּפָרָשַׁת נְדָרִים. אַחַר קְרִיאַת הַתּוֹרָה, אוֹמְרִים חֲצִי קַדִּישׁ, וּמַכְנִיסִין אֶת סִפְרֵי הַתּוֹרָה וְאוֹמְרִים עָלֵינוּ.

aravah of the *lulav* [bundle] also disqualifies this *aravah*. Therefore, a Jew should not cut it himself for his own use. (as I have written in ch. 136:7 above); the only difference [of the special *aravah*] is that even if most of the leaves fell off, it is valid. Even if there is only one leaf left on one branch, it is valid. However, the beauty of the mitzvah is enhanced when the *aravah* has many leaves and a long branch. It is a beautiful custom to take five branches [for the special *aravah*] and tie them together with a leaf of a *lulav*.

3) You should not take this *aravah* together with the *lulav*, but when you begin to say *Ta'aneh emunim* [Answer the faithful][1] you put down the *lulav* and the *esrog* and take the *aravah*, for then we pray for water. At the conclusion of the *Hoshanos*, you wave the *aravah* and beat it on the ground five times, and it is sufficient, even if no leaves fall off in the process. After beating the *aravah*, you should not throw it on the floor, because it shows contempt of the mitzvah. It is best to put save it and cast it into the fire of [the oven] when you bake matzos (for Pesach), since it was used for one mitzvah it should be used for another mitzvah.

4) On the night of *Shemini Atzeres* you should wait [and be sure] not to say the *Kiddush* before nightfall. In the *Kiddush* you should say *Shehecheyanu*, because it is a Yom Tov in itself. You should not say *Leisheiv basukkah*, because in the *Shemoneh Esrei* and in the *Kiddush*, we say *Yom hashemini chag ha'atzeres hazeh* [the Eighth Day, this Festival of Assembly], and if you said *Leisheiv basukkah*, you would be contradicting yourself.

5) The night of *Shemini Atzeres* and the whole day, you should eat in the *sukkah*, but you should not say the berachah [*Leisheiv basukkah*], as we have mentioned. When you take final leave of the *sukkah* you should say *Yehi ratzon*, [May it be favorable] etc. Regarding sleeping in the *sukkah*, some authorities take a lenient view, and this is the accepted custom; but it is proper to follow the stricter view.

6) On the eighth day near dark, you may remove the vessels from the *sukkah* into the house; but you should not arrange them in proper order while it is still day,[2] for that is considered preparing on one Yom Tov for another.

7) The last day of Yom Tov, which is also *Shemini Atzeres*, is called *Simchas Torah*, because on this day we conclude [the reading of] the Torah, and we rejoice with it. In the evening, after *Maariv*, we make [seven] *Hakafos* [circuits] carrying the *Sifrei Torah* around the *bimah*, after which the *Sifrei Torah* are replaced in the Ark. We leave one *Seifer Torah* from which we read for three people[3] from the portion *Vezos haberachah* [This is the blessing], (Deuteronomy 33). In some communities it is customary to read the portions dealing with vows. After the reading of the Torah, the *half-kaddish* is said, the *Seifer Torah* is replaced in the Ark, and *Aleinu* is said.

---

1. This is according to *Sheloh*, but according to *Ari Zal*, this is done after the final, whole *Kaddish*.

2. However, if they will cause the house to look unkempt, it is permitted to put them away neatly. (*Mishnah Berurah* 667:6)

3. In some communities five people are called to read from the Torah.

ח) בְּיוֹם שִׂמְחַת־תּוֹרָה, נוֹהֲגִין בְּהַרְבֵּה מְקוֹמוֹת, שֶׁהַכֹּהֲנִים נוֹשְׂאִים כַּפֵּיהֶם בִּתְפִלַּת שַׁחֲרִית וְלֹא בַּמּוּסָף, מִשּׁוּם דְּבַמּוּסָף יֵשׁ חֲשַׁשׁ שִׁכְרוּת. וְאֵין אוֹמְרִים וְתֶעֱרַב בִּתְפִלַּת שַׁחֲרִית.

ט) בַּיּוֹם אַחַר הַהַקָּפוֹת, מְשַׁיְּרִין שְׁלֹשָׁה סִפְרֵי תוֹרָה וּמַרְבִּים בִּקְרוּאִים בְּסֵפֶר־תּוֹרָה אֶחָד בְּפָרָשַׁת וְזֹאת הַבְּרָכָה כַּמָּה פְּעָמִים עַד מְעֹנָה, וּבְסוֹף קוֹרְאִין כָּל הַנְּעָרִים. וְהַנָּכוֹן, שֶׁהַגָּדוֹל שֶׁבָּהֶם יְבָרֵךְ וְהַשְּׁאָר יִשְׁמְעוּ. וְקוֹרִין לָהֶם פָּסוּק הַמַּלְאָךְ הַגּוֹאֵל וְגוֹ'. אַחַר כָּךְ קוֹרְאִין לַחֲתַן־תּוֹרָה, וְקוֹרֵא מִן מְעֹנָה עַד גְּמִירָא. וּבְסֵפֶר הַתּוֹרָה הַשֵּׁנִי, קוֹרֵא חֲתַן־בְּרֵאשִׁית, וְאוֹמְרִים חֲצִי קַדִּישׁ, וְקוֹרִין בַּשְּׁלִישִׁי מַפְטִיר (וְעַיֵּן לְעֵיל סִימָן עט סָעִיף א). וְנוֹהֲגִין בְּהַרְבֵּה מְקוֹמוֹת לְדַקְדֵּק לִקְרוֹת לַחֲתַן־תּוֹרָה אָדָם חָשׁוּב. וַאֲפִלּוּ מִי שֶׁעָלָה כְּבָר בְּפָרָשַׁת וְזֹאת הַבְּרָכָה, מִכָּל מָקוֹם עוֹלֶה לַחֲתַן־תּוֹרָה אוֹ לַחֲתַן־בְּרֵאשִׁית. בְּמָקוֹם שֶׁאֵין לָהֶם אֶלָּא שְׁנֵי סִפְרֵי תוֹרָה, קוֹרִין בָּרִאשׁוֹן וְזֹאת הַבְּרָכָה, וּבַשֵּׁנִי בְּרֵאשִׁית, וְחוֹזְרִין וְלוֹקְחִין אֶת הָרִאשׁוֹן לַמַּפְטִיר.

י) נוֹהֲגִין שֶׁחֲתַן־הַתּוֹרָה וַחֲתַן־בְּרֵאשִׁית נוֹדְרִין נְדָבוֹת, וְקוֹרִין לְכָל מֵרֵעֵיהֶם וְעוֹשִׂין מִשְׁתֶּה וְשִׂמְחָה לְסִיּוּמָהּ שֶׁל תּוֹרָה וּלְהַתְחָלָתָהּ. דְּאִיתָא בַּמִּדְרָשׁ (תְּחִלַּת קֹהֶלֶת), וַיָּבֹא יְרוּשָׁלַיִם וַיַּעֲמֹד לִפְנֵי אֲרוֹן בְּרִית־ה' וְגוֹ' וַיַּעַשׂ מִשְׁתֶּה לְכָל־עֲבָדָיו, אָמַר רַבִּי יִצְחָק, מִכָּאן, שֶׁעוֹשִׂין סְעוּדָה לִגְמָרָהּ שֶׁל תּוֹרָה.

סִימָן קלט
הִלְכוֹת חֲנֻכָּה

א) בְּבַיִת הַשֵּׁנִי, כְּשֶׁמָּלְכָה מַלְכוּת יָוָן, גָּזְרוּ גְזֵרוֹת עַל יִשְׂרָאֵל, וּבִטְּלוּ דָּתָם, וְלֹא הִנִּיחוּ אוֹתָם לַעֲסֹק בַּתּוֹרָה וּבַמִּצְוֹת, וּפָשְׁטוּ יְדֵיהֶם בְּמָמוֹנָם וּבִבְנוֹתֵיהֶם, וְנִכְנְסוּ לַהֵיכָל וּפָרְצוּ בוֹ פְּרָצוֹת, וְטִמְּאוּ אֶת הַטְּהָרוֹת, וְצַר לָהֶם לְיִשְׂרָאֵל מְאֹד מִפְּנֵיהֶם, וּלְחָצוּם לַחַץ גָּדוֹל, עַד שֶׁרִחֵם עֲלֵיהֶם אֱלֹהֵי אֲבוֹתֵינוּ וְהוֹשִׁיעָם מִיָּדָם וְהִצִּילָם וְגָבְרוּ בְּנֵי חַשְׁמוֹנָאִי הַכֹּהֲנִים הַגְּדוֹלִים וַהֲרָגוּם, וְהוֹשִׁיעוּ אֶת יִשְׂרָאֵל מִיָּדָם, וְהֶעֱמִידוּ מֶלֶךְ מִן הַכֹּהֲנִים,

8) On the day of *Simchas Torah* it is the custom in many communities that the *Kohanim* bless the people in the *Shacharis* service and not in *Musaf,* since during *Musaf* the *Kohanim* may be intoxicated. We do not say *Vesei'areiv* [May our entreaties be pleasing] when the *Kohanim* bless the people at *Shacharis* prayers.

9) In the daytime, after the *Hakafos,* three *Sifrei Torah* are left out, and many people are called up to one *Seifer Torah,* to read the portion *Vezos haberachah* up to *Me'onah* (Deut. 33:27) repeating it many times. At the end, all the young boys are called up. It is proper that a boy who is *bar mitzvah* should say the berachah and that the others should listen.[4] The verse *Hamalach hagoel* is read for them[5] [The angel who delivered me] etc. (Genesis 48:16). After that, the *Chasan Torah* is called up and he reads from *Me'onah* to the end [of the Torah]. In the second *Seifer Torah,* the *Chasan Bereishis* reads. Then *half-kaddish* is said. In the third *Seifer Torah, Maftir* is read. (see chapter 79:1 above) It is the custom in many communities to be mindful to call up an eminent person for *Chasan Torah*. Even a person who was called up already for the reading of *Vezos haberachah,* may still be called up as *Chasan Torah* or as *Chasan Bereishis.* Where there are only two *Sifrei Torah, Vezos haberachah* should be read in one, and *Bereishis* in the other one, and the first *seifer* is taken again for *Maftir.*

10) It is customary for the *Chasan Torah* and the *Chasan Bereishis* to make donations to charity,[6] and to invite all their friends to a joyous meal in honor of the completion of the Torah and its beginning. As it is written in the *Midrash,* (At the beginning of *Koheles* [Ecclesiastes], "He came to Jerusalem and he stood in front of the Ark of the Covenant of Hashem" etc. ". . . and he made a banquet for all his servants." Rabbi Yitzchak said, "From this we can infer, that you should make a festive meal upon the completion of the Torah."

Chapter 139

Laws of Chanukah

1) During the era of the Second *Beis Hamikdash* when the Greek kingdom was in power, they imposed evil decrees against the Jewish people, designed to put an end to their religion. They did not permit them to study the Torah or to perform the mitzvos; they plundered their property, [abducted] their daughters, entered the Temple, violating its sanctity and defiling its purity. Yisrael was in great distress because of them, for they oppressed them bitterly, until the God of our fathers took pity on them and delivered them from their dominion, and rescued them. The Hasmoneans, the sons of the *Kohein Gadol* defeated and killed them, and delivered Yisrael from their dominion. They appointed as king one of the *Kohanim,* and the

---

4. They will be exempt with his berachah.

5. According to *Levush* this verse is recited over them as an oral blessing, but it is not read. (*Ibid* 669:14)

6. It is a proper custom for all who are called to the Torah, to contribute for the support of the *Beis Hamedrash* and for the support of those who study the Torah. (*Ibid* 669:7)

וְחָזְרָה מַלְכוּת יִשְׂרָאֵל יוֹתֵר מִמָּאתַיִם שָׁנָה עַד הַחֻרְבָּן הַשֵּׁנִי. וּכְשֶׁגָּבְרוּ יִשְׂרָאֵל עַל אוֹיְבֵיהֶם וְאִבְּדוּם, בַּחֲמִשָּׁה וְעֶשְׂרִים בְּחֹדֶשׁ כִּסְלֵו הָיָה, וְנִכְנְסוּ לַהֵיכָל, וְלֹא מָצְאוּ שֶׁמֶן טָהוֹר בַּמִּקְדָּשׁ אֶלָּא פַּךְ אֶחָד, שֶׁהָיָה מֻנָּח בְּחוֹתָמוֹ שֶׁל כֹּהֵן־גָּדוֹל, וְלֹא הָיָה בוֹ לְהַדְלִיק אֶלָּא יוֹם אֶחָד בִּלְבָד, וְהִדְלִיקוּ מִמֶּנּוּ נֵרוֹת־הַמַּעֲרָכָה שְׁמוֹנָה יָמִים, עַד שֶׁכָּתְשׁוּ זֵיתִים וְהוֹצִיאוּ שֶׁמֶן טָהוֹר. וּמִפְּנֵי זֶה הִתְקִינוּ חֲכָמִים שֶׁבְּאוֹתוֹ הַדּוֹר, שֶׁיִּהְיוּ שְׁמוֹנַת הַיָּמִים הָאֵלּוּ שֶׁמַּתְחִילִין בַּחֲמִשָּׁה וְעֶשְׂרִים בְּכִסְלֵו, יְמֵי שִׂמְחָה וְהַלֵּל, וּמַדְלִיקִים בָּהֶם הַנֵּרוֹת בָּעֶרֶב עַל פִּתְחֵי הַבָּתִּים בְּכָל לַיְלָה וָלַיְלָה בִּשְׁמוֹנַת הַלֵּילוֹת, לְהַרְאוֹת וּלְגַלּוֹת הַנֵּס. וְהַיָּמִים הָאֵלּוּ, נִקְרָאִים חֲנֻכָּה, רוֹצֶה לוֹמַר, חָנוּ כ״ה, שֶׁבְּיוֹם כ״ה חָנוּ מֵאוֹיְבֵיהֶם. וְעוֹד, מִפְּנֵי שֶׁבַּיָּמִים הָאֵלּוּ עָשׂוּ חֲנֻכַּת הַבַּיִת שֶׁהַצּוֹרְרִים טִמְּאוּהוּ. וְלָכֵן יֵשׁ אוֹמְרִים, שֶׁמִּצְוָה לְהַרְבּוֹת קְצָת בִּסְעוּדָה בַּחֲנֻכָּה. וְעוֹד, מִפְּנֵי שֶׁמְּלֶאכֶת הַמִּשְׁכָּן נִגְמְרָה בַּיָּמִים הָאֵלּוּ. וְיֵשׁ לְסַפֵּר לִבְנֵי בֵיתוֹ עִנְיַן הַנִּסִּים שֶׁנַּעֲשׂוּ לַאֲבוֹתֵינוּ בַּיָּמִים הָאֵלּוּ (עַיֵּן יוֹסִיפוֹן). וּמִכָּל מָקוֹם לֹא הֲוֵי סְעוּדַת מִצְוָה, אֶלָּא אִם כֵּן אוֹמְרִים בַּסְּעוּדָה שִׁירוֹת וְתִשְׁבָּחוֹת. וּמַרְבִּים בִּצְדָקָה בִּימֵי חֲנֻכָּה, כִּי הֵם מְסֻגָּלִים לְתַקֵּן בָּהֶם פְּגָמֵי נַפְשׁוֹ עַל יְדֵי הַצְּדָקָה, וּבְיִחוּד לְלוֹמְדֵי תוֹרָה הָעֲנִיִּים לְהַחֲזִיקָם.

ב) אֵין מִתְעַנִּין בִּימֵי חֲנֻכָּה. אֲבָל בַּיּוֹם שֶׁלִּפְנֵיהֶם וּבַיּוֹם שֶׁלְּאַחֲרֵיהֶם, מֻתָּרִין בְּהֶסְפֵּד וּבְתַעֲנִית.

ג) בַּחֲנֻכָּה, מֻתָּר בַּעֲשִׂיַּת מְלָאכָה. אַךְ הַנָּשִׁים נוֹהֲגוֹת שֶׁלֹּא לַעֲשׂוֹת מְלָאכָה כָּל זְמַן שֶׁהַנֵּרוֹת בַּבַּיִת דּוֹלְקִים, וְאֵין לְהָקֵל לָהֶן. וְהַטַּעַם שֶׁהַנָּשִׁים מַחְמִירוֹת יוֹתֵר, מִפְּנֵי שֶׁהַגְּזֵרָה הָיְתָה קָשָׁה עַל בְּנוֹת יִשְׂרָאֵל, שֶׁגָּזְרוּ, בְּתוּלָה הַנִּשֵּׂאת, תִּבָּעֵל לַהֶגְמוֹן תְּחִלָּה. וְעוֹד, מִפְּנֵי שֶׁהַנֵּס נַעֲשָׂה עַל יְדֵי אִשָּׁה, בַּת יוֹחָנָן כֹּהֵן־גָּדוֹל הָיְתָה יְפַת־תֹּאַר מְאֹד, וּבִקֵּשׁ הַמֶּלֶךְ הַצּוֹרֵר שֶׁתִּשְׁכַּב עִמּוֹ, וְאָמְרָה לוֹ, שֶׁתְּמַלֵּא בַקָּשָׁתוֹ, וְהֶאֱכִילַתּוּ תַּבְשִׁילֵי גְבִינָה, כְּדֵי שֶׁיִּצְמָא וְיִשְׁתֶּה יַיִן וְיִשְׁתַּכֵּר וְיִישַׁן וְיֵרָדֵם. וְכֵן הָיָה, וְחָתְכָה אֶת רֹאשׁוֹ וֶהֱבִיאַתּוּ לִירוּשָׁלַיִם. וְכִרְאוֹת שַׂר צְבָאָם כִּי אָבַד מַלְכָּם,

1. In his responsa, *Maharshal* writes that it is fitting and proper that this festivity be combined and saturated with the spirit and joy of Torah. *Biur Halachah* writes: "Adding to our

Kingdom of Yisrael returned to power and [endured] for more than two hundred years, until the destruction of the Second *Beis Hamikdash.* When Yisrael triumphed over their enemies and destroyed them, —this happened on the twenty-fifth of Kislev—, they entered the *Beis Hamikdash,* and found of the pure oil in the *Beis Hamikdash* only one jar, that was stamped with the seal of the *Kohein Gadol.* This oil was sufficient to burn for only one day, but they lit the lights of the *Menorah* with it [and it lasted] for eight days, until they crushed olives and extracted pure oil. For this reason the Sages of that generation ordained that these eight days, beginning on the twenty-fifth of *Kislev,* should be days of rejoicing and praise. We kindle lights in the evening near the entrance to the house every night, during these eight nights, in order to display and reveal the miracle. These days are called *Chanukah,* which means [it is a contraction of] *chanu chaf-hei* [they rested on the twenty-fifth]. For on the twenty-fifth of *Kislev* they rested from their enemies [onslaughts]. Another reason [for the name *Chanukah*] is that during these days they dedicated the *Beis Hamikdash* [*Chanukas habayis*], that had been defiled by the oppressors. Some authorities say, therefore, that it is a mitzvah to somewhat embellish the meals on *Chanukah.* Another reason for celebrating *Chanukah* is that the construction of the *Mishkan* was completed during these days. You should tell your family the story of the miracles that were performed for our forefathers, during these days (see Flavius Josephus). Nevertheless, a *Chanukah* feast is not considered a mitzvah, unless you sing hymns and praises to Hashem during the meal.[1] On *Chanukah* you should give charity generously, for the days of *Chanukah* are auspicious to correct flaws of the soul through the giving of charity,[2] especially when it is given to support poor, Torah scholars.

2) Fasting is not permitted on *Chanukah.* However, on the day before *Chanukah* and on the day after *Chanukah,* it is permitted to deliver a eulogy[3] and to fast.

3) You are permitted to work on *Chanukah.* But women follow the custom, not to do any work during the time the *Chanukah* lights are burning, and you should not [cause them] to treat this matter lightly. The reason that women are more stringent about this [than men], is that the cruelty of the evil decree was directed mainly at Jewish women. For [the Greeks] decreed that a virgin girl before her wedding must first cohabit with the general. Another reason for this is that the miracle came about through a woman. The daughter of Yochanan the *Kohein Gadol* was a very beautiful girl, and the ruthless king wanted her to lie with him. She told him that she would fulfill his request; and she served him cheese dishes, so that he would be thirsty, and drink wine; then become intoxicated, and fall asleep. That is precisely what happened. Then she cut off his head and brought it to Jerusalem. When the

---

grave sins, there are those who have substituted card playing and other secular frivolities instead of hymns and praises [at their so called *Chanukah* parties]." (*Biur Halachah* 670:2)

2. It has always been a custom for the poor to ask for charity during the days of *Chanukah.* (*Mishnah Berurah* 670:1)

3. Eulogies are forbidden on the days of *Chanukah* itself.

וַיָּנוּסוּ. וְלָכֵן קְצָת נוֹהֲגִין לֶאֱכֹל מַאַכְלֵי חָלָב בַּחֲנֻכָּה, זֵכֶר לַנֵּס שֶׁנַּעֲשָׂה עַל יְדֵי חָלָב.

ד) כָּל הַשְּׁמָנִים, כְּשֵׁרִים לְנֵר חֲנֻכָּה. וּמִכָּל מָקוֹם מִצְוָה מִן הַמֻּבְחָר לִקַּח שֶׁמֶן זַיִת דְּמְיָא דְנֵס שֶׁבַּמִּקְדָּשׁ, שֶׁהָיָה בְּשֶׁמֶן זַיִת. וְאִם אֵינוֹ מָצוּי, יִבְרוֹר שְׁאָר שֶׁמֶן שֶׁאוֹרוֹ זַךְ וְנָקִי, אוֹ נֵרוֹת שֶׁל שַׁעֲוָה, שֶׁגַּם כֵּן אוֹרָן זָךְ. וְלֹא יִהְיוּ שְׁנַיִם קְלוּעִים בְּיַחַד, מִשּׁוּם דַּהֲוֵי כִּמְדוּרָה, אֶלָּא כָּל נֵר, יְחִידִי. וְלֹא יַעֲשֶׂה מִשַּׁעֲוָה שֶׁל בָּתֵּי עֲבוֹדָה־זָרָה, מִשּׁוּם דְּמָאִיס. וְכֵן כָּל הַפְּתִילוֹת כְּשֵׁרוֹת לְנֵר חֲנֻכָּה, וּמִצְוָה מִן הַמֻּבְחָר, לִקַּח צֶמֶר גֶּפֶן. וְאֵין צָרִיךְ בְּכָל לַיְלָה פְּתִילוֹת חֲדָשׁוֹת, אֶלָּא מַדְלִיק גַּם בָּרִאשׁוֹנוֹת, עַד שֶׁיִּכְלוּ.

ה) אִם מַדְלִיק בְּנֵר שֶׁל חֶרֶס, כֵּיוָן שֶׁהִדְלִיק בּוֹ לַיְלָה אֶחָד, נַעֲשָׂה יָשָׁן, וְאֵין מַדְלִיקִין בּוֹ בַּלַּיְלָה הַשֵּׁנִי, מִשּׁוּם דְּמָאִיס. וְעַל כֵּן תִּהְיֶה לוֹ מְנוֹרָה נָאָה שֶׁל מִינֵי מַתֶּכֶת. וּמִי שֶׁיָּדוֹ מַשֶּׂגֶת, יִקְנֶה מְנוֹרָה שֶׁל כֶּסֶף לְהִדּוּר מִצְוָה.

ו) מִנְהָג פָּשׁוּט בִּמְדִינָתֵנוּ כִּמְהַדְּרִין מִן הַמְהַדְּרִין, שֶׁמַּדְלִיקִין כָּל אֶחָד וְאֶחָד מִבְּנֵי הַבַּיִת בַּלַּיְלָה הָרִאשׁוֹן נֵר אֶחָד, וּבַשֵּׁנִי, שְׁנֵי נֵרוֹת. וְכֵן מוֹסִיפִין, עַד שֶׁבְּלֵיל שְׁמִינִי מַדְלִיק שְׁמוֹנָה. וּצְרִיכִין לִזָּהֵר, שֶׁיִּתֵּן כָּל אֶחָד וְאֶחָד נֵרוֹתָיו בְּמָקוֹם מְיֻחָד, כְּדֵי שֶׁיִּהְיֶה הֶכֵּר כַּמָּה נֵרוֹת מַדְלִיקִין. וְלֹא יַדְלִיקוּ בְּמָקוֹם שֶׁמַּדְלִיקִין נֵרוֹת כָּל הַשָּׁנָה. כְּדֵי שֶׁיִּהְיֶה הֶכֵּר שֶׁהֵם נֵרוֹת חֲנֻכָּה.

ז) מִצְוַת נֵר חֲנֻכָּה, לְהַדְלִיק בַּפֶּתַח הַסָּמוּךְ לִרְשׁוּת הָרַבִּים, מִשּׁוּם פִּרְסוּמֵי נִסָּא, וְכָךְ הָיוּ עוֹשִׂין בִּזְמַן הַמִּשְׁנָה וְהַגְּמָרָא. וּבַזְּמַן הַזֶּה שֶׁאָנוּ דָּרִים בֵּין הָאֻמּוֹת, מַדְלִיקִין בַּבַּיִת שֶׁהוּא דָר בּוֹ. וְאִם יֵשׁ לוֹ חַלּוֹן לִרְשׁוּת הָרַבִּים, יַדְלִיקֵם שָׁם. וְאִם לָאו, מַדְלִיקָן אֵצֶל הַפֶּתַח. וּמִצְוָה שֶׁיַּנִּיחֵם בַּטֶּפַח הַסָּמוּךְ לַפֶּתַח מִשְּׂמֹאל, שֶׁתְּהֵא מְזוּזָה מִיָּמִין, וְנֵר חֲנֻכָּה מִשְּׂמֹאל, וְנִמְצָא שֶׁהוּא מְסֻבָּב בְּמִצְוֹת. וְיוֹתֵר טוֹב לְהַנִּיחָם בַּחֲלַל הַפֶּתַח.

ח) מִצְוָה לְהַנִּיחָם לְמַעְלָה מִשְּׁלֹשָׁה טְפָחִים מִן הַקַּרְקַע, וּלְמַטָּה מֵעֲשָׂרָה טְפָחִים. וְאִם הִנִּיחָם לְמַעְלָה מֵעֲשָׂרָה, יָצָא. אֲבָל אִם הִנִּיחָם לְמַעְלָה מֵעֶשְׂרִים אַמָּה, לֹא יָצָא, מִשּׁוּם דִּלְמַעְלָה מֵעֶשְׂרִים אַמָּה לָא

general saw that the king was dead, he [and his army] fled. Therefore, some people have the custom to eat dairy dishes on *Chanukah,* to commemorate the miracle achieved by means of a dairy product.

4) All kinds of oil are valid for the *Chanukah* lights. Nevertheless, the mitzvah done to perfection is to use olive oil, similar to the miracle in the *Beis Hamikdash,* which was achieved with olive oil. If this cannot be obtained you should select another kind of oil that gives a clear, bright flame, or wax candles, for they also produce clear light. You should not use two candles braided together, for that would be like a torch; but each candle should [burn] by itself. You should not make the candles from wax that comes from houses of idol worship, for that is repulsive. All wicks are valid for *Chanukah* lights. The mitzvah done to perfection is to use cotton. It is not necessary to take new wicks every night, but you may light the old wicks until they are used up.

5) If you light a *menorah* made of earthenware, after you light it one night it deteriorates and you should not light it again the following night, because it is repulsive. Therefore, you should possess a beautiful *menorah* made of metal. If you can afford it, you should buy a silver *menorah,* in order to adorn the mitzvah.

6) It is the widespread custom in our regions [to follow the practice] of the most scrupulously observant, whereby each member of the family kindles one light on the first night, two lights on the second, and keeps adding until on the eighth night, he kindles eight lights. You should be careful that each person places his *menorah* in a separate place, so that one can easily tell how many lights are lit [that night]. The *menorah* should not be lit in a place where candles are lit all year, in order to make it manifestly clear that these are *Chanukah* lights.

7) It is a mitzvah to light the *menorah* in the doorway that opens to the street, [public domain], in order to publicize the miracle; and it was done in this manner in the days of the Mishnah and the Talmud. Now, since we live among non-Jews, we light the *menorah* in the house, and if you have a window facing the street, you should light it there; if not, you should light it near the door. It is a mitzvah to place the *menorah* within a *tefach*[4] of the left side of the door so that the *mezuzah* will be on the right[5] and the *Chanukah* lights on the left, and in so doing you find yourself surrounded by mitzvos. It is preferable to place the *menorah* within the open space of the door.

8) The mitzvah requires that [the *menorah*] be placed higher than three *tefachim*[4] above the floor and lower than ten *tefachim.* But if you placed it higher than ten *tefachim* you have fulfilled your obligation. However, if you placed it higher than

---

4. See glossary.
5. If for whatever reason there is no *mezuzah,* the *Chanukah menorah* should be placed on the right side of the door. (*Shulchan Aruch* 671:7)

שָׁלְטָא עֵינָא. וּמִי שֶׁהוּא דָר בַּעֲלִיָּה, יָכוֹל לְהַנִּיחָם בַּחַלּוֹן, אַף־עַל־פִּי שֶׁהוּא גָבוֹהַּ מֵעֲשָׂרָה טְפָחִים. אֲבָל אִם הַחַלּוֹן לְמַעְלָה מֵעֶשְׂרִים אַמָּה מִקַּרְקַע רְשׁוּת הָרַבִּים, דְּלָא שָׁלְטָא בְּהוּ עֵינָא מֵהַהוֹלְכִים בִּרְשׁוּת הָרַבִּים, אֲזַי טוֹב יוֹתֵר לְהַנִּיחָם אֵצֶל הַפֶּתַח.

ט) הַנֵּרוֹת, יִהְיוּ בְּשׁוּרָה אַחַת בְּשָׁוֶה, לֹא אֶחָד גָּבוֹהַּ וְאֶחָד נָמוּךְ. וְיִהְיֶה הֶפְסֵק בֵּין נֵר לְנֵר, שֶׁלֹּא יִתְקָרֵב הַלַּהַב שֶׁל זֶה לָזֶה וְיִהְיֶה כְּמוֹ מְדוּרָה. וּבְנֵרוֹת שֶׁל שַׁעֲוָה, יִהְיֶה הֶפְסֵק, שֶׁלֹּא יִתְחַמֵּם זֶה מִזֶּה וְתִטֹּף הַשַּׁעֲוָה וְיִתְקַלְקְלוּ. מִלֵּא קְעָרָה שֶׁמֶן וְהִקִּיפָהּ פְּתִילוֹת, אִם כָּפָה עָלֶיהָ כְּלִי, כָּל פְּתִילָה עוֹלָה בִּשְׁבִיל נֵר אֶחָד. לֹא כָּפָה עָלֶיהָ כְּלִי, אֲפִלּוּ לְנֵר אֶחָד, אֵינָהּ עוֹלָה, לְפִי שֶׁהִיא כִּמְדוּרָה. נֵר שֶׁיֵּשׁ לוֹ שְׁנֵי פִּיּוֹת אוֹ יוֹתֵר, לֹא יַדְלִיקוּ בוֹ שְׁנַיִם אֲפִלּוּ בַּלַּיְלָה הָרִאשׁוֹן, מִשּׁוּם דְּלֵיכָּא הֶכֵּר כַּמָּה נֵרוֹת מַדְלִיקִין.

י) זְמַן הַדְלָקָתָן, מִיָּד בְּצֵאת הַכּוֹכָבִים, וְלֹא יְאַחֵר. וְאָסוּר לַעֲשׂוֹת שׁוּם דָּבָר קֹדֶם הַהַדְלָקָה, אֲפִלּוּ לִלְמֹד. רַק אִם לֹא הִתְפַּלֵּל מַעֲרִיב, יִתְפַּלֵּל תְּחִלָּה וְאַחַר כָּךְ יַדְלִיק. וְקֹדֶם שֶׁיַּדְלִיק, יְקַבֵּץ כָּל בְּנֵי בֵיתוֹ לְפִרְסוּמֵי מִלְּתָא. וְצָרִיךְ לָתֵת שֶׁמֶן, שֶׁיִּדְלְקוּ לְכָל־הַפָּחוֹת חֲצִי שָׁעָה. וּבְדִיעֲבַד אִם לֹא הִדְלִיק מִיָּד, יָכוֹל לְהַדְלִיק בִּבְרָכָה כָּל זְמַן שֶׁבְּנֵי בֵיתוֹ נֵעוֹרִים. אֲבָל לְאַחַר שֶׁבְּנֵי בֵיתוֹ יְשֵׁנִים, תּוּ לֵיכָּא פִּרְסוּמֵי נִסָּא, וְיַדְלִיק בְּלֹא בְרָכָה. אִם לֹא יִהְיֶה לוֹ פְּנַאי לְהַדְלִיק בַּלַּיְלָה, יָכוֹל לְהַקְדִּים אֶת עַצְמוֹ וּלְהַדְלִיק מִפְּלַג הַמִּנְחָה וּלְמַעְלָה, דְּהַיְנוּ שָׁעָה וּרְבִיעִית קֹדֶם צֵאת הַכּוֹכָבִים, (וְהַיְנוּ שָׁעָה זְמַנִּית, לְפִי עֶרֶךְ הַיּוֹם, עַיֵּן לְעֵיל סִימָן סט סָעִיף ב. וּבִימֵי חֲנֻכָּה שֶׁהַיָּמִים קְצָרִים, אִם הַיּוֹם אָרֹךְ רַק עֶשֶׂר שָׁעוֹת (לְפִי הַשָּׁעוֹן), אֲזַי פְּלַג הַמִּנְחָה, הֲוֵי שָׁעָה אַחַת, וּשְׁתֵּי דַקּוֹת וָחֵצִי). וּבִלְבַד שֶׁיִּתֵּן שֶׁמֶן כְּדֵי שֶׁיִּהְיוּ דוֹלְקִים עַד חֲצִי שָׁעָה לְאַחַר צֵאת הַכּוֹכָבִים. וְאִם אֵינָם דוֹלְקִים כָּךְ, לֹא קִיֵּם הַמִּצְוָה.

---

4. See glossary.
6. The space should be the width of a finger. (*Mishnah Berurah* 671:18)
7. This is true only when the cover was in place before the wicks were lit but if they were lit and then covered, they must be extinguished, covered and then relit. (*Ibid* 671:13)
8. *Mishnah Berurah* comments that this is true when there are only two branches in the *Menorah*. Our *Menorohs,* however, have eight branches and may be used simultaneously by two persons, each lighting at opposite ends. (*Ibid* 671:12)
9. Those who follow the *halachic* decisions of the *Vilna Gaon,* customarily light the candles at sunset.

twenty *amos*[4] you have not fulfilled your obligation, because when it is placed higher than twenty *amos* it is out of the range of vision. If you live on an upper floor you may place [the *menorah*] in the window, even though it is higher than ten *tefachim* from the ground. But if the window is higher than twenty *amos* from the ground of the public domain, where it is out of visual range of the people walking in the street, then it is preferable to place the lights near the door.

9) The lights should be placed in an even row; one should not be higher than the other. Space should be left between the lights,[6] so that the flames will not merge and look like a torch. Wax candles should be separated,[6] so they will not become heated from each other and cause the wax to melt, and become spoiled. If you fill a dish with oil and put wicks around it, and you place a [perforated] cover on it, each wick counts as a separate light.[7] If you did not place such a cover on it, it does not even count as one light, because it resembles a torch. A lamp that has two or more branches should not be kindled by two persons, even on the first night, because there is no way to tell how many candles were lit [for that night].[8]

10) The time to light [the *menorah*] is immediately after the stars appear,[9] and you should not delay it. It is forbidden to do anything before lighting the *menorah,* even to study Torah.[10] Except, if you have not prayed *Maariv,* you should first pray and then light the *menorah.*[11] Before lighting the *menorah,* you should gather the entire family, in order to proclaim the event publicly. You should pour in enough oil to burn at least half an hour.[12] If, inadvertently, you did not light them immediately, you may light them and say the *berachos,* as long as the members of your family are still awake.[13] However, after the family is asleep it is no longer considered a public event, and you should light them without saying the *berachos.* If you will not have time to light the *menorah* at night, you may do it before that time and light the *menorah* from *pelag haMinchah*[14], which is one and one-fourth hour before the stars come out, (these are "time-variable" hours, measured according to the length of daylight, see chapter 69:2 above. And in the season of *Chanukah,* when the days are short, the day is only ten hours long (measured by the clock), then *pelag haMinchah,* is one hour and two and one-half minutes before the stars appear). [You may kindle the *menorah* then] provided you pour in enough oil to burn until one-half hour after the stars become visible. If the lights do not burn that long you have not fulfilled the mitzvah.[15]

---

10. It is forbidden to do any work from one half hour before the actual time for lighting. See (*Shaar Hatzion* 672:14) who indicates that this does not apply to Torah study.

11. Those who pray *Maariv* before lighting should have the *menorah* completely prepared with oil and wicks in order to be able to light them immediately after *Maariv.* (*Mishnah Berurah* 672:1)

12. If you do not have sufficient oil to burn a half hour, you should light them without saying the berachah. (*Biur Halachah* 672:2)

13. It is permitted in this situation only until day-break. (*Mishnah Berurah* 672:11)

14. You are also permitted to say the berachah. (*Ibid* 672:3)

15. In this case, you must light candles anew but without a berachah. (*Biur Halachah* 672:2)

יא) סֵדֶר הַדְלָקָתָן כְּפִי מִנְהָגֵנוּ, בַּלַּיְלָה הָרִאשׁוֹן מַדְלִיק הַנֵּר שֶׁכְּנֶגֶד יְמִינוֹ, וּבַלַּיְלָה הַשֵּׁנִי מוֹסִיף עָלָיו נֵר כְּנֶגֶד שְׂמֹאלוֹ, וְכֵן בְּכָל לַיְלָה מוֹסִיף כְּנֶגֶד שְׂמֹאלוֹ. וְזֶה שֶׁהוּא מוֹסִיף, מַדְלִיק בָּרִאשׁוֹנָה וּפוֹנֶה וְהוֹלֵךְ לִימִינוֹ.

יב) בַּלַּיְלָה הָרִאשׁוֹן מְבָרֵךְ הַמַּדְלִיק קֹדֶם הַהַדְלָקָה שָׁלֹשׁ בְּרָכוֹת, לְהַדְלִיק, שֶׁעָשָׂה נִסִּים, שֶׁהֶחֱיָנוּ. וּבִשְׁאָר הַלֵּילוֹת, אֵינוֹ מְבָרֵךְ שֶׁהֶחֱיָנוּ. לְאַחַר שֶׁבֵּרַךְ הַבְּרָכוֹת, מַדְלִיק נֵר אֶחָד. וּבְעוֹד שֶׁמַּדְלִיק הָאֲחֵרִים, אוֹמֵר, הַנֵּרוֹת הַלָּלוּ וְכוּ'. גֵּר אוֹמֵר, שֶׁעָשָׂה נִסִּים לְיִשְׂרָאֵל. וְאִם אָמַר לַאֲבוֹתֵינוּ, יָצָא. אוֹנֵן, רַחֲמָנָא לִצְלַן, אִם יֵשׁ אַחֵר, יַדְלִיק הָאַחֵר בִּבְרָכוֹת וְהוּא יַעֲנֶה אָמֵן. וְאִי לֵיכָּא אַחֵר, יַדְלִיק הוּא בְּלֹא בְּרָכוֹת.

יג) קַיְמָא לָן, הַדְלָקָה עוֹשָׂה מִצְוָה, פֵּרוּשׁ, הַהַדְלָקָה הִיא הַמִּצְוָה, וּבִשְׁעַת הַהַדְלָקָה, צְרִיכִין לִהְיוֹת הַנֵּרוֹת בִּמְקוֹמָן הָרָאוּי וְכַשִּׁעוּר הָרָאוּי, לְאַפּוּקֵי אִם הִדְלִיקָן לְמַטָּה מִשְּׁלשָׁה טְפָחִים אוֹ לְמַעְלָה מֵעֶשְׂרִים אַמָּה וְאַחַר כָּךְ כְּשֶׁהֵן דּוֹלְקִים הִנִּיחָן בִּמְקוֹמָן, פְּסוּלִים. וְכֵן אִם בִּשְׁעַת הַהַדְלָקָה לֹא הָיָה שֶׁמֶן כַּשִּׁעוּר וְאַחַר כָּךְ הוֹסִיף, לָא מַהֲנֵי. וְכֵן אִם הֶעֱמִידָן בְּמָקוֹם שֶׁהָרוּחַ שׁוֹלֵט וְעוֹמְדִין לִכְבּוֹת, לֹא קִיֵּם הַמִּצְוָה, וְחַיָּב לְהַדְלִיקָן שֵׁנִית, אֲבָל לֹא יְבָרֵךְ. אֲבָל אִם הֶעֱמִידָן כָּרָאוּי וְעַל יְדֵי מִקְרֶה כָּבוּ, כְּבָר קִיֵּם הַמִּצְוָה. וּמִכָּל מָקוֹם נוֹהֲגִין שֶׁחוֹזֵר וּמַדְלִיקָן. וְנוֹהֲגִין לְהַחְמִיר שֶׁלֹּא לְהַדְלִיק נֵר מִנֵּר, אֶלָּא מַדְלִיקָן מִן הַשַּׁמָּשׁ אוֹ מִנֵּר אַחֵר.

יד) כָּל זְמַן מִצְוָתָן, דְּהַיְנוּ חֲצִי שָׁעָה, אָסוּר לֵהָנוֹת מֵאוֹרָן. וְלָכֵן נוֹהֲגִין לְהַנִּיחַ אֶצְלָן אֶת הַשַּׁמָּשׁ שֶׁהִדְלִיקוּ בּוֹ, כְּדֵי שֶׁאִם יִשְׁתַּמֵּשׁ אֶצְלָן, יִשְׁתַּמֵּשׁ

---

16. However, if for whatever reason you did not say *Shehecheyanu* on the first night, you should say it on the next night or whenever you are reminded. On the first night, however, if you remember after lighting the candles, you should not say *Shehecheyanu* on that night but rather wait until the next night and say it when lighting the candles. (*Mishnah Berurah* 671:2, *Shaar Hatzion* 3)

17. *Mishnah Berurah* rules that a convert may say [even initially] the berachah: "Who has performed miracles for our fathers," like any other Jew. (*Mishnah Berurah* 675:14)

18. The *Poskim* have written that even when the *Menorah* was lit in a proper place, it should

11) According to our custom, the order of lighting the *menorah* is as follows: On the first night you kindle the light facing your right hand, on the second night you add one light to the left [of the previous night's light]; similarly, on each subsequent night you add one light to the left. The light that is added is always kindled first, and you continue lighting towards the right.

12) On the first night, you recite three *berachos* before lighting the *menorah: Lehadlik* [To kindle the *Chanukah* light], *She'asa nisim* [Who has performed miracles], and *Shehecheyanu.* On the other nights you do not say *Shehecheyanu.*[16] After you say the *berachos* you kindle one light, and while kindling the others, you says, *Haneiros halalu* [These lights] etc. A convert to Judaism should say, "Who has performed miracles for Yisrael,"[17] but if he said "*la'avoseinu,*" [for our forefathers], he has fulfilled his obligation. An *onein* [a mourner before the burial], [should not light the *menorah*], but he should let someone else light the *menorah*, and say the *berachos,* and [the *onein*] should respond *Amein.* But if there is no one else, then he should light the *menorah* himself but without saying the *berachos.*

13) It is a *halachic* rule that the act of lighting the *menorah* creates the mitzvah, which means, that the kindling is the essence of the mitzvah, and when you light the *menorah* the lights must be in their proper place and must have the proper amount [of oil]. Accordingly if you lit them when they were lower than three *tefachim* [off the ground] or higher than twenty *amos,* and after they were already burning you placed them in their proper place, they are not valid.[18] Similarly, if, when you lit them, they did not have the required amount of oil, and afterwards you added [oil], it is of no avail.[19] Similarly if you set the *menorah* in a place where the wind is blowing and the lights are bound to be extinguished, you have not fulfilled the mitzvah, and you must light them again, but you should not say a berachah. But if you put them in the proper place and they were extinguished by accident, you have fulfilled the mitzvah. Nevertheless, it is customary to kindle them again. It is the custom to be strict and not rekindle an extinguished light with another *Chanukah* light, but you should light it with the *shamash* or with some other candle.

14) During the time [they are burning] in fulfillment of the mitzvah, that is, one-half hour,[20] it is forbidden to have any benefit from their light. It is the custom therefore, to place the *shamash* near them so that if you use the light, [for any

---

not be moved to another [proper] place until after the candles had burned at least a half hour. This applies even to the *Menorah* that is lit in the synagogue. Others are more stringent, maintaining that the *menorah* should not be moved at all while it is burning. (*Mishnah Berurah* 675:6, See also *Shaar Hatzion* 672:12)

19. You must extinguish the candles, add the proper amount of oil, and rekindle the candles, but without a berachah. (*Ibid* 675:8)

20. Others are stringent, maintaining that this prohibition applies during the entire time they are burning. (*Ibid* 672:8)

לְאוֹר הַשַּׁמָּשׁ. וּצְרִיכִין לְהַנִּיחוֹ קְצָת לְמַעְלָה מִן הַנֵּרוֹת, שֶׁיְּהֵא נִכָּר שֶׁאֵינוֹ מִמִּנְיַן הַנֵּרוֹת.

טו) מַדְלִיקִין נֵרוֹת בְּבֵית־הַכְּנֶסֶת מִשּׁוּם פִּרְסוּמֵי נִסָּא, וּמְבָרְכִין עֲלֵיהֶן. וּמַנִּיחָן בְּכֹתֶל דָּרוֹם, וּמַדְלִיקָן בֵּין מִנְחָה לְמַעֲרִיב. וְאֵין אָדָם יוֹצֵא בְּנֵרוֹת שֶׁל בֵּית־הַכְּנֶסֶת, וְצָרִיךְ לַחֲזוֹר וּלְהַדְלִיק בְּבֵיתוֹ. וּמִי שֶׁהוּא אָבֵל, רַחֲמָנָא לִצְלָן, לֹא יַדְלִיק בַּלַּיְלָה הָרִאשׁוֹן בְּבֵית־הַכְּנֶסֶת, מִשּׁוּם דְּצָרִיךְ לוֹמַר שֶׁהֶחֱיָנוּ. וְאָבֵל, אֵין לוֹ לוֹמַר שֶׁהֶחֱיָנוּ בְּצִבּוּר. אֲבָל בְּבֵיתוֹ, מְבָרֵךְ שֶׁהֶחֱיָנוּ.

טז) נָשִׁים חַיָּבוֹת בְּנֵר חֲנֻכָּה, שֶׁאַף הֵן הָיוּ בְּאוֹתוֹ הַנֵּס (עַיֵּן לְעֵיל סָעִיף ג). וִיכוֹלָה הָאִשָּׁה לְהַדְלִיק בְּעַד כָּל בְּנֵי בֵיתָהּ. וְקָטָן שֶׁהִגִּיעַ לְחִנּוּךְ, גַּם כֵּן חַיָּב. סוֹמֵא, אִם יָכוֹל לְהִשְׁתַּתֵּף עִם אַחֵר בִּפְרוּטָה, מוּטָב. וְאִם יֵשׁ לוֹ אִשָּׁה, הִיא מַדְלֶקֶת בִּשְׁבִילוֹ. וְאִם אֵין לוֹ אִשָּׁה וְיֵשׁ לוֹ דִירָה מְיֻחֶדֶת, שֶׁאֵין לוֹ עִם מִי לְהִשְׁתַּתֵּף, מַדְלִיק עַל יְדֵי סִיּוּעַ אַחֵר.

יז) בְּעֶרֶב שַׁבָּת, מַדְלִיקִין תְּחִלָּה נֵר חֲנֻכָּה, וְאַחַר כָּךְ נֵר שַׁבָּת, וּבִלְבַד שֶׁיְּהֵא לְאַחַר פְּלַג־הַמִּנְחָה. וּמִתְפַּלְּלִין תְּחִלָּה מִנְחָה. וְצָרִיךְ שֶׁיִּתֵּן שֶׁמֶן כְּדֵי שֶׁיִּדְלְקוּ עַד חֲצִי שָׁעָה לְאַחַר צֵאת הַכּוֹכָבִים. דְּאִם לֹא כֵן, הֲוֵי לֵהּ בְּרָכָה לְבַטָּלָה. וְאִם מַדְלִיק אֵצֶל הַפֶּתַח, צָרִיךְ לִזָּהֵר לְהַפְסִיק בְּאֵיזֶה דָבָר בֵּינָם לְבֵין הַדֶּלֶת, שֶׁלֹּא יְכַבֶּם הָרוּחַ בִּפְתִיחַת וּנְעִילַת הַדֶּלֶת.

יח) בְּמוֹצָאֵי־שַׁבָּת, מַבְדִּילִין וְאַחַר כָּךְ מַדְלִיקִין נֵר חֲנֻכָּה. וּבְבֵית־הַכְּנֶסֶת, מַדְלִיקִין קֹדֶם וַיִּתֶּן־לְךָ.

יט) מִי שֶׁהוּא אֵינוֹ בְּבֵיתוֹ, אֶלָּא בְּמָקוֹם אַחֵר, אִם יוֹדֵעַ שֶׁאִשְׁתּוֹ מַדְלֶקֶת בְּבֵיתוֹ, יַדְלִיק הוּא בְּמָקוֹם שֶׁהוּא בְּלֹא בְרָכוֹת. וְטוֹב אִם אֶפְשָׁר שֶׁיִּשְׁמַע תְּחִלָּה אֶת הַבְּרָכוֹת מִמִּי שֶׁמַּדְלִיק שָׁם, וִיכַוֵּן לָצֵאת בְּבִרְכוֹתָיו וְיַעֲנֶה אָמֵן, וְאַחַר כָּךְ יַדְלִיק הוּא בְּלֹא בְרָכוֹת. וְאִם אֵין אִשְׁתּוֹ מַדְלֶקֶת בְּבֵיתוֹ, וְכֵן הַבַּחוּרִים בְּאַכְסַנְיָא שֶׁלָּהֶן, צְרִיכִין לְהַדְלִיק בִּבְרָכוֹת, אוֹ

21. This applies even to the person who lights the *Menorah* in the synagogue. (*Ibid* 671:45)

22. A mourner refers to one whose parents died within the past twelve months or within thirty days if he mourns for his wife, son, daughter, brother, or sister.

23. He should, however, not say the *berachos*. (*Ibid* 675:10)

24. According to most *Poskim*, however, if you have not yet accepted the Shabbos [mentally], even though you lit the Shabbos candles, you may still light the *Chanukah* candles. A woman who usually accepts the Shabbos when lighting candles, should not light *Chanukah*

personal purpose] you will be using the light of the *shamash*. You must place [the *shamash*] a little higher than the other lights, so that it is recognized that it is not one of the required number of lights.

15) The *menorah* is lit in the synagogue in order to herald the miracle publicly and the *berachos* are said over them. The *menorah* is placed near the southern wall, and it is kindled between *Minchah* and *Maariv.* But you cannot fulfill your obligation with the lighting of the *menorah* in the synagogue.[21] You must light them yourself at home. A mourner[22] should not light the *menorah* in the synagogue on the first night, because he has to say *Shehecheyanu,* and a mourner should not say *Shehecheyanu* publicly; but he may say *Shehecheyanu* in his house.

16) Women are obligated to kindle the *Chanukah* lights, because they were involved in the miracle of *Chanukah,* (see paragraph 3 above). A woman may light the *menorah* on behalf of her entire family. A child who has reached the age to be trained [for mitzvos] must also light the *menorah*. If a blind person can become someone's partner by contributing towards buying the *Chanukah* lights, fulfilling his obligation through his partner's lighting that would be best. If he has a wife, she should light the *menorah* for him; but if he has no wife and lives by himself, so that he cannot become anyone's partner, he should light it with someone's assistance.[23]

17) On *erev Shabbos* you should first kindle the *Chanukah* lights, then the Shabbos candles[24] but it should be after *pelag haMinchah.*[25] Before lighting them you should pray *Minchah.* You must put in enough oil to keep them burning until one-half hour after the stars come out, otherwise the *berachos* you say over them are in vain. If you light the *menorah* near the door, you must be careful[26] to place something between it and the door, so that the wind will not blow it out when the door is opened and closed.

18) On Shabbos night you should recite *Havdalah*[27] and then kindle the *Chanukah* lights. In the synagogue the lights are kindled before *Veyiten lecha* is said.

19) If you are away from home,—out of town; if you know that your wife[28] lights the *menorah* at home, you should light it wherever you are without saying the *berachos.* If possible, it is best to hear the *berachos* from someone who is lighting the *menorah* there, and have in mind to fulfill your obligation with his *berachos,* respond Amein, and after that, kindle the *menorah,* without saying the *berachos.* But if your wife does not light the *menorah* at home; similarly, yeshivah students boarding with a family must light the *menorah* and say the *berachos* or else, they should become

---

candles after she lit the Shabbos candles. (*Ibid* 679:1; See also *Shaar Hatzion* 679:2; See also *Kitzur Shulchan Aruch* 75:5)

25. See *Kitzur Shulchan Aruch* Chapter 69:2.

26. This ruling applies to weekdays as well. (See *Mishnah Berurah* 680:1)

27. According to *Ramah,* the precedure is reversed—the *Chanukah* lights are kindled before the *Havdalah* is said. Everyone should adhere to the custom of the community. (*Mishnah Berurah* 681:3)

28. This is true only if you are certain that she is lighting them, but if you have any doubt, you should light them and say the *berachos.* (*Mishnah Berurah* 677:8)

יִשְׁתַּתְּפוּ עִם בַּעַל הַבַּיִת שֶׁיִּתְּנוּ לוֹ אֵיזֶה פְּרוּטָה, שֶׁיִּהְיֶה לָהֶם גַּם כֵּן חֵלֶק בְּשֶׁמֶן וּפְתִילָה. וּבַעַל־הַבַּיִת, יוֹסִיף קְצָת שֶׁמֶן עַל הַשִּׁעוּר בִּשְׁבִיל הַשִּׁתּוּף. אֲבָל יֵשׁ לָהֶם לְהַדֵּר שֶׁיַּדְלִיקוּ כָּל אֶחָד בִּפְנֵי עַצְמוֹ. וּמִי שֶׁהוּא בְּעִירוֹ אֶלָּא בְּבֵית אַחֵר, כְּשֶׁהִגִּיעַ זְמַן הַהַדְלָקָה, צָרִיךְ לָשׁוּב לְבֵיתוֹ וּלְהַדְלִיק.

כ) הַשֶּׁמֶן שֶׁנִּשְׁאַר בַּמְּנוֹרָה לְאַחַר חֲנֻכָּה וְכֵן הַפְּתִילוֹת, עוֹשֶׂה לָהֶן מְדוּרָה וְשׂוֹרְפָן, מִשּׁוּם דְּהֻקְצוּ לְמִצְוָתָן. וְאָסוּר לֵהָנוֹת מֵהֶן, אֶלָּא אִם כֵּן הִתְנָה מִתְּחִלָּה שֶׁאֵינוֹ מַקְצֶה מַה שֶּׁיִּשָּׁאֵר.

כא) כָּל שְׁמוֹנַת יְמֵי חֲנֻכָּה, אוֹמְרִים בִּשְׁמוֹנֶה־עֶשְׂרֵה, עַל הַנִּסִּים, וְאִם שָׁכַח וְלֹא אֲמָרוֹ, אִם נִזְכַּר קֹדֶם שֶׁאָמַר אֶת הַשֵּׁם מִן בִּרְכַּת הַטּוֹב שִׁמְךָ וְכוּ', חוֹזֵר וּמַתְחִיל עַל הַנִּסִּים. אֲבָל אִם לֹא נִזְכַּר עַד לְאַחַר שֶׁאָמַר אֶת הַשֵּׁם, גּוֹמֵר אֶת הַבְּרָכָה וְאֵינוֹ חוֹזֵר. (וּבְבִרְכַּת הַמָּזוֹן, עַיֵּן לְעֵיל סִימָן מד, סָעִיף טז).

כב) כָּל שְׁמוֹנַת יְמֵי חֲנֻכָּה, גּוֹמְרִים אֶת הַהַלֵּל, וְאֵין אוֹמְרִים, לֹא תַחֲנוּן, וְלֹא אֵל אֶרֶךְ אַפַּיִם, וְלֹא לַמְנַצֵּחַ, וְלֹא צִדְקָתְךָ צֶדֶק. (דִּין הַלֵּל בְּבֵית הָאָבֵל, רַחֲמָנָא לִצְלַן, עַיֵּן לְקַמָּן סִימָן רז, סָעִיף ו).

כג) קוֹרִין בְּכָל יוֹם תְּלָתָא גַּבְרֵי בְּקָרְבְּנוֹת הַנְּשִׂיאִים שֶׁבְּפָרָשַׁת נָשֹׂא. בַּיּוֹם הָרִאשׁוֹן מַתְחִילִין לַכֹּהֵן מִן וַיְהִי בְּיוֹם כַּלּוֹת מֹשֶׁה, עַד לַחֲנֻכַּת הַמִּזְבֵּחַ. לַלֵּוִי, וַיְהִי הַמַּקְרִיב בַּיּוֹם הָרִאשׁוֹן וְגוֹ, עַד מְלֵאָה קְטֹרֶת. וּלְיִשְׂרָאֵל, פַּר אֶחָד וְגוֹ', עַד בֶּן־עַמִּינָדָב. בַּיּוֹם הַשֵּׁנִי, לַכֹּהֵן וְלַלֵּוִי, בַּיּוֹם הַשֵּׁנִי וְגוֹ'. וּלְיִשְׂרָאֵל, בַּיּוֹם הַשְּׁלִישִׁי וְגוֹ'. וְכֵן בְּכָל יוֹם, לַכֹּהֵן וְלַלֵּוִי, הַיּוֹם שֶׁעוֹמְדִים בּוֹ. וּלְיִשְׂרָאֵל, הַיּוֹם שֶׁלְּאַחֲרָיו. וּבַיּוֹם הַשְּׁמִינִי, לַכֹּהֵן וְלַלֵּוִי, בַּיּוֹם הַשְּׁמִינִי. וּלְיִשְׂרָאֵל, מַתְחִילִים בַּיּוֹם הַתְּשִׁיעִי, וְגוֹמְרִים כָּל הַסֵּדֶר וְגַם בְּפָרָשַׁת בְּהַעֲלֹתְךָ, עַד כֵּן עָשָׂה אֶת־הַמְּנֹרָה.

כד) בְּשַׁבַּת־חֲנֻכָּה, מוֹצִיאִין שְׁנֵי סִפְרֵי־תוֹרָה. בָּרִאשׁוֹן, קוֹרִין פָּרָשַׁת הַשָּׁבוּעַ. וּבַשֵּׁנִי, הַמַּפְטִיר בְּשֶׁל חֲנֻכָּה יוֹמוֹ, וּמַפְטִירִין רָנִּי וְשִׂמְחִי. וְאִם

29. *Mishnah Berurah* based on *Magein Avrohom* writes that if they have a private room it is best that they light themselves rather than joining in partnership with the head of household. (*Mishnah Berurah* 677:7, 8)

partners[29] with the head of the household by giving him several coins, and thus they will also own a share of the oil and the wick. The head of the household should add a bit more oil than is required for the partner [or partners]. They should, however, make an effort to light their own *menorah.* If you are in town but in someone else's house, when it is time to light the *menorah* you must return home and light it.

20) The oil that is left in the *menorah* after *Chanukah,* as well as the wicks, should be burnt in a bonfire, because they were set aside for a mitzvah. It is forbidden to derive any benefit from them, unless you had made a provision beforehand that you do not set aside what will be left [after *Chanukah*].

21) During the eight days of *Chanukah* we say in the *Shemoneh Esreih Al hanisim* [For the miracles]. If you forgot to say it, and become aware of it before you said the Name of God in the berachah *Hatov shimecha* ["The Beneficent is Your Name," etc.], you should turn back and start *Al hanisim.* But if you became aware of it after you pronounced the Name of God, you should conclude the berachah and not turn back [to *Al hanisim*].[30] (Concerning *Birkas Hamazon* see Chapter 44:16 above.)

22) During the eight days of *Chanukah* we recite the complete *Halleil,* and we do not say *Tachanun,* nor *Keil erech apayim,* nor *Lamenatzei'ach* nor *Tzidkasecha tzedek.* (For the *halachah* concerning the saying of *Halleil* in a mourner's house, see Chapter 207:6 below).

23) Each day [of *Chanukah*] we call up three men [for the reading of the Torah] from the chapter "The Offerings of the Princes" in the weekly portion of *Naso.* On the first day we begin to read for the *kohein,* from *Vayehi beyom kalos Moshe,* [On the day that Moses completed] (Numbers 7:1) until *Lachanukas hamizbei'ach,* [For the dedication of the altar]; for the Levi, *Vayehi hamakriv bayom harishon,* [The one to bring his offering on the first day] etc. until *melei'ah ketores* [Filled with incense]. For the *Yisrael, Par echad,* [One young bull] etc., until *Ben Aminadav.* On the second day for the *kohein* and the *Levi,* we read, *Bayom hasheini* [On the second day] etc., and for the *Yisrael, Bayom hashelishi,* [On the third day] etc. Similarly, on each subsequent day for the *kohein* and the *Levi* we read of the current day's offering, and for the *Yisrael,* the offering of the next day. On the eighth day, for the *kohein* and the *Levi,* we read, *Bayom hashemini* [On the eighth day] etc., and for the *Yisrael* we begin with *Bayom hatesh'i,* [On the ninth day], completing the entire parashah, and we continue in *parashas Beha'alosecha,* until *kein asa es hamenorah,* [So did he make the *menorah*] (Numbers 8:4).

24) On *Shabbos Chanukah,* two *sifrei Torah* are taken out of the Ark. In the first one we read the weekly portion;[31] and in the other we read the *Maftir* the "day"

---

30. However, after concluding *Shemoneh Esrei,* before saying, *Yehe Leratzon* (May there be pleased acceptance), you should say a prayer that the Almighty should perform miracles and wonders for us as He did for our ancestors in those days in this time, in the days of Matisyahu etc. (*Ibid* 682:4)

31. At least seven men should be called up to read from the first *seifer Torah.* (*Ibid* 684:5)

יֵשׁ עוֹד שַׁבָּת אַחַת, מַפְטִירִין בָּהּ בִּמְלָכִים, בַּנֵּרוֹת דִּשְׁלֹמֹה. בְּרֹאשׁ־חֹדֶשׁ טֵבֵת בַּחֹל, מוֹצִיאִין שְׁנֵי סִפְרֵי־תוֹרָה. בָּרִאשׁוֹן קוֹרִין תְּלָתָא גַבְרֵי בְּשֶׁל רֹאשׁ־חֹדֶשׁ, וְאַחַר כָּךְ הָרְבִיעִי בְּסֵפֶר־תּוֹרָה הַשֵּׁנִי בְּשֶׁל חֲנֻכָּה יוֹמוֹ, מִשּׁוּם דְּרֹאשׁ־חֹדֶשׁ תָּדִיר טְפֵי, וְקַיְמָא לָן תָּדִיר וְשֶׁאֵינוֹ תָדִיר, תָּדִיר קוֹדֵם, וְלָכֵן מַקְדִּימִין רֹאשׁ־חֹדֶשׁ. וְאִם טָעוּ וְהִתְחִילוּ לִקְרוֹת בְּשֶׁל חֲנֻכָּה, וַאֲפִלּוּ עֲדַיִן לֹא הִתְחִילוּ לִקְרוֹת, אֶלָּא שֶׁכְּבָר בֵּרַךְ הָעוֹלֶה, אֵין צְרִיכִין לְהַפְסִיק, אֶלָּא הָעוֹלֶה גוֹמֵר קְרִיאָתוֹ, וְאַחַר כָּךְ קוֹרִין לַנִּשְׁאָרִים בְּשֶׁל רֹאשׁ־חֹדֶשׁ. אִם קָרְאוּ בָרִאשׁוֹנָה בְּשֶׁל רֹאשׁ־חֹדֶשׁ כָּרָאוּי, אֶלָּא שֶׁטָּעוּ וְקָרְאוּ גַּם אֶת הָרְבִיעִי בְּשֶׁל רֹאשׁ־חֹדֶשׁ, אֲפִלּוּ נִזְכְּרוּ מִיָּד לְאַחַר שֶׁבֵּרַךְ הַקּוֹרֵא, אִם לֹא הוֹצִיאוּ רַק סֵפֶר־תּוֹרָה אֶחָד, אֵין צְרִיכִין לִקְרוֹת יוֹתֵר. אֲבָל אִם הוֹצִיאוּ שְׁנֵי סִפְרֵי תוֹרָה, שֶׁיֵּשׁ כָּאן חֲשָׁשׁ מִשּׁוּם פְּגָמוֹ שֶׁל סֵפֶר הַתּוֹרָה, שֶׁלֹּא יֹאמְרוּ פָּסוּל הוּא, צְרִיכִין לִקְרוֹת בּוֹ חֲמִישִׁי בְּשֶׁל חֲנֻכָּה, וְאַחַר הַחֲמִישִׁי יֹאמְרוּ חֲצִי קַדִּישׁ.

כה) חָל רֹאשׁ־חֹדֶשׁ טֵבֵת בַּשַּׁבָּת, מוֹצִיאִין שְׁלשָׁה סִפְרֵי תוֹרָה, בָּרִאשׁוֹן קוֹרִין שִׁשָּׁה גַבְרֵי בְּפָרָשַׁת הַשָּׁבוּעַ. בַּשֵּׁנִי, שְׁבִיעִי בְּשֶׁל רֹאשׁ־חֹדֶשׁ, וּמַתְחִילִין וּבְיוֹם הַשַּׁבָּת (וְעַיֵּן לְעֵיל סִימָן עח סָעִיף א וְסִימָן עט סָעִיף א), וְאוֹמְרִים חֲצִי קַדִּישׁ. וּבַשְּׁלִישִׁי מַפְטִיר בְּשֶׁל חֲנֻכָּה יוֹמוֹ, וּמַפְטִירִין רָנִּי וְשִׂמְחִי. וְאַף־עַל־גַּב דְּתָדִיר קוֹדֵם, זֶה בַּקְּרִיאָה, שֶׁקּוֹרִין שְׁנֵיהֶם. אֲבָל בְּהַפְטָרָה שֶׁאֵין מַפְטִירִין אֶלָּא אַחַת, דּוֹחִין שֶׁל רֹאשׁ־חֹדֶשׁ וְקוֹרִין שֶׁל חֲנֻכָּה, מִשּׁוּם פִּרְסוּמֵי נִסָּא.

כו) בַּחֲמִשָּׁה עָשָׂר בִּשְׁבָט, רֹאשׁ־הַשָּׁנָה לָאִילָנוֹת. אֵין אוֹמְרִים בּוֹ תַּחֲנוּן. וְנוֹהֲגִין לְהַרְבּוֹת בּוֹ בְּמִינֵי פֵּרוֹת אִילָנוֹת.

סִימָן קמ
סֵדֶר אַרְבַּע פָּרָשִׁיּוֹת

א) שַׁבָּת שֶׁלִּפְנֵי רֹאשׁ־חֹדֶשׁ אֲדָר הַסָּמוּךְ לְנִיסָן, הִיא שַׁבָּת פָּרָשַׁת שְׁקָלִים. וְאִם חָל רֹאשׁ־חֹדֶשׁ בַּשַּׁבָּת, אֲזַי הִיא שַׁבָּת שְׁקָלִים. וּמוֹצִיאִין

32. If he said: *Baruch ata Hashem,* but if he had not said Hashem, it is not yet considered a berachah. (*Biur Halachah* 684:3)

that corresponds to the current day of *Chanukah.* We read the *Haftarah, Roni vesimchi* [Sing and rejoice] (Zechariah 2:14). If another Shabbos occurs on *Chanukah,* we read for *Maftir* [on the second *Shabbos Chanukah*] from *Melachim I* (First Kings) 7:40 where the *menorohs* of Solomon [are mentioned]. If *Rosh Chodesh Teiveis* occurs on a weekday, two *sifrei Torah* are taken out of the Ark. In the first one we read the portion of *Rosh Chodesh* for three men; we then read for the fourth person in the other *seifer Torah* the reading of the current day of *Chanukah,* because *Rosh Chodesh* is more frequent [than *Chanukah*], and it is an *halachic* rule, when a regular practice [conflicts with] an occasional practice the regular practice takes precedence. Therefore, the the *Rosh Chodesh* reading takes precedence. If, by mistake, the portion of *Chanukah* is read first; and even if the reading has not yet begun, but the one called up had already said the berachah,[32] there is no need to interrupt, and the reading should be concluded. After that, they should read for the other *aliyos* the portion of *Rosh Chodesh.* If they read the portion of *Rosh Chodesh* in the first [*seifer Torah*], as indeed they should, but by mistake, they called up the fourth person also to the portion of *Rosh Chodesh,* even if they became aware of it immediately after he said the [concluding] berachah, then, if only one *seifer Torah* was taken out, no further reading is required. But if two *sifrei Torah* were taken out, and there is reason to fear that the [unused] *seifer Torah* will be slighted, because people will wrongly conclude that it is defective, a fifth person must be called for whom the portion of *Chanukah* is read. After this fifth *aliyah,* the *half-kaddish* is recited.

25) If *Rosh Chodesh Teiveis* occurs on Shabbos, three *sifrei Torah* are taken out. In the first one, six men are called up for the reading of the *parashah* of the week. To the second *seifer Torah,* a seventh person is called for the reading of *Rosh Chodesh,* beginning from *Uveyom haShabbos* [And on the Sabbath day] (see Chapter 78:1 and Chapter 79:1 above). Then [half-kaddish] is said. In the third *seifer Torah, Maftir* is read, from the *nasi* of the current *Chanukah* day. For the *Haftarah* we read *Roni vesimchi.* Although the more frequent takes precedence, this rule applies only to Torah reading, where both [*Rosh Chodesh* and *Chanukah*] are read, but in the case of the *Haftarah* where only one is read, we put aside *Rosh Chodesh* and read the *Haftarah* of *Chanukah,* to publicize the miracle.

26) The fifteenth day of *Shevat* is "*Rosh Hashanah* for Trees." We do not say *Tachanun* on that day, and it is the custom to eat many different kinds of tree-grown fruit.

Chapter 140

The Order of the Four Parshiyos

1) The Shabbos before *Rosh Chodesh Adar* that is closest to the month of *Nisan,* is [called] Shabbos, *Parashas Shekalim.* If *Rosh Chodesh* occurs on Shabbos, then that

שְׁלֹשָׁה סִפְרֵי תוֹרָה, בָּרִאשׁוֹן קוֹרִין שִׁשָּׁה בְּפָרָשַׁת הַשָּׁבוּעַ. בַּשֵּׁנִי, קוֹרִין לַשְּׁבִיעִי בְּשֶׁל רֹאשׁ־חֹדֶשׁ, וּמַתְחִילִין וּבְיוֹם הַשַּׁבָּת, וְאוֹמְרִים חֲצִי קַדִּישׁ (עַיֵּן לְעֵיל סִימָן עח סָעִיף א וְסִימָן עט סָעִיף א). וּבַשְּׁלִישִׁי, קוֹרִין מַפְטִיר בְּפָרָשַׁת שְׁקָלִים, וּמַפְטִירִין הַפְטָרַת שְׁקָלִים. אִם טָעוּ וְהִתְחִילוּ לִקְרוֹת תְּחִלָּה בְּפָרָשַׁת שְׁקָלִים, גּוֹמְרִים, וְהַמַּפְטִיר קוֹרֵא בְּשֶׁל רֹאשׁ־חֹדֶשׁ, וּמַפְטִיר גַּם כֵּן הַפְטָרַת שַׁבָּת וְרֹאשׁ־חֹדֶשׁ.

ב) שַׁבָּת שֶׁלִּפְנֵי פּוּרִים הִיא שַׁבָּת פָּרָשַׁת זָכוֹר. וְהַשַּׁבָּת שֶׁלִּפְנֵי רֹאשׁ־חֹדֶשׁ נִיסָן, הִיא שַׁבָּת פָּרָשַׁת הַחֹדֶשׁ, וְאִם חָל רֹאשׁ־חֹדֶשׁ בַּשַּׁבָּת, אָז הִיא פָּרָשַׁת הַחֹדֶשׁ, וְדִינָהּ כְּמוֹ רֹאשׁ־חֹדֶשׁ אֲדָר שֶׁחָל בַּשַּׁבָּת. וְהַשַּׁבָּת שֶׁלִּפְנֵי פָּרָשַׁת הַחֹדֶשׁ, הִיא שַׁבָּת פָּרָשַׁת פָּרָה.

ג) יֵשׁ אוֹמְרִים, כִּי פָּרָשַׁת זָכוֹר וּפָרָשַׁת פָּרָה, חַיָּבִים לִקְרוֹתָן מִדְּאוֹרַיְתָא, וְאֵין קוֹרִין בָּהֶם קָטָן לַמַּפְטִיר. וּבְנֵי הַיִּשּׁוּבִים שֶׁאֵין לָהֶם מִנְיָן, צְרִיכִין שֶׁיָּבוֹאוּ לְמָקוֹם שֶׁיֵּשׁ בּוֹ מִנְיָן. וְאִם אִי אֶפְשָׁר לָהֶם, לְכָל־הַפָּחוֹת יִקְרְאוּ אוֹתָן בִּנְגִינוֹת כָּרָאוּי.

סִימָן קמא
הִלְכוֹת מְגִלָּה

א) מִשֶּׁנִּכְנַס אֲדָר, מַרְבִּים בְּשִׂמְחָה. וְיִשְׂרָאֵל שֶׁיֵּשׁ לוֹ דִּין וּדְבָרִים עִם גּוֹי, יִשָּׁפֵט עִמּוֹ בְּחֹדֶשׁ זֶה.

ב) בִּימֵי מָרְדְּכַי וְאֶסְתֵּר, נִקְהֲלוּ הַיְּהוּדִים בִּשְׁלֹשָׁה עָשָׂר לְחֹדֶשׁ אֲדָר לַעֲמֹד עַל נַפְשָׁם וּלְהִנָּקֵם מֵאוֹיְבֵיהֶם, וְהָיוּ צְרִיכִין לְבַקֵּשׁ רַחֲמִים מֵאֵת ה' יִתְבָּרַךְ שְׁמוֹ, שֶׁיַּעְזְרֵם. וּמָצִינוּ שֶׁכַּאֲשֶׁר הָיוּ יִשְׂרָאֵל בַּמִּלְחָמָה, הִתְעַנּוּ שֶׁיַּעַזְרֵם ה'. וְגַם מֹשֶׁה רַבֵּנוּ עָלָיו הַשָּׁלוֹם, בְּיוֹם שֶׁנִּלְחַם עִם עֲמָלֵק, הִתְעַנָּה. וְאִם כֵּן, מִסְתָמָא גַּם אָז בִּימֵי מָרְדְּכַי וְאֶסְתֵּר, הִתְעַנּוּ בְּיוֹם שְׁלֹשָׁה עָשָׂר בַּאֲדָר. וְלָכֵן קִבְּלוּ עֲלֵיהֶם כָּל יִשְׂרָאֵל יוֹם זֶה לְתַעֲנִית צִבּוּר. וְנִקְרָא תַּעֲנִית אֶסְתֵּר, כְּדֵי לִזְכֹּר שֶׁהַבּוֹרֵא יִתְבָּרַךְ שְׁמוֹ, רוֹאֶה וְשׁוֹמֵעַ תְּפִלַּת כָּל אִישׁ בְּעֵת צָרָתוֹ, כַּאֲשֶׁר יִתְעַנֶּה וְיָשׁוּב אֶל ה' בְּכָל לְבָבוֹ, כְּמוֹ שֶׁעָשָׂה לַאֲבוֹתֵינוּ בַּיָּמִים הָהֵם. וּמִכָּל מָקוֹם אֵין תַּעֲנִית זוֹ חוֹבָה כָּל כָּךְ

1. The third *seifer Torah* is placed next to the second one when the *half-kaddish* is said. (*Mishnah Berurah* 685:5)

Shabbos is *Parashas Shekalim.* We take out three *sifrei Torah.* We call six persons to the first *seifer Torah,* for the reading of the weekly portion. In the second *seifer Torah* we call a seventh person for the reading of *Rosh Chodesh,* beginning with *Uve'yom haShabbos.* Then *half-kaddish* is said[1] (see Chaper 78:1 and 79:1 above). In the third *seifer Torah* we read the *Maftir* of *Parashas Shekalim,* [Exodus 30:11–16], and the *Haftarah* of *Parashas Shekalim* is read. If by mistake they began to read the section of *Parashas Shekalim* first, they should finish reading it,[2] and for *Maftir* they should read the section of *Rosh Chodesh,* and the *Haftarah,* too, is that of Shabbos *Rosh Chodesh.*

2) The Shabbos before *Purim* is [called] Shabbos, *Parashas Zachor.* The Shabbos before *Rosh Chodesh Nisan* is Shabbos, *Parashas Hachodesh.* If *Rosh Chodesh Nisan* occurs on Shabbos, then that Shabbos is *Parashas Hachodesh,* and it is governed by the same *Halachos* as apply when *Rosh Chodesh Adar* occurs on Shabbos. The Shabbos before *Parashas Hachodesh* is Shabbos, *Parashas Parah.*

3) Some authorities maintain that *Parashas Zachor* and *Parashas Parah*[3] are obligated to be read, according to Scriptural law, and a minor should not be called for the *maftir* [reading of those *parshiyos*]. People living in villages who have no *minyan*[4] are required to go to a place where there is a *minyan.* If that is impossible, they should at least read these [special portions] with the proper cantillation chant.

Chapter 141

Laws Concerning the Reading of the Megillah

1) The Month of *Adar* brings much joy to our people. If a Jew has a lawsuit against a non-Jew he should bring the case to court during this month.

2) In the days of Mordechai and Esther, the Jews joined together on the thirteenth day of *Adar* to defend themselves and take revenge against their enemies. They had to ask for compassion from God, blessed is His Name, that He should help them. And we find that whenever the Jewish people were at war they fasted, in order to invoke Divine assistance. Moshe Rabeinu, peace be upon him, also fasted on the day he went into battle against Amalek. This being the case, we may assume, that in the days of Mordechai and Esther, they also fasted on the thirteenth day of *Adar.* Therefore, all Jews have accepted this day as a public fast day. It is called *Ta'anis Esther* [Fast of Esther]. It is meant to remind us that the Creator, blessed is His Name, sees and hears the prayers of every person in his time of trouble, when he fasts and repents with all his heart, as He answered our forefathers in those days. Nevertheless, this fast is not as obligatory as the four fast days

---

2. This ruling applies to Shabbos, *Parashas Hachodesh* as well. (*Ibid*)
3. Many of the later *Poskim* agree that the obligation to read *Parashas Parah* is not ordained by Scriptural law. (*Ibid* 685:15)
4. This applies even if they have a *seifer Torah.* (*Ibid* 685:16)

כְּמוֹ אַרְבַּע הַתַּעֲנִיּוֹת שֶׁכְּתוּבוֹת בַּמִּקְרָא (עַיֵּן לְעֵיל סִימָן קכא), וְלָכֵן יֵשׁ לְהָקֵל בָּהּ בְּעֵת הַצֹּרֶךְ, כְּגוֹן מְעֻבָּרוֹת וּמֵינִיקוֹת אוֹ אֲפִלּוּ חוֹלֶה קְצָת בִּכְאֵב עֵינַיִם, שֶׁאִם מִצְטַעֲרִים הַרְבֵּה, לֹא יִתְעַנּוּ. וְכֵן יוֹלֶדֶת כָּל שְׁלֹשִׁים יוֹם, וְכֵן חָתָן בְּתוֹךְ שִׁבְעַת יְמֵי הַמִּשְׁתֶּה שֶׁלּוֹ, אֵינָן צְרִיכִין לְהִתְעַנּוֹת, וְיִפְרְעוּ אֶת הַתַּעֲנִית אַחַר כָּךְ. אֲבָל שְׁאָר הַבְּרִיאִים, לֹא יִפְרְשׁוּ (אֶת) עַצְמָם מִן הַצִּבּוּר. וַאֲפִלּוּ מִי שֶׁהוֹלֵךְ בַּדֶּרֶךְ וְקָשֶׁה עָלָיו הַתַּעֲנִית, מִכָּל מָקוֹם צָרִיךְ לְהִתְעַנּוֹת.

ג) בְּיוֹם אַרְבָּעָה עָשָׂר לְחֹדֶשׁ אֲדָר, הוּא פּוּרִים (לְעָרֵי הַפְּרָזוֹת). וְאִם חָל פּוּרִים בְּיוֹם רִאשׁוֹן, מַקְדִּימִין לְהִתְעַנּוֹת בַּיּוֹם הַחֲמִישִׁי. וְאִם יֵשׁ אָז בְּרִית מִילָה, יַעֲשׂוּ אֶת הַסְּעוּדָה בַּלַּיְלָה. אֲבָל הַסַּנְדָּק וַאֲבִי־הַבֵּן, מֻתָּרִין לֶאֱכֹל בַּיּוֹם, וְאֵין צְרִיכִין לְהִתְעַנּוֹת בַּיּוֹם הַשִּׁשִּׁי. אֲבָל אָדָם אַחֵר שֶׁשָּׁכַח וְאָכַל בַּיּוֹם הַחֲמִישִׁי, יִתְעַנֶּה בַּיּוֹם הַשִּׁשִּׁי.

ד) לִכְבוֹד הַמְּגִלָּה, יֵשׁ לִלְבּוֹשׁ בִּגְדֵי שַׁבָּת מִבָּעֶרֶב. וּכְשֶׁבָּא מִבֵּית־הַכְּנֶסֶת, יִמְצָא בְּבֵיתוֹ נֵרוֹת דּוֹלְקִים וְשֻׁלְחָן עָרוּךְ וּמִטָּה מֻצַּעַת. עַרְבִית, לְאַחַר שְׁמוֹנֶה־עֶשְׂרֵה, אוֹמְרִים קַדִּישׁ שָׁלֵם עִם תִּתְקַבֵּל, וְקוֹרִין אֶת הַמְּגִלָּה. אַחַר כָּךְ אוֹמְרִים וְאַתָּה קָדוֹשׁ וְגוֹ' (שֶׁהוּא בְּמִזְמוֹר לַמְנַצֵּחַ עַל אַיֶּלֶת הַשַּׁחַר, שֶׁנֶּאֱמַר עַל אֶסְתֵּר, וְשָׁם נֶאֱמַר, אֱלֹהַי אֶקְרָא וְגוֹ', דְּנֶאֱמַר עַל מִקְרָא מְגִלָּה, דְּאָמַר רַבִּי יְהוֹשֻׁעַ בֶּן לֵוִי, חַיָּב אָדָם לִקְרוֹת אֶת הַמְּגִלָּה בַּלַּיְלָה וְלִשְׁנוֹתָהּ בַּיּוֹם, שֶׁנֶּאֱמַר, אֱלֹהַי אֶקְרָא יוֹמָם וְלֹא תַעֲנֶה וְלַיְלָה וְלֹא דוּמִיָּה לִי, וְסָמִיךְ לֵהּ, וְאַתָּה קָדוֹשׁ וְגוֹ'), וְאַחַר כָּךְ קַדִּישׁ שָׁלֵם בְּלֹא תִּתְקַבֵּל. וּבְמוֹצָאֵי שַׁבָּת, וִיהִי נֹעַם, וְאַתָּה קָדוֹשׁ, וְקַדִּישׁ שָׁלֵם בְּלֹא תִּתְקַבֵּל, וְיִתֶּן־לְךָ, וּמַבְדִּילִין עַל הַכּוֹס, עָלֵינוּ.

ה) נוֹהֲגִין לִתֵּן קֹדֶם פּוּרִים מַחֲצִית מִן הַמַּטְבֵּעַ הַקָּבוּעַ בְּאוֹתוֹ מָקוֹם וּבְאוֹתוֹ זְמָן, זֵכֶר לְמַחֲצִית הַשֶּׁקֶל שֶׁהָיוּ נוֹתְנִים בַּאֲדָר לְצֹרֶךְ קָרְבְּנוֹת הַצִּבּוּר. וּמִנְהָג לִתֵּן שָׁלֹשׁ מַחֲצִיּוֹת, מִשּׁוּם דִּבְפָרָשַׁת כִּי תִשָּׂא כְּתִיב שָׁלֹשׁ פְּעָמִים תְּרוּמָה, וְנוֹתְנִין בָּעֶרֶב לִפְנֵי קְרִיאַת הַמְּגִלָּה, וּמְחַלְּקִין אוֹתָם לַעֲנִיִּים. קָטָן, פָּטוּר. וְאִם אָבִיו נָתַן בִּשְׁבִילוֹ פַּעַם אַחַת, חַיָּב לְעוֹלָם. בֶּן־שְׁלֹשׁ־עֶשְׂרֵה שָׁנָה, יֵשׁ אוֹמְרִים דְּחַיָּב, וְיֵשׁ אוֹמְרִים דְּפָטוּר, עַד שֶׁיְּהֵא בֶּן עֶשְׂרִים.

---

1. This refers only to one who has an eye irritation, but a pregnant or nursing woman need not fast even though they feel no discomfort. This is the opinion of *Yeshuos Yaakov,* but

mentioned in *Tanach* (see Chapter 121 above). Therefore, you may be lenient when it is necessary. Thus pregnant and nursing women, or even a person who is slightly ill with an eye irritation should not fast, if fasting would be greatly discomforting to them.[1] A woman within thirty days after giving birth, and a bridegroom during his seven days of *Sheva berachos,* do not have to fast, but they should make up for it later.[2] But all others who are in good health should not separate themselves from the community. Even if you are traveling and fasting is difficult, nevertheless, you are required to fast.

3) On the fourteenth day of *Adar, Purim* is celebrated in unwalled cities. If *Purim* occurs on a Sunday, the fast is moved up to Thursday. If there is a *bris* [circumcision] on [Thursday], the *bris* meal should be held at night, but the *sandek* and the father of the infant[3] are permitted to eat during the day, and they do not have to fast on Friday. But if anyone else forgets and eats on Thursday, he must fast on Friday.

4) In honor of [reading] the *Megillah* you should wear Shabbos clothes in the evening, and when returning from the synagogue, you should find the house brightly lit, the table set, and the beds made. In the evening, after the *Shemoneh Esrei,* the *Full Kaddish* with *Tiskabbeil* is said, then the *Megillah* is read. After that, *Ve'ata kadosh* etc. is said. (This verse is found in Psalm 22:4, "For the Conductor; on the *ayeles hashachar,"* which refers to Esther. It is said (verse 3), "My God, I call . . ." etc. which refers to the reading of the *Megillah.* Rabbi Yehoshua ben Levi said, Every man must read the *Megillah* at night and repeat it in the daytime, for it is said, "My God, I call by day, but you do not answer, and at night I am not silent." This is followed by [the verse], "You are the Holy One" etc.). After that, the *Full Kaddish,* is said, omitting *Tiskabbeil.* If it is Shabbos night [we say], *Vihi no'am, Ve'ata kadosh,* the *Full Kaddish* omitting *Tiskabbeil, Veyiten lecha;* and we say *Havdalah* over a cup of wine, [and conclude with] *Aleinu.*

5) It is customary to donate a coin, equal to half of the standard monetary unit currently in use in the country before *Purim,* as a reminder of the half-*shekel,* the Jews used to give in *Adar* to buy the communal offerings. It is customary to give three half-*shekels,* because in *Parashas Ki Sisa,* the word *terumah* [offering] is mentioned three times. These coins are given in the evening before the reading of the *Megillah,* and then distributed to the poor. A minor is exempt [from giving the half-*shekel*]; but if his father once contributed for him, it remains his obligation for life. According to some authorities, a thirteen year old boy must give [a half-*shekel*], while others hold that he is exempt until he reaches the age of twenty.

Eliyahu Rabbah disagrees and maintains that they are exempt only when they feel discomfort. However, regarding a woman within thirty days after childbirth, even *Eliyahu Rabbah* is lenient and agrees with *Yeshuos Yaakov.* (*Mishnah Berurah* 686:4, 5)

2. This refers only to one who did not fast because of an eye irritation. See note 1 above.

3. According to *Mishnah Berurah* the mother of the child and the *Mohel* are also permitted to eat during the day. (See *Shaar Hatzion* 686:15)

ו) בַּפּוּרִים, עַרְבִית שַׁחֲרִית וּמִנְחָה, אוֹמְרִים עַל הַנִּסִּים. וְאִם שָׁכַח, דִּינוֹ כְּמוֹ בַּחֲנֻכָּה (עַיֵּן לְעֵיל סִימָן קלט סָעִיף כא).

ז) חַיָּב כָּל אָדָם, בֵּין אִישׁ בֵּין אִשָּׁה, לִשְׁמֹעַ קְרִיאַת הַמְּגִלָּה בַּלַּיְלָה וּבַיּוֹם. וְלָכֵן גַּם הַבְּתוּלוֹת, יֵשׁ לָהֶן לָלֶכֶת לְבֵית־הַכְּנֶסֶת. וְאִם אֵינָן הוֹלְכוֹת, צְרִיכִין לִקְרוֹת לִפְנֵיהֶן בַּבַּיִת. וְגַם אֶת הַקְּטַנִּים חַיָּבִים לְחַנֵּךְ אוֹתָם שֶׁיִּשְׁמְעוּ קְרִיאַת הַמְּגִלָּה. וּמִכָּל מָקוֹם לֹא יָבִיאוּ לְבֵית־הַכְּנֶסֶת קְטַנִּים בְּיוֹתֵר, שֶׁמְּבַלְבְּלִים דַּעַת הַשּׁוֹמְעִים.

ח) מְגִלָּה שֶׁל לַיְלָה, אָסוּר לִקְרוֹת קֹדֶם צֵאת הַכּוֹכָבִים, אַף־עַל־פִּי שֶׁמִּצְטַעֵר הַרְבֵּה מֵחֲמַת הַתַּעֲנִית. אַךְ יָכוֹל לִטְעֹם קְצָת קֹדֶם הַמְּגִלָּה, כְּגוֹן קָפֶה וְכַדּוֹמֶה, כְּדֵי לְהִתְחַזֵּק מְעַט מֵחֻלְשַׁת הַתַּעֲנִית.

ט) מִצְוָה מִן הַמֻּבְחָר לִשְׁמוֹעַ אֶת הַמְּגִלָּה בְּבֵית־הַכְּנֶסֶת בְּמָקוֹם שֶׁיֵּשׁ רֹב אֲנָשִׁים, מִשּׁוּם דִּבְרָב־עָם הַדְרַת־מֶלֶךְ. וּלְכָל־הַפָּחוֹת יִשְׁתַּדֵּל לִשְׁמֹעַ אוֹתָהּ בְּמִנְיַן עֲשָׂרָה. וְאִם אִי אֶפְשָׁר לִקְרוֹתָהּ בְּמִנְיָן, יִקְרָא אוֹתָהּ כָּל יָחִיד מִתּוֹךְ מְגִלָּה כְּשֵׁרָה עִם הַבְּרָכוֹת שֶׁלְּפָנֶיהָ. וְאִם אֶחָד יוֹדֵעַ לִקְרוֹתָהּ וְהַשְּׁאָר אֵינָם יוֹדְעִים, יִקְרָא זֶה שֶׁיּוֹדֵעַ, וְהֵם יִשְׁמְעוּ וְיוֹצְאִין, אַף־עַל־פִּי שֶׁאֵינָם עֲשָׂרָה. אֲבָל בְּרָכָה שֶׁלְּאַחֲרֶיהָ, אֵין אוֹמְרִים רַק בַּעֲשָׂרָה. וְאַף בְּלֹא שֵׁם וּמַלְכוּת, יָכוֹל גַּם יָחִיד לְאָמְרָהּ.

י) מִנְהַג בְּכָל יִשְׂרָאֵל, שֶׁהַקּוֹרֵא אֵינוֹ קוֹרֵא מִתּוֹךְ מְגִלָּה כְּרוּכָה, אֶלָּא פּוֹשֵׁט אוֹתָהּ וְכוֹפְלָהּ דַּף עַל דַּף כְּמוֹ אִגֶּרֶת, מִפְּנֵי שֶׁנִּקְרֵאת אִגֶּרֶת הַפּוּרִים. אֲבָל הַשּׁוֹמְעִים, אֵינָם צְרִיכִים לְפָשְׁטָהּ.

יא) הַקּוֹרֵא אֶת הַמְּגִלָּה, בֵּין בַּיּוֹם בֵּין בַּלַּיְלָה, מְבָרֵךְ לְפָנֶיהָ שָׁלֹשׁ בְּרָכוֹת, עַל מִקְרָא מְגִלָּה, שֶׁעָשָׂה נִסִּים, וְשֶׁהֶחֱיָנוּ. וּלְאַחַר קְרִיאָתָהּ, כּוֹרְכָהּ כֻּלָּהּ וּמַנִּיחָהּ לְפָנָיו, וּמְבָרְכִין בִּרְכַּת הָרָב אֶת רִיבֵנוּ וְכוּ'. אִם אֲבָל קוֹרֵא אֶת הַמְּגִלָּה, יְבָרֵךְ אַחֵר אֶת הַבְּרָכוֹת, מִשּׁוּם בִּרְכַּת שֶׁהֶחֱיָנוּ.

---

4. *Mishnah Berurah* writes: "Presently in our times the result of bringing children to the synagogue has had a reverse effect. Not only do they not listen to the reading of the *Megillah,* they create such a tumult that the adults are unable to hear the reading properly. Their purpose in coming is only to make noise at the mention of Haman's name, and as such, the father does not fulfill his obligation of *chinuch,* (training his child to perform mitzvos.) In truth, therefore, a father must keep his children near him and to see that they actually listen to the *Megillah* reading, and though they are permitted to make noise at the mention of Haman's name, this should not be the primary reason for their coming to the synagogue. (*Ibid* 689:18)

6) On *Purim,* in the *Shemoneh Esrei* of *Maariv, Shacharis,* and *Minchah,* we recite *Al hanisim* [For the miracles]. If you forgot to say it, the same *Halachah* applies as on *Chanukah.* [See Chapter 139:21)

7) It is an obligation upon everyone, both men and women, to hear the reading of the *Megillah* in the evening and during the day. Therefore, girls too, should go to the synagogue. If they do not go someone must read for them at home. Children too, must be trained to hear the reading of the *Megillah.*[4] Nevertheless, you should not bring very young children to the synagogue since they disturb the congregation.

8) At night it is forbidden to read the *Megillah* before the stars come out, even if you suffer great discomfort because of the fast. But you may taste something[5] before the reading of the *Megillah,* such as coffee, and similar beverages, to strengthen yourself from the exhaustion of the fast.

9) The mitzvah done to perfection is to hear the *Megillah* in the synagogue, where there is a large number of people,[6] for "In the multitude of people is the splendor of the King" (Proverbs 14:28). You should at least make an effort to hear it read with a *minyan.* If it is impossible to have it read with a *minyan,* each individual should read it from a valid *Megillah,* and recite the *berachos* before the reading. If one of them knows how to read it and the others do not, then the one who knows it should read and the others should listen and fulfill their obligation in this manner, even though they are not a *minyan.* However, the berachah after the *Megillah* reading should be said only when there is a *minyan.* However, without mentioning God's name and Kingship [i.e., *Elokeinu melech ha'olam*], even an individual may recite the berachah.

10) It is a custom, accepted in all Yisrael, that the reader does not read from a rolled up *Megillah,* but he spreads it out and folds it, section over section,[7] like a letter, because the *Megillah* is called *Igeres haPurim* [the letter of Purim]; but those who listen, do not have to spread out their *Megillos.*

11) The person who reads the *Megillah,* whether in the daytime or at night, recites three *berachos* before the reading: *Al mikra Megillah* [. . . concerning the mitzvah of reading the *Megillah*], *She'asa nisim,* [Who made miracles] and *Sheheche-yanu* [Who kept us alive]. After the reading, he rolls it up completely and places it in front of him. Then [everyone] says the berachah *Harav es riveinu,* [Who fights for us] etc. If a mourner reads the *Megillah,* someone else should say the *berachos,*

---

5. You may eat a *kebeitzah* of bread or cake, or liquid in the same quantity. (*Ibid* 692:14)

6. *Mishnah Berurah* quotes *Chayei Adam* who wrote that if you pray all year with a specific *minyan,* you need not leave it to go to a synagogue where there are more people. *Mishnah Berurah* comments that *Chayei Adam's* ruling applies only when the *minyan* is held in a *Beis Midrash,* but if the minyan is held in a private home, it would seem that you should leave and go to the synagogue to hear the *Megillah.* (*Ibid* 687:7)

7. This should be done before he says the *berachos* so that there will be no interruption between the *berachos* and the reading. (*Ibid* 690:56)

יב) בְּבִרְכַּת שֶׁהֶחֱיָנוּ שֶׁל יוֹם, יְכַוְּנוּ גַּם עַל מִצְוַת מִשְׁלוֹחַ מָנוֹת וּמַתָּנוֹת לָאֶבְיוֹנִים וּסְעוּדַת פּוּרִים. וְכֵן שְׁלִיחַ־הַצִּבּוּר, צָרִיךְ שֶׁיְּכַוֵּן לְהוֹצִיא אֶת הַצִּבּוּר גַּם עַל מִצְוֹת אֵלּוּ.

יג) הַקּוֹרֵא אֶת הַמְּגִלָּה, צָרִיךְ לְכַוֵּן לְהוֹצִיא אֶת כָּל הַשּׁוֹמְעִים, וְגַם הַשּׁוֹמֵעַ צָרִיךְ לְכַוֵּן לָצֵאת וְלִשְׁמֹעַ כָּל תֵּבָה וְתֵבָה, שֶׁאֲפִלּוּ אִם רַק תֵּבָה אַחַת לֹא שָׁמַע, אֵינוֹ יוֹצֵא. וְלָכֵן צָרִיךְ הַקּוֹרֵא לְהַשְׁגִּיחַ מְאֹד, שֶׁבְּשָׁעָה שֶׁמַּרְעִישִׁין וּמְבַלְבְּלִין בְּהַכָּאַת הָמָן, יִשְׁתֹּק עַד יַעֲבֹר הָרַעַשׁ לְגַמְרֵי. וּמִכָּל מָקוֹם רָאוּי וְנָכוֹן שֶׁיִּהְיֶה לְכָל אֶחָד מְגִלָּה כְּשֵׁרָה, כְּדֵי שֶׁיֹּאמַר בְּעַצְמוֹ מִלָּה בְּמִלָּה בְּלַחַשׁ, פֶּן לֹא יִשְׁמַע תֵּבָה אַחַת מִן הַקּוֹרֵא. וְכֵן כָּל אִשָּׁה חַכְמַת לֵב שֶׁעוֹמֶדֶת בְּעֶזְרַת נָשִׁים, אִם אֶפְשָׁר, מַה טּוֹב לִהְיוֹת לָהּ מְגִלָּה כְּשֵׁרָה לִקְרוֹת מִתּוֹכָהּ, כִּי שָׁם קָשֶׁה לִשְׁמֹעַ, וְהַנָּשִׁים חַיָּבוֹת כְּמוֹ הָאֲנָשִׁים. (אִם לֹא קִדְּשׁוּ אֶת הַלְּבָנָה וְנִרְאֲתָה בִּשְׁעַת קְרִיאַת הַמְּגִלָּה, עַיֵּן לְעֵיל סוֹף סִימָן צז).

יד) הַקּוֹרֵא צָרִיךְ שֶׁיֹּאמַר אֶת עֲשֶׂרֶת בְּנֵי הָמָן וְגַם תֵּבַת עֲשֶׂרֶת, הַכֹּל בִּנְשִׁימָה אַחַת, לְהוֹדִיעַ שֶׁכֻּלָּם נֶהֶרְגוּ וְנִתְלוּ כְּאֶחָד. וְנוֹהֲגִין לְכַתְּחִלָּה לוֹמַר מִן חֲמֵשׁ מֵאוֹת אִישׁ, הַכֹּל בִּנְשָׁמָה אֶחָת. וּבְדִיעֲבַד, אֲפִלּוּ הִפְסִיק בֵּין עֲשֶׂרֶת בְּנֵי הָמָן, יָצָא. וּמַה שֶּׁנּוֹהֲגִין בִּקְצָת מְקוֹמוֹת שֶׁכָּל הַקָּהָל אוֹמְרִים עֲשֶׂרֶת בְּנֵי הָמָן. אֵינוֹ מִנְהָג נָכוֹן, אֶלָּא הַקּוֹרֵא לְבַד יֹאמְרֵם, וְהַקָּהָל יִשְׁמְעוּ כְּמוֹ כָּל הַמְּגִלָּה. כְּשֶׁאוֹמֵר הַקּוֹרֵא בַּלַּיְלָה הַהוּא נָדְדָה וְגוֹ', יַגְבִּיהַּ קוֹלוֹ, כִּי שָׁם מַתְחִיל עִקַּר הַנֵּס, וּכְשֶׁאוֹמֵר הָאִגֶּרֶת הַזֹּאת, יְנַעְנֵעַ אֶת הַמְּגִלָּה.

טו) מִי שֶׁיֵּשׁ לְפָנָיו מְגִלָּה פְּסוּלָה אוֹ חֻמָּשׁ, לֹא יִקְרָא עִם שְׁלִיחַ־הַצִּבּוּר. כִּי אִם הוּא קוֹרֵא, אֵינוֹ יָכוֹל לְכַוֵּן לִשְׁמֹעַ מִן שְׁלִיחַ־הַצִּבּוּר. וַאֲפִלּוּ אִם הוּא יְכַוֵּן, שֶׁמָּא יִשְׁמַע אַחַר מַה שֶּׁהוּא קוֹרֵא, וְלֹא יְכַוֵּן לִקְרִיאַת שְׁלִיחַ־הַצִּבּוּר. וְכֵן לֹא יְסַיֵּעַ שׁוּם אָדָם בְּעַל־פֶּה לִשְׁלִיחַ־הַצִּבּוּר. וְלָכֵן אוֹתָן אַרְבָּעָה פְּסוּקֵי גְאֻלָּה שֶׁאוֹמְרִים הַקָּהָל בְּקוֹל רָם, צָרִיךְ שְׁלִיחַ־הַצִּבּוּר לַחֲזוֹר וְלִקְרוֹתָם מִתּוֹךְ הַמְּגִלָּה הַכְּשֵׁרָה.

---

8. If you have no valid handwritten *Megillah,* you should at least have a printed *Megillah* to read from. (*Ibid* 690:19)

because of the *Shehecheyanu* [which a mourner should not say publicly]. (See 139:15)

12) When *Shehecheyanu* is said in the daytime you should also have in mind [to exempt with this berachah] the mitzvos of sending *Mishloach Manos* [gifts of food], *Matanos La'evyonim* [gifts to the poor], and *Se'udas Purim* [the *Purim* feast]. The reader, too, [when saying *Shehecheyanu*], should have the congregation in mind for these mitzvos as well.

13) The reader of the *Megillah* must have in mind to fulfill the mitzvah on behalf of all the listeners. The listeners, too, must have in mind to fulfill their obligation [with his reading] and they must listen to every word. If you failed to hear even one word you have not fulfilled your obligation. The reader, therefore, must be very alert, during the noise making and the confusion, when the name of *Haman* is mentioned, to remain silent until the commotion has passed completely. Nevertheless, it is proper and fitting to have a valid [handwritten] *Megillah,*[8] so that you can say word for word quietly, in case you do not hear one word from the reader. Also, every intelligent woman who is in the women's section is encouraged, if possible, to obtain a valid *Megillah*[8] from which to read, for in the [women's section] it is difficult to hear [the reading]; and women are obligated [to hear the *Megillah]* the same as men. (If *kiddush levanah* [Sanctification of the Moon] has not yet been said, and it became visible during the reading of the *Megillah,* see the end of Chapter 97 above [for instructions].)

14) The reader must recite the names of the ten sons of *Haman,* including the word *aseres* [ten], all in one breath, to make it known that they were all killed and hanged simultaneously. It is customary [at least] initially to recite from *chameish meios ish* [Five hundred men] all in one breath. If he has already read the names, then even if he paused while reciting the names of the ten sons of *Haman,* he has fulfilled his obligation. The custom followed in some communities, that the entire congregation says the names of the sons of *Haman,* is not correct. Rather the reader should recite them, and the congregation should listen as they do for the entire *Megillah.* When the reader says the verse, "That night the king could not sleep well" (6:1) he should raise his voice, for there the actual miracle begins; and when he says *"Ha'igeres hazos,"* [this letter] (9:26) he should [gently] shake the *Megillah.*

15) If you have a *Megillah* that is invalid, or a *Chumash,* you should not say the words along with the reader, because if you say the words while reading, you cannot concentrate on listening to the reader. And even if you, yourself, could concentrate [on the reader's recitation], someone else might listen to your reading and not concentrate on the reader's recitation. For the same reason, no one should assist the reader from memory. Therefore, the four "verses of redemption" [Verse 2:5, *Ish Yehudi*—There was a Jewish man, v. 8:15, *uMordechai yatzah*—Mordechai left, v. 8:16, *LaYehudim hayesa*—The Jews had light, v. 10:3, *Ki Mordechai HaYehudi*—For Mordechai the Jew,] which the congregation recites in a loud voice, must be repeated by the reader and read from the valid *Megillah.*

טז) מִי שֶׁכְּבָר יָצָא בִּקְרִיאַת הַמְּגִלָּה, וְקוֹרֵא לְהוֹצִיא אַחֵר, אִם זֶה שֶׁצָּרִיךְ לָצֵאת יוֹדֵעַ בְּעַצְמוֹ לְבָרֵךְ אֶת הַבְּרָכוֹת, יְבָרֵךְ בְּעַצְמוֹ. וְאִם הִיא אִשָּׁה, טוֹב יוֹתֵר שֶׁהַקּוֹרֵא יְבָרֵךְ, וְאוֹמֵר, אֲשֶׁר קִדְּשָׁנוּ בְּמִצְוֹתָיו וְצִוָּנוּ לִשְׁמֹעַ מְגִלָּה.

יז) בְּשַׁבָּת (שֶׁאֵינוֹ פּוּרִים), מֻתָּרִין לְטַלְטֵל אֶת הַמְּגִלָּה. וּמִכָּל מָקוֹם אִם חָל פּוּרִים בַּיּוֹם הָרִאשׁוֹן, אֵין לְהָבִיא בַּשַּׁבָּת אֶת הַמְּגִלָּה לְבֵית־הַכְּנֶסֶת, וַאֲפִלּוּ בְּעִיר שֶׁהִיא מְתֻקֶּנֶת בְּעֵרוּבִין, מִשּׁוּם דַּהֲוֵי מֵכִין מִשַּׁבָּת לַחֹל.

יח) צִבּוּר שֶׁאֵין לָהֶם שְׁלִיחַ־צִבּוּר שֶׁיָּכוֹל לִקְרוֹת אֶת הַמְּגִלָּה עִם הַטְּעָמִים כָּרָאוּי, יָכוֹל לִקְרוֹת גַּם בְּלֹא טְעָמִים, רַק שֶׁיִּקְרָא אֶת הַתֵּבוֹת כָּרָאוּי, שֶׁלֹּא יִשְׁתַּנֶּה הָעִנְיָן. שֶׁאִם קָרָא בִּמְקוֹם וּמָרְדְּכַי יוֹשֵׁב, יָשַׁב, אוֹ בְּמָקוֹם וְהָמָן נוֹפֵל, נָפַל וְכַדּוֹמֶה, אֲפִלּוּ בְּדִיעֲבַד אֵינוֹ יוֹצֵא. וִיכוֹלִין לַעֲשׂוֹת בַּמְּגִלָּה נְקֻדּוֹת וּטְעָמִים, שֶׁיִּקְרָא כְּהֹגֶן, כֵּיוָן שֶׁהִיא שְׁעַת הַדְּחָק, וְהָכִי עָדִיף טְפֵי מִמַּה שֶׁיִּקְרָא אֶחָד מִתּוֹךְ הַחֻמָּשׁ בְּלַחַשׁ, דְּכֵיוָן שֶׁזֶּה הַקּוֹרֵא מִתּוֹךְ הַחֻמָּשׁ, אֲפִלּוּ הוּא קוֹרֵא בְּלַחַשׁ, אֵינוֹ יָכוֹל לְכַוֵּן דַּעְתּוֹ שֶׁיִּשְׁמַע מִשְּׁלִיחַ־הַצִּבּוּר, וְנִמְצָא שֶׁקָּרָא רַק מִתּוֹךְ הַחֻמָּשׁ, וְאֵינוֹ יוֹצֵא, וְאִם אֵרַע כָּךְ, צָרִיךְ לַחֲזוֹר וּלְשָׁמְעָהּ מִתּוֹךְ מְגִלָּה כְּשֵׁרָה.

יט) צִבּוּר שֶׁאֵין לָהֶם מְגִלָּה כְּשֵׁרָה כְּדִינָהּ, מִכָּל מָקוֹם אִם הִיא כְּתוּבָה עַל קְלָף כְּהִלְכָתָהּ, רַק שֶׁחֲסֵרוֹת אֵיזוֹ תֵּבוֹת בְּאֶמְצָעָהּ, כֵּיוָן שֶׁלֹּא חָסֵר בָּהּ עִנְיָן אֶחָד שָׁלֵם, יְכוֹלִין לִקְרוֹת מִתּוֹכָהּ עִם הַבְּרָכוֹת, וְהַטָּעוּת יִקְרָא הַקּוֹרֵא בְּעַל־פֶּה, אוֹ יֹאמַר לְפָנָיו [אַחֵר] בְּלַחַשׁ מִתּוֹךְ הַחֻמָּשׁ. אֲבָל אִם אֵין מְגִלָּה כְּלָל אוֹ שֶׁחָסֵר בָּהּ עִנְיָן אֶחָד שָׁלֵם אוֹ שֶׁחָסֵר בָּהּ בַּתְּחִלָּה אוֹ בַסּוֹף, קוֹרִין מִתּוֹךְ הַחֻמָּשׁ כָּל אֶחָד בִּפְנֵי עַצְמוֹ וְאֵין מְבָרְכִין. וְיָחִיד שֶׁאֵין לוֹ רַק מְגִלָּה פְּסוּלָה, קוֹרֵא בָהּ בְּלֹא בְרָכוֹת.

כ) אָבֵל תּוֹךְ שִׁבְעָה, נוֹהֵג בְּכָל דִּינֵי אֲבֵלוּת, וְאָסוּר לִרְאוֹת כָּל מִינֵי שִׂמְחָה. אַךְ בִּנְעִילַת הַסַּנְדָּל וִישִׁיבָה עַל גַּבֵּי סַפְסָל, מֻתָּר, מִפְּנֵי שֶׁהֵם דְּבָרִים הַנִּרְאִים לַכֹּל. בַּלַּיְלָה, אִם יָכוֹל לֶאֱסוֹף מִנְיָן בְּבֵיתוֹ לִקְרוֹת הַמְּגִלָּה, מוּטָב. וְאִם לָאו, יִתְפַּלֵּל בְּבֵיתוֹ וְיֵלֵךְ לְבֵית־הַכְּנֶסֶת לִשְׁמוֹעַ

9. In such a case, the *Megillah* must be re-read from the place the mistake was made, but

16) Someone who has already fulfilled the Mitzvah of reading the *Megillah,* may read in order to exempt someone else. If the one for whose benefit he reads knows how to say the *berachos,* then he should say the *berachos.* If [he reads it for] a woman, it is preferable that the reader says the following berachah: *Asher kiddeshanu bemitzvosav vetzivanu lishmo'a megillah.* [Who has sanctified us with His commandments and has commanded us to hear the *Megillah*].

17) On Shabbos (on which *Purim* never occurs) it is permissible to handle the *Megillah.* Nevertheless, if *Purim* occurs on Sunday, you should not bring the *Megillah* to the synagogue on Shabbos even in a city which has an *eiruv,* because it is preparing on Shabbos for a weekday.

18) If a congregation has no reader capable of reading the *Megillah* with the proper cantillation chant, it may be read without the chant, provided the words are properly pronounced, so that the meaning is not changed. For, if instead of reading *uMordechai yosheiv* (is sitting) [it was read] *yashav* (sat) or instead of [reading] *veHaman nofeil* [Haman is falling], it was read *nafal* [fell], or the like, even post facto, the mitzvah is not fulfilled.[9] It is permissible to insert vowels and cantillation marks in the *Megillah,* so that it should be read correctly, since it is an extreme circumstance; and this is better than having someone prompt [the reader] from of a *chumash,* whispering quietly, because the prompter, who is reading out of a *chumash,* even if he reads in an undertone, cannot concentrate on listening to the reader's recitation. The result is, that he only reads it out of a *chumash,* and has not fulfilled the mitzvah. If this happened [the prompter] must hear it again read out of a valid *Megillah.*

19) If a congregation does not have a *halachically* valid *Megillah,* nevertheless, if it is written on parchment according to *Halachah,* except that some words are missing in mid text, since no complete subject is missing, it may be read from, and the *berachos* may be said over it. The reader should say the missing words from memory or someone should prompt him quietly from a *chumash.* But if they have no *Megillah* at all, or if an entire subject is missing, or if the first or last [verses] are missing, then each person should read from a *chumash* without saying the *berachos.* An individual who has only a *Megillah* that is not valid should read in it, without saying the *berachos.*

20) A mourner during the *shivah* should observe all the *Halachos* of mourning, and he is forbidden to attend any kind of celebration; but wearing shoes and sitting on a chair are permitted [to him on *Purim*], because these are things that everyone can see.[10] At night, if he can gather a *minyan* in his house to read the *Megillah,* that is preferable; if not, he should pray at home and go to the synagogue to hear the

---

a new berachah is not said. This rule also applies if an entire word was omitted. (*Biur Halachah* 690:14)

10. Only very private practices of mourning are permitted on *Purim.*

הַמְּגִלָּה. וְאִם חָל בְּמוֹצָאֵי־שַׁבָּת, יֵלֵךְ לְבֵית־הַכְּנֶסֶת לְאַחַר סְעוּדָה שְׁלִישִׁית בְּעוֹד יוֹם. וּבַיּוֹם, הוֹלֵךְ לְבֵית־הַכְּנֶסֶת לַתְּפִלָּה וְלַמְּגִלָּה.

כא) מִי שֶׁמֵּת לוֹ מֵת בְּתַעֲנִית אֶסְתֵּר וּבַלַּיְלָה הוּא אוֹנֵן קֹדֶם הַקְּבוּרָה, יִשְׁמַע קְרִיאַת הַמְּגִלָּה מֵאַחֵר. וְלֹא יֹאכַל בָּשָׂר וְלֹא יִשְׁתֶּה יַיִן, כִּי בַּלַּיְלָה אֵינוֹ חַיָּב בְּמִשְׁתֶּה. וּבַיּוֹם לְאַחַר יְצִיאָה מִבֵּית־הַכְּנֶסֶת, קוֹבְרִין אֶת הַמֵּת וְאַחַר כָּךְ יִתְפַּלֵּל וְיִקְרָא אֶת הַמְּגִלָּה אוֹ יִשְׁמַע מֵאַחֵר. וְאִם שָׁמַע קְרִיאַת הַמְּגִלָּה קֹדֶם הַקְּבוּרָה, יָצָא. וּמִכָּל מָקוֹם נָכוֹן שֶׁיַּחֲזוֹר וְיִקְרָאֶהָ בְּלֹא בְרָכוֹת. וּתְפִלִּין לֹא יַנִּיחַ אֲפִלּוּ אַחַר הַקְּבוּרָה, כֵּיוָן שֶׁהוּא יוֹם רִאשׁוֹן בְּאֶבְלוֹ. וְאוֹנֵן בְּפוּרִים בַּיּוֹם, מֻתָּר בְּבָשָׂר וָיַיִן.

כב) שַׁחֲרִית, מַשְׁכִּימִין לְבֵית־הַכְּנֶסֶת. לְאַחַר שְׁמוֹנֶה־עֶשְׂרֵה אוֹמְרִים חֲצִי קַדִּישׁ, וְקוֹרִין בַּתּוֹרָה בְּפָרָשַׁת וַיָּבֹא עֲמָלֵק תְּלָתָא גַבְרֵי, וְאַחַר כָּךְ חֲצִי קַדִּישׁ. וּלְאַחַר שֶׁמַּכְנִיסִין אֶת סֵפֶר־הַתּוֹרָה, קוֹרִין אֶת הַמְּגִלָּה. לְאַחַר בְּרָכָה אַחֲרוֹנָה, אֵין אוֹמְרִים בְּשַׁחֲרִית אֲשֶׁר הֵנִיא. וּלְאַחַר שֶׁסִּיֵּם הָאֵל הַמּוֹשִׁיעַ, אוֹמְרִים שׁוֹשַׁנַּת יַעֲקֹב וְכוּ׳. וְאוֹמְרִים אַשְׁרֵי, וּבָא לְצִיּוֹן, קַדִּישׁ שָׁלֵם עִם תִּתְקַבֵּל. וְאֵין לַחֲלוֹץ אֶת הַתְּפִלִּין עַד לְאַחַר קְרִיאַת הַמְּגִלָּה, מִשּׁוּם דִּכְתִיב בָּהּ, וִיקָר, וְדָרְשִׁינָן, אֵלּוּ תְּפִלִּין. אִם יֵשׁ מִילָה, מָלִין קֹדֶם קְרִיאַת הַמְּגִלָּה, מִשּׁוּם דִּכְתִיב, וְשָׂשׂוֹן, זוֹ מִילָה.

כג) עִיר שֶׁהִיא מֻקֶּפֶת חוֹמָה מִימוֹת יְהוֹשֻׁעַ בִּן־נוּן, קוֹרִין בָּהּ בַּחֲמִשָּׁה עָשָׂר (וְלֹא שְׁכִיחֵי בִּמְדִינוֹתֵינוּ).

סִימָן קמב
הִלְכוֹת מִשְׁלוֹחַ מָנוֹת אִישׁ לְרֵעֵהוּ וּמַתָּנוֹת לָאֶבְיוֹנִים וּסְעוּדַת פּוּרִים

א) חַיָּב כָּל אָדָם לִשְׁלוֹחַ לְכָל הַפָּחוֹת לְאָדָם אֶחָד שְׁתֵּי מָנוֹת, דִּכְתִיב, וּמִשְׁלוֹחַ מָנוֹת אִישׁ לְרֵעֵהוּ, מַשְׁמַע שְׁתֵּי מַתָּנוֹת לְאֶחָד. וְכָל הַמַּרְבֶּה לִשְׁלוֹחַ מָנוֹת לְרֵעִים, הֲרֵי זֶה מְשֻׁבָּח. וּמִכָּל מָקוֹם מוּטָב

---

11. However, before the burial he is exempt from the mitzvah to read *Kerias Shemah* and to pray the *Shemoneh Esrei.* (*Kitzur Shulchan Aruch* 196:7)

12. *Mishnah Berurah* disagrees with this ruling, maintaining that he is not permitted to eat meat or drink wine even by day. (*Shaar Hatzion* 696:28)

Megillah. If *Purim* occurs on Shabbos night, he should go to the synagogue after *Shalosh Seudos* [the third meal] while it is still day. On *Purim*-day he may go to the synagogue to pray and to hear the *Megillah.*

21) If someone lost a close relative on the Fast of Esther and at night he is an *onein,* since the burial has not yet taken place, he should hear the *Megillah* read by someone else; and he should not eat meat nor drink wine, since at night feasting is not mandatory. In the daytime, after leaving the synagogue, the dead should be buried. Afterwards he should pray,[11] and either read the *Megillah* himself or hear someone else read it. If he heard the reading of the *Megillah* before the burial, he has fulfilled his obligation. Nevertheless, it is proper that he read it again without saying the *berachos.* He should not put on the *tefillin* even after the burial, because it is the first day of mourning. An *onein,* on *Purim* during the daytime, is permitted to eat meat and drink wine.[12]

22) In the morning [it is proper] to get up early to go to the synagogue. After the *Shemoneh Esrei, half-kaddish* is said. We call up three persons for the Torah-reading of *Parashas Vayavo Amalek* [And Amelek came] [Ex. 17:8), after which *half-kaddish* is said. After the *seifer Torah* is placed in the Ark, the *Megillah* is read. After the last berachah [over the *Megillah*], in the morning, we do not say *Asher heini* [Who annuls the counsel of the nations]. After concluding the berachah with *hakeil hamoshia* [the God Who brings salvation] we say *Shoshanas Yaakov* [The rose of Jacob] etc. then *Ashrei, Uva leTzion, Full-Kaddish* including *Tiskabbeil.* You should not take off the *tefillin* until after the reading of the *Megillah,* because in the *Megillah* it is written, *Vikar* [and honor] (8:16), and [our Rabbis] expound that this refers to the *tefillin.* If there is a *bris,* it is performed before[13] the reading of the *Megillah,* because it is written *vesason* [gladness], which refers to *bris milah.*

23) In a city that has been surrounded by a wall since the days of Joshua the son of Nun, the *Megillah* is read on the fifteenth of *Adar* (such cities do not exist in our regions).

Chapter 142

Laws Concerning the Sending of Gifts of Food, Gifts to the Needy and the Seudas Purim, Purim Feast

1) [On Purim] everyone is required to send[1] no less than two gifts to one person; as it is written, "And sending gifts of food to one another" (9:22); which implies two gifts to one person. The more gifts you send to your friends the more praiseworthy

---

13. According to *Pri Chadosh* and *Vilna Gaon,* the *Megillah* is read before the *bris.* (*Mishnah Berurah* 693:12)

1. *Mishnah Berurah* questions if the mitzvah is fulfilled if you give the gift directly to the recipient, without a messenger. (*Mishnah Berurah* 695:18)

לְהַרְבּוֹת בְּמַתָּנוֹת לָאֶבְיוֹנִים מִלְּהַרְבּוֹת בִּסְעוּדָתוֹ וּבְמִשְׁלוֹחַ מָנוֹת לְרֵעִים, כִּי אֵין שִׂמְחָה גְּדוֹלָה וּמְפֹאֶרֶת לִפְנֵי הַקָּדוֹשׁ בָּרוּךְ־הוּא אֶלָּא לְשַׂמֵּחַ לֵב עֲנִיִּים וִיתוֹמִים וְאַלְמָנוֹת. וְהַמְשַׂמֵּחַ לֵב הָאֻמְלָלִים הָאֵלּוּ, דּוֹמֶה לַשְּׁכִינָה, שֶׁנֶּאֱמַר, לְהַחֲיוֹת רוּחַ שְׁפָלִים וּלְהַחֲיוֹת לֵב נִדְכָּאִים.

ב) לֹא נִקְרָא מָנוֹת אֶלָּא דָּבָר שֶׁרָאוּי לֶאֱכוֹל כְּמוֹת שֶׁהוּא בְּלִי תִּקּוּן, כְּגוֹן בָּשָׂר וְדָגִים מְבֻשָּׁלִים וְלֹא חַיִּים, אוֹ מִינֵי מְתִיקָה אוֹ פֵּרוֹת, אוֹ כּוֹס יַיִן וּמֵי־דְבַשׁ וְכַיּוֹצֵא בָּהֶם.

ג) כָּל אָדָם אֲפִלּוּ עָנִי שֶׁבְּיִשְׂרָאֵל הַמְקַבֵּל צְדָקָה, חַיָּב לִתֵּן לְכָל הַפָּחוֹת שְׁתֵּי מַתָּנוֹת לִשְׁנֵי עֲנִיִּים, דְּהַיְנוּ מַתָּנָה אַחַת לְכָל אֶחָד, דִּכְתִיב, וּמַתָּנוֹת לָאֶבְיֹנִים, מַשְׁמַע שְׁתֵּי מַתָּנוֹת לִשְׁנֵי עֲנִיִּים. וְאֵין מְדַקְדְּקִים בִּמְעוֹת פּוּרִים, אֶלָּא כָּל הַפּוֹשֵׁט יָד לִטּוֹל, נוֹתְנִים לוֹ. וּמִי שֶׁהוּא בְּמָקוֹם שֶׁאֵין שָׁם עֲנִיִּים, יְעַכֵּב אֶת הַמָּעוֹת אֶצְלוֹ, עַד שֶׁיִּזְדַּמְּנוּ לוֹ עֲנִיִּים אוֹ יִשְׁלָחֵם לָהֶם.

ד) גַּם הַנָּשִׁים חַיָּבוֹת בְּמִשְׁלוֹחַ מָנוֹת וּמַתָּנוֹת לָאֶבְיוֹנִים. מִשְׁלוֹחַ מָנוֹת, תִּשְׁלַח אִשָּׁה לְאִשָּׁה וְאִישׁ לְאִישׁ. אֲבָל מַתָּנוֹת לָאֶבְיוֹנִים, יְכוֹלָה גַּם אִשָּׁה לִשְׁלוֹחַ לְאִישׁ, וְכֵן בְּהֵפֶךְ. קְצָת נָשִׁים סוֹמְכוֹת עַל בַּעֲלֵיהֶן שֶׁהֵם שׁוֹלְחִים גַּם בִּשְׁבִילָן, וְאֵינוֹ נָכוֹן, אֶלָּא יֵשׁ לְהַחְמִיר.

ה) חַיָּבִים לֶאֱכוֹל וְלִשְׁתּוֹת וְלִשְׂמוֹחַ בַּפּוּרִים. גַּם בְּלֵיל אַרְבָּעָה עָשָׂר יִשְׂמַח וְיַרְבֶּה קְצָת בִּסְעוּדָה. וּכְשֶׁחָל בְּמוֹצָאֵי שַׁבָּת, אַף שֶׁצָּרִיךְ לַעֲשׂוֹת בַּשַּׁבָּת סְעוּדָה שְׁלִישִׁית, יְמַעֵט קְצָת בַּאֲכִילָתוֹ בַּיּוֹם, לִתֵּן מָקוֹם לִסְעוּדַת לֵיל פּוּרִים. וּמִכָּל מָקוֹם בִּסְעוּדָה שֶׁעוֹשִׂין בַּלַּיְלָה, אֵין יוֹצְאִין יְדֵי חוֹבָתָן, דְּעִקַּר הַסְּעוּדָה מִצְוָתָהּ שֶׁתְּהֵא בַּיּוֹם, דִּכְתִיב, יְמֵי מִשְׁתֶּה. וְיֵשׁ לְהַדְלִיק נֵרוֹת דֶּרֶךְ שִׂמְחָה וְיוֹם־טוֹב גַּם כְּשֶׁעוֹשִׂים הַסְּעוּדָה בַּיּוֹם. וְגַם בְּלֵיל חֲמִשָּׁה עָשָׂר, צָרִיךְ לִשְׂמוֹחַ קְצָת. גַּם מַתָּנוֹת לָאֶבְיוֹנִים וּמָנוֹת לְרֵעֵהוּ, צָרִיךְ לִהְיוֹת בַּיּוֹם. וּמִשּׁוּם דִּטְרִידֵי בְּמִשְׁלוֹחַ מָנוֹת, עוֹשִׂים מִקְצָת סְעוּדָה בַּלַּיְלָה. וּמִתְפַּלְּלִים מִנְחָה בְּעוֹד הַיּוֹם גָּדוֹל, וְעוֹשִׂין אֶת הַסְּעוּדָה לְאַחַר מִנְחָה. וּצְרִיכִין לַעֲשׂוֹת עַל־כָּל־פָּנִים רֹב הַסְּעוּדָה בַּיּוֹם. וּכְשֶׁחָל בְּעֶרֶב

2. Some *Poskim* rule that since raw meat or chicken is ready for the pot, it is permitted. (*Ibid* 695:20)

3. One article of food and a beverage is sufficient for the fulfillment of the mitzvah. (*Ibid*)

you are. Nevertheless, it is much better to give generously to the poor than to have a lavish feast and to send extravagant gifts to your friends; for there is no greater and more glorious joy before the Holy One, blessed is He, than to gladden the hearts of the poor, the orphans and the widows. Whoever gladdens the hearts of these unfortunates is compared to the Divine Presence, for it is said, (Isaiah 57:15) "To revive the spirit of the humble and revive the heart of the crushed."

2) The term *Mishlo'ach manos* implies only food that is ready-to-eat without preparation [by the recipient], such as cooked meat or fish, but not if it is uncooked.[2] Candy, fruits, wine, mead,[3] or similar [delicacies are acceptable].

3) Everybody, even the poorest in Yisrael, who is a recipient of charity, is required to give at least two gifts to two poor persons, that is, one gift to each person, for it is written, *Matanos l'evyonim* "And gifts to the poor," (9:22) [*leveyonim* is a plural] which implies, two gifts to two poor people. You should not be selective when giving charity on *Purim;* whoever holds out his hand to ask for charity should be given a donation. If you are in a community where there are no poor people, you should either keep the money until you meet needy persons, or send it to them.

4) Women, too, are required to send *mishlo'ach manos* [gifts of food] and to give gifts to the poor. Women should send *mishlo'ach manos* to women and men to men. But regarding donations to the poor, women may send to men, and conversely, [men may send to women]. Some women rely that their husbands give on their behalf as well, but this is not proper; rather they should be stringent about this.

5) It is an obligation to eat, drink and to rejoice on *Purim.*[4] Also on the night of the fourteenth you should rejoice and have a more elaborate meal [than usual]. If *Purim* occurs on Shabbos night, although you must have a third meal on Shabbos, you should eat a little less during the day[5] to leave some appetite for the meal of *Purim* night. Nevertheless, by having a meal at night you have not fulfilled the mitzvah [of *se'udas Purim,* the *Purim* feast]; for the mitzvah if to have the main *Purim* feast during the daytime, for it is written, "*Days* of feasting." You should light candles as you do on joyous occasions and Yom Tov, even when the meal is held in the daytime. Also on the night of the fifteenth you should celebrate a little. Giving gifts to the poor and sending *mishlo'ach manos* to friends must be done during the daytime. Since people are busy [preparing and delivering] *mishlo'ach manos,* part of the *Purim se'udah* may extend into the night. You should pray *Minchah* while it is still the middle of the day, and have the *se'udah* after *Minchah.* At any rate, you should have the greater part of the *se'udah* while it is still day. When *Purim* occurs on *erev*

---

4. It is proper to gather your family and friends because it is impossible to rejoice yourself. It must, however, be a joy that is in the spirit of Torah. (*Ibid* 695:9)

5. This ruling is not mentioned in *Mishnah Berurah,* on the contrary he writes (*Ibid* 695:3) "Even though you had a large meal for *Shalosh Seudos,* nevertheless, you should have a larger than usual meal at night."

שַׁבָּת, עוֹשִׂין אוֹתָהּ בְּשַׁחֲרִית, מִפְּנֵי כְּבוֹד שַׁבָּת. וְטוֹב לַעֲסֹק קְצָת בַּתּוֹרָה קֹדֶם שֶׁמַּתְחִיל הַסְּעוּדָה. וְסֶמֶךְ לַדָּבָר, לַיְּהוּדִים הָיְתָה אוֹרָה, וְדָרְשִׁינָן, אוֹרָה, זוֹ תּוֹרָה. יֵשׁ אוֹמְרִים, שֶׁיֵּשׁ לֶאֱכֹל מִינֵי זֵרְעוֹנִין בְּפוּרִים, זֵכֶר לְזֵרְעוֹנִין שֶׁאָכְלוּ דָּנִיֵּאל וַחֲבֵרָיו בְּבָבֶל, וְזֵכֶר לְזֵרְעוֹנִין שֶׁאָכְלָה אֶסְתֵּר. דְּאִיתָא בַּגְּמָרָא, וַיְשַׁנֶּהָ וְאֶת־נַעֲרוֹתֶיהָ לְטוֹב, שֶׁהֶאֱכִילָהּ זֵרְעוֹנִים. (דִּינֵי עַל הַנִּסִּים בְּבִרְכַּת הַמָּזוֹן, עַיֵּן סִימָן מד סָעִיף טז, יז).

ו) כֵּיוָן שֶׁכָּל הַנֵּס הָיָה עַל יְדֵי הַיַּיִן, וַשְׁתִּי נִטְרְדָה בְּמִשְׁתֵּה הַיַּיִן וּבָאָה אֶסְתֵּר בִּמְקוֹמָהּ, וְכֵן עִנְיַן הָמָן וּמַפַּלְתּוֹ הָיָה עַל יְדֵי יַיִן, לָכֵן חִיְּבוּ רַבּוֹתֵינוּ זִכְרוֹנָם לִבְרָכָה, לְהִשְׁתַּכֵּר בְּיַיִן, וְאָמְרוּ, חַיָּב אֱנָשׁ לְבַסּוּמֵי בְּפוּרְיָא עַד דְּלָא יָדַע בֵּין אָרוּר הָמָן לְבָרוּךְ מָרְדְּכָי. וְלַפָּחוֹת יִשְׁתֶּה יוֹתֵר מֵהֶרְגֵּלוֹ, כְּדֵי לִזְכֹּר אֶת הַנֵּס הַגָּדוֹל, וְיִישַׁן. וּמִתּוֹךְ שֶׁיָּשֵׁן, אֵינוֹ יוֹדֵעַ בֵּין אָרוּר הָמָן לְבָרוּךְ מָרְדְּכָי. וְאוּלָם מִי שֶׁהוּא חָלוּשׁ בְּטִבְעוֹ, וְכֵן מִי שֶׁיּוֹדֵעַ בְּעַצְמוֹ שֶׁעַל יְדֵי כֵן יְזַלְזֵל חַס־וְשָׁלוֹם בְּאֵיזוֹ מִצְוָה, בִּבְרָכָה, אוֹ בִתְפִלָּה, אוֹ שֶׁיָּבוֹא חַס־וְשָׁלוֹם לְקַלּוּת־רֹאשׁ, מוּטָב שֶׁלֹּא יִשְׁתַּכֵּר, וְכָל מַעֲשָׂיו יִהְיוּ לְשֵׁם־שָׁמָיִם.

ז) הָאָבֵל, אֲפִלּוּ תּוֹךְ שִׁבְעָה, חַיָּב בְּמַתָּנוֹת לָאֶבְיוֹנִים, וְגַם לִשְׁלוֹחַ מָנוֹת לְרֵעֵהוּ. וּמִכָּל מָקוֹם לֹא יִשְׁלַח דָּבָר שֶׁל שִׂמְחָה. אֲבָל לָאָבֵל, אֵין שׁוֹלְחִין מָנוֹת כָּל שְׁנֵים־עָשָׂר חֹדֶשׁ, אֲפִלּוּ דָּבָר שֶׁאֵינוֹ שֶׁל שִׂמְחָה. אִם הוּא עָנִי, מֻתָּר לִשְׁלוֹחַ לוֹ מָעוֹת אוֹ שְׁאָר דָּבָר שֶׁאֵינוֹ שֶׁל שִׂמְחָה. וְאִם אֵין בַּמָּקוֹם הַהוּא רַק הָאָבֵל עִם אַחֵר, חַיָּב לִשְׁלוֹחַ לוֹ, כְּדֵי לְקַיֵּם מִצְוַת מִשְׁלוֹחַ מָנוֹת (דִּין הָאוֹנֵן, עַיֵּן לְעֵיל סִימָן קמא סָעִיף כא).

ח) אֵין לַעֲשׂוֹת מְלָאכָה בְּפוּרִים. וּמִי שֶׁעוֹשֶׂה בוֹ מְלָאכָה, אֵינוֹ רוֹאֶה מֵאוֹתָהּ מְלָאכָה סִימָן בְּרָכָה לְעוֹלָם. וְעַל יְדֵי גוֹי, מֻתָּר. וּמֻתָּר לַעֲסֹק בְּפְרַקְמַטְיָא. וְכֵן מֻתָּר לִכְתֹּב אֲפִלּוּ אִגֶּרֶת שָׁלוֹם, וְכֵן חוֹבוֹתָיו וְכָל דָּבָר שֶׁאֵינוֹ צָרִיךְ עִיּוּן גָּדוֹל, וְכָל־שֶׁכֵּן לִכְתֹּב דְּבַר מִצְוָה אוֹ לַעֲשׂוֹת שְׁאָר דְּבַר מִצְוָה. וְכֵן לְצֹרֶךְ פּוּרִים, מֻתָּר לַעֲשׂוֹת אֲפִלּוּ מְלָאכוֹת גְּמוּרוֹת.

---

6. This refers only to a mourner for his father or mother. *Mishnah Berurah* rules this applies only where it is customary not to greet a mourner during the twelve months of mourning. However, where it is the custom to greet mourners you may also send them

Shabbos, you should have the *se'udah* in the morning, out of respect for Shabbos. It is commendable to devote some time to Torah study, before beginning the *se'udah.* This is based [on the verse] "The Jews had light," (8:16) and [our Rabbis] expound, "light" means Torah. Some authorities, say that you should eat different kinds of seeds on *Purim,* to commemorate the seeds Daniel and his friends ate in Babylon, and also to remember the seeds that Esther ate. For the Talmud (*Maseches Megillah* 16b) states, [it is written] "He favored her and her maids with preferential treatment . . ." (2:9) [this means], that he gave her seeds for her food. (For the laws of *Al hanisim* in *Birkas Hamazon,* see Chapter 44:16, 17.)

6) Since the entire miracle of *Purim* was brought about through wine: Vashti was banished at the wine party, and Esther took her place; also the episode of Haman's downfall came about through wine; therefore, our Rabbis of blessed memory mandated that everyone should become intoxicated with wine, and they said, "It is an obligation to become intoxicated on *Purim,* until you cannot tell the difference between 'Cursed be Haman' and 'Blessed be Mordechai.'" At least you should drink more than you usually do, to recall the great miracle, until you fall asleep; and once you are asleep, you can no longer tell the difference between "Cursed is Haman" and "Blessed is Mordechai." However, if a person is physically frail, and similarly, if you know that as a result of [drinking] you will, God forbid, ignore a mitzvah, a berachah, or a prayer, or that it would lead to lightheaded exuberance, it is better not to become drunk. All your deeds should be for the sake of Heaven.

7) A mourner, even during the week of *shivah* is required to give gifts to the poor, and to send *mishlo'ach manos* to his friends. Nevertheless, he should not send anything that generates happiness. But you should not send *mishlo'ach manos* to a mourner the entire twelve months [of mourning],[6] [this includes] even things that do not generate joyousness. If [the mourner] is a poor person you may send him money or anything that will not produce joy. If in an area where the only residents are a mourner and one other person, he must send *mishlo'ach manos* to [the mourner] in order to fulfill the mitzvah of *mishlo'ach manos.* (For the laws of *onein* see Chapter 141:21 above).

8) You should not do any work on *Purim.* Whoever performs work on that day, will never see any blessing from that work. But it is permitted to have a non-Jew work for you. You are allowed to attend to business.[7] You may write even a social letter, and [make an entry of] money you owe, or [write] anything that does not require much concentration. You are certainly [permitted] to write for the sake of a mitzvah or to do any work for the purpose of a mitzvah. For the needs of *Purim,* you are permitted to do even full-scale labor.

---

mishlo'ach manos on Purim during the twelve months. During the first thirty days of mourning it is definitely not permitted to send them *mishlo'ach manos.* (*Ibid* 696:20, 21)

7. For this is a source of joy. In the case of one who must work in order to provide for his family's needs, he too is permitted to work. (*Ibid* 696:2, 3)

ט) יוֹם חֲמִשָּׁה־עָשָׂר בַּאֲדָר נִקְרָא אֶצְלֵנוּ שׁוּשַׁן פּוּרִים. אֵין אוֹמְרִים בּוֹ תַּחֲנוּן, וְלֹא אֵל אֶרֶךְ אַפַּיִם, וְלֹא לַמְנַצֵּחַ. וְאָסוּר גַּם כֵּן בְּהֶסְפֵּד וְתַעֲנִית. וְנוֹהֲגִין בּוֹ קְצָת מִשְׁתֶּה וְשִׂמְחָה, אֲבָל אֵין אוֹמְרִים עַל הַנִּסִּים. וּמֻתָּרִין לַעֲשׂוֹת בּוֹ נִשּׂוּאִין, כֵּיוָן שֶׁאֵין אָנוּ קוֹרִין בּוֹ אֶת הַמְּגִלָּה. אֲבָל בְּיוֹם שֶׁקּוֹרִין אֶת הַמְּגִלָּה, שֶׁאָז עִקַּר הַשִּׂמְחָה, אֵין עוֹשִׂין בּוֹ נִשּׂוּאִין, מִשּׁוּם דְּאֵין מְעָרְבִין שִׂמְחָה בְּשִׂמְחָה.

י) יוֹם אַרְבָּעָה עָשָׂר וַחֲמִשָּׁה עָשָׂר שֶׁבַּאֲדָר הָרִאשׁוֹן גַּם כֵּן אֵין אוֹמְרִים בָּהֶם לֹא תַּחֲנוּן, וְלֹא אֵל אֶרֶךְ אַפַּיִם, וְלֹא לַמְנַצֵּחַ, וַאֲסוּרִין בְּהֶסְפֵּד וְתַעֲנִית. וּבְיוֹם אַרְבָּעָה עָשָׂר, מַרְבִּים קְצָת בִּסְעוּדָה.

סִימָן קמג
הִלְכוֹת כִּבּוּד אָב וָאֵם

א) צָרִיךְ לִזָּהֵר מְאֹד בִּכְבוֹד אָבִיו וְאִמּוֹ וּבְמוֹרָאָם, שֶׁהִשְׁוָה אוֹתָן הַכָּתוּב לִכְבוֹדוֹ וּלְמוֹרָאוֹ, יִתְבָּרַךְ שְׁמוֹ. כְּתִיב, כַּבֵּד אֶת־אָבִיךָ וְאֶת־אִמֶּךָ. וּכְתִיב, כַּבֵּד אֶת־ה׳, מֵהוֹנֶךָ. בְּאָבִיו וְאִמּוֹ כְּתִיב, אִישׁ אִמּוֹ וְאָבִיו תִּירָאוּ. וּכְתִיב, אֶת־ה׳ אֱלֹהֶיךָ תִּירָא. כְּדֶרֶךְ שֶׁצִּוָּה עַל כִּבּוּד שְׁמוֹ הַגָּדוֹל וּמוֹרָאוֹ, כֵּן צִוָּה עַל כִּבּוּדָם וּמוֹרָאָם. שְׁלֹשָׁה שֻׁתָּפִין הֵם בָּאָדָם, הַקָּדוֹשׁ־בָּרוּךְ־הוּא וְאָבִיו וְאִמּוֹ. (אִישׁ מַזְרִיעַ לֹבֶן שֶׁבּוֹ, אִשָּׁה מַזְרַעַת אֹדֶם שֶׁבּוֹ, וְהַקָּדוֹשׁ־בָּרוּךְ־הוּא נוֹפֵחַ בּוֹ נְשָׁמָה, מַרְאֵה עַיִן, וּשְׁמִיעַת אֹזֶן, וְדִבּוּר). בִּזְמַן שֶׁאָדָם מְכַבֵּד אֶת אָבִיו וְאֶת אִמּוֹ, אוֹמֵר הַקָּדוֹשׁ־בָּרוּךְ־הוּא, מַעֲלֶה אֲנִי עֲלֵיהֶם כְּאִלּוּ דַּרְתִּי בֵּינֵיהֶם וְכִבְּדוּנִי.

ב) אֵיזֶהוּ מוֹרָא. לֹא יַעֲמֹד בִּמְקוֹמוֹ הַמְיֻחָד לוֹ לַעֲמֹד שָׁם בְּסוֹד זְקֵנִים עִם חֲבֵרָיו אוֹ מָקוֹם הַמְיֻחָד לוֹ לְהִתְפַּלֵּל, וְלֹא יֵשֵׁב בְּמָקוֹם הַמְיֻחָד לוֹ לְהָסֵב בְּבֵיתוֹ, וְלֹא יִסְתֹּר אֶת דְּבָרָיו, וְלֹא יַכְרִיעַ אֶת דְּבָרָיו בְּפָנָיו, אֲפִלּוּ לוֹמַר, נִרְאִין דִּבְרֵי אַבָּא. עַד הֵיכָן מוֹרָאָם. הָיָה הַבֵּן לָבוּשׁ חֲמוּדוֹת וְיוֹשֵׁב בְּרֹאשׁ הַקָּהָל, וּבָאוּ אָבִיו אוֹ אִמּוֹ וְקָרְעוּ אֶת בְּגָדָיו, וְהִכּוּהוּ עַל רֹאשׁוֹ, וְיָרְקוּ בְּפָנָיו, לֹא יַכְלִים אוֹתָם וְלֹא יְצַעֵר בִּפְנֵיהֶם וְלֹא יִכְעַס כְּנֶגְדָּם, אֶלָּא יִשְׁתֹּק וְיִירָא מִמֶּלֶךְ מַלְכֵי הַמְּלָכִים הַקָּדוֹשׁ־בָּרוּךְ־הוּא שֶׁצִּוָּה בְּכָךְ. אֲבָל יָכוֹל לִתְבֹּעַ אוֹתָם לַדִּין עַל הַהֶפְסֵד.

1. *Exodus* 20:12.

9) The fifteenth day of *Adar* is called *Shushan Purim.* We do not say *Tachanun* on that day, nor *Keil erech apayim* nor *Lamenatzei'ach.* On this day it is also forbidden to deliver eulogies or to fast. It is the custom to celebrate on that day by feasting and rejoicing in moderation; but we do not say *Al hanisim,* and weddings may be performed because the *Megillah* is not read [on *Shushan Purim.*] However, [on *Purim*], when the *Megillah* is read which is the paramount time of joy, weddings should not be held, because we do not merge one joyous event with another.

10) On the fourteenth and fifteenth day of the first *Adar* (in a leap year), likewise, we do not say *Tachanun,* nor *Keil erech apayim,* nor *Lamenatzei'ach,* and it is forbidden to deliver eulogies or fast on these days, and on the fourteenth our meal should be a little more elaborate.

Chapter 143

Honoring Father and Mother

1) You must be extremely careful to honor and revere your father and mother for Scripture compares their honor and reverence to the honor and reverence you must have for the Almighty. It is written, "Honor your father and mother;"[1] It is also written, "Honor Hashem with your substance."[2] With regards to your father and mother it is written, "Every man must revere his mother and his father;"[3] and it is written, "You shall fear Adonoy your God."[4] Just as He commanded us to honor and fear His great Name so He commanded us to honor and revere them. Three partners share in the formation of man: The Holy One, Blessed is He, his father, and his mother. (The man contributes, the woman contributes, and the Holy One, Blessed is He, breathes a soul into him, endows him with eye sight, hearing and speech.) When man honors his father and mother, the Holy One, Blessed is He, says, "I account it to them as though I dwelt among them, and they honored Me."

2) How are they to be revered? You must not occupy his [your father's] designated place in the council of elders and with his friends, or the designated place in which he prays, and you must not sit in his designated place at his dining table. You must not contradict his words, or even corroborate his words in his presence, even to say "Father is right." To what extent must you revere them? If you were dressed in costly clothing and presiding over the assembly and your father or mother came and tore your clothing, struck you on the head and spat in your face, you must not embarrass them, or show distress in their presence or anger towards them; but you must be silent and fear the King who is King of Kings, the Holy One, Blesed is He, Who so commanded.[5] But you may summon them to Beis Din for the damages they inflicted on you.

---

2. *Proverbs* 3:9.
3. *Leviticus* 19:3.
4. *Deuteronomy* 6:13.
5. Nevertheless, if you are able to prevent them from doing these things, you are permitted to do so. (*Rema* 240:8)

ג) אֵיזֶהוּ כִּבּוּד. מַאֲכִילוֹ וּמַשְׁקֵהוּ, מַלְבִּישׁ וּמְכַסֶּה, מַכְנִיס וּמוֹצִיא וְיִתְּנֶנּוּ לוֹ בְּסֵבֶר פָּנִים יָפוֹת. שֶׁאֲפִלּוּ מַאֲכִילוֹ בְּכָל יוֹם פְּטוּמוֹת, וְהֶרְאָה לוֹ פָּנִים זוֹעֲפוֹת, נֶעֱנָשׁ עָלָיו.

ד) הָיוּ אָבִיו אוֹ אִמּוֹ יְשֵׁנִים וּמַפְתֵּחַ חֲנוּתוֹ שֶׁל הַבֵּן תַּחַת רָאשֵׁיהֶם, אָסוּר לַהֲקִיצָם מִשְּׁנָתָם, אַף־עַל־פִּי שֶׁיַּפְסִיד רֶוַח הַרְבֵּה. אֲבָל אִם יַגִּיעַ רֶוַח לְאָבִיו אִם יְקִיצוֹ, וְאִם לֹא יְקִיצוֹ יִצְטַעֵר עַל מְנִיעַת הָרֶוַח, מִצְוָה לַהֲקִיצוֹ, כֵּיוָן שֶׁיִּשְׂמַח בָּזֶה. וְכֵן מִצְוָה לַהֲקִיצוֹ לָלֶכֶת לְבֵית־הַכְּנֶסֶת אוֹ לִשְׁאָר דְּבַר מִצְוָה, מִפְּנֵי שֶׁכֻּלָּם חַיָּבִים בִּכְבוֹד הַמָּקוֹם בָּרוּךְ הוּא.

ה) הָיָה צָרִיךְ לְאֵיזֶה דָּבָר בָּעִיר, וְיוֹדֵעַ שֶׁיַּשְׁלִימוּ חֶפְצוֹ בִּשְׁבִיל אָבִיו, אַף־עַל־פִּי שֶׁיּוֹדֵעַ שֶׁגַּם בִּשְׁבִילוֹ יַעֲשׂוּהוּ לוֹ, לֹא יֹאמַר, עֲשׂוּ לִי בִּשְׁבִילִי, אֶלָּא יֹאמַר, עֲשׂוּ לִי בִּשְׁבִיל אַבָּא, כְּדֵי לִתְלוֹת הַכָּבוֹד בְּאָבִיו.

ו) אָמְרָה לוֹ אִמּוֹ, עֲשֵׂה זֹאת וְעָשָׂה, וְאַחַר כָּךְ בָּא אָבִיו וְשָׁאַל אוֹתוֹ, מִי אָמַר לְךָ לַעֲשׂוֹת זֹאת. וְהוּא מַרְגִּישׁ, שֶׁאִם יֹאמַר שֶׁאִמּוֹ אָמְרָה לוֹ, יִכְעַס אָבִיו עַל אִמּוֹ, אַל יֹאמַר לוֹ שֶׁאִמּוֹ אָמְרָה לוֹ לַעֲשׂוֹת הַדָּבָר, אַף־עַל־פִּי שֶׁעַל יְדֵי כֵן יִכְעַס הָאָב עָלָיו.

ז) חַיָּב לַעֲמֹד בִּפְנֵי אָבִיו וּבִפְנֵי אִמּוֹ.

ח) חַיָּב לְכַבְּדָם גַּם לְאַחַר מוֹתָם. וְאִם מַזְכִּירָם בְּתוֹךְ שְׁנֵים־עָשָׂר חֹדֶשׁ בַּפֶּה אוֹ בִכְתָב, אוֹמֵר אוֹ כּוֹתֵב, הֲרֵינִי כַּפָּרַת מִשְׁכָּבוֹ. (פֵּרוּשׁ, עָלַי יְהֵא כָּל רַע הָרָאוּי לָבוֹא עַל נַפְשׁוֹ) אוֹ מִשְׁכָּבָהּ. וּלְאַחַר שְׁנֵים עָשָׂר חֹדֶשׁ (כְּבָר קִבֵּל מַה שֶּׁקִּבֵּל, שֶׁאֵין מִשְׁפַּט רִשְׁעֵי יִשְׂרָאֵל בְּגֵיהִנֹּם אֶלָּא שְׁנֵים עָשָׂר חֹדֶשׁ) אוֹמֵר אוֹ כּוֹתֵב, זִכְרוֹנוֹ לִבְרָכָה לְחַיֵּי הָעוֹלָם הַבָּא אוֹ זִכְרוֹנָהּ לִבְרָכָה לְחַיֵּי הָעוֹלָם הַבָּא.

ט) אֲפִילּוּ אָבִיו רָשָׁע וּבַעַל עֲבֵרוֹת, מְכַבְּדוֹ וּמִתְיָרֵא מִמֶּנּוּ. וַאֲפִלּוּ מַמְזֵר, חַיָּב בִּכְבוֹד אָבִיו וּמוֹרָאוֹ. וְיֵשׁ אוֹמְרִים, דְּאֵינוֹ מְחֻיָּב לְכַבֵּד אָבִיו רָשָׁע כָּל זְמַן שֶׁלֹּא עָשָׂה תְּשׁוּבָה. וְאַךְ לְצַעֲרוֹ אָסוּר. וְיֵשׁ לְהַחְמִיר כִּסְבָרָא הָרִאשׁוֹנָה.

י) רָאָה לְאָבִיו שֶׁעוֹבֵר עַל דִּבְרֵי־תוֹרָה, לֹא יֹאמַר לוֹ, עָבַרְתָּ עַל דִּבְרֵי

3) How are they to be honored? You should provide them with food and drink, with clothing and shelter, escort them to their home and escort them from their home. You must provide these services cheerfully, for even if you provide them daily with choice poultry but do so with ill grace you will incur Divine punishment.

4) If your father or mother is asleep and the key to your store is under their pillow, it is forbidden to awaken them even if it means losing a large profit. However, if your father would profit by being awakened and if not awakened will be distressed by the loss of profit, it is a mitzvah to wake him since that will make him happy. Likewise, it is a mitzvah to waken him to go to the synagogue or to perform any other mitzvah because everyone is obligated to honor the Holy One, Blessed is He.

5) If you need a favor from the townsmen and you know they will grant your wish for your father's sake, even though you know that they would also do it for your sake, you should not say, "Do it for my sake," but rather, "Do it for me for my father's sake," in order to attribute the honor to your father.

6) If you did something your mother told you to do and subsequently your father asks you, "Who told you to do this?" and you sense that if you said your mother told you, your father will be angry at your mother, you must not say to him that your mother told you to do it, even though as a result, your father will be angry with you.

7) You must stand up in the presence of your father and your mother.

8) You must honor your parents even after their death. If you mention them within twelve months after their passing, whether you do so orally or in writing you should say or write, "May I be an atonement in his stead" (i.e., I take (accept) upon myself all the evil [punishment] that would be inflicted upon his soul). or may I be an atonement in her stead. After twelve months have transpired (since he would have already received any punishment due him, for [even] the judgement in *Gehinom* of the wicked of Israel does not exceed twelve months), you should say or write, "May his memory be a blessing in the life of the World to Come" or "May her memory be a blessing in the life of the World to Come."

9) Even if your father is wicked and a sinner you must honor and fear him.[6] Even a bastard is obligated to honor and fear his father. Others say[7] you need not honor your father, if he is wicked, so long as he did not repent, but you are forbidden to cause him grief. You should be stringent and follow the first opinion.

10) If you see your father transgress a Scriptural [Torah] Law, you must not say to him, "You transgressed a Scriptural [Torah] Law." Rather say to him, "Father, is

6. *Shulchan Aruch* 240:18.
7. *Tur, Rema.*

תּוֹרָה, אֶלָּא יֹאמַר לוֹ, אַבָּא, כְּתִיב בַּתּוֹרָה כָּךְ וְכָךְ, כְּאִלּוּ הוּא שׁוֹאֵל מִמֶּנּוּ, וְלֹא כְּמַזְהִירוֹ, וְהָאָב יָבִין מֵעַצְמוֹ וְלֹא יִתְבַּיֵּשׁ.

יא) אָמַר לוֹ אָבִיו לַעֲבֹר עַל דִּבְרֵי תוֹרָה, בֵּין עַל מִצְוַת עֲשֵׂה בֵּין עַל מִצְוַת לֹא תַעֲשֶׂה, אֲפִלּוּ עַל מִצְוָה שֶׁל דִּבְרֵיהֶם, לֹא יִשְׁמַע לוֹ, דִּכְתִיב, אִישׁ אִמּוֹ וְאָבִיו תִּירָאוּ וְאֶת־שַׁבְּתוֹתַי תִּשְׁמֹרוּ, אֲנִי ה׳ אֱלֹהֵיכֶם, סָמַךְ שַׁבָּת לְמוֹרָא אָב וָאֵם, לוֹמַר, אַף־עַל־פִּי שֶׁהִזְהַרְתִּיךָ עַל מוֹרָא אָב וָאֵם, אִם אָמַר לְךָ חַלֵּל אֶת הַשַּׁבָּת, אַל תִּשְׁמַע לוֹ. וְכֵן בִּשְׁאָר כָּל הַמִּצְוֹת. אֲנִי ה׳ אֱלֹהֵיכֶם, אַתָּה וְאָבִיךָ חַיָּבִים בִּכְבוֹדִי. לְפִיכָךְ לֹא תִשְׁמַע לוֹ לְבַטֵּל אֶת דְּבָרַי. וְגַם מִצְוֹת דְּרַבָּנָן, דִּבְרֵי הַשֵּׁם יִתְבָּרַךְ שְׁמוֹ הֵן, דִּכְתִיב, לֹא תָסוּר וְגוֹ׳. אָמַר לוֹ אָבִיו, שֶׁלֹּא יְדַבֵּר עִם פְּלוֹנִי וְשֶׁלֹּא יִמְחוֹל לוֹ, וְהַבֵּן הָיָה רוֹצֶה לְהִתְפַּיֵּס, אֵין לוֹ לָחוּשׁ לִפְקֻדַּת אָבִיו, כִּי אָסוּר לִשְׂנֹא שׁוּם יְהוּדִי אִם לֹא כְּשֶׁרוֹאֵהוּ שֶׁהוּא עוֹבֵר עֲבֵרָה, וְנִמְצָא שֶׁהָאָב צִוָּהוּ לַעֲבוֹר עַל דִּבְרֵי תוֹרָה.

יב) אִם הַבֵּן רוֹצֶה לָלֶכֶת לְאֵיזֶה מָקוֹם לִלְמֹד תּוֹרָה, מִפְּנֵי שֶׁשָּׁם תִּהְיֶה לוֹ תּוֹעֶלֶת יוֹתֵר מִבְּכָאן, וְהָאָב מוֹחֶה בְּיָדוֹ מֵאֵיזֶה טַעַם, אֵינוֹ חַיָּב לִשְׁמֹעַ לְאָבִיו, דְּתַלְמוּד־תּוֹרָה גָּדוֹל מִכִּבּוּד אָב וָאֵם, (כִּדְמָצִינוּ בְּיַעֲקֹב אָבִינוּ עָלָיו הַשָּׁלוֹם, כְּשֶׁהָלַךְ מִיִּצְחָק, נִטְמַן בְּבֵית־הַמִּדְרָשׁ שֶׁל עֵבֶר אַרְבַּע־עֶשְׂרֵה שָׁנָה וְעָסַק בַּתּוֹרָה, וְאַחַר כָּךְ הָלַךְ לְבֵית לָבָן וְנִשְׁתָּהָה שָׁם וּבַדֶּרֶךְ עֶשְׂרִים וּשְׁתַּיִם שָׁנָה, וְנֶעֱנַשׁ עַל אֵלּוּ עֶשְׂרִים וּשְׁתַּיִם שָׁנָה, שֶׁלֹּא קִיֵּם כִּבּוּד אָב, וְנֶעְלַם מִמֶּנּוּ יוֹסֵף עֶשְׂרִים וּשְׁתַּיִם שָׁנָה. וְעַל אֵלּוּ אַרְבַּע עֶשְׂרֵה שָׁנָה שֶׁעָסַק בַּתּוֹרָה, לֹא נֶעֱנַשׁ). וְכֵן אִם הַבֵּן רוֹצֶה לִשָּׂא אִשָּׁה, וְהָאָב אֵינוֹ מִתְרַצֶּה, אֵין הַבֵּן חַיָּב לִשְׁמֹעַ לוֹ.

יג) אֶחָד הָאִישׁ וְאֶחָד הָאִשָּׁה, חַיָּבִים בְּכִבּוּד אָב וָאֵם, אֶלָּא שֶׁהָאִשָּׁה הַנְּשׂוּאָה לְבַעַל, כֵּיוָן שֶׁהִיא מְשֻׁעְבֶּדֶת לַבַּעַל, לְפִיכָךְ הִיא פְּטוּרָה מִכִּבּוּד אָב וָאֵם. וְאַךְ אִם בַּעְלָהּ אֵינוֹ מַקְפִּיד עָלֶיהָ, מְחֻיֶּבֶת בְּכָל דָּבָר שֶׁאֶפְשָׁר לָהּ.

יד) כָּל הַמְבַזֶּה אָבִיו אוֹ אִמּוֹ, וַאֲפִלּוּ בִּדְבָרִים, וַאֲפִלּוּ בִּרְמִיזָה, הֲרֵי זֶה בִּכְלַל אָרוּר מִפִּי הַגְּבוּרָה, שֶׁנֶּאֱמַר, אָרוּר מַקְלֶה אָבִיו וְאִמּוֹ.

טו) הָיָה קוֹץ תָּחוּב לְאָבִיו אוֹ לְאִמּוֹ, לֹא יוֹצִיאֶנּוּ, שֶׁמָּא יַעֲשֶׂה בָּהֶם חַבּוּרָה, (שֶׁהוּא בְּאִסּוּר חִיּוּב חֶנֶק). וְכֵן אִם הַבֵּן הוּא רוֹפֵא, לֹא יַקִּיז

such and such not written in the Torah," as though you are asking him a question and not as though you are admonishing him. Your father will then himself realize [his error] and thus will not be humiliated.

11) If your father told you to transgress a Scriptural Law whether it be a positive or negative command or even a Rabbinical injunction, you must not obey him, for it is written, "Every man shall revere his mother and father and you shall preserve My Shabbos, I am Adonoy your God."[8] Shabbos is positioned in the same verse [that instructs you to fear] your father and mother to teach: "Even though I command you to fear your father and mother, if your parent tells you to desecrate the Shabbos you must not listen to him. This is true for all the mitzvos. [For] I am Adonoy your God. Both you and your father are bound to honor Me. You must therefore not listen to him to disregard My word." Rabbinical injunctions are also the commands of Hashem, Blessed be His Name, as it is written, "You shall not turn aside," etc. If your father told you not to speak to a certain person, and not to forgive him; but you would like to be reconciled; you should not be concerned with your father's order, as you are forbidden to hate any Jew unless you see him commit a sin. Thus your father has ordered you to transgress a law of the Torah.

12) If you want to go to a certain place to study Torah because there you will accomplish more than you will here, and your father disapproves for some reason, you do not have to listen to your father, for learning Torah is greater than the precept of honoring father and mother. (Similarly, we find that when our father Yaakov, peace unto him, went away from [his father] Yitzchok, he secreted himself in the *Beis Midrash* of Eiver for 14 years and immersed himself in Torah study. Afterwards, he went to Lavan's house and stayed away twenty two years, including journey time. He was punished for the twenty two years during which he did not fulfill the mitzvah of honoring his father, and Joseph's whereabouts was concealed from Him for twenty-two years, but for the fournteen years during which he studied Torah, he was not punished.) If the son wishes to get married and the father disapproves he need not listen to him.

13) Both men and women are obligated to respect their father and mother. However, a married woman owes her devotion to her husband and is thus exempt from honoring her father and mother. But if her husband has no objection, she is obligated to honor them as much as possible.

14) Whoever disgraces his father or mother even by words or gesture is among those whom the Almighty has cursed. As it said,[9] "Cursed is one who disgraces his father or mother."

15) If your parent has a splinter you should not remove it for you might thereby make a wound (which is a prohibition punishable by strangulation). Also, if the son

---

8. *Leviticus* 19,3.
9. *Deuteronomy* 27:16.

לָהֶם דָּם, וְלֹא יַחְתֹּךְ בָּהֶם אֵבֶר, אַף־עַל־פִּי שֶׁהוּא מְכַוֵּן לִרְפוּאָה. בַּמֶּה דְּבָרִים אֲמוּרִים, כְּשֶׁיֵּשׁ אַחֵר לַעֲשׂוֹת. אֲבָל אִם אֵין שָׁם אַחֵר לַעֲשׂוֹת וְהֵן מִצְטַעֲרִין, הֲרֵי הוּא מַקִּיז וְחוֹתֵךְ כְּפִי צֹרֶךְ הָרְפוּאָה.

טז) מִי שֶׁנִּטְרְפָה דַּעְתּוֹ שֶׁל אָבִיו אוֹ שֶׁל אִמּוֹ, מִשְׁתַּדֵּל לִנְהֹג עִמָּהֶם כְּפִי דַעְתָּם, עַד שֶׁיְּרַחֵם ה׳ עֲלֵיהֶם. וְאִם אִי אֶפְשָׁר לוֹ לַעֲמֹד, מִפְּנֵי שֶׁנִּשְׁתַּטּוּ בְּיוֹתֵר, יַנִּיחֵם וְיֵלֵךְ לוֹ וִיצַוֶּה לַאֲחֵרִים לְהַנְהִיגָם כָּרָאוּי לָהֶם.

יז) אָסוּר לְאָדָם לְהַכְבִּיד עֻלּוֹ עַל בָּנָיו וּלְדַקְדֵּק בִּכְבוֹדוֹ עִמָּהֶם, שֶׁלֹּא יְבִיאֵם לִידֵי מִכְשׁוֹל, אֶלָּא יִמְחוֹל וְיַעְלִים עֵינָיו מֵהֶם. שֶׁהָאָב שֶׁמָּחַל עַל כְּבוֹדוֹ, כְּבוֹדוֹ מָחוּל.

יח) אָסוּר לְהַכּוֹת אֶת בְּנוֹ הַגָּדוֹל. וְאֵין גַּדְלוּת זוֹ תְּלוּיָה בְּשָׁנִים, אֶלָּא הַכֹּל לְפִי טִבְעוֹ שֶׁל הַבֵּן, כֹּל שֶׁיֵּשׁ לָחוּשׁ שֶׁיִּתְרִיס כְּנֶגְדּוֹ בְּדִבּוּר אוֹ בְמַעֲשֶׂה, אֲפִלּוּ אֵינוֹ בַּר־מִצְוָה, אָסוּר לְהַכּוֹתוֹ, אֶלָּא יוֹכִיחוֹ בִדְבָרִים. וְכָל הַמַּכֶּה אֶת בְּנוֹ הַגָּדוֹל, מְנַדִּין אוֹתוֹ, שֶׁהֲרֵי הוּא עוֹבֵר עַל לִפְנֵי עִוֵּר לֹא תִתֵּן מִכְשׁוֹל.

יט) חַיָּב אָדָם לְכַבֵּד אֵשֶׁת אָבִיו, אַף־עַל־פִּי שֶׁאֵינָהּ אִמּוֹ, כָּל זְמַן שֶׁאָבִיו קַיָּם. וְכֵן חַיָּב לְכַבֵּד בַּעַל אִמּוֹ, כָּל זְמַן שֶׁאִמּוֹ קַיֶּמֶת. וְדָבָר הָגוּן הוּא לְכַבְּדָם גַּם לְאַחַר מִיתַת אָבִיו וְאִמּוֹ.

כ) חַיָּב אָדָם בִּכְבוֹד אָחִיו הַגָּדוֹל מִמֶּנּוּ, בֵּין שֶׁהוּא אָחִיו מִן הָאָב בֵּין מִן הָאֵם. וְחַיָּב אָדָם בִּכְבוֹד חָמִיו וַחֲמוֹתוֹ, (כִּדְמָצִינוּ בְּדָוִד הַמֶּלֶךְ עָלָיו הַשָּׁלוֹם, שֶׁחָלַק כָּבוֹד לְשָׁאוּל הַמֶּלֶךְ שֶׁהָיָה חָמִיו וּקְרָאוֹ אָבִי, שֶׁאָמַר לוֹ, אָבִי רְאֵה גַּם רְאֵה). וְחַיָּב בִּכְבוֹד אֲבִי־אָבִיו. אֶלָּא שֶׁכְּבוֹד אָבִיו, גָּדוֹל מִכְּבוֹד אֲבִי־אָבִיו.

כא) מִי שֶׁהוּא רוֹצֶה בֶּאֱמֶת לְכַבֵּד אֶת אָבִיו וְאֶת אִמּוֹ, יַעֲסֹק בַּתּוֹרָה וּבְמַעֲשִׂים טוֹבִים, שֶׁזֶּהוּ הַכָּבוֹד הַגָּדוֹל לָאָבוֹת, שֶׁאוֹמְרִים הַבְּרִיּוֹת, אַשְׁרֵי לְאָב וָאֵם שֶׁגִּדְּלוּ בֵּן כָּזֶה. אֲבָל אִם אֵין הַבֵּן הוֹלֵךְ בַּדֶּרֶךְ הַיָּשָׁר, הֲרֵי אֲבוֹתָיו יִשְׂאוּ חֶרְפָּה עָלָיו, וְהוּא מְבַיֵּשׁ אוֹתָם בְּבוּשָׁה שֶׁאֵין גְּדוֹלָה הֵימֶנָּה. וְכֵן הָאָב שֶׁרוֹצֶה לְרַחֵם עַל בָּנָיו בֶּאֱמֶת, יַעֲסֹק בַּתּוֹרָה וּבְמַעֲשִׂים

10. Even if he waives his honor, you still are rewarded for the mitzvah if you honor him. (*Radvaz* Response 554)

is a doctor, he may not bleed them and may not perform surgery on them, even though his intent is to cure them. This is true only when someone else can do it. But if no one else is available to do it, and they are suffering, he may bleed them and operate, as is required for healing.

16) If senility or insanity should effect the mind of your father or mother, you should try to deal with them in accordance with their mental status until Hashem will have mercy on them. But if it is impossible for you to endure because of their severe retardation, you may leave them, and delegate others to take proper care of them.

17) It is forbidden to place a burdensome yoke on your children, and be exacting in demanding honor from them, so as not to cause them to sin. You should rather forgive them, and overlook things, for if a father waives his honor his honor is waived.[10]

18) It is forbidden to hit your grown up son. Grown up, in this context, does not refer to age but on the nature of your son. If there is reason to believe he will attack you either verbally or physically, even if he is not yet Bar Mitzvah, you are forbidden to hit him.[11] Instead you should admonish him with words. Anyone who hits his grown up son is to be excommunicated[11] for he transgresses the Divine Command, "Do not place a stumbling block before the blind."[12]

19) You must honor your father's wife even though she is not your mother, so long as your father is alive. You are also obligated to honor your mother's husband during your mother's lifetime, and it is proper to honor them even after the passing of your father or mother.

20) You must honor your older brother, regardless if he is a brother from your paternal or maternal parent. You must honor your father-in-law and your mother-in-law (as we find that King David, peace be upon him, honored King Saul, who was his father-in-law and called him, "My father," as he said to him, "My father, see and observe"). You must honor your father's father[13] but honor due your father exceeds that of your grandfather.

21) One who truly wishes to honor his father and his mother should involve himself in Torah study and good deeds, for the greatest honor to parents is when people say, "Fortunate are the father and mother who have reared such a son." If the son does not walk in the right path, his parents suffer humiliation because of him, and he embarrasses them with the utmost embarrassment. Also, the father who truly has compassion on his children will involve himself in Torah study and

---

11. *Birkei Yosef-Ritvah.* But the *Rema* 240:20 says this applies only to a son who is at least 22 or 24 years old. The *Rashal* says that only if he is 24 years old is the father excommunicated.

12. *Leviticus* 19,14.

13. *Rema* 240:24. The *Gra* says you must honor your father's father but not your mother's father.

טוֹבִים, וִיהֵא נוֹחַ לַשָּׁמַיִם וְנוֹחַ לַבְּרִיּוֹת, וְיִתְכַּבְּדוּ בָּנָיו בּוֹ. אֲבָל מִי שֶׁאֵינוֹ הוֹלֵךְ בַּדֶּרֶךְ הַיָּשָׁר, גַּם זַרְעוֹ מְגֻנֶּה אַחֲרָיו. וְגַם בַּעֲוֹן אָבוֹת, בָּנָיו מֵתִים, כְּדִכְתִיב, פּוֹקֵד עֲוֹן אָבוֹת עַל בָּנִים. וְאֵין אַכְזְרִיּוּת גְּדוֹלָה מִזֹּאת, שֶׁהוּא גּוֹרֵם בַּחֲטָאָיו שֶׁיָּמוּתוּ בָּנָיו. וְאֵין לְךָ מְרַחֵם עַל בָּנָיו, יוֹתֵר מִן הַצַּדִּיק, כִּי זְכוּתוֹ עוֹמֶדֶת לְאֶלֶף דּוֹר.

כב) גֵּר, אָסוּר לְקַלֵּל אָבִיו הַגּוֹי וְלֹא יְבַזֵּהוּ שֶׁלֹּא יֹאמְרוּ, בָּאנוּ מִקְּדֻשָּׁה חֲמוּרָה לִקְדֻשָּׁה קַלָּה, אֶלָּא נוֹהֵג בָּהֶם מִקְצָת כָּבוֹד.

סִימָן קמד

הִלְכוֹת כְּבוֹד רַבּוֹ וְזָקֵן וְתַלְמִיד־חָכָם וְכֹהֵן

א) חַיָּב אָדָם בִּכְבוֹד רַבּוֹ וְיִרְאָתוֹ יוֹתֵר מִבְּשֶׁל אָבִיו, כִּי אָבִיו הֱבִיאוֹ לְחַיֵּי הָעוֹלָם הַזֶּה, וְרַבּוֹ מְבִיאוֹ לְחַיֵּי הָעוֹלָם הַבָּא.

ב) כְּתִיב, מִפְּנֵי שֵׂיבָה תָּקוּם וְהָדַרְתָּ פְּנֵי זָקֵן. זָקֵן זֶה, פֵּרוּשׁוֹ תַּלְמִיד־חָכָם, כְּמוֹ שֶׁנֶּאֱמַר, אֶסְפָה־לִּי שִׁבְעִים אִישׁ מִזִּקְנֵי יִשְׂרָאֵל, (וְהָתָם וַדַּאי בְּחָכְמָה תַּלְיָא מִלְּתָא, כְּדִכְתִיב, אֲשֶׁר יָדַעְתָּ כִּי הֵם זִקְנֵי הָעָם וְשֹׁטְרָיו). לָכֵן מִצְוַת עֲשֵׂה לָקוּם מִפְּנֵי תַלְמִיד־חָכָם מֻפְלָג בַּתּוֹרָה, אֲפִלּוּ אֵינוֹ זָקֵן בְּשָׁנִים וְאֵינוֹ רַבּוֹ. וְכֵן מִצְוָה לָקוּם מִפְּנֵי שֵׂיבָה, דְּהַיְנוּ בֶּן שִׁבְעִים שָׁנָה, וַאֲפִלּוּ הוּא עַם־הָאָרֶץ, וּבִלְבַד שֶׁלֹּא יְהֵא רָשָׁע. וַאֲפִלּוּ זָקֵן גּוֹי, מְהַדְּרִים אוֹתוֹ בִּדְבָרִים וְנוֹתְנִים לוֹ יָד לְסָמְכוֹ.

ג) שְׁלשָׁה שֶׁהָיוּ מְהַלְּכִין בַּדֶּרֶךְ, הָרַב בָּאֶמְצַע, וְהַשְּׁנַיִם לַאֲחוֹרָיו, וְכָל אֶחָד מְצַדֵּד עַצְמוֹ לִצְדָדִין, הַגָּדוֹל לַיָּמִין וְהַקָּטָן לַשְּׂמֹאל.

ד) עָוֹן גָּדוֹל הוּא לְבַזּוֹת תַּלְמִידֵי חֲכָמִים אוֹ לְשַׂנְאוֹתָן. לֹא חָרְבָה יְרוּשָׁלַיִם, עַד שֶׁבִּזּוּ בָהּ תַּלְמִידֵי חֲכָמִים, שֶׁנֶּאֱמַר, וַיִּהְיוּ מַלְעִיבִים בְּמַלְאֲכֵי הָאֱלֹהִים וּבוֹזִים דְּבָרָיו וּמִתַּעְתְּעִים בִּנְבִיאָיו, כְּלוֹמַר, בּוֹזִים מְלַמְּדֵי דְבָרָיו. וְכֵן זֶה שֶׁאָמְרָה תוֹרָה, וְאִם בְּחֻקֹּתַי תִּמְאָסוּ, מְלַמְּדֵי

14. Exodus 34:7.
1. *Leviticus* 19:32.

good deeds, and will please God and mankind, and his children will be proud of him. But he who does not walk in the right path brings disgrace on his children. Also children die because of the iniquity of their fathers as it is written,[14] "Visiting the iniquity of fathers on children." There is no greater cruelty than causing his children to die of his sins. Nobody has more compassion on his children than the righteous man, for his merit endures for a thousand generations.

22) A convert must not curse his non-Jewish father and he must not humiliate him; in order that they not say: "We came from a holiness [religion] that is significant to a holiness that is inferior." He should treat them with some degree of respect.

Chapter 144

Honor Due the Rebbe the Aged, the Scholar, and the Kohein.

1) You must honor and fear your *Rebbe* [teacher] more than your father, because your father [only] brought you to life in this world, but your *Rebbe* brings you to life in the World to Come.

2) It is written, "In the presence of the elderly you shall rise and you shall respect an elder."[1] "An elder," in this context refers to a Torah scholar as it is said, "Gather to me seventy men from the elders of Yisrael"[2] (and there certainly the situation called for wisdom as it is written, "Whom you know to be the elders of the people and its officers.")[2] Therefore, it is a positive command to rise before a Torah scholar who is distinguished in the knowledge of Torah, even if he is not advanced in years and is not your teacher. It is also a mitzvah to rise before an elderly person if he is at least seventy years old, even if he is an ignorant person, provided he is not a wicked person. Even to an elderly person who is not Jewish, you should talk respectfully and give him a helping hand.

3) When three people, (one of whom is a Rav,) are walking together, the Rav should walk in the middle. The other two should fall back slightly and walk at his side, the older one on the right and the younger one on the left.

4) It is a grave sin to humiliate *talmidei chachomim* or to hate them. Jerusalem was not destroyed until they began to humiliate *talmidei chachomim,* as it is said, "But they mocked the messengers of God and disgraced His words, and scoffed at His prophets."[3] That is to say they humiliated those who teach His words. This is also what the Torah says, "And if you will despise My statutes,"[4] [that is to say] "If you despise those who teach My statutes." And anyone who humiliates Torah

2. *Numbers* 11:16.
3. *Chronicles II* 36:16.
4. *Leviticus* 26:15.

חֻקּוֹתַי תִּמְאָסוּ. וְכָל הַמְבַזֶּה אֶת הַחֲכָמִים, אֵין לוֹ חֵלֶק לָעוֹלָם הַבָּא, וְהוּא בִּכְלַל כִּי דְבַר ה' בָּזָה. וְאָסוּר לְשַׁמֵּשׁ בְּמִי שֶׁהוּא שׁוֹנֶה הֲלָכוֹת.

ה) תַּלְמִיד־חָכָם שֶׁיֵּשׁ לוֹ סְחוֹרָה לִמְכֹּר, אֵין מַנִּיחִין לְשׁוּם אָדָם לִמְכֹּר מֵאוֹתָהּ סְחוֹרָה עַד שֶׁיִּמְכֹּר הוּא תְּחִלָּה אֶת שֶׁלּוֹ. וְדַוְקָא בִּדְלֵיכָּא גּוֹיִם דִּמְזַבְּנֵי, אֲבָל אִי אִכָּא גּוֹיִם דִּמְזַבְּנֵי לָא, דְּהָא לֵית לֵהּ רַוְחָא לַתַּלְמִיד־חָכָם, וְאַפְסוּדֵי לְהַנָּךְ בִּכְדִי לָא מַפְסְדֵינַן.

ו) מִי שֶׁהוּא מַחְזִק לְתַלְמִיד־חָכָם בְּדוֹרוֹ, דְּהַיְנוּ שֶׁיּוֹדֵעַ לִשָּׂא וְלִתֵּן בַּתּוֹרָה, וּמֵבִין מִדַּעְתּוֹ בְּרֹב מְקוֹמוֹת הַשַּׁ"ס וּפוֹסְקִים, וְתוֹרָתוֹ אֻמָּנוּתוֹ, וַאֲפִלּוּ יֵשׁ לוֹ מְעַט אֻמָּנוּת אוֹ מְעַט מַשָּׂא וּמַתָּן לְהִתְפַּרְנֵס בּוֹ כְּדֵי צָרְכֵי בְּנֵי בֵיתוֹ וְלֹא לְהִתְעַשֵּׁר, וּבְכָל שָׁעָה שֶׁהוּא פָּנוּי מֵעֲסָקָיו הוּא עוֹסֵק בַּתּוֹרָה, מִצַּד הַדִּין הוּא פָּטוּר מִכָּל מִינֵי מִסִּים וּמְכָסִים, וְאַף־עַל־פִּי שֶׁהוּא עָשִׁיר. וַאֲפִלּוּ מַס הַמֻּטָּל עַל כָּל אִישׁ בִּפְרָטוּת, חַיָּבִים בְּנֵי הָעִיר לְשַׁלֵּם עֲבוּרוֹ. וְהַכֹּל תָּלוּי בִּרְאוּת עֵינֵי טוּבֵי־הָעִיר.

ז) תַּלְמִיד־חָכָם הַמְזַלְזֵל בַּמִּצְוֹת וְאֵין בּוֹ יִרְאַת־שָׁמַיִם, הֲרֵי הוּא כְּקַל שֶׁבַּצִּבּוּר.

ח) כֹּהֵן וְיִשְׂרָאֵל שֶׁהֵם שָׁוִים בְּחָכְמָה מִצְוַת עֲשֵׂה מִן הַתּוֹרָה לְהַקְדִּים אֶת הַכֹּהֵן, שֶׁנֶּאֱמַר, וְקִדַּשְׁתּוֹ, וְדָרְשׁוּ רַבּוֹתֵינוּ זִכְרוֹנָם לִבְרָכָה, לְכָל דָּבָר שֶׁבִּקְדֻשָּׁה. כְּלוֹמַר, בְּכָל דָּבָר שֶׁיֵּרָאֶה גָדוֹל הוּא מְקֻדָּשׁ, לִהְיוֹת רִאשׁוֹן לִקְרִיאַת הַתּוֹרָה, וְלִהְיוֹת רֹאשׁ הַמְדַבְּרִים בְּכָל קִבּוּץ עָם, לְדַבֵּר וְלִדְרוֹשׁ תְּחִלָּה. וְכֵן בִּישִׁיבָה יְדַבֵּר בָּרֹאשׁ. וְכֵן בִּסְעוּדָה הוּא קוֹדֵם לְבָרֵךְ הַמּוֹצִיא וּבִרְכַּת־הַמָּזוֹן, וְלִתֵּן לוֹ מָנָה יָפָה תְּחִלָּה לְכָל הַמְסֻבִּין, אֶלָּא אִם כֵּן יֵשׁ יִשְׂרָאֵל גָּדוֹל מִמֶּנּוּ בְּחָכְמָה, אֲזַי יִתְּנוּ לְהֶחָכָם הַמָּנָה הַיָּפָה תְּחִלָּה. אֲבָל כְּשֶׁהַכֹּהֵן חוֹלֵק אֵיזוֹ שֻׁתָּפוּת עִם חֲבֵרוֹ יִשְׂרָאֵל, אֵינוֹ צָרִיךְ לִתֵּן לוֹ הַחֵלֶק הַיָּפֶה, שֶׁאֵין זֶה דֶרֶךְ כָּבוֹד שֶׁיִּטּוֹל אֶת הַחֵלֶק הַיָּפֶה. שֶׁכָּל הַנּוֹתֵן עֵינָיו בְּחֵלֶק הַיָּפֶה, אֵינוֹ רוֹאֶה סִימַן בְּרָכָה לְעוֹלָם. בְּמָקוֹם שֶׁאֵין כֹּהֵן, טוֹב לְהַקְדִּים הַלֵּוִי לְיִשְׂרָאֵל בְּכָל אֵלּוּ, אִם הֵם שָׁוִים בְּחָכְמָה.

---

5. *Numbers* 15:31.
6. And certainly not to do so to a student of the Talmud. (*Rema* 243:6)

scholars has no portion in the World to Come, and he is included among those of whom it is said: "For He has denigrated the word of Adonoy."[5] It is forbidden to make servile use of one who studies Torah laws.[6]

5) If a Torah scholar has merchandise to sell we do not permit anyone to sell such merchandise until he sells his merchandise. This is true only when there is no gentile selling such merchandise. But if a gentile is selling [such merchandise] this is not so because the Torah scholar will not profit from this, and it will needlessly cause loss to the other Jews.

6) To be accepted as a Torah scholar in his generation,[7] one must be competent to discuss and debate topics of [the Written and Oral] Torah, and have proper understanding of most of the Talmud and Codes of Law, and Torah study is his main occupation. Even if he has a profession or a business with which to support himself, and provide the needs of his family, but not [necessarily] to amass wealth; and whenever he is free from his occupation he studies Torah; [if all these requirements apply to him then] according to the Law he is exempt from all forms of taxes and levies even if he is wealthy. And even the personal tax that is incumbent upon each person, the townsmen are obligated to pay for him. [However] everything is dependent on the discretion of the elected town leaders.[8]

7) A scholar who slights the mitzvos and is not God-fearing, is to be treated like the insignificant men of the community.

8) When a *kohein* and an Israelite are equal in Torah scholarship it is a positive Scriptural mitzvah to give precedence to the *kohein,* as it is said, "You shall sanctify Him."[9] And our Rabbis, of blessed memory, explained that it refers to all matters of sanctity; that in all matters of importance he should be sanctified. He is to be called first to the Torah reading, and to be the first speaker at all public gatherings, and to speak first and expound on the Torah. He should also speak first in the yeshivah. Also at a meal, he is first to say the *Berachah* of *Hamotzi* and to lead the *Birkas Hamazon.* He should be given the choice portion before the others who are dining, unless an Israelite is present who is greater than him in Torah [learning], in which case you should give the scholar the choice portion.[10] But when a *kohein* divides a partnership with his friend, an Israelite, the Israelite need not give him the better share, for it is not honorable for the *kohein* to take the better share, for one who covets the better share will never see a sign of blessing. When a *kohein* is not present it is best to give preference to a Levi before an Israelite in all things mentioned here, if they are equal in Torah scholarship.

---

7. Even he is not as great as the scholars in other cities, because we go according to the level of the scholars in his city. (*Shach* 243:8)

8. If he is an accepted Rosh Yeshiva or an *halachic* authority, etc., he is exempt regardless of what the elected town leaders say. (*Knesses Yechezkiel* Response 95)

9. *Leviticus* 21:8.

10. If they are both Torah scholars, but the Israelite is the greater scholar, it is proper to honor the Kohein. (*Mishnah Berurah* 201:12)

ט) אָסוּר לְהִשְׁתַּמֵּשׁ בְּכֹהֵן אֲפִלּוּ בִּזְמַן הַזֶּה, וּכְמוֹעֵל בַּהֶקְדֵּשׁ הוּא, שֶׁנֶּאֱמַר, וְקִדַּשְׁתּוֹ כִּי אֶת־לֶחֶם אֱלֹהֶיךָ הוּא מַקְרִיב. וְאַף עַכְשָׁו, שֶׁאֵין לָנוּ קָרְבָּנוֹת, בִּקְדֻשָּׁתוֹ הוּא עוֹמֵד. וְאִם הַכֹּהֵן מוֹחֵל עַל כְּבוֹדוֹ, מֻתָּר, כִּי הַכְּהֻנָּה שֶׁלּוֹ הִיא, וְיָכוֹל לִמְחוֹל עַל כְּבוֹדָהּ וְלִתֵּן רְשׁוּת לְיִשְׂרָאֵל לְהִשְׁתַּמֵּשׁ בּוֹ. וּמִכָּל־שֶׁכֵּן שֶׁיָּכוֹל לַחֲלוֹק כָּבוֹד לְיִשְׂרָאֵל לְהַקְדִּימוֹ בַּדְּבָרִים הַנֶּאֱמָרִים לְעֵיל.

סִימָן קמה
הִלְכוֹת אִישׁוּת

א) חַיָּב כָּל אָדָם לִשָּׂא אִשָּׁה, כְּדֵי לִפְרוֹת וְלִרְבּוֹת. וּמִצְוָה זוֹ חָלָה עַל הָאָדָם מִשֶּׁנִּכְנַס לִשְׁנַת הַשְּׁמוֹנֶה־עֶשְׂרֵה. וְעַל־כָּל־פָּנִים לֹא יַעֲבוֹר מֵעֶשְׂרִים שָׁנָה בְּלֹא אִשָּׁה, רַק אִם עוֹסֵק בַּתּוֹרָה בְּהַתְמָדָה וּמִתְיָרֵא לִשָּׂא אִשָּׁה, כְּדֵי שֶׁלֹּא יִתְבַּטֵּל עַל יְדֵי כָּךְ מִלִּמּוּדוֹ, מֻתָּר לוֹ לְהִתְאַחֵר. וְהוּא, כְּשֶׁאֵין יִצְרוֹ מִתְגַּבֵּר עָלָיו.

ב) כֵּיוָן שֶׁהוֹלִיד בֵּן וּבַת, קִיֵּם מִצְוַת פְּרִיָּה וּרְבִיָּה. וְהוּא, שֶׁלֹּא יְהֵא הַבֵּן סָרִיס אוֹ הַבַּת אַיְלוֹנִית. נוֹלְדוּ לוֹ בֵּן וּבַת וָמֵתוּ, אִם הִנִּיחוּ בָּנִים, הֲרֵי זֶה קִיֵּם מִצְוַת פְּרִיָּה וּרְבִיָּה. בַּמֶּה דְּבָרִים אֲמוּרִים, כְּשֶׁהָיוּ בְּנֵי הַבָּנִים בֵּן וּבַת, וְנוֹלְדוּ מִן הַבֵּן וּמִן הַבַּת. אַף־עַל־פִּי שֶׁבְּנוֹ הוֹלִיד בַּת וּבִתּוֹ יָלְדָה בֵּן, הוֹאִיל וּבָאִים מִבְּנוֹ וּבִתּוֹ, קִיֵּם מִצְוַת פְּרִיָּה וּרְבִיָּה. אֲבָל אִם אֶחָד מֵהֶם לֹא הִנִּיחַ זֶרַע, אַף־עַל־פִּי שֶׁהַשֵּׁנִי הִנִּיחַ כַּמָּה בָנִים וּבָנוֹת, לֹא קִיֵּם הַמִּצְוָה.

ג) אַף־עַל־פִּי שֶׁקִּיֵּם מִצְוַת פְּרִיָּה וּרְבִיָּה, אָסוּר לוֹ לַעֲמֹד בְּלֹא אִשָּׁה. וְצָרִיךְ שֶׁיִּשָּׂא אִשָּׁה בַּת בָּנִים אִם אֶפְשָׁר לוֹ. אַךְ אִם הוּא מֵבִין בְּעַצְמוֹ שֶׁאֵינוֹ רָאוּי עוֹד לְהוֹלִיד, טוֹב לוֹ יוֹתֵר לִשָּׂא אִשָּׁה שֶׁאֵינָהּ בַּת בָּנִים. וְכֵן אִם יֵשׁ לוֹ בָּנִים הַרְבֵּה, וּמִתְיָרֵא שֶׁאִם יִשָּׂא אִשָּׁה בַּת בָּנִים, יָבוֹאוּ קְטָטוֹת וּמְרִיבוֹת בֵּין הַבָּנִים וּבֵין אִשְׁתּוֹ, מֻתָּר לוֹ לִשָּׂא אִשָּׁה שֶׁאֵינָהּ בַּת בָּנִים. אֲבָל אָסוּר לוֹ לֵישֵׁב בְּלֹא אִשָּׁה מִשּׁוּם חֲשָׁשָׁא זֹאת.

ד) נָשָׂא אִשָּׁה וְשָׁהֲתָה עִמּוֹ עֶשֶׂר שָׁנִים וְלֹא יָלְדָה, יֵשׁ לוֹ לְגָרְשָׁהּ, וְיֵשׁ בָּזֶה כַּמָּה חִלּוּקֵי דִינִים.

9) It is forbidden to make servile use of a *kohein*. This applies even in our time, and it is like taking unwarranted benefit of a sacred object. As it is said, "You shall sanctify him for he offers the bread of your God."[11] And even now though we have no sacrifices, he retains his sanctity. If the *kohein* wants to forego the honors due him, he may do so for the *kehunah* is his possession and he may forego its honors, and permit an Israelite to use him as a servant.[12] And certainly he may give the Israelite the honor of preceding him in the aforementioned matters.

Chapter 145

Laws Concerning Marriage

1) Every man is obligated to get married in order to fulfill the mitzvah of propagation. This mitzvah is incumbent on a man from the beginning of his eighteenth year[1]. At any rate, you should not pass your twentieth year without getting married. Only if you are diligently studying Torah and are afraid to marry in order not to be disrupted from learning Torah, are you permitted to delay marrying; and this is so, provided you are not overwhelmed with lustful desire.

2) When you have begotten a son and a daughter, you have fulfilled the mitzvah of propagation, provided the son is not impotent or the daughter sterile. If you had a son and a daughter who died, and they left surviving children, you have fulfilled the mitzvah of propagation. This is true only when the surviving grandchildren are a son and a daughter and were begotten from your son and your daughter, so that even if your son begot only a daughter, and your daughter begot only a son, since they come from your son and daughter, you have fulfilled the mitzvah of propagation. But if one of your children left no surviving children even though your other child left many surviving sons and daughters, you [the grandfather] have not fulfilled the mitzvah of propagation.

3) Even though you have fulfilled the mitzvah of propagation, you are forbidden to remain without a wife. You should marry a woman capable of bearing children if it is possible. But if you are aware that you are unable to have children, it is preferable that you marry a woman that is not able to bear children. Similarly, if you have many children, and you fear if you marry a woman capable of bearing children there will be bickering and quarrels between your children and your wife, you are permitted to marry a woman who is not capable of bearing children, but it is forbidden to remain unmarried because of this concern.

4) If a man takes a wife and she was with him ten years without bearing children, he should divorce her. Concerning this practice, there are many *halachic* details.

---

11. *Leviticus* 21:8.

12. *Mishnah Berurah* 128:175 maintains that you should be careful to follow the opinion of the *Taz* that this is not permitted unless the *kohein* derives a benefit from serving you.

1. *Magid Mishnah* rules that it means eighteen complete years.

ה) אִשָּׁה, אֵינָהּ מְצֻוָּה עַל פְּרִיָּה וּרְבִיָּה. וּמִכָּל מָקוֹם לֹא תַעֲמֹד בְּלֹא בַעַל, מִשּׁוּם חֲשָׁדָא.

ו) יִשְׁתַּדֵּל כָּל אָדָם לִקַּח אִשָּׁה הֲגוּנָה מִמִּשְׁפָּחָה הֲגוּנָה. שְׁלשָׁה סִימָנִים יֵשׁ לָהֶם לְיִשְׂרָאֵל, בַּיְשָׁנִים, רַחֲמָנִים, גּוֹמְלֵי חֲסָדִים. וּמִי שֶׁאֵין לוֹ סִימָנִים אֵלוּ, אֵינוֹ רָאוּי לְדָבֵק בּוֹ.

ז) אִשָּׁה כְּשֵׁרָה, אַף־עַל־פִּי שֶׁהוּא נוֹשֵׂא אוֹתָהּ בִּשְׁבִיל הַמָּמוֹן שֶׁיֵּשׁ לָהּ, מֻתָּר. וְדַוְקָא כְּשֶׁנּוֹתְנִים לוֹ אֶת הַמָּמוֹן בְּרָצוֹן טוֹב. אֲבָל אִם מְעַגֵּן אֶת עַצְמוֹ וּמַמְתִּין עַד שֶׁיִּמְצָא אִשָּׁה עִם מָמוֹן כְּחֶפְצוֹ, אוֹ שֶׁעָשָׂה שִׁדּוּכִין וּפָסְקוּ לוֹ מָמוֹן הַרְבֵּה וְחָזְרוּ בָהֶם וְהוּא מְעַגֵּן אֶת כַּלָּתוֹ בִּשְׁבִיל זֶה, אוֹ שֶׁהוּא מִתְקוֹטֵט בַּעֲבוּר זֶה, כָּל הָעוֹשֶׂה כֵּן, מִקְרֵי נוֹשֵׂא אִשָּׁה לְשֵׁם מָמוֹן, דַּהֲוָיָן לוֹ בָּנִים שֶׁאֵינָם מְהֻגָּנִים, וְאֵינוֹ מַצְלִיחַ, וְאֵין זִוּוּגוֹ עוֹלֶה יָפֶה. כִּי הַמָּמוֹן שֶׁהָאָדָם לוֹקֵחַ עִם אִשְׁתּוֹ, אֵינוֹ מָמוֹן שֶׁל יֹשֶׁר, אֶלָּא כָּל מַה שֶׁיִּתֵּן לוֹ חָמִיו וַחֲמוֹתוֹ, יִקַּח בְּעַיִן טוֹבָה, וְאָז יַצְלִיחַ.

ח) עַם־הָאָרֶץ, לֹא יִשָּׂא בַּת־כֹּהֵן, שֶׁאֵין זִוּוּגָם עוֹלֶה יָפֶה. וּמַאן דְּקָפֵיד, יֵשׁ לוֹ לְדַקְדֵּק שֶׁלֹּא יִשָּׂא אִשָּׁה שֶׁשְּׁמָהּ כְּשֵׁם אִמּוֹ.

ט) מִצְוָה לִשָּׂא בַּת אֲחוֹתוֹ אוֹ בַּת אָחִיו. אֲבָל שְׁאָר קְרוֹבָה, בֵּין שֶׁהִיא קְרוֹבָה לוֹ אוֹ לְאִשְׁתּוֹ שֶׁמֵּתָה אוֹ שֶׁגֵּרְשָׁהּ אוֹ שֶׁהִיא קְרוֹבָה לְאִשָּׁה שֶׁחָלַץ לָהּ, לֹא יִשָּׂא בְּלִי שְׁאֵלַת חָכָם.

י) לְעוֹלָם יְהֵא אָדָם זָהִיר בִּכְבוֹד אִשְׁתּוֹ שֶׁאֵין בְּרָכָה מְצוּיָה בְּבֵיתוֹ שֶׁל אָדָם אֶלָּא בִּשְׁבִיל אִשְׁתּוֹ, וְכָךְ אָמְרוּ חֲכָמִים לִבְנֵי דוֹרָם, כַּבְּדוּ אֶת נְשׁוֹתֵיכֶם כְּדֵי שֶׁתִּתְעַשְּׁרוּ.

יא) אָסוּר לִשְׁהוֹת עִם אִשְׁתּוֹ אֲפִלּוּ שָׁעָה אַחַת בְּלֹא כְּתֻבָּה. וְאִם אָבְדָה הַכְּתֻבָּה, צָרִיךְ לִזָּהֵר מְאֹד, שֶׁיֵּלֵךְ מִיָּד לְבֵית־הַדִּין לִכְתֹּב לָהּ כְּתֻבָּה אַחֶרֶת.

יב) כֹּהֵן אָסוּר בִּגְרוּשָׁה, בְּזוֹנָה, בַּחֲלָלָה, וּבַחֲלוּצָה. זוֹנָה, הַיְנוּ אֲפִלּוּ

---

2. Most *poskim* consider this a binding *halachah* but *Be'er Hetev* 1:27—considers this as just good advice.

3. The *Chavos Yair* Responsa 70 rules that this *halachah* does not apply to a man who is

5) A woman is not commanded to fulfill the mitzvah of propagation. Nevertheless, she should not remain unmarried[2] so as not to be subject to suspicion.

6) Every man should try to marry a worthy woman from a respectable family. The Jewish people have three traits: they are modest, compassionate, and benevolent. A person lacking these traits is not a commendable partner for marriage.

7) If a woman is suitable, even if you marry her because of her wealth, it is permitted, but only when the money is given willingly. But if you defer marriage and wait until you find a woman with the money you desire; or if you agreed to a marriage and was promised a great deal of money, and the promise was retracted, and you abandon your bride because of this, or you quarrel over this, you are referred to as "One who marries for money." You will have unworthy children, and will not be successful. Such a marriage will not be a happy one, for money that a man takes for marrying his wife is money not properly earned. But, rather, whatever is given to you by your father-in-law or mother-in-law you should accept graciously, and then you will be successful.

8) A man ignorant in Torah knowledge[3] should not marry the daughter of a *kohein* for such a marriage will not be a happy one. A scrupulous person should be particular not to marry a woman who has the same name as his mother.[4]

9) It is a mitzvah to marry your sister's daughter or your brother's daughter. You should not marry any other relative, whether she is related to you or to your deceased or divorced wife, or she is related to the woman to whom you have given *chalitzah,*[5] without consulting an *halachic* authority

10) You should be ever careful to honor your wife, for blessing is not found in a person's home but for the wife's sake. And so the Sages said to the men of their time, "Honor your wives so that you may be blessed with wealth."[6]

11) You may not dwell with your wife even for a short time without a *kesubah.*[7] If the *kesubah* is lost you must be very concerned and go immediately to the *Beis Din* to write another *kesubah* for her.

12) A *kohein* is forbidden to marry a divorcée, a harlot, a *chalalah*[8] or one to whom *chalitzah* was given. A woman is considered a harlot in this instance even if

---

ignorant in Torah knowledge but only to one who also fosters an extraordinary contempt for Torah scholars.

4. From the will of *Rabeinu Yehudah Hachassid.* When the situation arises, most authorities agree that it is sufficient to change the name of one of them by adding another name. Some prefer to change the names of both women.

5. *Chalitzah* means removing. Here it refers to a ritual that includes removing the sandal of her brother-in-law, in reference to the Law of Levirate. (*Yevomah*)

6. *Maseches Baba Metziah* (59a).

7. Marriage contract.

8. A *chalalah* is a woman who was born of a marriage between a *kohein* and a woman whom he was not permitted to marry, such as a divorcée etc. (see below)

נִבְעֲלָה בְּאֹנֶס בְּעִילַת אִסּוּר, נַעֲשְׂתָה זוֹנָה וַאֲסוּרָה לַכֹּהֵן. וַחֲלָלָה, הַיְנוּ שֶׁנּוֹלְדָה מִכֹּהֵן שֶׁנָּשָׂא אִשָּׁה הָאֲסוּרָה לוֹ.

יג) כָּל אִשָּׁה שֶׁנִּתְאַלְמְנָה אוֹ שֶׁנִּתְגָּרְשָׁה, לֹא תִנָּשֵׂא לְאִישׁ אַחֵר עַד שֶׁתַּמְתִּין תִּשְׁעִים יוֹם, חוּץ מִיּוֹם הַגֵּרוּשִׁין אוֹ מִיתַת בַּעְלָהּ, וְחוּץ מִיּוֹם הַנִּשּׂוּאִין, וַאֲפִלּוּ אִם הִיא אִשָּׁה שֶׁאֵינָהּ רְאוּיָה לָלֶדֶת. וַאֲפִלּוּ הָיָה בַּעְלָהּ הָרִאשׁוֹן בִּמְדִינַת הַיָּם אוֹ חָבוּשׁ בְּבֵית הָאֲסוּרִין, אֵין חִלּוּק. וַאֲפִלּוּ הִפִּילָה נֵפֶל בֵּינְתַיִם, לָא מַהֲנֵי לָהּ. וַאֲפִלּוּ לְהִתְקַשֵּׁר בְּשִׁדּוּכִין, אֲסוּרָה, אֶלָּא אִם כֵּן יִשָּׁבַע הַמְשַׁדֵּךְ, שֶׁלֹּא יִכָּנֵס לְתוֹךְ בֵּיתָהּ תּוֹךְ הַזְּמַן. אֲבָל הַמַּחֲזִיר גְּרוּשָׁתוֹ, אֵינוֹ צָרִיךְ לְהַמְתִּין.

יד) אִם הִיא מְעֻבֶּרֶת אוֹ מֵינִיקָה, לֹא תִנָּשֵׂא לְאִישׁ אַחֵר, עַד שֶׁיִּהְיֶה לַוָּלָד אַרְבָּעָה וְעֶשְׂרִים חֹדֶשׁ. וַאֲפִלּוּ יָלְדָה לְאַחַר שֶׁנִּתְגָּרְשָׁה אוֹ שֶׁנִּתְאַלְמְנָה, וְלֹא הִתְחִילָה לְהָנִיק, צְרִיכָה לְהַמְתִּין. וְאִם יֵשׁ אֵיזֶה עִנְיָן גָּדוֹל בַּדָּבָר, יַעֲשׂוּ שְׁאֵלַת חָכָם.

טו) אִשָּׁה שֶׁמֵּתוּ לָהּ שְׁנֵי אֲנָשִׁים, לֹא תִנָּשֵׂא לַשְּׁלִישִׁי בְּלִי שְׁאֵלַת חָכָם.

טז) אִשָּׁה שֶׁשָּׁמְעָה שֶׁמֵּת בַּעְלָהּ בְּמָקוֹם אַחֵר, אֲפִלּוּ שָׁמְעָה מִכַּמָּה אֲנָשִׁים כְּשֵׁרִים, לֹא תִנָּשֵׂא בְּלִי שְׁאֵלַת חָכָם.

יז) הַנֶּחְשָׁד עַל אֵשֶׁת־אִישׁ וְגֵרְשָׁהּ בַּעְלָהּ אוֹ שֶׁמֵּת, הֲרֵי זוֹ אֲסוּרָה לָזֶה הַנֶּחְשָׁד. שֶׁכְּשֵׁם שֶׁנֶּאֶסְרָה לַבַּעַל, כָּךְ נֶאֶסְרָה לַבּוֹעֵל. וַאֲפִלּוּ גֵּרְשָׁהּ בַּעְלָהּ רַק מֵחֲמַת דָּבָר מְכֹעָר שֶׁשָּׁמַע עָלֶיהָ עִם הַנֶּחְשָׁד, אָסוּר לְהַנֶּחְשָׁד שֶׁיִּשָּׂא אוֹתָהּ.

יח) הַנֶּחְשָׁד עַל הַנָּכְרִית וְנִתְגַּיְּרָה, לֹא יִשָּׂאֶנָּה.

יט) נָכְרִי הַבָּא עַל בַּת יִשְׂרָאֵל וְאַחַר כָּךְ נִתְגַּיֵּר, לֹא יִשָּׂאֶנָּה.

כ) הַמְגָרֵשׁ אֶת הָאִשָּׁה כְּדֵי שֶׁיִּשָּׂא אוֹתָהּ חֲבֵרוֹ, אֲפִלּוּ לֹא הִתְנָה עִמָּהּ בְּפֵרוּשׁ, אֶלָּא שֶׁנִּכָּר שֶׁנִּתְגָּרְשָׁה בִּשְׁבִיל זֶה, אָסוּר לוֹ שֶׁיִּשָּׂא אוֹתָהּ.

---

9. This is a Rabbinic injunction designed to eleminate any chance of someone marrying his sister. This can happen if there is doubt as to who is really the father; the first or the second husband. This waiting period leaves no room for doubt. See *Maseches Yevamos* (41B). *Beis Shmuel* 13:1.

10. It is a sign that perhaps this woman's lot causes her husbands to die.

11. Much depends on the circumstances surrounding their deaths.

she was forced to have illicit intercourse and is forbidden to a *kohein*. A *chalalah* is a woman born to a *kohein* who married a woman forbidden to him.

13) Any woman who was widowed or divorced must wait ninety days[9] excluding the day of her divorce or her husband's death and excluding her wedding day before marrying another man. This is the *halachah* even if she is a woman incapable of bearing a child. Even if her first husband was overseas; or incarcerated in prison, it makes no difference. Even if she miscarried in the interim, it is to no avail. She is forbidden even to get engaged [during this waiting period,] unless her intended husband vows not to enter her house during this waiting period. But one who remarries his divorcée need not wait.

14) If the aforementioned woman is pregnant or is nursing an infant, she may not marry *another* man until the child is twenty four months old. Even if she gave birth after she was divorced or widowed and has not yet begun to nurse, she must wait. If a very important matter is involved, they should consult an *halachic* authority.

15) A woman whose two husbands died, should not marry a third one[10] without consulting an *halachic* authority.[11]

16) If a woman heard that her husband died in some other place, even if she heard this from many trustworthy men, she should not remarry without consulting an *halachic* authority.

17) If a man is suspected of committing adultery with a married woman, and her husband divorced her or died, she is forbidden to [marry] that suspected man,[12] for just as she became forbidden to her husband, so too she is forbidden to the one who committed adultery with her. Even if her husband divorced her only because of improper conduct that was rumored about her regarding that suspected man, the suspect is forbidden to marry her.[13]

18) One who is suspected of having intercourse with a non-Jewess, who subsequently converted to Judaism, is forbidden to marry her.

19) A non-Jew who had intercourse with a Jewess, and subsequently converted to Judaism, is forbidden to marry her.

20) If one divorces his wife so that she can marry a particular man, even though he did not expressly make this conditional but it is evident that this is the objective of the divorce, it is forbidden for that individual to marry her.

---

12. This is a Biblical ordinance, and refers only when her husband had warned her that she not dare be alone with that man, and she was caught being alone with him. Although there were no witnesses that actual adultery had been committed, nonetheless, she is called a *sotah* and is forbidden to her husband (until she is proven innocent by the ritual involving drinking the *Sotah* water in the *Beis Hamikdash*). Subsequently, she is also forbidden to the suspect even after she is divorced or widowed.

13. In this case it is a Rabbinic injunction.

כא) אוֹתָן שֶׁאָמְרוּ רַבּוֹתֵינוּ זִכְרוֹנָם לִבְרָכָה, שֶׁלֹּא יִשָּׂא אוֹתָן, אֲפִלּוּ בְּאוֹתוֹ מָבוֹי שֶׁהוּא דָר, לֹא תָדוּר הִיא.

כב) מִי שֶׁשָּׁמַע עַל אִשְׁתּוֹ שֶׁזִּנְּתָה, אַף־עַל־פִּי שֶׁאֵין הַדָּבָר בָּרוּר לוֹ, צָרִיךְ לַעֲשׂוֹת שְׁאֵלַת חָכָם, אִם מֻתָּר לוֹ לָדוּר עִמָּהּ.

כג) אִשָּׁה שֶׁנִּתְגָּרְשָׁה מִשּׁוּם פְּרִיצוּת, אֵין רָאוּי לְאָדָם כָּשֵׁר שֶׁיִּשָּׂאֶנָּה.

כד) אִשָּׁה רָעָה בְּדֵעוֹתֶיהָ, שֶׁהִיא בַּעֲלַת מְרִיבָה, וְשֶׁאֵינָהּ צְנוּעָה כִּבְנוֹת יִשְׂרָאֵל הַכְּשֵׁרוֹת, מִצְוָה לְגָרְשָׁהּ, אֲפִלּוּ בְּזִוּוּג רִאשׁוֹן.

כה) מִצְוַת חֲכָמִים, שֶׁיַּשִּׂיא אָדָם בָּנָיו וּבְנוֹתָיו סָמוּךְ לְפִרְקָן, שֶׁאִם יַנִּיחֵן, יָבוֹאוּ לִידֵי זְנוּת אוֹ לִידֵי הִרְהוּר. וְעַל זֶה נֶאֱמַר, וּפָקַדְתָּ נָוְךָ וְלֹא תֶחֱטָא. וְכֵן מִצְוַת חֲכָמִים עַל בְּנֵי יִשְׂרָאֵל, שֶׁמִּי שֶׁרוֹאֶה שֶׁאִשְׁתּוֹ אֵינָהּ הוֹלֶכֶת בְּדֶרֶךְ יְשָׁרָה וְיֵשׁ לָהּ אֵיזוֹ קֻרְבוּת עִם אֲנָשִׁים אֲחֵרִים, שֶׁיּוֹכִיחַ אוֹתָהּ וְיַזְהִיר אוֹתָהּ בֵּינוֹ לְבֵינָהּ בְּנַחַת וּבְדֶרֶךְ טָהֳרָה, כְּדֵי לְהָסִיר אֶת הַמִּכְשׁוֹל וּלְהַדְרִיכָהּ בְּדֶרֶךְ יְשָׁרָה. אֲבָל אַל יֹאמַר לָהּ בְּפֵרוּשׁ, אַל תִּסָּתְרִי עִם פְּלוֹנִי, וַאֲפִלּוּ בֵּינוֹ לְבֵינָהּ, (מֵאַחַר שֶׁעַכְשָׁו אֵין לָנוּ מֵי סוֹטָה, וְיֵשׁ בָּזֶה מְבוּכָה). וְכָל מִי שֶׁאֵינוֹ מַקְפִּיד עַל אִשְׁתּוֹ וְעַל בָּנָיו וְעַל בְּנֵי בֵיתוֹ [וְאֵינוֹ] מַזְהִירָן וּפוֹקֵד דַּרְכֵיהֶם תָּמִיד עַד שֶׁיֵּדַע שֶׁהֵם שְׁלֵמִים מִכָּל חֵטְא וְעָוֹן — הֲרֵי זֶה חוֹטֵא, שֶׁנֶּאֱמַר, וְיָדַעְתָּ כִּי שָׁלוֹם אָהֳלֶךָ וּפָקַדְתָּ נָוְךָ וְלֹא תֶחֱטָא.

כו) אָסוּר לַעֲשׂוֹת שְׁתֵּי חֻפּוֹת לִשְׁנֵי אַחִים אוֹ לִשְׁתֵּי אֲחָיוֹת בְּיוֹם אֶחָד, מִשּׁוּם דְּאֵין מְעָרְבִין שִׂמְחָה בְּשִׂמְחָה. וְיֵשׁ אוֹמְרִים, דַּאֲפִלּוּ בְּשָׁבוּעַ אֶחָד אֵין לַעֲשׂוֹתָן, וּרְאָיָה מִיַּעֲקֹב אָבִינוּ, דִּכְתִיב, מַלֵּא שְׁבֻעַ זֹאת.

סִימָן קמו
מִנְהֲגֵי תַּעֲנִית חָתָן וְכַלָּה

א) נוֹהֲגִין שֶׁהֶחָתָן וְהַכַּלָּה מִתְעַנִּין בְּיוֹם חֻפָּתָן, מִפְּנֵי שֶׁבְּאוֹתוֹ־יוֹם מוֹחֲלִין לָהֶם עֲוֹנוֹתֵיהֶם. וְאוֹמְרִים בִּתְפִלַּת הַמִּנְחָה עֲנֵנוּ, כְּמוֹ בִּשְׁאָר תַּעֲנִיּוֹת. וְנוֹהֲגִין בִּמְדִינוֹת אֵלּוּ, שֶׁאֵין מִתְעַנִּין אֶלָּא עַד לְאַחַר הַחֻפָּה.

---

14. *Job* 5:24 נָוְךָ "Your habitation" refers to your wife.
15. See note 12.

21) Those women whom the Sages, of blessed memory, have forbidden one to marry, may not dwell even in the closed alley in which he dwells.

22) If a man heard that his wife committed adultery, even though he is not certain about it, he must consult an *halachic* authority if he is permitted to live with her.

23) It is not befitting for a respectable man to marry a woman who was divorced because of immodesty.

24) If a woman has bad character traits such as a quarrelsome disposition, or she is not modest as are respectable Jewish women, it is a mitzvah to divorce her, even if it is the first marriage.

25) The Sages have ordained that a man should marry off his sons and daughters when they reach maturity, for if he neglects to do so they may be tempted into prostitution, or to have lewd thoughts. Concerning this it says, "And you shall visit your habitation and you will not sin."[14] Also the Sages commanded the *Bnei Yisrael*, that whoever sees that his wife is not conducting herself properly, and is somewhat intimate with other men, he should admonish her and caution her, privately, gently, and in a pure way, to prevent her from stumbling, and to influence her to conduct herself properly. But he should not say to her expressly, "Do not meet in private with so and so." (You should not say this) even privately, (since presently we do not have *Mei sotah*[15] this can lead to serious problems). If you are not strict with your wife and your children, and all the members of your household to caution them and to constantly supervise their conduct until you are confident they are perfectly free of sin and iniquity, you are considered a sinner. For it is said, "And you shall know that peace is in your tent and you shall visit your habitation and not sin."[16]

26) It is forbidden to perform the marriage ceremonies of two brothers or of two sisters in the same day, because you may not join one festive event with another. Some [authorities] say that you may not perform both ceremonies even in the same week,[17] and they bring proof [of this from the marriage] of our father, Yaakov. For it is written, "Fulfill the week of this one."[18]

Chapter 146

The Fast of the Bridegroom and Bride

1) It is customary that the bridegroom and the bride fast on their wedding day because on that day their sins are forgiven. They should say *Aneinu*[1] at *Minchah* as on other fast days. In our area it is customary that they fast only until after the

---

16. *Job* 5:24. However, if there is no peace in your home, you will have then sinned.

17. *Taz* 548:1—*Rabbeinu Yehudah Hachassid.* See *Sha'ar Hatziyun* 546:3 who rules against this opinion, for *Rashal* stated it is a printing error as it contradicts the Talmud that permits one to marry less than a week before *Yom Tov.*

18. *Genesis* 29:27.

1. See Chapter 19.

וְאִם נִתְאַחֲרָה הַחֻפָּה בַּלַּיְלָה, אֲזַי לְאַחַר צֵאת הַכּוֹכָבִים, יְכוֹלִים לֶאֱכֹל אֵיזֶה דָבָר, וּבִלְבַד שֶׁלֹּא יִשְׁתּוּ מַשְׁקֶה הַמְשַׁכֵּר.

ב) בְּרֹאשׁ־חֹדֶשׁ, וּבְאִסְרוּ־חַג דְּשָׁבוּעוֹת, וּבַחֲמִשָּׁה־עָשָׂר בְּאָב, וּבַחֲמִשָּׁה־עָשָׂר בִּשְׁבָט, וְכֵן בַּחֲנֻכָּה, וּבְשׁוּשַׁן פּוּרִים, אֵין מִתְעַנִּין. אֲבָל בְּנִיסָן, אֲפִלּוּ בְּרֹאשׁ־חֹדֶשׁ נִיסָן, מִתְעַנִּין. וְכֵן בְּל"ג בָּעֹמֶר, וּבְיָמִים שֶׁבֵּין רֹאשׁ־חֹדֶשׁ סִיוָן לְשָׁבוּעוֹת, וּבְיָמִים שֶׁבֵּין יוֹם הַכִּפּוּרִים לְסֻכּוֹת, מִתְעַנִּין.

ג) בְּיָמִים שֶׁאֵין מִתְעַנִּין, צְרִיכִין לִזָּהֵר שֶׁלֹּא לִרְדֹּף אַחֲרֵי מוֹתָרוֹת מַאֲכָל וּמִשְׁתֶּה. וּמִכָּל־שֶׁכֵּן שֶׁיִּזָּהֲרוּ מְאֹד מִמַּשְׁקֶה הַמְשַׁכֵּר, (כִּי יֵשׁ אוֹמְרִים, טַעַם הַתַּעֲנִית, מִשּׁוּם דְּחָיְשִׁינָן שֶׁמָּא יִשְׁתַּכְּרוּ וְלֹא תְהֵא דַעְתָּם מְיֻשֶּׁבֶת).

ד) צְרִיכִין הֶחָתָן וְהַכַּלָּה לְקַדֵּשׁ עַצְמָם בִּמְאֹד מְאֹד בְּהִכָּנְסָם לַחֻפָּה, וְיַעֲשׂוּ תְשׁוּבָה בַּיּוֹם הַהוּא, וִיפַשְׁפְּשׁוּ בְּמַעֲשֵׂיהֶם מִיּוֹם הִוָּלְדָם עַד הַיּוֹם הַזֶּה, וְיִתְוַדּוּ וִיבַקְשׁוּ מְחִילָה וּסְלִיחָה וְכַפָּרָה מֵהַשֵּׁם יִתְבָּרַךְ, וְיִהְיוּ מוֹדִים וְעוֹזְבִים, וְיִתְחָרְטוּ חֲרָטָה גְמוּרָה בְּשִׁבְרוֹן לֵב, וְיַעֲשׂוּ הַסְכָּמָה חֲזָקָה מֵהַיּוֹם וָהָלְאָה לַעֲבוֹד אֶת ה' בֶּאֱמֶת וּבְתָמִים וְלִהְיוֹתָם קְדוֹשִׁים וּטְהוֹרִים. וְאַחַר כָּךְ יִכָּנְסוּ לַחֻפָּה, וְיִתְפַּלְּלוּ שֶׁהַקָּדוֹשׁ־בָּרוּךְ־הוּא יַשְׁרֶה שְׁכִינָתוֹ בֵּינֵיהֶם, וּכְמוֹ שֶׁאָמְרוּ חֲכָמֵינוּ זִכְרוֹנָם לִבְרָכָה, אִישׁ וְאִשָּׁה, שְׁכִינָה בֵּינֵיהֶם וְנוֹהֲגִין שֶׁאוֹמְרִים הַוִּדּוּי בִּתְפִלַּת מִנְחָה, כְּמוֹ בְּעֶרֶב יוֹם־הַכִּפּוּרִים.

סִימָן קמז
מִנְהֲגֵי הַחֻפָּה

א) נוֹהֲגִין לַעֲשׂוֹת הַחֻפָּה תַּחַת הַשָּׁמַיִם לְסִימָן בְּרָכָה, כֹּה יִהְיֶה זַרְעֲךָ כְּכוֹכְבֵי הַשָּׁמָיִם. וְכֵן נוֹהֲגִין שֶׁאֵין נוֹשְׂאִין נָשִׁים אֶלָּא בְּמִלּוּי הַלְּבָנָה, לְסִימָן טוֹב.

ב) כָּשֵׁר הַדָּבָר שֶׁלֹּא תִנָּשֵׂא, עַד שֶׁתִּטְהָר. וְעַכְשָׁו הַמִּנְהָג שֶׁלֹּא לְדַקְדֵּק. וּמִכָּל מָקוֹם טוֹב לְהוֹדִיעַ לְהֶחָתָן קֹדֶם הַחֻפָּה, שֶׁהִיא נִדָּה.

---

2. It is best that they state before starting the fast, that they are fasting only until the marriage ceremony. (*Mishnah Berurah* 562:12).

3. *Mishnah Berurah* 573:7 rules that there is no difference between the day after *Shavuos*

marriage ceremony.[2] If the ceremony is delayed till the night, then, after the stars appear, they may eat something, provided they do not drink any intoxicating beverages.

2) On *Rosh Chodesh,* on the day after *Shavuos,*[3] on the fifteenth day of the month of *Av,* on the fifteenth day of the month of *Shevat,* and also on *Chanukah* and on *Shushan Purim,* they do not fast. But in the month of *Nissan,* even on *Rosh Chodesh (Nissan)* they do fast. And so too on the thirty-third day of the *Omer,*[4] and on the days between *Rosh Chodesh Sivan* and *Shavuos,* and on the days between *Yom Kippur* and *Sukkos,* they fast.[5]

3) On the days they do not fast, they must be careful not to indulge in excessive food and drink; and certainly they must be very careful to abstain from intoxicating beverages. (For some authorities say the very reason for the fast is because we are concerned they may become intoxicated and their minds would not be lucid).

4) The bridegroom and the bride must conduct themselves with utmost sanctity when they enter the *chupah,* and they should repent on that day. They should search [review] their deeds from the day of their birth until this day, and they should confess [their sins,] and seek forgiveness, pardon, and atonement from Hashem, Blessed is He. They should confess and forsake (their evil ways). Their absolute remorse should emanate from a contrite heart. They should firmly resolve from this day onward to serve Hashem honestly and sincerely, and to be holy and pure. They should then enter the *chupah* and pray that the Holy one, Blessed is He, rest His Divine Presence between them, as our Sages of blessed memory said, "A husband and wife, (if deserving), the Divine Presence is between them."[6] It is customary for them to say the confession at the *Minchah* prayer as is done the day before *Yom Kippur.*

Chapter 147

The Nuptial Ceremony

1) It is customary to have the *chupah* under the open sky as a good omen (as it is written),[1] "So will your children be, like the stars of the heavens." Similarly it is customary to marry only in the phase of the full moon as a good omen.

2) It is proper not to marry until the bride purifies herself. It is now the custom not to be exacting about this. However, it is best to inform the bridegroom before the *chupah,* that she is a *niddah.*[2]

---

and the day after *Pesach* or *Sukkos.* Also see *Kitzur Shulchan Aruch* 103:14 that this fast does not take place on the day after *Pesach* and *Sukkos.*

4. See Chapter 120.

5. *Rama* 573:1. *Mishnah Berurah* cites those *poskim* who are lenient and who rule that they need not fast on any day *Tachnun* is not said.

6. Maseches Sotah 17a.

1. *Genesis* 15:5.

2. Menstrually unclean.

ג) הַמִּנְהָג בִּמְדִינוֹת אֵלּוּ בְּנִשּׂוּאֵי בְתוּלָה, שֶׁחֲשׁוּבֵי הָעִיר פּוֹרְסִין סוּדָר עַל רֹאשׁ הַכַּלָּה, וּמְבָרְכִים אוֹתָהּ וְאוֹמְרִים לָהּ, אֲחוֹתֵנוּ, אַתְּ הֲיִי לְאַלְפֵי רְבָבָה. וְחֻפָּה קוֹרִין מַה שֶּׁאַחַר כָּךְ פּוֹרְסִין יְרִיעָה עַל גַּבֵּי כְּלוֹנְסָאוֹת, וּמַכְנִיסִין תַּחְתֶּיהָ הֶחָתָן וְהַכַּלָּה בָּרַבִּים, וּמְקַדְּשָׁהּ שָׁם, וּמְבָרְכִין שָׁם בִּרְכוֹת אֵרוּסִין וְנִשּׂוּאִין. אֲבָל עִקַּר הַחֻפָּה הוּא הַיִּחוּד, שֶׁיִּתְבָּאֵר אִם יִרְצֶה הַשֵּׁם בְּסִימָן שֶׁאַחַר זֶה.

ד) הַשּׁוֹשְׁבִינִים מַלְבִּישִׁים אֶת הֶחָתָן בְּקִיטֶל, כְּדֵי שֶׁיִּזְכֹּר אֶת יוֹם הַמִּיתָה וְיִתְעוֹרֵר בִּתְשׁוּבָה. גַּם נוֹהֲגִין לָתֵת אֵפֶר בְּרֹאשׁ הֶחָתָן בִּמְקוֹם הַנָּחַת הַתְּפִלִּין. גַּם נוֹהֲגִין שֶׁהָאָבוֹת וְהַקְּרוֹבִים אַנְשֵׁי צוּרָה מְבָרְכִים אֶת הֶחָתָן וְאֶת הַכַּלָּה וּמִתְפַּלְּלִים עֲלֵיהֶם, שֶׁזִּוּוּגָם יַעֲלֶה יָפֶה.

ה) אַחַר כָּךְ מוֹלִיכִין אֶת הֶחָתָן תַּחַת הַחֻפָּה, (שֶׁפּוֹרְסִין יְרִיעָה עַל גַּבֵּי כְּלוֹנְסָאוֹת, שֶׁאָנוּ קוֹרִין חֻפָּה), וּמַעֲמִידִין אוֹתוֹ פָּנָיו לַמִּזְרָח, וּשְׁלִיחַ־הַצִּבּוּר מְנַגֵּן כְּמִנְהַג הַמָּקוֹם, וְהַשּׁוֹשְׁבִינוֹת מוֹלִיכוֹת אֶת הַכַּלָּה, וְהַשּׁוֹשְׁבִינִים וַאֲנָשִׁים חֲשׁוּבִים הוֹלְכִים לִקְרָאתָהּ. וּכְשֶׁמִּתְקָרְבִים אֵלֶיהָ, חוֹזְרִים לַאֲחוֹרֵיהֶם לַחֻפָּה, וְהַשּׁוֹשְׁבִינוֹת מְבִיאוֹת אֶת הַכַּלָּה וּמְסוֹבְבוֹת עִמָּהּ שֶׁבַע פְּעָמִים אֶת הֶחָתָן, וּשְׁלִיחַ־הַצִּבּוּר מְנַגֵּן גַּם כֵּן כְּפִי הַמִּנְהָג. אַחַר כָּךְ מַעֲמִידִין אֶת הַכַּלָּה לִימִין הֶחָתָן, וְהַמְבָרֵךְ מְצַדֵּד אֶת עַצְמוֹ וּפָנָיו לַמִּזְרָח.

סִימָן קמח
יִחוּד שֶׁאַחַר הַקִּדּוּשִׁין

א) עִקַּר הַחֻפָּה הוּא מַה שֶּׁאַחַר הַקִּדּוּשִׁין מוֹלִיכִין אֶת הֶחָתָן וְהַכַּלָּה לְחֶדֶר מְיֻחָד, וְאוֹכְלִים שָׁם יַחַד בְּמָקוֹם צָנוּעַ. וְיֵשׁ לִמְנֹעַ, שֶׁלֹּא יִכָּנֵס לְשָׁם שׁוּם אָדָם, כְּדֵי שֶׁיִּהְיֶה יִחוּד גָּמוּר, וְזוֹהִי הַחֻפָּה הַקּוֹנָה וְעוֹשָׂה נִשּׂוּאִין.

ב) בִּבְתוּלָה, קוֹנֶה יִחוּד זֶה, אַף־עַל־גַּב דְּאֵינוֹ רָאוּי לְבִיאָה, כְּגוֹן שֶׁהִיא נִדָּה, אוֹ שֶׁבְּנֵי אָדָם נִכְנָסִין וְיוֹצְאִין שָׁם. (וּכְשֶׁהִיא נִדָּה,

---

3. *Genesis* 25:60.
4. A white shroud like garment.

3) It is the custom in our areas that at the marriage of a virgin, the distinguished persons of the community spread a veil over the bride's head, and bless her, saying, "Our sister, be the mother of thousands and myriads."[3] We refer to the *chupah* as the next sequence when a cloth is spread upon poles, under which the groom and bride enter in public, and where he consecrates her to himself. This is where the *berachos* of betrothal and marriage are recited. However, the most essential part of the *chupah* is the intimate privacy, which will be explained, God willing, in the following chapter.

4) The groomsmen [or the father] enrobe the bridegroom with a *kittle*[4], so that he is reminded of the day of death, and be inspired to repent. It is also customary[5] to place ashes on the groom's head on the place where the *tefillin shel rosh* is worn. It is also customary that the parents and prominent relatives bless the groom and the bride and pray that their union be successful.

5) Thereafter the groom is led under the *chupah* (canopy) (for we spread a cloth upon poles which is what we refer to as *chupah*), and we place him [under the *chupah*] facing East, while the *chazan* chants whatever chant is customary in that community. Then the bridesmaids lead the bride (to the *chupah*). The groomsmen and prominent men walk toward the bride, and as they approach her, they turn around and proceed to the *chupah*. Then the bridesmaids bring the bride [under the *chupah*], and together with her, walk around the groom seven times. The *chazan* again chants in accordance with the custom. After that, they place the bride to the right of the groom, and the one who recites the *berachos* stands to the side and faces the East.

Chapter 148

The Privacy Following the Marriage Ceremony

1) The most essential part of the *chupah* is bringing the groom and the bride to a designated private room,[1] where they eat together in privacy following the *kidushin*[2]. You must prevent anybody from entering that room so that there may be absolute privacy. This is the real *chupah* that consummates and completes the marriage.[3]

2) In the case of a virgin, this *yichud* (privacy) consummates the marriage even if it is not fit for cohabitation, if for example, she is a *niddah,* or if people are going in and out of the room. (When she is a *niddah* it is mandatory that people should

---

5. *Shulchan Aruch* 560:2. It is difficult to understand why many are not accustomed to do so. (*Biur Halachah* 560—*Chayei Adam*)

1. It must be designated specifically for the groom, so that it is like his house, into which he is bringing his wife. (*Mishnah Berurah* 339:32)

2. The act of consecrating the woman to be his wife.

3. *Beis Shmuel* 55:5.

בְּעַל־כָּרְחָם צְרִיכִין שֶׁיִּהְיוּ בְּנֵי אָדָם נִכְנָסִין וְיוֹצְאִין שָׁם, דְּאִם לֹא כֵן, אֲסוּרִין לְהִתְיַחֵד קֹדֶם בִּיאָה רִאשׁוֹנָה).

ג) אֲבָל בְּאַלְמָנָה, אֵינוֹ קוֹנֶה אֶלָּא יִחוּד הָרָאוּי לַבִּיאָה, דְּהַיְנוּ שֶׁהִיא טְהוֹרָה וְאֵין אָדָם נִכְנָס לְשָׁם.

ד) אֵין עוֹשִׂין קִנְיָן בַּשַּׁבָּת. וְלָכֵן אִם הַנִּשּׂוּאִין בְּעֶרֶב שַׁבָּת, צְרִיכִין לִזָּהֵר מְאֹד שֶׁיִּהְיֶה יִחוּד הַקּוֹנֶה קֹדֶם שַׁבָּת. וַאֲזַי כְּשֶׁנַּעֲשָׂה הַיִּחוּד הַקּוֹנֶה מִבְּעוֹד יוֹם, מֻתָּר לָבוֹא עָלֶיהָ בִּיאָה רִאשׁוֹנָה בַּשַּׁבָּת, בֵּין בִּבְתוּלָה בֵּין בְּאַלְמָנָה. אֲבָל אִם לֹא נַעֲשָׂה הַיִּחוּד הַקּוֹנֶה מִבְּעוֹד יוֹם, אָז אָסוּר לָבוֹא עָלֶיהָ בַּשַּׁבָּת בִּיאָה רִאשׁוֹנָה, מִשּׁוּם דְּהַבִּיאָה עוֹשָׂה אֶת הַקִּנְיָן, וְאֵין קוֹנִין בַּשַּׁבָּת.

סִימָן קמט
דִּינֵי בִּרְכַּת־הַמָּזוֹן בַּנִּשּׂוּאִין וּמִצְוַת שִׂמְחַת חָתָן וְכַלָּה

א) קֹדֶם בִּרְכַּת־הַמָּזוֹן בַּעֲשָׂרָה אוֹמֵר הַמְבָרֵךְ, דְּוַי הָסֵר וְכוּ'. וְאוֹמְרִים שֶׁהַשִּׂמְחָה בִּמְעוֹנוֹ. וְיֵשׁ לוֹמַר, שֶׁאָכַלְנוּ מִשֶּׁלּוֹ בְּלֹא וָא"ו, וְלֹא וְשֶׁאָכַלְנוּ מִשֶּׁלּוֹ. וְאַחַר בִּרְכַּת־הַמָּזוֹן לוֹקֵחַ כּוֹס שֵׁנִי וְאוֹמֵר עָלָיו שֵׁשׁ בְּרָכוֹת, וְאַחַר כָּךְ מְבָרֵךְ עַל הַכּוֹס שֶׁל בִּרְכַּת־הַמָּזוֹן בּוֹרֵא פְּרִי הַגָּפֶן. וְטוֹב שֶׁלֹּא לְמַלֹּאת אֶת הַכּוֹס לְשֵׁשׁ הַבְּרָכוֹת עַד לְאַחַר בִּרְכַּת־הַמָּזוֹן. צְרִיכִין לִזָּהֵר שֶׁלֹּא יֹאכְלוּ אֲנָשִׁים וְנָשִׁים בְּחֶדֶר אֶחָד. שֶׁאִם אוֹכְלִים אֲנָשִׁים וְנָשִׁים בְּחֶדֶר אֶחָד, אֵין אוֹמְרִים שֶׁהַשִּׂמְחָה בִּמְעוֹנוֹ, כִּי אֵין שִׂמְחָה כְּשֶׁיֵּצֶר־הָרַע שׁוֹלֵט.

ב) בָּחוּר שֶׁנָּשָׂא בְתוּלָה אוֹ אַלְמָנָה, וְכֵן אַלְמָן שֶׁנָּשָׂא בְתוּלָה, מְבָרְכִין כֵּן בַּסְּעוּדָה הָרִאשׁוֹנָה שֶׁאַחֲרֵי הַנִּשּׂוּאִין, אֲפִלּוּ לֹא אֲכָלוּהָ בַּיּוֹם, רַק בַּלַּיְלָה שֶׁלְּאַחַר יוֹם הַנִּשּׂוּאִין, אוֹ אֲפִלּוּ בַּיּוֹם שֶׁלְּאַחֲרָיו, (מִשּׁוּם דְּהַסְּעוּדָה הָרִאשׁוֹנָה הֲוֵי כְּפָנִים חֲדָשׁוֹת). אֲבָל אַחַר הַסְּעוּדָה הָרִאשׁוֹנָה, וְכֵן בְּכָל שִׁבְעַת יְמֵי הַמִּשְׁתֶּה, אִם בָּאוּ פָּנִים חֲדָשׁוֹת, מְבָרְכִין כֵּן.

ג) וּכְשֶׁאֵין פָּנִים חֲדָשׁוֹת, אִם סוֹעֲדִים עִם הֶחָתָן אֲנָשִׁים שֶׁאֵינָם מִבְּנֵי־בֵיתוֹ מֵחֲמַת שִׂמְחַת מֵרֵעוּת, אֵין אוֹמְרִים דְּוַי הָסֵר וְכוּ', וְאוֹמְרִים נוֹדֶה לְשִׁמְךָ וְכוּ', וְהַשִּׂמְחָה בִּמְעוֹנוֹ. וְאַחַר בִּרְכַּת־הַמָּזוֹן, לוֹקֵחַ כּוֹס שֵׁנִי וְאוֹמֵר בִּרְכַּת אֲשֶׁר בָּרָא שָׂשׂוֹן וְשִׂמְחָה וְכוּ', וְאַחַר כָּךְ לוֹקֵחַ הַכּוֹס שֶׁל

be going in and out of the room for if not, they are forbidden to have privacy prior to their first cohabitation.)

3) In the case of a widow the marriage is consummated only when their privacy is appropriate for cohabitation, which means she must be menstrually clean, and no one is able to enter the room.

4) An acquisition may not be made on Shabbos, and therefore if the wedding took place on Friday, great care must be taken that the *yichud* consummating the marriage be made before Shabbos sets in. And then, when the *yichud* consummating the marriage was made while it was yet day, he is permitted to have the initial marital relations on Shabbos, regardless if she is a virgin or a widow. But if the *yichud* was not made while it was yet day (before Shabbos), then he is forbidden to approach her on Shabbos, for their initial marital relations. This is because cohabitation completes the acquisition, and it is forbidden to make an acquisition on Shabbos.

Chapter 149

The Laws of Birkas Hamazon for Weddings and the Mitzvah to Gladden the Bride and Groom

1) Before saying *Birkas Hamazon*, in the company of ten adult males, the leader says *Dvai Hoser* etc. (banish sorrow etc.), and *Shehasimcha bimono* (In Whose abode is joy). *Sheachalnu mishelo* (We have eaten of His bounty) is said without the letter *vav* as a conjunction, and not *vesheachalnu mishelo.* After concluding the *Birkas Hamazon* the leader takes a second cup (of wine) over which he recites six *berachos.* After this, he says over the (first cup), which is the cup of *Birkas Hamazon*, the berachah *Borei peri Hagaffen* (Creator of the fruit of the vine). It is best not to fill the cup for the six *berachos* until the conclusion of *Birkas Hamazon.* Care should be taken that men and women should not eat [together] in one room, for if men and women eat [together] in one room *Shehasimcha Bimono* cannot be said, because there is no joy [in the Heavens] where the evil inclination reigns.

2) If a young man [one who was never married] married a virgin or a widow, or if a widower married a virgin, the above mentioned *berachos* are said after the first meal following the wedding, even if they did not eat it on that day, but only at night following the day of the wedding, or even on the following day (because the first meal is considered as if new guests are participating). But after this first meal, and during the entire seven days of the wedding week, only if new guests come to participate is *Birkas Hamazon* recited in this manner.

3) When a new guest does not come to participate, and the men dining with the groom are not members of his family, but come to celebrate as friends, *Dvai Hoser* is not said, but *nodeh leshimecha* is said as well as *shehasimcha bimono.* After concluding *Birkas Hamazon*, the leader takes a second cup, and recites the berachah *asher bara sassone vesimcha* etc. After that he again takes the cup that was used for *Birkas*

בִּרְכַּת־הַמָּזוֹן וְאוֹמֵר עָלָיו בּוֹרֵא פְּרִי הַגָּפֶן, וְלָזֶה אֵינוֹ צָרִיךְ עֲשָׂרָה, רַק גַּם בִּשְׁלֹשָׁה, מְבָרְכִין. אֲבָל אִם אֵינוֹ סוֹעֵד רַק עִם בְּנֵי־בֵיתוֹ לְבַד, אֵינוֹ אוֹמֵר כְּלוּם מִזֶּה.

ד) אַלְמָן שֶׁנָּשָׂא אַלְמָנָה, אִם אָכְלוּ סְעוּדָה הָרִאשׁוֹנָה בְּיוֹם הַנִּשּׂוּאִין, אַף־עַל־פִּי שֶׁנִּמְשְׁכָה הַסְּעוּדָה גַּם בַּלַּיְלָה, מְבָרְכִין, כְּמוֹ שֶׁכָּתַבְתִּי בְּסָעִיף א. אֲבָל אִם לֹא אָכְלוּ עַד הַלַּיְלָה, אִי אִכָּא אֲנָשִׁים שֶׁאוֹכְלִים מֵחֲמַת שִׂמְחַת מֵרֵעוּת, מְבָרְכִין, כְּמוֹ שֶׁכָּתַבְתִּי בְּסָעִיף ג (וַאֲפִלּוּ אִכָּא פָּנִים חֲדָשׁוֹת), וְכֵן בְּכָל הַסְּעוּדוֹת שְׁלֹשָׁה הַיָּמִים הָרִאשׁוֹנִים.

ה) פָּנִים חֲדָשׁוֹת מִקְרֵי, אִם בָּא לְשָׁם אָדָם מֵחֲמַת שִׂמְחַת מֵרֵעוּת, וְרוֹצִים לְהַרְבּוֹת בִּשְׁבִילוֹ, וְאַף־עַל־פִּי שֶׁאֵינוֹ אוֹכֵל. שַׁבָּת וְיוֹם־טוֹב רִאשׁוֹן וְיוֹם־טוֹב שֵׁנִי, הָוֵי כְּפָנִים חֲדָשׁוֹת. וְדַוְקָא סְעוּדַת הַלַּיְלָה וּסְעוּדַת שַׁחֲרִית. אֲבָל סְעוּדָה שְׁלִישִׁית, לֹא הָוֵי כְּפָנִים חֲדָשׁוֹת, אֶלָּא אִם הֶחָתָן דּוֹרֵשׁ.

ו) אִם אָדָם מַזְמִין אֶת הֶחָתָן וְאֶת הַכַּלָּה לֶאֱכֹל שָׁם, אִם מְיַחֲדִין לָהֶם שָׁם חֶדֶר בִּפְנֵי עַצְמָם, שֶׁיְּכוֹלִין לִהְיוֹת בְּיַחַד לְבַד וּלְשַׂמֵּחַ שָׁם, הָוֵי שָׁם כְּמוֹ חֻפָּה דִּידְהוּ וּמְבָרְכִין שָׁם שֶׁבַע בְּרָכוֹת. וְאִם לָאו, אֵין מְבָרְכִין אֲפִלּוּ אֲשֶׁר בָּרָא וְכוּ׳, וְשֶׁהַשִּׂמְחָה בִּמְעוֹנוֹ.

ז) בְּנֵי הַחֻפָּה שֶׁנֶּחְלְקוּ לַחֲבוּרוֹת הַרְבֵּה, אֲפִלּוּ לְבָתִּים שֶׁאֵינָם פְּתוּחִים לַמָּקוֹם שֶׁהֶחָתָן שָׁם, מִכָּל מָקוֹם מְבָרְכִים בְּכָל חֲבוּרָה וַחֲבוּרָה בְּרָכוֹת אֵלּוּ, כֵּיוָן שֶׁאוֹכְלִים מִסְּעוּדָה שֶׁהִתְקִינוּ לַחֻפָּה. אֲבָל הַשַּׁמָּשִׁים הָאוֹכְלִים אַחַר סְעוּדַת נִשּׂוּאִין, אֵין מְבָרְכִין בְּרָכוֹת אֵלּוּ.

ח) מַחֲזִיר גְּרוּשָׁתוֹ, אֵין אוֹמְרִים שֶׁהַשִּׂמְחָה בִּמְעוֹנוֹ. וּבַסְּעוּדָה הָרִאשׁוֹנָה בְּיוֹם הַנִּשּׂוּאִין, אוֹמְרִים שֶׁבַע בְּרָכוֹת, וּמִכָּאן וְאֵילַךְ אֵין אוֹמְרִים כְּלוּם.

ט) מִצְוָה לְשַׂמֵּחַ חָתָן וְכַלָּה וְלִרְקֹד לְפָנֶיהָ וְלוֹמַר, שֶׁהִיא נָאָה וַחֲסוּדָה (מִלָּשׁוֹן וַתִּשָּׂא חֵן וָחֶסֶד לְפָנָיו). וּמָצִינוּ, שֶׁרַבִּי יְהוּדָה בַּר אִלְעַי הָיָה מְרַקֵּד לִפְנֵי הַכַּלָּה.

---

1. *Taz* (*Even Ha'ezer* 62:9). But the *Shulchan Aruch* rules that they should recite the *berachos.*

Hamazon, and recites over it *Borei peri Haggafen.* For this ten men are not necessary, and even the presence of three is sufficient for saying *Birkas Hamazon* in this manner. However, if the groom eats only with family members, these things are not said.

4) When a widower marries a widow, if they ate the first meal on the day of the wedding, even if the meal lasted into the night, *Birkas Hamazon* is recited as stated in paragraph 1. But if they did not begin the meal until nightfall, if there are men dining [with them] to celebrate as friends, *Birkas Hamazon* should be recited as stated in paragraph 3. (This is true even if there is a new guest participating.) This applies to all the meals during the first three days (after the wedding).

5) The term "new guest" applies to a person who has come to celebrate as a friend, and for whom they want to prepare extra food even though he does not eat (with them). Shabbos, the first day Yom Tov and the second day Yom Tov are considered as new guests. But this applies only to the meal at night and the meal in the morning, but the third meal is not considered as a new guest unless the groom expounds on a Torah topic.

6) If one invites the groom and the bride to dine with him, and he assigns a private room for them where they can be alone and rejice together, it is considered as [a part of] their wedding and the seven *berachos* are recited. But if this is not the case, even the beracha *asher bara* is not recited, (nor do we say) *shehasimcha bimono.*

7) When the wedding guests break up into many groups [to feast], even in houses that do not face the place of the groom. Nevertheless, each group recites these (seven) *berachos,* since they are eating from the feast that was prepared for the wedding. However, the waiters, who eat after the wedding feast is over, do not recite these *berachos.*[1]

8) When one remarries his divorced wife, *shehasimcha bimono* is omitted. At the first meal on the wedding day the seven *berachos* are recited.[2] But from then on none of the *berachos* are said.[3]

9) It is a mitzvah to rejoice the groom and bride, and to dance before her and say that she is beautiful and gracious, (from the expression, "She found grace and favour before him");[4] and we find that Rabbi Yehuda Bar Illai used to dance before the bride.[5]

---

2. *Radvaz. Mishpat Shalom* in the name of *Rav Hai Gaon* rules that even under their *chupah* the seven *berachos* are not recited.

3. This is the law when a widower marries a widow.

4. *Esther* 2:17.

5. Maseches Kesubos 17a.

י) אָסוּר לְהִסְתַּכֵּל בַּכַּלָּה, אֲבָל מֻתָּר לְהִסְתַּכֵּל בַּתַּכְשִׁיטִין שֶׁעָלֶיהָ וּבִפְרִיעַת רֹאשָׁהּ.

יא) יֵשׁ נוֹהֲגִין, שֶׁאִם הַכַּלָּה הָיְתָה טְמֵאָה בִּשְׁעַת הַנִּשּׂוּאִין, אָז אַחַר כָּךְ בְּלֵיל טְבִילָתָהּ עוֹשִׂין סְעוּדָה וּמַזְמִינִים גַּם אֲנָשִׁים אֲחֵרִים. וְאֵין זֶה נָכוֹן. וְיֵשׁ לְבַטֵּל מִנְהָג זֶה, מִשּׁוּם צְנִיעוּת. אַךְ אִם עוֹשִׂים קְצָת סְעוּדָה לְאַנְשֵׁי־הַבַּיִת וְאוֹמְרִים שֶׁהַשִּׂמְחָה בִּמְעוֹנוֹ, אֵין לִמְחוֹת. אֲבָל שֶׁבַע בְּרָכוֹת, אָסוּר לְבָרֵךְ, רַק בְּאֹפֶן שֶׁנִּתְבָּאֵר לְעֵיל.

יב) הַנּוֹשֵׂא בְּתוּלָה, צָרִיךְ לִשְׂמֹחַ עִמָּהּ שִׁבְעָה יָמִים, וְנִקְרָאִים שִׁבְעַת יְמֵי מִשְׁתֶּה. לֹא יַעֲשֶׂה מְלָאכָה, וְלֹא יִשָּׂא וְיִתֵּן בַּשּׁוּק, אֶלָּא אוֹכֵל וְשׁוֹתֶה וְשָׂמֵחַ עִמָּהּ, בֵּין אִם הוּא בָּחוּר אוֹ אַלְמָן. וַאֲפִלּוּ הִיא מוֹחֶלֶת, מִכָּל מָקוֹם אָסוּר בַּעֲשִׂיַּת מְלָאכָה. וְאָסוּר לָצֵאת יְחִידִי בַּשּׁוּק. וְהַנּוֹשֵׂא בְּעוּלָה, אִם הוּא אַלְמָן, לְכֻלֵּי עָלְמָא אֵינוֹ צָרִיךְ שִׂמְחָה אֶלָּא שְׁלֹשָׁה יָמִים. וְאִם הוּא בָּחוּר, יֵשׁ אוֹמְרִים דְּצָרִיךְ לִשְׂמוֹחַ עִמָּהּ שִׁבְעָה יָמִים, כֵּיוָן שֶׁמְּבָרְכִין בִּשְׁבִילוֹ שֶׁבַע בְּרָכוֹת. וּמִכָּל מָקוֹם בָּזֶה אִשָּׁה יְכוֹלָה לִמְחֹל עַל שִׂמְחָתָהּ. (חָתָן שֶׁחָלָה תַּעֲנִית צִבּוּר בְּשִׁבְעַת יְמֵי הַמִּשְׁתֶּה שֶׁלּוֹ, עַיֵּן לְעֵיל סִימָן קכא סָעִיף ז וְסִימָן קמא סָעִיף ב).

יג) הַנּוֹשֵׂא אִשָּׁה, צָרִיךְ לַעֲמוֹד בְּעִירוֹ שָׁנָה תְמִימָה לִשְׂמוֹחַ עִמָּהּ, שֶׁנֶּאֱמַר, לֹא יֵצֵא בַּצָּבָא וְגוֹ', נָקִי יִהְיֶה לְבֵיתוֹ שָׁנָה אֶחָת וְשִׂמַּח אֶת־אִשְׁתּוֹ. אֲבָל הָאִשָּׁה, יְכוֹלָה לִמְחוֹל.

סִימָן קנ
הִלְכוֹת צְנִיעוּת

א) רָאוּי לְאָדָם לְהַרְגִּיל אֶת עַצְמוֹ בִּקְדֻשָּׁה יְתֵרָה וּבְמַחֲשָׁבָה טְהוֹרָה וּבְדַעַת נְכוֹנָה בִּשְׁעַת תַּשְׁמִישׁ. לֹא יָקֵל רֹאשׁוֹ עִם אִשְׁתּוֹ, וְלֹא יְנַבֵּל פִּיו בְּדִבְרֵי הֲבַאי אֲפִלּוּ בֵּינוֹ לְבֵינָהּ. הֲרֵי הַכָּתוּב אוֹמֵר, וּמַגִּיד לְאָדָם מַה־שֵּׂחוֹ, וְאָמְרוּ רַבּוֹתֵינוּ זִכְרוֹנָם לִבְרָכָה, אֲפִלּוּ שִׂיחָה קַלָּה שֶׁבֵּין אִישׁ לְאִשְׁתּוֹ, מַגִּידִין לוֹ בִּשְׁעַת הַדִּין. לֹא יְסַפֵּר עִמָּהּ בִּשְׁעַת תַּשְׁמִישׁ וְלֹא קֹדֶם לָכֵן, אֶלָּא מַה שֶּׁהוּא צָרִיךְ בְּעִנְיַן תַּשְׁמִישׁ. וְאִם הָיוּ בְּכַעַס שֶׁאָסוּר לְשַׁמֵּשׁ אָז עִמָּהּ, יָכוֹל לְדַבֵּר עִמָּהּ לְרַצּוֹתָהּ שֶׁתִּתְפַּיֵּס. וִישַׁמֵּשׁ בְּהַצְנֵעַ הָאֶפְשָׁרִי. הוּא לְמַטָּה וְהִיא לְמַעְלָה, זֶהוּ דֶּרֶךְ עַזּוּת. שִׁמְּשׁוּ שְׁנֵיהֶם כְּאֶחָד, זֶהוּ

10) It is forbidden to stare at the bride, but you are allowed to look at her jewelry, and at her uncovered hair.

11) Some people have a custom that if the bride was menstrually unclean at the time of the wedding, then afterwards, on the night of her ritual immersion, they make a feast and invite guests. This is improper, and this custom should be abolished because it is a breach of modesty. But if they make a small feast for the household and they say *shehasimcha bimono,* one need not protest. But the seven *berachos* must not be said, other than in the manner described above.[6]

12) One who marries a virgin must rejoice with her for seven days, which are called "The seven days of feasting." (During this time) he should not do work, and should not do business in the marketplace; but should eat and drink and rejoice with her regardless if he was a bachelor or a widower. Even if she waives this right he is still forbidden to do work. He is forbidden to go alone in the street. If one marries a previously married woman, if he is a widower, all authorities agree he need not rejoice more than three days. If he was never married, some authorities rule that he must rejoice with her seven days since because of him they recite the seven *berachas.* Nevertheless, in this case the woman may waive her right to be rejoiced.[7] If a public fast occurs during "The seven days of feasting" see chapter 121:7 and chapter 141:2.

13) One who takes a wife to himself must remain in his city a full year to rejoice with her; as it is said, "He shall not go out with the army; he shall be free for his home one year, and he shall cheer his wife."[8] But the woman can waive this right.

Chapter 150

Laws of Modesty

1) It is fitting that man conduct himself with great holiness, pure thoughts, and a correct attitude when having marital relationship. He should not indulge in frivolity with his wife, nor defile his mouth with indecent jests, even in private conversation with her, for the Scriptures say, "And declare to man what is his conversation."[1] And our Rabbis, of blessed memory, said, "Even the light conversation between a man and his wife are recalled to him on the day of Judgement."[2] He should not converse with her during the marital act, nor immediately before it, except what is necessary for marital relations. When she is angry and he is forbidden to have marital relations with her, he may speak kind words to her to appease her. The marital act should be in the most possible modest manner. He underneath and she above him, is considered an impudent manner. Both at the same level, is an act

---

6. Only during the seven days of the feast.
7. *Ramah* 62:. This applies to his being allowed to do work also.
8. *Deuteronomy* 24:5.
1. *Amos* 4:13.
2. Maseches *Hagigah* 5b.

דֶּרֶךְ עִקֵּשׁ. אָמְרוּ עָלָיו עַל רַבִּי אֱלִיעֶזֶר, שֶׁכָּל כָּךְ הָיָה מְשַׁמֵּשׁ בְּאֵימָה וּבְיִרְאָה, עַד שֶׁהָיָה דוֹמֶה כְּאִלּוּ כְּפָאוֹ שֵׁד.

ב) בִּשְׁעַת הַזִּוּוּג, יֵשׁ לוֹ לְהַרְהֵר בְּדִבְרֵי תוֹרָה וּבִשְׁאָר דָּבָר שֶׁבִּקְדֻשָּׁה. וְאַף־עַל־פִּי שֶׁאָסוּר לִקְרוֹת בְּפִיו, הִרְהוּר מֻתָּר וּמִצְוָה, כִּי הִרְהוּר אֵינוֹ כְּדִבּוּר לְעִנְיָן זֶה. אַף־עַל־פִּי דְּבַמְּבוֹאוֹת הַמְטֻנָּפִים אָסוּר אֲפִלּוּ לְהַרְהֵר בְּדָבָר שֶׁבִּקְדֻשָּׁה, זֶהוּ מִשּׁוּם דִּבְעִינָן וְהָיָה מַחֲנֶיךָ קָדוֹשׁ. אֲבָל הֵיכָא דְּהָאִסּוּר הוּא מִשּׁוּם עֶרְוָה, מִדִּכְתִיב עֶרְוַת דָּבָר דָּרְשׁוּ רַבּוֹתֵינוּ, זִכְרוֹנָם לִבְרָכָה, דִּבּוּר אָסוּר, הִרְהוּר מֻתָּר.

ג) אָסוּר לְשַׁמֵּשׁ לְאוֹר הַנֵּר, אַף־עַל־פִּי שֶׁמַּאֲפִיל בְּטַלִּיתוֹ. אֲבָל אִם עוֹשֶׂה מְחִצָּה גְּבוֹהָה עֲשָׂרָה טְפָחִים לִפְנֵי הַנֵּר, מֻתָּר. וְכֵן אָסוּר לְשַׁמֵּשׁ בַּיּוֹם, אֶלָּא בְּבַיִת אָפֵל. וּבַלַּיְלָה, אִם הַלְּבָנָה מְאִירָה עֲלֵיהֶם לְהֶדְיָא, אָסוּר. אֲבָל אִם אֵינָהּ מְאִירָה עֲלֵיהֶם, אַף־עַל־פִּי שֶׁמְּאִירָה לְתוֹךְ הַבַּיִת, מַאֲפִיל בְּטַלִּיתוֹ וּמֻתָּר. וְכֵן אִם יֵשׁ נֵר בְּחֶדֶר אַחֵר וּמֵאִיר לְחֶדֶר זֶה, צָרִיךְ הָאֲפָלַת טַלִּית.

ד) אָסוּר לְאָדָם לְשַׁמֵּשׁ מִטָּתוֹ בִּפְנֵי כָּל אָדָם אִם הוּא נֵעוֹר, וַאֲפִלּוּ עַל יְדֵי הֶפְסֵק מְחִצַּת עֲשָׂרָה. וּבִפְנֵי תִינוֹק שֶׁאֵינוֹ יוֹדֵעַ לְדַבֵּר, מֻתָּר.

ה) אָסוּר לְהִסְתַּכֵּל בְּאוֹתוֹ מָקוֹם, שֶׁכָּל הַמִּסְתַּכֵּל שָׁם, אֵין לוֹ בֹּשֶׁת פָּנִים, וְעוֹבֵר עַל וְהַצְנֵעַ לֶכֶת, וּמַעֲבִיר הַבּוּשָׁה מֵעַל פָּנָיו. שֶׁכָּל הַמִּתְבַּיֵּשׁ, אֵינוֹ חוֹטֵא, דִּכְתִיב, וּבַעֲבוּר תִּהְיֶה יִרְאָתוֹ עַל פְּנֵיכֶם, זוֹ הַבּוּשָׁה, לְבִלְתִּי תֶחֱטָאוּ. וְעוֹד, דְּקָא מְגָרֶה יֵצֶר־הָרַע בְּנַפְשֵׁהּ. וְכָל־שֶׁכֵּן הַנּוֹשֵׁק שָׁם, שֶׁעוֹבֵר עַל כָּל אֵלֶּה, וְעוֹבֵר גַּם עַל בַּל־תְּשַׁקְּצוּ אֶת־נַפְשׁוֹתֵיכֶם.

ו) בַּיִת שֶׁיֵּשׁ בּוֹ סֵפֶר־תּוֹרָה, אָסוּר לְשַׁמֵּשׁ שָׁם, אֶלָּא צָרִיךְ שֶׁיּוֹצִיאוֹ לְחֶדֶר אַחֵר. וְאִם אֵין לוֹ חֶדֶר אַחֵר, יַעֲשֶׂה לְפָנָיו מְחִצָּה גְּבוֹהָה עֲשָׂרָה

---

3. Maseches *Nedarim* 20b.

4. *Deuteronomy* 22:15.

5. *Maseches Shabbos* 150a. the word דָּבָר indicates actual speech.

6. See glossary. The partition must also be secured at the bottom to the extent it would not blow to and fro in a usual outdoor wind. (*Magein Avraham, Mishnah Berurah* 240:40). If the partition completely covers the source of the light, it does not have to be ten *tefachim* high, but our case refers to where the candle or bulb is visible above the partition. The partition merely creates a separate domain and thus marital relations are permitted, providing the light is dimmed with a garment. (*Magein Avraham, Mishnah Berurah* 325:10). However, if the light

of perversion. It is said of Rabbi Eliezer, that the marital act was done with such awe and terror, that it appeared as if a demon was forcing him to do it.[3]

2) While engaged in the marital act, you should think about Torah subjects or other sacred subjects. Even though [during the act itself] it is forbidden to speak words of Torah, thinking about them is permitted and meritorious, for thought is not likened to speech in this case. Even though in filthy alleys it is forbidden to even think about sacred subjects, this is because of the Divine command, "And your camp shall be holy;"[4] but where it is forbidden because of body nakedness, concerning which it is written, *ervas davar* (unseemingly thing), our Sages of blessed memory inferred from this that speaking *davar* (words of Torah) is forbidden, but thinking about them is permitted.[5]

3) The marital act is forbidden in a lighted room, even if the light is dimmed with a garment. But if you make a partition ten *tefachim* high[6] in front of the light, it is permissible. Marital relations are also forbidden by day unless the room is darkened. At night, if the moon is shining directly on you it is forbidden. However if it is not shining [directly] on you, even though it is shining into the room, you may shut out its light with a garment [or window shade], and it is then permitted. Also, if there is a light in another room and it shines into this room, you must shut out this light with a garment.

4) Marital relations are forbidden in the presence of any person who is awake,[7] even with a partition of ten *tefachim*.[8] In the presence of a child who is unable to speak, it is permitted.

5) It is forbidden to look at the genitals of your wife. Anyone who does look there, is devoid of shame. He violates [the Scriptural verse], "And walk humbly (or modestly) before Adonoy,"[9] and removes the sign of shame from his face. A bashful person is not apt to sin, as it is written, "So that His fear be on your face,"[10] which refers to bashfulness, "So that you do not sin."[10] Also, (by looking there); you stimulate evil desire within yourself. Certainly one who kisses that place violates all these admonitions, and in addition he violates [the Scriptural verse,] "Do not make yourselves repulsive."[11]

6) In a room in which there is a *seifer Torah,*[12] marital relations are forbidden until it is removed to another room. If there is no other room you must make a

---

source is in another room, everyone permits it if the light is dimmed with a garment. See *Sh'ar Hatziyun* 240:24–26.

7. Even if he is asleep, it is still preferable to have a partition as well. (*Biur Halachah* 240:6).

8. Unless it is done in a way that nobody will know. (*Mishnah Berurah* 240:22)

9. *Micah* 6:8.

10. *Exodus* 20:20.

11. *Leviticus* 11:43.

12. Or any other Scriptural scroll, written on parchment. (*Mishnah Berurah* 240:23)

טְפָחִים. וּתְהֵא מְחִצָּה סְתוּמָה, שֶׁלֹּא יֵרָאֶה סֵפֶר־הַתּוֹרָה. וְהַיְרִיעָה שֶׁסְּבִיב הַמִּטָּה לָא חֲשִׁיבָה מְחִצָּה, כֵּיוָן שֶׁהִיא נָדָה, אֶלָּא אִם כֵּן קָשַׁר אוֹתָהּ מִלְּמַטָּה. וּבִתְפִלִּין וְחֻמָּשִׁים וּשְׁאָר כִּתְבֵי הַקֹּדֶשׁ, כְּגוֹן גְּמָרָא וּמִדְרָשִׁים וּמְפָרְשֵׁיהֶם, בֵּין שֶׁהֵם בִּכְתָב בֵּין שֶׁהֵם בִּדְפוּס, יָכוֹל לְהַנִּיחָן בִּכְלִי תּוֹךְ כֶּלִי. וְדַוְקָא כְּשֶׁהַכְּלִי הַשֵּׁנִי אֵינוֹ מְיֻחָד לָהֶם. אֲבָל כֵּלִים הַמְיֻחָדִים לָהֶם, אֲפִלּוּ הֵם עֲשָׂרָה, כֻּלָּם כְּחַד חֲשִׁיבֵי. וְאִם פָּרַשׂ אֵיזֶה מִכְסֶה עַל הָאַרְגָּז שֶׁהַסְּפָרִים בּוֹ חָשׁוּב כִּכְלִי בְּתוֹךְ כֶּלִי. וְכֵן הַמְּזוּזָה, אִם הִיא קְבוּעָה בִּפְנִים הַחֶדֶר, צְרִיכִין לְכַסּוֹתָהּ בִּשְׁנֵי כִסּוּיִין, שֶׁתְּהֵא בִּכְלִי תּוֹךְ כֶּלִי, וְהַשֵּׁם יְהֵא גַּם כֵּן מְכֻסֶּה. וְכִסּוּי זְכוּכִית, לָא מַהֲנֵי, דְּצָרִיךְ שֶׁלֹּא יְהֵא נִרְאֶה.

ז) לֹא יְהֵא רָגִיל בְּיוֹתֵר עִם אִשְׁתּוֹ, אֶלָּא בְּעוֹנָה, שֶׁהוּא חַיָּב לִפְרֹעַ לָהּ עוֹנָתָהּ, דִּכְתִיב, וְעוֹנָתָהּ לֹא יִגְרָע. הָאֲנָשִׁים הַבְּרִיאִים וְהַמְּעֻנָּגִים שֶׁפַּרְנָסָתָן בִּמְקוֹמָם בְּרֶוַח וְאֵין פּוֹרְעִין מַס, עוֹנָתָן בְּכָל לַיְלָה. הַפּוֹעֲלִים שֶׁעוֹשִׂים מְלָאכָה בְּעִירָם, עוֹנָתָן שְׁתֵּי פְעָמִים בְּכָל שָׁבוּעַ. וְאִם עוֹשִׂין מְלָאכָה בְּעִיר אַחֶרֶת, עוֹנָתָן פַּעַם אַחַת בַּשָּׁבוּעַ. וְכֵן הַסּוֹחֲרִים שֶׁיּוֹצְאִין לַכְּפָרִים עִם חֲמוֹרִים לְהָבִיא תְבוּאָה לִמְכּוֹר וְכֵן כַּיּוֹצֵא בָהֶם, עוֹנָתָן פַּעַם אַחַת בַּשָּׁבוּעַ. וְהַמְּבִיאִים חֲבִילוֹת עַל הַגְּמַלִּים מִמָּקוֹם רָחוֹק, עוֹנָתָן פַּעַם אַחַת בִּשְׁלֹשִׁים יוֹם. וְעוֹנַת תַּלְמִידֵי־חֲכָמִים מִלֵּיל שַׁבָּת לְלֵיל שַׁבָּת. וְצָרִיךְ לְקַיֵּם אֶת הָעוֹנָה גַּם כְּשֶׁהִיא מְעֻבֶּרֶת אוֹ מֵינִיקָה. וְלֹא יְבַטֵּל עוֹנָתָהּ, אֶלָּא מִדַּעְתָּהּ כְּשֶׁהִיא מוֹחֶלֶת לוֹ וּכְבָר קִיֵּם מִצְוַת פְּרִיָּה וּרְבִיָּה. וְאִם מוֹנֵעַ עוֹנָתָהּ כְּדֵי לְצַעֲרָהּ, עוֹבֵר בְּלֹא תַעֲשֶׂה, שֶׁנֶּאֱמַר, וְעוֹנָתָהּ לֹא יִגְרָע.

ח) כָּל אָדָם צָרִיךְ לִפְקֹד אֶת אִשְׁתּוֹ בְּלֵיל טְבִילָתָהּ וּבַלַּיְלָה שֶׁלִּפְנֵי יְצִיאָתוֹ לַדֶּרֶךְ, אִם אֵינוֹ הוֹלֵךְ לִדְבַר מִצְוָה. וְכֹל שֶׁרוֹאֶה שֶׁאִשְׁתּוֹ מְשַׁדַּלְתּוֹ וּמְרַצָּה אוֹתוֹ וּמְקַשֶּׁטֶת עַצְמָהּ לְפָנָיו כְּדֵי שֶׁיִּתֵּן דַּעְתּוֹ עָלֶיהָ, חַיָּב לְפָקְדָהּ אֲפִלּוּ שֶׁלֹּא בִּשְׁעַת עוֹנָתָהּ, וְהַוְיָן לָהּ בָּנִים הֲגוּנִים. אֲבָל אִם תְּבָעַתּוּ בַּפֶּה מַמָּשׁ, הִיא חֲצוּפָה וַהֲרֵי הִיא כְּזוֹנָה וְאָסוּר לְקַיְּמָהּ.

ט) וְאַף כְּשֶׁהוּא אֶצְלָהּ, לֹא יְכַוֵּן לַהֲנָאָתוֹ, אֶלָּא כְּאָדָם שֶׁהוּא פּוֹרֵעַ

---

13. *Taz* (*Yoreh Deiah* 271:8) rules that there is no difference between printed and written *seforim*, but *Eliyohu Rabba* and *Chavos Yair*, responsa 187, rule that you may be lenient if you have nothing with which to cover the printed *seforim*.

partition in front of it that is ten *tefachim* high. The partition should be totally closed up, so that the *seifer Torah* cannot be seen. The curtain around the bed is not considered a partition since it is movable; unless it is tied at the bottom. *Tefillin, Chumashim,* or other sacred writings, such as the Talmud, Midrash and their commentaries, whether they are written or printed[13] should be placed into a vessel within a vessel.[14] This is valid only when the second vessel [or covering] is not especially made for such holy works, but if they are especially made for them, even ten such vessels are all considered as only one vessel. If you spread a cover over the chest containing these books, it is considered like a vessel within a vessel. Also a *mezuzah,* when affixed on the inside of the room, must be covered it with two covers, so it should be a vessel within a vessel. The Name (*Shaddai,* on the outer face of the *mezuzah*) must also be covered. A glass covering is of no avail for the covering must not be transparent.[15]

7) You must not be excessive in marital relations with your wife, except at the time you are required to fulfil her conjugal rights, as it is written, "And he shall not diminish her conjugal rights."[16] Men who are healthy, who enjoy the pleasures of life, who have profitable businesses in their home town, and are not burdened with taxes, should perform their marital duty nightly. Laborers who work in the city in which they reside, should perform their marital duty twice a week. If they are employed in another city, their marital duty is once a week. Also the merchants who travel to the villages with their mules to buy grain to be sold in town, and those who have similar pursuits, their marital duty is once a week. Men who carry freight on camels to distant places, their marital duty is once in thirty days. The marital duty of Torah scholars is from Shabbos eve to Shabbos eve. You must perform your marital duty even when your wife is pregnant or nursing. You may not deprive her of her conjugal rights unless she consents to it willingly, and only after you have already fulfilled the Divine commandment of propogation. If you deprive her conjugal rights in order to afflict her, you violate a negative command, as it is said, "And he shall not diminish her conjugal rights."

8) Every husband is required to be with his wife on the night of her ritual immersion, and on the night before he sets out on a journey, unless he is going to perform a mitzvah. When a husband sees that his wife is enticing him, trying to please him, and beautifying herself in front of him, in order to attract his intention, he is obligated to be with her even if it is not the appointed time; and from such a union will come worthy children. However, if she demands it openly, she is a brazen woman, and she is considered like a harlot; and he is forbidden to keep her for a wife.

9) When engaging in marital relations, your intention should not be to satisfy

---

14. They may be covered with two covers. (*Mishnah Berurah* 40:7.
15. Thus if only one of the covers is made of glass it is permitted (*Mishnah Berurah* 40:7)
16. *Exodus* 21:10.

חוֹבוֹ, שֶׁהוּא חַיָּב בְּעוֹנָתָהּ, וּלְקַיֵּם מִצְוַת בּוֹרְאוֹ, שֶׁיִּהְיוּ לוֹ בָּנִים עוֹסְקִים בַּתּוֹרָה וּמְקַיְּמִים מִצְוֹת בְּיִשְׂרָאֵל. וְכֵן אִם הוּא מְכַוֵּן לְתִקּוּן הַוָּלָד, דְּאָמְרוּ רַבּוֹתֵינוּ זִכְרוֹנָם לִבְרָכָה, שְׁלֹשָׁה חֳדָשִׁים הָרִאשׁוֹנִים (מֵהֵרָיוֹן), תַּשְׁמִישׁ קָשֶׁה לְאִשָּׁה וְקָשֶׁה לַוָּלָד. אֶמְצָעִים, קָשֶׁה לָאִשָּׁה וְיָפֶה לַוָּלָד. אַחֲרוֹנִים, יָפֶה לָאִשָּׁה וְיָפֶה לַוָּלָד, שֶׁמִּתּוֹךְ כָּךְ יֵצֵא מְלֻבָּן וּמְזֹרָז – שַׁפִּיר דָּמֵי. וְאִם הוּא מְכַוֵּן לִגְדֹּר עַצְמוֹ בָּהּ כְּדֵי שֶׁלֹּא יִתְאַוֶּה לַעֲבֵרָה, כִּי רוֹאֶה יִצְרוֹ גּוֹבֵר וּמִתְאַוֶּה אֶל הַדָּבָר הַהוּא, גַּם בָּזֶה יֵשׁ קִבּוּל שָׂכָר. אַךְ יוֹתֵר טוֹב הָיָה לוֹ לִדְחוֹת אֶת יִצְרוֹ וְלִכְבּוֹשׁ אוֹתוֹ, כִּי אֵבֶר קָטָן יֵשׁ בָּאָדָם. מַרְעִיבוֹ, שָׂבֵעַ. מַשְׂבִּיעוֹ, רָעֵב, אֲבָל מִי שֶׁאֵינוֹ צָרִיךְ לַדָּבָר, אֶלָּא שֶׁמְּעוֹרֵר תַּאֲוָתוֹ כְּדֵי לְמַלֹּאת תַּאֲוָתוֹ, זוֹ הִיא עֲצַת יֵצֶר־הָרָע.

י) מִי שֶׁנּוֹחַ לוֹ, יֵשׁ לוֹ לִזָּהֵר, שֶׁלֹּא לְשַׁמֵּשׁ לֹא בִּתְחִלַּת הַלַּיְלָה וְלֹא בְּסוֹפוֹ אֶלָּא בְּאֶמְצָעִיתוֹ. לֹא יִגַּע בְּאַמָּה אֲפִלּוּ לְצֹרֶךְ זִוּוּג, עַד שֶׁיִּטּוֹל יָדָיו כָּרָאוּי, דְּהַיְנוּ שָׁלשׁ פְּעָמִים בְּסֵרוּגִין, כִּמְבֹאָר בְּסִימָן ב.

יא) אָסוּר לְשַׁמֵּשׁ בַּשְּׁוָקִים וּבָרְחוֹבוֹת וּבַגַּנִּים וּבַפַּרְדֵּסִים, אֶלָּא בְּבֵית דִּירָה, שֶׁלֹּא יִהְיֶה כְּדֶרֶךְ זְנוּת.

יב) כְּשֶׁיֵּשׁ חַס־וְשָׁלוֹם רָעָב בַּמְּדִינָה, שֶׁהוּקְרָה הַתְּבוּאָה בְּכֶפֶל, אַף־עַל־פִּי שֶׁהוּא יֵשׁ לוֹ תְּבוּאָה בְּתוֹךְ בֵּיתוֹ, אוֹ שֶׁיֵּשׁ חַס־וְשָׁלוֹם שְׁאָר צָרָה, אָסוּר לְשַׁמֵּשׁ מִטָּתוֹ כִּי אִם בְּלֵיל טְבִילָתָהּ. וְלַחֲשׂוּכֵי בָנִים, מֻתָּר בְּכָל עוֹנָה.

יג) לֹא יְשַׁמֵּשׁ עִם אִשְׁתּוֹ אֶלָּא מֵרְצוֹנָהּ. אֲבָל כְּשֶׁאֵינָהּ מְרֻצָּה, לֹא יְשַׁמֵּשׁ עִמָּהּ, וּמִכָּל־שֶׁכֵּן דְּאָסוּר לְאָנְסָהּ. וְכֵן לֹא יְשַׁמֵּשׁ כְּשֶׁהִיא שְׂנוּאָה לוֹ אוֹ שֶׁהוּא שָׂנוּי לָהּ דְּאָמְרָה לֵהּ לָא בָּעֵינָא לָךְ, אַף־עַל־פִּי שֶׁרְצוּיָה בַּתַּשְׁמִישׁ. וְכֵן אִם גָּמַר בְּלִבּוֹ לְגָרְשָׁהּ וְהִיא אֵינָהּ יוֹדַעַת, אַף־עַל־פִּי

17. *Maseches Niddah* 31a.

18. *Maseches Sukkah* 52b.

19. Or any other opening in the body.

20. If food is generally available, it is permitted, no matter how much it costs. (*Birkei Yosef, Sha'arei Teshuva* 574.)

21. *Ramah* 240:12. *Sha'arei Tzion* rules that in case of other calamaties it is not prohibited, but it is a matter of individual piety. This law generally only refers to such calamities that have a resultant effect similar to famine.

your personal pleasure but as one fulfilling his obligation to satisfy her conjugal rights; and also to fulfill the command of your Creator, (and) to have children who engage in Torah study, and fulfill the *mitzvos* of the Jewish people. It is also proper if your intent is to improve the fetus; as our Rabbis, of blessed memory, said, "During the first trimester of pregnancy cohabitation is difficult for the woman and the child. During the middle trimester, it is difficult for the woman but good for the child. During the last trimester, it is good both for the woman and the child, for it will cause the child at his birth to be strong and healthy."[17] This too is a proper intention. If your purpose of being with her is to restrain yourself against sinful lust, when you are overwhelmed by desire, and have a craving for it—if this is your intention, you will also be rewarded. However, it is better that you push off your desire and overcome it; for (as the Sages said), "A man has a small organ, if he starves it, it is contented, and if he pampers it, it is hungry."[18] But one who has no need for it, but deliberately arouses his desire in order to satisfy that desire, is following the counsel of the evil impulse.

10) If possible you should be careful not to have marital relations in the beginning or at the end of the night, but rather in the middle of the night. [If you were asleep before this] you may not touch the penile orifice[19] even for the sake of cohabitation, before washing your hands properly, that is, three times alternately, as stated in Chapter 2.

11) Marital relations are forbidden in the market places, in streets, in gardens, or in orchards. It is permitted only in dwellings so that it does not resemble prostitution.

12) If, God forbid, there is [such] famine in the land that the price of grain [food] doubled,[20] even though you have sufficient grain [food] in your house, or if, God forbid, there is some other calamity [in the country],[21] marital relations are forbidden except on the night of her ritual immersion. Those who are childless[22] are permitted to have marital relations on each appointed time of marital duty.

13) You should not have marital relations with your wife unless she is willing. But if she is not willing you should not have marital relations with her, and it is certainly forbidden to force her. Also, you should not have marital relations with her if you hate her,[23] or if she hates you and tells you she does not want you, although she consents to marital relations. Also, if you have decided to divorce her, and she is unaware of it; even though you do not hate her, you are forbidden to have

---

22. This refers to one who has not yet fulfilled the mitzvah of propagation, which is fulfilled with the birth of a boy and a girl (*Eliyohu Rabba*). One whose children desecrate the Shabbos is probably considered childless with regard to this halachah. (*Mishnah Berurah* 574:12).

23. At the time of cohabitation. But if generally speaking you hate her, but at *that* time you do not, it is permitted. (*Mishnah Berurah* 240:15)

שֶׁאֵינָהּ שְׂנוּאָה לוֹ, אָסוּר לְשַׁמֵּשׁ עִמָּהּ. גַּם לֹא יְשַׁמֵּשׁ עִמָּהּ כְּשֶׁהִיא יְשֵׁנָה מַמָּשׁ. גַּם לֹא יְשַׁמֵּשׁ כְּשֶׁהוּא שִׁכּוֹר אוֹ הִיא שִׁכּוֹרָה.

יד) אַכְסְנַאי, אָסוּר לְשַׁמֵּשׁ. וְאִם יִחֲדוּ לוֹ וּלְאִשְׁתּוֹ בַּיִת מְיֻחָד, מֻתָּר, וּבִלְבַד שֶׁלֹּא יִישַׁן עַל סָדִין שֶׁל בַּעַל־הַבַּיִת.

טו) מִדַּרְכֵי הָרְפוּאָה, שֶׁלֹּא לִבְעֹל לֹא כְּשֶׁהוּא שָׂבֵעַ וְלֹא כְּשֶׁהוּא רָעֵב, אֶלָּא כְּשֶׁיִּתְעַכֵּל הַמָּזוֹן שֶׁבְּמֵעָיו. וְלֹא יִבְעַל מְעֻמָּד, וְלֹא מְיֻשָּׁב, וְלֹא בְּיוֹם שֶׁנִּכְנַס לַמֶּרְחָץ, וְלֹא בְּיוֹם הַקָּזָה, וְלֹא בְּיוֹם יְצִיאָה לַדֶּרֶךְ אוֹ בִּיאָה מִן הַדֶּרֶךְ כְּשֶׁהוֹלֵךְ בְּרַגְלָיו, וְלֹא לִפְנֵיהֶם וְלֹא לְאַחֲרֵיהֶם.

טז) לֹא יְשַׁמֵּשׁ עַל מִטָּה שֶׁיֵּשׁ שָׁם תִּינוֹק לְרַגְלֵיהֶם, כְּשֶׁאֵין הַתִּינוֹק בֶּן שָׁנָה. כְּשֶׁיּוֹצֵא מִבֵּית־כִּסֵּא קָבוּעַ, לֹא יְשַׁמֵּשׁ עַד לְאַחַר שָׁעָה. אִשָּׁה מֵינִיקָה, לֹא תְשַׁמֵּשׁ אֶלָּא בְּשָׁעָה שֶׁהַתִּינוֹק יָשֵׁן, וְאַחַר כָּךְ לֹא תֵּינִיקֵהוּ עַד לְאַחַר שְׁנֵי שְׁלִישֵׁי שָׁעָה, אִם לֹא כְּשֶׁהַתִּינוֹק בּוֹכֶה.

יז) שִׁכְבַת־זֶרַע הִיא כֹּחַ הַגּוּף וּמְאוֹר הָעֵינָיִם. וּכְשֶׁתֵּצֵא בְּיוֹתֵר, הַגּוּף כָּלֶה וְחַיָּיו אוֹבְדִים. וְכָל הַשָּׁטוּף בִּבְעִילָה, זִקְנָה קוֹפֶצֶת עָלָיו, וְכֹחוֹ תָּשֵׁשׁ, וְעֵינָיו כֵּהוֹת, וְרֵיחַ רַע נוֹדֵף מִפִּיו, וּשְׂעַר רֹאשׁוֹ וְגַבּוֹת עֵינָיו וְרִיסֵי עֵינָיו נוֹשְׁרִים, וּשְׂעַר זְקָנוֹ וְשֶׁחְיוֹ וּשְׂעַר רַגְלָיו רָבֶה, וְשִׁנָּיו נוֹשְׁרוֹת, וְהַרְבֵּה כְּאֵבִים חוּץ מֵאֵלּוּ בָּאִים עָלָיו. אָמְרוּ חַכְמֵי הָרוֹפְאִים, אֶחָד מֵאֶלֶף, מֵת מִשְּׁאָר חֳלָאִים, וְהָאֶלֶף מֵרֹב תַּשְׁמִישׁ. לְפִיכָךְ צָרִיךְ הָאָדָם לִזָּהֵר.

סִימָן קנא

אִסּוּר הוֹצָאַת זֶרַע לְבַטָּלָה וְתִקּוּנִים לְמִי שֶׁנִּכְשַׁל בּוֹ

א) אָסוּר לְהוֹצִיא זֶרַע לְבַטָּלָה. וְעָוֹן זֶה חָמוּר מִכָּל עֲבֵרוֹת שֶׁבַּתּוֹרָה. וְאֵלּוּ שֶׁמְּנָאֲפִים בַּיָּד וּמוֹצִיאִים זֶרַע לְבַטָּלָה, לֹא דַי לָהֶם שֶׁאִסּוּר גָּדוֹל הוּא, אֶלָּא שֶׁהָעוֹשֶׂה זֹאת, הוּא בְּנִדּוּי, וַעֲלֵיהֶם נֶאֱמַר, יְדֵיכֶם דָּמִים מָלֵאוּ

24. This probably refers to a steam bath and is merely a hygenic rule but not a *halachah*.
25. *Mishnah Berurah* 240:54.
26. *Zohar.* See *Mishnah Berurah* 240:54—*Yad Ephraim* says that the *Zohar* does not mean an hour, but rather a period of time. This time is half an hour.
27. *Zohar* says the amount of time it takes to walk two *mil*. That is 36 minutes.
28. Even then, you should wait at least one *mil* (eighteen minutes). (*Mishnah Berurah* 240:54).

marital relations with her. You should also not have marital relations with your wife when she is actually asleep. You also may not have marital relations when either of you are intoxicated.

14) House guests are forbidden to have marital relations. But if you and your wife were given private quarters, it is permitted, provided you do not sleep on sheets that belong to the host.

15) According to the rules of good health, you should not have marital relations when you are satiated, and not when you are hungry, but only when your food has been digested. You should not have marital relations while standing, and not in a sitting position, not on a day you had a bath,[24] and not on a day you let blood; not on the day you set out on a journey, or return from a journey[25] by foot; and not on the day before nor on the day following any of the above.

16) You should not have marital relations on a bed where an infant lies at your feet if the baby is less than one year old. After leaving the bathroom, you should wait an hour before having marital relations.[26] A nursing woman should not indulge in marital relations unless the baby is asleep. After marital relations she should not nurse him before two thirds of an hour transpires,[27] unless the baby is crying.[28]

17) Semen is the vitality of man's body and the light of his eyes, and when issued in excess, the body weakens and life is shortened. Anyone who overindulges in marital relations, ages prematurely, his strength ebbs, his eyes dim, his breath becomes foul; the hair on his head, his eyebrows, and his eye lashes fall out. The hair of his beard and armpits, the hair on his legs, increase, his teeth fall out and many other aches besides these befall him. Great physicians said one out of a thousand dies from other diseases, the rest of the thousand (999) die from sexual indulgence. Therefore, man should avoid such indulgence.

Chapter 151

The Prohibition of Discharging Semen in Vain And the Ways of Ammendment for One Who has Succumbed to this Sin

1) It is forbidden to discharge semen in vain. This is a graver sin than any other in the Torah.[1] Those who masturbate and thus discharge semen in vain, not only do they commit a grave sin, but also one who does this is placed under a ban. Concerning such people it is said, "Your hands are full of blood,"[2] and it is likened

1. *Zohar, Shulchan Aruch, Even Ha'Ezer* 23:1. *Beis Shmuel* explains this is not meant to be taken literally. Any sin that carries a penalty of death or *koreis* is a graver sin. This is meant to impress man with the severity of this sin.
2. *Isaiah* 1:15.

וּכְאִלּוּ הוֹרֵג אֶת הַנֶּפֶשׁ. וּרְאֵה מַה שֶּׁכָּתַב רַשִׁ"י בְּפָרָשַׁת וַיֵּשֶׁב בְּעֵר וְאוֹנָן שֶׁמֵּתוּ בְּחֵטְא זֶה. וְלִפְעָמִים בְּעֹנֶשׁ זֶה, חַס־וְשָׁלוֹם, בָּנָיו מֵתִים כְּשֶׁהֵם קְטַנִּים, אוֹ שֶׁיִּהְיוּ רְשָׁעִים, וְהוּא בָא לִידֵי עֲנִיּוּת.

ב) אָסוּר לְאָדָם שֶׁיְּקַשֶּׁה אֶת עַצְמוֹ לָדַעַת, אוֹ שֶׁיָּבִיא אֶת עַצְמוֹ לִידֵי הִרְהוּר אִשָּׁה. וְאִם בָּא לוֹ אֵיזֶה הִרְהוּר, יַסִּיעַ אֶת לִבּוֹ מִדִּבְרֵי הֲבַאי לְדִבְרֵי תוֹרָה, שֶׁהִיא אַיֶּלֶת אֲהָבִים וְיַעֲלַת חֵן. וְאֵין מַחֲשֶׁבֶת עֲרָיוֹת מִתְגַּבֶּרֶת אֶלָּא בְּלֵב פָּנוּי מִן הַחָכְמָה. וְיִזָּהֵר מְאֹד שֶׁלֹּא יָבוֹא לִידֵי קִשּׁוּי. לְפִיכָךְ אָסוּר לְאָדָם לִישׁוֹן עַל עָרְפּוֹ וּפָנָיו לְמַעְלָה, אוֹ לִישׁוֹן וּפָנָיו לְמַטָּה, אֶלָּא יִישַׁן עַל הַצְּדָדִין, שֶׁלֹּא יָבוֹא לִידֵי קִשּׁוּי. וְלֹא יִישְׁנוּ שְׁנֵי רַוָּקִים יַחַד. וְלֹא יִסְתַּכֵּל בִּבְהֵמָה חַיָּה וָעוֹף כְּשֶׁמִּזְדַּקְקִין זָכָר לִנְקֵבָה. וְאָסוּר לִרְכֹּב עַל בְּהֵמָה בְּלֹא אֻכָּף.

ג) כְּשֶׁמַּשְׁתִּין, אָסוּר לֶאֱחֹז בַּמִּילָה לְהַשְׁתִּין. וְאִם הוּא נָשׂוּי וְאִשְׁתּוֹ עִמּוֹ בָּעִיר וְהִיא טְהוֹרָה, מִצַּד הַדִּין מֻתָּר לוֹ, דְּכֵיוָן שֶׁיֵּשׁ לוֹ פַּת בְּסַלּוֹ, אֵינוֹ בָא לִידֵי הִרְהוּר וְחִמּוּם. אַךְ מִמִּדַּת חֲסִידוּת לְהַחְמִיר. וְשֶׁלֹּא לְצֹרֶךְ הַשְׁתָּנָה גַּם מִצַּד הַדִּין אָסוּר לוֹ.

ד) בִּסְעוּדַת הַלַּיְלָה, לֹא יַרְבֶּה בַּאֲכִילָה וּבִשְׁתִיָּה, וְלֹא יֹאכַל דְּבָרִים הַמְחַמְּמִים אֶת הַגּוּף, כְּגוֹן בָּשָׂר שָׁמֵן וְכָל מַאַכְלֵי חָלָב וּגְבִינָה וּבֵיצִים וָשׁוּם. גַּם לֹא יִשְׁתֶּה מַשְׁקֶה הַמְחַמֵּם, כִּי דְבָרִים אֵלּוּ גּוֹרְמִים לְחֵטְא זֶה.

ה) מִי שֶׁרָאָה, חַס־וְשָׁלוֹם, קֶרִי בַּלַּיְלָה, כְּשֶׁנֵּעוֹר מִשְּׁנָתוֹ, יִטּוֹל יָדָיו וְיֹאמַר בְּשִׁבְרוֹן לֵב, רִבּוֹנוֹ שֶׁל עוֹלָם, עָשִׂיתִי זֹאת שֶׁלֹּא בְּכַוָּנָה, רַק בְּהִרְהוּרִים רָעִים וּבְמַחֲשָׁבוֹת רָעוֹת. לָכֵן יְהִי רָצוֹן מִלְּפָנֶיךָ, ה' אֱלֹהַי וֵאלֹהֵי אֲבוֹתַי, מְחֹק בְּרַחֲמֶיךָ הָרַבִּים עָוֹן זֶה, וְתַצִּילֵנִי מֵהִרְהוּרִים רָעִים וְכַיּוֹצֵא בָהֶם לְעוֹלָם וָעֶד, אָמֵן וְכֵן יְהִי רָצוֹן.

ו) הָרוֹצֶה לִשְׁמֹר אֶת עַצְמוֹ מֵחֵטְא זֶה, יִשְׁמֹר אֶת פִּיו מִנִּבּוּל פֶּה, מִשְּׁקָרִים, מֵרְכִילוּת וּמִלָּשׁוֹן הָרָע וּמִלֵּצָנוּת. וְכֵן יִשְׁמֹר אֶת אָזְנוֹ מִשְּׁמֹעַ דְּבָרִים כָּאֵלּוּ. גַּם יְהֵא זָהִיר לְקַיֵּם נְדָרָיו, וְלֹא יַרְבֶּה בִּדְאָגָה, וְגַם יְהֵא זָהִיר מֵהִרְהוּרִים רָעִים, וְקֹדֶם שֶׁהוֹלֵךְ לִישׁוֹן, יַעֲסֹק בַּתּוֹרָה, אוֹ יֹאמַר אַרְבָּעָה מִזְמוֹרֵי תְהִלִּים הָרִאשׁוֹנִים וְיִזָּהֵר שֶׁלֹּא לִישׁוֹן בַּחֶדֶר יְחִידִי.

to killing a person. See what *Rashi* wrote in the *Sidrah* of *Vayeishev*[3] concerning Er and Onan, who died because of committing this sin. Occasionally, as a punishment for this sin, God forbid, one's children die when young,[4] or grow up to be wicked, while the sinner is reduced to poverty.

2) It is forbidden to bring on an erection (in vain), or to cause yourself to think about women. If a [lewd] thought comes spontaneously, you should divert your attention from nonsense to words of Torah, which is likened to, "A lovely hind and a graceful doe." Lewd thoughts prevail only in a heart devoid of (Torah) wisdom. You should be extremely careful to avoid an erection. Therefore, it is forbidden to sleep on your back facing upward, or to sleep (on your stomach) facing downward, but you should sleep on your side to avoid an erection. Two bachelors should not sleep in one bed. You should not watch animals, beasts, or fowl when the male and female copulate. It is forbidden to ride on an animal without a saddle.

3) When urinating, it is forbidden to hold the penis[5] even to facilitate urination. If you are married and your wife is also with you in town, and she is clean (menstrually), from the *halachic* standpoint it is permitted; for when a person has the possibility, he will usually not succumb to lustful thoughts and stimulation. But it is a matter of piety to be stringent even in this situation.[6] When not for the purpose of urinating, even *halachically* the above mentioned things are forbidden.

4) At supper you should not eat or drink excessively nor eat any foods that tend to heat the body, such as fat meats, all milk products, cheese, eggs, and garlic. Neither should you drink a beverage that tends to heat the body, for these things cause the committing of this sin.

5) If, God forbid, you had a seminal emission at night, upon waking up from your sleep you should wash your hands and say with a contrite heart, "Master of the Universe I have done this unwittingly but it was due to sinful thoughts and sinful reflections; therefore, may it be Your will Adonoy, my God, and the God of my fathers, to erase this iniquity through your great mercy, and save me from sinful thoughts, and from similar occurrences forever and ever. *Amein,* so may it be Your will."

6) If you wish to avoid this sin, guard your mouth against obscene language, lies, talebearing, slander, and mockery. You should also guard your ears from hearing such talk. You must also be careful to fulfill your vows, not to worry too much about things, and be careful to guard yourself against lewd thoughts. Before going to sleep you should study Torah or say the first four Chapters of the Psalms,[7] and be careful not to sleep alone in a room.

---

3. *Genesis* 38:7.
4. Under the age of Bar or Bas-Mitzvah.
5. From the glans and downward is permitted even while erect. (*Mishnah Berurah* 3:25)
6. If you are standing in a place where you are afraid of falling, it is not even piety to be strict, provided you are married. (*Mishnah Berurah* 3:28)
7. See *Kitzur Shulchan Aruch* 132:5.

ז) תִּקּוּנִים לְמִי שֶׁנִּכְשַׁל בְּחֵטְא זֶה כְּתוּבִים בַּסֵּפֶר יְסוֹד יוֹסֵף, אֲשֶׁר לִקֵּט וְאָסַף מִסְּפָרִים קְדוֹשִׁים וְקַדְמוֹנִים. וְאֶכְתֹּב פֹּה קְצָת מֵהֶם בְּקִצּוּר, לְהַדֵּר לִהְיוֹת סַנְדָּק, שֶׁיִּמּוֹלוּ יְלָדִים עַל בִּרְכָּיו, וּבִפְרָט לִהְיוֹת סַנְדָּק אֵצֶל עֲנִיִּים, לְהַרְבּוֹת בִּצְדָקָה לַעֲנִיִּים, לִשְׁמֹר שַׁבָּת כְּהִלְכָתָהּ וּלְעָנְגָהּ וּלְהַדְלִיק נֵרוֹת הַרְבֵּה, לְכַבֵּד וְלֶאֱהֹב לוֹמְדֵי תוֹרָה, לְהִתְפַּלֵּל בְּכַוָּנָה וּבְבֶכִי, לִבְחוֹר בְּמִדַּת הָעֲנָוָה. וְכַאֲשֶׁר יִשְׁמַע שֶׁמְּחָרְפִים אוֹתוֹ, יִשְׁתֹּק וְיִמְחֹל. כַּאֲשֶׁר יַעֲשֶׂה אֵיזוֹ מִצְוָה, יַעֲשֶׂהָ בְּכֹחַ וּבִזְרִיזוּת עַד שֶׁיִּתְחַמֵּם בָּהּ, וּבִפְרָט בַּעֲשִׂיַּת הַמַּצּוֹת לַפֶּסַח. לְגַדֵּל בָּנָיו לְתַלְמוּד תּוֹרָה וּלְהַדְרִיכָם בְּיִרְאַת־שָׁמַיִם. לְגַדֵּל יָתוֹם בְּתוֹךְ בֵּיתוֹ, וְיִתְנַהֵג עִמּוֹ כְּמוֹ עִם בְּנוֹ. לַעֲסֹק בְּמִצְוַת הַכְנָסַת כַּלָּה. לַעֲלוֹת לַתּוֹרָה לְכָל־הַפָּחוֹת פַּעַם אַחַת בְּכָל חֹדֶשׁ, וִיבָרֵךְ הַבְּרָכוֹת בְּקוֹל רָם. גַּם יִסְתַּכֵּל בַּתּוֹרָה וְיִקְרָא בְלַחַשׁ עִם הַקּוֹרֵא. לִהְיוֹת מִן הָעֲשָׂרָה הָרִאשׁוֹנִים בְּבֵית־הַכְּנֶסֶת. לַעֲמֹד בַּחֲצוֹת לַיְלָה לַעֲשׂוֹת תִּקּוּן חֲצוֹת בִּבְכִי. וְאִם אִי אֶפְשָׁר לוֹ לָקוּם בַּחֲצוֹת הַלַּיְלָה, יַעֲשֶׂה אַחַר כָּךְ תִּקּוּן חֲצוֹת. לֶאֱהֹב שָׁלוֹם וְלִרְדֹּף שָׁלוֹם.

סִימָן קנב
אִסּוּר יִחוּד וּשְׁאָר קֻרְבוֹת בְּנָשִׁים

א) אָסוּר לְהִתְיַחֵד עִם שׁוּם אִשָּׁה, בֵּין יַלְדָּה בֵּין זְקֵנָה, בֵּין יִשְׂרְאֵלִית בֵּין גּוֹיָה, בֵּין קְרוֹבָתוֹ בֵּין אֵינָהּ קְרוֹבָתוֹ, חוּץ מִן הָאָב שֶׁמֻּתָּר לְהִתְיַחֵד עִם בִּתּוֹ, וְהָאֵם עִם בְּנָהּ, וְהַבַּעַל עִם אִשְׁתּוֹ, אַף־עַל־פִּי שֶׁהִיא נִדָּה. (וְכַלָּה שֶׁהִיא נִדָּה, עַיֵּן לְקַמָּן סִימָן קנז).

ב) אִם הָיְתָה אִשְׁתּוֹ שָׁמָּה, מֻתָּר לוֹ לְהִתְיַחֵד גַּם עִם אַחֶרֶת, מִפְּנֵי שֶׁאִשְׁתּוֹ מְשַׁמַּרְתּוֹ. אֲבָל יִשְׂרְאֵלִית, לֹא תִתְיַחֵד עִם גּוֹי, אֲפִלּוּ אִשְׁתּוֹ עִמּוֹ. וַאֲפִלּוּ הֵם הַרְבֵּה גּוֹיִם וּנְשׁוֹתֵיהֶם עִמָּהֶם, לֹא תִתְיַחֵד עִמָּהֶם.

ג) אִשָּׁה אַחַת, מִתְיַחֶדֶת עִם שְׁנֵי אֲנָשִׁים כְּשֵׁרִים. וְדַוְקָא בָּעִיר וּבַיּוֹם. אֲבָל בַּשָּׂדֶה, אוֹ בַלַּיְלָה אֲפִלּוּ בָעִיר, בָּעֵינַן שְׁלֹשָׁה אֲנָשִׁים כְּשֵׁרִים.

---

8. See *Kitzur Shulchan Aruch* 1:5.

9. See also *Kitzur Shulchan Aruch* 198:7.

1. *Tur* rules that *yichud* with a Jewish relative with whom relations would be considered incest is a Scriptural prohibition. According to *Rambam* it is *Divrei Kabalah,* and the penalty is flogging in the same manner as for violation of Rabbinic ordinances. *Yichud* with an unmarried girl is prohibited by decree of King David and his court. However, once they have menstru-

7) Means of amendment for a person who has succumbed to this sin, are recorded in the book, *Yesod Yosef,* which the author culled and gathered from holy and ancient books. Here I will cite some of them briefly: He should try to be *sandeik,* that is, to have babies circumcised on his knees (lap), and in particular to be a *sandeik* for poor families. He should increase his charity to the poor, observe Shabbos properly and honor it delightfully, and light many Shabbos candles. He should honor and love those who learn Torah. He should pray with fervor and tears. He should adopt the character of humility, and if he hears people insult him, he should be quiet and forgiving. When performing a mitzvah, he should do it energetically and with quickness until it warms him, particularly when preparing the *matzos* for Pesach. He should raise his children to study Torah. and train them to be God-fearing. He should raise an orphan in his home, and should treat him as he treats his own son. He should engage in the mitzvah of dowering poor brides. He should be called up to the reading of the Torah at least once a month, and recite the *berachos* aloud. He should look in the Torah, and read quietly along with the reader. He should try to be among the first ten to come to the Synagogue. He should arise in the middle of the night to recite *tikun chatzos*[8] with tears. And if it is impossible for him to get up in the middle of the night, he should recite *tikun chatzos* later in the night. He should love peace and should pursue peace.[9]

Chapter 152

Prohibition Against Being Secluded with Women and Other Forbidden Associations with Them.

1) It is forbidden to be secluded with any woman whether young or old, a Jewess or a non-Jewess,[1] whether she is a relative or not a relative, with the exception of a father who may be alone with his daughter,[2] and a mother with her son,[3] and a husband with his wife, even though she is menstrually unclean.[4] (Concerning a bride who is menstrually unclean see Chapter 157, below).

2) If your wife is [also] present, you are permitted to be alone even with another woman because your wife is a chaperon. But a Jewess may not be alone with a non-Jew, even in the presence of his wife. Even if there are many non-Jews accompanied by their wives, she may not be alone with them.

3) One woman may be alone with two virtuous men, but only in town, and in the daytime. But in a field, or at night even in the city, there must be [at least] three

---

ated, they are always in a state of *niddah* (for unmarried girls are not accustomed to purify themselves from menstrual uncleanliness. See *Kitzur Shulchan Aruch* 159–162), and therefore *yichud* with them is prohibited as with relatives. *Yichud* with a non-Jewess is prohibited by decree of *Shamai* and *Hillel* and their courts. See *Shulchan Aruch Even Ha'Ezer* 22:1,2.

2. Or with his granddaughter, great grand etc. (*Bach*)

3. The issue of *yichud* with a grandmother requires further deliberation. (*Ezer Mikodesh*)

4. You may be alone with your sister temporarily (*Rosh*). However, *Beis Shmuel* says the *Rambam* and *Tur* possibly disagree.

וְעִם פְּרִיצִים, לְעוֹלָם לֹא תִתְיַחֵד אֲפִלּוּ הֵם כַּמָּה, אֶלָּא אִם כֵּן נְשׁוֹתֵיהֶם עִמָּהֶם. וְאִישׁ אֶחָד, עִם שְׁתֵּי נָשִׁים אָסוּר לְהִתְיַחֵד. וְעִם שָׁלֹשׁ אוֹ יוֹתֵר, יֵשׁ מַתִּירִין אִם אֵין אֻמָּנוּתוֹ אוֹ סְחוֹרָתוֹ בִּדְבָרִים הַמְיֻחָדִים לְנָשִׁים. וְיֵשׁ אוֹסְרִין בְּכָל עִנְיָן.

ד) אִשָּׁה שֶׁבַּעְלָהּ בָּעִיר, אֵין חוֹשְׁשִׁין לְהִתְיַחֵד עִמָּהּ, מִפְּנֵי שֶׁאֵימַת בַּעְלָהּ עָלֶיהָ.

ה) בַּיִת שֶׁפִּתְחוֹ פָּתוּחַ לִרְשׁוּת הָרַבִּים, אֵין שָׁם אִסּוּר יִחוּד בַּיּוֹם וּבִתְחִלַּת הַלַּיְלָה, כָּל זְמַן שֶׁבְּנֵי אָדָם עוֹבְרִים וְשָׁבִים בָּרְחוֹב וְאִם הָיָה זֶה רָגִיל בָּהּ, כְּגוֹן שֶׁגָּדְלָה עִמּוֹ, אוֹ שֶׁהִיא קְרוֹבָתוֹ, אוֹ שֶׁבַּעְלָהּ הִזְהִיר אוֹתָהּ שֶׁלֹּא תִתְיַחֵד עִמּוֹ, הֲרֵי זוֹ לֹא תִתְיַחֵד עִמּוֹ, אֲפִלּוּ בַּעְלָהּ בָּעִיר, וַאֲפִלּוּ בְּבַיִת שֶׁהַפֶּתַח פָּתוּחַ לִרְשׁוּת הָרַבִּים.

ו) תִּינֹקֶת שֶׁהִיא פְּחוּתָה מִשָּׁלֹשׁ שָׁנִים, מֻתָּרִין לְהִתְיַחֵד עִמָּהּ. וְכֵן תִּינוֹק פָּחוּת מִתֵּשַׁע שָׁנִים, מֻתָּר לְאִשָּׁה שֶׁתִּתְיַחֵד עִמּוֹ.

ז) מִי שֶׁאֵין לוֹ אִשָּׁה, לֹא יְהֵא מְלַמֵּד תִּינוֹקוֹת, מִפְּנֵי שֶׁאִמּוֹתֵיהֶן בָּאוֹת לְבֵית־הַסֵּפֶר, וְנִמְצָא מִתְיַחֵד עִם אִשָּׁה וְאֵינוֹ צָרִיךְ שֶׁתִּהְיֶה אִשְׁתּוֹ שְׁרוּיָה עִמּוֹ בְּבֵית־הַסֵּפֶר, אֶלָּא שֶׁתְּהֵא עִמּוֹ בָּעִיר, אֲפִלּוּ הִיא בְּבֵיתָהּ וְהוּא מְלַמֵּד בִּמְקוֹמוֹ. אֲבָל אִשָּׁה לֹא תְלַמֵּד תִּינוֹקוֹת אֲפִלּוּ יֵשׁ לָהּ בַּעַל בָּעִיר, אֶלָּא אִם הוּא דָר עִמָּהּ בְּאוֹתוֹ בַּיִת מִפְּנֵי אֲבִיהֶם שֶׁמְּבִיאִים אֶת בְּנֵיהֶם.

ח) צָרִיךְ הָאָדָם לְהִתְרַחֵק מִן הַנָּשִׁים מְאֹד מְאֹד. אָסוּר לִקְרֹץ בְּיָדָיו אוֹ בְּרַגְלָיו וְלִרְמֹז בְּעֵינָיו לְאִשָּׁה. וְאָסוּר לִשְׂחוֹק עִמָּהּ, לְהָקֵל רֹאשׁוֹ כְּנֶגְדָּהּ אוֹ לְהַבִּיט בְּיָפְיָהּ. וְאָסוּר לְהָרִיחַ בִּבְשָׂמִים הַמְיֻחָדִים לְאִשָּׁה. וְכָל־שֶׁכֵּן כְּשֶׁהִיא אוֹחַזְתָּן בְּיָדֶיהָ אוֹ שֶׁהֵן תְּלוּיִין עָלֶיהָ. וְאָסוּר לְהִסְתַּכֵּל בְּבִגְדֵי צִבְעוֹנִין שֶׁל אִשָּׁה שֶׁהוּא מַכִּיר אוֹתָהּ אֲפִלּוּ הַבְּגָדִים אֵינָם עָלֶיהָ, שֶׁמָּא יָבוֹא לְהַרְהֵר בָּהּ. פָּגַע אִשָּׁה בַּשּׁוּק, אָסוּר לְהַלֵּךְ אַחֲרֶיהָ, אֶלָּא רָץ, שֶׁתִּשָּׁאֵר לִצְדָדִין אוֹ לְאַחֲרָיו. וְלֹא יַעֲבוֹר בְּפֶתַח זוֹנָה, אֲפִלּוּ בְּרִחוּק אַרְבַּע אַמּוֹת. וְהַמִּסְתַּכֵּל אֲפִלּוּ בְּאֶצְבַּע קְטַנָּה שֶׁל אִשָּׁה וְנִתְכַּוֵּן לֵהָנוֹת מִמֶּנָּה, עֲוֹנוֹ גָּדוֹל מְאֹד. וְאָסוּר לִשְׁמֹעַ קוֹל זֶמֶר שֶׁל אִשָּׁה אוֹ לְהִסְתַּכֵּל בִּשְׂעָרָהּ.

---

5. Rashbah, Responsa 1,265 rules there is no *yichud* in such a case until the door is locked, however, *Beis Meir* and *Rabbi Akiva Eiger* Responsa 100 say that unless the door is opened, there is *yichud;* even if it is closed and not locked.

virtuous men present. With immoral men, she should never be alone, even if they are many, unless their wives are with them. One man is forbidden to be secluded with two women. Some authorities permit seclusion with three or more women, provided his vocation or trade is not specifically for women. Other authorities forbid it in any event.

4) If a woman's husband is in town, you need not be concerned about being secluded with her, because she is in fear of her husband.

5) In a room where the door is open[5] to a public thoroughfare,[6] there is no prohibition of *yichud* during the daytime and in the early evening, so long as people are passing by on the street. But if he is an intimate friend of hers, like one with whom she grew up, or if she is related to him, or if her husband warned her not to be alone with him, she may not be alone with him, even if her husband is in town, and not even in a room whose door is opened to a public thoroughfare.

6) If a girl is less than three years old, it is permitted to be secluded with her. Likewise, if a boy is less than nine years old a woman is permitted to be alone with him.

7) A man who does not have a wife should not teach children, because their mothers come to the school and at times he will be alone with a woman. [If he is married], it is not necessary that his wife be with him at the school, so long as she is in town; even if she is at home, and he teaches at the school. But a woman should not teach children even if her husband is in town, unless her husband lives with her in the house (where she teaches), because the fathers bring their children to school.

8) A man must diligently avoid women. It is forbidden to make gestures with your hands or with your feet, nor wink your eyes at a woman. It is forbidden to jest with her, to act with levity in her presence, or to gaze at her beauty. It is forbidden to smell perfumes designed specifically for a woman; especially when she is holding them in her hands, or when they are on her. It is forbidden to look at the colored garments of a woman with whom you are acquainted, although the garments are not upon her lest you come to think about her. If you encounter a woman on the street, it is forbidden to walk behind her, but you should hasten your steps so that she is alongside you or behind you. You should not pass by the door of a harlot, even at a distance of four cubits. He who gazes, even at the small finger of a woman in order to enjoy its sight[7], commits a very grave sin.[8] It is forbidden to listen to the voice [of a woman] singing[9] or to gaze at a woman's hair.[10]

---

6. *Chochmas Adam* 112:7 questions if three dwellers in a yard is considered a thoroughfare or not.

7. If she is a *niddah*. But just to look without deriving pleasure is permissible, but it is not proper to do so. (*Mishnah Berurah* 75:7)

8. "You shall not stray after your hearts and after your eyes." (*Mishnah Berurah* 75:7.

9. Even if she is a non-Jewess and single. (*Mishnah Berurah* 75:17—*Peri Megadim.*)

10. This applies also to single girls who do not have to cover their hair. It is also forbidden to gaze at the small amount of hair that sometimes protrudes from under the headpieces of many women (even in regions where they allow this little protrusion). (see *Mishnah Berurah* 75:13)

ט) אֵין שׁוֹאֲלִין בִּשְׁלוֹם אִשָּׁה כְּלָל. וַאֲפִלּוּ עַל יְדֵי בַעְלָהּ, אָסוּר לִשְׁלֹחַ לָהּ דִּבְרֵי שְׁלוֹמִים. וְלָכֵן כְּשֶׁכּוֹתֵב אִגֶּרֶת לַחֲבֵרוֹ אָסוּר לִכְתּוֹב, וְתֹאמַר שָׁלוֹם לְזוּגָתְךָ. אֲבָל מֻתָּר לִשְׁאֹל לְבַעְלָהּ אוֹ לְאַחֵר, אֵיךְ שְׁלוֹמָהּ. וְכֵן מֻתָּר לִכְתֹּב לַחֲבֵרוֹ, הוֹדִיעֵנִי מִשְּׁלוֹם זוּגָתְךָ.

י) הַמְחַבֵּק אוֹ הַמְנַשֵּׁק אֲפִלּוּ אַחַת מִן הַקְּרוֹבוֹת, שֶׁאֵין לוֹ שׁוּם הֲנָאָה, הֲרֵי זֶה עוֹשֶׂה אִסּוּר, שֶׁאֵין קְרֵבִים לְעֶרְוָה כְּלָל, חוּץ מִן הָאָב עִם בִּתּוֹ וְהָאֵם עִם בְּנָהּ, שֶׁהֵם מֻתָּרִין בְּחִבּוּק וְנִשּׁוּק.

יא) אֵין לִנְהֹג אֲפִלּוּ עִם אִשְׁתּוֹ בִּדְבָרִים שֶׁל חִבָּה, כְּגוֹן לְעַיֵּן בְּרֵישָׁהּ וְכַדּוֹמֶה בִּפְנֵי אֲחֵרִים, שֶׁלֹּא יָבוֹא הָרוֹאֶה לִידֵי הִרְהוּר.

יב) אָסוּר לְאִישׁ שֶׁיָּדוּר בְּבֵית חָמִיו, אֶלָּא כְּשֶׁיֵּשׁ לוֹ חֶדֶר מְיֻחָד לִשְׁכִיבָה.

יג) כְּבָר הֶאֱרִיכוּ גְדוֹלֵי יִשְׂרָאֵל זִכְרוֹנָם לִבְרָכָה בְּסִפְרֵיהֶם הַקְּדוֹשִׁים בְּתוֹכָחוֹת מוּסָרִים עַל הַמִּנְהָג הָרַע בְּאֵיזֶה מְקוֹמוֹת שֶׁאֵינָן בְּנֵי תוֹרָה וְיִרְאָה, שֶׁמִּתְקָרְבִים הֶחָתָן עִם הַכַּלָּה בְּחִבּוּק וְנִשּׁוּק, וְכֵן רִקּוּדִים בַּחוּרִים עִם בְּתוּלוֹת יַחַד. וּמִלְּבַד הָאִסּוּר הַגָּדוֹל, אִסּוּר נִדָּה, שֶׁהֲרֵי כָּל הַבְּתוּלוֹת מִסְתָמָא נִדּוֹת הֵן, וְאֵין חִלּוּק בְּאִסּוּר נִדָּה בֵּין פְּנוּיָה לִנְשׂוּאָה, וְכָל הַנּוֹגֵעַ בָּהּ דֶּרֶךְ חִבָּה, חַיָּב מַלְקוּת, עוֹד מְגָרֶה יֵצֶר־הָרַע בְּנַפְשֵׁהּ, וּמֵבִיא אֶת עַצְמוֹ לִידֵי קִשּׁוּי לָדַעַת וְהוֹצָאַת זֶרַע לְבַטָּלָה, רַחֲמָנָא לִצְּלָן. וּבְוַדַּאי כָּל מִי שֶׁיֵּשׁ בְּיָדוֹ לִמְחוֹת, צָרִיךְ לְהִתְאַמֵּץ בְּכָל כֹּחוֹ לִמְחוֹת. וּלְכָל־הַפָּחוֹת צָרִיךְ כָּל אִישׁ אֲשֶׁר יִרְאַת ה׳ בִּלְבָבוֹ, לִהְיוֹת שׂוֹרֵר בְּבֵיתוֹ וּלְהַשְׁגִּיחַ עַל בְּנֵי בֵיתוֹ, שֶׁיִּתְרַחֲקוּ מִן הַכִּעוּר הַגָּדוֹל הַזֶּה. וְכָל מִי שֶׁיֵּשׁ בְּיָדוֹ לִמְחוֹת וְאֵינוֹ מוֹחֶה, חַס־וְשָׁלוֹם, הוּא נִתְפָּס בְּעָוֹן זֶה. וְכָל הַמַּצִּיל אֶת אֲחֵרִים מִן הַחֵטְא, הִצִּיל אֶת נַפְשׁוֹ וְטוֹב לוֹ.

יד) אִשָּׁה שֶׁהוּא רוֹצֶה לִשָּׂא אוֹתָהּ, מֻתָּר לוֹ וְרָאוּי לוֹ לִרְאוֹתָהּ אִם הִיא לִרְצוֹנוֹ. אֲבָל לֹא יִסְתַּכֵּל בָּהּ דֶּרֶךְ זְנוּת. וְעַל זֶה נֶאֱמַר, בְּרִית כָּרַתִּי לְעֵינָי, וּמָה אֶתְבּוֹנֵן עַל בְּתוּלָה.

טו) מִי שֶׁגֵּרַשׁ אֶת אִשְׁתּוֹ מִן הַנִּשּׂוּאִין, לֹא תָדוּר עִמּוֹ בֶּחָצֵר. וְאִם הוּא כֹּהֵן, וְכֵן אֲפִלּוּ אִם הוּא יִשְׂרָאֵל, וְהִיא נִשֵּׂאת לְאַחֵר וְנִתְגָּרְשָׁה גַּם

9) You must refrain from showing interest in women. It is forbidden to send her regards even through her husband. Therefore, when writing a letter to your friend, it is forbidden to write, "Send regards to your wife." But it is permitted to inquire of her husband or of someone else about her welfare. It is also permitted to write to your friend, "Let me know how your wife is doing."

10) If you hug or kiss even one of your female relatives, even though you derive no pleasure from it, you are violating a prohibition, for you may not have any physical closeness with a near relative, with the exception of a father with his daughter, and a mother with her son, who are permitted to hug and kiss.

11) You must not engage in any intimate activities, even with your wife in the presence of others, so that on-lookers will not be led to sinful thoughts.

12) A man must not dwell in his father-in-law's house, unless he has a private bedroom.

13) The great men of Yisrael, of blessed memory, in their holy works, admonished against the evil custom prevailing in some communities, where there are no Torah scholars or God-fearing men, that the groom and bride become intimate with hugs and kisses; and they also allow dances, in which boys and girls dance together. All virgins are assumed to be menstrually unclean, and since the prohibition of *niddah* applies to married and single woman alike, whoever touches a woman in an intimate manner deserves punishment by lashing. Besides the grave sin of touching a *niddah,* he also stirs the evil impulse within himself, and causes himself to have an erection, and to discharge semen in vain, God forbid. Certainly anyone who is able to effectively protest [against this custom] must make every endeavor to protest. At least, it is the duty of every man who has the fear of God in his heart, to control his household, and to supervise the members of his family, so that they will keep themselves distant from this extremely abominable behavior. Anyone who is able to effectively protest and does not protest, God forbid, he too will be accountable for this very iniquity. Anyone who saves others from sin has saved himself (too), and it shall be well with him.

14) With regard to the woman whom you wish to marry, it is permissible and even desirable for you to look at her to see if she pleases you, but you may not gaze upon her in a lustful manner. Concerning this it is said, "I made a covenant with my eyes, how then can I ever gaze at a maiden."[11]

15) If you divorced the wife you married, she may not reside in the same courtyard as you do. If you are a *kohein,* or even a *Yisroeil*, but she has since married

11. *Job* 31:1.

מִמֶּנּוּ, וְכֵן מִי שֶׁגֵּרַשׁ אֶת אִשְׁתּוֹ מִשּׁוּם שֶׁהִיא אֲסוּרָה לוֹ, כָּל אֵלּוּ צְרִיכִין הַרְחָקָה יְתֵרָה, וְלֹא תָדוּר עִמּוֹ בְּמָבוֹי, אִם הוּא מָבוֹי סָתוּם. אֲבָל בְּמָבוֹי מְפֻלָּשׁ שֶׁדֶּרֶךְ הָרַבִּים עוֹבֵר בֵּינֵיהֶם, מֻתָּרִים לָדוּר. וּגְרוּשָׁה שֶׁנִּשֵּׂאת וְדָרָה עִם בַּעְלָהּ הַשֵּׁנִי, אֵלּוּ צְרִיכִין עוֹד הַרְחָקָה יְתֵרָה, וְלֹא תָדוּר עִם בַּעְלָהּ הָרִאשׁוֹן בְּכָל הַשְּׁכוּנָה. בְּכָל אֵלּוּ הַהַרְחָקוֹת, הִיא נִדְחֵית מִפָּנָיו. אַךְ אִם הָיְתָה הֶחָצֵר שֶׁלָּהּ, הוּא נִדְחֶה מִפָּנֶיהָ.

טז) מֻתָּר לְאָדָם לָזוּן גְּרוּשָׁתוֹ, וּמִצְוָה הִיא יוֹתֵר מִבִּשְׁאָר עָנִי, שֶׁנֶּאֱמַר, וּמִבְּשָׂרְךָ לֹא תִתְעַלָּם. וּבִלְבַד שֶׁלֹּא יְהֵא לוֹ עֵסֶק עִמָּהּ, רַק יְזוּנָהּ עַל יְדֵי שָׁלִיחַ.

יז) אָמַר רַב בְּרוּנָא אָמַר רַב, כָּל הַיָּשֵׁן בְּקִלְעָא (בְּחֶדֶר) שֶׁאִישׁ וְאִשְׁתּוֹ שְׁרוּיִין בָּהּ, עָלָיו הַכָּתוּב אוֹמֵר, נְשֵׁי עַמִּי תְּגָרְשׁוּן מִבֵּית תַּעֲנֻגֶיהָ (שֶׁבּוֹשִׁין הֵן מִמֶּנּוּ). וְאָמַר רַב יוֹסֵף, אֲפִלּוּ בְּאִשְׁתּוֹ נִדָּה.

סִימָן קנג
הִלְכוֹת נִדָּה

א) כָּל אִשָּׁה שֶׁנֶּעֶקְרָה מִמְּקוֹרָהּ טִפַּת דָּם, אֲפִלּוּ כָּל שֶׁהִיא, יִהְיֶה בְּאֵיזֶה אֹפֶן שֶׁיִּהְיֶה, בֵּין בְּטִבְעָהּ, כְּדֶרֶךְ הַנָּשִׁים לִרְאוֹת בִּזְמַנִּים יְדוּעִים, אוֹ שֶׁלֹּא בִּזְמַנָּהּ וַאֲפִלּוּ אֵרַע לָהּ אֵיזֶה אֹנֶס, אֲשֶׁר מֵחֲמַת זֶה יָצָא מִמְּקוֹרָהּ דָּם, הֲרֵי הִיא טְמֵאָה נִדָּה, עַד שֶׁתִּסְפֹּר שִׁבְעָה נְקִיִּים וְתִטְבֹּל כָּרָאוּי. וְכָל הַבָּא עָלֶיהָ בְּטֻמְאָתָהּ, חַיָּב כָּרֵת, וְכֵן הִיא חַיֶּבֶת כָּרֵת. וְעַל הַנְּגִיעָה דֶּרֶךְ חִבָּה, חַיָּבִים מַלְקוּת.

ב) אֲפִלּוּ לֹא הִרְגִּישָׁה שֶׁיָּצָא דָם מִמְּקוֹרָהּ, אֶלָּא שֶׁמָּצְאָה כֶּתֶם דָּם בִּבְשָׂרָהּ אוֹ בַּחֲלוּקָהּ אוֹ בִּסְדִינָהּ אוֹ בִּשְׁאָר מָקוֹם, וְאֵין לָהּ לִתְלוֹת שֶׁבָּא מִמָּקוֹם אַחֵר, אֶלָּא שֶׁבָּא מִמְּקוֹרָהּ, הֲרֵי הִיא טְמֵאָה. וְכָל אִשָּׁה שֶׁמָּצְאָה אֵיזֶה כֶּתֶם, אֲפִלּוּ אֵינוֹ אָדֹם מַמָּשׁ, אֶלָּא שֶׁאֵינוֹ לָבָן מַמָּשׁ, צְרִיכָה לַעֲשׂוֹת שְׁאֵלַת חָכָם, כִּי יֵשׁ בָּזֶה הַרְבֵּה חִלּוּקֵי דִינִים בְּעִנְיַן גַּדְלוּת

---

12. *Isaiah* 58:7.
13. *Michah* 2:8.
14. *Maseches Eruvin* 63:2.
1. The *koras* for this sin includes shortening of the life span to sixty years, and some say to fifty years (see *Tosafos Maseches Shabbos* 25a and *Tosafos Maseches Yevamos* 2a). Also his

another man, and was divorced from him too; or if you divorced her because she was forbidden to you; all of these require a greater measure of separation. And subsequently, she may not reside with you in the same alley if it comes to a dead-end. But if it is an open alley, through which there is traffic, they are permitted to live there. A divorced woman who remarried and lives with her second husband, they [she and her first husband] require an even greater measure of separation, and she may not dwell with her first husband in the same neighborhood. In all these cases of separation, the woman must move away from him. But if the courtyard belongs to her, he must move away from her.

16) A man is permitted to support his divorcee, and it is [even] a mitzvah to do so more than to another poor person, for it is said, "Do not hide from your own flesh."[12] But he may have no personal contact with her, and should send her support through an agent.

17) Said Rav Beruna in the name of Rav, "He who sleeps in a room in which a husband and wife reside, the Scripture says concerning him, "The women of My people you cast out of their pleasant houses",[13] (for they are ashamed to be intimate because of him). Rav Yosef said this applies even if his wife is menstrually unclean.[14]

Chapter 153

The Laws of a Woman Who is Menstrually Unclean

1) A woman from whose womb there issued a drop of blood, be it ever so small, regardless of the circumstances, whether it is in her nature, as some women, to have a regular period or an irregular period; even if she experienced some sort of accident which caused blood to issue from her womb, she is a *niddah* (menstrually unclean), until she counts seven clean days, and properly performs the ritual immersion. Anyone who cohabitates with her when she is menstrually unclean, receives the punishment of *koras.*[1] She too receives the punishment, *koras.* For touching in an intimate manner, their punishment is flagellation.[2]

2) Even if she did not feel the issue of blood from her womb, but found a stain of blood on her body, or garment, or sheet, or any other place, and she is unable to attribute its presence to any source other than from her womb, she is unclean.[3] A woman who finds a stain that is not actually red, but is not actually white either,[4] must consult a competent Rav, for concerning this there are many divergent laws

---

children die during his lifetime (*Tosafos Yevamos* 2a). And if he has no children now, he will never have any later (*Rashi* on *Leviticus* 20:20). Also see *Rambam* on *Maseches Sanhedrin* Chapt. 9 that when one dies he also receives a punishment for *koras* in the next world, as death is not an atonement for it.

2. This is *de'oraisa* according to the *Rambam.*

3. This, however, is a Rabbinic Law.

4. From this we deduct that if it is actually white, she is always clean. This is according to the ruling of *Taz* 188 who says if she saw a thick white stain within three hours of a bath,

וְקַטְנוּת הַכֶּתֶם וְגַם בְּעִנְיַן הַתְּלִיָּה, בַּמֶּה יְכוֹלִין לְתְלוֹתוֹ וּבַמֶּה אֵין יְכוֹלִין לְתְלוֹתוֹ, וְגַם יֵשׁ חִלּוּק בְּאֵיזֶה זְמַן שֶׁמָּצְאָה אוֹתוֹ, אִם בְּיָמִים שֶׁהִיא טְהוֹרָה אוֹ בַּיָּמִים הָרִאשׁוֹנִים מִשִּׁבְעָה נְקִיִּים.

ג) אִשָּׁה שֶׁהִרְגִּישָׁה שֶׁנִּפְתַּח מְקוֹרָהּ, אֲפִלּוּ בָּדְקָה אֶת עַצְמָהּ מִיָּד וְלֹא מָצְאָה כְלוּם, הֲרֵי הִיא טְמֵאָה. (וּצְרִיכִין לְהוֹדִיעַ זֹאת לַנָּשִׁים, כִּי הַרְבֵּה נָשִׁים אֵינָן יוֹדְעוֹת זֹאת). אֲבָל אִם מָצְאָה שֶׁיָּצְאָה מִמֶּנָּה אֵיזוֹ לֵחָה לְבָנָה בְּלִי שׁוּם תַּעֲרֹבֶת אַדְמוּמִית, הֲרֵי הִיא טְהוֹרָה.

ד) כְּתִיב, וְאֶל־אִשָּׁה בְּנִדַּת טֻמְאָתָהּ לֹא תִקְרַב. מִדִּכְתִיב לֹא תִקְרַב, דָּרְשִׁינָן, שֶׁכָּל מִינֵי קְרִיבָה אֲסוּרִים, שֶׁלֹּא יִשְׂחוֹק וְלֹא יָקֵל רֹאשׁוֹ עִמָּהּ אֲפִלּוּ בִדְבָרִים, [אִם] מַרְגִּילִין לַעֲבֵרָה. אֲבָל מֻתָּר לְהִתְיַחֵד עִמָּהּ, דְּכֵיוָן שֶׁכְּבָר בָּא עָלֶיהָ, וְגַם יֵשׁ לָהּ הֶתֵּר לְאַחַר שֶׁתִּטְבֹּל, לָא תַּקִּיף יִצְרֵהּ, וְלָא חָיְשִׁינָן שֶׁמָּא יָבוֹא עָלֶיהָ בְּאִסּוּר.

ה) לֹא יִגַּע בָּהּ אֲפִלּוּ בְּאֶצְבַּע קְטַנָּה, וְלֹא יוֹשִׁיט מִיָּדוֹ לְיָדָהּ אֲפִלּוּ דָּבָר אָרֹךְ, וְכֵן לֹא יְקַבֵּל מִיָּדָהּ. וְכֵן זְרִיקָה מִיָּדוֹ לְיָדָהּ אוֹ מִיָּדָהּ לְיָדוֹ, אֲסוּרָה.

ו) לֹא יֹאכַל עִמָּהּ עַל הַשֻּׁלְחָן, אֶלָּא אִם כֵּן יֵשׁ אֵיזֶה שִׁנּוּי, דְּהַיְנוּ שֶׁיִּהְיֶה אֵיזֶה דָּבָר מַפְסִיק בֵּין קְעָרָה שֶׁלּוֹ לִקְעָרָה שֶׁלָּהּ, דָּבָר שֶׁאֵין דַּרְכּוֹ לְהַנִּיחוֹ שָׁם בְּפַעַם אַחֶרֶת, אוֹ שֶׁתְּשַׁנֶּה אֶת מְקוֹמָהּ. וְאִם דַּרְכָּן שֶׁכְּשֶׁהִיא טְהוֹרָה אוֹכְלִין מִתּוֹךְ קְעָרָה אַחַת, וְעַתָּה אוֹכְלִין כָּל אֶחָד מִתּוֹךְ קְעָרָה אַחֶרֶת, סַגֵּי בְּהָכִי.

ז) לֹא יִשְׁתֶּה מִשְּׁיוּרֵי הַכּוֹס שֶׁשָּׁתְתָה הִיא. וְאִם הִפְסִיק אָדָם אַחֵר בֵּינֵיהֶם, אוֹ שֶׁהוּרַק אֶל כּוֹס אַחֵר, שָׁרֵי. וְאִם שָׁתְתָה וְהוּא אֵינוֹ יוֹדֵעַ, וְרוֹצֶה לִשְׁתּוֹת מִכּוֹס זֶה, אֵינָהּ צְרִיכָה לְהַגִּיד לוֹ שֶׁשָּׁתְתָה הִיא מִמֶּנּוּ. (אֲבָל אִם יָדַע שֶׁשָּׁתְתָה הִיא, אֶלָּא שֶׁלֹּא יָדַע שֶׁהִיא נִדָּה, נִרְאֶה דִּצְרִיכָה

---

she is clean. *Bach* and *Pardes Rimonim* say in such a case she must suspect it is blood that turned white because of her bath.

5. This is the consensus of virtually all *poskim* except the *Radvaz* Responsa 149 and *Ya'avetz* vol. 2 Responsa 5. If this occurred during pregnancy, or if she is a nursing mother, when normally she would not experience a menstrual flow, if she checked and found nothing, many *poskim* rule that she is clean. *Toras Hashlomim, Sidrei Taharah, Chochmas Adam* and

regarding the size of the stain. There are also many laws regarding to what it can be attributed and to what it cannot be attributed. There is also a distinction as to the time she found it, whether it was on her menstrually clean days or on the first days of her seven clean days.

3) If a woman senses that her womb has opened [i.e. she senses the beginning of mensruation], even if she examined herself immediately and found nothing, she is menstrually unclean.[5] (It is necessary to let women know this, for many women do not know it.) But if she found a white secretion from her body without any reddish admixture, she is clean.

4) It is written, "And to a woman who is menstrually unclean, you shall not approach."[6] Since it is written "You shall not approach," it is explained, that any kind of approach is forbidden. You should not jest (with her), and should not indulge in levity with her, or even speak words that may lead to sin.[7] However, you may be secluded with her, for since you have had marital relations with her, and she will be permitted to you after immersion, your impulse will not be that strong, and we are not concerned that you might cohabit with her when it is forbidden.

5) You may not touch your wife (during that period) even on the small finger, and you may not hand her anything,[8] not even a long object, nor may you receive anything from her hand. Also, throwing anything from your hand into her hand or from her hand to yours is forbidden.

6) You may not eat with her at the table[9] unless you make a noticeable change; for example, separating your plate from her plate, with something you do not usually place there at other times, or she should change her place. If you are accustomed, when she is menstrually clean, to eat together from one plate, and now when she is unclean you eat from separate plates, this change is sufficient.[10]

7) You are not allowed to drink what she leaves over in her cup. But if someone else drank from the cup after her, or it has been poured into another cup you are permitted to drink it. If she drank from it and you are unaware of it, and you want to drink from that cup, she need not tell you that she drank from it. (But if you know she drank from it but do not know that she is a *niddah,* it would seem that

---

Shulchan Aruch Harav. But many *poskim* hold she is considered unclean. *Nodah Beyehuda* (*Tinyana*) Responsa 120, *Chasam Sofer* Resp. 168, *Beis Lechem Yehuda, Rabbi Akiva Eiger.*

6. *Leviticus* 18:19.

7. But they may give gifts to one another. *Placey* 195.

8. This is a Rabbinic injunction. This applies even if you pass it in an unusual manner (*Bach*) and even in public (*Beis Yitzchok* Resp. 18). Even if she is embarrassed that people may realize she is a *niddah,* it is still forbidden. (*Igros Moshe* vol. 2 Resp. 77).

9. If there is someone else eating at the table, the prevailing custom is to permit it without any changes. *Massas Binyomin, Birkei Yosef* Sha'arei Deah.

10. This is valid only if they are eating the same menu. If not, the change is not noticeable. (*Sidrei Taharah* 195— *Maharashal*)

לְהַגִּיד לוֹ). הִיא מֻתֶּרֶת לִשְׁתּוֹת מִשִּׁיּוּרֵי כּוֹס שֶׁלּוֹ. יֵשׁ אוֹמְרִים, דִּכְשֵׁם שֶׁאָסוּר לִשְׁתּוֹת מִשִּׁיּוּרֵי כּוֹס שֶׁלָּהּ, כָּךְ אָסוּר לֶאֱכוֹל מִשִּׁיּוּרֵי מַאֲכָל שֶׁלָּהּ.

ח) לֹא יִישַׁן עִמָּהּ בְּמִטָּה אַחַת, אֲפִלּוּ אֵין הַמִּטָּה מְיֻחֶדֶת לָהּ. וַאֲפִלּוּ כָּל אֶחָד בְּבִגְדוֹ וְאֵין נוֹגְעִין זֶה בָּזֶה. וַאֲפִלּוּ יֵשׁ לְכָל אֶחָד מַצָּע בִּפְנֵי עַצְמוֹ. וַאֲפִלּוּ אִם שׁוֹכְבִים בִּשְׁתֵּי מִטּוֹת, וְהַמִּטּוֹת נוֹגְעוֹת זוֹ בָּזוֹ, אָסוּר. וְאִם שׁוֹכְבִין עַל הָאָרֶץ, לֹא יִשְׁכְּבוּ פָּנִים כְּנֶגֶד פָּנִים, אֶלָּא אִם כֵּן יֵשׁ מֶרְחָק רַב בֵּינֵיהֶם. וְהוּא הַדִּין אִם יְשֵׁנִים בִּשְׁתֵּי מִטּוֹת סְמוּכוֹת זוֹ לָזוֹ בְּאָרְכָּן בְּאֹפֶן שֶׁלִּפְעָמִים הֵם פָּנִים כְּנֶגֶד פָּנִים, אַף־עַל־פִּי שֶׁיֵּשׁ הֶפְסֵק בֵּין הַמִּטּוֹת, יֵשׁ לֶאֱסֹר, אֶלָּא אִם כֵּן יֵשׁ מֶרְחָק רַב בֵּינֵיהֶם. וְאָסוּר לַבַּעַל אֲפִלּוּ לֵישֵׁב עַל הַמִּטָּה הַמְיֻחֶדֶת לָהּ, וַאֲפִלּוּ שֶׁלֹּא בְּפָנֶיהָ. וְהִיא, אֲסוּרָה לִישַׁן עַל הַמִּטָּה הַמְיֻחֶדֶת לוֹ. אֲבָל לֵישֵׁב עָלֶיהָ, אֵין לְהַחְמִיר.

ט) אֲסוּרִין לֵישֵׁב עַל סַפְסָל אָרֹךְ שֶׁהוּא מִתְנַדְנֵד. וְאִם אָדָם אַחֵר מַפְסִיק בֵּינֵיהֶם, מֻתָּר. וְלֹא יֵלְכוּ בַּעֲגָלָה אַחַת אוֹ בִּסְפִינָה אַחַת, אִם הוֹלְכִין רַק דֶּרֶךְ טִיּוּל, כְּגוֹן לְגַנּוֹת וּלְפַרְדֵּסִים וְכַיּוֹצֵא בָּזֶה. אֲבָל אִם הוֹלְכִין מֵעִיר לְעִיר לְעִסְקֵיהֶם, מֻתָּר, אַף־עַל־פִּי שֶׁהֵן לְבַדָּם, וּבִלְבַד שֶׁיֵּשְׁבוּ בְּאֹפֶן שֶׁלֹּא יִגְּעוּ זֶה בָּזֶה.

י) לֹא יִסְתַּכֵּל בְּשׁוּם מָקוֹם מִגּוּפָהּ בְּמָקוֹם שֶׁדַּרְכָּהּ לְכַסּוֹת. אֲבָל בִּמְקוֹמוֹת הַגְּלוּיִים, מֻתָּר לוֹ לְהִסְתַּכֵּל, אַף־עַל־פִּי שֶׁהוּא נֶהֱנֶה. אָסוּר לְהָרִיחַ בִּבְשָׂמִים הַמְיֻחָדִים לָהּ, וְאָסוּר לִשְׁמֹעַ קוֹל זֶמֶר שֶׁלָּהּ.

יא) רָאוּי שֶׁתְּיַחֵד לָהּ בְּגָדִים לִימֵי נִדָּתָהּ, כְּדֵי שֶׁיִּהְיוּ שְׁנֵיהֶם זוֹכְרִים תָּמִיד שֶׁהִיא נִדָּה. וּבְקֹשִׁי הִתִּירוּ לָהּ שֶׁתִּכְחֹל וְתִפְקֹס וְתִתְקַשֵּׁט בְּבִגְדֵי צִבְעוֹנִין בִּימֵי נִדָּתָהּ, אֶלָּא כְּדֵי שֶׁלֹּא תִתְגַּנֶּה עַל בַּעְלָהּ.

יב) לֹא תִמְזֹג לוֹ כּוֹס יַיִן בְּפָנָיו אוֹ לַהֲבִיאוֹ לוֹ וּלְהַנִּיחוֹ לְפָנָיו עַל

---

11. All the conditions that make it possible for you to drink her leftovers make it possible for you to eat her leftovers.

12. Only if it is one piece of food. But if there are two pieces on a plate and she eats one, the second one is not considered her leftover (*Igros Moshe* Resp. 92). If it is a food made up of many small pieces (like cut-up salads etc.) the whole salad is like one piece and is considered her leftover.

13. The *Kav Hayashar—Ariz'l* says they have to be far enough apart that his blanket will not come in contact with his wife's bed at any time throughout the night. The *Taharas Yisroel* says they have to be far enough apart that they will not touch one another while asleep.

she has to inform you). She is permitted to drink the leftovers from your cup. Some authorities maintain that just as you are forbidden to drink the leftovers from her cup so too you are forbidden[11] to eat from her leftover food.[12]

8) You may not sleep together in the same bed, even if the bed is not exclusively hers, and even if you are both fully clothed and do not touch one another, and even if each of you have a separate mattress. And even to lie on two separate beds, if the beds touch one another it is forbidden. If you both lie on the ground, you should not lie facing one another unless there is a sizable distance between you and her. The same applies if you sleep in two separate beds placed parallel to one another, whereby sometimes you face one another. Even though there is space between the beds, it is forbidden unless there is a sizable space between the beds.[13] The husband is forbidden even to sit on the bed[14] reserved for her, even when she is not present. She is forbidden to sleep on the bed reserved for her husband. But so far as her sitting on it, you need not be stringent.

9) It is forbidden to sit together on a long bench, if it sways. If someone else sits[15] between you, it is permitted. You may not ride together in the same wagon or on the same boat, if it is just a pleasure trip, like riding through parks, orchards or similar excursions. But if you are travelling from city to city on business, it is permitted, even though you are by yourselves; provided you are seated in a way that you will not touch one another.

10) You must not look at any part of her body that she usually keeps covered.[16] But on those parts that are usually not covered, you are permitted to look even if you derive pleasure from it. You are forbidden to scent her personal perfume, and you are forbidden to hear her sing.

11) It is proper that she wear special clothes[17] on the days of her impurity, so that they will both always remember that she is menstrually unclean. With great *halachic* difficulty, the Sages permitted her to use cosmetics (rouge, lipstick etc.), and to dress in colorful (attractive) clothing[18] during her days of impurity, so that she will not become repulsive to her husband.

12) She may not pour a cup of wine for you in your presence,[19] nor may she

---

14. Or pillows (*Chochmas Adam*) or linens (*Pischei Teshuva*).

15. Even a baby.

16. I.e. in the house. However, those parts of the body she keeps covered only when she is out of the house you are permitted to see since you are accustomed to seeing it. (*Igros Moshe* Vol. 2 Responsa 75)

17. One item is enough. *Sidrei Taharah* 195:8.

18. If her husband doesn't mind, it is preferable that she does not do these things when she is a *niddah. Gra—Avos D'Rabbi Nosson, Sha'arei Tohar.*

19. *Rashba* and *Rav Hamaggid* say that this rule applies only to wine and not to anything else. This is also the opinion of the *Taz, Lechem V'Simla* (author of the *Kitzur*) and *Aruch Hashulchan.* However the *Bach* and *Shach* say it applies to all food and beverage (except water). *Chochmas Adam* says it is best to be strict if possible.

הַשֻּׁלְחָן, וְלֹא תַצִּיעַ לוֹ מִטָּתוֹ בְּפָנָיו. אֲבָל שֶׁלֹּא בְּפָנָיו, הַכֹּל מֻתָּר, אַף־עַל־פִּי שֶׁהוּא יוֹדֵעַ שֶׁהִיא עָשְׂתָה. וַאֲסוּרָה לִצוֹק לוֹ מַיִם לִרְחוֹץ פָּנָיו יָדָיו וְרַגְלָיו, וַאֲפִלּוּ מַיִם צוֹנְנִים.

יג) כְּשֵׁם שֶׁהִיא אֲסוּרָה לִמְזֹג לוֹ אֶת הַכּוֹס, כָּךְ הוּא אָסוּר לִמְזֹג לָהּ. וְלֹא עוֹד, אֶלָּא אֲפִלּוּ לִשְׁלֹחַ לָהּ כּוֹס יַיִן הַמְיֻחָד לָהּ, אֲפִלּוּ הוּא כּוֹס שֶׁל בְּרָכָה, אָסוּר.

יד) אִם הוּא חוֹלֶה וְאֵין לוֹ מִי שֶׁיְּשַׁמֵּשׁ אוֹתוֹ זוּלָתָהּ, מֻתֶּרֶת לְשַׁמְּשׁוֹ שִׁמּוּשׁ שֶׁאֵין בּוֹ נְגִיעָה, רַק עַל יְדֵי דָבָר אַחֵר, אֲפִלּוּ לַהֲקִימוֹ וּלְהַשְׁכִּיבוֹ וּלְתָמְכוֹ, רַק שֶׁתִּזָּהֵר בְּיוֹתֵר מֵהַרְחָצַת פָּנָיו יָדָיו וְרַגְלָיו וְהַצָּעַת הַמִּטָּה בְּפָנָיו. וְאִם הָאִשָּׁה חוֹלָה, אָסוּר לְבַעְלָהּ לְשַׁמְּשָׁהּ, אֲפִלּוּ בְּלֹא נְגִיעָה, אֶלָּא אִם כֵּן בִּשְׁעַת דְּחָק גָּדוֹל, שֶׁאִי אֶפְשָׁר לִמְצֹא מִי שֶׁיְּשַׁמְּשֶׁנָּה. וְאִם הַבַּעַל הוּא רוֹפֵא וְאֵין שָׁם רוֹפֵא אַחֵר מֻמְחֶה כָּמוֹהוּ, מֻתָּר לוֹ לְמַשֵּׁשׁ לָהּ אֶת הַדֹּפֶק, כֵּיוָן שֶׁאֵינוֹ עוֹשֶׂה דֶּרֶךְ תַּאֲוָה וְחִבָּה.

טו) בְּכָל הַהַרְחָקוֹת הַנִּזְכָּרוֹת, צְרִיכִין לִזָּהֵר גַּם בִּימֵי לִבּוּנָהּ, דְּהַיְנוּ בִּימֵי סְפִירַת שִׁבְעָה נְקִיִּים, וְגַם אַחַר כָּךְ, אִם נִתְאַחֲרָה מִלִּטְבֹּל בִּזְמַנָּהּ, אֲסוּרִים בְּכָל הַנִּזְכָּר עַד לְאַחַר שֶׁתִּטְבֹּל.

טז) אִשָּׁה נִדָּה, בִּימֵי רְאִיָּתָהּ קֹדֶם יְמֵי לִבּוּנָהּ, נוֹהֲגִין שֶׁאֵינָהּ נִכְנֶסֶת לְבֵית־הַכְּנֶסֶת וְאֵינָהּ מִתְפַּלֶּלֶת אַךְ בַּיָּמִים הַנּוֹרָאִים, דְּהַיְנוּ מִיּוֹם רִאשׁוֹן דִּסְלִיחוֹת וּלְהַלָּן שֶׁרַבִּים מִתְאַסְּפִים בְּבֵית־הַכְּנֶסֶת, וְיִהְיֶה לָהּ עִצָּבוֹן גָּדוֹל אִם לֹא תֵלֵךְ, מֻתֶּרֶת לָלֶכֶת וּלְהִתְפַּלֵּל. וְכֵן כְּשֶׁהִיא מַשִּׂיאָה אֶת בְּנָהּ אוֹ אֶת בִּתָּהּ אוֹ כְּשֶׁהִיא יוֹלֶדֶת שֶׁהִגִּיעַ זְמַנָּהּ לָלֶכֶת לְבֵית־הַכְּנֶסֶת, וְכַיּוֹצֵא בָּזֶה, מֻתֶּרֶת.

---

20. If she does so in an unusual manner, such as placing it down with her left hand or placing it somewhat away from him so that he will have to move it himself, it is permitted.

21. Some *poskim* say this refers to pouring water on any part of you or into the tub in which are now washing yourself (*Ramban, Ritvah, Tashbatz* 3:230, and *Taz*). However, *Rabbenu Yonah, Eshkol, Bach,* and *Shach* say this refers also to just preparing the water for you to wash. This is the opinion of the *Beis Meir, Chavos Da'as* and *Chochmas Adam.*

22. These laws must also be observed at the *seder* on Pesach.

23. With regard to wine from *Kiddush,* if you send her the cup you drank from, in an unusual manner, for instance, with your left hand; she is permitted to drink from it according

bring it and place it in front of you at the table;[20] nor may she make your bed in your presence. But when not in your presence, all these things are permitted, even though you know that she did them. She is forbidden to pour water[21] to wash your face and hands and feet, even if the water is cold.

13) Just as she is forbidden to pour a cup of wine for you, so are you forbidden to pour wine for her.[22] Furthermore, even to send her a cup of wine specially for her, even if it is a cup over which a berachah has been pronounced, is forbidden.[23]

14) If you are sick and there is no one but her to attend you, she is permitted to attend you[24] but without direct contact with your body,[25] but rather by means of some object. She may even raise you up, lay you down, and support you. But she must be very careful not to wash your face, hands, and feet, or make your bed in your presence. If the woman is sick (when she is a *niddah*), her husband is forbidden to attend her, even without touching her,[26] except in a case of extreme emergency, when it is impossible to find someone else to attend her. If the husband is a physician, and there is no other physician as competent as himself, he may feel her pulse, since he is not doing it out of desire or love.

15) All the foregoing precautionary measures must also be observed during the "white days," that is, the seven days after the flow has ceased, and even thereafter if she delays her immersion. They are forbidden in all that was mentioned previously, until after she immerses herself.

16) During the time a woman is a *niddah,* during her menstruation period before the white days, it is customary[27] for her not to enter a synagogue and not to pray. But on the Days of Awe, that is from the first day of *Selichot* when multitudes assemble at the synagogue, and she will be greatly distressed if she does not go, she is permitted to go and pray. Similarly at the marriage of her son, or daughter, or she has given birth and it is time for her to go to the synagogue, or for similar things, she is permitted to do so.

---

to *Prisha.* However, *Ya'avetz* (Responsa 126) rules even if it is the cup you drank from and did not pour it specially for her, you are still not allowed to send it to her. The best thing to do is to leave the cup in front of you and let her take it herself.

24. Even if you are not dangerously ill. But if you just have a minor illness, it is not permitted. (*Aruch Hashulchan*)

25. If this is not possible, she may do it even if she touches you.

26. *Shulchan Aruch* 185:15, *Beis Yosef. Trumas Hadeshen* and *Chochmas Adam* rule that it is forbidden only if you touch her. The source of the *Kitzur Shulchan Aruch* is unknown. According to the *Ramah, Chavos Da'as, Sidrei Taharah,* and *Chochmas Adam,* this is permitted only if her illness is dangerous to her life (or limb). However, the *Radvaz, Zerah Emess,* and *Lechem V'simla* permit this even when such dangers are not involved.

27. Nowadays they are accustomed to go but should not look at the *Seifer Torah* when they raise it and show it to the congregants. *Mishnah Berurah* 88:7—*Chayei Adam.*

סִימָן קנד

סֵדֶר קְבִיעַת הַוֶּסֶת וְדִין בְּדִיקָה לִפְנֵי תַשְׁמִישׁ וּלְאַחַר תַּשְׁמִישׁ

א) כָּל וֶסֶת נִקְבָּע בְּשָׁלֹשׁ פְּעָמִים רְצוּפוֹת, שֶׁאִם רָאֲתָה שָׁלֹשׁ פְּעָמִים רְצוּפוֹת בִּזְמַן שָׁוֶה כְּפַעַם בְּפַעַם, אֲזַי זְמַן זֶה הוּא לָהּ לְוֶסֶת קָבוּעַ. יֵשׁ נָשִׁים שֶׁהֵן קוֹבְעוֹת וֶסְתָּן בְּיָמִים שָׁוִים בַּחֹדֶשׁ, כְּגוֹן שֶׁרָאֲתָה שָׁלֹשׁ פְּעָמִים רְצוּפוֹת, כָּל פַּעַם בְּרֹאשׁ־חֹדֶשׁ, וַהֲוֵי לָהּ וֶסֶת קָבוּעַ בְּרֹאשׁ־חֹדֶשׁ. וְכֵן אִם רָאֲתָה שָׁלֹשׁ פְּעָמִים בַּחֲמִשָּׁה יָמִים בַּחֹדֶשׁ, אֲזַי יוֹם חֲמִישִׁי בַּחֹדֶשׁ הוּא יוֹם וֶסֶת קָבוּעַ שֶׁלָּהּ, וְזֶה נִקְרָא וֶסֶת הַיָּמִים, שֶׁקְּבָעָהּ בְּיוֹם יָדוּעַ בַּחֹדֶשׁ. וְאַף־עַל־פִּי שֶׁמִּסְפַּר הַיָּמִים אֲשֶׁר בֵּין רְאִיָּה לִרְאִיָּה אֵינָם שָׁוִים, כִּי יֵשׁ חֳדָשִׁים שֶׁאֵין לָהֶם רַק תִּשְׁעָה וְעֶשְׂרִים יוֹם, וְיֵשׁ מִשְּׁלֹשִׁים יוֹם, מִכָּל מָקוֹם כֵּיוָן שֶׁהִיא לְמוּדָה לִרְאוֹת בְּיוֹם קָבוּעַ בַּחֹדֶשׁ, הֲוֵי לָהּ יוֹם זֶה וֶסֶת קָבוּעַ.

ב) אֲבָל רֹב הַנָּשִׁים, דַּרְכָּן לִקְבֹּעַ וֶסְתָּן בְּהַפְלָגוֹת שָׁווֹת, דְּהַיְנוּ שֶׁהִיא מַפְלֶגֶת וּמְחַלֶּקֶת בֵּין רְאִיָּה לִרְאִיָּה יָמִים שָׁוִים בְּמִסְפָּר. כְּגוֹן שֶׁהִיא רוֹאָה פַּעַם אַחַת וּמַפְסֶקֶת חֲמִשָּׁה וְעֶשְׂרִים יוֹם אוֹ שְׁלֹשִׁים יוֹם אוֹ שְׁנַיִם וּשְׁלֹשִׁים יוֹם וְכַדּוֹמֶה, וְחוֹזֶרֶת וְרוֹאָה. אִם עָשְׂתָה שָׁלֹשׁ הַפְלָגוֹת שָׁווֹת וּרְצוּפוֹת, הֲוֵי לָהּ וֶסֶת קָבוּעַ, וְזֶה נִקְרָא וֶסֶת הַפְלָגוֹת. וּלְאַחַר שֶׁתַּפְלִיג שׁוּב יָמִים בְּמִסְפָּר אֵלּוּ, אֲזַי הַיּוֹם הַבָּא הוּא יוֹם וֶסֶת קָבוּעַ שֶׁלָּהּ. וְכֵיוָן שֶׁכָּל וֶסֶת אֵינוֹ נִקְבָּע בְּפָחוֹת מִשָּׁלֹשׁ פְּעָמִים, וְהַפְלָגָה אֵינָהּ נִכֶּרֶת אֶלָּא בִּשְׁתֵּי רְאִיּוֹת, לָכֵן לְוֶסֶת הַפְלָגוֹת צְרִיכוֹת אַרְבַּע רְאִיּוֹת, כְּגוֹן שֶׁרָאֲתָה הַיּוֹם, וְהִפְלִיגָה חֲמִשָּׁה וְעֶשְׂרִים יוֹם וְרָאֲתָה, וְשׁוּב הִפְלִיגָה חֲמִשָּׁה וְעֶשְׂרִים יוֹם וְרָאֲתָה, וְשׁוּב הִפְלִיגָה חֲמִשָּׁה וְעֶשְׂרִים יוֹם וְרָאֲתָה, הֲרֵי רָאֲתָה אַרְבַּע פְּעָמִים, אֲשֶׁר בֵּינֵיהֶן שָׁלֹשׁ הַפְלָגוֹת שָׁווֹת, וְקָבְעָה וֶסֶת.

ג) וְיֵשׁ נָשִׁים, שֶׁאֵין לָהֶן יוֹם קָבוּעַ לִרְאוֹת, לֹא בִּימֵי הַחֹדֶשׁ, וְלֹא בְּהַפְלָגוֹת שָׁווֹת, אֲבָל יֵשׁ לָהֶן סִימָנִים בְּגוּפָן. כְּגוֹן שֶׁדַּרְכָּהּ הִיא, שֶׁקֹּדֶם רְאִיָּתָהּ הִיא מְפַהֶקֶת, דְּהַיְנוּ, כְּאָדָם שֶׁפּוֹשֵׁט זְרוֹעוֹתָיו מֵחֲמַת כֹּבֶד, אוֹ כְּאָדָם שֶׁפּוֹתֵחַ פִּיו מֵחֲמַת כֹּבֶד, אוֹ כְּאָדָם שֶׁמּוֹצִיא קוֹל דֶּרֶךְ הַגָּרוֹן מֵחֲמַת הַמַּאֲכָל שֶׁאָכַל, כָּל אֵלּוּ עִנְיְנֵי פִּהוּק הֵן. וְכֵן אִם מִתְעַטֶּשֶׁת דֶּרֶךְ

1. If this sequence had been interrupted by a flow after a shorter interval elapsed, this does not upset the establishment of the longer interval. For example, if she perceived after

Chapter 154

Regulations Concerning the Menses, Laws of Examination Before and After Marital Relations

1) The date of the menses is established by three consecutive times. That is, if menstruation began three consecutive times, at a similar time, then this date is her established date of the menses. There are women who establish their periodic menses at certain days of the month. For instance, if she perceived the flow three consecutive times, each time on *Rosh Chodesh* (New Moon), then her established menses is on *Rosh Chodesh.* Also if she perceived it three consecutive times on the fifth of the Jewish-Hebrew month, then the fifth day of the Jewish-Hebrew month is the established day of her menses. This way of reckoning is referred to as "Menses determined by days," for it is consistently the same day in the month. And even though the number of days between one perception and the other is not always alike, for some months consist of only twenty-nine days, while others consist of thirty days, nevertheless, since she is accustomed to perceive on a certain day of the month, this day is her established day of the menses.

2) Most women, however, are accustomed to establish a mensal pattern of "equal intervals", which is a separation from one perception to another of an equal number of intervening days. For instance, if she perceives a flow and twenty-five days elapse, or thirty days or thirty-two days or the like, and following she again perceives a flow. If she had these perceptions on three consecutive equal[1] intervals, this is her established date of the menses, and is referred to as the menses of "equal intervals." And after another interruption of that number of days, the following day is her established date of the menses. Since the menses cannot be established by less than three times, and an interval cannot be recognized by less than two perceptions; therefore, establishment of the menses of equal intervals requires four perceptions. For instance, if she perceived a flow today, followed by an interval of twenty-five days, and she perceived, followed again by an interval of twenty-five days, and she perceived, followed again by an interval of twenty-five days, and she perceived, she has had four perceptions, between which there were three equal intervals, and has thereby established her menses.

3) There are some women who do not have an established date of perception, neither of the days of the month, nor of equal intervals, but do experience various physical symptoms.[2] For instance, it is charactaristic of her to yawn before menstruation, in the manner of one who stretches his arms from weariness, or like a person who opens his mouth (yawns) from drowsiness, or like a person who burps because of the food he has eaten—all of these are included in "yawning." Similarly,

---

twenty days on two consecutive occasions, and then perceived after a fifteen day interval, and then again after a twenty day interval, she has thus established a twenty day cycle. But if, instead of the fifteenth, she had seen on the twenty-fifth, she has not established her menses. *Chazon Ish* 85:34.

2. That are brought on by the oncoming menses.

מַטָּה אוֹ דֶּרֶךְ מַעְלָה, אוֹ מַרְגֶּשֶׁת אֵיזֶה מֵחוֹשׁ כְּנֶגֶד טַבּוּרָהּ אוֹ בְּבֵית הָרֶחֶם, אוֹ שֶׁאֲחָזוּהָ צִירֵי הַקַּדַּחַת, אוֹ סָמְרוּ שַׂעֲרוֹת בְּשָׂרָהּ, אוֹ שֶׁרֹאשָׁהּ וְאֵבָרֶיהָ כְּבֵדִים עָלֶיהָ, כֹּל שֶׁהֶחְזְקָה שָׁלֹשׁ פְּעָמִים רְצוּפוֹת שֶׁבָּא לָהּ אֶחָד מִן הַמִּקְרִים הַנִּזְכָּרִים, וְאַחַר כָּךְ רָאֲתָה דָם, הֲרֵי זוֹ קָבְעָה וֶסֶת, וְזֶה נִקְרָא וֶסֶת הַגּוּף. וְדַוְקָא פִּהוּק וְעִטּוּשׁ כַּמָּה פְּעָמִים זוֹ אַחַר זוֹ הֲוֵי סִימַן וֶסֶת, וְקָבְעָה בָּהֶם. אֲבָל מִשּׁוּם פִּהוּק וְעִטּוּשׁ פַּעַם אַחַת, אֵין הַוֶּסֶת נִקְבָּע, כִּי זֶה דֶּרֶךְ כָּל הָאָדָם. וְדַוְקָא שֶׁקָּבְעָה כָּל שָׁלֹשׁ הַפְּעָמִים עַל יְדֵי מִקְרֶה אֶחָד. אֲבָל אִם פַּעַם בְּמִקְרֶה זֶה וּפַעַם בְּמִקְרֶה זֶה, לֹא הֲוֵי קְבִיעוּת.

ד) וְיֵשׁ שֶׁקְּבִיעוּת לְיָמִים אוֹ לְהַפְלָגוֹת שָׁווֹת בְּצֵרוּף פִּהוּק וְעִטּוּשׁ וְכַדּוֹמֶה. דְּהַיְנוּ שֶׁבְּכָל חֲמִשָּׁה יָמִים בַּחֹדֶשׁ, הִיא מְפַהֶקֶת אוֹ מִתְעַטֶּשֶׁת וְאַחַר כָּךְ הִיא רוֹאָה, אוֹ כְּשֶׁהִיא מַפְלֶגֶת מֵרְאִיָּה חֲמִשָּׁה וְעֶשְׂרִים יוֹם, הִיא מְפַהֶקֶת אוֹ מִתְעַטֶּשֶׁת וְאַחַר כָּךְ הִיא רוֹאָה. וְזֶה נִקְרָא וֶסֶת הַמֻּרְכָּב, דְּהַיְנוּ שֶׁהוּא מֻרְכָּב מִיּוֹם שָׁוֶה עִם סִימַן הַגּוּף. אִם קָבְעָה כֵּן שָׁלֹשׁ פְּעָמִים, אֲזַי כְּשֶׁמַּגִּיעַ הַיּוֹם הַמְּגֻבָּל וְהִיא מְפַהֶקֶת אוֹ מִתְעַטֶּשֶׁת, חוֹשֶׁשֶׁת לוֹ. אֲבָל בְּיוֹם גְּרִידָא אוֹ בְּפִהוּק וְעִטּוּשׁ גְּרִידָא, אֵינָהּ צְרִיכָה לָחוּשׁ, כֵּיוָן שֶׁלֹּא קָבְעָה אֶלָּא בְּתַרְוַיְהוּ כַּהֲדָדֵי.

ה) כָּל אִשָּׁה שֶׁיֵּשׁ לָהּ וֶסֶת קָבוּעַ, הֲרֵי זוֹ שֶׁלֹּא בִּשְׁעַת וֶסְתָּהּ בְּחֶזְקַת טְהוֹרָה, וּבַעְלָהּ בָּא עָלֶיהָ, וְאֵינוֹ צָרִיךְ לִשְׁאֹל אוֹתָהּ כְּלוּם. וַאֲפִלּוּ הִיא יְשֵׁנָה קְצָת, יָכוֹל לָבוֹא עָלֶיהָ, וְאֵינָהּ צְרִיכָה בְּדִיקָה לֹא לִפְנֵי תַשְׁמִישׁ וְלֹא לְאַחַר תַּשְׁמִישׁ. וְאַדְּרַבָּא, אֵין לָהּ לִבְדֹּק אֶת עַצְמָהּ בִּפְנֵי בַעְלָהּ, שֶׁלֹּא יְהֵא לִבּוֹ נוֹקְפוֹ לַחְשֹׁב מִסְתָמָא הִרְגִּישָׁה, שֶׁאִם לֹא הִרְגִּישָׁה לֹא הָיְתָה בּוֹדֶקֶת וְלָכֵן אִם תִּבְדֹּק בְּפָנָיו לִפְנֵי תַשְׁמִישׁ, אִכָּא לְמֵיחַשׁ, שֶׁמָּא מֵחֲמַת שֶׁיִּהְיֶה לִבּוֹ נוֹקְפוֹ יִפְרוֹשׁ אֶת עַצְמוֹ מִמֶּנָּה. וְאִם תִּבְדֹּק בְּפָנָיו לְאַחַר תַּשְׁמִישׁ, אִכָּא לְמֵיחַשׁ, שֶׁמָּא יְהֵא לִבּוֹ נוֹקְפוֹ לַחְשֹׁב, דְּמִסְתָמָא הִרְגִּישָׁה בִּשְׁעַת תַּשְׁמִישׁ, וְיִפְרוֹשׁ אֶת עַצְמוֹ בְּפַעַם אַחֶרֶת. וְעַל כֵּן לֹא תִבְדֹּק בִּפְנֵי בַעְלָהּ. אֲבָל שֶׁלֹּא בִּפְנֵי בַעְלָהּ, כָּל אִשָּׁה שֶׁמַּרְבָּה לִבְדֹּק אֶת עַצְמָהּ, הֲרֵי זוֹ מְשֻׁבַּחַת.

3. During the onset (day or night) when she experiences one of these symptoms, she is forbidden to you. *Shulchan Aruch* 189:19. At that time she must examine herself to see if she

if she flatuates or sneezes, or feels some pain in the region of the navel or the womb, or she has an attack of chills and fever, or the hair of her body bristles, or her head and (her) limbs grow heavy. If she experienced any of these symptoms, on three consecutive periods, and immediately began menstruation, this symptom serves as her established date of menses. And this is referred to as "Menses regulated by physical symptoms."[3] Yawning and sneezing only when repeated many times consecutively are regarded as symptoms by which to establish a date of menses, but if she yawns or sneezes one time, the date of menses is not established for it is a natural and normal thing. The date of menses is established by symptoms only if she perceived each of the three times through one particular symptom. But if once it occurs through one symptom and once through another symptom, it is not considered established.

4) Some women establish their menstrual periods by monthly, or by equal intervals, combined with yawning, sneezing, or similar physical symptoms. For instance, every fifth day of the month she yawns or sneezes, and then perceives the flow, or when twenty-five days from perception elapse, she yawns or sneezes, and then perceives the flow. This is referred to as "menses regulated by combining factors." That is, it is a combination of a regular date and a physical symptom. If this pattern occurs three (consecutive) times, then, when that regular day arrives, and she yawns or sneezes, she must be concerned about her perception. But with the arrival of that day alone, or with yawning and sneezing alone, she need not be concerned, since she has regulated her term only with the two factors combined.

5) A woman whose periods are regular, is at all other times presumed to be menstrually clean, and her husband may have marital relations with her, and does not have to inquire about her status. Even if she is partly asleep he may have marital relations with her, and she does not need to examine herself, either before marital relations or afterwards. On the contrary, she should not examine herself in the presence of her husband,[4] so that he will not be apprehensive, thinking she probably felt something, for if she did not feel something she would not have examined herself. Therefore if she examines herself in his presence, before having marital relations, there is cause for concern, that perhaps because of his apprehension he might keep away from her.[5] And if she examines herself in his presence after having marital relations, there is cause for concern that perhaps he will be apprehensive, thinking that she probably felt something while having marital relations, and will keep away from her the next time. Therefore, she should not examine herself in her husband's presence. But if not in her husband's presence, the more a woman examines herself, the more praiseworthy she is.

---

is menstrually clean. *Eshkol* 34. If she did not examine herself, she remains forbidden until she does and finds herself menstrually clean. See *Shulchan Aruch* 184:9.

4. Not necessarily his presence but rather his knowledge.
5. And thus neglect the mitzvah of propagation. (*L'vush* 186)

ו) אִשָּׁה שֶׁאֵין לָהּ וֶסֶת קָבוּעַ כְּלָל, יֵשׁ לָהּ לִבְדֹּק אֶת עַצְמָהּ לִפְנֵי תַשְׁמִישׁ וּלְאַחַר תַּשְׁמִישׁ, וְגַם הַבַּעַל יֵשׁ לוֹ לְקַנֵּחַ אֶת עַצְמוֹ לְאַחַר תַּשְׁמִישׁ וְלִרְאוֹת אִם לֹא נִמְצֵאת אֵיזוֹ טִפַּת דָּם. וְאַךְ כְּשֶׁהִיא בְּחֶזְקַת מְסֻלֶּקֶת מִדָּמִים, כְּגוֹן מְעֻבֶּרֶת לְאַחַר שְׁלשָׁה חֳדָשִׁים, אוֹ מֵינִיקָה אוֹ זְקֵנָה, אֵלּוּ אֵינָן צְרִיכוֹת בְּדִיקָה.

ז) וְיֵשׁ נָשִׁים שֶׁאֵין לָהֶן וֶסֶת קָבוּעַ מַמָּשׁ, אֲבָל יֵשׁ לָהֶן עַל־כָּל־פָּנִים מִסְפַּר יָמִים יְדוּעִים שֶׁבָּהֶם אֵינָן רוֹאוֹת, כְּגוֹן אִשָּׁה שֶׁהִיא מֻחְזֶקֶת שֶׁבְּכָל חֲמִשָּׁה וְעֶשְׂרִים יוֹם לְאַחַר רְאִיָּתָהּ אֵינָהּ חוֹזֶרֶת וְרוֹאָה, אֶלָּא אַחַר כָּךְ, וְאָז אֵין לָהּ יוֹם קָבוּעַ, שֶׁלִּפְעָמִים הִיא מְאַחֶרֶת יוֹם אוֹ יוֹמַיִם אוֹ שְׁלשָׁה יָמִים, אִשָּׁה כָּזוֹ עַד חֲמִשָּׁה וְעֶשְׂרִים יוֹם כֵּיוָן שֶׁהֻחְזְקָה שָׁלשׁ פְּעָמִים שֶׁבְּיָמִים אֵלּוּ אֵינָהּ רוֹאָה, דִּינָהּ בַּיָּמִים הָאֵלּוּ כְּמוֹ אִשָּׁה שֶׁיֵּשׁ לָהּ וֶסֶת קָבוּעַ. וּבַיָּמִים שֶׁלְּאַחַר כָּךְ, שֶׁהִיא נְבוֹכָה בָהֶם וְאֵין לָהּ בָּהֶם חֶזְקַת טָהֳרָה, אֲסוּרָה לְבַעְלָהּ.

סִימָן קנה

דִּין פְּרִישָׁה סָמוּךְ לַוֶּסֶת וְהַחִלּוּקִים שֶׁבֵּין וֶסֶת קָבוּעַ לְאֵינוֹ קָבוּעַ

א) תָּנוּ רַבָּנָן, וְהִזַּרְתֶּם אֶת־בְּנֵי יִשְׂרָאֵל מִטֻּמְאָתָם, אָמַר רַבִּי יֹאשִׁיָּה, מִכָּאן אַזְהָרָה לִבְנֵי יִשְׂרָאֵל, שֶׁיִּפְרְשׁוּ מִנְּשׁוֹתֵיהֶן סָמוּךְ לְוֶסְתָּן. וְכַמָּה. אָמַר רָבָא, עוֹנָה. וְעוֹנָה הִיא אוֹ יוֹם אוֹ לַיְלָה. שֶׁאִם זְמַן וֶסְתָּהּ הוּא בַּיּוֹם, אַף־עַל־פִּי שֶׁרְגִילָה לִרְאוֹת בְּסוֹף הַיּוֹם, מִכָּל מָקוֹם נֶאֶסְרָה מִתְּחִלַּת הַיּוֹם. וְכֵן אִם רְגִילָה לִרְאוֹת בַּבֹּקֶר וְלֹא רָאֲתָה, מִכָּל מָקוֹם עֲדַיִן הִיא אֲסוּרָה כָּל הַיּוֹם עַד הַלַּיְלָה. וְכֵן אִם וֶסְתָּהּ בַּלַּיְלָה, אַף־עַל־פִּי שֶׁהִיא רְגִילָה לִרְאוֹת בִּתְחִלַּת הַלַּיְלָה, אוֹ שֶׁהִיא רְגִילָה לִרְאוֹת בְּסוֹף הַלַּיְלָה, מִכָּל מָקוֹם הִיא אֲסוּרָה כָּל הַלַּיְלָה. וּלְהַרְבֵּה פּוֹסְקִים, לֹא לְבַד בְּתַשְׁמִישׁ הִיא נֶאֶסְרָה, אֶלָּא גַּם בִּשְׁאָר מִינֵי קֵרְבוּת הִיא אֲסוּרָה. וְכֵן יֵשׁ לְהַחְמִיר.

ב) יֵשׁ אוֹמְרִים, דְּעוֹנָה זוֹ שֶׁהוּא צָרִיךְ לִפְרוֹשׁ אֶת עַצְמוֹ, זוֹהִי עוֹנָה

---

6. *Rambam,* but the *Rosh* maintains this is unnecessary; and this is the accepted custom.
1. *Maseches Shavuos* 18b.
2. *Leviticus* 15:31.

6) A woman whose periods are totally irregular should examine herself before and after having marital relations. The husband, too, should wipe himself[6] after marital relation's to ascertain whether there is a drop of blood. However, if her flow of blood is assumed to have ceased, for instance, a pregnant woman after the first three months of pregnancy, or one who nurses, or a woman who is old, these need not examine themselves.

7) There are women who do not have a regular cycle, but have, nevertheless, a certain number of days during which they do not perceive any flow. For instance, a woman who has ascertained that during the twenty-five days after her perception of a flow, she does not perceive another flow, but only after that, and then she has no definite date, because sometimes she delays one day, or two or three days. Since it has been established three times, that during these days she does not perceive, a woman until twenty-five days elapse, is regarded during these days like a woman who has a regular menstrual cycle. But on the days that follow when she is uncertain, and cannot be presumed to be menstrually clean, she is forbidden to her husband.

Chapter 155

Separation Before the Menstrual Term
Differences Between Regular and Irregular Menses

1) The Rabbis expounded[1] (on the verse) "You shall separate the Children of Yisrael from their impurities."[2] Rabbi Josiah said: "This verse is an admonition to the Children of Yisrael, that they must separate from their wives prior to their expected periods." How long before? Rava said,[3] "An *onah.*" An *onah* is either a day or a night. If she is accustomed to perceive the flow during the day, even though she is accustomed to perceive this flow at the end of the day, she is nevertheless forbidden to her husband from the beginning of the day. Likewise, if she is accustomed to perceive in the morning and has not yet perceived, nevertheless, she is forbidden the entire day until the night.[4] Likewise, if her periods occur at night, even if she is accustomed to perceive the flow in the beginning of the night, or if she is accustomed to perceive the flow at the end of the night, nevertheless she is forbidden to her husband the entire night. According to many authorities,[5] not only marital relations are forbidden at this time, but also every other type of intimacy is forbidden, and it is proper to heed this opinion.[6]

2) Some authorities[7] say that this *onah* during which you must separate (from

---

3. *Maseches Avodah Zara* 78a.

4. Most *poskim* agree that the length of each *onah* depends on the length of the day or night at that time and place (*Beis Yosef, Taz, Toras Hashelomim* and *Placey*). *Chochmas Adam* rules that it is no less than twelve hours at any time.

5. *Trumas Hadeshen* Responsa 250.

6. *Bach, Shach,* and *Toras Hashlomim* say that one who is strict in this will be blessed; but from the *Halachic* standpoint it is permitted. (*Shulchan Aruch, Ramah, Bach, Radvaz* etc.)

7. *Ohr Zaruah.*

שֶׁלִּפְנֵי הָעוֹנָה שֶׁהֻוֶּסֶת בָּהּ, דְּהַיְנוּ אִם וֶסְתָּהּ בַּלַּיְלָה, אֲסוּרָה גַּם כָּל הַיּוֹם שֶׁלְּפָנֶיהָ. וְאִם וֶסְתָּהּ בַּיּוֹם, אֲסוּרָה גַּם כָּל הַלַּיְלָה שֶׁלְּפָנֶיהָ. וְכֵן יֵשׁ לִנְהֹג. וְאַף כְּשֶׁהוּא יוֹצֵא לַדֶּרֶךְ, אוֹ שֶׁהוּא בָּא מִן הַדֶּרֶךְ, אוֹ שֶׁחָלָה טְבִילָתָהּ בַּלַּיְלָה שֶׁלִּפְנֵי עוֹנַת הַוֶּסֶת לֹא יַחְמִיר.

ג) אִשָּׁה שֶׁאֵין לָהּ וֶסֶת קָבוּעַ, אֲזַי תָּמִיד יוֹם שְׁלֹשִׁים שֶׁלְּאַחַר יוֹם רְאִיָּתָהּ, הוּא לָהּ כְּמוֹ וֶסֶת קָבוּעַ, וְנִקְרֵאת עוֹנָה בֵּינוֹנִית. כְּגוֹן שֶׁרָאֲתָה בְּיוֹם שֵׁנִי פָּרָשַׁת נֹחַ, אֲזַי יוֹם רְבִיעִי פָּרָשַׁת תּוֹלְדוֹת הוּא לָהּ כְּמוֹ וֶסֶת קָבוּעַ. וּמִלְּבַד זֹאת, עוֹד צְרִיכָה לָחוּשׁ לְכָל רְאִיָּה שֶׁתִּרְאֶה, אִם לְהַפְלָגוֹת אוֹ לִימֵי הַחֹדֶשׁ, כַּאֲשֶׁר יְבֹאַר אִם יִרְצֶה הַשֵּׁם. וְכָל זְמַן שֶׁהִיא צְרִיכָה לָחוּשׁ שֶׁמָּא תִרְאֶה, צָרִיךְ הַבַּעַל לִפְרוֹשׁ מִמֶּנָּה בָּעוֹנָה הַסְּמוּכָה, כָּאָמוּר.

ד) כָּל אִשָּׁה שֶׁרָאֲתָה דָם, צְרִיכָה הִיא לָחוּשׁ, שֶׁמָּא גַּם בְּפַעַם אַחֶרֶת תִּרְאֶה בַּיּוֹם הַהוּא וּבַזְּמַן הַזֶּה. לָא מִבַּעְיָא אִם אֵין לָהּ עַתָּה וֶסֶת קָבוּעַ, פְּשִׁיטָא שֶׁהִיא צְרִיכָה לָחוּשׁ, שֶׁמָּא תִרְאֶה עוֹד בִּזְמַן הַזֶּה וְתִקְבַּע וֶסֶת – אֶלָּא אֲפִלּוּ אִשָּׁה שֶׁיֵּשׁ לָהּ וֶסֶת קָבוּעַ, אִם אֵרַע לָהּ שֶׁשִּׁנְּתָה וֶסְתָּהּ וְרָאֲתָה שֶׁלֹּא בִשְׁעַת וֶסְתָּהּ, צְרִיכָה הִיא לָחוּשׁ גַּם לָרְאִיָּה הַזֹּאת, כִּי שֶׁמָּא תְּשַׁנֶּה וֶסְתָּהּ לִזְמַן אַחֵר. אֲבָל אִם לֹא שִׁנְּתָה וֶסְתָּהּ, אֶלָּא שֶׁאֵרַע לָהּ גַּם רְאִיָּה אַחֶרֶת שֶׁלֹּא בִשְׁעַת וֶסְתָּהּ, אָז אֵינָהּ צְרִיכָה לָחוּשׁ לָרְאִיָּה הַזֹּאת, דְּכֵיוָן דְּיֵשׁ לָהּ וֶסֶת קָבוּעַ, אֵינָהּ צְרִיכָה לָחוּשׁ לְוֶסֶת שֶׁאֵינוֹ קָבוּעַ.

ה) וְנִנְקֹט דֻּגְמָא בְּאִשָּׁה שֶׁאֵין לָהּ וֶסֶת. רָאֲתָה (יוֹם שֵׁנִי שֶׁל רֹאשׁ־חֹדֶשׁ אִיָּר וּבְיוֹם חֲמִשָּׁה וְעֶשְׂרִים בּוֹ, צְרִיכָה הִיא לָחוּשׁ לְרֹאשׁ־חֹדֶשׁ סִיוָן, כִּי יֵשׁ לָהּ לָחוּשׁ, שֶׁמָּא תִקְבַּע וֶסְתָּהּ לְרֹאשׁ־חֹדֶשׁ, (וְגַם בְּיוֹם שֵׁנִי שֶׁל סִיוָן צְרִיכָה לָחוּשׁ, מִשּׁוּם עוֹנָה בֵּינוֹנִית). בָּא רֹאשׁ־חֹדֶשׁ סִיוָן, (וְגַם יוֹם שֵׁנִי שֶׁל סִיוָן) וְלֹא רָאֲתָה, צְרִיכָה הִיא לָחוּשׁ, שֶׁמָּא תִקְבַּע לְהַפְלָגוֹת. וְכֵיוָן שֶׁהִפְלִיגָה בֵּין רְאִיָּה לִרְאִיָּה שְׁלֹשָׁה וְעֶשְׂרִים יוֹם (מִלְּבַד יוֹם הָרְאִיָּה הָרִאשׁוֹנָה וְיוֹם הָרְאִיָּה הַשְּׁנִיָּה), צְרִיכָה גַּם עַתָּה לִמְנוֹת שְׁלֹשָׁה וְעֶשְׂרִים יוֹם, וְאַחַר כָּךְ תָּחוּשׁ, וְהַיְנוּ בְּחֹדֶשׁ אִיָּר יֵשׁ לָהּ אַרְבָּעָה יָמִים, תּוֹסִיף תִּשְׁעָה עָשָׂר יוֹם מֵחֹדֶשׁ סִיוָן, וְחוֹשֶׁשֶׁת לְיוֹם עֶשְׂרִים בּוֹ. בָּא יוֹם עֶשְׂרִים

8. *Toras Hashlomim, Placey, Chochmas Adam, Maharsham* 3:258, and *Chazon Ish* rule that one may be lenient. With regard to other kinds of intimacies, it would seem that even the *Ohr Zaruah* permits them.

her), is the *onah* prior to the *onah* during which she expects her period. For instance, if she expects her period at night, she is also forbidden the entire day before. If she expects her period by day, she is also forbidden the entire night before. And this is the proper course to follow.[8] However, if you are setting out on a journey, or you have just returned from one, or if she has performed the ritual immersion[9] on the night preceding her expected period, you should not heed the stricter opinion.

3) If a woman does not have regular menstrual periods, then the thirtieth day[10] after her (last) perception is always considered her fixed period, and is termed "an average *onah.*" For instance, if she perceived the flow on Monday, of the week when the *sidrah* of *Noah* is read, then the Wednesday of the week when the *sidrah* of *Toldos* is read, is considered her fixed period. In addition, she must also pay attention to the other occasional times of perception, whether based on equal intervening days, or on certain days of the month, as will be explained hereafter, God-willing. Whenever she has reason to expect her period, her husband must separate from her on the *onah* before, as has been explained.

4) Whenever a woman perceives blood, she must suspect perhaps she may perceive it again on the same date and at the same time. It goes without saying, if she presently does not have a regular menstrual period, she definitely must suspect that it might occur again at a similar time, and thus establish her date of menses. But even a woman who has a regular menstrual period, and experienced a change in regularity and perceived the flow not at her fixed period, must also be concerned with this perception, lest this indicate a change of her regular period to a different time. But if her regular period has not changed, and she has an additional perception, not at her regular period, then she does not have to be concerned (in the future) about this (extra) perception, for since she (also) has her regular period, she does not need to be concerned about an irregular period.

5) Let us give an illustration of a woman who has no regular periods. If she perceived blood on the second day of *Rosh Chodesh*, of the month of *Iyar,* and again on the twenty-fifth of the same month, she must be mindful of *Rosh Chodesh* of the month of *Sivan*, for she should suspect she might establish her menses on *Rosh Chodesh.* (Also on the second day of the month of *Sivan*, she must be mindful, because it is the "average *onah* (period).") If *Rosh Chodesh* of *Sivan* came, (and the second day of *Sivan* too), and she has not yet perceived blood, she must suspect that she may establish her menses by equal intervening days. And since there was an interval of twenty-three days between perceptions, (exclusive of the day of the first perception and the second perception), she must now also count twenty-three days, and then expect another flow. That is, she has four remaining days of the month of *Iyar,* onto which she should add nineteen days from the month of *Sivan*, and expect a flow on the twentieth of the month. If the twentieth day of *Sivan* came, and she

9. In these circumstances you are obligated to visit her.
10. *Beis Yosef* (*Shulchan Aruch*), *Bach, Taz, Prisha, Chochmas Adam,* etc.

סִיוָן וְלֹא רָאֲתָה, חוֹשֶׁשֶׁת לְיוֹם חֲמִשָּׁה וְעֶשְׂרִים בּוֹ, שֶׁמָּא תִקְבַּע יוֹם חֲמִשָּׁה וְעֶשְׂרִים בַּחֹדֶשׁ, (וְגַם בְּיוֹם שִׁשָּׁה וְעֶשְׂרִים צְרִיכָה לָחוּשׁ, מִשּׁוּם עוֹנָה בֵּינוֹנִית). אֲבָל לְרֹאשׁ־חֹדֶשׁ תַּמּוּז אֵינָהּ צְרִיכָה לָחוּשׁ, כִּי רְאִיַּת רֹאשׁ־חֹדֶשׁ אִיָּר כְּבָר נֶעֶקְרָה עַל יְדֵי מַה שֶּׁלֹּא רָאֲתָה בְּרֹאשׁ־חֹדֶשׁ סִיוָן, (דְּכָל שֶׁלֹּא קָבְעָה בְּשָׁלֹשׁ פְּעָמִים, נֶעֱקָר בְּפַעַם אַחַת, כִּדְלְקַמָּן).

ו) וְדֻגְמָא לְאִשָּׁה שֶׁיֵּשׁ לָהּ וֶסֶת, הָיָה לָהּ וֶסֶת קָבוּעַ לִרְאוֹת בְּהַפְלָגָה לְיוֹם הַחֲמִשָּׁה וְעֶשְׂרִים, וְשִׁנְּתָה פַּעַם אַחַת, וְלֹא רָאֲתָה עַד יוֹם הַשְּׁמוֹנָה וְעֶשְׂרִים, צְרִיכָה הִיא לָחוּשׁ לְיוֹם חֲמִשָּׁה וְעֶשְׂרִים מֵרְאִיָּה זוֹ, מִשּׁוּם וֶסְתָּהּ. וְאִם בָּא יוֹם הַחֲמִשָּׁה וְעֶשְׂרִים וְלֹא רָאֲתָה צְרִיכָה לָחוּשׁ לְיוֹם הַשְּׁמוֹנָה וְעֶשְׂרִים מִשּׁוּם רְאִיָּה שֶׁעָבְרָה. רָאֲתָה גַּם עַתָּה בַּיּוֹם הַשְּׁמוֹנָה וְעֶשְׂרִים, עֲדַיִן הִיא אֲסוּרָה גַּם בְּיוֹם הַחֲמִשָּׁה וְעֶשְׂרִים לִרְאִיָּה זוֹ, מִשּׁוּם וֶסְתָּהּ. לֹא רָאֲתָה גַּם עַתָּה בְּיוֹם הַחֲמִשָּׁה וְעֶשְׂרִים, אֶלָּא בְּיוֹם הַשְּׁמוֹנָה וְעֶשְׂרִים, הֻקְבַּע יוֹם הַשְּׁמוֹנָה וְעֶשְׂרִים לְוֶסְתָּהּ, וְיוֹם הַחֲמִשָּׁה וְעֶשְׂרִים נֶעֱקַר (דְּהָא עֲקַרְתֵּהּ שָׁלֹשׁ פְּעָמִים) וְהֻתַּר. וְאִם לֹא הִשְׁוְתָה רְאִיּוֹתֶיהָ הָאַחֲרוֹנוֹת, כְּגוֹן שֶׁרָאֲתָה לִשְׁמוֹנָה וְעֶשְׂרִים, לְתִשְׁעָה וְעֶשְׂרִים, לְאֶחָד וּשְׁלֹשִׁים, עָקְרָה וֶסְתָּהּ הָרִאשׁוֹן, וְאֵין לָהּ וֶסֶת חָדָשׁ, וּצְרִיכָה תָּמִיד לָחוּשׁ מֵרְאִיָּה הָאַחֲרוֹנָה לְהַפְלָגָה וּלְיוֹם הַחֹדֶשׁ וּלְעוֹנָה בֵּינוֹנִית, עַד שֶׁתִּקְבַּע וֶסֶת חָדָשׁ.

ז) הַכְּלָל הוּא לְכָל יְרֵא־שָׁמַיִם, אִם הָאִשָּׁה אֵין לָהּ וֶסֶת קָבוּעַ, יֵשׁ לוֹ לִכְתֹּב תָּמִיד יוֹם רְאִיָּתָהּ, וְיִרְאֶה אֵיזֶה יוֹם בַּחֹדֶשׁ הוּא, וְכַמָּה יָמִים הֵם בֵּין רְאִיָּה לִרְאִיָּה, וְיָחוּשׁ תָּמִיד לְהַבָּא לְיוֹם הַפְלָגָה כְּהַפְלָגָה הָאַחֲרוֹנָה, וְכֵן לְיוֹם הַחֹדֶשׁ, כְּמוֹ שֶׁהָיְתָה הָרְאִיָּה הָאַחֲרוֹנָה, וְגַם צָרִיךְ לָחוּשׁ לְעוֹנָה בֵּינוֹנִית. כָּכָה יִנְהַג עַד שֶׁתִּקְבַּע לָהּ וֶסֶת קָבוּעַ. וּלְאַחַר שֶׁתִּקְבַּע וֶסֶת, אִם יֶאֱרַע שֶׁתְּשַׁנֶּה וֶסְתָּהּ, צָרִיךְ גַּם כֵּן לִזָּהֵר לָחוּשׁ לָרְאִיָּה הַחֲדָשָׁה, הֵן לְהַפְלָגָה הֵן לִימֵי הַחֹדֶשׁ. וְגַם צָרִיךְ לִזָּהֵר לִזְכֹּר יוֹם וֶסֶת קָבוּעַ שֶׁלָּהּ, כִּי הַוֶּסֶת הַקָּבוּעַ אֵינוֹ נֶעֱקָר אֶלָּא בְּשָׁלֹשׁ פְּעָמִים, כִּדְלְקַמָּן.

ח) אִשָּׁה שֶׁיֵּשׁ לָהּ וֶסֶת קָבוּעַ, אַף אִם הִגִּיעַ פַּעַם אַחַת אוֹ שְׁתֵּי פְעָמִים יוֹם וֶסְתָּהּ אוֹ סִימַן וֶסְתָּהּ וְלֹא רָאֲתָה, אַף־עַל־פִּי שֶׁבָּרוּר לָהּ בְּבֵרוּר גָּמוּר שֶׁלֹּא רָאֲתָה, כְּגוֹן שֶׁהָיָה לָהּ כָּל מֶשֶׁךְ הַוֶּסֶת מוֹךְ דָּחוּק,

did not perceive blood, she must be mindful of the twenty-fifth day, as she may establish her menses on the twenty-fifth day of the month. (She must also be mindful on the twenty-sixth day, because it is the "average *onah* (period).") However, for the *Rosh Chodesh* of *Tammuz* she need not be concerned, for her perception on *Rosh Chodesh Iyar*, has already been eliminated as a period by her failure to perceive blood on *Rosh Chodesh* of *Sivan*. (For whatever is not established by three (consecutive) occurrences, is nullified by a one-time failure to occur, as explained hereafter.)

6) An example of a woman who has a regular menses: she has an established menses of twenty-five day intervals, and one time a change occured, whereby she did not perceive until the twenty-eighth day. She must be mindful of the twenty-fifth day from this last perception, because this is her regular period. If the twenty-fifth day came and she has not perceived blood, she must take heed of the twenty-eighth day, because of her last perception. If she has perceived again on the twenty-eighth day, she is still forbidden (to her husband) on the twenty-fifth day after this last perception, because of her regular period. If now, too, she did not perceive blood on the twenty-fifth day, but rather on the twenty-eighth day, the twenty-eighth day is set as her fixed period while the twenty-fifth is eliminated, (for she has replaced it with another, three times,) and she is permitted [on the twenty fifth day]. If the last perceptions were not had at equal intervals, if she saw on the twenty eighth day, on the twenty ninth day, and on the thirty first day, her previous fixed period is eliminated, and now she has no established fixed period. She must, therefore, always be mindful of the equal interval from her last perception (31 days), and for the "day of the month," and for the "average period," until she establishes a new fixed period

7) This rule should guide every God-fearing person: If the woman has no regular period you should always write the date on which she perceived blood, the day of the month, and how many days elapsed between perceptions. You must always be mindful in the future of the intervening number of days between the last two periods. You must also be mindful of the day of the month, based on her last perception. You must also be mindful of the "average *onah* (period)." This is how you should conduct yourself until she establishes a regular period. After she establishes a regular period, if a change occurs in her period, you must also be careful to take notice of the new perception, with regard to both the number of intervening days, and the day of the month. You must also be careful to remember the day of her regular period because the regular period is eliminated only after three times, as stated hereafter.

8) A woman who has a fixed period, even if once or twice the date of her period (arrived), or her characteristic symptoms (arrived), and she did not perceive blood, even though she is certain beyond any doubt, that she did not perceive, for instance

מִכָּל מָקוֹם עֲדַיִן לֹא נֶעֱקַר וֶסְתָּהּ, וּצְרִיכָה עֲדַיִן לָחוּשׁ גַּם לַפַּעַם הַשְּׁלִישִׁית. אֲבָל אִם הִגִּיעָה גַּם הַפַּעַם הַשְּׁלִישִׁית וְלֹא רָאֲתָה, אִם בָּרוּר לָהּ בְּבֵרוּר גָּמוּר שֶׁלֹּא רָאֲתָה בְּכָל שְׁלֹשֶׁת הַפְּעָמִים, כְּגוֹן שֶׁבְּכָל פַּעַם הָיָה לָהּ מוֹךְ דָּחוּק כָּל מֶשֶׁךְ הַוֶּסֶת, מֵעַתָּה נֶעֱקַר וֶסְתָּהּ, וְאֵינָהּ צְרִיכָה לָחוּשׁ לוֹ עוֹד, כִּי כָל וֶסֶת נֶעֱקַר בְּשָׁלֹשׁ פְּעָמִים, אֲפִלּוּ הָיָה קָבוּעַ כַּמָּה שָׁנִים. אֲבָל וֶסֶת שֶׁאֵינוֹ קָבוּעַ, דְּהַיְנוּ רְאִיָּה שֶׁלֹּא קְבָעַתָּהּ רַק פַּעַם אַחַת אוֹ שְׁתֵּי פְּעָמִים, אִם הִגִּיעַ פַּעַם אַחַת הַיּוֹם הַזֶּה אוֹ הַסִּימָן הַזֶּה וְלֹא רָאֲתָה, וְאַף־עַל־פִּי שֶׁלֹּא בָּדְקָה אֶת עַצְמָהּ, אֶלָּא שֶׁלֹּא הִרְגִּישָׁה שׁוּם רְאִיָּה, שׁוּב אֵינָהּ צְרִיכָה לָחוּשׁ לָהּ, כִּי כָל מַה שֶּׁלֹּא נִקְבַּע בְּשָׁלֹשׁ פְּעָמִים, נֶעֱקָר בְּפַעַם אַחַת, וַאֲפִלּוּ בְּלֹא בְדִיקָה.

ט) אִשָּׁה שֶׁיֵּשׁ לָהּ וֶסֶת קָבוּעַ, קֹדֶם שֶׁבָּאָה לָהּ הַשָּׁעָה שֶׁהִיא רְגִילָה לִרְאוֹת, יֵשׁ לָהּ לְהַכְנִיס מוֹךְ דָּחוּק, לְמַעַן תֵּדַע בְּבֵרוּר, כִּי יֵשׁ לָחוּשׁ, שֶׁמָּא תֵצֵא מִמֶּנָּה אֵיזוֹ טִפַּת דָּם וְתֹאבַד, וְהִיא לֹא תֵדָע. וְאִם לֹא עָשְׂתָה כֵן, וְעָבַר זְמַן וֶסְתָּהּ, אֲסוּרָה לְבַעְלָהּ, עַד שֶׁתִּבְדֹּק אֶת עַצְמָהּ הֵיטֵב. וְאִם בְּתוֹךְ הַזְּמַן רָחֲצָה אֶת עַצְמָהּ, שׁוּב לָא מַהֲנֵי לָהּ בְּדִיקָה. וְיֵשׁ לָהּ לְהַחְמִיר וּלְהַחֲזִיק אֶת עַצְמָהּ טְמֵאָה, כִּי חֲזָקָה הִיא, שֶׁהַדָּם בָּא בִּזְמַנּוֹ הַקָּבוּעַ. אֲבָל אִם אֵין לָהּ וֶסֶת קָבוּעַ, אֶלָּא שֶׁהִיא חוֹשֶׁשֶׁת לְוֶסֶת שֶׁאֵינוֹ קָבוּעַ, אִם עָבַר הַזְּמַן וְלֹא הִרְגִּישָׁה, אַף־עַל־פִּי שֶׁלֹּא בָדְקָה אֶת עַצְמָהּ, הֲרֵי הִיא אַחַר כָּךְ בְּחֶזְקַת טְהוֹרָה. אַךְ עוֹנָה בֵּינוֹנִית, שֶׁהִיא יוֹם הַשְּׁלֹשִׁים, דִּינָהּ כְּמוֹ וֶסֶת קָבוּעַ, וּכְמוֹ שֶׁכָּתַבְתִּי לְעֵיל.

י) אִשָּׁה שֶׁרְאִיָּתָהּ נִמְשֶׁכֶת שְׁנַיִם אוֹ שְׁלֹשָׁה יָמִים, שֶׁהִיא שׁוֹפַעַת אוֹ מְזַלֶּפֶת, יוֹם הַתְחָלַת הָרְאִיָּה הוּא הָעִקָּר. וְיֵשׁ אוֹמְרִים, דְּמִכָּל מָקוֹם צְרִיכָה הִיא לָחוּשׁ תָּמִיד לְכָל הַיָּמִים עַד שֶׁיֵּעָקְרוּ.

יא) כְּשֵׁם שֶׁהָאִשָּׁה חוֹשֶׁשֶׁת לְוֶסֶת הַיָּמִים וּלְוֶסֶת הַהַפְלָגוֹת בְּפַעַם אַחַת, כְּמוֹ כֵן חוֹשֶׁשֶׁת גַּם לְוֶסֶת הַגּוּף וּלְוֶסֶת הַמֻּרְכָּב בְּפַעַם אֶחָת. וּכְשֵׁם שֶׁוֶּסֶת הַיָּמִים וְוֶסֶת הַהַפְלָגוֹת שֶׁאֵינָן קְבוּעִין, נֶעֱקָרִין בְּפַעַם אַחַת, כְּמוֹ

11. The *Kitzur Shulchan Aruch* rules like the *Chavas Da'as* who requires such a tampon in place throughout the entire *onah*. However, this is not the prevailing custom anywhere. The *Chazon Ish* 80:22 says she has to examine herself [only] one time during that *onah*. It is better to check once in the beginning and again at the end of the *onah*.

if during the entire period she had a cloth [or tampon] packed tightly in place,[11] still her regular period is not eliminated, and she must still be mindful of it even the third time. But if the third time also arrived and she did not perceive anything, if she is absolutely certain that she did not perceive anything on any of these three times; for instance, if at each time she had a cloth packed tightly into place throughout the date of her expected period, from then on her regular period has been eliminated, and she need not be concerned about it anymore. For every regular fixed period is eliminated after failing to happen three times, even if it was regular for many years. But a period which is not established, such as a perception that occured only once or twice, then if this day arrived, or this particular sign arrived one time, and she did not perceive her menstrual flow, even if she did not examine herself, as long as she did not feel anything, she no longer needs to observe this period. Whatever has not been established by three consecutive occurrences is eliminated by one time, even without examination.

9) If a woman has a regular fixed period, then before the time arrives when she regularly perceives, she should insert a cloth[11] so she will be sure (her menstrual flow has not begun), for otherwise, she must suspect that perhaps a drop of blood issued and disappeared without her being aware of it. If she failed to do so, and the time of her fixed period passed, she is forbidden to her husband[12] until she examines herself thoroughly. If during the time of her expected period, she bathed herself, the examination will be of no avail.[13] She must be stringent and consider herself to be in an unclean state, because it is presumed that the flux has come at its regular time. But if she does not have a regular period, but she is being mindful of an irregular period, if the time has passed and she has felt nothing even though she failed to examine herself, she is thereafter presumed to be menstrually clean. However, with regard to the average period, which is the thirtieth day, her status is like that of a regular (fixed) period, as has been stated above.

10) If a woman's flow continues two or three days, coming either in a flow or in drops, the day on which she begins to perceive is considered the principal day. Some authorities say that, nevertheless, she must always be mindful of all these days until they are eliminated.

11) Just as a woman must be mindful of the menstrual period as indicated by the monthly date of menstruation, and by the amount of intervening days, even after a single occurrence, so, too, must she be mindful of the menses indicated by physical symptoms alone, or in combination with (equal interval perceptions) after

---

12. *Tiferes L'Moshe* prohibits even other intimacies, but the *Sidrei Taharah* permits it and only forbids marital relations during this time.
13. *Prisha* and *Placey* 184. However, others say that bathing makes no differnce and she is permitted to her husband if she is clean on examination. The *Chazon Ish* also permits her, and such is the prevailing custom.

כֵּן וֶסֶת הַגּוּף וּוֶסֶת הַמֻּרְכָּב, נֶעֱקָרִין בְּפַעַם אֶחָת. וּכְשֵׁם שֶׁוֶּסֶת הַיָּמִים וּוֶסֶת הַהַפְלָגוֹת הַקְּבוּעִים אֵינָן נֶעֱקָרִין אֶלָּא בְּשָׁלֹשׁ פְּעָמִים, כָּךְ וֶסֶת הַגּוּף וּוֶסֶת הַמֻּרְכָּב הַקְּבוּעִים אֵינָן נֶעֱקָרִין אֶלָּא בְּשָׁלֹשׁ פְּעָמִים, דְּהַיְנוּ אִם הָיָה לָהּ וֶסֶת הַגּוּף גְּרִידָא, כֵּיוָן שֶׁפִּהֲקָה אַחַר כָּךְ שָׁלֹשׁ פְּעָמִים וְלֹא רָאֲתָה, שׁוּב אֵינָהּ צְרִיכָה לָחוּשׁ כַּאֲשֶׁר תְּפַהֵק. וְאִם הוּא וֶסֶת הַמֻּרְכָּב, כְּשֶׁהִגִּיעַ שָׁלֹשׁ פְּעָמִים יוֹם זֶה וּפִהֲקָה וְלֹא רָאֲתָה, אָז הַוֶּסֶת נֶעְקַר. אֲבָל הַיָּמִים בְּלֹא פִהוּק אוֹ פִהוּק בְּלֹא יָמִים, אֵינָן עוֹקְרִין אֶת הַוֶּסֶת הַמֻּרְכָּב, דְּבָעֵינָן עֲקִירָתוֹ דֻּמְיָא דִּקְבִיעָתוֹ.

יב) מְעֻבֶּרֶת, לְאַחַר שְׁלֹשָׁה חֳדָשִׁים מִתְּחִלַּת עִבּוּרָהּ וְכֵן מֵינִיקָה, הֵן בְּחֶזְקַת מְסֻלָּקוֹת מִדָּמִים וְאֵינָן חוֹשְׁשׁוֹת לְוֶסְתָּן, אַף־עַל־פִּי שֶׁהָיָה לָהֶן וֶסֶת קָבוּעַ. וּמִכָּל מָקוֹם חוֹשֶׁשֶׁת לִרְאִיָּה שֶׁתִּרְאֶה כְּדֶרֶךְ שֶׁחוֹשֶׁשֶׁת לְוֶסֶת שֶׁאֵינוֹ קָבוּעַ. עָבְרוּ יְמֵי הֲנָקָתָהּ, חוֹזֶרֶת לָחוּשׁ לְוֶסְתָּהּ הָרִאשׁוֹן כְּגוֹן אִם הָיָה לָהּ וֶסֶת לְרֹאשׁ חֹדֶשׁ, צְרִיכָה לָחוּשׁ מִיָּד לְרֹאשׁ־חֹדֶשׁ הָרִאשׁוֹן. אֲבָל אִם הָיָה לָהּ וֶסֶת לְהַפְלָגוֹת, אֵינָהּ חוֹשֶׁשֶׁת עַד שֶׁתִּרְאֶה פַּעַם אַחַת, וְאָז חוֹשֶׁשֶׁת לְהַפְלָגָה שֶׁהָיְתָה רְגִילָה לִרְאוֹת.

סִימָן קנו
דִּין רָאֲתָה דָּם מֵחֲמַת תַּשְׁמִישׁ

א) אִשָּׁה שֶׁרָאֲתָה דָּם מֵחֲמַת תַּשְׁמִישׁ, אֲפִלּוּ שֶׁלֹּא בִשְׁעַת תַּשְׁמִישׁ אֶלָּא אַחַר כָּךְ בְּאוֹתוֹ הַלַּיְלָה, מֻתֶּרֶת לְשַׁמֵּשׁ פַּעַם שֵׁנִית לְאַחַר שֶׁתִּטְהַר, אֲבָל מֵיחַשׁ חָיְשָׁא גַּם בַּחֲדָא זִמְנָא. שֶׁאִם אֵרַע לָהּ כֵּן בְּלֵיל טְבִילָה, אֲזַי כְּשֶׁתִּטְבֹּל, צָרִיךְ לִפְרוֹשׁ מִמֶּנָּה לֵיל טְבִילָה, כִּי חָיְשִׁינָן שֶׁמָּא הַטְּבִילָה בְּצֵרוּף הַתַּשְׁמִישׁ, גּוֹרְמִים לָהּ לִרְאוֹת דָּם, וְשֶׁמָּא תִרְאֶה בְּלֵיל טְבִילָה שֵׁנִית בִּשְׁעַת תַּשְׁמִישׁ מַמָּשׁ. אֲבָל בְּלֵיל טְבִילָה שְׁלִישִׁית, אֵין צָרִיךְ לִפְרוֹשׁ, מִשּׁוּם דְּעִקַּר הַחֲשָׁשׁ הָיָה מִשּׁוּם הַטְּבִילָה. וְכֵיוָן דִּבְטְבִילָה שְׁנִיָּה

a single occurrence. And just as the menses based on monthly perceptions, and by the number of intervening days, if they are not established (three consecutive times), are eliminated by a one-time failure to occur, so, too, the menses based on bodily symptoms alone, or in combination with one of the above, are eliminated by a one-time failure to occur. And just as the menses of monthly perceptions, and of equal interval perceptions that have been established by three occurrences, are eliminated only by three successive occurrences (to the contrary), so, too, the menses based on bodily symptoms alone, or in combination with one of the above, after being established by three occurrences, are eliminated only by three successive occurrences to the contrary. For instance, if she has established a period based only on physical symptoms, for example, if thereafter she yawned three times, and did not perceive a flow, she no longer has to be mindful when she yawns again. If it is a period based on a combination when the fixed day arrives three times, and she yawned and did not perceive any flow, then the term is eliminated. But a change of days without yawning, or a change in yawning without a change in days, do not eliminate the term established by a combination of factors, because we require that this process of its elimination be similar to the process through which it was established.

12) A pregnant woman, after three months from the beginning of her pregnancy, and a woman while nursing a child, are presumed to have ceased their flow, and need not be concerned about their periods, even if they have an established periods. Nevertheless she must take heed of every perception just as a woman is required to be mindful of an irregular period. When the period of nursing is over, she must continue to observe her former periods. For instance, if she had an established period on the day of *Rosh Chodesh*, she must immediately continue to expect its occurrence on the first *Rosh Chodesh.* But if she had a period of equal interval perceptions, she need not be concerned until she once again has a perception, and then she must be mindful of her customary interval between periods.

Chapter 156

Perception of Blood as a Result of Cohabitation

1) If a woman has an issue of blood as a result of marital intercourse, even if it did not occur during marital intercourse, but later that night, she is permitted to have marital relations again after she purifies herself, but they should be apprehensive of a repetition even after only one such occurrence. Thus if it occurred on the night of her immersion, then the next time she immerses, he must be separated from her on the night of her immersion, for we suspect that perhaps the immersion in conjuction with the intercourse, causes her to issue blood, and perhaps she will perceive blood on the night of the following immersion, during the very act of marital intercourse. But on the night of the third immersion, they are not bound to separate themselves, because the main cause for concern was due to the immersion, and since on the night of her second immersion she did not perceive any blood there is no cause for further concern. Likewise, if a perception occurred on the night

לֹא רָאֲתָה, תּוּ לָא חָיְשִׁינַן. וְכֵן אִם אֵרַע לָהּ שֶׁרָאֲתָה בְּלֵיל שֵׁנִי שֶׁל טְבִילָה, צָרִיךְ לִפְרוֹשׁ בִּטְבִילָה שְׁנִיָּה לֵיל שֵׁנִי וְלֹא בִטְבִילָה שְׁלִישִׁית.

ב) וְכֵיוָן דְּאִתְיְלִיד רֵיעוּתָא בְּאִשָּׁה זוֹ, לָכֵן אֲפִלּוּ אִם יֵשׁ לָהּ וֶסֶת קָבוּעַ, מִכָּל מָקוֹם כְּשֶׁתְּשַׁמֵּשׁ פַּעַם שֵׁנִית, צְרִיכָה בְדִיקָה לִפְנֵי תַשְׁמִישׁ וּלְאַחַר תַּשְׁמִישׁ, לְבָרֵר אִם לֹא רָאֲתָה עוֹד מֵחֲמַת תַּשְׁמִישׁ. וְתִזָּהֵר הָאִשָּׁה לַעֲסוֹק מִיָּד בִּרְפוּאוֹת. וּמִכָּל־שֶׁכֵּן אִם אֵרַע לָהּ שֶׁרָאֲתָה בִּשְׁעַת תַּשְׁמִישׁ מַמָּשׁ אוֹ בְסָמוּךְ לְאַחַר תַּשְׁמִישׁ. כִּי אִם יֶאֱרַע לָהּ כֵּן שָׁלֹשׁ פְּעָמִים רְצוּפוֹת, נָפְלָה בִּמְצוֹדָה גְדוֹלָה, וּבְקֹשִׁי גָדוֹל יִמָּצֵא לָהּ הֶתֵּר שֶׁתִּשָּׁאֵר אֵצֶל בַּעְלָהּ.

ג) אִשָּׁה שֶׁהִרְגִּישָׁה בִּשְׁעַת תַּשְׁמִישׁ שֶׁנִּטְמָאָה, מְחֻיֶּבֶת לוֹמַר מִיָּד לְבַעְלָהּ נִטְמֵאתִי, וְלֹא יִפְרוֹשׁ אֶת עַצְמוֹ מִיָּד בְּאֵבֶר חַי, כִּי גַם זֹאת הֲנָאָה הִיא לוֹ, אֶלָּא יִסְמוֹךְ עַל יָדָיו וְרַגְלָיו וְלֹא עָלֶיהָ, וְיִמָּלֵא פַחַד וּרְתֵת עַל הָעֲבֵרָה שֶׁבָּאָה לְיָדוֹ. וּכְשֶׁיָּמוּת הָאֵבֶר, יִפְרוֹשׁ אֶת עַצְמוֹ, וְיִשְׁאַל לְמוֹרֵה־הוֹרָאָה שֶׁיּוֹרֶה לוֹ תְשׁוּבָה עַל הָעֲבֵרָה.

סִימָן קנז
דִּינֵי כַּלָּה הַנִּכְנֶסֶת לַחֻפָּה

א) אִשָּׁה שֶׁהִיא מְכִינָה אֶת עַצְמָהּ לַנִּשּׂוּאִין, צְרִיכָה לִסְפֹּר תְּחִלָּה שִׁבְעָה נְקִיִּים, בֵּין שֶׁהִיא קְטַנָּה שֶׁעֲדַיִן לֹא רָאֲתָה דָם מֵעוֹלָם, בֵּין שֶׁהִיא זְקֵנָה שֶׁכְּבָר פָּסְקָה מִלִּרְאוֹת, מִכָּל מָקוֹם חָיְשִׁינַן, שֶׁמָּא מֵחֲמַת חִמּוּד יָצְאָה מִמֶּנָּה אֵיזוֹ טִפַּת דָּם וְנֶאֶבְדָה, לָכֵן מַחֲזִיקִים אוֹתָהּ כְּמוֹ נִדָּה מַמָּשׁ. וְגַם לְאַחַר סְפִירַת שִׁבְעָה נְקִיִּים, יֵשׁ לָהּ לִבְדֹּק אֶת עַצְמָהּ בְּכָל יוֹם עַד הַטְּבִילָה, וְכֵן לְאַחַר הַטְּבִילָה עַד בְּעִילַת מִצְוָה.

ב) אִם נִדְחוּ הַנִּשּׂוּאִין מֵחֲמַת אֵיזוֹ סִבָּה, וְאַחַר כָּךְ שׁוּב נִתְפַּשְּׁרוּ לַעֲשׂוֹת הַנִּשּׂוּאִין, אַף־עַל־פִּי שֶׁסָּפְרָה שִׁבְעָה נְקִיִּים בָּרִאשׁוֹנָה, מִכָּל מָקוֹם צְרִיכָה לִסְפֹּר מֵחָדָשׁ, כֵּיוָן שֶׁנּוֹלַד לָהּ חִמּוּד חָדָשׁ. וַאֲפִלּוּ בָּדְקָה אֶת

1. She becomes permanently forbidden to her husband if this happens three consecutive times immediately after cohabitation. The *Makor Chaim* says only if it happens within one half an hour after cohabitation; the *Peri Deah* suggests about fifteen seconds. In all cases, a competent Rav must be consulted.

following her immersion, they must separate themselves on the night following her second immersion but not after the third immersion.

2) However, since an unfavorable tendency has developed in this woman, therefore, even if she has regular periods, nevertheless, the next time she has marital intercourse, she must examine herself both before and after intercourse in order to ascertain whether she had a flow again as a result of marital intercourse. She should also be careful to immediately seek medical attention; and most certainly if it happened that she perceived blood during marital intercourse, or shortly thereafter, for if this occurs three successive times[1] she will be in a very perplexing position, and only with utmost difficulty can she be permitted to continue living with her husband.

3) If during marital intercourse, the woman feels that she has become menstrually unclean, she must immediately say to her husband, "I have become unclean." He should not separate himself from her immediately while his organ is rigid, for this act in itself affords pleasure, but he must support himself on his hands and feet, and not upon her. He should be filled with fear and trembling because of this sinful occurrence, and when his organ relaxes, he should separate from her. He should consult a Rav to instruct him regarding a proper penance for this sin.

Chapter 157

Pre-Nuptial Laws

1) A woman who is preparing herself for her wedding, must first count seven (menstrually) clean days, whether she is a minor who has never perceived blood, or whether she is an aged woman whose flow has long ceased. Nevertheless, we suspect that perhaps because of her anticipation, some drops of blood issued from her and disappeared. Therefore, we regard her as an actual *niddah.* After having counted the seven clean days, she must examine herself daily until she performs the ritual immersion and also after the immersion, until the ordained consummation of the marital act.[1]

2) If the wedding was cancelled[2] for some reason, and afterward they agreed to hold the wedding, even though she had already counted seven clean days the first time, nevertheless she must count them anew, because a new desire has been created in her. Even if she has examined herself daily during the interval, it is of no

---

1. Even after the wedding, she must examine herself daily until the consummation of the first marital act. (*Lechem V'simla*)

2. If the groom cancelled but the bride did not give up the idea and he was convinced to go through with it, she does not need to count anew (*Taz*). If the bride made up her mind not to marry him, and then changed her mind, she must count anew (*Aruch Hashulchan*). The *Makor Chaim* say she does not need to.

עַצְמָהּ בְּכָל הַיָּמִים שֶׁבֵּינְתַיִם, לָא מַהֲנֵי לָהּ. וְאִם לֹא הָיָה דִחוּי גָּמוּר, אֶלָּא שֶׁלֹּא יָכְלוּ לְהִשְׁתַּווֹת בְּעֵסֶק הַנְּדֻנְיָא וְכַדּוֹמֶה, וּמֵחֲמַת זֶה נִתְעַכְּבוּ עַד שֶׁנִּתְפַּשְּׁרוּ, אוֹ שֶׁמֵּרְצוֹנָם דָּחוּ הַנִּשּׂוּאִין מִיּוֹם שֶׁקְּבָעוּם וְהִגְבִּילוּ יוֹם אַחֵר, יַעֲשׂוּ שְׁאֵלַת חָכָם, אִם שִׁבְעָה נְקִיִּים הָרִאשׁוֹנִים מַהֲנֵי לָהּ. אִם נִתְקוֹטְטוּ בִּשְׁעַת הַנִּשּׂוּאִין, וְנִכְנַס חָתָן אַחֵר תַּחַת הָרִאשׁוֹן, פְּשִׁיטָא דְּלָא מַהֲנֵי לָהּ שִׁבְעָה נְקִיִּים שֶׁסָּפְרָה עַל דַּעַת חָתָן אַחֵר, אֶלָּא אֲפִלּוּ אִם לְאַחַר שֶׁנִּתְרַצּוּ לְחָתָן אַחֵר, שׁוּב נִתְפַּיֵּס הָרִאשׁוֹן, לָא מַהֲנֵי לָהּ שִׁבְעָה נְקִיִּים הָרִאשׁוֹנִים, כֵּיוָן שֶׁהִסִּיחָה דַעְתָּהּ מִמֶּנּוּ, אֶלָּא צְרִיכָה לִסְפֹּר מֵחָדָשׁ.

ג) יֵשׁ לִזָּהֵר שֶׁלֹּא תִנָּשֵׂא אִשָּׁה עַד שֶׁתִּטְהַר מִטֻּמְאָתָהּ. וְאִם הָעֵת דְּחוּקָה וּצְרִיכִין לַעֲשׂוֹת הַנִּשּׂוּאִין בְּעוֹדָהּ בְּטֻמְאָתָהּ, אוֹ אִם אֵרַע שֶׁפֵּרְסָה נִדָּה לְאַחַר הַחֻפָּה קֹדֶם שֶׁנִּבְעֲלָה, לֹא יִתְיַחֲדוּ בְּלִי שְׁמִירָה עַד שֶׁתִּטְבֹּל. וְנוֹהֲגִין לִקַּח קָטָן אֵצֶל הֶחָתָן וּקְטַנָּה אֵצֶל הַכַּלָּה, וְאֵין מִתְיַחֲדִין אֲפִלּוּ בַּיּוֹם בְּלֹא קָטָן אוֹ קְטַנָּה. וּצְרִיכִין שֶׁיִּהְיוּ גְדוֹלִים קְצָת שֶׁיּוֹדְעִין עִנְיְנֵי בִיאָה, וְלֹא גְדוֹלָה מַמָּשׁ שֶׁכְּבָר לָבְשָׁה יִצְרָא, שֶׁיֵּשׁ לָחוּשׁ שֶׁתִּתְפַּתֶּה, אֶלָּא בֵּינוֹנִים. וְאֵין חִלּוּק בָּזֶה בֵּין בָּחוּר לְאַלְמָן וּבֵין בְּתוּלָה לְאַלְמָנָה, שֶׁכֹּל שֶׁלֹּא בָעַל אִשָּׁה זוֹ מִיָּמָיו, חָיְשִׁינָן דְּתַקִּיף יִצְרֵהּ, וַאֲסוּרִין לְהִתְיַחֵד בְּלִי שְׁמִירָה.

ד) מַחֲזִיר גְּרוּשָׁתוֹ, צְרִיכָה לִסְפֹּר שִׁבְעָה נְקִיִּים, אֲפִלּוּ גֵּרְשָׁהּ כְּשֶׁהָיְתָה מְעֻבֶּרֶת וְהֶחֱזִירָהּ כְּשֶׁהִיא מְעֻבֶּרֶת, אוֹ גֵּרְשָׁהּ כְּשֶׁהִיא מֵינֶקֶת וְהֶחֱזִירָהּ כְּשֶׁהִיא מֵינֶקֶת. וְאִם עָבַר וּכְנָסָהּ קֹדֶם, מֻתָּרִין לְהִתְיַחֵד, דְּכֵיוָן שֶׁכְּבָר בָּא עָלֶיהָ, תּוּ לָא תַקִּיף יִצְרֵהּ כָּל כָּךְ.

ה) צְרִיכִין לִזָּהֵר בִּמְאֹד מְאֹד, שֶׁלֹּא יִשְׁכַּב הֶחָתָן אֵצֶל הַכַּלָּה עַד הַלַּיְלָה שֶׁהוּא רוֹצֶה לִבְעֹל.

ו) הַכּוֹנֵס אֶת הַבְּתוּלָה, בּוֹעֵל בְּעִילַת מִצְוָה. וְאַף־עַל־פִּי שֶׁהַדָּם שׁוֹתֵת וְיוֹרֵד, גּוֹמֵר בִּיאָתוֹ כִּרְצוֹנוֹ, וְאֵינוֹ חוֹשֵׁשׁ. אֲבָל לְאַחַר שֶׁגָּמַר בִּיאָתוֹ, פּוֹרֵשׁ אֶת עַצְמוֹ מִמֶּנָּה, וְהִיא טְמֵאָה. וַאֲפִלּוּ לֹא נִרְאָה שׁוּם דָּם, חָיְשִׁינָן שֶׁמָּא יָצְאָה טִפַּת דָּם וְנֶחְפְּתָה בְּשִׁכְבַת זֶרַע, וְעַל כֵּן מַחֲזִיקִין אוֹתָהּ כְּנִדָּה גְמוּרָה.

ז) בְּתוּלָה, שֶׁלְּאַחַר הַבְּעִילָה הָרִאשׁוֹנָה טָבְלָה, וְגַם בַּבְּעִילָה הַשְּׁנִיָּה

avail. If it was not a definite cancellation, but they were unable to agree about the amount of the dowry, or the like, and because of this the wedding was delayed until they came to terms, or if they postponed the wedding by mutual consent, from the original day to a different day, they should consult a *poseik* to determine if the first clean days are of avail. If they quarreled at the wedding, and another groom took the place of the first, it is self evident that there is no validity to the seven clean days that she counted for the first bridegroom. But even if after consenting to marry the second groom, she became reconciled with the first one, there is no validity to the first seven clean days, because her thoughts were diverted from him. She must count anew, seven clean days.

3) A woman should be careful not to marry before she purifies herself from her unclean menstrual status. If it is urgent and the wedding must be held when she is still unclean, or if it occurred that she became menstrually unclean after the wedding ceremony, but before the consummation of the marital act; they are forbidden to be alone together without supervision, until she has performed the rite of immersion. It is customary to place a male child with the groom, and a female child with the bride. They may not be alone even during the daytime, without the children. The children must be old enough to understand something about marital relations. The girl should not be fully mature already having desire, lest she permit herself to be seduced, but of average maturity. Regarding this law there is no distinction between a groom who has never been married and a widower, or between a virgin and a widow; for so long as he has never had marital relations with that woman, we fear he may succumb to his passions, and therefore, they are prohibited to be alone, without supervision.

4) When one remarries the woman he divorced, she must count seven clean days. [This rule applies] even if he divorced her while she was pregnant, and remarried her while she is still pregnant, or he divorced her while she was nursing a child, and remarried her while she is still nursing. If he violated this rule and remarried her before [her seven clean days and immersion], they are permitted to be alone together. Since he already had marital relations with her, his impulse will not be so overpowering.

5) Extreme care should be taken that the groom should not lie next to the bride until the night he wishes to consummate their marriage.

6) One who marries a virgin should perform the ordained marital act, and even if there is an issue of hymenal blood, he should conclude the act and need have no scruples about it. However, after concluding the act, he must separate himself from her, and she is regarded as unclean. And even if no blood is perceived, we suspect perhaps a drop of blood issued from her, and was covered up by the semen. Therefore we regard her as menstrually unclean.

7) A virgin, who performed the rite of immersion after the first marital act, and

רָאֲתָה דָם, וְכֵן בְּפַעַם שְׁלִישִׁית וּרְבִיעִית, יֵשׁ בָּזֶה שְׁאֵלָה אִם מֻתֶּרֶת לְהִשָּׁאֵר אֵצֶל בַּעְלָהּ.

ח) מֻתָּר לִבְעֹל בְּתוּלָה בְּשַׁבָּת, אַף־עַל־פִּי שֶׁהוּא עוֹשֶׂה חַבּוּרָה.

סִימָן קנח
דִּין יוֹלֶדֶת וּמַפֶּלֶת

א) יוֹלֶדֶת, בֵּין יָלְדָה וָלָד חַי בֵּין וָלָד מֵת, וַאֲפִלּוּ נֵפֶל, אֲפִלּוּ לֹא רָאֲתָה דָם, הֲרֵי הִיא טְמֵאָה טֻמְאַת לֵדָה. וּמִצַּד הַדִּין אִם הָיָה הַוָּלָד זָכָר, הִיא טְמֵאָה שִׁבְעַת יָמִים מִשּׁוּם לֵדָה, וְאַחַר כָּךְ יְכוֹלָה לִסְפֹּר שִׁבְעָה נְקִיִּים וְתִטְבֹּל. וְאִם הָיָה נְקֵבָה, הִיא טְמֵאָה אַרְבָּעָה עָשָׂר יוֹם מִשּׁוּם לֵדָה, וְאַחַר כָּךְ סוֹפֶרֶת שִׁבְעָה נְקִיִּים וְטוֹבֶלֶת. וְיֵשׁ מְקוֹמוֹת שֶׁנּוֹהֲגִין שֶׁאֵינָן טוֹבְלוֹת תּוֹךְ אַרְבָּעִים יוֹם לְזָכָר וּשְׁמוֹנִים יוֹם לִנְקֵבָה. וּבְמָקוֹם שֶׁהַמִּנְהָג הַזֶּה הוּא מֻסְכָּם אֵצֶל כֻּלָּם, אֵין לְהָקֵל, כִּי יֵשׁ קְצָת טַעַם בָּזֶה. וְעַל כָּזֶה נֶאֱמַר, שְׁמַע בְּנִי מוּסַר אָבִיךָ וְאַל תִּטֹּשׁ תּוֹרַת אִמֶּךָ. אֲבָל בִּמְדִינוֹתֵינוּ, אֵין בָּזֶה מִנְהָג קָבוּעַ. וּמַה שֶּׁיֵּשׁ בִּקְצָת מְקוֹמוֹת מִנְהָג, שֶׁלֹּא לִטְבֹּל עַד לְאַחַר שִׁשָּׁה שָׁבוּעוֹת לְזָכָר וְתִשְׁעָה שָׁבוּעוֹת לִנְקֵבָה וְכַדּוֹמֶה, לְמִנְהָגִים כָּאֵלּוּ אֵין לָהֶם שׁוּם טַעַם וּכְבָר נִתְבַּטְּלוּ בִּקְהִלּוֹת קְדוֹשׁוֹת עַל יְדֵי גְאוֹנִים זִכְרוֹנָם לִבְרָכָה.

ב) יֵשׁ אוֹמְרִים, שֶׁצָּרִיךְ לִפְרוֹשׁ מֵאִשְׁתּוֹ לֵיל אַרְבָּעִים וְאֶחָד לְזָכָר וְלֵיל שְׁמוֹנִים וְאֶחָד לִנְקֵבָה, מִפְּנֵי שֶׁאָז אִכָּא חֲשָׁשָׁא, שֶׁמָּא תִּרְאֶה דָם כְּמוֹ בִּשְׁעַת וֶסְתָּהּ, וְיֵשׁ חוֹלְקִין. וּבַעַל נֶפֶשׁ יָחוּשׁ לְעַצְמוֹ. וְאִם הִפִּילָה סָפֵק זָכָר סָפֵק נְקֵבָה, יִפְרוֹשׁ לֵיל אַרְבָּעִים וְאֶחָד וְלֵיל שְׁמוֹנִים וְאֶחָד.

ג) אִשָּׁה שֶׁהִפִּילָה אֵיזֶה דָּבָר, אֲפִלּוּ אֵין בּוֹ צוּרַת וָלָד כְּלָל, אֶלָּא כְּמוֹ חֲתִיכַת בָּשָׂר אוֹ עוֹר וְכַדּוֹמֶה, צְרִיכָה לְהַחְמִיר וּלְהַחֲזִיק אֶת עַצְמָהּ בְּטֻמְאַת לֵדַת נְקֵבָה, אוֹ תַּעֲשֶׂה שְׁאֵלַת חָכָם כִּי לִפְעָמִים יֵשׁ לְהָקֵל. וְכֵן אִם הִפִּילָה וָלָד וְאַחַר כָּךְ שִׁלְיָא, אַף־עַל־פִּי שֶׁהַוָּלָד הָיָה זָכָר, צְרִיכָה לָחוּשׁ לְטֻמְאַת לֵדַת נְקֵבָה מִשּׁוּם הַשִּׁלְיָא, אוֹ תַּעֲשֶׂה שְׁאֵלַת חָכָם.

---

3. If however the marital acts were painful to her, the blood may be the result of the wound caused by the loss of her virginhood. A Rav must be consulted in any case.

1. The *Placey, Nodah Beyehuda* Resp. 54 etc. were against this custom, as it can lead to very negative developments. If one's father did not have this custom, neither should he.

2. *Behag.*

3. Which may have contained a female fetus.

perceived blood after the second marital act, and also after the third and fourth times; it is questionable (*halachically*) if she is permitted to remain with her husband.[3]

8) It is permitted to perform the marital act with a virgin on *Shabbos* even though the act causes a bruise.

Chapter 158

Childbirth and Miscarriage

1) A woman who has given birth whether she bore a living child or a dead one, or even if it was a miscarriage, even if she perceived no blood, she is regarded as unclean with the uncleanliness ascribed to birthgiving. The law prescribes that if the child was a male, the mother is unclean for seven days, (because of her) birthgiving, after which she may count seven clean days and perform the rite of immersion. If the baby is female, the mother is unclean for fourteen days (because of her) birthgiving, after which she counts seven clean days and performs the rite of immersion. There are places where the accepted custom is that woman do not perform the immersion within forty days of giving birth to a male, and within eighty days of giving birth to a female. In a community where this custom is uniformly accepted, it should not be treated lightly, for there is some reason for this. Concerning such instances it is said, "Hear my son, the instruction of your father, and do not forsake the teaching of your mother." But in our regions, there is no established custom concerning this.[1] The custom prevailing in some communities that she should not immerse herself until six weeks after giving birth to a male, and nine weeks for a female, or similar customs, have no valid reason whatsoever, and have already been abolished in the holy communities by the *Geonim,* of blessed memory.

2) Some authorities maintain that you must separate from your wife the night of the forty-first day after having given birth to a male, and the night of the eighty-first day after having given birth to a female; for then there is the likelihood[2] she may perceive the flow the same as during her menses. Other authorities differ, but a scrupulous person should be strict about it. If she miscarried, and there is doubt if the fetus is male or female, you should separate from her the night of the forty-first day and the night of the eighty-first day.

3) If a woman suffered a miscarriage and expelled something even if it had no shape of a child, but looked like a piece of flesh or skin, or the like, she must be stringent and consider herself unclean as after the birth of a female, or she should consult a *poseik,* for sometimes it is possible to be lenient. Also, if she first miscarried a child, and thereafter dropped the afterbirth, although the child was a male, she must be observant of the uncleanliness due to birth of a female, because of the afterbirth[3] or seek the opinion of a *poseik.*

ד) אִשָּׁה שֶׁבָּרוּר לָהּ שֶׁאֵינָהּ מְעֻבֶּרֶת וְטָבְלָה לְבַעְלָהּ, וּבְתוֹךְ אַרְבָּעִים יוֹם הִפִּילָה, אֵינָהּ חוֹשֶׁשֶׁת לְלֵדָה כִּי אֵין הַוָּלָד נוֹצָר בְּפָחוֹת מֵאַרְבָּעִים יוֹם, אֲבָל טְמֵאָה נִדָּה. וַאֲפִלּוּ לֹא נִרְאָה דָם, מִסְתָמָא הָיָה קְצָת דָּם, אֶלָּא שֶׁנֶּאֱבַד, כִּי אִי אֶפְשָׁר לִפְתִיחַת הָרֶחֶם בְּלֹא דָם.

סִימָן קנט
דִּינֵי לְבִישַׁת הַלִּבּוּן וּסְפִירַת הַנְּקִיִּים

א) כָּל אִשָּׁה שֶׁרָאֲתָה דָם בִּימֵי טָהֳרָתָהּ, צְרִיכָה לִמְנוֹת חֲמִשָּׁה יָמִים עִם יוֹם זֶה, דְּהַיְנוּ יוֹם הָרְאִיָּה וְעוֹד אַרְבָּעָה יָמִים. וַאֲפִלּוּ רָאֲתָה בְּסוֹף הַיּוֹם לְאַחַר שֶׁהִתְפַּלְּלוּ הַקָּהָל וְגַם הִיא עַרְבִית, אוֹ קִבְּלוּ שַׁבָּת, אִם עֲדַיִן הוּא יוֹם, עוֹלֶה לָהּ יוֹם זֶה לְמִנְיָן. וּבַיּוֹם הַחֲמִשִׁי לְעֵת עֶרֶב קֹדֶם בֵּין־הַשְּׁמָשׁוֹת תִּבְדֹּק אֶת עַצְמָהּ הֵיטֵב וְתִרְחַץ לְכָל־הַפָּחוֹת פָּנֶיהָ שֶׁלְּמַטָּה, וְתִלְבַּשׁ כְּתֹנֶת לְבָנָה וּנְקִיָּה, וְגַם שְׁאָר בְּגָדֶיהָ יִהְיוּ נְקִיִּים, וְזֶה נִקְרָא הֶפְסֵק טָהֳרָה. וּבַלַּיְלָה, תַּצִּיעַ עַל מִטָּתָהּ גַּם כֵּן סָדִין לָבָן וְנָקִי וְגַם הַכָּרִים וְהַכְּסָתוֹת כֻּלָּם יִהְיוּ נְקִיִּים, וּמִיּוֹם הַמָּחֳרָת מַתְחֶלֶת לִסְפֹּר שִׁבְעָה נְקִיִּים. וְאֵין חִלּוּק בֵּין רְאִיָּה מְרֻבָּה לִרְאִיָּה מֻעֶטֶת, שֶׁאֲפִלּוּ לֹא רָאֲתָה אֶלָּא טִפָּה אַחַת, אוֹ שֶׁמָּצְאָה רַק כֶּתֶם בִּימֵי טָהֳרָתָהּ, לְעוֹלָם צְרִיכָה לְהַמְתִּין חֲמִשָּׁה יָמִים. וְכֵן אֲפִלּוּ רָאֲתָה דָם כָּל חֲמֵשֶׁת הַיָּמִים, אֶלָּא שֶׁפָּסְקָה קֹדֶם בֵּין הַשְּׁמָשׁוֹת, מִיָּד לְאַחַר שֶׁפָּסַק הַדָּם, יְכוֹלָה לְהַפְסִיק בְּטָהֳרָה.

ב) בִּשְׁעַת הַדְּחָק, כְּגוֹן שֶׁהִיא בַדֶּרֶךְ וְאֵין לָהּ מַיִם כְּלָל אֲפִלּוּ לִרְחוֹץ פָּנֶיהָ שֶׁלְּמַטָּה, אֵינוֹ מְעַכֵּב, רַק שֶׁתְּקַנֵּחַ אֶת עַצְמָהּ הֵיטֵב בְּכָל מַה דְּאֶפְשָׁר וְאִם יְכוֹלָה לִרְחוֹץ בְּמֵי־רַגְלַיִם, שַׁפִּיר דָּמֵי. וְאִם אֵין לָהּ כְּתֹנֶת לְבָנָה, יְכוֹלָה לִלְבּוֹשׁ גַּם כְּתֹנֶת יְשָׁנָה, רַק שֶׁתְּהֵא בְדוּקָה, שֶׁאֵין עָלֶיהָ כִּתְמֵי דָם.

ג) יֵשׁ אוֹמְרִים, דְּאִם הִתְפַּלְּלוּ הַקָּהָל עַרְבִית, אַף־עַל־פִּי שֶׁעוֹד הַיּוֹם גָּדוֹל, אֵינָהּ יְכוֹלָה עוֹד לְהַפְסִיק בְּטָהֳרָה, שֶׁתִּמְנֶה מִיּוֹם הַמָּחֳרָת, מֵאַחַר שֶׁהַקָּהָל כְּבָר עָשׂוּ אוֹתוֹ, לַיְלָה. וְיֵשׁ אוֹמְרִים, דְּמֻתֶּרֶת, וַאֲפִלּוּ עָשׂוּ הַקָּהָל

---

1. In the event she had waited only four days and then began her seven clean days she must add another clean day. If she had already performed the ritual immersion and thereafter had marital relations with her husband, she should not perform immersion again the next day

4) If a woman is certain she has not conceived, and performed the rite of immersion, and within forty days had a miscarriage, she need not deem it a birth, for the embryo is not formed in less than forty days. But she is menstrually unclean, even if no blood was perceived, for presumably there was some blood which may have disappeared, as it is impossible for the womb to have opened without issuing blood.

Chapter 159

Putting on White Linen and Counting the Clean Days

1) A woman who perceived blood during the days when she is menstrually clean, must count five days including the day on which she perceived, plus another four days. Even if she perceived it at the end of the day, after the congregation, and she herself have prayed the *maariv* service or ushered in the Shabbos; if it is still daytime, this day is counted as one of the five.[1] On the fifth day, towards evening before twilight, she should carefully examine herself, wash at least her pubic area and put on clean white undergarments. Her other garments should also be clean. This procedure is called *hefsek tarahah.* At night, she should spread a clean white sheet on her bed. The pillows and cushions should also be clean. The next day she should begin to count the seven clean days. It makes no difference whether she noticed much blood or little, for even if she saw only one drop, or she found only a stain during her period of purity, she must always wait another five days. Also, if she continues to bleed the entire five days, but the flow ceased before twilight (of the fifth day), immediately after the flow ceases, she may proceed with the *hefsek taharah.*

2) In case of emergency, as for instance, when she is traveling and cannot obtain water even to wash the pubic area, this does not delay (the *hefsek taharah*), but she must clean the area very well with whatever she can. If she is able to wash the area with urine, it is sufficient. If she does not have a fresh undergarment, she may put on an old one, provided it is first examined to ascertain that it is free from bloodstains.[2]

3) Some authorities are of the opinion that if the congregation had recited the *Maariv* prayer, although it is still daytime, she cannot perform the *hefsek taharah* (on that day), in order to start counting[3] from the next day; since the congregation has already accepted it as night. Other authorities hold she is permitted to do this,

---

(*Sidrei Taharah*). Even if she had immersed but had not yet had marital relations, the *Maharashaam* Responsa 40 rules that she should not repeat her immersion.

2. In the event that she had counted seven clean days, wearing a bloodstained undergarment, she need not count them over again. *Pischei Teshuva* 190:73—*Me'il Tzeddakah* Responsa 63.

3. The seven clean days.

שַׁבָּת. וְיֵשׁ לִזָּהֵר לְכַתְּחִלָּה. וּבְדִיעֲבַד אֵין לְהַחְמִיר, וִיכוֹלָה לְהַפְסִיק בְּטָהֳרָה כֹּל שֶׁעֲדַיִן אֵינוֹ בֵּין־הַשְּׁמָשׁוֹת. אֲבָל אִם גַּם הִיא הִתְפַּלְּלָה עַרְבִית, וּמִכָּל־שֶׁכֵּן כְּשֶׁהִדְלִיקָה נֵרוֹת לְשַׁבָּת אוֹ לְיוֹם־טוֹב, אַף־עַל־פִּי שֶׁעֲדַיִן הַיּוֹם גָּדוֹל, אֵינָהּ יְכוֹלָה עוֹד לְהַפְסִיק בְּטָהֳרָה. בַּקַּיִץ אֲשֶׁר בְּהַרְבֵּה קְהִלּוֹת מִתְפַּלְּלִין עַרְבִית בְּעוֹד הַיּוֹם גָּדוֹל, שֶׁהִיא צְרִיכָה לְכַתְּחִלָּה לְהַפְסִיק בְּטָהֳרָה קֹדֶם לָכֵן, כְּמוֹ שֶׁכָּתַבְתִּי, אֲזַי כְּשֶׁיַּגִּיעַ סָמוּךְ לְבֵין־הַשְּׁמָשׁוֹת, יֵשׁ לָהּ לִבְדֹּק אֶת עַצְמָהּ עוֹד הַפַּעַם, כִּי עִקַּר הֶפְסֵק טָהֳרָה הוּא בָּעֵת הַיּוֹתֵר סְמוּכָה לְבֵין־הַשְּׁמָשׁוֹת. וּבְדִיעֲבַד, אִם לֹא בָדְקָה אֶת עַצְמָהּ שֵׁנִית, אֵין לְהַקְפִּיד. וַאֲפִלּוּ לֹא בָדְקָה אֶת עַצְמָהּ אֶלָּא שַׁחֲרִית וּמָצְאָה טְהוֹרָה, בְּדִיעֲבַד סַגֵּי בְּכָךְ.

ד) לְעוֹלָם יְלַמֵּד אָדָם בְּתוֹךְ בֵּיתוֹ לְהַחְמִיר לְכַתְּחִלָּה, שֶׁתְּהֵא בְּדִיקַת הֶפְסֵק טָהֳרָתָהּ בְּמוֹךְ דָּחוּק, וְשֶׁיְּהֵא שָׁם כָּל בֵּין הַשְּׁמָשׁוֹת, שֶׁבְּדִיקָה זוֹ מוֹצִיאָה מִידֵי כָּל סָפֵק.

ה) יֵשׁ מְקוֹמוֹת שֶׁנּוֹהֲגִים, שֶׁאִם זְמַן לְבִישַׁת לְבָנִים הוּא בְּשַׁבָּת אוֹ בְּיוֹם־טוֹב, דּוֹחִין לְאַחַר כָּךְ, מִפְּנֵי שֶׁאֵין כָּל אִשָּׁה יוֹדַעַת לִזָּהֵר בְּאִסּוּר רְחִיצָה וְאִסּוּר סְחִיטָה. וּבִמְקוֹמוֹת שֶׁנּוֹהֲגִין לְהָקֵל, אִם רוֹחֶצֶת בְּצוֹנֵן, יְכוֹלָה לִרְחוֹץ אֲפִלּוּ כָּל גּוּפָהּ. אֲבָל בְּחַמִּין, צְרִיכָה לִזָּהֵר שֶׁלֹּא לִרְחוֹץ אֶלָּא בְּאוֹתוֹ מָקוֹם וּבֵין יְרֵכוֹתֶיהָ, וְדַוְקָא בְּחַמִּין שֶׁהוּחַמּוּ בְּעֶרֶב שַׁבָּת וּבְעֶרֶב יוֹם־טוֹב. גַּם צְרִיכָה לִזָּהֵר מֵאִסּוּר סְחִיטָה, שֶׁלֹּא תִרְחַץ בְּבֶגֶד, רַק בְּיָדֶיהָ. וּבְיוֹם־הַכִּפּוּרִים לֹא תִרְחַץ כְּלָל, רַק תְּקַנֵּחַ אֶת עַצְמָהּ יָפֶה יָפֶה, (דַּהֲוֵי שְׁעַת הַדְּחָק, כְּמוֹ שֶׁכָּתַבְתִּי בְּסָעִיף ב, דְּהָא אֲסוּרָה בִּרְחִיצָה), וְתִלְבַּשׁ כֻּתֹּנֶת לְבָנָה. וּבְתִשְׁעָה בְּאָב וְכֵן בְּשִׁבְעַת יְמֵי אֶבְלָהּ, גַּם כֵּן לֹא תִרְחַץ, רַק תְּקַנֵּחַ. וְגַם כֻּתֹּנֶת לְבָנָה לֹא תִלְבַּשׁ, רַק כֻּתֹּנֶת יְשָׁנָה, שֶׁהִיא בְדוּקָה שֶׁאֵין עָלֶיהָ כִּתְמֵי דָם אֲבָל לְאַחַר שִׁבְעָה, אַף־עַל־פִּי שֶׁאֲסוּרָה בִּרְחִיצָה כָּל שְׁלֹשִׁים, מִכָּל מָקוֹם יְכוֹלָה לִרְחוֹץ קְצָת לְצֹרֶךְ לְבִישַׁת לְבָנִים, וְתוּכַל לִלְבּוֹשׁ כֻּתֹּנֶת לְבָנָה.

ו) בְּכָל יוֹם מִשִּׁבְעַת יְמֵי הַסְּפִירָה, צְרִיכָה לִבְדֹּק אֶת עַצְמָהּ שְׁתֵּי פְעָמִים בְּכָל יוֹם, אַחַת שַׁחֲרִית וְאַחַת סָמוּךְ לְבֵין הַשְּׁמָשׁוֹת. וּבְדִיעֲבַד, אֲפִלּוּ לֹא בָדְקָה רַק פַּעַם אַחַת בַּיּוֹם הָרִאשׁוֹן וּפַעַם אַחַת בַּיּוֹם הַשְּׁבִיעִי,

---

4. *Ramah* 196:1.

5. Although the *Sidrei Taharah* and *Chochmas Adam* agree with this interpretation of the

even if the congregation already ushered in the *Shabbos.* It is best to be stringent about this, but if she had already done so, you need not be stringent, and she may perform the *hefsek taharah* so long as it is not yet twilight.[4] However, if she too had prayed *Maariv,* and certainly if she had already lit candles for *Shabbos* or *Yom Tov,* although it is still daytime, she can no longer perform the *hefsek taharah* (on that day.)[5] During the summer, when many congregations pray *Maariv* when it is still daytime, she should make her *hefsek taharah* before that time, as I have already stated. Then, when twilight draws near, she should examine herself again, for the principal time for *hefsek taharah* is as close to twilight as possible. In the event she did not examine herself that second time, you need not be concerned about it. Even if she only examined herself in the morning,[6] when she (checked and) found herself clean, post factum, this is sufficient.

4) You should always instruct your household to be scrupulous that the examination of *hefsek taharah* be performed by inserting cotton cloth; which should remain there during the entire twilight. Such an examination will remove her from all possible doubt.[7]

5) There is a custom in some communities, that if the time for putting on white linen is on *Shabbos* or *Yom Tov,* it is postponed until later; because not every woman knows how to observe the laws prohibiting washing and wringing. In communities where the custom is to be lenient and she washes with cold water, she may even wash her entire body. But when using warm water, she must be careful to wash only the pubic area and between her thighs; and such water must have been warmed before *Shabbos* and before *Yom Tov.* She must also be careful not to transgress the prohibition of wringing. She should, therefore, not wash herself with a cloth, but only with her bare hands. On *Yom Kippur,* she must not wash herself at all, but merely wipe herself thoroughly, (as this is considered an emergency, like the one stated in paragraph two, since she is forbidden to wash herself) and put on a freshly cleaned garment. On *Tisha B'Av,* and in the seven days of mourning, she should also not wash herself, but merely wipe herself (thoroughly). She should also not put on a fresh garment, but an old one that was examined and found to be free of bloodstains.[8] But after the seven days of mourning, although washing is forbidden the entire first thirty days (of mourning), nevertheless, she is permitted to wash herself lightly, for the purpose of wearing white (for the clean days), and she is allowed to put on a fresh gown.

6) Every day of the seven clean days, it is preferable that she examine herself twice daily; once in the morning and once near twilight. Post factum, even if she did not examine herself but once on the first day and once on the seventh day, you

---

Ramah, the prevailing custom is to be lenient and allow her to make the *hefsek taharah* so long as it is before sunset (*Igur, Maharil, Gra.* See *Aruch Hashulchan*).

6. Or even during the previous night. (*Chazon Ish*)

7. Sometimes this causes an irritation which can interfere with the very results of the examination. A competent Rav must be consulted.

8. If she has none, many *poskim* permit her to wear a white [fresh] one. (*Mishna Berurah* 551:31)

יֵשׁ לְהָקֵל. וְדַוְקָא בַּיּוֹם הָרִאשׁוֹן וּבַיּוֹם הַשְּׁבִיעִי. אֲבָל אִם בָּדְקָה בַּיּוֹם הָרִאשׁוֹן וּבַיּוֹם הַשְּׁמִינִי, אֵין לָהּ אֶלָּא יוֹם שְׁמִינִי בִּלְבָד, וּצְרִיכָה לְהוֹסִיף עוֹד שִׁשָּׁה יָמִים.

ז) כָּל בְּדִיקוֹת אֵלּוּ, בֵּין בְּהֶפְסֵק טָהֳרָה בֵּין בְּשִׁבְעַת יְמֵי נְקִיִּים, צְרִיכִין לִהְיוֹת בְּבֶגֶד פִּשְׁתָּן לָבָן יָשָׁן אוֹ בְּצֶמֶר־גֶּפֶן לָבָן, נָקִי וָרַךְ, וְתַכְנִיסֶנּוּ בְּעֹמֶק לְחוֹרִים וְלִסְדָקִים עַד מְקוֹם שֶׁהַשַּׁמָּשׁ דָּשׁ, וְתִרְאֶה אִם אֵין בּוֹ אֵיזֶה מַרְאֶה אַדְמוּמִית. וְאִם אִי אֶפְשָׁר לָהּ לְהַכְנִיס כָּל כָּךְ בְּעֹמֶק, תִּבְדֹּק עַל־כָּל־פָּנִים כְּפִי כֹחָהּ הָאֶפְשָׁרִי וְטוֹב שֶׁלְּכָל־הַפָּחוֹת בְּדִיקָה אַחַת תִּהְיֶה עַד מְקוֹם שֶׁהַשַּׁמָּשׁ דָּשׁ. (וְצָרִיךְ כָּל אִישׁ לְלַמֵּד אֶת אִשְׁתּוֹ דִּין הַבְּדִיקוֹת כִּי הַרְבֵּה אֵינָן יוֹדְעוֹת). וּבְתוּלוֹת שֶׁבּוֹדְקוֹת קֹדֶם הַנִּשּׂוּאִין, יִבְדְּקוּ גַּם כֵּן כְּפִי כֹחָן הָאֶפְשָׁרִי.

ח) הַבְּדִיקוֹת צְרִיכוֹת לִהְיוֹת לְאוֹר הַיּוֹם, וְלֹא לְאוֹר הַנֵּר. וְיֵשׁ מַחְמִירִין אֲפִלּוּ בְדִיעֲבַד אִם לֹא הָיְתָה לְכָל־הַפָּחוֹת בְּדִיקָה אַחַת בַּיּוֹם הָרִאשׁוֹן וּבְדִיקָה אַחַת בַּיּוֹם הַשְּׁבִיעִי לְאוֹר הַיּוֹם.

ט) אִם מָצְאָה כֶּתֶם בִּימֵי סְפִירַת הַנְּקִיִּים, אוֹ אֲפִלּוּ רָאֲתָה דָּם מַמָּשׁ, יְכוֹלָה לְהַפְסִיק בְּטָהֳרָה וְלִלְבּוֹשׁ לְבָנִים גַּם בְּיוֹם זֶה, כֹּל שֶׁפָּסְקָה קֹדֶם בֵּין הַשְּׁמָשׁוֹת, וּמִיּוֹם הַמָּחֳרַת תִּסְפֹּר שִׁבְעָה נְקִיִּים מֵחָדָשׁ.

י) וְכֵן כַּלָּה שֶׁרָאֲתָה דָּם קֹדֶם הַנִּשּׂוּאִין, וְאִם תַּמְתִּין חֲמִשָּׁה יָמִים, יִהְיֶה יוֹם הַנִּשּׂוּאִין קֹדֶם טְבִילָתָהּ וְקָשֶׁה לָהֶם לִדְחוֹת הַנִּשּׂוּאִין, אֲזַי תּוּכַל לְהַפְסִיק בְּטָהֳרָה מִיָּד בְּיוֹם שֶׁפָּסְקָה קֹדֶם בֵּין־הַשְּׁמָשׁוֹת וְלִסְפֹּר מִמָּחֳרַת שִׁבְעָה נְקִיִּים, כְּדֵי שֶׁתּוּכַל לִטְבֹּל קֹדֶם הַחֻפָּה וְזֶה עָדִיף טְפֵי מִלַּעֲשׂוֹת הַחֻפָּה בְּעוֹדָהּ נִדָּה.

---

9. However, if she already immersed and was with her husband, it is valid even if she had examined herself only on either the first or seventh day. (*Chasam Sofer* Responsa 178)

10. Old cloth is softer than new cloth and are more reliable for the examination. If only new cloth is available, she may use it. (*Hagaos Maimonee*)

11. However, she must check the crevices, as this is essential according to most *poskim*. If the examination is very painful to her, or if examinations cause her irritations that can make

may be lenient about it. This is true only (if she examined herself) on the first and seventh days, but if she examined herself on the first and eighth days, then only the eighth day is counted and she is required to add another six days.[9]

7) All these examinations, whether of the *hefsek taharah,* or during the seven clean days, must be made with an[10] old white linen cloth, or with a clean, soft, white cotton cloth. She must insert it deeply, and into the crevices, to a depth that the male organ penetrates, and then see if there is any reddish spot on it. If it is impossible for her to insert it to such a depth, she should at least examine herself to the best of her ability.[11] It is important that at least one[12] examination[13] be made to the depth the male organ penetrates. (It is the duty of every husband to instruct his wife about the laws of examination, for many women are not familiar with them). Virgins who examine themselves before the wedding, should also examine themselves to the best of their ability.

8) The examinations must be made[14] by the light of day and not by candle (artificial) light.[15] Some stringent authorities void the purification if she had not made at least one examination on the first day and one examination on the seventh day by the light of day.

9) If she found a stain during the seven clean days, or even if she perceived a flow of blood, she may perform a *hefsek taharah* and put on the white garments on that very day, so long as it ceased before twilight; and on the following day she may start to count seven days anew.

10) Also a bride who perceived blood before her wedding, and if she must wait five days, the day of the wedding will be before the time of her ritual immersion, and it is difficult to postpone the wedding, she is allowed to make her *hefsek taharah* immediately, on the day the flow ceases, before twilight, and count seven clean days from the following day, in order to be able to immerse herself before the wedding. This is preferable to having the marriage ceremony take place when she is still menstrually unclean.

---

a spot of blood on the cloth, it is sufficient if she makes a *hefsek* and examines herself once on the first clean day and once on the seventh clean day. (*Nodah Beyhudah Tinyana* Responsa 129)

12. Besides the *hefsek taharah.* (see *Shulchan Aruch* 196:6)

13. The best day to choose is the first day. If she did not do this on the first, she should do it on the second, if not, then on the third etc. (*Ramah* 196:6). (see *Chasam Sofer* Responsa 178)

14. This means she must check the cloth by daylight. Some women wait until the morning to check the cloth (which until then must be protected from foreign material).

15. See *Seifer Baadei Hashulchan* in reference to today's electric lighting facilities.

סִימָן קס
הִלְכוֹת חֲפִיפָה

א) בַּיּוֹם הַשְּׁבִיעִי בְּעוֹד יוֹם קֹדֶם בֵּין הַשְּׁמָשׁוֹת תִּרְחַץ בְּחַמִּין כָּל גּוּפָהּ הֵיטֵב, וּבִפְרָט בִּמְקוֹמוֹת הַקְּמָטִין וּבְבֵית הַסְּתָרִים תִּרְחַץ הֵיטֵב, וְתִבְדֹּק כָּל גּוּפָהּ בְּמָקוֹם שֶׁיְּכוֹלָה לִרְאוֹת וּלְמַשְׁמֵשׁ בְּיָדֶיהָ הֵיטֵב, שֶׁלֹּא יִשָּׁאֵר עָלֶיהָ שׁוּם חֲצִיצָה אוֹ שׁוּם לִכְלוּךְ, וְגַם תָּחֹף וְתִסְרֹק הֵיטֵב בְּמַסְרֵק כָּל שַׂעֲרוֹתֶיהָ וּתְפַסְפְּסֵן, שֶׁלֹּא תִהְיֶינָה מְדֻבָּקוֹת אוֹ קְשׁוּרוֹת. וְזֹאת נִקְרֵאת חֲפִיפָה. וּצְרִיכָה לַעֲסֹק בַּחֲפִיפָה עַד שֶׁתֶּחְשַׁךְ, שֶׁתִּטְבֹּל מִיָּד לְאַחַר הַחֲפִיפָה, כִּי לְכַתְּחִלָּה צְרִיכָה לִהְיוֹת הַחֲפִיפָה סָמוּךְ לַטְּבִילָה, וְגַם שֶׁתְּהֵא הַחֲפִיפָה בַּיּוֹם. עַל כֵּן הַמִּנְהָג הַכָּשֵׁר הוּא, שֶׁתַּתְחִיל בַּחֲפִיפָה בְּעוֹד יוֹם וְתַמְשִׁיךְ עַד הַלַּיְלָה.

ב) חֲפִיפָה שֶׁבִּמְקוֹם הַשְּׂעָרוֹת, לֹא תְהֵא בְּדָבָר שֶׁמְּסַבֵּךְ אֶת הַשְּׂעָרוֹת. וּבְבוֹרִית שֶׁאָנוּ קוֹרִין זֵייף [סַבּוֹן], נוֹהֲגִין לְהָקֵל, שֶׁהוּא מְנַקֶּה הֵיטֵב וְאֵינוֹ מְסַבֵּךְ.

ג) בְּמָקוֹם שֶׁאֵין מֶרְחָץ בְּבֵית־הַטְּבִילָה, אֶלָּא שֶׁחוֹפֶפֶת בְּבֵיתָהּ וְאַחַר כָּךְ הוֹלֶכֶת לִטְבֹּל, תִּשָּׂא עִמָּהּ מַסְרֵק וְתִסְרֹק שָׁמָּה שַׂעֲרוֹתֶיהָ עוֹד הַפָּעַם.

ד) בִּשְׁעַת הַדְּחָק שֶׁאִי אֶפְשָׁר לָהּ לַעֲשׂוֹת הַחֲפִיפָה בַּיּוֹם, תּוּכַל לַעֲשׂוֹתָהּ בַּלַּיְלָה, רַק תִּזָּהֵר לָחוֹף כָּרָאוּי וְלֹא תְמַהֵר. וְכֵן אִם אִי אֶפְשָׁר לָהּ לָחֹף גַּם בַּלַּיְלָה, תּוּכַל לַעֲשׂוֹת כָּל הַחֲפִיפָה בַּיּוֹם.

ה) חָלָה טְבִילָתָהּ בְּלֵיל שַׁבָּת, תַּעֲשֶׂה הַחֲפִיפָה בַּיּוֹם, וְתִזָּהֵר מְאֹד לִגְמֹר כָּל הַחֲפִיפָה קֹדֶם בֵּין הַשְּׁמָשׁוֹת, שֶׁלֹּא תָבוֹא חַס וְשָׁלוֹם לִידֵי חִלּוּל שַׁבָּת. וּלְעִנְיַן הַדְלָקַת הַנֵּרוֹת, הַמֻּבְחָר הוּא, אִם אֶפְשָׁר, שֶׁתֵּלֵךְ לְבֵיתָהּ לְאַחַר הַחֲפִיפָה, אוֹ שֶׁתַּעֲשֶׂה הַחֲפִיפָה בְּבֵיתָהּ, וּלְאַחַר הַחֲפִיפָה קֹדֶם בֵּין הַשְּׁמָשׁוֹת תַּדְלִיק אֶת הַנֵּרוֹת, וְאַחַר כָּךְ תִּטְבֹּל. וְאִם אִי אֶפְשָׁר, יַדְלִיק הַבַּעַל. וְאִם גַּם זֹאת אִי אֶפְשָׁר, תַּדְלִיק וּתְבָרֵךְ עַל הַנֵּרוֹת בְּעוֹד הַיּוֹם גָּדוֹל, וְתֹאמַר קֹדֶם הַהַדְלָקָה שֶׁאֵינָהּ מְקַבֶּלֶת שַׁבָּת בְּהַדְלָקָה זֹאת, כִּי בִּמְקוֹם הַצֹּרֶךְ, מַהֲנֵי תְנַאי. אֲבָל מַה שֶּׁקְּצָת נוֹהֲגוֹת לְבָרֵךְ אַחַר הַטְּבִילָה עַל נֵרוֹת דּוֹלְקִים, צְרִיכִין לְבַטֵּל, כִּי הִיא מְבָרֶכֶת בְּרָכָה לְבַטָּלָה.

Chapter 160

How to Shampoo the Hair

1) On the seventh day [of purification,] during the daytime, before sunset, she should wash herself thoroughly with warm water, especially in places where there are wrinkles, and her hidden parts. She should wash thoroughly and examine her whole body in a room where she can see and feel efficiently with her hands. There should not remain any interposing[1] particle or any dirt on her body. She must also thoroughly cleanse and comb all of her hair with a comb,[2] and disentangle them so that they will not be matted together or knotted. This whole process is called *chafifah.* She must engage in *chafifah* until nightfall, in order to perform immersion immediately after *chafifah;* for preferably the *chafifah* should take place close to the [time of] immersion, and the *chafifah* should also take place in the daytime. Therefore, the proper procedure is to start the *chafifah* while it is yet day, and prolong it till nightfall.

2) The *chafifah* on places where there is hair, should not be done with anything that tends to entangle the hair.[3] With regard to using soap, our custom is to be lenient because it cleanses well, and does not entangle the hair.

3) When there is no bath in the *mikvah,* and she must make *chafifa* at home and afterwards go to perform the immersion, she should take a comb with her, and comb her hair again at the *mikvah.*

4) In an emergency, when it is impossible for her to make the *chafifah* during the daytime, she can make it at night, but she must do it properly and not hurriedly. Also, if it is impossible for her to prolong the *chafifah* into the night, she may perform the entire *chafifah* in the daytime.

5) If her time for immersion is on Friday night, she should make the *chafifah* during the day. She must be very careful to complete the entire *chafifah* before twilight, and not, God forbid, violate the Shabbos. With regard to Shabbos candle lighting, it is best, if possible, for her to return home after the *chafifah*, or to make the *chafifah* at home, and after the *chafifah,* before twilight, she should light the candles and after that perform the immersion.[4] If this is not possible, then her husband should light the candles instead. If this too is impossible, she should light the candles, and say the *berachah* over the candles while there is still plenty of time remaing in the day. Before lighting them she should declare that she is not assuming the [holiness of] Shabbos with the lighting; for when necessary such a stipulation is valid. But the practice of some women to say the *berachah* over the burning candles after their immersion, should be voided, for they are saying a *berachah* in vain.

---

1. Between her body and the water of the *mikvah* (see chapt. 161)

2. This is an injunction enacted by *Ezra Hasofer.* Checking her body for a *chatsitsah* before immersion, is a *de'oraisa*. Failure to perform either, totally invalidates her immersion. (see *Chochmas Adam* 120:12.)

3. For this reason cold water should not be used. (*Shulchan Aruch* 199:2)

4. After nightfall.

ו) בְּמָקוֹם שֶׁנּוֹהֲגִין לִטְבֹּל בְּמוֹצָאֵי שַׁבָּת וּבְמוֹצָאֵי יוֹם־טוֹב, צְרִיכִין לִשְׁאֹל לְמוֹרֵה־הוֹרָאָה אֵיךְ יִתְנַהֲגוּ בַּחֲפִיפָה.

סִימָן קסא
דִּינֵי חֲצִיצָה

א) צְרִיכָה שֶׁתִּטְבֹּל כָּל גּוּפָהּ עִם כָּל שַׂעֲרוֹתֶיהָ בְּפַעַם אֶחָת. וְלָכֵן צְרִיכָה לְהַשְׁגִּיחַ בִּמְאֹד מְאֹד, שֶׁלֹּא יְהֵא עָלֶיהָ בִּשְׁעַת טְבִילָה שׁוּם דָּבָר הַחוֹצֵץ, שֶׁאֲפִלּוּ אִם הוּא מַשֶּׁהוּ, לִפְעָמִים הוּא חוֹצֵץ, וְלֹא עָלְתָה לָהּ טְבִילָה. לָא מִבַּעְיָא עַל גּוּפָהּ מִבַּחוּץ שֶׁצְּרִיכִין הַמַּיִם לָבוֹא שָׁמָּה, וְכֵיוָן שֶׁיֵּשׁ חֲצִיצָה, הֲרֵי אֵין הַמַּיִם בָּאִים שָׁמָּה, אֶלָּא אֲפִלּוּ בְּבֵית־הַסְּתָרִים, שֶׁאֵין הַמַּיִם בָּאִים שָׁמָּה, מִכָּל מָקוֹם צְרִיכִין שֶׁיִּהְיוּ רְאוּיִים לְבִיאַת מָיִם. דֶּרֶךְ מָשָׁל, הַשִּׁנַּיִם, אַף־עַל־פִּי שֶׁאֵין צְרִיכִין שֶׁיָּבוֹאוּ הַמַּיִם לְתוֹךְ פִּיהָ, מִכָּל מָקוֹם אִם יֵשׁ חֲצִיצָה בֵּין שִׁנֶּיהָ, לֹא עָלְתָה לָהּ טְבִילָה, כַּאֲשֶׁר יְבֹאַר אִם יִרְצֶה הַשֵּׁם. וּצְרִיכָה כָּל אִשָּׁה לָדַעַת כְּלָל זֶה, שֶׁכָּל הַמְּקוֹמוֹת שֶׁבְּגוּפָהּ, צְרִיכִין שֶׁיִּהְיוּ נְקִיִּים וּרְאוּיִין לְבִיאַת הַמַּיִם בִּשְׁעַת טְבִילָה.

ב) צוֹאַת הָעַיִן שֶׁחוּץ לָעַיִן, חוֹצֶצֶת אַף־עַל־פִּי שֶׁהִיא לַחָה. וְשֶׁבְּתוֹךְ הָעַיִן, לַחָה אֵינָהּ חוֹצֶצֶת וִיבֵשָׁה שֶׁהִתְחִילָה לְהוֹרִיק, חוֹצֶצֶת.

ג) הַדָּם הַיָּבֵשׁ שֶׁעַל הַמַּכָּה, חוֹצֵץ. וְרִיר שֶׁבְּתוֹכָהּ, אֵינוֹ חוֹצֵץ. יָצָא הָרִיר, אִם לַח, אֵינוֹ חוֹצֵץ. יָבֵשׁ, חוֹצֵץ. לְפִיכָךְ אִשָּׁה בַּעֲלַת חֲטָטִים, צְרִיכָה לָחֹף אוֹתָם בְּמַיִם עַד שֶׁיִּתְרַכְּכוּ. וְכֵן גֶּלֶד שֶׁעַל גַּבֵּי הַמַּכָּה, אֲפִלּוּ אִם הִיא מִצְטַעֶרֶת לַהֲסִירוֹ, אוֹ אֲבַעְבּוּעוֹת שְׁחִין, צְרִיכָה לַהֲסִירָן אוֹ לְרַכְּכָן הֵיטֵב בְּמַיִם.

ד) רְטִיָּה שֶׁעַל גַּבֵּי הַמַּכָּה, חוֹצֶצֶת. וְגַם רְטִיּוֹת שֶׁמַּנִּיחִין אוֹתָן לִזְמַן שְׁלֹשָׁה אוֹ אַרְבָּעָה חֳדָשִׁים וְאַחַר כָּךְ נוֹפְלוֹת מֵעַצְמָן וּבְתוֹךְ הַזְּמַן אִי אֶפְשָׁר לַהֲסִירָן אֶלָּא בִּקְרִיעַת הָעוֹר עִמָּהֶן וְהָאִשָּׁה אוֹמֶרֶת שֶׁהֻרְגְּלָה עִמָּהֶן וְאֵינָהּ מַקְפֶּדֶת, מִכָּל מָקוֹם חוֹצְצוֹת. וְכֵן אִשָּׁה שֶׁיֵּשׁ לָהּ מַכָּה וְנִפְתְּחָה, וְנוֹתְנִים בְּתוֹךְ הַנֶּקֶב תַּחַת הָרְטִיָּה גֶּרֶר מִבְּגָדִים עִדִּים שֶׁל פִּשְׁתָּן, וְאַף כְּשֶׁמְּסִירִין אֶת הָרְטִיָּה אֵינוֹ נִרְאֶה כִּי הוּא בָּעֹמֶק, מִכָּל מָקוֹם חוֹצֵץ. (תשובה מאהבה)

ה) לִכְלוּכֵי צוֹאָה שֶׁעַל הַבָּשָׂר שֶׁנַּעֲשׂוּ מֵחֲמַת זֵעָה, אִם נִתְיַבְּשׁוּ,

6) In communities where it is customary to perform the ritual immersion after the close of *Shabbos* or *Yom Tov*, a Rav should be consulted as to how they should perform the *chafifah.*

Chapter 161

What Constitutes a *Chatsitsah* (interposition)

1) She must immerse her entire body, and all her hair at one time. She must, therefore, be extremely careful while immersing, that there be nothing on her that would interpose [between the water and her body.] For even the slightest particle, at times is considered a *chatsitsah* (an interposition), and renders her immersion invalid. Not only must the water reach the external part of her body, but even the internal parts of the body, which the water does not penetrate, must nevertheless be fit for the penetration of water. For example, although it is not necessary that the water enter her mouth, nevertheless, if there is an intervening particle between her teeth, her immersion is invalid, as will be explained, God willing. Every woman must know this rule: All parts of her body must be clean, and fit for the water to reach them during immersion.

2) When mucous is outside the eye, it is a *chatsitsah* (interposition) even if it is moist. Mucous inside the eye, it is not a *chatsitsah,* if it is moist but if it is dry, and has begun to turn green, it is considered a *chatsitsah.*[1]

3) The dried blood on a wound is considered a *chatsitsah,* but the matter (pus etc.) that is inside the wound, is not considered a *chatsitsah.* Discharged matter is not a *chatsitsah* when wet,[2] but when dry, it is a *chatsitsah.* Therefore, a woman who has scabs, must rub them in water until they soften. Even if it is painful to remove the crust of a wound, or if she has blisters, she must either remove them, or soften them well in water.

4) The plaster on a wound is considered a *chatsitsah.* Sometimes plasters are applied to last for three or four months, and then fall off. During this time they cannot be removed without tearing the skin, and even if the woman says she is used to them and does not mind them, nevertheless, they are considered a *chatsitsah.* A woman had a wound which opened, and gauze made of worn linen clothing was inserted into the hole (of the wound) underneath the bandage. Even if the bandage is removed and the gauze is not visible because it is deep inside, it is, nevertheless considered a *chatsitsah.* (*Teshuva Ma'ahava*)

5) Filth on the body that resulted from perspiration, is considered a (*chatsitsah*)

---

1. Most *poskim* maintain this does not apply to the laws of family purity, rather to laws of purity pertaining to sacrifices, food etc. (which at present are not possible to implement). The *Shach* 198:13 says if she cannot repeat her immersion, she may rely on this majority opinion and is permitted to her husband.
2. The first three days it is considered wet (*Shulchan Aruch* 198:9).

חוֹצְצִין. מִלְמוּלִין שֶׁעַל הַבָּשָׂר, וְהוּא מַה שֶּׁלִּפְעָמִים יָדָיו שֶׁל אָדָם מְלֻכְלָכוֹת בְּטִיט אוֹ בְּבָצֵק אוֹ בְזֵעָה, וּמוֹלֵל יָדוֹ הָאַחַת עַל חֲבֶרְתָּהּ וְנַעֲשִׂים כְּעֵין גַּרְגְּרִין, חוֹצְצִין.

ו) הַדְּיוֹ, הֶחָלָב וְהַדְּבַשׁ, שְׂרַף הַתְּאֵנָה וּשְׂרַף הַתּוּת וּשְׂרַף הֶחָרוּב וּשְׂרַף הַשִּׁקְמָה (הוּא מִין תְּאֵנָה), יְבֵשִׁים, חוֹצְצִין, לַחִים, אֵינָן חוֹצְצִין. וּשְׁאָר כָּל הַשְּׂרָפִים, אֲפִלּוּ לַחִים, חוֹצְצִין. וְכֵן הַדָּם, אֲפִלּוּ לַח, חוֹצֵץ.

ז) צֶבַע שֶׁצּוֹבְעוֹת הַנָּשִׁים פְּנֵיהֶן וִידֵיהֶן וּשְׂעַר רֹאשָׁן, אֵינוֹ חוֹצֵץ. וְכֵן אִשָּׁה שֶׁאֻמָּנוּת שֶׁלָּהּ לִצְבֹּעַ בְּגָדִים וְכַדּוֹמֶה וּמֵחֲמַת זֶה יָדֶיהָ צְבוּעוֹת וְכָל הַנָּשִׁים שֶׁיֵּשׁ לָהֶן אֻמָּנוּת זוֹ דַּרְכָּן שֶׁלֹּא לְהַקְפִּיד בְּכָךְ, אֵינוֹ חוֹצֵץ.

ח) בְּצוֹאָה שֶׁתַּחַת הַצִּפֹּרֶן, יֵשׁ חִלּוּקִים. וּכְבָר נָהֲגוּ לַחְתֹּךְ צִפָּרְנֵי יְדֵיהֶן וְרַגְלֵיהֶן קֹדֶם הַטְּבִילָה. וְתִזָּהֵר לְשָׂרְפָן, כִּי אִם יִדְרֹךְ עֲלֵיהֶן בַּעְלָהּ אוֹ אָדָם אַחֵר, מְסֻכָּן. וּבְשַׁבָּת וְיוֹם־טוֹב אִם שָׁכְחָה לְחָתְכָן קֹדֶם, יֵשׁ מַתִּירִין לְחָתְכָן עַל יְדֵי גוֹיָה. אִם יֵשׁ לָהּ נֶפַח עַל מְקוֹם הַצִּפֹּרֶן, וְאֵינָהּ יְכוֹלָה לֹא לְחָתְכוֹ וְלֹא לְנַקֵּר תַּחְתָּיו, אִם נָפוּחַ כָּל כָּךְ שֶׁאֵין הַטִּיט שֶׁתַּחְתָּיו נִרְאֶה אֵינוֹ חוֹצֵץ. אִשָּׁה שֶׁשָּׁכְחָה לַחְתֹּךְ צִפֹּרֶן וְטָבְלָה כָּךְ, אִם נִזְכְּרָה קֹדֶם שֶׁנִּזְקְקָה לְבַעְלָהּ, צְרִיכָה טְבִילָה אַחֶרֶת. וְאִם לֹא נִזְכְּרָה עַד לְאַחַר שֶׁנִּזְקְקָה לְבַעְלָהּ, תַּעֲשֶׂה שְׁאֵלַת חָכָם.

ט) תִּזָּהֵר לְהָסִיר קֹדֶם טְבִילָה, הַנְּזָמִים וְהַטַּבָּעוֹת.

י) צְרִיכָה לְנַקֵּר שִׁנֶּיהָ קֹדֶם טְבִילָה, מִשּׁוּם דִּמְצוּי הוּא שֶׁיִּמָּצְאוּ בֵּין שִׁנֶּיהָ שִׁיּוּרֵי מַאֲכָל. וְאִם טָבְלָה וְנִמְצָא אֵיזֶה דָּבָר בֵּינֵיהֶן אוֹ דָבוּק בָּהֶן, לֹא עָלְתָה לָהּ טְבִילָה וְיֵשׁ נוֹהֲגוֹת שֶׁלֹּא לֶאֱכֹל בָּשָׂר בְּיוֹם לֶכְתָּן לְבֵית הַטְּבִילָה, מִפְּנֵי שֶׁהַבָּשָׂר נִכְנָס בֵּין הַשִּׁנַּיִם יוֹתֵר מִשְּׁאָר אֹכֶל, וְיֵשׁ לָחוּשׁ, שֶׁאֲפִלּוּ תְּנַקֵּר שִׁנֶּיהָ, שֶׁמָּא יִשָּׁאֵר מִמֶּנּוּ, וּמִנְהָג יָפֶה הוּא. וּבְשַׁבָּת וְיוֹם־טוֹב שֶׁאוֹכְלִין בָּשָׂר תִּזָּהֵר לְנַקֵּר בְּיוֹתֵר. וּצְרִיכָה כָּל אִשָּׁה לִזָּהֵר, שֶׁלֹּא תֹאכַל שׁוּם מַאֲכָל בֵּין הַחֲפִיפָה לַטְּבִילָה. וְכָל יוֹם הַטְּבִילָה לֹא

3. Only if it has begun to congeal so that if you touch it, it sticks to you and draws like a string. (*Rashi, Maseches Menachos* 21a.)

4. *Taz* 198:21 forbids this and says she should immerse without having them cut, but should clean under them. *Biur Halacha* 340:1 rules like *Magein Avrohom, Nekudos Hakessef,* and

when dry. When a persons hands are soiled with mud, dough or perspiration, and he rubs them together, crumb-like particles are formed, and they are considered a *chatsitsah.*

6) Ink, milk, honey, fig juice, berry juice, carob resin, juice of the fruit of the sycamore (which is a type of fig), are considered a *chatsitsah* when dry, but are not a *chatsitsah* when moist. All other juices, even when moist are a *chatsitsah.* Also blood, even when moist,[3] is a *chatsitsah.*

7) The coloring used by women to color their faces, hands, and hair on their heads, is not considered a *chatsitsah.* Also, a woman whose occupation is dyeing clothes, or similar work, and as a result her hands are colored, and all other women engaged in this occupation, usually do not mind this, it is not considered a *chatsitsah.*

8) Concerning dirt under the nails, there are a number of factors involved. It is already the established custom to cut the nails of the hands and the feet before the ritual immersion. She must be careful to burn them afterward, for if her husband should step on them, or if another man should step on them it is dangerous. (When she immerses) on Shabbos or Yom Tov, and has forgotten to cut them beforehand, some authorities permit her to have them cut[4] (on Shabbos) by a non-Jewess. If she has a swelling over the nail, and is thus unable to cut it or to clean underneath it, and the swelling is so large that the dirt underneath it is not visible, it is not a *chatsitsah.* If a woman forgot to cut her nails and performed the ritual immersion, and became aware of it before having marital relations with her husband, she must have another immersion. If she did not become aware of it until after having marital relations with her husband, she should consult a Rav.

9) She should be careful to remove her earrings and rings before the ritual immersion.

10) She must clean her teeth before immersing because it is common that remnants of food are found between the teeth. If she immersed herself and then found something between them or adhering to them, her immersion is invalid. Some women are accustomed not to eat meat the day they are to go to the *mikvah,* because meat gets between the teeth more so than other foods, and it is to be feared that even after cleaning some of it may remain; this is an excellent custom. On Shabbos and Yom Tov when we do eat meat, she must be careful to clean them very well. Every woman must be careful not to eat any food[5] between the *chafifah* and the immersion. During the entire day of her immersion, she should not knead

---

Shevus Yaakov Vol. 2 Responsa 8 that if need be she may have a non-Jewess cut them even with a clipper. The *Chacham Tzvi* does not permit having them cut with a tool. Toe nails should just be cleaned, rather than cut by a non-Jewess on Shabbos. (*Biur Halachah*)

5. The *Zerah Emess* Vol. 3 Responsa 118 permits her to drink, in opposition to the *Mekor Chaim.*

תַּעֲסֹק בְּבָצֵק אוֹ בְּנֵרוֹת שֶׁל שַׁעֲוָה, שֶׁלֹּא יִדָּבֵק בָּהּ שׁוּם דָּבָר. אַךְ בְּעֶרֶב שַׁבָּת, אִם דַּרְכָּהּ לָלוּשׁ בְּעַצְמָהּ לִכְבוֹד שַׁבָּת, אַל תִּמָּנַע, רַק תִּזָּהֵר לִרְחוֹץ אַחַר כָּךְ יָדֶיהָ יָפֶה יָפֶה.

יא) אִשָּׁה שֶׁיֵּשׁ לָהּ שֵׁן תּוֹתֶבֶת, תִּשְׁאַל לְמוֹרֵה־הוֹרָאָה אֵיךְ תִּתְנַהֵג בִּטְבִילָה. אִשָּׁה שֶׁיֵּשׁ לָהּ סְתִימַת אֵבֶר בְּנִקְבֵי שִׁינֶיהָ, וְכֵן אִשָּׁה שֶׁהִיא מֻכָּה בְּשֶׁבֶר וְנוֹשֵׂאת טַבַּעַת בְּרַחְמָהּ, תַּעֲשֶׂה שְׁאֵלַת חָכָם.

יב) לֹא תֹּאחַז בָּהּ חֲבֶרְתָּהּ בִּשְׁעַת טְבִילָה, לְפִי שֶׁלֹּא יָבוֹאוּ הַמַּיִם בִּמְקוֹם הָאֲחִיזָה. וּבִשְׁעַת הַדְּחָק, הָאִשָּׁה, שֶׁהִיא רוֹצָה לֶאֱחוֹז אוֹתָהּ תַּטְבִּיל תְּחִלָּה יָדֶיהָ בַּמִּקְוֶה, וְאַחַר כָּךְ תֹּאחַז אוֹתָהּ, לֹא בְּכֹחַ וּבְדִבּוּק חָזָק. אֶלָּא בְּדִבּוּק בֵּינוֹנִי כְּדֶרֶךְ כָּל אָדָם.

יג) הֵיכָא דְּאֶפְשָׁר, אֵין לִטְבֹּל בְּמָקוֹם שֶׁיֵּשׁ בְּקַרְקָעִיתוֹ טִיט, מִשּׁוּם חֲשַׁשׁ חֲצִיצָה. וּבִשְׁעַת הַדְּחָק נוֹהֲגִין לְהָקֵל, מִשּׁוּם דִּסְתָם טִיט שֶׁבַּמַּיִם אֵינוֹ עָב כָּל כָּךְ. אֲבָל הַטִּיט שֶׁעַל שְׂפַת הַנָּהָר שֶׁמִּתְדַּבֵּק בְּרַגְלֶיהָ הֲוֵי חֲצִיצָה. וְלָכֵן צְרִיכָה לִזָּהֵר, שֶׁבְּבוֹאָהּ אֶל תּוֹךְ הַנָּהָר, קֹדֶם שֶׁתִּטְבֹּל, תָּדִיחַ הֵיטֵב רַגְלֶיהָ מִן הַטִּיט שֶׁנִּדְבַּק בָּהּ בִּשְׂפַת הַנָּהָר. אִם תִּרְצֶה לְהַנִּיחַ בְּתוֹךְ הַנָּהָר תַּחַת כַּפּוֹת רַגְלֶיהָ אֵיזֶה דָּבָר שֶׁתַּעֲמֹד עָלָיו בִּשְׁעַת טְבִילָה, צְרִיכָה לִשְׁאֹל לְמוֹרֵה־הוֹרָאָה כִּי יֵשׁ הַרְבֵּה דְּבָרִים שֶׁאָסוּר לַעֲמֹד עֲלֵיהֶם בִּשְׁעַת טְבִילָה.

יד) לֹא תִּטְבֹּל בְּקוֹמָה זְקוּפָה, מִפְּנֵי שֶׁיֵּשׁ מְקוֹמוֹת שֶׁמִּסְתַּתְּרִים בָּהּ עַל יְדֵי כָּךְ. וְאַל תִּשְׁחֶה הַרְבֵּה עַד שֶׁיִּדְבְּקוּ סְתָרֶיהָ זֶה בָּזֶה, אֶלָּא שׁוֹחָה מְעַט, עַד שֶׁיִּהְיוּ סִתְרֵי בֵּית־הָעֶרְוָה נִרְאִים, כְּדֶרֶךְ שֶׁנִּרְאִים בְּשָׁעָה שֶׁהִיא לָשָׁה אֶת הַפַּת שֶׁמְּפַסֶּקֶת רַגְלֶיהָ מְעַט לְהִתְחַזֵּק וְלָלוּשׁ בְּחֹזֶק. וְתַחַת דַּדֶּיהָ יְהֵא נִרְאֶה, כְּדֶרֶךְ שֶׁנִּרְאֶה בְּשָׁעָה שֶׁהִיא מֵינִיקָה אֶת הַתִּינוֹק. וְאֵינָהּ צְרִיכָה לְהַרְחִיק יַרְכוֹתֶיהָ זֶה מִזֶּה יוֹתֵר מִדַּי, וְגַם לֹא לְהַרְחִיק זְרוֹעוֹתֶיהָ מֵהַגּוּף יוֹתֵר מִדַּי אֶלָּא יִהְיוּ כְּדֶרֶךְ שֶׁהֵם בְּעֵת הִלּוּכָהּ. וְאִם שָׁחֲחָה בְּיוֹתֵר

6. As a general rule, if it is a permanent tooth it is not a *chatsitsah;* if it is removable (for cleaning purposes, etc., it is a *chatsitsah.* (see *Avnei Nezer* Responsa 258, *Shoel V'maishiv Tinyana* V,ol. 3 Responsa 108, *Igros Moshe* Responsa 92.)

7. Today's fillings are not a *chatsitsah.* See footnote 6. Some *poskim* permit immersion

dough, or make wax candles, so that nothing will cling to her. But on Friday if it is her custom to knead the dough herself, in honor of Shabbos, she should not refrain from doing so; however, she must be careful to wash her hands thoroughly afterward.

11) A woman who has an artificial tooth, should consult a competent *poseik* concerning how to perform the immersion.[6] A woman who has a lead filling[7] in her dental cavities, and also a woman who is ruptured and wears a ring in her womb, should consult a competent *poseik.*

12) Another woman should not hold her during the immersion, because the water will not penetrate to the place within her grasp. In case of emergency, the woman who must hold her should first dip her own hands into the *mikvah,*[8] and afterward hold her. She should not hold her tightly with a strong grip, but with a moderate grip[9] that people usually use.

13) Whenever possible she should not immerse in a place where there is mud on the bottom because it might be a *chatsitsah.* In case of emergency, it is the custom to be lenient as the mud generally found in water is not very thick. But the mud found at the edge of a river which clings to the feet is considered a *chatsitsah.* Therefore, she must be careful when going to immerse herself in the river to wash her feet well from the mud that stuck to her, from the edge of the river. If she wants to set something in the river under her feet upon which to stand during the immersion, she must consult a competent *poseik,* for there are many things upon which it is forbidden to stand during immersion.

14) She should not stand erect during immersion, because certain parts of her body are concealed by this posture; nor should she bend over so much that her hidden parts will be pressed together. But she must bend slightly, until the hidden places of her lower limbs are exposed as they are when she kneads dough, when she spreads her legs slightly in order to stand firm and knead briskly. Also, the space under her breasts should appear as it appears when she nurses a baby. She does not have to separate her thighs to any great extent, nor to extend her arms from her body too much, but they should be like they are when she walks. If she bends over

---

while having temporary fillings, for there is a set time in which they must be left in. Also even after their removal, the tooth is covered again by the new filling. See *Igros Moshe* Responsa 97. Some are stringent about this and require that the temporary filling be scheduled to remain in place at least for thirty days from the time of her immersion.

8. Wetting the hands in other water does not help. *Ramah* 120. Even if she wet her hands in the *mikvah*, and took her hands out of the *mikvah* and grasped her friend's arm outside the *mikvah*, it does not help, and is considered a *chatsitsah— Levush* and *Sidrei Taharah.* However, the *Gra* says all water is valid, and even if she grasps her outside the *mikvah,* and even if she grasps her tightly, it is still valid. *Taz* says it need not be *mikvah* water, but he maintains it does not help if she holds her with a tight grip.

9. This is done only in case of emergency, for we are not all experts to differentiate between an average grip and a strong one. (see *Sidrei Taharah*)

אוֹ זָקְפָה בְּיוֹתֵר, לֹא עָלְתָה לָהּ טְבִילָה, מִפְּנֵי שֶׁנַּעֲשִׂים קְמָטִים בְּגוּפָהּ וְאֵין הַמַּיִם בָּאִים שָׁמָּה. וְלָכֵן צְרִיכִין לְהַשְׁגִּיחַ שֶׁיִּהְיוּ הַמַּיִם לְמַעְלָה מִטַּבּוּרָהּ שְׁלֹשָׁה טְפָחִים, דִּבְעִנְיָן זֶה יְכוֹלָה לִטְבּוֹל כָּרָאוּי. וּבִשְׁעַת הַדְּחָק שֶׁאֵין הַמַּיִם גְּבוֹהִים כָּל כָּךְ, תֵּשֵׁב מִתְּחִלָּה לְאַט לְאַט בַּמַּיִם עַד צַוָּארָהּ, וְאַחַר כָּךְ תִּטְבֹּל, בְּאֹפֶן שֶׁלֹּא יִתְהַוֶּה תְּחִלָּה בְּגוּפָהּ שֶׁחוּץ לַמַּיִם שׁוּם קֶמֶט. וּמַה שֶּׁנַּעֲשָׂה אַחַר כָּךְ אֵיזֶה קֶמֶט בְּגוּפָהּ שֶׁבְּתוֹךְ הַמַּיִם, אֵינוֹ מַזִּיק, מִפְּנֵי שֶׁכְּבָר קָדְמוּ הַמַּיִם שָׁם. וְאִם הַמַּיִם נְמוּכִים מְאֹד, בִּשְׁעַת הַדְּחָק תִּטְבֹּל בִּשְׁכִיבָה כְּמוֹ דָג, רַק שֶׁיִּתְכַּסֶּה כָּל גּוּפָהּ עִם שַׂעֲרוֹתֶיהָ בְּפַעַם אַחַת בַּמַּיִם.

טו) אֵינָהּ צְרִיכָה לִפְתּוֹחַ פִּיהָ כְּדֵי שֶׁיִּכָּנְסוּ הַמַּיִם, וְלֹא תִקְפֹּץ אוֹתוֹ יוֹתֵר מִדַּי. וְאִם קָפְצָה, לֹא עָלְתָה לָהּ טְבִילָה, אֶלָּא תַּשִּׁיק שִׂפְתוֹתֶיהָ זוֹ לָזוֹ דִּבּוּק בֵּינוֹנִי. נָתְנָה שְׂעָרָהּ בְּפִיהָ וְטָבְלָה, לֹא עָלְתָה לָהּ טְבִילָה, מִפְּנֵי שֶׁלֹּא בָאוּ הַמַּיִם עַל שְׂעָרָהּ.

טז) לֹא תַעֲצוֹם עֵינֶיהָ בְּיוֹתֵר, כִּי עַל יְדֵי זֶה נַעֲשִׂים קְמָטִים לְמַטָּה. וְגַם לֹא תִפְתַּחֵן בְּיוֹתֵר, כִּי נַעֲשִׂים קְמָטִים לְמַעְלָה, אֶלָּא תִּסְגְּרֵן בְּרִפְיוֹן.

יז) צְרִיכָה לְהָסִיר הַצּוֹאָה מִשְּׂפַת הַחֹטֶם גַּם מִבִּפְנִים. אֲבָל מַה שֶּׁהִיא לְמַעְלָה בְּתוֹךְ הַחֹטֶם, לֹא חָיְיץ. וְכֵן צְרִיכָה לְהוֹצִיא צוֹאַת הָאֹזֶן. יֵשׁ אוֹמְרִים, שֶׁהָאִשָּׁה צְרִיכָה לְהַטִּיל מַיִם קֹדֶם טְבִילָה אִם הִיא צְרִיכָה לְכָךְ. גַּם צְרִיכָה לִבְדּוֹק עַצְמָהּ בַּגְּדוֹלִים וּבַקְּטַנִּים, שֶׁלֹּא תְהֵא צְרִיכָה לַעֲצוֹר עַצְמָהּ וְלֹא יִהְיוּ רְאוּיִים לְבִיאַת מָיִם. וּבְדִיעֲבַד, אֵינוֹ מְעַכֵּב.

יח) לֹא תִטְבֹּל בְּאָבָק שֶׁעַל רַגְלֶיהָ. וְאִם טָבְלָה, אִם הָיָה אָבָק דַּק שֶׁהֶעֱבִירוּהוּ הַמַּיִם, עָלְתָה לָהּ טְבִילָה.

יט) סְתָם כִּנִּים וּפַרְעוֹשִׁים, אֵינָם נִדְבָּקִים בַּגּוּף, וְהַמַּיִם נִכְנָסִים שָׁמָּה וְלָא חָיְצֵי. אֲבָל מִין כִּנִּים הַדְּבוּקִים בַּבָּשָׂר וְנוֹשְׁכִים בָּעוֹר בִּמְקוֹם שֵׂעָר וְנִדְבָּקִים בְּחֹזֶק בַּבָּשָׂר, צְרִיכָה לַהֲסִירָן עַל יְדֵי חַמִּין וּלְגָרְרָן בְּצִפֹּרֶן. וְאִם אֵינָהּ יְכוֹלָה לַהֲסִירָן, אֵינָן חוֹצְצִין. וְאוֹתָן כִּנִּים קְטַנִּים הַדְּבוּקִים בַּשְּׂעָרוֹת, צְרִיכָה לַהֲסִירָן, מִשּׁוּם דַּהֲוְיָן חֲצִיצָה.

כ) אִשָּׁה שֶׁיֵּשׁ לָהּ קְלִיעוֹת שְׂעָרוֹת דְּבוּקוֹת זוֹ בָזוֹ, שֶׁקּוֹרִין בִּלְשׁוֹן אַשְׁכְּנַז מַאָהר־צֶעפּ אוֹ מַאָהר־לַאקֶען וּבִלְשׁוֹן פּוֹלִין וְרוּסְיָא קַאלְטוּנִים,

too much, or stands up too erect, her immersion is invalid,[10] because folds will have been formed in her body, and the water will not penetrate there. Therefore, it is necessary to watch that the water level be higher than three *tefachim* above her navel, for in such a manner, she will be able to immerse properly. In case of emergency, when the water level is not so high, she should slowly sit herself down in the water until it reaches her neck, and then immerse herself in a way that initially the part of her body still out of the water will not form any folds. The folds that form afterwards on her body while in the water do not matter, because the water has already penetrated there. If the water level is very low, then in an emergency, she may immerse herself in a prostrate position like a fish provided that her entire body and hair are submerged in the water at the same time.

15) She does not need to open her mouth to let the water in, nor should she close it too tightly. If she closed it tightly her immersion is invalid. Rather she should close her lips together in a natural way. If she put strands of her hair into her mouth when immersing, her immersion is invalid, because the water did not reach her hair.

16) She should not close her eyes tightly because folds will be formed under them, nor should she open them too much because folds will be formed above them, but she should keep them lightly closed.

17) She must remove the mucus from around the nose as well as from inside, but whatever is higher up in the nose, is not considered a *chatsitsah.* Similarly, she must remove the wax from the ears. Some authorities say that she should pass water before immersing, if she needs to. She must also check if she needs to ease herself from stool or water, so she will not need to restrain herself and render that area impenetrable to water. If she did not do so, it does not invalidate the immersion.

18) She should not immerse herself with dust on her feet. If she did immerse herself and the dust was that thin that the water washed it away, the immersion is valid.

19) Ordinary lice and fleas do not cling to the body. Therefore the water penetrates and they are not considered a *chatsitsah.* But the kind of lice that cling to the skin, and bite the skin where there is hair, and cling tightly to the skin, must be removed by means of hot water, or scraped off with the fingernail. If she is unable to remove them they do not constitute a *chatsitsah.* The small lice that cling to the hair, must be removed because they do constitute a *chatsitsah.*

20) If a woman has elf-locks, called in Ashkenaz "moertzep," or "moer locken," and in Polish-Russian, "kaaltanis," and it is dangerous to cut them, they do not

---

10. *Ra'avad.* However, the *Sidrei Taharah, Chochmas Adam, Aruch Hashulchan* etc. are lenient in this event. Therefore, if she already spent the night at home, she need not go back to repeat her immersion.

וְיֵשׁ סַכָּנָה לְגַלְּחָן, לָא חָיְצֵי. וַאֲפִלּוּ יֵשׁ בְּתוֹכָן אֵיזֶה חוּטִין שֶׁאִי אֶפְשָׁר לַהֲסִירָן, אִם אֵינָן נִרְאִין מִבַּחוּץ לָא חָיְצֵי.

סִימָן קסב
הִלְכוֹת טְבִילָה

א) אִם בַּעְלָהּ בָּעִיר, מִצְוָה עַל הָאִשָּׁה שֶׁתִּטְבֹּל בִּזְמַנָּהּ, שֶׁלֹּא לְבַטֵּל מִפְּרִיָּה וּרְבִיָּה אֲפִלּוּ לַיְלָה אֶחָד, שֶׁהֲרֵי מָצִינוּ בִּיהוֹשֻׁעַ שֶׁנֶּעֱנַשׁ עַל שֶׁבִּטֵּל אֶת יִשְׂרָאֵל מִפְּרִיָּה וּרְבִיָּה לַיְלָה אֶחָד. וְאִשָּׁה שֶׁמִּתְאַחֶרֶת מִלִּטְבֹּל כְּדֵי לְצַעֵר אֶת בַּעְלָהּ, עָנְשָׁהּ גָּדוֹל מְאֹד, רַחֲמָנָא לִצְּלַן.

ב) אֲסוּרָה לִטְבֹּל בַּיּוֹם הַשְּׁבִיעִי עַד צֵאת הַכּוֹכָבִים. וַאֲפִלּוּ לִטְבֹּל סָמוּךְ לַחֲשֵׁכָה בְּאֹפֶן שֶׁלֹּא תָבוֹא לְבֵיתָהּ עַד שֶׁתֶּחְשַׁךְ, נַמִּי אָסוּר. וַאֲפִלּוּ נִתְאַחֲרָה שֶׁלֹּא טָבְלָה בַּלַּיְלָה שֶׁלְּאַחַר יוֹם הַשְּׁבִיעִי, וְטוֹבֶלֶת אַחַר כָּךְ, אֲסוּרָה גַם כֵּן לִטְבֹּל בַּיּוֹם. וְגַם בְּעִנְיָן זֶה, יֵשׁ לְהַחְמִיר שֶׁלֹּא תִטְבֹּל אֲפִלּוּ סָמוּךְ לַחֲשֵׁכָה, וְשֶׁלֹּא תָבוֹא לְבֵיתָהּ עַד שֶׁתֶּחְשַׁךְ אֶלָּא תִטְבֹּל דַּוְקָא בַּלַּיְלָה. וְהַכַּלּוֹת הַטּוֹבְלוֹת קֹדֶם הַחֻפָּה, יְכוֹלוֹת לִטְבֹּל בַּיּוֹם הַשְּׁמִינִי אוֹ אַחַר כָּךְ בַּיּוֹם. וּבִשְׁעַת הַדְּחָק אֲפִלּוּ אִם טוֹבֶלֶת בַּיּוֹם הַשְּׁבִיעִי יְכוֹלָה גַם כֵּן לִטְבֹּל בַּיּוֹם, וַאֲפִלּוּ בַּבֹּקֶר לְאַחַר הָנֵץ הַחַמָּה, אֲבָל לֹא יַעֲמִידוּ אֶת הַחֻפָּה עַד צֵאת הַכּוֹכָבִים. אֲבָל אִם טוֹבֶלֶת לְאַחַר הַחֻפָּה, אַף־עַל־פִּי שֶׁהִיא טְבִילָה הָרִאשׁוֹנָה לְבַעְלָהּ, דִּינָהּ כְּמוֹ שְׁאָר אִשָּׁה.

ג) הֵיכָא דְאִכָּא אֹנֶס, כְּגוֹן שֶׁיְּרֵאָה לִטְבֹּל בַּלַּיְלָה מֵחֲמַת צִנָּה אוֹ פַּחַד אוֹ שֶׁבֵּית הַטְּבִילָה הוּא חוּץ לָעִיר וְשַׁעֲרֵי הָעִיר נִנְעָלִין בַּלַּיְלָה, יְכוֹלָה לִטְבֹּל בַּשְּׁמִינִי בְּעוֹד יוֹם. אֲבָל בַּשְּׁבִיעִי, לֹא תִטְבֹּל בַּיּוֹם אֲפִלּוּ בְּמָקוֹם אֹנֶס. וְהָא דְמֻתֶּרֶת לִטְבֹּל בִּמְקוֹם אֹנֶס בַּשְּׁמִינִי בַּיּוֹם, דַּוְקָא שֶׁתַּעֲשֶׂה גַּם הַחֲפִיפָה אָז סָמוּךְ לַטְּבִילָה. אֲבָל אִם יוֹם הַשְּׁמִינִי הוּא שַׁבָּת אוֹ יוֹם־טוֹב שֶׁתִּצְטָרֵךְ לַעֲשׂוֹת הַחֲפִיפָה בַּיּוֹם שֶׁקֹּדֶם הַטְּבִילָה וְגַם תִּטְבֹּל בַּיּוֹם, זֶהוּ אָסוּר, מִשּׁוּם דִּתְרֵי קֻלֵּי בַּהֲדָדֵי לָא מְקִלִּינַן (דְּהַיְנוּ טְבִילָה בַּיּוֹם וְגַם הַרְחָקַת חֲפִיפָה מִטְּבִילָה).

ד) לֹא תַעֲמֹד עַל שׁוּם דָּבָר בִּשְׁעַת טְבִילָה. וְאִם מֵי הַמִּקְוֶה עֲמֻקִּים וּצְרִיכָה לַעֲמֹד עַל שְׁלִיבָה, תַּעֲשֶׂה שְׁאֵלַת חָכָם.

constitute a (*chatsitsah.*) Even if there are some threads entangled in them, which cannot be removed, if they are not visible from the outside, they do not constitute a *chatsitsah.*

Chapter 162

Immersion

1) If her husband is in town, it is the duty of a woman to immerse herself at the proper time, in order not to delay the mitzvah of propogation even for one night; for Joshua was punished for causing Yisrael to delay the mitzvah of propogation for one night. A woman who delays her immersion in order to torment her husband, will be severely punished, God forbid.

2) She is forbidden to immerse[1] herself on the seventh (clean) day before the stars appear (nightfall). Even if she immerses close to nightfall, and will be unable to return home before dark, it is also forbidden. Even if she was delayed and did not immerse herself on the night following the seventh day, but is immersing herself afterwards, she is also forbidden to immerse in the daytime. In such a case, too, she should be strict and not immerse even shortly before dark,[2] and not return home until dark. She should immerse herself only at night. Brides who immerse before the *chupah*, may immerse themselves on the eighth day or thereafter, during the daytime. In case of emergency, even if the bride must immerse on the seventh day, she may also immerse during the daytime, even in the morning after sunrise. But they should not make the *chupah* until the stars appear. If the bride immerses after the *chupah*, even though it is the first immersion of her married life, she is subject to the same laws as apply to any other woman.

3) In case of emergency, as when she is afraid to immerse at night on account of the cold or some other fear, or if the *mikvah* is outside the city, and the gates of the city are locked at night, she is allowed to immerse on the eighth day during the daytime. But on the seventh day, she is not allowed to immerse in the daytime even in the event of an emergency.[3] She is permitted to immerse in the daytime on the eighth day in case of an emergency, only if she makes the *chafifah* then, immediately before the immersion. But if the eighth day is Shabbos or Yom Tov, in which case she would have to make the *chafifa* a day before her immersion, and then do the immersion in the daytime, such practice is forbidden, for two concessions may not be made in one case. (The concessions being, immersion in the daytime and a long interval between *chafifa* and immersion).

4) She should not stand on anything during the immersion. If the water of the *mikvah* is deep, and she must stand on a step, she must consult a *poseik.*

---

1. *Maseches Eruvin* 63.
2. *Shulchan Aruch* 197:3. *Chochmas Adam* says she should not leave the house to go to the *mikvah* at a time when she would arrive there before nightfall.
3. If she immerses on the seventh day before nightfall. *Shulchan Aruch* 197:5 says she need not repeat her immersion after nightfall. *Shach—Maharam* rule that she must repeat it.

ה) לֹא תִטְבֹּל בְּמָקוֹם שֶׁיֵּשׁ חֲשָׁשׁ שֶׁיִּרְאוּ אוֹתָהּ בְּנֵי אָדָם, מִפְּנֵי שֶׁמִּתּוֹךְ כָּךְ הִיא מְמַהֶרֶת לִטְבֹּל, וְחָיְשִׁינָן שֶׁמָּא לֹא תִטְבֹּל יָפֶה. וּבְדִיעֲבַד אִם טָבְלָה וְיָדְעִינָן בְּבֵרוּר שֶׁטָּבְלָה כָּרָאוּי, עָלְתָה לָהּ טְבִילָה.

ו) כְּשֶׁהִיא טוֹבֶלֶת, צְרִיכָה לַעֲמֹד אֶצְלָהּ אִשָּׁה יְהוּדִית גְּדוֹלָה יוֹתֵר מִשְּׁתֵּים־עֶשְׂרֵה שָׁנָה וְיוֹם אֶחָד, שֶׁתִּרְאֶה שֶׁלֹּא יִשָּׁאֵר מִשְּׂעַר רֹאשָׁהּ צָף עַל פְּנֵי הַמָּיִם. וְאִם אֵין לָהּ אִשָּׁה, יָכוֹל גַּם בַּעְלָהּ לַעֲמֹד אֶצְלָהּ לִרְאוֹת שֶׁתִּטְבֹּל יָפֶה.

ז) מֻתֶּרֶת לִטְבֹּל בְּלֵיל שַׁבָּת אִם עַתָּה הִגִּיעַ זְמַן טְבִילָתָהּ שֶׁלֹּא יָכְלָה לִטְבֹּל מִקֹּדֶם, וּבַעְלָהּ בָּעִיר. אֲבָל אִם אֵין בַּעְלָהּ בָּעִיר, אוֹ שֶׁהָיְתָה יְכוֹלָה לִטְבֹּל קֹדֶם, אֲסוּרָה לִטְבֹּל בְּלֵיל שַׁבָּת. וְאִם הִיא אַחַר לֵדָה, יֵשׁ חִלּוּקֵי דִינִים אִם מֻתֶּרֶת לִטְבֹּל בְּלֵיל שַׁבָּת אוֹ לֹא, וְתַעֲשֶׂה שְׁאֵלַת חָכָם. וְאִשָּׁה שֶׁזְּמַן טְבִילָתָהּ בָּא קֹדֶם, אֶלָּא שֶׁלֹּא טָבְלָה, מֵחֲמַת שֶׁלֹּא הָיָה בַעְלָהּ בָּעִיר וּבָא בְּעֶרֶב שַׁבָּת, יֵשׁ מְקוֹמוֹת שֶׁמַּחְמִירִין שֶׁלֹּא לִטְבֹּל בְּלֵיל שַׁבָּת. וּבְמָקוֹם שֶׁאֵין מִנְהָג קָבוּעַ, אֵין לְהַחְמִיר. וּבִמְקוֹמוֹת שֶׁנּוֹהֲגִין לְהַחְמִיר בְּלֵיל שַׁבָּת, גַּם בְּמוֹצָאֵי־שַׁבָּת לֹא תִטְבֹּל. וְאַלְמָנָה שֶׁנִּשֵּׂאת, אֲסוּרָה לִטְבֹּל טְבִילָה הָרִאשׁוֹנָה בְּלֵיל שַׁבָּת, דְּהָא אָסוּר לָבוֹא עָלֶיהָ בִּיאָה רִאשׁוֹנָה בַּשַּׁבָּת. וּבְמוֹצָאֵי־שַׁבָּת יֵשׁ מְקִלִּין שֶׁתִּטְבֹּל.

ח) לְאַחַר שֶׁטָּבְלָה כָּרָאוּי, בְּעוֹדָהּ עוֹמֶדֶת תּוֹךְ הַמַּיִם, תְּבָרֵךְ אֲשֶׁר קִדְּשָׁנוּ בְּמִצְוֹתָיו וְצִוָּנוּ עַל הַטְּבִילָה. וְיֵשׁ לְהַחְמִיר שֶׁקֹּדֶם הַבְּרָכָה תְּכַסֶּה אֶת עַצְמָהּ לְמַטָּה בְּאֵיזוֹ מִטְפַּחַת, אוֹ לְכָל־הַפָּחוֹת תְּחַבֵּק זְרוֹעוֹתֶיהָ עַל גּוּפָהּ לְהַפְסִיק. וְלֹא תִסְתַּכֵּל לְתוֹךְ הַמַּיִם בְּשָׁעָה שֶׁהִיא מְבָרֶכֶת. וְאִם

---

4. According to the *Sidrei Taharah,* this is a *de'oraisa. Rabbi Akiva Eiger* Responsa 114 is undecided if this is a *de'oraisa* or *de'rabonon.*

5. This would totally invalidate her immersion.

6. If she would prefer, she may loosely wrap her hair in woolen strings or use a loose hair net. (*Bach, Ra'avad*)

7. Or if accidently she was delayed—*Nodah Beyehudah Tinyana* 131. Or if she had immersed before, and found dirt under her nails etc, for which she must repeat the immersion—*Shach—Maharah Lublin.* Or if she was slightly ill—*Levushei Sarad,* or if this water was too cold for her. (*Imrei Binah,* Chapter 9)

8. This is a custom (*Ramah* 197:2). *Bach* and *Taz* rule that it is a *halachah. Sidrei Taharah* says if she postponed her day of immersion for no reason, she may not immerse on Shabbos. *Chachmas Adam, Aruch Hashulchan, Taharas Yisroel* etc. maintain that the prevailing custom

5) She must not immerse in a place where people might see her, for this might cause her to immerse hastily, and thus she may not immerse properly. If she has already performed the immersion, and she is positive she immersed properly, her immersion is valid.

6) When she immerses herself, she must have in attendance[4] a Jewish woman, older than twelve years and one day, to see that none of her hair remains floating on the water.[5] If there is no woman available, her husband may stand by her to see to it that she immerses properly.[6]

7) She is permitted to immerse on Friday night if it is the proper time for her immersion, and she was unable to immerse before this,[7] and provided her husband is in town. But if her husband is out of town, or if she was able to immerse before, she is forbidden to immerse on Friday night.[8] If it is after she had given birth, there are many intricate laws regarding if she is permitted to immerse on Friday night or not, so she should consult a *poseik.* A woman whose date of immersion was before Friday night, but she failed to immerse because her husband was out of town, and he arrived on Friday, in some communities they are strict and do not allow such an immersion on Friday night. In a community without an established custom one should not be strict about this. In communities where the custom is to be strict about Friday night immersions, she may not immerse even[9] at the conclusion of Shabbos.[10] A widow who got married (while menstrually unclean), is forbidden to immerse for her first time on Friday night since he is forbidden to have initial marital relations with her on Shabbos.[11] (However) on the conclusion of Shabbos, some authorities are lenient and permit her to immerse.

8) After immersing properly, while she is still standing in the water, she should recite the *berachah: Asher kideshanu bemitzvosav vetzivanu al hatevillah.* ("Who has sanctified us with His commandments, and has commanded us concerning immersion.") She should be strict,[12] and before reciting the *berachah*, she should cover her lower limbs with a cloth, or at least hold her arms together on her body, to serve as a separation from her lower limbs. She should not look into the water while

---

is that she may go to the (*mikvah*) on Friday night, even if there is no reason why she could not have gone before.

9. Because according to *Rashi, the chafifah* should be done by day; and if she immerses *motzei Shabbos* she has to make her *chafifah erev Shabbos.* The *chafifah* must be close to the time of immersion if possible; therefore, if she is able to immerse close to the *chafifah,* she may not postpone it for a time when she will not be able to perform the immersion shortly after the *chafifah.* This is consistent with the view that does not allow her to immerse on Shabbos night, if she was able to do so before.

10. The prevailing custom is that all women may immerse on *motzei Shabbos.* (see footnote 8)

11. See *Kitzur Shulchan Aruch* 148:4.

12. This is according to *Bach* who says that women, too, should abide by the concept of separating the heart from the nakedness (the *Taz* and *Shach*). *Shulchan Aruch* maintain that this does not apply to women.

טוֹבֶלֶת בְּמָקוֹם שֶׁתּוּכַל לַעֲכֹר אֶת הַמַּיִם בְּרַגְלֶיהָ, טוֹב לַעֲשׂוֹת כֵּן קֹדֶם הַבְּרָכָה. יֵשׁ נוֹהֲגוֹת שֶׁלְּאַחַר הַבְּרָכָה טוֹבֶלֶת עוֹד פַּעַם אַחַת, וּמִנְהָג נָכוֹן הוּא, רַק תַּשְׁגִּיחַ שֶׁגַּם הַטְּבִילָה הַשְּׁנִיָּה תִּהְיֶה כְּהֹגֶן.

ט) לְאַחַר שֶׁטָּבְלָה בְּמִקְוֶה כָּרָאוּי, מֻתֶּרֶת לִכָּנֵס לְבֵית־הַמֶּרְחָץ לְחַמֵּם אֶת עַצְמָהּ, וַאֲפִלּוּ הוּא מֶרְחָץ שֶׁל זֵעָה. אֲבָל לַחֲזוֹר וְלִרְחוֹץ בְּאַמְבַּטִי, יֵשׁ אוֹסְרִים, וְכֵן נָהֲגוּ. וְלִשְׁפֹּךְ עָלֶיהָ מַיִם חַמִּים לְחַמֵּם אֶת גּוּפָהּ, יֵשׁ לְהָקֵל. אַךְ בְּמָקוֹם שֶׁנָּהֲגוּ לֶאֱסֹר גַּם זֹאת, אֵין לְהָקֵל.

י) יֵשׁ לָאִשָּׁה לִהְיוֹת צְנוּעָה בִּטְבִילָתָהּ לְהַסְתִּיר לֵיל טְבִילָתָהּ, וְלֹא תֵּלֵךְ בִּפְנֵי הַבְּרִיּוֹת, שֶׁלֹּא יַרְגִּישׁוּ בָהּ בְּנֵי אָדָם וּמִי שֶׁאֵינָהּ עוֹשָׂה כֵן, נֶאֱמַר עָלֶיהָ, אָרוּר שֹׁכֵב עִם כָּל־בְּהֵמָה. עוֹד יֵשׁ לָהּ לִזָּהֵר, כְּשֶׁתֵּצֵא מִן הַטְּבִילָה, שֶׁתִּפְגַּע בָּהּ חֲבֶרְתָּהּ וְתִגַּע בָּהּ, שֶׁלֹּא יִפְגַּע בָּהּ תְּחִלָּה דָּבָר טָמֵא, כְּגוֹן כֶּלֶב אוֹ חֲמוֹר אוֹ חֲזִיר אוֹ סוּס אוֹ מְצֹרָע וְכַיּוֹצֵא בָהֶן, אוֹ עַם־הָאָרֶץ אוֹ גוֹי. וְאִם פָּגְעוּ בָהּ דְּבָרִים אֵלּוּ, אִם הִיא יִרְאַת־שָׁמַיִם, תַּחֲזוֹר וְתִטְבּוֹל. מִי שֶׁפָּגַע בְּאִשָּׁה יוֹצֵאת מִן הַטְּבִילָה, אִכָּא לְמֵיחַשׁ, חַס־וְשָׁלוֹם, לְתַקָּלָה. וְהַתַּקָּנָה הִיא שֶׁיֹּאמַר שְׁנֵי פְּסוּקִים אֵלּוּ, שֹׁפֵךְ בּוּז עַל־נְדִיבִים וַיַּתְעֵם בְּתֹהוּ לֹא־דָרֶךְ, שׁוֹפֵךְ בּוּז עַל־נְדִיבִים וּמְזִיחַ אֲפִיקִים רִפָּה.

יא) לְחַמֵּם אֶת מֵי הַמִּקְוֶה, יֵשׁ אוֹסְרִין וְיֵשׁ מַתִּירִין. וּכְבָר נִתְפַּשֵּׁט הַמִּנְהָג בְּהַרְבֵּה מְקוֹמוֹת לְהֶתֵּר. אֲבָל בְּמָקוֹם שֶׁאֵין מִנְהָג, אֵין לְהָקֵל וּבְמָקוֹם שֶׁנָּהֲגוּ לְהָקֵל, צְרִיכִין לְהַשְׁגִּיחַ שֶׁבְּלֵיל שַׁבָּת כְּשֶׁטּוֹבְלִין, לֹא יִהְיוּ הַמַּיִם חַמִּין מַמָּשׁ, אֶלָּא פּוֹשְׁרִים.

יב) בְּעִנְיַן הַטְּבִילָה בִּנְהָרוֹת, לְדַעַת הַרְבֵּה גְּדוֹלֵי הַפּוֹסְקִים זִכְרוֹנָם לִבְרָכָה, אֵין הַטְּבִילָה מוֹעֶלֶת בְּנָהָר אֶלָּא בִּזְמַן שֶׁהוּא קָטָן כָּל כָּךְ, שֶׁיָּדוּעַ בְּבֵרוּר שֶׁלֹּא נִתְגַּדֵּל מֵחֲמַת מֵי גְשָׁמִים אוֹ מֵי שְׁלָגִים, כִּי מֵי גְשָׁמִים וּמֵי שְׁלָגִים אֵינָם מְטַהֲרִין אֶלָּא בִּזְמַן שֶׁהֵם נִקְוִים וְעוֹמְדִים כַּמִּקְוֶה. אֲבָל כְּשֶׁהֵם זוֹחֲלִים עַל הָאָרֶץ, אֵינָם מְטַהֲרִין, אֶלָּא מֵי מַעְיָן מְטַהֲרִין גַּם בְּזוֹחֲלִין וְאַף בִּשְׁעַת הַדְּחָק, בְּמָקוֹם שֶׁאֵין מִקְוֶה, נוֹהֲגִין לְהָקֵל וְלִסְמֹךְ עַל הַפּוֹסְקִים דִּסְבִירָא לְהוּ כְּמַאן דְּאָמַר, דַּאֲפִלּוּ רוֹאִים שֶׁהַנָּהָר מִתְגַּדֵּל

13. So that people will not think that the bath purifies her, rather than the (*mikvah.*)

reciting the *berachah*. If she immerses in a place where she is able to make the water opaque by stirring it with her feet, it is best to do so before reciting the *berachah*. Some women are accustomed after reciting the *berachah* to immerse one more time, and this is a proper custom. If she does so, she must take care that the second immersion also be done properly.

9) After she has properly immersed in the mikvah she is permitted to enter the bath-house to warm herself, even if it is a steam bath. But according to some Poskim it is forbidden to wash again in a tub,[13] and this is the prevailing custom. As far as pouring hot water on herself to warm her body, she may be lenient. But in a community where custom forbids this too, she may not be lenient.

10) A woman should be modest about her immersion, and conceal the date of her immersion. She should not go to the (*mikvah*) when people are about. [She should arrange it] so that people will not notice her. Concerning a woman who does not act modestly, it is said, "Cursed be he who lies with any kind of animal."[14] She should also take care when leaving the (*mikvah*) that her friend should meet her and touch her, so that she not be met first by an unclean thing such as a dog, a donkey, a pig, a horse, a *metzorah*, or similar things, or by a person, ignorant in Torah, and not God-fearing or a non-Jew. If any of these meet her (first), if she is God-fearing, she will return and immerse again. If one meets a woman leaving the (*mikvah*) after her immersion, he may expect some mishap, God forbid. To prevent this he should recite these two verses: "He pours contempt upon nobles and causes them to wander, in the wasteland, where there is no path"[15] and, "He pours contempt upon nobles and he loosens the belt of the mighty."[16]

11) With regard to heating the water of the *mikvah*, some authorities forbid it and some authorities permit it. The prevailing custom in many communities is to permit it, but where no such custom prevails, one should not be lax about it. In a place where it is customary to permit immersion on Friday night, care must be taken that the water should not be hot, but lukewarm.[17]

12) With regard to immersion in rivers, according to many great *halachic* authorities, of blessed memory, the immersion in a river is valid only when it is so small that it is certain that the river did not increase due to rainwater or melted snow, because rainwater and melted snow purify only when they are gathered together and standing as a *mikvah*. But when they are flowing on the ground they do not purify. Only spring waters purify [even] when flowing on the ground. However, in an emergency, as when there is no *mikvah*, it is customary to be lenient, and to rely on the *poskim* who rule according to the *poseik* who says even when we see that the river was increased from the rain water, nevertheless, the major increase

14. *Deuteronomy* 27:21.
15. *Psalms* 107:40.
16. *Job* 12:21.
17. See *Kitzur Shulchan Aruch* 86:1.

מִן הַגְּשָׁמִים מִכָּל מָקוֹם עִקַּר גִּדּוּלוֹ הוּא מִמְּקוֹרוֹ מִן הַתְּהוֹם, כִּי בְּעֵת הַגְּשָׁמִים, הָאֲוִיר מְלַחְלֵחַ וּמְקוֹרֵי הַמַּעְיָנוֹת מִתְרַבִּים וּמִתְגַּבְּרִים, וְנִמְצָא לְעוֹלָם שֶׁהַמַּיִם שֶׁבַּנָּהָר רֻבָּם מִמַּעְיָן, וּמֵי הַגְּשָׁמִים מִתְבַּטְּלִים בְּתוֹכוֹ, וּמְטַהֲרִין גַּם בְּזוֹחֲלִין. אֲבָל בְּמָקוֹם שֶׁיֵּשׁ מִקְוֶה, חָלִילָה לְהָקֵל. וְגַם בְּמָקוֹם שֶׁאֵין מִקְוֶה, אִם בְּאֶפְשָׁרִי, יֵשׁ לְהַחְמִיר, שֶׁאִם הַנָּהָר נִתְרַבָּה מִמֵּי גְשָׁמִים, תַּמְתִּין בִּטְבִילָתָהּ שְׁנַיִם אוֹ שְׁלֹשָׁה יָמִים, עַד שֶׁיָּשׁוּב לְאֵיתָנוֹ. וְטוֹב אִם בְּאֶפְשָׁרִי, שֶׁלֹּא תִטְבּוֹל בְּמָקוֹם שֶׁנִּתְרַחֵב, אֶלָּא בְּמָקוֹם שֶׁהוֹלֵךְ תָּמִיד, דְּבָזֶה יֵשׁ קְצָת לְהָקֵל טְפֵי.

יג) וּבְנָהָר שֶׁמִּתְהַוֶּה לְגַמְרֵי עַל יְדֵי גְשָׁמִים וְלִפְעָמִים מִתְיַבֵּשׁ, אַף־עַל־פִּי שֶׁבִּשְׁעַת הַגְּשָׁמִים גַּם שְׁאָר נְהָרוֹת שׁוֹפְכִים לְתוֹכוֹ מִכָּל מָקוֹם הוֹאִיל וְלִפְעָמִים פּוֹסֵק לְגַמְרֵי אֵין שׁוּם הֶתֵּר לִטְבּוֹל בּוֹ כְּשֶׁהוּא זוֹחֵל עַד שֶׁיִּקָּווּ הַמַּיִם וְיַעַמְדוּ.

יד) דִּינֵי הַמִּקְוֶה, רַבִּים הֵם מְאֹד. וּבְכָל מָקוֹם שֶׁעוֹשִׂין מִקְוֶה, אֵין לַעֲשׂוֹתוֹ כִּי אִם עַל יְדֵי רַב מֻמְחֶה לָרַבִּים, גָּדוֹל בַּתּוֹרָה וּבְיִרְאָה. וְכַאֲשֶׁר יִתְהַוֶּה בּוֹ אֵיזֶה שִׁנּוּי גָּדוֹל אוֹ קָטָן, יַעֲשׂוּ מִיָּד שְׁאֵלַת חָכָם. וְכֵן כַּאֲשֶׁר יִצְטָרְכוּ לִשְׁאֹב אוֹתוֹ לְנַקּוֹתוֹ, יִשְׁאֲלוּ אֵיךְ יִתְנַהֲגוּ.

סִימָן קסג
הִלְכוֹת מִילָה

א) מִצְוַת עֲשֵׂה עַל הָאָב לָמוּל אֶת בְּנוֹ, אוֹ לְכַבֵּד וְלַעֲשׂוֹת שָׁלִיחַ לְיִשְׂרָאֵל אַחֵר שֶׁיָּמוּל אוֹתוֹ. וְיֵשׁ לוֹ לְהָאָב לָתֵת אֶת הַיֶּלֶד עַל בִּרְכֵּי הַסַּנְדָּק וּלְהוֹשִׁיט אֶת הָאִזְמֵל לִידֵי הַמּוֹהֵל, וְלַעֲמֹד אֶצְלוֹ בִּשְׁעַת הַמִּילָה לְהַרְאוֹת שֶׁהוּא שְׁלוּחוֹ. וּבֵין חִתּוּךְ לִפְרִיעָה, מְבָרֵךְ הָאָב אֲשֶׁר קִדְּשָׁנוּ בְּמִצְוֹתָיו וְצִוָּנוּ לְהַכְנִיסוֹ וְכוּ'. וְיֵשׁ לְאָדָם לַחֲזוֹר וּלְהַדֵּר אַחַר מוֹהֵל וְסַנְדָּק הַיּוֹתֵר טוֹב וְצַדִּיק. נוֹהֲגִין שֶׁאֵין נוֹתְנִין סַנְדְּקָאוֹת לְאִישׁ אֲשֶׁר כְּבָר הָיָה אֶצְלוֹ סַנְדָּק בְּבֵן אַחֵר. אִם כִּבֵּד לְמוֹהֵל אֶחָד אָסוּר לַחֲזוֹר בּוֹ וּלְכַבֵּד לְאַחֵר, שֶׁנֶּאֱמַר, שְׁאֵרִית יִשְׂרָאֵל לֹא יַעֲשׂוּ עַוְלָה וְלֹא יְדַבְּרוּ כָזָב.

18. The *Chassam Sofer* Responsa 202, *Sharei Taharah* and *Peri Hadaseh* say she must go to another city where there is a *mikvah*, even if it means immersing on the eighth day.

is from its source under the ground. For in time of rain, the air is full of moisture, and the sources of the springs increase and becomes stronger. Consequently, the water in the river is always mostly from underground springs, and the rainwater is nullified within it, and therefore it purifies even though it contains water that flowed on the ground. However, in a place where there is a *mikvah,*[18] far be it from anyone to be lenient about it. Even where there is no *mikvah,* if possible, it is best to be strict and if the river increased from rain water, she should postpone her immersion two or three days, until it resumes its normal level. It is best, if possible, not to immerse in the place where the river was widened, but rather in the place where it flows continuously; for in that case there is somewhat more ground for leniency.

13) With regard to a river which is formed entirely by rain and at times completely dries up, although during the rainfall some other streams empty into it, nevertheless, since occasionally it dries up completely, there are no grounds to permit immersion in it while the water is flowing on the ground, until the water gathers and remains standing.

14) The laws regarding *mikvah* are very numerous. Wherever a *mikvah* is being made, it should be constructed only under the supervision of a very renowned *poseik,* great in Torah and in fear of God. When any change occurs (in the *mikvah*), whether a minor or major (change), a competent *poseik* should be consulted immediately. Also, when it becomes necessary to draw the water in order to clean it, a *poseik* should be consulted about the proper way to do it.

Chapter 163

The Laws of Circumcision

1) It is a positive mitzvah for the father to circumcise his son, or to grant the honor and appoint another Jew as his agent to circumcise him. The father should place the infant on the knees of the *sandek,* hand over the knife to the *mohel,* and stand by him during the circumcision, to indicate that the *mohel* is his agent. In the interval between the cutting of the foreskin and its laceration, the father recites the *berachah, Asher kideshanu bemitzvosav vetzivanu lehachniso* etc. "Who has sanctified us with His commandments and has commanded us to induct him into the covenant of our father *Avrohom.*" You should make an effort to find the best and most righteous *mohel* and *sandek.* It is customary not to select as *sandek,* a man who had already been *sandek* at the circumcision of another one of his sons.[1] If you have invited a *mohel,* it is forbidden to retract and invite another one, for it is said, "The remnant of Yisrael will do no injustice and will speak no falsehood."[2] If you

1. See *Ramah* 265:11—*Maharil.* Also *Tzava'as Rabbeinu Yehuda Hachassid.* However, the *Nodah Beyehuda Kama* Responsa 86 says the custom is to permit it. See *Chasam Sofer* (*Orach Chaim*) Responsa 158 that you may give the honor more than once to the Rabbi of the city.

2. *Tzefanya* 3:13.

וְאִם כִּבֵּד לְאֶחָד וּבְתוֹךְ כָּךְ הָלַךְ זֶה הַמּוֹהֵל מִן הָעִיר וְחָשַׁב הָאָב כִּי לֹא יָבוֹא לִזְמַן הַמִּילָה וְעַל כֵּן כִּבֵּד לְאַחֵר וּבְתוֹךְ כָּךְ בָּא הָרִאשׁוֹן, יְמוֹלֶנּוּ הָרִאשׁוֹן.

ב) נוֹהֲגִין שֶׁכָּל הָעָם שֶׁאֵצֶל הַמִּילָה, עוֹמְדִים, שֶׁנֶּאֱמַר, וַיַּעֲמֹד כָּל־הָעָם בַּבְּרִית, מִלְּבַד הַסַּנְדָּק שֶׁהוּא תּוֹפֵס אֶת הַתִּינוֹק, וְהוּא יוֹשֵׁב. וּלְאַחַר שֶׁבֵּרַךְ הָאָב לְהַכְנִיסוֹ וְעָנוּ אָמֵן, אוֹמְרִים כֻּלָּם, כְּשֵׁם שֶׁנִּכְנַס לַבְּרִית, כֵּן יִכָּנֵס לַתּוֹרָה וְלַחֻפָּה וּלְמַעֲשִׂים טוֹבִים.

ג) הַמּוֹהֵל צָרִיךְ שֶׁיֵּדַע הִלְכוֹת מִילָה. וְצָרִיךְ שֶׁיַּחְקֹר אִם הַיֶּלֶד הוּא בָּרִיא. וְגַם לְהַמְיַלֶּדֶת יֵשׁ לְהַזְהִיר, שֶׁאִם תִּרְאֶה אֵיזֶה מֵחוֹשׁ בַּיֶּלֶד, תּוֹדִיעַ.

ד) וּצְרִיכִין לִזָּהֵר בִּמְאֹד מְאֹד שֶׁלֹּא לָמוּל וָלָד שֶׁיֵּשׁ בּוֹ חֲשַׁשׁ חֹלִי, כִּי סַכָּנַת נְפָשׁוֹת דּוֹחָה אֶת הַכֹּל, שֶׁאֶפְשָׁר לוֹ לָמוּל לְאַחַר זְמַן, וְאִי־אֶפְשָׁר לְהַחֲזִיר נֶפֶשׁ אַחַת מִיִּשְׂרָאֵל לְעוֹלָם. וְעַיֵּן יוֹרֶה דֵעָה סִימָן רסב וְסִימָן רסג, מָתַי מָלִין תִּינוֹק שֶׁהָיָה חוֹלֶה וְהִבְרִיא. וּמִיָּד כְּשֶׁהַתִּינוֹק רָאוּי לָמוּל, אָסוּר לְעַכֵּב אֶת הַמִּצְוָה מֵאֵיזֶה טַעַם לְהַרְבּוֹת שִׂמְחָה וְכַדּוֹמֶה, אֶלָּא יָמוּל מִיָּד כְּשֶׁהוּא רָאוּי. אַךְ לֹא בְּשַׁבָּת וְלֹא בְּיוֹם־טוֹב, כְּמוֹ שֶׁכָּתוּב בְּיוֹרֶה דֵעָה סִימָן רסו.

ה) אִשָּׁה שֶׁמֵּתוּ שְׁנֵי בָנֶיהָ מֵחֲמַת מִילָה, שֶׁנִּרְאֶה כִּי הַמִּילָה הִכְחִישָׁה אֶת כֹּחָם אֵין מָלִין אֶת הַשְּׁלִישִׁי, עַד שֶׁיִּגְדַּל וְיִתְחַזֵּק כֹּחוֹ. וְכֵן אִשָּׁה שֶׁמֵּת לָהּ יֶלֶד אֶחָד מֵחֲמַת מִילָה וְגַם לַאֲחוֹתָהּ אֵרַע כֵּן, אֲזַי גַּם שְׁאָר הָאֲחָיוֹת לֹא יָמוּלוּ בְּנֵיהֶן, עַד שֶׁיִּגְדְּלוּ וְיִתְחַזְּקוּ.

ו) תִּינוֹק שֶׁנּוֹלַד בֵּין־הַשְּׁמָשׁוֹת אוֹ קְצָת קֹדֶם, יַעֲשׂוּ שְׁאֵלַת חָכָם, מָתַי יִמּוֹל.

ז) תִּינוֹק שֶׁמֵּת קֹדֶם שֶׁנִּמּוֹל (בֵּין בְּתוֹךְ שְׁמוֹנָה יָמִים בֵּין אַחַר כָּךְ) מָלִין אוֹתוֹ אֵצֶל קִבְרוֹ לְהָסִיר חֶרְפָּתוֹ מִמֶּנּוּ, שֶׁלֹּא יִקָּבֵר בְּעָרְלָתוֹ, כִּי חֶרְפָּה הִיא לוֹ. וְאֵין מְבָרְכִין עַל הַמִּילָה אֲבָל קוֹרְאִין לוֹ שֵׁם לְזֵכֶר שֶׁיְּרַחֲמוּהוּ מִן הַשָּׁמַיִם וְיִחְיֶה בִּתְחִיַּת הַמֵּתִים, וְתִהְיֶה בּוֹ דֵעָה לְהַכִּיר אָבִיו וְאִמּוֹ. אִם שָׁכְחוּ לְמוּלוֹ וּקְבָרוּהוּ בְּעָרְלָתוֹ, אִם נִזְכְּרוּ מִיָּד, שֶׁעֲדַיִן

---

3. II Kings 23:3.

appointed a *mohel,* and in the meantime the *mohel* left the city, and the father, thinking that he would not return in time for the circumcision, appointed another (in his stead), but in the meantime the original *mohel* returned, he should perform the circumcision.

2) It is customary that all those attending a circumcision, stand throughout the ceremony, for it is said, "And all the people stood in the covenant,"[3] excepting the *sandek,* who holds the baby while seated. After the father recites the *berachah, Lehachniso,* and those assembled answer *amein,* they all say, "Just as he was initiated into the covenant, so may he be initiated into the study of Torah, to the *Chupah,* and to the performance of good deeds."

3) It is essential that the *mohel* be versed in the laws of circumcision, and he must examine the child to see if he is healthy. The midwife (nurses etc.) should be alerted that in case she observes some weakness or illness in the child, she should notify the *mohel.*

4) Extreme care must be taken not to circumcise a child who is possibly ill, for danger to human life overrides all other consideration. Moreover, the circumcision can be performed at a later date, but it is impossible to ever restore one Jewish life. See *Yoreh Deiah,* Chapters 262,263 as to when to circumcise an infant who had been ill and recovered. As soon as the infant is fit for circumcision, it is forbidden to defer the mitzvah for any reason, such as to elaborate the festivities or the like. You must circumcise him immediately when he is fit, but you may not do so on Shabbos or on Yom Tov, as is stated in *Yoreh Deiah* Chapter 266.

5) If a woman has lost two sons from the effect of circumcision, as it appears that the circumcision had weakened their strength, you may not circumcise the third son until he gets older and stronger. Also a woman who lost a child from the effect of circumcision, and the same thing happened to her sister's son, then the other sisters, too, should not have their sons circumcised until they get older and stronger.

6) If a baby is born during twilight, or close to it, you must consult a competent *poseik* as to when he should be circumcised.

7) An infant who dies before circumcision (whether within the eight days or thereafter,) is circumcised at the grave in order to remove (the foreskin) which is a disgrace to him, so he should not be buried with his foreskin which is considered a disgrace to him.[4] No *berachah* is recited on this circumcision, but a name is given to him as a remembrance that mercy will be shown him from Heaven and he will be included in the resurrection of the dead, and that he may then have sufficient understanding to recognize his father and his mother. If they forgot to circumcise him, and they had already buried him with his foreskin, if they became aware of it immediately, when there is as yet no reason to suspect that the body has begun to

4. *Kolbo.*

אֵין לָחוּשׁ שֶׁנִּתְנַוֵּל בַּקֶּבֶר, צְרִיכִין לִפְתֹּחַ אֶת הַקֶּבֶר וּלְמוּלוֹ. אֲבָל אִם לֹא נִזְכְּרוּ עַד אֵיזֶה יָמִים לְאַחַר מוֹתוֹ, אֵין לִפְתֹּחַ אֶת הַקֶּבֶר.

ח) נוֹהֲגִין לַעֲשׂוֹת סְעוּדָה בְּיוֹם הַמִּילָה. שֶׁכָּל מִצְוָה שֶׁקִּבְּלוּ יִשְׂרָאֵל בְּשִׂמְחָה (כְּמוֹ מִצְוַת מִילָה), עֲדַיִן עוֹשִׂין בְּשִׂמְחָה. וּכְתִיב, שָׂשׂ אָנֹכִי עַל אִמְרָתֶךָ וְגוֹ׳, וְדָרְשִׁינָן, זוֹ מִילָה. וּמִי שֶׁאֶפְשָׁר לוֹ לַעֲשׂוֹת סְעוּדָה הֲגוּנָה וּמְקַמֵּץ וְאֵינוֹ עוֹשֶׂה אֶלָּא בְּקָפֶה וּמִינֵי מְתִיקָה וְכַדּוֹמֶה, לֹא יָפֶה עוֹשֶׂה. מִי שֶׁמְּזַמְּנִין אוֹתוֹ לִסְעוּדַת בְּרִית מִילָה, וְיוֹדֵעַ שֶׁיֵּשׁ שָׁם אֲנָשִׁים מְהֻגָּנִים, מְחֻיָּב גַּם הוּא לָלֶכֶת. עוֹד נוֹהֲגִין לַעֲשׂוֹת סְעוּדָה בְּמִינֵי פֵּרוֹת וּמַשְׁקִין בְּלֵיל שַׁבָּת שֶׁקֹּדֶם הַמִּילָה, וְגַם זוֹהִי סְעוּדַת מִצְוָה. עוֹד נוֹהֲגִין, שֶׁבַּלַּיְלָה שֶׁלִּפְנֵי הַמִּילָה, מִתְקַבְּצִין בְּבֵית הַתִּינוֹק וְעוֹסְקִין בַּתּוֹרָה וְעוֹשִׂין קְצָת סְעוּדָה, וְזוֹ אֵין לָהּ דִּין סְעוּדַת מִצְוָה, שֶׁאֵינָהּ אֶלָּא מִנְהָג בְּעָלְמָא.

סִימָן קסד
הִלְכוֹת פִּדְיוֹן בְּכוֹר

א) מִצְוַת עֲשֵׂה עַל כָּל אִישׁ מִיִּשְׂרָאֵל, שֶׁיִּפְדֶּה מִכֹּהֵן אֶת בְּנוֹ שֶׁהוּא בְּכוֹר לְאִמּוֹ בַּחֲמִשָּׁה סְלָעִים. וּבְמַטְבְּעוֹת שֶׁלָּנוּ צָרִיךְ שֶׁיִּהְיוּ כָּל־כָּךְ עַד שֶׁיְּהֵא בְּכֻלָּם חֲמִשָּׁה לוֹיט וּשְׁלִישׁ כֶּסֶף צָרוּף. וְיָכוֹל לִתֵּן לַכֹּהֵן, אֲפִלּוּ שְׁאָר חֲפָצִים שֶׁיִּהְיוּ שָׁוִים כָּךְ, אֲבָל לֹא קַרְקָעוֹת אוֹ שְׁטָרוֹת. וְלָכֵן אֵין פּוֹדִין [בִּשְׁטָרוֹת־כֶּסֶף]. וְנוֹהֲגִין לַעֲשׂוֹת סְעוּדָה לְמִצְוָה זֹאת.

ב) אָמַר לְכֹהֵן אֶחָד שֶׁיִּפְדֶּה מִמֶּנּוּ אֶת בְּנוֹ, אָסוּר לַחֲזוֹר בּוֹ. וְאִם חָזַר וּפָדָה אוֹתוֹ מִכֹּהֵן אַחֵר, הֲרֵי זֶה פָּדוּי.

ג) אֵין פּוֹדִין אֶת הַבְּכוֹר, עַד שֶׁיַּעַבְרוּ עָלָיו שְׁלֹשִׁים יוֹם. וּבְיוֹם שְׁלֹשִׁים וְאֶחָד יִפְדּוּהוּ מִיָּד, שֶׁלֹּא לְהַשְׁהוֹת אֶת הַמִּצְוָה. וְאֵין פּוֹדִין בְּשַׁבָּת וּבְיוֹם־טוֹב. אֲבָל בְּחֹל־הַמּוֹעֵד פּוֹדִין. נוֹהֲגִין לַעֲשׂוֹת אֶת הַפִּדְיוֹן בַּיּוֹם. וּמִכָּל מָקוֹם אִם עָבַר יוֹם שְׁלֹשִׁים וְאֶחָד וְלֹא פָּדָה, אוֹ שֶׁחָל בְּשַׁבָּת אוֹ בְּיוֹם־טוֹב אוֹ בְּתַעֲנִית, יֵשׁ לִפְדּוֹתוֹ תֵּכֶף בַּלַּיְלָה שֶׁלְּאַחֲרָיו וְלֹא יַמְתִּינוּ עַד לְמָחָר לְהַשְׁהוֹת הַמִּצְוָה יוֹתֵר.

5. *Psalms* 119:162.
6. *Maseches Shabbos* 130a.
7. See *Tosafos Maseches Baba Kama* 80a.
8. *Remah* 262:12.

decompose in the grave, they should open the grave and circumcise him. But if they had not become aware of it until several days after his death, his grave should not be opened (*Nodah Beyehudah Tinyana* No. 164).

8) It is customary to make a feast on the day of the circumcision; for every mitzvah which Jews accepted with joy, (like the precept of circumcision), they still perform with joy. It is written, "I am happy with your word"[5] etc. and the Sages[6] explain that this refers to circumcision. He who can afford to make a proper feast, but economizes, and makes it only with coffee and sweets, or the like, does not act properly. If you are invited to a circumcision feast, and you know that worthy men will be present, you are obligated to attend. It is also customary to make a feast of various fruits and drinks on the Friday night before the circumcision.[7] This feast is also considered a mitzvah.[8] It is also customary that the night prior to the circumcision, people assemble in the house where the baby is, and study Torah. Some refreshments are served, but this feast is not considered a mitzvah, for it is merely a custom.

Chapter 164

The Redemption of The Firstborn

1) It is a positive mitzvah incumbent on every Jewish man to redeem his son from a *kohein*, if his son is the mother's firstborn child. This is done by giving the *kohein* five *selaim*. Our coinage must be of sufficient value, so that their sum equals five and one-third *loit* of refined silver.[1] You may give the *kohein* even other articles of that value, but not real property or notes. Therefore you may not redeem your son with paper money. It is customary to make a feast when performing this mitzvah.

2) If you told a particular *kohein* that you will redeem your son from him, you are forbidden to retract your word, but if you did retract and redeemed him from another *kohein*, the redemption is valid.

3) You cannot redeem the firstborn before he is fully thirty days old, and on the thirty-first day you should redeem him immediately, and not postpone the performance of the mitzvah. You may not redeem him on Shabbos or Yom Tov,[2] but you may redeem him on *Chol Hamoed.*[3] It is customary to do the redemption during the daytime. However, if the thirty-first day has passed, and you have not yet redeemed the infant, or if that day is on Shabbos or Yom Tov or on a fast day, you should redeem him immediately on the following night, and not wait until the next day, thus, further postponing the mitzvah.

---

1. This is an old measure. In todays measure it is 96 grams or its equivilent at the time of the Redemption. When old coins are going to be used, their silver content must be verified.
2. Because it is similar to buying and selling, which is forbidden on Shabbos and Yom Tov. (Shach 305:12, Rivash, Responsa 152)
3. *Ramah* 305:11.

ד) הָאָב מַיְיתֵי לֵהּ לִבְכוֹר קַמֵּי כֹּהֵן, וּמוֹדִיעַ לוֹ שֶׁהוּא בְּכוֹר פֶּטֶר רֶחֶם לְאִמּוֹ הַיִּשְׂרְאֵלִית. וּמַיְיתֵי כֶּסֶף אוֹ שָׁוֶה־כֶּסֶף חֲמִשָּׁה סְלָעִים וּמַנִּיחַ לִפְנֵי הַכֹּהֵן, וְאוֹמֵר לַכֹּהֵן, זֶה בְּנִי בְכוֹרִי וְכוּ', וְאַחַר כָּךְ מַנִּיחוֹ לִפְנֵי הַכֹּהֵן, וְהַכֹּהֵן שׁוֹאֵל אוֹתוֹ, בְּמַאי בָּעִית טְפֵי. וְהוּא מֵשִׁיב לוֹ וְאוֹמֵר חָפֵץ אֲנִי לִפְדּוֹת אֶת בְּנִי וְכוּ'. וּבְעוֹד שֶׁהָאָב מַחֲזִיק אֶת הַמַּטְבְּעוֹת בְּיָדוֹ, קֹדֶם שֶׁיִּתְּנֵם לַכֹּהֵן, מְבָרֵךְ, אֲשֶׁר קִדְּשָׁנוּ בְּמִצְוֹתָיו וְצִוָּנוּ עַל פִּדְיוֹן הַבֵּן וְגַם שֶׁהֶחֱיָנוּ, וְנוֹתֵן מִיָּד אֶת הַמַּטְבְּעוֹת לַכֹּהֵן, וְהַכֹּהֵן נוֹטֵל אֶת הַכֶּסֶף וּמוֹלִיכוֹ בְּיָדוֹ עַל רֹאשׁ הַבֵּן, וְאוֹמֵר, זֶה תַּחַת זֶה וְכוּ'. וְאַחַר כָּךְ נוֹתֵן אֶת יָדוֹ עַל רֹאשׁ הַבֵּן וּמְבָרְכוֹ וְאוֹמֵר, יְשִׂימְךָ אֱלֹהִים וְגוֹ', יְבָרֶכְךָ ה' וְיִשְׁמְרֶךָ וְגוֹ', כִּי אֹרֶךְ יָמִים וּשְׁנוֹת חַיִּים וְגוֹ', ה' יִשְׁמָרְךָ מִכָּל רָע וְגוֹ'. וְאַחַר כָּךְ מְבָרֵךְ הַכֹּהֵן עַל כּוֹס יַיִן. וְאִם אֵין יַיִן, מְבָרֵךְ עַל שְׁאָר מַשְׁקֶה שֶׁרְגִילִין לִשְׁתּוֹת שָׁם, אֲבָל אָז צְרִיכִין לַעֲשׂוֹת הַפִּדְיוֹן קֹדֶם נְטִילַת יָדַיִם לַסְּעוּדָה, כִּי בְּתוֹךְ הַסְּעוּדָה אֵין מְבָרְכִין עַל שְׁאָר מַשְׁקִים, מַה שֶּׁאֵין כֵּן כְּשֶׁיֵּשׁ יַיִן, שֶׁאָז עוֹשִׂין הַפִּדְיוֹן אַחַר בִּרְכַּת הַמּוֹצִיא.

ה) אִם אֵין הָאָב בִּמְקוֹם הַיֶּלֶד, יָכוֹל גַּם כֵּן לִפְדּוֹתוֹ מִכֹּהֵן בַּאֲשֶׁר הוּא שָׁם. וְאוֹמֵר לַכֹּהֵן, יֵשׁ לִי בֵּן בְּכוֹר לִפְדּוֹתוֹ. וְהַכֹּהֵן אוֹמֵר לוֹ, בְּמַאי בָּעִית טְפֵי וְכוּ'.

ו) בְּעִנְיַן מַה שֶּׁנּוֹהֲגִין, שֶׁהַכֹּהֵן מַחֲזִיר אַחַר כָּךְ אֶת דְּמֵי הַפִּדְיוֹן כֻּלּוֹ אוֹ מִקְצָתוֹ לָאָב, כָּתַב טוּרֵי זָהָב טַעַם (וְצָרִיךְ עִיּוּן). וּמִי שֶׁרוֹצֶה לַעֲשׂוֹת הַמִּצְוָה כִּדְבָעֵי לְמֶהֱוֵי, יִבְחַר לוֹ כֹּהֵן עָנִי בַּעַל תּוֹרָה וְיִרְאָה, וְהָאָב וְגַם הַכֹּהֵן יִגְמְרוּ בְּדַעְתָּם שֶׁלֹּא לְהַחֲזִיר אוֹ יִתֵּן לוֹ בְּמַתָּנָה עַל מְנָת לְהַחֲזִיר.

ז) הָאֵם, אֵינָהּ חַיֶּבֶת לִפְדּוֹת אֶת בְּנָהּ. וְאִם מֵת הָאָב, בֵּית־הַדִּין פּוֹדִין אוֹתוֹ.

ח) עָבַר הָאָב וְלֹא פָּדָה אֶת בְּנוֹ, אוֹ שֶׁמֵּת הָאָב וּבֵית־הַדִּין לֹא פָּדוּ אוֹתוֹ, חַיָּב הוּא בְּעַצְמוֹ לִפְדּוֹת אֶת עַצְמוֹ כְּשֶׁיִּגְדַּל, וּמְבָרֵךְ, אֲשֶׁר קִדְּשָׁנוּ בְּמִצְוֹתָיו וְצִוָּנוּ עַל פִּדְיוֹן בְּכוֹר, וְשֶׁהֶחֱיָנוּ.

ט) כֹּהֲנִים וּלְוִיִּם, פְּטוּרִים מִפִּדְיוֹן הַבֵּן. וַאֲפִלּוּ בַּת־כֹּהֵן אוֹ בַּת־לֵוִי שֶׁנִּשֵּׂאָה לְיִשְׂרָאֵל, הַבֵּן פָּטוּר מִפִּדְיוֹן. וְאִם בַּת־כֹּהֵן נִבְעֲלָה לְגוֹי וְנִתְעַבְּרָה

4. If the father had in mind that the *kohein* will return it but the *kohein* was not aware of it, the redemption is invalid, even if the *kohein* returns the money.

4) The father brings the firstborn before the *kohein* and informs him that the infant is the firstborn to his mother, who is an Israelite (i.e. she is not the daughter of a *kohein* or Levi). He brings the money, or goods worth five *selaim*, and places it before the *kohein*, and says to the *kohein*, "This is my firstborn son," etc. and then places the infant before the *kohein*. The *kohein* asks him, "What would you rather," etc., and the father responds, "I want to redeem my son," etc. While the father still holds the coins in his hand, before giving them to the *kohein*, he recites the *berachah: Asher kideshanu bemitzvosav vetzivanu al pidyon habben* "Who has sanctified us with His commandments, and has commanded us concerning redemption of the firstborn son." He also recites the *berachah, Shecheyanu,* and then immediately gives the coins to the *kohein*. The *kohein* takes the money, and revolves it over the child's head, and says, *Zeh tachas zeh* etc. "This (money) instead of this (child)." Afterwards he places his hand on the boy's head and blesses him, saying, *Yesimcha Elokim* etc. "May God make you etc;" *Yevarechechah Hashem Veyishmerechah,* May God bless you and keep you; *Ki orech yomim ushnos chaim* etc. "For length of days and years of life," etc. *Adonoy Yisumarchah mikol rah* etc. "God shall guard you from all evil" etc.). Thereafter the *kohein* recites a *berachah* over a cup of wine. If no wine is available, he may recite a *berachah* over some other beverage which is commonly used in the region. But if so, the redemption should take place before the hands are washed for the meal, for during the meal, it is not permitted to recite a *berachah* over any beverage (other than wine). This is not the case when there is wine, for then the redemption takes place after the *Hamotzi* has been recited over the bread.

5) If the father is not with his son, he may redeem his son from a *kohein* wherever he is. In such an event he says to the *kohein*, "I have a firstborn son to redeem," whereupon the *kohein* inquires: "What would you rather," etc.

6) The *Turei Zahav* gives a reason for the custom of having the *kohein* return all the redemption money or part of it to the father, (and [even] this requires further deliberation). He who desires to perform the mitzvah properly, should choose a *kohein* who is poor, who is learned in Torah and is God-fearing, and both the father and the *kohein* should agree that the money is not to be returned,[4] or else the father should give it explicitly as a gift on condition that the *kohein* return it to him.

7) The mother is not obligated to redeem her son; and if the father has died, the *Beis Din* (Jewish court) redeems him.

8) If the father violated the law, and did not redeem his son, or if the father died and the *Beis Din* failed to redeem him, he himself is obligated to redeem himself when he becomes Bar Mitzvah, at which time he recites the *berachah, Asher kideshanu bemitzvosav vetzivanu al pidyon bechor* "Who has sanctified us with His commandments and commanded us concerning the redemption of the firstborn." He also recites the *berachah, Shehecheyanu.*

9) *Kohanim* and Levites are exempt from redeeming their firstborn sons. Even if the daughter of a *kohein* or a Levite is married to an Israelite, the son is exempt from redemption. If the daughter of a *kohein* had sexual relations with a non-Jew and has

מִמֶּנּוּ, אוֹ אֲפִלּוּ נִתְעַבְּרָה אַחַר כָּךְ בְּהֶתֵּר, הַבֵּן חַיָּב בְּפִדְיוֹן, שֶׁהֲרֵי אִמּוֹ נִתְחַלְּלָה מִן הַכְּהֻנָּה עַל יְדֵי בְּעִילַת גּוֹי. וְכֵן עַל יְדֵי שְׁאָר בְּעִילַת אִסּוּר, שֶׁהִיא מִתְחַלֶּלֶת.

י) אִשָּׁה שֶׁהִפִּילָה וְאַחַר כָּךְ יָלְדָה בֶּן־קַיָּמָא, צְרִיכִין לַעֲשׂוֹת שְׁאֵלָה.

סִימָן קסה

דִּין חִנּוּךְ קְטַנִּים וּקְצָת דִּינֵי מְלַמֵּד

א) כָּל אָב, חַיָּב לְחַנֵּךְ אֶת בָּנָיו הַקְּטַנִּים בְּכָל הַמִּצְוֹת, בֵּין בְּמִצְוָה דְּאוֹרַיְתָא בֵּין בְּמִצְוָה דְּרַבָּנָן, כָּל מִצְוָה וּמִצְוָה לְפִי דַּעַת הַקָּטָן וְהַקְּטַנָּה. וְכֵן לְהַפְרִישָׁם מִכָּל דְּבַר אִסּוּר, כְּמוֹ שֶׁאָמַר הַכָּתוּב, חֲנֹךְ לַנַּעַר עַל פִּי דַרְכּוֹ וְגוֹ'. וְאִם לֹא יִוָּסֵר בִּדְבָרִים, יַכֵּהוּ בַּשֵּׁבֶט וְכַדּוֹמֶה, אֲבָל לֹא יַכֵּהוּ מַכּוֹת אַכְזָרִיּוֹת כְּמוֹ הַשּׁוֹטִים. וְכָל עָרוּם יַעֲשֶׂה בְדָעַת. וּבְיוֹתֵר צְרִיכִים לְהַשְׁגִּיחַ עֲלֵיהֶם שֶׁלֹּא יְדַבְּרוּ שְׁקָרִים, וּלְלַמֵּד לְשׁוֹנָם דִּבְרֵי אֱמֶת, וּלְהַרְחִיקָם מִן הַשְּׁבוּעוֹת. וּדְבָרִים אֵלּוּ מֻטָּלִים עַל הָאָבוֹת וְעַל הַמְלַמְּדִים.

ב) הַגָּעַת זְמַן הַחִנּוּךְ לְמִצְוֹת עֲשֵׂה, הִיא בְּכָל תִּינוֹק לְפִי חָכְמָתוֹ וַהֲבָנָתוֹ. כְּגוֹן הַיּוֹדֵעַ מֵעִנְיַן שַׁבָּת, חַיָּב לִשְׁמוֹעַ קִדּוּשׁ וְהַבְדָּלָה, וְכָל כַּיּוֹצֵא בָזֶה. וְהַחִנּוּךְ בְּמִצְוֹת לֹא תַעֲשֶׂה, בֵּין בִּדְאוֹרַיְתָא בֵּין בִּדְרַבָּנָן, הוּא בְּכָל תִּינוֹק שֶׁהוּא בַר־הֲבָנָה שֶׁמֵּבִין כְּשֶׁאוֹמְרִים לוֹ שֶׁזֶּה אָסוּר לַעֲשׂוֹת אוֹ אָסוּר לֶאֱכוֹל. וְיֵשׁ לְחַנֵּךְ הַקְּטַנִּים שֶׁיַּעֲנוּ בְּבֵית־הַכְּנֶסֶת אָמֵן וּשְׁאָר הַדְּבָרִים. וּמִשָּׁעָה שֶׁהַתִּינוֹק עוֹנֶה אָמֵן, יֵשׁ לוֹ חֵלֶק לָעוֹלָם הַבָּא. וּצְרִיכִים לְחַנְּכָם שֶׁיַּעַמְדוּ בְּבֵית־הַכְּנֶסֶת בְּאֵימָה וּבְיִרְאָה. אֲבָל אוֹתָן שֶׁהֵם רָצִים וְשָׁבִים וּמְבַלְבְּלִים, מוּטָב שֶׁלֹּא לַהֲבִיאָם.

ג) אֲפִלּוּ מִי שֶׁאֵינוֹ אָבִיו שֶׁל קָטָן, אָסוּר לוֹ שֶׁיִּתֵּן לוֹ דְּבַר אִסּוּר

1. Some say every mother too. See *Mishna Berurah* 343:5. Others say if he has no father, his mother and *Beis Din* are responsible to train him. (see *Mishna Berurah* 640:5)

2. After his Bar Mitzvah, you are as responsible for him as you are for your fellow Jew and must reprimand him when necessary and direct him to do what is right. (see *Mishna Berurah* 225:7)

3. Even from violating a Rabbinic injunction.

4. *Proverbs* 22:6.

5. The *Gra,* in his *Igeres,* says to deal severely with children when they tell a lie.

become pregnant from him, or even if she had thereafter become pregnant from a legal marriage, the son must be redeemed, for his mother was disqualified from the *kehunah* (priesthood) by having cohabitation with a non-Jew. (This also applies to any illicit cohabitation through which his mother's priesthood is profaned.)

10) If a woman had a miscarriage and thereafter has given birth to a viable child, a Rav should be consulted (regarding his redemption).

Chapter 165

The Training of Children

1) Every[1] father is obligated to train his young children[2] in the practice of all the *mitzvos,* both Biblical *mitzvos*, and *mitzvos* that are Rabbinically ordained. They should be trained to do each mitzvah, in accordance with his or her intelligence. It is also his obligation to prevent them from doing any forbidden act,[3] as is said in the Scriptures, "Train a child in the way he should go,"[4] etc. If words are of no avail, you should chastise him with a rod, or the like. But you should not strike him severely as some fools do; a wise person will act intelligently. It is especially important to watch that they tell no lies,[5] and to train them to speak the truth, and to avoid oaths. The above things are mandatory upon fathers as well as teachers.

2) The time for training a child in the performance of positive commandments is set for each child according to his wisdom and understanding. For example, when he knows the significance of Shabbos, it is his duty[6] to hear *kiddush* and *havdalah,* and other similar things. Training the child to keep the prohibitive commandments, whether Biblical or Rabbinical, applies to every child, who understands when he is told that something is forbidden to do or forbidden to eat.[7] Young children should be trained to answer *Amein* in the synagogue, and to participate in other aspects of synagogue prayer. From the time a child answers *Amein* [to a berachah] he has a share in the World to Come.[8] They must be trained to behave in the synagogue with awe and reverence. Children who run about to and fro, and disturb the prayers, should not be brought to the synagogue.[9]

3) Even one who is not the father of the child is forbidden[10] to give him[11]

---

6. Some say that it is not the child who is obligated, but, rather, it is the father who has the obligation to train him. *Rashi, Meseches Berachos* 48a. However, *Tosafos* disagrees and maintains that the child, too, is obligated to keep the *mitzvos.*

7. If he does not have this much understanding, you do not have to stop him from acts that violate those *mitzvos.* (*Mishna Berurah* 343:2)

8. *Ramah* (Orach Chaim) 124:7.

9. *Magain Avraham* 124:11.

10. See *Mishna Berurah* 343:4.

11. Placing it in front of them is like feeding them according to *Magein Avraham* 616:2. *Zichron Yosef,* Responsa disagrees. On a fast day, it is best that children take their own food.

לְאָכְלוֹ אוֹ לְצַוּוֹתוֹ שֶׁיַּעֲשֶׂה אֵיזֶה אִסּוּר. וּלְרֹב הַפּוֹסְקִים, אֲפִלּוּ דָּבָר הָאָסוּר רַק מִדְּרַבָּנָן, אָסוּר לִתֵּן לוֹ לֶאֱכוֹל אוֹ לְצַוּוֹתוֹ שֶׁיַּעֲשֶׂה. וְאִם הַתִּינוֹק חוֹלֶה קְצָת וְצָרִיךְ לֶאֱכוֹל דְּבַר אִסּוּר, יֵשׁ לְהַתִּיר לָתֵת לוֹ עַל יְדֵי גוֹי דָּבָר שֶׁאֵינוֹ אָסוּר רַק מִדְּרַבָּנָן.

ד) דָּבָר שֶׁאֵין בּוֹ אִסּוּר מִצַּד עַצְמוֹ אֶלָּא שֶׁהַיּוֹם גּוֹרֵם, אֵין בּוֹ מִצְוַת חִנּוּךְ. וּלְפִיכָךְ מֻתָּר לִתֵּן לְתִינוֹק לֶאֱכוֹל קֹדֶם קִדּוּשׁ, אַף־עַל־גַּב דְּחַיָּב לְחַנְּכוֹ בְּקִדּוּשׁ. אֲבָל אָסוּר לִתֵּן לוֹ לֶאֱכֹל חוּץ לַסֻּכָּה. דְּדַוְקָא בְּקִדּוּשׁ שֶׁהוּא כְּמוֹ אִסּוּר לָאו, שֶׁאָסוּר לֶאֱכֹל קֹדֶם קִדּוּשׁ, בָּזֶה קִיל. אֲבָל לַעֲבוֹר עַל עֲשֵׂה, אָסוּר לִתֵּן לוֹ.

ה) אָסוּר לִתֵּן לְתִינוֹק, אֲפִלּוּ הוּא פָּחוֹת מִתֵּשַׁע שָׁנִים, שֶׁיּוֹצִיא אֵיזֶה דָּבָר בַּשַּׁבָּת אֲפִלּוּ לְצֹרֶךְ מִצְוָה, כְּגוֹן סִדּוּר וְחֻמָּשׁ לְבֵית־הַכְּנֶסֶת וְכַדּוֹמֶה.

ו) קָטָן שֶׁגָּנַב אֵיזֶה דָּבָר, אִם הוּא בָּעַיִן, מְחַיְּבִין לְהַחֲזִירוֹ. וְאִם אֵינוֹ בָּעַיִן, פָּטוּר מִדִּינֵי אָדָם אַף לְאַחַר שֶׁיִּגְדַּל. אַךְ לָצֵאת יְדֵי שָׁמַיִם, חַיָּב לְשַׁלֵּם כְּשֶׁיִּגְדַּל. וְכֵן אִם עָשָׂה שְׁאָר עֲבֵרוֹת בְּקַטְנוּתוֹ כְּשֶׁהוּא בַּר־הֲבָנָה, טוֹב שֶׁיְּקַבֵּל עָלָיו אֵיזֶה דָּבָר לִתְשׁוּבָה. וְעַל זֶה נֶאֱמַר, גַּם בְּלֹא דַעַת נֶפֶשׁ לֹא טוֹב.

ז) לֹא יְאַיֵּם עַל הַתִּינוֹק שֶׁיַּכֵּהוּ לְאַחַר זְמַן. אֶלָּא אִם רוֹאֵהוּ עוֹשֶׂה אֵיזֶה מַעֲשֶׂה יַכֵּהוּ מִיָּד אוֹ יִשְׁתֹּק לְגַמְרֵי. מַעֲשֶׂה בְּתִינוֹק שֶׁבָּרַח מִבֵּית־הַסֵּפֶר, וְהִפְחִידוֹ אָבִיו שֶׁיַּכֵּהוּ, הָלַךְ הַתִּינוֹק וְהֵמִית אֶת עַצְמוֹ. אָמְרוּ רַבּוֹתֵינוּ זִכְרוֹנָם לִבְרָכָה, יֵצֶר, תִּינוֹק, וְאִשָּׁה, תְּהֵא שְׂמֹאל דּוֹחָה וְיָמִין מְקָרֶבֶת. לֹא יַעֲשֶׂה מוֹרָא לְתִינוֹק בְּדָבָר טָמֵא.

ח) מִדִּינָא, מֻתָּר לְתִינוֹק יִשְׂרָאֵל. לִינֹק מִגּוֹיָה. מִכָּל מָקוֹם אִם אֶפְשָׁר עַל יְדֵי יִשְׂרְאֵלִית, לֹא יַנִּיחוּהוּ לִינֹק מִגּוֹיָה, מִשּׁוּם דִּמְטַמְטֵם אֶת הַלֵּב וּמוֹלִיד מֶזֶג רָע. וְכֵן מֵינֶקֶת יִשְׂרְאֵלִית שֶׁצְּרִיכָה לֶאֱכֹל מַאַכְלֵי אִסּוּר לִרְפוּאָה, אִם אֶפְשָׁר, לֹא תָּנִיק בַּיָּמִים הָהֵם אֶת הַתִּינוֹק.

---

12. However, if it is for the child's own benefit, as for example if he will use the *Siddur* or *Chumash* to read or pray with, it is permitted (Biyur Halachah 243) as long as it is not a public domain by Torah standards.

forbidden food to eat, or to tell him to do something that is forbidden. According to most *poskim,* it is forbidden to give him food that is Rabbinically prohibited, or to command him to do something that is Rabbinically prohibited. If the child is somewhat ill and must eat forbidden food, he may be fed by a non-Jew with food which was forbidden only by Rabbinic Law.

4) Something which is not forbidden in and of itself, but is forbidden because of the special day, is not included in the mitzvoh of training. Therefore, it is permitted to give a child food, to eat before *kiddush* even though it is your duty, to train him to make *kiddush,* but it is forbidden to give him food [to eat] outside the *sukkah.* Only (in cases like) not eating before *kiddush,* which is similar to a negative commandment, since it is forbidden to eat before *kiddush,* is the law more lenient; but where a violation of a positive command is involved, it is forbidden to give it to him.

5) It is forbidden to tell a child even if he is under the age of nine, to carry anything out on Shabbos, even for the purpose of doing a mitzvah, like taking a Siddur (prayer book) or a Chumash (Bible) to the synagogue, or similar things.[12]

6) If a child steals something, if it is still intact, you are obligated to return it; but if it is no longer intact, he is legally exempt from making restitution even after he becomes of age. But in order to fulfill his obligation before the judgement in Heaven, he must make restitution when he becomes of age. Similarly, if he committed other sins in his youth [before Bar Mitzvah], it is advisable that he accept upon himself some sort of repentance when he reaches an age of understanding. Concerning this it is said, "For the soul to be without knowledge is not good."[13]

7) You should not threaten a child that you will hit him after a while, but if you see him misbehave, either hit him at once or ignore it. A story is told about a child who ran away from school, and his father threatened to hit him.[14] The child committed suicide. Our Rabbis, of blessed memory, said,[14] In dealing with your impulse, your child or your wife; your left hand should repel [reject] and your right hand should bring near [accept]. You should not threaten a child with an unclean object.[15]

8) *Halachically,* it is permitted to allow a Jewish child to be nursed by a gentile woman. Nevertheless, if it is possible to have him nurse from a Jewess, you should not let him nurse from a gentile, for it dulls the spiritual sensitivities of the heart, and causes bad temperament. Also, a Jewish woman who is nursing and must eat forbidden foods as a remedy for illness, if possible, she should not nurse the child on those days.

---

13. *Proverbs* 19:2.
14. *Maseches Semachos* Chapter 2.
15. See *Kitzur Shulchan Aruch* 33:14.

ט) כָּל אָב, מְחֻיָּב לְלַמֵּד אֶת בְּנוֹ תּוֹרָה, שֶׁנֶּאֱמַר, וְלִמַּדְתֶּם אֹתָם אֶת־בְּנֵיכֶם לְדַבֵּר בָּם. וּכְשֵׁם שֶׁמִּצְוָה לְלַמֵּד אֶת בְּנוֹ, כָּךְ מִצְוָה לְלַמֵּד אֶת בֶּן בְּנוֹ, שֶׁנֶּאֱמַר, וְהוֹדַעְתָּם לְבָנֶיךָ וְלִבְנֵי בָנֶיךָ.

י) מִיָּד כְּשֶׁהַתִּינוֹק מַתְחִיל לְדַבֵּר, יְלַמְּדוֹ הַפָּסוּק תּוֹרָה צִוָּה לָנוּ מֹשֶׁה מוֹרָשָׁה וְגוֹ׳, וְכֵן פָּסוּק שְׁמַע יִשְׂרָאֵל וְגוֹ׳, (רַק יִזָּהֵר מְאֹד שֶׁיְּהֵא הַתִּינוֹק נָקִי בְּשָׁעָה שֶׁהוּא מְלַמֵּד אוֹתוֹ.) וְכֵן מְלַמְּדוֹ מְעַט מְעַט אֵיזֶה פְסוּקִים עַד שֶׁיַּגִּיעַ בְּכֹחוֹ לָלֶכֶת אֶל בֵּית־הַסֵּפֶר, וְאָז יַשְׂכִּיר לוֹ מְלַמֵּד. וִידַקְדֵּק לִבְחוֹר מְלַמֵּד שֶׁהוּא יְרֵא־שָׁמַיִם, לְמַעַן יַרְגִּיל אֶת הַתִּינוֹק מִנְּעוּרָיו בְּיִרְאַת־שָׁמַיִם. וּכְשֶׁהִגִּיעַ הַתִּינוֹק לִלְמֹד מִקְרָא, נוֹהֲגִין לְהַתְחִיל עִמּוֹ פָּרָשַׁת וַיִּקְרָא, שֶׁהִיא פָּרָשַׁת הַקָּרְבָּנוֹת, דְּאָמְרוּ רַבּוֹתֵינוּ זִכְרוֹנָם לִבְרָכָה, יָבֹאוּ טְהוֹרִים (דְּהַיְנוּ תִּינוֹקוֹת שֶׁל בֵּית רַבָּן) וְיַעַסְקוּ בִּטְהוֹרִים.

יא) הַמְלַמֵּד, צָרִיךְ לֵישֵׁב וּלְלַמֵּד אֶת הַתִּינוֹקוֹת כָּל הַיּוֹם וּקְצָת מִן הַלַּיְלָה, כְּדֵי לְחַנְּכָם לִלְמֹד בַּיּוֹם וּבַלַּיְלָה. וְלֹא יְבַטְּלוּ הַתִּינוֹקוֹת כְּלָל, חוּץ מֵעֶרֶב שַׁבָּת וְעֶרֶב יוֹם־טוֹב בְּסוֹף הַיּוֹם. אֵין מְבַטְּלִין אֶת הַתִּינוֹקוֹת אֲפִלּוּ לְבִנְיַן בֵּית הַמִּקְדָּשׁ.

יב) מְלַמֵּד תִּינוֹקוֹת שֶׁמַּנִּיחַ אֶת הַתִּינוֹקוֹת וְיוֹצֵא, אוֹ שֶׁעוֹשֶׂה מְלָאכָה אַחֶרֶת עִמָּהֶם, אוֹ שֶׁמִּתְרַשֵּׁל בְּתַלְמוּדוֹ, הֲרֵי זֶה בִּכְלַל אָרוּר עוֹשֶׂה מְלֶאכֶת ה׳ רְמִיָּה. לְפִיכָךְ אֵין לְהוֹשִׁיב מְלַמֵּד אֶלָּא בַּעַל יִרְאָה, מָהִיר לִקְרֹא וּלְדַקְדֵּק. וְאֵין לַמְלַמֵּד לִהְיוֹת נֵעוֹר בַּלַּיְלָה יוֹתֵר מִדַּי, שֶׁלֹּא יִהְיֶה עָצֵל בַּיּוֹם לְלַמֵּד. וְכֵן לֹא יִתְעַנֶּה אוֹ יַעֲצֹר אֶת עַצְמוֹ מִמַּאֲכָל וּמִשְׁתֶּה אוֹ יֹאכַל יוֹתֵר מִדַּי, כִּי כָּל אֵלּוּ הַדְּבָרִים, גּוֹרְמִים שֶׁלֹּא יוּכַל לְלַמֵּד הֵיטֵב. וְכָל הַמְשַׁנֶּה, יָדוֹ עַל הַתַּחְתּוֹנָה וּמְסַלְּקִין לֵהּ.

יג) לֹא יַכֶּה אוֹתָם מַכַּת אוֹיֵב, מוּסָר אַכְזָרִי, לֹא בְשׁוֹטִים וְלֹא בְמַקֵּל, אֶלָּא בִּרְצוּעָה קְטַנָּה.

יד) אֵין מְלַמְּדִין אֶת הַתִּינוֹקוֹת בַּשַּׁבָּת דָּבָר חָדָשׁ מַה שֶּׁלֹּא לָמְדוּ עֲדַיִן, מִשּׁוּם טֹרַח שַׁבָּת. אֲבָל מַה שֶּׁקָּרְאוּ פַּעַם אַחַת, שׁוֹנִים אוֹתוֹ לָהֶם בַּשַּׁבָּת.

16. *Deuteronomy* 11:19.
17. *Deuteronomy* 4:9.

9) Every father is obligated to teach his son Torah, as it is said, "And you shall teach them to your children to speak of them."[16] Just as it is a mitzvah to teach your son, so too it is a mitzvah to teach your son's son, as it is said,[17] "And you shall make them known to your sons and to your son's son.[18]

10) As soon as the child begins to talk, you should teach him (the verse), "The Torah that Moses has commanded us is a heritage for the community of Jacob,"[19] and, also the verse of *Shema Yisrael*[20] etc. (However you must be very careful that the child is clean when you are teaching him.) Likewise you should teach him other verses little by little, until he is strong enough to attend school, at which time you should engage a teacher for him. You should be careful to choose a teacher who is God-fearing, in order that he accustom the child from his youth to be God-fearing. When the child has advanced to the study of the Scriptures, it is customary to begin teaching him the *Sidrah* of *Vayikra,* which is the *Sidrah* containing the laws of sacrificial offerings, for our Sages of blessed memory said, Let those who are pure (the children) come and engage in the study of purity.[21]

11) The teacher must teach the children the entire day and part of the evening, in order to train them to study Torah by day and by night. He must not interrupt the childrens' learning except on *erev* Shabbos and on *erev* Yom Tov at the end of the day. The children are not to be interrupted from their learning even for the purpose of building the Beis HaMikdosh

12) A teacher who leaves the children to themselves and goes out, or does some other work with them, or who teaches carelessly, is included in, "Cursed be he who does the work of God with a slack hand."[22] Therefore, you should appoint as a teacher, only a person who is God-fearing, fluent in his reading as well as exacting. A teacher should not stay awake at night more than necessary, so that he will not be lazy while teaching during the day. He should also not fast or eat and drink too sparingly. Nor should he eat and drink excessively, for all these things prevent him from teaching efficiently. Any teacher who deviates from these rules, forfeits his rights and should be dismissed.

13) A teacher should not strike his pupils as one strikes an enemy, [or with] malice and cruelty, nor with a whip or a stick, but with a light strap.

14) You should not teach the children anything new on Shabbos, i. e. something they have never learned before, because it is too burdensome to do on Shabbos. But something they once read, should be reviewed with them on Shabbos.

---

18. *Maseches Kidushin* 69b.
19. *Deuteronomy* 33:4.
20. *Deuteronomy* 6:4.
21. *Midrash* (*Vayikra* 6:3).
22. *Jeremiah* 48:10.

טו) קָטָן שֶׁמָּצָא מְצִיאָה, וּמִכָּל־שֶׁכֵּן אִם נָתַן לוֹ אַחֵר אֵיזֶה דָבָר בְּמַתָּנָה, אָסוּר לְגָזְלוֹ מִמֶּנּוּ.

טז) אֵין מוֹסְרִין תִּינוֹק יִשְׂרָאֵל לַגּוֹי לְלַמְּדוֹ סֵפֶר אוֹ לְלַמְּדוֹ אֻמָּנוּת, וּמִכָּל־שֶׁכֵּן דְּאָסוּר לְמָסְרוֹ לְאֶפִּיקוֹרוֹס יִשְׂרָאֵל, דְּגָרַע טְפֵי וְאִכָּא לְמֵיחַשׁ דִּלְמָא מַמְשִׁיךְ אֲבַתְרֵהּ.

סִימָן קסו
שֶׁלֹּא לְנַחֵשׁ לְעוֹנֵן וּלְכַשֵּׁף

א) כְּתִיב, לֹא תְנַחֲשׁוּ וְלֹא תְעוֹנֵנוּ. כֵּיצַד הוּא מְנַחֵשׁ. הָאוֹמֵר, הוֹאִיל וְנָפְלָה פִּתִּי מִפִּי, אוֹ נָפַל מַקְלִי מִיָּדִי אוֹ בְּנִי קָרָא לִי מֵאֲחוֹרַי, עוֹרֵב קָרָא לִי, צְבִי הִפְסִיקַנִי בַּדֶּרֶךְ, נָחָשׁ מִימִינִי, שׁוּעָל מִשְּׂמֹאלִי, לֹא אֵלֵךְ בַּדֶּרֶךְ הַזֶּה כִּי לֹא אַצְלִיחַ; וְכֵן אֵלּוּ שֶׁשּׁוֹמְעִים צִפְצוּף הָעוֹף וְאוֹמְרִים, יִהְיֶה כָּךְ אוֹ לֹא יִהְיֶה כָּךְ, טוֹב לַעֲשׂוֹת דָּבָר זֶה, וְרַע לַעֲשׂוֹת דָּבָר זֶה; וְכֵן מִי שֶׁמְּבַקְשִׁין מִמֶּנּוּ מָעוֹת, וְאוֹמֵר, בְּבַקָּשָׁה מִמְּךָ הַנִּיחֵנִי, עַתָּה שַׁחֲרִית הִיא, וְלֹא אַתְחִיל תְּחִלַּת הַיּוֹם בְּפֵרָעוֹן, אוֹ מוֹצָאֵי־שַׁבָּת הוּא, אוֹ רֹאשׁ־חֹדֶשׁ הוּא; וְכֵן אֵלּוּ שֶׁאוֹמְרִים צְרִיכִין לִשְׁחוֹט תַּרְנְגוֹל זֶה, מִפְּנֵי שֶׁקָּרָא עַרְבִית, אוֹ תַּרְנְגֹלֶת זֹאת, מִפְּנֵי שֶׁקָּרְאָה כְּמוֹ תַרְנְגוֹל, וְכֵן כָּל כַּיּוֹצֵא בִּדְבָרִים אֵלּוּ — הַכֹּל אָסוּר. וְהָעוֹשֶׂה דָבָר מִדְּבָרִים אֵלּוּ, עוֹבֵר בְּלָאו. יֵשׁ אוֹמְרִים, דְּאִם אֵינוֹ אוֹמֵר הַטַּעַם לָמָּה הוּא מְצַוֶּה לִשְׁחוֹט אֶת הַתַּרְנְגֹלֶת אוֹ אֶת הַתַּרְנְגוֹל, אֶלָּא אוֹמֵר סְתָם, שַׁחֲטוּ תַּרְנְגֹלֶת זֹאת אוֹ תַּרְנְגוֹל זֶה, מֻתָּר לְשָׁחֲטָם. וְכֵן הוּא הַמִּנְהָג.

ב) בַּיִת, תִּינוֹק, וְאִשָּׁה, אַף־עַל־פִּי שֶׁאֵין נִחוּשׁ, יֵשׁ סִימָן. פֵּרוּשׁ, שֶׁאִם בָּנָה בַיִת, אוֹ נוֹלַד לוֹ תִינוֹק, אוֹ נָשָׂא אִשָּׁה, אִם הִצְלִיחַ אַחַר כָּךְ שָׁלֹשׁ פְּעָמִים אוֹ לֹא, הוּא סִימָן לוֹ לְהַבָּא, וְיָכוֹל לוֹמַר, בַּיִת זֶה מַצְלִיחַ לִי וְכוּ׳. וְכֵן מֻתָּר לִשְׁאֹל לְתִינוֹק, אֵיזֶה פָּסוּק לָמַד, וְלִסְמֹךְ עָלָיו לַעֲשׂוֹת מַעֲשֶׂה, דְּחָשִׁיב קְצָת כְּמוֹ נְבוּאָה. יֵשׁ אוֹמְרִים, דְּמֻתָּר לַעֲשׂוֹת לוֹ סִימָן בְּדָבָר שֶׁיָּבוֹא לֶעָתִיד, כְּמוֹ שֶׁעָשָׂה אֱלִיעֶזֶר עֶבֶד אַבְרָהָם אוֹ יְהוֹנָתָן בֶּן שָׁאוּל, וְיֵשׁ אוֹסְרִין. וְהַהוֹלֵךְ בְּתֹם וּבוֹטֵחַ בַּה׳, חֶסֶד יְסוֹבְבֶנּוּ.

---

1. *Leviticus* 19:26.
2. *Rashi, Ramah* 179:4. However, *Rambam* and *Smag* maintain that you can only say these are signs, but you may not base any future plans and actions on them.

15) If a minor finds something, and certainly if someone gave him something as a gift, it is forbidden to rob him of it.

16) You may not give a Jewish child to a non-Jew to instruct him in reading and writing or to teach him a trade, and needless to say, that it is forbidden to give him to a Jewish heretic, which is much worse (than giving him to a non-Jew), for there is concern the child may follow in his footsteps.

Chapter 166

Prohibition of Omens and Auspicious Times

1) It is written, "You must not practice superstition nor attribute significance to [auspicious] times."[1] What constitutes superstition? He who says, "Since the bread fell from my mouth;" or "The cane fell from my hand;" or "My son called me from behind;" "A raven croaked at me;" "A deer crossed my path;" "A snake passed on my right;" "A fox passed on my left, therefore, I will not go on this journey because I will not be successful." Similarly, those who on hearing the chirping of a bird, say: "May it mean this and not that;" "(Now I know) it is good to do this, or it is bad to do this;" Similarly, when asked to repay a loan, he says: "Please leave me alone for now it is morning, and I do not want to start the day by making a payment;" or "It is the close of the Shabbos;" or "It is the New Moon." Similarly those who say, "We must slaughter this rooster because he crowed in the evening;" or "This hen (should be slaughtered) because she crowed like a rooster." Everything similar to these things, are forbidden. Anyone who practices any of these things, violates a negative command. Some *poskim* say that if you do not state the reason why you ordered the slaughter of the hen or the rooster, but simply say, "Slaughter this hen" or "This rooster," it is permissible to slaughter them, and such is the prevailing custom.

2) Although no superstition may be practiced through a house, a child, and a woman, they may be regarded as omens. For example, if someone built a house, or had a child born to him, or taken a wife, and afterwards he was successful on three occasions, or was unsuccessful, he may regard this as an omen for the future,[2] and say: "This house brings me good luck" etc. It is also permitted to inquire of a child about the verse he studied (that day), and rely on it to do a certain thing, for it is regarded somewhat like a prophecy. Some *Poskim*[3] say it is permitted to designate a sign for the future (and to act accordingly): as Eliezer the servant of Abraham,[4] or Yonason the son of Saul; while other *Poskim* forbid it.[5] However, he who walks in integrity; "And trusts in God, kindness surrounds him."[6]

---

3. *Tur* 179.
4. Who used a sign to determine who would be the right girl for Yitzchok to marry.
5. *Rambam, Smag* etc. Eliezer and Yonason were permitted to rely on signs, for they were signs based on logic and reason. (*Yeraim, Prisha* etc.)
6. *Psalms* 32:10.

ג) אֵיזֶהוּ מְעוֹנֵן. זֶה שֶׁנּוֹתֵן עִתִּים, שֶׁאוֹמֵר בְּאִצְטַגְנִינוּת, יוֹם פְּלוֹנִי טוֹב וְיוֹם פְּלוֹנִי רָע, יוֹם פְּלוֹנִי רָאוּי לַעֲשׂוֹת בּוֹ מְלָאכָה פְלוֹנִית, שָׁנָה פְלוֹנִית אוֹ חֹדֶשׁ פְּלוֹנִי רַע לְדָבָר פְּלוֹנִי. וּמַה שֶּׁנּוֹהֲגִין שֶׁאֵין נוֹשְׂאִין נָשִׁים אֶלָּא בְּמִלּוּי הַלְּבָנָה, אֵין זֶה בִּכְלַל מְנַחֵשׁ וּמְעוֹנֵן, שֶׁאֵין עוֹשִׂין זֹאת אֶלָּא לְסִימָן טוֹב, כְּדֶרֶךְ שֶׁמּוֹשְׁחִין אֶת הַמְּלָכִים עַל הַמַּעְיָן לְסִימָן שֶׁתִּמָּשֵׁךְ מַלְכוּתָם, כֵּן עוֹשִׂין לְסִימָן טוֹב כְּמוֹ שֶׁהַלְּבָנָה הוֹלֶכֶת וּמִתְמַלֵּאת. וּמִכָּל מָקוֹם אֵין לְעַכֵּב אֶת הַנִּשּׂוּאִין בִּשְׁבִיל זֶה, וּמִכָּל־שֶׁכֵּן שֶׁאֵין לַעֲשׂוֹת חֻפַּת נִדָּה בַּעֲבוּר זֶה. וְכֵן נוֹהֲגִין לְהַתְחִיל לִלְמֹד בְּרֹאשׁ־חֹדֶשׁ. וּמַה שֶּׁנּוֹהֲגִין שֶׁאֵין מַתְחִילִין בְּשֵׁנִי וּבִרְבִיעִי, יֵשׁ מַתִּירִין גַּם כֵּן.

ד) עוֹד אָמְרוּ רַבּוֹתֵינוּ זִכְרוֹנָם לִבְרָכָה, אֵיזֶהוּ מְעוֹנֵן, זֶה הָאוֹחֵז אֶת הָעֵינָיִם. פֵּרוּשׁ, שֶׁהוּא כְּאִלּוּ אוֹחֵז עֵינֵי בְנֵי אָדָם וְסוֹגְרָן, שֶׁהוּא מַטְעֶה אוֹתָן, שֶׁנִּדְמֶה לָהֶם כְּאִלּוּ עוֹשֶׂה דְבָרִים נִפְלָאִים חוּץ מִדֶּרֶךְ הַטֶּבַע, וּבֶאֱמֶת אֵינוֹ עוֹשֶׂה כְלוּם, אֶלָּא בְּקַלּוּת יָדָיו וּבְתַחְבּוּלוֹת הוּא מַטְעֶה אוֹתָן. וְהַבַּדְחָנִין שֶׁעוֹשִׂין כְּמַעֲשִׂים אֵלּוּ בַּחֲתֻנּוֹת, עוֹבְרִים בְּלָאו. וְהַמְּצַוֶּה לַעֲשׂוֹתָן, עוֹבֵר עַל לִפְנֵי עִוֵּר. וְלָכֵן מִי שֶׁיֵּשׁ בְּיָדוֹ לִמְחוֹת, מְחֻיָּב לִמְחוֹת, וְכָל־שֶׁכֵּן שֶׁאָסוּר לְהִסְתַּכֵּל וְלִרְאוֹתָן. אֲבָל אִם נָכְרִי עוֹשֶׂה כֵּן, מֻתָּר לִרְאוֹת.

ה) אָסוּר לִדְרוֹשׁ בִּמְכַשְּׁפִים אֶלָּא בִּמְקוֹם סַכָּנַת נְפָשׁוֹת, אוֹ אִם בָּא לוֹ אֵיזֶה חֳלִי עַל יְדֵי כִשּׁוּף אוֹ מִקְרֶה וְרוּחַ רָעָה, מֻתָּר לְהִתְרַפְּאוֹת עַל יְדֵי מְכַשֵּׁף גּוֹי.

סִימָן קסז
הִלְכוֹת עֲבוֹדָה־זָרָה

א) עֲבוֹדָה־זָרָה, אֲסוּרָה בַהֲנָאָה, הִיא וְתַשְׁמִישֶׁהָ וְנוֹיָהּ וְתִקְרָבְתָּהּ. וְאִם נִתְעָרֵב מִדְּבָרִים אֵלּוּ אֲפִלּוּ אֶחָד בְּאֶלֶף שֶׁל הֶתֵּר, אוֹסֵר אֶת כָּל הַתַּעֲרוֹבוֹת בַּהֲנָאָה. אֵיזֶהוּ תַשְׁמִישֶׁהָ. הַכֵּלִים שֶׁהַכֹּהֵן מַקְטִיר בָּהֶם לְפָנֶיהָ, כְּגוֹן הַמַּחְתָּה וְהַגְּבִיעִים, וְכֵן הַבַּיִת שֶׁמְּיַחֲדִים לָהּ, וְהַבָּסִיס שֶׁמַּעֲמִידִין אוֹתָהּ עָלָיו, וְכֵן כְּלֵי הַשִּׁיר שֶׁמְּזַמְּרִים בָּהֶם לְפָנֶיהָ וְכַדּוֹמֶה. וְאֵיזֶהוּ נוֹיָהּ. כְּגוֹן הַנֵּרוֹת שֶׁמַּדְלִיקִין לְפָנֶיהָ, וְהַמַּלְבּוּשִׁים שֶׁמַּלְבִּישִׁים אוֹתָהּ, אוֹ שֶׁשָּׁטַח

3) What is meant by "auspicious times?" One who believes in astrology and thus says, "This day is good and this day is bad;" or this day is a good day to do this work; or this year or this month is bad for such and such a thing. Regarding our custom to hold marriages only on the days when the moon, progresses to its fullness, this is not considered superstition or auspicious, for this is done only as a favorable sign, as the coronation of Kings which were held at springs to symbolize the permanency of his rule. Similarly, it is a good sign to make a wedding on a day when the moon (progresses) to its fullness. Nevertheless it is not proper to postpone a wedding on this account, and needless to say, you should certainly not make the wedding when the bride is menstrually unclean, on the account of this custom. It is also customary to begin to study on the New Moon. The custom of not starting anything on Monday or Wednesday, is permissible according to some authorities.[7]

4) Our Rabbis, of blessed memory, also said, "What is meant by *meonein?* It refers to one who deceives the eyes. [a magician] In other words, it is as though he holds peoples eyes and closes them, for he deceives them. It seems to them as though he is performing wondrous, supernatural feats, while in reality he is doing nothing, but with slight of hand and cunning, he deceives them. The entertainers who perform these things at weddings, are violating a negative command. He who engages them, is guilty of transgressing (the negative command), "Before the blind you shall not place a stumbling block."[8] Therefore whoever is able to prevent this, is obligated to prevent it. And it is certainly forbidden to view these things but if a non-Jew performs these things, it is permitted to view it.

5) It is forbidden to consult sorcerers unless there is danger to human life,[9] or if someone fell ill due to witchcraft, or some mishap or evil spirit, then he is permitted to be cured by a non-Jewish sorcerer.

Chapter 167

Laws Concerning Idolatry

1) It is forbidden to benefit from idols, from its vestments, ornaments and sacrifices. If any of these things are mingled with even one thousand legitimate items, it is forbidden to derive benefit from the entire lot. What are considered its vestments? The vessels that the priest uses for sacrificial purposes, such as pans and goblets, also the house (church) that is used exclusively for its worship, the base upon which the idol stands, also, the musical instruments that are used to play music before it. What are considered its ornaments? The candles that are lit before

7. *Zohar* (*Raiya Mehemna*) 273A. *Shulchan Aruch Yonah Deiah* 179:2. The *Zohar* mentions not starting on Monday and not ending on Wednesday.

8. Leviticus 19:14.

9. Loss of limb is not a reason to permit this. (*Shach* 179— *Maharshal*)

לְפָנֶיהָ בְּגָדִים וְכֵלִים נָאִים לְנוֹי וְכֵן הָאִילָנוֹת שֶׁרְגִילִין לִטַּע לִפְנֵי עֲבוֹדָה זָרָה לִהְיוֹת לָהּ לְנוֹי, הֲוָיִן נוֹיֶיהָ וַאֲסוּרִין בַּהֲנָאָה וְלָכֵן אָסוּר לֵישֵׁב בְּצִלָּן. וְאֵיזוֹהִי תִקְרָבְתָּהּ, כְּגוֹן מִינֵי מַאֲכָל שֶׁמַּנִּיחִין לְפָנֶיהָ.

ב) עֲבוֹדָה־זָרָה שֶׁל גּוֹי, וְכֵן תַּשְׁמִישָׁהּ וְנוֹיָהּ, יֵשׁ לָהֶן בִּטּוּל. כְּשֶׁמְּבַטֵּל אוֹתָהּ הַגּוֹי בְּיָדַיִם, שֶׁלֹּא תְהֵא עוֹד עֲבוֹדָה־זָרָה אוֹ תַשְׁמִישׁ אוֹ נוֹי לַעֲבוֹדָה־זָרָה, הֻתְּרוּ. וְשֶׁל יִשְׂרָאֵל מוּמָר, אֵין לָהֶם בִּטּוּל.

ג) נֵרוֹת שֶׁהִדְלִיקוּ לְפָנֶיהָ, וְאַחַר כָּךְ כִּבָּן הַגּוֹי לְצֹרֶךְ עַצְמוֹ וּמְכָרָן לְיִשְׂרָאֵל, מֻתָּרִין, דְּכֵיוָן שֶׁכִּבָּן לְצֹרֶךְ עַצְמוֹ, זֶהוּ בִּטּוּלָן. וּמִכָּל מָקוֹם אֵין לַעֲשׂוֹת מֵהֶן נֵרוֹת שֶׁל מִצְוָה. וְכֵן כָּל דָּבָר שֶׁל עֲבוֹדָה־זָרָה, אַף־עַל־פִּי שֶׁנִּתְבַּטֵּל וּמֻתָּר לְהֶדְיוֹט, אָסוּר לִדְבַר מִצְוָה, מִשּׁוּם דְּמָאִיסֵי לַגָּבוֹהַּ.

ד) הַמַּלְבּוּשִׁים שֶׁלּוֹבְשִׁים הַכֹּהֲנִים כְּשֶׁנִּכְנָסִים לְבֵית עֲבוֹדָה־זָרָה, יֵשׁ אוֹמְרִים, דְּנוֹי שֶׁלָּהֶם הֵן, וְלֹא נוֹי שֶׁל עֲבוֹדָה־זָרָה, וְאֵינָן צְרִיכִין בִּטּוּל. וְיֵשׁ מִי שֶׁמַּצְרִיךְ בִּטּוּל.

ה) צוּרַת שְׁתִי־וָעֵרֶב שֶׁמִּשְׁתַּחֲוִים לָהּ, אֲסוּרָה בְּלֹא בִטּוּל. אֲבָל שְׁתִי־וָעֵרֶב שֶׁתּוֹלִין בַּצַּוָּאר לְזִכָּרוֹן בְּעָלְמָא מֻתָּר.

ו) אָסוּר לַעֲשׂוֹת שׁוּם דָּבָר לְצֹרֶךְ עֲבוֹדָה־זָרָה. וַאֲפִלּוּ חַלּוֹנוֹת לְהַבָּיִת. וְאָסוּר לִמְכֹּר לָהֶם סְפָרִים הַמְיֻחָדִים לַעֲבוֹדָה־זָרָה. [וְכֵן סִפְרֵי תנ"ך הַמֻּעְתָּקִים בְּשִׁנּוּיִים, כְּדֵי לְפַקְּרָם וּלְהַחֲזִיק אֱמוּנָתָם]. וְכֵן לִמְכֹּר לָהֶם דָּבָר לְצֹרֶךְ עֲבוֹדָתָם, אָסוּר אִם לֹא יוּכְלוּ לִקְנוֹת בְּמָקוֹם אַחֵר. וְיֵשׁ אוֹסְרִין אֲפִלּוּ אִם יוּכְלוּ לִקְנוֹת בְּמָקוֹם אַחֵר. וְכָל בַּעַל־נֶפֶשׁ, יַחְמִיר לְעַצְמוֹ.

ז) אָסוּר לְהִסְתַּכֵּל בָּאֱלִיל וּבְנוֹי שֶׁלּוֹ, שֶׁנֶּאֱמַר, אַל־תִּפְנוּ אֶל־הָאֱלִילִים. וּצְרִיכִין לְהִתְרַחֵק מִן הַבַּיִת וּמִכָּל־שֶׁכֵּן מִן הָאֱלִיל עַצְמוֹ אַרְבַּע אַמּוֹת, שֶׁלֹּא לַעֲבֹר שָׁם. וְאָסוּר לִשְׁמֹעַ כְּלֵי הַשִּׁיר אוֹ לְהָרִיחַ בְּרֵיחַ שֶׁלָּהֶם. וְאִם שׁוֹמֵעַ כְּלֵי הַשִּׁיר, יֶאְטֹם אָזְנָיו. וְכֵן אִם בָּא רֵיחַ, יְכַוֵּן שֶׁלֹּא לֵהָנוֹת מִמֶּנּוּ.

1. Its sacrifices cannot be annulled. (*Shulchan Aruch* 139:2)
2. This is only true if they can buy it from a non-Jew, but if they can only buy it from a

it, the garments that are used to clothe it, or those used to spread before it for beauty, and the trees that they are accustomed to plant in front of the idols to beautify them. These are its ornaments and it is forbidden to benefit from them, and it is therefore forbidden to sit in the shade of these trees. What are its sacrifices? The various kinds of food that are placed before it.

2) The idols of a non-Jew, its vestments and ornaments,[1] can be annulled. Thus, if the heathen actually defaces them so that they can no longer be used as idols, or as vestments or ornaments to idols, it is permitted to benefit from them. But for idols of a Jewish heretic, the law of annullment does not apply.

3) It is permitted to benefit from candles that were lit (in front of an idol), and thereafter extinguished by a heathen, to be used for his own benefit, and were subsequently sold to a Jew. Since the heathen extinguished them to use for his own purpose, this act constitutes their annulment. Nevertheless, such candles should not be used for the performance of a *mitzvah.* Similarly, everything that was used for an idol, although it has been annulled, and is permitted for common use, is forbidden to be used for a *mitzvah* because they are abominable to the Almighty.

4) Regarding the clothing that the priests wear when they enter the house of idol worship, some *Poskim* maintain that they are ornaments of the priests and not ornaments of the idols, and therefore do not require annulment; while other *Poskim* require their annullment.

5) A cross to which they bow down, is a forbidden object unless it is annulled, but a cross that is hung around the neck, as a momento is a permitted object [from which profit may be derived].

6) It is forbidden to make anything that is needed for idols; even windows for the house of idol worship. It is forbidden to sell books that are exclusive to idol worship, [or books of Biblical Scriptures, that were copied with alterations designed to make them heretical and to strengthen their beliefs.] Similarly, selling them something that they need for their worship is forbidden, if they cannot purchase them elsewhere.[2] Some *Poskim* forbid this even when they are able to purchase the same thing elsewhere, and a righteous person, should be strict regarding this.[3]

7) It is forbidden to gaze at an idol or at its ornaments, as it is said, "Do not turn to idols."[4] You must keep a distance of four *amohs* from a house of idolatry, and certainly from the idol itself so as not to pass by them. It is forbidden to listen to their musical instruments, or to smell their incense. If you hear their musical instruments, you should plug your ears, and if the aroma of their incense comes to you, have in mind not to derive pleasure from it.

Jew, you may not sell it to them. Also you may not sell to them for less money than the competition.

3. *Ramah* 151:1.

4. *Leviticus* 19:4.

ח) הָרוֹאֶה בָּתֵּי עֲבוֹדָה־זָרָה בְּיִשּׁוּבָן, אוֹמֵר, בֵּית גֵּאִים יִסַּח ה'. בְּחֻרְבָּנָן, אוֹמֵר, אֵל נְקָמוֹת ה', אֵל נְקָמוֹת הוֹפִיעַ.

ט) יָשַׁב לוֹ קוֹץ בְּרַגְלוֹ, אוֹ נִתְפַּזְּרוּ לוֹ מָעוֹת בִּפְנֵי עֲבוֹדָה־זָרָה, לֹא יָשֹׁחַ לְהָסִיר אֶת הַקּוֹץ אוֹ לִטּוֹל אֶת הַמָּעוֹת, מִפְּנֵי שֶׁנִּרְאֶה כְּמִשְׁתַּחֲוֶה לָהּ. וַאֲפִלּוּ אֵין אָדָם רוֹאֶה, מִכָּל מָקוֹם אָסוּר, אֶלָּא יֵשֵׁב אוֹ יַפְנֶה אֲחוֹרָיו אוֹ צִדּוֹ לְצַד הָעֲבוֹדָה־הַזָּרָה, וְאַחַר כָּךְ יִטּוֹל.

י) יֵשׁ מִי שֶׁאוֹמֵר, שֶׁאָסוּר לְהַלְווֹת לְצֹרֶךְ בִּנְיַן עֲבוֹדָה־זָרָה אוֹ לְתַכְשִׁיטֶיהָ אוֹ לִמְשַׁמְּשֶׁיהָ, וְכָל־שֶׁכֵּן דְּאָסוּר לִמְכֹּר לָהֶם תַּשְׁמִישִׁים. וְהַנִּמְנָע, מַצְלִיחַ. וְאֵין לִכְרֹךְ סִפְרֵי עֲבוֹדָה־זָרָה, חוּץ מִסִּפְרֵי הַדַּיָּנִים וְהַסּוֹפְרִים. וְאִם חוֹשֵׁשׁ מִשּׁוּם אֵיבָה, עַל־כָּל־פָּנִים כָּל מַה שֶּׁיָּכוֹל לְהִשָּׁמֵט, יִשָּׁמֵט.

יא) מָקוֹם שֶׁמִּתְקַבְּצִים גּוֹיִם וְאוֹמְרִים שֶׁשָּׁם מוֹחֲלִים לָהֶם עֲוֹנוֹתֵיהֶם, אָסוּר לָשֵׂאת וְלָתֵת שָׁם עִמָּהֶם.

יב) אָסוּר לְהַזְכִּיר שֵׁם עֲבוֹדָה־זָרָה, בֵּין לְצֹרֶךְ, כְּגוֹן לוֹמַר לַחֲבֵרוֹ, הַמְתֵּן לִי בְּצַד עֲבוֹדָה־זָרָה פְּלוֹנִית בֵּין שֶׁלֹּא לְצֹרֶךְ, שֶׁנֶּאֱמַר, וְשֵׁם אֱלֹהִים אֲחֵרִים לֹא תַזְכִּירוּ. וְאָסוּר לִגְרֹם לַגּוֹי, שֶׁיַּזְכִּיר שֵׁם עֲבוֹדָה־זָרָה, שֶׁנֶּאֱמַר, לֹא יִשָּׁמַע עַל פִּיךָ, לֹא יִשָּׁמַע בִּגְרָמָא שֶׁלָּךְ. וְאִם נִתְחַיֵּב לוֹ הַגּוֹי שְׁבוּעָה, יֵשׁ מְקִלִּין לְהַנִּיחַ לוֹ לִשָּׁבַע. שֵׁם הַחַגִּים שֶׁלָּהֶם שֶׁהֵם כִּשְׁמוֹת בְּנֵי־אָדָם, אֵין חֲשָׁשׁ לְהַזְכִּירָם וְהוּא, שֶׁלֹּא יִקְרָאֵם כְּמוֹ שֶׁהַגּוֹיִם מַזְכִּירִים אוֹתָם בִּלְשׁוֹן חֲשִׁיבוּת.

יג) כָּל לֵיצְנוּתָא אֲסִירָא, חוּץ מִלֵּיצְנוּתָא דַּעֲבוֹדָה־זָרָה דִּשְׁרְיָא.

יד) אָסוּר לִתֵּן מַתְּנַת חִנָּם לְגוֹי שֶׁאֵינוֹ מַכִּירוֹ, וְיֵשׁ אוֹסְרִין אֲפִלּוּ אִם יוּכְלוּ לִקְנוֹת בְּמָקוֹם אַחֵר. וְכָל בַּעַל־נֶפֶשׁ, אֲבָל אִם הוּא מַכִּירוֹ, לֹא

---

5. *Rashi* explains that this refers to places where idol worshippers live in peace and prosperity. The *Rif* explains this to mean a place of idol worship.

6. *Proverbs* 15:25.

7. *Psalms* 94:1.

8. If it is a matter of life or death, you may do these things, since you are not actually bowing to the idol. *Ramah* 150:3— *Ran*. However, the *Gra—Rashba* disagree.

9. *Taz* 150:4. *Chochmas Adam* 87:5 says this might be permitted according to the *Shach* 148:13 who says that nowadays it is unusual for them to go and thank their idols.

8) If you see houses of idolatry in a settled state[5] you should say: "God will uproot the house of the haughty."[6] (If you see them) in a state of destruction, you should say: "Almighty of vengeance, God, Almighty of vengeance, reveal Yourself."[7]

9) If a splinter has lodged in your foot, or if your coins were scattered, in front of an idol, you must not bend down to remove the splinter, or to gather the coins, because it would appear as though you are bowing to the idol. Even if there is no one to witness it, it is nevertheless forbidden. You should rather sit down, or turn your back, or your side to the idol and then take whatever you need.[8]

10) There is an authority who says that it is forbidden to lend money for the purpose of building a house of idolatry, or for their ornaments or for their staff. And you most certainly are forbidden to sell them ornaments. He who refrains from doing these things will prosper. You should not bind books dealing with idolatry; except for their law books and literature. [Even] if you fear this will incur their hatred, nevertheless, whatever you can do to evade doing so, you must evade it.

11) In a place where Gentiles assemble, and say that there they are forgiven their iniquities, it is forbidden to do business with them there.[9]

12) It is forbidden to mention the name of an idol, whether for some purpose, like saying to your friend: "Wait for me near such and such idol," or without a purpose, as it is said, "And the name of other gods you shall not mention."[10] It is forbidden to cause a Gentile to mention the name of an idol, as it is said, "It shall not be heard by your mouth,"[11] that is, it should not be heard because of you. However, if a Gentile is obligated to you to take an oath (as in a law suit), some Poskim are lenient and permit him to swear [by his idol.][12] The names of their holidays, which are named after people, may be mentioned without reservation; this is provided you do not refer to them in the same way the Gentiles do, in a manner indicative of respect.

13) All kinds of mockery are forbidden, except mockery of idols which is permitted.[13]

14) It is forbidden to give a gift to a Gentile that is not your acquaintance,[14]

---

10. *Exodus* 23:13.

11. Ibid.

12. In order to protect your money. Even so, you may not tell him to swear in the name of the idol, rather simply ask him to swear. (*Radvaz* Responsa 166)

13. *Maseches Sanhedrin* 63B.

14. All Gentiles are included in the prohibition, even Moslems. *Beis Yosef* (*Choshen Mishpat* 249). *Shach* 151:18.

הֲוֵי מַתְּנַת חִנָּם, שֶׁגַּם הוּא יְשַׁלֵּם גְּמוּלוֹ, אוֹ כְּבָר שִׁלֵּם לוֹ, וַהֲוֵי כְּמוֹ מְכִירָה.

טו) אָסוּר לְסַפֵּר בְּשִׁבְחָן, אֲפִלּוּ לוֹמַר, כַּמָּה נָאֶה גּוֹי זֶה בְּצוּרָתוֹ. וּמִכָּל־שֶׁכֵּן שֶׁלֹּא לְסַפֵּר בְּשֶׁבַח מַעֲשָׂיו אוֹ שֶׁיְּחַבֵּב דָּבָר מִדְּבָרָיו, שֶׁזֶּהוּ גַּם כֵּן בִּכְלַל וְלֹא תְחָנֵּם, לֹא תִתֵּן לָהֶם חֵן. אֲבָל אִם מְכַוֵּן בְּשִׁבְחוֹ לְהוֹדוֹת לְהַקָּדוֹשׁ־בָּרוּךְ־הוּא שֶׁבָּרָא בְּרִיָּה נָאָה כָּזוֹ, מֻתָּר.

טז) מֻתָּר לְפַרְנֵס עֲנִיֵּיהֶם וּלְבַקֵּר חוֹלֵיהֶם וְלִקְבּוֹר מֵתֵיהֶם וּלְהַסְפִּידָן וּלְנַחֵם אֲבֵלֵיהֶם, מִשּׁוּם דַּרְכֵי שָׁלוֹם.

יז) לֹא יִתְיַחֵד יִשְׂרָאֵל עִם גּוֹי, מִפְּנֵי שֶׁהֵם חֲשׁוּדִים עַל שְׁפִיכוּת דָּמִים.

יח) גּוֹיָה לֹא תֵנִיק לְיֶלֶד יִשְׂרָאֵל בְּבֵיתָהּ, וַאֲפִלּוּ אֲחֵרִים עוֹמְדִים עַל גַּבָּהּ. אֲבָל בְּבֵית יִשְׂרָאֵל, מֻתֶּרֶת לְהֵנִיקוֹ אִם אֲחֵרִים עוֹמְדִים עַל גַּבָּהּ אוֹ נִכְנָסִים וְיוֹצְאִים. וְהוּא שֶׁלֹּא יַנִּיחֶנּוּ עִמָּהּ לְבַדּוֹ בַּלָּיְלָה.

יט) יִשְׂרְאֵלִית לֹא תְיַלֵּד לַגּוֹיָה, אֶלָּא אִם כֵּן הִיא יְדוּעָה לִמְיַלֶּדֶת, שֶׁאָז מֻתֶּרֶת (מִשּׁוּם אֵיבָה). וְדַוְקָא בְּשָׂכָר וּבַחֹל. וְלֹא תֵנִיק יִשְׂרְאֵלִית לְבֶן גּוֹיָה אֲפִלּוּ בְּשָׂכָר, אֶלָּא אִם כֵּן יֵשׁ לָהּ חָלָב הַרְבֵּה וּמְצַעֵר אוֹתָהּ, אָז מֻתֶּרֶת לְהֵנִיקוֹ.

כ) אָסוּר לְלַמֵּד אֻמָּנוּת לַגּוֹי.

סִימָן קסח
צוּרוֹת הָאֲסוּרוֹת

א) כְּתִיב לֹא תַעֲשׂוּן אִתִּי אֱלֹהֵי כֶסֶף וְגוֹ' וְקִבְּלוּ רַבּוֹתֵינוּ זִכְרוֹנָם לִבְרָכָה, דְּזוֹהִי אַזְהָרָה שֶׁלֹּא לְצַיֵּר צוּרוֹת שֶׁבַּמָּדוֹר הָעֶלְיוֹן וְשֶׁבַּמָּדוֹר הַתַּחְתּוֹן, וְהַיְנוּ, לֹא תַעֲשׂוּן כִּדְמוּת שַׁמָּשַׁי הַמְשַׁמְּשִׁין לְפָנָי. וְלָכֵן אָסוּר לְצַיֵּר צוּרוֹת אַרְבָּעָה פָּנִים שֶׁבַּמֶּרְכָּבָה וְצוּרוֹת שְׂרָפִים וְאוֹפַנִּים וּמַלְאֲכֵי הַשָּׁרֵת, וְכֵן אָסוּר לְצַיֵּר צוּרוֹת חַמָּה וּלְבָנָה וְכוֹכָבִים. וַאֲפִלּוּ אֵינָן בּוֹלְטוֹת, אָסוּר לַעֲשׂוֹתָן, וַאֲפִלּוּ בִּשְׁבִיל גּוֹי. אֲבָל לְהַשְׁהוֹתָן בַּבַּיִת, אִם

---

15. *Deuteronomy* 7:2. the word תְחָנֵּם is interpreted as grace and also חִנָּם which means for no reason.

1. *Exodus* 20:23.
2. *Maseches Avodah Zara* 43b.
3. See *Yechezkiel* 1.

as it is written, "You shall not show them grace;"[15] and this is explained, "You shall not give them a free gift." But, if he is an acquaintance, it is not considered a free gift, for in time he will return this favor, or he has already compensated for it, and it is like a sale (and not a gift).

15) It is forbidden to praise them, even as much as to say, "How handsome that Gentile is," and certainly you are not to speak in praise of his deeds, or to cherish any of his utterances, for this is also included [in the negative command] "You shall not show them grace," that is, do not ascribe any grace to them. But if your intention by praising him, is to give thanks to the Holy One, Blessed be He, for having created such a handsome being, it is permissible.

16) It is permitted to help their poor, visit their sick, bury their dead, eulogize them, and console their mourners, for the purpose of maintaining peaceful relations with them.

17) A Jew should not be alone with a Gentile, because they are suspect to commit homicide.

18) A non-Jewess must not be allowed to nurse a Jewish child in her own house, even in the presence of others. But in the house of a Jew, she is permitted to nurse him when others are present, [or at least if they are] going in and out, provided that they do not leave him alone with her at night.

19) A Jewess should not act as midwife for a non-Jewess, unless she is known to be a [professional] midwife, for then it is permitted (so as not to incur hated). This too is permitted only if she is compensated and only on a weekday. A Jewess should not nurse a non-Jewish child, even if she is compensated. If she is engorged with milk and it is causing her discomfort; she is permitted to nurse him.

20) It is forbidden to teach a trade to a Gentile.

Chapter 168

Images That are Forbidden

1) It is written: "You shall not make with Me gods of silver."[1] Our Rabbis, of blessed memory, received by tradition[2] that this verse is a command not to draw pictures of objects of the heavens above or the spheres below. You shall not make anything resembling My "attendants" that minister before Me. Therefore, it is forbidden to draw a picture of the "four faces" on the Chariot,[3] the images of the *Seraphim,*[4] *Ophanim,*[4] and the ministering angels. It is also forbidden to draw pictures of the sun, the moon, and the stars. Even if they are not in relief, it is forbidden to make them,[5] even when made for a non-Jew. However, it is permissible

---

4. Various types of angels.

5. *Ramban, Ran, Taz, Shulchan Aruch* 141:4 maintains that these are only forbidden when in relief.

אֵינָן בּוֹלְטוֹת, מֻתָּר רַק שֶׁלֹּא יֹאמַר לְגוֹי לַעֲשׂוֹתָן, מִשּׁוּם דַּאֲמִירָה לְגוֹי, אֲסוּרָה בְּכָל הָאִסּוּרִין כְּמוֹ בְּאִסּוּרֵי שַׁבָּת.

ב) וְכֵן אָסוּר לְצַיֵּר צוּרַת אָדָם. וַאֲפִלּוּ רַק פַּרְצוּף פְּנֵי אָדָם לְחוּד, נַמִּי אָסוּר. וַאֲפִלּוּ לְהַשְׁהוֹתָהּ, אָסוּר, עַד שֶׁיְּקַלְקֵל אוֹתָהּ קְצָת. וְדַוְקָא בְּצוּרָה שְׁלֵמָה, דְּהַיְנוּ בִּשְׁתֵּי עֵינַיִם וְחֹטֶם שָׁלֵם. אֲבָל אִם אֵינָהּ רַק חֲצִי הַצּוּרָה מִצַּד אֶחָד, כְּדֶרֶךְ קְצָת הַמְצַיְּרִים צַד אֶחָד שֶׁל הַצּוּרָה, זֶהוּ אֵינוֹ אָסוּר.

ג) טַבַּעַת שֶׁיֵּשׁ עָלֶיהָ חוֹתָם שֶׁהוּא צוּרַת אָדָם, אִם הָיְתָה הַצּוּרָה בּוֹלֶטֶת, אָסוּר לְהַשְׁהוֹתָהּ, וּמֻתָּר לַחְתֹּם בָּהּ, מִפְּנֵי שֶׁנַּעֲשֵׂית שְׁקוּעָה. וְאִם הָיְתָה הַצּוּרָה שׁוֹקַעַת, מֻתָּר לְהַשְׁהוֹתָהּ, וְאָסוּר לַחְתֹּם בָּהּ, מִפְּנֵי שֶׁנַּעֲשֵׂית בּוֹלֶטֶת.

ד) אָסוּר לְהִסְתַּכֵּל בְּצוּרַת אָדָם, שֶׁהֲרֵי נִקְרָא פֶּסֶל, וְעוֹבֵר מִשּׁוּם אַל תִּפְנוּ אֶל הָאֱלִילִים. אֲבָל בְּצוּרוֹת שֶׁעַל הַמַּטְבְּעוֹת, כֵּיוָן שֶׁרְגִילִין בָּהֶן, מֻתָּר. וְהֶחָסִיד נִזְהָר גַּם בָּזֶה.

ה) אָסוּר לַעֲשׂוֹת בַּיִת תַּבְנִית הֵיכָל כְּשִׁעוּר אָרְכּוֹ וְגָבְהוֹ וְרָחְבּוֹ, אַכְסַדְרָה תַּבְנִית אוּלָם, חָצֵר תַּבְנִית עֲזָרָה, שֻׁלְחָן תַּבְנִית הַשֻּׁלְחָן שֶׁהָיָה בְּבֵית־הַמִּקְדָּשׁ, מְנוֹרָה תַּבְנִית הַמְּנוֹרָה שֶׁהָיְתָה בְּבֵית־הַמִּקְדָּשׁ. אֲבָל עוֹשֶׂה שֶׁל חֲמִשָּׁה קָנִים אוֹ שֶׁל שִׁשָּׁה אוֹ שֶׁל שְׁמוֹנָה. אֲבָל שֶׁל שִׁבְעָה לֹא יַעֲשֶׂה, אֲפִלּוּ מִשְּׁאָר מִינֵי מַתָּכוֹת וַאֲפִלּוּ בְּלֹא גְבִיעִים וְכַפְתּוֹרִים וּפְרָחִים, וַאֲפִלּוּ אֵינָהּ גְּבוֹהָה שְׁמוֹנָה עָשָׂר טְפָחִים, מִשּׁוּם דְּכָל אֵלּוּ הַדְּבָרִים, גַּם בַּמְּנוֹרָה שֶׁבַּמִּקְדָּשׁ לֹא הָיוּ מְעַכְּבִין.

ו) יֵשׁ נוֹהֲגִין לַעֲשׂוֹת מְנוֹרָה לְשִׁבְעָה נֵרוֹת, דְּהַיְנוּ שִׁשָּׁה בְּעִגּוּל וְאֶחָד בְּאֶמְצַע. אֲבָל הַרְבֵּה פּוֹסְקִים אוֹסְרִים זֹאת. וְיֵשׁ לְהַחְמִיר בִּסְפֵק אִסּוּר דְּאוֹרַיְתָא.

ז) הָעוֹשֶׂה שֶׁמֶן הַמִּשְׁחָה בְּמַעֲשֶׂה וּבְמִשְׁקַל הָאָמוּר בַּתּוֹרָה, חַיָּב כָּרֵת. וּבְשׁוֹגֵג, חַיָּב חַטָּאת, וְהוּא שֶׁעוֹשֶׂה אוֹתוֹ כְּדֵי לְהִמָּשֵׁחַ. וְהָעוֹשֶׂה

---

6. With regard to the sun etc., also, only when full is it forbidden. (*Taz*)
7. The *Ramah* 141:7 says the prevailing custom is to permit sculpturing the image of a

to keep them in your house, if they are not in relief. You must not tell a non-Jew to make them, because telling a non-Jew (to do a prohibited act) is forbidden in regard to all prohibited acts, as it is pertaining to acts prohibited on Shabbos.

2) It is also forbidden to sculpture the image of a person. It is prohibited to sculpture even the face of a person, and it is even forbidden to keep it in your house, unless you disfigure it to some extent. However, only a full face is forbidden,[6] that is, when it has two eyes and a complete nose,[7] but if it is only half a face, a profile, like some artists who form one side of the (picture) face, it is not forbidden.

3) If a ring has a seal on it, consisting of a person's image, and the image was made in relief, you are forbidden to keep it; but it is permissible to seal with it because then the signature becomes depressed. If the image on the ring is depressed, you may keep the ring, but you are forbidden to seal with it, because it comes out in relief.

4) It is forbidden to gaze at the image of a person, for it is called a *pessel* (idol), and this is in violation of the Scripture, "Do not turn to idols." However, with regard to the images on coins, since everyone is accustomed to them, it is permitted. A very pious person is even careful about this.[8]

5) It is forbidden to make a house modeled after the sanctuary of the Bais HaMikdosh, having the same length, height, and width, or a vestibule modeled after the *ulam* in the Bais HaMikdosh or a court modeled after the *azarah* in the Bais HaMikdosh or a table modeled after the Table that was in the Bais HaMikdosh, nor a candelabra modeled after the *menorah* that was in the Bais HaMikdosh. But you may make one with five stems, or of six or eight (stems), but not of seven stems, even if it is made of metals other than gold,[9] and even without cups, knobs, and flowers, and even if it is not eighteen *tefachim* high, because all these things were not essential even in the Bais HaMikdosh *Menorah*.

6) Some are accustomed to make a seven-branched candelabra by shaping six in a circle and one in the middle. But many *Poskim* forbid this, and the stricter opinion should be followed when there is doubt regarding a Scriptural prohibition.

7) Anyone who prepares anointment oil with the same formula and weight as prescribed in the Torah, is liable to the penalty of excisement. If he did it unknowingly, he is liable for a sin-offering, providing he had prepared it with the intention to anoint himself with it. Anyone who prepares incense with the eleven ingredients

---

person so long as some part of the body is incomplete, but a head without a body or a body without a head is permitted. The *Sheloh* says its better not to permit it. The *Shach* 141:32 says one who is strict about it will be blessed.

8. See *Tosafos Avodah Zara* 50a.

9. You are allowed to make one out of wood or pottery, for these are not fitting for the *menorah* in the Bais HaMikdosh. (*Shach* 141:35—*Rambam* etc.)

קְטֹרֶת מֵאַחַד עָשָׂר סַמְמָנִין שֶׁבַּתּוֹרָה לְפִי הַמִּשְׁקָל, אֲפִלּוּ לֹא עָשָׂה אֶלָּא חֶצְיָהּ אוֹ שְׁלִישִׁיתָהּ, חַיָּב כָּרֵת. עָשָׂה לְהִתְלַמֵּד בָּהּ, פָּטוּר.

סִימָן קסט

אִסּוּר כְּתֹבֶת קַעֲקַע וְקָרְחָה עַל מֵת

א) כָּתוּב בַּתּוֹרָה, וּכְתֹבֶת קַעֲקַע לֹא תִתְּנוּ בָּכֶם. מַהִי כְּתֹבֶת קַעֲקַע. כְּתָב הַמְחֻקֶּה וְשָׁקוּעַ שֶׁאֵינוֹ נִמְחָק לְעוֹלָם זֶהוּ הַשּׂוֹרֵט עַל בְּשָׂרוֹ וּמְמַלֵּא מְקוֹם הַשְּׂרִיטָה בִּכְחוֹל אוֹ בִּדְיוֹ אוֹ בִּשְׁאָר צִבְעוֹנִים הָרוֹשְׁמִים. וְכֵן אִם צוֹבֵעַ תְּחִלָּה בְּצֶבַע וְאַחַר כָּךְ שׂוֹרֵט בִּמְקוֹם הַצֶּבַע, עוֹבֵר בְּלָאו. וּמִכָּל מָקוֹם מֻתָּר לִתֵּן אֵפֶר וּשְׁאָר דְּבָרִים עַל הַמַּכָּה לִרְפוּאָה, אַף־עַל־פִּי שֶׁיִּשָּׁאֵר הָרֹשֶׁם, כִּי גַם מִמַּכָּתוֹ יִשָּׁאֵר רֹשֶׁם הַמּוֹכִיחַ עָלָיו, שֶׁלֹּא עָשָׂה מִשּׁוּם כְּתֹבֶת קַעֲקַע.

ב) כְּתִיב, וְשֶׂרֶט לָנֶפֶשׁ לֹא תִתְּנוּ בִּבְשַׂרְכֶם. וּכְתִיב, לֹא תִתְגֹּדְדוּ וְלֹא תָשִׂימוּ קָרְחָה בֵּין עֵינֵיכֶם לָמֵת. וּגְדִידָה וּשְׂרִיטָה אַחַת הֵן, וַאֲסוּרוֹת בֵּין בִּפְנֵי הַמֵּת בֵּין שֶׁלֹּא בִּפְנֵי הַמֵּת. וַאֲפִלּוּ לְהַכּוֹת בְּיָדוֹ עַל בְּשָׂרוֹ עַד שֶׁדָּם יוֹצֵא, אָסוּר. וַאֲפִלּוּ עַל צַעַר אַחֵר, אָסוּר.

ג) קָרְחָה, הוּא שֶׁתּוֹלֵשׁ מִשְּׂעַר רֹאשׁוֹ עַל מֵת. וַאֲפִלּוּ בְּשַׂעֲרָה אַחַת, אִכָּא אִסּוּרָא. וְגַם הַנָּשִׁים מֻזְהָרוֹת בְּבַל יִקְרְחוּ, וּמִכָּל־שֶׁכֵּן בְּבַל יִשְׂרְטוּ.

סִימָן קע

אִסּוּר גִּלּוּחַ פְּאוֹת הָרֹאשׁ וְהַזָּקָן

א) פְּאוֹת הָרֹאשׁ הֵן שְׁתַּיִם בְּסוֹף הָרֹאשׁ, וְהוּא מְקוֹם חִבּוּרוֹ לַלֶּחִי מִיָּמִין וּמִשְּׂמֹאל אֵצֶל הָאֹזֶן. וַאֲפִלּוּ לְגַלְּחָן בְּמִסְפָּרַיִם כְּעֵין תַּעַר, דְּהַיְנוּ סָמוּךְ לַבָּשָׂר, שֶׁאֵינוֹ מְשַׁיֵּר כְּלוּם מִן הַשְּׂעָרוֹת סָמוּךְ לַבָּשָׂר, יֵשׁ אוֹסְרִין. וְלָכֵן אִם צָרִיךְ לְגַלְּחָן לִרְפוּאָה, יִזָּהֵר שֶׁלֹּא לְגַלְּחֵן סָמוּךְ לַבָּשָׂר מַמָּשׁ. וְשִׁעוּר הַפֵּאָה – מִכְּנֶגֶד שֵׂעָר שֶׁעַל פַּדַּחְתּוֹ וְעַד לְמַטָּה מִן הָאֹזֶן, מְקוֹם שֶׁהַלֶּחִי הַתַּחְתּוֹנָה יוֹצֵאת וּמִתְפָּרֶדֶת שָׁם.

---

1. *Leviticus* 19:28.
2. Ibid.
3. *Deuteronomy* 14:1.
4. *Rosh.* The *Ramban,* however, permits it. The *Rosh* says it is permitted only when done over the loss of Torah, as on the passing away of a great Torah Scholar.

prescribed in the Torah, and in the same proportion, even if he prepared only one-half, or one-third of that quantity, is liable to the penalty of *karess* (excisement). If he prepared it for the purpose of making a study of it, he is guiltless.

Chapter 169

The Prohibition of Tatooing, and Making Gashes of Mourning

1) It is written in the Torah, "You shall not imprint marks upon yourself."[1] What is meant by "imprint marks"? A mark which is absorbed and sunken into the skin, so that it can never be erased. He who makes an incision in his skin and fills the incision with stirium, or ink, or other dyes that leave a mark; likewise, if he first dyes (the skin), and then makes an incision on the dyed area, is guilty of transgressing a negative command. Nevertheless, it is permitted to put ashes and other things on a wound for medical purposes, even if a mark will remain; for (in such cases) the wound will also leave a mark, and it will be apparent that you did not do it for the purpose of tattooing.

2) It is written; "You shall not cut into your flesh for the dead."[2] It is also written: "You shall not cut yourselves nor make any baldness between your eyes for the dead."[3] *Gedidah* and *seritah* [the Hebrew terms used in the Scriptural text respectively] are one and the same, and are forbidden whether in the presence of the dead, or not in the presence of the dead. Even to strike your hand onto your flesh so that blood comes out is forbidden. And to do this even for any other kind of grief is also forbidden.[4]

3) "Baldness" refers to plucking out hair of the head in mourning for the dead. Even the plucking out of a single hair is forbidden. Women, are included in the prohibition of making baldness, and certainly in the prohibition of cutting.

Chapter 170

The Prohibition of Shaving the Hair of the Temples and Beard

1) There are two "corners" of the head,[1] located at the base of the (sides of) the head, at the juncture of the temple and the cheek, on both right and left sides near the ears. Even shaving [cutting these corners] with a scissors close to the skin as with a razor, so that nothing remains of the hair close to the skin, is forbidden according to some *Poskim*. Therefore, if it is necessary to shave them for medical reasons, you should be careful not to shave close to the skin. The area of the corners that are forbidden to shave includes the hair from the top of the forehead to below the ear, at the point where the bottom jaw widens and spreads outward.

1. See Leviticus 19:27.

ב) פְּאוֹת הַזָּקָן לֹא אָסְרָה תוֹרָה לְהַשְׁחִית אֶלָּא בְּתַעַר. וְהַפֵּאוֹת הֵן חָמֵשׁ וְרַבּוּ בָּהֶן הַדֵּעוֹת, לְפִיכָךְ יְרֵא־שָׁמַיִם לֹא יַעֲבִיר תַּעַר עַל כָּל זְקָנוֹ כְּלָל, וַאֲפִלּוּ עַל הַשָּׂפָה הָעֶלְיוֹנָה אוֹ תַּחַת הַגָּרוֹן. וְאֵין חִלּוּק בֵּין תַּעַר לְאֶבֶן חַדָּה שֶׁחוֹתֶכֶת אֶת הַשְּׂעָרוֹת, כְּגוֹן פִּיגְמאֶנְט אוֹ פִּימְסֶענְשְׁטֵיין, שֶׁאָסוּר גַּם כֵּן. וְאוֹתָן שֶׁמְּסִירִין שְׂעַר הַזָּקָן עַל יְדֵי מִשְׁחָה מִסִּיד עִם אַוִירעם, יֵשׁ לָהֶם לִזָּהֵר, שֶׁלֹּא לִגְרֹר אֶת הַמִּשְׁחָה בְּסַכִּין, שֶׁמָּא יַחְתֹּךְ שֵׂעָר, רַק יִגְרְרוּ בְּקֵיסָם וְכַדּוֹמֶה.

סִימָן קעא
דְּבָרִים הָאֲסוּרִים מִשּׁוּם לֹא יִלְבַּשׁ גֶּבֶר שִׂמְלַת אִשָּׁה

א) אָסוּר לְאִישׁ לִלְבּוֹשׁ אֲפִלּוּ מַלְבּוּשׁ אֶחָד שֶׁל אִשָּׁה, אַף־עַל־פִּי שֶׁהוּא נִכָּר בִּשְׁאָר מַלְבּוּשָׁיו שֶׁהוּא אִישׁ. וְכֵן אָסוּר לְאִשָּׁה לִלְבּוֹשׁ אֲפִלּוּ מַלְבּוּשׁ אֶחָד שֶׁל אִישׁ. וְלֹא לְבַד מַלְבּוּשִׁים אֲסוּרִים, אֶלָּא אֲפִלּוּ כָּל תַּכְשִׁיט וְכָל תִּקּוּן נוֹי וְיֹפִי הַמְיֻחָד לְאִשָּׁה לְפִי מִנְהַג הַמָּקוֹם, אָסוּר לְאִישׁ שֶׁיִּתְקַשֵּׁט וְיִתְיַפֶּה בּוֹ. וְכֵן כָּל מַה שֶּׁמְּיֻחָד לְאִישׁ, אָסוּר לְאִשָּׁה.

ב) אָסוּר לְאִישׁ לְהַעֲבִיר שְׂעַר בֵּית־הַשֶּׁחִי וּבֵית־הָעֶרְוָה אֲפִלּוּ בְּמִסְפָּרַיִם כְּעֵין תַּעַר, דְּהַיְנוּ שֶׁמְּגַלְּחָן סָמוּךְ לַבָּשָׂר מַמָּשׁ, מִפְּנֵי שֶׁזֶּהוּ תִּקּוּן לַנָּשִׁים. וְאָסוּר לָחֹךְ בְּיָדוֹ בִּשְׂעַר בֵּית־הַשֶּׁחִי וּבֵית־הָעֶרְוָה כְּדֵי לְהַשִּׁירָן. אֲבָל עַל יְדֵי בִגְדוֹ, מֻתָּר. וּמִי שֶׁיֵּשׁ לוֹ חֲטָטִין בְּבֵית־הַשֶּׁחִי וּבְבֵית־הָעֶרְוָה וּמִצְטַעֵר מֵחֲמַת הַשְּׂעָרוֹת, מֻתָּר לְהַעֲבִירָן.

ג) אָסוּר לְאִישׁ לְלַקֵּט אֲפִלּוּ שַׂעֲרָה אַחַת לְבָנָה מִתּוֹךְ הַשְּׁחוֹרוֹת, שֶׁזֶּהוּ נוֹי אִשָּׁה, וְאָסוּר מִשּׁוּם לֹא יִלְבַּשׁ גֶּבֶר. וְכֵן אָסוּר לוֹ לִצְבּוֹעַ אֲפִלּוּ שַׂעֲרָה אַחַת לְבָנָה שֶׁתְּהֵא שְׁחוֹרָה. וְכֵן אָסוּר לְאִישׁ לְהִסְתַּכֵּל בַּמַּרְאָה. וְאִם רוֹאֶה מִשּׁוּם רְפוּאָה, אוֹ שֶׁמְּסַפֵּר אֶת עַצְמוֹ, אוֹ כְּדֵי לְהָסִיר הַכְּתָמִים מֵעַל פָּנָיו אוֹ הַנּוֹצוֹת מֵרֹאשׁוֹ, מֻתָּר. וּבְמָקוֹם שֶׁהַדֶּרֶךְ הוּא שֶׁגַּם הָאֲנָשִׁים רוֹאִים בַּמַּרְאָה, בְּכָל עִנְיָן מֻתָּר.

---

2. Ibid.

1. *Ramah* (*Orach Chaim* 696:8) says that it is customary to dress in this way on Purim for merry making. *Mishna Berurah* 596:30—*Be'er Hagolah*—*Taz*—*Bach* say that this custom should be abolished.

2. *Deuteronomy* 22:5.

2) The Torah forbids shaving the corners of the beard,[2] only when done with a razor. The beard has five "corners" and there are many opinions as to what they are. Therefore, a God-fearing Jew, should not use a razor on any part of the beard, even on his upper lip or under the chin. There is no difference between a razor and a sharp stone which cuts the hair, such as pigment or pumice stone, which are also forbidden. Those who remove their beard by means of a cream prepared from lime and avirem, should be careful not to scrape off the cream with a knife, which might cut the hair; but they should scrape it with a strip of wood or something similar.

Chapter 171

Things that are Forbidden Because A Man Should Not Wear a Woman's Garb

1) A man is forbidden to wear even one garment worn by women, even though he can be recognized as a male by his other garments.[1] Likewise a woman is forbidden to wear even one garment worn by men. Not only are feminine garments forbidden to men, but also every ornament and all toiletries and cosmetics that are used exclusively by women, of that region, are forbidden to a man for purposes of adornment or enhancement. Likewise, everything used exclusively by men, is forbidden for use by a woman.

2) A man is forbidden to remove the hair from his armpits and the genital area, even with a pair of scissors when it is cut close to the skin, if it appears that it was done with a razor, for this is the custom of women. It is forbidden to rub the hairs of the armpits or of the genital area with the hands, so that they should fall out, but it is permitted when done with a garment. One who has scabs in his armpits, or in the genital area, and the hair causes him discomfort, is allowed to remove them.

3) A man is forbidden to pick even one white hair from among the black ones, for this is the way women beautify themselves, and is forbidden because of the enjoinder that "A man shall not wear (a woman's garment)."[2] It is also forbidden to dye even one white hair to make it black. A man is also forbidden to look into a mirror. However, if you look into it for medical purposes, or when you are cutting your own hair, or wish to remove stains from your face, or remove feathers from your head, it is permitted (to use a mirror). In a region where it is customary for men, to look into mirrors, it is permissible for any reason.

סִימָן קעב
הִלְכוֹת חָדָשׁ

א) כְּתִיב, וְלֶחֶם וְקָלִי וְכַרְמֶל לֹא תֹאכְלוּ עַד עֶצֶם הַיּוֹם הַזֶּה וְגוֹ'. פֵּרוּשׁ, שֶׁאֲסוּרִין לֶאֱכֹל מִתְּבוּאָה חֲדָשָׁה מֵחֲמֵשֶׁת הַמִּינִים עַד לְאַחַר הַקְרָבַת הָעֹמֶר שֶׁהִקְרִיבוּ בְּשִׁשָּׁה עָשָׂר בְּנִיסָן. וּבִזְמַן שֶׁאֵין עֹמֶר, כָּל הַיּוֹם אֲסוּרִין. וְלִבְנֵי חוּץ־לָאָרֶץ שֶׁעוֹשִׂין יוֹם־טוֹב שְׁנֵי יָמִים מֵחֲמַת סְפֵקָא גַּם כָּל יוֹם שִׁבְעָה־עָשָׂר, אָסוּר עַד תְּחִלַּת לֵיל שְׁמוֹנָה־עָשָׂר. וּתְבוּאָה שֶׁנִּזְרְעָה וְנִשְׁרְשָׁה קֹדֶם שִׁשָּׁה־עָשָׂר בְּנִיסָן, הָעֹמֶר הַזֶּה הִתִּירָהּ, וּמֻתֶּרֶת מִיָּד לְאַחַר קְצִירָתָהּ. אֲבָל אִם לֹא נִשְׁרְשָׁה קֹדֶם שִׁשָּׁה־עָשָׂר בְּנִיסָן, אֲסוּרָה עַד שֶׁיָּבוֹא הָעֹמֶר הַבָּא.

ב) לְדַעַת רֹב גְּדוֹלֵי הַפּוֹסְקִים, אִסּוּר זֶה גַּם בְּחוּץ־לָאָרֶץ הוּא מִן הַתּוֹרָה. וְלָכֵן צְרִיכִין לְהַשְׁגִּיחַ מְאֹד בִּתְבוּאָה שֶׁנִּזְרְעָה לִפְעָמִים אַחַר הַפֶּסַח אוֹ סָמוּךְ לִפְנֵי הַפֶּסַח, שֶׁלֹּא הִשְׁרִישָׁה קֹדֶם שִׁשָּׁה־עָשָׂר בְּנִיסָן, כְּגוֹן שְׂעוֹרִים וְשִׁבֹּלֶת־שׁוּעָל, וּבִקְצָת מְקוֹמוֹת גַּם חִטִּין, שֶׁהֵן אֲסוּרוֹת עַד לְאַחַר שִׁבְעָה־עָשָׂר בְּנִיסָן הַבָּא. (וְאִם הִשְׁרִישָׁה בְּיוֹם שִׁשָּׁה עָשָׂר, מֻתֶּרֶת בִּתְחִלַּת לֵיל שִׁבְעָה עָשָׂר בְּנִיסָן הַבָּא, מִכֹּחַ מִמָּה נַפְשָׁךְ). וְגַם הַשֵּׁכָר שֶׁנַּעֲשָׂה מִתְּבוּאָה זוֹ, אָסוּר עַד לְאַחַר הַפֶּסַח הַבָּא. וְכֵן הַשְּׁמָרִים, אֲסוּרִים. וְאִם חִמְּצוּ בָּהֶם עִסָּה, אֲפִלּוּ מִתְּבוּאָה יְשָׁנָה, כָּל הָעִסָּה אֲסוּרָה מֵחֲמַת הַשְּׁמָרִים. תְּבוּאָה שֶׁמִּסְתַּפְּקִים בָּהּ אִם הִיא יְשָׁנָה אוֹ חֲדָשָׁה, יַעֲשׂוּ עָלֶיהָ שְׁאֵלַת חָכָם.

ג) יֵשׁ אוֹמְרִים, דְּאֵין אִסּוּר חָדָשׁ אֶלָּא בִּתְבוּאָה שֶׁגָּדְלָה בִּרְשׁוּת יִשְׂרָאֵל. וַאֲפִלּוּ הַשָּׂדֶה שַׁיֶּכֶת לַגּוֹי, אֶלָּא שֶׁהַיִּשְׂרָאֵל שְׂכָרָהּ, יֵשׁ בִּתְבוּאָה זוֹ אִסּוּר חָדָשׁ. אֲבָל בִּתְבוּאָה שֶׁגָּדְלָה בִּרְשׁוּת הַגּוֹי, אֵין בָּהּ אִסּוּר חָדָשׁ. וְעַל זֶה סוֹמְכִים הַרְבֵּה בִּשְׁעַת הַדְּחָק. וּמִכָּל מָקוֹם בִּתְבוּאָה שֶׁגָּדְלָה בִּרְשׁוּת יִשְׂרָאֵל, אֵין שׁוּם הֶתֵּר. אֲבָל רַבּוּ הַחוֹלְקִים וְאוֹמְרִים, דְּגַם בְּשֶׁל גּוֹי אִכָּא אִסּוּר חָדָשׁ. וְהַמַּחְמִיר תָּבוֹא עָלָיו בְּרָכָה.

---

1. *Leviticus* 23:14.

2. The *Chinuch* says "*carmel*" is grain roasted in its stalks.

3. *Rif, Rambam, Smag, Rosh, Ittur, Mordecai—Ravia, Hagahos Maimonee, Ritvah, Shulchan Aruch,* etc. However, the *Ohr Zarua* is inclined, when there is a doubt about a particular product from outside *Eretz Yisrael,* to consider it a Rabbinical injunction and is lenient. The *Trumas Hadeshen* says grain of a non-Jew's fields outside *Eretz Yisroel* is "*chodosh*" only as a Rabbinical injunction and *Bach-Riva* permit it entirely. Anyone who can, should be strict with

Chapter 172

Laws Concerning New Crops

1) It is written:[1] "And bread, and roasted grain and fresh grain[2] you shall not eat until this very day" etc. This means that it is forbidden to eat of any of the five species [of grain] [wheat, barley, oats, spelt, rye] from the new grain crop until after the offering of the *omer*, which was offered on the sixteenth day of *Nissan*. In a time when there is no *omer* [as in our times], it is forbidden to eat the new crop the entire day. In countries outside *Eretz Yisroel*, where two days of Yom Tov are celebrated, because of the doubt (of the actual day of Yom Tov,) it is also forbidden the entire seventeenth day until the beginning of the night of the eighteenth day. Grain which had been sown and taken root before the sixteenth day of *Nissan*, is made valid for use by (bringing) the *omer*, and it may be eaten immediately after it is harvested. However, if it did not take root before the sixteenth of *Nissan*, it is forbidden until next year's *omer* is brought.

2) According to most of the greatest *Poskim*,[3] the above prohibition, even outside *Eretz Yisroel*, is a Scriptural prohibition. Therefore we must pay careful attention to grain crops that are sometimes sown after *Pesach* or so close to *Pesach* that it has not taken root before the sixteenth of *Nissan*, such as barley and oats. and in some places also wheat, for they are forbidden until after the seventeenth of *Nissan* of the next year. (If it had taken root on the sixteenth day of *Nissan*, it is permitted at the beginning of the seventeenth night of *Nissan* of the next year in any event.) Also the beer[4] made from this grain, is forbidden until after the next Pesach. Also the lees are forbidden. If dough was leavened with it, even if the dough was made from the old grain crops, the entire dough is forbidden due to the yeast. Concerning crops about which there is a doubt whether it is old or new, you should consult a *Poseik*.

3) Some *Poskim* maintain that the prohibition of eating the new crops applies only to grain that grew in the field of a Jew. Even if the field belongs to a non-Jew, but it has been leased by a Jew, the law of new crops applies to this grain. However, if the grain grew in the field of a non-Jew, the prohibition of new crops does not apply. Many people rely on this in difficult circumstances.[5] Nevertheless, if the grain grew in the field of a Jew, it is not permitted at all. Most *Poskim* disagree, and maintain that even grain that grew in the field of a non-Jew is subject to the prohibition of new crops; and a blessing will come upon one who is strict about it.[6]

---

regard to "*chodosh*" outside *Eretz Yisroel*, as most *poskim* hold it is *de'oraisa*, and certainly if you know it is "*chodosh*," you should not eat it, since, even most of those who say it is not a *de'oraisa*, say it is a Rabbinical injunction (*Biur Halacha* 489:10)

4. Some *Poskim* are lenient with regard to beer and all malt products.

5. See footnote 3.

6. All discussion of leniency pertaining to "*chodosh*" is only if grown outside *Eretz Yisroel*, i.e., "*chodosh*" in *Eretz Yisroel* is unequivocally prohibited *de'oraisa*, with all the ramifications.

סִימָן קעג
הִלְכוֹת עָרְלָה

א) כָּל עֵץ מַאֲכָל, בֵּין שֶׁל יִשְׂרָאֵל בֵּין שֶׁל גּוֹי, וַאֲפִלּוּ בְּעָצִיץ שֶׁאֵינוֹ נָקוּב, שָׁלֹשׁ שָׁנִים הָרִאשׁוֹנוֹת מִנְּטִיעָתוֹ, הַפֵּרוֹת וְהַגַּרְעִינִין וְהַקְּלִפּוֹת, הַכֹּל אָסוּר בַּהֲנָאָה. וְשָׁלֹשׁ שָׁנִים אֵלּוּ, אֵין מוֹנִים מִיּוֹם לְיוֹם אֶלָּא אִם נָטַע קֹדֶם שִׁשָּׁה־עָשָׂר בְּאָב, כֵּיוָן שֶׁיֵּשׁ אַרְבָּעָה וְאַרְבָּעִים יוֹם עַד רֹאשׁ הַשָּׁנָה, נֶחְשֶׁבֶת לוֹ הַשָּׁנָה, מִשּׁוּם דְּאַרְבָּעָה עָשָׂר יוֹם הֵמָּה יְמֵי קְלִיטָה, וְאַחַר כָּךְ שְׁלֹשִׁים יוֹם בַּשָּׁנָה נֶחְשָׁבִים שָׁנָה וְשׁוּב מוֹנֶה שְׁתֵּי שָׁנִים מִתִּשְׁרֵי. אֲבָל אִם נָטַע מִיּוֹם שִׁשָּׁה עָשָׂר בְּאָב וְאֵילָךְ, לֹא נֶחְשֶׁבֶת שָׁנָה זֹאת לִכְלוּם, וּמוֹנֶה מִתִּשְׁרֵי שָׁלֹשׁ שָׁנִים.

ב) בַּשָּׁנָה הָרְבִיעִית, נִקְרָאוּ הַפֵּרוֹת נֶטַע רְבָעִי, וּצְרִיכִין פִּדְיוֹן. כֵּיצַד פּוֹדֶה אוֹתָן. תּוֹלְשָׁן לְאַחַר שֶׁנִּגְמְרוּ כָּל צָרְכָּן, וְנוֹטֵל מַטְבֵּעַ כֶּסֶף אוֹ פֵּרוֹת שֶׁל הֶתֵּר שָׁוִין פְּרוּטָה, וְאוֹמֵר, בָּזֶה אֲנִי פּוֹדֶה פֵּרוֹת נֶטַע רְבָעִי אֵלּוּ. וְנוֹטֵל הַמַּטְבֵּעַ אוֹ הַפֵּרוֹת וְשׁוֹחֲקָן וְזוֹרְקָן בַּנָּהָר. וְאֵין מְבָרְכִין בְּחוּץ־לָאָרֶץ עַל הַפִּדְיוֹן.

ג) אֶחָד הַנּוֹטֵעַ גַּרְעִין אוֹ עָנָף אוֹ שֶׁעָקַר אִילָן וּנְטָעוֹ בְּמָקוֹם אַחֵר, חַיָּבִים בְּעָרְלָה. אֲבָל הַמַּרְכִּיב עָנָף בְּאִילָן אַחֵר, וְכֵן הַמַּבְרִיךְ, דְּהַיְנוּ שֶׁעוֹשֶׂה גּוּמָא בָּאָרֶץ וּמַשְׁפִּיל אֶחָד מֵעַנְפֵי הָאִילָן וּמַטְמִין אֶמְצָעוּתוֹ בָּאָרֶץ וְרֹאשׁוֹ יוֹצֵא מִצַּד אַחֵר, אַף־עַל־פִּי שֶׁחֲתָכוֹ מֵעִקַּר הָאִילָן, בְּחוּץ־לָאָרֶץ אֵין בּוֹ מִשּׁוּם עָרְלָה.

ד) אִילָן שֶׁנִּקְצַץ, אִם נִשְׁאַר גָּבוֹהַּ מֵהָאָרֶץ טֶפַח, אֲזַי מַה שֶּׁגָּדַל אַחַר כָּךְ, אֵינוֹ חַיָּב בְּעָרְלָה. אֲבָל אִם לֹא נִשְׁאַר טֶפַח, חַיָּב בְּעָרְלָה. וּמוֹנִין הַשָּׁנִים מִשְּׁעַת הַקְּצִיצָה. וְאִילָן שֶׁנֶּעֱקַר וְנִשְׁאַר מִשָּׁרָשָׁיו מְחֻבָּר, אֲפִלּוּ רַק כְּעֹבִי הַמַּחַט שֶׁמּוֹתְחִין בָּהּ הַבֶּגֶד לְאַחַר אֲרִיגָה בְּיָדוּעַ שֶׁיָּכוֹל לִחְיוֹת בְּלִי תּוֹסֶפֶת עָפָר וּפָטוּר, וַאֲפִלּוּ הוֹסִיף עָלָיו עָפָר הַרְבֵּה.

1. Of pottery or wood—*Rambam, Shulchan Aruch, Gra* 294:64. But *Rashi, Rosh* and *Tur* hold this is true only for pottery and not for wood.
2. They are not permitted until after the 15th of Shevat.

Chapter 173

Law of Orlah (Fruits of the First Three Years)

1) It is forbidden to derive benefit from the fruit of a fruit tree, whether of a Jew or of a non-Jew, even if they grow in a flower pot[1] without a hole on the bottom, until after three years from its planting. It is also forbidden to derive benefit from their pits and skins. These three years are not reckoned from day (of planting) to day. Rather if you planted a tree before the sixteenth day of the month of *Av,* since there are still forty-four days to *Rosh Hashanah,* they are counted as one year, because it takes fourteen days for it to take root, and thereafter, the thirty remaining days of the year are counted as a full year. We then count two more years from the month of *Tishrei* (from *Rosh Hashana*).[2] But if the tree was planted after the sixteenth of *Av,* that part of the year is not counted at all, and you must count three years from *Tishrei.*[3]

2) The fruit of the fourth year's growth are called *neta revai* (growth of the fourth year) and must be redeemed. How does one redeem them? You pick them after they are fully ripe, and take a silver coin or produce that is permitted to eat, to the value of a *perutah,*[4] and say: "With this I redeem these fruits of the fourth year." You then take the coin or the produce, destroy it and throw it into a river. You do not recite a berachah on the redemption of *neta revai* that grew outside of *Eretz Yisroel.*

3) Whether you have planted a seed, or a branch or transplanted a tree you must consider the fruit as *orlah.* However, if you graft a branch upon a tree, or if you are *mavrich,* which means making a hole in the ground, and bending one of the branches of the tree, and inserting the middle of the branch in the ground, leaving the end protrude above the ground; even if it was (later) cut off from the trunk of the tree; in lands outside *Eretz Yisroel,* the laws of *orlah* do not apply.

4) If a tree was cut down, and one *tefach* of stump remains above the ground, then whatever grew out of that stump is not subject to the laws of *orlah.* But if the stump is less than a *tefach* high, whatever grows out is subject to the law of *orlah,* and we count its years from the time the tree was cut down. If a tree was uprooted and some of its roots remained attached to the ground, even if they are as thin as a needle used for stretching the garment after weaving, it is a fact that it can sustain itself without additional earth, and its fruit is not subject to the law of *orlah,* even if you added much more dirt.

---

3. According to *Shach* 294:10 they are permitted immediately. According to *Chazon Ish* they are not permitted until the 15th Shevat.

4. See *Shulchan Aruch* 294:17 and *Sheilas Ya'avetz* vol. 2 Responsa 19–20.

סִימָן קעד
הִלְכוֹת כִּלְאֵי אִילָן

א) כִּלְאֵי אִילָנוֹת, הֲרֵי הֵם בִּכְלַל מַה שֶּׁנֶּאֱמַר, שָׂדְךָ לֹא תִזְרַע כִּלְאָיִם. וְעַל כֵּן אָסוּר לְהַרְכִּיב מִין בְּשֶׁאֵינוֹ מִינוֹ, כְּגוֹן עָנָף שֶׁל תַּפּוּחַ בְּאֶתְרוֹג, אוֹ אֶתְרוֹג בְּתַפּוּחַ. וַאֲפִלּוּ מִינִים הַדּוֹמִים זֶה לָזֶה, כְּגוֹן תַּפּוּחַ בְּתַפּוּחַ יַעֲרִי וְכַיּוֹצֵא, כֵּיוָן שֶׁהֵם שְׁנֵי מִינִים, אֲסוּרִים זֶה בָּזֶה. וְאָסוּר לְיִשְׂרָאֵל לְהַנִּיחַ לַגּוֹי שֶׁיַּרְכִּיב לוֹ אִילָנוֹ כִּלְאָיִם.

ב) אָסוּר לְקַיֵּם הַמֻּרְכָּב כִּלְאָיִם. אֲבָל הַפְּרִי הַגָּדֵל מִמֶּנּוּ, מֻתָּר. וּמֻתָּר לִקַּח עָנָף מִן הַמֻּרְכָּב וּלְנָטְעוֹ בְּמָקוֹם אַחֵר.

ג) כִּלְאֵי הַכֶּרֶם וְכִלְאֵי זְרָעִים אֵינָם אֲסוּרִים בְּחוּץ־לָאָרֶץ אֶלָּא אִם כֵּן זָרַע שְׁנֵי מִינֵי תְבוּאָה אוֹ שְׁנֵי מִינֵי יָרָק עִם זֶרַע הַכֶּרֶם בְּיַחַד.

סִימָן קעה
הִלְכוֹת כִּלְאֵי בְהֵמָה

א) אָסוּר לְהַרְכִּיב זָכָר עַל נְקֵבָה מִשְּׁנֵי מִינִים בֵּין בִּבְהֵמוֹת בֵּין בְּחַיּוֹת בֵּין בְּעוֹפוֹת. וַאֲפִלּוּ לִגְרוֹם שֶׁיַּרְכִּיבוּ, אָסוּר.

ב) אָסוּר לַעֲשׂוֹת מְלָאכָה בִּשְׁנֵי מִינִים, כְּגוֹן לַחֲרוֹשׁ אוֹ שֶׁיִּמְשְׁכוּ אֶת הַקָּרוֹן. וַאֲפִלּוּ לְהַנְהִיגָם בְּקוֹל בִּלְבַד שֶׁהוּא צוֹעֵק עֲלֵיהֶם, אָסוּר, אִם הֵם קְשׁוּרִים יַחַד. וְלָכֵן עֲגָלָה שֶׁל גּוֹי שֶׁכִּלְאַיִם מוֹשְׁכִים אוֹתָהּ, וּמַשָּׂא שֶׁל יִשְׂרָאֵל עַל הָעֲגָלָה, אָסוּר לְיִשְׂרָאֵל שֶׁיֵּלֵךְ סָמוּךְ לְהָעֲגָלָה דְּחָיְשִׁינָן שֶׁמָּא יִצְעַק עֲלֵיהֶם שֶׁיֵּלְכוּ מַהֵר, וְזֶהוּ אָסוּר מִשּׁוּם מַנְהִיג בְּכִלְאָיִם.

ג) עֲגָלָה שֶׁהַכִּלְאַיִם מוֹשְׁכִים אוֹתָהּ, אָסוּר לֵישֵׁב בָּהּ, אֲפִלּוּ אֵינוֹ מַנְהִיג.

---

1. *Leviticus* 19:19.
2. Even outside of *Eretz Yisroel—Shulchan Aruch* 295:1.
3. *Ramah* 295:6 (and *Shach* 295:3) permit the grafting of a fruitless tree onto a different kind of a fruitless tree. *Chasam Sofer* Responsa 288 says it is best to refrain from this as well. However, you may not graft a fruit tree with a fruitless tree. (*Shulchan Aruch* 295:3)
4. *Levushei Sarad* Chapter 106 says these are different species because their taste is very different. However, the *Mishkanos Yaakov* Responsa 66 reinforces the prevailing custom that permits grafting an apple tree with a wild apple tree because they are one species and this does not depend on their taste.

Chapter 174
The Laws of Tree Grafting

1) The prohibition against the grafting of diverse tree species is implied in the verse: "You shall not sow your field with diverse seeds."[1] Therefore it is forbidden to graft a branch of one kind of tree upon another,[2] such as the branch of an apple tree upon a citron tree,[3] or a branch of citron upon an apple tree. Even between similar species, like a branch of a [cultivated] apple tree upon a wild apple tree,[4] since they are two varieties of apples,[5] they are forbidden to be grafted with one another.[6] A Jew is forbidden to allow a non-Jew to graft two diverse kinds of trees for him.

2) It is forbidden to maintain a tree upon which another kind has been grafted, but it is permitted to eat its fruit. It is permitted to take a branch of a grafted tree and plant it elsewhere.

3) Sowing a vineyard with two kinds of seeds, or sowing a field with two kinds of seeds, is not prohibited outside of *Eretz Yisroel*[7] unless you have sown two kinds of grain or two kinds of vegetables together with the seeds of the vineyard.

Chapter 175
The Laws of Interbreeding Animals

1) It is forbidden to breed a male and female of two diverse kinds of animals, beasts or fowl. Even to merely cause cross-breeding is forbidden.

2) It is forbidden to do work with two diverse kinds of animals, such as ploughing with them or let them pull a wagon. Even to drive them merely by sound, such as yelling at them is forbidden, if they are harnessed together. Therefore if the cart of a non-Jew is being drawn by diverse kinds of animals, and the cargo of a Jew is on the cart, that Jew is forbidden to walk alongside the cart, for it is likely that he will yell at them, to make them go faster, which is forbidden as it constitutes driving diverse kinds of animals.

3) If a cart is being drawn by diverse kinds of animals, it is forbidden to sit on it even if you do not drive them.

---

5. If one variety is not edible, *Levushei Sarad* Chapter 10 says it is considered like a fruitless tree and it is forbidden to graft it with an edible variety. *Mishkanos Yaakov* Responsa 66 disagrees, and considers them one species.

6. *Ramah* 295:6 says it is best to refrain from grafting any two trees that are not exactly the same kind because not everyone is knowledgeable if they are the same species or not.

7. This refers to both sowing and eating the produce. (See *Shulchan Aruch* 296:69)

ד) עֲגָלָה שֶׁמּוֹשֵׁךְ אוֹתָהּ מִין אֶחָד, לֹא יִקְשֹׁר מִין אַחֵר לֹא בְּצִדָּהּ וְלֹא לְאַחֲרֶיהָ.

ה) אָסוּר לִקְשֹׁר שְׁנֵי מִינִים יַחַד, אֲפִלּוּ רַק מִשּׁוּם שְׁמִירָה שֶׁלֹּא יִבְרְחוּ. וְיֵשׁ לִזָּהֵר בָּזֶה בְּעוֹפוֹת, שֶׁלֹּא לִקְשֹׁר שְׁנֵי מִינִים יַחַד, שֶׁקְּצָת טוֹעִין בָּזֶה.

ו) פֶּרֶד, הוּא הַבָּא מִן הַסּוּס וְהַחֲמוֹר, וְיֵשׁ בּוֹ שְׁנֵי מִינִים. יֵשׁ שֶׁאָבִיו סוּס וְאִמּוֹ חֲמוֹרָה, וְיֵשׁ שֶׁאִמּוֹ סוּסָה וְאָבִיו חֲמוֹר, וְהֵם כִּלְאַיִם זֶה בָּזֶה. וְלָכֵן הַבָּא לִקְשֹׁר שְׁתֵּי פְּרָדוֹת, בּוֹדֵק בְּסִימָנֵי אָזְנַיִם וְזָנָב וְקוֹל, אִם דּוֹמִין זֶה לָזֶה בְּיָדוּעַ שֶׁאִמָּן מִמִּין אֶחָד וּמֻתָּרוֹת. וְיֵשׁ אוֹמְרִים, דַּאֲפִלּוּ פֶּרֶד אֶחָד, הֲוֵי כִּלְאַיִם, מִשּׁוּם דְּבָא מִשְּׁנֵי מִינִים, וְאָסוּר לַעֲשׂוֹת בּוֹ מְלָאכָה אוֹ לִרְכֹּב עָלָיו.

סִימָן קעו
הִלְכוֹת כִּלְאֵי בְגָדִים (שַׁעַטְנֵז)

א) צֶמֶר רְחֵלִים וְאֵילִים עִם פִּשְׁתָּן, אָסוּר מִשּׁוּם כִּלְאַיִם, בֵּין שֶׁתָּפַר בֶּגֶד צֶמֶר עִם בֶּגֶד פִּשְׁתָּן אֲפִלּוּ בְּחוּטֵי מֶשִׁי אוֹ בְּחוּטֵי קַנְבּוֹס, בֵּין שֶׁתָּפַר בֶּגֶד צֶמֶר בְּחוּטֵי פִּשְׁתָּן אוֹ בְּהִפּוּךְ, בֵּין שֶׁקָּשַׁר חוּטֵי פִּשְׁתָּן עִם חוּטֵי צֶמֶר אוֹ שֶׁקְּלָעָן יַחַד, כָּל אֵלּוּ אֲסוּרִין מִשּׁוּם כִּלְאַיִם. הַתּוֹכֵף תְּכִיפָה אַחַת וְקָשַׁר אוֹ שֶׁתָּכַף שְׁתֵּי תְכִיפוֹת אַף־עַל־פִּי שֶׁלֹּא קָשַׁר, הֲוֵי חִבּוּר לְכִלְאָיִם. וְעַל כֵּן אָסוּר לְחַבֵּר בֶּגֶד צֶמֶר בְּבֶגֶד פִּשְׁתָּן אֲפִלּוּ עַל יְדֵי מַחַט בְּלֹא חוּט.

ב) עוֹרוֹת הַכְּבָשִׂים שֶׁעוֹשִׂין מֵהֶן בְּגָדִים, מֻתָּר לְתָפְרָן בְּחוּטֵי פִּשְׁתָּן וְאֵין חוֹשְׁשִׁין לְנִימוֹת שֶׁל צֶמֶר, אַף־עַל־פִּי שֶׁמִּתְחַבְּרִין בְּחוּט הַפִּשְׁתָּן, מִשּׁוּם דְּאֵלּוּ הַנִּימוֹת שֶׁל הַצֶּמֶר אֵינָן חוּטִין, וְלָא חֲשִׁבֵי, וּבָטְלֵי.

ג) לְחַבֵּר צֶמֶר וּפִשְׁתָּן עַל יְדֵי אֶמְצָעִי, דְּהַיְנוּ חֲתִיכַת עוֹר, לִתְפֹּר אוֹ לִקְשֹׁר מִצִּדּוֹ הָאֶחָד צֶמֶר וּמִצִּדּוֹ הַשֵּׁנִי פִּשְׁתָּן, לְהָרַמְבַּ"ם אָסוּר מִן הַתּוֹרָה, וְיֵשׁ מְקִלִּין. וְלָכֵן לְדִידְהוּ עוֹרוֹת הַתְּפוּרִין יַחַד בְּחוּטֵי פִּשְׁתָּן, מֻתָּר לְחַבְּרָם תַּחַת בֶּגֶד צֶמֶר, (וְאַף־עַל־פִּי שֶׁאֶפְשָׁר שֶׁהַחוּט שֶׁל קַנְבּוֹס, שֶׁהוּא תּוֹפֵר אֶת הָעוֹרוֹת תַּחַת הַבֶּגֶד שֶׁל צֶמֶר, יִכָּנֵס בְּתוֹךְ חוּטֵי פִּשְׁתָּן

4) If a wagon is being drawn by one kind of animal, you may not tie another kind of animal to the side of the cart or behind it.

5) It is forbidden to tie two diverse kinds of animals together even if only to prevent them from running away.[1] You must be careful about this with regard to fowl, not to tie them together, as some people are in error concerning this.

6) A mule is bred by a horse and a donkey, and it has two species. One is bred by a stallion and a she-donkey and the other by a mare and a donkey. These mules are considered diverse kinds of beasts. Therefore, if you wish to hitch two mules together, first examine the features of their ears, tails, and voices. If these are similar, it indicates that their mothers are of the same kind and it is permitted to hitch them together. Some *Poskim* maintain that even a single mule is considered a mixture since it was bred from two species, and it is forbidden to do work with it or to ride on it.

Chapter 176

Laws Concerning Shaatnez (Wool Mixed with Linen)

1) [A garment made of] wool of ewes or rams, mixed with linen is forbidden, for it is *kelayim* (*shaatnez*). Whether a woolen garment was sewn to a linen garment even with silk or hemp thread, or whether a woolen garment was sewn with linen thread or vice versa, whether linen thread was tied with woolen thread or braided together, all of these are forbidden for they are *shaatnez.* Sewing one stitch and tying it, or sewing two stitches even without tying them is enough of a connection to make it *shaatnez.* Therefore, it is forbidden to join a woolen garment with a linen garment even with a needle [pin] without thread.

2) Sheepskins from which clothing is made, may be sewn with linen threads, and we are not concerned with the woolen hairs although they are joined with linen thread, because these woolen hairs are not considered threads and are of no use and are considered non-existent.

3) To join wool and linen (flax) with something between them, for example, to take a piece of leather and sew or fasten a piece of wool on one side and a piece of linen on the other side, is forbidden by Scriptural law, according to the *Rambam*; but some *Poskim* permit it.[1] Therefore, according to the latter opinion, skins sewed together with linen threads may be used as a lining for a woolen garment. (And though it is possible that the hemp thread, with which the skins are sewn to line the woolen garment, will penetrate among the flax threads with which the skin were

1. *Taz* 297:5.
1. *Rosh.*

שֶׁתְּפוּרִין בָּהֶן הָעוֹרוֹת לֵית לָן בָּהּ), וְהָכִי נוֹהֲגִין. אֲבָל בַּעַל נֶפֶשׁ, יֵשׁ לוֹ לְהַחְמִיר כְּדַעַת הָרַמְבַּ"ם.

ד) אֲפִלּוּ עֲשָׂרָה מַצָּעוֹת זֶה עַל גַּב זֶה, וְהַתַּחְתּוֹן כִּלְאַיִם, אָסוּר לֵישֵׁב עַל הָעֶלְיוֹן.

ה) בֶּגֶד גָּדוֹל, שֶׁכִּלְאַיִם בְּקָצֶה אֶחָד מִמֶּנּוּ, אָסוּר לְכַסּוֹת עַצְמוֹ בּוֹ אֲפִלּוּ בְּקָצֶה הַשֵּׁנִי, אַף־עַל־פִּי שֶׁהַכִּלְאַיִם מֻנָּחִים עַל הָאָרֶץ.

ו) הַתּוֹפֵר כְּסוּת כִּלְאַיִם בִּשְׁבִיל גּוֹי, תּוֹפְרוֹ כְּדַרְכּוֹ, אַף־עַל־פִּי שֶׁהַכְּסוּת מֻנַּחַת עַל אַרְכּוּבוֹתָיו, וּבִלְבַד שֶׁלֹּא יְכַוֵּן לֵהָנוֹת מִמַּה שֶּׁמֻּנַּחַת עָלָיו. וְכֵן מוֹכְרֵי כְסוּת שֶׁנּוֹשְׂאִין אוֹתָן עַל כִּתְפֵיהֶן לְמָכְרָן, מֻתָּר, וּבִלְבַד שֶׁלֹּא יְכַוְּנוּ שֶׁיָּגֵנּוּ עֲלֵיהֶם מִפְּנֵי הַצִּנָּה אוֹ מִפְּנֵי הַגְּשָׁמִים. וּמִכָּל מָקוֹם, הַיְרֵאִים נוֹשְׂאִין אוֹתָן עַל גַּבֵּי מַקֵּל.

ז) מִטְפַּחַת הַיָּדַיִם, וְכֵן מִטְפַּחַת שֶׁמְּקַנְּחִין בָּהּ אַחַר הָרְחִיצָה, וּמִטְפַּחַת הַשֻּׁלְחָן שֶׁאוֹכְלִין עָלָיו וְכַיּוֹצֵא בָזֶה, וְכֵן מַפָּה שֶׁעַל הַשֻּׁלְחָן בְּבֵית־הַכְּנֶסֶת שֶׁקּוֹרִין עָלָיו, אֲסוּרוֹת מִשּׁוּם כִּלְאַיִם. וְכֵן וִילוֹן, אָסוּר לַעֲשׂוֹת מִכִּלְאַיִם. אֲבָל פָּרֹכֶת שֶׁלִּפְנֵי אֲרוֹן הַקֹּדֶשׁ מֻתָּר.

ח) עֲגָלוֹת שֶׁיֵּשׁ לָהֶן מִכְסֶה שֶׁהַשָּׂרִים הוֹלְכִין בָּהֶן, וְיֵשׁ מֵהֶן מְחֻפּוֹת מִבִּפְנִים בְּבִגְדֵי צֶמֶר שֶׁהֵם כִּלְאַיִם, כִּי מִסְתָמָא נִתְפְּרוּ בְּחוּטֵי פִשְׁתָּן, מֻתָּר לָלֶכֶת בָּהֶם, וּבִלְבַד שֶׁיִּזָּהֵר שֶׁלֹּא לְהִשָּׁעֵן בַּצְּדָדִים שֶׁיֵּשׁ שָׁם כִּלְאַיִם וּמִכָּל־שֶׁכֵּן שֶׁיִּזָּהֵר שֶׁלֹּא לָשֶׁבֶת עַל הַכָּרִים, שֶׁהֵן כִּלְאַיִם. וְיֵשׁ מַתִּירִין אֲפִלּוּ לֵישֵׁב עַל הַכָּרִים, כֵּיוָן שֶׁעֲשׂוּיִים בְּאֹפֶן שֶׁאֵינָם נִכְפָּפִים עַל צִדְדֵי הָאָדָם.

סִימָן קעז
הִלְכוֹת בְּכוֹר בְּהֵמָה טְהוֹרָה

א) יִשְׂרָאֵל שֶׁיָּלְדָה לוֹ בְּהֵמָה שֶׁלּוֹ בְּכוֹר, מִצְוָה לְהַקְדִּישׁוֹ וְלוֹמַר, הֲרֵי זֶה קֹדֶשׁ, שֶׁנֶּאֱמַר, תַּקְדִּישׁ לַה׳ אֱלֹהֶיךָ. וְאִם לֹא הִקְדִּישׁוֹ, מִתְקַדֵּשׁ מֵאֵלָיו מֵרֶחֶם. וְנוֹתְנִים אוֹתוֹ לַכֹּהֵן, בֵּין שֶׁהוּא תָם, בֵּין שֶׁנָּפַל בּוֹ מוּם, וַאֲפִלּוּ נוֹלַד בְּמוּמוֹ. אֲבָל לֹא יִתְּנֵהוּ לַכֹּהֵן בְּעוֹדוֹ קָטָן מְאֹד, שֶׁאֵין זוֹ גְדֻלָּה לַכֹּהֵן, אֶלָּא הַבְּעָלִים מְטַפְּלִים בּוֹ עַד שֶׁיִּגְדַּל מְעַט, דְּהַיְנוּ, בְּדַקָּה שְׁלֹשִׁים

sewn, we are not concerned about it). And this is the prevailing custom.[2] Nevertheless, one who is spiritially sensitive, should be strict and heed the opinion of the *Rambam.*

4) Even if ten mats [lie] one on top of the other, and the bottom one is *shaatnez*, it is forbidden to sit on the top one.[3]

5) If a large garment contains *shaatnez* at one end, it is forbidden to cover yourself even with the other end, even if the *shaatnez* part is resting on the ground.

6) If you sew a garment of *shaatnez* for a gentile, you may sew it in the regular manner, even though the garment rests upon your knees, provided you do not have intention to derive pleasure from its resting on you. Also clothing dealers, who carry [coats] on their shoulders to sell them, are permitted (to carry them) provided they do not intend to use them for protection from the cold or the rain. Nevertheless, God-fearing people carry them on a stick.[4]

7) Handkerchiefs, and bath towels, tablecloths and similar things, also the cover of the lectern in the synagogue on which the Torah is read, are subject to the law of *shaatnez.* It is also forbidden to have curtains containing *shaatnez,* but the curtain covering the Holy Ark may be made of *shaatnez.*

8) It is permitted to ride in covered wagons, (coaches) which are upholstered on the inside, with woolen cloth containing *shaatnez,* providing you are careful not to lean on the sides that contain *shaatnez.* You must be especially careful not to sit on cushions containing *shaatnez.* Some *Poskim* even permit to sit on such cushions, since they are made in such a way that they do not bend over the sides of the person.

Chapter 177

The Firstborn of Clean Animals

1) If a Jew's, clean [kosher] animal gives birth to a firstborn,[1] it is a mitzvah (for the owner) to sanctify it and say "This is holy;" for it is said, "You shall sanctify it to Adonoy, your God."[2] If he did not sanctify it, it is holy on its own accord from the womb, and it must be given to the *kohein* regardless if it is perfect, or if it received a defect after its birth, or even if it was born with a defect. However, it should not be given to the *kohein* when it is very young, because this does not do honor to the *kohein.* The owner should raise it until it is somewhat grown up, that is thirty days

---

2. *Ramah* 299:2.
3. Sitting on *Shaatnez* is a Rabbinic prohibition, and is only forbidden if the mat is soft, so that when you sit on it, it is possible that at least one thread will fold over under you. (See *Shulchan Aruch* 301:1)
4. If there is a doubt whether the garment contains *Shaatnez,* it is nevertheless permitted to try it on for size etc. If it definitely has *Shaatnez,* you must consult a Rav.
1. Male.
2. *Deuteronomy* 15:19.

יוֹם, וּבְגַסָּה חֲמִשִּׁים יוֹם. וְאִם אֵין לוֹ כֹּהֵן מָצוּי, חַיָּב לְטַפֵּל בּוֹ עַד שֶׁיִּזְדַּמֵּן לוֹ כֹּהֵן.

ב) אָמַר לוֹ הַכֹּהֵן תּוֹךְ הַזְּמָן, תְּנֵהוּ לִי וַאֲנִי אֲטַפֵּל בּוֹ, אִם אֵין בּוֹ מוּם, אֵינוֹ רַשַּׁאי לִתְּנוֹ לוֹ, מִפְּנֵי שֶׁזֶּהוּ כְּמוֹ שֶׁעוֹשֶׂה לוֹ טוֹבָה לְיִשְׂרָאֵל, (שֶׁהוּא יְטַפֵּל בּוֹ תַּחְתָּיו), בִּשְׁבִיל שֶׁיִּתְּנֵהוּ לוֹ, וְזֶה אָסוּר, דַּהֲוֵי כְּגוֹזֵל אֲחֵרִים. אֲבָל אִם נָפַל בּוֹ מוּם תּוֹךְ הַזְּמָן וְאָמַר לוֹ הַכֹּהֵן תְּנֵהוּ לִי שֶׁאֹכְלֶנּוּ, מֻתָּר, שֶׁהֲרֵי יָכוֹל לְשָׁחֲטוֹ מִיָּד.

ג) אִם הַכֹּהֵן אֵינוֹ רוֹצֶה לְקַבְּלוֹ, מִפְּנֵי כִּי בַּזְּמַן הַזֶּה יֵשׁ בּוֹ טֹרַח גָּדוֹל לְגַדְּלוֹ עַד שֶׁיִּפּוֹל בּוֹ מוּם, אֵינוֹ רַשַּׁאי, מִפְּנֵי שֶׁנִּרְאֶה כִּמְבַזֶּה מַתְּנוֹת כְּהֻנָּה. וּמִכָּל מָקוֹם הַיִּשְׂרָאֵל אָסוּר לוֹ לִתְּנוֹ לַכֹּהֵן כְּדֵי לְהַקְנִיטוֹ אוֹ לִנְקֹם מִמֶּנּוּ. וְאִם עוֹשֶׂה כֵן, אֵין הַכֹּהֵן צָרִיךְ לְקַבְּלוֹ. וְכֵן אִם פָּשַׁע הַיִּשְׂרָאֵל, שֶׁהָיָה יָכוֹל לִמְכֹּר אֶת הַבְּהֵמָה לַגּוֹי קֹדֶם שֶׁיָּלְדָה וְלֹא מְכָרָהּ, אֵין הַכֹּהֵן צָרִיךְ לְקַבֵּל אֶת הַבְּכוֹר, אֶלָּא הוּא בְעַצְמוֹ יְטַפֵּל בּוֹ עַד שֶׁיִּפּוֹל בּוֹ מוּם, וְאָז יִתְּנֵהוּ לַכֹּהֵן.

ד) הַבְּכוֹר בַּזְּמַן הַזֶּה, צְרִיכִין לְהַשְׁהוֹתוֹ עַד שֶׁיִּפּוֹל בּוֹ מוּם. וּכְשֶׁנָּפַל בּוֹ מוּם, מַרְאִין אוֹתוֹ לִשְׁלֹשָׁה בַּעֲלֵי תוֹרָה, וְאֶחָד מֵהֶם יִהְיֶה בָקִי לָדַעַת אִם הוּא מוּם קָבוּעַ, וּמַתִּירִין אוֹתוֹ, וְאַחַר כָּךְ שׁוֹחֲטִין אוֹתוֹ. וְאִם הוּא כָּשֵׁר, אוֹכְלִין אוֹתוֹ, וּמֻתָּר גַּם לְיִשְׂרָאֵל. אֲבָל אֵינוֹ נִמְכָּר בְּמָקוּלִין, וְאֵינוֹ נִשְׁקָל בְּלִיטְרָא, וְאֵין נוֹתְנִין מִמֶּנּוּ לַכְּלָבִים, וְאֵין מוֹכְרִין אוֹ נוֹתְנִין מִמֶּנּוּ לַגּוֹי.

ה) הַבְּכוֹר שֶׁנּוֹלַד בּוֹ מוּם, אִם יֵשׁ בַּמָּקוֹם הַהוּא אֲנָשִׁים הָרְאוּיִים לְהַתִּירוֹ, מַרְאִין אוֹתוֹ לָהֶם מִיָּד. וּמִשֶּׁהֻתַּר, אֵין מַשְׁהִין אוֹתוֹ הַרְבֵּה, אֶלָּא אִם הֻתַּר תּוֹךְ שְׁנָתוֹ, יְכוֹלִין לְהַשְׁהוֹתוֹ עַד שֶׁתְּהֵא לוֹ שָׁנָה. וְאִם הֻתַּר סָמוּךְ לִשְׁנָתוֹ אוֹ לְאַחַר שְׁנָתוֹ, אֵין מַשְׁהִין אוֹתוֹ יוֹתֵר מִשְּׁלֹשִׁים יוֹם. עָבַר וְהִשְׁהָה אוֹתוֹ יוֹתֵר, אֵינוֹ נִפְסָל בְּכָךְ.

ו) הַכֹּהֵן צָרִיךְ לְגַדֵּל אֶת הַבְּכוֹר עַד שֶׁיִּפֹּל בּוֹ מוּם. וְיָכוֹל לְמָכְרוֹ לְיִשְׂרָאֵל, בֵּין שֶׁיֵּשׁ בּוֹ מוּם בֵּין שֶׁאֵין בּוֹ מוּם, רַק שֶׁהַיִּשְׂרָאֵל יִנְהַג בּוֹ בִּקְדֻשַּׁת בְּכוֹרָה, וְגַם לֹא יִקְנֵהוּ לִסְחוֹרָה.

for a small animal (sheep or goat), and fifty days for a large animal (cow). If a *kohein* cannot be found, the owner must care for it until a *kohein* comes along.

2) If, within this time the *kohein* said to the owner: "Give it to me and I will raise it," if it does not have a defect, he is not permitted to give it to him, because this would appear as if the *kohein* is doing the Yisroel (owner) a favor (that he is tending it for him) in consideration of his giving the animal to him. And this is forbidden, for it is tantamount to robbing the other *kohanim*. However, if the animal was blemished during this time, and the *kohein* said to the owner, "Give it to me so that I may eat it," it is permitted to give it to him since he may slaughter it immediately.

3) At present if the *kohein* does not want to accept the animal, because it is too bothersome to raise it until it is blemished, he is not allowed to refuse it because it looks as though he is showing contempt for the priestly gifts. Nevertheless, the Yisroel is forbidden to give it to the *kohein* in order to vex him or to take revenge on him. If he does so with this intention, the *kohein* need not accept it. Similarly, if the Yisroel was negligent in that he was able to sell the animal to a Gentile before it gave birth and he did not sell it, the *kohein* need not accept that firstborn; rather the owner himself must raise it until it becomes blemished, and then give it to the *kohein*.

4) In our times, the firstborn must be kept until it is blemished, and upon receiving the blemish, it must be shown to three Torah scholars one of whom must be an expert, to know if it is a permanent blemish, and, if it is, they permit its use. Afterwards it is slaughtered and if found to be kosher, it may be eaten even by a Yisroel ([and certainly by a *kohein*]). However, it should not be sold in the meat market, or weighed out by the pound and no part of it may be given to the dogs, and you may not sell, or give, any part of it to a Gentile.

5) When a firstborn sustains a blemish, and there are men in the area who are competent to rule that it is permitted, it should be shown to them immediately. Once it has been permitted, it should not be kept a long time. If it was permitted during its first year, it may be kept until it is a year old. If it was permitted near the end of its first year, or after its first year, it should not be kept for longer than thirty days. If the owner transgressed and kept it longer, it is not disqualified because of this.

6) The *kohein* must raise the firstborn until it sustains a blemish. He may sell it to a Yisroel whether it has a blemish or whether it does not have a blemish, providing the Yisroel treats it in a manner befitting the holiness of a firstborn, and is also not buying it for commercial purposes.

ז) אֵין מַרְגִּילִין בַּבְּכוֹר, דְּהַיְנוּ לְהַפְשִׁיט עוֹרוֹ שָׁלֵם דֶּרֶךְ מַרְגְּלוֹתָיו, דְּנִרְאֶה כְּבִזָּיוֹן, שֶׁבְּעוֹד שֶׁהָעוֹר עַל הַקֳּדָשִׁים, חוֹשֵׁב לַעֲשׂוֹת מִמֶּנּוּ מַפּוּחַ.

ח) שְׁחָטוֹ וְנִמְצָא טְרֵפָה, עוֹרוֹ וּבְשָׂרוֹ אֲסוּרִים בַּהֲנָאָה, וְטָעוּן קְבוּרָה. וְהוּא הַדִּין אִם מֵת מֵעַצְמוֹ טָעוּן קְבוּרָה. וְנוֹהֲגִין שֶׁכּוֹרְכִין אוֹתוֹ בְּסָדִין וְקוֹבְרִין אוֹתוֹ בְּבֵית הַקְּבָרוֹת בָּעֹמֶק.

ט) הַבְּכוֹר, בֵּין תָּם בֵּין בַּעַל מוּם, אָסוּר בְּגִזָּה וַעֲבוֹדָה. וַאֲפִלּוּ נִתְלַשׁ מִמֶּנּוּ צֶמֶר מֵעַצְמוֹ, אוֹתוֹ הַצֶּמֶר, אָסוּר בַּהֲנָאָה לְעוֹלָם. אֲבָל הַצֶּמֶר שֶׁעַל גּוּפוֹ, אִם נִשְׁחַט בְּמוּמוֹ, הַשְּׁחִיטָה מַתֶּרֶת גַּם אֶת הַצֶּמֶר, כְּמוֹ שֶׁהִיא מַתֶּרֶת אֶת הַבָּשָׂר וְאֶת הָעוֹר.

י) הַבְּכוֹר, אֵין לוֹ הֶתֵּר אֶלָּא בְּמוּם. וְאָסוּר לְכָנְסוֹ לְכִפָּה כְּדֵי שֶׁיָּמוּת מֵעַצְמוֹ מִשּׁוּם דְּמַפְסִיד קָדָשִׁים.

יא) אָסוּר לַעֲשׂוֹת מוּם בַּבְּכוֹר. וַאֲפִלּוּ לִגְרֹם לוֹ מוּם, כְּגוֹן לִתֵּן בָּצֵק עַל גַּבֵּי אָזְנוֹ כְּדֵי שֶׁיִּטְּלֶנּוּ הַכֶּלֶב מִשָּׁם וְיִקְטַע אָזְנוֹ עִמּוֹ וְכַיּוֹצֵא בָזֶה, אוֹ שֶׁיֹּאמַר לַגּוֹי לַעֲשׂוֹת בּוֹ מוּם, אָסוּר. וּמֻתָּר לִתְּנוֹ לַגּוֹי לְגַדְּלוֹ אוֹ לְשָׁמְרוֹ.

יב) הַלּוֹקֵחַ בְּהֵמָה מִן הַגּוֹי, וְאֵין יָדוּעַ אִם כְּבָר יָלְדָה אוֹ לֹא, וְיָלְדָה עַתָּה בְּבֵית יִשְׂרָאֵל, הֲרֵי זֶה סְפֵק בְּכוֹר. וַאֲפִלּוּ הַגּוֹי מֵסִיחַ לְפִי תֻמּוֹ שֶׁכְּבָר יָלְדָה, לָא מַהֲנֵי. וְגַם הַסִּימָנִים שֶׁבְּסִדְקֵי קַרְנַיִם, לָא מַהֲנֵי וַאֲפִלּוּ אִם הִיא חוֹלֶבֶת, לָא מַהֲנֵי, אֶלָּא אִם כֵּן רוֹאִין שֶׁמֵּנִיקָה עֵגֶל. וְאִם הִיא חוֹלֶבֶת וְגַם הַגּוֹי מֵסִיחַ לְפִי תֻמּוֹ שֶׁלֹּא לְהַשְׁבִּיחַ אֶת מִקָּחוֹ וְאוֹמֵר שֶׁכְּבָר יָלְדָה, מַהֲנֵי בְּפָרוֹת, אֲבָל לֹא בְּעִזִּים.

יג) כֹּהֲנִים וּלְוִיִּם, חַיָּבִים גַּם כֵּן בִּבְכוֹר בְּהֵמָה טְהוֹרָה אֶלָּא שֶׁהַכֹּהֵן מַפְרִישׁוֹ וּמְעַכְּבוֹ לְעַצְמוֹ וּמַחֲזִיקוֹ בִּקְדֻשַּׁת בְּכוֹר.

יד) אִם יֵשׁ לַגּוֹי שֻׁתָּפוּת עִם יִשְׂרָאֵל בִּבְהֵמָה, וְכֵן הַמְקַבֵּל בְּהֵמָה מִן הַגּוֹי לְגַדְּלָהּ וְשֶׁיַּחְלְקוּ בִּוְלָדוֹת, פְּטוּרִין מִן הַבְּכוֹרָה, שֶׁנֶּאֱמַר, פֶּטֶר

7) It is not permitted to be *margil* the firstborn.[3] This means it must not be skinned in one piece, from its feet upward, for it would appear disgraceful to skin the sacred [animal], with the intention of making bellows of it (the skin).

8) If the firstborn is slaughtered and found to be a *treifa,* [4] it is forbidden to benefit from its hide and its meat, and it must be buried. Similarly, if it dies a natural death it must be buried. It is customary to wrap it in a sheet, and bury it deep in the ground of the cemetery.

9) It is forbidden to fleece or to do work with the first born regardless if it is blemished or not. Even if some wool came off by itself, no benefit may ever be derived from that wool. However, the wool that is on its body, when slaughtered after receiving a blemish, is permitted for the slaughtering permits the wool for use just as it permits the use of the meat and the hide.

10) The firstborn is not permitted to be eaten unless it sustains a blemish. It is forbidden to close it up in a vault so that it should die of its own, for this would be destroying a sacred thing.

11) It is forbidden to make a blemish in a firstborn, or even to cause a blemish indirectly; for example, to put dough on its ear, in order for a dog to grab it and bite off its ear with it; or to cause a blemish in some similar way. It is forbidden to tell a Gentile to make a blemish in a firstborn, but it is permitted to give it to a Gentile to raise it or watch it.

12) If an animal is purchased from a Gentile, and it is not known if it has given birth before or not, and now it has given birth while in the possession of the Jew, its status as a firstborn is doubtful, and even if the Gentile innocently volunteers the information that it had previously given birth, it is of no avail. Even the characteristic signs in the cracks of its horns are of no avail. And even if she was being milked, it is of no avail, unless we see her nursing a calf. If she is being milked, and the Gentile innocently volunteers, (not for the purpose of promoting the sale,) and states that she has previously given birth, these two things together are proof with regards to cows, but not with regards to goats.[5]

13) *Kohanim* and Levites are also subject to the laws regarding the firstborn of clean animals, except that the *kohein* sets it aside, and keeps it for himself and maintains it in the state of holiness that is due a firstborn.[6]

14) If a Gentile and a Jew are partners in an animal, or a Jew agrees to raise an animal of a Gentile, and share equally in the offspring, they are exempt from the laws of the firstborn for it is said: "Whatever opens the womb among the Children

---

3. Not even if it has a blemish. (*Taz* 307:1.)

4. A *treifa* is an animal that has one or more of the eighteen categories of wounds and defects that render it prohibited for eating.

5. It is the nature of many goats to give milk, although they did not give birth.

6. He keeps it until it gets blemished, whereby he slaughters and eats it.

כָּל־רֶחֶם בִּבְנֵי יִשְׂרָאֵל, עַד שֶׁיִּהְיֶה הַכֹּל מִיִּשְׂרָאֵל. וְגוֹי הַמְקַבֵּל בְּהֵמָה מִיִּשְׂרָאֵל לְגַדְּלָהּ וְשֶׁיַּחְלְקוּ בִּוְלָדוֹת, לְהַרְבֵּה פּוֹסְקִים לָא מַהֲנֵי אֶלָּא צָרִיךְ הַיִּשְׂרָאֵל לִמְכֹּר אֶת הָאֵם לַגּוֹי.

טו) מִצְוָה לִמְכֹּר לַגּוֹי אֶת הַבְּהֵמָה הַטְּהוֹרָה אוֹ לְהִשְׁתַּתֵּף עִמּוֹ בָּהּ קֹדֶם שֶׁתֵּלֵד כְּדֵי לְפָטְרָהּ מֵהַבְּכוֹרָה. וְאַף־עַל־פִּי שֶׁמַּפְקִיעַ קְדֻשַּׁת הַבְּכוֹר, הָכִי עָדִיף טְפֵי, שֶׁלֹּא יָבוֹא לִידֵי מִכְשׁוֹל בְּגִזָּה וַעֲבוֹדָה. וְאִם יַקְנֶה לַגּוֹי אֶת הָעֻבָּר, לֹא מַהֲנֵי, כֵּיוָן דַּהֲוֵי דָּבָר שֶׁלֹּא בָא לָעוֹלָם, אֶלָּא צָרִיךְ לְהַקְנוֹת לוֹ אֶת הָאֵם. וְהַקִּנְיָן יִהְיֶה בְּאֹפֶן זֶה, יִשְׁתַּוֶּה עִם הַגּוֹי עַל מְחִיר הַפָּרָה, וְגַם יַשְׂכִּיר לוֹ אֶת הַמָּקוֹם אֲשֶׁר הַפָּרָה עוֹמֶדֶת שָׁם, וְהַגּוֹי יִתֵּן לוֹ פְּרוּטָה, וְיֹאמַר לוֹ הַיִּשְׂרָאֵל, בְּזוֹ הַפְּרוּטָה, תִּקְנֶה אֶת הַמָּקוֹם אֲשֶׁר הַפָּרָה עוֹמֶדֶת שָׁמָּה, וְהַמָּקוֹם הַזֶּה יַקְנֶה לְךָ אֶת הַפָּרָה. אוֹ יַעֲשֶׂה כֵּן, שֶׁלְּאַחַר שֶׁהִשְׁתַּוּוּ עַל מְחִיר הַפָּרָה, יִתֵּן לוֹ הַגּוֹי פְּרוּטָה, וְגַם יִמְשֹׁךְ הַגּוֹי אֶת הַפָּרָה לִרְשׁוּתוֹ אוֹ לְסִמְטָא, וְקוֹנֶה אוֹתָהּ בִּמְשִׁיכָה וּמָעוֹת. וַאֲפִלּוּ אִם מַחֲזִירָהּ אַחַר כָּךְ לִרְשׁוּת יִשְׂרָאֵל, לֹא אִכְפַּת לָן.

סִימָן קעח
הִלְכוֹת פֶּטֶר חֲמוֹר

א) יִשְׂרָאֵל שֶׁיֵּשׁ לוֹ חֲמוֹרָה וְיָלְדָה בְכוֹר, מִצְוָה לִפְדּוֹתוֹ. וּבַמֶּה פּוֹדֶה אוֹתוֹ. בְּשֶׂה מִן הַכְּבָשִׂים אוֹ מִן הָעִזִּים, בֵּין זָכָר בֵּין נְקֵבָה, בֵּין גָּדוֹל בֵּין קָטָן, בֵּין תָּם בֵּין בַּעַל מוּם, וּבִלְבַד שֶׁלֹּא יְהֵא טְרֵפָה וְלֹא שָׁחוּט וְלֹא בֶן־פְּקוּעָה, וְיִתֵּן אֶת הַשֶּׂה לַכֹּהֵן. וּמֵאֵימָתַי חַיָּב לִפְדּוֹתוֹ. מִשֶּׁיִּוָּלֵד עַד שְׁלֹשִׁים יוֹם, אֶלָּא שֶׁמִּצְוָה לִפְדּוֹתוֹ מִיָּד, שֶׁלֹּא לְהַשְׁהוֹת אֶת הַמִּצְוָה. וּלְאַחַר שֶׁפָּדָה אוֹתוֹ, הֲרֵי הוּא בְּיַד הַיִּשְׂרָאֵל חֻלִּין גְּמוּרִים, וְגַם הַשֶּׂה הוּא בְּיַד הַכֹּהֵן חֻלִּין גְּמוּרִים.

ב) מִיָּד כְּשֶׁהִפְרִישׁ אֶת הַטָּלֶה שֶׁיְּהֵא תַּחַת פֶּטֶר הַחֲמוֹר, נַעֲשָׂה פֶּטֶר הַחֲמוֹר חֻלִּין, אֲפִלּוּ קֹדֶם שֶׁנְּתָנוֹ אֶת הַטָּלֶה לַכֹּהֵן. לְפִיכָךְ מִיָּד כְּשֶׁמַּפְרִישׁוֹ, מְבָרֵךְ אֲשֶׁר קִדְּשָׁנוּ בְּמִצְוֹתָיו וְצִוָּנוּ עַל פִּדְיוֹן פֶּטֶר חֲמוֹר.

---

7. *Exodus* 13:2.
8. This applies only now, since there is no *Beis Hamikdash*. (*Taz* 320:5)
9. Therefore, transfer of ownership cannot be accomplished.
10. A *perutah* was a coin of minimal value.
11. The yard thus acquires its own contents for its owner. This is called *kinyan chatzer*.

of Yisrael,"[7] meaning, all of it must belong to a Jew. If a Gentile agrees to raise an animal of a Jew, and share equally in the offspring, according to many *Poskim* it is of no avail, but the Jew must sell the mother to the Gentile.

15) It is a mitzvah to sell to a Gentile the clean animal (before it gives birth), or to form a partnership with him before it gives birth, in order to exempt it from the laws of the firstborn.[8] And although (by doing this), it circumvents the holiness of the firstborn, it is, nevertheless, preferable so that no violations will be committed with regard to its wool and its use for work. Transferring the title (of the calf) to the Gentile when the calf is yet unborn is of no avail, since it is something that has not come into existence;[9] but the title of the mother must be transferred as well. The transfer of the title should be done in this manner: the owner should come to terms with the Gentile regarding the price of the cow, and also rent him the place that the cow now occupies; the Gentile should give him a *perutah,*[10] and the Jew should say to him, "With this *perutah* you shall acquire the place that the cow now occupies, and this place will acquire the title of the cow for you.[11] It can also be done in this manner: after they come to terms about the price of the cow, the Gentile should give him a *perutah,* and then lead the cow into his own premises, or into an alleyway, whereby he acquires title both by *meshicha* (actual transfer) and with money. Even if he returns the cow afterwards to the premises of the Jew it does not matter.

Chapter 178
The Firstborn of a Donkey

1) If a Jew has a female-donkey that gives birth to a firstborn male, it is a mitzvah to redeem it. With what do you redeem it? With the young of sheep or goats whether male or female, whether large or small, whether perfect or blemished; provided it is not a *treifa,*[1] it is not slaughtered, and is not a *ben pekuah.*[2] This lamb must then be given to the *kohein.* From when are you obliged to redeem it? At anytime from the day it was born until it dies. However, it is a mitzvah to redeem it immediately, in order not to delay the performance of the mitzvah. After it has been redeemed it remains in the owner's possession, and is no longer considered sacred. Also the lamb in the possession of the *kohein* is not considered sacred.

2) Immediately, upon setting aside the lamb to be exchanged for the firstborn donkey, the firstborn donkey is considered a secular item even before the lamb is given to the *kohein.* Therefore, as soon as the lamb is set aside, this *berachah* is recited: *Asher kidishanu bemitzvosav vetzivanu al pidyon petter chamor* "Who has sanctified us with His commandments, and has commanded us concerning redemption of the firstborn donkey."

---

1. See Chapter 177, footnote 4.
2. When a cow carries an unborn calf, the slaughter of the cow is considered the slaughter of the calf as well, and thus the calf, although alive, does not require further slaughtering. This type of calf is called a *ben pekuah.*

ג) קֹדֶם שֶׁנִּפְדָּה, אָסוּר בַּהֲנָאָה, וַאֲפִלּוּ נְתָנוֹ לַכֹּהֵן. גַּם הַכֹּהֵן אָסוּר לְהִשְׁתַּמֵּשׁ בּוֹ, עַד שֶׁיִּפְדֶּה אוֹתוֹ וְיִקַּח אֶת הַשֶּׂה לְעַצְמוֹ. וְאִם מֵת קֹדֶם שֶׁנִּפְדָּה, יִקָּבֵר.

ד) אִם אֵינוֹ רוֹצֶה לִפְדּוֹתוֹ, מַכֵּהוּ בְּקוֹפִיץ בְּעָרְפּוֹ עַד שֶׁיָּמוּת וְיִקְבְּרֶנּוּ, מִפְּנֵי שֶׁאָסוּר בַּהֲנָאָה. וּמִצְוַת פְּדִיָּה, קוֹדֶמֶת לְמִצְוַת עֲרִיפָה.

ה) כֹּהֲנִים וּלְוִיִּם, פְּטוּרִים מִפֶּטֶר חֲמוֹר. וְכֵן בַּת־כֹּהֵן וּבַת לֵוִי. אֲבָל בַּעֲלֵיהֶן, חַיָּבִים כְּפֶטֶר חֲמוֹר שֶׁלָּהֶם. וְשֻׁתָּפוּת כֹּהֵן וְלֵוִי וְכֵן שֻׁתָּפוּת גּוֹי, גַּם כֵּן פּוֹטֶרֶת. אֲבָל אָסוּר לְהִשְׁתַּתֵּף עִמָּהֶם אוֹ לִמְכֹּר לָהֶם כְּדֵי לְהַפְקִיעַ קְדֻשָּׁתוֹ, כֵּיוָן דְּאֶפְשָׁר בִּפְדִיָּה אוֹ בַעֲרִיפָה.

סִימָן קעט
הִלְכוֹת הַלְוָאָה

א) מִצְוַת עֲשֵׂה לְהַלְווֹת לַעֲנִיֵּי יִשְׂרָאֵל, שֶׁנֶּאֱמַר, אִם כֶּסֶף תַּלְוֶה אֶת־עַמִּי אֶת־הֶעָנִי עִמָּךְ וְגוֹ׳. וְאַף־עַל־גַּב דִּכְתִיב, אִם, קִבְּלוּ חֲכָמֵינוּ זִכְרוֹנָם לִבְרָכָה, דְּאִם זֶה, אֵינוֹ רְשׁוּת אֶלָּא חוֹבָה. הָכִי אָמְרִינָן בִּמְכִלְתָּא, אִם־כֶּסֶף תַּלְוֶה אֶת עַמִּי, חוֹבָה. אַתָּה אוֹמֵר חוֹבָה אוֹ אֵינוֹ אֶלָּא רְשׁוּת (מִדִּכְתִיב אִם) תַּלְמוּד לוֹמַר, הַעֲבֵט תַּעֲבִיטֶנּוּ, חוֹבָה וְלֹא רְשׁוּת. וְהָא דִּכְתִיב בִּלְשׁוֹן אִם, פֵּרוּשׁוֹ, אִם־כֶּסֶף תַּלְוֶה, אֶת עַמִּי תַּלְוֵהוּ וְלֹא לַגּוֹי. וּלְאֵיזֶה מֵעַמִּי, לְאוֹתוֹ שֶׁעִמָּךְ. מִכָּאן אָמְרוּ, עָנִי שֶׁהוּא קְרוֹבוֹ, קוֹדֵם לַעֲנִיִּים אֲחֵרִים. וַעֲנִיֵּי עִירוֹ, קוֹדְמִים לַעֲנִיֵּי עִיר אַחֶרֶת. וּגְדוֹלָה מִצְוַת הַהַלְוָאָה לְעָנִי, יוֹתֵר מִמִּצְוַת צְדָקָה לְעָנִי הַשּׁוֹאֵל, שֶׁזֶּה כְּבָר נִצְרַךְ לִשְׁאֹל, וְזֶה עֲדַיִן לֹא הִגִּיעַ לְמִדָּה זוֹ. וְהַתּוֹרָה הִקְפִּידָה עַל מִי שֶׁהוּא נִמְנָע מִלְּהַלְווֹת לְעָנִי, שֶׁנֶּאֱמַר, וְרָעָה עֵינְךָ בְּאָחִיךָ הָאֶבְיוֹן וְגוֹ׳. וְהַמַּלְוֶה לְעָנִי בִּשְׁעַת דָּחְקוֹ, עָלָיו הַכָּתוּב אוֹמֵר, אָז תִּקְרָא וַה׳ יַעֲנֶה.

ב) אֲפִלּוּ עָשִׁיר, אִם צָרִיךְ לִלְווֹת, מִצְוָה לְהַלְווֹת לוֹ וּלְהַנּוֹתוֹ אַף בִּדְבָרִים וּלְיָעֲצוֹ עֵצָה הַהוֹגֶנֶת לוֹ.

---

1. *Exodus* 22:24. This applies only if you have ready cash. It is also a mitzvah to lend him vessels or other thing. (*Ahavas Chesed* 1:2, 3)
2. *Deuteronomy* 15:8.

3) Before it is redeemed, it is forbidden to have any benefit from it, even if it was already given to the *kohein*. Even the *kohein* is forbidden to use it until it is redeemed and has taken the lamb for himself. If it died before it was redeemed, it must be buried

4) If the owner chooses not to redeem it, he strikes it with a hatchet on the back of its head, until it dies, and then buries it, as it is forbidden for use. The mitzvah of redemption takes preference over the mitzvah of breaking its neck.

5) *Kohanim* and Levites are exempt from the mitzvah of redeeming the firstborn of their donkeys. The daughter of a *kohein* or Levi are also exempt, but their husbands are obligated to redeem the firstborn of their donkeys. Partnerships with a *kohein* or a Levite, and also partnership with a Gentile, are exempt from the mitzvah; but it is forbidden to form a partnership with them, or to sell it to them in order to nullify its sacredness, since this may be achieved through redemption or by breaking its neck.

Chapter 179
Laws Concerning Loans

1) It is a mitzvah to lend money to Jews who are in need, as it is said, "If you lend money to My people, to the poor amongst you," etc.[1] Although it is written "if", our Sages of blessed memory, received the tradition that this "if" is not an option, but an obligation. The *Mechilta* states that the verse, "If you lend money to my people," denotes an obligation. Why do you say it is an obligation? Perhaps it is really optional (since it states "if")? Because we can infer from the verse, "And you shall surely lend him," [2] that it is obligatory and not optional. The word "if" written here means, when you lend money, you should lend it to *My* people, and not to heathens. And to whom of My people? To him that is with you. From this they inferred that your poor relatives take precedence over other poor people, and the poor of your city take precedence over the poor of other cities.[3] The *mitzvah* of lending money to a poor person is greater than giving charity to a poor beggar,[4] for the latter has already been reduced to begging, while the former has not yet reached this stage. The Torah is provoked with one who refuses to lend money to the poor, as it is said, "And your eye be evil against your needy brother"[5] etc. Concerning the one who lends to the needy in time of his distress, the Scripture says, "Then you shall call and God will answer."[6]

2) Even if a rich man needs to borrow money, it is a *mitzvah* to lend it to him, and to cheer him with kind words, and to give him proper advice.

3. *Maseches Baba Metzia* 21a.
4. *Maseches Shabbos* 63a.
5. *Deuteronomy* 15:9.
6. *Isaiah* 58:9.

ג) אָסוּר לְהַלְווֹת בְּלֹא עֵדִים וַאֲפִלּוּ לְתַלְמִיד־חָכָם, אֶלָּא אִם כֵּן מַלְוֵהוּ עַל הַמַּשְׁכּוֹן. וְהַמַּלְוֶה בִּשְׁטָר, מְשֻׁבָּח יוֹתֵר.

ד) אָסוּר לִנְגֹּשׂ אֶת הַלֹּוֶה כְּשֶׁיּוֹדֵעַ שֶׁאֵין לוֹ לִפְרֹעַ. וַאֲפִלּוּ לַעֲבוֹר לְפָנָיו, אָסוּר, מִפְּנֵי שֶׁהוּא נִכְלָם בִּרְאוֹתוֹ לַמַּלְוֶה וְאֵין יָדוֹ מַשֶּׂגֶת לִפְרֹעַ, וְעַל זֶה נֶאֱמַר, לֹא תִהְיֶה לוֹ כְּנשֶׁה.

ה) וּכְשֵׁם שֶׁאָסוּר לַמַּלְוֶה לִנְגֹּשׂ אֶת הַלֹּוֶה, כָּךְ אָסוּר לַלֹּוֶה לִכְבּוֹשׁ מָמוֹן חֲבֵרוֹ שֶׁבְּיָדוֹ וְלוֹמַר לוֹ, לֵךְ וָשׁוּב, כְּשֶׁיֵּשׁ לוֹ, שֶׁנֶּאֱמַר, אַל־תֹּאמַר לְרֵעֲךָ לֵךְ וָשׁוּב.

ו) אָסוּר לַלֹּוֶה לִקַּח אֶת הַהַלְוָאָה וּלְהוֹצִיאָהּ שֶׁלֹּא לְצֹרֶךְ עַד שֶׁתּוּכַל לְהֵאָבֵד וְלֹא יִמְצָא הַמַּלְוֶה מִמָּה לִגְבּוֹת, וַאֲפִלּוּ אִם הַמַּלְוֶה הוּא עָשִׁיר גָּדוֹל. וְהָעוֹשֶׂה כֵּן, נִקְרָא רָשָׁע, שֶׁנֶּאֱמַר, לֹוֶה רָשָׁע וְלֹא יְשַׁלֵּם. וְצִוּוּ חֲכָמִים, יְהִי מָמוֹן חֲבֵרְךָ חָבִיב עָלֶיךָ כְּשֶׁלָּךְ. וּכְשֶׁהַמַּלְוֶה מַכִּיר אֶת הַלֹּוֶה שֶׁהוּא בַּעַל מִדָּה זֹאת שֶׁלֹּא לְהַשְׁגִּיחַ עַל מָמוֹן אֲחֵרִים, מוּטָב שֶׁלֹּא לְהַלְווֹת לוֹ, מִמָּה שֶׁיַּלְוֵהוּ וְיִצְטָרֵךְ לְנָגְשׂוֹ אַחַר כָּךְ וְיַעֲבוֹר בְּכָל פַּעַם מִשּׁוּם לֹא תִהְיֶה לוֹ כְּנשֶׁה.

ז) הַמַּלְוֶה עַל הַמַּשְׁכּוֹן, צָרִיךְ לִזָּהֵר שֶׁלֹּא יִשְׁתַּמֵּשׁ בּוֹ, מִפְּנֵי שֶׁהוּא כְּמוֹ רִבִּית. וְאִם הִלְוָה לְעָנִי עַל מָרָא [אֵת] וְקַרְדֹּם וְכַיּוֹצֵא בּוֹ, שֶׁשְּׂכָרוֹ מְרֻבֶּה וְאֵינוֹ נִפְחָת אֶלָּא מְעַט, יָכוֹל לְהַשְׂכִּירוֹ אַף בְּלִי נְטִילַת רְשׁוּת מֵהַלֹּוֶה, וּלְנַכּוֹת לוֹ דְּמֵי הַשְּׂכִירוּת בְּחוֹבוֹ, דְּמִסְתָּמָא נִיחָא לֵהּ לַלֹּוֶה בְּכָךְ. וְיֵשׁ מִי שֶׁאוֹמֵר דְּדַוְקָא לַאֲחֵרִים יָכוֹל לְהַשְׂכִּירוֹ, אֲבָל לֹא לְעַצְמוֹ, שֶׁלֹּא יַחְשְׁדוּהוּ דְּמִשְׁתַּמֵּשׁ בּוֹ בְּחִנָּם, רַק בִּשְׁבִיל הַהַלְוָאָה.

ח) אִם רוֹצֶה הַמַּלְוֶה לָקַחַת מַשְׁכּוֹן מִן הַלֹּוֶה שֶׁלֹּא בִּשְׁעַת הַהַלְוָאָה אֶלָּא אַחַר כָּךְ, לֹא יַעֲשֶׂה כִּי אִם עַל פִּי בֵּית־דִּין.

---

7. *Maseches Baba Metzia* 75b. *Shulchan Aruch* 70:1. The reason is because you are placing a stumbling block in front of a person, who might be tempted to deny that you lent him. Also you may cause yourself to be cursed, for people may suspect you of lodging a false claim. Today people are not careful about this, and the *Peri Yitzchok* Vol. 1 Responsa 48 explains why. However, he, too, confirms that you should be careful to follow this *halacha,* as brought in *Rif, Rambam, Rosh, Shulchan Aruch* etc. without question.

3) It is forbidden to lend money without witnesses,[7] not even to a Torah scholar,[8] unless you are lending against a security. To lend money with legal documentation is the best course to take.

4) It is forbidden to demand payment from the borrower, when you know that he is unable to pay. It is forbidden even to appear before him, for he may be ashamed to see the lender, at a time when he is unable to repay the loan.[9] Concerning this it is said, "You shall not be unto him like a creditor."[10]

5) Just as the lender is forbidden to demand payment from the borrower, so, too, is the borrower forbidden to withhold his friend's money, and tell him, "Go away and return later," when he actually has the money; as it is said, "Do not tell your friend, "Go away and return later."[11]

6) A borrower is forbidden to take the loan, and spend it unnecessarily, and possibly lose it, and thus the lender will be unable to collect it. This applies even if the lender is very wealthy. One who does this is called a wicked person, as it is said, "The wicked borrow and do not repay."[12] The Sages have commanded: "Your friend's property should be as dear to you as your own."[13] If the lender recognizes that the borrower has this character, that he has no consideration for other people's property, it is better not to lend him, than to lend him and be compelled to press him later, thereby violating on each occasion the precept, "You shall not be to him like a creditor."

7) If you lend money on a security, you must refrain from using the security, for this is like taking interest. If you lend a poor man money on [the security of] a shovel, or on an axe, or a similar thing, which can be rented out at a good fee, and is only slightly depreciated by use, you may rent it out without obtaining the owner's permission, and deduct the proceeds from the debt, as it may be assumed that the borrower would agree to it. Some *Poskim* say you may rent out these articles only to others, but not to yourself,[14] lest you be suspected of using them free of charge merely because of the loan.

8) If the lender wants to take a security from the borrower, after the loan had been made, he should not do so by himself,[15] but rather through *Beis Din*.

---

8. Because he is engrossed in his Torah learning, he might forget that he borrowed the money.

9. If he is able to secure another loan with which to pay you, he must do so, and you may press him to do it. *Steipler Rav Z'l.* This is generally the situation nowadays.

10. *Exodus* 22:24.

11. *Proverbs* 3:28.

12. *Psalms* 37:21.

13. *Avos* 2:17.

14. Unless you made the loan on condition that you may use it and deduct payment from the loan. *Ramah* 72:1. *Smah* says this condition helps only if made at the time of loan and not later. The *Taz* disagrees. *Shach* questions the use of it under any condition, for you may still be suspected of using it free of charge.

15. It is a negative command (*de'oraisa*). *Shulchan Aruch* 97:6, as it is written, "You shall not enter his house." *Nesivos.*

ט) לְעוֹלָם יַרְחִיק אָדָם אֶת עַצְמוֹ מִן הָעֲרֵבוּת וּמִן הַפִּקְדוֹנוֹת בְּכָל מַה דְּאֶפְשָׁר.

י) מִי שֶׁיֵּשׁ לוֹ שְׁטַר־חוֹב עַל חֲבֵרוֹ, וְהַשְּׁטָר בָּלֶה וְהוֹלֵךְ לְהִמָּחֵק, יָבוֹא לְבֵית־דִּין וְיַעֲשׂוּ לוֹ קִיּוּם.

יא) אָסוּר לְהַשְׁהוֹת שְׁטָר פָּרוּעַ בְּתוֹךְ בֵּיתוֹ, שֶׁנֶּאֱמַר, וְאַל־תַּשְׁכֵּן בְּאֹהָלֶיךָ עַוְלָה.

יב) כְּמוֹ שֶׁצָּרִיךְ לִזָּהֵר בִּשְׁמִירַת פִּקָּדוֹן, כָּךְ צָרִיךְ לִזָּהֵר בִּשְׁמִירַת הַמַּשְׁכּוֹן בְּיוֹתֵר, מִפְּנֵי שֶׁהוּא כְּמוֹ שׁוֹמֵר שָׂכָר עַל הַמַּשְׁכּוֹן. וּכְשֵׁם שֶׁהַנִּפְקָד אֵינוֹ רַשַּׁאי לִמְסֹר אֶת הַפִּקָּדוֹן לְאַחֵר לְשָׁמְרוֹ, כְּמוֹ שֶׁיִּתְבָּאֵר בְּסִימָן קפח, כָּךְ אֵין הַמַּלְוֶה רַשַּׁאי לְהַפְקִיד אֶת הַמַּשְׁכּוֹן בְּיַד אַחֵר אוֹ לְמַשְׁכְּנוֹ שֶׁלֹּא מִדַּעַת הַבְּעָלִים.

יג) הַמַּלְוֶה אֶת חֲבֵרוֹ עַל הַמַּשְׁכּוֹן, שֶׁאִם לֹא יִפְרָעֶנּוּ לִזְמַן פְּלוֹנִי, יְהֵא הַמַּשְׁכּוֹן חָלוּט לוֹ, יִזָּהֵר לוֹמַר לוֹ בִּשְׁעַת הַלְוָאָה, אִם לֹא תִפְדֶּה אוֹתוֹ עַד זְמַן פְּלוֹנִי, יְהֵא קָנוּי לִי מֵעַכְשָׁו.

יד) מִי שֶׁהוּא יוֹדֵעַ שֶׁחַיָּב לַחֲבֵרוֹ, וַחֲבֵרוֹ אוֹמֵר לוֹ, וַדַּאי לִי שֶׁאֵינְךָ חַיָּב לִי, פָּטוּר מִלְּשַׁלֵּם לוֹ, שֶׁהֲרֵי מָחַל לוֹ.

טו) לֹוֶה שֶׁבָּא לִפְרוֹעַ לַמַּלְוֶה עַל יְדֵי שָׁלִיחַ, מִיָּד כְּשֶׁמָּסַר אֶת הַמָּעוֹת לִידֵי הַשָּׁלִיחַ, זָכָה הַשָּׁלִיחַ בַּמָּעוֹת עֲבוּר הַמַּלְוֶה, וּכְשֶׁהַלֹּוֶה מִתְחָרֵט וְרוֹצֶה לְקַחְתָּן מִיַּד הַשָּׁלִיחַ וְשֶׁיִּפְרַע לוֹ אַחַר כָּךְ, אָסוּר, מִשּׁוּם דַּהֲוֵי לֵהּ שֶׁלֹּא מִדַּעַת, וְגַם עַל הַשָּׁלִיחַ יֵשׁ אִסּוּר לְהַחֲזִירָן לַלֹּוֶה.

סִימָן קפ
הִלְכוֹת שְׁמִטַּת כְּסָפִים

א) הַסְכָּמַת רֹב הַפּוֹסְקִים דִּשְׁמִטַּת כְּסָפִים נוֹהֶגֶת גַּם בַּזְּמַן הַזֶּה, וַאֲפִלּוּ בְּחוּץ לָאָרֶץ. וְהָעוֹלָם נָהֲגוּ לְהָקֵל. וּכְבָר הִרְעִישׁוּ עַל זֹאת גְּדוֹלֵי

---

16. *Maseches Yevamos* 109a.

17. If it has totally faded, you may still have it certified if you furnish witnesses who saw the document before and remember its content. *Ramah* 41:1—*Rashbam, Smah.* Some disagree. (see *Nesivos*)

9) You should avoid becoming a guarantor, or a trustee whenever possible.[16]

10) If you hold a note of indebtedness against your friend, and the document is worn out, and its script is fading[17] you should go to a *Beis Din* and have it certified.

11) It is forbidden to keep a paid note in your possession, for it is said,[18] "Do not let unrighteousness dwell in your tents."[19]

12) Just as you must be careful to guard a deposited article, you must be careful to guard the security even more so; because you are like a paid watchman[20] of the article. And just as a trustee is not permitted to give the article to another person to watch, as will be explained in chapter 188, so is the lender not permitted to deposit the security with someone else, or to give it as a security without the consent of the owner.

13) If you lend money to your friend on a security on condition that if he does not repay the loan at a certain date, he will forfeit the security, then you must be sure to tell the borrower when the loan is made, "If you do not redeem the security by such and such a date, it shall become mine retroactive to the present time."

14) If you know you owe your friend money, and your friend says to you: "I am certain you owe me nothing," you need not pay him, because he has apparently forgiven the debt.[21]

15) When a borrower chooses to repay the lender via a messenger, as soon as he gives the money to the messenger, the messenger acquires the money for the lender. Thereafter, if the borrower has regrets, and wishes to take back the money from the messenger, and repay the loan later, he is forbidden to do so; because this is borrowing without the owner's knowledge. The messenger is equally forbidden to return the money to the borrower.

Chapter 180

Cancellation of Debts in the Sabbatical Year

1) Most *Poskim* [*halachic* authorities] agree that the cancellation of debts on the *shemitah* year, is effective even in our time,[1] and even in lands outside *Eretz Yisroel.* The general public is lenient about this, and have been censured on this account by

---

18. *Job* 11:14.

19. If it is partially repaid, *Shulchan Aruch* 57:1 says you must write a receipt for the amount paid. *Shach* 57:6 argues that even if you do not write a receipt for that part, you may keep the document until it is fully paid.

20. Since you are engaged in the performance of a mitzvoh at the time you lend him, you are exempt from giving charity at that moment. This is considered a benefit, and makes you a paid watchman. (*Gaonim, Rif, Smah* 72:9, *Shach* 72:11)

21. And he does not have the right to say later that he had made a mistake about it. (*Smah* 75:28, *Shach* 75:33. The *Bach* disagrees.)

1. Today it is a Rabbinical injunction. When the *Yoveil* (Jubilee Year) was observed (as in the era of the first Beis Hamikdash, and some say during the second as well), the cancellation of debts on the *Shemitah* year was a *de'oraisa.* (see *Shulchan Aruch* 67:1)

יִשְׂרָאֵל זִכְרוֹנָם לִבְרָכָה, וּקְצָת מֵהֶם טָרְחוּ לְלַמֵּד זְכוּת עַל הַמִּנְהָג שֶׁסּוֹמְכִין עַל קְצָת מְקִלִּין. אֲבָל מִי שֶׁרוֹצֶה לְדַקְדֵּק בַּמִּצְוֹת, בְּוַדַּאי מְחֻיָּב לַעֲשׂוֹת כְּדַעַת רֹב הַפּוֹסְקִים זִכְרוֹנָם לִבְרָכָה. וּבִפְרָט שֶׁיּוּכַל לְתַקֵּן אֶת הַדָּבָר עַל יְדֵי פְּרוֹזְבּוּל וְלֹא יָבוֹא לִידֵי פְסִידָא. וּשְׁנַת הַשְּׁמִטָּה הָיְתָה בִּשְׁנַת תרל"ה, וְתִהְיֶה אִם יִרְצֶה הַשֵּׁם בִּשְׁנַת תרמ"ב.

ב) שְׁבִיעִית, מְשַׁמֶּטֶת כָּל מִלְוֶה, בֵּין מִלְוֶה עַל־פֶּה, בֵּין מִלְוֶה בִּשְׁטָר, וַאֲפִלּוּ יֵשׁ בּוֹ אַחֲרָיוּת נְכָסִים. וּמִי שֶׁנָּתַן לַחֲבֵרוֹ מָעוֹת בְּתוֹרַת עִסְקָא, שֶׁהַדִּין הוּא שֶׁחֶצְיָן מִלְוֶה וְחֶצְיָן פִּקָּדוֹן, הַחֵצִי שֶׁהוּא מִלְוֶה מְשַׁמֵּט, וְהַחֵצִי שֶׁהוּא פִּקָּדוֹן אֵינוֹ מְשַׁמֵּט.

ג) הַמַּלְוֶה אֶת חֲבֵרוֹ עַל הַמַּשְׁכּוֹן, אֵינוֹ מְשַׁמֵּט. וְאִם הִלְוָהוּ עַל מַשְׁכּוֹן קַרְקַע, יֵשׁ בָּזֶה חִלּוּקֵי דִינִים.

ד) עָרֵב שֶׁפָּרַע לַמַּלְוֶה וְקֹדֶם שֶׁפָּרַע לוֹ הַלֹּוֶה לְהֶעָרֵב הִגִּיעָה שְׁנַת הַשְּׁמִטָּה, מְשַׁמֵּט.

ה) מִי שֶׁנִּתְחַיֵּב לַחֲבֵרוֹ שְׁבוּעָה עַל מָמוֹן, שֶׁאִלּוּ הָיָה מוֹדֶה לוֹ הָיְתָה שְׁבִיעִית מְשַׁמֶּטֶת אֶת הַמָּמוֹן, מְשַׁמֶּטֶת גַּם כֵּן אֶת הַשְּׁבוּעָה.

ו) מִי שֶׁהָיָה חַיָּב לַחֲבֵרוֹ מָמוֹן וְכָפַר, וְעָמְדוּ לַדִּין וְנִתְחַיֵּב, וְכָתְבוּ בֵּית־הַדִּין פְּסַק דִּין וּנְתָנוּהוּ לִידֵי הַמַּלְוֶה, אֵין הַשְּׁבִיעִית מְשַׁמַּטְתּוֹ.

ז) הַמַּלְוֶה אֶת חֲבֵרוֹ וְהִתְנָה עִמּוֹ שֶׁלֹּא תְשַׁמְּטֶנּוּ שְׁבִיעִית, אֲפִלּוּ הָכִי מְשַׁמַּטְתּוֹ. אֲבָל אִם הִתְנָה עִמּוֹ שֶׁלֹּא יַשְׁמִיט הוּא חוֹב זֶה, אֲפִלּוּ הָיָה זֶה בִּשְׁנַת הַשְּׁמִטָּה, אֵינָהּ מְשַׁמַּטְתּוֹ. וְכֵן אִם כָּתַב בִּשְׁטָר לְשׁוֹן פִּקָּדוֹן, אֵינָהּ מְשַׁמֶּטֶת.

ח) הַמַּלְוֶה אֶת חֲבֵרוֹ לְאֵיזֶה שָׁנִים וְהִגִּיעַ זְמַן הַפֵּרָעוֹן לְאַחַר שְׁמִטָּה. אֵינָהּ מְשַׁמַּטְתּוֹ, כֵּיוָן שֶׁלֹּא הָיָה יָכוֹל לְתָבְעוֹ קֹדֶם.

ט) הַמּוֹסֵר שְׁטָרוֹתָיו לְבֵית־דִּין וְאָמַר לָהֶם, אַתֶּם גְּבוּ לִי חוֹבִי, אֵינוֹ נִשְׁמָט.

---

2. Ba'al Hamaor.
3. As an update, the most recent one occured in the year 5754.
4. *Rambam, Ramban, Rashba,* etc. The *Maharik* disagrees on this point.

the great Torah scholars of Yisrael, of blessed memory. A few of them have tried to justify this [lax] custom by relying on a few [authorities][2] who are lenient about this. However, a person who wishes to observe *mitzvos* meticulously is certainly obligated to follow the opinion of the majority of *poskim* of blessed memory. Particularly so, when the problem can be solved by means of the *prosbol,* (see paragraph 15) without any monetary loss. The last Sabbatical Year was in 5635,[3] and will occur, God willing, in the year 5642.[3]

2) The Sabbatical Year (*shemitah*) cancels every type of loan, whether it is an oral loan, or on a note, or even on a property mortgage.[4] If you gave your friend money, as a business partnership, (described in Chapter 66), whereby half of it is a loan and the other half is a deposit, the half that is considered a loan is cancelled, but the half that is a deposit is not cancelled.

3) If you lend someone on the security of a pledge [collateral], it is not cancelled[5] (on *shemitah*); but if you lent him on the security of real estate, there are various halachic opinions regarding the cancellation of the debt.

4) If a guarantor paid the lender, and before the borrower had paid the guarantor, the Sabbatical Year intervened, *shemitah* cancels this debt.

5) If someone is obliged to another, [to take] an oath concerning a monetary claim, and if he were to admit his liability, the *shemitah* would cancel his debt, then *shemitah* cancels the oath as well.

6) If a man owes someone money and denies it, (and as a result) the claim was presented to *Beis Din* and he was charged, once the *Beis Din* recorded the verdict, and gave it to the lender, the *shemitah* does not cancel this debt.

7) If you lend money to someone on condition that *shemitah* will not cancel the debt, even so, *shemitah* cancels it. However, if a condition was made that the *borrower* shall not cancel this debt, even if this is during the *shemitah* year, it does not cancel it. Also, if the note was written with reference as a deposit, *shemitah* does not cancel this debt.

8) If you lend money to someone for a certain number of years, and the debt is due after the *shemitah* year, the debt is not cancelled, because you were unable to demand payment earlier.

9) If you present your notes of indebtedness to *Beis Din* and say to them: "Collect my debts for me," they are not cancelled in the *shemitah* year.[6]

---

5. Some say only the amount equivalent to the value of the pledge is not cancelled, while others say the entire debt is not cancelled. *Shulchan Aruch* 67:12. The latter is the opinion of the majority of *Rishonim*.

6. The *Rambam, Smag, Chinuch* etc. explain that it is not you, but the *Beis Din,* that is claiming the debt; and that is permitted.

י) הַמּוֹכֵר אֵיזֶה דָּבָר לַחֲבֵרוֹ בְּהַקָּפָה, הֲוֵי לֵהּ כְּאִלּוּ הִלְוָהוּ מָעוֹת, וּמְשַׁמֵּט. אֲבָל חֶנְוָנִי הַמּוֹכֵר לַאֲחֵרִים בְּהַקָּפָה, וְאֵין דַּרְכּוֹ לִתְבֹּעַ עַד שֶׁמִּתְקַבֵּץ אֵיזֶה סַךְ, אֵינוֹ מְשַׁמֵּט. וְאִם זְקָפָן עָלָיו בְּמִלְוָה, דְּהַיְנוּ, שֶׁחָשַׁב הַכֹּל בְּיַחַד וְכָתַב בְּפִנְקָסוֹ סַךְ הַכּוֹלֵל, אֲזַי הֲוֵי כְּהַלְוָאָה וּמְשַׁמֵּט.

יא) שְׂכַר שָׂכִיר, אֵינוֹ מְשַׁמֵּט. וְאִם זְקָפוֹ עָלָיו בְּמִלְוָה, מְשַׁמֵּט.

יב) הַבָּא מִכֹּחַ הַגּוֹי, הֲרֵי הוּא כַּגּוֹי. לָכֵן מִי שֶׁקָּנָה מִגּוֹי שְׁטַר־חוֹב עַל יִשְׂרָאֵל, אֵינוֹ מְשַׁמֵּט, שֶׁהֲרֵי הַגּוֹי הָיָה גוֹבֶה בִּשְׁטָרוֹ לְעוֹלָם. וְכֵן מִי שֶׁעָרַב לַגּוֹי בְּעַד יִשְׂרָאֵל, וְלֹא פָּרַע הַיִּשְׂרָאֵל, וְהֻצְרַךְ הַיִּשְׂרָאֵל הֶעָרֵב לִפְרֹעַ לַגּוֹי, וְנָטַל מִן הַגּוֹי אֶת הַשְּׁטָר שֶׁעַל הַלֹּוֶה, אֵינוֹ מְשַׁמֵּט. אֲבָל אִם לֹא הָיָה שְׁטָר, אֶלָּא שֶׁתּוֹבֵעַ לַחֲבֵרוֹ בְּעַל־פֶּה, עַל שֶׁהֻצְרַךְ לִפְרֹעַ בַּעֲדוֹ לַגּוֹי, הֲרֵי זֶה פָּטוּר.

יג) אֵין שְׁבִיעִית מְשַׁמֶּטֶת כְּסָפִים, אֶלָּא בְּסוֹפָהּ. לְפִיכָךְ הַמַּלְוֶה אֶת חֲבֵרוֹ בִּשְׁנַת הַשְּׁמִטָּה עַצְמָהּ, גּוֹבֶה חוֹבוֹ כָּל הַשָּׁנָה. וּכְשֶׁתִּשְׁקַע הַחַמָּה בְּעֶרֶב רֹאשׁ־הַשָּׁנָה, אָבַד הַחוֹב.

יד) לֹוֶה שֶׁבָּא לִפְרֹעַ לַמַּלְוֶה חוֹב שֶׁעָבַר עָלָיו שְׁמִטָּה, יֹאמַר לוֹ הַמַּלְוֶה, מְשַׁמֵּט אֲנִי אֶת הַחוֹב וּכְבָר נִפְטַרְתָּ מִמֶּנִּי. אִם אָמַר לוֹ הַלֹּוֶה, אַף־עַל־פִּי־כֵן רוֹצֶה אֲנִי שֶׁתְּקַבֵּל מִמֶּנִּי, מֻתָּר לַמַּלְוֶה לְקַבְּלוֹ מִמֶּנּוּ. וְאַל יֹאמַר הַלֹּוֶה, בְּחוֹבִי אֲנִי נוֹתֵן לְךָ, אֶלָּא יֹאמַר לוֹ, שֶׁלִּי הֵם וּבְמַתָּנָה אֲנִי נוֹתְנָם לְךָ. וְיָכוֹל הַמַּלְוֶה לַעֲשׂוֹת הִשְׁתַּדְּלוּת וְהִתְפַּעֲלוּת, שֶׁיֹּאמַר הַלֹּוֶה שֶׁהוּא נוֹתְנָם לוֹ בְּמַתָּנָה. וְאִם אֵינוֹ יָכוֹל לִפְעֹל זֹאת, אַל יִקָּחֵם.

טו) פְּרוֹזְבּוּל אֵינוֹ מְשַׁמֵּט. וּמַהוּ פְּרוֹזְבּוּל. הַמַּלְוֶה הוֹלֵךְ אֵצֶל שְׁלֹשָׁה בְּנֵי תוֹרָה שֶׁיִּהְיוּ בֵּית־דִּין, וְיֹאמַר אֲלֵיהֶם, אַתֶּם דַּיָּנִים, מוֹסֵר אֲנִי לָכֶם, שֶׁכָּל חוֹב שֶׁיֶּשׁ לִי עַל פְּלוֹנִי וְעַל פְּלוֹנִי, שֶׁאֶגְבֶּה אוֹתָן חוֹבוֹת כָּל זְמַן שֶׁאֶרְצֶה. וְהֵמָּה כּוֹתְבִים לוֹ פְּרוֹזְבּוּל בְּזוֹ הַלָּשׁוֹן, בְּמוֹתַב תְּלָתָא כַּחֲדָא הֲוֵינָא, וַאֲתָא פְּלוֹנִי הַמַּלְוֶה וְאָמַר לְפָנֵינוּ, מוֹסֵר אֲנִי וְכוּ׳. וּשְׁלָשְׁתָּן חוֹתְמִין לְמַטָּה, בִּלְשׁוֹן דַּיָּנִים אוֹ בִּלְשׁוֹן עֵדִים. וִיכוֹלִין לַעֲשׂוֹת זֹאת גַּם

---

7. Or to a certain amount of time that extends beyond the Sabbatical year. (*Beis Yosef, Smah*)

8. *Ramah—Rosh* and *Tur* maintain that if a day was designated for payment, it is like a loan.

9. Because when he paid for him, it is as though he had lent it to him and *Shemitah* cancels loans. (*Smah* 67:35.

10) If you sell something to someone on credit, the money is considered a loan and *shemitah* cancels it. However, a storekeeper who sells to people on credit, and it is not his custom to demand payment until a certain amount accumulates,[7] these debts are not cancelled. If, however, he charged them as a loan, that is, he totalled all the items, and entered the sum total in his ledger, then it is considered a loan,[8] and *shemitah* cancels it.

11) The wages of a laborer are not cancelled, but if they were converted into a loan, they are cancelled by *shemitah.*

12) Claims acquired from a non-Jew are treated as claims of a non-Jew. Therefore, if you purchase a note of indebtedness from a non-Jew, against a Jew, *shemitah* does not cancel it, for the non-Jew was able to collect with his note under all circumstances. Also, if one has become a guarantor to a non-Jew, on behalf of a Jew, and the Jew failed to pay his debt, so that the Jewish guarantor had to pay the non-Jew, and thus took the note that the non-Jew held against the borrower, *shemitah* does not cancel this note. However, if there is no note, but the guarantor sues the borrower orally, because he had to pay the non-Jew for him; then the borrower is exempt from payment.[9]

13) *Shemitah* cancels monetary loans only at the end of the *shemitah* year. Therefore, if you lend someone money during the *shemitah* year, you may collect the debt during the entire year, but at sunset the eve of *Rosh Hashana,* the debt is cancelled.

14) If a borrower comes to pay his debt to the lender after the *shemitah* had passed, the lender should say to him: "I have cancelled your debt, and you are released from my claims." If the borrower says: "Even so, I want you to accept the money," the lender is permitted to accept it. However, the borrower should not say, "I am paying this on the account of my debt;" rather, he should say to him: "The money is mine, and I am giving it to you as a gift." The lender is [even] permitted to make an effort to persuade the borrower to say "I am giving you the money as a gift." However, if he is unable to [persuade him] he may not accept the money from him.

15) If there is a *prosbol, shemitah* does not cancel the debt. What is a *prosbol* and how is it obtained? The lender goes before three men, learned in Torah,[10] who constitute a *Beis Din.* He says to them: "To you judges, I hand over all the claims I have against so and so, etc. so that I am able to collect these debts whenever I desire." They then write for him a *prosbol* which reads: "We were sitting together, as three [judges], and so-and-so the lender came and said in our presence, "I hand over etc." All three judges sign at the bottom of the document, either as judges or as

---

10. *Rambam* 9:17 states that they must be *very* great in Torah. *Shulchan Aruch* 67:18 adds they must be the accepted authorities of that city. The *Ramah* 67:18 is lenient and says nowadays three ordinary (observant) Jews are sufficient for making a *prosbol.*

בְּסוֹף הַשָּׁנָה, דְּהַיְנוּ בְּעֶרֶב רֹאשׁ־הַשָּׁנָה קֹדֶם שְׁקִיעַת הַחַמָּה. וְיֵשׁ אוֹמְרִים, שֶׁאֵינָן צְרִיכִין דַּוְקָא לִכְתֹּב אֶת הַפְּרוֹזְבּוּל, אֶלָּא דַּי בְּמַה שֶּׁהוּא אוֹמֵר לִפְנֵיהֶם. וַאֲפִלּוּ אִם אֵין בִּמְקוֹמוֹ בֵּית־דִּין, יָכוֹל לוֹמַר, אֲנִי מוֹסֵר שְׁטָרוֹתַי לְבֵית־דִּין שֶׁבִּמְקוֹם פְּלוֹנִי.

טז) לֹא מַהֲנֵי פְּרוֹזְבּוּל אֶלָּא אִם יֵשׁ לַלֹּוֶה קַרְקַע. וַאֲפִלּוּ כָּל שֶׁהוּא, סַגֵּי. וַאֲפִלּוּ אֵין לוֹ אֶלָּא עָצִיץ נָקוּב, סַגֵּי. וַאֲפִלּוּ אֵין לַלֹּוֶה כְּלוּם, אֶלָּא שֶׁיֵּשׁ לֶעָרֵב אוֹ שֶׁיֵּשׁ לְמִי שֶׁהוּא חַיָּב לוֹ לְלֹוֶה זֶה, נַמֵּי מַהֲנֵי. וְאִם גַּם לְאֵלּוּ אֵין לָהֶם כְּלָל, אִם יֵשׁ לַמַּלְוֶה קַרְקַע כָּל־שֶׁהוּא יָכוֹל לְזַכּוֹת לוֹ לַלֹּוֶה, וַאֲפִלּוּ עַל יְדֵי אַחֵר, וַאֲפִלּוּ שֶׁלֹּא בְּפָנָיו, וּמַהֲנֵי לִפְרוֹזְבּוּל.

סִימָן קפא
הִלְכוֹת טוֹעֵן וְנִטְעָן וְעֵדוּת

א) כְּשֶׁנָּפַל בֵּין שְׁנֵי בְנֵי אָדָם אֵיזֶה סִכְסוּךְ רָאוּי לָהֶם לְהִתְפַּשֵּׁר בְּטוֹב וְשֶׁיְּוַתֵּר כָּל אֶחָד נֶגֶד חֲבֵרוֹ, כְּדֵי לְהִתְרַחֵק מִזִּילוּתָא דְבֵי דִינָא בְּכָל מַה דְּאֶפְשָׁר.

ב) אִם אִי אֶפְשָׁר לָהֶם לְהִתְפַּשֵּׁר בְּטוֹב, וּמֻכְרָחִים לָבוֹא בְּמִשְׁפָּט, יָבוֹאוּ לִפְנֵי בֵית־דִּין יִשְׂרָאֵל. וְאָסוּר לָדוּן בִּפְנֵי דַיָּנֵי גוֹיִם וּבְעַרְכָּאוֹת שֶׁלָּהֶם, אֲפִלּוּ בְּדִין שֶׁדָּנִים כְּדִינֵי יִשְׂרָאֵל. וַאֲפִלּוּ נִתְרַצּוּ שְׁנֵי בַעֲלֵי דִינִים לָדוּן בִּפְנֵיהֶם, אָסוּר. וַאֲפִלּוּ נִתְקַשְּׁרוּ בְּקִנְיָן עַל זֶה אוֹ שֶׁכָּתְבוּ כֵן בִּשְׁטָר, אֵינוֹ כְלוּם. וְכָל הַבָּא לָדוּן בִּפְנֵיהֶם הֲרֵי זֶה רָשָׁע, וּכְאִלּוּ חֵרֵף וְגִדֵּף וְהֵרִים יָד בְּתוֹרַת משֶׁה רַבֵּנוּ עָלָיו הַשָּׁלוֹם. וַאֲפִלּוּ בְּדָבָר הַמֻּתָּר לְמֶעְבַּד דִּינָא לְנַפְשֵׁהּ, כַּאֲשֶׁר יִתְבָּאֵר אִם יִרְצֶה הַשֵּׁם בְּסָעִיף ט, מִכָּל מָקוֹם אָסוּר לַעֲשׂוֹתוֹ עַל יְדֵי גוֹיִם. וַאֲפִלּוּ אֵינוֹ דָן לִפְנֵי הַגּוֹיִם, אֶלָּא שֶׁכּוֹפֵהוּ עַל יְדֵי גוֹי שֶׁיַּעֲמֹד עִמּוֹ לְדִין יִשְׂרָאֵל, רָאוּי לְמַתְּחוֹ עַל הָעַמּוּד.

ג) הָיְתָה יָדָם תַּקִּיפָה וּבַעַל דִּינוֹ גֶּבֶר אַלָּם, יִתְבָּעֶנּוּ לְדַיָּנֵי יִשְׂרָאֵל תְּחִלָּה. אִם לֹא רָצָה לָבוֹא, נוֹטֵל רְשׁוּת מִבֵּית־דִּין וּמַצִּיל בְּדִינֵיהֶם.

ד) מִי שֶׁתּוֹבְעִים אוֹתוֹ מָמוֹן שֶׁהוּא מֻחְזָק בּוֹ, אָסוּר לוֹ לְבַקֵּשׁ

11. But you cannot transfer it to him against his will. (*Ramah* 67:22—*Ran*)

witnesses. This can also be done at the end of the year, that is, on the eve of Rosh Hashana before sunset. Some *Poskim* say it is not necessary to write the *prosbol,* but it is sufficient if he declares this before the *Beis Din.* Even if there is no *Beis Din* in your town, you can declare: "I hand over my notes to the *Beis Din* which is in such and such a place.

16) The *prosbol* is of no avail unless the borrower possesses some real estate, be it ever so small; even if he has only a flower pot with a hole in the bottom, it is sufficient. Even if the borrower has none, but the guarantor has some real estate, or someone who is indebted to the borrower has some, this too is sufficient. If none of these people possess any real estate, and the lender possesses some real estate, be it ever so small, he may transfer it to the borrower, even through a third party, and even in the borrower's absence,[11] and this is sufficient to validate the *prosbol.*

Chapter 181
Laws of Litigation and Testimony

1) When there is a controversy between two persons, it is best for them to agree to an acceptable compromise, with each side yielding somewhat, in order to avoid the humiliation of a lawsuit. They should make every effort to do so.

2) If it is impossible for them to reach an acceptable compromise, and they are forced to go to court, they should go before a Jewish *Beis Din.* It is forbidden to bring a suit before secular judges, and in their courts; even if their decision would be in accordance with the Torah law.[1] Even if both litigants are willing to bring the case before them, it is forbidden to do so. Even if they had made a binding agreement, or they had a written agreement to that effect, it is of no avail. Whoever brings a case before them is a wicked person, and it is considered as if he had insulted, blasphemed, and rebelled against the Torah of *Moshe Rabbeinu,* peace be on him. Even in a case where a man is permitted to take the law into his own hands, as will be explained, God willing, in paragraph 9, it is forbidden to do so through non-Jews. Even if he does not bring the case before a secular tribunal, but uses non-Jews to force his opponent to go with him to a Jewish court, he deserves to be flogged.

3) When the defendant is a difficult person, and you live in a society governed by non-Jews; you should first summon him to appear in *Beis Din.* If he refuses to go, you may obtain the consent of *Beis Din,* and save your property in the secular courts.

4) If you are sued on a monetary claim, that you really owe, it is forbidden to

---

1. When Jewish courts base their decisions on secular laws, it is also forbidden to appear before them. (*Chazon Ish* 55:15 *Tzitz Eliezer* II 82).

צְדָדִים לְהִשָּׁמֵט, כְּדֵי שֶׁיִּתְרַצֶּה הַלָּה לַעֲשׂוֹת עִמּוֹ פְּשָׁרָה וְיִמְחוֹל לוֹ עַל הַשְּׁאָר. וְאִם עָבַר וְעָשָׂה כֵן, אֵינוֹ יוֹצֵא יְדֵי שָׁמַיִם, עַד שֶׁיִּתֵּן לוֹ אֶת שֶׁלּוֹ.

ה) אָסוּר לְבַעַל־דִּין לְסַפֵּר עִנְיַן הַמִּשְׁפָּט לִפְנֵי הַדַּיָּן שֶׁלֹּא בִּפְנֵי בַעַל־הַדִּין חֲבֵרוֹ. וְלֹא יַקְדִּים אֶת עַצְמוֹ לָבוֹא לִפְנֵי הַדַּיָּן קֹדֶם לַחֲבֵרוֹ, שֶׁלֹּא יְהֵא נֶחְשָׁד שֶׁמַּקְדִּים כְּדֵי לְסַדֵּר טַעֲנוֹתָיו שֶׁלֹּא בִּפְנֵי חֲבֵרוֹ.

ו) כְּשֵׁם שֶׁהַדַּיָּן הַלּוֹקֵחַ שֹׁחַד אֲפִלּוּ לְזַכּוֹת אֶת הַזַּכַּאי עוֹבֵר בְּלֹא תַעֲשֶׂה, כָּךְ הַנּוֹתֵן אֶת הַשֹּׁחַד עוֹבֵר בְּלֹא תַעֲשֶׂה דְלִפְנֵי עִוֵּר לֹא תִתֵּן מִכְשֹׁל.

ז) אָסוּר לִטְעֹן שֶׁקֶר בְּכָל עִנְיָן. וַאֲפִלּוּ אִם יוֹדֵעַ בְּעַצְמוֹ שֶׁהוּא זַכַּאי, וְאִם יִטְעַן הָאֱמֶת יִתְחַיֵּב בַּדִּין, מִכָּל מָקוֹם לֹא יִטְעַן שֶׁקֶר. הָכִי אִיתָא בַּגְּמָרָא, תָּנוּ רַבָּנָן, מִנַּיִן לְנוֹשֶׁה בַּחֲבֵרוֹ מָנֶה, שֶׁלֹּא יֹאמַר אֶטְעָנֶנּוּ בְּמָאתַיִם כְּדֵי שֶׁיּוֹדֶה לִי בְּמָנֶה וְיִתְחַיֵּב לִי שְׁבוּעָה וַאֲגַלְגֵּל עָלָיו שְׁבוּעָה מִמָּקוֹם אַחֵר תַּלְמוּד לוֹמַר, מִדְּבַר שֶׁקֶר תִּרְחָק. מִנַּיִן לְנוֹשֶׁה בַּחֲבֵרוֹ מָנֶה וּטְעָנוֹ מָאתַיִם, שֶׁלֹּא יֹאמַר הַלֹּוֶה, אֶכְפְּרֶנּוּ בְּבֵית־דִּין וְאוֹדֶה לוֹ חוּץ לְבֵית־הַדִּין כְּדֵי שֶׁלֹּא אֶתְחַיֵּב לוֹ שְׁבוּעָה וְלֹא יְגַלְגֵּל עָלַי שְׁבוּעָה מִמָּקוֹם אַחֵר תַּלְמוּד לוֹמַר, מִדְּבַר שֶׁקֶר תִּרְחָק. מִנַּיִן לִשְׁלֹשָׁה שֶׁנּוֹשִׁין מָנֶה בְּאֶחָד, שֶׁלֹּא יְהֵא אֶחָד בַּעַל־דִּין וּשְׁנַיִם עֵדִים כְּדֵי שֶׁיּוֹצִיאוּ הַמָּנֶה וְיַחְלְקוּ תַּלְמוּד לוֹמַר, מִדְּבַר שֶׁקֶר תִּרְחָק.

ח) לִפְעָמִים בַּעֲלֵי־הַדִּין בּוֹרְרִים לָהֶם אֲנָשִׁים שֶׁיַּעֲשׂוּ פְּשָׁרָה בֵּינֵיהֶם, אִם בְּצֵרוּף בֵּית־הַדִּין אוֹ שֶׁלֹּא בְּבֵית־דִּין. וְדָבָר זֶה, הָגוּן הוּא, שֶׁכָּל אֶחָד הוּא מְצַדֵּד בִּזְכוּתוֹ שֶׁל זֶה אֲשֶׁר בְּחָרוֹ וְיֵצֵא הַפֶּשֶׁר כָּרָאוּי. וְדַוְקָא לְצַדֵּד בְּדֶרֶךְ הַיָּשָׁר. אֲבָל חָלִילָה־לּוֹ לְעַוֵּת אֶת הַפֶּשֶׁר. שֶׁכְּשֵׁם שֶׁמַּזְהִירִין שֶׁלֹּא לְהַטּוֹת אֶת הַדִּין, כָּךְ מַזְהִירִין שֶׁלֹּא לְהַטּוֹת אֶת הַפֶּשֶׁר.

ט) יָכוֹל אָדָם לַעֲשׂוֹת דִּין לְעַצְמוֹ. אִם רוֹאֶה חֵפֶץ שֶׁלּוֹ בְּיַד אַחֵר שֶׁגְּזָלוֹ, יָכוֹל לְקַחְתּוֹ מִיָּדוֹ. וְאִם הָאַחֵר עוֹמֵד כְּנֶגְדּוֹ, יָכוֹל לְהַכּוֹתוֹ עַד שֶׁיַּנִּיחֶנּוּ, אִם לֹא יוּכַל לְהַצִּיל בְּעִנְיָן אַחֵר, אֲפִלּוּ הוּא דָּבָר שֶׁאֵין בּוֹ

---

2. *Leviticus* 19:14.
3. *Maseches Shavuos* 31a.
4. That he owes no more than one hundred.

seek ways of evasion, in order to force the creditor to compromise, and forgo the remainder of the debt. If you transgressed and did so, you are not discharged of your obligation before the judgement of Heaven, until you pay the claimant what is rightfully his.

5) A litigant is forbidden to present his case to the judge in the absence of his opponent. Therefore, one litigant should not present himself to the judge before the other, lest he be suspected of coming early in order to present his case in the absence of his opponent.

6) Just as the judge who accepts a bribe, even to acquit the innocent, transgresses a negative precept, so does he who offers the bribe transgress the negative precept, "You shall not put a stumbling block before the blind."[2]

7) It is forbidden to enter a false plea. Even if you know you have a just claim, and if you tell the truth, the judgement will be against you, nevertheless, you may not enter a false plea. This is stated in the Talmud:[3] "Our Rabbis have taught, from where do we know that one who has lent his friend one hundred *shekalim*, should not say I will claim two hundred, so that when he admits to owing one hundred, he will be obliged to take an oath,[4] and then I will force him to take an oath[5] with regard to some other matter? We learn it from the verse: "Keep far away from anything false."[6] From where do we know that if one has a claim against another for one hundred *shekalim*, but demands two hundred *shekalim*, that the borrower should not say, I will deny the whole claim in *Beis Din*, and will admit (to one hundred) out of *Beis Din*, in order not to be obliged to take an oath, and to prevent him from making me take an oath as regards some other matter? We learn it from the verse: "Keep far away from anything false."[6] From where do we know that if three people have a claim of one hundred *shekalim* against one person, that one of them must not be the plaintiff and the other appear as witnesses, in order to obtain the one hundred *shekalim*, and divide it among themselves? We learn from the verse: "Keep far away from anything false."[6]

8) Occasionally, the litigants choose men [arbitrators] to effect a compromise between them, either jointly with the *Beis Din*, or without *Beis Din*. This is a proper procedure, because each [arbitrator] promotes the cause of the one who has chosen him, and thus a just settlement will be reached. But the arbitration must be conducted in a just manner, [and not] Heaven forbid pervert the process of compromise. For just as we are commanded not to pervert judgement, so, too, we are commanded not to pervert the process of compromise.

9) A man may [sometimes] take the law into his own hands. If you see an article of yours in the possession of someone who had robbed it, you may take it away from him. If the latter tries to stop you, you may even strike him until he releases it, if

5. Once someone is obliged to you for an oath, you may force him to take an oath with regard to all other claims you have against him.

6. *Exodus* 23:7.

הֶפְסֵד, אִם יַמְתִּין עַד שֶׁיַּעֲמִידֶנּוּ בַּדִּין. וְאִם יֵשׁ עֵדִים הָרוֹאִים שֶׁהוּא תּוֹפֵס אֶת הַחֵפֶץ מִיַּד הָאַחֵר, אֵינוֹ יָכוֹל לְתָפְסוֹ עַל יְדֵי הַכָּאָה, אֶלָּא אִם כֵּן יָכוֹל לְבָרֵר אַחַר כָּךְ שֶׁנָּטַל אֶת שֶׁלּוֹ. כִּי אִם לֹא יְבָרֵר, לֹא מַהֲנֵי לֵהּ תְּפִיסָתוֹ, כֵּיוָן שֶׁהָיוּ עֵדִים בַּדָּבָר. אֲבָל אִם אֵין עֵדִים, דְּאָז מַהֲנֵי תְּפִיסָתוֹ, יָכוֹל לַעֲשׂוֹת כֵּן, אַף־עַל־פִּי שֶׁלֹּא יוּכַל לְבָרֵר.

י) בְּנֵי הָעִיר שֶׁמַּעֲמִידִין לָהֶם בֵּית־דִּין, צְרִיכִין לֵידַע שֶׁיֵּשׁ בְּכָל אֶחָד מֵהֶם שִׁבְעָה דְּבָרִים אֵלּוּ, חָכְמָה בַּתּוֹרָה, עֲנָוָה, יִרְאָה, שִׂנְאַת מָמוֹן אֲפִלּוּ שֶׁלָּהֶם, אַהֲבַת הָאֱמֶת, אַהֲבַת הַבְּרִיּוֹת לָהֶם, בַּעֲלֵי שֵׁם טוֹב בְּמַעֲשֵׂיהֶם. וְכָל הַמַּעֲמִיד דַּיָּן שֶׁאֵינוֹ הָגוּן, עוֹבֵר בְּלֹא־תַעֲשֶׂה, שֶׁנֶּאֱמַר, לֹא תַכִּירוּ פָנִים בַּמִּשְׁפָּט, כְּלוֹמַר, לֹא תַכִּירוּ פְּנֵי הָאִישׁ, לוֹמַר, פְּלוֹנִי עָשִׁיר הוּא, קְרוֹבִי הוּא, אוֹשִׁיבֶנּוּ בַּדִּין. וְכָל דַּיָּן שֶׁנִּתְמַנָּה בִּשְׁבִיל כֶּסֶף וְזָהָב, אָסוּר לַעֲמֹד לְפָנָיו אוֹ לְכַבְּדוֹ בִּשְׁאָר כִּבּוּד, וְעָלָיו דָּרְשׁוּ רַבּוֹתֵינוּ זִכְרוֹנָם לִבְרָכָה אֱלֹהֵי כֶסֶף וֵאלֹהֵי זָהָב לֹא תַעֲשׂוּ לָכֶם.

יא) עֲיָרוֹת שֶׁאֵין בָּהֶם חֲכָמִים הָרְאוּיִים לִהְיוֹת דַּיָּנִים מְמַנִּים הַטּוֹבִים וְהַחֲכָמִים שֶׁבָּהֶם לְדַעַת אַנְשֵׁי הָעִיר, וְהֵם יָדוּנוּ אַף־עַל־פִּי שֶׁאֵינָם רְאוּיִים לְדַיָּנִים, כְּדֵי שֶׁלֹּא יֵלְכוּ לִפְנֵי עַרְכָּאוֹת שֶׁל גּוֹיִם. וְכֵיוָן שֶׁקִּבְּלוּם עֲלֵיהֶם בְּנֵי הָעִיר, אֵין אַחֵר יָכוֹל לְפָסְלָן. וְכָל מַעֲשֵׂיהֶם יִהְיוּ לְשֵׁם־שָׁמָיִם.

יב) כָּל מִי שֶׁיּוֹדֵעַ עֵדוּת לַחֲבֵרוֹ וְרָאוּי לַהֲעִידוֹ וְיֵשׁ לַחֲבֵרוֹ תּוֹעֶלֶת בְּעֵדוּתוֹ וְהוּא תּוֹבְעוֹ שֶׁיָּעִיד לוֹ בִּפְנֵי בֵּית־דִּין חַיָּב לְהָעִיד לוֹ, בֵּין שֶׁיֵּשׁ עוֹד עֵד אַחֵר עִמּוֹ, בֵּין שֶׁהוּא לְבַדּוֹ. וְאִם כָּבַשׁ עֵדוּתוֹ, חַיָּב בְּדִינֵי שָׁמָיִם. וְאָסוּר לְאָדָם לְהָעִיד בְּדָבָר שֶׁאֵינוֹ יוֹדֵעַ, אַף־עַל־פִּי שֶׁאָמַר לוֹ אָדָם שֶׁיּוֹדֵעַ בּוֹ שֶׁאֵינוֹ מְשַׁקֵּר. וַאֲפִלּוּ אָמַר לוֹ בַּעַל־הַדִּין, בּוֹא וַעֲמֹד עִם עֵד אֶחָד שֶׁיֵּשׁ לִי וְלֹא תָעִיד, רַק שֶׁיִּפְחַד בַּעַל חוֹבִי וְיִסְבּוֹר שֶׁיֵּשׁ לִי שְׁנֵי עֵדִים, וְיוֹדֶה לִי לֹא יִשְׁמַע לוֹ, שֶׁנֶּאֱמַר, מִדְּבַר שֶׁקֶר תִּרְחָק.

יג) הָא דְּעֵד אֶחָד מֵעִיד, זֶהוּ דַּוְקָא בְּדָבָר שֶׁבְּמָמוֹן, דְּמַהֲנֵי גַּם עֵד אֶחָד לְעִנְיַן שְׁבוּעָה. וְכֵן בִּדְבַר אִסּוּר, אִם עֲדַיִן לֹא נַעֲשָׂה הָאִסּוּר, יָעִיד

7. *Deuteronomy* 1:17.
8. *Maseches Sanhedrin* 7b.

you are unable to get it by other means. You may do so even if it is an article that will not depreciate if you wait until you summon him to *Beis Din.* If there are witnesses who [will] see you seize the article from this other's possession, you may not seize it by forceful means, unless you will be able to verify later that you took what is yours. For if you are unable to prove your ownership, your seizure is of no avail since there are witnesses that you took it by force. However, if there are no witnesses, whereby the seizure will be effective, you may seize it forcefully even though you will be unable to verify your ownership.

10) When the people of a city appoint a *Beis Din* for the community, they must ascertain that each one of the judges possesses the following seven qualities: wisdom in Torah, humility, fear of God, abhorence of money—even their own, love of truth, loved by their fellow men, and a reputation for good deeds. Whoever appoints a judge who is unfit for the position, transgresses a negative precept, as it is said, "You shall not respect persons in judgement."[7] This means, you shall not favor anyone and say, "So-and-so is wealthy, or is my relative, I will appoint him as a judge." It is forbidden to rise before a judge who was appointed through the influence of money, or to show him any other honor. With reference to such a person, our Rabbis, of blessed memory,[8] applied the verse: "Gods of silver and gods of gold you shall not make for yourselves."[9]

11) In communities where there are no scholars who are qualified to be judges, they should appoint the best and wisest among themselves according to the understanding of the townsmen, and they should judge even though they are not qualified to be judges. We permit this so that people will not go to the secular courts. Since they were accepted by their townsmen, no one can disqualify them. All their activities should be for the glory of Heaven.

12) If you are able to bear witness for your neighbor and are qualified to testify, and your neighbor would benefit from your testimony, and asks you to testify on his behalf in the presence of *Beis Din,* you are obliged to testify, whether there is another witness besides you or you are the only one. If you withhold such testimony, you will have to answer to the Heavenly Court. It is forbidden to testify about anything you do not know (firsthand), and not even if the man who told you is someone you are certain that tells no lies. Even if the litigant says to you, "Come and stand next to the one witness that I have, not to testify, but just to intimidate my debtor, so he will think that I have two witnesses, and he will consequently admit (his obligation to me)," you must not listen to him, as it is said, "Keep far away from anything false."

13) The law that states that the testimony of one witness is valid, is only when money matters are involved; for then, the testimony of even one witness is sufficient to require the administration of an oath. Similarly, with regard to a sinful act, if the

9. *Exodus* 20:23.

כְּדֵי לְאַפְרוּשֵׁי מֵאִסּוּרָא. אֲבָל אִם כְּבָר נַעֲשָׂה הָאִסּוּר, לֹא יָעִיד עֵד אֶחָד. דְּכֵיוָן דְּעֵד אֶחָד אֵינוֹ נֶאֱמָן, אֵינוֹ אֶלָּא כְּמוֹצִיא שֵׁם רָע עַל חֲבֵרוֹ.

יד) הַנּוֹטֵל שָׂכָר לְהָעִיד, עֵדוּתוֹ בְּטֵלָה. וְדַוְקָא כְּשֶׁכְּבָר רָאָה הַמַּעֲשֶׂה דִּמְחֻיָּב לְהָעִיד בְּחִנָּם. אֲבָל לֵילֵךְ לִרְאוֹת אֶת הָעִנְיָן שֶׁיִּהְיֶה אַחַר כָּךְ עֵד בַּדָּבָר, מֻתָּר לוֹ לִקַּח שָׂכָר אֲבָל רַק שָׂכָר הָרָאוּי לְפִי הַטִּרְחָא שֶׁלּוֹ וְלֹא יוֹתֵר וְכֵן אִם יֵשׁ לוֹ טִרְחָא לָלֶכֶת לִפְנֵי בֵּית־הַדִּין, יָכוֹל לִטּוֹל שְׂכַר טִרְחָא כְּפִי הָרָאוּי בְּעַד טִרְחָא זוֹ, וְלֹא יוֹתֵר.

טו) כָּל עֵדוּת שֶׁיֵּשׁ לְאָדָם הֲנָאָה בָהּ, וְאֵיזֶה צַד נְגִיעָה אֲפִלּוּ בְּדֶרֶךְ רְחוֹקָה, פָּסוּל לְהָעִיד.

טז) כְּתִיב, וַאֲשֶׁר לֹא־טוֹב עָשָׂה בְּתוֹךְ עַמָּיו, וְדָרְשִׁינָן, זֶה הַבָּא בְּהַרְשָׁאָה וּמִתְעַבֵּר עַל־רִיב לֹא־לוֹ. וְדַוְקָא כְּשֶׁשְּׁנֵי בַּעֲלֵי־הַדִּין הֵמָּה בָּעִיר, אֶלָּא כְּגוֹן שֶׁהַלֹּוֶה הוּא אַלָּם וּבַעַל טְעָנוֹת, וְיָרֵא הַמַּלְוֶה לִטְעֹן עִמּוֹ וּמַרְשֶׁה לְאַחֵר, זֶהוּ מִתְעַבֵּר עַל רִיב לֹא לוֹ. אֲבָל אִם הַנִּתְבָּע הוּא בְּעִיר אַחֶרֶת, וְהַתּוֹבֵעַ אֵינוֹ יָכוֹל לְהַטְרִיחַ אֶת עַצְמוֹ וּמַרְשֶׁה לְאַחֵר, זֶה הַמֻּרְשֶׁה – מִצְוָה קָעָבֵיד לְהַצִּיל עָשׁוּק מִיַּד עוֹשְׁקוֹ. וְיֵשׁ אוֹמְרִים, דְּהַבָּא בְּהַרְשָׁאָה כְּדֵי לֵהָנוֹת מִן הַשָּׂכָר וְלֹא בִּשְׁבִיל אַלָּמוּת מֻתָּר.

יז) לְעוֹלָם יַרְחִיק אָדָם אֶת עַצְמוֹ אֲפִלּוּ מִשְּׁבוּעַת אֱמֶת בְּכָל מַה דְּאֶפְשָׁר.

יח) מִי שֶׁחֲבֵרוֹ נִתְחַיֵּב לוֹ שְׁבוּעָה, וְרוֹאֶה בּוֹ שֶׁהוּא רוֹצֶה לִשָּׁבַע לַשֶּׁקֶר חַס־וְשָׁלוֹם יִתְפַּשֵּׁר עִמּוֹ כְּפִי הָאֶפְשָׁרִי וְלֹא יַנִּיחֶנּוּ לִשָּׁבַע לַשֶּׁקֶר, שֶׁנֶּאֱמַר, שְׁבֻעַת ה׳ תִּהְיֶה בֵּין שְׁנֵיהֶם, וְדָרְשִׁינָן, מְלַמֵּד שֶׁהַשְּׁבוּעָה חָלָה עַל שְׁנֵיהֶם.

יט) יִשְׂרָאֵל הַיּוֹדֵעַ עֵדוּת לְגוֹי שֶׁיֵּשׁ לוֹ דִּין עִם יִשְׂרָאֵל בְּעַרְכָּאוֹתֵיהֶם, אִם יִגְרֹם בְּעֵדוּתוֹ לְחַיֵּב אֶת הַיִּשְׂרָאֵל יוֹתֵר מִמַּה שֶּׁהָיָה חַיָּב בְּדִינֵי יִשְׂרָאֵל, אָסוּר לְהָעִיד לוֹ. וְאִם לָאו, מֻתָּר לְהָעִיד לוֹ. וְאִם מִתְּחִלָּה יִחֲדוּ

10. *Yecheskiel* 18:18.
11. *Maseches Shavuos* 31a.
12. *Shach* 123:32. However, the *Tumim* argues that if the borrower is a strongman, it is a *mitzvah* to assist the lender.

prohibition was not yet violated, the singular witness may testify in order to prevent him from sinning. However, if the sinful act had already been committed one witness should not testify to it; since one witness is not believed, he will only be spreading an evil report about another person.

14) If you accept a reward for your testimony, your testimony is null and void. This is true only after you had already witnessed the facts, for then it is your duty to testify free of charge. However, (if you are asked) to witness a certain transaction in order to subsequently testify, you are permitted to take compensation. It is permitted to take compensation only to the extent that you were inconvenienced and no more. Also, if it is an inconvenience for you to go to *Beis Din,* you are entitled to compensation for your inconvenience, but only to the extent that it is proper for this inconvenience, and no more.

15) Any testimony from which you derive benefit, or in which you have a personal interest, even if remote, disqualifies you as a witness.

16) It is written, "And that which is not good, he did among his people."[10] This is homiletically interpreted to refer to a person who comes with power of attorney, and argues about a quarrel that is not his.[11] This applies only when both litigants are in town, but the borrower is a strong man, and a good pleader, and the lender fears the confrontation with him, and thus gives power of attorney to someone else. This is the case of someone arguing about a quarrel that is not his.[12] However, if the defendant is in another city, and the plaintiff cannot trouble himself (to go personally), and gives someone the power of attorney, then the latter is doing a meritorious deed in rescuing the wronged person from the hand of the one exploiting him. Some *Poskim* maintain that if you accept a power of attorney in order to receive a fee, and not because you are a quarrelsome person, it is permitted.

17) You should distance yourself from taking an oath, even if it is a truthful one. You should make every effort to refrain from it.[13]

18) If your opponent is obliged to you for an oath, and you realize that he is prepared to swear falsely, Heaven forbid, you should reach the best possible compromise with him, and not permit him to swear falsely, for it is said, "an oath to Adonoy shall be between them."[14] And this is expounded to teach, that [the punishment of] the oath rests on both of them.[15]

19) If a Jew knows of evidence that favors a Gentile who has a lawsuit with a Jew in the secular courts, and his testimony will cause his fellow Jew to be liable for a larger amount than he would have been liable to according to Jewish law, he is forbidden to testify for him;[16] but if not, he is permitted to testify for him. If

13. *Midrash Tanchuma (Vayikra).*
14. *Exodus* 22:10.
15. *Maseches Shavuos* 39b.
16. If he did so, he should be banished for thirty days, (*Shulchan Aruch* 28:3) unless he agrees to pay him the money he lost in court. (*Maharshal, Shach*)

הַגּוֹי לְהַיִּשְׂרָאֵל שֶׁיִּהְיֶה לוֹ עֵד, הוֹאִיל וְיִהְיֶה חִלּוּל הַשֵּׁם אִם לֹא יָעִיד לוֹ, יָעִיד לוֹ בְּכָל עִנְיָן.

כ) כָּל זְמַן שֶׁהָאָדָם זוֹכֵר, יָכוֹל לְהָעִיד לְעוֹלָם, וְאֵינוֹ חוֹשֵׁשׁ שֶׁמָּא מִתּוֹךְ שֶׁנִּתְיַשֵּׁן הַדָּבָר הַרְבֵּה אֵינוֹ זוֹכְרוֹ עַל בֻּרְיוֹ. וַאֲפִלּוּ אֵינוֹ נִזְכָּר לָעֵדוּת אֶלָּא מִתּוֹךְ הַכְּתָב, שֶׁכְּשֶׁמְּסָרוּהוּ לוֹ, כְּתָבוֹ בְּפִנְקָסוֹ לְזִכְרוֹן דְּבָרִים וְשָׁכַח אֶת הַדָּבָר וְאֵינוֹ נִזְכָּר אֶלָּא מִתּוֹךְ הַכְּתָב יָכוֹל לְהָעִיד. וְדַוְקָא שֶׁכַּאֲשֶׁר רָאָה אֵת הַכְּתָב נִזְכַּר בַּדָּבָר. וְכֵן אִם נִזְכַּר בַּדָּבָר עַל יְדֵי אַחֵר שֶׁהִזְכִּירוֹ לוֹ, יָכוֹל לְהָעִיד, וַאֲפִלּוּ הָיָה הַמַּזְכִּיר הָעֵד הַשֵּׁנִי. אֲבָל אִם בַּעַל הַדִּין בְּעַצְמוֹ מַזְכִּירוֹ וְנִזְכַּר, לֹא יָעִיד. אַךְ יָכוֹל בַּעַל הַדִּין לִמְסֹר אֶת הַדְּבָרִים לְאַחֵר וְהוּא יַזְכִּירוֹ, דַּהֲוֵי לֵהּ נִזְכָּר עַל יְדֵי אַחֵר.

כא) עֵד שֶׁהוּא קָרוֹב לְאֶחָד מִבַּעֲלֵי הַדִּין, אוֹ לְאֶחָד מֵהַדַּיָּנִים, אוֹ שֶׁהָעֵדִים קְרוֹבִים זֶה לָזֶה, וַאֲפִלּוּ קֻרְבָה עַל יְדֵי נְשׁוֹתֵיהֶם לִפְעָמִים פְּסוּלִים לְהָעִיד. וַאֲפִלּוּ קְרוֹבִים רַק לֶעָרֵב וְלֹא לַלֹּוֶה, גַּם כֵּן פְּסוּלִים לְהָעִיד לַלֹּוֶה. וְזֶה שֶׁפָּסְלָה הַתּוֹרָה עֵדוּת הַקְּרוֹבִים, לֹא מִפְּנֵי שֶׁחֶזְקָתָם אוֹהֲבִים זֶה אֶת זֶה, שֶׁהֲרֵי פְּסוּלִים לְהָעִיד, בֵּין לִזְכוּתוֹ בֵּין לְחוֹבָתוֹ, אֶלָּא גְּזֵרַת הַכָּתוּב הִיא. וַאֲפִלּוּ מֹשֶׁה וְאַהֲרֹן, לֹא הָיוּ כְּשֵׁרִים לְהָעִיד זֶה לָזֶה. לָכֵן כָּל עֵד שֶׁיֵּשׁ לוֹ אֵיזֶה קֻרְבָה לְאֶחָד מִן הַנִּזְכָּרִים אוֹ שֶׁהָיָה קָרוֹב וְנִתְרַחֵק וְהַדַּיָּנִים אֵינָם יוֹדְעִים, צָרִיךְ לְהוֹדִיעַ לָהֶם, וְהֵם יַגִּידוּ לוֹ עַל פִּי הַתּוֹרָה אִם יֵשׁ בְּקֻרְבָה זוֹ כְּדֵי לְפָסְלוֹ אוֹ לֹא.

כב) שְׁנֵי עֵדִים, שֶׁאֶחָד יוֹדֵעַ בַּחֲבֵרוֹ שֶׁהוּא רָשָׁע וּפָסוּל לְעֵדוּת מִן הַתּוֹרָה וְאֵין הַדַּיָּנִים מַכִּירִים בְּרִשְׁעוֹ, אָסוּר לוֹ לְהָעִיד עִמּוֹ, אַף־עַל־פִּי שֶׁהִיא עֵדוּת אֱמֶת, שֶׁנֶּאֱמַר, אַל תָּשֶׁת יָדְךָ עִם רָשָׁע לִהְיוֹת עֵד חָמָס, וּגְזֵרַת הַכָּתוּב הִיא, שֶׁכָּל הָעֵדוּת בְּטֵלָה אֲפִלּוּ הֵם רַבִּים, אִם אֶחָד בֵּינֵיהֶם פָּסוּל. וְאֵיזֶהוּ רָשָׁע שֶׁפָּסוּל לְעֵדוּת מִן הַתּוֹרָה. כֹּל שֶׁעָבַר עַל דָּבָר שֶׁפָּשַׁט בְּיִשְׂרָאֵל שֶׁהוּא עֲבֵרָה, וְהוּא דָבָר שֶׁבְּלֹא־תַעֲשֶׂה מִן הַתּוֹרָה, וְעָבַר בְּזָדוֹן וְלֹא עָשָׂה תְשׁוּבָה. אֲבָל אִם יֵשׁ לִתְלוֹת שֶׁעָשָׂה בִשְׁגָגָה אוֹ בְטָעוּת, שֶׁלֹּא יָדַע אֶת הָאִסּוּר לֹא נִפְסַל לְעֵדוּת.

initially the Gentile arranged for the Jew to testify for him, since the Name of God will be desecrated if he does not testify (as he had agreed to), he should testify under all circumstances.

20) So long as you remember the facts, you may testify at any time and you need not fear that because it happened long ago, you do not remember clearly. Even if you only remember the testimony from the record you made. If for example when they gave you [a document etc.] you wrote the information in your book, in order to have a record of it, and you had forgotten the facts and only remember them from your records, even in such an event you may testify. This is true only if upon reading the records, your memory is refreshed. Also, if your memory is refreshed by someone else who reminded you, you may testify; even if the one who reminded you is the second witness. However, if the litigant himself[17] reminded you and refreshed your memory, you may not testify. The litigant, however, may present the facts to someone else, and that person may in turn remind you, for then your memory will have been refreshed by a third party.

21) A witness who is related to one of the litigants, or to one of the judges; or witnesses who are related to one another, even if the relationship is on their wives side, may sometimes be disqualified to testify. Even if they are related only to the guarantor, and not to the borrower, they are also disqualifed from testifying on behalf of the borrower. The Torah has disqualified the testimony of relatives, not because of the love they have for one another, for they are disqualified to testify whether it is in his favor or against him; but rather, it is a Divine decree. Even Moses and Aaron were not qualified to testify for one another. Therefore, any witness who is related to any one of the above mentioned individuals, or was once related, but the relationship no longer exists—should the judges be unaware of the situation, the witness must inform them, and they will tell him if in accordance with Torah law, the relationship is significant enough to disqualify him, or not.

22) If there are two witnesses and one of them knows that the other is a sinful man, and is not qualified to testify according to the law of the Torah, and the judges are unaware of his wickedness, it is forbidden to testify with him, even though the testimony is true, for it is said: "Do not join your hand with a wicked man to be a corrupt witness.[18] It is a Divine decree that the entire testimony be invalidated even if there are many witnesses, should one of them be disqualified to testify. Who is considered sinful enough to be disqualified as a witness by decree of the Torah? Whoever transgresses in a matter which has been accepted by the Jewish people as a sin, and which is a Divine prohibition, that he violated intentionally and has not (been known to have) repented. However, if it is possible to assume that he did it unintentionally, or in ignorance, not being aware of the prohibition, he is not disqualified to bear testimony.

---

17. Or his wife or his children (but other relatives are like strangers in this regard). (*Shevus Ya'akov* 2:147)

18. *Exodus* 23:1.

סִימָן קפב
הִלְכוֹת גְּנֵבָה וּגְזֵלָה

א) אָסוּר לִגְזוֹל אוֹ לִגְנוֹב אֲפִלּוּ כָּל־שֶׁהוּא, בֵּין מִיִּשְׂרָאֵל בֵּין מִגּוֹי. אִיתָא בְּתַנָּא דְבֵי אֵלִיָּהוּ, מַעֲשֶׂה בְּאֶחָד שֶׁסִּפֵּר לִי, שֶׁעָשָׂה עַוְלָה לַגּוֹי בִּמְדִידַת הַתְּמָרִים שֶׁמָּכַר לוֹ, וְאַחַר כָּךְ קָנָה בְּכָל הַמָּעוֹת שֶׁמֶן, וְנִשְׁבַּר הַכַּד וְנִשְׁפַּךְ הַשֶּׁמֶן. וְאָמַרְתִּי, בָּרוּךְ הַמָּקוֹם שֶׁאֵין לְפָנָיו מַשּׂוֹא פָנִים. הַכָּתוּב אוֹמֵר, לֹא תַעֲשֹׁק אֶת רֵעֲךָ וְלֹא תִגְזֹל. וְגֶזֶל הַנָּכְרִי, גָּזֵל.

ב) אִם הוּא דָבָר מֻעָט כָּל־כָּךְ שֶׁאֵין מִי שֶׁיַּקְפִּיד עָלָיו כְּלָל, כְּגוֹן לִטּוֹל מֵהַחֲבִילָה קֵיסָם לַחֲצוֹץ בּוֹ שִׁנָּיו, מֻתָּר. וּמִדַּת חֲסִידוּת לְהִמָּנַע גַּם מִזֶּה.

ג) אֲפִלּוּ לִגְנוֹב עַל דַּעַת לְהַחֲזִיר, אֶלָּא שֶׁרוֹצֶה לְצַעֲרוֹ קְצָת אוֹ בְּדֶרֶךְ שְׂחוֹק גַּם כֵּן אָסוּר.

ד) אָסוּר לַעֲשֹׁק אֶת חֲבֵרוֹ אֲפִלּוּ כָּל־שֶׁהוּא, שֶׁנֶּאֱמַר, לֹא תַעֲשֹׁק אֶת־רֵעֲךָ. וְאֵיזֶהוּ עוֹשֵׁק. זֶה שֶׁבָּא מָמוֹן חֲבֵרוֹ לְיָדוֹ בִּרְצוֹן חֲבֵרוֹ, כְּגוֹן שֶׁיֵּשׁ לוֹ בְּיָדוֹ הַלְוָאָה אוֹ שְׂכִירוּת, וְאֵינוֹ רוֹצֶה לְשַׁלֵּם לוֹ, אוֹ שֶׁמְּדַחֵהוּ בְּלֵךְ וָשׁוּב, לֵךְ וָשׁוּב. וְכֵיוָן דִּכְתִיב רֵעֲךָ, אֵינוֹ אָסוּר בְּגוֹי. וְהוּא שֶׁאֵין חִלּוּל הַשֵּׁם בַּדָּבָר, כְּגוֹן שֶׁלָּוָה מִגּוֹי וָמֵת, רַשַּׁאי לְכַחֵשׁ לִבְנוֹ, שֶׁאֵינוֹ יוֹדֵעַ בְּבֵרוּר שֶׁהוּא מְשַׁקֵּר. אֲבָל כְּשֶׁהַגּוֹי יוֹדֵעַ שֶׁהוּא מְשַׁקֵּר, אָסוּר, מִפְּנֵי חִלּוּל־הַשֵּׁם. וְאַף בְּמָקוֹם שֶׁאֵינוֹ יוֹדֵעַ, אֵינוֹ רַשַּׁאי אֶלָּא לְהַפְקִיעַ הַלְוָאָתוֹ אוֹ שְׁאָר חוֹב שֶׁהוּא חַיָּב לוֹ. אֲבָל חֵפֶץ שֶׁהוּא בָעַיִן, אָסוּר לִכְפּוֹר, שֶׁהֲרֵי זֶה הָוֵי גָּזֵל מַמָּשׁ. וְלֹא עוֹד, אֶלָּא אֲפִלּוּ קָנָה מִמֶּנּוּ חֵפֶץ, אָסוּר לְהַטְעוֹת אוֹתוֹ בְּחֶשְׁבּוֹן בִּנְתִינַת הַמָּעוֹת, כְּמוֹ שֶׁנֶּאֱמַר, וְחִשַּׁב עִם קוֹנֵהוּ, דְּמַיְרֵי בְּגוֹי, שֶׁהֲרֵי אֵינוֹ מַקְנֶה לוֹ הַחֵפֶץ אֶלָּא בְּעַד הַסְּכוּם שֶׁהִשְׁתַּוּוּ. וְהַמַּטְעֵהוּ בְּחֶשְׁבּוֹן הַמָּעוֹת, הֲרֵי זֶה כְּגוֹנֵב אֶת הַחֵפֶץ וְלֹא כְּמַפְקִיעַ חוֹבוֹ. וַאֲפִלּוּ גְּנֵבַת דַּעַת שֶׁאֵין בָּהּ חֶסְרוֹן מָעוֹת, אָסוּר בְּמַשָּׂא וּמַתָּן, כְּמוֹ שֶׁכָּתַבְתִּי בְּסִימָן סג. וּמִכָּל מָקוֹם אִם הַגּוֹי טָעָה בְּעַצְמוֹ, מֻתָּר אִם לֹא יִהְיֶה חִלּוּל־הַשֵּׁם בַּדָּבָר, שֶׁלֹּא יִוָּדַע לוֹ. וְנָכוֹן שֶׁיֹּאמַר לוֹ הַיִּשְׂרָאֵל, רְאֵה שֶׁעַל חֶשְׁבּוֹנְךָ אֲנִי סוֹמֵךְ.

Chapter 182

Laws Concerning Theft and Robbery

1) It is forbidden to rob or to steal even an article of trivial value from a Jew or from a non-Jew. It is recorded in *Tanna Devei Eliyohu:*[1] It happened that a man told me [Eliyah] that he had wronged a non-Jew in measuring dates that he sold to him. Thereafter, he bought oil with all that money and the jug broke and the oil spilled. I said, "Blessed is the Omnipotent that shows no favoritism." The Torah says, "Do not cheat your fellow, nor rob him,"[2] and robbery of a non-Jew also constitutes robbery.

2) Taking a thing of such trivial value, that no one would mind, like taking a splinter from a bundle [of wood], in order to use it as a toothpick, is permitted. However, it is an act of piousness to refrain from this as well.

3) Even stealing with the intention of returning it, but just for the sake of annoying someone, or to tease someone, is also forbidden.

4) It is forbidden to cheat your fellow even in the slightest degree, as it is said, "Do not cheat your neighbor."[3] What is cheating? If your neighbor's money comes into your possession with his consent; for example, if he lent you money, or you owe him wages (or rent), and you do not wish to pay him, or you put him off by saying, "Go," "and return [later]." Since the verse states: your [*Jewish*] neighbor, it is not forbidden to do so with a non-Jew. This is true only if this will not cause the Name of God to be desecrated; for example if you borrowed from a non-Jew and he died, it is permitted to deny the loan to his son, because he does not know for sure that you are lying. However, if the non-Jew knows you are lying, it is forbidden because of the desecration of God's Name. And even if the son is not sure, it is only permitted to deny a loan, or any other such debt you owed him. If you have in your possession an article you received from a non-Jew which is intact, you are forbidden to deny it, for this constitutes actual robbery. Moreover, even if you buy something from a non-Jew, you are forbidden to fool him in counting out the money, as it is said, "And he shall reckon with his buyer,"[4] which refers to a non-Jew. For he is only conveying the article to you in consideration of the sum agreed upon, and if you fool him in the payment, it is tantamount to stealing the article, and not merely denying a debt.[5] Even deception not involving any loss of money is forbidden in business dealing, as was explained in Chapter 63. Nevertheless, if the non-Jew makes a mistake, it is permitted to benefit from it, provided there will be no desecration of God's Name, [for example] in such a case where he remains unaware of his mistake. It is best to say to him, "I am relying on your estimate or your bill."

---

1. Chapter 15.
2. *Leviticus* 19:13.
3. *Leviticus* 19:13.
4. *Leviticus* 25:50.
5. Which is permitted in a situation when it will not cause profanity of God's name. (*Ramah* 348:2)

ה) כָּל הַחוֹמֵד בֵּיתוֹ אוֹ כֵּלָיו שֶׁל חֲבֵרוֹ, אוֹ כָּל דָּבָר שֶׁאֵין בְּדַעַת חֲבֵרוֹ לְמָכְרוֹ, וְהוּא הִרְבָּה עָלָיו רֵעִים אוֹ שֶׁהִפְצִיר בּוֹ בְּעַצְמוֹ עַד שֶׁמְּכָרוֹ לוֹ, הֲרֵי זֶה עוֹבֵר בְּלֹא תַחְמֹד. וּמִשָּׁעָה שֶׁנִּפְתָּה בְלִבּוֹ וְחָשַׁב אֵיךְ יִקְנֶה חֵפֶץ זֶה, עָבַר בְּלֹא תִתְאַוֶּה, כִּי אֵין תַּאֲוָה אֶלָּא בַלֵּב בִּלְבָד, וְהַתַּאֲוָה מְבִיאָה לִידֵי חִמּוּד. וְהַקּוֹנֶה אֶת הַדָּבָר שֶׁהִתְאַוָּה לוֹ, עוֹבֵר בִּשְׁנֵי לָאוִין. וּלְכָךְ נֶאֱמַר, לֹא תַחְמֹד וְלֹא תִתְאַוֶּה.

ו) מִצְוַת-עֲשֵׂה עַל הַגּוֹזֵל לְהַחֲזִיר אֶת הַגְּזֵלָה עַצְמָהּ אִם הִיא בְעֵינָהּ וְלֹא נִשְׁתַּנֵּית, שֶׁנֶּאֱמַר, וְהֵשִׁיב אֶת-הַגְּזֵלָה אֲשֶׁר גָּזָל. וְהוּא הַדִּין לְגַנָּב. וְאֵינוֹ יוֹצֵא יְדֵי חוֹבָתוֹ בִּנְתִינַת דָּמִים, אֲפִלּוּ אִם כְּבָר נִתְיָאֲשׁוּ הַבְּעָלִים. אֲבָל אִם אָבְדָה אוֹ שֶׁנִּשְׁתַּנֵּית בְּשִׁנּוּי שֶׁאֵינוֹ חוֹזֵר לִבְרִיָּתוֹ אוֹ שֶׁשִּׁקְּעָהּ בְּבִנְיָן, שֶׁיִּהְיֶה לוֹ הֶפְסֵד גָּדוֹל לִסְתֹּר אֶת הַבִּנְיָן, יוֹצֵא יְדֵי חוֹבָתוֹ בִּנְתִינַת דָּמִים, כְּמוֹ שֶׁהָיְתָה שָׁוָה בִּשְׁעַת הַגְּזֵלָה. וְאִם הַנִּגְזָל הוּא בְּמָקוֹם אַחֵר, אֵינוֹ צָרִיךְ לִשְׁלוֹחַ אֶת הַמָּעוֹת לִמְקוֹמוֹ, אֶלָּא מוֹדִיעוֹ שֶׁיָּבוֹא וִישַׁלֵּם לוֹ. אִם מֵת הַנִּגְזָל, יַחֲזִיר לְיוֹרְשָׁיו.

ז) הַגּוֹזֵל אֶת הָרַבִּים, כְּגוֹן שֶׁהָיָה חֶנְוָנִי וּמָדַד בְּמִדָּה חֲסֵרָה אוֹ שֶׁשָּׁקַל בְּמִשְׁקָל חָסֵר וְכַדּוֹמֶה, אוֹ שֶׁהָיָה מְמֻנֶּה בַּקָּהָל וְהֵקֵל עַל קְרוֹבָיו וְהִכְבִּיד עַל אֲחֵרִים, וְכֵן מִי שֶׁנָּטַל רִבִּית מֵרַבִּים, תְּשׁוּבָתוֹ קָשָׁה. לְפִיכָךְ יַעֲשֶׂה צָרְכֵי רַבִּים, שֶׁגַּם הַנִּגְזָלִים יֵהָנוּ מֵהֶם. וּמִכָּל מָקוֹם לָאֵלֶּה שֶׁהוּא יוֹדֵעַ שֶׁגָּזַל מֵהֶם, מְחֻיָּב לְהַחֲזִיר לָהֶם, וְאֵינוֹ יוֹצֵא יְדֵי חוֹבָתוֹ בַּמֶּה שֶׁעָשָׂה צָרְכֵי רַבִּים.

ח) אָסוּר לִקְנוֹת מֵהַגַּנָּב אוֹ מֵהַגַּזְלָן אֶת הַחֵפֶץ שֶׁגָּנַב אוֹ גָּזַל. וְאֵין חִלּוּק בֵּין שֶׁהוּא יִשְׂרָאֵל אוֹ נָכְרִי, כִּי גַם הַנָּכְרִי נִצְטַוָּה עַל אִסּוּר גְּנֵבָה וּגְזֵלָה אֲפִלּוּ מִנָּכְרִי חֲבֵרוֹ, וְהוּא מִשֶּׁבַע מִצְוֹת שֶׁנִּצְטַוּוּ עֲלֵיהֶם. וְעָוֹן גָּדוֹל הוּא לִקְנוֹת מִן הַגַּנָּב אוֹ מִן הַגַּזְלָן, שֶׁהֲרֵי הוּא מַחֲזִיק יְדֵי עוֹבְרֵי עֲבֵרָה. וְעַל זֶה נֶאֱמַר, חוֹלֵק עִם גַּנָּב שׂוֹנֵא נַפְשׁוֹ, וְגוֹרֵם לַגַּנָּב שֶׁיִּגְנוֹב עוֹד גַּם גְּנֵבוֹת אֲחֵרוֹת, וְאִם לֹא יִמְצָא לוֹקֵחַ, לֹא יִגְנוֹב. וְאַף-עַל-פִּי שֶׁאֶפְשָׁר לוֹ לְהוֹלִיךְ אֶת הַגְּנֵבָה לְמָקוֹם שֶׁאֵין מַכִּירִין אוֹתוֹ, אֵין זֶה מָצוּי לוֹ כָּל-כָּךְ.

---

6. *Exodus* 20:14.
7. *Deuteronomy* 5:18.
8. These are two separate negative commands.

5) If you covet the house or the vessels of your neighbor, or anything which your neighbor has no intention of selling, and you ask his friends to influence him, or if you, yourself, pressure him until he agrees to sell it to you, you have violated the injunction, "You shall not covet."[6] From the moment you were tempted, and began to think, how will you acquire this item, you have violated the command, "You shall not desire";[7] for desire is only in the heart, and desire leads one to covet. If you ultimately buy that which you had desired, you will have transgressed two negative commands. That is why it is said, "You shall not covet" and "You shall not desire."[8]

6) The robber is enjoined by a positive command, to return the stolen article if it is in its original state, and has not been altered. As it is said, "He shall return *that* which he robbed."[9] The same law applies to a thief.[10] This obligation cannot be fulfilled merely with the return of money to the owner, even when he had already given up hope of getting it back. However, if the stolen article was lost or altered in such a way that it cannot be restored to its original state, or it was sunk into a building, and will cause him a great loss to tear down the building, the obligation may be fulfilled by paying a sum of money equivalent to its worth at the time of the robbery. If the victim of the robbery is in another town, the robber is not required to send the money to him, but he should notify him to come and get it. If the victim died, the robber must pay the restitution to his heirs.

7) He who robs the public—such as a shopkeeper who gives a short measure, or weighs with a short weight, or the like, or a public official who is lenient towards his relatives, and exacting towards others, or one who took usury from the public, will find it difficult to repent adequately. Therefore, he should establish a community service, so that his victims, too, might benefit from them.[11] Nevertheless, if the identity of his victims are known to him, he is obligated to make restitution, and he does not fulfill this obligation merely by contributing to a public service.

8) It is forbidden to buy from a thief, or a robber, any article that was stolen or robbed. There is no difference if he is a Jew or a non-Jew, for the non-Jew is also commanded not to steal or rob even from another non-Jew; and this is one of the seven precepts which they have been commanded. It is a serious sin to buy from a thief or a robber, for in doing so you are abetting evildoers. With reference to this it is said, "He who is a partner with a thief, hates his own soul,"[12] and he causes the thief to commit other acts of stealing; for if he will find no buyer he will not steal. Although it is possible for the thief to take the stolen article to a place where he is not known, this course is not always available to him. If the buyer's intention is for

---

9. *Leviticus* 5:23.

10. The Robber (*gazlan*) steals openly, in the presence of others, the thief (*ganav*) steals when no one is looking.

11. This is the best he can do, but is still not a complete repentance. (*Shulchan Aruch* 231:19, *Smah*)

12. *Proverbs* 29:24.

וְאִם הַקּוֹנֶה מִתְכַּוֵּן לְטוֹבַת הַבְּעָלִים לְהַחֲזִירוֹ לָהֶם כְּשֶׁיַּחֲזִירוּ לוֹ מְעוֹתָיו, מֻתָּר. וְדַוְקָא כְּשֶׁלֹּא הָיָה אֶפְשָׁרִי לַבְּעָלִים בְּעַצְמָם לְהַצִּיל. וְכֵן אָסוּר לְקַבֵּל בְּפִקָּדוֹן דָּבָר שֶׁנִּרְאֶה שֶׁהוּא גָנוּב אוֹ גָזוּל.

ט) אֲפִלּוּ לֵהָנוֹת שׁוּם הֲנָאָה מִן הַגְּנֵבָה אוֹ מִן הַגְּזֵלָה כָּל זְמַן שֶׁהִיא בְּיַד הַגַּנָּב אוֹ הַגַּזְלָן, אָסוּר. וַאֲפִלּוּ הֲנָאָה מֻעֶטֶת שֶׁגַּם בְּעָלֶיהָ לֹא הָיוּ מַקְפִּידִים עָלֶיהָ, כְּגוֹן חִלּוּף מַטְבְּעוֹת בְּשָׁוְיָן, אָסוּר בְּמָעוֹת גְּנוּבוֹת אוֹ גְזוּלוֹת. וְכֵן לִכָּנֵס לְבַיִת גָּזוּל, בַּחַמָּה מִפְּנֵי הַחַמָּה וּבַגְּשָׁמִים מִפְּנֵי הַגְּשָׁמִים, אוֹ לַעֲבוֹר בְּשָׂדֶה גְזוּלָה, אָסוּר.

י) וְלָכֵן מִי שֶׁהוּא גַנָּב אוֹ גַזְלָן מְפֻרְסָם, שֶׁאֵין לוֹ מְלָאכָה אַחֶרֶת אֶלָּא זֹאת, וְכָל מָמוֹנוֹ בְּחֶזְקַת גָּנוּב אוֹ גָזוּל, אָסוּר לֵהָנוֹת מִמֶּנּוּ, וְאָסוּר לְעָנִי לָקַחַת מִמֶּנּוּ צְדָקָה.

יא) וְכֵן אִם אֶחָד רוֹצֶה לִמְכֹּר אֵיזֶה חֵפֶץ שֶׁנִּרְאֶה שֶׁהוּא גָנוּב, כְּגוֹן שׁוֹמְרֵי פֵרוֹת שֶׁמּוֹכְרִים פֵּרוֹת בְּמָקוֹם צָנוּעַ, אוֹ מוֹכֵר אַחֵר שֶׁנּוֹשֵׂא אֵיזֶה דָבָר בְּהַצְנֵעַ לְמָכְרוֹ, אוֹ שֶׁאוֹמֵר לְהַקּוֹנֶה, הַטְמֵן, אָסוּר לִקְנוֹת. וַאֲפִלּוּ לִקְנוֹת מֵאִשָּׁה אֵיזֶה דָבָר שֶׁיֵּשׁ לָחוּשׁ שֶׁהִיא מוֹכֶרֶת שֶׁלֹּא מִדַּעַת בַּעְלָהּ, אוֹ לִקְנוֹת מֵאִישׁ דָּבָר מִתַּכְשִׁיטֵי הָאִשָּׁה וּמַלְבּוּשֶׁיהָ, שֶׁיֵּשׁ לָחוּשׁ שֶׁהוּא מוֹכְרוֹ שֶׁלֹּא מִדַּעַת אִשְׁתּוֹ, אָסוּר.

יב) מִי שֶׁנִּתְחַלְּפוּ לוֹ כֵּלָיו בְּבֵית הַמִּשְׁתֶּה וְכַדּוֹמֶה, הֲרֵי זֶה לֹא יִשְׁתַּמֵּשׁ בְּכֵלִים אֵלּוּ שֶׁבָּאוּ לְיָדוֹ וְאֵינָם שֶׁלּוֹ. וּכְשֶׁיָּבוֹא בַּעַל הַחֵפֶץ, צָרִיךְ לְהַחֲזִירוֹ לוֹ, וְאַף־עַל־פִּי שֶׁהַחֵפֶץ שֶׁלּוֹ נֶאֱבָד. וְכֵן כּוֹבֶסֶת הַמְכַבֶּסֶת לָרַבִּים וְהֵבִיאָה לוֹ חָלוּק שֶׁאֵינוֹ שֶׁלּוֹ, אָסוּר לְלָבְשׁוֹ, אֶלָּא צָרִיךְ לְהַחֲזִירוֹ לִבְעָלָיו, וְאַף־עַל־פִּי שֶׁשֶּׁלּוֹ נֶאֱבָד. אַךְ אִם מֻנָּח אֶצְלוֹ יָמִים רַבִּים, עַד שֶׁאִי אֶפְשָׁר שֶׁלֹּא חָקְרוּ הַבְּעָלִים בֵּינְתַיִם אַחַר שֶׁלָּהֶם, אָז מֻתָּר לוֹ לְלָבְשׁוֹ, כִּי מִסְתָמָא סִלְּקָה הַכּוֹבֶסֶת אֶת בְּעָלָיו וְשִׁלְּמָה בְּעַד הֶחָלוּק הַזֶּה.

יג) אָסוּר לֵהָנוֹת מִשּׁוּם דָּבָר שֶׁל חֲבֵרוֹ שֶׁלֹּא מִדַּעְתּוֹ. אַף־עַל־פִּי שֶׁבָּרוּר לוֹ שֶׁכְּשֶׁיִּוָּדַע לִבְעָלָיו יִשְׂמְחוּ וְיָגִילוּ מִפְּנֵי אַהֲבָתָם אוֹתוֹ, מִכָּל מָקוֹם אָסוּר. לְפִיכָךְ הַנִּכְנָס לְפַרְדֵּס אוֹ לְגִנַּת חֲבֵרוֹ, אָסוּר לוֹ לִלְקֹט פֵּרוֹת שֶׁלֹּא מִדַּעַת הַבְּעָלִים. אַף־עַל־פִּי שֶׁבַּעַל הַפַּרְדֵּס וּבַעַל הַגִּנָּה אוֹהֲבוֹ וְרֵעוֹ אֲשֶׁר כְּנַפְשׁוֹ, וּבְוַדַּאי יִשְׂמַח וְיָגִיל כְּשֶׁיִּוָּדַע לוֹ שֶׁנֶּהֱנָה זֶה מִפֵּרוֹתָיו, מִכָּל מָקוֹם כֵּיוָן שֶׁעַכְשָׁו אֵינוֹ יוֹדֵעַ מִזֶּה, הֲרֵי הוּא נֶהֱנֶה בְּאִסּוּר. וְצָרִיךְ לְהַזְהִיר לָרַבִּים, שֶׁנִּכְשָׁלִין בָּזֶה מֵחֲמַת חֶסְרוֹן יְדִיעָה.

the owner's benefit, in order to restore it to him, upon payment of the money he advanced, it is permissible; provided it is impossible for the owner himself to recover it. It is also forbidden to accept for safekeeping, anything which appears to be stolen.

9) It is forbidden to derive the slightest benefit from property that was stolen or robbed while it is in the possession of the thief or robber. Even a trivial benefit that its owner would not mind, such as exchanging the money for an equal amount of another denomination is forbidden in the case of money that was stolen or robbed. It is also forbidden to enter a stolen house to [protect yourself] from the hot sun or from the rain, or to pass through a stolen field.

10) It is forbidden to derive benefit from the possessions of one who is a known thief or robber, who has no other occupation, and whose entire property is presumed to have been acquired by theft or robbery, and a poor man is forbidden to accept charity from him.

11) Similarly, it is forbidden to buy something from someone who wishes to sell an article that apparently had been stolen as when fruit watchmen sell fruit in a secluded spot, or when a salesman conceals the merchandise he is trying to sell, or when he says to the buyer, "Hide it." It is forbidden to buy something from a woman when there is reason to suspect that she is selling it without her husband's consent, or to buy women's jewelry or clothing from a man, when there is reason to suspect that he is selling them without his wife's consent.

12) If you inadvertently exchanged coats at a wedding hall or another public place, you are not allowed to use these items that came into your possession, and are not yours. When the rightful owner appears you must return it to him, even if yours had been lost there. Also, in case a commercial launderer gave you someone else's garment, you are forbidden to wear it, but must return it to its rightful owner; even though yours was lost. However, if the article was with you so long that it is impossible the owner did not inquire after his things during this time, then you are permitted to wear it, for you may assume that the launderer satisfied the owner, and paid him for this garment.

13) It is forbidden to use anything belonging to your fellow without his knowledge. Even if you are certain that when the owner finds out he will be happy and elated that you used it, because of his good feelings towards you; nevertheless it is forbidden. Therefore, if you enter the orchard or garden belonging to your neighbor, it is forbidden to pluck fruit without the owner's knowledge, even though the owner of the orchard and the owner of the garden is truly a dear, cherished friend, and will certainly be happy and elated when finding out that you enjoyedhis fruit. Nevertheless, since at the present time he knows nothing of this, you are enjoying it unlawfully.[13] It is necessary to warn the public regarding this; for they break this rule for lack of knowledge.

---

13. *Tosafos Baba Metziah* 22a, *Ashri, Mordechai.* The *Shach* 358:1.

יד) וּמִכָּל מָקוֹם מֻתָּר לְבֶן־בֵּיתוֹ שֶׁל אָדָם לִתֵּן פְּרוּסָה לְעָנִי אוֹ לִבְנוֹ שֶׁל אוֹהֲבוֹ שֶׁל בַּעַל־הַבַּיִת שֶׁלֹּא מִדַּעְתּוֹ, לְפִי שֶׁכָּךְ נָהֲגוּ בַּעֲלֵי הַבָּתִּים. וְאֵין זֶה נִקְרָא שֶׁלֹּא מִדַּעַת הַבְּעָלִים, כֵּיוָן שֶׁכָּךְ נָהֲגוּ, וְהַבְּעָלִים יוֹדְעִין מִזֶּה הַמִּנְהָג. וּמִטַּעַם זֶה, מֻתָּר לְקַבֵּל צְדָקָה מִן הַנָּשִׁים דָּבָר מֻעָט שֶׁלֹּא מִדַּעַת הַבְּעָלִים, הוֹאִיל וְדַרְכָּן בְּכָךְ, וְיוֹדְעִין הַבְּעָלִים שֶׁדַּרְכָּן בְּכָךְ. וְכֵן בְּפַרְדֵּס, אִם הוּא רָגִיל בּוֹ לֶאֱכֹל מִפֵּרוֹתָיו מִדַּעַת הַבְּעָלִים מֻתָּר. וְכֵן כָּל כַּיּוֹצֵא בָזֶה.

טו) הַמּוֹצֵא פֵּרוֹת בַּדֶּרֶךְ תַּחַת אִילָן שֶׁהוּא נוֹטֶה עַל הַדֶּרֶךְ, אִם הֵם פֵּרוֹת שֶׁדַּרְכָּן לִפּוֹל מִן הָאִילָן וּבִנְפִילָתָם הֵם נִמְאָסִים, אוֹ אֲפִלּוּ אֵינָם נִמְאָסִים אֶלָּא שֶׁרֹב הָעוֹבְרִים שָׁמָּה הֵמָּה גוֹיִם, אוֹ שֶׁהֵם פֵּרוֹת שֶׁדֶּרֶךְ הַבְּהֵמוֹת לֶאֱכֹל אוֹתָם, וְהֵן עוֹבְרוֹת דֶּרֶךְ שָׁם, הֲרֵי הַבְּעָלִים כְּבָר נִתְיָאֲשׁוּ מֵהֶם וּמֻתָּרִים. אֲבָל אִם הֵם פֵּרוֹת שֶׁאֵינָם נִמְאָסִים בִּנְפִילָתָם, וְרֹב הָעוֹבְרִים שָׁמָּה הֵמָּה יִשְׂרְאֵלִים, אֲסוּרִים מִשּׁוּם גָּזֵל. וְאִם הֵם שֶׁל יְתוֹמִים קְטַנִּים, אֲסוּרִים בְּכָל עִנְיָן, כִּי הַקְּטַנִּים, אֵין הַיֵּאוּשׁ וְהַמְּחִילָה שֶׁלָּהֶם כְּלוּם.

טז) דִּינָא דְמַלְכוּתָא דִּינָא.

סִימָן קפג
הִלְכוֹת נִזְקֵי מָמוֹן

א) אָסוּר לְהַזִּיק מָמוֹן חֲבֵרוֹ, אֲפִלּוּ עַל דַּעַת לְשַׁלֵּם, כְּמוֹ שֶׁאָסוּר לִגְנֹב וְלִגְזֹל עַל דַּעַת לְשַׁלֵּם. וַאֲפִלּוּ לִגְרֹם נֶזֶק לַחֲבֵרוֹ, בֵּין בְּמַעֲשֶׂה בֵּין בְּדִבּוּר, אָסוּר, כְּגוֹן רְאוּבֵן שֶׁמּוֹכֵר סְחוֹרָה לַגּוֹי, וּבָא שִׁמְעוֹן וְאוֹמֵר לוֹ, שֶׁאֵינָהּ שָׁוָה כָּל כָּךְ, אַף־עַל־פִּי שֶׁהָאֱמֶת כֵּן, אָסוּר. וְכָל הַגּוֹרֵם נֶזֶק לַחֲבֵרוֹ, אֲפִלּוּ בְּעִנְיָן שֶׁפָּטוּר מִדִּינֵי אָדָם, חַיָּב בְּדִינֵי שָׁמַיִם, עַד שֶׁיְּפַיֵּס אֶת חֲבֵרוֹ.

ב) אֲפִלּוּ שֶׁבָּא אֵיזֶה נֶזֶק עָלָיו, אָסוּר לְסַלְּקוֹ מֵעָלָיו, אִם עַל יְדֵי זֶה יִגְרוֹם שֶׁיָּבוֹא עַל חֲבֵרוֹ, כִּי אָסוּר לְהַצִּיל אֶת עַצְמוֹ אֲפִלּוּ בִּגְרַם נֶזֶק

14) However, it is permitted for a member of your household to give a slice of bread to a poor man, or to the owner's friend's son without his knowledge, for this is customary among people, and is not considered as something done without the owner's knowledge since this is customary, and the owner is aware of this custom. For this reason it is permitted to accept charity from women, if it is a small contribution, even without her husband's knowledge, since this is the general custom, and husbands are aware of this custom. Also, with regard to an orchard, if you are generally acustomed to eat of its fruit with the owner's knowledge, you are permitted to do so (even without his knowledge). And so it is in all similar cases.

15) If you find fruit on the road underneath a tree, that overhangs the road, if it is the type of fruit that usually falls from the tree, and becomes spoiled after falling, or even it it does not become spoiled, but most people who pass by are non-Jews, or if it is the type of fruit that animals are accustomed to eat, and animals do pass by, [it may be assumed that] the owner has already abandoned his ownership, and you are permitted to take them. However, if it is fruit that does not become spoiled by the fall, and if most of the people passing by are Jews, it is forbidden to take them because it is considered robbery, If the fruit belongs to minor orphans, it is forbidden to take it in any case, because minors cannot waive their rights of ownership.

16) The law of existing government must be recognized as the law (in civil matters).[14]

Chapter 183
The Laws of Property Damages

1) It is forbidden to damage someone's property even with the intention of making reparation, just as it is forbidden to steal or to rob with the intention of making restitution. It is even forbidden to cause damage to your neighbor, either by deed or by word. For example, if Reuven sold merchandise to a non-Jew, and Shimon came along and told the non-Jew that it is not worth so much money, although it is really true, it is forbidden to do so. He who indirectly causes damage to his neighbor, although he is exempt in the court of Beis Din, he is liable in the (Heavenly Court) until he placates his neighbor.

2) Even if you sustain a loss, you are forbidden to remove the cause of your damage if by doing so you will cause damage to your neighbor, for it is forbidden

14. This too applies only to laws that are designed for the benefit of the government or of its citizens. However, it does not apply to laws of inheritance or similar circumstances relative to individual or family obligations. (*Ramah* 369:11)

מָמוֹן שֶׁל חֲבֵרוֹ. אֲבָל קֹדֶם שֶׁבָּא הַנֶּזֶק עָלָיו, מֻתָּר לִדְחוֹתוֹ שֶׁלֹּא יָבוֹא עָלָיו, אַף־עַל־פִּי שֶׁעַל יְדֵי זֶה יָבוֹא עַל חֲבֵרוֹ. כְּגוֹן אַמַּת הַמַּיִם שֶׁבָּאָה לִשְׁטֹף שָׂדֵהוּ, עַד שֶׁלֹּא נִכְנְסָה לְשָׂדֵהוּ, מֻתָּר לִגְדֹּר בְּפָנֶיהָ, אַף־עַל־פִּי שֶׁעַל יְדֵי זֶה הִיא שׁוֹטֶפֶת שְׂדֵה חֲבֵרוֹ. אֲבָל מִשֶּׁנִּכְנְסָה לְשָׂדֵהוּ, אָסוּר לְהוֹצִיאָהּ בְּעִנְיָן שֶׁתַּגִּיעַ לִשְׂדֵה חֲבֵרוֹ, שֶׁכֵּיוָן שֶׁהַנֶּזֶק מֻטָּל עָלָיו, אֵינוֹ רַשַּׁאי לְסַלְּקוֹ מֵעָלָיו וּלְהַטִּילוֹ עַל חֲבֵרוֹ.

ג) וְכֵן חֵיל מֶלֶךְ שֶׁבָּא לָעִיר, וּבְנֵי הָעִיר מְחֻיָּבִים לָתֵת לָהֶם אַכְסַנְיָא, אָסוּר לְאֶחָד לִתֵּן שָׂכָר לְשַׂר הַחַיִל לְפָטְרוֹ, כִּי עַל יְדֵי זֶה יִגְרֹם נֶזֶק לְיִשְׂרָאֵל אַחֵר. וְכֵן בְּכָל שְׁאָר עִנְיְנֵי מִסִּים, אָסוּר לְהִשְׁתַּדֵּל אֵצֶל הַשַּׂר לְפָטְרוֹ, אִם עַל יְדֵי זֶה יַכְבִּיד עַל אֲחֵרִים. וְהָעוֹשֶׂה כֵּן, נִקְרָא מָסוּר.

ד) אָסוּר לִמְסֹר יִשְׂרָאֵל בְּיַד גּוֹיִם, בֵּין גּוּפוֹ בֵּין מָמוֹנוֹ, בֵּין בְּמַעֲשֶׂה בֵּין בְּדִבּוּר, לְהַלְשִׁין עָלָיו אוֹ לְגַלּוֹת מַצְפּוּנָיו. וְכָל הַמּוֹסֵר, אֵין לוֹ חֵלֶק לָעוֹלָם הַבָּא. וַאֲפִלּוּ רָשָׁע וּבַעַל עֲבֵרוֹת, אָסוּר לְמָסְרוֹ לֹא גּוּפוֹ וְלֹא מָמוֹנוֹ, וַאֲפִלּוּ הוּא מֵצֵר לוֹ וּמְצַעֲרוֹ תָּמִיד בִּדְבָרִים. אֲבָל אִם חֲבֵרוֹ מוֹסֵר אוֹתוֹ וְאִי־אֶפְשָׁר לְהַצִּיל אֶת עַצְמוֹ אֶלָּא עַל יְדֵי שֶׁיִּמְסֹר אוֹתוֹ, מֻתָּר.

ה) אָסוּר לִכָּנֵס לְתוֹךְ שְׂדֵה נִיר שֶׁל חֲבֵרוֹ, מִפְּנֵי שֶׁהוּא דָשׁ נִירוֹ וּמְקַלְקְלוֹ.

ו) אָסוּר לַעֲמֹד עַל שְׂדֵה חֲבֵרוֹ לְהִסְתַּכֵּל בָּהּ בְּשָׁעָה שֶׁהִיא עוֹמֶדֶת בְּקָמוֹתֶיהָ, שֶׁלֹּא יַזִּיקֶנָּה בְּעַיִן הָרָע. וּמִכָּל־שֶׁכֵּן שֶׁאָסוּר לְהִסְתַּכֵּל בַּחֲבֵרוֹ בְּעִנְיָן שֶׁיֵּשׁ לָחוּשׁ שֶׁיַּזִּיקֶנּוּ בְּעַיִן הָרָע. וַאֲפִלּוּ בַּעֲסָקָיו וּבְמַעֲשָׂיו שֶׁאֵין בָּהֶם חֲשַׁשׁ הֶזֵּק עַיִן הָרָע, אִם עוֹשֶׂה בְּבֵיתוֹ וּבִרְשׁוּתוֹ, אָסוּר לִרְאוֹת שֶׁלֹּא מִדַּעְתּוֹ, כִּי שֶׁמָּא אֵינוֹ חָפֵץ שֶׁיֵּדְעוּ אֲחֵרִים מִמַּעֲשָׂיו וַעֲסָקָיו. וְדֶרֶךְ־אֶרֶץ הוּא כְּשֶׁאֶחָד רוֹאֶה שֶׁחֲבֵרוֹ עוֹסֵק בִּמְלַאכְתּוֹ, יְבָרְכֶנּוּ וְיֹאמַר לוֹ, תַּצְלִיחַ בְּמַעֲשֶׂיךָ.

ז) אֲפִלּוּ לַעֲשׂוֹת בִּרְשׁוּת שֶׁלּוֹ דָּבָר שֶׁהוּא מַזִּיק לִשְׁכֵנוֹ, אָסוּר. לֹא יַנִּיחַ בַּחֲצֵרוֹ סָמוּךְ לְכֹתֶל שֶׁל חֲבֵרוֹ כָּל דָּבָר שֶׁיֵּשׁ בּוֹ חֲמִימוּת וּמוֹצִיא הֶבֶל וּמַזִּיק אֶת הַחוֹמָה, כְּגוֹן זֶבֶל וְכַדּוֹמֶה, אֶלָּא אִם כֵּן הִרְחִיק שְׁלֹשָׁה טְפָחִים. וְכֵן צָרִיךְ לְהַרְחִיק שֶׁלֹּא לִשְׁפֹּךְ מַיִם סָמוּךְ לְכֹתֶל חֲבֵרוֹ. וְלָכֵן צִנּוֹר הַמְקַלֵּחַ מִן הַגַּג, צָרִיךְ לְהַרְחִיקוֹ מִכֹּתֶל חֲבֵרוֹ שְׁלֹשָׁה טְפָחִים.

to salvage your property by causing damage to another even indirectly. However, before the damage is done to you, it is permitted to forestall it so that it doesn't occur, even though by doing so, it will cause a loss to your neighbor. For example, if a stream of water is threatening to flood your field, before the water reaches your field, you are permitted to construct a dam in its path, even though this will cause it to flood your neighbor's field.[1] But if the water had already entered your field, you are forbidden to divert it to your neighbor's field. For since the damage has already occured, you are not permitted to divert it from your field, and direct it to your neighbor's field.

3) Also, if an army arrived in town, and the townspeople are obliged to provide them with room and board, it is forbidden to offer a bribe to the commanding officer for an exemption; because this will cause a loss to other Jews. Also, in all cases of taxes, it is forbidden to influence the officer to exempt you, if by doing so, you make the burden heavier for others. One who does such a thing is called an *informer.*

4) It is forbidden to surrender a Jew or his property into the hands of non-Jews. [It is also forbidden] whether by deed or by word to inform on [a Jew] or to divulge his hiding place. Whoever acts as an informer has no share in the World to Come. Even if the person is an evildoer and a sinner, it is forbidden to surrender him or his property; even if he troubles you, and constantly provokes you with words. However, if someone informed on you, and you cannot save yourself unless you inform on your informer, you are permitted to do so.

5) It is forbidden to enter the ploughed field of your neighbor because you will spoil it by trampling upon it.

6) It is forbidden to stand at your neighbor's field, to gaze at it at the time the crops are standing (ready for harvest), so as not to harm them with an "evil eye." It is certainly forbidden to gaze at someone in a way that might damage him personally, [as a result] of an "evil eye." Even with regard to his business and occupation where there is no cause to fear an "evil eye", if he works in his own house or property, it is forbidden to watch him without his knowledge, for he may not want others to know of his business and occupation. It is good manners, when seeing someone engaged at his work, to bless him and say to him, "May you be successful at your task."

7) Even on your own premises it is forbidden to engage in an activity that may cause damage to your neighbor. Thus, you must avoid placing in your yard, near your neighbor's wall, anything that generates heat or releases warm gasses or vapors, and damages the wall, such as manure and similar things, unless you keep them at a distance of three *tefachim.* You must also keep a distance not to spill water near

1. *Yerushalmi.*

וּמִכָּל־שֶׁכֵּן שֶׁלֹּא לִשְׁפֹּךְ עָבִיט שֶׁל מֵי רַגְלַיִם סָמוּךְ לְכֹתֶל חֲבֵרוֹ. וּלְהַשְׁתִּין מַיִם סָמוּךְ לְכֹתֶל חֲבֵרוֹ, אִם הוּא כֹּתֶל שֶׁל אֲבָנִים אוֹ שֶׁל עֵץ בְּלִי טִיט, דַּי כְּשֶׁמַּרְחִיק טֶפַח אֶחָד. וְאִם הָיוּ הָאֲבָנִים צְחִיחַ סֶלַע, אֵינוֹ צָרִיךְ לְהַרְחִיק כְּלָל, וּמַשְׁתִּין אֲפִלּוּ עַל הַכֹּתֶל. וְאִם הוּא כֹּתֶל שֶׁל לְבֵנִים אוֹ שֶׁל עֵץ מְחֻפֶּה בְּטִיט, צָרִיךְ לְהַרְחִיק שְׁלֹשָׁה טְפָחִים.

סִימָן קפד
הִלְכוֹת נִזְקֵי הַגּוּף

א) אָסוּר לְאָדָם לְהַכּוֹת אֶת חֲבֵרוֹ. וְאִם הִכָּהוּ, עוֹבֵר בְּלֹא תַעֲשֶׂה, שֶׁנֶּאֱמַר, וְהָיָה אִם־בִּן הַכּוֹת הָרָשָׁע וְגוֹ׳, אַרְבָּעִים יַכֶּנּוּ לֹא יֹסִיף פֶּן־יֹסִיף וְגוֹ, אִם הִקְפִּידָה הַתּוֹרָה בְּהַכָּאַת הָרָשָׁע שֶׁלֹּא לְהַכּוֹתוֹ יוֹתֵר עַל רִשְׁעוֹ, קַל־וָחֹמֶר בְּהַכָּאַת צַדִּיק. וְכָל הַמֵּרִים יָד עַל חֲבֵרוֹ לְהַכּוֹתוֹ, אַף־עַל־פִּי שֶׁלֹּא הִכָּהוּ, נִקְרָא רָשָׁע, שֶׁנֶּאֱמַר, וַיֹּאמֶר לָרָשָׁע לָמָּה תַכֶּה רֵעֶךָ, לָמָּה הִכִּיתָ לֹא נֶאֱמַר, אֶלָּא לָמָּה תַכֶּה, אַף־עַל־פִּי שֶׁעֲדַיִן לֹא הִכָּהוּ, נִקְרָא רָשָׁע. וְכָל מִי שֶׁהִכָּה אֶת חֲבֵרוֹ, הֲרֵי הוּא מֻחֲרָם בְּחֵרֶם הַקַּדְמוֹנִים, וְאֵין לְצָרְפוֹ לְמִנְיַן עֲשָׂרָה לְכָל דָּבָר שֶׁבִּקְדֻשָּׁה, עַד שֶׁיַּתִּירוּ לוֹ בֵּית־דִּין אֶת הַחֵרֶם, כְּשֶׁמְּקַבֵּל עָלָיו לִשְׁמֹעַ דִּינָם. וְאִם אֶחָד מַכֶּה אוֹתוֹ אוֹ לְיִשְׂרָאֵל אַחֵר וְאִי־אֶפְשָׁר לְהַצִּיל אֶת עַצְמוֹ אוֹ אֶת חֲבֵרוֹ מִיַּד מַכֵּהוּ אֶלָּא עַל יְדֵי שֶׁיַּכֶּה אוֹתוֹ, מֻתָּר לְהַכּוֹתוֹ.

ב) אֲפִלּוּ מְשָׁרְתוֹ שֶׁאֵינוֹ שׁוֹמֵעַ בְּקוֹלוֹ, אָסוּר לְהַכּוֹתוֹ. אֲבָל מֻתָּר לְהַכּוֹת בָּנָיו הַקְּטַנִּים אוֹ יָתוֹם שֶׁהוּא מְגַדֵּל בְּתוֹךְ בֵּיתוֹ, כְּדֵי לְהַדְרִיכָם בְּדֶרֶךְ יְשָׁרָה, שֶׁזּוֹהִי טוֹבָתָם.

ג) צָרִיךְ לִזָּהֵר שֶׁלֹּא לְהַשְׁלִיךְ שִׁבְרֵי כְּלֵי זְכוּכִית וְכַדּוֹמֶה בְּמָקוֹם שֶׁיּוּכְלוּ לְהַזִּיק.

ד) אִם יֵשׁ לִשְׁכֵנוֹ חֳלִי הָרֹאשׁ, רַחֲמָנָא לִצְּלַן, וְקוֹל הַהַכָּאָה מַזִּיק לוֹ, לֹא יִכְתּוֹשׁ אֲפִלּוּ בְּבֵיתוֹ רִיפוֹת וְכַיּוֹצֵא בָהֶן, דְּבָרִים שֶׁקּוֹל הַכָּאָתָם מַגִּיעַ לְבֵית שְׁכֵנוֹ וּמַזִּיק לוֹ.

---

1. *Deuteronomy* 25:2,3.
2. *Exodus* 2:13.
3. *Ramah* 420:1. *Smah* 420:4 says that from the *Ramah* we learn that even now, one who does this is automatically excommunicated, by virtue of this ancient ruling, and requires a *Beis*

your neighbor's wall. Therefore, the (outlet of) the roof's drain pipe must be kept a distance of three *tefachim* from your neighbor's wall. You most certainly may not spill a pot of urine close to your neighbor's wall. With regard to urinating close to your neighbor's wall, if the wall is of stone, or of wood, without plaster, a distance of one *tefach* is sufficient. If the wall is of bare rock, you need not distance yourself at all, and may urinate on the wall itself. If the wall is brick, or of wood covered with plaster, you must keep a distance of three *tefachim*.

Chapter 184
The Laws of Physical Injury

1) It is forbidden to strike your fellow Jew, and if you do strike him you are transgressing a Divine negative command, as it is said, "If the wicked man deserves to be beaten etc., he should be given forty stripes, he shall not exceed, lest he exceed."[1] If the Torah is concerned not to strike a wicked person more than prescribed for his evil, all the more so does this apply to the striking of the righteous. Whoever raises his hand against another to strike him, even if he does not actually strike him, is called a *rasha* (wicked person) as it is said, "And he said to the *rasha:* 'Why will you strike your neighbor?'"[2] It is not said, "Why have you struck," but "Why will you strike;" although he did not actually strike him, he is called a *rasha.* Whoever strikes his fellow Jew has been excommunicated by the early Sages. He can not be counted as one of a quorum of ten required for the performance of sacred rituals, until *Beis Din* releases him from excommunication, upon his acceptance to abide by their decisions.[3] However, if someone strikes you or a fellow Jew, and you are unable to save yourself or your fellow Jew from the attacker unless you strike him, you are permitted to strike him.

2) Even if your servant disobeys you, you are forbidden to strike him. However, you are permitted to strike your young children, or [even] an orphan whom you are raising in your home, in order to admonish them and guide them on the proper way, as this is for their ultimate benefit.

3) You must be careful not to throw pieces of broken glass and the like in any place where they may cause harm to anyone.

4) If your neighbor suffers from a headache, which may be aggravated by the noise of hammering, you are forbidden to pound grits even in your own house, or anything similar to them, should the sound of their pounding carry to your neighbor's house and cause him harm.[4]

Din of three to annull it. *Chasam Sofer* Responsa 182 says that nowadays if we were to follow the example of the early Sages, we would not be able to deal with the majority of the population.

4. This is included among the things that are not permitted, even if you were living in your house before your neighbor moved there. *Ashri* says the reason is because it is easier for you to remove the causative factor, than it is for him to move.

ה) יֵשׁ עוֹד הַרְבֵּה דְּבָרִים בְּעִנְיַן נִזְקֵי שְׁכֵנִים אוֹ לִבְנֵי רְשׁוּת־הָרַבִּים. וְהַכְּלָל הוּא, שֶׁאָסוּר לַעֲשׂוֹת שׁוּם דָּבָר אֲפִלּוּ בִּרְשׁוּתוֹ, וּמִכָּל־שֶׁכֵּן בִּרְשׁוּת־הָרַבִּים, דָּבָר שֶׁיָּכוֹל לְהַגִּיעַ מִמֶּנּוּ אֵיזֶה הֶזֵּק לִשְׁכֵנוֹ אוֹ לָעוֹבְרִים בִּרְשׁוּת־הָרַבִּים, אִם לֹא בְדָבָר שֶׁפָּשַׁט הַמִּנְהָג שֶׁעוֹשֶׂה כֵּן כָּל מִי שֶׁרוֹצֶה, שֶׁהֲרֵי זֶה, כְּאִלּוּ מָחֲלוּ כָּל אַנְשֵׁי הָעִיר, כְּדֵי שֶׁיּוּכַל כָּל אֶחָד לַעֲשׂוֹת כֵּן כְּשֶׁיִּצְטָרֵךְ לָזֶה, הוּא אוֹ בָנָיו אַחֲרָיו.

ו) הַמַּבְעִית אֶת חֲבֵרוֹ, כְּגוֹן שֶׁצָּעַק עָלָיו מֵאַחֲרָיו אוֹ שֶׁנִּרְאָה לוֹ בָּאֲפֵלָה וְכַיּוֹצֵא בָזֶה, חַיָּב בְּדִינֵי שָׁמָיִם.

ז) הַחוֹבֵל בַּחֲבֵרוֹ, אַף־עַל־פִּי שֶׁנָּתַן אֶת הַמָּמוֹן לַנֶּחְבָּל מַה שֶּׁנִּתְחַיֵּב לוֹ עֲבוּר הַחֲבָלָה, וְכֵן גַּנָּב אוֹ גַזְלָן, אַף־עַל־פִּי שֶׁהֶחֱזִירוּ אוֹ שִׁלְּמוּ, מִכָּל מָקוֹם אֵין מִתְכַּפֵּר לָהֶם עַד שֶׁיְּבַקְשׁוּ מְחִילָה מֵאֵת הַנֶּחְבָּל אוֹ הַנִּגְזָל אוֹ הַנִּגְנָב עַל הַצַּעַר שֶׁהָיָה לָהֶם. וְהֵם יִמְחֲלוּ וְלֹא יִהְיוּ אַכְזָרִים.

ח) הָרוֹאֶה אֶת חֲבֵרוֹ בְּצָרָה, רַחֲמָנָא לִצְלַן, וְיָכוֹל לְהַצִּילוֹ הוּא בְּעַצְמוֹ אוֹ לִשְׂכֹּר אֲחֵרִים לְהַצִּילוֹ, חַיָּב לִטְרֹחַ וְלִשְׂכֹּר וּלְהַצִּילוֹ, וְחוֹזֵר וְנִפְרָע מִמֶּנּוּ אִם יֵשׁ לוֹ. וְאִם אֵין לוֹ, מִכָּל מָקוֹם לֹא יִמָּנַע בִּשְׁבִיל זֶה, וְיַצִּילֶנּוּ בְּמָמוֹן שֶׁלּוֹ. וְאִם נִמְנַע, עוֹבֵר עַל לֹא תַעֲמֹד עַל דַּם רֵעֶךָ. וְכֵן אִם שָׁמַע מֵאֵיזֶה רְשָׁעִים מְחַשְּׁבִים רָעָה עַל חֲבֵרוֹ אוֹ טוֹמְנִים לוֹ פַּח וְלֹא גִלָּה אָזְנוֹ לְהוֹדִיעוֹ, אוֹ שֶׁיָּכוֹל לְפַיְּסָם בְּמָמוֹן בִּגְלַל חֲבֵרוֹ וּלְהָסִיר מַה שֶּׁבִּלְבָבָם וְלֹא פִיְּסָם, וְכַיּוֹצֵא בִּדְבָרִים אֵלּוּ, עוֹבֵר עַל לֹא תַעֲמֹד עַל דַּם רֵעֶךָ. וְכָל הַמְקַיֵּם נֶפֶשׁ אַחַת מִיִּשְׂרָאֵל, כְּאִלּוּ קִיֵּם עוֹלָם מָלֵא.

ט) מִי שֶׁעוֹסֵק בְּזִיּוּפִים וְיֵשׁ לָחוּשׁ שֶׁיְּסַכֵּן בָּזֶה רַבִּים דִּינוֹ כְּמוֹ רוֹדֵף, וּמַתְרִין בּוֹ שֶׁלֹּא יַעֲשֶׂה. וְאִם אֵינוֹ מַשְׁגִּיחַ, מֻתָּר לְמָסְרוֹ לַמַּלְכוּת וְלוֹמַר, שֶׁאֵין אַחֵר מִתְעַסֵּק בָּזֶה אֶלָּא פְּלוֹנִי לְבַדּוֹ. וְכֵן יָחִיד שֶׁמַּעֲלִילִים עָלָיו בִּגְלָלוֹ, יָכוֹל לוֹמַר לָהֶם, אֲנִי אֵינִי עוֹשֶׂה, אֶלָּא פְּלוֹנִי לְבַדּוֹ.

י) נוֹהֲגִין שֶׁשִּׁבְעָה טוּבֵי הָעִיר דָּנִין דִּינֵי קְנָסוֹת, כְּגוֹן עַל חֲבָלוֹת וְחֵרוּפִים וְכַדּוֹמֶה, וְאֵין לָהֶם לַעֲשׂוֹת דָּבָר בְּלִי בֵית־דִּין, כִּי יֵשׁ בְּעִנְיָנִים

---

5. If you touched him while you did it, you are obliged to pay in *Beis Din*. (*Shulchan Aruch* 420:32)
6. *Leviticus* 19:16.

5) There are many more things that are forbidden because they cause harm to your neighbors, or to the public. The general principle is that it is forbidden to do anything, even on your own premises, and especially on a public domain, that may cause damage to your neighbor or to passers by in a public domain, unless it is generally accepted that whoever wishes to do this activity may do so. For in such case, it is as if all the townspeople sanctioned this activity, so that each of them has the privilege to do so whenever he needs to; he, or his children (etc.).

6) If you frighten someone, such as by suddenly screaming behind him, or by appearing suddenly before him in the dark, or anything similar, you will be answerable to the Heavenly court.[5]

7) If you injure your neighbor, although you paid the injured person all that you owe him for his injury; also a thief or a robber, although he had returned the article, or made restitution for it, nevertheless, there cannot be atonement until you seek forgiveness from the injured, or from the victim for the pain you caused them. They, for their part, should forgive and not be harsh in refusing.

8) If you see that your neighbor is in trouble, and you are able to save him, or to hire others to save him, you are obliged to trouble yourself or to hire others to save him. If he has the money to pay, you may ask him to repay the money you spent to save him. If he does not have the money, nevertheless, you may not shirk your duty because of this, and you must save him at your own expense. If you refuse to do so, you are guilty of transgressing the negative command, "Do not stand idly by when the blood of your neighbor [is in danger]."[6] Likewise, if you hear wicked people devising a plot against your fellow Jew, or setting a trap for him, and you did not reveal it to him, or if you were able to appease them with money on his behalf, and thereby cause them to discard their plot, and you did not appease them, and other matters similar to this, you are guilty of transgressing the negative command, "Do not stand idly by when the blood of your neighbor" is in danger.[6] He who saves one Jewish life is considered as if he had saved the whole world.[7]

9) A person who is involved in counterfeiting (money) and it is feared he will jeopardize others,[8] is considered as one who is endangering the lives of others. He must be warned to give up this activity. If he does not heed the warning, it is permitted to denounce him to the government, and to declare that no one else is engaged in this practice aside from him. Also, if a person is falsely accused because of him [the counterfeiter], he may tell them, "I am not involved in this, but so and so is the only one involved".

10) It had been the custom for the seven elders of the city[9] to set fines in cases of injuries, insults, and the like. (However,) they must not do anything independ-

7. *Maseches Sanhedrin* 37a.
8. Because of collective punishment, anti-semitism, etc.
9. These people were elected directly by the people of the city.

אֵלּוּ הַרְבֵּה חִלּוּקֵי דִינִים, וְאֵין לַעֲשׂוֹת יוֹתֵר מִן הָרָאוּי עַל פִּי הַדָּת, וְאַל יְהִי קַל בְּעֵינֵיהֶם כְּבוֹד הַבְּרִיּוֹת.

יא) מְעֻבֶּרֶת שֶׁהִיא מַקְשָׁה לֵילֵד, כָּל זְמַן שֶׁהָעֻבָּר בְּתוֹךְ מֵעֶיהָ, מֻתָּרִין לְחַתְּכוֹ בֵּין בְּסַם בֵּין בְּיָד, שֶׁכֹּל שֶׁלֹּא יָצָא לַאֲוִיר הָעוֹלָם, אֵין שֵׁם נֶפֶשׁ עָלָיו. וּבִשְׁבִיל לְהַצִּיל אֶת הָאֵם, מֻתָּרִין לְחַתְּכוֹ, מִשּׁוּם דַּהֲוֵי לֵהּ כְּמוֹ רוֹדֵף אַחַר חֲבֵרוֹ לְהָרְגוֹ. אֲבָל כְּשֶׁהוֹצִיא רֹאשׁוֹ, אֵין נוֹגְעִין בּוֹ, שֶׁאֵין דּוֹחִין נֶפֶשׁ מִפְּנֵי נֶפֶשׁ, וְזֶהוּ טִבְעוֹ שֶׁל עוֹלָם.

סִימָן קפה
הִלְכוֹת שְׁאֵלָה וּשְׂכִירוּת

א) הַשּׁוֹאֵל אוֹ הַשּׂוֹכֵר בְּהֵמָה אוֹ מִטַּלְטְלִין מֵחֲבֵרוֹ, אֵינוֹ רַשַּׁאי, לֹא לְהַשְׁאִילָם וְלֹא לְהַשְׂכִּירָם לְאַחֵר שֶׁלֹּא מִדַּעַת בְּעָלִים. אֲפִלּוּ סְפָרִים שֶׁיֵּשׁ מִצְוָה בְּהַשְׁאָלָתָן, אֵין אוֹמְרִים, מִן הַסְּתָם נִיחָא לַבְּעָלִים שֶׁתֵּעָשֶׂה מִצְוָה בְּמָמוֹנָם, כִּי שֶׁמָּא אֵין רְצוֹנָם שֶׁיְּהֵא דָּבָר שֶׁלָּהֶם בְּיַד אַחֵר שֶׁאֵינוֹ נֶאֱמָן בְּעֵינֵיהֶם. אֲבָל מֻתָּר לַשּׁוֹאֵל סֵפֶר לְהַנִּיחַ לְאַחֵר לִלְמֹד בּוֹ בְּתוֹךְ בֵּיתוֹ, וּבִלְבַד שֶׁלֹּא יִלְמַד, רַק יְחִידִי, וְלֹא שְׁנֵיהֶם בְּיַחַד. וְאִם יָדוּעַ שֶׁדַּרְכָּן שֶׁל הַבְּעָלִים לְהַאֲמִין לָזֶה הַשֵּׁנִי בִּדְבָרִים כָּאֵלּוּ, מֻתָּר הַשּׁוֹאֵל לְהַשְׁאִיל לוֹ וְהַשּׂוֹכֵר לְהַשְׂכִּיר לוֹ.

ב) מִצְוָה לָתֵת שְׂכַר פְּעֻלַּת שָׂכִיר בִּזְמַנּוֹ. וְאִם אִחַר, עוֹבֵר בְּלֹא־תַעֲשֶׂה, שֶׁנֶּאֱמַר, בְּיוֹמוֹ תִתֵּן שְׂכָרוֹ וְלֹא תָבוֹא עָלָיו הַשֶּׁמֶשׁ. וּכְמוֹ כֵן מִצְוָה לָתֵת שְׂכַר בְּהֵמָה אוֹ כְלִי בִּזְמַנּוֹ. וְאִם אֵחֲרוֹ, עוֹבֵר בְּלָאו, שֶׁנֶּאֱמַר, לֹא תַעֲשֹׁק שָׂכִיר עָנִי וְאֶבְיוֹן וְגוֹ' בְּיוֹמוֹ תִתֵּן שְׂכָרוֹ. וְאֵיזֶהוּ זְמַנּוֹ. אִם כָּלְתָה הַמְּלָאכָה בַּיּוֹם, זְמַנּוֹ כָּל הַיּוֹם. וְאִם עָבַר הַיּוֹם וְלֹא נָתַן לוֹ, עוֹבֵר עַל בְּיוֹמוֹ תִתֵּן שְׂכָרוֹ וְלֹא תָבוֹא עָלָיו הַשֶּׁמֶשׁ. וְאִם כָּלְתָה הַמְּלָאכָה לְאַחַר שֶׁיָּצָא הַיּוֹם וְנִכְנַס הַלַּיְלָה, זְמַנּוֹ כָּל הַלָּיְלָה. עָבַר הַלַּיְלָה וְלֹא נָתַן לוֹ, עוֹבֵר עַל לֹא תָלִין פְּעֻלַּת שָׂכִיר אִתְּךָ עַד־בֹּקֶר. וְכֵן שְׂכִיר

---

10. It is permitted to kill the attacker in order to save the life of the victim.

11. If the feet emerged first, the birth of most of its body is the criteria. (*Punim Meiros* Responsa Vol. 3:8.)

ently of the *Beis Din,* since in regard to these matters, there are many diverse laws, and they may not impose a fine greater than what the *halachah* imposes. They should also not treat the dignity of the people lightly.

11) When a woman has severe complications in childbirth, so long as the fetus is unborn, it may be destroyed, either with medicine or with instruments; for as long as it is unborn it is not considered a living soul; and in order to save the [life of the] mother, it is permitted to destroy it; for it is like someone attempting to take the life of another.[10] However, as soon as its head protrudes, [11] it must not be touched, for one life is not to be sacrificed to save another, and this is the way of nature.[12]

Chapter 185
Laws of Borrowing and Hiring

1) If you borrow or rent an animal or other articles from your neighbor, you are not permitted to lend them or rent them to another party without the consent of the owner. Even in the case of sacred books, the lending of which is a meritorious act, we do not assume that the owner would want to have a mitzvah done with his property, for it is possible he does not want his property in the possession of someone who may not be trustworthy in his eyes. However, if you borrow a book, you may allow someone else to study from it in your house, provided he studies from it alone and not two [of you] together. If it is known that the owner is accustomed to trust this other party in such matters, the borrower is permitted to lend it to him, and the renter is permitted to rent it to him.

2) It is a mitzvah to pay the wages of a hired workman on time, and if you delay such payment, you are transgressing a negative commandment, as it is said, "On the same day you shall give him his wages, and the sun shall not go down on it."[1] It is also a mitzvah to pay for the hire of an animal or a utensil at the proper time, and if you delay such payment, you are transgressing a negative command, as it is said "You shall not oppress a hired worker who is poor and needy etc., in the same day you must give his wage."[2] What is the proper time? If he finished his work during the day, he should be paid before the end of that day. If the day has passed and you still did not pay him, you are transgressing the mitzvah of "In the same day you should give him his wage, and the sun shall not go down on it."[1] If he finished his work during the evening, he should be paid during that night. If the night passed and you had not paid him, you are transgressing the negative command, "The wages of your worker shall not abide with you (all the night) until the morning."[3]

---

12. Therefore, we do not view this as an attack of the child on its mother's life. (See *Rambam, Smah* 425:8.)

1. *Deuteronomy* 24:15.
2. *Deuteronomy* 24:14.
3. *Leviticus* 19:13.

שָׁבוּעַ, שְׂכִיר חֹדֶשׁ, שְׂכִיר שָׁנָה, יָצָא מִמְּלַאכְתּוֹ בַּיּוֹם, יֵשׁ לוֹ זְמַן כָּל הַיּוֹם. יָצָא מִמְּלַאכְתּוֹ בַּלַּיְלָה, יֵשׁ לוֹ זְמַן כָּל הַלַּיְלָה וְלֹא יוֹתֵר.

ג) וְכֵן אִם נָתַן טַלִּיתוֹ לְאֻמָּן לְתַקְּנָהּ בְּקַבְּלָנוּת וֶהֱבִיאָהּ לוֹ בַּיּוֹם, יֵשׁ לוֹ זְמַן כָּל הַיּוֹם בִּלְבַד. הֱבִיאָהּ לוֹ בַּלַּיְלָה, יֵשׁ לוֹ זְמַן כָּל הַלַּיְלָה בִּלְבַד. אֲבָל כָּל זְמַן שֶׁהַטַּלִּית בְּיַד הָאֻמָּן, אַף־עַל־פִּי שֶׁנִּגְמְרָה וְכָלְתָה מְלַאכְתָּהּ, אֵין בַּעַל־הַבַּיִת עוֹבֵר, אֲפִלּוּ הִיא אֵצֶל הָאֻמָּן כַּמָּה יָמִים. וַאֲפִלּוּ הוֹדִיעוֹ שֶׁיָּבִיא לוֹ מָעוֹת וְיִטּוֹל אֶת שֶׁלּוֹ, מִכָּל מָקוֹם אֵינוֹ עוֹבֵר.

ד) אֵינוֹ עוֹבֵר מִשּׁוּם בַּל תָּלִין וְלֹא תָבוֹא עָלָיו הַשֶּׁמֶשׁ, אֶלָּא אִם כֵּן תְּבָעוֹ הַשָּׂכִיר וְיֵשׁ לוֹ מָעוֹת לִתֵּן לוֹ. אֲבָל אִם לֹא תְבָעוֹ הַשָּׂכִיר, אוֹ שֶׁתְּבָעוֹ וְאֵין לוֹ מָעוֹת, אֵינוֹ עוֹבֵר. וּמִכָּל מָקוֹם מִדַּת חֲסִידוּת הִיא לִלְווֹת וְלִפְרֹעַ לַשָּׂכִיר בִּזְמַנּוֹ, כִּי הוּא עָנִי וְאֵלָיו הוּא נוֹשֵׂא אֶת נַפְשׁוֹ. וּמִי שֶׁדַּרְכּוֹ שֶׁלֹּא לִפְרֹעַ לַפּוֹעֲלִים עַד לְאַחַר הַחֶשְׁבּוֹן, אֲפִלּוּ תְבָעוּ מִמֶּנּוּ דָּבָר מְעַט שֶׁבְּוַדַּאי מַגִּיעַ לָהֶם, מִכָּל מָקוֹם אֵינוֹ עוֹבֵר, שֶׁכֵּיוָן שֶׁיָּדוּעַ שֶׁדַּרְכּוֹ כֵן, עַל דַּעַת כֵּן נִשְׂכְּרוּ אֶצְלוֹ.

ה) שָׂכִיר שֶׁעָשָׂה מְלָאכָה לְבַעַל־הַבַּיִת וְהִפְסִידָהּ, אֲפִלּוּ בִּפְשִׁיעָה, בְּאֹפֶן שֶׁעַל פִּי הַדִּין הוּא חַיָּב בְּתַשְׁלוּמִין, מִצְוָה עַל בַּעַל־הַבַּיִת לְהִכָּנֵס עִמּוֹ לִפְנִים מִשּׁוּרַת הַדִּין וְלִמְחוֹל לוֹ, שֶׁנֶּאֱמַר, לְמַעַן תֵּלֵךְ בְּדֶרֶךְ טוֹבִים. וְאִם הַשָּׂכִיר עָנִי הוּא וְאֵין לוֹ מַה יֹּאכַל, מִצְוָה לִתֵּן לוֹ שְׂכָרוֹ, שֶׁנֶּאֱמַר וְאָרְחוֹת צַדִּיקִים תִּשְׁמֹר. וְזֶה הוּא אֹרַח צַדִּיקִים, לִשְׁמֹר דֶּרֶךְ ה' לַעֲשׂוֹת צְדָקָה וּמִשְׁפָּט לִפְנִים מִשּׁוּרַת הַדִּין.

ו) כְּדֶרֶךְ שֶׁבַּעַל־הַבַּיִת מֻזְהָר שֶׁלֹּא לִגְזֹל שְׂכַר הֶעָנִי וְלֹא לְאַחֲרוֹ, כָּךְ הֶעָנִי מֻזְהָר שֶׁלֹּא יְבַטֵּל מִמְּלֶאכֶת בַּעַל־הַבָּיִת. וְחַיָּב לַעֲבוֹד בְּכָל כֹּחוֹ, כְּמוֹ שֶׁאָמַר יַעֲקֹב אָבִינוּ עָלָיו הַשָּׁלוֹם, כִּי בְּכָל־כֹּחִי עָבַדְתִּי אֶת־אֲבִיכֶן. לְפִיכָךְ אֵין הַפּוֹעֵל רַשַּׁאי לַעֲשׂוֹת מְלָאכָה בַּלַּיְלָה וּלְהַשְׂכִּיר עַצְמוֹ בַּיּוֹם, (שֶׁכְּבָר נֶחֱלַשׁ מֵהַלַּיְלָה), וְכֵן אֵינוֹ רַשַּׁאי לַעֲשׂוֹת מְלָאכָה בִּבְהֶמְתּוֹ בַּלַּיְלָה וּלְהַשְׂכִּירָהּ בַּיּוֹם. וְאֵין הַפּוֹעֵל רַשַּׁאי לְהַרְעִיב וּלְסַגֵּף עַצְמוֹ, שֶׁהֲרֵי מַחֲלִישׁ כֹּחוֹ וְלֹא יוּכַל לַעֲשׂוֹת מְלֶאכֶת בַּעַל־הַבַּיִת כָּרָאוּי. וְכֵן הוּא דִּין הַמְלַמֵּד.

---

4. *Shulchan Aruch Horav—Ariz'l.*
5. *Proverbs* 2:20.

Similarly, a workman who is hired by the week, or month, or year, if he has finished his work during the day, he should be paid during that day; if he finished during the night, he should be paid during that night and not later.

3) Also, if you gave your garment to a tailor to repair, for a set price, and the tailor returns it to you during the day, you must pay him during that day. And if he returned it to you at night, you must pay him during that night. However, so long as the garment remains with the tailor, although the garment is finished, and the work has been completed, you are not in violation of the law, even if it is in the tailor's possession for many days, and even if the tailor has notified you to bring the money and take the garment nevertheless, you are not in violation of the law.

4) You have not transgressed the law of: "The wages of your worker shall not abide with you"[3] [or the law of] "That the sun shall not go down on it,"[1] unless the worker demands his wages, and you have the money to pay him. But if the worker did not demand his wages, or he demanded his wages but you do not have the money, you are not in violation of the law. Nevertheless,[4] a scrupulous person will borrow money to pay his worker in the proper time, for he is poor and sets his heart upon his wage. If your system is not to pay the workers until after a certain sum is due, even if they demand a small sum, which they have undoubtedly already earned, nevertheless, (if you refuse to give it to them), you are not guilty of transgressing the law, since it is known that this is your system of payment, and on such condition they hired themselves out to you.

5) If a hired workman was working for you, and spoiled the article on which he had worked, even if it was caused by his negligence, in a manner in which he is legally bound to make reparation, it is a mitzvah for you to waive your legal rights, and release him from liability, as it is said: "That you may walk in the way of good men."[5] If the worker is a poor man, and has no food, it is a mitzvah to give him his wages, as it is said, "And keep the paths of the righteous."[5] and the path of the righteous is to keep the way of Hashem, to practice charity and justice, to an even greater degree than is required by law.[6]

6) Just as the employer is admonished not to rob the worker of his wages, and not to delay payment, so is the worker admonished not to cheat his employer by wasting time at work. He must work with all his strength [ability,] as our father, Jacob, peace unto him, said, "That I served your father with all my strength."[7] Therefore, a worker is not permitted to work all night, and hire himself out during the day because he has been weakened by the night work. Similarly, it is not permitted to work your animal at night and hire it out for work during the day. A worker is not permitted to starve or afflict himself, for this weakens his physical strength, and he will not be able to do the work for his employer properly. This law applies also to a teacher. (see Chapter 165:12)

---

6. See *Maseches Baba Metziah* 83a.
7. *Genesis* 31:6.

סִימָן קפו

הִלְכוֹת לֹא תַחְסֹם

א) כָּל הַמּוֹנֵעַ אֶת הַבְּהֵמָה מִלֶּאֱכֹל בִּשְׁעַת מְלַאכְתָּהּ, לוֹקֶה, שֶׁנֶּאֱמַר, לֹא תַחְסֹם שׁוֹר בְּדִישׁוֹ. אֶחָד שׁוֹר וְאֶחָד כָּל מִינֵי בְהֵמָה וְחַיָּה, בֵּין טְמֵאִים בֵּין טְהוֹרִים, וְאֶחָד הַדִּישָׁה וְאֶחָד כָּל שְׁאָר מְלָאכוֹת שֶׁל גִּדּוּלֵי קַרְקַע. וְלֹא נֶאֱמַר שׁוֹר בְּדִישׁוֹ, אֶלָּא בַּהֹוֶה. וַאֲפִלּוּ חֲסָמָהּ בְּקוֹל, דְּהַיְנוּ שֶׁצָּעַק עָלֶיהָ וְעַל יְדֵי זֶה לֹא תֹאכַל, חַיָּב מַלְקוּת.

ב) יִשְׂרָאֵל הַדָּשׁ אֲפִלּוּ בְּפָרָתוֹ שֶׁל גּוֹי וּתְבוּאָה שֶׁל גּוֹי, עוֹבֵר מִשּׁוּם לֹא־תַחְסֹם.

ג) אִם הַבְּהֵמָה אֵינָהּ יְכוֹלָה לֶאֱכֹל, מִפְּנֵי שֶׁהִיא צְמֵאָה, צָרִיךְ לְהַשְׁקוֹתָהּ.

ד) בְּהֵמָה שֶׁהִיא עוֹשָׂה בְּדָבָר שֶׁהוּא רַע לִבְנֵי מֵעֶיהָ, מֻתָּר לְחָסְמָהּ, שֶׁלֹּא הִקְפִּידָה הַתּוֹרָה אֶלָּא עַל הֲנָאָתָהּ, וַהֲרֵי אֵינָהּ נֶהֱנֵית.

סִימָן קפז

הִלְכוֹת אֲבֵדָה וּמְצִיאָה

א) הָרוֹאֶה אֲבֵדַת יִשְׂרָאֵל, חַיָּב לְטַפֵּל בָּהּ לַהֲשִׁיבָהּ לִבְעָלֶיהָ, שֶׁנֶּאֱמַר, הָשֵׁב תְּשִׁיבֵם. וְכֵן כָּל מָמוֹן שֶׁל חֲבֵרוֹ שֶׁאָדָם יָכוֹל לְהַצִּיל שֶׁלֹּא יֹאבַד, חַיָּב לְהַצִּיל, וְהוּא בִּכְלַל הֲשָׁבַת אֲבֵדָה.

ב) אַף־עַל־פִּי שֶׁמִּן הַדִּין בְּמָקוֹם שֶׁרֹב גּוֹיִם מְצוּיִים, אֲפִלּוּ נָתַן בָּהּ יִשְׂרָאֵל סִימָן, אֵינוֹ חַיָּב לְהַחֲזִיר, מִשּׁוּם דְּמִסְתָמָא כְּבָר נִתְיָאֵשׁ הֵימֶנָּה, מִכָּל מָקוֹם טוֹב וְיָשָׁר לַעֲשׂוֹת לִפְנִים מִשּׁוּרַת הַדִּין לְהַחֲזִיר לְיִשְׂרָאֵל שֶׁנָּתַן בָּהּ סִימָן. וְכוֹפִין עַל זֶה. וְאִם הַמּוֹצֵא הוּא עָנִי, וּבַעַל הָאֲבֵדָה הוּא עָשִׁיר, אֵינוֹ צָרִיךְ לַעֲשׂוֹת לִפְנִים מִשּׁוּרַת הַדִּין. וּבְמָקוֹם שֶׁיֵּשׁ דִּינָא דְמַלְכוּתָא לְהַחֲזִיר אֲבֵדָה, חַיָּב בְּכָל עִנְיָן לְהַחֲזִיר.

ג) כָּל הַמּוֹצֵא אֲבֵדָה, בֵּין שֶׁיֵּשׁ בָּהּ סִימָן בֵּין שֶׁאֵין בָּהּ סִימָן, אִם מְצָאָהּ דֶּרֶךְ הַנָּחָה, כְּגוֹן טַלִּית וְקַרְדֹּם בְּצַד הַגָּדֵר, וַאֲפִלּוּ יֵשׁ לְהִסְתַּפֵּק אִם הִנִּיחָם שָׁם בְּכַוָּנָה אוֹ אִבְּדָם שָׁם, אָסוּר לִגַּע בָּהֶם.

1. *Deuteronomy* 25:4.
2. This, however, is not punishable by flogging. (*Shulchan Aruch* 338:6)

Chapter 186
The Laws of Muzzling Animals

1) Anyone who prevents an animal from eating while working is liable to be punished by flogging as it is said, "You shall not muzzle the ox when it is threshing."[1] It is immaterial whether it is an ox, or any other animal or beast, whether unclean or clean, whether it is threshing or any other work concerned with produce of the ground. The Torah mentions the ox and threshing only because it speaks of the usual circumstance. Even if it is muzzled by voice, that is, it is shouted at, and is thus prevented from eating, it is punishable by flogging.

2) A Jew who threshes (grain) even with an animal belonging to a non-Jew, and even if the grain belongs to a non-Jew, transgresses the commandment "You shall not muzzle."

3) If the animal is unable to eat because it is thirsty, you must give it to drink.[2]

4) If an animal is working with something which would be harmful to its intestines, you are permitted to muzzle it; for the Torah is concerned with the benefit of the animal, and in such case it would not be to its benefit.

Chapter 187
The Laws of Articles Lost and Found

1) If you see an article that was lost by a Jew, it is your duty to care for it, and return it to its owner, as it is said, "You shall surely return them."[1] Similarly, any of your neighbor's property, that you are able to save from destruction, you are obliged to do so, for this is included in the mitzvah of returning a lost article.

2) Although according to *halachah,* in a place where the majority of the people are non-Jewish, even if the Jew identifies it you are not obliged to return it to him, because we assume he already had despaired of its recovery, nevertheless, it is good and proper to do more than the *halachah* requires, and return it to the Jew who identifies it; and we force him to do this.[2] If the finder is a poor man, and the owner of the article is wealthy, the finder is not obligated to do more than the *halachah* requires. In a place where you are required by civil law to return a lost article, you must return it in all circumstances.

3) If you find an article regardless if it has an identification mark or not, if upon finding it, it was apparent that it had been placed there, such as a garment or an ax, that was left at the side of a fence;[3] and even if it is doubtful whether they were purposely placed there, or lost there, it is forbidden to touch them.

---

1. *Deuteronomy* 22:1.
2. *Shach* 259—*Raviah*
3. Or any other place where it is protected. *Ramah* 260:10, *Shach-Poskim.* Otherwise, if it is in a totally unprotected place and bears a mark of identification, you must take it and return it to its owner. If it bears no mark, you may take it for yourself. If you found it in a place that is partially protected, if it bears a mark, you must take it and return it to its owner. If it bears

ד) מִי שֶׁהוּא זָקֵן מְכֻבָּד, וּמָצָא אֲבֵדָה וְהוּא דָּבָר מְבֻזֶּה, שֶׁאֲפִלּוּ הָיָה שֶׁלּוֹ, לֹא הָיָה נוֹטְלוֹ לַהֲבִיאוֹ לְבֵיתוֹ, מִשּׁוּם דַּהֲוֵי לֵהּ בִּזָּיוֹן, אֵינוֹ חַיָּב לְטַפֵּל בָּהּ. וּמִכָּל מָקוֹם יֵשׁ לוֹ לַעֲשׂוֹת לִפְנִים מִשּׁוּרַת הַדִּין וְלִטַּפֵּל בָּהּ, אַף־עַל־פִּי שֶׁאֵינָהּ לְפִי כְבוֹדוֹ.

ה) מָצָא מְצִיאָה וְאֵינוֹ יוֹדֵעַ מִי אִבְּדָהּ, בֵּין שֶׁיֵּשׁ בָּהּ סִימָן בֵּין שֶׁאֵין בָּהּ סִימָן, יֵשׁ בְּעִנְיָנִים אֵלּוּ הַרְבֵּה חִלּוּקֵי דִינִים, וְיַעֲשֶׂה שְׁאֵלַת חָכָם אֵיךְ יַעֲשֶׂה.

סִימָן קפח

הִלְכוֹת פִּקָּדוֹן

א) הַמַּפְקִיד מָעוֹת אֵצֶל חֲבֵרוֹ, עַתָּה בַּזְּמַן הַזֶּה שֶׁכָּל עֲסָקֵינוּ בְּמַשָּׂא וּמַתָּן וְהַכֹּל צְרִיכִין לְמָעוֹת, מִן הַסְּתָם נִתְרַצָּה הַמַּפְקִיד, שֶׁהַנִּפְקָד יוֹצִיאֵן כְּשֶׁיִּצְטָרֵךְ. וְלָכֵן מֻתָּר לוֹ לְהוֹצִיאָן, וַהֲרֵי הֵן אֶצְלוֹ כְּמוֹ מִלְוָה, אֶלָּא אִם כֵּן גִּלָּה הַמַּפְקִיד דַּעְתּוֹ שֶׁאֵין רְצוֹנוֹ בְּכָךְ, כְּגוֹן שֶׁחֲתָמָן אוֹ קְשָׁרָן בְּקֶשֶׁר מְשֻׁנֶּה, אָז אֵין הַנִּפְקָד רַשַּׁאי לְהוֹצִיאָן.

ב) הַמַּפְקִיד שְׁאָר חֵפֶץ אֵצֶל חֲבֵרוֹ, אָסוּר לְהַנִּפְקָד לְהִשְׁתַּמֵּשׁ בְּחֵפֶץ זֶה לְצָרְכּוֹ. וְאַף־עַל־פִּי שֶׁאֵין הַחֵפֶץ מִתְקַלְקֵל כְּלָל בְּתַשְׁמִישׁ זֶה, מִכָּל מָקוֹם הֲוֵי שׁוֹאֵל שֶׁלֹּא מִדַּעַת. וְשׁוֹאֵל שֶׁלֹּא מִדַּעַת, גַּזְלָן הוּא. וְאִם יָדוּעַ בְּבֵרוּר שֶׁאֵין הַמַּפְקִיד מַקְפִּיד עָלָיו, מֻתָּר. וְיֵשׁ אוֹסְרִין גַּם בָּזֶה, מִשּׁוּם דְּפִקָּדוֹן אֲפִלּוּ בְּדָבָר שֶׁאֵין דֶּרֶךְ בְּנֵי אָדָם לְהַקְפִּיד, אָסוּר, מִשּׁוּם דַּהֲוֵי שׁוֹלֵחַ יָד בַּפִּקָּדוֹן גַּם בְּכַהַאי גַּוְנָא. וְיֵשׁ לְהַחְמִיר.

ג) חַיָּב לִשְׁמֹר אֶת הַפִּקָּדוֹן בְּאֹפֶן הַיּוֹתֵר טוֹב כְּפִי הַדֶּרֶךְ לִשְׁמֹר חֲפָצִים כָּאֵלּוּ. וַאֲפִלּוּ אִם הוּא אֵינוֹ מְדַקְדֵּק כָּל כָּךְ בִּשְׁמִירַת חֲפָצִים שֶׁלּוֹ בַּפִּקָּדוֹן, חַיָּב לְדַקְדֵּק יוֹתֵר.

ד) אֵין הַנִּפְקָד רַשַּׁאי לְהַפְקִיד אֶת הַפִּקָּדוֹן בְּיַד אֲחֵרִים, אֲפִלּוּ כְּשֵׁרִים וְנֶאֱמָנִים יוֹתֵר מִמֶּנּוּ, אֶלָּא אִם כֵּן הַמַּפְקִיד גַּם כֵּן רָגִיל לְהַפְקִיד דְּבָרִים כָּאֵלּוּ אֶצְלָם.

ה) כְּשֶׁבָּא לְהַחֲזִיר אֶת הַפִּקָּדוֹן, לֹא יַחֲזִירֶנּוּ לְאֶחָד מִבְּנֵי בֵיתוֹ שֶׁל הַמַּפְקִיד שֶׁלֹּא מִדַּעְתּוֹ. וְכֵן כְּשֶׁבָּא לְהַחֲזִיר לוֹ אֵיזֶה חֵפֶץ שֶׁהִשְׁאִיל לוֹ אוֹ לִפְרֹעַ חוֹבוֹ. אֲבָל יָכוֹל לְהַחֲזִיר לְאִשְׁתּוֹ, כִּי מִן הַסְּתָם הִיא נוֹשֵׂאת וְנוֹתֶנֶת בְּתוֹךְ הַבַּיִת, וְהַבַּעַל מַפְקִיד כָּל אֲשֶׁר לוֹ בְּיָדָהּ.

4) If an old, respected man finds a lost article, that it is so shabby that even if it were his own, he would not carry it home, because it would be disgraceful to him, he is not obligated to bother with it. He should, nevertheless, do more than the *halachah* requires, and bother with it, even though it is beneath his dignity.

5) If you find an article and you do not know who lost it, whether it has a mark of identification, or does not have a mark of identification, these matters involve many divergent laws, and you should consult a Rav as to what you should do.

Chapter 188
Laws Concerning Bailments

1) If you deposit money with your neighbor, since most of us are involved in business, and we always need money, it is assumed that you agree that the depositary may use that money if he needs it. Therefore, the despositary is permitted to use the money, and the money is considered by him as a loan, unless you indicate to him that you do not wish it to be used. For instance, if you put the money in a sealed package, or tied it up with a special knot, the depositary is not permitted to use it.

2) If someone deposits an article with you, you are forbidden to use that article for your own needs even though the article will not spoil in the least by such use. Nevertheless, you would be borrowing it without the owner's knowledge, and he who borrows without the owner's knowledge is considered a robber. If you know definitely that your depositer would not object to your using it, you are permitted to use it. Some *Poskim* prohibit this too, because with regard to a deposit, it is forbidden to use even something whose use people generally do not object to, because it is considered a fraudulent use of a deposit even in such circumstances. You should follow the stricter opinion.

3) It is your duty to safeguard the deposit in the most effective manner, in accordance with the accepted manner of safeguarding such articles. Even though you are not so particular to guard your own property so carefully, nevertheless with property entrusted to you, you must take special care.

4) You are not permitted to entrust the deposit with other people, even though they are more fit and trustworthy than yourself, unless the depositor is also accustomed to entrust these kinds of things with them.

5) When you return the deposit, you should not return it to any member of the depositor's household without his consent. This is also true when you return any article that was lent to you, or when you pay a debt. However, you may return it to his wife, as it may be assumed that she manages the household, and her husband entrusts everything with her.

---

no mark, you must not touch it; just leave it there (*Ramah* 260:10). If in the last instance you picked it up, the *Ramah* says you must hold it until *Eliyohu,* the prophet, comes and reveals who the owner is. (*Shach* 260:32)

סִימָן קפט
הִלְכוֹת פְּרִיקָה וּטְעִינָה

א) מִי שֶׁפָּגַע בַּחֲבֵרוֹ בַּדֶּרֶךְ וּבְהֶמְתּוֹ רוֹבֶצֶת תַּחַת מַשָּׂאָהּ, בֵּין שֶׁהָיָה עָלֶיהָ מַשָּׂא הָרָאוּי לָהּ, בֵּין שֶׁהָיָה עָלֶיהָ יוֹתֵר מִמַּה שֶּׁרָאוּי לָהּ, הֲרֵי זֶה מִצְוָה לְסַיְּעוֹ לִפְרֹק מֵעָלֶיהָ, שֶׁנֶּאֱמַר, עָזֹב תַּעֲזֹב עִמּוֹ. וּלְאַחַר שֶׁפָּרַק, לֹא יַנִּיחַ אֶת חֲבֵרוֹ בְּצַעַר וְיֵלֵךְ לוֹ, אֶלָּא יַעֲזוֹר לוֹ לַחֲזוֹר וְלִטְעוֹן עָלֶיהָ שֶׁנֶּאֱמַר, הָקֵם תָּקִים. וְאִם הִנִּיחַ אֶת חֲבֵרוֹ וְלֹא פָרַק וְלֹא טָעַן, בִּטֵּל מִצְוַת־עֲשֵׂה וְעָבַר עַל מִצְוַת־לֹא־תַעֲשֶׂה, שֶׁנֶּאֱמַר, לֹא תִרְאֶה אֶת־חֲמוֹר אָחִיךָ וְגוֹ׳.

ב) פָּרַק וְטָעַן וְחָזַר וְנָפַל, חַיָּב לִפְרֹק וְלִטְעֹן פַּעַם אַחֶרֶת, וַאֲפִלּוּ מֵאָה פְעָמִים, שֶׁנֶּאֱמַר, עָזֹב תַּעֲזֹב, הָקֵם תָּקִים עִמּוֹ. לְפִיכָךְ צָרִיךְ לֵילֵךְ עִמּוֹ עַד פַּרְסָה, שֶׁמָּא יִצְטָרֵךְ לוֹ, אֶלָּא אִם כֵּן אוֹמֵר לוֹ בַּעַל הַמַּשָּׂא, אֵינִי צָרִיךְ לָךְ.

ג) מִצְוַת פְּרִיקָה, צָרִיךְ לַעֲשׂוֹת בְּחִנָּם. אֲבָל לִטְעֹן, אֵינוֹ מְחֻיָּב אֶלָּא בְּשָׂכָר, וְכֵן בְּעַד מַה שֶּׁהוֹלֵךְ עִמּוֹ, מְחֻיָּב לְשַׁלֵּם לוֹ.

ד) בֶּהֱמַת גּוֹי, אִם הָיָה הַגּוֹי מְחַמֵּר אַחַר בְּהֶמְתּוֹ, בֵּין שֶׁהַמַּשָּׂא הוּא שֶׁל יִשְׂרָאֵל בֵּין שֶׁהוּא שֶׁל גּוֹי, אֵינוֹ חַיָּב, רַק לִפְרֹק, מִשּׁוּם צַעַר בַּעֲלֵי־חַיִּים, וְיָכוֹל לְקַבֵּל שָׂכָר עַל זֶה. אֲבָל לִטְעֹן, אֵינוֹ חַיָּב כְּלָל, רַק אִי אִכָּא מִשּׁוּם אֵיבָה. וְאִם אֵין שָׁם גּוֹי, אֶלָּא יִשְׂרָאֵל מְחַמֵּר אַחַר הַבְּהֵמָה, חַיָּב גַּם כֵּן לִטְעֹן מִשּׁוּם צַעַר הַיִּשְׂרָאֵל. וְכֵן בֶּהֱמַת יִשְׂרָאֵל וְהַמַּשָּׂא שֶׁל גּוֹי, חַיָּב לִפְרֹק וְלִטְעֹן מִשּׁוּם צַעַר הַיִּשְׂרָאֵל.

ה) כְּתִיב, כִּי תִרְאֶה חֲמוֹר שֹׂנַאֲךָ רֹבֵץ תַּחַת מַשָּׂאוֹ וְגוֹ׳, שׂוֹנֵא זֶה לֹא מֵהַגּוֹיִם הוּא, (שֶׁהֲרֵי אֵינָם בְּמִצְוַת טְעִינָה וּפְרִיקָה, אֶלָּא מִשּׁוּם צַעַר בַּעֲלֵי חַיִּים), אֶלָּא מִיִּשְׂרָאֵל. וְהֵיאַךְ יִהְיֶה יִשְׂרָאֵל שׂוֹנֵא לְיִשְׂרָאֵל, וְהַכָּתוּב אוֹמֵר, לֹא תִשְׂנָא אֶת־אָחִיךָ בִּלְבָבֶךָ. אָמְרוּ חֲכָמִים, כְּגוֹן שֶׁהוּא לְבַדּוֹ רָאָהוּ שֶׁעָבַר עֲבֵרָה, וְהִתְרָה בוֹ וְלֹא חָזַר, הֲרֵי מִצְוָה לְשָׂנְאוֹתוֹ עַד שֶׁיַּעֲשֶׂה תְשׁוּבָה וְיָשׁוּב מֵרִשְׁעָתוֹ. וְאַף־עַל־פִּי שֶׁעֲדַיִן לֹא עָשָׂה תְשׁוּבָה. אִם מְצָאוֹ בְּצַעַר עַל מַשָּׂאוֹ, מִצְוָה לִפְרֹק וְלִטְעֹן עִמּוֹ וְלֹא יַנִּיחֶנּוּ כָּךְ, כִּי שֶׁמָּא

Chapter 189
Laws of Unloading and Loading

1) If you meet your neighbor on the road and his animal is lying underneath its load, whether its burden was a proper load for it, or it was burdened with a load that was too heavy for it, it is a mitzvah to assist him to unload the burden, as it is said, "You shall surely help him."[1] After you have helped unload the burden, you should not leave your neighbor in distress, and go on your way, but you should help him reload it, as it is said, "You shall surely help him lift it up again."[2] If you leave your neighbor, and did not help him in unloading and loading, you have neglected to perform an affirmative command, and have transgressed a negative command, as it is said, "You shall not see the donkey of your neighbor [or his ox fallen down by the way and conceal yourself.]"[2]

2) If after you helped to unload and reload, the animal fell down again, you must help unload and reload again, even a hundred times, as it is said, "You shall surely help"[1] (and) "You shall surely help him lift it up."[2] Therefore, you must go with him a distance of a *parsah,*[3] as he might need your help again, unless the owner of the load tells you, "I no longer need your help."

3) The unloading must be done gratis, but you are not obliged to reload unless he is willing to compensate you and he must also compensate you for accompanying him.

4) If the animal belongs to a non-Jew, and the non-Jew was driving the animal, whether the load belongs to a Jew, or it belongs to a non-Jew, you are only obliged to help unload because of the suffering of the animal, and you may receive compensation for it. But you are not at all obliged to help him reload, unless it would cause animosity. If the non-Jew is not present, and a Jew drives the animal, you must also help him reload, because of the distress to the Jew. If the animal belongs to a Jew and the load belongs to a non-Jew, you are obliged to help unload and reload because of the distress of the Jew.

5) It is written,[4] "If you see the donkey of your enemy lying under its burden," etc. This "enemy" does not refer to a non-Jew. (They are not included in the command regarding loading and unloading, unless the animal suffers), but it refers to a Jew. And how can one Jew hate another Jew since the Torah states, "You shall not hate your brother in your heart"?[5] The Sages said: "For instance: if you actually saw him transgress a law, and warned him against it, and he did not desist, it is a mitzvah to hate him until he repents,[6] and abandons his wickedness. Even though he has not yet repented, if you find him in distress on the account of his load, it is a mitzvah to help him unload and reload, and not leave him without help, for he

1. *Exodus* 23:5.
2. *Deuteronomy* 22:4.
3. See Glossary.
4. *Exodus* 23:5.
5. *Leviticus* 19:17.
6. See *Maseches Pesachim* 113b.

יִשְׁהֶה בִּשְׁבִיל מָמוֹנוֹ וְיָבוֹא לִידֵי סַכָּנָה וְהַתּוֹרָה הִקְפִּידָה עַל נַפְשׁוֹת יִשְׂרָאֵל, בֵּין רְשָׁעִים בֵּין צַדִּיקִים, מֵאַחַר שֶׁהֵם נִלְוִים אֶל ה׳ וּמַאֲמִינִים בְּעִקַּר הַדָּת, שֶׁנֶּאֱמַר, אֱמוֹר אֲלֵיהֶם חַי אָנִי נְאֻם ה׳ אֱלֹהִים אִם אֶחְפֹּץ בְּמוֹת הָרָשָׁע כִּי אִם בְּשׁוּב רָשָׁע מִדַּרְכּוֹ וְחָיָה.

ו) בְּנֵי חֲבוּרָה שֶׁאֵרַע לְאֶחָד מֵהֶם שֶׁרַגְלֵי חֲמוֹרוֹ רְעוּעוֹת, אֵין בְּנֵי חֲבוּרָה רַשָּׁאִים לִפָּרֵד עִם חֲמוֹרֵיהֶם וּלְהַנִּיחוֹ לְבַדּוֹ בַּדֶּרֶךְ. אֲבָל אִם נָפַל חֲמוֹרוֹ וְאֵינוֹ יָכוֹל עוֹד לֵילֵךְ כְּלָל, רַשָּׁאִים לִפָּרֵד מִמֶּנּוּ, וְאֵין צְרִיכִין לְהִתְעַכֵּב בִּשְׁבִילוֹ יוֹתֵר מִדַּי. וְכֵן בְּנֵי חֲבוּרָה שֶׁנּוֹסְעִין בַּעֲגָלוֹת, וְאֵרַע לְאֶחָד מֵהֶם אֵיזֶה קִלְקוּל, שֶׁצָּרִיךְ לִשְׁהוֹת מְעַט לְתַקֵּן, אֵין חֲבֵרָיו רַשָּׁאִים לִפָּרֵד מִמֶּנּוּ, אֶלָּא אִם כֵּן צָרִיךְ לְהִתְעַכֵּב הַרְבֵּה יוֹתֵר מִדַּי.

סִימָן קצ
הִלְכוֹת [מַעֲקֶה] שְׁמִירַת הַגּוּף וּבַל תַּשְׁחִית

א) מִצְוַת־עֲשֵׂה לַעֲשׂוֹת מַעֲקֶה לְגַגּוֹ, שֶׁנֶּאֱמַר, וְעָשִׂיתָ מַעֲקֶה לְגַגֶּךָ. גֹּבַהּ הַמַּעֲקֶה אֵינוֹ פָּחוֹת מֵעֲשָׂרָה טְפָחִים, וִיהֵא חָזָק כְּדֵי שֶׁיִּשָּׁעֵן אָדָם עָלָיו וְלֹא יִפּוֹל. גַּגּוֹת שֶׁלָּנוּ שֶׁאֵין מִשְׁתַּמְּשִׁין בָּהֶם, פְּטוּרִין. וְאָמְנָם לֹא הַגַּג בִּלְבַד חַיָּב בְּמַעֲקֶה, אֶלָּא כָּל דָּבָר שֶׁיֵּשׁ בּוֹ סַכָּנָה, שֶׁיִּכָּשֵׁל בּוֹ אָדָם וְיָמוּת, חַיָּב בְּמַעֲקֶה וְתִקּוּן. וְכָל הַמַּנִּיחוֹ בְּלִי מַעֲקֶה, בִּטֵּל מִצְוַת־עֲשֵׂה וְעָבַר עַל לֹא־תַעֲשֶׂה, שֶׁנֶּאֱמַר, וְלֹא תָשִׂים דָּמִים בְּבֵיתֶךָ. כְּגוֹן מִי שֶׁיֵּשׁ לוֹ בּוֹר בְּתוֹךְ חֲצֵרוֹ, חַיָּב לַעֲשׂוֹת לוֹ חֻלְיָא [גָּדֵר] גְּבוֹהָה עֲשָׂרָה טְפָחִים אוֹ לַעֲשׂוֹת לוֹ כִּסּוּי שֶׁלֹּא יִפּוֹל בּוֹ אָדָם.

ב) וְכֵן כָּל מִכְשׁוֹל שֶׁיֵּשׁ בּוֹ סַכָּנַת נְפָשׁוֹת, מִצְוַת־עֲשֵׂה לַהֲסִירוֹ וּלְהִשָּׁמֵר מִמֶּנּוּ וּלְהִזָּהֵר בַּדָּבָר יָפֶה, שֶׁנֶּאֱמַר, הִשָּׁמֶר לְךָ וּשְׁמֹר נַפְשְׁךָ מְאֹד. וְאִם הִנִּיחַ וְלֹא הֵסִיר אֶת הַמִּכְשׁוֹלִים הַמְּבִיאִים לִידֵי סַכָּנָה, בִּטֵּל מִצְוַת־עֲשֵׂה וְעָבַר בְּלֹא תָשִׂים דָּמִים, כְּגוֹן אִם סֻלָּם רָעוּעַ עוֹמֵד בְּבֵיתוֹ וַחֲצֵרוֹ, וְכֵן הַמְגַדֵּל כֶּלֶב רָע.

ג) כְּשֵׁם שֶׁצָּרִיךְ הָאָדָם לְהִזָּהֵר בְּגוּפוֹ שֶׁלֹּא לְאַבְּדוֹ וְשֶׁלֹּא לְקַלְקְלוֹ וְשֶׁלֹּא לְהַזִּיקוֹ, כְּמוֹ שֶׁנֶּאֱמַר, הִשָּׁמֶר לְךָ וּשְׁמֹר נַפְשְׁךָ מְאֹד, כָּךְ צָרִיךְ

may stay there out of concern for his money and may endanger his life." The Torah is concerned regarding Jewish lives, whether they are wicked or righteous, so long as they cleave to Hashem, and believe in the principal tenets of our religion, as it is said, "Say to them: as I live says *Hashem Elokim,* I do not desire the death of the wicked, but that the wicked turn from his way and live." [7]

6) If a group was traveling together, and it happened to one of them that the legs of his donkey became lame, the other members of the group are not permitted to depart with their donkeys and leave him alone on the road. However, if his donkey fell down, and is unable to continue the journey, they are permitted to leave him, and need not tarry for his sake longer than is reasonable. Also, a group traveling in vehicles, if one of them broke down, and requires a short time to repair, the rest of the group are not permitted to depart from him, unless they would be detained beyond a reasonable amount of time.

Chapter 190
Laws of Protection of Life and Property

1) It is an affirmative mitzvah to make a fence around the rooftop of your house, as it is said, "And you shall make a fence for your roof."[1] The height of the fence must not be less than ten *tefachim* [high],[2] and it should be so strong that if a man leans against it, it will not fall. The roofs of our houses, which we do not use, are exempt from this law. Indeed, not only rooftops require a fence, but any place where there is danger that a person could meet a fatal accident must have a fence and or other protection. Anyone who leaves it without a fence violates an affirmative precept and transgresses a negative precept, as it is said, "You shall not bring blood upon your house."[3] For instance, if there is a hole (well) in your property, you are obligated to make a fence around it, [that is at least] ten *tefachim* high, or you must cover it so that no one will fall in to it.

2) Similarly, it is a mitzvah to remove any obstacle that represents a possible danger to life. You must also take care to protect yourself from it, as it is said, "Preserve yourself, and preserve your soul (life) diligently."[4] If you neglect and do not remove potentially dangerous objects, you will have violated the affirmative mitzvah, and transgressed the negative command, "You shall not bring blood upon your house."[5] This is applicable if you allow a broken ladder to remain in your house or property, or if you keep a vicious dog.

3) Just as you must guard your body, and not allow it to deteriorate, to be damaged or to be injured, as it is said, "Preserve (guard) yourself, and preserve your

---

7. *Ezekiel* 33:11.
1. *Deuteronomy* 22:8.
2. See Glossary.
3. *Deuteronomy* 22:8.
4. Ibid 4:9.
5. Ibid 22:8.

לְהִזָּהֵר בְּמָמוֹנוֹ שֶׁלֹּא לְאַבְּדוֹ וְשֶׁלֹּא לְקַלְקְלוֹ וְשֶׁלֹּא לְהַזִּיקוֹ. וְכָל הַמְשַׁבֵּר כְּלִי, אוֹ קוֹרֵעַ בֶּגֶד, אוֹ מְאַבֵּד מַאֲכָל אוֹ מַשְׁקֶה אוֹ מְמָאֲסָם, אוֹ זוֹרֵק מָעוֹת לְאִבּוּד, וְכֵן הַמְקַלְקֵל שְׁאָר כָּל דָּבָר שֶׁהָיָה רָאוּי שֶׁיֵּהָנוּ בוֹ בְּנֵי אָדָם, עוֹבֵר בְּלֹא־תַעֲשֶׂה, שֶׁנֶּאֱמַר, לֹא תַשְׁחִית אֶת־עֵצָהּ וְגוֹ'.

סִימָן קצא
אִסּוּר צַעַר בַּעֲלֵי־חַיִּים וְאִסּוּר סֵרוּס

א) אָסוּר מִן הַתּוֹרָה לְצַעֵר כָּל בַּעַל חָי. וְאַדְּרַבָּא, חַיָּב לְהַצִּיל כָּל בַּעַל־חַי מִצַּעַר, אֲפִלּוּ שֶׁל הֶפְקֵר, וַאֲפִלּוּ שֶׁל נָכְרִי. אַךְ אִם הֵם מְצַעֲרִין לְאָדָם, אוֹ שֶׁצָּרִיךְ הָאָדָם לָהֶם לִרְפוּאָה אוֹ לִשְׁאָר דָּבָר, מֻתָּר אֲפִלּוּ לְהָרְגָן, וְאֵין חוֹשְׁשִׁין לְצַעֲרָן, שֶׁהֲרֵי הַתּוֹרָה הִתִּירָה שְׁחִיטָה. וְלָכֵן מֻתָּר לִמְרֹט נוֹצוֹת מֵאֲוָזוֹת חַיּוֹת אִם אֵין לוֹ נוֹצָה אַחֶרֶת, רַק שֶׁהָעוֹלָם נִמְנָעִים מִשּׁוּם אַכְזְרִיּוּת.

ב) סוּסִים הַמּוֹשְׁכִים בַּעֲגָלָה וְהִגִּיעוּ לְמָקוֹם מְקֻלְקָל אוֹ לְהַר גָּבוֹהַּ, וְאֵינָן יְכוֹלִין לִמְשֹׁךְ בְּלִי עֵזֶר, מִצְוָה לַעֲזוֹר אַף לְנָכְרִי מִשּׁוּם צַעַר בַּעֲלֵי חַיִּים, שֶׁלֹּא יַכֶּה אוֹתָם הַנָּכְרִי מַכָּה רַבָּה לִמְשֹׁךְ יוֹתֵר מֵאֲשֶׁר בְּכֹחָם.

ג) אָסוּר לִקְשֹׁר רַגְלֵי בְּהֵמָה חַיָּה וָעוֹף בְּעִנְיָן שֶׁיִּהְיֶה לָהֶם צַעַר.

ד) אָסוּר לְהוֹשִׁיב עוֹף עַל בֵּיצִים מִשֶּׁאֵינוֹ מִינוֹ, מִשּׁוּם צַעַר בַּעֲלֵי־חַיִּים.

ה) אָסוּר לְסָרֵס בֵּין אָדָם וּבֵין בְּהֵמָה חַיָּה וָעוֹף, אֶחָד טְמֵאִים וְאֶחָד טְהוֹרִים, בֵּין בְּאֶרֶץ־יִשְׂרָאֵל בֵּין בְּחוּץ־לָאָרֶץ. וְכָל הַמְסָרֵס, חַיָּב מַלְקוּת. וַאֲפִלּוּ לְהַשְׁקוֹת כּוֹס שֶׁל עִקְּרִין לְאִישׁ אוֹ לִשְׁאָר בַּעֲלֵי חַיִּים הַזְּכָרִים, אָסוּר.

ו) אָסוּר לוֹמַר לְגוֹי לְסָרֵס בְּהֵמָה שֶׁלָּנוּ. וְיֵשׁ אוֹמְרִים, דַּאֲפִלּוּ לְמָכְרָהּ לְגוֹי אוֹ לִתְּנָהּ לוֹ לְמַחֲצִית שָׂכָר, אִם יָדוּעַ שֶׁיְּסָרְסֶנָּה, אָסוּר. מִשּׁוּם דְּגוֹי גַּם כֵּן מְצֻוֶּה עַל אִסּוּר סֵרוּס, וְאִם כֵּן הַיִּשְׂרָאֵל עוֹבֵר עַל לִפְנֵי עִוֵּר. וּמִיהוּ אִם אֵין הַגּוֹי הַקּוֹנֶה מְסָרֵס בְּעַצְמוֹ, רַק נוֹתֵן לְגוֹי אַחֵר לְסָרֵס, לְכֻלֵּי עָלְמָא שָׁרֵי, דְּאָז הָוֵי לִפְנֵי דְלִפְנֵי וּמֻתָּר.

soul (life) diligently;"[6] so, too, you must guard your property against destruction, ruin, or damage. Anyone who breaks a vessel, tears a garment, or destroys food or drink, or pollutes them, or throws away money, or spoils anything that is fit for man's enjoyment, violates a negative precept, as it is said, "You shall not destroy its trees" etc.[7]

Chapter 191
Prohibition of Cruelty to Animals

1) The Torah forbids us to inflict suffering on any living creature. On the contrary, it is an obligation to remove the suffering of any creature, even if it is ownerless, and even if it belongs to a non-Jew. However, if they are troublesome to mankind, or if they are needed for medical purposes, or for any other purpose, it is permitted even to kill them, and we disregard their pain; for the Torah permits us to slaughter them. Therefore, it is permitted to pluck feathers from living geese [to use as a quill], if you have no other feather [with which to write]. However, people abstain from doing so because of cruelty.

2) When horses pull a wagon and come to a rough road, or to a steep hill, and cannot draw it further without help, it is a mitzvah to help, even if they belong to a non-Jew, because of the suffering of the animals, lest the non-Jew strike them harshly to force them to pull more than they are able.

3) It is forbidden to tie the legs of an animal, beast, or fowl, in a manner that causes them pain.[1]

4) It is forbidden to set a bird on eggs of a different species, for this is cruelty to animals.

5) It is forbidden to castrate a person, or an animal, beast, or fowl, whether unclean or clean, whether in *Eretz Yisroel* or outside of *Eretz Yisroel.* Anyone who castrates is punishable by flogging. Even to cause sterility through medical means to man or to any other male creature, is forbidden.

6) It is forbidden to tell a non-Jew to castrate our animals. According to some *Poskim,* it is forbidden even to sell an animal to a non-Jew, or to give it to him on condition to share the profits, if it is known that he will castrate it. Because a non-Jew is also included in the prohibition against castrating, thus in doing so, the Jew transgresses the precept, not to place a stumbling block before the blind. However, if the non-Jewish buyer will not castrate it himself, but will give it to another non-Jew, for castration, all *Poskim* permit the transaction, for it is an indirect stumbling block and is permitted.

---

6. Ibid 4:9.
7. Ibid 20:19.
1. See above Chapter 87:7.

סִימָן קצב

דִּין הַחוֹלֶה וְהָרוֹפֵא וּבַמֶּה מִתְרַפְּאִין

א) אָמַר רַב יִצְחָק בְּרֵהּ דְּרַב יְהוּדָה, לְעוֹלָם יְבַקֵּשׁ אָדָם רַחֲמִים שֶׁלֹּא יֶחֱלֶה. שֶׁאִם חָלָה, אוֹמְרִים לוֹ, הָבֵא זְכוּת וְהִפָּטֵר. אָמַר מַר עֻקְבָא, מַאי קְרָאָהּ. כִּי יִפֹּל הַנֹּפֵל מִמֶּנּוּ, מִמֶּנּוּ לְהָבִיא רְאָיָה. פֵּרוּשׁ, מֵאַחַר שֶׁהוּא נוֹפֵל, צָרִיךְ לִמְצוֹא מִמֶּנּוּ וּמִמַּעֲשָׂיו רְאָיָה לִזְכוּת. עוֹד אִיתָא בַּגְּמָרָא, חָשׁ בְּרֹאשׁוֹ, יְהִי דוֹמֶה בְעֵינָיו כְּמִי שֶׁנְּתָנוּהוּ בְקוֹלָר. עָלָה לַמִּטָּה וְנָפַל לְמִשְׁכָּב, יְהִי דוֹמֶה בְעֵינָיו כְּמִי שֶׁהֶעֱלוּהוּ לַגַּרְדּוֹם לִדּוֹן, שֶׁכָּל הָעוֹלֶה לַגַּרְדּוֹם לִדּוֹן, אִם יֵשׁ לוֹ פְּרַקְלִיטִין גְּדוֹלִים, נִצּוֹל. וְאִם לָאו, אֵינוֹ נִצּוֹל. וְאֵלּוּ הֵן פְּרַקְלִיטִין שֶׁל אָדָם, תְּשׁוּבָה וּמַעֲשִׂים טוֹבִים. וַאֲפִלּוּ תְּשַׁע מֵאוֹת וְתִשְׁעִים וְתִשְׁעָה מְלַמְּדִים עָלָיו חוֹבָה, וְאֶחָד מְלַמֵּד עָלָיו זְכוּת, נִצּוֹל, שֶׁנֶּאֱמַר, אִם יֵשׁ עָלָיו מַלְאָךְ מֵלִיץ אֶחָד מִנִּי־אָלֶף לְהַגִּיד לְאָדָם יָשְׁרוֹ, וַיְחֻנֶּנּוּ וַיֹּאמֶר, פְּדָעֵהוּ מֵרֶדֶת שַׁחַת וְגוֹ'.

ב) דָּרַשׁ רַבִּי פִּינְחָס בַּר חָמָא, כָּל מִי שֶׁיֵּשׁ לוֹ חוֹלֶה בְּתוֹךְ בֵּיתוֹ, יֵלֵךְ אֵצֶל חָכָם וִיבַקֵּשׁ עָלָיו רַחֲמִים, שֶׁנֶּאֱמַר, חֲמַת מֶלֶךְ מַלְאֲכֵי מָוֶת, וְאִישׁ חָכָם יְכַפְּרֶנָּה. וְנוֹהֲגִין לָתֵת צְדָקָה לַעֲנִיִּים בַּעֲדוֹ, כִּי תְּשׁוּבָה וּתְפִלָּה וּצְדָקָה, מַעֲבִירִין אֶת רֹעַ הַגְּזֵרָה. גַּם נוֹהֲגִין לְבָרֵךְ אֶת הַחוֹלִים בְּבֵית־הַכְּנֶסֶת. וְאִם הוּא מְסֻכָּן, מְבָרְכִין אוֹתוֹ אֲפִלּוּ בְּשַׁבָּת וְיוֹם־טוֹב. וְלִפְעָמִים מְשַׁנִּים אֶת שֵׁם הַחוֹלֶה, כִּי גַּם שִׁנּוּי הַשֵּׁם, קוֹרֵעַ גְּזַר־דִּינוֹ.

ג) הַתּוֹרָה נָתְנָה רְשׁוּת לָרוֹפֵא שֶׁיְּרַפֵּא, שֶׁנֶּאֱמַר, וְרַפֹּא יְרַפֵּא. וְלָכֵן אֵין לוֹ לַחוֹלֶה לִסְמֹךְ עַל הַנֵּס, אֶלָּא חַיָּב לְהִתְנַהֵג בְּדֶרֶךְ הָעוֹלָם לִקְרוֹא לָרוֹפֵא שֶׁיְּרַפְּאֵהוּ. וּכְבָר כַּמָּה חֲסִידֵי עוֹלָם נִתְרַפְּאוּ עַל יְדֵי רוֹפְאִים. וּמִי שֶׁמּוֹנֵעַ אֶת עַצְמוֹ מִלִּקְרוֹא לָרוֹפֵא, שְׁתַּיִם רָעוֹת הִנֵּהוּ עוֹשֶׂה, הָאַחַת, דְּאָסוּר לִסְמֹךְ עַל הַנֵּס בְּמָקוֹם שֶׁיֵּשׁ סַכָּנָה, וְדָבָר זֶה גּוֹרֵם שֶׁיִּזָּכְרוּ עֲוֹנֹתָיו בִּשְׁעַת חָלְיוֹ. וְעוֹד, דַּהֲוֵי יוֹהֲרָא וְגַאֲוַת שֶׁסּוֹמֵךְ עַל צִדְקָתוֹ שֶׁיִּתְרַפֵּא בְּדֶרֶךְ הַנֵּס. וְיֵשׁ לוֹ לִקְרוֹא לָרוֹפֵא הַיּוֹתֵר מֻמְחֶה. וּבְכָל זֹאת לִבּוֹ יְהֵא לַשָּׁמַיִם, וִיבַקֵּשׁ רַחֲמִים מֵאֵת הָרוֹפֵא הַנֶּאֱמָן יִתְבָּרַךְ שְׁמוֹ, וְאַךְ בּוֹ יִבְטַח לִבּוֹ.

ד) וּמִצְוָה הוּא עַל הָרוֹפֵא הַבָּקִי לְרַפֵּא, וּבִכְלָל פִּקּוּחַ־נֶפֶשׁ הוּא. וְאִם

---

1. Deuteronomy 22:8.
2. Maseches Shabbos 32a.

Chapter 192

Laws of The Sick, the Physician, and Remedies

1) Said *Rav Yitzchok* the son of *Rav Yehudah*, "One should always plead for mercy that he should not get sick, for if one falls sick, he is told, 'Demonstrate your merit and you will be acquitted.'" Said *Mar Ukva*, "From which verse in the Torah is this inferred?" From the verse, "Lest any man fall from (*mimenu*) there."[1] From within himself (*mimenu*) he must produce evidence; which means, since he has fallen, he must produce from within himself and from his deeds, evidence of his merit."[2] It is also stated in the Talmud,[2] "If a person has a headache he should view it as if he were put in chains. If he becomes ill and is confined to bed, he should view it as if he were placed onto a scaffold, (a place where capital cases are tried) for trial. Anyone who is placed onto the scaffold for trial, if he has great advocates, may be saved. But if he has none, he cannot be saved. These are the advocates of man: repentance and good deeds. Even if nine hundred and ninety-nine accuse him, and only one advocate defends him, he is saved, as it is said, "If there be for him an angel, an advocate, [even] one among a thousand, to vouch for man's uprightness, then he is gracious unto him, and says, 'Redeem him from going down to the pit.'"[3]

2) Rabbi Pinchas, the son of Chama, expounded,[4] "Anyone who has a sick person in his house, should go to a Sage and ask him to plead for mercy on his behalf, as it is said, "The wrath of a king is like messengers of death. But a wise man will pacify it."[5] It is customary to give charity to the poor on a sick person's behalf, for repentance, prayer, and charity, avert the evil decree. It is also customary to bless the sick person in the synagogue, and if he is critically ill, we bless him even on Shabbos and Yom Tov. At times the name of the sick person is changed, for a change of name may also nullify the decree.

3) The Torah permits a doctor to heal the sick, as it is said "And he shall [pay] to have him healed properly."[6] Therefore, a sick person should not rely on a miracle, but is obliged to follow the accepted procedure and call a physician to heal him. Many of the world's pious men have been cured by physicians. A person who refrains from calling in a physician (for himself) commits two wrongs: For one, it is forbidden to rely on a miracle in a life-threatening situation. This behavior causes one's sins to be remembered at a time of illness. Secondly, it is arrogant and presumptuous to rely on your righteousness that you will be healed in some miraculous manner. You should call the most competent physician but with all that, your heart should be turned to Heaven, and pray for mercy from the Faithful Healer, blessed is His Name trusting in Him alone.

4) It is a mitzvah for the competent physician to heal and is included in the

3. *Job* 33:23, 24.
4. *Maseches Bava Basrah* 116.
5. *Proverbs* 16:14.
6. *Exodus* 21:19.

מוֹנֵעַ אֶת עַצְמוֹ, הֲרֵי זֶה שׁוֹפֵךְ דָּמִים, וַאֲפִלּוּ יֵשׁ לַחוֹלֶה רוֹפֵא אַחֵר, כִּי לֹא מִן כָּל אָדָם זוֹכֶה לְהִתְרַפֵּא, וְאוּלַי הוּא מִן הַשָּׁמַיִם שֶׁיִּתְרַפֵּא עַל יָדוֹ. אֲבָל לֹא יִתְעַסֵּק בִּרְפוּאוֹת, אֶלָּא אִם כֵּן הוּא בָקִי, וְאֵין שָׁם גָּדוֹל מִמֶּנּוּ, שֶׁאִם לֹא כֵן, הֲרֵי זֶה שׁוֹפֵךְ דָּמִים.

ה) חוֹלֶה שֶׁאֵין בּוֹ סַכָּנָה, אִם יוּכַל לְהִתְרַפְּאוֹת בְּדָבָר הֶתֵּר, אַף־עַל־פִּי שֶׁצְּרִיכִין לִשְׁהוֹת קְצָת עַד שֶׁיַּשִּׂיגוּהוּ, אֵין מַתִּירִין לוֹ שׁוּם דְּבַר אִסּוּר. וְאִם צָרִיךְ דַּוְקָא לִדְבַר אִסּוּר, אִם צָרִיךְ לְאָכְלוֹ כְּמוֹ שֶׁהַדֶּרֶךְ הוּא לֶאֱכֹל דָּבָר זֶה, אָסוּר לוֹ לְאָכְלוֹ, אֲפִלּוּ הוּא רַק אִסּוּר דְּרַבָּנָן, כֵּיוָן שֶׁאֵין בּוֹ סַכָּנָה. אֲבָל שֶׁלֹּא כְּדֶרֶךְ הֲנָאָתוֹ, כְּגוֹן שֶׁמְּעָרֵב בּוֹ דָּבָר מַר, וְכֵן לַעֲשׂוֹת מִמֶּנּוּ רְטִיָּה וְכַדּוֹמֶה, מֻתָּר, אֲפִלּוּ הוּא דָּבָר הָאָסוּר בַּהֲנָאָה מִדְּאוֹרָיְתָא, חוּץ מִכִּלְאֵי הַכֶּרֶם וּבָשָׂר בְּחָלָב, שֶׁאֲסוּרִין אֲפִלּוּ שֶׁלֹּא כְּדֶרֶךְ הֲנָאָתָן בְּמָקוֹם שֶׁאֵין סַכָּנָה. (דִּין הַבְּרָכָה עַל מַה שֶּׁאוֹכֵל אוֹ שׁוֹתֶה לִרְפוּאָה, עַיֵּן לְעֵיל סִימָן נ׳ סְעִיף ח׳ וְסִי׳ ס״א סְעִיף ד׳. וְדִין תִּינוֹק שֶׁצָּרִיךְ לֶאֱכוֹל חָמֵץ בְּפֶסַח, עַיֵּן לְעֵיל סוֹף סִימָן קי״ז.)

ו) יֵשׁ אוֹמְרִים, דְּכָל אִסּוּרֵי הֲנָאָה מִדְּרַבָּנָן מֻתָּר לְהִתְרַפְּאוֹת בָּהֶן, אֲפִלּוּ חוֹלֶה שֶׁאֵין בּוֹ סַכָּנָה, וַאֲפִלּוּ כְּדֶרֶךְ הֲנָאָתָן וּבִלְבַד שֶׁלֹּא יֹאכַל וְלֹא יִשְׁתֶּה אֶת הָאִסּוּר.

ז) חוֹלֶה שֶׁיֵּשׁ בּוֹ סַכָּנָה, מִתְרַפֵּא בְּכָל הָאִסּוּרִין, שֶׁאֵין לְךָ דָּבָר הָעוֹמֵד בִּפְנֵי פִּקּוּחַ נֶפֶשׁ, חוּץ מֵעֲבוֹדָה־זָרָה, גִּלּוּי־עֲרָיוֹת, וּשְׁפִיכוּת־דָּמִים, שֶׁהֵן בְּיֵהָרֵג וְאַל יַעֲבוֹר, וְאֵין מִתְרַפְּאִין בָּהֶן.

ח) מֻתָּר לָרוֹפֵא לְהַקִּיז דָּם וּלְמַשֵּׁשׁ הַדֹּפֶק וּשְׁאָר מְקוֹמוֹת שֶׁבָּאִשָּׁה, אֲפִלּוּ בְּאֵשֶׁת אִישׁ, וַאֲפִלּוּ בִּמְקוֹם תָּרְפָּהּ כְּדֶרֶךְ הָרוֹפְאִים, כֵּיוָן שֶׁאֵינוֹ עוֹשֶׂה דֶּרֶךְ תַּאֲוָה וְחִבָּה, אֶלָּא שֶׁבִּמְלַאכְתּוֹ הוּא עוֹסֵק. וְאַךְ בְּאִשְׁתּוֹ נִדָּה, יֵשׁ לְהַחְמִיר כְּשֶׁאֵין סַכָּנָה בַּדָּבָר וְיֵשׁ שָׁם רוֹפֵא אַחֵר בָּקִי כָּמוֹהוּ. (וְעַיֵּן לְעֵיל סִימָן קנ״ג סְעִיף י״ד וְשָׁם מְבֹאָר אִם אִשָּׁה נִדָּה יְכוֹלָה לְשַׁמֵּשׁ אֶת בַּעֲלָהּ כְּשֶׁהוּא חוֹלֶה אוֹ הוּא אוֹתָהּ. וְעַיֵּן לְעֵיל סִימָן קמ״ג סְעִיף ט״ו אִם הַבֵּן מוּתָּר לְהָקִיז דָּם לְאָבִיו, וְכַיּוֹצֵא בּוֹ).

ט) בְּחָלְיֵ מֵעַיִם, אֵין הָאִישׁ מְשַׁמֵּשׁ אֶת הָאִשָּׁה, פֶּן יִתְגַּבֵּר יִצְרוֹ, כֵּיוָן שֶׁהוּא בָרִיא. אֲבָל הָאִשָּׁה, מְשַׁמֶּשֶׁת אֶת הָאִישׁ, כֵּיוָן שֶׁהוּא חוֹלֶה.

7. A product of diverse species sown in a vineyard.

mitzvah of saving a life. If he refrains from doing so, he is guilty of shedding blood, even if the patient has another physician, because not through every physician does a person merit to be cured, and it is perhaps Heavenly ordained that he shall be cured through him. However, one should not practice medicine unless he is an expert and there is no one more competent than him. For otherwise, he is guilty of bloodshed.

5) A person who is not critically ill, and can possibly be cured by permissable medication, is forbidden to take anything that is prohibited; although he must wait until he can obtain it, we do not permit him to take anything that is prohibited. If he specifically requires a prohibited article, if he must eat it in the way it is usually eaten, he is forbidden to eat it; even if it is only prohibited by Rabbinical ordinance, since his life is not in danger. However [if it can be eaten] in a manner by which he will not derive the usual pleasure, for instance, if a bitter substance is mixed with it, it is permitted. It is permitted to make a plaster of it or something similar, even if it is something the enjoyment of which is forbidden by the Torah, with the exception of *kilayei hakerem*[7] and meat cooked with milk, which is forbidden to use even in a manner that it is not usual. These laws apply so long as no danger to life is involved. Regarding the laws of *berachos* upon eating and drinking medication, refer to Chapter 50:5 and Chapter 61:4. (Regarding the law when a child must eat *chametz* on *Pesach,* see the end of Chapter 117.)

6) Some *Poskim* say[8] that all things, the enjoyment of which is Rabbinically prohibited, are permitted to be used for a cure, even for one who is not critically ill, and even in the manner by which they are regularly enjoyed, provided he does not eat or drink the forbidden article.

7) A person who is critically ill may use any forbidden article for his cure, for nothing can stand in the way of saving a life except idolatry, incest, and murder; for which one must give up his life and not transgress. Thus man may not cure himself by transgressing these sins.

8) A physician is permitted to let blood, and feel the pulse, or other parts of a woman even if she is married, and he may feel her vulnerable area, as is customary with physicians, since he does not do so in a sensual and immoral manner, but is merely practicing his profession. However, if his own wife is menstrually unclean, he should be stringent (and refrain from any of the above), if she is not critically ill and there is another doctor available who is as competent as he is. (See Chapter 153:14 where it is explained, whether a woman who is menstrually unclean is permitted to attend her husband when he is sick, or if he may attend her if she is sick, and see Chapter 143:15 if a son is permitted to let blood from his father, and similar laws.)

9) In case of abdominal illness, a man may not attend a woman, lest he will be overcome by desire, since he is healthy [and capable.] But a woman may attend a man since he is sick [and incapable.]

---

8. See *Shulchan Aruch Yoreh Deiah* 154:3 and see *Shach*, note 14.

י) מִי שֶׁיֵּשׁ לוֹ סַמְמָנִים, וַחֲבֵרוֹ חוֹלֶה וְצָרִיךְ לָהֶם, אָסוּר לוֹ לְהַעֲלוֹת בְּדָמֵיהֶם יוֹתֵר מִן הָרָאוּי.

סִימָן קצג
הִלְכוֹת בִּקּוּר חוֹלִים

א) כְּשֶׁחָלָה הָאָדָם, מִצְוָה עַל כָּל אָדָם לְבַקְּרוֹ, שֶׁכֵּן מָצִינוּ בְּהַקָּדוֹשׁ־בָּרוּךְ־הוּא שֶׁמְּבַקֵּר חוֹלִים, כְּמוֹ שֶׁדָּרְשׁוּ רַבּוֹתֵינוּ, זִכְרוֹנָם לִבְרָכָה בְּפָסוּק וַיֵּרָא אֵלָיו ה' בְּאֵלוֹנֵי מַמְרֵא, מְלַמֵּד שֶׁבָּא אֵלָיו לְבַקֵּר הַחוֹלֶה. הַקְּרוֹבִים וְהַחֲבֵרִים שֶׁרְגִילִים לִכָּנֵס לְבֵיתוֹ תָּמִיד, הֵמָּה הוֹלְכִים לְבַקְּרוֹ מִיָּד כְּשֶׁשָּׁמְעוּ שֶׁהוּא חוֹלֶה. אֲבָל הָרְחוֹקִים שֶׁאֵינָם רְגִילִים בְּבֵיתוֹ, לֹא יִכָּנְסוּ מִיָּד, כִּי הֵיכִי דְּלָא לִתְּרַע מַזָּלֵהּ לְהַטִּיל עָלָיו שֵׁם חוֹלֶה. וְאֵינָם נִכְנָסִים עַד לְאַחַר שְׁלֹשָׁה יָמִים. וְאִם קָפַץ עָלָיו הַחֹלִי, גַּם הָרְחוֹקִים נִכְנָסִים מִיָּד. אֲפִלּוּ הַגָּדוֹל, יֵלֵךְ לְבַקֵּר אֶת הַקָּטָן, וַאֲפִלּוּ כַּמָּה פְּעָמִים בַּיּוֹם. וְכָל הַמּוֹסִיף, הֲרֵי זֶה מְשֻׁבָּח, וּבִלְבַד שֶׁלֹּא יִהְיֶה לְטֹרַח עַל הַחוֹלֶה. הַשּׂוֹנֵא לֹא יְבַקֵּר אֶת שׂוֹנְאוֹ הַחוֹלֶה, וְלֹא יְנַחֲמֶנּוּ כְּשֶׁהוּא אָבֵל, שֶׁלֹּא יַחְשֹׁב שֶׁשָּׂמֵחַ לְאֵידוֹ. אֲבָל מֻתָּר לְלַוּוֹתוֹ, וְלֵיכָּא לְמֵיחַשׁ, שֶׁיֹּאמְרוּ כִּי הוּא שָׂמֵחַ לְאֵידוֹ, בַּאֲשֶׁר זֶהוּ סוֹף כָּל אָדָם. (עַיֵּן לְקַמָּן סִימָן רז סָעִיף ב, דְּהַחוֹלֶה אֵינוֹ צָרִיךְ לַעֲמֹד אֲפִלּוּ מִפְּנֵי נָשִׂיא. וְאִם רוֹצֶה לַעֲמֹד, אֵין אוֹמְרִים לוֹ שֵׁב).

ב) כְּשֶׁהַחוֹלֶה שׁוֹכֵב עַל הָאָרֶץ, לֹא יֵשֵׁב הַמְּבַקֵּר עַל גַּבֵּי כִּסֵּא שֶׁגָּבֹהַּ מִמֶּנּוּ, לְפִי שֶׁהַשְּׁכִינָה לְמַעְלָה מְרַאֲשׁוֹתָיו שֶׁל חוֹלֶה, שֶׁנֶּאֱמַר, ה' יִסְעָדֶנּוּ עַל עֶרֶשׂ דְּוָי. אֲבָל כְּשֶׁהַחוֹלֶה שׁוֹכֵב בְּמִטָּה, מֻתָּר לַמְּבַקֵּר לֵישֵׁב עַל כִּסֵּא וְסַפְסָל.

ג) עִקַּר מִצְוַת בִּקּוּר חוֹלִים הוּא לְעַיֵּן בְּצָרְכֵי הַחוֹלֶה מַה הוּא צָרִיךְ לַעֲשׂוֹת לוֹ, וְשֶׁיִּמְצָא נַחַת רוּחַ עִם חֲבֵרָיו, וְגַם שֶׁיִּתֵּן דַּעְתּוֹ עָלָיו וִיבַקֵּשׁ רַחֲמִים עָלָיו. וְאִם בִּקֵּר וְלֹא בִקֵּשׁ, לֹא קִיֵּם אֶת הַמִּצְוָה. וְלָכֵן אֵין מְבַקְּרִין בְּשָׁלֹשׁ שָׁעוֹת הָרִאשׁוֹנוֹת שֶׁל הַיּוֹם, מִפְּנֵי שֶׁאָז כָּל חוֹלֶה מֵקֵל עָלָיו חָלְיוֹ וְלֹא יָחוּשׁ לְבַקֵּשׁ עָלָיו רַחֲמִים. וְלֹא בְשָׁלֹשׁ שָׁעוֹת הָאַחֲרוֹנוֹת שֶׁל הַיּוֹם, שֶׁאָז מַכְבִּיד עָלָיו חָלְיוֹ וְיִתְיָאֵשׁ מִלְּבַקֵּשׁ עָלָיו רַחֲמִים.

10) If you possess medication and your neighbor is ill and needs them, you are forbidden to raise their price unreasonably.

Chapter 193

The Laws of Visiting the Sick

1) When a person is ill it is a mitzvah for everyone to visit him, for we find that the Holy One, Blessed is He, visits the sick, as our Sages of blessed memory,[1] explained the verse, "And God appeared unto him [Abraham] in the plains of *Mamre,*"[2] teaching us that He came to visit Abraham when he was sick.[3] Relatives and friends who are accustomed to visit him often, should go to visit him as soon as they hear of his illness. But casual acquaintances, who are not accustomed to visit him often, should not visit him immediately, so as not to deter his chances of recovery by labeling him a a sick person. They should therefore not visit Him until after three days. If, however, one becomes suddenly ill, even casual acquaintances should visit at once. Even a great man should visit a less important person, and even many times a day. The more often one visits, the more praiseworthy it is, providing it is not bothersome for the sick person. You should not visit your sick enemy, nor should you comfort him in his mourning, lest he think that you are rejoicing at his calamity. However, you may attend his funeral, for there is no concern that people will say that you are rejoicing at his downfall, since this is the end of every mortal. (In chapter 207:2 we learn that a sick person need not rise even before the *Nasi,*[4] but if he wishes to stand we do not tell him to remain seated.)

2) When the patient lies on the ground, the visitor may not sit upon a chair which is more elevated than he is, because the Divine Presence is above the head of the sick, as it is said, "*Hashem* will support him on the bed of his illness."[5] But when the patient lies in bed, the visitor may sit on a chair or a bench.

3) The essence of the *mitzvah* to visit the sick, is to determine the needs of the patient to see what has to be done for him, and to make him comfortable with his friends. You must also bear in mind to pray for mercy on his behalf. If you visited him and did not pray for his recovery, you have not fulfilled the mitzvah. Therefore, you should not visit the sick during the first three hours of the day, because during this time every sick person has some relief from his illness, and as a result, you will not be concerned to pray for mercy on his behalf. Nor should you visit him during the three final hours of the day, for then the illness becomes more severe, and you might despair of his recovery and will not pray for mercy on his behalf.

---

1. *Maseches Bava Metzia* 86b.
2. *Genesis* 18:1.
3. After Abraham was circumcised he was ill.
4. The *Nasi* was recognized as the leader of all Jewry.
5. *Psalms* 41:4.

ד) כְּשֶׁמְּבַקֵּשׁ עָלָיו רַחֲמִים, אִם מְבַקֵּשׁ בְּפָנָיו, יָכוֹל לְבַקֵּשׁ בְּכָל לָשׁוֹן שֶׁיִּרְצֶה, שֶׁהֲרֵי מְבַקֵּשׁ כִּבְיָכוֹל לִפְנֵי הַשְּׁכִינָה, שֶׁהִיא אֵצֶל הַחוֹלֶה. אֲבָל כְּשֶׁמְּבַקֵּשׁ שֶׁלֹּא בְּפָנָיו, דְּאָז מַלְאֲכֵי הַשָּׁרֵת נִזְקָקִין לְהַעֲלוֹת תְּפִלָּתוֹ, וְאֵינָם נִזְקָקִין לְכָל הַלְּשׁוֹנוֹת, עַל כֵּן יְבַקֵּשׁ בִּלְשׁוֹן־הַקֹּדֶשׁ, וְיִכְלוֹל אוֹתוֹ בְּתוֹךְ כָּל חוֹלֵי יִשְׂרָאֵל, שֶׁמִּתּוֹךְ שֶׁכּוֹלְלוֹ עִם הָאֲחֵרִים, תְּפִלָּתוֹ נִשְׁמַעַת יוֹתֵר בִּזְכוּתָן שֶׁל רַבִּים. וְיֹאמַר, הַמָּקוֹם יְרַחֵם עָלֶיךָ בְּתוֹךְ כָּל חוֹלֵי יִשְׂרָאֵל. וּבְשַׁבָּת יֹאמַר, שַׁבָּת הִיא מִלִּזְעֹק, וּרְפוּאָה קְרוֹבָה לָבוֹא, וְרַחֲמָיו מְרֻבִּים, וְשִׁבְתוּ בְּשָׁלוֹם.

ה) הַמְבַקְּרִים יְדַבְּרוּ אִתּוֹ בְּהַשְׂכֵּל וָדַעַת, וְיֹאמְרוּ לוֹ, לֹא דְּבָרִים מְחַיִּים, וְלֹא דְּבָרִים מְמִיתִים. וְיֹאמְרוּ לוֹ, שֶׁיִּתֵּן דַּעְתּוֹ עַל עִנְיָנָיו, אִם הִלְוָה אוֹ הִפְקִיד אֵצֶל אֲחֵרִים אוֹ אֲחֵרִים אֶצְלוֹ, וְאַל יְפַחֵד מִפְּנֵי זֶה מֵהַמָּוֶת.

ו) אֵין לִתֵּן נְכָסָיו בְּמַתָּנָה לַאֲחֵרִים וַאֲפִלּוּ לִצְדָקָה וּלְהַנִּיחַ אֶת הַיּוֹרְשִׁים בְּלֹא כְלוּם. וְכָל הָעוֹשֶׂה כֵּן, אֵין רוּחַ חֲכָמִים נוֹחָה הֵימֶנּוּ, וַאֲפִלּוּ אֵין הַיּוֹרְשִׁים נוֹהֲגִין כַּשּׁוּרָה. אֲבָל אִם מַנִּיחַ גַּם לַיּוֹרְשִׁים דָּבָר הַמַּסְפִּיק לָהֶם, מֻתָּר. וּמִדַּת חֲסִידוּת, שֶׁלֹּא לַחְתֹּם אֶת עַצְמוֹ עֵד וְלֹא לִהְיוֹת בְּעֵצָה בְּצַוָּאָה שֶׁמַּעֲבִירִין בָּהּ אֶת הַיְרֻשָּׁה מֵהַיּוֹרֵשׁ, אֲפִלּוּ מִבֵּן שֶׁאֵינוֹ נוֹהֵג כַּשּׁוּרָה, לְאָחִיו חָכָם וְנוֹהֵג כַּשּׁוּרָה, כִּי שֶׁמָּא יֵצֵא מִמֶּנּוּ זֶרַע טוֹב וְהָגוּן. וַאֲפִלּוּ לְמַעֵט מִזֶּה וּלְהַרְבּוֹת לָזֶה, יֵשׁ מִי שֶׁאוֹסֵר, וְרָאוּי לָחוּשׁ לִדְבָרָיו. עַיֵּן סוֹף סִימָן כו.

ז) אִם יֵשׁ לוֹ בָּנִים קְטַנִּים אוֹ קְטַנִּים וּגְדוֹלִים, אוֹ שֶׁאִשְׁתּוֹ מְעֻבֶּרֶת, צָרִיךְ לְמַנּוֹת אַפּוֹטְרוֹפּוֹס שֶׁיִּתְעַסֵּק בִּשְׁבִיל הַקְּטַנִּים עַד שֶׁיִּגְדְּלוּ.

ח) חוֹלֶה שֶׁבִּקֵּשׁ לַעֲשׂוֹת קַבָּלַת קִנְיָן לְחַזֵּק אֶת הַצַּוָּאָה, קוֹנִין מִמֶּנּוּ אֲפִלּוּ בְּשַׁבָּת. וְכֵן אִם מְבַקֵּשׁ לִשְׁלֹחַ לִקְרוֹבָיו, מֻתָּר לִשְׂכֹּר גּוֹי בְּשַׁבָּת וּלְשָׁלְחוֹ.

ט) חוֹלֶה שֶׁמֵּת לוֹ מֵת, אֵין מוֹדִיעִין לוֹ, שֶׁלֹּא תִטָּרֵף דַּעְתּוֹ עָלָיו. וַאֲפִלּוּ נוֹדַע לוֹ, אֵין אוֹמְרִים לוֹ לִקְרֹעַ, שֶׁמָּא תִגְדַּל דַּאֲגָתוֹ. וְאֵין בּוֹכִין וְאֵין מַסְפִּידִין בְּפָנָיו, בֵּין עַל מֵתוֹ בֵּין עַל מֵת אַחֵר, אַף־עַל־פִּי שֶׁאֵינוֹ קְרוֹבוֹ, פֶּן יִפְחַד שֶׁגַּם הוּא יָמוּת. וּמַשְׁתִּיקִין אֶת הַמְנַחֲמִים בְּפָנָיו.

4) When you pray for mercy on his behalf, if you are praying in his presence, you may pray in any language you wish, for you are, so to speak, praying before the Divine Presence, Who is at the bedside of the sick. If, however, you are not praying in his presence, for then the ministering angels are needed to uplift your prayer, and since they are not bound [to regard] all languages, you should pray in the Holy Tongue, and include him among all the sick of Yisrael. For by including him with the others, your prayer will be more readily heard because of the collective merit of the many sick ones. You should say to the sick man, "May the Almighty have mercy on you, among all the sick of Yisrael." On Shabbos you should say, "This is Shabbos, we are forbidden to wail, healing is soon to come, His mercy is great, rest in peace."

5) The visitors must speak to him with wisdom and intelligence. They should tell him that words do not determine life, nor do words determine death. They should tell him to give thought to his affairs and state whether he has loaned to others or deposited anything with others, or others with him. You should explain to him that imparting this information is no reason to fear death

6) He should not bequeath [all] his property to strangers, not even to charity, and leave his natural heirs with nothing. Whoever does so should realize that the spirit of the Sages is not content with him. This applies even if the heirs do not conduct themselves properly. However, if he also leaves the heirs, enough to provide sufficiently for them, he is permitted to leave the rest to others. A pious man should not sign as a witness, and should not give counsel in making a will in which the natural heirs are disinherited; even when the son who is being disinherited does not act properly, and the inheritance is left to his brother who is a Torah scholar, who acts properly; because it is possible that the worthless son will have good and decent children. Even to give less to one child and more to the other, is forbidden, according to one *Poseik,* and it is proper to heed his opinion. See the end of Chapter 26.

7) If the sick man has young children, or if he has both young and grown-up children, or if his wife is pregnant, he should appoint a guardian to act on behalf of the minor children, until they come of age.

8) If the sick person wants to make a *Kinyan*[6] in order to confirm his will, it may be done even on Shabbos. Also, if he wants to send for his relatives, it is permitted to hire a non-Jew on Shabbos, and to send him to bring them.

9) If a close relative of the patient dies, he should not be told about it, lest he become distressed. Even if he becomes aware of it, he should not be told to tear [his garment], lest it causes him greater anxiety. One should not cry or lament in his presence, whether the deceased was his relative, or even someone who was not a member of his family, lest he will fear that he too is dying. Those who comfort mourners in his presence must be silenced.

---

6. *Kinyan* is a legal form which binds an agreement. It is usually done by handing over an object from one to the other of the two contracting individuals.

י) אֵין מְבַקְּרִין לֹא לְחוֹלֵי מֵעַיִם, מִשּׁוּם כִּסּוּפָא, וְלֹא לְחוֹלֵי הָעַיִן, וְלֹא לְחוֹלֵי הָרֹאשׁ. וְכֵן כָּל חוֹלֶה דְּתַקִּיף לֵהּ עָלְמָא וְקָשֶׁה לֵהּ דִּבּוּרָא, אֵין מְבַקְּרִין אוֹתוֹ בְּפָנָיו, אֶלָּא נִכְנָסִין לַבַּיִת הַחִיצוֹן וְשׁוֹאֲלִין וְדוֹרְשִׁין בּוֹ אִם צָרִיךְ לְאֵיזֶה דָּבָר, וְשׁוֹמְעִין צַעֲרוֹ, וּמְבַקְשִׁים עָלָיו רַחֲמִים.

יא) מִי שֶׁיֵּשׁ לְפָנָיו שְׁתֵּי מִצְוֹת, בִּקּוּר חוֹלִים וְנִחוּם אֲבֵלִים, אִם אֶפְשָׁר לוֹ לְקַיֵּם שְׁתֵּיהֶן, בִּקּוּר חוֹלִים קוֹדֵם, כְּדֵי לְבַקֵּשׁ רַחֲמִים עָלָיו. וְאִם אִי אֶפְשָׁר לוֹ לְקַיֵּם שְׁתֵּיהֶן, נִחוּם אֲבֵלִים קוֹדֵם, שֶׁהוּא גְּמִילוּת־חֶסֶד עִם הַחַיִּים וְעִם הַמֵּתִים.

יב) מְבַקְּרִין חוֹלֶה גּוֹי, מִפְּנֵי דַּרְכֵי שָׁלוֹם.

יג) תַּנְיָא בְּסִפְרֵי, רַבִּי נָתָן אוֹמֵר, וְאָשְׁמָה הַנֶּפֶשׁ הַהִיא וְהִתְוַדָּה, זֶה בָּנָה אָב עַל כָּל הַמֵּתִים שֶׁיִּטָּעֲנוּ וִדּוּי. וְאִיתָא בַּמִּשְׁנָה, שֶׁכָּל הַמִּתְוַדֶּה יֵשׁ לוֹ חֵלֶק לָעוֹלָם־הַבָּא, שֶׁכֵּן מָצִינוּ בְּעָכָן, שֶׁאָמַר לוֹ יְהוֹשֻׁעַ, בְּנִי, שִׂים נָא כָבוֹד לַה׳ אֱלֹהֵי יִשְׂרָאֵל וְתֶן־לוֹ תוֹדָה וְהַגֶּד־נָא לִי מֶה עָשִׂיתָ אַל־תְּכַחֵד מִמֶּנִּי. וַיַּעַן עָכָן אֶת־יְהוֹשֻׁעַ וַיֹּאמַר, אָמְנָה אָנֹכִי חָטָאתִי לַה׳ אֱלֹהֵי יִשְׂרָאֵל וְכָזֹאת וְכָזֹאת עָשִׂיתִי. וּמִנַּיִן שֶׁכִּפֵּר לוֹ וִדּוּיוֹ. שֶׁנֶּאֱמַר, וַיֹּאמֶר יְהוֹשֻׁעַ מֶה עֲכַרְתָּנוּ, יַעְכָּרְךָ ה׳ בַּיּוֹם הַזֶּה, בַּיּוֹם הַזֶּה אַתָּה עָכוּר, וְאִי אַתָּה עָכוּר לָעוֹלָם־הַבָּא. לָכֵן חוֹלֶה שֶׁרוֹאִין בּוֹ שֶׁהוּא נוֹטֶה לָמוּת, מְסַבְּבִים עִמּוֹ בִּדְבָרִים וְאוֹמְרִים לוֹ, הִתְוַדֵּה וְאַל תִּדְאַג מִזֶּה, הַרְבֵּה הִתְוַדּוּ וְעָמְדוּ מֵחָלְיָם וְהֵמָּה בַּחַיִּים, וְהַרְבֵּה שֶׁלֹּא הִתְוַדּוּ וּמֵתוּ. וּבִשְׂכַר שֶׁאַתָּה מִתְוַדֶּה, אַתָּה חַי, וְכָל הַמִּתְוַדֶּה, יֵשׁ לוֹ חֵלֶק לָעוֹלָם־הַבָּא. וְאִם אֵינוֹ יָכוֹל לְהִתְוַדּוֹת בְּפִיו, יִתְוַדֶּה בְּלִבּוֹ. וְאִם יָכוֹל לְדַבֵּר אַךְ מְעַט, אוֹמְרִים לוֹ, אֱמֹר, תְּהֵא מִיתָתִי כַּפָּרָה עַל כָּל עֲוֹנוֹתָי. וְגַם יֹאמְרוּ לוֹ, שֶׁיְּבַקֵּשׁ מְחִילָה מִכָּל אָדָם שֶׁחָטָא כְּנֶגְדּוֹ, בֵּין בְּמָמוֹן בֵּין בִּדְבָרִים. וְכָל אֵלּוּ הַדְּבָרִים, אֵין אוֹמְרִים לוֹ, לֹא בִּפְנֵי עַמֵּי הָאָרֶץ, וְלֹא בִּפְנֵי נָשִׁים, וְלֹא בִּפְנֵי קְטַנִּים, שֶׁמָּא יִבְכּוּ וְיִשְׁבְּרוּ לִבּוֹ.

יד) סֵדֶר הַוִּדּוּי בְּקִצָּרָה, מוֹדֶה אֲנִי לְפָנֶיךָ, ה׳ אֱלֹהַי וֵאלֹהֵי אֲבוֹתַי, שֶׁרְפוּאָתִי בְּיָדֶךָ וּמִיתָתִי בְּיָדֶךָ. יְהִי רָצוֹן מִלְּפָנֶיךָ שֶׁתְּרַפְּאֵנִי רְפוּאָה שְׁלֵמָה. וְאִם אָמוּת, תְּהֵא מִיתָתִי כַּפָּרָה עַל כָּל חֲטָאִים וַעֲוֹנוֹת וּפְשָׁעִים, שֶׁחָטָאתִי וְשֶׁעָוִיתִי וְשֶׁפָּשַׁעְתִּי לְפָנֶיךָ, וְתֵן חֶלְקִי בְּגַן־עֵדֶן, וְזַכֵּנִי לָעוֹלָם־

10) A person who has stomach problems should not be visited, because he may be embarrassed. A person who has an eye ailment, or one who has a headache, and also one who is critical, and to whom conversation is difficult, should not be visited personally. Rather you should enter an outer room and inquire there if he needs anything. You should be concerned of his pain and pray for mercy on his behalf.

11) If you have two *mitzvos* to perform, to visit the sick and to comfort a mourner, if you are able to do both, you should first visit the sick, so that you will pray for mercy on his behalf. If you cannot do both, comforting a mourner takes precedence, as this is an act of loving kindness toward both the living and the dead.

12) A non-Jew may be visited during his illness, for the sake of maintaining harmonious relationships.

13) It is taught in the *Sifrei,*[7] Rabbi Nossan says, "The verse, 'and that person is guilty, they shall confess,'[8] teaches that all dying persons must confess." It is said in the *Mishnah,*[9] "Everyone who confesses has a share in the World to Come, for so we find with Achar, to whom Joshua said, 'My son, please give glory to *Adonoy,* God of Yisrael, and confess to Him. Tell me what you have done, do not hide anything from me.'[10] Achar answered Joshua, and he said, 'Indeed I have sinned against *Adonoy,* God of Yisrael, and this is what I have done.'[11] How do we know his confession atoned for him? As it is said, 'Joshua said, "Why have you afficted us? *Adonoy* will afflict you *this day.*"'[12] *This day* you will be afflicted, but you will not be afflicted in the World to Come." Therefore if the visitors notice that the patient is near death, they should tactfully turn the conversation and say to him, "Make confession but don't be disturbed about it, for many have confessed and have recovered, and are alive, and many who did not confess have died. As a reward for your confession, you will be granted life, and all who confess have a share in the World to Come." If he cannot confess by word of mouth, he should confess with his heart. If he is able to speak only a few words, he should be told to say, "May my death be an atonement for all my sins." He should also be told to ask the forgiveness of all he had wronged, whether in money matters or with words. None of these words should be said to him in the presence of the unlearned, or in the presence of women or children, for it may cause them to weep and thereby break the heart of the sick man.

14) A brief form of confession [is as follows]: I avow unto You *Adonoy,* my God, and the God of my fathers, that my recovery as well as my death are in Your hands. May it be Your will to heal me with a complete recovery; and if I am to die, may my death be an atonement for all my sins, iniquities and transgressions which I have sinned, perpetrated and transgressed before you. Grant me a share in *Gan Eiden*, and

---

7. *Sifrei, Numbers* 5:6.
8. *Numbers* 5:6.
9. *Maseches Sanhedrin* 43a.
10. *Joshua* 7:19.
11. Ibid 7:20.
12. Ibid 7:25.

הַבָּא הַצָּפוּן לַצַּדִּיקִים. וְאִם רוֹצֶה לְהַאֲרִיךְ כְּוִדּוּי יוֹם־הַכִּפּוּרִים, הָרְשׁוּת בְּיָדוֹ. וּכְבָר מְסֻדָּרִים הַוִּדּוּיִים בְּסֵפֶר הַיָּקָר מַעֲבַר יַבֹּק. וּבְסֵפֶר חָכְמַת אָדָם הֶעְתִּיק גַּם כֵּן סֵדֶר הַוִּדּוּי מֵהָרַמְבַּ"ן זִכְרוֹנוֹ לִבְרָכָה.

סִימָן קצד
דִּינֵי גּוֹסֵס וּשְׁמִירַת הַמֵּת

א) הַגּוֹסֵס הֲרֵי הוּא כְּחַי לְכָל דְּבָרָיו. וְלָכֵן אָסוּר לִגַּע בּוֹ, שֶׁכָּל הַנּוֹגֵעַ בּוֹ, הֲרֵי זֶה שׁוֹפֵךְ דָּמִים. לְמָה הַדָּבָר דּוֹמֶה. לְנֵר מְטַפְטֵף, שֶׁכֵּיוָן שֶׁנּוֹגֵעַ בּוֹ אָדָם, מִיָּד נִכְבֶּה. וְאַף־עַל־פִּי שֶׁהוּא גּוֹסֵס זְמַן אָרֹךְ וְיֵשׁ צַעַר גָּדוֹל לוֹ וְלִקְרוֹבָיו, מִכָּל מָקוֹם אָסוּר לִגְרֹם שֶׁיָּמוּת מְהֵרָה, כְּגוֹן לְהַשְׁמִיט הַכַּר וְהַכֶּסֶת מִתַּחְתָּיו, מֵחֲמַת שֶׁאוֹמְרִים, שֶׁיֵּשׁ נוֹצוֹת מִקְצָת עוֹפוֹת שֶׁגּוֹרְמִים לְעַכֵּב אֶת הַמִּיתָה, אוֹ לָשׂוּם מַפְתְּחוֹת בֵּית־הַכְּנֶסֶת תַּחַת רֹאשׁוֹ, כָּל זֶה אָסוּר. אֲבָל אִם יֵשׁ שָׁם דָּבָר שֶׁגּוֹרֵם עִכּוּב יְצִיאַת הַנֶּפֶשׁ, כְּגוֹן קוֹל דּוֹפֵק וְכַיּוֹצֵא בָּזֶה, מֻתָּר לַהֲסִירוֹ, דְּאֵין בָּזֶה מַעֲשֶׂה, אֶלָּא שֶׁמֵּסִיר אֶת הַמּוֹנֵעַ וְאֵינוֹ נוֹגֵעַ בּוֹ.

ב) אַף־עַל־פִּי שֶׁאָסוּר לִגַּע בְּגוֹסֵס, מִכָּל מָקוֹם אִם נָפְלָה דְלֵקָה, אֵין מַנִּיחִין אוֹתוֹ בַּבַּיִת, אֶלָּא מוֹצִיאִין אוֹתוֹ. וְהוּא קוֹדֵם לְהַצָּלַת סִפְרֵי קֹדֶשׁ.

ג) הָעוֹמְדִים אֵצֶל הַגּוֹסֵס, יַשְׁגִּיחוּ שֶׁלֹּא יוֹצִיא שׁוּם אֵבֶר חוּץ לַמִּטָּה, כְּמוֹ שֶׁנֶּאֱמַר בְּיַעֲקֹב, וַיֶּאֱסֹף רַגְלָיו אֶל הַמִּטָּה. וְלָכֵן יַעֲמִידוּ כִּסְאוֹת אֵצֶל הַמִּטָּה, שֶׁלֹּא יוּכַל לְהוֹצִיא יָד אוֹ רָגֶל. וּמִכָּל מָקוֹם אִם לֹא עָשׂוּ כֵן וְהוֹצִיא, אָסוּר לִגַּע בּוֹ לְהַחֲזִירוֹ.

ד) כֵּיוָן שֶׁנָּטָה אָדָם לָמוּת, אֵין שׁוּם אָדָם רַשַּׁאי לִפָּרֵד מִמֶּנּוּ, שֶׁלֹּא תֵּצֵא נַפְשׁוֹ וְהוּא יְחִידִי, מִפְּנֵי שֶׁהַנֶּפֶשׁ מִשְׁתּוֹמֶמֶת בְּשָׁעָה שֶׁיּוֹצֵאת מִן הַגּוּף. וּמִצְוָה לַעֲמֹד עַל הָאָדָם בִּשְׁעַת יְצִיאַת נְשָׁמָה, שֶׁנֶּאֱמַר, וִיחִי עוֹד לָנֶצַח לֹא יִרְאֶה הַשָּׁחַת כִּי יִרְאֶה חֲכָמִים יָמוּתוּ וְגוֹ'. וְרָאוּי לְקַבֵּץ עֲשָׂרָה, שֶׁיִּהְיוּ בִּשְׁעַת יְצִיאַת נְשָׁמָה, וְלֹא יַעַסְקוּ, חַס־וְשָׁלוֹם, בִּדְבָרִים בְּטֵלִים,

---

1. Nevertheless, a *kohein* is forbidden to enter the house of a dying person. See Chapter 205:1 for details.

2. There is a question if it is permitted to give him a drastic, medicine that could either cure him or perhaps hasten his death. According to *Shevus Yaakov* Volume III Response 75, it is permitted to do so only if the majority of the doctors concur and the chief *Poseik* agrees.

cause me to merit [the life of] the World to Come, which is reserved for the righteous. If he [the sick one] wants to make a lengthy confession, like the confession of Yom Kippur, he may do so. The forms of confession are found in the worthy *seifer, Maavar Yaabok*. The *seifer, Chochmas Adom*, has copied the confession form of the *Ramban* (Nachmanides), of blessed memory.

Chapter 194

Laws Pertaining To A Person Near Death, And Guarding The Body Of The Deceased.

1) A person who is very near death is considered as a living being in every respect.[1] It is, therefore, forbidden to touch him, for anyone who touches him is considered like one who sheds blood. To what can this be compared? To a dripping [flickering] candle, which becomes extinguished as soon as someone touches it. Even if he is critical over a long period, and he and his family are in great agony, it is, nevertheless, forbidden to hasten his death in any way.[2] [It is forbidden] for example to remove a feathered pillow from under him, because some people say that feathers of certain birds defer death, or for example to place the keys to the synagogue under his head; all these things are forbidden. However, if there is something which prevents the departure of the soul, such as a pounding noise or something similar, it is permitted to remove it since this is not a direct act, but merely the removal of the deterrent [to his death], without touching the dying person.

2) Although it is forbidden to touch a dying person, nevertheless, if a fire breaks out, he should not be left in the house, rather he should be taken out of the house. His removal takes precedence over the rescue of sacred books.

3) Those who are attending the dying person, should see to it that no limb of his projects from his bed, as it is said concerning Jacob, "And he gathered up his feet to the bed."[3] Therefore, they should place chairs at [the side of] the bed, so that he cannot extend a hand or foot outside it. Nevertheless, if this was not done, and his hand or foot was extended, it is forbidden to touch him in order to put it back.

4) From the moment that his death is imminent, no one is permitted to leave him, so that his soul does not depart when he is alone, because the soul is shocked as it departs from the body. It is a mitzvah to stand by a person, as the soul is departing from him, as it is said, "Shall he then live forever, shall he never see the grave? For he sees that wise men die, etc."[4] It is proper to gather ten adult males to be present at the departure of the soul. They must not God forbid engage in idle

3. *Genesis* 49:33.
4. *Psalms* 49:10–11.

אֶלָּא יַעַסְקוּ בַּתּוֹרָה וּבַתְּהִלִּים וּבִשְׁאָר מִזְמוֹרִים, כִּמְסֻדָּר בְּסֵפֶר מַעֲבַר יַבֹּק. וְנוֹהֲגִין לְהַדְלִיק נֵרוֹת בִּפְנֵי הַגּוֹסֵס.

ה) לְאַחַר יְצִיאַת נְשָׁמָה, מַנִּיחִין אֵצֶל חָטְמוֹ נוֹצָה קַלָּה, וְאִם אֵינָהּ מִתְנַדְנֶדֶת, בְּיָדוּעַ שֶׁמֵּת, וְאָז פּוֹתְחִין אֶת הַחַלּוֹנוֹת, וְהָאֲבֵלִים אוֹמְרִים צִדּוּק הַדִּין, וּכְשֶׁמַּגִּיעִים לְבָרוּךְ דַּיַּן הָאֱמֶת, אוֹמְרִים בְּשֵׁם וּמַלְכוּת וְקוֹרְעִין, כְּדִין שֶׁיִּתְבָּאֵר בְּסִימָן שֶׁלְּאַחַר זֶה.

ו) וְכָל הָעוֹמְדִין עַל הַמֵּת בִּשְׁעַת יְצִיאַת נְשָׁמָה, חַיָּבִין לִקְרֹעַ. הָא לְמַה זֶּה דּוֹמֶה, לְסֵפֶר־תּוֹרָה שֶׁנִּשְׂרָף, שֶׁאֵין רֵיק בְּיִשְׂרָאֵל שֶׁאֵין בּוֹ תּוֹרָה וּמִצְוֹת. וַאֲפִלּוּ עַל קָטָן שֶׁלָּמַד מִקְרָא אוֹ עַל אִשָּׁה, חַיָּבִין לִקְרֹעַ. וַאֲפִלּוּ הָיָה זֶה הַמֵּת לִפְעָמִים עוֹשֶׂה עֲבֵרָה לְתֵאָבוֹן חַיָּבִין לִקְרֹעַ עָלָיו. אֲבָל אִם הָיָה רָגִיל לַעֲשׂוֹת עֲבֵרָה, אֲפִלּוּ רַק לְתֵאָבוֹן, הֲרֵי זֶה בִּכְלַל הַפּוֹרְשִׁים מִדַּרְכֵי הַצִּבּוּר, שֶׁאֵין קוֹרְעִין עָלָיו. וּקְרִיעָה זוֹ שֶׁעַל הַמֵּת שֶׁאֵין מִתְאַבְּלִים עָלָיו אֶלָּא שֶׁקּוֹרְעִין מִפְּנֵי שֶׁעוֹמְדִין בִּשְׁעַת יְצִיאַת נְשָׁמָה, סַגֵּי בִּקְרִיעָה מֻעֶטֶת. וַאֲפִלּוּ מִן הַצַּד אוֹ בְּשׁוּלֵי הַבֶּגֶד, סַגֵּי.

ז) מְעַצְּמִין עֵינָיו שֶׁל מֵת. וּמִי שֶׁיֵּשׁ לוֹ בָּנִים, יַעֲשֶׂה זֹאת בְּנוֹ, כְּמוֹ שֶׁנֶּאֱמַר, וְיוֹסֵף יָשִׁית יָדוֹ עַל עֵינֶיךָ. וְאִם יֵשׁ בְּכוֹר, יַעֲשֶׂה הוּא.

ח) כְּשֶׁנּוֹשְׂאִין אוֹתוֹ מִמִּטָּתוֹ לְהַשְׁכִּיבוֹ עַל הָאָרֶץ, יַשְׁגִּיחוּ שֶׁיְּהֵא מְכֻסֶּה, כִּי כֹּל מַה שֶּׁנּוֹהֵג בַּחַי מִשּׁוּם צְנִיעוּת, נוֹהֵג גַּם בַּמֵּת.

ט) מִנְהָג לִשְׁפֹּךְ כָּל הַמַּיִם הַשְּׁאוּבִים שֶׁבִּשְׁכוּנַת הַמֵּת, דְּהַיְנוּ שְׁלֹשָׁה בָּתִּים (עִם הַבַּיִת אֲשֶׁר שָׁם הַמֵּת), וַאֲפִלּוּ מֵת יֶלֶד בְּתוֹךְ שְׁלֹשִׁים יוֹם לְלֵדָתוֹ. וּבְשַׁבָּת, אֵין צְרִיכִין לִשְׁפֹּךְ. (וְהַ„בִּרְכֵּי יוֹסֵף" כָּתַב, דְּיֵשׁ לְהַחְמִיר גַּם בְּשַׁבָּת).

י) הַמְשַׁמֵּר אֶת הַמֵּת אֲפִלּוּ אֵינוֹ מֵתוֹ פָּטוּר מִקְּרִיאַת־שְׁמַע וּמִתְּפִלָּה וּמִכָּל מִצְוֹת הָאֲמוּרוֹת בַּתּוֹרָה, כִּי הָעוֹסֵק בְּמִצְוָה, פָּטוּר מִמִּצְוָה אַחֶרֶת. הָיוּ שְׁנַיִם, זֶה מְשַׁמֵּר, וְזֶה קוֹרֵא וּמִתְפַּלֵּל.

---

5. According to *Zchor L'Avrohom,* our custom is that those who are present when the soul departs *do not tear* their garments. The reason is that we do not want the person to die alone, as people will not want to be present if it means tearing their garments.

6. *Genesis* 46:4.

7. The deceased must be guarded from rodents. See *Mishnah Beruch* 71:12.

8. He is not permitted to be stringent in this matter. *Mishnah Berurah,* Ibid.

talk, rather they should engage in Torah subjects, and in the recitation of Psalms and other supplication, as arranged in the *seifer, Maavar Yabbok.* It is customary to light candles in the presence of a dying person.

5) After the departure of the soul, a light feather is placed at his nostrils. If it does not move, it is certain that he is dead. The windows should then be opened, and the mourners should recite the prayer, *Tzidduk Ha Din,* (The righteousness of Divine judgement.) When they say the *berachah, Baruch Dayan ha-emes* [Blessed is the true Judge], they should include in it, the Divine Name, (*Adonoy Elokeinu*) and the mention of His kingdom, (*Melech haolam*). [The complete *berachah* is thus: *Baruch atah Adonoy, Elokeinu, Melech haolam, Dayan ha-emes.*] They then tear their garments, according to the laws stated in the next chapter.

6) All those attending the deceased when the soul departs, must tear their garments.[5] To what is this [death] compared? To the burning of a *Seifer* Torah, for there is no one in Yisrael who is [totally] void of Torah knowledge and the performance of mitzvos. Even at the death of a child who studied Scriptures, or at the death of a woman, the garments must be torn. Even if the deceased had at times committed a sin to satisfy his lustful desire, the garments must be torn at his death. However if the person committed a sin regularly, even though he did so only to satisfy his lustful desire, he is considered among those who have departed from the ways of the community, and the garments are not torn at his death. Regarding the tearing of the garments at the death of one for whom you are not a mourner, and you are tearing your garment only because you are present at the time of the soul's departure, it is sufficient if you make a slight tear, even at the side or at the hem.

7) The eyes of the deceased must be closed. If there are sons, it should be done by his son, as it is said, "Joseph shall place his hand upon your eyes."[6] If there is a firstborn son, he should do it.

8) When lifting the deceased from his bed to lay him on the floor, care must be taken to keep him covered, for all the customs of modesty that apply to the living, apply also to the dead

9) It is customary to pour out all the water from the vessels in the vicinity of the deceased, which is three houses (including the one in which the deceased lies.) This is done even for an infant who died within thirty days of its birth. If death occurs on Shabbos the water need not be poured out. (*Birkei Yoseif* writes, that one should be stringent and pour out the water even on Shabbos.)

10) The person who guards the deceased,[7] even if he is not a mourner, is exempt from *Kerias Shema* and *Shemoneh Esrei,* and from all other mitzvos of the Torah,[8] for he who is engaged in the performance of a mitzvah is exempt from performing another mitzvah.[9] If there are two two watchmen, [they should alternate] one of them should guard, while the other says *Krias Shema* and *Shemoneh Esrei.*

---

9. This general rule applies only if the second mitzvah involves some extra effort, but if

יא) אָסוּר לֶאֱכֹל בְּחֶדֶר שֶׁהַמֵּת שָׁם, אִם לֹא עַל יְדֵי מְחִצָּה. וַאֲפִלּוּ אֲכִילַת אַרְעַי. וַאֲפִלּוּ אֲכִילַת פֵּרוֹת אוֹ שְׁתִיַּת מַיִם, אָסוּר. וּצְרִיכִין לְהַזְהִיר אֶת הַשּׁוֹמְרִים עַל זֹאת. וְגַם אָסוּר לְבָרֵךְ שָׁם אֵיזוֹ בְּרָכָה.

יב) אָסוּר לְטַלְטֵל אֶת הַמֵּת בְּשַׁבָּת אֲפִלּוּ לְצֹרֶךְ כֹּהֲנִים אוֹ לְצֹרֶךְ מִצְוָה, רַק עַל יְדֵי גוֹיִם, אִם הַקְּרוֹבִים רוֹצִים.

סִימָן קצה
הִלְכוֹת קְרִיעָה

א) מִי שֶׁמֵּת לוֹ מֵת שֶׁהוּא חַיָּב לְהִתְאַבֵּל עָלָיו, חַיָּב לִקְרֹעַ עָלָיו. וְחַיָּב לִקְרֹעַ מְעֻמָּד, שֶׁנֶּאֱמַר, וַיָּקָם הַמֶּלֶךְ וַיִּקְרַע אֶת בְּגָדָיו. וְאִם קָרַע מְיֻשָּׁב, לֹא יָצָא, וְצָרִיךְ לַחֲזוֹר וְלִקְרֹעַ מְעֻמָּד. לְכַתְּחִלָּה צָרִיךְ לִקְרֹעַ קֹדֶם שֶׁיִּסָּתְמוּ פְּנֵי הַמֵּת בַּקֶּבֶר בְּעוֹד חִמּוּם צַעֲרוֹ.

ב) עַל הַמֵּתִים שֶׁהוּא מִתְאַבֵּל עֲלֵיהֶם, צָרִיךְ לִקְרֹעַ בְּבֵית הַצַּוָּאר לְפָנָיו. וְצָרִיךְ לִקְרֹעַ מִן הַשָּׂפָה וּלְמַטָּה, וְלֹא לְרֹחַב הַבֶּגֶד. וְצָרִיךְ לִקְרֹעַ בְּמָקוֹם שֶׁהַבֶּגֶד שָׁלֵם מִתְּחִלָּתוֹ, וְלֹא בִּמְקוֹם הַתֶּפֶר.

ג) חִלּוּקִים יֵשׁ בֵּין הַקְּרִיעָה שֶׁעַל אָבִיו וְאִמּוֹ לַקְּרִיעָה שֶׁעַל שְׁאָר קְרוֹבִים. עַל כָּל הַמֵּתִים, קוֹרֵעַ טֶפַח בַּבֶּגֶד הָעֶלְיוֹן וְדַיּוֹ, וְאֵין לִקְרֹעַ יוֹתֵר, מִשּׁוּם בַּל תַּשְׁחִית. וְעַל אָבִיו וְאִמּוֹ, צָרִיךְ לִקְרֹעַ כָּל הַבְּגָדִים עַד כְּנֶגֶד לִבּוֹ, (וְעַיֵּן לְעֵיל סִימָן י סָעִיף ג, שֶׁהַלֵּב הוּא כְּנֶגֶד הַבָּשָׂר הַגָּבוֹהַּ שֶׁעַל הַזְּרוֹעַ), חוּץ מִן הַכֻּתֹּנֶת שֶׁאֵינוֹ קוֹרֵעַ. וְכֵן הַבֶּגֶד שֶׁהוּא לוֹבֵשׁ רַק לְעִתִּים לְמַעְלָה מִכָּל בְּגָדָיו, וְלִפְעָמִים הוּא יוֹצֵא לַשּׁוּק גַּם בִּלְעָדָיו, בֶּגֶד זֶה גַּם כֵּן אֵינוֹ צָרִיךְ לִקְרֹעַ. וְאִם לֹא קָרַע כָּל בְּגָדָיו שֶׁהוּא צָרִיךְ לִקְרֹעַ, לֹא יָצָא. וְהָאִשָּׁה, מִשּׁוּם צְנִיעוּת תִּקְרַע תְּחִלָּה אֶת הַבֶּגֶד הַתַּחְתּוֹן לְפָנֶיהָ, וְתַחֲזִיר אֶת הַקֶּרַע לִצְדָדִין, וְאַחַר כָּךְ תִּקְרַע אֶת הַבֶּגֶד הָעֶלְיוֹן, שֶׁלֹּא יִתְגַּלֶּה לִבָּהּ, (וְאַף שֶׁהִיא לְבוּשָׁה חָלוּק, מִכָּל מָקוֹם אִכָּא מִשּׁוּם פְּרִיצוּת).

ד) נוֹהֲגִין שֶׁעַל שְׁאָר קְרוֹבִים, קוֹרְעִין בְּצַד יָמִין, וְעַל אָבִיו וְאִמּוֹ

---

they can both be done without extra effort, both mitzvos should be performed. (*Rema* 38:8, See *Mishnah Berurah*.)

10. It is also forbidden to smoke in that room. (*Sdei Chemed*, Laws of mourning, 116.)

1. II Samuel 13:31.

2. The custom among certain "liberated" Jews to pin a black cloth on their garment and

11) It is forbidden to eat [a meal] in the room where the deceased lies,[10] unless there is a partition. It is even forbidden to have a snack, even to eat fruit or drink water is forbidden. It is necessary to instruct the guards about this. It is also forbidden to recite a berachah there.

12) It is forbidden to move the deceased on Shabbos, even for the sake of [vacating the place for] *kohanim,* or for the sake of performing some mitzvah. It may be done however by a non-Jews, if the relatives consent to it.

Chapter 195

The Laws of Tearing the Garments

1) When a person suffers the loss [the death] of one for whom he is obligated to mourn, he must tear his garments because of it. He must tear his garments while standing, as it is said, "And the king arose and tore his garments."[1] If he tore his garments while sitting, he has not fulfilled his obligation, and he must again tear his garments while standing. Initially he should tear them before the deceased is covered in the grave, when his sorrow is still intense.

2) For the dead for whom one must observe laws of mourning, the tear in the garment must be made near the front of the neck. It must be made from the top, downward, and not in the width of the garment. The tear must be made in the very cloth of the garment,[2] and not at the seam.

3) There are differences between tearing garments upon the death of a father or mother, and the tearing of garments upon the death of other relatives. For all deceased relatives, tearing a *tefach*[3] of the outer garment is sufficient, and tearing it more than that is a transgression of, "You shall not destroy."[4] For a father or a mother, all the garments must be torn that are over against his heart, (see above Chapter 10:3 that the area of the heart is that which is opposite the bicep of the arm) except the undershirt which is not torn. Similarly, a garment that is worn only on occassions, over other garments, and at times one goes out without it, such as an overcoat, such a garment also does not need to be torn. If the mourner did not tear all the garments that he was required to tear, he has not fulfilled his obligation. Because of modesty, a woman should first tear her inner-garment in private, and turn the tear to the side, and then tear her outer garment, so as not to expose herself. (Even though she is covered by her undershirt, nevertheless, it would be immodest to do otherwise.)

4) Upon the death of other relatives, it is the custom to tear the right side of the garments, and upon the death of a father or a mother, [it is the custom] to tear the

---

to tear it instead of the actual garment, certainly does not meet the requirements of Jewish law.

3. See glossary.
4. Deuteronomy 20:19.

בְּצַד שְׂמֹאל, לְפִי שֶׁצָּרִיךְ לְגַלּוֹת אֶת לִבּוֹ שֶׁהוּא בְּצַד שְׂמֹאל. וּבְדִיעֲבַד, אֵין זֶה מְעַכֵּב.

ה) עַל כָּל הַמֵּתִים, רָצָה קוֹרֵעַ בַּיָּד, רָצָה קוֹרֵעַ בִּכְלִי. עַל אָבִיו וְאִמּוֹ, דַּוְקָא בַּיָּד. וְהַמִּנְהָג שֶׁאֶחָד מֵאַנְשֵׁי חֶבְרָא־קַדִּישָׁא חוֹתֵךְ קְצָת בְּסַכִּין, וְהָאָבֵל תּוֹפֵס בִּמְקוֹם הַחֲתָךְ וְקוֹרֵעַ. וְצָרִיךְ לְהַשְׁגִּיחַ, שֶׁיִּקְרַע בְּאֹרֶךְ הַבֶּגֶד וְלֹא בְּרָחְבּוֹ.

ו) עַל כָּל הַמֵּתִים, אִם מַחֲלִיף בְּגָדָיו בְּתוֹךְ שִׁבְעָה, אֵינוֹ צָרִיךְ לִקְרֹעַ בְּאֵלּוּ שֶׁהוּא לוֹבֵשׁ עַתָּה. וְעַל אָבִיו וְאִמּוֹ, אִם הוּא מַחֲלִיף בְּגָדָיו בִּימֵי הַחֹל שֶׁבְּתוֹךְ שִׁבְעָה, צָרִיךְ לִקְרֹעַ בָּהֶם. אַךְ לִכְבוֹד שַׁבָּת, יַחֲלִיף בְּגָדָיו וְלֹא יִלְבַּשׁ אֶת הַבֶּגֶד הַקָּרוּעַ. וְאִם אֵין לוֹ בְּגָדִים אֲחֵרִים לְהַחֲלִיף, יַחֲזִיר אֶת הַקֶּרַע לַאֲחוֹרָיו. וְהָא דְּמַחֲלִיף בְּשַׁבָּת, הַיְנוּ שֶׁלּוֹבֵשׁ בִּגְדֵי חֹל אֲחֵרִים. אֲבָל לִלְבּוֹשׁ בִּגְדֵי שַׁבָּת, אָסוּר.

ז) עַל כָּל הַמֵּתִים, (מִצַּד הַדִּין) שׁוֹלֵל לְאַחַר שִׁבְעָה, וּמְאַחֶה לְאַחַר שְׁלֹשִׁים. עַל אָבִיו וְאִמּוֹ, שׁוֹלֵל לְאַחַר שְׁלֹשִׁים, וְאֵינוֹ מְאַחֶה לְעוֹלָם. וַאֲפִלּוּ אִם בָּא לַחְתֹּךְ סְבִיבוֹת הַקְּרִיעָה וְלָשׂוּם שָׁם חֲתִיכַת בֶּגֶד אַחֵר וּלְתָפְרוֹ אָסוּר אֲבָל נוֹהֲגִין, כִּי בְּתוֹךְ שְׁלֹשִׁים, אֲפִלּוּ עַל שְׁאָר מֵתִים, אֲפִלּוּ לִשְׁלֹל, אָסוּר. וַאֲפִלּוּ לְחַבֵּר רָאשֵׁי הַקְּרִיעָה עַל יְדֵי מַחַט, אָסוּר. וְאִשָּׁה, אֲפִלּוּ עַל אָבִיהָ וְאִמָּהּ, שׁוֹלֶלֶת לְאַלְתַּר, מִפְּנֵי הַצְּנִיעוּת. וְכָל הַקְּרָעִים שֶׁאֲסוּרִין לְתָפְרָן אֲפִלּוּ אִם מָכַר אֶת הַבֶּגֶד לְאַחֵר אָסוּר הַלּוֹקֵחַ לְתָפְרוֹ. וְלָכֵן צָרִיךְ הַמּוֹכֵר לְהוֹדִיעַ לַלּוֹקֵחַ. וְאָסוּר לְמָכְרוֹ לַגּוֹי.

ח) עַל כָּל הַמֵּתִים, אִם לֹא שָׁמַע עַד לְאַחַר שְׁלֹשִׁים, אֵינוֹ קוֹרֵעַ. עַל אָבִיו וְאִמּוֹ, קוֹרֵעַ לְעוֹלָם בִּבְגָדָיו שֶׁהֵם עָלָיו בִּשְׁעַת שְׁמִיעָה. אַךְ הַבְּגָדִים שֶׁהוּא מַחֲלִיף אַחַר כָּךְ, אֵינוֹ צָרִיךְ לִקְרֹעַ.

ט) הָרֶגֶל מְבַטֵּל גְּזֵרַת שְׁלֹשִׁים גַּם לְעִנְיַן קְרִיעָה. וְלָכֵן אִם פָּגַע הָרֶגֶל בְּתוֹךְ שְׁלֹשִׁים, בִּשְׁאָר קְרוֹבִים יָכוֹל לִתְפֹּר לְגַמְרֵי בְּעֶרֶב הָרֶגֶל לְאַחַר מִנְחָה וְעַל אָבִיו וְאִמּוֹ, יָכוֹל לִשְׁלוֹל.

5. The seven days of mourning.

6. Today the prevailing custom is to wear regular Shabbos clothing even on the first Shabbos of the *Shivah*. *Radvaz* II 693, *Birkei Yosef* 400, Gra.

Chapter 196

The Laws Of An Onein* Regarding Weekdays, Shabbos And Yom Tov.

1) When a person suffers the loss [death] of a relative for whom he is obligated to observe the ritual mourning,[1] he is considered an *onein* until after the burial.[2] An *onein* must avoid [all kinds of] levity, lest his conduct lead people to say that the deceased was a worthless person, and therefore he is not bothered about his burial, and his mourning, and is not concerned about his death. This is a tremendous disgrace to the deceased, and such a person is included among those "Who ridicule the poor." Rather he should manifest to all that he is distressed and concerned about the deceased and his burial. He should not eat in the room where the deceased lies, but in another room. If there is no other room, he should eat in his neighbor's house. If he has no neighbor, he should put up a partition in front of the deceased, that is at least ten *tefachem* high,[3] and the open space below [the partition] should be less than three tefachim. It should be strong enough to resist the wind. If he has no material with which to make a partition, he should turn his face aside and eat. Under all circumstances, and even if he happens to be in another city, he should not have an elaborate meal, but only a simple snack, and he must not eat meat or drink wine.

2) An *onein* is exempt[4] from all mitzvos of the Torah, even if it is not necessary for him to be occupied with the arrangements for the deceased, as he has others to do so in his behalf. Even if he wants to be stringent [and perform mitzvos] he is not permitted to do so,[5] out of respect to the deceased.[6] He should not say the *berachah* of *Hamotzei* on bread nor recite *Birkas Hamazon* after eating. Even if others eat and recite *berachos,* he should not respond *Amein* [to their *berachos*]. He cannot be included in a quorum of three for *Birkas Hamazon,* or in quorum of ten (a *minyan*) for prayers. However, prohibitory mitzvos, even those enacted by the Sages, are forbidden even to an *onein.* Therefore if he wants to eat bread, he must wash his hands, but he must not say the *berachah, Al Netilas Yadayim,* just as he must not say the *Hamotzi.* Regarding the washing of hands upon arising in the morning, he should wash his three times as customary but without saying the *berachah.*

3) If the *onein* had eaten before the burial, and after the burial, the food was not yet digested, he should say *Birkas Hamazon.* Similarly, if he had gone to the toilet before the burial, he should say the *berachah, Asher Yatzar,* at anytime during the whole day.

---

5. If he said *Kerias Shema* etc. while he was an *onein,* he did not fulfil his obligation and must repeat his prayers after the burial (Ibid 71:3).

6. When there are others who are occupied with the burial arrangements, the son is permitted to go to the synagogue to say *Kaddish,* as this is a mark of respect. This is certainly true on Shabbos and Yom Tov when there is no burial. (*Mishna Berurah* 71:7)

ד) אִם הָאוֹנֵן הוּא בְּעִיר אַחֶרֶת, וּבִמְקוֹם הַמֵּת יֵשׁ גַּם כֵּן קְרוֹבִים שֶׁחַיָּבִים לְהִתְאַבֵּל, אֲזַי עַל זֶה שֶׁהוּא בְּמָקוֹם אַחֵר, אֵין עָלָיו דִּין אוֹנֵן. אֲבָל אִם אֵין קְרוֹבִים בִּמְקוֹם הַמֵּת, חָל עַל זֶה דִּין אוֹנֵן.

ה) בְּמָקוֹם שֶׁיֵּשׁ חֶבְרָא קַדִּישָׁא, וּלְאַחַר שֶׁהַקְּרוֹבִים נִתְעַסְּקוּ בְּצָרְכֵי הַקְּבוּרָה וְהִתְפַּשְּׁרוּ עִם אַנְשֵׁי חֶבְרָא קַדִּישָׁא, אֵין עֲלֵיהֶם שׁוּם דָּבָר לַעֲשׂוֹת, אַךְ אַנְשֵׁי חֶבְרָא קַדִּישָׁא עוֹשִׂין הַכֹּל, אֲזַי אֵין עוֹד עַל הַקְּרוֹבִים דִּין אוֹנֵן, וּמֻתָּרִין בְּבָשָׂר וָיַיִן, וּמִכָּל־שֶׁכֵּן שֶׁמֻּתָּרִין וְחַיָּבִין בִּקְרִיאַת־שְׁמַע וּבִתְפִלָּה וּבְכָל הַמִּצְוֹת. וּמִכָּל מָקוֹם נוֹהֲגִין שֶׁאֵין הָאוֹנְנִין מִתְפַּלְּלִין עַד לְאַחַר הַקְּבוּרָה, וְהַיְנוּ מִפְּנֵי שֶׁגַּם הֵם הוֹלְכִין וּמְלַוִּין אֶת הַמֵּת עַד בֵּית הַקְּבָרוֹת. וְהָרוֹצֶה לְהַחְמִיר וּלְהִתְפַּלֵּל תֵּכֶף לְאַחַר שֶׁמָּסַר אֶת הַמֵּת לְאַנְשֵׁי חֶבְרָא קַדִּישָׁא, יָכוֹל לְהַחְמִיר עַל עַצְמוֹ.

ו) כָּל זְמַן שֶׁלֹּא נִקְבַּר הַמֵּת, אֵינוֹ חוֹלֵץ מִנְעָלָיו, וּמֻתָּר לָצֵאת מִבֵּיתוֹ לְצָרְכֵי הַמֵּת. אֲבָל אָסוּר לֵישֵׁב אוֹ לִישֹׁן עַל כִּסֵּא אוֹ מִטָּה, וְכָל־שֶׁכֵּן שֶׁאָסוּר בְּתַשְׁמִישׁ־הַמִּטָּה, וְאָסוּר בִּרְחִיצָה וְסִיכָה וְשִׂמְחָה וּשְׁאִילַת שָׁלוֹם וּבְתִסְפֹּרֶת וּבְתַלְמוּד תּוֹרָה, וְאָסוּר בִּמְלָאכָה אֲפִלּוּ עַל יְדֵי אֲחֵרִים, וַאֲפִלּוּ בְּדָבָר הָאָבֵד. וּבְהֶפְסֵד גָּדוֹל, יַעֲשֶׂה שְׁאֵלַת חָכָם.

ז) מִי שֶׁהוּא אוֹנֵן בִּשְׁעַת קְרִיאַת־שְׁמַע וּתְפִלָּה, וּלְאַחַר שֶׁנִּקְבַּר הַמֵּת עָבְרָה רְבִיעִית הַיּוֹם (שֶׁהִיא זְמַן קְרִיאַת־שְׁמַע), מִכָּל מָקוֹם אוֹמֵר גַּם קְרִיאַת־שְׁמַע וּבִרְכוֹתֶיהָ (בְּלֹא תְפִלִּין) עַד שְׁלִישׁ הַיּוֹם. אֲבָל אִם עָבַר גַּם שְׁלִישׁ הַיּוֹם, אוֹמֵר קְרִיאַת־שְׁמַע בְּלֹא הַבְּרָכוֹת. וּתְפִלַּת שְׁמוֹנֶה־עֶשְׂרֵה, מֻתָּר לְהִתְפַּלֵּל עַד חֲצוֹת הַיּוֹם. וּמוּסָף בְּרֹאשׁ־חֹדֶשׁ, יָכוֹל לְהִתְפַּלֵּל גַּם אַחַר כָּךְ, שֶׁזְּמַנָּהּ כָּל הַיּוֹם. וּמִבִּרְכוֹת הַשַּׁחַר לֹא יֹאמַר כִּי אִם שָׁלשׁ בְּרָכוֹת, שֶׁלֹּא עָשַׂנִי גּוֹי, שֶׁלֹּא עָשַׂנִי עָבֶד, שֶׁלֹּא עָשַׂנִי אִשָּׁה, וּבִרְכוֹת הַתּוֹרָה, שֶׁאֵלּוּ זְמַנָּן כָּל הַיּוֹם. וּשְׁאָר הַבְּרָכוֹת, לֹא יֹאמַר לְאַחַר שֶׁעָבַר זְמַנָּן, כֵּיוָן שֶׁבִּשְׁעַת חוֹבָתָן, הַיְנוּ בַּבֹּקֶר, הָיָה פָּטוּר. וְאִם נִקְבַּר הַמֵּת קֹדֶם שְׁלִישׁ הַיּוֹם וּבֵיתוֹ רָחוֹק מִבֵּית הַקְּבָרוֹת שֶׁעַד שֶׁיַּגִּיעַ לְבֵיתוֹ יַעֲבֹר שְׁלִישׁ הַיּוֹם טוֹב יוֹתֵר שֶׁיִּכָּנֵס לְאֵיזֶה בַּיִת סָמוּךְ לְבֵית הַקְּבָרוֹת לִקְרוֹא קְרִיאַת־שְׁמַע וּלְהִתְפַּלֵּל בִּזְמַן הָרָאוּי, אוֹ אֲפִלּוּ בַּחוּץ בְּמָקוֹם נָקִי. וּמִיָּד

4) If the *onein* is in another city, and there are relatives in the city where the dead lies, and they too are obligated to observe the rules of mourning, then the one who is in the other city, is not considered an *onein.* However if there are no relatives where the dead lies, he assumes all the laws of an *onein.*

5) In a place where there is a Burial Society, after the relatives have made arrangements for the burial with the burial society and have come to terms with them, they have nothing further to do since the members of the Burial Society will do everthing. Then the relatives are not subject to the laws of *onein,* and they are permitted to eat meat and to drink wine. They are certainly permitted, even obligated, to recite *Kerias Shema* and *Shemoneh Esrei,* and to observe all the *mitzvos.* Nevertheless, it is customary for the *oneinin* not to pray until after the burial, because they too follow and accompany the deceased to the cemetery. If he [the *onein*] wishes to be stringent and pray immediately after handing over the deceased to the Burial Society, he may be stringent [and do so].

6) So long as the deceased is not buried, the *onein* does not remove his shoes, and is permitted to leave the house to make arrangements for the burial. However, he is forbidden to sit or sleep on a chair or bed. He is certainly forbidden to have marital relations. He is forbidden to bathe, to annoint himself, to participate in joyous events, to greet people, to have his hair cut, and to study Torah. He is forbidden to work, or even allow others to do work for him, even where a loss is involved. Where the loss would be substantial, he should consult a *Poseik.*

7) If a person is an *onein,* when it is time to recite *Krias Shema*[7] and *Shemoneh Esrei,* and by the time the burial is finished, a fourth of the day will have passed, (which is the time limit for saying *Krias Shema*), he may say *Kerias Shema* and its *berachos* without Tefillin until the third of the day. If a third of the day had passed before the burial he may still say *Kerias Shema,* [but] without its *berachos.* [However] the prayer of *Shemoneh Esrei* may be said until midday; and the *Musaph* service of *Rosh Chodesh* may be said even later, for it may be said the entire day. Of the morning *berachos* he should say only three: "Who did not make me a gentile," "Who did not make me a slave," "Who not make me a woman." He should also say the *berachos* over the Torah as they may be said the entire day. The other *berachos* should not be said after their time has passed, since at the proper time, which is the morning, he was exempt. If the deceased was buried before a third of the day, and his house is far away from the cemetery, so that by the time he reaches his house, a third of the day will have passed, it is best that he should enter a house near the cemetery, to say *Kerias Shema* and *Shemoneh Esrei,* at the proper time, or he may do so even in the open in a clean place. As soon as they begin to throw earth on the body, he may

---

7. If he sees that the period of *oneenas* will extend right up to end of the time of *Kerias Shema*, which is a fourth of the day, and if he begins his prayers in proper order, he will pass the time of *Kerias Shema,* he should first say *Kerias Shema* without its *berachos,* and then begin to pray in the proper order and repeat the *Kerias Shema* with its *berachos*. (*Mishnah Berurah* 71:4)

כְּשֶׁמַּתְחִילִין לְהַשְׁלִיךְ עָפָר עַל הַמֵּת, יָכוֹל לִקְרוֹא קְרִיאַת־שְׁמַע וּלְהִתְפַּלֵּל, אַף־עַל־פִּי שֶׁהָאֲבֵלוּת עֲדַיִן אֵינָהּ חָלָה.

ח) מִי שֶׁמֵּת לוֹ מֵת, וְנַעֲשָׂה אוֹנֵן לְאַחַר שֶׁכְּבָר הִגִּיעַ זְמַן תְּפִלַּת שַׁחֲרִית אוֹ מִנְחָה אוֹ עַרְבִית, וְהוּא לֹא הִתְפַּלֵּל מִקֹּדֶם שֶׁנַּעֲשָׂה אוֹנֵן, וְנִמְשְׁכָה הָאֲנִינוּת עַד לְאַחַר זְמַן הַתְּפִלָּה, אַף־עַל־פִּי־כֵן אֵינוֹ צָרִיךְ תַּשְׁלוּמִין לְהִתְפַּלֵּל בִּתְפִלָּה שֶׁלְּאַחֲרֶיהָ שְׁתַּיִם.

ט) מִי שֶׁמֵּת לוֹ מֵת בְּשַׁבָּת, כֵּיוָן דְּאָסוּר לְקָבְרוֹ הַיּוֹם, לֹא חָלָה עָלָיו אֲנִינוּת, וּמֻתָּר בְּבָשָׂר וָיַיִן, וְחַיָּב בְּכָל הַמִּצְוֹת, חוּץ מִתַּשְׁמִישׁ־הַמִּטָּה שֶׁאָסוּר לוֹ וְגַם אָסוּר בְּתַלְמוּד תּוֹרָה, דַּהֲוָיִן דְּבָרִים שֶׁבִּצְנְעָא. וְאִם הוּא שְׁלִיחַ־צִבּוּר, אִם יֵשׁ אַחֵר לְהִתְפַּלֵּל, לֹא יִתְפַּלֵּל הוּא. וְאִי לֵיכָּא אַחֵר, יִתְפַּלֵּל הוּא. אִם הַמֵּת הוּא אָבִיו אוֹ אִמּוֹ, יָכוֹל לוֹמַר קַדִּישׁ בִּמְקוֹם שֶׁאֵין שְׁאָר אֲבֵלִים. אֲבָל בִּמְקוֹם שְׁאָר אֲבֵלִים, לֹא יֹאמַר קַדִּישׁ קֹדֶם הַקְּבוּרָה. וְאִם הָאוֹנֵן הוּא אָבֵל מִכְּבָר עַל אָבִיו אוֹ עַל אִמּוֹ, אוֹ שֶׁיֵּשׁ לוֹ יָאר־צַייט, יֹאמַר קַדִּישׁ כְּמוֹ שְׁאָר אָבֵל אוֹ יָאר־צַייט.

י) סָמוּךְ לָעֶרֶב, קוֹרֵא קְרִיאַת־שְׁמַע בְּלֹא בְרָכוֹת, וְאֵינוֹ מִתְפַּלֵּל עַרְבִית, וְאֵינוֹ מַבְדִּיל בְּמוֹצָאֵי־שַׁבָּת, וּמֻתָּר לוֹ לֶאֱכֹל בְּלֹא הַבְדָּלָה. וּלְאַחַר שֶׁיִּקָּבֵר הַמֵּת, יַבְדִּיל עַל הַכּוֹס. וַאֲפִלּוּ לֹא נִקְבַּר עַד לְמָחָר, יָכוֹל לְהַבְדִּיל עַל הַכּוֹס, וְלֹא יְבָרֵךְ עַל הַנֵּר וְהַבְּשָׂמִים, דְּמֻתָּר לְהַבְדִּיל עַד יוֹם שְׁלִישִׁי בְּשַׁבָּת. וּבִתְפִלַּת שַׁחֲרִית שֶׁהוּא מִתְפַּלֵּל כְּשֶׁלֹּא עָבַר זְמַנָּהּ, אֵינוֹ אוֹמֵר אַתָּה חוֹנַנְתָּנוּ.

יא) אִם צָרִיךְ לְעֵת עֶרֶב לָלֶכֶת מִבֵּיתוֹ עַד סָמוּךְ לִתְחוּם שַׁבָּת כְּדֵי שֶׁיֵּלֵךְ בְּמוֹצָאֵי־שַׁבָּת לְמָקוֹם אַחֵר בִּשְׁבִיל צָרְכֵי הַמֵּת, אוֹ שֶׁהוּא צָרִיךְ לְעֵת עֶרֶב לֶאֱסֹף אֶת הַגַּבָּאִים דְּחֶבְרָא קַדִּישָׁא לְהִשְׁתַּוּוֹת עִמָּהֶם בְּעַד מְקוֹם הַקְּבוּרָה, אֲזַי מִיָּד כְּשֶׁהִתְחִיל לָלֶכֶת וְלַעֲסֹק בְּצָרְכֵי הַמֵּת, חָלָה עָלָיו אֲנִינוּת.

יב) מֵת בְּעֶרֶב שַׁבָּת לְעֵת מִנְחָה, בְּעִנְיָן שֶׁאִי אֶפְשָׁר לְקָבְרוֹ קֹדֶם שַׁבָּת, מִתְפַּלֵּל גַּם מִנְחָה בְּעֶרֶב שַׁבָּת.

---

8. See below, Chapter 204.
9. See above, Chapter 21.

recite the *Kerias Shema* and *Shemoneh Esrei* even though the period of mourning has not yet begun.[8]

8) If the death occured, and he became an *onein* after the time for the *Shacharis* prayers, or after the time for the *Mincha* or *Maariv* prayers, and he had not prayed before he became an *onein,* and he remained an *onein* until after the time of prayer had passed, nevertheless, he need not make up for them by reciting the *Shemoneh Esrei* twice in the next prayer.[9]

9) If death occurs on Shabbos, since it is forbidden to bury him on that day, the mourner is not restricted by the laws of *onein,* and is permitted to eat meat and to drink wine, He must fulfil all the mitzvos,[10] except that of having marital relations which is forbidden to him. He is also forbidden to study Torah,[11] because these two are private activities. If he is the Chazzan of the synagogue, and there is someone else to lead the prayers, he should not lead the prayers. If there is no one else, he may lead the prayers. If the deceased is his father or his mother, he may say the *Kaddish,* if there are no other mourners, but if there are other mourners, he should not say *Kaddish* before the burial.[12] If the *onein* had already been in mourning for his father or his mother, or if he was observing *Yahrtseit,*[13] he may recite *Kaddish,* as any other mourner or *Yahrtseit* observer.

10) Towards evening (Saturday night) he should say *Kerias Shema* without its *berachos*, but he does not pray *Maariv,* nor does he recite the *Havdalah* for *Motzi Shabbos.* He is permitted to eat without saying *Havdalah.* After the burial, he should say *Havdalah* with a cup of wine. Even if the burial is on Sunday, he may say *Havdalah* with a cup of wine, but without saying the *berachos* over the candle and the spices; because it is permitted to say *Havdalah* until Tuesday (as stated in Chapter 96 above). If he prays *Shacharis* before the time has passed for saying *Havdalah*, he need not say *"Attah Chonantanu"* in the *Shemneh Esrei.*

11) If towards evening it is necessary for the mourner to walk from his house to the Shabbos boundary line in order to go immediately after Shabbos to a place to attend to matters concerning the deceased, or if towards evening he needs to gather together the officers of the Burial Society to negotiate the price of the grave, then as soon as begins to walk and to engage in arrangements in behalf of the deceased, he becomes an *onein.*

12) If the death occured *erev* Shabbos before *Minchah,* when it was impossible to bury him before Shabbos, the mourner must even pray *Minchah erev* Shabbos.

---

10. He is also permitted to go to the synagogue to pray. (*Mishnah Berurah* 71:8)

11. It is forbidden to call him to the Torah for an *Aliyah.* (*Magein* Avrohom). *Bigdei Yeishah,* question this ruling. Since the person is not yet considered an *onein,* why should he be forbidden to study Torah?

12. See note 6.

13. *Yahrtseit* is the yearly observance of the anniversary of the death of a parent or relative.

יג) מֵת בְּיוֹם רִאשׁוֹן שֶׁל יוֹם־טוֹב, אִם רוֹצֶה לְקָבְרוֹ הַיּוֹם עַל יְדֵי גוֹי, חָלָה עָלָיו מִיָּד אֲנִינוּת. וּמִכָּל־שֶׁכֵּן בְּיוֹם שֵׁנִי, שֶׁיָּכוֹל לְקָבְרוֹ גַּם בְּעַצְמוֹ, דְּחָלָה עָלָיו מִיָּד אֲנִינוּת, וַאֲפִלּוּ הוּא אֵינוֹ רוֹצֶה לְקָבְרוֹ הַיּוֹם.

יד) מִי שֶׁמֵּתוֹ מוּטָל לְפָנָיו בְּלֵיל יוֹם־טוֹב שֵׁנִי, מָקוֹם שֶׁנָּהֲגוּ לְקָבְרוֹ עַל יְדֵי יִשְׂרָאֵל, נוֹהֵג דִּין אֲנִינוּת אֲפִלּוּ בַּלַּיְלָה, וְאֵינוֹ אוֹמֵר קִדּוּשׁ, וְאֵינוֹ אוֹכֵל בָּשָׂר, וְאֵינוֹ שׁוֹתֶה יַיִן. אֲבָל בְּלֵיל יוֹם־טוֹב רִאשׁוֹן, אוֹ אֲפִלּוּ בְּלֵיל יוֹם־טוֹב שֵׁנִי בְּמָקוֹם שֶׁנָּהֲגוּ לְהִתְעַסֵּק גַּם בְּיוֹם־טוֹב שֵׁנִי דַּוְקָא עַל יְדֵי גוֹיִם, אֵין לִנְהֹג דִּין אֲנִינוּת בַּלָּיְלָה.

טו) מִי שֶׁהָיָה אוֹנֵן בְּמוֹצָאֵי יוֹם־טוֹב, יַבְדִּיל בְּיוֹם שֶׁלְּאַחֲרָיו, אֲבָל לֹא אַחַר כָּךְ, כִּי הַבְדָּלָה שֶׁל יוֹם־טוֹב אֵין זְמַנָּהּ אֶלָּא עַד סוֹף הַיּוֹם שֶׁלְּאַחֲרָיו.

טז) אוֹנֵן שֶׁיֵּשׁ לוֹ בֵּן לָמוּל, אִם אֶפְשָׁר לִקְבֹּר אֶת הַמֵּת קֹדֶם שֶׁיֵּצְאוּ מִבֵּית־הַכְּנֶסֶת שַׁחֲרִית, אֲזַי יִתְפַּלְּלוּ הַקַּבְּרָנִים תְּחִלָּה, וְיִקְבְּרוּ אֶת הַמֵּת, וְיָמוּלוּ אֶת הַתִּינוֹק. וְאִם אִי אֶפְשָׁר, מִכָּל מָקוֹם יָמוּלוּ אֶת הַתִּינוֹק שַׁחֲרִית בְּבֵית־הַכְּנֶסֶת, וְהַסַּנְדָּק יְבָרֵךְ בִּרְכַּת לְהַכְנִיסוֹ, מִשּׁוּם דְּמֵת וּמִילָה, מִילָה קוֹדֶמֶת.

יז) אוֹנֵן בְּאוֹר לְאַרְבָּעָה עָשָׂר בְּנִיסָן, יַעֲשֶׂה שָׁלִיחַ לִבְדֹּק אֶת הֶחָמֵץ, וְכָל חֲמִירָא וְכוּ' יֹאמַר בְּעַצְמוֹ.

יח) אוֹנֵן בְּלֵיל סְפִירַת הָעֹמֶר, לֹא יִסְפֹּר בַּלַּיְלָה, אֶלָּא בַּיּוֹם לְאַחַר הַקְּבוּרָה יִסְפֹּר בְּלֹא בְרָכָה. וּבִשְׁאָר הַלֵּילוֹת, יִסְפֹּר אַחַר כָּךְ בִּבְרָכָה. וְאִם רוֹאֶה בַּיּוֹם כִּי הָאֲנִינוּת תִּמָּשֵׁךְ עַד הַלַּיְלָה, יִסְפֹּר אֲפִלּוּ בַּאֲנִינוּת בְּלֹא בְרָכָה, כְּדֵי שֶׁיִּסְפֹּר שְׁאָר הַלֵּילוֹת בִּבְרָכָה.

יט) מִי שֶׁמֵּת בִּתְפִיסָה וְהַמּוֹשֵׁל אֵינוֹ רוֹצֶה לִתְּנוֹ לִקְבוּרָה עַד שֶׁיִּתְּנוּ לוֹ מָמוֹן הַרְבֵּה, לֹא חָלָה עַל הַקְּרוֹבִים אֲנִינוּת, וְגַם אֲבֵלוּת לֹא חָלָה

14. This is true only when it is possible to bury the deceased but the mourner does not want to, but if it is impossible because of a secular holiday or some other emergency, he does not yet become an *onein*. (*Mishnah Berurah* 71:11)
15. See Chapter 203.

13) If the death occured on the first day of Yom Tov, and the mourner wants to bury him on that day using the services of non-Jews, he immediately becomes subject to the laws of *onein.* This is certainly true when death occurs on the second day of Yom Tov, when the mourner himself is permitted to bury him. He immediately becomes subject to the laws of *onein,* even if he does not intend to bury him on that day.[14]

14) If his dead[15] lies before him on the night of the second day of Yom Tov, when the custom of the community is to bury the deceased using the services of Jews, the mourner is subject to the laws of *onein* even at night. He therefore should not recite *Kiddush,* nor should he eat meat or drink wine.[16] However, on the night of the first day of Yom Tov, or even on the night of the second day of Yom Tov, when the custom of the community is that even on the second day of Yom Tov, burial is made only through the services of non-Jews, the mourner is not subject to the laws of *onein* at night.

15) If one is an *onein* at the conclusion of Yom Tov, he may recite *Havdalah* on the day after [Yom Tov,] but not after that, because the proper time for *Havdalah* after Yom Tov, is only until the end of the day after Yom Tov.

16) If an *onein* has a son that must be circumcised, and it is possible to bury the deceased before the men leave the synagogue after the *Shacharis* prayers, those who are involved in the burial should first pray *Shacharis,* then bury the deceased, and the child is then circumcised. If that is impossible, the child should nevertheless be circumcised in the morning at the synagogue, and the *sandeik*[17] should say the *berachah, "Lehachniso,"* because circumcision has preference over burial.

17) If a person is an *onein* on the night of the fourteenth day of *Nisan,* he should appoint an agent to search for *chametz,* but he himself should recite, "*Kol Chamirah.*[18]

18) If a person is an *onein* on a night when the *omer* is counted, he should not count at night, rather on the following day after the burial, he should count the *omer* without a *berachah.* [However], on the following nights, he may count the *omer* with a *berachah.* If he sees during the day that he will retain the status of an *onein* until night, he may count the *omer* even while he is an *onein* but without a *berachah,* so that on the following nights he may count the *omer* with a *berachah*

19) If a man dies in prison, and the warden refuses to release the body for burial unless he is given a large sum of money, the relatives are not subject to the laws of *onein,* nor are they subject to the laws of mourning, since they have not despaired

---

16. *Mishna Berurah* writes that many of the later *poskim* agreed that since it is not customary to have burials at night, the mourner should say *Kiddush,* pray as always, and is permitted to do everything except to study Torah which is a source of joy. (*Mishna Berurah* 71:11)

17. The *sandeik* is the person who holds the child on his knees during the circumcision. The father who is an *onein* cannot say the *berachah.*

18. *Kol Chamirah* is the declaration whereby a person nulifies all leaven in his possession and causes it to be ownerless.

עֲלֵיהֶם, כֵּיוָן שֶׁלֹּא נִתְיָאֲשׁוּ מִלְּקָבְרוֹ, וּמְצַפִּים לְהִתְפַּשֵּׁר עִם הַמּוֹשֵׁל. וְכֵן אִם קְרוֹבֵי הַמֵּת הֵם בִּתְפִיסָה וְאֵינָם יְכוֹלִים לַעֲסֹק בְּצָרְכֵי הַמֵּת אֵין אֲנִינוּת חָלָה עֲלֵיהֶם.

כ) בִּמְקוֹמוֹת אֲשֶׁר נִתְּנָה הַדָּת שֶׁלֹּא לִקְבּוֹר אֶת הַמֵּת עַד לְאַחַר אַרְבָּעִים וּשְׁמוֹנֶה שָׁעוֹת, אַף־עַל־פִּי־כֵן לֹא נִפְטָר הָאוֹנֵן מִדִּין אֲנִינוּת, כֵּיוָן שֶׁלְּאַחַר עֲבוֹר הַזְּמַן וַדַּאי יִקְבְּרוּהוּ, מֻטָּל עֲלֵיהֶם בֵּינְתַיִם לְהִתְעַסֵּק בִּכְבוֹדוֹ, לְהָכִין תַּכְרִיכִין וְאָרוֹן, וּלְהָכִין אֲנָשִׁים. אַךְ בְּיוֹם־טוֹב שֵׁנִי, יֵשׁ לְהָקֵל וּלְפָטְרוֹ מִדִּין אֲנִינוּת בָּזֶה שֶׁאִי אֶפְשָׁר לְקָבְרוֹ מֵחֲמַת פְּקֻדַּת הַמַּלְכוּת.

כא) בִּמְקוֹמוֹת הַנִּזְכָּרִים, לְפִי שֶׁחוֹשְׁשִׁין שֶׁלֹּא יִמְצְאוּ אֲנָשִׁים לְטַהֵר אֶת הַמֵּת בְּקָרוֹב שְׁנֵי־מֵעֵת־לְעֵת לְאַחַר מוֹתוֹ וְעַל כֵּן הִמְצִיאוּ לְטַהֲרוֹ תֵּכֶף לְאַחַר מוֹתוֹ וּלְשׂוּמוֹ בְּאָרוֹן שָׁלֵם וְנָקוּב מִלְּמַטָּה, אֲזַי לְאַחַר שֶׁהוּשַּׂם בָּאָרוֹן, פְּטוּרִין מִדִּין אֲנִינוּת, וְנוֹהֵג דִּין אֲבֵלוּת. וּמִכָּל מָקוֹם צְרִיכִין לִמְנוֹת שִׁבְעָה יָמִים מִשָּׁעָה שֶׁיִּסָּתֵם הַגּוֹלֵל בַּקֶּבֶר.

כב) מִי שֶׁמֵּת לוֹ מֵת וְהוּא אֵינוֹ יוֹדֵעַ, אִם אֵין מִי שֶׁיִּתְעַסֵּק בּוֹ, צְרִיכִין לְהַגִּיד לוֹ. אֲבָל אִם יֵשׁ מִתְעַסְּקִין אֲחֵרִים, אֵין לְהַגִּיד לוֹ עַד לְאַחַר שֶׁיִּתְפַּלֵּל. וּמִי שֶׁלְּאִשְׁתּוֹ מֵת לָהּ מֵת, וְהִיא אֵינָהּ יוֹדַעַת, יֵשׁ לוֹ לְהַבַּעַל לְהַחְמִיר שֶׁלֹּא לְשַׁמֵּשׁ עִמָּהּ.

סִימָן קצז

דִּין הַתַּכְרִיכִין וְהַטָּהֳרָה, וְאִסּוּר הֲנָאָה בַּמֵּת

א) נוֹהֲגִין לְהַדֵּר אַחַר בִּגְדֵי פִּשְׁתָּן לְבָנִים לְתַכְרִיכִין, וְיִהְיוּ נָאִים, לְסִימָן שֶׁמּוֹדִים בִּתְחִיַּת הַמֵּתִים, דְּאָמַר רַב חִיָּא בַּר יוֹסֵף, עֲתִידִין הַצַּדִּיקִים שֶׁיַּעַמְדוּ בִּלְבוּשֵׁיהֶן. אֲבָל לֹא יִהְיוּ חֲשׁוּבִים יוֹתֵר מִדַּי, כִּי זֶה אָסוּר. אֵין לַעֲשׂוֹת בַּתַּכְרִיכִין לֹא אִמְרָא וְלֹא שׁוּם קֶשֶׁר, הֵן בְּחוּטִין שֶׁתּוֹפְרִין בָּהֶם, הֵן בִּלְבִישָׁה קוֹבְרִין אֶת הָאִישׁ בְּטַלִּית שֶׁיֵּשׁ בָּהּ צִיצִית, אַךְ פּוֹסְלִין אֶחָת. וְהַיּוֹתֵר נָכוֹן, שֶׁכְּשֶׁמֻּנָּח בַּקֶּבֶר, אָז יַכְנִיסוּ צִיצָה אַחַת בְּתוֹךְ הַכָּנָף. אִם הָיְתָה טַלִּית נָאָה שֶׁהִתְפַּלֵּל בָּהּ בְּחַיָּיו, אֵינוֹ רָאוּי

of being able to bury him and hope to reach an agreement with the warden. Likewise, if the relatives of the deceased are in prison, and are unable to tend the needs of the deceased [burial etc.] they are not subject to the laws of *onein.*

20) In countries where the law forbids burial of the dead until after forty-eight hours, nevertheless, the *onein* is still subject to the laws of *onein*. Since at the end of the forty-eight hours time limit, they will definitely bury him, they [the relatives] must in the meantime be occupied in the honor of the deceased; to prepare shrouds, and a coffin, and to engage men of the Burial Society. However, on the second day of Yom Tov, there is a leniency, and they may be exempt from the laws of *onein,* since it is impossible to bury the dead [anyway] because of the civil law.

21) In the above mentioned places, since the relatives are concerned that they may not find men to cleanse the body once forty-eight hours have passed since the death, and therefore they had the body cleansed immediately after death, and had it placed in a coffin having holes at the bottom; then in such a case, as soon as it is placed in the coffin, they are exempt from the laws of *onein,* and they begin to observe the laws of mourning. Nevertheless, they must count the seven days of mourning from the time the grave is closed.

22) If a death occured, and the relative is unaware of it, if there is no one else to arrange the burial, he should be told. If there are others to arrange the burial, he should not be told, until after he has concluded his prayers. If one's wife lost a relative, and she is unaware of it, the husband should be strict, and abstain from marital relations with her.

Chapter 197

The Laws of the Shrouds, and Purification. The Prohibition of Deriving Pleasure from Belongings of the Deceased.

1) It is a custom of respect to make garments of white linen for shrouds.[1] They should be made nicely to indicate our belief in the resurrection of the dead, for Rav Chiya bar Yosef said, "The righteous will arise with their garments on them."[2] However they should not be too elaborate, for that is forbidden. One should not make the shrouds with a hem, or a knot of any sort, either when sewing the shrouds or when dressing the deceased with them. A man should be buried in a *tallis* with *tzitzis* [fringes], but one [of the four *tzitzis*] should be invalidated. The better procedure however is to insert one of the *tzitzis* in a corner pocket of the *tallis* when the body is in the grave. If he had a beautiful *tallis* [3] in which he prayed during his

1. Linen is preferable because it deteriorates quickly and therefore does not delay the deterioration of the body. (*Tzelach* to *Maseches Berachos* 28b)

2. *Maseches Kesubos* 11b. However if the deceased was not dressed in shrouds, it is forbidden to open the grave and to dress him. Rather the grave is opened and the shrouds placed on the casket. (*Beir Heitiv* 355)

3. This also applies if he had a beautiful *Kittel* in which he prayed on *Yom Kippur.*

לְהַחֲלִיפָהּ לְאַחַר מוֹתוֹ בְּטַלִּית אַחֶרֶת שֶׁאֵינָהּ נָאָה, כִּי נִיחָה לוֹ לָאָדָם לְהִקָּבֵר בְּטַלִּית שֶׁהִתְפַּלֵּל בָּהּ בְּחַיָּיו. כְּשֶׁמַּלְבִּישִׁין אֶת הַמֵּת, יְכַוְּנוּ שֶׁכְּשֵׁם שֶׁהֵם מַלְבִּישִׁים אֶת הַגּוּף, כָּךְ תִּתְלַבֵּשׁ נִשְׁמָתוֹ בְּמַלְבּוּשִׁים רוּחָנִיִּים בְּגַן־עֵדֶן.

ב) סֵדֶר הַטָּהֳרָה, מַרְחִיצִין בְּמַיִם חַמִּים כָּל גּוּפוֹ וְרֹאשׁוֹ, וּמְנַקִּין אוֹתוֹ הֵיטֵב בֵּין אֶצְבְּעוֹת יָדָיו וְרַגְלָיו וּבְכָל מָקוֹם, וְחוֹפְפִין אֶת רֹאשׁוֹ, וְסוֹרְקִין וְגוֹזְזִין שַׂעֲרוֹת רֹאשׁוֹ, וְנוֹטְלִין צִפָּרְנֵי יָדָיו וְרַגְלָיו (וּבִמְדִינָתֵנוּ אֵין נוֹהֲגִין זֹאת). וּצְרִיכִין לִזָּהֵר שֶׁלֹּא יַהַפְכוּ אֶת הַמֵּת עַל פָּנָיו, שֶׁהוּא דֶּרֶךְ בִּזָּיוֹן, אֶלָּא יַטּוּ אוֹתוֹ עַל צִדּוֹ, וְאַחַר כָּךְ עַל צִדּוֹ הַשֵּׁנִי. לְאַחַר שֶׁנִּקּוּ אוֹתוֹ הֵיטֵב, שׁוֹפְכִין עָלָיו תִּשְׁעָה קַבִּין מַיִם, דְּהַיְנוּ שֶׁמַּעֲמִידִין אֶת הַמֵּת עַל הַקַּרְקַע אוֹ עַל גַּבֵּי קַשׁ וְשׁוֹפְכִין הַמַּיִם עַל רֹאשׁוֹ שֶׁיֵּרְדוּ עַל כָּל גּוּפוֹ.

ג) שִׁעוּר תִּשְׁעָה קַבִּין יֵשׁ בּוֹ מַחֲלֹקֶת. (וְיֵשׁ לִקַּח לְעֵרֶךְ עֶשְׂרִים וְאַרְבָּעָה קְוָוארְט [=לִיטֶר] פּוֹלִישׁ). וְאֵין צְרִיכִין שֶׁיִּהְיוּ כֻּלָּם בִּכְלִי אֶחָד דַּוְקָא, אֶלָּא גַּם מִשְּׁנֵי כֵלִים אוֹ מִשְּׁלֹשָׁה, מִצְטָרְפִין, רַק שֶׁהַשֵּׁנִי יַתְחִיל לִצוֹק בְּעוֹד שֶׁלֹּא הִפְסִיק הָרִאשׁוֹן, וְכֵן הַשְּׁלִישִׁי בְּעוֹד שֶׁלֹּא הִפְסִיק הַשֵּׁנִי. וְגַם אִם מְעָרֶה מִכְּלִי אֶחָד, לֹא יַפְסִיק הַקִּלּוּחַ. וּמִתּוֹךְ אַרְבָּעָה כֵלִים, אֲפִלּוּ שׁוֹפְכִין בְּפַעַם אַחַת, אֵין מִצְטָרְפִין.

ד) אַחַר כָּךְ טוֹרְפִין בֵּיצָה עִם יַיִן בְּיַחַד, וְטוֹרְפִין הַבֵּיצָה בִּקְלִפָּתָהּ, לְרַמֵּז שֶׁגַּלְגַּל הוּא שֶׁחוֹזֵר בָּעוֹלָם, (וּבְמָקוֹם שֶׁאֵין יַיִן מָצוּי, לוֹקְחִין מַיִם) וּמַרְחִיצִין בּוֹ רֹאשׁוֹ. וּמַה שֶּׁנּוֹהֲגִין בְּאֵיזֶה מְקוֹמוֹת שֶׁכָּל אֶחָד לוֹקֵחַ מְעַט וּמַזֶּה עַל הַמֵּת, אֵין זֶה נָכוֹן, וְיֵשׁ לְבַטֵּל מִנְהָג זֶה, כִּי דוֹמֶה לְחֻקּוֹת הָעַמִּים, אֶלָּא יִרְחֲצוּ בּוֹ רֹאשׁוֹ.

ה) צְרִיכִין לְהַשְׁגִּיחַ שֶׁלֹּא יִקְמֹץ הַמֵּת אֶצְבְּעוֹת יָדָיו. וּמַה שֶּׁבִּקְצָת מְקוֹמוֹת נוֹהֲגִין לִקְמֹץ אֶת הָאֶצְבָּעוֹת, יֵשׁ לְבַטֵּל מִנְהָג זֶה. וּמַה שֶּׁקְּצָת אוֹמְרִים, שֶׁמְּרַמְּזִים בָּזֶה שֵׁמוֹת קְדוֹשִׁים, דָּבָר בָּדוּי הוּא. גַּם מַה שֶּׁנּוֹתְנִין בְּיָדוֹ שַׁרְבִיטִין שֶׁקּוֹרִין גֶּעפְּלִיךְ, מִנְהַג שְׁטוּת הוּא. וְאִם רוֹצִים דַּוְקָא לָתֵת אוֹתָן, יַנִּיחוּם אֶצְלוֹ.

ו) לְאַחַר שֶׁטִּהֲרוּ אֶת הַמֵּת, לֹא יַנִּיחוּ אוֹתוֹ בְּאוֹתוֹ מָקוֹם שֶׁטִּהֲרוּהוּ,

lifetime, it is not proper to exchange it after his death with a *tallis* that is not as beautiful, for a person is desirous of being buried in the *tallis* in which he prayed during his lifetime.[4] When dressing the deceased, they should think: "Just as his body is being clothed, so may his soul be attired in spiritial garments in *Gan Eiden.*"

2) The purification of the body is done in this manner: His entire body and head is washed with warm water. He should be thoroughly cleansed between his fingers and toes, as well as all other parts of his body. His head should be shampooed, his hair should be combed and trimmed, and his finger and toe nails should be cut (it is not the custom to do so in our countries). Care should be taken not to place the deceased with his face downwards as that is disrespectful, rather he should be inclined on one side, and then on the other side. After he is thoroughly cleansed, we pour nine *kavvim* of water over him. This is done in the following manner: The deceased is placed in a standing position on the ground, or on straw, and the water is poured on his head, so that it runs down his entire body.

3) Regarding the capacity of nine *kavvim,*[5] there are diverse opinions (It is best to take about twenty four quarts, one liter according to the Polish measurements.) It is not necessary that all the water be contained in one vessel; but even two or three vessels can be combined to make up nine *kavvim*. It is however necessary that the second vessel be poured before the first is emptied, and the third one be poured before the second is emptied. Even when pouring from one vessel, the flow must not be interrupted. However, four vessels, even if they are poured simultaneously, cannot be combined.

4) Afterwards, an egg is beaten with wine. The egg is beaten together with its shell, to symbolize that fortune is like a revolving wheel in the world. (Where wine is not available water may be used.) The head of the deceased is washed with this mixture. The custom in some places that each one takes a little of the mixture and sprinkles it upon the deceased is improper, and the custom should be abolished because it resembles the customs of the gentiles. Rather it should be used only to wash his head.

5) Care should be taken that the fingers of the deceased do not remain closed. The custom in some places to close his fingers, should be abolished. The belief of those who say that by doing so, they symbolize sacred names, is a mere fabrication. Similarly the custom of placing twigs in his hand generally called forks, is a foolish custom.[6] If they insist on placing them, they should be put alongside the deceased.

6) After the deceased has been cleansed he should not be left in the place where

---

4. When an unmarried person dies, who did not pray with a *tallis* in his lifetime, there are various customs regarding dressing him with a *tallis.* If the deceased was a Torah scholar and a God-fearing person, it is the custom in some places to dress him with a *tallis,* while others have the custom to dress him with a *tallis kattan.* (*Mishmeres Sholom* 27)

5. A *Kav* is equal to 24 *Kabeitza* or 16 *Revi'is* . See Glossary.

6. According to *Chassam Sofer* the custom should be upheld as it is an old, accepted custom. See *Chassam Sofer Yora Deiah* 175.

אֶלָּא יַשְׁכִּיבוּהוּ כְּנֶגֶד הַפֶּתַח, לִפְנִים מִן הַבַּיִת. וְאֵין מְהַפְּכִין אֶת הַדַּף שֶׁטִּהֲרוּהוּ עָלָיו, כִּי יֵשׁ סַכָּנָה בַּדָּבָר.

ז) לֹא יְנַשֵּׁק אָדָם יְלָדָיו שֶׁמֵּתוּ, כִּי הִיא סַכָּנָה גְּדוֹלָה. וּמִכָּל־שֶׁכֵּן שֶׁלֹּא יֹאחַז בְּיָדוֹ שֶׁל מֵת וְיֹאמַר שֶׁיּוֹלִיכֵהוּ עִמּוֹ.

ח) כְּשֶׁמּוֹצִיאִין אֶת הַמֵּת מִן הַבַּיִת, יֵשׁ לִזָּהֵר שֶׁלֹּא יֵצֵא אָדָם רִאשׁוֹן. אַךְ הַמִּתְעַסְּקִים שֶׁצְּרִיכִין לֵילֵךְ רִאשׁוֹן מִן הַבַּיִת כְּדֵי לְנָשְׂאוֹ, אֵין קְפִידָא.

ט) מִי שֶׁנָּפַל מֵאֵלָיו וּמֵת מִיָּד, אִם יֵשׁ פְּצָעִים בְּגוּפוֹ וְיָצָא מִמֶּנּוּ דָם, וְאִם כֵּן יֵשׁ לָחוּשׁ שֶׁמָּא נִבְלַע דַּם הַנֶּפֶשׁ בִּבְגָדָיו וּבְמִנְעָלָיו, לָכֵן אֵין מְטַהֲרִין אוֹתוֹ, אֶלָּא קוֹבְרִין אוֹתוֹ בִּבְגָדָיו וּבְמִנְעָלָיו, רַק לְמַעְלָה מִבְּגָדָיו כּוֹרְכִין אוֹתוֹ בְּסָדִין שֶׁקּוֹרִין סוֹבֵב. וְנוֹהֲגִין לַחְפֹּר בַּקַּרְקַע שֶׁנָּפַל שָׁם אִם יֵשׁ שָׁם דָּם, וְכֵן בְּקָרוֹב לוֹ, וְקוֹבְרִין עִמּוֹ אֶת כָּל הֶעָפָר שֶׁיֵּשׁ בּוֹ דָם. וְדַוְקָא בְּגָדָיו שֶׁהָיָה לָבוּשׁ בָּהֶם, קוֹבְרִין עִמּוֹ. אֲבָל אִם נִתַּז מִן הַדָּם עַל שְׁאָר בְּגָדִים שֶׁאֵינוֹ מְלֻבָּשׁ בָּהֶם, וְכֵן אִם הִנִּיחוּהוּ עַל כָּרִים וּכְסָתוֹת וַעֲדַיִן הַדָּם יוֹצֵא, אֵינָן צְרִיכִין קְבוּרָה, אֶלָּא יְכַבְּסוּם הֵיטֵב עַד שֶׁלֹּא יִשָּׁאֵר בָּהֶם רֹשֶׁם דָּם, וְהַמַּיִם יִשְׁפְּכוּ לְתוֹךְ קִבְרוֹ. אִם לֹא יָצָא מִמֶּנּוּ דָם, פּוֹשְׁטִין בְּגָדָיו, וּמְטַהֲרִין אוֹתוֹ, וּמַלְבִּישִׁין אוֹתוֹ תַכְרִיכִין כִּשְׁאָר מֵתִים. וְכֵן מִי שֶׁנִּטְבַּע בַּיָּם, פּוֹשְׁטִין בְּגָדָיו, וְדִינוֹ כִּשְׁאָר מֵתִים. וְיֵשׁ מְקוֹמוֹת שֶׁנּוֹהֲגִין לִקְבֹּר גַּם הַנִּטְבָּעִים בְּבִגְדֵיהֶם שֶׁנִּמְצְאוּ בָהֶם, וְהֵיכָא דְנָהוּג, נָהוּג.

י) אֲפִלּוּ יָצָא מִמֶּנּוּ דָם, אֶלָּא שֶׁכְּבָר פָּסַק, וּפָשְׁטוּ אֶת בְּגָדָיו, וְחַי אַחֲרֵי זֶה אֵיזֶה יָמִים, וְאַחַר כָּךְ מֵת, מְטַהֲרִין אוֹתוֹ, וְעוֹשִׂין לוֹ תַכְרִיכִין. וְאַף־עַל־פִּי שֶׁהוּא מְלֻכְלָךְ מִדָּם שֶׁיָּצָא מִמֶּנּוּ, אֲפִלּוּ הָכִי מְטַהֲרִין אוֹתוֹ, כִּי אֵין לָחוּשׁ לְדָם שֶׁיָּצָא מִמֶּנּוּ בְּחַיִּים, אֶלָּא לְדָם שֶׁיָּצָא מִמֶּנּוּ בִּשְׁעַת מִיתָה, חָיְשִׁינָן שֶׁמָּא הוּא דַּם הַנֶּפֶשׁ, אוֹ שֶׁמָּא נִתְעָרֵב בּוֹ דַּם הַנֶּפֶשׁ.

יא) יוֹלֶדֶת שֶׁמֵּתָה מֵחֲמַת לֵדָה, דִּינָהּ כְּהָרוּג, שֶׁאִם יָדוּעַ שֶׁיָּצְאוּ מִמֶּנָּה דָּמִים מְרֻבִּים, אֵין מְטַהֲרִין אוֹתָהּ. אֲבָל אִם כְּבָר כָּלוּ הַדָּמִים לָצֵאת, וְאַחַר כָּךְ מֵתָה, שֶׁאֵין לְהִסְתַּפֵּק בְּדַם הַנֶּפֶשׁ, עוֹשִׂין לָהּ כְּמוֹ לִשְׁאָר מֵתִים. וּבְהַרְבֵּה קְהִלּוֹת נוֹהֲגִין לְטַהֵר כָּל יוֹלֶדֶת, וְעוֹד יֵשׁ אֵיזֶה מִנְהָגִים בְּיוֹלֶדֶת, וְהֵיכָא דְנָהוּג, נָהוּג.

the purification took place, but should be placed opposite the door inside the house. One should not turn over the board upon which the deceased has been washed, for it may be dangerous to do so.

7) A parent should not kiss his dead children, as it is very dangerous. All the more so, one should not grasp the hand of the deceased and say that he should take him along.

8) When the deceased is being taken from the house, care must be exercised that no one should walk out ahead of him. The pallbearers, however, who must exit the house first, in order to carry him out, need not be concerned about this.

9) If a person collapses and dies instantly, if his body was injured, and blood flowed from the wound, and there is reason to fear that perhaps his lifeblood was absorbed in his clothes and his shoes, he should not be ritually cleansed, but he should be buried in his clothing and his shoes. Over his clothing, he should be wrapped in a sheet. The sheet is called *soveir,* (wrapping). It is customary to scoop up the earth from the spot where he fell, if any blood is there. The earth nearby that spot should also be dug up, and he should be buried with all the earth that contains blood. Only the clothing he wore when he fell should be buried with him, but if the blood splashed on other garments that he was not wearing at that time, or if he was placed upon pillows and cushions while still bleeding, these need not be buried but should be thoroughly washed until no trace of blood remains. The water is then poured into his grave. If he did not bleed, his clothing should be removed, his body ritually cleansed, and dressed in shrouds as is done in cases of natural death. Likewise, the clothing of a person who drowned in water should be removed, and he should be treated as one who died a natural death. In some places, it is customary to bury those who drowned with the clothing in which they were found. Where this is the custom it should be upheld.

10) Even if blood issued from his body but it stopped, and his clothes were removed, after which he lived for a few days and died, his body must be ritually cleansed and dressed in shrouds. Even though his body is stained from the blood which issued from him, he still must be cleansed, because we are not concerned [about washing off the blood] that issued when he was alive. We are concerned only about the blood which issued from him while he was dying because it may have been his lifeblood, or that his lifeblood was mixed with it.

11) If a woman dies while giving birth, we apply to her the same law as that of a slain person, and if it is known that she had lost a great deal of blood, she is not to be cleansed. If the flow of blood had ceased and she died later, in which case there is no doubt about lifeblood, she should be treated as any other person who died naturally. In many communities, it is the custom to cleanse the body of any woman who dies at childbirth. There are many other customs pertaining to a woman who dies at childbirth; where they prevail they should be observed.

יב) הַנֶּהֱרָג עַל יְדֵי גוֹיִם, אֲפִלּוּ לֹא יָצָא מִמֶּנּוּ דָם כְּלָל, כְּגוֹן שֶׁנֶּחֱנַק, קוֹבְרִין אוֹתוֹ כְּמוֹ שֶׁנִּמְצָא, כְּדֵי לְהַעֲלוֹת חֵמָה.

יג) מֵת, בֵּין גּוֹי בֵּין יִשְׂרָאֵל, וְתַכְרִיכָיו, אֲסוּרִין בַּהֲנָאָה. וְכֵן נוֹיֵי הַמֵּת הַמְחֻבָּרִים לְגוּפוֹ, כְּגוֹן פֵּאָה נָכְרִית שֶׁהִיא קְשׁוּרָה אוֹ קְלוּעָה בְּתוֹךְ שַׂעֲרוֹתָיו, אֲסוּרִין בַּהֲנָאָה. וְכֵן אִם הָיְתָה לוֹ שֵׁן תּוֹתֶבֶת, תִּקָּבֵר עִמּוֹ. אֲבָל נוֹי שֶׁאֵינוֹ מְחֻבָּר לְגוּפוֹ, מֻתָּר. וְכֵן נוֹי שֶׁאֵינוֹ כְּעֵין גּוּפוֹ, כְּגוֹן הַתַּכְשִׁיטִין וְהַבְּגָדִים, מֻתָּרִים בְּכָל עִנְיָן.

סִימָן קצח
הִלְכוֹת הוֹצָאַת הַמֵּת וְהַלְוָיָתוֹ וְצִדּוּק הַדִּין

א) אִם יֵשׁ מֵת בָּעִיר, כָּל בְּנֵי הָעִיר אֲסוּרִין בִּמְלָאכָה. וְאִם יֵשׁ בָּעִיר מְמֻנִּים לְהִתְעַסֵּק בַּמֵּת, אֵלּוּ שֶׁאֵינָן צְרִיכִין לְהִתְעַסֵּק בּוֹ, מֻתָּרִין בִּמְלָאכָה.

ב) בִּכְפָר קָטָן, אִם יֵשׁ שָׁם מֵת, אֵין שׁוֹאֲלִין בִּשְׁלוֹם זֶה לָזֶה, וּמִכָּל־שֶׁכֵּן שֶׁאֵין שׁוֹאֲלִין בִּשְׁלוֹם בְּבֵית הַקְּבָרוֹת, כְּשֶׁיֵּשׁ שָׁם מֵת, אֲפִלּוּ בְּעִיר גְּדוֹלָה. אֲבָל כְּשֶׁאֵין שָׁם מֵת, שׁוֹאֲלִין בְּרִחוּק אַרְבַּע אַמּוֹת מִן הַקְּבָרִים.

ג) אָסוּר לְהָלִין אֶת הַמֵּת, שֶׁנֶּאֱמַר, לֹא תָלִין וְגוֹ׳ כִּי קָבוֹר תִּקְבְּרֶנּוּ בַּיּוֹם הַהוּא. וְאִם מְלִינוֹ מִשּׁוּם כְּבוֹדוֹ לְהָבִיא לוֹ אָרוֹן וְתַכְרִיכִין אוֹ שֶׁיָּבוֹאוּ קְרוֹבָיו אוֹ סַפְדָּנִים, מֻתָּר, דְּלֹא אָסְרָה תוֹרָה אֶלָּא דֻמְיָא דְתָלוּי, שֶׁהוּא דֶרֶךְ בִּזָּיוֹן. אֲבָל לֹא כְּשֶׁהוּא לִכְבוֹדוֹ. וְכֵן אִם נִמְצָא אֵיזֶה מֵת וְלֹא נוֹדַע בְּבֵרוּר מִי הוּא, מֻתָּר לַהֲלִינוֹ עַד שֶׁיָּבוֹאוּ עֵדִים אוֹ אִשְׁתּוֹ לְהַכִּירוֹ.

ד) בְּכָל הַמֵּתִים, הַמְמַהֵר לְהוֹצִיאוֹ לִמְנוּחָתוֹ, הֲרֵי זֶה מְשֻׁבָּח. אֲבָל בְּאָבִיו וְאִמּוֹ שֶׁחַיָּב לְהַסְפִּידָם וּלְקוֹנֵן עֲלֵיהֶם הַרְבֵּה, הַמְמַהֵר לְהוֹצִיאָם, הֲרֵי זֶה מְגֻנֶּה, אֶלָּא אִם כֵּן הָיָה עֶרֶב שַׁבָּת אוֹ עֶרֶב יוֹם־טוֹב, אוֹ שֶׁהָיוּ גְשָׁמִים מְזַלְּפִים עַל הַמִּטָּה.

ה) אִם יֵשׁ שְׁנֵי מֵתִים, זֶה שֶׁמֵּת תְּחִלָּה מוֹצִיאִין אוֹתוֹ תְּחִלָּה, וְאַחַר

1. *Deuteronomy* 21:23.

12) One who is murdered by a non-Jew, even if he did not bleed at all, for example if he was strangled to death, he should be buried as he was found, in order to arouse wrath against the killer.

13) The deceased, whether gentile or Jew, and his shrouds, are forbidden to be used for any benefit. Also ornaments of the dead that are attached to his body, such as a wig that is tied to, or woven into his hair, are forbidden to be used for any benefit. Also, if he has an artificial tooth, it should be buried with him, but ornaments that are not attached to the body are permitted. Also ornaments that are not considered of the body, such as jewelry and clothing, may be used in any event.

Chapter 198

The Removal of the Deceased
The Funeral and Burial Services.

1) If a death occurs in town all the inhabitants are forbidden to do work. If there are people in the town appointed to take care of the dead, those whose services are not required, are permitted to work.

2) If a death occurs in a small village, the inhabitants should not exchange greetings; and certainly one should not extend greetings in a cemetery, when the deceased is there, awaiting burial. This applies even in a large city. But if there is no deceased awaiting burial, greetings may be exchanged at a distance of four *amos* from the graves.

3) It is forbidden to allow the deceased to remain overnight, as it is said, "You shall not let it remain etc., but you shall surely bury him the same day."[1] To let him remain for his honor, to arrange for a coffin, or shrouds, or to await the arrival of relatives, or eulogizers, is permitted.[2] For the Torah forbids delaying the burial only in such a case as when one is hanged, for it leads to disgrace of the dead, but not when it is for his honor. Likewise, if a corpse was found and his identity has not been established, it is permitted to keep the body until witnesses come, or until his wife comes to identify him.

4) With regard to other relatives who die, the sooner they are brought to their rest the more praiseworthy it is, but in the case of one's father or mother whom he is obligated to eulogize and to mourn abundantly, he who hastens to bring them to rest is despised, unless it is the day before Shabbos, or the day before Yom Tov, or if it is raining on the coffin.

5) If there are two persons awaiting burial, the one who died first should be

---

2. There are later *Poskim* who maintain that even for the honor of the deceased it is forbidden to delay the burial for more than twenty four hours. *Divrei Malkiel* Volume II 95, *Chamisha Mamuros* folio 129

כָּךְ אֶת הַשֵּׁנִי. וּלְאַחַר שֶׁקְּבָרוּ אֶת הָרִאשׁוֹן, אֵין עוֹמְדִין עָלָיו בְּשׁוּרָה, וְאֵין אוֹמְרִים עָלָיו בִּרְכַּת אֲבֵלִים וְתַנְחוּמֵי אֲבֵלִים, כְּדֵי שֶׁלֹּא לְעַכֵּב קְבוּרַת הַשֵּׁנִי. אִם רוֹצִים לְהָלִין אֶת הָרִאשׁוֹן מִפְּנֵי כְבוֹדוֹ, אֵין מְעַכְּבִין אֶת הַשֵּׁנִי בִּשְׁבִיל זֶה, אֶלָּא קוֹבְרִין אוֹתוֹ מִיָּד.

ו) אִם אֶחָד תַּלְמִיד־חָכָם וְאֶחָד עַם־הָאָרֶץ, מוֹצִיאִין אֶת הַתַּלְמִיד־חָכָם תְּחִלָּה, אֲפִלּוּ אִם עַם־הָאָרֶץ מֵת תְּחִלָּה. אִישׁ וְאִשָּׁה, מוֹצִיאִין אֶת הָאִשָּׁה תְּחִלָּה, אֲפִלּוּ אִם הָאִישׁ מֵת תְּחִלָּה, דִּכְתִיב, וַתָּמָת שָׁם מִרְיָם וַתִּקָּבֵר שָׁם, סָמוּךְ לְמִיתָה קְבוּרָה.

ז) כָּל הַמּוֹרִיד דְּמָעוֹת עַל אָדָם כָּשֵׁר שֶׁמֵּת, הַקָּדוֹשׁ־בָּרוּךְ־הוּא סוֹפְרָן וּמַנִּיחָן בְּבֵית גְּנָזָיו, וְיֵשׁ בָּזֶה תִּקּוּן לַעֲוֹן קֶרִי, וְהַצָּלָה לְבָנָיו הַקְּטַנִּים מִן הַמִּיתָה רַחֲמָנָא לִצְּלָן.

ח) הָרוֹאֶה אֶת הַמֵּת וְאֵינוֹ מְלַוֶּה אוֹתוֹ, עוֹבֵר מִשּׁוּם לוֹעֵג לָרָשׁ, וּבַר נִדּוּי הוּא. וּלְפָחוֹת יְלַוֵּהוּ אַרְבַּע אַמּוֹת. וּבְמָקוֹם שֶׁאֵינוֹ צָרִיךְ לְלַוּוֹתוֹ, מִכָּל מָקוֹם צָרִיךְ לַעֲמֹד בְּפָנָיו. וְלֹא לִפְנֵי הַמֵּת הוּא עוֹמֵד, אֶלָּא מִפְּנֵי הָעוֹסְקִים בּוֹ, שֶׁהֵם עֲסוּקִים בְּמִצְוָה. וְכֵן הַדִּין בְּכָל דְּבַר מִצְוָה שֶׁהָאָדָם עוֹסֵק בּוֹ, צְרִיכִין לַעֲמֹד בְּפָנָיו. וְכֵן הָיוּ בַּעֲלֵי אֻמָּנִיּוֹת עוֹמְדִין בִּפְנֵי מְבִיאֵי בִכּוּרִים.

ט) בִּזְמַן הַזֶּה מִסְתָמָא כָּל אִישׁ יִשְׂרָאֵל לָמַד מִקְרָא וּמִשְׁנָה. וְלָכֵן כְּשֶׁמֵּת, מְבַטְּלִין אֲפִלּוּ תַלְמוּד תּוֹרָה כְּדֵי לְלַוּוֹת אוֹתוֹ. אַךְ לְאִשָּׁה אוֹ לְתִינוֹק, נוֹהֲגִין לְהָקֵל, שֶׁלֹּא לְבַטֵּל תַּלְמוּד תּוֹרָה בִּשְׁבִיל הַלְוָיָה. וְתִינוֹקוֹת שֶׁל בֵּית רַבָּן, לְעוֹלָם אֵין מְבַטְּלִין כְּלָל, דַּאֲפִלּוּ לְבִנְיַן בֵּית־הַמִּקְדָּשׁ אֵין מְבַטְּלִין אוֹתָם.

י) צְרִיכִין לִזָּהֵר מְאֹד, לְבַל יִתְרָאוּ הַנָּשִׁים עִם הָאֲנָשִׁים כְּשֶׁהוֹלְכִין לְבֵית־הַקְּבָרוֹת וּמִכָּל־שֶׁכֵּן בַּחֲזָרָתָן, כִּי יֵשׁ, חַס וְשָׁלוֹם, סַכָּנָה בַּדָּבָר.

יא) נוֹשְׂאֵי הַמִּטָּה, אֵין לָהֶם לִנְעוֹל בְּרַגְלֵיהֶם סַנְדְּלִים, (שֶׁהֵם בְּלֹא עָקֵב, וִיכוֹלִין לִפּוֹל בְּקַל מֵעַל הָרֶגֶל). אֲבָל בְּמִנְעָלִים, אֵין קְפִידָא.

יב) כְּשֶׁמַּגִּיעִים עִם הַמֵּת לְעֵרֶךְ שְׁלֹשִׁים אַמָּה מִן הַקֶּבֶר יַעַמְדוּ עִמּוֹ כָּל אַרְבַּע אַמּוֹת, כְּדֵי שֶׁיַּעַמְדוּ שֶׁבַע פְּעָמִים כְּנֶגֶד שִׁבְעָה מַעֲמָדוֹת, שֶׁהֵם

taken out for burial first, and then the second. After burial of the first one, they should not arrange themselves in rows, nor should they say the *beracha* of mourners, or console the mourners, so as not to delay the burial of the second. If they wish to delay the burial of the first one, in order to do him honor, the burial of the second should not be delayed because of him, but he should be buried immediately.

6) If one of the deceased persons is a Torah scholar, and the other is an ignorant man, the Torah scholar should be taken out for burial first, even though the ignorant man died first. If there is a man and a woman, the woman should be buried first, even if the man died first, for it is written, "And Miriam died there, and was buried there,"[3] (which means) the burial was immediately after her death.

7) When a person sheds tears over the death of a virtuous person, the Holy One, blessed is He, counts the tears, and stores them in His treasure house.[4] This is also an atonement for the sin of pollution, and prevents the death of his small children, God forbid.

8) If a person sees the funeral procession, and fails to join the procession, he is guilty of *mocking the poor,* and is deserving of excommunication. He should accompany the dead at least a distance of four *Amos.* Even when one is exempt from accompanying the dead (as in paragraph 9), he, nevertheless, must rise before the procession. He does not rise in deference to the dead, but to those attending to the dead, for they are engaged in performing a mitzvah. This is the law with regard to every mitzvah in which a person is engaged. It is required that all must rise before him; and, therefore, workmen used to rise before those bringing *Bikkurim.*[5]

9) Nowadays, it is assumed that every Jew has studied [some] Scripture and some *Mishnah.* Therefore, when he dies, even the study of Torah must be interrupted in order to participate in his funeral procession. However, for a woman or a child, the custom is to be lenient, and not to interrupt Torah study in order to attend their funeral. School children, should never be interrupted from Torah study. Even for the purpose of building the *Beis Hamikdash,* they must not be interrupted.

10) Great care must be taken that men and women should not mingle together when going to the cemetery and especially upon returning from the cemetery, for this could be dangerous, God forbid.

11) The pallbearers should not wear sandals on their feet (the kind without heels that can easily slip off their feet), but they may wear shoes.

12) At approximately thirty *amos* from the grave the pallbearers should halt with the coffin every four *amos,* so that they can halt seven times. These seven stops are symbolic of the seven *maamados*[6] which are equal to the seven times that *vanity* is

3. Numbers 20:1
4. *Maseches Shabbos* 105b.
5. See *Maseches Bikurim* 3:3.
6. See Maseches Taanis 27b.

כְּנֶגֶד שִׁבְעָה הֲבָלִים שֶׁבְּקֹהֶלֶת, וְשִׁבְעָה מְדוֹרֵי גֵיהִנָּם, וְשִׁבְעָה דִינִים הַחוֹלְפִים עַל הַמֵּת, וְיֶשְׁנוֹ מְעַט שָׁם, שֶׁזּוֹהִי קְצָת כַּפָּרָה לַמֵּת. וּבְיוֹם שֶׁאֵין אוֹמְרִים תַּחֲנוּן, אֵין צְרִיכִין לְהַעֲמִיד, כִּי אָז אֵין הַדִּין קָשֶׁה.

יג) כְּשֶׁבָּאִים לְבֵית־הַקְּבָרוֹת, מִי שֶׁלֹּא רָאָה אֶת הַקְּבָרִים שְׁלֹשִׁים יוֹם, צָרִיךְ לְבָרֵךְ אֲשֶׁר יָצַר אֶתְכֶם בַּדִּין וְכוּ', וְאַחַר כָּךְ אוֹמְרִים אַתָּה גִּבּוֹר וְכוּ' עַד לְהַחֲיוֹת מֵתִים.

יד) אַחַר כָּךְ אוֹמְרִים צִדּוּק הַדִּין, הַצּוּר תָּמִים פָּעֳלוֹ וְכוּ'. אֶחָד מִן הָאֲבֵלִים מַתְחִיל. וְאִם אֵין שָׁם אָבֵל, הַמֻּפְלָא אֲשֶׁר שָׁם מַתְחִיל. וּבַיָּמִים שֶׁאֵין אוֹמְרִים בָּהֶם תַּחֲנוּן, אֵין אוֹמְרִים צִדּוּק הַדִּין. וְלָכֵן אֵין אוֹמְרִים בְּעֶרֶב שַׁבָּת לְאַחַר חֲצוֹת הַיּוֹם, וְכֵן בְּעֶרֶב יוֹם־טוֹב. אֲבָל בְּעֶרֶב רֹאשׁ־חֹדֶשׁ וְעֶרֶב חֲנֻכָּה וְעֶרֶב פּוּרִים, אוֹמְרִים גַּם לְאַחַר חֲצוֹת הַיּוֹם. וְעַל תַּלְמִיד־חָכָם אוֹמְרִים גַּם בְּלַ"ג בָּעֹמֶר, וּבַיָּמִים שֶׁלְּאַחַר רֹאשׁ־חֹדֶשׁ סִיוָן עַד שָׁבוּעוֹת, וּבְתִשְׁעָה בְּאָב, וּבְעֶרֶב רֹאשׁ־הַשָּׁנָה קֹדֶם חֲצוֹת הַיּוֹם.

טו) בַּלַּיְלָה, אֵין אוֹמְרִים לֹא צִדּוּק־הַדִּין וְלֹא קַדִּישׁ בְּבֵית־הַקְּבָרוֹת.

טז) עַל תִּינוֹק פָּחוֹת מִשְּׁלֹשִׁים יוֹם, אֵין אוֹמְרִים צִדּוּק־הַדִּין.

סִימָן קצט
דִּין הַקְּבוּרָה וּבֵית־הַקְּבָרוֹת

א) קְבוּרָה הָאֲמוּרָה בַּתּוֹרָה, הִיא שֶׁיִּתֵּן אֶת הַמֵּת בַּקַּרְקַע מַמָּשׁ. וּבְהַרְבֵּה מְקוֹמוֹת נוֹהֲגִין לְהַנִּיחַ אֶת הַמֵּת בְּאָרוֹן הֶעָשׂוּי מִנְּסָרִים וְכָךְ קוֹבְרִין אוֹתוֹ, דְּאִי אֶפְשָׁר שֶׁלֹּא יִהְיוּ נְקָבִים בְּאָרוֹן זֶה, וְסַגֵּי בְּהָכִי. וְיֵשׁ מְקוֹמוֹת שֶׁקּוֹבְרִין בְּלֹא אָרוֹן, אֶלָּא מַנִּיחִין אוֹתוֹ עַל הַקַּרְקַע מַמָּשׁ בְּלֹא דַף תַּחְתָּיו, אֶלָּא מִן הַצְּדָדִין נוֹתְנִים שְׁנֵי דַפִּים, וְעַל אֵלּוּ נוֹתְנִים עוֹד דַּף אֶחָד, כְּדֵי שֶׁלֹּא יִפּוֹל הֶעָפָר עַל גּוּף הַמֵּת, שֶׁזֶּה בִּזָּיוֹן לוֹ. וְיֵשׁ עוֹד מְקוֹמוֹת שֶׁקּוֹבְרִין שְׁאָר מֵתִים כָּךְ בְּלֹא אָרוֹן, וְרַק לְכֹהֲנִים וּבְכוֹרִים שֶׁהֵם חֲשׁוּבִים, עוֹשִׂים אָרוֹן. כְּשֶׁעוֹשִׂין אָרוֹן, יֵשׁ לִזָּהֵר בְּשִׁיּוּרֵי הַנְּסָרִים

7. See *Kitzur Shulchan Aruch* Chapter 22:8.

8. Excluding the day in which he last saw a grave and excluding the present day. (*Mishnah Berurah* 218:11) According to *Birkei Yosef*, if one sees graves from a window in his house that is near a cemetery, nevertheless when he enters the cemetery he still says the *berachah*. (See

mentioned in *Koheles,* and to the seven portals of Gehenom, and to the seven judgements that are passed upon the dead. They should wait a little at each stop, for the delay atones, somewhat, for the dead. On a day that *tachanun*[7] is not recited, these halts are not necessary, for on those days the judgement is not that severe.

13) Upon reaching the cemetery, those who have not seen graves in thirty days[8] must say the *berachah, "Asher Yatzar Esschem Baddin"* etc. ("Who has created you in judgement"), after which, is said: *"Attah Gibbor"* ("You are mighty") etc. until, *"Lehachayos meisim"* ("To restore the dead to life").

14) Afterwards, *Tzidduk Haddin* is recited, beginning with *"Hatzur Tamim Paalo"* etc. ("The Rock is perfect in His ways"). This prayer is begun by one of the mourners. If there is no mourner present, it is begun by the most distinguished person present. On days that *Tachanun* is not said, *Tzidduk Haddin* is not said. Therefore, it is not said on *erev* Shabbos, after midday, and not on *erev* Yom Tov. But on *erev Rosh Chodesh, erev* Chanukah, and *erev* Purim, it is said, even after midday. If the deceased is a Torah scholar, it is also said on *Lag Be'omer,* and on the days between *Rosh Chodesh Sivan* and *Shavuos,* on the ninth day of *Av,* and on *erev Rosh Hoshana* before noon.

15) At night, there is no recitation of *Tzidduk Haddin* or *Kaddish* at the cemetery.

16) For an infant less than thirty days old, *Tzidduk Haddin* is not recited.

Chapter 199

Laws of Burial And The Cemetery

1) The burial mentioned in the Torah, means actually placing the body in the earth.[1] In many places it is customary to place the deceased in a wooden coffin, and he is buried in that manner. Since it is impossible that such a coffin is without holes [at the bottom], it is sufficient to bury him is such a way. In some places the body is buried without a coffin, rather it is placed actually on the earth, without a board underneath, but with one board placed on each side, and one more board on top of them to prevent any dirt from falling upon the body, which would be a dishonor to him. In other communities, ordinary men are buried without a coffin, and only for *kohanim* and firstborn males, who are of special importance, are coffins made. When making a coffin, care must be taken that the remnants of the boards not be used

---

Shaarei Teshuvah Ohr Hachaim 224:9.) If one saw only the tombstones but not the graves, he can still recite the *berachah*. (*Halachah L'Moshe* 9.)

1. Cremation of the body is forbidden and those who ask to be cremated are considered transgressors and heretics as they deny the resurrection. Their ashes are forbidden to be interred in a Jewish cemetery and there should be no mourning over them. (See *Yora Deiah* 345:5)

שֶׁלֹּא לַעֲשׂוֹת מֵהֶם אֵיזֶה תַּשְׁמִישׁ, וְיֵשׁ לְהַסִּיק בָּהֶן תַּחַת הַכְּלִי שֶׁמְּחַמְּמִים אֶת הַמַּיִם לְטָהֳרָה. טוֹבֵי לֵבָב שֶׁהֶאֱכִילוּ עֲנִיִּים עַל שֻׁלְחָנָם, יֵשׁ לַעֲשׂוֹת לָהֶם אָרוֹן מִן הַשֻּׁלְחָן, כְּמוֹ שֶׁכָּתוּב, וְהָלַךְ לְפָנֶיךָ צִדְקֶךָ.

ב) מַנִּיחִין אֶת הַמֵּת עַל גַּבָּיו וּפָנָיו לְמַעְלָה, וּמִי שֶׁיֵּשׁ לוֹ עֲפַר אֶרֶץ־יִשְׂרָאֵל, מְפַזְּרִין קְצָת תַּחְתָּיו וּקְצָת עָלָיו, עַל שֵׁם, וְכִפֶּר אַדְמָתוֹ עַמּוֹ. וְהָעִקָּר לָתֵת עַל בְּרִית־הַקֹּדֶשׁ, וְגַם עַל פִּיו וְעַל עֵינָיו וְעַל כַּפָּיו.

ג) אֵין קוֹבְרִין אֶת הַמֵּתִים זֶה אֵצֶל זֶה, אֶלָּא אִם כֵּן הָיָה הַדֹּפֶן הַמַּפְסִיק בֵּינֵיהֶם יָכוֹל לַעֲמֹד בִּפְנֵי עַצְמוֹ, וְהוּא לְפָחוֹת שֵׁשׁ אֶצְבָּעוֹת. וְאִם אֶפְשָׁר, יֵשׁ לְהַחֲמִיר שֶׁיִּהְיוּ שִׁשָּׁה טְפָחִים בֵּין זֶה לָזֶה. אֲבָל הָאִישׁ אוֹ הָאִשָּׁה, נִקְבָּרִים עִם בְּנָם אוֹ בִתָּם, אוֹ עִם בֶּן אוֹ בַּת־בְּנָם וּבִתָּם. זֶה הַכְּלָל, כָּל קָטָן שֶׁיָּשֵׁן עִמּוֹ בְּחַיָּיו, נִקְבָּר עִמּוֹ בְּמוֹתוֹ. אֲבָל בֵּן גָּדוֹל עִם אָבִיו אוֹ בַּת גְּדוֹלָה עִם אִמָּהּ, אֵינָם נִקְבָּרִים יַחַד. וַאֲפִלּוּ בִּקְטַנִּים, דַּוְקָא לִקְבֹּר שְׁנֵיהֶם בְּבַת אַחַת, אֲבָל אִם כְּבָר נִקְבַּר אֶחָד, אָסוּר לִקְבֹּר אֶצְלוֹ אֶת הָאַחֵר.

ד) כְּבָר מְבֹאָר בְּסִימָן קסג סָעִיף ז, דְּתִינוֹק שֶׁמֵּת, מָלִין אוֹתוֹ אֵצֶל קִבְרוֹ וְקוֹרְאִין לוֹ שֵׁם, וְכֵן לְתִינֹקֶת גַּם כֵּן צְרִיכִין לִקְרוֹא לָהּ שֵׁם. וּצְרִיכִין לְהַזְהִיר אֶת הַקַּבְּרָנִים עַל זֶה.

ה) אֵין נוֹתְנִים שְׁנֵי אֲרוֹנוֹת זֶה עַל זֶה, אֶלָּא אִם יֵשׁ בֵּינֵיהֶן עָפָר שִׁשָּׁה טְפָחִים.

ו) אֵין קוֹבְרִים רָשָׁע אֵצֶל צַדִּיק, שֶׁנֶּאֱמַר, אַל תֶּאֱסֹף עִם חַטָּאִים נַפְשִׁי. וַאֲפִלּוּ רָשָׁע חָמוּר אֵצֶל רָשָׁע קַל, אֵין קוֹבְרִים. וְכֵן אֵין קוֹבְרִין צַדִּיק וְכָל־שֶׁכֵּן בֵּינוֹנִי וְכָשֵׁר אֵצֶל חָסִיד מֻפְלָג. שְׁנַיִם שֶׁהָיוּ שׂוֹנְאִים זֶה לָזֶה, אֵין לְקָבְרָם יַחַד, שֶׁגַּם בְּמוֹתָם אֵין לָהֶם מְנוּחָה יָחַד.

ז) הַמִּנְהָג לְהַקְפִּיד שֶׁלֹּא לִקַּח מָרָא אוֹ חֲצִינָא מִיַּד חֲבֵרוֹ כְּשֶׁקּוֹבְרִין אֶת הַמֵּת, אֶלָּא זֶה זוֹרְקוֹ מִיָּדוֹ וְזֶה נוֹטְלוֹ.

ח) לְאַחַר שֶׁהִנִּיחוּ אֶת הַמֵּת בַּקֶּבֶר, מְהַפְּכִין אֶת הַמִּטָּה שָׁלֹשׁ פְּעָמִים, כִּי מִטָּה בְּגִימַטְרִיָּא דִין, לְרַמֵּז שֶׁיִּתְהַפֵּךְ הַדִּין לְרַחֲמִים וְהַהֶסְפֵּד

2. *Isaiah* 58:8.

for any other purpose. They should be burned for fuel to heat the cauldron in which water is warmed for the ritual purification of the deceased. Benevolent people, who in their lifetime fed the poor at their table, should be buried in a coffin made of boards from the table, as it is written, "And your righteousness shall go before you."[2]

2) The body is laid on its back, its face upward. If the deceased had prepared earth from *Eretz Yisroel,* some of it is spread underneath his body and some on top of it, as it is said "And His land shall atone His people."[3] The main place to put this earth is on the "holy covenant" (of circumcision) and also on his mouth, his eyes, and his hands.

3) Two persons should not be buried close to each other, unless the wall that separates them can stand by itself, and is at least six finger breadths thick. If possible, it is best to be strict, so that the thickness of the separation is six *tefachim.* However, a man or woman may be buried with their son or daughter, or with their grandson or granddaughter. This is the rule: A minor who may sleep with him in his lifetime, may be buried with him after his death. However, an adult son with his father, or an adult daughter with her mother, should not be buried together. Even the burial of a minor [with his parent] is permissible only when they are buried at the same time, but if one of them had already been buried, it is forbidden to bury the other with him.

4) It has been explained in chapter 163:7, that if an uncircumcised infant dies, he should be circumcised at his grave, and a name given to him. A female infant should also be given a name; and the Burial Society must be informed of this law.

5) Two coffins must not be placed one atop the other, unless there is at least six *tefachim* of earth between them.

6) A wicked person should not be buried next to a righteous person, as it is said, "Do not gather my soul with sinners."[4] Even a very wicked man, should not be buried next to a less wicked man. Similarly, a righteous man should not be buried, and certainly a man of average piety and virtue, should not be buried next to a man who excelled in saintliness. Two people who hated one another should not be buried next to each other, for even in their death they will have no peace together.

7) One should be mindful of the custom not to take a shovel or a pick axe from the hand of another when burying the dead; rather the one who used it lays it down, and the other picks it up.

8) After the body is laid in the grave, the bier is turned over three times, for the numerical value of the word *mittah* (bed, bier) is the same as that of the word *Din* (judgement). This is an omen that the judgement will be turned into mercy, and the

---

3. *Deuteronomy* 32:43.
4. *Psalms* 26:9.

לְמָחוֹל. זֵכֶר לַדָּבָר, הָפַכְתָּ מִסְפְּדִי לְמָחוֹל לִי. וּבְיוֹם שֶׁאֵין אוֹמְרִים תַּחֲנוּן, אֵין עוֹשִׂין זֹאת.

ט) אִם יֵשׁ יָתוֹם בְּבֵית־הַקְּבָרוֹת, אֲזַי לְאַחַר הַקְּבוּרָה (אִם הוּא יוֹם), מַרְחִיקִין לְכָל־הַפָּחוֹת אַרְבַּע אַמּוֹת מֵהַקְּבָרִים, וְאוֹמְרִים אֶת הַמִּזְמוֹר לַמְנַצֵּחַ וְגוֹ׳ שִׁמְעוּ זֹאת וְגוֹ׳. וּבְיוֹם שֶׁאֵין אוֹמְרִים תַּחֲנוּן, אוֹמְרִים מִכְתָּם לְדָוִד וְגוֹ׳, וְהַיָּתוֹם אוֹמֵר קַדִּישׁ דְּהוּא עָתִיד לְאִתְחַדָּתָא, וְהַקָּהָל אוֹמְרִים עִמּוֹ עַד וִיקָרֵהּ. וְיֵשׁ מְקוֹמוֹת נוֹהֲגִין שֶׁגַּם הַקַּדִּישׁ אוֹמְרִים תְּחִלָּה קֹדֶם הַקְּבוּרָה לְאַחַר צִדּוּק־הַדִּין. וְיֵשׁ מְקוֹמוֹת, שֶׁגַּם צִדּוּק־הַדִּין אֵין אוֹמְרִים עַד לְאַחַר הַקְּבוּרָה.

י) נוֹהֲגִין שֶׁכְּשֶׁהוֹלְכִין מִבֵּית־הַקְּבָרוֹת, תּוֹלְשִׁין עֲשָׂבִים וּמַשְׁלִיכִין אַחֲרֵי גֵוָם וְאוֹמְרִים, זָכוּר כִּי עָפָר אֲנָחְנוּ. וְגַם הוּא רֶמֶז לִתְחִיַּת הַמֵּתִים, שֶׁיִּחְיוּ מֵעֲפָרָם, עַל דֶּרֶךְ, וְיָצִיצוּ מֵעִיר כְּעֵשֶׂב הָאָרֶץ. וִיכוֹלִין לַעֲשׂוֹת כֵּן גַּם בְּחֹל־הַמּוֹעֵד. וְרוֹחֲצִין יְדֵיהֶם. וְיֵשׁ רֶמֶז, שֶׁאֵין טֻמְאָה זֹאת נִטְהֶרֶת אֶלָּא בִּשְׁלֹשָׁה דְבָרִים אֵלּוּ, מַיִם וְאֵפֶר־פָּרָה וְאֵזוֹב. אֵין לִרְחוֹץ אֶת הַיָּדַיִם בְּנָהָר אֶלָּא מִכֶּלִי. וְאֵין לִטּוֹל אֶת הַכְּלִי מִיַּד מִי שֶׁרָחַץ, אֶלָּא זֶה מַעֲמִידוֹ וְזֶה נוֹטְלוֹ. וְאֵין לְנַגֵּב אֶת הַיָּדַיִם. יֵשׁ אוֹמְרִים, שֶׁיּוֹשְׁבִים שֶׁבַע פְּעָמִים, מִפְּנֵי שֶׁהָרוּחוֹת מְלַוּוֹת אוֹתוֹ, וְכָל זְמַן שֶׁיּוֹשְׁבִין, בּוֹרְחִין מִמֶּנּוּ. וּבִקְצָת מְקוֹמוֹת נוֹהֲגִין לֵישֵׁב רַק שָׁלֹשׁ פְּעָמִים לְאַחַר שֶׁרָחֲצוּ אֶת הַיָּדַיִם, וְאוֹמְרִים בְּכָל פַּעַם וִיהִי נֹעַם וְגוֹ׳. וְגַם כְּשֶׁנִּקְבַּר הַמֵּת בְּיוֹם־טוֹב, יְכוֹלִין לֵישֵׁב כָּךְ שָׁלֹשׁ פְּעָמִים כְּמוֹ בַּחֹל. וְנוֹהֲגִין לְהַקְפִּיד, אִם יִכָּנֵס אָדָם לְבֵיתוֹ קֹדֶם שֶׁיִּרְחַץ יָדָיו וְיֵשֵׁב. וּמִנְהַג אֲבוֹתֵינוּ, תּוֹרָה.

יא) אֵין מוֹלִיכִין אֶת הַמֵּת מֵעִיר שֶׁיֵּשׁ בָּהּ קְבָרוֹת לְעִיר אַחֶרֶת, מִשּׁוּם דַּהֲוֵי לֵהּ בִּזָּיוֹן לְטַלְטְלוֹ מִמָּקוֹם לְמָקוֹם, אֶלָּא מִחוּץ־לָאָרֶץ לְאֶרֶץ־יִשְׂרָאֵל אוֹ שֶׁמּוֹלִיכִין אוֹתוֹ לִמְקוֹם קִבְרוֹת אֲבוֹתָיו. וְכֵן אִם הוּא צִוָּה לְהוֹלִיכוֹ מִמָּקוֹם לְמָקוֹם, מֻתָּר.

יב) אָסוּר לִפְתֹּחַ קֶבֶר לְאַחַר שֶׁנִּסְתַּם הַגּוֹלֵל, דְּהַיְנוּ שֶׁכְּבָר נָתְנוּ עָפָר עַל כִּסּוּי הָאָרוֹן. אֲבָל כָּל זְמַן שֶׁלֹּא נָתְנוּ עָפָר, מֻתָּר לְפָתְחוֹ מִשּׁוּם אֵיזֶה

---

5. *Psalms* 30:12.
6. *Psalms* 49.
7. *Psalms* 16.

mourning into joy. The verse alludes to this, "You turned my mourning into dancing."[5] On a day when *Tachanun* is not said, this is not done.

9) If an orphan is present in the cemetery, then, after the burial, (if it is still day) the people should step away a distance of at least four *amos* from the graves and recite the psalm, "*Lamenatzaich*" ("To the chief musician") etc. "*Shimu Zos*" ("Hear this") etc.[6] On a day when *Tachanun* is not said, "*Michtam Le'Dovid*" etc. is said.[7] The orphan then says the *Kaddish*: "*D'Hu Assid Lehischadetah*" ("That he will renew"), and those present recite with him up to "*Vikarei*" (And may this happen). In some communities it is customary that the *Kaddish* is recited first before the burial, following *Tzidduk Haddin*. There are communities where even *Tzidduk Haddin* is not said until after the burial.

10) It is customary, upon leaving the cemetery to pluck some grass[8] and throw it behind your back and say, "He is mindful that we are dust."[9] This is also symbolic of the resurrection of the dead, who will emerge living from their dust, as it is said, "And may they blossom out of the city like grass of the earth."[10] This may also be done on *Chol Hamoed*.[11] They should then wash their hands. There is a symbolic allusion to this practice, for this impurity (death) can be purified only by means of these three things: water, ashes of the *Red Cow*, and the hyssop. This handwashing should not be done in a river, but with water poured from a vessel. You should not take the vessel from the hand of another who washed; rather the first one puts it down and the others take it, and the hands should not be wiped. Some say that one should sit down seven times, because of the evil spirits that accompany him, and when one sits, they flee. In some places they are accustomed to sit only three times after they wash their hands, and they say each time: "*Vehi Noam*" etc. [And may the pleasantness (of our master etc.)][12] Even when the burial takes place on Yom Tov they can sit three times, as on the weekdays. It is our custom to be mindful that a person should not enter his house before washing his hands and sitting down. The customs of our ancestors have the validity of Torah law.

11) The deceased should not be brought from a city where there is a cemetery to another city, because it is degrading to transport him from place to place, unless it is from the diaspora to *Eretz Yisroel*, or if they are transporting him to the burial ground of his ancestors. Also, if he had instructed that he should be brought from place to place, it is permissible to do so.

12) It is forbidden to open a grave after it was closed, that is after earth had been placed over the lid of the coffin; but as long as earth has not been placed there,

---

8. According to *Shulchan Aruch*, 547:12, this should not be done when a burial takes place on *Chol Hamoed*.
9. *Psalms* 103:14.
10. *Psalms* 72:16.
11. See note 8.
12. *Psalms* 90:17.

דָּבָר. וְאִם מֵחֲמַת אֵיזֶה דָבָר צְרִיכִין לְפַנּוֹת אֶת הַמֵּת מִקִּבְרוֹ, יַעֲשׂוּ שְׁאֵלַת חָכָם.

יג) אִם חָפְרוּ קֶבֶר, לֹא יַנִּיחוּהוּ פָּתוּחַ בַּלַּיְלָה, כִּי יֵשׁ סַכָּנָה בַּדָּבָר. וְאִם אֵין פְּנַאי לִקְבֹּר אֶת הַמֵּת, עַד לְמָחָר, יְמַלְאוּ אֶת הַקֶּבֶר בֶּעָפָר.

יד) אָסוּר לִדְרוֹךְ עַל גַּבֵּי קְבָרִים, מִשּׁוּם דְּיֵשׁ אוֹמְרִים, דְּאָסוּר בַּהֲנָאָה. וּמִכָּל מָקוֹם אִם צָרִיךְ לְאֵיזֶה קֶבֶר וְאֵין לוֹ דֶרֶךְ אֶלָּא אִם כֵּן יִדְרוֹךְ עַל גַּבֵּי קְבָרִים, מֻתָּר.

טו) לֹא יֵלֵךְ בְּבֵית־הַקְּבָרוֹת אוֹ בְּתוֹךְ אַרְבַּע אַמּוֹת שֶׁל מֵת וְכֵן בְּכָל הַחֶדֶר שֶׁהַמֵּת הוּא שָׁם כְּשֶׁתְּפִלִּין בְּרֹאשׁוֹ אוֹ צִיצִית בְּבִגְדוֹ, מִשּׁוּם לוֹעֵג לָרָשׁ. וְאִם הֵם מְכֻסִּים, מֻתָּר. וְכֵן לֹא יִתְפַּלֵּל שָׁם וְלֹא יֹאמַר שָׁם מִזְמוֹרִים, אֶלָּא מַה שֶּׁהוּא לִכְבוֹד הַמֵּת.

טז) בֵּית־הַקְּבָרוֹת, אֵין נוֹהֲגִין בּוֹ קַלּוּת־רֹאשׁ, מִפְּנֵי כְּבוֹדָן שֶׁל הַמֵּתִים, כְּגוֹן לֶאֱכֹל וְלִשְׁתּוֹת שָׁם אוֹ לְהִפָּנוֹת שָׁם. וְאֵין מַרְעִין שָׁם בְּהֵמוֹת, וְלֹא יְלַקֵּט מִמֶּנּוּ עֲשָׂבִים. אֲבָל אִילָנוֹת הַנְּטוּעִין בְּבֵית־הַקְּבָרוֹת וְאֵינָן עַל הַקְּבָרִים, מֻתָּר לְלַקֵּט פֵּרוֹתֵיהֶן.

יז) יֵשׁ מְקוֹמוֹת שֶׁנּוֹהֲגִין שֶׁאֵין מַצִּיבִין מַצֵּבָה עַד לְאַחַר שְׁנֵים עָשָׂר חֹדֶשׁ, מִשּׁוּם דְּהַמַּצֵּבָה נִרְאֵית לַחֲשִׁיבוּתָא, וּבְתוֹךְ שְׁנֵים עָשָׂר חֹדֶשׁ יֵשׁ לוֹ צַעַר. וְעוֹד, טַעַם הַמַּצֵּבָה, שֶׁלֹּא יִשָּׁכַח מִן הַלֵּב, וְהַמֵּת אֵינוֹ נִשְׁכָּח, עַד לְאַחַר שְׁנֵים עָשָׂר חֹדֶשׁ. וְיֵשׁ מְקוֹמוֹת שֶׁאֵין מְדַקְדְּקִין בָּזֶה.

סִימָן ר
דִּין הַקְּבוּרָה בְּיוֹם־טוֹב

א) מֵת הַמֻּטָּל לְקָבְרוֹ בְּיוֹם־טוֹב, בַּיּוֹם הָרִאשׁוֹן לֹא יִתְעַסְּקוּ בוֹ יִשְׂרָאֵל. אֲפִלּוּ אִם אִי אֶפְשָׁר לְקָבְרוֹ עַל יְדֵי גוֹיִם וְיֵשׁ חֲשַׁשׁ שֶׁמָּא יַסְרִיחַ עַד לְמָחָר, מִכָּל מָקוֹם לֹא יִקְבְּרוּהוּ יִשְׂרָאֵל בַּיּוֹם הָרִאשׁוֹן. אַךְ אִם

13. This applies even within four *amos* of the entrance to the cemetery unless there is a separation between the entrance and the actual cemetery. According to *Magin Avrohom* it is

it is permitted to open it for any reason. If for any reason it becomes necessary to remove a body from its grave, a *Poseik* should be consulted.

13) If a grave has been dug, it should not be left open overnight, because there is danger in this. If there is no time to bury the deceased until the following day, the grave must be refilled with earth.

14) It is forbidden to step upon graves because some *Poskim* maintain that it is forbidden to derive benefit from them. However, if you have to visit a certain grave, and have no way of getting there unless you step upon other graves, it is permitted.

15) You may not go to the cemetery,[13] or within four *amos* of the deceased, or in a room where the deceased lies while wearing *Tefillin* upon your head or *tzitzit* in your garment, for it seems as if you are "mocking the poor."[14] But if they[15] are covered, it is permitted. Likewise, you are not allowed to pray there,[16] or to recite Psalms, unless it is in honor of the dead.

16) In the cemetery, you should not indulge in levity, out of respect to the dead. This means you may not eat or drink there, or respond to nature's call. And you may not allow cattle to graze there, and not gather the vegetation that grows there. However, if trees are planted in a cemetery and do not grow over the graves, it is permitted to pick their fruit.

17) It is customary in some communities not to put up a tombstone until after twelve months, because a tombstone is a mark of distinction, and within these twelve months the deceased is in grief. Also, because the reason for putting up a tombstone is so that the dead not be forgotten, and, as a rule, the deceased is not forgotten until after twelve months. There are communities where no heed is paid to this custom.

Chapter 200

Laws of Burial on Yom Tov

1) If the deceased awaits burial on the first day of (Yom Tov,) a Jew is not allowed to bury him. Even if it is impossible to have it done by non-Jews, and there is concern that decay might set in before the next day, nevertheless, a Jew may not

---

forbidden to wear them in the cemetery itself, even if you are more than four *amos* away from a grave. Others are lenient in their respect.

14. *Poor* refers to their inabilty to perform *mitzvos*. (See *Mishnah Berurah* 45:1.) This applies even regarding the grave of a child for his soul may be that of a great person. This does not apply to a grave of a woman for even in her lifetime she was poor (exempt) from *mitzvos*. *Mishnah Berurah* 23:5.

15. If the *Tefillin* are covered. The straps of the *Tefillin* must also be covered.

16. It is also forbidden to recite the *Krias Shema*. *Mishnah Berurah* 71:15, 17.

אֶפְשָׁר, לְקָבְרוֹ עַל יְדֵי גוֹיִם, דְּהַיְנוּ שֶׁהַגּוֹיִם יַעֲשׂוּ אֶת הַקֶּבֶר וְיַחְתְּכוּ אֶת הַדַּפִּין שֶׁל עֵץ, אוֹ יַעֲשׂוּ אָרוֹן בְּמָקוֹם שֶׁנָּהֲגוּ, וְגַם יִתְפְּרוּ אֶת הַתַּכְרִיכִין אִם צְרִיכִין. אֲבָל לְהַלְבִּישׁוֹ וּלְחַמֵּם מַיִם וּלְטַהֲרוֹ וּלְהוֹצִיאוֹ וּלְשׂוּמוֹ בַּקֶּבֶר, מֻתָּר עַל יְדֵי יִשְׂרָאֵל. וְהַכִּסּוּי בְּעָפָר, יַעֲשׂוּ גַּם כֵּן עַל יְדֵי גוֹיִם. וְאִם אֶפְשָׁר, יֵשׁ לִזָּהֵר לְטַהֲרוֹ בְּלֹא בֶּגֶד, שֶׁלֹּא יָבוֹאוּ לִידֵי סְחִיטָה.

ב) יֵשׁ אוֹמְרִים, דְּאִם אֶפְשָׁר לַעֲשׂוֹת עַל יְדֵי גוֹיִם, כְּמוֹ שֶׁנִּתְבָּאֵר, אָסוּר לְהַשְׁהוֹתוֹ עַד לְמָחָר כְּדֵי שֶׁיִּתְעַסְּקוּ בּוֹ יִשְׂרָאֵל. וַאֲפִלּוּ מֵת הַיּוֹם וִיכוֹלִין לְהַשְׁהוֹתוֹ עַד לְמָחָר, שֶׁלֹּא יַסְרִיחַ, מִכָּל מָקוֹם יִקְבְּרוּהוּ הַיּוֹם עַל יְדֵי גוֹיִם. אַךְ יֶלֶד שֶׁמֵּת, אַף־עַל־פִּי שֶׁחַי יוֹתֵר מִשְּׁלֹשִׁים יוֹם שֶׁיָּדוּעַ שֶׁאֵינוֹ נֵפֶל, מִכָּל מָקוֹם אִם הָעֵת קָרָה וְאֵין בִּזָּיוֹן לְהַשְׁהוֹתוֹ, דְּלָא אִשְׁתְּהֵי, אֵין לְקָבְרוֹ בְּיוֹם־טוֹב רִאשׁוֹן, אֶלָּא מַשְׁהִינָן לֵהּ עַד יוֹם־טוֹב שֵׁנִי. וְיֵשׁ אוֹמְרִים, דְּגַם בְּגָדוֹל אִי לָא אִשְׁתְּהֵי, מַשְׁהִינָן לֵהּ עַד יוֹם־טוֹב שֵׁנִי. וּבְמָקוֹם שֶׁאֵין מִנְהָג יָדוּעַ, נִרְאֶה דְּיֵשׁ לִנְהֹג כֵּן.

ג) בְּיוֹם שֵׁנִי שֶׁל יוֹם־טוֹב, וַאֲפִלּוּ שֶׁל רֹאשׁ־הַשָּׁנָה, אִם אֶפְשָׁר לַעֲשׂוֹת בְּלִי שִׁהוּי עַל יְדֵי גוֹיִם דְּבָרִים הַנִּזְכָּרִים לְעֵיל, יַעֲשׂוּ עַל יְדֵי גוֹיִם, וּשְׁאָר הַדְּבָרִים יַעֲשׂוּ יִשְׂרְאֵלִים, כְּמוֹ שֶׁנִּתְבָּאֵר לְעֵיל. וִיכוֹלִין לְטַהֲרוֹ גַּם עַל יְדֵי בְּגָדִים וּסְדִינִים, רַק שֶׁיִּזָּהֲרוּ שֶׁלֹּא לַעֲשׂוֹת סְחִיטָה בְּיָדַיִם. וְאִם אִי אֶפְשָׁר עַל יְדֵי גוֹיִם, יִתְעַסְּקוּ בּוֹ יִשְׂרָאֵל לְכָל מַה שֶּׁצָּרִיךְ כְּדַרְכָּם בַּחֹל, כִּי יוֹם־טוֹב שֵׁנִי לְגַבֵּי מֵת, כַּחֹל שַׁוְיוּהוּ רַבָּנָן. וּמִכָּל מָקוֹם אִם יֵשׁ בַּמָּקוֹם הַהוּא מִי שֶׁהֵכִין לְעַצְמוֹ תַּכְרִיכִין, יִקְחוּ אוֹתָן הַמְתֻקָּנִים, שֶׁלֹּא יִצְטָרְכוּ לִתְפֹּר. וְהָא דְּמֻתָּרִין לְהִתְעַסֵּק בּוֹ, דַּוְקָא כְּשֶׁרוֹצִין לְקָבְרוֹ בּוֹ בַּיּוֹם. אֲבָל אִם אֵין רוֹצִין לְקָבְרוֹ בּוֹ בַּיּוֹם, אֵין עוֹשִׂין בּוֹ שׁוּם דָּבָר. וַאֲפִלּוּ בְּטִלְטוּל, אָסוּר.

ד) הָא דְּשַׁוְיוּהוּ רַבָּנָן יוֹם־טוֹב שֵׁנִי לְגַבֵּי מֵת כַּחֹל, זֶהוּ מִפְּנֵי כְּבוֹדוֹ שֶׁל מֵת, שֶׁלֹּא יְהֵא מֻטָּל בְּבִזָּיוֹן. אֲבָל לַעֲשׂוֹת שְׁאָר דָּבָר, אָסוּר. וְלָכֵן אָסוּר לִקְצֹץ עִם בַּעַל הַחֲנוּת דְּמֵי הַפִּשְׁתָּן שֶׁלּוֹקְחִין לְתַכְרִיכִין, אִם לֹא כְּשֶׁאִי אֶפְשָׁר בְּעִנְיָן אַחֵר, כְּגוֹן שֶׁלּוֹקְחִין מִגּוֹי. וְהַקַּבְּרָנִים אֲסוּרִין לִקַּח שְׂכַר קַבְּרָנוּת בְּיוֹם־טוֹב, כִּי שְׂכַר שַׁבָּת וּשְׂכַר יוֹם־טוֹב, אָסוּר. וְאִם אֵינָם

1. Many earlier *poskim* (*Rishonim*) disagree with this ruling. They maintain that since the major part of the burial will be done through non-Jews, it is best to have them do everything. This is also the opinion of *Radvaz* and the *Gra*. See *Mishnah Berurah* 526:12.

bury him on the first day of Yom Tov. But if it is possible to have non-Jews bury him, that is to have non-Jews dig the grave, and cut the wooden planks, or make the coffin, where it is customary, and sew the shrouds if necessary; then dressing him, heating the water, washing him, removing him, and placing him into the grave, are permitted to be done by a Jew.[1] Covering him with earth must also be done only by non-Jews. If possible, care should be taken to cleanse and purify him without using a cloth, in order not to wring out the water.

2) Some *Poskim* say, if it is possible to have the burial performed by non-Jews, as stated above, it is forbidden to keep the body till the next day in order that Jews may attend to it. And even if he died that day, and his body could be kept till the next day without decay setting in, nevertheless, he should be buried that day by non-Jews. In the case of an infant who died, even if he lived for more than thirty days, whereby we know that he is not an aborted fetus, nonetheless, if the weather is cold and it is not a dishonor to keep him, as he has not become malodorous, he should not be buried on the first day of Yom Tov, but should be kept until the second day of Yom Tov. Some say, even in the case of an adult, if he has not become malodorous, his burial should be delayed until the second day of Yom Tov. In a place where there is no fixed custom, it is proper to follow the latter opinion.

3) On the second day of Yom Tov, even the second day of *Rosh Hoshana*, if it is possible to accomplish the above mentioned things without delay through non-Jews. they should be done by non-Jews. The other things should be done by Jews, as was previously stated. The purification may be performed with cloths and sheets, but care must be taken not to wring the water out of them directly. If it is impossible to have those other things done by non-Jews, Jews may attend to all his needs as though it were a weekday, because the second day of *Yom Tov*, with reference to the dead, was regarded by the Sages as a weekday. Nevertheless, if someone in that area had previously prepared shrouds for themselves, those shrouds should be used in order to avoid the need of sewing. It is permitted to attend his needs only when they intend to bury him on that day. But if they do not intend to bury him on that day, no preparations should be made for his burial; and it is even forbidden to handle the body.

4) The Sages considered the second day of Yom Tov as a weekday, with regard to the dead in order to honor the dead and not permit him to lie in disgrace. However, to do anything unconnected to his burial is forbidden. Therefore, it is forbidden to negotiate with the shopkeeper about the price of linen for the shrouds, unless it is impossible to obtain it otherwise, as when it can be bought from a non-Jew. Jewish gravediggers are forbidden to accept renumeration for their work on a Yom Tov, because wages for work done on Shabbos or Yom Tov are forbidden. If they refuse to work without pay, they may be paid, but they will have to face the

---

Please note *Igros Moshe, Orach Chaim,* Responsa 76. In America, one should not make a funeral on the second day of Yom Tov. One must not do anything without consultation with a competent Rav.

רוֹצִים לַעֲשׂוֹת בְּחִנָּם, יִתְּנוּ לָהֶם שְׂכָרָם, וְהֵם עֲתִידִים לִתֵּן אֶת הַדִּין. וְאַנְשֵׁי חֶבְרָא קַדִּישָׁא, בְּעַד הַקַּרְקַע לֹא יִקְחוּ מָעוֹת, רַק מַשְׁכּוֹנוֹת בְּלִי קְצִיצַת דָּמִים.

ה) אִם אֵין בְּעִירוֹ בֵּית־קְבָרוֹת יִשְׂרָאֵל, אַף־עַל־פִּי שֶׁיְּכוֹלִין לִקְבֹּר שָׁם זֶה הַמֵּת, מִכָּל מָקוֹם מֻתָּר לְהוֹלִיכוֹ לְעִיר אַחֶרֶת, בְּיוֹם־טוֹב רִאשׁוֹן עַל יְדֵי גוֹי, וּבְיוֹם־טוֹב שֵׁנִי גַּם עַל יְדֵי יִשְׂרָאֵל, לְקָבְרוֹ בְּקִבְרוֹת יִשְׂרָאֵל. אֲבָל אִם לֹא יִקְבְּרוּהוּ הַיּוֹם, אָסוּר לְיִשְׂרָאֵל לְהוֹלִיכוֹ בְּיוֹם־טוֹב לְקָבְרוֹ לְאַחַר יוֹם־טוֹב.

ו) מֻתָּר לְלַווֹת אֶת הַמֵּת בְּיוֹם־טוֹב רִאשׁוֹן בְּתוֹךְ הַתְּחוּם, וּבְיוֹם־טוֹב שֵׁנִי אֲפִלּוּ חוּץ לַתְּחוּם, וּמֻתָּרִין גַּם כֵּן לַחֲזוֹר לְבֵיתָם בּוֹ בַּיּוֹם. אֲבָל אָסוּר לִרְכֹּב עַל גַּבֵּי בְהֵמָה כְּדֵי לְלַווֹת אֶת הַמֵּת בְּיוֹם־טוֹב, אֲפִלּוּ בְּיוֹם־טוֹב שֵׁנִי, וַאֲפִלּוּ הָאֲבֵלִים. אֲבָל הַקַּבְּרָנִים, אִם אִי אֶפְשָׁר לָהֶם לֵילֵךְ בְּרַגְלֵיהֶם, מֻתָּרִים לִרְכֹּב בְּיוֹם־טוֹב שֵׁנִי. וּמִכָּל מָקוֹם לֹא יִרְכְּבוּ בְּתוֹךְ הָעִיר.

ז) מֵת בְּלֵיל יוֹם־טוֹב שֵׁנִי, דְּמִתְעַסְּקִין בּוֹ יִשְׂרָאֵל אִם אֵין גּוֹי, מַשְׁכִּימִין עֲשָׂרָה בְּנֵי אָדָם, וְקוֹבְרִים אוֹתוֹ בְּשָׁעָה שֶׁשְּׁלִיחַ־הַצִּבּוּר אוֹמֵר פִּיּוּטִים. וְאִם הוּא אָדָם חָשׁוּב שֶׁרַבִּים צְרִיכִין לְלַווֹתוֹ, קוֹבְרִין אוֹתוֹ לְאַחַר הַיְּצִיאָה מִבֵּית־הַכְּנֶסֶת קֹדֶם הָאֲכִילָה, דְּאִיתָא בַּמִּדְרָשׁ, לֹא תֹאכְלוּ עַל הַדָּם, שֶׁאָסוּר לֶאֱכֹל סְעוּדָה קְבוּעָה קֹדֶם שֶׁנִּקְבַּר הַמֵּת. וְאִם אִי אֶפְשָׁר לְהָכִין כָּל צָרְכֵי הַקְּבוּרָה עַד הַזְּמַן הַהוּא, קוֹבְרִין אוֹתוֹ לְאַחַר הָאֲכִילָה.

ח) יֶלֶד שֶׁמֵּת לְאַחַר שְׁלֹשִׁים יוֹם, שֶׁיָּדוּעַ שֶׁאֵינוֹ נֵפֶל, דִּינוֹ כְּמוֹ שְׁאָר מֵת. אַךְ אִם הוּא זָכָר וּמֵחֲמַת אֵיזוֹ סִבָּה עֲדַיִן לֹא נִמּוֹל, אַף־עַל־גַּב דְּאִשְׁתְּהֵי, אֵין קוֹבְרִים אוֹתוֹ בְּיוֹם־טוֹב רִאשׁוֹן, מִשּׁוּם דִּצְרִיכִין לְהָסִיר עָרְלָתוֹ, וְאֵין לַעֲשׂוֹת זֹאת עַל יְדֵי גוֹי, אֶלָּא מַשְׁהִינָן לֵהּ עַד יוֹם־טוֹב שֵׁנִי, דְּמֻתָּר לַהֲלִינוֹ לִכְבוֹדוֹ, וּבְיוֹם־טוֹב שֵׁנִי מְסִירִין עָרְלָתוֹ וְקוֹבְרִין אוֹתוֹ.

ט) תִּינוֹק שֶׁמֵּת כְּשֶׁהוּא סְפֵק נֵפֶל, אִי לָא אִשְׁתְּהֵי, אֵין קוֹבְרִין אוֹתוֹ בְּיוֹם־טוֹב רִאשׁוֹן אֲפִלּוּ עַל יְדֵי גוֹי, וּמַשְׁהִינָן לֵהּ עַד יוֹם־טוֹב שֵׁנִי, וְקוֹבְרִין אוֹתוֹ עַל יְדֵי גוֹי וְלֹא עַל יְדֵי יִשְׂרָאֵל. וְאִי אִשְׁתְּהֵי, קוֹבְרִין אוֹתוֹ

judgement of the Heavenly Court. The Burial Society should not take money for the grave on Yom Tov, but they may accept pledges (collateral) without stipulating the price of the grave.

5) If there is no Jewish cemetery in town, although there is a place where this deceased can be buried, nevertheless, it is permitted to take him to another city on the first day of Yom Tov, by a non-Jew, and on the second day of Yom Tov, even by a Jew, in order to bury him in a Jewish cemetery. But if the burial will not take place on that day, it is forbidden for a Jew to move him on Yom Tov in order to bury him after Yom Tov.

6) It is permitted to accompany the deceased within the *t'chum,* on the first day of Yom Tov, and on the second day of Yom Tov, even outside the *t'chum.* It is also permitted to return home on that very day. However, it is forbidden to ride upon an animal in order to accompany the dead on Yom Tov, even on the second day of Yom Tov. Even the mourners are not permitted. If it is impossible for the gravediggers to go by foot, they are permitted to ride on an animal on the second day of Yom Tov. Nevertheless, they should not ride in the city.

7) If one dies on the night of the second day of Yom Tov, when it is permitted for Jews to attend to the burial if there are no non-Jews to do so, ten men should rise in the morning and bury him at the time the *Chazan* recites the *Piyutim* [festival hymns]. If he was a distinguished person, so that a multitude of people are obligated to accompany him, he should be buried after people leave the synagogue before the meal is eaten, for the Midrash states, "(It is written) 'You shall not eat with the blood' (which signifies) that it is forbidden to eat a regular meal before the deceased is buried." If it is impossible to make all the preparations for the burial by that time, he should be buried after the meal.

8) If an infant dies after thirty days, so that it is certain that it is not an abortive fetus, the same law applies to him as to an adult. However, if he is a male, and for some reason he was not yet circumcised, even though decay is setting in, he should not be buried on the first day of Yom Tov, because his foreskin must be removed, (as stated above, Chapter 163:7) and that cannot be done by a non-Jew. Rather it should be held over until the second day of Yom Tov, for it is permitted to delay [the burial] for his honor; and on the second day, his foreskin should be removed, and he should be buried.

9) If an infant dies and there is doubt if it is an abortive fetus, if decay has not yet set in, it may not be buried on the first day of Yom Tov, even by a non-Jew, and it is held over till the second day of Yom Tov, and then buried by a non-Jew, and not by a Jew. If decay has set in, it should be buried on the first day of Yom Tov by a non-Jew. If it died on the second day of Yom Tov, it should be buried on that very day by a non-Jew and not by a Jew. If he is a male, and was not yet circumcised,

בְּיוֹם־טוֹב רִאשׁוֹן עַל יְדֵי גוֹי. וְאִם מֵת בְּיוֹם־טוֹב שֵׁנִי, קוֹבְרִין אוֹתוֹ בּוֹ בַּיּוֹם עַל יְדֵי גוֹי וְלֹא עַל יְדֵי יִשְׂרָאֵל. אִם הוּא זָכָר וַעֲדַיִן לֹא נִמּוֹל, אֲפִלּוּ אִשְׁתָּהֵי, אֵין קוֹבְרִין אוֹתוֹ אֲפִלּוּ בְּיוֹם־טוֹב שֵׁנִי, אֲפִלּוּ עַל יְדֵי גוֹי, אֶלָּא מַשְׁהֵינָן לֵהּ עַד לְאַחַר יוֹם־טוֹב, וּמְסִירִין עָרְלָתוֹ וְקוֹבְרִין אוֹתוֹ.

י) בְּשַׁבָּת וּבְיוֹם־הַכִּפּוּרִים, לֹא יִתְעַסְּקוּ בַּמֵּת כְּלָל, אֲפִלּוּ עַל יְדֵי גוֹי.

יא) בְּחֹל־הַמּוֹעֵד, אֵין לְהוֹצִיא אֶת הַמֵּת לְבֵית־הַקְּבָרוֹת, עַד שֶׁהַקֶּבֶר מְתֻקָּן, שֶׁלֹּא יִצְטָרְכוּ לְהַעֲמִיד אֶת הַמִּטָּה.

סִימָן רא

דִּין הַמְאַבֵּד עַצְמוֹ לָדַעַת וּשְׁאָר רָשָׁע שֶׁמֵּת

א) הַמְאַבֵּד עַצְמוֹ לָדַעַת, הוּא רָשָׁע שֶׁאֵין לְמַעְלָה מִמֶּנּוּ, שֶׁנֶּאֱמַר, וְאַךְ אֶת־ דִּמְכֶם לְנַפְשֹׁתֵיכֶם אֶדְרשׁ. וּבִשְׁבִיל יָחִיד, נִבְרָא הָעוֹלָם. וְכָל הַמְאַבֵּד נֶפֶשׁ אַחַת מִיִּשְׂרָאֵל, מְאַבֵּד עוֹלָם מָלֵא. וְלָכֵן אֵין מִתְעַסְּקִין עִמּוֹ לְכָל דָּבָר. לֹא קוֹרְעִין וְלֹא מִתְאַבְּלִין עָלָיו, וְאֵין מַסְפִּידִין אוֹתוֹ. אֲבָל קוֹבְרִין אוֹתוֹ וּמְטַהֲרִין אוֹתוֹ, וּמַלְבִּישִׁין אוֹתוֹ תַּכְרִיכִין. כְּלָלוֹ שֶׁל דָּבָר, כֹּל שֶׁהוּא מִשּׁוּם כְּבוֹד הַחַיִּים, עוֹשִׂין לוֹ.

ב) מִסְתָמָא, לָא מַחֲזְקִינָן אֱנָשֵׁי בְּרַשִׁיעֵי. וְלָכֵן אִם נִמְצָא אֶחָד חָנוּק אוֹ תָלוּי וְכַדּוֹמֶה, כֹּל שֶׁאֶפְשָׁר לִתְלוֹת שֶׁמָּא אַחֵר עָשָׂה לוֹ זֹאת, לָא תָלֵינָן בֵּהּ.

ג) קָטָן הַמְאַבֵּד אֶת עַצְמוֹ, חָשׁוּב כְּשֶׁלֹּא לָדַעַת. וְכֵן גָּדוֹל אִם נִרְאֶה שֶׁעָשָׂה הַדָּבָר מֵחֲמַת רוּחַ רָעָה אוֹ שִׁגָּעוֹן וְכַדּוֹמֶה, הֲוֵי שֶׁלֹּא לָדַעַת. וְכֵן אִם עָשָׂה אֶת הַדָּבָר מֵחֲמַת אֹנֶס, שֶׁהָיָה מִתְיָרֵא מֵעִנּוּיִים קָשִׁים, כְּמוֹ שָׁאוּל שֶׁהָיָה מִתְיָרֵא שֶׁמָּא יַעֲשׂוּ בוֹ הַפְּלִשְׁתִּים כִּרְצוֹנָם, הֲרֵי הוּא כִּשְׁאָר מֵת, וְאֵין מוֹנְעִין מִמֶּנּוּ שׁוּם דָּבָר.

ד) כָּל הַפּוֹרְשִׁים מִדַּרְכֵי הַצִּבּוּר, וְהֵם הָאֲנָשִׁים שֶׁפָּרְקוּ עֹל הַמִּצְוֹת מֵעַל צַוָּארָם, וְאֵין נִכְלָלִים בִּכְלַל יִשְׂרָאֵל בַּעֲשִׂיָּתָם, אֶלָּא הֲרֵי הֵם כִּבְנֵי חוֹרִין לְעַצְמָן, וְכֵן הַמּוּמָרִים וְהַמּוֹסְרִים וְהָאֶפִּיקוֹרוֹסִים, כָּל אֵלּוּ, אֵין אוֹנְנִים וְאֵין מִתְאַבְּלִים עֲלֵיהֶם אֶלָּא אֲחֵיהֶם וּשְׁאָר קְרוֹבֵיהֶם לוֹבְשִׁים לְבָנִים וּמִתְעַטְּפִים לְבָנִים, וְאוֹכְלִים וְשׁוֹתִים וּשְׂמֵחִים עַל שֶׁאָבְדוּ שׂוֹנְאוֹ

even if decay has set in, he should not be buried even on the second day of Yom Tov and not even by a non-Jew, but he should be held over until after Yom Tov. His foreskin should then be removed, and he should be buried.

10) On Shabbos and *Yom Kippur,* it is not permitted to attend the dead in any way, even by means of a non-Jew.

11) On *Chol Hamoed,* the deceased should not be brought to the cemetery before the grave is ready, so that it is not necessary for the bier to remain waiting.

Chapter 201

The Laws of Suicide and the Wicked

1) A person who commits suicide is unsurpassed in wickedness, as it is said, "However of the blood of your souls, I will demand an account."[1] The world was created for a single person, (to indicate that) anyone who destroys one Jewish life is considered to have destroyed a whole world.[2] He should, therefore, not be attended in any way. Garments should not be torn for him, he should not be mourned, nor should he be eulogized. However, he should be buried, ritually purified and dressed in shrouds. The rule is: anything that is done out of respect to the living, should be done for him.[3]

2) Without proof to the contrary, a man is not presumed to be wicked. Therefore, if a person if found asphyxiated, hanged, or the like, so long as it is possible to assume that he was murdered, it should not be considered a suicide.

3) A minor who committed suicide is considered like one who had taken his life unintentionally. Similarly, an adult who committed suicide, and it appears he did so because of severe depression, or madness, and the like, it is considered unintentional. Similarly, if he did so under duress, because he was afraid of torture, like King Saul, who feared what the Philistines might do to him, he is like any other deceased person, and nothing should be withheld from him.

4) All those who separate themselves from the ways of the community, such as those people who have cast off the yoke of *mitzvos* from themselves, and do not include themselves among the Jewish people with regard to observance of the *mitzvos,* but are like a liberated sect of their own; for all these, including apostates, informers, and heretics, the laws of *Onein* are not observed, and their death is not mourned. Their brothers and other relatives dress in white and adorn themselves in white, eat, drink, and rejoice that the enemies of the Almighty have perished.

---

1. *Genesis* 9:5.
2. *Maseches Sanhedrin* 37a.
3. Regarding the saying of *Kaddish,* see *Chassam Sofer* Section *Yorah Deiah* 326.

שֶׁל מָקוֹם. וַעֲלֵיהֶם הַכָּתוּב אוֹמֵר, הֲלֹא מְשַׂנְאֶיךָ ה', אֶשְׂנָא. וְאוֹמֵר, וּבַאֲבֹד רְשָׁעִים רִנָּה.

ה) אִם נֶהֱרַג, בֵּין בְּדִינָא דְמַלְכוּתָא בֵּין בְּעִנְיָן אַחֵר, אֲפִלּוּ הָיָה מוּמָר, מִתְאַבְּלִין עָלָיו, דְּכֵיוָן שֶׁנֶּהֱרַג בִּידֵי אָדָם וְלֹא מֵת כְּדֶרֶךְ כָּל הָאָרֶץ, הֲוֵי לֵהּ כַּפָּרָה.

ו) מִי שֶׁהָיָה רָגִיל לַעֲשׂוֹת עֲבֵרָה אַחַת, אֲפִלּוּ רַק לְתֵאָבוֹן, וּמֵת, אִם לֹא הִתְוַדָּה קֹדֶם מוֹתוֹ, אֵין מִתְאַבְּלִין עָלָיו. אֲבָל אִם הִתְוַדָּה, מִתְאַבְּלִין עָלָיו, אֲפִלּוּ הָיָה גַּנָּב אוֹ גַּזְלָן.

ז) קָטָן בֶּן שָׁנָה אוֹ שְׁנָתַיִם שֶׁהֵמִיר עִם אָבִיו אוֹ עִם אִמּוֹ, וּמֵת, אֵין מִתְאַבְּלִין עָלָיו.

סִימָן רב
הִלְכוֹת טֻמְאַת כֹּהֵן

א) הַכֹּהֵן מֻזְהָר שֶׁלֹּא לִטַּמֵּא לְמֵת. וַאֲפִלּוּ נֵפֶל שֶׁעֲדַיִן לֹא נִתְקַשְּׁרוּ אֵבָרָיו בְּגִידִין, חָשׁוּב מֵת. (אַךְ אִם הִפִּילָה תּוֹךְ אַרְבָּעִים יוֹם, לָא חָשִׁיב אֶלָּא כְּמַיָּא בְעָלְמָא). וְלָאו דַּוְקָא לְמֵת שָׁלֵם, אֶלָּא אֲפִלּוּ לִדְבָרִים שֶׁנִּפְרָשִׁים מִמֶּנּוּ, כְּמוֹ דָם וְכַדּוֹמֶה. וְכֵן אָסוּר לְטַמֵּא לְאֵבֶר שֶׁנֶּחְתַּךְ מִן הַחַי, אִם יֵשׁ עָלָיו בָּשָׂר כָּל כָּךְ, שֶׁאִם הָיָה מְחֻבָּר, הָיָה רָאוּי לְהַעֲלוֹת אֲרוּכָה. וַאֲפִלּוּ לְאֵבֶר שֶׁל עַצְמוֹ, אָסוּר לוֹ לְטַמֵּא. וְאָסוּר לְכֹהֵן לִכָּנֵס לְבַיִת שֶׁיֵּשׁ שָׁם גּוֹסֵס. וְאַף־עַל־פִּי שֶׁהַגּוֹסֵס הֲרֵי הוּא כְּחַי לְכָל דָּבָר וְאֵינוֹ מְטַמֵּא, מִכָּל מָקוֹם עוֹבֵר הַכֹּהֵן עַל לֹא יְחַלֵּל, שֶׁהוּא מֻזְהָר שֶׁיִּשְׁמֹר כְּהֻנָּתוֹ שֶׁלֹּא תִתְחַלֵּל, וְשֶׁמָּא יָמוּת זֶה תֵּכֶף.

ב) אָסוּר לַכֹּהֵן לִכָּנֵס תַּחַת אֹהֶל שֶׁיֵּשׁ מֵת תַּחְתָּיו, אֲפִלּוּ הוּא אֹהֶל גָּדוֹל מְאֹד. וַאֲפִלּוּ יֵשׁ שְׁנֵי חֲדָרִים, אֲשֶׁר בְּחֶדֶר אֶחָד יֵשׁ מֵת וְיֵשׁ בַּמְּחִצָּה הַמַּפְסֶקֶת נֶקֶב שֶׁיֵּשׁ בּוֹ טֶפַח עַל טֶפַח, אָסוּר לִכָּנֵס גַּם לַחֶדֶר הַשֵּׁנִי, כִּי נֶקֶב טֶפַח עַל טֶפַח, מֵבִיא אֶת הַטֻּמְאָה. וְכֵן אִם אֵצֶל הַחֶדֶר הַשֵּׁנִי יֵשׁ עוֹד חֶדֶר שְׁלִישִׁי וּבֵינֵיהֶם גַּם כֵּן נֶקֶב טֶפַח עַל טֶפַח, הוֹלֶכֶת הַטֻּמְאָה גַּם לַחֶדֶר הַשְּׁלִישִׁי, וְכֵן לְעוֹלָם. וְנֶקֶב הֶעָשׂוּי לְאוֹרָה, אֲפִלּוּ אֵין בּוֹ אֶלָּא כְּפוּנְדְּיוֹן, מֵבִיא אֶת הַטֻּמְאָה.

4. *Psalms* 139:21.
5. *Proverbs* 11:10.

Concerning such people, the Scripture says,[4] "Behold those who hate you Adonoy, I hate" also it is said, "When the wicked perish there is joy."[5]

5) If one was executed either by the government or otherwise, even if he was an apostate, his relatives should mourn over him. For since he was killed by man and did not die naturally, he had an atonement.

6) If the deceased was an habitual sinner whose sins were motivated by lustful desire, and he made no confession before his death, mourning should not be observed for him. But if he did confess, he should be mourned, even if he had been a thief or a robber.

7) In the case of a child, one or two years old, who was converted[6] with his father or with his mother, and died, no mourning should be observed for him.

Chapter 202

The Laws Of Defilement Of A Kohein

1) The *Kohein* is commanded not to defile himself through any form of contact with the deceased. Even an abortive fetus, whose limbs have not yet been connected with ligamentous tissue, is considered in this regard as a dead body. (If, however, the abortion occurred within forty days from conception, it is considered like water). The dead body need not be in its entirety, for this law applies even to things that have separated from the corpse such as blood and the like. He is also forbidden to defile himself through contact with the severed limb of a living person, if there is enough flesh on it that were it still connected, it would have possibly healed. Even if it is his own limb, he is forbidden to defile himself by touching it. A *Kohein* is forbidden to enter a house where a person is close to death, and even though a *gosseis* (dying person) is considered alive with regard to everything else, and he is not considered impure, nevertheless, the *Kohein* [by entering such a house] violates the command, "You shall not desecrate,"[1] for he is commanded to guard his priesthood so that it does not become profaned, and the *gosseis* may die at any moment.

2) A *Kohein* is forbidden to enter a dwelling where there is a dead body, even if the dwelling is very large. Even if there are two rooms, and there is a dead body in one of them, and in the wall that separates them, there is a hole one *tefach* square, he is forbidden to enter even the second room, because the hole of one *tefach* square conducts the impurity into the second room. Likewise, if next to the second room, there is yet a third room, and between them, too, there is a hole one *tefach* square, the impurity passes also to the third room, and so ad infinitum. If the hole was made to admit light, even if it is only the size of a small coin, the impurity passes through.

---

6. To a non-Jewish religion.

1. *Leviticus* 21:12. A *Kohein* is forbidden to attend Medical School. See *Igros Moshe, Yorah Deiah* III 155.

ג) וְלָכֵן בִּמְדִינוֹתֵינוּ שֶׁגַּגּוֹת הַבָּתִּים בּוֹלְטִין לַחוּץ בְּרֹחַב טֶפַח, וְקַיְמָא לָן דְּרֹחַב טֶפַח מֵבִיא אֶת הַטֻּמְאָה, וְאִם כֵּן זֶה הַקָּצֶה מִן הַגַּג, הֲוֵי אֹהֶל לְהָבִיא אֶת הַטֻּמְאָה. לְפִי זֶה שְׁנֵי בָתִּים סְמוּכִין זֶה לָזֶה, אִם יֵשׁ מֵת בְּאֶחָד מֵהֶן, הוֹלֶכֶת הַטֻּמְאָה דֶּרֶךְ פֶּתַח אוֹ חַלּוֹן תַּחַת הַקְּצָווֹת מִן הַגַּגִּין שֶׁבּוֹלְטִין לַחוּץ, וְנִכְנֶסֶת גַּם לְתוֹךְ הַבַּיִת הַשֵּׁנִי דֶּרֶךְ חַלּוֹן אוֹ פֶּתַח פָּתוּחַ, וְאָסוּר לַכֹּהֵן לִכָּנֵס גַּם לְתוֹךְ הַבַּיִת הַשֵּׁנִי. וְכֵן אֲפִלּוּ כַּמָּה בָתִּים הַסְּמוּכִים זֶה אֵצֶל זֶה.

ד) וַאֲפִלּוּ הַגַּגִּין אֵינָן שָׁוִין, אֶלָּא זֶה לְמַעְלָה מִזֶּה, וַאֲפִלּוּ הַגַּג שֶׁהַטֻּמְאָה שָׁם בַּבַּיִת הוּא גָבוֹהַּ הַרְבֵּה מִן הַגַּג הַשֵּׁנִי אוֹ בְּהִפּוּךְ, הֲלָכָה לְמשֶׁה מִסִּינַי הִיא, דְּאָמְרִינַן, חָבוּט רָמֵי. פֵּרוּשׁ, שֶׁאָנוּ רוֹאִים כְּאִלּוּ הָעֶלְיוֹן נֶחְבָּט וְנִשְׁפָּל עַד לְמָטָה. וּמֵאַחַר שֶׁאִם הָיָה נִשְׁפָּל עַד הַתַּחְתּוֹן, הָיָה נוֹגֵעַ בּוֹ, עַל כֵּן הוֹלֶכֶת הַטֻּמְאָה מִזֶּה לָזֶה. אֲבָל אִם יֵשׁ הֶפְסֵק בֵּינֵיהֶם אֲפִלּוּ כָּל־שֶׁהוּא, שׁוּב אֵינָהּ הוֹלֶכֶת הַטֻּמְאָה.

ה) וְכֵן כְּשֶׁיֵּשׁ קוֹרָה מֻנַּחַת עַל הַמָּבוֹי כְּמוֹ שֶׁעוֹשִׂין לְעֵרוּב, וְהִיא רְחָבָה טֶפַח וְהַגַּגִּין מַאֲהִילִין עָלֶיהָ טֶפַח מִכָּאן וְטֶפַח מִכָּאן, אִם כֵּן בָּאָה הַטֻּמְאָה מִן תַּחַת הַגַּג אֶל תַּחַת הַקּוֹרָה, וְהִיא מְבִיאָה אֶת הַטֻּמְאָה אֶל תַּחַת גַּג הַבַּיִת שֶׁמִּצַּד הַשֵּׁנִי, וּמִתְפַּשֶּׁטֶת בְּכָל מָקוֹם שֶׁיֵּשׁ אֹהֶל טֶפַח עַד הַמָּקוֹם שֶׁיֵּשׁ הֶפְסֵק. וְכֵן כְּשֶׁיֵּשׁ בֵּין שְׁנֵי בָתִּים כִּפָּה מִבִּנְיָן כְּדֶרֶךְ שֶׁעוֹשִׂין לְשַׁעַר הֶחָצֵר, הַדִּין כֵּן הוּא. וְאַף־עַל־פִּי שֶׁאֵין עַל הַכִּפָּה גַּג בּוֹלֵט, מִכָּל מָקוֹם הֲרֵי בָאָה הַטֻּמְאָה מִתַּחַת גַּג הַבַּיִת לְתַחַת הַכִּפָּה. וְאוּלָם לִפְעָמִים בּוֹנִין אֶת הַכִּפָּה שֶׁיֵּשׁ לָהּ כְּמוֹ רַגְלַיִם מִן הַקַּרְקַע וּלְמַעְלָה, וְאִם כֵּן יֵשׁ סְתִימָה אֵצֶל כָּתְלֵי הַבָּתִּים אִם אֵין עָלֶיהָ גַּג בּוֹלֵט, וְהַסְּתִימָה שֶׁמִּן הַצַּד נִמְשֶׁכֶת יוֹתֵר מִן הַגַּג שֶׁלְּמַעְלָה, בְּזֶה הָעִנְיָן אֵין מָקוֹם לַטֻּמְאָה שֶׁתָּבוֹא, כֵּיוָן שֶׁיֵּשׁ קְצָת הֶפְסֵק בְּלִי אֹהֶל. וְלִפְעָמִים יֵשׁ בֵּין בַּיִת לְבַיִת כֹּתֶל סָתוּם בְּלִי פֶתַח, אֶלָּא שֶׁיֵּשׁ עָלָיו גַּג בּוֹלֵט, וְהַטֻּמְאָה בָּאָה מִגַּג לְגַג. וְיֵשׁ תַּקָּנָה לְעֵת הַצֹּרֶךְ לְהָסִיר אֶת הָרְעָפִים בְּמָקוֹם אֶחָד שֶׁיִּהְיֶה קְצָת הֶפְסֵק בְּלִי אֹהֶל טֶפַח. וּצְרִיכִין לְהַשְׁגִּיחַ אִם אֵין מֵהַחוֹמָה עַצְמָהּ בּוֹלֵט טֶפַח כְּדֶרֶךְ שֶׁעוֹשִׂין לִפְעָמִים בְּלִיטָה לַחוֹמָה.

ו) הֲלָכָה לְמשֶׁה מִסִּינַי הִיא שֶׁהַפֶּתַח אֲשֶׁר עֲתִידִים לְהוֹצִיא דֶּרֶךְ שָׁם אֶת הַמֵּת מִן הָאֹהֶל אֲשֶׁר הוּא שָׁם, שֶׁעַל יְדֵי הוֹצָאָה זֹאת יִטְהַר הָאֹהֶל,

3) Therefore, in our regions, where the roofs project towards the outside with a width of no less than one *tefach,* and since we know that the width of one *tefach* conveys impurity, this projecting roof is considered a tent which conveys impurity. Hence, when two houses are close to each other, if the deceased is in one of them, the impurity passes through the door, or open window, beneath the ends of the projecting rooftop, and enters into the second house, through the open window or door. Thus the *Kohein* is forbidden to enter even the second house. This is true even if there are many houses closely adjoining one another.

4) Even if the roofs are not of the same height, but one is higher than the other, even if the roof of the house where the impurity is found is much higher than the second roof or vice versa, there is a *halachah* handed down by Moshe from [Mount] Sinai, that the height is considered as lowered, that is, we consider as though the height was pressed down and lowered until it reaches the lower one. And since if it were lowered to the level of the bottom one, they would touch, therefore, the impurity passes from one to the other. But if there would be a space between them, even if ever so small, the impurity does not pass from one to the other.

5) Similarly if a beam lies across an alley as is done for a *eiruv,* (and) is a *tefach* wide, and is covered by the roofs projecting above it to the extent of *tefach* on each side. (Like this:)

In such a case, the impurity passes from underneath the roof to underneath the beam, which conveys the impurity to underneath the roof of the house on the opposite side. From there it spreads to any place where there is a dwelling no less than one *tefach* wide, until it reaches a barrier or open space. Also, if between the two houses, there is an arch constructed on the style of a court entrance, like this:

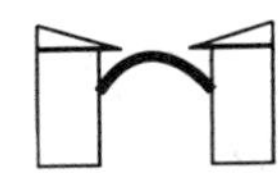

the same law applies. And although the arch has no projecting roof, nevertheless, the impurity is transmitted from beneath the roof to underneath the arch. However, at times an arch is constructed on posts from the ground up, which close up the space between the arch and the walls of the house. Then, if the arch has no projecting roof covering it, and the closed spaces on the sides extend further than the roofs that are above it, in such a case, there is no space through which the impurity may pass, since there is some open space without a tent covering. At times, between the houses there is a solid closed wall without an opening (like this:)

but there is a projecting roof over it. Then the impurity is conveyed from one roof to another. When necessary, this can be remedied by removing the tiles of the roof in one place to create an interrupting [open] space of a *tefach* wide without a tent. You must be certain that the wall itself does not project a *tefach,* as sometimes they make a projection (to adorn) the wall.

6) There is a *halachah* transmitted to Moshe from Sinai, concerning the door through which the deceased will be carried from the house. Since after the removal

אַף־עַל־פִּי שֶׁהַפֶּתַח הַזֶּה הוּא סָתוּם, מִכָּל מָקוֹם נִדּוֹן כְּאִלּוּ הוּא פָּתוּחַ, וְלָכֵן אָסוּר לַכֹּהֵן שֶׁיַּעֲמֹד שָׁם תַּחַת הַמַּשְׁקוֹף, אַף־עַל־פִּי שֶׁהַדֶּלֶת נְעוּלָה מִבִּפְנִים. וְכֵן אִם יֵשׁ שָׁם גַּג בּוֹלֵט טֶפַח נֶגֶד הַפֶּתַח, מֵבִיא אֶת הַטֻּמְאָה לְכָל מָקוֹם שֶׁאֶפְשָׁר, כְּאִלּוּ הָיָה הַפֶּתַח פָּתוּחַ. אַךְ אִם נִפְתַּח מִצַּד אַחֵר פֶּתַח אוֹ חַלּוֹן שֶׁהוּא אַרְבָּעָה טְפָחִים עַל אַרְבָּעָה טְפָחִים, אָז לֹא נֶחְשָׁב הַפֶּתַח הַסָּתוּם כְּאִלּוּ הָיָה פָּתוּחַ, וּמֻתָּר לַכֹּהֵן לַעֲמוֹד שָׁם אִם אֵין הַטֻּמְאָה יְכוֹלָה לְהַגִּיעַ אֵלָיו דֶּרֶךְ הַפֶּתַח אוֹ הַחַלּוֹן הַפָּתוּחַ.

ז) כֹּהֵן שֶׁהוּא בְּבַיִת אוֹ בְּחֶדֶר שֶׁהַדְּלָתוֹת וְהַחַלּוֹנוֹת סְגוּרִין בְּאֹפֶן שֶׁאֵין בְּפֶתַח פָּתוּחַ טֶפַח וּבְחַלּוֹן אֵין נֶקֶב כְּפוּנְדְּיוֹן, וְשָׁמַע שֶׁיֵּשׁ בִּשְׁכוּנָתוֹ מֵת, בְּאֹפֶן שֶׁאִם יִפְתַּח פֶּתַח אוֹ חַלּוֹן, יְהֵא מָקוֹם לַטֻּמְאָה שֶׁתָּבוֹא עָלָיו, אָסוּר לִפְתּוֹחַ, אֶלָּא יִשָּׁאֵר שָׁם כְּמוֹ שֶׁהוּא עַד שֶׁיּוֹצִיאוּ אֶת הַמֵּת. כִּי כָּל זְמַן שֶׁאֵין פּוֹתֵחַ טֶפַח, אֵין הַטֻּמְאָה נִכְנֶסֶת, וּכְשֶׁיִּפְתַּח, תִּכָּנֵס.

ח) אָסוּר לַכֹּהֵן לִקְרַב בְּתוֹךְ אַרְבַּע אַמּוֹת שֶׁל מֵת אוֹ שֶׁל קֶבֶר. וְדַוְקָא כְּשֶׁהַמֵּת מֻנָּח בִּמְקוֹם קְבִיעָתוֹ. אֲבָל כְּשֶׁהוּא בַּמִּטָּה שֶׁמּוֹצִיאִין אוֹתוֹ וּבְעֵת אֲמִירַת צִדּוּק הַדִּין אַף כְּשֶׁמַּעֲמִידִין אוֹתוֹ, אֵין שָׁם קְבִיעָתוֹ, וְאֵין צְרִיכִין לְהִתְרַחֵק כִּי אִם אַרְבָּעָה טְפָחִים.

ט) כֹּהֵן שֶׁהוּא יָשֵׁן בְּאֹהֶל שֶׁיֵּשׁ בּוֹ מֵת שֶׁהַטֻּמְאָה נִכְנֶסֶת בּוֹ וְאִי אֶפְשָׁר לִסְגּוֹר בַּעֲדוֹ לִמְנוֹעַ אֶת הַטֻּמְאָה, צְרִיכִין לַהֲקִיצוֹ וּלְהַפְרִישׁוֹ שֶׁיֵּלֵךְ מִשָּׁם. וְאִם הוּא שׁוֹכֵב עָרוֹם אֵין לְהַגִּיד לוֹ, אֶלָּא יִקְרְאוּ לוֹ סְתָם שֶׁיֵּצֵא, בִּכְדֵי שֶׁיַּלְבִּישׁ אֶת עַצְמוֹ תְּחִלָּה, דְּגָדוֹל כְּבוֹד הַבְּרִיּוֹת. וּמִכָּל מָקוֹם לְאַחַר שֶׁנּוֹדַע לוֹ מִן הַטֻּמְאָה, אָסוּר לִשְׁהוֹת שָׁמָּה עַד שֶׁיַּלְבִּישׁ אֶת עַצְמוֹ, אֶלָּא צָרִיךְ לָצֵאת מִיָּד.

י) יֵשׁ אוֹמְרִים, דְּגַם מֵת גּוֹי מְטַמֵּא בָּאֹהֶל. וְיֵשׁ לִזָּהֵר כְּדִבְרֵיהֶם שֶׁלֹּא לֵילֵךְ עַל קֶבֶר גּוֹי. וּמִכָּל שֶׁכֵּן כְּשֶׁיֵּשׁ לָחוּשׁ שֶׁמָּא גַּם מוּמָר נִקְבַּר שָׁם, שֶׁהַמּוּמָר דִּינוֹ כְּיִשְׂרָאֵל. וְגַם הַוָּלָד שֶׁיְּלָדָה מוּמֶרֶת מִגּוֹי, דִּינוֹ כְּמוֹ יִשְׂרָאֵל.

יא) מֻתָּר הַכֹּהֵן לְטַמֵּא לַקְּרוֹבִים, וּמִצְוָה לוֹ לְטַמֵּא לָהֶם. וְאֵלּוּ הֵן הַקְּרוֹבִים: אִשְׁתּוֹ הָרְאוּיָה לוֹ, אָבִיו וְאִמּוֹ, בְּנוֹ וּבִתּוֹ, וְאָחִיו וַאֲחוֹתוֹ מֵאָבִיו שֶׁהָיוּ בְּנֵי קַיָּמָא. אֲבָל לִסְפֵק נְפָלִים אֵינוֹ מְטַמֵּא. וְאֵינוֹ מְטַמֵּא לַאֲחוֹתוֹ שֶׁנִּתְקַדְּשָׁה לְאִישׁ. יֵשׁ אוֹמְרִים, הָא דְּמֻתָּר וּמִצְוָה לְטַמֵּא

the house will again be ritually pure, although the door is now closed, nevertheless according to *halachah,* it is considered as though it is open, and therefore a *Kohein* is forbidden to stand under the lintel, even though the door is closed. Also, if there is a roof projecting a *tefach* over the door, it conveys the impurity to every possible place, as though the door were open. However, if there was an open door or window on another side measuring four square *tefachim,* the closed door is not considered as being open, and a *Kohein* is permitted to stand there provided the impurity cannot reach him through the open door or window.

7) If a *Kohein* is in a house or a room, the doors and windows of which are closed in such manner that the door is not opened a *tefach,* and the window does not have an opening the size of a *pundyon* (coin), and he hears that there is a corpse in the vicinity, so that if the door or window were to be opened, the impurity would reach him, he is forbidden to open either of them, but he should remain there as is, until the deceased is carried out; for so long as there is not an opening of a *tefach,* the impurity cannot penetrate, but when it is opened, it can penetrate.

8) A *kohein* is forbidden to approach within four *amos* of a deceased person or a grave. This applies only when the deceased lies in his permanent place. But when he lies on the bier during the funeral procession, or when they are saying *Tzidduk Haddin,* even when they stop with the bier, since this is not his permanent place, the *Kohein* need keep away only a distance of four *tefachim.*

9) If a *Kohein* is asleep in a house where there is a deceased person, where the impurity of the deceased penetrates, and it is impossible to shut him in, in order to prevent the access of the impurity, he should be awakened and told to leave the premises. If he is undressed, he should not be told about the impurity, but merely called outside so that he may get dressed first; for a person's dignity is very important. However, as soon as he is aware of the impurity, he is forbidden to wait there until he gets dressed, but he must leave immediately.

10) Some *Poskim* maintain that even the corpse of a non-Jew causes impurity in a house. A *Kohein* should be mindful of this opinion and not walk over the grave of a non-Jew. Especially when there is reason to believe that an apostate may have been buried there (too), for an apostate is like a Jew (in this regard). Also the child born by an apostate woman from a non-Jew, is like in Jew in this regard.

11) A *Kohein* is permitted to defile himself at the death of his relatives, and it is a *mitzvah* for him to do so. These are the relatives for which he may defile himself: his wife whom he was permitted to marry, his father, his mother, his son or his daughter, his brother and sister born from his father, provided they were born full term, but for a child who may have been aborted, a *Kohein* may not defile himself. He may not defile himself for a married sister. [2] Some *Poskim* maintain that which a *Kohein* is permitted and is a *mitzvah* to defile himself for relatives is only for the

2. Even if she was divorced or widowed and no longer married.

לַקְּרוֹבִים, דַּוְקָא לְצֹרֶךְ קְבוּרָה אוֹ לְהָבִיא לוֹ אָרוֹן וְתַכְרִיכִין וְכַדּוֹמֶה. וְלָכֵן בְּשַׁבָּת שֶׁאִי־אֶפְשָׁר לְקָבְרוֹ בּוֹ־בַיּוֹם, אָסוּר לְטַמְּאוֹת לוֹ אֲפִלּוּ כְּדֵי לְשָׁמְרוֹ, וְנָכוֹן לְהַחְמִיר כֵּן. מִיהוּ לְצָרְכֵי קְבוּרָה, וַדַּאי מִצְוָה לְטַמֵּא לָהֶם. וַאֲפִלּוּ יֵשׁ חֶבְרָא קַדִּישָׁא הַמִּתְעַסְּקִים וְהוּא אֵינוֹ מִתְעַסֵּק כְּלָל, מֻתָּר לוֹ לִהְיוֹת שָׁם בַּבַּיִת, שֶׁמָּא יִצְטָרְכוּ לְאֵיזֶה דָּבָר. וְאֵינוֹ מְטַמֵּא לַקְּרוֹבִים אֶלָּא עַד שֶׁיִּסָּתֵם הַגּוֹלֵל וְלֹא אַחַר כָּךְ.

יב) כֹּהֵן שֶׁפֵּרְשׁוּ אֲבוֹתָיו מִדַּרְכֵי הַצִּבּוּר, אֵינוֹ מְטַמֵּא לָהֶם, וְלֹא לְמִי שֶׁאִבֵּד עַצְמוֹ לָדַעַת. וְכֵן כָּל מִי שֶׁאֵין מִתְאַבְּלִין עָלָיו אֵין הַכֹּהֵן מְטַמֵּא לוֹ.

יג) אֵין הַכֹּהֵן מְטַמֵּא לְקָרוֹב אֶלָּא כְּשֶׁהוּא שָׁלֵם וְלֹא כְּשֶׁהוּא חָסֵר. וְלָכֵן יֵשׁ אוֹמְרִים, דְּאֵינוֹ מְטַמֵּא לְהָרוּג, דְּמִקְרֵי חָסֵר. וְנָכוֹן לְהַחְמִיר.

יד) יֵשׁ כֹּהֲנִים הֶדְיוֹטִים נוֹהֲגִין לָלֶכֶת עַל קִבְרֵי צַדִּיקִים, בְּאָמְרָם שֶׁקִּבְרֵי צַדִּיקִים אֵינָם מְטַמְּאִים, וְטָעוּת הִיא בִידֵיהֶם, וּצְרִיכִין לְמַחוֹת בָּהֶם.

טו) כְּשֵׁם שֶׁהַכֹּהֵן מֻזְהָר שֶׁלֹּא לְטַמֵּא, כָּךְ מֻזְהָרִים הַגְּדוֹלִים עַל הַקְּטַנִּים, שֶׁנֶּאֱמַר, אֱמֹר אֶל־הַכֹּהֲנִים. וְאָמַרְתָּ. וּמִדִּכְתִיב שְׁתֵּי אֲמִירוֹת, דָּרְשׁוּ רַבּוֹתֵינוּ, זִכְרוֹנָם לִבְרָכָה, לְהַזְהִיר גְּדוֹלִים עַל הַקְּטַנִּים. וְדַוְקָא לְטַמְּאוֹתָן בְּיָדַיִם. דְּהַיְנוּ לְהַכְנִיסָן לְאֹהֶל הַמֵּת. אֲבָל אִם הַקָּטָן מְטַמֵּא מֵעַצְמוֹ, אֵין צְרִיכִין לְהַפְרִישׁוֹ. אַךְ אִם הִגִּיעַ לְחִנּוּךְ, יֵשׁ לְהַפְרִישׁוֹ. וְאֵשֶׁת כֹּהֵן מְעֻבֶּרֶת, מֻתֶּרֶת לִכָּנֵס בְּאֹהֶל הַמֵּת.

טז) הַכֹּהֲנִים אֵינָם יְכוֹלִים לָכוֹף קְרוֹבֵי הַמֵּת שֶׁיְּמַהֲרוּ לְהוֹצִיא אֶת הַמֵּת מִמְּקוֹמוֹ כְּדֵי שֶׁיִּכָּנְסוּ לְבָתֵּיהֶם, אִם לֹא כְּשֶׁהַכֹּהֵן הוּא חוֹלֶה שֶׁאֵינוֹ יָכוֹל לָצֵאת מִבֵּיתוֹ, כּוֹפִין אֶת הַקְּרוֹבִים לְהוֹצִיא אֶת הַמֵּת, כְּדֵי שֶׁלֹּא יָבֹא הַחוֹלֶה לִידֵי אִסּוּר דְּאוֹרַיְתָא. וְאִם הַמֵּת הוּא נֵפֶל, כּוֹפִין אוֹתוֹ בְּכָל עִנְיָן וַאֲפִלּוּ בְּשַׁבָּת, לְהוֹצִיאוֹ עַל יְדֵי גוֹי.

---

3. *Leviticus* 21:1.
4. *Maseches Yevomos* 114a.
5. Even if it seems she will give birth there, because perhaps it will be a girl; and if not, it may not be a viable child. *Mishnah Berurah* 343:3.

needs of burial, or to bring a coffin, or shrouds, or the like. Consequently, on Shabbos, a day when he may not be buried, a *Kohein* is forbidden to defile himself even in order to guard the deceased. It is proper to follow this strict opinion. However, concerning things necessary for burial, it is certainly a *mitzvah* for him to defile himself. Even if there is a Burial Society to take care of all the arrangements, and he has nothing to take care of, he is permitted to be in the house in case they might need something. He may defile himself for these relatives only until the grave is closed, and not thereafter.

12) A *Kohein* is forbidden to defile himself for parents who abandoned the practices of the Jewish people, and not for one who committed suicide. Similarly, a *Kohein* is forbidden to defile himself for anyone for whom the rules of mourning need not be observed.

13) A *Kohein* may not defile himself for a relative unless the body is complete but not if it is missing a limb. Therefore some *Poskim* maintain that a *Kohein* may not defile himself for a slain relative, for his body is considered incomplete; and it is proper to heed this strict opinion.

14) Some ignorant *Kohanim* are accustomed to visit the graves of the righteous, maintaining that the graves of the righteous do not defile. They are in error, and such practice should be protested.

15) Just as an [adult] *Kohein* is warned against defiling himself, so too are adult *Kohanim* warned concerning minors, as it is said, "Say to the *Kohanim*. . . and say (to them)."[3] Because the word "say" is written twice, our Sages, of blessed memory,[4] inferred from this that the adults are warned concerning the minors. They must not be the direct cause of their defilement by bringing them into a house where there is a deceased person, but if the minor defiles himself on his own, there is no need to remove him. However, if he has reached the age of training, he should be removed. The pregnant wife of a *Kohein* is permitted to enter a house containing a corpse.[5]

16) The *Kohanim* cannot force[6] the relatives of the deceased to hasten the removal of the deceased from its place so that they may enter their homes,[7] unless the *Kohein* is ill and is unable to leave the house. In that case the relatives are forced to remove the deceased, so as not to cause the sick [*Kohein*] to transgress a law of the Torah. If the deceased is an aborted fetus, its relatives can be forced, in any event, to remove it, even on Shabbos through a non-Jew.

---

6. If it was customary to remove the body quickly to the place where they wash it, you may force them. *Mishnah Berurah* 311:13.

7. Even if the synagogue is under the same roof and the *Kohanim* are prevented from entering. *Mishnah Berurah* 311.13

סִימָן רג
עַל אֵיזֶה קָרוֹב וְתִינוֹק מִתְאַבְּלִים

א) עַל שִׁבְעָה קְרוֹבִים חַיָּבִים לְהִתְאַבֵּל, אָבִיו וְאִמּוֹ, בְּנוֹ וּבִתּוֹ, אָחִיו וַאֲחוֹתוֹ בֵּין מִן הָאָב בֵּין מִן הָאֵם, וַאֲפִלּוּ הָיְתָה אֲחוֹתוֹ נְשׂוּאָה לְאִישׁ: הָאִישׁ עַל אִשְׁתּוֹ, וְהָאִשָּׁה עַל בַּעְלָהּ.

ב) נוֹהֲגִין שֶׁגַּם שְׁאָר קְרוֹבִים, מַרְאִים קְצָת אֲבֵלוּת בְּעַצְמָם שָׁבוּעַ הָרִאשׁוֹן עַד אַחַר הַשַּׁבָּת, שֶׁאֵין רוֹחֲצִין בְּחַמִּין, וְאֵין מְשַׁנִּין קְצָת בִּגְדֵיהֶם כְּמוֹ בִּשְׁאָר שַׁבָּת. וְאֵין כָּל הַקְּרוֹבִים שָׁוִין בָּזֶה. אִם הָיוּ שֵׁנִי בְּשֵׁנִי, אוֹ בֶּן־בְּנוֹ אוֹ בֶּן־בִּתּוֹ, לוֹבֵשׁ כָּל בִּגְדֵי שַׁבָּת, חוּץ מִבֶּגֶד הָעֶלְיוֹן. וְעַל חָמִיו וַחֲמוֹתוֹ, אוֹ עַל אֲבִי־אָבִיו וַאֲבִי־אִמּוֹ, וְכֵן הָאִשָּׁה עַל חָמִיהָ וַחֲמוֹתָהּ, וַאֲבִי־אָבִיהָ אוֹ אֲבִי־אִמָּהּ, אֵינָן לוֹבְשִׁין רַק כְּתֹנֶת לְבָנָה, וְהָאִשָּׁה גַּם צָעִיף לָבָן. וְכֵן הַמִּנְהָג שֶׁלֹּא לֵילֵךְ לְבֵית־הַמֶּרְחָץ, וְלֹא לָחֹף אֶת הָרֹאשׁ. גַּם אֵין לֶאֱכוֹל חוּץ לְבֵיתוֹ לֹא בִסְעוּדַת מִצְוָה וְלֹא בִסְעוּדַת מֵרֵעִים. וּלְאַחַר שַׁבָּת, מֻתָּר בְּכָל דָּבָר.

ג) תִּינוֹק, שֶׁאֵינוֹ יָדוּעַ אִם כָּלוּ חֳדָשָׁיו אִם לֹא, אִם מֵת בְּתוֹךְ שְׁלֹשִׁים יוֹם וַאֲפִלּוּ בַּיּוֹם הַשְּׁלֹשִׁים, אֲפִלּוּ גָּמְרוּ שַׂעֲרוֹ וְצִפָּרְנָיו, אֵין קוֹרְעִין עָלָיו, וְאֵין אוֹנְנִין עָלָיו, וְאֵין מִתְאַבְּלִין עָלָיו, מִשּׁוּם דַּהֲוֵי סְפֵק נֵפֶל. וְאִם מֵת לְאַחַר שְׁלֹשִׁים יוֹם וַאֲפִלּוּ בְּיוֹם שְׁלֹשִׁים וְאֶחָד קֹדֶם הַשָּׁעָה שֶׁנּוֹלַד בָּהּ, קוֹרְעִין עָלָיו, וְאוֹנְנִין עָלָיו, וּמִתְאַבְּלִין עָלָיו, אֶלָּא אִם כֵּן נוֹדַע בְּבֵרוּר שֶׁהוּא רַק בֶּן שְׁמוֹנָה חֳדָשִׁים (דְּלָאו בַּר־קַיָּמָא הוּא). וְאִם יָדוּעַ בְּבֵרוּר שֶׁהוּא בֶּן תִּשְׁעָה חֳדָשִׁים, כְּגוֹן שֶׁבָּעַל וּפֵרַשׁ וְנוֹלַד חַי לְתִשְׁעָה חֳדָשִׁים גְּמוּרִים, אֲפִלּוּ מֵת בְּיוֹם שֶׁנּוֹלַד בּוֹ, קוֹרְעִין עָלָיו, וְאוֹנְנִין עָלָיו וּמִתְאַבְּלִין עָלָיו.

ד) תְּאוֹמִים שֶׁמֵּת אֶחָד מֵהֶם תּוֹךְ שְׁלֹשִׁים וַאֲפִלּוּ בַּיּוֹם הַשְּׁלֹשִׁים, וְהַשֵּׁנִי חַי לְאַחַר שְׁלֹשִׁים, לֹא אָמְרִינָן מִדְּזֶה חַי לְאַחַר שְׁלֹשִׁים, גַּם הָרִאשׁוֹן הָיָה בֶּן קַיָּמָא, אֶלָּא אֵין מִתְאַבְּלִין עָלָיו.

ה) גֵּר אוֹ גִּיֹּרֶת שֶׁנִּתְגַּיְּרוּ עִם בְּנֵיהֶם, אֵין מִתְאַבְּלִין זֶה עַל זֶה, דְּגֵר שֶׁנִּתְגַּיֵּר, כְּקָטָן שֶׁנּוֹלַד דָּמֵי, וְקֻרְבָה שֶׁהָיְתָה בְּגֵיוּתָם אֵינָהּ קֻרְבָה.

Chapter 203

Relatives and Infants
For Whom Mourning Must Be Observed

1) One is obligated to mourn for seven relatives: his father and mother, his son and daughter, his brother and sister, whether from a common father or mother, and even a married sister, a husband for his wife, and a wife for her husband.

2) It is customary for other relatives too, to observe partial mourning during the first week until after Shabbos. It is therefore customary not to bathe in warm water, and not to change their clothing as they do every other Shabbos. Not all relatives are alike in this respect. For a first cousin, a son's son or a daughter's son, one should wear all his Shabbos clothing except for his outer garment. For a father-in-law, a mother-in-law, or for a paternal or maternal grandfather; also a woman for her father-in-law, her mother-in-law, and for her paternal or maternal grandfather, they should wear only a white Shabbos shirt, and a woman may also wear her white scarf. It is also customary not to bathe, and not to shampoo the hair. One should also not eat out of the house at a religious feast or at any social gatherings. After Shabbos, all of these activities are permitted.[1]

3) When it is not known if a child was born at term or prematurely, if he died within thirty days after birth, or even on the thirtieth day, even if his hair and nails were fully grown, one does not tear his garments for him, nor does he observe the laws of *onein.* Neither does he mourn for him, because it may have been an aborted child. If he died after thirty days, even on the thirty-first day at an earlier hour than that on which he was born, one must tear his garments, observe the laws of *onein,* and mourn over him, unless it is known for sure, that he was born in the eighth month of pregnancy (and is not a viable child). If it was known for sure that he was born in the ninth month, for example, if after cohabitation, the father was separated from his wife, and he was born alive, nine full months later, even if he dies on the day he was born, one must tear his garments, observe the laws of *onein* and mourn over him.

4) If one of twin children dies within thirty days after birth or even on the thirtieth day, and the other survives after thirty days, we do not draw the conclusion, that since one lived after thirty days, the other one, too, was a viable child. Therefore mourning is not observed for him.

5) A male or female proselyte who converted to Judaism with their children, do not observe mourning for one another; for a proselyte is considered like a new-born infant, and their kinship when they were Gentiles is no longer recognized as kinship.

---

1. All these things depend on the prevailing customs. *Shach* 374:7.

סִימָן רד
אֵימָתַי מַתְחִילָה הָאֲבֵלוּת

א) מִשֶּׁנִּקְבַּר הַמֵּת וְנִגְמְרָה סְתִימַת הַקֶּבֶר בֶּעָפָר מִיָּד מַתְחִילָה הָאֲבֵלוּת, וְחוֹלֵץ הַמִּנְעָלִים שָׁם בְּבֵית־הַקְּבָרוֹת וְאִם צָרִיךְ לֵילֵךְ לְבֵיתוֹ בֵּין שְׁכוּנַת גּוֹיִם, יָכוֹל לְנָעֳלָם, אֶלָּא שֶׁיִּתֵּן בָּהֶם קְצָת עָפָר.

ב) אִם בֵּית־הַקְּבָרוֹת סָמוּךְ לָעִיר, וְהָאָבֵל לֹא הָלַךְ שָׁמָּה אֶלָּא חָזַר לְבֵיתוֹ, אֵינוֹ צָרִיךְ לִנְהוֹג אֲבֵלוּת, אֶלָּא מִשָּׁעָה שֶׁאוֹמְרִים לוֹ שֶׁנִּסְתַּם הַקֶּבֶר. וּמִכָּל מָקוֹם אִם הוּא סָמוּךְ לַלַּיְלָה וְרוֹצֶה שֶׁיַּעֲלֶה לוֹ יוֹם זֶה, אֲזַי מִשָּׁעָה שֶׁהוּא מְשַׁעֵר שֶׁנִּסְתַּם הַקֶּבֶר, יָכוֹל לִנְהוֹג אֲבֵלוּת. וְאִם יֹאמְרוּ לוֹ אַחַר כָּךְ שֶׁנִּסְתַּם הַקֶּבֶר קֹדֶם הַלַּיְלָה, עוֹלֶה לוֹ זֶה הַיּוֹם. וְאִם הוּא עֶרֶב הָרֶגֶל, מְבַטֵּל הָרֶגֶל אֶת הָאֲבֵלוּת שֶׁל שִׁבְעָה.

ג) בִּמְקוֹמוֹת שֶׁשּׁוֹלְחִים אֶת הַמֵּת לְקָבְרוֹ בְּעִיר אַחֶרֶת וְאֵינָם יוֹדְעִים מָתַי יִקְבְּרוּהוּ, אֲזַי הָאֲבֵלִים הַנִּשְׁאָרִים בְּעִירָם מִיָּד כְּשֶׁחָזְרוּ מִן הַלַּיְלָה, מַתְחִילִין לְהִתְאַבֵּל, וּמוֹנִים מֵאָז שִׁבְעָה וְגַם שְׁלֹשִׁים. וְהַהוֹלְכִים עִם הַמֵּת עַד מְקוֹם קְבוּרָתוֹ, מוֹנִים מִשֶּׁיִּקָּבֵר. וְיֵשׁ אוֹמְרִים, דְּאִם גָּדוֹל הַבַּיִת הוֹלֵךְ עִם הַמֵּת, אֲזַי גַּם הַנִּשְׁאָרִים אֵינָם מוֹנִים אֶלָּא מִשֶּׁיִּקָּבֵר. וּמְשַׁעֲרִין לְפִי אֹמֶד הַדַּעַת מָתַי נִקְבַּר, וּמַתְחִילִין לְהִתְאַבֵּל. (וְהַיָּמִים שֶׁבֵּינְתַיִם, דִּינָם כִּדְלְעֵיל סִימָן קצו סָעִיף ה׳ וְסָעִיף ו׳). וַדְוְקָא לְחֻמְרָא אָזְלִינָן בָּתַר גָּדוֹל הַבַּיִת דְּגַם הַנִּשְׁאָרִים אֵינָם מוֹנִים אֶלָּא מִשֶּׁיִּקָּבֵר. אֲבָל אִם גָּדוֹל הַבַּיִת נִשְׁאַר בְּבֵיתוֹ, הַהוֹלְכִים עִם הַמֵּת אֵינָן נִגְרָרִין אַחֲרָיו, אֶלָּא מוֹנִין מִשֶּׁנִּקְבַּר.

ד) מִי שֶׁטָּבַע בַּמַּיִם אוֹ שֶׁהֲרָגוּהוּ גוֹיִם וְאֵינוֹ נִמְצָא לְקָבְרוֹ, כָּל זְמַן שֶׁלֹּא נִתְיָאֲשׁוּ מִלְּבַקְּשׁוֹ, לֹא חָלָה לֹא אֲנִינוּת וְלֹא אֲבֵלוּת, וּמֻתָּרִין אֲפִלּוּ בְּתַשְׁמִישׁ. וּמִשָּׁעָה שֶׁנִּתְיָאֲשׁוּ מִלְּבַקְּשׁוֹ עוֹד, מַתְחִילִין לְהִתְאַבֵּל. וְאִם לְאַחַר יְמֵי הָאֵבֶל נִמְצָא וְהוּבָא לִקְבוּרָה, אֵינָן צְרִיכִין לִנְהוֹג אֲבֵלוּת עוֹד, אֶלָּא שֶׁאִם הוּא אָבִיו אוֹ אִמּוֹ, צָרִיךְ לִקְרוֹעַ. וּמִי שֶׁטָּבַע בַּמַּיִם וְיֵשׁ לוֹ אִשָּׁה וְהוּא בְּעִנְיָן שֶׁאֵין מַתִּירִין אוֹתָהּ לְהִנָּשֵׂא, אֵין נוֹהֲגִין עָלָיו אֲבֵלוּת,

1. *Shvuss Yaakov* Responsa I:103. However, the *Maharam Habib* and *Shach* 375:7 maintain even if he is not married one may not observe the rites of mourning for we fear people will exterpolate from this to other cases and subsequently will permit the wife of such a person to

Chapter 204

When Does The Mourning Period Begin?

1) The mourning period begins from the time the deceased is buried, and the grave is filled with earth. The mourner must remove his shoes at the cemetery. If he has to walk home through a non-Jewish neighborhood, he may wear his shoes, but should place a little earth in them.

2) If the cemetery is close to the city, and the mourner did not go [to the cemetery] but went straight home after the funeral service, he does not observe the laws of mourning until he is told that the grave has been filled. However, if night is approaching and he wants this day counted as one of the seven days of mourning, then, from the time he assumes that the grave was filled, he may begin to observe mourning. If he is informed thereafter that the grave was filled before nightfall, he may count that day as one of the seven, and if it was the day preceding a Festival, the Festival cancels the remainder of the seven days of mourning.

3) In places where the deceased are sent to another city for burial, and they do not know when he will be buried, the mourners who remain in the city should begin to observe the period of mourning immediately upon returning from the funeral, and count from that time the seven days and the thirty days of mourning. The mourners who accompany the deceased to the place of burial count from the time he was buried. Some *poskim* maintain that if the head of the family accompanies the deceased, then also those who remain behind count from the time he was buried. They have to estimate the time he was buried, and begin to observe the laws of mourning. (Regarding the intervening days, See above Chapter 196:5, 6) It is only regarding a more strict application that the other mourners follow the head of the family, and even those who remain at home start counting from the time of burial, but if the head of the family remained at home, those mourners who accompany the deceased are not subject to him, rather they begin to count from the time of the burial.

4) If a person drowned, or was murdered by non-Jews, and his body was not found for burial, so long as the search has not been abandoned, the laws of *onein* and mourning do not apply, and even marital relations are permitted. From the time the search is finally abandoned, they begin to observe the laws of mourning. If, after they finish the period of mourning, the body is found, and brought to burial they need not observe another mourning period. However, if the deceased is his father or mother, he must tear his garments. If a man drowned and left a wife,[1] and proof of his death is so unsubstantiated[2] that she cannot be permitted to remarry,

---

remarry. And this is forbidden. The *Chassam Sofer*, Responsa 344, says one may rely on the *Shvuss Yaakov*.

2. As when he drowned in a sea where he possibly came out and was just not noticed.

וְאֵין אוֹמְרִים אַחֲרָיו קַדִּישׁ. וּמִכָּל מָקוֹם יִשְׁתַּדְּלוּ לַעֲשׂוֹת נַחַת־רוּחַ לַנְּשָׁמָה לְהִתְפַּלֵּל לִפְרָקִים לִפְנֵי הַתֵּבָה, וְלִקְרוֹת הַהַפְטָרָה, וּלְבָרֵךְ בְּזִמּוּן וְלִתֵּן צְדָקָה, וְלִלְמוֹד אוֹ לִשְׂכּוֹר מִי שֶׁיִּלְמַד עֲבוּרוֹ.

ה) מִי שֶׁמֵּת לוֹ קָרוֹב וְהוּא אֵינֶנּוּ שָׁם וְנוֹדַע לוֹ בְּמָקוֹם אֲשֶׁר הוּא שָׁם, מוֹנֶה לְעַצְמוֹ מִשָּׁעָה שֶׁנּוֹדַע לוֹ. וַאֲפִלּוּ בָּא אַחַר כָּךְ לִמְקוֹם הַמֵּת אֶל שְׁאָר הָאֲבֵלִים שֶׁהִתְחִילוּ מִקֹּדֶם לְהִתְאַבֵּל, לֹא יְקַצֵּר אֲבֵלוּתוֹ בִּשְׁבִיל זֶה. וְכֵן אֲפִלּוּ אִם לֹא נוֹדַע לוֹ עַד שֶׁבָּא אֶל הָאֲבֵלִים, אֶלָּא שֶׁהָאֲבֵלִים אֵינָם בִּמְקוֹם שֶׁמֵּת הַמֵּת וְלֹא בִּמְקוֹם הַקְּבוּרָה, גַּם כֵּן מוֹנֶה לְעַצְמוֹ מִשָּׁעָה שֶׁנּוֹדַע לוֹ.

ו) אֲבָל אִם לֹא נוֹדַע לוֹ עַד שֶׁבָּא אֶל הָאֲבֵלִים שֶׁהֵם בִּמְקוֹם הַמֵּת אוֹ בִּמְקוֹם הַקְּבוּרָה, אֲזַי אִם הָיָה בִּשְׁעַת קְבוּרָה בְּמָקוֹם קָרוֹב, דְּהַיְנוּ לֹא יוֹתֵר מִמַּהֲלַךְ עֶשֶׂר פַּרְסָאוֹת שֶׁהוּא מַהֲלַךְ יוֹם אֶחָד, הֲרֵי זֶה כְּאִלּוּ הָיָה כָּאן בִּשְׁעַת קְבוּרָה וּמוֹנֶה עִמָּהֶם. וַאֲפִלּוּ בָּא בְּיוֹם שְׁבִיעִי קֹדֶם יְצִיאַת בֵּית־הַכְּנֶסֶת, כֵּיוָן שֶׁעֲדַיִן נוֹהֲגִין קְצָת אֲבֵלוּת, מוֹנֶה עִמָּהֶם שִׁבְעָה וּשְׁלֹשִׁים. וְדַוְקָא כְּשֶׁגָּדוֹל הַבַּיִת אֶצְלָם שֶׁכֻּלָּם נִגְרָרִין אַחֲרָיו. אֲבָל אִם לֹא הָיָה שָׁם גְּדוֹל הַבַּיִת, מוֹנֶה לְעַצְמוֹ. וְכֵן אִם בָּא מִמָּקוֹם רָחוֹק, אַף־עַל־פִּי שֶׁיֵּשׁ שָׁם גְּדוֹל הַבַּיִת, מִכָּל מָקוֹם מוֹנֶה לְעַצְמוֹ.

ז) זֶה שֶׁהוּא מוֹנֶה עִם הַנִּמְצָאִים, אֲפִלּוּ הוּא חוֹזֵר לְבֵיתוֹ, מִכָּל מָקוֹם מוֹנֶה עִמָּהֶם.

ח) גְּדוֹל הַבַּיִת שֶׁבָּא מִמָּקוֹם קָרוֹב, אֵינוֹ נִגְרָר אַחַר הַקְּטַנִּים, וּמוֹנֶה לְעַצְמוֹ.

ט) מִי הוּא נִקְרָא גְּדוֹל הַבַּיִת. זֶה אֲשֶׁר עַל פִּי הָאֹמֶד, אִם הָיוּ עוֹסְקִין בְּעִזְבוֹן הַמֵּת, הָיוּ הַדְּבָרִים נֶחְתָּכִין עַל פִּיו, וְהָיוּ כֻּלָּם הוֹלְכִין אַחַר עֲצָתוֹ אֲפִלּוּ הוּא קָטָן בַּשָּׁנִים, נִקְרָא גְּדוֹל הַבַּיִת. וַאֲפִלּוּ אֵינוֹ יוֹרֵשׁ, כְּגוֹן שֶׁהָאַלְמָנָה בְּכָאן וְהִיא מַנְהֶגֶת אֶת הַבַּיִת, הִיא נִקְרֵאת גְּדוֹל הַבַּיִת. מִי שֶׁהוּא דָר אֵצֶל חָמִיו וּמֵתָה אִשְׁתּוֹ, חָמִיו הוּא הַגָּדוֹל.

י) מִי שֶׁשָּׁמַע שֶׁמֵּת לוֹ מֵת, וּכְבָר הִתְפַּלְּלוּ הַצִּבּוּר עַרְבִית וַעֲדַיִן הוּא

---

3. So as not to mistakenly allow his wife to remarry. (For someone may testify in *Beis Din*, on this basis, that her husband died.) This law is the opinion of the *Rif* and *Beis Yoseif.* But the

mourning should not be observed for him,[3] and *Kaddish*[4] should not be recited for him. Nevertheless, his kin should try to ease his soul by occasionally leading the prayers at services in the synagogue, by reading the *Haftorah,* by leading the *Birkas Hamazon,*[5] by giving charity, and by learning Torah, or by hiring someone else to learn Torah in his memory.

5) If a person lost a relative, and he was not there at the time of death but learned about it later at the place where he is, he should count the days of mourning from the time he became aware of it. Even though afterwards he arrives at the place of the deceased, where the other mourners reside, who began their mourning before he did, he must not abreviate his mourning period because of this. Similarly, even if he was not aware of it until he came to the mourners, but the mourners are neither at the place where the death occurred, nor where he was buried, he too, begins to count [the days of mourning] from the time he became aware of it.

6) However if he was not aware of it, until he came to the mourners, and they are at the place where the death occured, or at the place where he was buried, then if at the time of the burial he was near by, that is not further than ten *parasangs,* which is a day's walk, it is considered though he was present at the time of the burial and he counts together with them. Even if he came on the seventh day, before the people leave the Synagogue, since the mourners are still observing some mourning, he counts the seven and thirty days of mourning with them. This is so only when the head of the family is with them, as they all follow him, but if the head of the family is not there, he counts on his own, or if he came from far away, even if the head of the family is there, nevertheless he must count on his own.

7) If a person began counting with the mourners who were present, even if he returns to his home, nevertheless he continues counting with them.

8) The head of the family who is close by does not follow the younger members, but counts on his own.

9) Who is called the head of the family? It is the one whose judgement would be accepted and whose advice everyone would follow, if they were engaged in dividing the inheritance. Even if he is young in years and even if he is not an heir, he is called the head of the family. For example, if the widow is present, and she manages the household, she is called the head of the family. If a person lives with his father-in-law, and his wife dies, his father-in-law is the head of the family.

10) If one becomes aware of the death of his relative after the congregation had prayed the *Maariv* service, but it is still day, [6] if he has not yet prayed *Maariv,* he is

---

majority permit mourning (*Rashba, Ra'avan, Rambam, Tur, Mordecai,* etc.) However, we are strict like the *Rif.*

4. *Chinuch Beis Yehudah* Responsa 91. But the *Knessess Yechezel,* Responsa 53, and *Mishkenos Yaakov* Responsa 69 permit the son to say *Kaddish.*

5. See *Kitzur Shulchan Aruch,* Chapter. 45.

6. See *Kitzur Shulchan Aruch,* Chapter. 70:1.

יוֹם, אִם הוּא עֲדַיִן לֹא הִתְפַּלֵּל עַרְבִית, אֵינוֹ נִגְרָר אַחַר הַצִּבּוּר, וְאוֹתוֹ הַיּוֹם עוֹלֶה לוֹ. אֲבָל אִם הִתְפַּלֵּל עַרְבִית, שׁוּב אֵינוֹ עוֹלֶה לוֹ אוֹתוֹ הַיּוֹם, וּמוֹנֶה שִׁבְעָה וּשְׁלֹשִׁים מִיּוֹם הַמָּחֳרָת. וְדַוְקָא לְחֻמְרָא אָמְרִינָן הָכִי, וְלָא לְקֻלָּא. שֶׁאִם שָׁמַע בַּיּוֹם הַשְּׁלֹשִׁים לְאַחַר שֶׁהִתְפַּלֵּל עַרְבִית לָא אָמְרִינָן שֶׁכְּבָר הוּא לַיְלָה וַהֲוֵי לֵהּ שְׁמוּעָה רְחוֹקָה לְהָקֵל עָלָיו, אֶלָּא חָשְׁבִינָן לֵהּ לְיוֹם, וַהֲוֵי לֵהּ שְׁמוּעָה קְרוֹבָה, וְיוֹם זֶה עוֹלֶה לוֹ בְּמִמָּה־נַפְשָׁךְ. וּלְעִנְיַן תְּפִלִּין בִּשְׁאָר הַיָּמִים, אִם שָׁמַע לְאַחַר שֶׁהִתְפַּלֵּל עַרְבִית וַעֲדַיִן הוּא יוֹם, יַנִּיחֵם לְמָחָר בְּלֹא בְרָכָה וִיכַסֶּה אוֹתָם. וְאִם הָיָה כֵּן בַּיּוֹם הַשְּׁלֹשִׁים, מַנִּיחַ לְמָחָר תְּפִלִּין וּמְבָרֵךְ עֲלֵיהֶם בְּמִמָּה־נַפְשָׁךְ. וְאִשָּׁה שֶׁשָּׁמְעָה שֶׁמֵּת לָהּ מֵת וּכְבָר הִתְפַּלְּלוּ הַצִּבּוּר עַרְבִית, אֶלָּא שֶׁעֲדַיִן הוּא יוֹם, אִם אֵין דַּרְכָּהּ לְהִתְפַּלֵּל עַרְבִית, נִגְרֶרֶת אַחַר הַצִּבּוּר לְחֻמְרָא, וְאוֹתוֹ הַיּוֹם אֵינוֹ עוֹלֶה לָהּ.

יא) בִּשְׁעַת הַדֶּבֶר, רַחֲמָנָא לִצְלַן, נוֹהֲגִין שֶׁאֵין מִתְאַבְּלִין, מִשּׁוּם בַּעֲתוּתָא. וְאִם עָבַר הַזַּעַם בְּתוֹךְ שְׁלֹשִׁים, צָרִיךְ לְהִתְאַבֵּל אָז. אֲבָל אִם לֹא עָבַר עַד לְאַחַר שְׁלֹשִׁים אוֹ שֶׁהִפְסִיק רֶגֶל בֵּינְתַיִם אֵינוֹ צָרִיךְ לְהִתְאַבֵּל אַחַר כָּךְ.

סִימָן רה
דִּין סְעוּדַת הַבְרָאָה

א) הָאָבֵל, בַּיּוֹם הָרִאשׁוֹן, אָסוּר לוֹ לֶאֱכוֹל סְעוּדָה הָרִאשׁוֹנָה מִשֶּׁלוֹ. וּמִצְוָה עַל שְׁכֵנָיו שֶׁיִּשְׁלְחוּ לוֹ לִסְעוּדָה הָרִאשׁוֹנָה, וְנִקְרֵאת סְעוּדַת הַבְרָאָה. וּתְחִלַּת הַסְּעוּדָה, תְּהֵא בְּבֵצִים אוֹ עֲדָשִׁים שֶׁהֵן עֲגֻלּוֹת וְאֵין לָהֶן פֶּה, כְּמוֹ שֶׁהָאָבֵל אֵין לוֹ פֶּה. וְאַחַר זֹאת, מֻתָּר לוֹ לֶאֱכוֹל כָּל מַאֲכָל וַאֲפִלּוּ בָשָׂר. וּמֻתָּר לִשְׁתּוֹת קְצָת יַיִן בְּתוֹךְ הַסְּעוּדָה כְּדֵי לִשְׁרוֹת הַמַּאֲכָל בְּמֵעָיו, אֲבָל לֹא לִרְווֹת. (יֵשׁ אוֹמְרִים, דְּכָל הַיּוֹם הָרִאשׁוֹן, אָסוּר לוֹ לֶאֱכוֹל מִשֶּׁלוֹ, אֲפִלּוּ אוֹכֵל כַּמָּה פְּעָמִים בַּיּוֹם).

ב) אִם אֵינוֹ רוֹצֶה לֶאֱכוֹל בַּיּוֹם עַד הַלַּיְלָה, כֵּיוָן שֶׁעָבַר הַיּוֹם, הֻתַּר לוֹ לֶאֱכוֹל מִשֶּׁלוֹ. וְלָכֵן מִי שֶׁהוּא דָר יְחִידִי בִּכְפָר וְאֵין מִי שֶׁיִּשְׁלַח לוֹ סְעוּדַת הַבְרָאָה, נָכוֹן שֶׁיִּתְעַנֶּה עַד הַלַּיְלָה. וּמִכָּל מָקוֹם אִם אֵינוֹ יָכוֹל לְהִתְעַנּוֹת, אֵינוֹ מְחֻיָּב לְצַעֵר אֶת עַצְמוֹ וּמֻתָּר לוֹ לֶאֱכוֹל מִשֶּׁלוֹ.

not drawn after the congregation, and he can include that day in his mourning period. If, however, he too had already prayed *Maariv,* that day is not counted, and he must count the seven days of mourning and the thirty days of mourning from the following day. This rule is applied only for stricter observance and not for leniency. Thus if he becomes aware of the death on the thirtieth day after the burial, after he has already prayed *Maariv,* we do not say that it is already night and it is delayed news[7] to make it lenient for him, but we consider it as day, and thus it is a timely news. Either way this day counts towards the mourning period. With regard to *Tefillin* on the other days, if he heard of the death after he has prayed *Maariv* but it is still daytime, he should put them on the next day without reciting the *berachah* and he should cover them. If this happened on the thirtieth day, he should put on *Tefillin* the following day, and should recite the *berachah* regardless. If a woman heard of the death of a relative, after the congregation prayed the *Maariv* service, but it is still daytime, if she usually does not pray *Maariv,* she is drawn after the congregation for the strict application of the law, and that day is not counted as one of the days of mourning.[8]

11) During a plague, God forbid, it is customary not to observe any mourning, because of the prevailing fear and panic. If the plague passed within thirty days from the day of death, the laws of mourning must be observed. However, if the plague did not pass, until after thirty days from the day of death, or if a Festival had intervened in the meantime, mourning need not be observed.

Chapter 205

The Meal of Condolence

1) On the first day of mourning, the mourner is forbidden to eat his first meal from his own food. It is a *mitzvah* for his neighbors to send him food for his first meal, which is called the meal of condolence. This meal should begin with eggs or lentils, for they are round and have no mouth, just as the mourner has no mouth (speech). After this course he may eat all foods, even meat. He is permitted to drink a little wine during the meal, in order to help digest the food in his stomach, but not enough to satisfy his desire. (Some *Poskeim* maintain that he is forbidden to eat of his own food the entire first day, even if he eats many meals on that day).

2) If the mourner does not wish to eat that day until nightfall, since the day has passed, he is permitted to eat of his own food. Therefore, if he lives alone in a village, and there is nobody to send him the meal of condolence, it is proper for him to fast until nightfall. Nevertheless, if he cannot fast, he is not obliged to afflict himself, and he may eat of his own food.

---

7. See Chapter 206.
8. *Maharshal.* But the *Shach* 375:14 disagrees.

ג) אִשָּׁה נְשׂוּאָה שֶׁאֵרְעָהּ אֵבֶל, אָסוּר לָהּ לֶאֱכוֹל סְעוּדָה הָרִאשׁוֹנָה מִשֶּׁל בַּעְלָהּ, דְּכֵיוָן שֶׁהוּא מְחֻיָּב לְזוּנָהּ, שֶׁלָּהּ הִיא. וְכֵן מִי שֶׁיֵּשׁ לוֹ שָׂכִיר, אִם אוֹכֵל בִּשְׂכָרוֹ וְאֵרְעוֹ אֵבֶל, לֹא יֹאכַל סְעוּדָה הָרִאשׁוֹנָה מִשֶּׁל בַּעַל־הַבַּיִת שֶׁלּוֹ. אֲבָל מִי שֶׁהוּא זָן יָתוֹם אוֹ בְנוֹ אוֹ בִתּוֹ בְּלֹא תְנַאי וְאֵרְעָם אֵבֶל, יְכוֹלִים לֶאֱכוֹל מִשֶּׁלּוֹ, שֶׁאֵין זֹאת מִשֶּׁלָּהֶם.

ד) אִשָּׁה, אֵין לַאֲנָשִׁים לְהַבְרוֹת אוֹתָהּ, אֶלָּא נָשִׁים מַבְרוֹת אוֹתָהּ.

ה) אִם נִקְבַּר הַמֵּת בַּלַּיְלָה, אִם רוֹצֶה לֶאֱכוֹל בַּלַּיְלָה, אָסוּר לוֹ לֶאֱכוֹל מִשֶּׁלּוֹ, אֶלָּא מַבְרִין אוֹתוֹ. וְאִם אֵינוֹ רוֹצֶה לֶאֱכוֹל בַּלַּיְלָה, אָסוּר לוֹ לֶאֱכוֹל בַּיּוֹם סְעוּדָה הָרִאשׁוֹנָה מִשֶּׁלּוֹ, מִשּׁוּם דְּהַיּוֹם הוֹלֵךְ אַחַר הַלַּיְלָה, וַהֲוֵי לֵהּ יוֹם רִאשׁוֹן.

ו) אִם נִקְבַּר הַמֵּת בְּעֶרֶב שַׁבָּת מִתֵּשַׁע שָׁעוֹת וּלְמַעְלָה שֶׁאָז אָסוּר לִקְבּוֹעַ סְעוּדָה, אֵין מַבְרִין אוֹתוֹ, מִפְּנֵי כְּבוֹד שַׁבָּת, וְלֹא יֹאכַל כְּלוּם עַד הַלָּיְלָה.

ז) מַבְרִין עַל שְׁמוּעָה קְרוֹבָה וְאֵין מַבְרִין עַל שְׁמוּעָה רְחוֹקָה. שָׁמַע שְׁמוּעָה קְרוֹבָה בַּשַּׁבָּת, אֵין מַבְרִין אוֹתוֹ, וְאוֹכֵל מִשֶּׁלּוֹ. וְגַם בְּיוֹם רִאשׁוֹן שֶׁלְּאַחֲרָיו, אֵין מַבְרִין אוֹתוֹ, מִפְּנֵי שֶׁכְּבָר נִדְחָה יוֹם הַשְּׁמוּעָה.

ח) וְכֵן מִי שֶׁמֵּת לוֹ מֵת וְנִקְבַּר בְּיוֹם־טוֹב, אֵין מַבְרִין אוֹתוֹ. וְגַם לְאַחַר יוֹם־טוֹב אֵין מַבְרִין אוֹתוֹ, כֵּיוָן שֶׁכְּבָר נִדְחָה. אֲבָל אִם נִקְבַּר בְּחֹל־הַמּוֹעֵד, מַבְרִין אוֹתוֹ, אֶלָּא שֶׁאוֹכֵל כְּשֶׁהוּא יוֹשֵׁב עַל הַסַּפְסָל אֵצֶל הַשֻּׁלְחָן כְּדַרְכּוֹ, כִּי אֵין אֲבֵלוּת בְּחֹל־הַמּוֹעֵד.

ט) הָיוּ נוֹהֲגִין לְהִתְעַנּוֹת בְּיוֹם מִיתַת תַּלְמִיד־חָכָם.

סִימָן רו

דִּין שְׁמוּעָה קְרוֹבָה וּשְׁמוּעָה רְחוֹקָה

א) מִי שֶׁבָּאָה לוֹ שְׁמוּעָה שֶׁמֵּת לוֹ קָרוֹב שֶׁהוּא חַיָּב לְהִתְאַבֵּל עָלָיו, אִם בָּאָה לוֹ בְּתוֹךְ שְׁלֹשִׁים וַאֲפִלּוּ בְּיוֹם הַשְּׁלֹשִׁים עַצְמוֹ, הֲרֵי זוֹ שְׁמוּעָה קְרוֹבָה, וְקוֹרֵעַ. וְחַיָּב לִנְהוֹג שִׁבְעָה יְמֵי אֲבֵלוּת מִיּוֹם שֶׁהִגִּיעָה לוֹ הַשְּׁמוּעָה. וְגַם אֲבֵלוּת שֶׁנּוֹהֵג בִּשְׁלֹשִׁים, מוֹנֶה מִיּוֹם הַשְּׁמוּעָה. וְיוֹם הַשְּׁמוּעָה, דִּינוֹ כְּיוֹם הַקְּבוּרָה לְכָל דָּבָר. וְאוֹתָן שְׁלֹשִׁים יוֹם שֶׁנִּקְרְאָה בָהֶן שְׁמוּעָה קְרוֹבָה, מוֹנֶה מִיּוֹם הַקְּבוּרָה וְלֹא מִיּוֹם הַמִּיתָה.

3) If a married woman became a mourner, she is forbidden to eat her first meal from her husband's food, for since it is his duty to support her, it is considered as her own food. Similarly, if a hired person works for someone and his meals are part of his wages, and he became a mourner, he should not eat his first meal from his employers's food. However, if a person supports an orphan, or his own grownup son or daughter without any legal commitment to do so, and they became mourners, they may eat their first meal from his food for it is not considered as their own.

4) A woman should not be provided with the condolence meal by men, rather women should provide her with the meal.

5) If the deceased was buried at night and the mourner wishes to eat at night, he is forbidden to eat of his own food, but it must be provided for him by others. If he does not wish to eat that night, he is forbidden to eat his first meal from his own food during the daytime, for since the daytime follows the night, it is still the first day of his mourning.

6) If the burial took place on Friday, after the ninth hour of the day, when it is forbidden to eat a regular meal, he should not be sent the meal of condolence out of respect for the Shabbos and the mourner should eat nothing until the evening.

7) The meal of condolence is sent only to one who received timely news, but it is not sent to one who received delayed news. If one received timely news on Shabbos, the condolence meal is not sent to him for he may eat his own food. Also on the following day (Sunday) the condolence meal is not sent to him, because the need for it was cancelled on the day he received the news.

8) Also, if one's relative dies, and was buried on Yom Tov, the condolence meal is not sent to him. After Yom Tov you also do not send him this meal because the need for it was already cancelled. However, if the burial took place on *Chol Ha'moed,* the condolence meal should be sent to him, but he should eat it while sitting on a chair, at the table, in his usual manner, because there is no mourning on *Chol Ha'moed.*

9) It was the custom to fast on the day a Torah scholar passed away.

Chapter 206

The Laws of Timely and Delayed News

1) If a person heard of the death of a relative for whom he is obliged to observe mourning, within thirty days of his death or even on the thirtieth day itself, such tidings are timely and he must tear his garments. He is obliged to observe the seven days of mourning from the day he received the news. The thirty days of mourning are also counted from the day he received the news. And the day he received the news is like the day of burial with regard to all its laws. The thirty-day period during which the news is considered timely is counted from the day of burial, and not from the day of death.

ב) בָּאָה לוֹ הַשְּׁמוּעָה לְאַחַר שְׁלֹשִׁים יוֹם, זוֹהִי שְׁמוּעָה רְחוֹקָה, וְאֵינוֹ צָרִיךְ לִנְהוֹג אֲבֵלוּת רַק שָׁעָה אֶחָת. לָא שְׁנָא שָׁמַע בַּיּוֹם, וְלָא שְׁנָא שָׁמַע בַּלַּיְלָה וְנָהַג שָׁעָה אַחַת, דַּיּוֹ, וַאֲפִלּוּ עַל אָבִיו וְאִמּוֹ. אַךְ דְּבָרִים שֶׁנּוֹהֲגִין עַל אָבִיו וְעַל אִמּוֹ כָּל שְׁנֵים עָשָׂר חֹדֶשׁ, נוֹהֵג גַּם בִּשְׁמוּעָה רְחוֹקָה, וּמוֹנֶה שְׁנֵים עָשָׂר חֹדֶשׁ מִיּוֹם הַמִּיתָה. וְאִם בָּאָה לוֹ הַשְּׁמוּעָה עַל אָבִיו וְאִמּוֹ לְאַחַר שְׁנֵים עָשָׂר חֹדֶשׁ, אֵינוֹ נוֹהֵג אֲבֵלוּת אֶלָּא שָׁעָה אַחַת גַּם בַּדְּבָרִים שֶׁנּוֹהֲגִין כָּל שְׁנֵים עָשָׂר חֹדֶשׁ.

ג) הַשּׁוֹמֵעַ שְׁמוּעָה רְחוֹקָה, אֵינוֹ צָרִיךְ לִנְהוֹג כָּל דִּין אֲבֵלוּת, אֶלָּא דַּיּוֹ בַּחֲלִיצַת מִנְעָל לְבַד, וּמֻתָּר בִּמְלָאכָה וּרְחִיצָה וְסִיכָה וְתַשְׁמִישׁ־הַמִּטָּה וְתַלְמוּד־תּוֹרָה. וְאִם אֵין מִנְעָלִים בְּרַגְלָיו בִּשְׁעַת שְׁמוּעָה, צָרִיךְ לַעֲשׂוֹת מַעֲשֶׂה אַחֵר שֶׁיְּהֵא נִכָּר שֶׁהוּא עוֹשֶׂה מִשּׁוּם אֲבֵלוּת, כְּגוֹן שֶׁיֵּשֵׁב עַל הַקַּרְקַע שָׁעָה אֶחָת.

ד) בָּאָה לוֹ שְׁמוּעָה קְרוֹבָה בְּשַׁבָּת, יוֹם הַשַּׁבָּת עוֹלֶה לוֹ לְיוֹם אֶחָד, וּלְמוֹצָאֵי שַׁבָּת קוֹרֵעַ, וּמוֹנֶה לוֹ עוֹד שִׁשָּׁה יָמִים.

ה) בָּאָה לוֹ שְׁמוּעָה קְרוֹבָה בְּשַׁבָּת אוֹ בְּרֶגֶל, וּלְמוֹצָאֵי שַׁבָּת אוֹ לְמוֹצָאֵי הָרֶגֶל נַעֲשֵׂית רְחוֹקָה, אָסוּר בְּיוֹם הַשַּׁבָּת אוֹ בִימֵי הָרֶגֶל בִּדְבָרִים שֶׁבְּצִנְעָא. וּלְמוֹצָאֵי שַׁבָּת וְהָרֶגֶל, נוֹהֵג שָׁעָה אַחַת אֲבֵלוּת כְּמוֹ בִּשְׁמוּעָה רְחוֹקָה.

ו) בָּאָה לוֹ שְׁמוּעָה קְרוֹבָה בְּשַׁבָּת וְהוּא עֶרֶב יוֹם־טוֹב, כֵּיוָן שֶׁדְּבָרִים שֶׁבְּצִנְעָא נוֹהֵג בּוֹ, מְבַטֵּל הָרֶגֶל אֶת הַשִּׁבְעָה.

ז) הַשּׁוֹמֵעַ שְׁמוּעָה רְחוֹקָה בְּשַׁבָּת אוֹ בְּרֶגֶל, אֵינוֹ נוֹהֵג אֲבֵלוּת. וַאֲפִלּוּ בִּדְבָרִים שֶׁבְּצִנְעָא מֻתָּר. וּלְמוֹצָאֵי שַׁבָּת וָרֶגֶל, נוֹהֵג שָׁעָה אַחַת וְדַיּוֹ.

ח) מִי שֶׁשָּׁמַע לְאַחַר הָרֶגֶל שֶׁמֵּת לוֹ מֵת קֹדֶם הָרֶגֶל, אַף־עַל־גַּב דִּלְאוֹתָן שֶׁנָּהֲגוּ אֲבֵלוּת קֹדֶם הָרֶגֶל בָּא הָרֶגֶל וְהִפְסִיק, מִכָּל מָקוֹם לְדִידֵהּ כֵּיוָן שֶׁלֹּא נָהַג כְּלָל קֹדֶם הָרֶגֶל, כֹּל שֶׁשָּׁמַע אֲפִלּוּ בַּיּוֹם הַשְּׁלֹשִׁים מִיּוֹם הַקְּבוּרָה, הֲוֵי אֶצְלוֹ שְׁמוּעָה קְרוֹבָה, וְצָרִיךְ לִנְהוֹג שִׁבְעָה וּשְׁלֹשִׁים.

ט) מִי שֶׁמֵּת לוֹ מֵת וְלֹא נוֹדַע לוֹ, אֵין לְהַגִּיד לוֹ. וְעַל הַמַּגִּיד נֶאֱמַר, וּמוֹצִיא דִּבָּה הוּא כְסִיל. וּמֻתָּרִין לְהַזְמִינוֹ לִסְעוּדַת אֵרוּסִין וּלְכָל שִׂמְחָה,

2) If he received the news after thirty days, it is delayed news, and he needs to observe the laws of mourning for only one hour. Whether he received the news by day or he received it at night, one hour of mourning is sufficient. This is true even for one's parents. However, the mourning which is observed for one's father or mother during the entire twelve months applies even when the news of the death was delayed. These twelve months are counted from the day of death. If one received word of the death of his father or mother, after twelve months, he need observe only one hour of mourning, even with regard to things that are usually observed throughout the twelve months.

3) One who receives delayed news need not observe all the laws of mourning, and removal of his shoes is sufficient. He is permitted to work, bathe, anoint himself, to have marital relations and to study Torah. If he was not wearing shoes when he received the news, he must do something else to indicate that he is doing so to observe mourning such as sitting on the ground for an hour.

4) If he received timely news on Shabbos, the Shabbos is counted as one day, and at the conclusion of Shabbos he must tear his garments and observe six days of mourning.

5) If he received timely news on Shabbos or on Yom Tov, but at the conclusion of Shabbos or Yom Tov it will become delayed news, he must observe all the laws of private mourning on Shabbos or Yom Tov and at the conclusion of Shabbos or *Yom Tov* he should observe one hour's mourning as is done for delayed tidings.

6) If he received timely news on Shabbos and it is the eve of a Yom Tov, since he must observe mourning in privacy, the Yom Tov cancels the seven days of mourning.

7) If one received delayed news on Shabbos or Yom Tov, he should not observe any mourning, not even in private matters. At the conclusion of Shabbos or Yom Tov, he should observe one hour of mourning, and that is sufficient.

8) If one found out after Yom Tov that a relative had died before Yom Tov, although for those who observed mourning before Yom Tov, the Yom Tov cancels the remaining days, nevertheless, since he did not observe any mourning before Yom Tov, the remaining days are not cancelled. [In such a case] if he received the news even on the thirtieth day after the burial, it is timely news for him, and he must observe the seven and thirty-day periods of mourning.

9) If a person lost a relative and does not know about it, you should not inform him of it. Concerning one who bears such news it is said, "He who utters a report is a fool."[1] You are permitted to invite him to a betrothal feast and to any other

1. *Proverbs* 10:18.

כִּי כָּל זְמַן שֶׁהוּא אֵינוֹ יוֹדֵעַ, הֲרֵי הוּא כִּשְׁאָר כָּל אָדָם. וְכֵן בַּעַל שֶׁיּוֹדֵעַ שֶׁמֵּת אֵיזֶה קָרוֹב לְאִשְׁתּוֹ, מֻתָּר לוֹ לְשַׁמֵּשׁ עִמָּהּ, כֵּיוָן שֶׁהִיא אֵינָהּ יוֹדַעַת.

י) אָבֵל אִם אֶחָד שׁוֹאֵל אוֹתוֹ עַל קְרוֹבוֹ (שֶׁמֵּת) אִם הוּא חַי, אֵין לוֹ לְשַׁקֵּר וְלוֹמַר, חַי הוּא, שֶׁנֶּאֱמַר, מִדְּבַר־שֶׁקֶר תִּרְחָק. אֶלָּא יֹאמַר בְּלָשׁוֹן דְּמִשְׁתְּמַע בִּתְרֵי אַנְפִּין, וְישַׁעֵר בְּעַצְמוֹ שֶׁמֵּת.

יא) לְבָנִים זְכָרִים, נוֹהֲגִין לְהוֹדִיעַ כְּשֶׁמֵּת הָאָב אוֹ הָאֵם, כְּדֵי שֶׁיֹּאמְרוּ קַדִּישׁ.

סִימָן רז
דִּינֵי נִחוּם אֲבֵלִים

א) מִצְוָה גְדוֹלָה לְנַחֵם אֲבֵלִים. וּמָצִינוּ בְּהַקָּדוֹשׁ־בָּרוּךְ־הוּא שֶׁנִּחֵם אֲבֵלִים, דִּכְתִיב, וַיְהִי אַחֲרֵי מוֹת אַבְרָהָם, וַיְבָרֶךְ אֱלֹהִים אֶת־יִצְחָק בְּנוֹ. וְהוּא גְמִילוּת־חֶסֶד עִם הַחַיִּים וְעִם הַמֵּתִים. אֵין הַמְנַחֲמִים רַשָּׁאִים לִפְתּוֹחַ פִּיהֶם עַד שֶׁיִּפְתַּח הָאָבֵל תְּחִלָּה, כִּדְמָצִינוּ בְּאִיּוֹב, שֶׁנֶּאֱמַר, וְאֵין־דֹּבֵר אֵלָיו דָּבָר. וּכְתִיב, אַחֲרֵי־כֵן פָּתַח אִיּוֹב אֶת־פִּיהוּ, וַהֲדַר, וַיַּעַן אֱלִיפַז הַתֵּימָנִי. כְּשֶׁרוֹאִים הַמְנַחֲמִים שֶׁהָאָבֵל פּוֹטֵר אוֹתָם, אֵינָן רַשָּׁאִים לֵישֵׁב אֶצְלוֹ.

ב) אָבֵל אוֹ חוֹלֶה, אֵינָן צְרִיכִין לַעֲמוֹד אֲפִלּוּ מִפְּנֵי נָשִׂיא. דֶּרֶךְ־אֶרֶץ הוּא שֶׁאִם אֶחָד רוֹצֶה לְכַבֵּד אֶת חֲבֵרוֹ וְלָקוּם מִפָּנָיו, אוֹמֵר לוֹ חֲבֵרוֹ, שֵׁב. אֲבָל לְאָבֵל אוֹ לְחוֹלֶה, לֹא יֹאמַר כֵּן, מִשּׁוּם דְּמַשְׁמָע, שֵׁב בַּאֲבֵלוּת שֶׁלְּךָ, שֵׁב בָּחֳלִי שֶׁלְּךָ.

ג) לֹא יֹאמַר אָדָם, לֹא נִפְרַעְתִּי כְּפִי מַעֲשַׂי הָרָעִים, וְכַיּוֹצֵא בִּדְבָרִים אֵלּוּ, שֶׁלֹּא יִפְתַּח פֶּה לְשָׂטָן.

ד) לֹא יֹאמַר אָדָם לְאָבֵל, מַה לְּךָ לַעֲשׂוֹת, אִי־אֶפְשָׁר לְשַׁנּוֹת מַה שֶׁעָשָׂה הַקָּדוֹשׁ בָּרוּךְ־הוּא, כִּי זֶהוּ כְּעֵין גִּדּוּף, דְּמַשְׁמַע, הָא אִם הָיָה אֶפְשָׁר לְשַׁנּוֹת, הָיָה מְשַׁנֶּה. אֶלָּא צָרִיךְ הָאָדָם לְקַבֵּל עָלָיו גְּזֵרַת הַשֵּׁם, יִתְבָּרַךְ שְׁמוֹ, בְּאַהֲבָה.

joyful gathering, for as long as he is uninformed, he is like any other person. Also, if a husband knows that his wife's relative died, he is permitted to have marital relations with her, since she does not know about it.

10) However, if you are asked if a relative is alive, you should not lie and say he is alive, for it says, "Keep far from a false matter,"[2] but you should answer him in an ambiguous way, so that he will understand himself that he had died.

11) It is customary to notify sons when their mother or father pass away so that they may say the *Kaddish.*

Chapter 207

Laws of Consoling The Mourners

1) It is a great mitzvah to console mourners. We find that the Holy One blessed is He, consoled mourners, as it is written, "And it came to pass after the death of Avraham, that God blessed his son,"[1] Yitchak, This is an act of kindness to the living as well as to the deceased.[2] The comforters are not allowed to speak before the mourner begins to speak, as it is said concerning Job, "And none spoke a word to him;"[3] and it is written, "And after this Job opened his mouth;"[4] and later it is written "*Eliphaz Hateimani* answered."[5] If the comforters perceive that the mourner wishes them to leave, they are not allowed to remain there.

2) A mourner or a sick person is not required to rise even before a *Nasi.*[6] [Under normal circumstances] it is mannerly, when someone wants to honor his friend, and rise before him, his friend should say, "Sit." However to a mourner or to a sick person, he should not say this, for it might be construed as "Sit in your mourning" or "Sit in your illness".

3) A person should not say, "I have not been punished sufficiently for my evil deeds," or similar expressions, so as not to open the mouth of the Satan.[7]

4) You should not say to the mourner, "What can you do? It is impossible to change what the Holy One blessed is He has done," for this is like blasphemy, for it implies that were it possible to change it, he would do so. Rather a person must accept upon himself the decree of the Almighty, blessed is He, with love.[8]

---

2. *Exodus* 23:7.
1. *Genesis* 25:11.
2. *Maseches Sotah* 14a.
3. *Job* 2:13.
4. *Job* 3:11.
5. See *Maseches Mo'ed Kattan* 25b.
6. The head of the great Sanhedrin.
7. See *Kitzur Shulchan Aruch* chapter 33:14; note 7.
8. See *Kitzur Shulchan Aruch* chapter 59:2.

ה) הָאֲבֵלִים, יֵשׁ לָהֶם לְהִתְאַבֵּל בִּמְקוֹם שֶׁיָּצְאָה נִשְׁמָתוֹ שֶׁל הַמֵּת, כִּי בְּאוֹתוֹ מָקוֹם, נֶפֶשׁ הַמֵּת מִתְאַבֶּלֶת וְשָׁם צְרִיכִין לִתֵּן לָהּ תַּנְחוּמִין. וּמִצְוָה לְהִתְפַּלֵּל שָׁם בַּעֲשָׂרָה שַׁחֲרִית וְעַרְבִית, וַאֲפִלּוּ אֵין שָׁם אָבֵל, כִּי יֵשׁ בָּזֶה נַחַת רוּחַ לַנְּשָׁמָה. וְאִם יֵשׁ שָׁם אָבֵל, מִצְטָרֵף לַמִּנְיָן. וְיָבִיאוּ לְשָׁם סֵפֶר־תּוֹרָה מִקֹּדֶם, וְיָכִינוּ לוֹ מָקוֹם כָּרָאוּי עַל זְמַן שֶׁיִּתְפַּלְּלוּ שָׁם. אִם יֵשׁ בִּשְׁנֵי בָתִּים מֵתִים, בְּאֶחָד יֵשׁ שָׁם אָבֵל וּבְאֶחָד אֵין שָׁם אָבֵל וְאֵין בָּעִיר הַהִיא כְּדֵי לְחַלֵּק שֶׁיִּתְפַּלְּלוּ כָּאן וְכָאן בַּעֲשָׂרָה, יִתְפַּלְּלוּ בְּבַיִת שֶׁאֵין שָׁם אָבֵל. נוֹהֲגִין לוֹמַר בְּבֵית הַנִּפְטָר לְאַחַר תְּפִלַּת שַׁחֲרִית וּמִנְחָה, אֶת הַמִּזְמוֹר לַמְנַצֵּחַ וְגוֹ׳ שִׁמְעוּ זֹאת כָּל־הָעַמִּים וְגוֹ׳. וּמַה טּוֹב לִלְמוֹד שָׁם מִשְׁנָיוֹת לְתִקּוּן הַנְּשָׁמָה.

ו) אֵין אוֹמְרִים הַלֵּל בְּבֵית הַנִּפְטָר אִם יֵשׁ שָׁם אָבֵל תּוֹךְ שִׁבְעָה (מִשּׁוּם דַּהֲוֵי כְּמוֹ לוֹעֵג לָרָשׁ, שֶׁאוֹמְרִים בּוֹ, לֹא הַמֵּתִים יְהַלְלוּ יָהּ). וְאִם יֵשׁ שָׁם חֶדֶר אַחֵר, יֵלֵךְ הָאָבֵל לְחֶדֶר אַחֵר, וְהַצִּבּוּר יֹאמְרוּ הַלֵּל. וְאִם אֵין חֶדֶר אַחֵר, אֲזַי בְּרֹאשׁ־חֹדֶשׁ, אֵין צְרִיכִין לוֹמַר אַחַר כָּךְ הַלֵּל בְּבֵיתָם. אֲבָל בַּחֲנֻכָּה, צְרִיכִין לוֹמַר הַלֵּל בְּבֵיתָם. וְאִם מִתְפַּלְּלִים בְּבֵית הַנִּפְטָר וְאֵין שָׁם אָבֵל, אוֹ בְּבֵית הָאָבֵל שֶׁאֵינוֹ בְּבֵית הַנִּפְטָר, אוֹמְרִים גַּם בְּרֹאשׁ־חֹדֶשׁ הַלֵּל, אֶלָּא שֶׁהָאָבֵל לֹא יֹאמַר (מִשּׁוּם שֶׁנֶּאֱמַר בּוֹ, זֶה הַיּוֹם עָשָׂה ה׳ נָגִילָה וְנִשְׂמְחָה בוֹ). אִם יוֹם הַשְּׁבִיעִי הוּא בַּחֲנֻכָּה, אֲזַי לְאַחַר שֶׁהָלְכוּ הַמְנַחֲמִים שֶׁפָּסְקָה הָאֲבֵלוּת, יֹאמַר גַּם הָאָבֵל הַלֵּל, מִפְּנֵי שֶׁהוּא חִיּוּב. וְיֵשׁ אוֹמְרִים, דְּבַחֲנֻכָּה אוֹמְרִים הַלֵּל גַּם בְּבֵית הָאָבֵל בְּצִבּוּר. בְּרֹאשׁ־חֹדֶשׁ שֶׁחָל בְּשַׁבָּת, אוֹמְרִים הַלֵּל בַּצִּבּוּר גַּם בְּבֵית הָאָבֵל, דְּאֵין אֲבֵלוּת בְּשַׁבָּת.

ז) בִּרְכַּת אֲבֵלִים שֶׁבְּבִרְכַּת־הַמָּזוֹן, לָא נְהִיגֵי עַכְשָׁו, כִּי סוֹמְכִים עַל הַפּוֹסְקִים דִּסְבִירָא לְהוּ דְּלָא נִתְקְנָה אֶלָּא כְּשֶׁמְּבָרְכִין בַּעֲשָׂרָה.

5) Mourners should observe their mourning in the place where the soul of the deceased departed, for in that place, the soul of the deceased grieves, and that is the place to comfort it. It is a mitzvah to pray there with a *minyan* of ten men in the morning and evening, even if there is no mourner present, for it is a consolation for the soul. If there is a mourner present, he may be counted in the *minyan*. A *Seifer Torah* should be brought there earlier, and a suitable place should be prepared for it, for the entire time they will pray there. If two deaths occurred in two separate houses, in one of which there is a mourner, while in the other there is no mourner, and there are not enough worshipers in the city to have a *minyan* of ten pray in each house, they should pray in the house where there is no mourner. In the house of the deceased it is customary to say, *Psalm,*[9] "*Lamanetzeach,* etc. *Shimu Zoss Kol Ha'ammim*" etc. after *Shacharis* and *Minchah.* And it is certainly good to study *Mishnayos* there, for the benefit of the soul. (The Hebrew letters of the word *Mishnah.* are the same as the word *neshoma* (soul).)

6) *Hallel* is not said in the house where the death occured, if the mourner is present during the first seven days of mourning, (because it is considered like mocking the poor, for in *Hallel* we say, "The dead do not praise God.") If there is another room, the mourner should go into that room, and the congregation should say *Hallel.* And if there is no other room, then on *Rosh Chodesh,* those who prayed there need not say *Hallel* at home afterwards. But on Chanukah, they must say *Hallel* in their homes. And if they are praying in the house where the death occured but where there is no mourner present, or in the mourner's house, but the death did not occur there,[10] *Hallel* should be recited even on *Rosh Chodesh,* but the mourner should not recite it, (because in it, it is said, "This day was made by Adonoy; let us exult and rejoice in Him.") If the seventh day of mourning occurs during the days of Chanukah, then after the comforters leave, at which time mourning ceases, the mourner, too, must recite the *Hallel,* because it is obligatory. Other *Poskim* are of the opinion that on Chanukah, *Hallel* should be recited even in the house of a mourner[11] with the *Minyan*. If *Rosh Chodesh* occurs on Shabbos, *Hallel* should be recited with the *Minyan*, even in the house of a mourner, for on Shabbos, public mourning is not observed.

7) The special *berachos* for mourners in the *Birkas Hamazon* is not part of our custom today, because we rely on the opinion of the *Poskim* who maintain that these *berachos* were enacted to be said only when *Birkas Hamazon* is recited with a *minyan* of ten.

---

9. *Psalms* 49.
10. It appears the *Mishnah Berurah* 131:20 does not agree with this.
11. The mourner himself, however, certainly is not allowed to say *Hallel* in any case.

סִימָן רח
שֶׁהָאָבֵל אָסוּר בִּמְלָאכָה

א) אֵלּוּ דְבָרִים שֶׁהָאָבֵל אָסוּר בָּהֶם כָּל שִׁבְעָה: בִּמְלָאכָה, בִּרְחִיצָה, בְּסִיכָה, בִּנְעִילַת־הַסַּנְדָּל, וּבְתַשְׁמִישׁ־הַמִּטָּה. וְאָסוּר לִקְרוֹת בַּתּוֹרָה, וְאָסוּר בִּשְׁאִילַת שָׁלוֹם, וְאָסוּר בְּגִהוּץ וּבְתִסְפֹּרֶת וּבְכָל מִינֵי שִׂמְחָה. וְאָסוּר לְהָנִיחַ תְּפִלִּין בַּיּוֹם הָרִאשׁוֹן.

ב) מְלָאכָה כֵּיצַד. כָּל שְׁלֹשָׁה יָמִים הָרִאשׁוֹנִים, אָסוּר בִּמְלָאכָה, אֲפִלּוּ הוּא עָנִי הַמִּתְפַּרְנֵס מִן הַצְּדָקָה. מִיּוֹם הָרְבִיעִי וְאֵילָךְ, אִם הוּא עָנִי וְאֵין לוֹ מַה יֹּאכַל, עוֹשֶׂה בְּצִנְעָא בְּתוֹךְ בֵּיתוֹ. וְכֵן הָאִשָּׁה עוֹשָׂה מְלַאכְתָּהּ בְּתוֹךְ בֵּיתָהּ בְּצִנְעָא כְּדֵי פַּרְנָסָתָהּ. אֲבָל אָמְרוּ חֲכָמִים, תָּבוֹא מְאֵרָה לִשְׁכֵנָיו שֶׁהִצְרִיכוּהוּ לְכָךְ, כִּי עֲלֵיהֶם מֻטָּל לְהַשְׁגִּיחַ עַל הֶעָנִי, וּמִכָּל שֶׁכֵּן בִּימֵי אֶבְלוֹ.

ג) אֲפִלּוּ לַעֲשׂוֹת מְלַאכְתּוֹ עַל יְדֵי אֲחֵרִים וַאֲפִלּוּ עַל יְדֵי גוֹי, אָסוּר. וְאִם הַמְּלָאכָה דָּבָר נָחוּץ מְאֹד וְיָכוֹל לָבוֹא לִידֵי הֶפְסֵד, יַעֲשֶׂה שְׁאֵלַת חָכָם.

ד) כְּשֵׁם שֶׁאָסוּר בִּמְלָאכָה, כָּךְ אָסוּר לוֹ לִשָּׂא וְלִתֵּן בִּסְחוֹרָה. וְאִם יֵשׁ לוֹ סְחוֹרָה שֶׁאִם לֹא יִמְכְּרֶנָּה עַכְשָׁו יִהְיֶה לוֹ הֶפְסֵד מִן הַקֶּרֶן, יַעֲשֶׂה גַּם כֵּן שְׁאֵלַת חָכָם. וְאִם בָּאוּ שַׁיָּרוֹת אוֹ סְפִינוֹת שֶׁמּוֹכְרִים עַתָּה בְּזוֹל וְאַחַר כָּךְ לֹא יִמְצָא וְכֵן אִם הוּא בַּיָּרִיד וְשָׁמַע שְׁמוּעָה קְרוֹבָה יָכוֹל לִמְכּוֹר וְלִקְנוֹת עַל יְדֵי אֲחֵרִים.

ה) מֻתָּר לְהַלְווֹת בְּרִבִּית עַל יְדֵי אֲחֵרִים לְגוֹיִם הָרְגִילִים לִלְווֹת מִמֶּנּוּ. וְהוּא הַדִּין לִמְכּוֹר סְחוֹרָה לָרְגִילִים אֶצְלוֹ, שֶׁלֹּא יַרְגִּילוּ אֶת עַצְמָם אֵצֶל אֲחֵרִים.

ו) מֻתָּר לוֹ לִשְׁלוֹחַ לִגְבּוֹת חוֹבוֹתָיו שֶׁיֵּשׁ בָּהֶם חֲשַׁשׁ שֶׁמָּא יִתְקַלְקְלוּ.

ז) כְּתִיבָה הַמֻּתֶּרֶת בְּחֹל־הַמּוֹעֵד, מֻתֶּרֶת גַּם לְאָבֵל אִם אִי־אֶפְשָׁר לוֹ עַל יְדֵי אַחֵר.

ח) אָבֵל, שֶׁשָּׂדֵהוּ בְּיַד אֲחֵרִים בַּאֲרִיסוּת (דְּהַיְנוּ לִשְׁלִישׁ אוֹ לִרְבִיעַ), אוֹ בַּחֲכִירוּת (שֶׁנּוֹתֵן הַמְקַבֵּל לְבַעַל־הַשָּׂדֶה סְכוּם קָצוּב מִפֵּרוֹת הַשָּׂדֶה),

Chapter 208

Work that a Mourner Is Forbidden To Perform

1) These are the things a mourner is forbidden to do during the first seven days: to work, to bathe, to anoint himself to wear shoes and to engage in marital relations. He is forbidden to study Torah, he is forbidden to offer greetings, he is forbidden to wear a pressed garment, cut his hair, or be present at any festivity. He is also forbidden to put on *Tefillin* the first day.

2) What are the rules concerning work? During the first three days[1] a mourner must not perform any work, even if he is a poor man who relies on charity. But after the fourth day if the mourner is a poor man, and has nothing to eat, he may work privately at home. A woman may also work privately in her own home to earn enough for her sustenance. But our Sages say:[2] "May a curse fall on the mourner's neighbors who made it necessary for him to do work," for it is their duty to provide for the poor, especially during the days of his mourning.

3) It is forbidden even to have his work done by others, and even by a non-Jew. If the work is very urgent and he might sustain a loss by not doing it, he should consult a competent Rav.

4) Just as he is forbidden to do work, so is he forbidden to transact business. If he possesses merchandise, which unless he sells now he will sustain a loss of the principle, he should consult a competent Rav. If caravans or ships arrived with merchandise, which is now being sold at a low price, and will be unavailable later, or, if he was at the market when he received *timely* news,[3] he may transact business through others.

5) He may lend money on interest through an agent to non-Jews who are accustomed to borrow from him. The same applies to selling merchandise to his regular customers, so that they should not become accustomed to trade elsewhere.

6) He is permitted to send someone to collect his debts, if he has reason to fear they might become uncollectable later.

7) Such writing that is permitted on *Chol Hamoed* is also permitted to a mourner, if it cannot be done by someone else.

8) If a mourner's field is occupied by a tenant either as a sharecropper, (e.g., a third or a quarter share) or on lease (whereby the tenant gives the owner a fixed amount of the field's produce), or on a rental basis (whereby he pays him an amount

1. With regard to this we do not say that part of the day is like the whole day. *Rabbi Akiva Eiger* (*Yoreh Deah* 380) *Matzevas Moshe*.
2. *Yerushalmi Maseches Moed Kattan* 3:5.
3. See *Kitzur Shulchan Aruch* chapter 208.

אוֹ בְקַבְּלָנוּת (שֶׁנּוֹתֵן לוֹ מָעוֹת בִּשְׂכִירוּת), הֲרֵי אֵלּוּ עוֹבְדִין כְּדַרְכָּן בִּימֵי הָאֵבֶל שֶׁל בַּעַל הַשָּׂדֶה, דְּכֵיוָן שֶׁהָעֲבוֹדָה הִיא לְתוֹעֶלֶת שֶׁלָּהֶם, אֵין לָהֶם לְהַפְסִיד בִּשְׁבִיל אֶבְלוֹ. אֲבָל אִם יֵשׁ לָאָבֵל שְׂכִיר־יוֹם לַעֲשׂוֹת בְּשָׂדֵהוּ, אָסוּר אֲפִלּוּ אִם הַשָּׂדֶה בְּעִיר אַחֶרֶת, כֵּיוָן שֶׁעֲבוֹדָה זֹאת, הִיא לְתוֹעֶלֶת הָאָבֵל וְהִיא בְּפַרְהֶסְיָא.

ט) אִם הָאָבֵל הוּא אָרִיס בְּשָׂדֶה שֶׁל אַחֵר, אָסוּר לוֹ לַעֲבוֹד בּוֹ בְּעַצְמוֹ. אֲבָל עַל יְדֵי אֲחֵרִים, מֻתָּר, מִשּׁוּם דְּאֵין זֹאת נִקְרֵאת מְלֶאכֶת הָאָבֵל אֶלָּא מְלֶאכֶת בַּעַל הַשָּׂדֶה. וְאִם יֵשׁ שְׁאָר דָּבָר שֶׁל אֲחֵרִים בְּיַד הָאָבֵל לַעֲשׂוֹתוֹ, לֹא יַעֲשֶׂה אֲפִלּוּ עַל יְדֵי אֲחֵרִים. אַךְ כְּשֶׁהוּא דָּבָר הָאָבֵד, יַעֲשֶׂה עַל יְדֵי אֲחֵרִים.

י) בְּהֵמוֹת שֶׁל הָאָבֵל הַמֻּשְׂכָּרִים לְאַחֵר, מֻתָּר הַשּׂוֹכֵר לַעֲשׂוֹת בָּהֶם מְלָאכָה, כֵּיוָן שֶׁשְּׂכָרָם קֹדֶם שֶׁנַּעֲשָׂה אָבֵל, וּשְׂכִירוּת קַנְיָא, וְהַוְיָן שֶׁל הַשּׂוֹכֵר. וּלְאַחַר כְּלוֹת יְמֵי הַשְּׂכִירוּת, אָסוּר.

יא) מֻתָּר לָאָבֵל לְקַבֵּל מְלָאכָה לַעֲשׂוֹתָהּ אַחַר יְמֵי אֶבְלוֹ, וּבִלְבַד שֶׁלֹּא יִשְׁקֹל וְלֹא יִמְדֹּד כְּדֶרֶךְ שֶׁהוּא עוֹשֶׂה בִּשְׁאָר פְּעָמִים.

יב) הָיְתָה לָאָבֵל אֵיזוֹ מְלָאכָה בְּיַד אַחֵר, כֵּיוָן שֶׁהִיא בְקַבְּלָנוּת וְקִבֵּל אֶת הַמְּלָאכָה קֹדֶם שֶׁנַּעֲשָׂה אָבֵל וְגַם הִיא בְּצִנְעָא בְּבֵיתוֹ שֶׁל בַּעַל הַמְּלָאכָה לָכֵן מֻתָּר לוֹ לַעֲשׂוֹתָהּ.

יג) מְלֶאכֶת בִּנְיָן שֶׁל הָאָבֵל, אֲפִלּוּ עַל יְדֵי גוֹי וּבְקַבְּלָנוּת וּבְמָקוֹם רָחוֹק שֶׁאֵין יִשְׂרְאֵלִים דָּרִים שָׁם, אָסוּר. וּמְלֶאכֶת שָׂדֵהוּ בְּיַד אֲחֵרִים בְּקַבְּלָנוּת, דְּהַיְנוּ שֶׁהוּא נוֹתֵן לַפּוֹעֵל שָׂכָר קָצוּב בְּעַד כָּל עֲבוֹדוֹת הַשָּׂדֶה, חֲרִישָׁה וּזְרִיעָה וּקְצִירָה וְכַדּוֹמֶה, יֵשׁ מַתִּירִין וְיֵשׁ אוֹסְרִין.

יד) מְלָאכוֹת הַבַּיִת, אֵין בָּהֶן מִשּׁוּם מְלָאכָה לָאָבֵל, וּמֻתָּר לְאִשָּׁה בִּימֵי אֶבְלָהּ לֶאֱפוֹת וּלְבַשֵּׁל וְלַעֲשׂוֹת כָּל צָרְכֵי הַבַּיִת מַה שֶּׁצָּרִיךְ לָהּ. אֲבָל מַה שֶּׁאֵינוֹ צָרִיךְ לָהּ, אָסוּר. וְכֵן מְשָׁרֶתֶת שֶׁאֵרַע לָהּ אֵבֶל, אַף־עַל־פִּי שֶׁהִיא מְשָׁרֶתֶת בְּשָׂכָר, מֻתָּר לָהּ לַעֲשׂוֹת כָּל צָרְכֵי הַבַּיִת. אֲבָל לֹא תַעֲשֶׂה מַה שֶּׁאֵינוֹ צָרְכֵי הַבַּיִת אֶלָּא לְהַרְוִיחַ, וְכָל־שֶׁכֵּן שֶׁלֹּא תֵצֵא מִן הַבַּיִת, כְּמוֹ שְׁאָר אָבֵל.

טו) שְׁנֵי שֻׁתָּפִים חֶנְוָנִים שֶׁאֵרַע אֵבֶל לְאֶחָד מֵהֶם, נוֹעֲלִים חֲנוּתָם,

of money for rent), they may work the field as usual, during the owner's time of mourning, for since the work is for their own benefit (profit), they need not suffer any loss on the account of the owner's mourning. However, if the mourner has a day laborer working in his field, he is forbidden to let him work, even if the field is in another city, since the work being done is for the benefit of the mourner, and it is done publicly.

9) If the mourner is a sharecropper in the field of another, he himself is forbidden to do the work, but he may employ others to do it, for it is not called the work of the mourner, but rather that of the owner of the field. If others have contracted work for the mourner to do, he is forbidden to do it even by employing others. But if it is work the delay of which will cause him to sustain a [substantial] loss, he may have it done by others.

10) When the animals of a mourner are hired out to another person, the renter is permitted to do work with them, since he rented them before the owner became a mourner, and through renting one acquires certain rights of ownership, and they are considered the property of the renter; but after expiration of the time for which they were rented, he is forbidden to use them.

11) A mourner is permitted to accept work to be done after his period of mourning, provided he does not weigh or measure as he would do at other times.

12) If the mourner had given work to a contractor, since it is on a contractual basis, and the work was received prior to his becoming a mourner, and it is being done privately at the home of the contractor, the contractor is permitted to do it.

13) Construction of a building belonging to a mourner, even if done by a non-Jew on a contractual basis, and in a far-away place where no Jews live, is forbidden. If the work in his field was given to others on a contractual basis, whereby he pays the worker a fixed wage for all the work in the field: ploughing, sowing, harvesting, and similar work, some *Poskim* permit the work to be done.

14) Domestic chores are not considered forbidden work for a mourner. Thus, a woman is permitted, during the period of her mourning, to bake, cook, and do all household chores that she finds necessary. But that which is not necessary is forbidden to do. Also, a domestic servant who is in mourning, even though she is a paid servant she is permitted to do all the housework. But she is not permitted to do work that is not necessary for the house, but only to earn extra money, and certainly she may not leave the house just as any other mourner is forbidden to do so.

15) If two people are partners in a store, and one of them became a mourner, they must close their store, so that the partner does not do work in public. But he

שֶׁלֹּא יַעֲשֶׂה הַשֻּׁתָּף בְּפַרְהֶסְיָא. אֲבָל יָכוֹל לַעֲשׂוֹת בִּצְנְעָא בְּתוֹךְ בֵּיתוֹ אֲפִלּוּ בְּעֵסֶק הַשֻּׁתָּפוּת. וְאִם הָאָבֵל הוּא אָדָם חָשׁוּב וְהַשֻּׁתָּפוּת נִקְרֵאת עַל שְׁמוֹ שֶׁיֵּשׁ לָאָבֵל חֵלֶק בּוֹ, אָסוּר לַשֵּׁנִי לַעֲשׂוֹת אֲפִלּוּ בְּתוֹךְ בֵּיתוֹ. וּבִמְקוֹם שֶׁיֵּשׁ הֶפְסֵד גָּדוֹל אִם גַּם הַשֻּׁתָּף שֶׁל הָאָבֵל לֹא יִפְתַּח הֶחָנוּת יַעֲשׂוּ שְׁאֵלַת חָכָם אִם לְהַתִּיר לְאַחַר שְׁלשָׁה יָמִים.

סִימָן רט
אִסּוּר רְחִיצָה וְסִיכָה וּנְעִילַת־הַסַּנְדָּל וְתַשְׁמִישׁ־הַמִּטָּה

א) אָסוּר לִרְחוֹץ כָּל גּוּפוֹ אֲפִלּוּ בְּצוֹנֵן. אֲבָל פָּנָיו יָדָיו וְרַגְלָיו, בְּחַמִּין אָסוּר וּבְצוֹנֵן מֻתָּר. וּרְחִיצָה בְּחַמִּין, אֲסוּרָה כָּל שְׁלֹשִׁים, וַאֲפִלּוּ לָחֹף הָרֹאשׁ. וְגַם רְחִיצַת כָּל הַגּוּף בְּצוֹנֵן אִם הִיא לְתַעֲנוּג, אֲסוּרָה כָּל שְׁלֹשִׁים. וְאִשָּׁה לְצֹרֶךְ חֲפִיפָה שֶׁקֹּדֶם טְבִילָה, מֻתֶּרֶת לִרְחוֹץ בְּחַמִּין לְאַחַר שִׁבְעָה (וּלְעִנְיַן לְבִישַׁת לְבָנִים, עַיֵּן לְעֵיל סִימָן קנט סָעִיף ה׳).

ב) יוֹלֶדֶת שֶׁאֵרַע לָהּ אֵבֶל וְהִיא צְרִיכָה לִרְחוֹץ, מֻתֶּרֶת גַּם בְּתוֹךְ שִׁבְעָה. אַךְ בְּיוֹם רִאשׁוֹן, יֵשׁ לְהַחְמִיר אִם אֵין לָהּ צֹרֶךְ כָּל כָּךְ. וְכֵן מִי שֶׁהוּא אִסְטְנִיס שֶׁאִם לֹא יִרְחַץ, יִצְטַעֵר הַרְבֵּה וְיָבוֹא לִידֵי מֵחוֹשׁ, מֻתָּר לוֹ לִרְחוֹץ. וְכֵן מָאן דְּאִית לֵהּ עִרְבּוּבְיָא בְּרֵישֵׁהּ, מֻתָּר לוֹ לָחֹף רֹאשׁוֹ בְּחַמִּין.

ג) אָסוּר לָסוּךְ אֲפִלּוּ כָּל־שֶׁהוּא אִם מְכַוֵּן לְתַעֲנוּג. אֲבָל אִם הוּא מְכַוֵּן לְהַעֲבִיר הַזֻּהֲמָא, מֻתָּר. וּמִכָּל־שֶׁכֵּן מִשּׁוּם רְפוּאָה, כְּגוֹן שֶׁיֵּשׁ לוֹ חֲטָטִין בְּרֹאשׁוֹ.

ד) מִי שֶׁתְּכָפוּהוּ אֲבָלָיו, שֶׁאֵרְעוּ לוֹ שְׁתֵּי אֲבֵלִיּוֹת זוֹ אַחַר זוֹ, מֻתָּר לוֹ לִרְחֹץ בְּצוֹנֵן.

ה) אִסּוּר נְעִילַת־הַסַּנְדָּל, הוּא דַּוְקָא בְּשֶׁל עוֹר. אֲבָל שֶׁל בֶּגֶד אוֹ שֶׁל גֶּמִי אוֹ שֶׁל שֵׂעָר אוֹ שֶׁל עֵץ, מֻתָּר, דְּלָא מִקְרֵי מִנְעָל אֶלָּא שֶׁל עוֹר. מִנְעָל שֶׁל עֵץ וּמְחֻפֶּה עוֹר, אָסוּר. אַף־עַל־פִּי שֶׁהָאָבֵל אָסוּר בִּנְעִילַת־הַסַּנְדָּל, מִכָּל מָקוֹם מְבָרֵךְ בַּבֹּקֶר שֶׁעָשָׂה לִי כָּל צָרְכִּי.

ו) יוֹלֶדֶת, כָּל שְׁלֹשִׁים יוֹם לְלֵדָתָהּ, מֻתֶּרֶת בִּנְעִילַת־הַסַּנְדָּל, וְכֵן חוֹלֶה [וּמִי] שֶׁיֵּשׁ לוֹ מַכָּה בְּרַגְלוֹ, מִפְּנֵי שֶׁהַצִּנָּה קָשָׁה לָהֶם.

may do work in the privacy of his home, even in such matters in which both partners have an interest. If the mourner is a distinguished person, and the business bears his name, as he has a share in it, the partner is forbidden to conduct the business even in his own home. In the event a great loss would be sustained if the the mourner's partner, too, would not open the store, they should consult a competent Rav as to whether it may be opened after three days.

Chapter 209

The prohibition to Bathe, Anoint, Wear Shoes And to Engage In Marital Relations.

1) The mourner is forbidden to wash his entire body even with cold water; but his face, hands and feet are only forbidden to be washed with warm water, but are permitted to be washed with cold water. Bathing with warm water is forbidden during the entire thirty day mourning period, and even washing the head with warm water is forbidden. Similarly, bathing the entire body with cold water, if done for pleasure, is forbidden the entire thirty days. A woman, for the necessity of bathing before the ritual immersion, is permitted to bathe in warm water after the seven days of mourning have passed. With regard to wearing clean white garments, refer to Chapter 159:5.

2) If a woman becomes a mourner after giving birth, and she must bathe, she is permitted to bathe even during the seven days of mourning. However, on the first day she should be stringent and not bathe if it is not that necessary. Similarly, a person of delicate constitution, who would suffer greatly if he did not bathe, and his health might be affected, is permitted to bathe. Also, one who has disturbing head pains is permitted to wash his head with warm water.

3) A mourner is forbidden to anoint himself even in a minimal fashion if it is for the sake of pleasure. However, if his intention is to remove dirt, he is permitted to anoint himself. It is certainly permitted for medical purposes, as when he has scabs on his head.

4) A person who had multiple periods of mourning, such as two consecutive periods of mourning, is permitted to bathe with cold water.

5) The prohibition against wearing shoes applies only to leather shoes; but shoes of cloth, reeds, hair, or wood, are permitted, for the term "shoe" refers only to a shoe made of leather. A wooden shoe covered with leather is forbidden. Although the mourner is forbidden to wear shoes, nevertheless, in the morning he should say the *berachah*, " *She'assa Lee Kol Tzarkee*" ("Who provided me with all my needs").

6) A woman within thirty days after giving birth is permitted to wear shoes; so is an ill person, or one who has a wound on his foot, because the cold is harmful to them.

ז) אָבֵל שֶׁהוֹלֵךְ בַּדֶּרֶךְ, מֻתָּר בִּנְעִילַת־הַסַּנְדָּל, וְיָשִׂים קְצָת עָפָר בְּסַנְדָּלָיו. וְכֵן בְּכָל מָקוֹם שֶׁצָּרִיךְ לִנְעוֹל סַנְדָּל, יַעֲשֶׂה כֵּן.

ח) אָסוּר בְּתַשְׁמִישׁ־הַמִּטָּה וְגַם בְּחִבּוּק וְנִשּׁוּק. אֲבָל שְׁאָר דְּבַר קֻרְבָה, כְּגוֹן מְזִיגַת הַכּוֹס וְהַצָּעַת הַמִּטָּה וְכַדּוֹמֶה מֻתָּר, בֵּין בַּאֲבֵלוּת דִּידֵהּ בֵּין בַּאֲבֵלוּת דִּידָהּ.

סִימָן רי
אִסּוּר תַּלְמוּד־תּוֹרָה וּשְׁאִילַת שָׁלוֹם

א) אָסוּר בְּתַלְמוּד־תּוֹרָה, מִשּׁוּם דִּכְתִיב, פִּקּוּדֵי ה׳ יְשָׁרִים מְשַׂמְּחֵי־לֵב, וְאָבֵל אָסוּר בְּשִׂמְחָה. וְאָסוּר בַּתּוֹרָה נְבִיאִים וּכְתוּבִים, מִשְׁנָה, תַּלְמוּד, הֲלָכוֹת וְאַגָּדוֹת. אֲבָל מֻתָּר לִקְרוֹת בְּאִיּוֹב וּבְקִינוֹת, וּבִדְבָרִים הָרָעִים שֶׁבְּסֵפֶר יִרְמְיָה, וּבִגְמָרָא פֶּרֶק אֵלּוּ מְגַלְּחִין, דְּמַיְרֵי מִדִּינֵי מְנֻדֶּה וְאָבֵל, וּבְמַסֶּכֶת שְׂמָחוֹת וּבְסִפְרֵי פּוֹסְקִים, מֻתָּר לִלְמוֹד הִלְכוֹת אֲבֵלוּת. וְגַם בִּדְבָרִים שֶׁהוּא מֻתָּר לִלְמוֹד, אָסוּר לְעַיֵּן קֻשְׁיָא אוֹ תֵּרוּץ.

ב) מְלַמֵּד שֶׁהוּא אָבֵל, לְאַחַר שְׁלשָׁה יָמִים, מֻתָּר לוֹ לִלְמוֹד עִם הַתִּינוֹקוֹת כָּל הַדְּבָרִים שֶׁצְּרִיכִין, וְלֹא יִתְבַּטְּלוּ מִלִּמּוּדָם, כִּי תִינוֹקוֹת שֶׁל בֵּית־רַבָּן אֲשֶׁר הֶבֶל פִּיהֶם נְקִי מֵחֵטְא, חָבִיב יוֹתֵר מִלִּמּוּד שֶׁל גְּדוֹלִים. וְכֵן אָבֵל שֶׁיֵּשׁ לוֹ בָּנִים קְטַנִּים, לֹא יִתְבַּטְּלוּ מִלִּמּוּדָם, שֶׁהֲרֵי אֵינָם חַיָּבִים בַּאֲבֵלוּת.

ג) אֲפִלּוּ הָאָבֵל הוּא כֹּהֵן וְאֵין בְּבֵית־הַכְּנֶסֶת אַחֵר, אָסוּר לוֹ לַעֲלוֹת לַתּוֹרָה.

ד) בִּתְפִלָּתוֹ כָּל שִׁבְעָה, לֹא יֹאמַר פִּטּוּם הַקְּטֹרֶת, וְגַם לֹא יֹאמַר סֵדֶר מַעֲמָדוֹת. וּבְפֶרֶק אֵיזֶהוּ מְקוֹמָן, לֹא יֹאמַר יְהִי רָצוֹן כְּאִלּוּ הִקְרַבְתִּי וְכוּ׳ (דְּאָבֵל אֵינוֹ מְשַׁלֵּחַ קָרְבְּנוֹתָיו). וּכְשֶׁעוֹשֶׂה הַבְדָּלָה בְּמוֹצָאֵי־שַׁבָּת עַל הַכּוֹס, לֹא יֹאמַר פְּסוּקֵי שִׂמְחָה שֶׁקּוֹדְמִים לָהּ, אֶלָּא יַתְחִיל מִן הַבְּרָכוֹת.

ה) אָבֵל תּוֹךְ שִׁבְעָה, אֵין לוֹ לְהִתְפַּלֵּל לִפְנֵי הַתֵּבָה אֶלָּא אִם אֵין שָׁם אַחֵר שֶׁיִּתְפַּלֵּל. אַךְ אִם הוּא אָבֵל עַל אָבִיו אוֹ אִמּוֹ, נוֹהֲגִין שֶׁמִּתְפַּלְּלִין לִפְנֵי הַתֵּבָה, אַף־עַל־פִּי שֶׁיֵּשׁ שָׁם אַחֵר. וּבְשַׁבָּתוֹת וְיָמִים

7) A mourner who must travel on the road, is permitted to wear shoes. he should, however, put a bit of earth in his shoes. Similarly, in all other instances when a mourner must wear shoes, he should do this.

8) A mourner is forbidden to engage in marital relations. Embracing and kissing are also forbidden. But other acts of intimacy, such as filling a cup, making the bed and similar things, are permitted. [It makes no difference if] the husband is the mourner, or the wife is the mourner.

Chapter 210

The Prohibition To Study Torah And To Exchange Greetings

1) A mourner is forbidden to study Torah, for it is written, "The precepts of *Adonoy*, are upright, rejoicing the heart."[1] and a mourner is forbidden to rejoice. He is forbidden to study the Scriptures, the *Mishnah*, and the *Talmud*, including the laws and *Aggadah*. But he is permitted to read the book of *Job*, *Lamentations*, and the mournful sections of *Jeremiah*. In the *Talmud*, he may study chapter, *V'eelu Megalchin*,[2] dealing with the laws of the excommunicated and the mourner, and also *Maseches Semachos*. And in the *Seforim* (books) of *Halachah* (laws), he may study the laws concerning mourning. However, he is forbidden to probe and analyze even the subjects he is permitted to study.

2) After three days of mourning, one who teaches Torah to children is permitted to teach the children everything they need to learn, so that they are not interrupted from their studies; for the (study of) children whose mouths are pure of sin, is more precious than the study of adults. Likewise a mourner's young children should not be interrupted from their studies, for they are not obligated to observe mourning.

3) Even if the mourner is a *Kohein* and there is no other *Kohein* in the synagogue, he is forbidden to go up to read the Torah.

4) When he prays during all seven days of mourning, a mourner should not recite *Pittum Haketoress, Keitsad* [How was the incense compounded] nor should he say *Maamados*, and after the Chapter of *Eizehu Mekoman*,[3] he should not say *Yehi Ratzon* etc. [May it be Your will] (because a mourner may not send offerings). When reciting *Havdalah* at the conclusion of Shabbos over a cup [of wine], he should not say the introductary verses of joy, but should begin immediately with the *berachos*.

5) During his seven days of mourning a mourner should not officiate as *Chazzan* unless there is no one else to lead the prayers. But if he is in mourning for his father or mother, the custom is to permit him to be the *Chazzan* even if there is someone else capable of doing so. It is customary that a mourner not be the *Chazzan* on

1. *Psalms* 19:9.
2. The third chapter of *Masechess Moed Kattan*.
3. "Where are the offerings slaughtered." This chapter of *Mishnayos* is recited daily.

טוֹבִים, נוֹהֲגִין שֶׁאֵינוֹ מִתְפַּלֵּל לִפְנֵי הַתֵּבָה כָּל הַשָּׁנָה אֶלָּא בִּדְלֶגָא אַחֵר. וְאִם הָיָה דַּרְכּוֹ לְהִתְפַּלֵּל לִפְנֵי הַתֵּבָה גַּם קֹדֶם שֶׁנַּעֲשָׂה אָבֵל, יֵשׁ לְהַתִּיר בְּכָל עִנְיָן. וְעַיֵּן לְעֵיל סִימָן קכח סָעִיף ח.

ו) שְׁאִילַת שָׁלוֹם כֵּיצַד. שְׁלֹשָׁה יָמִים הָרִאשׁוֹנִים, אֵינוֹ שׁוֹאֵל בִּשְׁלוֹם כָּל אָדָם. וְאִם אֲחֵרִים שֶׁלֹּא יָדְעוּ שֶׁהוּא אָבֵל שָׁאֲלוּ בִּשְׁלוֹמוֹ, לֹא יְשִׁיבֵם שָׁלוֹם, אֶלָּא יוֹדִיעֵם שֶׁהוּא אָבֵל. וּלְאַחַר שְׁלֹשָׁה עַד שִׁבְעָה, אֵינוֹ שׁוֹאֵל. וְאִם אֲחֵרִים שֶׁלֹּא יָדְעוּ שָׁאֲלוּ בִּשְׁלוֹמוֹ, מֵשִׁיב לָהֶם. מִשִּׁבְעָה עַד שְׁלשִׁים, הוּא שׁוֹאֵל בִּשְׁלוֹם אֲחֵרִים, שֶׁהֲרֵי הָאֲחֵרִים שְׁרוּיִן בְּשָׁלוֹם. וְאֵין אֲחֵרִים שׁוֹאֲלִין בִּשְׁלוֹמוֹ, שֶׁהֲרֵי הוּא אֵינוֹ שָׁרוּי בְּשָׁלוֹם. וְאִם לֹא יָדְעוּ וְשָׁאֲלוּ, מֵשִׁיב לָהֶם. לְאַחַר שְׁלשִׁים, הֲרֵי הוּא כִּשְׁאָר כָּל אָדָם.

ז) כֵּיוָן שֶׁהוּא אָסוּר בִּשְׁאִילַת שָׁלוֹם, מִכָּל־שֶׁכֵּן שֶׁאָסוּר בִּשְׂחוֹק. וְלָכֵן כָּל שִׁבְעָה לֹא יֹאחֵז תִּינוֹק בְּיָדוֹ, כְּדֵי שֶׁלֹּא יְבִיאֶנּוּ לִידֵי שְׂחוֹק. וְכֵן אָסוּר לוֹ לְהַרְבּוֹת בִּדְבָרִים עִם הַבְּרִיּוֹת. אַךְ אִם עוֹשֶׂה לִכְבוֹד רַבִּים, כְּגוֹן שֶׁרַבִּים בָּאִים לְנַחֲמוֹ, מֻתָּר לוֹ לוֹמַר לָהֶם לְכוּ לְבָתֵּיכֶם לְשָׁלוֹם, דְּלִכְבוֹד רַבִּים שָׁרֵי.

ח) מָקוֹם שֶׁנָּהֲגוּ לִשְׁאוֹל בִּשְׁלוֹם אֲבֵלִים בַּשַּׁבָּת, שׁוֹאֲלִים. וְהָאָבֵל נוֹתֵן שָׁלוֹם לְכָל אָדָם בַּשַּׁבָּת, כִּי דָּבָר שֶׁבְּפַרְהֶסְיָא הוּא.

ט) מֻתָּר לְבָרֵךְ שֶׁהֶחֱיָנוּ אֲפִלּוּ תּוֹךְ שִׁבְעָה כְּשֶׁהוּא צָרִיךְ, כְּגוֹן בַּחֲנֻכָּה אוֹ עַל פְּרִי חָדָשׁ וְכַדּוֹמֶה.

סִימָן ריא
שְׁאָר דְּבָרִים שֶׁהָאָבֵל אָסוּר בָּהֶם

א) אָסוּר לֵישֵׁב כָּל שִׁבְעָה עַל גַּבֵּי סַפְסָל אוֹ עַל גַּבֵּי כָּרִים וּכְסָתוֹת, כִּי אִם עַל גַּבֵּי קַרְקַע. אַךְ חוֹלֶה וְזָקֵן שֶׁיֵּשׁ לָהֶם צַעַר בִּישִׁיבָה עַל גַּבֵּי קַרְקַע, מַתִּירִין לָשִׂים כַּר קָטָן תַּחְתֵּיהֶם. מִיהוּ יָכוֹל לֵילֵךְ וְלַעֲמוֹד וְאֵינוֹ

4. On days when *Lamanetzaiach* and *Kail Erech Appaim* are not said, a mourner should not be the *Chazzan*, except on the day before *Yom Kippur. Biur Halachah* 132. On *Rosh Chodesh* he may be the *Chazzan* for *Shacharis*, provided someone else continues with the *Hallel*. However, the *Chayei Adam* says that the *Gra* did not allow a mourner to be the *Chazzan* at *Shacharis* on

Shabbos and Yom Tov[4] during his entire year[5] [of mourning] unless there is no one else to do so.[6] If he was accustomed to be the *Chazzan* even before he became a mourner, he is permitted to do so in any event. See Chapter 128:8 above.

6)What is the rule concerning the exchange of greetings? During the first three days, a mourner must not greet anyone. If others who are unaware that he is a mourner greet him, he should not return the greeting, but should inform them that he is a mourner. From the third day until the seventh day, he must not greet anyone, but if others who unaware that he is a mourner greet him, he may respond to their greetings. From the seventh until the thirtieth day, he may extend greetings to others for they have peace of mind, but others should not greet him because he lacks peace of mind. If they did not know he is a mourner and they greeted him, he may respond to their greetings. After thirty days, he may exchange greetings like anyone else.

7) Since he is forbidden to greet anybody, he is certainly forbidden to laugh. Therefore, during the seven days of mourning, he must not take a child in his arms, so he should not be induced to laughter. He is also forbidden to engage in lengthy conversation with people.[7] However, if he does so out of respect for a group of people, as when many come together to console him, he is permitted to say (when they are leaving), "Go to your homes in peace," for out of respect for a group of people, it is permitted.

8) In a place where it is customary to greet the mourners on Shabbos, you may do so. The mourner may greet everybody on Shabbos since it is done publicly.

9) He is permitted to say the *berachah, Shehecheyanu* even during the seven days of mourning, when it is necessary, for instance on Chanukah, or when eating a new fruit and the like.

Chapter 211

Other Things A Mourner Is Forbidden To Do

1) During the seven days of mourning he is forbidden to sit on a bench or upon pillows and cushions. He must sit on the ground [floor]. But an ill or elderly person, who experience pain when sitting on the floor, may place a small pillow beneath them. However, the mourner may walk or stand, and is not compelled to sit down

---

Rosh Chodesh. Mishna Berurah 581:7. A mourner should not be the *Chazzan* at *Shacharis* on *Chanukah. Mishna Berurah* 683:1 A mourner is allowed to be *Chazzan* at *Mincha* and *Ma'ariv* on *Chanukah.* But not on *Chol Hamoed. Mishna Berurah* 671:44—*Peri Megadim.*

5. If he is mourning the loss of a parent, or thirty days if he is mourning the loss of another relative. *Mishnah Berurah* 581:7.

6. If no one else can read the *Megillah* as accurately as he, he should read it for everyone. *Mishnah Berurah* 696:12.

7. *Aruch HaShulchan* 384:9 writes, "It is obviously forbidden for a mourner to read secular books and certainly newspapers."

צָרִיךְ לֵישֵׁב כְּלָל, רַק כְּשֶׁהַמְנַחֲמִים אֶצְלוֹ צָרִיךְ לֵישֵׁב. וְכֵן אָסוּר לִישׁוֹן עַל גַּבֵּי מִטָּה אוֹ סַפְסָל, רַק עַל גַּבֵּי קַרְקַע. אֲבָל יָכוֹל לְהַצִּיעַ תַּחְתָּיו כָּרִים וּכְסָתוֹת עַל הַקַּרְקַע כְּמוֹ שֶׁהוּא רָגִיל לִשְׁכַּב בְּמִטָּה. וְיֵשׁ מַתִּירִין לִישׁוֹן בְּמִטָּה. וְכֵן נוֹהֲגִין קְצָת, מִפְּנֵי שֶׁטִּבְעָם חָלוּשׁ וְהַוְיָן כְּמוֹ חוֹלִים לְעִנְיָן זֶה.

ב) אֲבָל בַּיּוֹם הָרִאשׁוֹן אָסוּר לְהַנִּיחַ תְּפִלִּין, בֵּין שֶׁהוּא יוֹם מִיתָה וּקְבוּרָה, בֵּין שֶׁהוּא יוֹם קְבוּרָה לְחוּד. וְאִם נִקְבַּר בַּלַּיְלָה, אָסוּר לְהַנִּיחַ תְּפִלִּין בַּיּוֹם שֶׁלְּאַחֲרָיו, וּבַיּוֹם הַשֵּׁנִי מַנִּיחָן לְאַחַר הָנֵץ הַחַמָּה. וְיוֹם שְׁמוּעָה קְרוֹבָה, כְּיוֹם מִיתָה וּקְבוּרָה דָּמֵי. אֲבָל מִי שֶׁמֵּת לוֹ מֵת בָּרֶגֶל אוֹ שֶׁבָּאָה לוֹ שְׁמוּעָה קְרוֹבָה בָּרֶגֶל, אֲזַי בַּיּוֹם הָרִאשׁוֹן שֶׁלְּאַחַר הָרֶגֶל, מַנִּיחַ תְּפִלִּין.

ג) עֲטִיפַת הָרֹאשׁ, אֵין נוֹהֲגִין בִּמְדִינוֹת אֵלּוּ. וּמִכָּל מָקוֹם יֵשׁ לִנְהוֹג בַּעֲטִיפָה קְצָת, דְּהַיְנוּ לִמְשׁוֹךְ אֶת הַכּוֹבַע לְמַטָּה לִפְנֵי הָעֵינַיִם כָּל שִׁבְעָה, חוּץ מִשַּׁבָּת, מִשּׁוּם דַּהֲוֵי דָּבָר שֶׁבְּפַרְהֶסְיָא.

ד) אָסוּר לִלְבּוֹשׁ בֶּגֶד מְכֻבָּס וַאֲפִלּוּ כֻּתֹּנֶת, בְּתוֹךְ שִׁבְעָה, וַאֲפִלּוּ לִכְבוֹד שַׁבָּת. אֲפִלּוּ סְדִינִים וּמַצְּעוֹת־הַמִּטָּה וּמִטְפְּחוֹת־יָדַיִם, אָסוּר לְהַצִּיעַ הַמְכֻבָּסִין. אַךְ לִכְבוֹד שַׁבָּת, מֻתָּר לְהַצִּיעַ עַל הַשֻּׁלְחָן, מִטְפָּחוֹת מְכֻבָּסוֹת מִכְּבָר.

ה) לְכַבֵּס כְּסוּתוֹ בְּעַצְמוֹ, אֲפִלּוּ לְהַנִּיחָהּ לְאַחַר שִׁבְעָה, אָסוּר מִשּׁוּם מְלָאכָה. וְאִם הָיְתָה כְּסוּתוֹ בִּידֵי אֲחֵרִים, מֻתָּרִין לְכַבְּסָן כְּמוֹ שְׁאָר מְלָאכָה בְּקַבְּלָנוּת.

ו) מִי שֶׁתְּכָפוּהוּ אֲבֵלִיּוֹת זוֹ אַחַר זוֹ, מֻתָּר לְכַבֵּס כְּסוּתוֹ בְּמַיִם לְבַד (אֲבָל לֹא בְּאֵפֶר וּבוֹרִית וְכַדּוֹמֶה) וּלְלָבְשָׁהּ.

ז) לְאַחַר שִׁבְעָה עַד שְׁלֹשִׁים, מִדִּינָא אֵינוֹ אָסוּר לִלְבּוֹשׁ אוֹ לְהַצִּיעַ תַּחְתָּיו אֶלָּא בֶּגֶד מְגֹהָץ, (וְיֵשׁ אוֹמְרִים, דְּהַיְנוּ כָּבוּס בְּמַיִם וָאֵפֶר אוֹ בְּנֶתֶר וּבוֹרִית). וְהוּא שֶׁיְּהֵא לָבָן וְחָדָשׁ. אֲבָל נוֹהֲגִין לֶאֱסוֹר גַּם בִּמְכֻבָּס אֲפִלּוּ בְּלֹא גִהוּץ, אֶלָּא אִם כֵּן לוֹבְשׁוֹ אָדָם אַחֵר תְּחִלָּה זְמַן מָה. אַךְ אִם אֵינוֹ מְכֻבָּס אֶלָּא בְּמַיִם לְבַד, אֵין צָרִיךְ שֶׁיִּלְבָּשֶׁנּוּ אַחֵר תְּחִלָּה.

ח) אִם אֵינוֹ מַחֲלִיף לְתַעֲנוּג אֶלָּא לְצֹרֶךְ, כְּגוֹן שֶׁהַכֻּתֹּנֶת שֶׁעָלָיו

at all. Only in the presence of the consolers is he required to be seated. He is also forbidden to sleep in a bed or on a bench; he must sleep on the floor. But he may spread pillows and cushions on the floor as he usually does in his bed. Some *Poskim* permit him to sleep in a bed. And some are accustomed to do so because they have frail constitutions, and are considered ill in this regard.

2) On the first day, a mourner is forbidden to put on *Tefillin,* whether it is the day of death and burial or the day of burial alone. If the burial took place at night, he may not put on *Tefillin* the following day. On the second day of mourning, he should put them on after sunrise. The day on which one receives timely news is like the day of death and burial. But if the death occurs on a Festival, or he receives timely news on a Festival, then, on the first day after the Festival, he should put on *Tefillin*.

3) Wrapping the head is not customary in our regions. Nevertheless, one should make a token wrapping, by pulling down the hat close to the eyes during the seven days of mourning. This is not done on Shabbos because this is a public manifestation of mourning.

4) A mourner is forbidden to wear a freshly washed garment, even a shirt, during the seven days of mourning and not even in the honor of Shabbos. Even sheets, bedspreads, and hand-towels, are forbidden if they are freshly washed. However, in honor of Shabbos it is permitted to cover the table with tablecloths that were washed before the period of mourning began.

5) Washing his own garments, even if he intends to leave them until after the seven days of mourning, is forbidden, because it is considered work. However, if his garments are in the hands of others, they are permitted to wash them, like any other type of work which they had contracted to do for him.

6) If one is in a second consecutive period of mourning, he is permitted to wash his garments with water only (not with ash, soap or the like), and to wear them.

7) After the seven days of mourning until the thirtieth day, the *halacha* that forbids the mourner to wear or spread beneath himself a freshly washed garment is applicable only if it is ironed (some say this does not mean ironing, but washing with water and ash or with soda and soap), and is white and new. But it is the custom to forbid wearing even washed garments, even if they were not ironed, unless someone else had worn them for a short time previously. If, however, they were merely washed with water, it is not necessary that another person wear them first.

8) If he does not change his garments for pleasure, rather out of necessity, as

מְלֻכְלֶכֶת אוֹ מִשּׁוּם עִרְבּוּבְיָא, מֻתָּר אֲפִלּוּ תּוֹךְ שִׁבְעָה, וּבִלְבַד, אִם לְבָשָׁהּ אַחֵר תְּחִלָּה.

ט) מֻתָּר לְכַבֵּס וּלְגַהֵץ לְאַחַר שִׁבְעָה לְלָבְשָׁם לְאַחַר שְׁלֹשִׁים, אוֹ לְלָבְשָׁם אֲפִלּוּ תּוֹךְ שְׁלֹשִׁים לְאַחַר שֶׁיִּלְבָּשֵׁם אַחֵר.

י) אָסוּר לִלְבּוֹשׁ תּוֹךְ שְׁלֹשִׁים בִּגְדֵי שַׁבָּת אֲפִלּוּ בַּשַּׁבָּת, וּמִכָּל־שֶׁכֵּן לִלְבּוֹשׁ בְּגָדִים חֲדָשִׁים. וְעַל אָבִיו וְאִמּוֹ, נָהֲגוּ אִסּוּר לִלְבּוֹשׁ בְּגָדִים חֲדָשִׁים כָּל שְׁנֵים עָשָׂר חֹדֶשׁ. אַךְ אִם צָרִיךְ לָהֶם, יִתֵּן לְאַחֵר לְלָבְשָׁם תְּחִלָּה שְׁנַיִם אוֹ שְׁלֹשָׁה יָמִים.

יא) אִשָּׁה בְּתוֹךְ שְׁלֹשִׁים וַאֲפִלּוּ בְּתוֹךְ שִׁבְעָה לְאֶבְלָהּ, שֶׁהִגִּיעַ זְמַנָּהּ לָלֶכֶת בַּשַּׁבָּת לְבֵית־הַכְּנֶסֶת לְאַחַר לֵדָתָהּ, וְנוֹהֲגוֹת שֶׁאוֹתָהּ שַׁבָּת הִיא לָהּ כְּמוֹ יוֹם־טוֹב לִלְבּוֹשׁ בִּגְדֵי־יְקָר וַעֲדִי־זָהָב, מֻתֶּרֶת לִלְבּוֹשׁ בְּשַׁבָּת זוֹ בִּגְדֵי שַׁבָּת, אַךְ לֹא בִגְדֵי יוֹם־טוֹב, שֶׁלֹּא תָזוּחַ דַּעְתָּהּ וְתִשְׁכַּח הָאֲבֵלוּת. וְאֵינָהּ צְרִיכָה לְשַׁנּוֹת מְקוֹמָהּ.

יב) אָסוּר לְגַלֵּחַ שְׂעָרוֹ כָּל שְׁלֹשִׁים, בֵּין שְׂעַר רֹאשׁוֹ, בֵּין שְׂעַר זְקָנוֹ, בֵּין שְׂעַר כָּל מָקוֹם. וְעַל אָבִיו וְאִמּוֹ, אָסוּר לְגַלֵּחַ עַד שֶׁיִּגְעֲרוּ בוֹ חֲבֵרָיו. וְשִׁעוּר גְּעָרָה, יֵשׁ בּוֹ מַחֲלֹקֶת הַפּוֹסְקִים. וְנוֹהֲגִין בִּמְדִינוֹת אֵלּוּ, שֶׁאֵין מְגַלְּחִין כָּל שְׁנֵים עָשָׂר חֹדֶשׁ אִם לֹא לְצֹרֶךְ, כְּגוֹן שֶׁהִכְבִּיד עָלָיו שְׂעָרוֹ אוֹ שֶׁהוֹלֵךְ בֵּין הַגּוֹיִם וּמִתְנַוֵּל בֵּינֵיהֶם בְּשַׂעֲרוֹתָיו, אָז מֻתָּר לְגַלְּחָם, כִּי אֵין צְרִיכִים גְּעָרָה בְּפֵרוּשׁ, אֶלָּא כְּשֶׁיִּגַּדֵּל שְׂעָרוֹ עַד שֶׁיִּהְיֶה מְשֻׁנֶּה מֵחֲבֵרָיו שֶׁרָאוּי לוֹמַר עָלָיו כַּמָּה מְשֻׁנֶּה זֶה, אָז מֻתָּר לְגַלֵּחַ, וּבִלְבַד שֶׁיְּהֵא לְאַחַר שְׁלֹשִׁים.

יג) כְּשֵׁם שֶׁאָסוּר לְגַלֵּחַ כָּל שְׁלֹשִׁים, כָּךְ אָסוּר לִקְצוֹץ צִפָּרְנָיו בִּכְלִי. אֲבָל בְּיָדָיו אוֹ בְשִׁנָּיו, מֻתָּר אֲפִלּוּ תּוֹךְ שִׁבְעָה. וְאִם הוּא מוֹהֵל, אָסוּר לוֹ לְתַקֵּן אֶת הַצִּפָּרְנַיִם לְצֹרֶךְ הַפְּרִיעָה אֶלָּא אִם כֵּן שֶׁאֵין כָּאן מוֹהֵל אַחֵר, וְאָז מֻתָּר אֲפִלּוּ תּוֹךְ שִׁבְעָה. וְאִשָּׁה שֶׁאֵרְעָה טְבִילָתָהּ לְאַחַר שִׁבְעָה תּוֹךְ שְׁלֹשִׁים, תֹּאמַר לְאִשָּׁה נָכְרִית שֶׁתָּקוּץ צִפָּרְנֶיהָ. וְאִי לֵכָּא נָכְרִית, תָּקוּץ לָהּ יִשְׂרְאֵלִית.

יד) מֻתָּר לִסְרוֹק רֹאשׁוֹ בְּמַסְרֵק וַאֲפִלּוּ תּוֹךְ שִׁבְעָה.

when the shirt he is wearing is soiled, or because of a rash, he is permitted to change his garments even during the first seven days, and even on a weekday, provided someone had previously worn them.

9) He is permitted to wash and and iron his garments after the seven days of mourning in order to wear them after the thirty days, or to wear them during the thirty days, after they will have been worn by someone else.

10) During the first thirty days he is forbidden to wear Shabbos clothes even on Shabbos,[1] and he certainly may not wear new clothing. When mourning the loss of his father or mother, he is by custom forbidden to wear new clothes during the entire twelve months. If, however, he needs them, he should let another person wear them first, for two or three days.

11) A woman, during the first thirty days of mourning, or even during the first seven days of mourning, whose time has come, to go to the synagogue on the Shabbos, after giving birth, customarily considers this Shabbos like a Yom Tov by wearing expensive clothing and gold jewelry. She is permitted to wear Shabbos clothing, but not her Yom Tov clothing, lest her mind be diverted, and she forget she is in mourning. She does not need to change her seat in the synagogue.

12) A mourner is forbidden to have his hair cut during the first thirty days of mourning, whether it is the hair of his head, the beard, or any other part of the body. If he mourns the loss of his father or mother, he is forbidden to cut his hair until he is admonished by his friends. The estimated time of admonishment is a subject of controversy between the *Poskim*. The custom in our regions is not to cut the hair the entire year unless it is necessary, as when his hair is burdensome to him, or if he mingles with people of different nationalities, who would look upon him with scorn because of his hair. In such instances he is allowed to have it cut, for actual admonishment is not required. But if his hair grew to such proportions, that he looks different from his friends, so that people would be apt to say, "How different he is," then he is allowed to have it cut, provided it is after thirty days of mourning.

13) Just as he is forbidden to have his hair cut during the first thirty days of mourning, so too is he forbidden to cut his nails with an instrument. But with his hands or teeth, it is permitted even during the first seven days. If he is a *Mohel*, he is forbidden to cut his nails in order to perform the laceration of the foreskin, unless there is no other *Mohel* available, and then he is permitted to do so even during the first seven days. A woman who needs to perform the ritual immersion after the first seven days of mourning, but within the thirty days, should ask a non-Jewess to cut her nails. If a non-Jewess in unavailable, a Jewess may do it.

14) A mourner is permitted to comb his hair with a comb even during the first seven days of mourning.

1. The prevailing custom today is to permit Shabbos clothing even during the first week. (*Gesher HaChaim,* Chapter 21:10:4).

טו) נוֹהֲגִין שֶׁהָאָבֵל מְשַׁנֶּה מְקוֹמוֹ בְּבֵית־הַכְּנֶסֶת כָּל שְׁלֹשִׁים, וּלְאַחַר אָבִיו וְאִמּוֹ שְׁנֵים־עָשָׂר חֹדֶשׁ. וְשִׁנּוּי מָקוֹם, הַיְנוּ לְכָל הַפָּחוֹת רָחוֹק אַרְבַּע אַמּוֹת מִמְּקוֹמוֹ, וְלִמְקוֹם שֶׁהוּא יוֹתֵר רָחוֹק מֵאֲרוֹן־הַקֹּדֶשׁ מִמְּקוֹמוֹ.

סִימָן ריב
דְּבָרִים הָאֲסוּרִים מִשּׁוּם שִׂמְחָה גַּם לְאַחַר שִׁבְעָה

א) אָסוּר לֶאֱכוֹל בִּסְעוּדַת בְּרִית־מִילָה אוֹ פִּדְיוֹן־הַבֵּן וְסִיּוּם מַסֶּכְתָּא וְכָל־שֶׁכֵּן בִּסְעוּדַת נִשּׂוּאִין כָּל שְׁלֹשִׁים עַל שְׁאָר קְרוֹבָיו, וְכָל שְׁנֵים עָשָׂר חֹדֶשׁ עַל אָבִיו וְאִמּוֹ (וַאֲפִלּוּ בְּשָׁנָה מְעֻבֶּרֶת, סַגֵּי בִּשְׁנֵים עָשָׂר חֹדֶשׁ). וּבְתוֹךְ בֵּיתוֹ, אִם יֵשׁ סְעוּדַת מִצְוָה מֻתָּר לוֹ לֶאֱכוֹל. אַךְ בִּסְעוּדַת נִשּׂוּאִין, יֵשׁ לְהַחְמִיר אֲפִלּוּ בְּתוֹךְ בֵּיתוֹ, אִם לֹא כְּשֶׁהוּא מַשִּׂיא יָתוֹם אוֹ יְתוֹמָה, שֶׁאִם לֹא יֹאכַל שָׁם, יִתְבַּטֵּל הַמַּעֲשֶׂה, אָז מֻתָּר לוֹ לֶאֱכוֹל אֲפִלּוּ אֵינָהּ בְּבֵיתוֹ. וְגַם לִלְבּוֹשׁ בִּגְדֵי שַׁבָּת, לְאַחַר הַמַּעֲשֶׂה, אָז מֻתָּר לוֹ לֶאֱכוֹל אֲפִלּוּ אֵינָהּ בְּבֵיתוֹ. וְגַם לִלְבּוֹשׁ בִּגְדֵי שַׁבָּת לְאַחַר שְׁלֹשִׁים וַאֲפִלּוּ עַל אָבִיו וְאִמּוֹ, וְלִשְׁאָר קְרוֹבִים גַּם תּוֹךְ שְׁלֹשִׁים.

ב) אֵינוֹ רַשַּׁאי לְהַזְמִין אֲחֵרִים אוֹ לְהִזָּמֵן עִם אֲחֵרִים. לֹא יִשְׁלַח מָנוֹת לַאֲחֵרִים, וַאֲחֵרִים לֹא יִשְׁלְחוּ לוֹ, כָּל שְׁלֹשִׁים. וְהוּא הַדִּין כָּל שְׁנֵים עָשָׂר חֹדֶשׁ עַל אָבִיו וְאִמּוֹ. וּבְשַׁבָּת, תַּלְיָא בְּמִנְהָג דִּלְעֵיל סִימָן רי סָעִיף ח.

ג) אָבֵל שֶׁהוּא סַנְדָּק אוֹ מוֹהֵל לְאַחַר שְׁלֹשִׁים (אֲפִלּוּ עַל אָבִיו וְאִמּוֹ), יִלְבַּשׁ בִּגְדֵי שַׁבָּת עַד לְאַחַר הַמִּילָה, וְיָכוֹל לֶאֱכוֹל גַּם בַּסְּעוּדָה.

ד) אָסוּר לִכָּנֵס לְבֵית־נִשּׂוּאִין כָּל שְׁלֹשִׁים עַל שְׁאָר קְרוֹבִים, וּשְׁנֵים עָשָׂר חֹדֶשׁ עַל אָבִיו וְאִמּוֹ, אֲפִלּוּ לִשְׁמוֹעַ אֶת הַבְּרָכוֹת שֶׁמְּבָרְכִין שָׁם. אֲבָל בַּחֻפָּה שֶׁעוֹשִׂין בַּחֲצַר בֵּית־הַכְּנֶסֶת וּמְבָרְכִין שָׁם בִּרְכַּת אֵרוּסִין וְנִשּׂוּאִין, מֻתָּר לַעֲמוֹד וְלִשְׁמוֹעַ אֶת הַבְּרָכוֹת לְאַחַר שְׁלֹשִׁים אֲפִלּוּ עַל אָבִיו וְאִמּוֹ. וְגַם הוּא בְּעַצְמוֹ יָכוֹל לְבָרֵךְ אֶת הַבְּרָכוֹת. וְגַם יָכוֹל לִהְיוֹת שׁוֹשְׁבִין לְהַכְנִיס אֶת הֶחָתָן תַּחַת הַחֻפָּה. וְיָכוֹל לִלְבּוֹשׁ בִּגְדֵי שַׁבָּת, וּבִלְבַד

1. Where it is customary to offer greetings to a mourner on Shabbos, you may send him

15) If it customary for a mourner to change his place in the synagogue during the first thirty days of mourning, and after the loss of his father or mother, for twelve months. The change of place should be at least four *amos* away from his original place, and should be to a place that is farther from the *Aron HaKodesh* than his original place.

Chapter 212

Things that are Forbidden Because of "Rejoicing" After the Seven Days.

1) A mourner is forbidden to eat at the feasts of either a circumcision, redemption of a firstborn, or completion of a *Talmudic* tractate, and especially a wedding feast, during the thirty days of mourning for a relative, and during the entire twelve months of mourning for his father or mother. (Even during a leap-year, twelve months are sufficient). However, in his own house, when there is a feast in honor of a mitzvah, he is permitted to participate. However with regard to a wedding feast. he should be strict [and abstain] even though it is celebrated at his own house, unless it is a wedding in which he is giving an orphaned groom or bride to marriage, and his lack of participation may cause the match to break off. In that case, he is permitted to eat even if the feast is held in another house. He may then also wear his Shabbos clothing after thirty days of mourning for his father or mother, or within thirty days of mourning for other relatives.

2) He is not permitted to invite others or to accept invitations from others. He may not send gifts to others, and others should not send gifts to him during the entire thirty days of mourning, or during the twelve months of mourning for his father or mother. Concerning Shabbos, it depends on the custom,[1] see Chapter 210:8.

3) If a mourner has been asked to serve as either a *Sandek* or a *Mohel*, after the thirty days of mourning even for his father or mother, he may wear his Shabbos clothing until after the circumcision, and he may even partake of the feast.[2]

4) He is forbidden to enter a house where a wedding feast is being held, during the entire thirty days of mourning for a relative, or the twelve months of mourning for his father or mother, even to hear the *berachos* that are said there. However, during a wedding ceremony that is held in the court of the synagogue, where they are reciting, the *berachos* of betrothal and marriage, he is permitted to stand there and listen to the *berachos* after thirty days of mourning even for his father or mother. He is even permitted to recite the *berachos,* and may even act as best man to escort the bridegroom under the *chupah.* He may wear his Shabbos clothing, provided it is

---

gifts on Shabbos as well, and if not, not. *Rama* 385:3. This formula applies to *Purim* as well. *Magen Avraham* 656. *Taz* disagrees regarding Purim and forbids sending him *Mishloach Monos*.

2. Even if it takes place out of his home.

שֶׁיְּהֵא לְאַחַר שְׁלֹשִׁים. אֲבָל לֹא יִכָּנֵס לֶאֱכוֹל עַל הַסְּעוּדָה. וְיֵשׁ מְקִלִּין גַּם לֶאֱכוֹל עַל הַסְּעוּדָה.

ה) מֻתָּר לָאָבֵל לָלֶכֶת אֶל הַמִּשְׁתֶּה לְשַׁמֵּשׁ וְאוֹכֵל בְּבֵיתוֹ מַה שֶּׁשּׁוֹלְחִין לוֹ מִן הַסְּעוּדָה.

סִימָן רִיג
שֶׁהָאָבֵל אָסוּר לִשָּׂא אִשָּׁה, וְדִין חָתָן אוֹ כַּלָּה שֶׁנַּעֲשׂוּ אֲבֵלִים

א) כָּל שְׁלֹשִׁים, אָסוּר לִשָּׂא אִשָּׁה. וְכֵן אִשָּׁה שֶׁהִיא אֲבֵלָה, אֲסוּרָה שֶׁתִּנָּשֵׂא עַד לְאַחַר שְׁלֹשִׁים. וּלְאַחַר שְׁלֹשִׁים, מֻתָּרִין אֲפִלּוּ עַל אָב וָאֵם. אֲבָל לְהִתְקַשֵּׁר בְּשִׁדּוּכִין וּבְלֹא סְעוּדָה, מֻתָּר אֲפִלּוּ תּוֹךְ שִׁבְעָה.

ב) מֵתָה אִשְׁתּוֹ, לֹא יִשָּׂא אַחֶרֶת, עַד לְאַחַר שָׁלֹשׁ רְגָלִים, כְּדֵי שֶׁעַל יְדֵי שִׂמְחַת הָרְגָלִים, תִּשְׁתַּכַּח מִמֶּנּוּ אַהֲבַת הָרִאשׁוֹנָה בְּשָׁעָה שֶׁיִּהְיֶה עִם הַשְּׁנִיָּה, שֶׁלֹּא יִשְׁתֶּה בְּכוֹס זֶה וְיִתֵּן דַּעְתּוֹ עַל הָרִאשׁוֹנָה. וְרֹאשׁ־הַשָּׁנָה וְיוֹם־הַכִּפּוּרִים, אֵינָם חֲשׁוּבִים כִּרְגָלִים לְעִנְיָן זֶה. וְגַם שְׁמִינִי־עֲצֶרֶת אֵינוֹ נֶחְשָׁב לְרֶגֶל בִּפְנֵי עַצְמוֹ לְעִנְיָן זֶה. וְאִם עֲדַיִן לֹא קִיֵּם מִצְוַת פְּרִיָּה וּרְבִיָּה, אוֹ שֶׁיֵּשׁ לוֹ בָּנִים קְטַנִּים, אוֹ שֶׁאֵין לוֹ מִי שֶׁיְּשַׁמְּשֶׁנּוּ, אֵינוֹ צָרִיךְ לְהַמְתִּין שָׁלֹשׁ רְגָלִים. וּמִכָּל מָקוֹם נִרְאֶה דְּיֵשׁ לְהַמְתִּין עַד לְאַחַר שְׁלֹשִׁים. וְאִשָּׁה שֶׁמֵּת בַּעְלָהּ, צְרִיכָה לְהַמְתִּין תִּשְׁעִים יוֹם.

ג) מִי שֶׁהֵכִין צָרְכֵי חֻפָּתוֹ, וּמֵת אֶחָד מִן הַקְּרוֹבִים שֶׁל הֶחָתָן אוֹ שֶׁל הַכַּלָּה, וַאֲפִלּוּ אֲבִי הֶחָתָן וְאֵם הַכַּלָּה, בַּזְּמַן הַזֶּה שֶׁיְּכוֹלִים גַּם אֲחֵרִים לְהָכִין צָרְכֵי נִשּׂוּאִין, דּוֹחִין אֶת הַנִּשּׂוּאִין עַד לְאַחַר יְמֵי הָאֵבֶל.

ד) וַאֲפִלּוּ מֵתוּ לְאַחַר שֶׁהֶעֱמִידוּ אֶת הַחֻפָּה, אָסוּר לוֹ לִבְעוֹל עַד לְאַחַר שִׁבְעַת יְמֵי הָאֵבֶל. וְכֵיוָן שֶׁעֲדַיִן לֹא בָעַל וְאָסוּר לוֹ לִבְעוֹל, אֲסוּרִין לְהִתְיַחֵד בְּלִי שׁוֹמֵר. וּלְאַחַר שִׁבְעַת יְמֵי הָאֵבֶל, בּוֹעֵל בְּעִילַת מִצְוָה, וְנוֹהֵג שִׁבְעַת יְמֵי מִשְׁתֶּה.

ה) אֲבָל אִם לְאַחַר שֶׁבָּעַל, מֵת קְרוֹבוֹ שֶׁל הֶחָתָן אוֹ שֶׁל הַכַּלָּה, כְּבָר

---

3. *Taz* 391:4.

1. *Rabbi Akiva Eiger* (see *Chassam Sofer* resp. 350), but the *Dagul Marevava* says it is counted as a separate Festival in this regard.

after the thirty days of mourning. However, he is not allowed to enter [the house or hall] to partake of the feast.[3] Some *Poskim* are lenient, and even permit him to partake of the feast.

5) A mourner may attend a wedding feast if he serves as a waiter. He may also eat in his own house of what is sent to him from the feast.

Chapter 213

A Mourner is Forbidden to Marry
Laws of a Groom or Bride Who Becomes Mourners

1) During the thirty days of mourning it is forbidden for a man to marry. Likewise, a woman who is a mourner is forbidden to get married until after the thirty days of mourning are over. After thirty days, they are permitted even if they are in mourning for a parent. However, an engagement without a feast, is permitted even during the first seven days of mourning.

2) If one's wife dies, he should not remarry until the three Festivals have passed (*Pesach, Shavuos, Sukkos*). Rejoicing on the Festivals will help him forget his love for his first wife when he marries the second, so that he will not drink from this cup and have his mind on the first cup. *Rosh Hashanah* and *Yom Kippur* are not considered Festivals in this respect. *Shemini Atzeress*, too, is[1] not considered a separate Festival in this respect. If he has not yet fulfilled the mitzvah of propagation,[2] or if he has young children, or if he has no one to look after him, he need not wait for the passage of three Festivals. Nevertheless, it seems [proper] that he should wait until after thirty days have passed. A woman whose husband died, must wait ninety days before remarrying.[3]

3) When everything had been prepared for the wedding, and one of the relatives of the bridegroom died, or one of the bride's relatives died, even if it was the groom's father or the bride's mother, in our times, since others are able to prepare what is needed for the wedding, the wedding must be postponed until after the days of mourning.[4]

4) Even if the death occurred after the *chupah*, the mourner is forbidden to have marital relations until after the seven days of mourning. Since he has not yet had marital relations with her and he is forbidden to have marital relations with her, they are forbidden to be alone without a chaperone. After the seven days of mourning, he may have marital relations with her, and celebrate the seven days of wedding feasts.

5) However, if after they had marital relations a relative of the groom or bride

---

2. See *Kitzur Shulchan Aruch* 145:2.
3. See *Kitzur Shulchan Aruch* 145:13.
4. *Nekudos Hakeseff* 342:1.

חָלוּ עֲלֵיהֶם יְמֵי הַמִּשְׁתֶּה, וְהֵמָּה לָהֶם כְּמוֹ רֶגֶל שֶׁאֵין אֲבֵלוּת נוֹהֶגֶת בָּהֶם, וְעוֹד קַלִּים יוֹתֵר שֶׁמֻּתָּרִים בְּגִהוּץ וְתִסְפֹּרֶת, וְאֵין אֲסוּרִים אֶלָּא בִּדְבָרִים שֶׁבְּצִנְעָא. וּלְאַחַר שִׁבְעַת יְמֵי הַמִּשְׁתֶּה, אָז מַתְחִילִים שִׁבְעַת יְמֵי אֲבֵלוּת. וְגַם שְׁלֹשִׁים אֵינוֹ מוֹנֶה אֶלָּא מִימֵי הָאֲבֵלוּת וְאֵילָךְ. (וְאַף־עַל־גַּב דְּרֶגֶל עוֹלֶה לְמִנְיַן שְׁלֹשִׁים כִּדְלְקַמָּן סִימָן ריט סְעִיף ז, שִׁבְעַת יְמֵי הַמִּשְׁתֶּה אֵינָן עוֹלִין, כֵּיוָן שֶׁמֻּתָּר בְּתִסְפֹּרֶת).

סִימָן ריד
מָתַי הָאָבֵל יָכוֹל לָצֵאת מִבֵּיתוֹ

א) כָּל שִׁבְעָה, אֵינוֹ יוֹצֵא מִבֵּיתוֹ. אַךְ אִם מֵת לוֹ מֵת, אוֹ אֲפִלּוּ אֵצֶל אַחֵר, אֶלָּא שֶׁאֵין שָׁם כְּדֵי מִטָּה וְקוֹבְרֶיהָ, יוֹצֵא אֲפִלּוּ בַּיּוֹם הָרִאשׁוֹן. אִם שָׁלַח הַמּוֹשֵׁל לִקְרוֹא לוֹ, אוֹ שֶׁצָּרִיךְ לָלֶכֶת לִשְׁאָר דָּבָר שֶׁצָּרִיךְ לוֹ הַרְבֵּה, כְּגוֹן דְּבַר הָאָבֵד, מֻתָּר לוֹ לָצֵאת, וְיִתֵּן עָפָר בְּמִנְעָלָיו.

ב) אֲפִלּוּ לְבֵית־הַכְּנֶסֶת לְהִתְפַּלֵּל, אֵינוֹ יוֹצֵא בְּתוֹךְ שִׁבְעָה, רַק בַּשַּׁבָּת. אַךְ אִם אִי־אֶפְשָׁר לֶאֱסוֹף עֲשָׂרָה וִיהֵא מֻכְרָח לְהִתְפַּלֵּל בִּיחִידוּת וּבִשְׁכוּנָתוֹ יֵשׁ מִנְיָן, יָכוֹל לָצֵאת לָלֶכֶת לְהִתְפַּלֵּל שָׁם, שֶׁלֹּא לְהִתְבַּטֵּל מִתְּפִלָּה בְּצִבּוּר.

ג) אִם הָאָבֵל צָרִיךְ לָמוּל אֶת בְּנוֹ, הוֹלֵךְ לְבֵית־הַכְּנֶסֶת אֲפִלּוּ תּוֹךְ שְׁלֹשָׁה יָמִים. וְאִם הָאָבֵל הוּא סַנְדָּק אוֹ מוֹהֵל, לֹא יֵצֵא תּוֹךְ שְׁלֹשָׁה, וּלְאַחַר שְׁלֹשָׁה יִתְפַּלֵּל בְּבֵיתוֹ, וּכְשֶׁמְּבִיאִין אֶת הַתִּינוֹק לָמוּל, הוֹלֵךְ לְבֵית־הַכְּנֶסֶת. וְאִם אֵין מוֹהֵל אַחֵר בָּעִיר, הוֹלֵךְ אֲפִלּוּ בַּיּוֹם הָרִאשׁוֹן.

סִימָן רטו
שֶׁלֹּא לְהִתְקַשּׁוֹת עַל הַמֵּת יוֹתֵר מִדַּי

א) אֵין מִתְקַשִּׁין עַל הַמֵּת יוֹתֵר מִדַּי, שֶׁנֶּאֱמַר, אַל־תִּבְכּוּ לְמֵת וְאַל־תָּנֻדוּ לוֹ. וְאָמְרוּ חֲכָמֵינוּ, זִכְרוֹנָם לִבְרָכָה, וְכִי אֶפְשָׁר לוֹמַר כֵּן. אֶלָּא אַל־תִּבְכּוּ לְמֵת יוֹתֵר מִדַּי, וְאַל־תָּנֻדוּ לוֹ יוֹתֵר מִכַּשִּׁעוּר. הָא כֵּיצַד. שְׁלֹשָׁה יָמִים לִבְכִי, שִׁבְעָה לְהֶסְפֵּד, וּשְׁלֹשִׁים לְגִהוּץ וּלְתִסְפֹּרֶת. מִכָּאן וְאֵילָךְ,

died, they are already subject to the laws pertaining to the week of wedding feasts, which is for them like a Yom Tov, and thus the laws of mourning are not to be observed. These days are even more lenient than a Festival, for they are permitted to put on pressed clothing, and they may have their hair cut. They are forbidden only such things that are done privately. After the seven days of wedding feasts, the seven days of mourning begin. Even the first thirty days of mourning are to be counted only from the beginning of the seven days of mourning. (Although the days of a Yom Tov are always included in the first thirty days of mourning as stated in chapter 219:7, the wedding week is not included since they are permitted to have their hair cut.)

Chapter 214

When a Mourner May Leave His House.

1) During the first seven days of mourning, the mourner may not leave his house. However, if a death occurs in his family, or even if a stranger dies, and there are not enough people to attend the funeral and burial, he is permitted to leave his house even on the first day of mourning. If he is summoned by the authorities, or if he must attend to something very urgent to him as otherwise he will sustain a great loss, he is permitted to leave his house, but he should put some earth in his shoes.

2) Even for the purpose of going to the synagogue to pray, the mourner is not allowed to leave his house during the seven days of mourning, except on Shabbos. However, if he is unable to gather a quorum of ten men for a *minyan* and would be compelled to pray alone, and there is a *minyan* in his neighborhood, he may leave his house to go and pray there, in order not to miss praying with a *minyan*.

3) If a mourner has to circumcise his son, he may go to the synagogue for this purpose even during the first three days of mourning. If the mourner is the *Sandek* or *Mohel*, he may not leave the house on that account, during the first three days of mourning. After the first three days, he should pray at home, and when the infant is brought to the synagogue to be circumcised, he may then go to the synagogue. If there is no other *Mohel* in the city. he may go even on the first day of mourning.

Chapter 215

Excessive Grief is Forbidden

1) It is forbidden to grieve excessively over the dead, as it is said, "Do not weep for the dead, and do not bemoan him."[1] Our Sages of blessed memory, said,[2] "Is it possible to say so? But it means, "Do not weep for the dead excessively, and do not bemoan him inordinately." How should one mourn? Three days are appropriate for weeping, seven days for mourning, and thirty days for abstaining from wearing

---

1. *Jeremiah* 22:10.
2. *Masechess Moed Kattan* 27b.

אָמַר הַקָּדוֹשׁ־בָּרוּךְ־הוּא, אִם אַתֶּם רַשָּׁאִים לְרַחֵם עָלָיו יוֹתֵר מִמֶּנִּי. וְאָמְרוּ חֲכָמֵינוּ, זִכְרוֹנָם לִבְרָכָה, כָּל הַמִּתְקַשֶּׁה עַל הַמֵּת יוֹתֵר מִדַּי, עַל מֵת אַחֵר הוּא בוֹכֶה. בַּמֶּה דְבָרִים אֲמוּרִים, בִּשְׁאָר הָעָם. אֲבָל תַּלְמִיד־חָכָם, הַכֹּל לְפִי חָכְמָתוֹ. וּמִכָּל מָקוֹם, אֵין בּוֹכִין עָלָיו יוֹתֵר מִשְּׁלשִׁים יוֹם, דְּלָא עָדִיף מִמֹּשֶׁה רַבֵּנוּ, עָלָיו הַשָּׁלוֹם, דִּכְתִיב בּוֹ, וַיִּבְכּוּ בְנֵי־יִשְׂרָאֵל אֶת מֹשֶׁה וְגוֹ׳ שְׁלשִׁים יוֹם.

ב) אָמְרוּ רַבּוֹתֵינוּ, זִכְרוֹנָם לִבְרָכָה, אֶחָד מִבְּנֵי הַמִּשְׁפָּחָה שֶׁמֵּת, יִדְאֲגוּ כָּל הַמִּשְׁפָּחָה. מָשָׁל לְמָה הַדָּבָר דּוֹמֶה, לְכִפָּה שֶׁל אֲבָנִים, כֵּיוָן שֶׁנִּזְדַּעְזְעָה אַחַת מֵהֶן, נִזְדַּעְזְעוּ כֻּלָּן. כְּלוֹמַר, שֶׁמִּדַּת־הַדִּין מְתוּחָה כְּנֶגְדָּם עַל שֶׁתִּתְרַפֶּה מְעַט מְעַט. כִּי כָּל שִׁבְעָה, הַחֶרֶב שְׁלוּפָה. וְעַד שְׁלשִׁים, הִיא רוֹפֶפֶת, וְאֵינָהּ חוֹזֶרֶת לְתַעְרָהּ עַד אַחַר שְׁנֵים עָשָׂר חֹדֶשׁ. לְפִיכָךְ שְׁלשָׁה יָמִים הָרִאשׁוֹנִים, יִרְאֶה הָאָבֵל אֶת עַצְמוֹ, כְּאִלּוּ חֶרֶב מֻנַּחַת לוֹ בֵּין כְּתֵפָיו. מִשְּׁלשָׁה וְעַד שִׁבְעָה, כְּאִלּוּ זְקוּפָה כְּנֶגְדּוֹ בְּקֶרֶן זָוִית. מִשִּׁבְעָה וְעַד שְׁלשִׁים, כְּאִלּוּ עוֹבֶרֶת לְפָנָיו בַּשּׁוּק. וְאַחַר כָּךְ כָּל אוֹתָהּ הַשָּׁנָה, עֲדַיִן מִדַּת־הַדִּין מְתוּחָה כְּנֶגֶד אוֹתָהּ הַמִּשְׁפָּחָה. וְאִם נוֹלַד בֵּין זָכָר בְּאוֹתָהּ מִשְׁפָּחָה. נִתְרַפְּאָה כָּל הַמִּשְׁפָּחָה. וְדַוְקָא זָכָר. דְּזָכָר בָּא לָעוֹלָם, שָׁלוֹם בָּא לָעוֹלָם. וְכֵן אֶחָד מֵהַחֲבוּרָה שֶׁמֵּת, מִדַּת־הַדִּין מְתוּחָה כְּנֶגֶד כָּל הַחֲבוּרָה, וְיִדְאֲגוּ כֻּלָּם.

ג) כָּל מִי שֶׁאֵינוֹ מִתְאַבֵּל כְּמוֹ שֶׁצִּוּוּ חֲכָמִים, הֲרֵי זֶה אַכְזָר. אֶלָּא יְעוֹר מִשְּׁנָתוֹ, וְיִפְחַד וְיִדְאַג וִיפַשְׁפֵּשׁ בְּמַעֲשָׂיו, וְיַחֲזֹר בִּתְשׁוּבָה, אוּלַי יִנָּצֵל מֵחַרְבּוֹ שֶׁל מַלְאַךְ־הַמָּוֶת. הֲרֵי הוּא אוֹמֵר, הִכִּיתָה אֹתָם וְלֹא־חָלוּ, מִכְּלָל שֶׁצָּרִיךְ לְהָקִיץ וְלָחוּל וְלַחֲזוֹר בִּתְשׁוּבָה.

סִימָן רטז

דִּין מִקְצָת יוֹם שְׁבִיעִי וּמִקְצָת יוֹם שְׁלשִׁים וְדִין שְׁנֵים עָשָׂר חֹדֶשׁ

א) בַּיּוֹם הַשְּׁבִיעִי לְאַחַר שֶׁהָלְכוּ הַמְנַחֲמִים מִן הָאָבֵל, מֻתָּר בְּכָל הַדְּבָרִים שֶׁהָיָה אָסוּר תּוֹךְ שִׁבְעָה, דְּאָמְרִינָן מִקְצָת הַיּוֹם כְּכֻלּוֹ. חוּץ מִתַּשְׁמִישׁ־הַמִּטָּה שֶׁאָסוּר כָּל הַיּוֹם (אֲפִלּוּ בְּבַיִת אָפֵל). וּבִמְדִינוֹת אֵלּוּ שֶׁאֵין הַמְנַחֲמִים רְגִילִים לָבוֹא בַּיּוֹם הַשְּׁבִיעִי, צָרִיךְ לְהַמְתִּין עַד שָׁעָה

ironed clothes, and from having the hair cut. Thereafter the Holy One, blessed is He, says, "You are not permitted to show him more compassion than I do." Our Sages, of blessed memory, said,[3] "One who grieves excessively over the dead, will have cause to weep over another death." This applies only when the deceased was an ordinary person, but if he was a Torah scholar, he is mourned in proportion to his wisdom. Nevertheless, you should not weep over him more than thirty days, for he is not greater than Moshe *Rabbeinu*, peace unto him, of whom it is written, "And the Children of Yisrael wept for Moshe thirty days."[4]

2) Our Rabbis of blessed memory, said,[5] "When a family member dies, the entire family has cause for concern." To what can this be compared? To an arch made of stone, when one stone shakes all of them are insecure. In other words, severe judgement hovers over them, until it is gradually diminished. For during the first seven days of mourning the sword is drawn, and up to thirty days it is gradually withdrawn, and is not returned to its sheath until after twelve months. Therefore, during the first three days the mourner should perceive himself as if the sword is resting between his shoulders; from the third day to the seventh day, as if it were standing in a corner, facing him; from the seventh day to the thirtieth as if it were passing before him in the street. And thereafter during the entire year, the severe judgement still hangs over that family. If a son is born in that family, the entire family is healed [saved]. This is true only if a male child was born; for when a male comes to this world, peace comes to the world. Likewise when a member of a group dies, judgement hangs over the entire group, and they all have cause to be concerned.

3) He who does not mourn, in the manner the Sages have ordained, is considered a heartless person. But he should arouse himself from his sleep, examine his deeds with fear and anxiety, and repent and then, perhaps he may be spared from the sword of the angel of death. For it is said, "You have smitten them, but they were not greived,"[6] which indicates that a person must awaken, examine [his deeds] and repent.

Chapter 216

Parts of the Seventh and Thirtieth Days and Laws of the Twelve Months

1) On the seventh day, after the consolers have left the mourner, he is permitted to do all the things that were forbidden during the seven days. because we say that a part of the day is considered like the entire day, except with regard to marital relations, which is forbidden the entire seventh day (even in a dark room). In those places where the consolers are not accustomed to come on the seventh day, he must

3. Ibid.
4. *Deuteronomy* 34:8.
5. See *Yerushalmi Moed Kattan* 3:7, and *Maseches Shabbos* 105b.
6. *Jeremiah* 5:3.

שֶׁרְגִילִין לָבוֹא בִּשְׁאָר הַיָּמִים, דְּהַיְנוּ לְאַחַר יְצִיאָה מִבֵּית־הַכְּנֶסֶת, שֶׁרְגִילִין לָבוֹא מְנַחֲמִים. וְכֵן אִם חָל יוֹם הַשְּׁבִיעִי בְּשַׁבָּת, אֲזַי לְאַחַר יְצִיאָה מִבֵּית־הַכְּנֶסֶת שַׁחֲרִית, מֻתָּר בְּתַלְמוּד־תּוֹרָה.

ב) בְּיוֹם שְׁלשִׁים, אָמְרִינָן גַּם כֵּן מִקְצָת הַיּוֹם כְּכֻלּוֹ. וְכֵיוָן שֶׁאָז אֵין בָּאִים מְנַחֲמִים, לָכֵן תֵּכֶף כְּשֶׁתָּנֵץ הַחַמָּה, בָּטְלָה מִמֶּנּוּ גְּזֵרַת שְׁלשִׁים. חָל יוֹם שְׁלשִׁים בְּשַׁבָּת, מֻתָּר לוֹ לִרְחוֹץ בְּעֶרֶב־שַׁבָּת בְּחַמִּין לִכְבוֹד שַׁבָּת, וְלוֹבֵשׁ בִּגְדֵי שַׁבָּת, וְחוֹזֵר לִמְקוֹמוֹ בְּבֵית־הַכְּנֶסֶת, אֲבָל אָסוּר בְּגִלּוּחַ (דְּחָמִיר טְפֵי).

ג) בִּשְׁנֵים עָשָׂר חֹדֶשׁ שֶׁעַל אָבִיו וְאִמּוֹ, לָא אָמְרִינָן מִקְצָת הַיּוֹם כְּכֻלּוֹ, וְאַדְּרַבָּא נוֹהֲגִין לְהוֹסִיף גַּם יוֹם הַיָּארְצֵייט לִנְהוֹג בּוֹ כָּל דִּין שְׁנֵים־עָשָׂר חֹדֶשׁ, וַאֲפִלּוּ חָל בְּשַׁבָּת. אַךְ אִם הָיְתָה הַשָּׁנָה מְעֻבֶּרֶת, גַּם כֵּן אֵין נוֹהֲגִין בַּאֲבֵלוּת שֶׁלִּכְבוֹד אָבִיו וְאִמּוֹ, כִּי אִם שְׁנֵים־עָשָׂר חֹדֶשׁ. וּמֵאַחַר שֶׁכְּבָר כָּלוּ שְׁנֵים־עָשָׂר הַחֳדָשִׁים קֹדֶם הַיָּארְצֵייט, אָז בְּיוֹם הַיָּארְצֵייט, אֵינוֹ חוֹזֵר עוֹד לַאֲבֵלוּת.

סִימָן רי״ז
דִּין מִי שֶׁלֹּא נָהַג אֲבֵלוּת

א) אָבֵל שֶׁלֹּא נָהַג אֲבֵלוּת תּוֹךְ שִׁבְעָה, בֵּין בְּשׁוֹגֵג בֵּין בְּמֵזִיד, מַשְׁלִים אוֹתָהּ כָּל שְׁלשִׁים, חוּץ מִן הַקְּרִיעָה, שֶׁאִם לֹא קָרַע בִּשְׁעַת חִמּוּם, אֵינוֹ קוֹרֵעַ אֶלָּא בְּתוֹךְ שִׁבְעָה, דְּחָשִׁיב שְׁעַת חִמּוּם. וְעַל אָבִיו וְאִמּוֹ, קוֹרֵעַ לְעוֹלָם.

ב) קָטָן שֶׁמֵּת לוֹ מֵת, אֲפִלּוּ גָּדַל תּוֹךְ שִׁבְעָה, כֵּיוָן שֶׁבִּשְׁעַת מִיתָה הָיָה פָּטוּר בָּטֵל מִמֶּנּוּ כָּל דִּין אֲבֵלוּת, אַךְ בַּאֲבֵלוּת דִּשְׁנֵים עָשָׂר חֹדֶשׁ עַל אָבִיו וְאִמּוֹ שֶׁהִיא מִשּׁוּם כְּבוֹדָם, יֵשׁ לוֹ לִנְהוֹג.

ג) חוֹלֶה שֶׁמֵּת לוֹ מֵת שֶׁחַיָּב לְהִתְאַבֵּל עָלָיו וְנוֹדַע לוֹ, אִם הִבְרִיא תּוֹךְ שִׁבְעָה, גּוֹמֵר הַיָּמִים הַנִּשְׁאָרִים. וְכֵן תּוֹךְ שְׁלשִׁים, גּוֹמֵר הַיָּמִים הַנִּשְׁאָרִים. אֲבָל אֵינוֹ צָרִיךְ לְהַשְׁלִים הַיָּמִים שֶׁעָבְרוּ בְּחָלְיוֹ, מִשּׁוּם דְּאָז נָהַג גַּם כֵּן מִקְצָת אֲבֵלוּת, וְדוֹמֶה לְשַׁבָּת דְּעוֹלָה וְאֵינָהּ מַפְסֶקֶת. וְכֵן

wait until the time they used to come on the other days, which is after people leave the synagogue in the morning. If the seventh day of mourning occurs on Shabbos, then after people leave the synagogue in the morning, he is permitted to study Torah.

2) Regarding the thirtieth day we also say that part of the day is considered like the entire day. And since no consolers come then, therefore, immediately after sunrise he is absolved of the laws governing the thirty days of mourning. If the thirtieth day occurs on a Shabbos the mourner is permitted to bathe on Friday, with warm water, in honor of the Shabbos. He may put on Shabbos clothes and return to his regular seat in the synagogue; but he may not have his hair cut.

3) Regarding the twelve month period of mourning for a father or mother we do not say part of the day is considered like the entire day. On the contrary, it is customary to add the *Yahrzeit* (anniversary of death) day in which to observe all the laws of mourning that pertain to the twelve months of mourning, even if it occurs on Shabbos. However, if it was a leap year, the custom is to observe mourning for the honor of a father and mother only twelve months. Since the twelve months expired before the *Yahrzeit* day, therefore, on the *Yahrzeit* day he is not required to resume mourning.

Chapter 217

The Law if One Neglected to Observe Mourning.

1) A mourner who neglected to observe mourning during the first seven days, whether inadvertently or intentionally, may fulfill his obligation during the thirty day period, with the exception of tearing his garments. If he did not tear his garments, at his moment of grief, he should not tear them, for tearing the garments are of no avail except during the first seven days which are considered a time of grief. For his father or mother one must tear his garments at any time.

2) If a child under thirteen years loses a relative, even if he becomes thirteen years of age during the first seven days of mourning, since he was exempt at the time of death, the laws of mourning are cancelled for him.[1] However he should observe the twelve month period of mourning for his father or mother, which is for their honor.

3) If a sick person was notified about the death of a relative for whom he must mourn, and he recovered during the first seven days, he should complete the remaining days. Similarly, with regard to the thirty days of mourning, he should complete the remaining days. But he does not have to make up the days that passed when he was ill, because then, too, he had observed partial mourning. This is comparable to Shabbos, which is included in the seven days of mourning, and does

1. Some *Poskim* disagree and prevailing custom is that he should observe the remaining days. See *Gesher HaChaim* 19:3:3. A Rav should be consulted.

הַיּוֹלֶדֶת גַּם כֵּן אֵינָהּ צְרִיכָה לְהַשְׁלִים הַיָּמִים שֶׁעָבְרוּ עָלֶיהָ בְּלֵדָתָהּ, רַק גּוֹמֶרֶת הַיָּמִים הַנִּשְׁאָרִים.

סִימָן ריח
דִּין עֵדוּת לַאֲבֵלוּת

א) מִתְאַבְּלִין עַל פִּי עֵד אֶחָד, וְעֵד מִפִּי עֵד, וּבְנָכְרִי מֵסִיחַ לְפִי תֻמּוֹ.

ב) מִי שֶׁקִּבֵּל אִגֶּרֶת שֶׁמֵּת קְרוֹבוֹ וְאֵין מְבֹאָר בָּהּ אִם הוּא עֲדַיִן תּוֹךְ שְׁלשִׁים אוֹ לְאַחַר שְׁלשִׁים, אִם הַכּוֹתֵב אֵינוֹ בַּעַל־תּוֹרָה, מוֹקְמִינָן לְאָדָם בְּחֶזְקַת חַי, וְאָמְרִינָן שֶׁלֹּא מֵת עַד סָמוּךְ לִכְתִיבַת הָאִגֶּרֶת, וְחַיָּב לְהִתְאַבֵּל. אֲבָל אִם הַכּוֹתֵב הוּא בַּעַל־תּוֹרָה, אָמְרִינָן מִסְתָמָא הוּא לְאַחַר שְׁלשִׁים. דְּאִם אִיתָא שֶׁהָיָה אֶפְשָׁר שֶׁתַּגִּיעַ הָאִגֶּרֶת לְיָדוֹ תּוֹךְ שְׁלשִׁים, לֹא הָיָה כּוֹתֵב בִּסְתָם. אַךְ אִם הוּא אָבִיו אוֹ אִמּוֹ, כֵּיוָן שֶׁהַמִּנְהָג הוּא לְהוֹדִיעַ מִיָּד חַיָּב לְהִתְאַבֵּל.

סִימָן ריט
דִּין אֲבֵלוּת בְּשַׁבָּת וְיוֹם־טוֹב

א) שַׁבָּת שֶׁבְּתוֹךְ הַשִּׁבְעָה, נוֹהֵג בָּהּ דְּבָרִים שֶׁבְּצִנְעָא, דְּהַיְנוּ שֶׁאָסוּר בְּתַשְׁמִישׁ הַמִּטָּה וּבִרְחִיצָה. אֲבָל דְּבָרִים שֶׁבְּפַרְהֶסְיָא, אֵינוֹ נוֹהֵג. וְלָכֵן קֹדֶם מִזְמוֹר שִׁיר לְיוֹם הַשַּׁבָּת. נוֹעֵל אֶת הַמִּנְעָלִים, וְיוֹשֵׁב עַל כִּסֵּא, וּמַחֲלִיף אֶת הַבֶּגֶד הַקָּרוּעַ, כִּדְלְעֵיל סִימָן קצה, סָעִיף ו. וְתַלְמוּד־תּוֹרָה, הֲוֵי דָּבָר שֶׁבְּצִנְעָא. אֲבָל לַחֲזוֹר אֶת הַפָּרָשָׁה שְׁנַיִם מִקְרָא וְאֶחָד תַּרְגּוּם, מֻתָּר, דְּכֵיוָן שֶׁחַיָּב אָדָם לְהַשְׁלִים פָּרְשִׁיּוֹתָיו, הֲוֵי לֵהּ כְּקוֹרֵא אֶת שְׁמַע וְכַדּוֹמֶה מִסֵּדֶר הַיּוֹם.

ב) אִם קָרְאוּ אֶת הָאָבֵל לַעֲלוֹת לַתּוֹרָה, צָרִיךְ לַעֲלוֹת. כִּי אִם הָיָה נִמְנָע, הֲוֵי דָּבָר שֶׁבְּפַרְהֶסְיָא. וְרַבֵּינוּ תָּם הָיוּ קוֹרִין אוֹתוֹ בְּכָל שַׁבָּת לִשְׁלִישִׁי, וְאֵרַע לוֹ אֵבֶל וְלֹא קְרָאוֹ הַחַזָּן, וְעָלָה הוּא מֵעַצְמוֹ וְאָמַר, כֵּוָן

---

1. Any testimony that is sufficient to permit one's wife to remarry is certainly sufficient for the laws of mourning. *Ramban*.
2. *Bach, Shach*.
3. So that he can say *Kaddish*.

not suspend it. Similarly, a woman who had given birth does not need to make up the days that passed during her confinement, but merely completes the remaining days of mourning.

Chapter 218

The Law of Testimony Relating to Mourning

1) A person must observe the laws of mourning on the testimony of one witness, or the testimony of a witness who heard about is from another witness, or by the disinterested statement of a non-Jew.[1]

2) How should one who receives a letter notifying him of the death of his relative conduct himself when it is not clear whether it is still within thirty days of the death, or after thirty days. If the writer is not learned in Torah, we assume that the relative was alive, and did not die until right before the letter was written, and thus he must observe mourning for him. However, if the writer is learned in Torah, we assume it is after the thirty days, for if it were possible that the letter would arrive during the first thirty days, he would not have written it without specifiying the date.[2] If however, he was informed of the death of his father or his mother, since it is customary to notify [the son] immediately,[3] he must observe the laws of mourning.[4]

Chapter 219

The Law of Mourning on a Shabbos or Yom Tov

1) On Shabbos during the seven days of mourning, the mourner must observe the laws that concern his private life. This means he is forbidden to have marital relations, and to bathe.[1] But he should not observe any mourning in public. Therefore, before saying " *Mizmor Shir Leyom Ha'Shabbos*" he should put on his shoes, sit on a chair, and change his torn garment, as stated above, Chapter 195:6. Torah study is considered a private matter,[2] but, to review the weekly portion of the Torah, the Scripture twice, and the Targum once,[3] is permissible. Since it is the duty of every Jew to complete the weekly portion of the Torah, it is likened to the reading of the *Shema*, and other such portions of the daily prayers.

2) If the mourner was called to the reading of the Torah, he must go up, for if he were to refuse, it would constitute a public display of mourning. *Rabbeinu Tam* used to be called to the Torah to the reading of the third portion every Shabbos; and

---

4. *Sh'vuss Yaakov* vol. 1 Responsa 98.

1. In warm water. *Mishnah Berurah* 548:16.

2. And is forbidden. *Ritva* and *Ran, Masechess Moed Kattan* 22. The *Maharil* used to learn the laws of mourning (on Shabbos when he was in mourning), and Rabbi Yosef S. Natanzohn in his *Yosef Da'as,* resp. 376 permits the learning of the sad things in Scripture, and everything one may learn on *Tisha B'av.*

3. He may do this even on Friday afternoon. *Kerem Shlomo. Maharil* forbids this even on Shabbos.

שֶׁהֻרְגַּל לִקְרוֹת שְׁלִישִׁי בְּכָל שַׁבָּת, הָרוֹאֶה שֶׁאֵינוֹ עוֹלֶה הַיּוֹם, יֵדַע שֶׁהוּא מֵחֲמַת אֲבֵלוּת, וַהֲוֵי פַּרְהֶסְיָא. וְכֵן אִם הַכֹּהֵן הוּא אָבֵל וְאֵין כֹּהֵן אַחֵר בְּבֵית־הַכְּנֶסֶת, צְרִיכִין לִקְרוֹתוֹ. אֲבָל יוֹתֵר טוֹב שֶׁיֵּצֵא מִבֵּית־הַכְּנֶסֶת קֹדֶם הוֹצָאַת סֵפֶר־הַתּוֹרָה. וְכֵן אִם יֵשׁ לְאָבֵל בֵּן לָמוּל וְהַמִּנְהָג שֶׁהוּא חִיּוּב לַעֲלוֹת לַתּוֹרָה, יִקְרָאוּהוּ. דְּאִם לֹא יִקְרָאוּהוּ, הֲוֵי פַּרְהֶסְיָא, וְיוֹתֵר טוֹב שֶׁלֹּא יְהֵא בְּבֵית־הַכְּנֶסֶת בִּשְׁעַת קְרִיאַת הַתּוֹרָה. (אִשָּׁה שֶׁהִגִּיעַ זְמַנָּהּ לָלֶכֶת לְבֵית־הַכְּנֶסֶת בְּשַׁבָּת שֶׁבִּימֵי אֶבְלָהּ, עַיֵּן לְעֵיל סִימָן רי״א סָעִיף י״א).

ג) הַמְמֻנֶּה מֵהַקָּהָל לִהְיוֹת קוֹרֵא בַּתּוֹרָה בְּבֵית־הַכְּנֶסֶת בְּשַׁבָּת וְאֵרַע לוֹ אֵבֶל, לֹא יֵלֵךְ בְּשַׁבָּת שֶׁבְּתוֹךְ שִׁבְעָה לְבֵית־כְּנֶסֶת זֶה. כִּי אִם יִהְיֶה שָׁם, יֵשׁ לְהִסְתַּפֵּק אִם יִקְרָא אוֹ לֹא.

ד) שַׁבָּת עוֹלָה לְמִנְיַן שִׁבְעָה. וַאֲפִלּוּ שָׁמַע שְׁמוּעָה קְרוֹבָה בְּיוֹם שַׁבָּת, שֶׁלֹּא הִתְחִיל עֲדַיִן כְּלָל בַּאֲבֵלוּת, עוֹלֶה לוֹ גַּם כֵּן, וּבְמוֹצָאֵי שַׁבָּת קוֹרֵעַ.

ה) הַקּוֹבֵר אֶת מֵתוֹ אוֹ שָׁמַע שְׁמוּעָה קְרוֹבָה בָּרֶגֶל, בֵּין בְּיוֹם־טוֹב בֵּין בְּחֹל־הַמּוֹעֵד, לֹא חָלָה עָלָיו אֲבֵלוּת עַד לְאַחַר הָרֶגֶל. וְהַנֵּי מִלֵּי בִּדְבָרִים שֶׁל פַּרְהֶסְיָא. אֲבָל דְּבָרִים שֶׁבִּצְנְעָא, נוֹהֵג גַּם בָּרֶגֶל. לֹא יַחֲלִיף בְּגָדָיו, דְּזֶה הֲוֵי פַּרְהֶסְיָא. (וְאַף־עַל־גַּב דִּשְׁאָר אָבֵל מְשַׁנֶּה בְגָדָיו גַּם בָּרֶגֶל, מִכָּל מָקוֹם זֶה שֶׁלֹּא הִתְחִיל עֲדַיִן אֲבֵלוּת אֵין לוֹ לְשַׁנּוֹת בָּרֶגֶל). וּמִי שֶׁמַּנִּיחַ תְּפִלִּין בְּחֹל־הַמּוֹעֵד יַנִּיחַ גַּם בַּיּוֹם הָרִאשׁוֹן שֶׁלְּאַחַר הַקְּבוּרָה.

ו) לְאַחַר הָרֶגֶל, מַתְחִיל לִמְנוֹת שִׁבְעָה יְמֵי אֲבֵלוּת, וְיוֹם הָאַחֲרוֹן שֶׁל יוֹם־טוֹב עוֹלֶה לוֹ לְמִנְיָן, וּמוֹנֶה אַחֲרָיו שִׁשָּׁה יָמִים. וַאֲפִלּוּ יוֹם שֵׁנִי שֶׁל רֹאשׁ־הַשָּׁנָה גַּם כֵּן עוֹלֶה לוֹ לְמִנְיָן.

---

4. This is true only if it is the accepted practice for the *Kohein* to leave in order for a *Yisroel* to be called up. See *Chassam Sofer* resp. *Yoreh* Deah 352. *Tashbatz* 2:276 states he should not go out, because doing so constitutes public display of mourning. And so the *Rabbeinu Tam* did not go out either.

5. *Halachos Ketanos* 1:289, *Aish Dos* resp. 7. The *Maharshal* responsa 71 says not to call him.

6. *Eliyohu Rabba* 132:4.

7. However he should light a candle, as is done on the seven days of mourning. It should

when he happened to be in mourning and the *Chazzan* failed to call him, he went up himself. He said that since he had been accustomed to read the third portion every Shabbos, those who would see that he did not go up this day would understand that it was due to his mourning, and this would be a public display of mourning. Also, if a *Kohein* is a mourner, and there is no other *Kohein* in the synagogue, they must call him up to the reading of the Torah. However, it is preferable that he leave the synagogue[4] before the *Seifer Torah* is taken out of the *Aron HaKodesh*. Also, if the mourner has a son to be circumcised and it is the custom that he must go up to the Torah reading, they should call him up. For if they do not call him, it constitutes a public display of mourning.[5] But it is preferable that he not be in the synagogue during the reading of the Torah.[6] (As for a woman whose time has come to go to the synagogue occurs on the Shabbos during her mourning, see chapter 211:11, above.)

3) If one is officially appointed by the congregation to be the reader of the Torah in the synagogue on Shabbos, and he became a mourner on the Shabbos of the first seven days, he should not go to *that* synagogue; for if he is present there, it will raise the question if he should read or not.

4) Shabbos is included in the seven days of mourning. Even if he received *timely* news of the death of a relative on Shabbos, when he had not yet begun mourning, it is still counted as one of the seven days, and at the conclusion of the Shabbos, he must tear his garments.

5) If he buried his dead, or received *timely* news of his relatives death, on a *Yom Tov*, whether on Yom Tov itself, or on *Chol Hamoed*, he is not subject to the laws of mourning, [7] until after the Yom Tov. This rule applies to the observance of mourning in public. But the laws concerning his private life must be observed even on a *Yom Tov*. He should not change his garments,[8] [9] for this would constitute a public display of mourning. (Although every other mourner must change his clothing during a Yom Tov, nevertheless, this person who has not yet begun to mourn, should not change his garments during the Festival). One who puts on *Tefillin* during *Chol Hamoed*, should also put them on on the first day after the burial.[10]

6) At the conclusion of Yom Tov, he begins to count the seven days of mourning. The last day of Yom Tov is counted as one of the seven days and he counts six days after it. Even the second day of Rosh Hashanah is included in the seven days.

---

not be lit where he eats and not where the person died. On Yom Tov it must be lit by a non-Jew, because the candle is not for his personal needs for Yom Tov.

8. He should not remove his Yom Tov garments. With regard to new clothing, the *Peri Megadim* is doubtful. *Sha'ar Hatziyon* 548:9.

9. He should also not change his place in the synagogue. *Mishnah Berurah* 548:15.

10. The *Peri Megadim* is doubtful about this. *Mishnah Berurah* 38:16.

ז) אַף־עַל־פִּי שֶׁאֵין אֲבֵלוּת בְּיוֹם־טוֹב וּבְחֹל־הַמּוֹעֵד, וַאֲפִלּוּ גְּזֵרַת שְׁלֹשִׁים אֵין בָּהֶם, וּמֻתָּר לוֹ לִלְבּוֹשׁ בְּגָדִים מְגֹהָצִים, מִכָּל מָקוֹם כֵּיוָן דְּאָסוּר בָּהֶם בְּגִלּוּחַ מֵחֲמַת הַמּוֹעֵד, לָכֵן עוֹלִין לְמִנְיַן שְׁלֹשִׁים, וּמוֹנֶה שְׁלֹשִׁים מִיּוֹם הַקְּבוּרָה. וְיוֹם שְׁמִינִי־עֲצֶרֶת, אַף־עַל־פִּי שֶׁהוּא רֶגֶל בִּפְנֵי עַצְמוֹ, מִכָּל מָקוֹם כֵּיוָן שֶׁלֹּא הִתְחִיל עֲדַיִן בַּאֲבֵלוּת, אֵינוֹ מְבַטֵּל, וְגַם בְּמִנְיַן הַשְּׁלֹשִׁים אֵינוֹ נִמְנֶה רַק לְיוֹם אֶחָד.

ח) אֲבָל חָתָן שֶׁנָּשָׂא אִשָּׁה קֹדֶם הָרֶגֶל, וּבָא הָרֶגֶל תּוֹךְ שִׁבְעַת יְמֵי הַמִּשְׁתֶּה, וּמֵת לוֹ מֵת בְּתוֹךְ הָרֶגֶל, אֲזַי כָּל שִׁבְעַת יְמֵי הַמִּשְׁתֶּה שֶׁלּוֹ, אֵינָן עוֹלִין לוֹ לְמִנְיַן שְׁלֹשִׁים.

ט) אַף־עַל־פִּי שֶׁאֵין אֲבֵלוּת בָּרֶגֶל, מִתְעַסְּקִין בּוֹ לְנַחֲמוֹ (וְאֵין בָּזֶה מִשּׁוּם אֲבֵלוּת, כֵּיוָן דְּהָאָבֵל לָאו מִדֵּי קָעָבֵד). וּלְאַחַר הָרֶגֶל כְּשֶׁיִּכְלוּ שִׁבְעָה מִיּוֹם הַקְּבוּרָה, אַף־עַל־פִּי שֶׁעֲדַיִן לֹא כָלוּ שִׁבְעַת יְמֵי הָאֲבֵלוּת, מְלַאכְתּוֹ נַעֲשֵׂית עַל יְדֵי אֲחֵרִים בְּבָתֵּיהֶם, וַעֲבָדָיו עוֹשִׂין לוֹ בְּצִנְעָא בְּתוֹךְ בֵּיתוֹ. וְאֵין צְרִיכִין לְנַחֲמוֹ אַחַר הָרֶגֶל מִנְּיַן הַיָּמִים שֶׁנִּחֲמוּהוּ בָּרֶגֶל, אֲבָל מַרְאִין לוֹ פָּנִים.

סִימָן רכ
דִּין שֶׁהָרְגָלִים מְבַטְּלִין גְּזֵרַת שִׁבְעָה וּשְׁלֹשִׁים

א) הָרֶגֶל, מְבַטֵּל גְּזֵרַת שִׁבְעָה וּגְזֵרַת שְׁלֹשִׁים. כֵּיצַד. הַקּוֹבֵר אֶת מֵתוֹ קֹדֶם הָרֶגֶל וְנָהַג אֲבֵלוּת, כֵּיוָן שֶׁבָּא הָרֶגֶל, מַפְסִיק אֶת הָאֲבֵלוּת. וַאֲפִלּוּ נִקְבַּר בְּעֶרֶב־יוֹם־טוֹב לְעֵת עֶרֶב בְּעִנְיָן שֶׁחָלָה עָלָיו אֲבֵלוּת, אֲפִלּוּ שֶׁחָלַץ מִנְעָלָיו רַק שָׁעָה מֻעֶטֶת קֹדֶם יוֹם־טוֹב. מַפְסִיק אֶת הָאֲבֵלוּת וְנֶחְשָׁב לוֹ כְּאִלּוּ כְּבָר נָהַג אֲבֵלוּת כָּל שִׁבְעָה, וְיוֹם־טוֹב הָרִאשׁוֹן הוּא שְׁמִינִי, וּמַשְׁלִים עַד שְׁלֹשִׁים וַאֲפִלּוּ אִם הָיָה עֶרֶב־יוֹם־טוֹב בְּיוֹם שַׁבָּת וְשָׁמַע שְׁמוּעָה קְרוֹבָה סָמוּךְ לָעֶרֶב, אַף־עַל־פִּי שֶׁבְּשַׁבָּת אֵין נוֹהֵג אֶלָּא דְּבָרִים שֶׁבְּצִנְעָא כֵּיוָן שֶׁנָּהַג אֲפִלּוּ רַק בָּזֶה, גַּם כֵּן הָרֶגֶל מְבַטֵּל אֶת הַשִּׁבְעָה.

ב) שָׁגַג אוֹ הֵזִיד וְלֹא נָהַג אֲבֵלוּת קֹדֶם הָרֶגֶל אוֹ שֶׁנִּקְבַּר הַמֵּת סָמוּךְ

---

11. Even though they did not recieve the work before his becoming a mourner.

12. If he cannot find workers to do it, and he will suffer a loss, perhaps he may do it himself as the *Levush* permits it even if he could find others to do it. *Mishnah Berurah* 548:22.

7) Although the laws of mourning do not apply on Yom Tov and *Chol Hamoed*, and even the laws of the thirty days of mourning do not apply, and he is permitted to wear pressed garments; nevertheless, since he is forbidden to have his hair cut because of the Yom Tov, the days of the Yom Tov are included in the thirty days and the thirty days are counted from the day the burial took place. Although *Shemini Atzeress* is a Yom Tov by itself, nevertheless, since he has not yet begun mourning, it does not cancel the period of mourning and in the total of thirty days, it counts as only one day.

8) However, if a bridegroom marries before a Yom Tov, and the Yom Tov occurs in the middle of the wedding week, and his relative died during the Yom Tov, then the days of his wedding week, are not included in the total of thirty days.

9) Although no mourning is observed on a Yom Tov, it is still proper to console the mourner (this does not constitute mourning, since the mourner himself does nothing). After the Yom Tov, at the end of seven days from the burial, although, as yet, the seven days of mourning have not expired, he may employ[11] others to do his work[12] in their homes, and his servants may work for him privately in his home. It is not necessary to console him after the Yom Tov, for as many days as they comforted him during the Yom Tov, but they should visit him during those days.

Chapter 220

The Mourning Period is Cancelled By a Festival

1) A Festival cancels the seven-day and the thirty day periods of mourning. Thus, if one buries his dead before a Festival, and observed some time in mourning, as soon as the Festival begins, his mourning is suspended. Even if the burial took place on the eve of Yom Tov, toward the close of the day, so that the laws of mourning pertained to him, even if he merely removed his shoes for just a short time before Yom Tov, the Festival suspends the mourning, and we consider it as though he had observed the entire seven days of mourning. The first day of the Yom Tov is counted as the eighth day,[1] and he then completes the thirty day mourning period. Even if the eve of Yom Tov is Shabbos, and he received *timely* news towards the evening, although on Shabbos the only laws of mourning observed are those concerning his private life, since at least these laws were observed, the Festival cancels the seven days of mourning.

2) If the mourner either inadvertently or intentionally neglected to observe any mourning[2] before the Festival, or if the burial took place close to nightfall, whereby

1. Although it is a Festival, since it is during the thirty days of mourning he may not wear freshly pressed garments. *Ramban, Mishnah Berurah* 548:22.

2. If however he observed some aspect of mourning, the Festival does cancel the rest of the mourning (Sha'ar Hatzion 548:18).

לַחֲשֵׁכָה וְלֹא הָיָה יָכוֹל לִנְהוֹג אֲבֵלוּת, אֵין הָרֶגֶל מְבַטֵּל, וְדִינוֹ כְּדִין קוֹבֵר מֵתוֹ בָּרֶגֶל.

ג) אִם חָל אֶחָד מִימֵי הָאֲבֵלוּת חוּץ מִיּוֹם הַשְּׁבִיעִי בְּעֶרֶב הָרֶגֶל, יֵשׁ מַתִּירִין לְכַבֵּס כְּסוּתוֹ, וְלֹא יִלְבָּשֶׁנָּה עַד הַלַּיְלָה, כֵּיוָן דְּהָרֶגֶל יְבַטֵּל גְּזֵרַת שִׁבְעָה. וְטוֹב לִזָּהֵר מִלְּכַבֵּס עַד לְאַחַר חֲצוֹת, כְּדֵי שֶׁיִּהְיֶה נִכָּר שֶׁמִּפְּנֵי הָרֶגֶל הוּא מְכַבֵּס. וְלִרְחוֹץ, אָסוּר עַד הַלַּיְלָה. וְיֵשׁ מַתִּירִין לִרְחוֹץ אַחַר תְּפִלַּת מִנְחָה סָמוּךְ לַחֲשֵׁכָה. וְהֵיכָא דְנָהוּג, נָהוּג. וּבְגִלּוּחַ, לְכֻלֵּי עָלְמָא, אָסוּר.

ד) קָבַר אֶת מֵתוֹ שִׁבְעָה יָמִים לִפְנֵי הָרֶגֶל, כֵּיוָן שֶׁנָּהַג שִׁבְעָה קֹדֶם הָרֶגֶל, הָרֶגֶל מְבַטֵּל גְּזֵרַת שְׁלֹשִׁים. וַאֲפִלּוּ הָיָה יוֹם הַשְּׁבִיעִי בְּעֶרֶב יוֹם־טוֹב, כֵּיוָן דְּאָמְרִינָן מִקְצָת הַיּוֹם כְּכֻלּוֹ, הֲרֵי לְאַחַר יְצִיאָה מִבֵּית־הַכְּנֶסֶת, נִשְׁלְמוּ הַשִּׁבְעָה, וּשְׁאָר הַיּוֹם הוּא בְּתוֹרַת שְׁלֹשִׁים, וּבָא הָרֶגֶל וּמַפְסִיק, וּמֻתָּר לְכַבֵּס וְלִרְחוֹץ וּלְגַלֵּחַ בְּעֶרֶב הָרֶגֶל סָמוּךְ לַחֲשֵׁכָה, כֵּיוָן שֶׁהוּא עוֹשֶׂה לִכְבוֹד הָרֶגֶל, וְהָרֶגֶל מְבַטֵּל גְּזֵרַת שְׁלֹשִׁים. וּבְעֶרֶב פֶּסַח, כֵּיוָן דִּלְאַחַר חֲצוֹת שֶׁהוּא זְמַן שְׁחִיטַת הַפֶּסַח, נֶחְשָׁב קְצָת כְּמוֹ יוֹם־טוֹב, מֻתָּר בִּרְחִיצָה תֵּכֶף לְאַחַר חֲצוֹת, וּבְגִלּוּחַ קֹדֶם חֲצוֹת (כֵּיוָן דִּלְאַחַר חֲצוֹת אָסוּר לְאַחֵר שֶׁיְּגַלֵּחַ אוֹתוֹ).

ה) חָל שְׁבִיעִי שֶׁלּוֹ בְּעֶרֶב־שַׁבָּת, וְיוֹם הַשַּׁבָּת יִהְיֶה עֶרֶב־יוֹם־טוֹב, מֻתָּר לְכַבֵּס וְלִרְחוֹץ וּלְגַלֵּחַ בְּעֶרֶב־שַׁבָּת.

ו) אִם לֹא גִלַּח אֶת עַצְמוֹ בְּעֶרֶב־שַׁבָּת אוֹ בְעֶרֶב־יוֹם־טוֹב, אָסוּר לוֹ לְגַלֵּחַ בְּחֹל־הַמּוֹעֵד, כֵּיוָן שֶׁהָיָה יָכוֹל לְגַלֵּחַ מִקֹּדֶם. אֲבָל מֻתָּר לוֹ לְגַלֵּחַ לְאַחַר יוֹם־טוֹב. וְאִם חָל שְׁבִיעִי שֶׁלּוֹ בַּשַּׁבָּת שֶׁהוּא עֶרֶב־יוֹם־טוֹב, כֵּיוָן שֶׁמִּצַּד הָאֲבֵלוּת הָיָה יָכוֹל לְגַלֵּחַ אֶלָּא שֶׁהַשַּׁבָּת עִכְּבוֹ, אִם כֵּן הֲוֵי לֵהּ אָנוּס, וּמֻתָּר לְגַלֵּחַ אֶת עַצְמוֹ גַּם בְּחֹל־הַמּוֹעֵד.

ז) הָא דְרֶגֶל מְבַטֵּל גְּזֵרַת שְׁלֹשִׁים, דַּוְקָא עַל שְׁאָר מֵתִים. אֲבָל עַל אָבִיו וְאִמּוֹ שֶׁאָסוּר לְגַלֵּחַ עַד שֶׁיִּגְעֲרוּ בוֹ חֲבֵרָיו, אֵין הָרֶגֶל מְבַטֵּל זֹאת.

---

3. The *Kitzur Shulchan Aruch* in the following paragraph says not to wash until near the evening. This is also the ruling of the *Mishnah Berurah* 548:37.

4. Only bathing, but all other laws of mourning are observed until nightfall. *Mishna Berurah* 548:39.

5. Only after he already prayed the Minchah service. *Mogein Avraham.* Even then, he is permitted only near twilight. *Yeshuos Yaakov, Mishnah Berurah* 548:40.

he was unable to observe any mourning, the Festival does not cancel it, and he is subject to the same law as one who buries his dead during a Festival.

3) If one of the days of mourning, except the seventh day, occurs on the eve of a Festival, since the Festival will cancel the seven-day mourning period, some *Poskim* permit him to wash his clothes, provided he does not wear them until nightfall. It is best to take care not to wash them until the afternoon,[3] so that it is evident that he is washing them on account of the Festival. He is forbidden to bathe until nightfall, but some *Poskim* permit bathing[4] after the *Minchah* service,[5] close to nightfall. In places where this custom prevails one may follow it. With regard to having his hair cut, all *Poskim* agree that it is forbidden.

4) If he buried his dead seven days before the Festival, since he observed seven days of mourning before the Festival, the Festival cancels the thirty day mourning period. This is true even when the seventh day occurs on the day before Yom Tov; since we maintain that part of the day is like an entire day; as soon as the people leave the synagogue (in the morning), the seven day mourning period has been completed, and the remainder of the day is counted as part of the thirty-day mourning period, which is cancelled by the Festival. The mourner may wash his clothing, bathe, and have his hair cut on the eve of the Festival towards nightfall.[6] since he is doing it in honor of the Festival, and the Festival cancels the thirty-day mourning period. If the seventh day occurs on the eve of *Pesach*, since the afternoon which is the time the Pascal lamb was offered, is regarded somewhat as a Yom Tov, he is permitted to bathe immediately after midday and to have his hair cut before noon (since after midday, another person is forbidden to cut his hair for him).

5) If the seventh day of mourning occurs on Friday, and Shabbos will be the eve of Yom Tov, he is permitted to wash his clothing, bathe, and have his hair cut on the eve of Shabbos.[7]

6) If a mourner neglected to have his hair cut on the eve of Shabbos, or on the eve of Yom Tov, he is forbidden to have his hair cut on *Chol Hamoed*, since he was able to have his hair cut before then. He is, however, permitted to have his hair cut after Yom Tov. If the seventh day of mourning occurred on Shabbos, which is the eve of Yom Tov, since from the standpoint of the laws of mourning he was allowed to have his hair cut then, but was prevented because of Shabbos, it is considered as though he was prevented by an accident, and he is, therefore, permitted to have his hair cut even on *Chol Hamoed*.

7) A Festival cancels the thirty-day mourning period, only if the mourning is for other relatives; but if he is mourning for his father or mother, since he is forbidden to have his hair cut until his friends reprove him,[8] the Festival does not cancel this regulation.

---

6. *Ramah* 548. In case of emergency one can rely on the *Shulchan Aruch* and do these things in the afternoon. *Mishnah Berurah* 548:31.

7. In this case he may do it even before he says the *Minchah* prayer. See *Biur Halacha* 548:8.

8. If they reprove him, he is permitted on the thirtieth day of mourning. *Mishnah Berurah* 548:34.

ח) נָהַג שָׁעָה אַחַת (לָאו דַּוְקָא שָׁעָה אֶלָּא אֲפִלּוּ פָּחוֹת) לִפְנֵי פֶּסַח, אוֹתָהּ שָׁעָה חֲשׁוּבָה כְּמוֹ שִׁבְעָה, וּשְׁמוֹנָה יְמֵי פֶּסַח, הֲרֵי לוֹ חֲמִשָּׁה עָשָׂר יוֹם, וּמַשְׁלִים עוֹד חֲמִשָּׁה עָשָׂר לְמִנְיַן שְׁלֹשִׁים. נָהַג שָׁעָה אַחַת לִפְנֵי שָׁבוּעוֹת, אוֹתָהּ שָׁעָה הִיא כְּמוֹ שִׁבְעָה, וְיוֹם הָרִאשׁוֹן שֶׁל שָׁבוּעוֹת נֶחְשָׁב גַּם כֵּן שִׁבְעָה יָמִים (כֵּיוָן שֶׁקָּרְבְּנוֹתָיו יֵשׁ לָהֶם תַּשְׁלוּמִין כָּל שִׁבְעָה). וְיוֹם שֵׁנִי שֶׁל שָׁבוּעוֹת הוּא לוֹ יוֹם חֲמִשָּׁה־עָשָׂר, וּמַשְׁלִים אַחַר כָּךְ גַּם כֵּן עוֹד חֲמִשָּׁה־עָשָׂר יוֹם. נָהַג שָׁעָה אַחַת לִפְנֵי חַג הַסֻּכּוֹת, הֲרֵי שִׁבְעָה. וְשִׁבְעָה יְמֵי סֻכּוֹת, הֲרֵי אַרְבָּעָה־עָשָׂר יוֹם. וּשְׁמִינִי־עֲצֶרֶת נֶחְשָׁב גַּם כֵּן לְשִׁבְעָה (שֶׁהוּא רֶגֶל בִּפְנֵי עַצְמוֹ, וְיֵשׁ לְקָרְבְּנוֹתָיו תַּשְׁלוּמִין) הֲרֵי עֶשְׂרִים וְאֶחָד יוֹם. וְיוֹם שִׂמְחַת־תּוֹרָה, יוֹם הָעֶשְׂרִים וּשְׁנַיִם. וּמַשְׁלִים עוֹד שְׁמוֹנָה יָמִים.

ט) רֹאשׁ־הַשָּׁנָה וְיוֹם־הַכִּפּוּרִים, נֶחְשָׁבִים גַּם כֵּן כִּרְגָלִים לְעִנְיַן בִּטּוּל שִׁבְעָה וּשְׁלֹשִׁים. נָהַג שָׁעָה אַחַת לִפְנֵי רֹאשׁ־הַשָּׁנָה, בִּטֵּל רֹאשׁ־הַשָּׁנָה גְּזֵרַת שִׁבְעָה, וְיוֹם־הַכִּפּוּרִים מְבַטֵּל גְּזֵרַת שְׁלֹשִׁים. נָהַג שָׁעָה אַחַת לִפְנֵי יוֹם־הַכִּפּוּרִים, בִּטֵּל יוֹם־הַכִּפּוּרִים שִׁבְעָה, וְחַג הַסֻּכּוֹת מְבַטֵּל שְׁלֹשִׁים.

י) אַף־עַל־גַּב דְּרֶגֶל מְבַטֵּל שִׁבְעָה, מִכָּל מָקוֹם מַה שֶּׁנּוֹהֲגִין לְהַדְלִיק נֵר בְּמָקוֹם שֶׁמֵּת לִכְבוֹד הַנְּשָׁמָה, יַדְלִיקוּ גַּם בְּיוֹם־טוֹב. וּמִכָּל מָקוֹם טוֹב יוֹתֵר לְהַדְלִיק בְּבֵית־הַכְּנֶסֶת.

סִימָן רכא

דִּין תַּעֲנִית יָארְצַייט

א) מִצְוָה לְהִתְעַנּוֹת בְּכָל שָׁנָה יוֹם שֶׁמֵּת בּוֹ אָבִיו אוֹ אִמּוֹ, כְּדֵי לְהִתְעוֹרֵר לִתְשׁוּבָה, לְפַשְׁפֵּשׁ בְּמַעֲשָׂיו בְּאוֹתוֹ הַיּוֹם וּלְהִתְחָרֵט עֲלֵיהֶם, וְעַל יְדֵי זֶה יְזַכֶּה אֶת אָבִיו וְאִמּוֹ שֶׁיִּתְעַלּוּ בְּגַן־עֵדֶן. וְלָעֶרֶב בִּתְפִלַּת הַמִּנְחָה, אוֹמֵר עֲנֵנוּ כְּמוֹ בְּכָל תַּעֲנִית יָחִיד. אִם הִתְעַנָּה פַּעַם אַחַת, מִסְתָמָא הָיְתָה דַעְתּוֹ לְהִתְעַנּוֹת כָּל יָמָיו. וְאִם כֵּן הֲרֵי הוּא עָלָיו כְּמוֹ

---

9. Amends actually cannot be made for its sacrifices, but since all the Festivals are compared to one another, *Shemini Atzeress*, too, counts as seven days. *Mishnah Berurah* 548:46.

10. If the burial took place the day before *Yom Kippur*, he is permitted to wash in warm water

8) If one had observed mourning for one hour, (not exactly, but even less than an hour) before *Pesach*, that hour is considered like seven days, which together with the eight days of *Pesach,* make a total of fifteen days, to which he must add another fifteen days to complete the thirty-day mourning period. If he observed mourning for one hour before *Shavuos,* that hour is regarded as seven days, and the first day of *Shavuos* is also regarded as seven days (since its sacred offerings can be brought on any of the following seven days,) and the second day of *Shavuos* is counted as his fifteenth day, after which he must add another fifteen days. If he observed mourning for one hour before the Festival of *Sukkos*, it is counted as seven days, which together with the seven days of *Sukkos* make a total of fourteen days. The Festival of *Shemini Atzeress* is also counted as seven days (for it is a Festival in its own right, and amends[9] can be made for its sacrifices), making it a total of twenty-one days. The day of *Simchas Torah* counts as the twenty-second day, and he must add another eight days.

9) *Rosh Hashanah* and *Yom Kippur* are also considered Festivals with regard to canceling the seven and thirty-day mourning periods. Thus, if one observed mourning for one hour before *Rosh Hashanah, Rosh Hashanah* cancels the seven day period, and *Yom Kippur* cancels the thirty-day period. If he observed mourning for one hour before *Yom Kippur, Yom Kippur* cancels the seven day period,[10] and *Sukkos* cancels the thirty-day period.

10) Although a Festival cancels the seven-day mourning period, nevertheless, the candle that is customarily lit in the place where the death occurred, to honor the soul of the deceased, should also be lit on Yom Tov. However, it is better to light it in the synagogue.

Chapter 221

The Law of Fasting on the Day of Yahrzeit

1) It is a *Mitzvah* to fast, every year, on the anniversary of the death of one's father or mother, as an inspiration to repentance, to examine his deeds on that day and lament his wrong doings. By doing this, he will bring merit to his father and mother, so that they will be exalted in *Gan Eiden*. Towards evening, in the *Shemoneh Esreh* of *Minchah,* he should say *Aneinu* (Answer us) just as on any private fast day. If a person fasted on one *Yahrzeit*, it is presumed that it was his intention to fast that day all his lifetime, and therefore it becomes like a vow, which is binding upon him

---

that very day, because immersion in a *mikvah* on the day before Yom Kippur is a mitzvah. He is permitted to do so even though he usually does not do so on the day before a Festival. Since he must immerse in the *mikveh* the day before *Yom Kippur,* he is also permitted to bathe to remove any interposition. See *Mishnah Berurah* 606:23–27. The *Mogein Avraham* maintains in this case he should not bathe more than an hour or two before nightfall. If it is the last day of the seven days of mourning, he may bathe earlier (in the afternoon) *Mishnah Berurah* 548:24.

נֶדֶר, שֶׁהוּא מִן הַתּוֹרָה, וְצָרִיךְ לְהִתְעַנּוֹת לְעוֹלָם. וּכְשֶׁהוּא חוֹלֶה אוֹ שֶׁהוּא בְּעִנְיָן אַחֵר שֶׁהוּא צָרִיךְ לֶאֱכוֹל, צָרִיךְ הַתָּרָה. וְאִם פֵּרֵשׁ שֶׁאֵינוֹ מְקַבֵּל עָלָיו בְּנֶדֶר, אֵינוֹ צָרִיךְ הַתָּרָה. נוֹהֲגִין לְהַדְלִיק נֵר יָאר־צֵייט.

ב) מִתְעַנִּין לְעוֹלָם בְּיוֹם הַמִּיתָה, וַאֲפִלּוּ בַּשָּׁנָה הָרִאשׁוֹנָה. וַאֲפִלּוּ מֵת בְּסוֹף הַיּוֹם לְאַחַר שֶׁהִתְפַּלְּלוּ עַרְבִית, אִם עֲדַיִן הוּא יוֹם, נִקְבַּע זֶה הַיּוֹם לְיָארצֵייט. אַךְ אִם הַקְּבוּרָה נִמְשְׁכָה מִן הַמִּיתָה אֵיזֶה יָמִים, אֲזַי יִתְעַנֶּה שָׁנָה הָרִאשׁוֹנָה בְּיוֹם הַקְּבוּרָה, וְאַחַר כָּךְ תָּמִיד בְּיוֹם הַמִּיתָה.

ג) אִם מֵת לוֹ מֵת בְּשָׁנָה מְעֻבֶּרֶת בַּאֲדָר רִאשׁוֹן אוֹ בַּאֲדָר שֵׁנִי, אֲזַי בְּשָׁנָה פְּשׁוּטָה מִתְעַנֶּה כֵּן בַּאֲדָר, וּבְשָׁנָה מְעֻבֶּרֶת מִתְעַנֶּה בְּזֶה הָאֲדָר שֶׁמֵּת. אִם בָּרִאשׁוֹן, בָּרִאשׁוֹן. וְאִם בַּשֵּׁנִי, בַּשֵּׁנִי. וְאִם מֵת בְּשָׁנָה פְּשׁוּטָה, אֲזַי בְּשָׁנָה מְעֻבֶּרֶת, יִתְעַנֶּה בַּאֲדָר רִאשׁוֹן, וְגַם בַּאֲדָר שֵׁנִי יֹאמַר קַדִּישׁ, אַךְ אַל יַסִּיג גְּבוּל אֲחֵרִים.

ד) חֹדֶשׁ חֶשְׁוָן, לִפְעָמִים הוּא מָלֵא, דְּהַיְנוּ שֶׁיֵּשׁ לוֹ שְׁלֹשִׁים יוֹם, וְאָז רֹאשׁ־חֹדֶשׁ כִּסְלֵו שֶׁלְּאַחֲרָיו הוּא שְׁנֵי יָמִים. יוֹם רִאשׁוֹן דְּרֹאשׁ־חֹדֶשׁ הוּא יוֹם הַשְּׁלֹשִׁים שֶׁל חֶשְׁוָן וְשַׁיָּךְ לוֹ, וְיוֹם שֵׁנִי דְּרֹאשׁ־חֹדֶשׁ הוּא יוֹם הָרִאשׁוֹן שֶׁל כִּסְלֵו (וְכֵן בְּכָל רֹאשׁ־חֹדֶשׁ שֶׁהוּא שְׁנֵי יָמִים, יוֹם הָרִאשׁוֹן הוּא יוֹם הַשְּׁלֹשִׁים שֶׁל חֹדֶשׁ שֶׁעָבַר וְשַׁיָּךְ לוֹ). וְלִפְעָמִים הוּא חָסֵר, דְּהַיְנוּ שֶׁאֵין לוֹ אֶלָּא תִּשְׁעָה וְעֶשְׂרִים יוֹם. וְרֹאשׁ־חֹדֶשׁ כִּסְלֵו שֶׁלְּאַחֲרָיו הוּא אֵינוֹ אֶלָּא יוֹם אֶחָד. וְכֵן חֹדֶשׁ כִּסְלֵו לִפְעָמִים מָלֵא, וְרֹאשׁ־חֹדֶשׁ טֵבֵת שֶׁלְּאַחֲרָיו שְׁנֵי יָמִים. וְלִפְעָמִים חָסֵר, וְרֹאשׁ־חֹדֶשׁ טֵבֵת שֶׁלְּאַחֲרָיו הוּא רַק יוֹם אֶחָד וּמִי שֶׁמֵּת לוֹ מֵת בְּרֹאשׁ־חֹדֶשׁ כִּסְלֵו כְּשֶׁהָיָה רַק יוֹם אֶחָד, אֲזַי בְּשָׁנָה שֶׁיִּהְיֶה רֹאשׁ־חֹדֶשׁ כִּסְלֵו שְׁנֵי יָמִים, יַחֲזִיק אֶת הַיָּארצֵייט בְּיוֹם שֵׁנִי דְּרֹאשׁ־חֹדֶשׁ שֶׁהוּא יוֹם רִאשׁוֹן שֶׁל חֹדֶשׁ כִּסְלֵו, שֶׁגַּם הַמִּיתָה הָיְתָה בְּאֶחָד בְּכִסְלֵו. וְאָמְנָם מִי שֶׁמֵּת לוֹ מֵת בְּיוֹם רִאשׁוֹן דְּרֹאשׁ־חֹדֶשׁ כִּסְלֵו כְּשֶׁהָיָה רֹאשׁ־חֹדֶשׁ שְׁנֵי יָמִים, הִנֵּה בְּשָׁנָה שֶׁרֹאשׁ־חֹדֶשׁ כִּסְלֵו אֵינוֹ רַק יוֹם אֶחָד, יֵשׁ לְהִסְתַּפֵּק מָתַי יַחֲזִיק אֶת הַיָּארצֵייט, אִם בְּתִשְׁעָה וְעֶשְׂרִים בְּחֶשְׁוָן כֵּיוָן שֶׁמֵּת בְּסוֹף חֶשְׁוָן, אוֹ כֵּיוָן דִּבִנְדָרִים הוֹלְכִין אַחַר לְשׁוֹן בְּנֵי־אָדָם, יַחֲזִיק אֶת הַיָּארצֵייט בְּרֹאשׁ־חֹדֶשׁ כִּסְלֵו כְּמוֹ שֶׁקּוֹרִין אוֹתוֹ. וְיֵשׁ לִנְהוֹג כֵּן: אִם בַּשָּׁנָה הָרִאשׁוֹנָה הַבָּאָה רֹאשׁ־חֹדֶשׁ כִּסְלֵו הוּא

1. The *Mishnah Berurah* 568:44 brings two opinions on this matter.

as a Scriptual obligation, and he is obligated to fast on that day forever. If he becomes ill, or if he is in some other situation where he must eat, he must have his vow annulled. However, if he distinctly declared that his fasting is not an acceptance of a vow, annulment is not necessary. It is customary to light a *Yahrzeit* candle.

2) The *Yahrzeit* fast is always observed on the day of death even in the first year. Even if the death occurred towards the end of the day, after the congregation said the *Maariv* prayer, if it is still day, that day is fixed as the day of *Yahrzeit.* However, if the burial took place several days after the death occurred, the *Yahrzeit* fast should be observed the first year on the date of the burial,[1] but in subsequent years on the day of death.

3) If death occurs during a leap year, either in the first or second month of *Adar,* then, in a regular year, the *Yahrzeit* fast is observed on that day of *Adar.* And in a leap year it should be observed in the month when the death occurred; if in the first *Adar,* it is observed in the first, and if in the second, it is observed in the second.[2] If the death occurred in (*Adar* of) a regular year, then, during a leap year it is observed in the first *Adar.*[3] In the second *Adar,* too, he should say *Kaddish* but he may not encroach upon the rights of others.

4) The month of *Cheshvan* is sometimes full, that is, it consists of thirty days, and then, *Rosh Chodesh Kislev* that follows, is two days. The first day of this *Rosh Chodesh* [*Kislev*] is the thirtieth day of *Cheshvan* and belongs to it (*Cheshvan*), and the second day of *Rosh Chodesh* is the first of *Kislev.* (This is true of every *Rosh Chodesh* which consists of two days; the first day is the thirtieth of the previous month, and belongs to it.) Sometimes the month of *Cheshvan* is lacking, that is, it consists of only twenty-nine days, and *Rosh Chodesh Kislev* that follows is only one day. Also the month of *Kislev* is full sometimes, and *Rosh Chodesh Teives* that follows is two days, and other times it is lacking, and *Rosh Chodesh Teives* that follows consists of only one day. If someone dies on *Rosh Chodesh Kislev* when it was only one day, then, in a year when *Rosh Chodesh Kislev* will be two days, the *Yahrzeit* should be observed on the second day of *Rosh Chodesh,* which is the first day of *Chodesh Kislev,* for the death occurred on the first day of *Kislev.* However, if someone died on the first day of *Rosh Chodesh Kislev* when *Rosh Chodesh* was two days, then in a year when *Rosh Chodesh Kislev* is only one day, there is a question when the *Yahrzeit* is to be observed; if on the twenty-ninth of *Cheshvan,* since he died at the end of *Cheshvan,* or, perhaps, since as regards the law of vows, we are guided by colloquial language, the *Yahrzeit* should be observed on *Rosh Chodesh Kislev* as the first day of *Rosh Chodesh* is usually called. The following is the proper procedure: If in the first year (after the death occurred) *Rosh Chodesh Kislev* is only one day, the

---

2. If he does not know which, he should fast on the second *Adar* . *Sha'ar Hatziyun* 568:38.

3. *Maharik, Ramah* etc., and this is the custom. If it is not too difficult, he should fast on both. If he vowed to fast on the *Yahrzeit* he must fast on both. See *Mogen Avraham, Gra, Mishnah Berurah* 568:42.

רַק יוֹם אֶחָד, יַחֲזִיק אֶת הַיָּארְצַייט בְּתִשְׁעָה וְעֶשְׂרִים בְּחֶשְׁוָן, וְכֵן לְעוֹלָם כְּשֶׁיִּהְיֶה חֶשְׁוָן חָסֵר. וּמִכָּל מָקוֹם אִם לְמָחֳרָתוֹ בְּיוֹם רֹאשׁ־חֹדֶשׁ אֵין שָׁם אֲבֵלִים, יֵשׁ לוֹ גַּם כֵּן לוֹמַר קַדִּישׁ וּלְהִתְפַּלֵּל לִפְנֵי הַתֵּבָה, רַק לֹא יַסִּיג גְּבוּל אֲחֵרִים. אֲבָל אִם גַּם בַּשָּׁנָה הָרִאשׁוֹנָה הַבָּאָה רֹאשׁ־חֹדֶשׁ כִּסְלֵו הוּא שְׁנֵי יָמִים, אֲזַי קוֹבֵעַ אֶת הַיָּארְצַייט לְרֹאשׁ־חֹדֶשׁ כִּסְלֵו וְיַחֲזִיקֶנּוּ כֵּן לְעוֹלָם. וְגַם כְּשֶׁיִּהְיֶה רֹאשׁ־חֹדֶשׁ רַק יוֹם אֶחָד, יַחֲזִיקֶנּוּ אָז בְּרֹאשׁ־חֹדֶשׁ. וְהוּא הַדִּין לְרֹאשׁ־חֹדֶשׁ טֵבֵת.

ה) וְכֵיוָן שֶׁרֹאשׁ־חֹדֶשׁ טֵבֵת הוּא לִפְעָמִים רַק יוֹם אֶחָד, דְּהַיְנוּ יוֹם שִׁשִּׁי דַּחֲנֻכָּה, וַהֲוֵי יוֹם שִׁשִּׁי דַּחֲנֻכָּה אֶחָד בְּטֵבֵת יוֹם שְׁבִיעִי שְׁנַיִם בְּטֵבֵת, וְיוֹם שְׁמִינִי שְׁלֹשָׁה בְּטֵבֵת, וְלִפְעָמִים שְׁנֵי יָמִים, דְּהַיְנוּ יוֹם שִׁשִּׁי וְיוֹם שְׁבִיעִי דַּחֲנֻכָּה, וְאָז הֲוֵי יוֹם שְׁבִיעִי דַּחֲנֻכָּה אֶחָד בְּטֵבֵת, וְיוֹם שְׁמִינִי שְׁנַיִם בְּטֵבֵת, לָכֵן מִי שֶׁיֵּשׁ לוֹ יָארְצַייט בְּיָמִים אֵלּוּ, לֹא יִטְעֶה לִמְנוֹת לִימֵי חֲנֻכָּה כִּי צָרִיךְ לִמְנוֹת לִימֵי הַחֹדֶשׁ.

ו) בְּיוֹם שֶׁאֵין אוֹמְרִים בּוֹ תַּחֲנוּן, אֵין מִתְעַנִּין תַּעֲנִית יָארְצַייט. וְכֵן בְּיוֹם מִילָה, הָאָב וְהַסַּנְדָּק וְהַמּוֹהֵל אֵין מִתְעַנִּין. וְכֵן בְּפִדְיוֹן הַבֵּן, הָאָב וְהַכֹּהֵן אֵין מִתְעַנִּין. וְכֵן הֶחָתָן בְּשִׁבְעַת יְמֵי הַמִּשְׁתֶּה, אֵינוֹ מִתְעַנֶּה. אֲבָל בִּסְעוּדַת סִיּוּם, אָסוּר לֶאֱכוֹל בְּיוֹם הַיָּארְצַייט. וּבְיָמִים שֶׁאֵינוֹ מִתְעַנֶּה, עַל־כָּל־פָּנִים יַעֲסֹק בַּתּוֹרָה וּבְמִצְוֹת וּבִשְׁאָר מַעֲשִׂים טוֹבִים לִזְכוּת נִשְׁמַת אָבִיו וְאִמּוֹ.

ז) בַּלַּיְלָה אֲשֶׁר בְּיוֹם הַמָּחֳרַת יִהְיֶה לוֹ יָארְצַייט, אֵין לוֹ לֶאֱכוֹל בִּסְעוּדַת חֲתֻנָּה שֶׁיֵּשׁ שָׁם מְזֻמּוּטֵי חָתָן וְכַלָּה וְיֵשׁ בָּהּ שִׂמְחָה. אֲבָל בִּסְעוּדַת בְּרִית מִילָה וּפִדְיוֹן הַבֵּן וְסִיּוּם מַסֶּכֶת, מֻתָּר.

ח) מִי שֶׁאֵינוֹ יוֹדֵעַ יוֹם מִיתַת אָבִיו אוֹ אִמּוֹ, יִבְרֹר לוֹ יוֹם אֶחָד בַּשָּׁנָה לְהִתְעַנּוֹת. אֲבָל לֹא יַסִּיג גְּבוּל אֲחֵרִים בְּקַדִּישִׁים. בִּלַּע הַמָּוֶת לָנֶצַח, וּמָחָה ה' אֱלֹהִים דִּמְעָה מֵעַל כָּל־פָּנִים בָּרוּךְ הַנּוֹתֵן לַיָּעֵף כֹּחַ, וּלְאֵין אוֹנִים עָצְמָה יַרְבֶּה

---

4. If they want, they may fast a half a day.

5. *Mishnah Berurah* 568:46 *Sha'arei Teshuvah* 568:19. But the *Ponim Meiros* 2:99 says the *Kohein* must fast.

6. If either the groom or the bride are married for the first time. *Mishna Berurah* 550:12. He does, however, need an annulment of his vow to fast. *Biur Halacha* 559:9-*Chochmas Shlomo*.

Yahrzeit should be observed on the twenty-ninth of *Cheshvan*, and similarly when ever *Cheshvan* is lacking. Nevertheless, if the next day, on *Rosh Chodesh,* there are no mourners present, he should recite *Kaddish* and lead the services on that day, but he may not encroach upon the rights of others. If, however, also in the first year following the death, *Rosh Chodesh Kislev* is two days, then the *Yahrzeit* is established to be observed on *Rosh Chodesh Kislev,* and he should forever observe it on that day. Even when *Rosh Chodesh* will be only one day, the *Yahrzeit* should be observed on *Rosh Chodesh*. This applies also to the month of *Teivis.*

5) Since *Rosh Chodesh Teives* is sometimes only one day, that is, on the sixth day of *Chanukah*, when the sixth day of *Chanukah* is the first day of the month of *Teives* and the seventh day of *Chanukah* is the second day of *Teives,* and the eighth day of *Chanukah* is the third day of *Teives*, and at other times (*Rosh Chodesh Teives*) is two days, that is, on the sixth and seventh day of *Chanukah*, when the seventh day of *Chanukah* is the first day of *Teives*, and the eighth day (of *Chanukah*) is the second day of *Teives*. Therefore, one who has a *Yahrzeit* to observe on one of these days, should not err by calculating according to the days of *Chanukah*, for it must be calculated according to the day of the month.

6) On days that *Tachanun* is not said fasting should not be observed on the *Yahrzeit*. Also, on the day of a circumcision, the father, the *Sandek*, and the *Mohel* should not observe the *Yahrzeit* fast.[4] Also, on the day of redemption of the firstborn, the father and *Kohein*[5] should not observe the *Yahrzeit* fast. Also, a bridegroom, during the wedding week, should not observe a *Yahrzeit* fast.[6] But it is forbidden to partake of a meal at a *Siyum*[7] on the day of a *Yahrzeit*. On the days when fasting is not observed, he should at least devote his time to study Torah and to practice *Mitzvos* and good deeds to bring merit to the souls of his father and mother.

7) In the night preceding the day when one must observe *Yahrzeit*, he should not partake of a wedding meal, for there is music for the groom and bride and there is merriment. But to partake of a meal in honor of a circumcision, or the redemption of the firstborn or *siyum* is permitted.[8]

8) If one does not know the date of his parent's death, he should select one day on which to observe the *Yahrzeit* fast, but he may not encroach upon the rights of others with regard to reciting the *Kaddish.* "He will swallow up death forever; and *Adonoy,* God will wipe away tears from all faces." "Blessed be He who gives strength to the weary; and to Him who increases strength to the powerless."

---

7. A *Siyum* is the completion of a *Masechess* of the Talmud. If he also took part in learning the *Masechess*, he may definitely partake of the meal at the *Siyum*. *Maharam Shick* Responsa *Yoreh Deah* 367.

8. *Mekom Shmuel* Responsa 80. However, the *Eliyohu Rabba* 568 :15 forbids attending the meal of a circumcision.

Glossary

	Rabbi Moshe Feinstein זצ״ל			Chazon Ish זצ״ל		
	Lenient View	**Stringent View**	**Rabbinic Laws**	**Lenient View**	**Stringent View**	**Accepted Practice**
Agudal **אגודל**	0.89 inches 2.26 cm	0.91 inches 2.31 cm		0.95 inches 2.4 cm	0.98 inches 2.48 cm	
Amah **אמה**	21.25 inches 53.975 cm	21.7 inches 55.11 cm		22.7 inches 57.66 cm	23.5 inches 59.7 cm	
Kabeitza **כביצה**		2.92 fl. oz. 86.23 ml	1.94 fl. oz 57.29 ml	3.4 fl. oz. 100 ml		
Kazayis **כזית**		1.5 fl. oz. 44.29 ml	.97 fl. oz. 28.64 ml	1.7 fl. oz 50 ml		
Mil **מיל**	0.7 miles (3,542 feet) 1.079 km			0.75 miles (3,784 feet) 1.16 km		as a unit of time: 18 minutes
Parsah **פרסה**	2.7 miles (14,167 feet) 4.31 km			2.8 miles (15,134 feet) 4.62 km		as a unit of time: 72 minutes
Pras* **פרס**				4 minutes	2 minutes	
Revi'is **רביעית**		4.42 fl. oz. 130.52 ml	2.9 fl. oz. 85.64 ml	5.1 fl. oz. 150 ml		
Tefach **טפח**	3.6 inches 9.14 cm	3.7 inches 9.39 cm		3.79 inches 9.61 cm	3.92 inches 9.95 cm	

Lechem mishneh The two loaves that are placed on the table at each Shabbos meal.

*For one who must eat on Yom Kippur the measure of *Pras* is 9 minutes.

GW00392141